THE SUPER Book of
HOME REPAIRS
REMODELING
AND BUILDING

THIS BOOK IS DEDICATED TO BRINY-MARLIN

Eisinger Publications, Incorporated, P.O. Box 19765, Sarasota, FL 34276

LARRY EISINGER	LARRY EISINGER, Jr.	FRANCES EISINGER
Publisher	Vice President/Director of Marketing	Treasurer

ISBN 0-9637349-0-3

Some of the material appearing in the Carpentry, Plumbing, Electrical and Concrete sections was initially published in The Homeowner Handbook of Carpentry and Woodworking, The Homeowner Handbook of Plumbing and Heating, The Homeowner Handbook of Electrical Repairs and The Homeowner Handbook of Concrete and Masonry Copyright MCMLXXIV Eisinger Publications, Inc. For this publication the material selected was completely updated, with new page design and typography.

A WORD OF CAUTION...

All repair, remodeling and building projects represent a risk of personal injury, the degree of which is dependent upon the nature of the job, the experience of the individual and working conditions at the job site. The editors and authors have made ever effort to provide accurate, tested information but the responsibility of selecting the material and executing the job is that of the individual. Carefully evaluate each do-it-yourself project and proceed with caution. Adhere to all building codes and always follow the instructions of the manufacturer when using materials and tools. If you feel a project is beyond your capability it is wise to consult a professional.

ABOUT THIS BOOK...

Many years in development, this book reflects the talent and expertise of scores of individuals—authors, editors, illustrators, photographers, researchers and writers. Here is a brief background on the major contributors

RICHARD DAY—Like the fellow writers who helped make this book possible, Rich Day is an inveterate do-it-yourselfer who has written 19 books on home maintenance, repairs, improvements and construction. His latest Merideth Press book "Building Patios, Decks & Fences" won the first Stanley Tools Award for the Best How-to-Do-It-Yourself Book of 1991-1992. His other books have been published by Fawcett Publications, the Outdoor Life/Popular Science Book Club, Home Owner Publications and Eisinger Publications. A former consulting Home and Shop editor for Popular Science magazine as well as consultant on numerous Time-Life Home Repair books and the original Reader's Digest Complete Do-It-Yourself Manual, Rich has built several houses, the current one a California Palomar mountainside home, complete with well, diesel generator and other amenities including a cellular phone in that regular telephone service is not available in his wilderness site.

For the past 40 years Rich has written and illustrated how-to articles and currently produces video tapes on home maintenance subjects. He is a charter member and former president of the National Association of Home Workshop Writers.

ROBERT BRIGHTMAN—Bob Brightman was the Home and Shop Editor of Mechanix Illustrated (now Home Mechanix) for twenty six years before he became the Technical Editor of the famous Reader's Digest Complete Do-It-Yourself Manual that has sold in excess of 11 million copies. After his Reader's Digest stint, Bob taught Industrial Arts at the Great Neck High School in Long Island, New York. Bob is happily married to his wife, Mollie, a retired New York City high school history teacher; they have a son, Kenneth, an IBM trained computer expert.

Bob practices what he preaches and takes care of all the work in his ranch style home in Great Neck, Long Island, New York. He currently teaches Home Maintenance and Repair for the Adult Center in Great Neck.

ROBERT HERTZBERG—Bob was Editor-in-Chief of Mechanix Illustrated just prior to and after World War II. He joined the U. S. Army Signal Corp immediately after Pearl Harbor and was on active duty and stationed in England on the staff of General Omar Bradley. Bob retired from the Service as a full Colonel, rejoined Mechanix Illustrated for a short time and continued his writing career by producing books on electrical repairs for Fawcett Publications. A pioneer electronic and early radio and TV experimenter, Bob helped popularize ham radio with his best selling book, "So You Want to be a Ham."

WALTER GOZDAN—Walt is Technical Director of the Rohm and Haas Paint Quality Institute in New Jersey, and oversees testing and developing paint formulas to improve the quality and performance of paint. With a full time staff of ten professionals, including four scientists, technical assistants, the Research Center to which the Paint Quality Institute is attached operates on a year-round basis to study what happens to different paint formulas exposed to elements over time. These findings are regularly disseminated by Walt in the form of articles for magazines, trade journals, radio and TV appearances—and in the Painting section of this book.

HENRY CLARK—Of all the how-to illustrators in the publishing industry, Hank probably had more how-to-illustrations published in the past 40 years than any other illustrator! Most of the illustrations in this book were created by Hank—and not on the computer. Hank Clark illustrations are unique because his building methods and tools knowledge, including safety recommendations, are always reflected in his art.

The aforementioned creative do-it-yourself authors were responsible for the major sections representing their specialty but in addition other individuals made meaningful contributions…David Rowenkamp of The Wooster Brush Company in Wooster, Ohio, authored our story on paint brushes and rollers, in addition to supplying technical advice. In the development of the Wallcovering section, we thank Jack Ford, Sales Director of Evans Adhesive of Columbus, Ohio for his help…Seymour Buckbine, Manager of Quality Assurance PSC Wallcovering of New York…Jeff Keelan, Founder and Owner of the Paperhanging Institute, Fairfield, New Jersey…Jeannie Byington, Public Information Director, Wallcoverings Association, Chicago, Illinois. Jeannie is also a Vice President with Sumner Rider Associates, Inc. of New York and Washington…Mary Ann Whitney of the Wallpaper Warehouse of Sarasota, Florida.

In reading the background of the major authors who helped make this book possible, if you have concluded the major players were Fawcett Publications and Mechanix Illustrated oriented you are absolutely correct—because for five years I was the Home and Shop Editor of Mechanix Illustrated, transferring within Fawcett Publications to become Editor-in-Chief of Fawcett Books where we produced a new magazine or how-to book every 4 1/2 days. For 20 years!

To keep current in the do-it-yourself field, for the past 15 years I have been publishing How-to books and writing a nationally syndicated weekly newspaper column called Home Workshop for Tribune Media Services, a subsidiary of The Tribune Company (of Chicago).

Larry Eisinger
Publisher

CREDITS

SARASOTA MACINTOSH SPECIALISTS
Steve Smith, Marty Smith
NEW YORK MACINTOSH SPECIALISTS
Gary Kroman, Joe Ianelli

SARASOTA LINOTRONIC OUTPUT
Win Remley, ArtType Publishing
STRIPPING FOR WEB PRINTING by SERBIN
PRINTING, INC.-Harry Allen,
Linda Houston, Linda Kretlew,
Lori Hayes, Bob Phillips, and
Cliff Scully
EDITORIAL RESEARCH by Bonnie Heleen

COVER LAYOUT ENHANCEMENT by
Sam Donato, Brooke Lyon, Jamie King of
the Ringling School of Art and Design
Sarasota, Florida
COPY EDITING
John Graboski, Betty Geigel, Maj Eisinger,
Trudy Martineau, Sheila Johnston
INDEX PREPARED by Sheila Johnston
FILM COVER LAMINATION by
BCS Laminating, Ruskin, Florida
SPECIAL PHOTOGRAPHY by Alan Cook
Escondido, CA
COPY PREPARATION by Jeremy Lourde

TEXT PRINTED BY QUEBECOR PRINTING SEMLINE , INC . WESTWOOD , MA
BINDING BY QUEBECOR PRINTING BOOK PRESS , INC . BRATTLEBORO , VT
COVER PRINTED BY SERBIN PRINTING, INC . SARASOTA , FL

BOOK 1 CARPENTRY CONTENTS PAGE 7

BOOK 2 PLUMBING CONTENTS PAGE 97

98 Basics of Your Plumbing System
104 Pipe and Fittings
106 Galvanized Steel Pipe
108 Black Iron Pipe
109 Threaded Brass Pipe
110 Copper Tubing
114 Plastic Water Supply Pipe
118 Plastic Drain-Waste-Vent Pipe
120 Other Types of Pipe

WORKING WITH PIPE

122 Cast Iron Pipe
126 Copper Tubing
128 How to Sweat Solder
130 Working with Flare Fittings
132 Working with Threaded Pipe

136 Working with Plastic Tubing

PROJECTS

142 Installing a Water Heater
144 Replacing a Kitchen or Bathroom Sink
150 Changing a Toilet
154 Changing Faucets
160 Private Water Supply
166 Plumbing Tips for an Add-On Room
174 Fixing Faucets
178 Fixing Toilets
184 Washing Machine Plumbing
186 Stopping Leaks
188 Tips on Unclogging

BOOK 3 ELECTRICAL CONTENTS PAGE 193

194 Basic Facts About Electricity
198 Electrical Safety
206 How to Read a Meter
208 Fuses vs. Circuit Breakers
212 Tools and Testers
218 Successful Soldering
220 Making Wire Nut Connections
222 GFCI Ground Fault Circuit Interrupter
226 Installing Outlets and Switches
230 Wiring Techniques
238 Wiring Tricks You Can Use
242 Amperage Requirements
244 ENT: The Do-It-Yourself Conduit
248 All About Fluorescent Lamps
254 Door Chimes, Bells and Buzzers
258 Dramatic Lighting
262 Landscape Lighting Ideas
268 Lighting for Security and Safety

272 What to do Before a Storm
274 Lamp Repair
275 Hanging a Swag Lamp

TELEPHONE INSTALLATION

276 Installing Your Telephones
277 Your Telephone Company
278 The Point of Demarcation
280 Pulse and Tone Dialing Telephones
281 Safety Tips when Running Your Lines
282 Apartment Telephone Layout
283 Two-Story Telephone Layout
284 Major Accessories for Running Telephone Lines
286 Converting Hard Wired to Modular
287 Tapping into a Junction Box
288 The Ringer Equivalence Number

BOOK 4 CONCRETE CONTENTS PAGE 289

290	The Basics of Concrete	340	Unusual Surfaces
294	Tools & Techniques	346	Pattern Stamping
302	Mixing Concrete	348	Concrete Can Be Colored
308	Buying Ready-Mix Concrete	350	Making Mortar
312	How Much to Order	352	How to Lay Blocks
316	Using Sacked Concrete	360	Building a Retaining Wall
318	The Importance of Curing	364	Masonry Fences
320	All About Footings	366	Cement Plastering
324	Plain and Fancy Walks	368	How to Lay Bricks
330	Build a Floor	374	The Art of Repointing Bricks
334	Repairing Walks and Drives	376	How to Lay Stone
336	Pour a Driveway	380	Make a Patio

BOOK 5 PAINTING/WALLCOVERING PAGE 385
CONTENTS

PAINTING

386	The Pros and Cons of Painting Your Home	418	What Makes Paint Durable?
		418	Answers to Painting Problems
388	Enemies of Paint	420	Unusual Rollers, Mitts and Pads
390	Comparing Oil & Latex Paints	422	Masking Around Windows and Doors
392	How to Estimate Paint Quantities		
392	Paint when Weather is Right	424	Cleaning Brushes and Rollers
394	Primers Solve Paint Problems	426	Paint with a Roller that does not need a Tray
396	Selecting Interior Paint		
396	Solid Color Latex Stains	428	Power Rollers
398	Surface Preparation: Wood, Metal, Stucco	428	Cordless Roller
		430	Power Sprayers
398	Painting Concrete Floors		
400	Painting Aluminum/Vinyl Siding		WALLCOVERING
400	Safety Rules when Painting		
400	Elastomeric Coatings for Masonry	432	History
402	Storing Latex Paint	433	Selecting Ideas
402	Painting an Older Home	434	Choosing the Right Wallcovering
402	Understanding Paint Terminology		
404	Diagnosing Paint Failures	436	Special Effects
404	Future Trends in Paint Technology	437	Innovative Use
406	All About Paint Brushes	438	Wallcovering Wizardry
412	All About Paint Rollers	442	Home Decorator's Dictionary
416	Three Ways to Apply Paint	444	How to Hang Wallcovering
		446	Unusual Glamour Wallcoverings
		448	Tools and Equipment Required

BOOK 5 PAINTING/WALLCOVERING CONTENTS *(Continued)* PAGE 385

450	All About Patterns	466	Covering Around Windows and Doors
452	Working with Adhesives	468	Covering Behind Sinks and Radiators
454	Estimating Number of Rolls		
456	Must you Remove the Old Covering?	470	How to Hang a Ceiling
458	Treating Painted/Unpainted Walls	472	Techniques: Pasting the Wall
		474	Working with Pre-Pasted Rolls
460	Do You Need a Lining Paper?	476	Trimming Untrimmed Rolls
		478	Correcting Common Faults
462	Hanging Instructions	480	Wallcovering Glossary

BOOK 6 PROJECTS CONTENTS PAGE 481

482	Types of Suspended Tile	509	Translucent Roof Construction
483	Recessing Fluorescent Lights	510	Extra Patio Door Lock
484	Install a Dropped Ceiling Without a Helper	511	How to Cut Glass
		512	Tips for Building a Fence
486	Metal Clip Ceiling Installation	513	Birdbath Mounted on a Stump
488	Replacing Screening: Aluminum Door	514	Installing Bi-Fold Doors
		515	Build a Stone Column
489	Replacing Screening: Wood Door	516	Riveting with Blind Rivets
490	Winterizing Your Attic Fan	517	The Unique Blind Rivet-Nut
491	Aluminum Soffit Insulation	518	Outdoor Coffee Table/Planter
494	Installing Aluminum Siding	519	Shelves for Your Laundry Room
495	Aluminum Fascia	520	Combination Mail Box and Planter
496	Insulating Your Home	521	Desk and Chair for Your Tyke
500	Insulating a Beamed Ceiling	522	Take-Apart Dining Table
501	Attic Ventilation is Important	523	Modern Dog House
502	Tips on Installing Roll Roofing	524	Choosing Waterproof Shower Walls
503	Asphalt Shingles are Easy to Apply	525	Finishing the Edges of Plywood
		526	Mounting Heavy Duty Drapery Rods
504	How to Cut Roof Shingles	527	Ceiling Fan Must be Braced for Safety
506	How to Flash Your Chimney		
507	A Reel for Extension Cords	528	Lead Downspout Rain Water Away from Your Foundation
508	Nailing Translucent Roofing		
		530	Underground Sprinkler System

BOOK 1 CARPENTRY

Prime Author: ROBERT BRIGHTMAN

CONTENTS

HAND TOOLS

8 Hammers
10 Crosscut and Ripsaws
12 Utility Saws
14 Screwdrivers
16 Planes
17 Squares
18 Rulers
19 Levels
20 Chisels
21 Drills
22 Miter Boxes
24 Clamps
25 Vises
26 Miscellaneous Hand Tools

PORTABLE POWER TOOLS

30 The Drill
32 The Circular Saw
34 The Sander
36 The Saber Saw
38 The Utility Saw
39 The Plane
40 The Router
42 Cordless Tools

STATIONARY POWER TOOLS

44 The Table Saw
46 The Radial Arm Saw
48 The Miter Saw
49 The Band Saw
50 The Drill Press
51 The Sander and The Grinder
52 The Jig Saw
53 The Shaper
54 The Jointer-Planer
55 The Lathe

CARPENTRY PROJECTS

56 Lumber and Plywood
62 All About Wall Paneling
74 Building a Workbench
76 Four Ways to Install Ceiling Tile
77 Three Ways to Arrange Ceiling Tile
78 How to Work with Wallboard
80 Nails and Screws
82 Splices and Joints
88 Pressure Treated Lumber

DECK CONSTRUCTION TECHNIQUES

90 Hardware and Fastening Devices
91 Deck Ledger
92 Locating Deck Piers
93 Mounting Floor Joists
94 Attaching Deck Planks
95 Deck Railing
96 Add a Built-In Bench

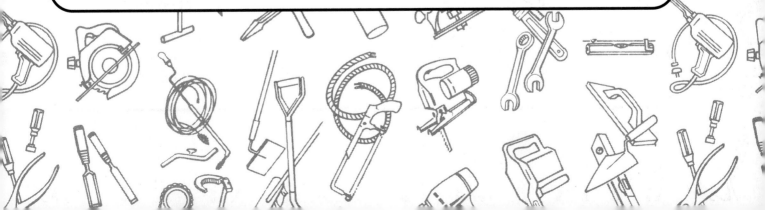

TWELVE PRIMARY HAND TOOLS) 1. HAMMERS

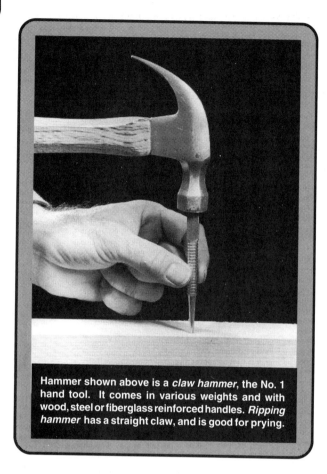

Hammer shown above is a *claw hammer*, the No. 1 hand tool. It comes in various weights and with wood, steel or fiberglass reinforced handles. *Ripping hammer* has a straight claw, and is good for prying.

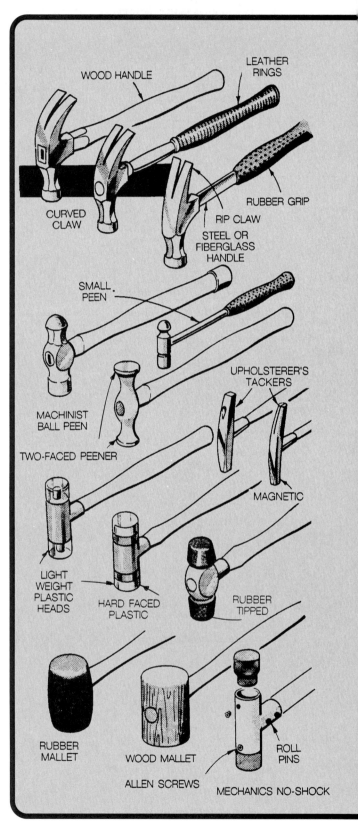

1. Hammers. The basic tool for the carpenter, as well as the homeowner, is the hammer. The *claw hammer* is used for nailing, nail pulling and dismantling work. Its face is usually bell-faced (convex) to minimize marring when a nail is driven flush to a surface. A good hammer will have a tempered rim to reduce the chances of chipping. The *ripping hammer* is equally useful. This has a comparatively straight claw and is very handy for removing floor boards and similar work requiring a prying action. Avoid cheap hammers made of cast iron; they are bound to shatter under severe strain. Hammers come in various sizes and weights. Most homeowners involved in carpentry work use a 16-ounce hammer, although many who have a muscular arm prefer a 20-ounce head. And the popularity of adding a deck has brought about a heavier hammer with a longer handle hammer, appropriately called a *deck hammer*.

Twelve essential hand tools can take care of most of your woodworking tasks. Use this comprehensive guide on how to choose and use them.

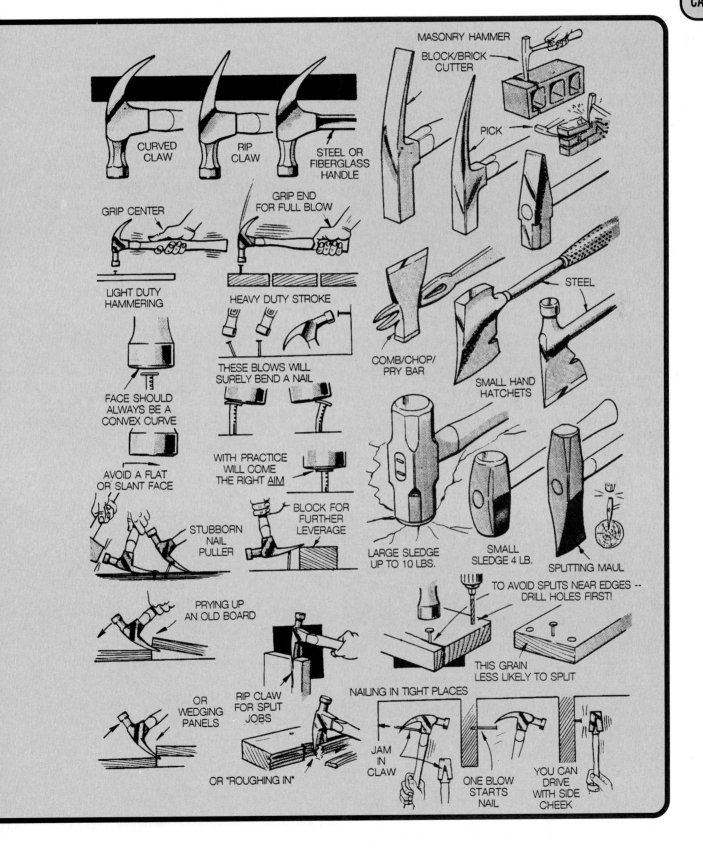

- CURVED CLAW
- RIP CLAW
- STEEL OR FIBERGLASS HANDLE
- MASONRY HAMMER
- BLOCK/BRICK CUTTER
- PICK
- GRIP CENTER
- GRIP END FOR FULL BLOW
- LIGHT DUTY HAMMERING
- HEAVY DUTY STROKE
- FACE SHOULD ALWAYS BE A CONVEX CURVE
- THESE BLOWS WILL SURELY BEND A NAIL
- COMB/CHOP/PRY BAR
- STEEL
- SMALL HAND HATCHETS
- AVOID A FLAT OR SLANT FACE
- WITH PRACTICE WILL COME THE RIGHT AIM
- STUBBORN NAIL PULLER
- BLOCK FOR FURTHER LEVERAGE
- LARGE SLEDGE UP TO 10 LBS.
- SMALL SLEDGE 4 LB.
- SPLITTING MAUL
- PRYING UP AN OLD BOARD
- TO AVOID SPLITS NEAR EDGES -- DRILL HOLES FIRST!
- THIS GRAIN LESS LIKELY TO SPLIT
- OR WEDGING PANELS
- RIP CLAW FOR SPLIT JOBS
- NAILING IN TIGHT PLACES
- OR "ROUGHING IN"
- JAM IN CLAW
- ONE BLOW STARTS NAIL
- YOU CAN DRIVE WITH SIDE CHEEK

TWELVE PRIMARY HAND TOOLS) 2. SAWS

The No. 2 hand tool, after the hammer, is the saw. Your first choice should be a crosscut saw; the next, a ripsaw.

2. Saws. Despite the fact that portable electric saws are relatively inexpensive and are used more than hand saws, there are certain jobs where a hand saw is the best tool to use. Ideally, you should have two saws—a crosscut saw for cutting across the grain and a ripsaw for cutting with the grain. The number of teeth, or points, determines the smoothness of the cut—the greater number of teeth the smoother the cut. For cutting across the grain, a saw with eight teeth per inch is adequate. Incidentally, two types of crosscut saws are now

available. The regular style and the newer 60 degree deep tooth saw that cuts faster than the conventional crosscut because the teeth are sharpened in such a manner that they cut on both the up and down stroke.

Ripsaws were originally designed to cut with the grain and have larger and fewer teeth per inch. However, the portable electric saw all but made the ripsaw obsolete because cutting lumber with the grain with a handsaw is both time consuming and strenuous.

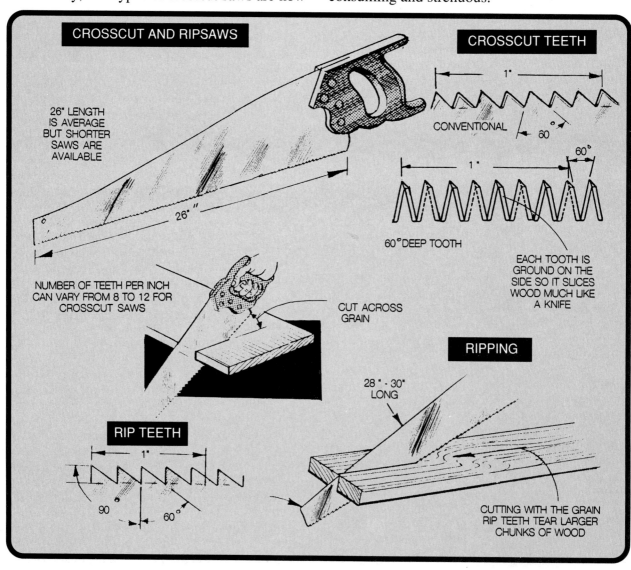

CROSSCUT AND RIPSAWS

CROSSCUT TEETH

26" LENGTH IS AVERAGE BUT SHORTER SAWS ARE AVAILABLE

26" "

CONVENTIONAL 60°

1"

60°

60° DEEP TOOTH

EACH TOOTH IS GROUND ON THE SIDE SO IT SLICES WOOD MUCH LIKE A KNIFE

NUMBER OF TEETH PER INCH CAN VARY FROM 8 TO 12 FOR CROSSCUT SAWS

CUT ACROSS GRAIN

RIPPING

28" - 30" LONG

RIP TEETH

1"

90° 60°

CUTTING WITH THE GRAIN RIP TEETH TEAR LARGER CHUNKS OF WOOD

THE HAND SAW

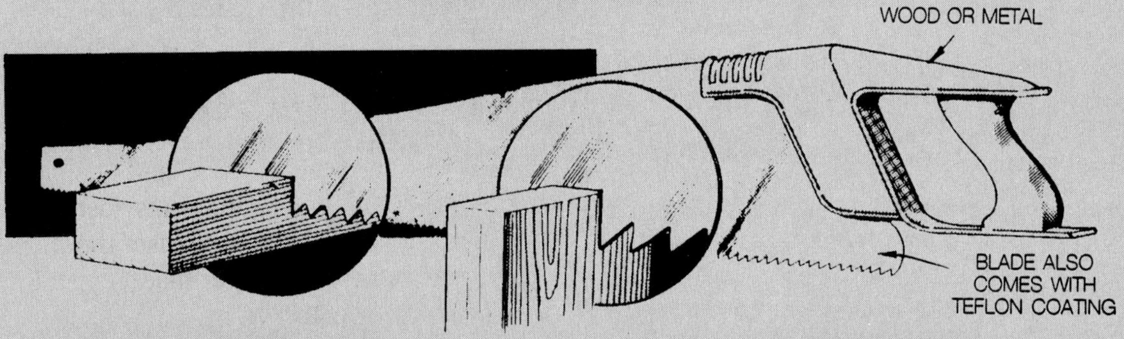

WOOD OR METAL

BLADE ALSO
COMES WITH
TEFLON COATING

CROSSCUT TEETH

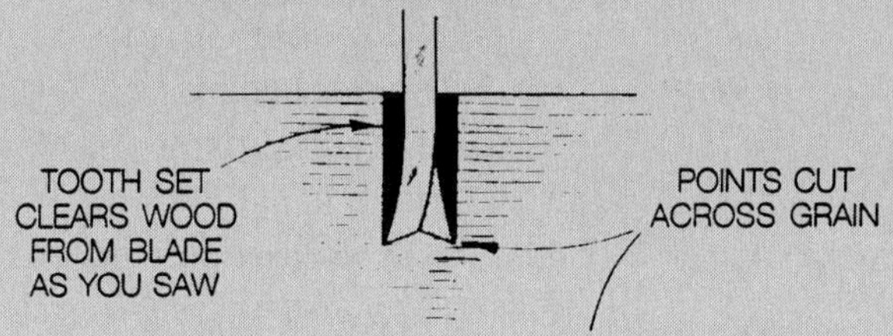

TOOTH SET
CLEARS WOOD
FROM BLADE
AS YOU SAW

POINTS CUT
ACROSS GRAIN

RIP TEETH

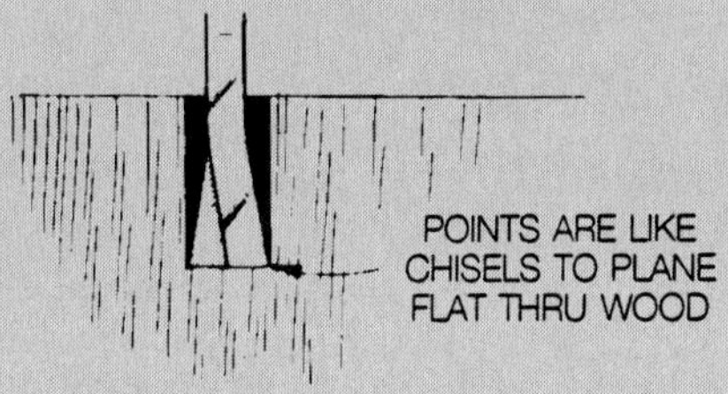

POINTS ARE LIKE
CHISELS TO PLANE
FLAT THRU WOOD

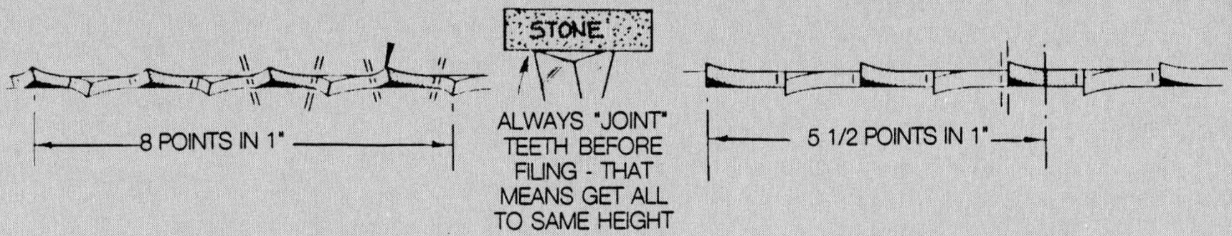

STONE

8 POINTS IN 1"

ALWAYS "JOINT"
TEETH BEFORE
FILING - THAT
MEANS GET ALL
TO SAME HEIGHT

5 1/2 POINTS IN 1"

CROSSCUT TEETH

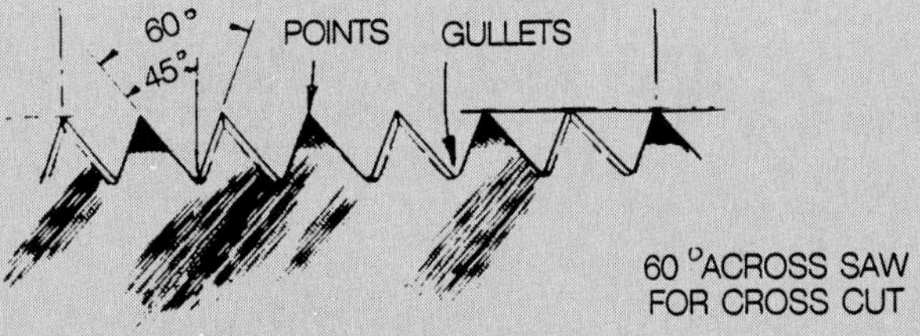

60°
45°
POINTS   GULLETS

60° ACROSS SAW
FOR CROSS CUT

RIP TEETH

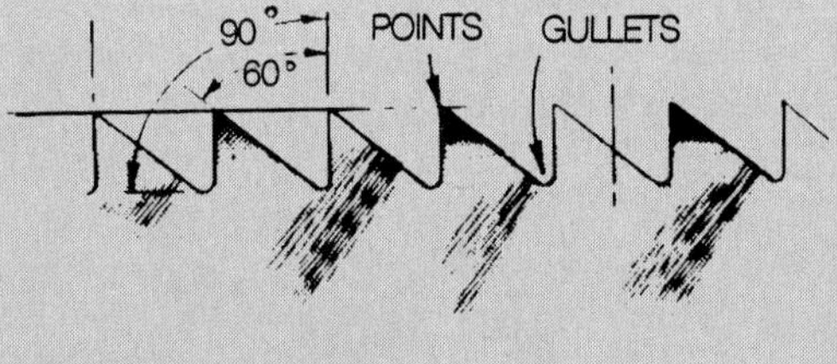

90°
60°
POINTS   GULLETS

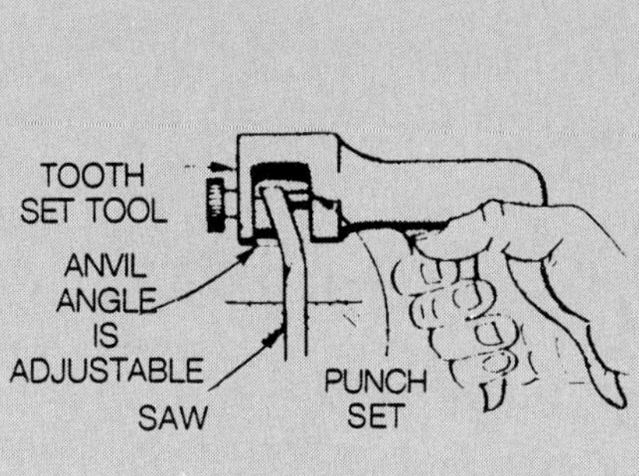

TOOTH
SET TOOL

ANVIL
ANGLE
IS
ADJUSTABLE
SAW

PUNCH
SET

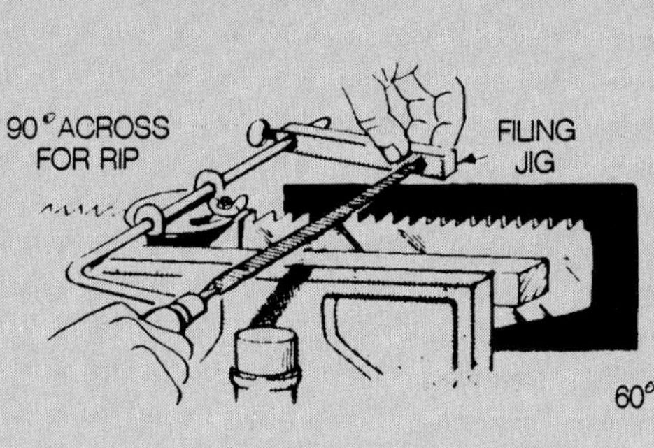

90° ACROSS
FOR RIP

FILING
JIG

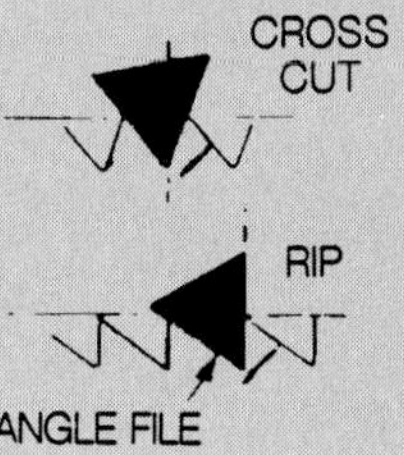

CROSS
CUT

RIP

60° TRIANGLE FILE

TWELVE PRIMARY HAND TOOLS
UTILITY SAWS

Illustrated below are some of the many different kinds of hand saws designed for special purposes

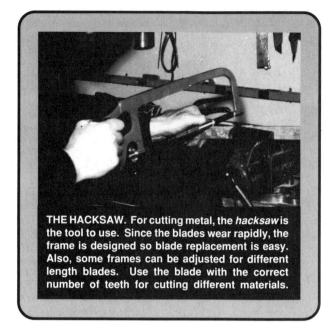

THE HACKSAW. For cutting metal, the *hacksaw* is the tool to use. Since the blades wear rapidly, the frame is designed so blade replacement is easy. Also, some frames can be adjusted for different length blades. Use the blade with the correct number of teeth for cutting different materials.

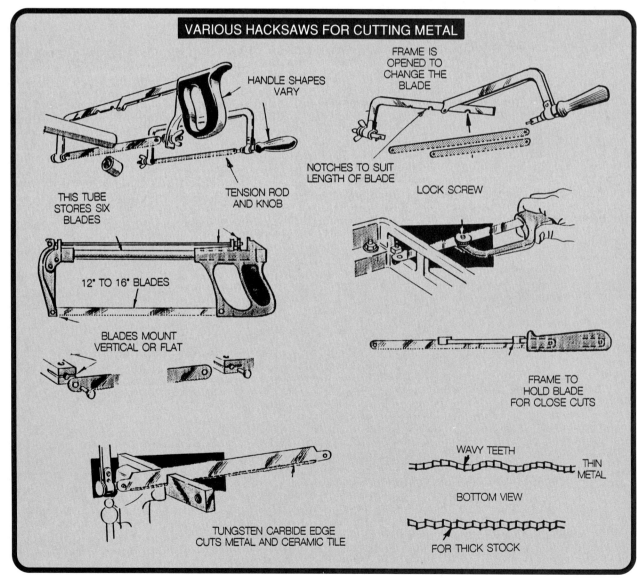

VARIOUS HACKSAWS FOR CUTTING METAL

HANDLE SHAPES VARY

FRAME IS OPENED TO CHANGE THE BLADE

NOTCHES TO SUIT LENGTH OF BLADE

THIS TUBE STORES SIX BLADES

TENSION ROD AND KNOB

LOCK SCREW

12" TO 16" BLADES

BLADES MOUNT VERTICAL OR FLAT

FRAME TO HOLD BLADE FOR CLOSE CUTS

TUNGSTEN CARBIDE EDGE CUTS METAL AND CERAMIC TILE

WAVY TEETH
THIN METAL

BOTTOM VIEW

FOR THICK STOCK

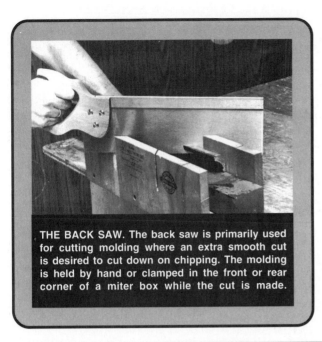

THE BACK SAW. The back saw is primarily used for cutting molding where an extra smooth cut is desired to cut down on chipping. The molding is held by hand or clamped in the front or rear corner of a miter box while the cut is made.

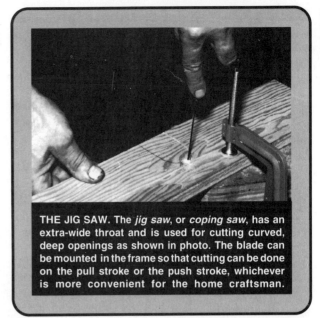

THE JIG SAW. The *jig saw*, or *coping saw*, has an extra-wide throat and is used for cutting curved, deep openings as shown in photo. The blade can be mounted in the frame so that cutting can be done on the pull stroke or the push stroke, whichever is more convenient for the home craftsman.

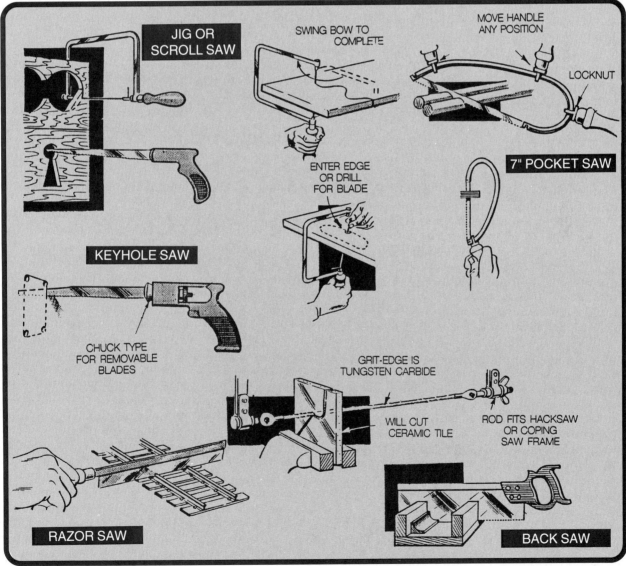

JIG OR SCROLL SAW

SWING BOW TO COMPLETE

MOVE HANDLE ANY POSITION

LOCKNUT

ENTER EDGE OR DRILL FOR BLADE

7" POCKET SAW

KEYHOLE SAW

CHUCK TYPE FOR REMOVABLE BLADES

GRIT-EDGE IS TUNGSTEN CARBIDE

WILL CUT CERAMIC TILE

ROD FITS HACKSAW OR COPING SAW FRAME

RAZOR SAW

BACK SAW

TWELVE PRIMARY HAND TOOLS **3. SCREWDRIVERS**

No longer is the screwdriver a simple tool. Many different types are available for driving the Phillips, Hex, Clutch, Torx and Square head screws.

3. Screwdrivers. Despite the fact that the cordless screwdriver with a wide assortment of interchangeable bits — Phillips, Hex, Clutch, Square, Torx — along with different size blade bits for slotted screws, has virtually replaced the hand-driven screwdriver, the well-equipped workshop has a wide selection of screwdrivers for use where the cordless screwdriver is impractical. Here is just a small sampling of what is available from your local hardware store, home center, etc.

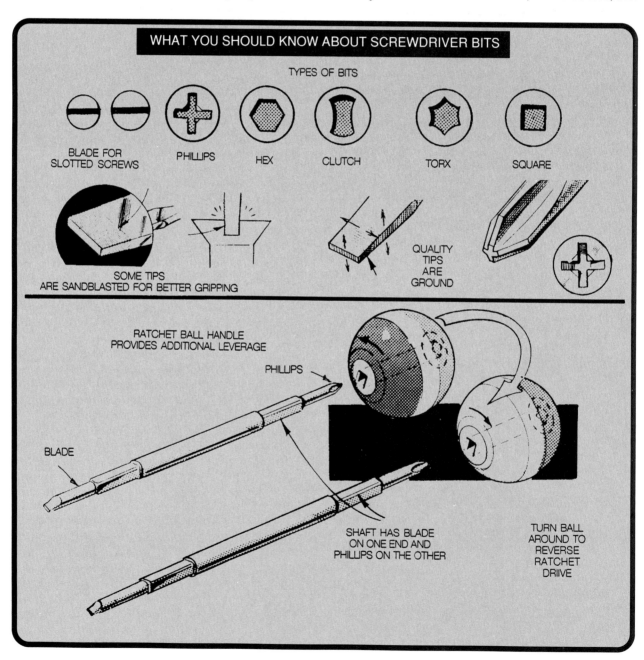

WHAT YOU SHOULD KNOW ABOUT SCREWDRIVER BITS

TYPES OF BITS

BLADE FOR SLOTTED SCREWS   PHILLIPS   HEX   CLUTCH   TORX   SQUARE

SOME TIPS ARE SANDBLASTED FOR BETTER GRIPPING

QUALITY TIPS ARE GROUND

RATCHET BALL HANDLE PROVIDES ADDITIONAL LEVERAGE

PHILLIPS

BLADE

SHAFT HAS BLADE ON ONE END AND PHILLIPS ON THE OTHER

TURN BALL AROUND TO REVERSE RATCHET DRIIVE

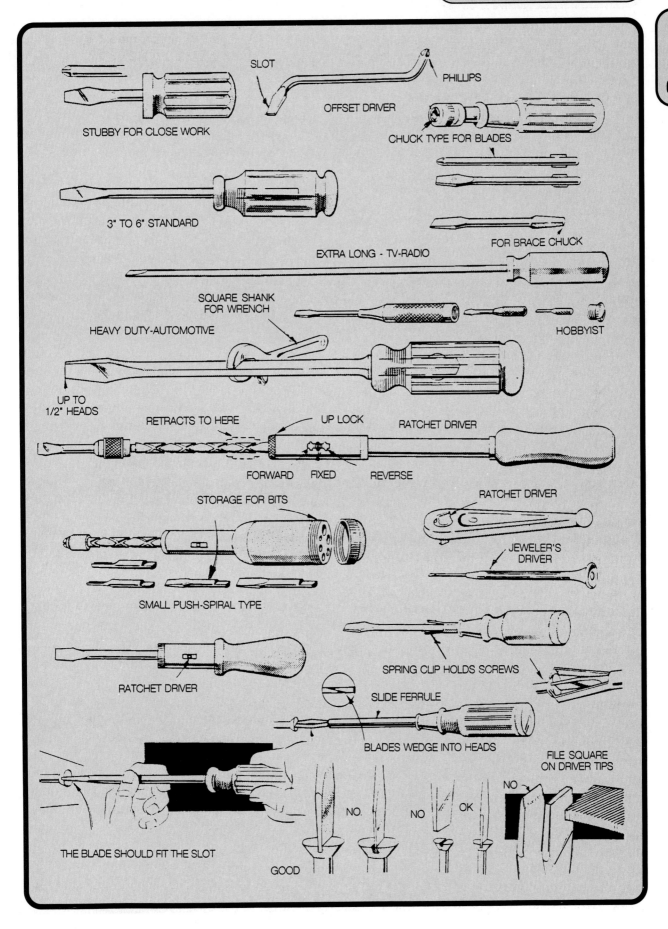

STUBBY FOR CLOSE WORK

SLOT

PHILLIPS

OFFSET DRIVER

CHUCK TYPE FOR BLADES

3" TO 6" STANDARD

FOR BRACE CHUCK

EXTRA LONG - TV-RADIO

SQUARE SHANK
FOR WRENCH

HEAVY DUTY-AUTOMOTIVE

HOBBYIST

UP TO
1/2" HEADS

RETRACTS TO HERE

UP LOCK

RATCHET DRIVER

FORWARD   FIXED   REVERSE

STORAGE FOR BITS

RATCHET DRIVER

JEWELER'S
DRIVER

SMALL PUSH-SPIRAL TYPE

RATCHET DRIVER

SPRING CLIP HOLDS SCREWS

SLIDE FERRULE

BLADES WEDGE INTO HEADS

FILE SQUARE
ON DRIVER TIPS

NO

THE BLADE SHOULD FIT THE SLOT

NO.   NO   OK

GOOD

4. PLANES

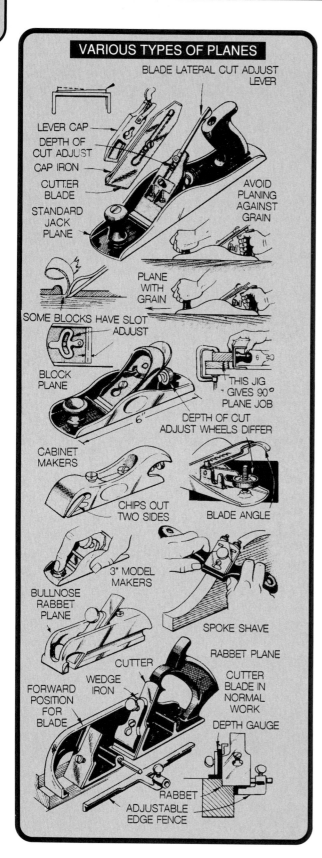

VARIOUS TYPES OF PLANES

BLADE LATERAL CUT ADJUST LEVER

LEVER CAP

DEPTH OF CUT ADJUST

CAP IRON

CUTTER BLADE

STANDARD JACK PLANE

AVOID PLANING AGAINST GRAIN

PLANE WITH GRAIN

SOME BLOCKS HAVE SLOT ADJUST

BLOCK PLANE

THIS JIG GIVES 90° PLANE JOB

6"

DEPTH OF CUT ADJUST WHEELS DIFFER

CABINET MAKERS

CHIPS OUT TWO SIDES

BLADE ANGLE

3" MODEL MAKERS

BULLNOSE RABBET PLANE

SPOKE SHAVE

RABBET PLANE

CUTTER

WEDGE IRON

FORWARD POSITION FOR BLADE

CUTTER BLADE IN NORMAL WORK

DEPTH GAUGE

RABBET

ADJUSTABLE EDGE FENCE

4. **Planes**. Planes are used to trim wood to an exact size, to bevel edges, to smooth out irregularities and even to make moldings. This is an essential tool if you are building furniture. A major use in home building is to trim a door to fit the jamb. The *block plane* is about 6 inches long, is always held in one hand (while the other hand is used to steady the work), and has a blade mounted at a shallow angle so that it can cut across the grain without splitting the wood. Next in size comes the *bench plane,* about 10 inches long (usually the first choice of the do-it-yourselfer); then the *jack plane*, about 14 inches in length; and finally the *jointer plane,* 18 to 22 inches in length. In addition, there are many specialty planes used to cut rabbets and grooves in boards. There is even a tiny plane suitable for the model-maker called a *trimming plane*. It has a narrow blade, that is 1 inch in width.

When planing an edge, tilt the plane at an angle on the surface to develop a slicing action rather than a straight cut. Also, always plane with the grain.

TWELVE PRIMARY HAND TOOLS 5. SQUARES

5. **Squares** come in many sizes and types. The most common, and the most useful for the handyman, is the *combination square*. The combination square, which can also be used as a ruler and a level, has an overall length of 12 inches, a built-in scratch awl, and both 45° and 90° settings. The blade is grooved so that it can be set and locked at any desired length to measure and indicate depth. The *try square* is used to determine exact right angles and the "levelness" of work. The *miter square* is similar to the try square, but its handle at the point where it meets the blade is cut at a 45° angle for measuring, marking and testing 45° miter joints. One of the most important squares for the carpenter and builder is the *rafter or roofing square*. This is a steel square with one leg 24 inches long and the other leg (the tongue) 16 inches long. It is an extremely useful tool for marking rafter cuts according to roof pitch, determining brace length between two points, finding the center of a circle, laying off angles, and performing other calculations in building construction.

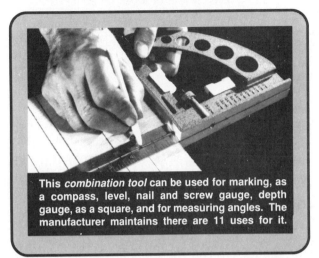

This *combination tool* can be used for marking, as a compass, level, nail and screw gauge, depth gauge, as a square, and for measuring angles. The manufacturer maintains there are 11 uses for it.

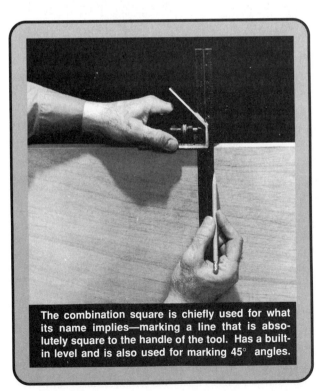

The combination square is chiefly used for what its name implies—marking a line that is absolutely square to the handle of the tool. Has a built-in level and is also used for marking 45° angles.

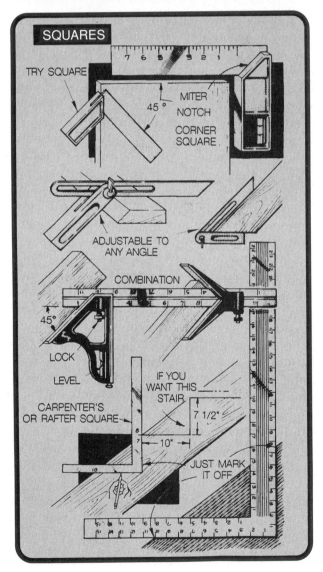

SQUARES

TRY SQUARE

MITER NOTCH

CORNER SQUARE

45°

ADJUSTABLE TO ANY ANGLE

COMBINATION

45°

LOCK

LEVEL

CARPENTER'S OR RAFTER SQUARE

IF YOU WANT THIS STAIR

7 1/2"

10"

JUST MARK IT OFF

TWELVE PRIMARY HAND TOOLS 6. RULERS

TYPES OF RULERS

WHEN WORKING ALONE, WOOD FOLDING RULE IS BEST FOR LONG SPANS

HERE BRASS EXTENSION SLIDES OUT FOR

INSIDE INCHES

STEEL 8' TO 16' POCKET TAPE

OUTSIDE MEASURE

SELF-ADJUST END CLIP

INSIDE

12"

2" ADD.

20 FT. TAPE HAS LOCK

POCKET CLIP

NYLON CLAMP

UNLOCK

STUD MARK EVERY 16"

INCHES UP TO 240"

ONE FOOT 2" UP TO 19 FT. 11"

3/4"

MM 10 20 30 40 50

INCHES

12 FT.- 365 METERS

THIS TAPE GIVES INCHES-METRIC EQUIVALENTS

6. **Rulers.** A good, all purpose measuring device is the *flexible steel tape*. Purchase one at least 10 feet long and make sure that the right angle clip at the end is self-adjusting for inside as well as outside measurements. *Folding wooden rules,* extend to 6 or 8 feet. Some have a sliding brass extension for determining inside measurements; whereas some are marked off at 16-inch intervals to expedite stud placement. The advantage of the folding *zig-zag ruler* is that it is stiff enough to measure across horizontal openings without collapsing.

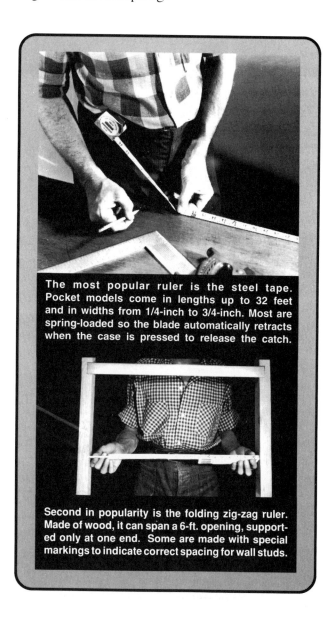

The most popular ruler is the steel tape. Pocket models come in lengths up to 32 feet and in widths from 1/4-inch to 3/4-inch. Most are spring-loaded so the blade automatically retracts when the case is pressed to release the catch.

Second in popularity is the folding zig-zag ruler. Made of wood, it can span a 6-ft. opening, supported only at one end. Some are made with special markings to indicate correct spacing for wall studs.

TWELVE PRIMARY HAND TOOLS 7. LEVELS

7. Levels come in dozens of different types and sizes. A good level for the do-it-yourselfer is the 24-inch *carpenter's level*. It has at least two vials. One vial determines the true horizontal level and the other determines the "uprightness" (plumb) of a vertical member. Other levels useful for the carpenter and handyman are the *torpedo level* which is about 9 inches long: the *line level* (suspended on a string to span a long distance); and the *pocket level*, usually about 4 inches long and hexagonal in cross section. It clips to your pocket.

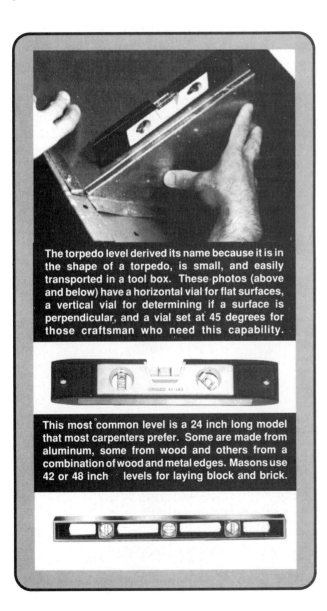

The torpedo level derived its name because it is in the shape of a torpedo, is small, and easily transported in a tool box. These photos (above and below) have a horizontal vial for flat surfaces, a vertical vial for determining if a surface is perpendicular, and a vial set at 45 degrees for those craftsman who need this capability.

This most common level is a 24 inch long model that most carpenters prefer. Some are made from aluminum, some from wood and others from a combination of wood and metal edges. Masons use 42 or 48 inch levels for laying block and brick.

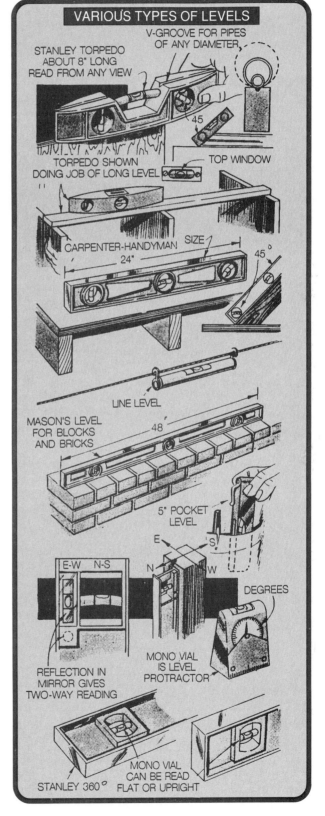

VARIOUS TYPES OF LEVELS

STANLEY TORPEDO ABOUT 8" LONG READ FROM ANY VIEW

V-GROOVE FOR PIPES OF ANY DIAMETER

45

TORPEDO SHOWN DOING JOB OF LONG LEVEL

TOP WINDOW

CARPENTER-HANDYMAN SIZE 24"

45°

LINE LEVEL

MASON'S LEVEL FOR BLOCKS AND BRICKS

48"

5" POCKET LEVEL

E-W   N-S

E   S

N   W

DEGREES

REFLECTION IN MIRROR GIVES TWO-WAY READING

MONO VIAL IS LEVEL PROTRACTOR

STANLEY 360°

MONO VIAL CAN BE READ FLAT OR UPRIGHT

Use a wood chisel to clean out the wood between two parallel saw cuts. The beveled side of the chisel should always face up. Use one hand to guide the chisel and other hand for driving it.

8.   Wood Chisels. A set of chisels is essential, and far more practical than purchasing them individually. A 1/4-, 1/2- 3/4- and l-inch chisel will take care of most carpentry needs. Always purchase chisels in a plastic wrap-up case so that their edges will be protected during storage. Do not confuse *"wood" chisels* with *"cold" chisels.* Wood chisels have their cutting edge ground from one side, while cold chisels have their edge ground from both sides to form a V. Cold chisels are used for cutting metal and chipping concrete, though there are also all-steel chisels made for woodworking. Chisels should be sharp and well-honed before use. It is the dull tool which requires unnecessary force that causes accidents.

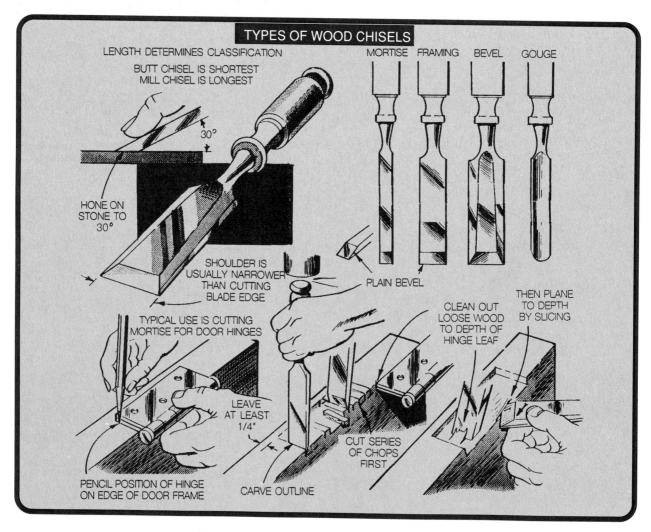

TYPES OF WOOD CHISELS

LENGTH DETERMINES CLASSIFICATION

BUTT CHISEL IS SHORTEST
MILL CHISEL IS LONGEST

MORTISE   FRAMING   BEVEL   GOUGE

30°

HONE ON STONE TO 30°

SHOULDER IS USUALLY NARROWER THAN CUTTING BLADE EDGE

PLAIN BEVEL

TYPICAL USE IS CUTTING MORTISE FOR DOOR HINGES

LEAVE AT LEAST 1/4"

CLEAN OUT LOOSE WOOD TO DEPTH OF HINGE LEAF

THEN PLANE TO DEPTH BY SLICING

CUT SERIES OF CHOPS FIRST

PENCIL POSITION OF HINGE ON EDGE OF DOOR FRAME

CARVE OUTLINE

TWELVE PRIMARY HAND TOOLS) **9. DRILLS**

9. **H**and **Drills** and **Braces**. The electric drill, and more recently the cordless drill-driver, has to a large extent replaced the *hand drill* and the *carpenter's brace*. However, the latter two tools are still useful. Their chief advantage, of course, is the absence of need for an electric cord. Another advantage of the carpenter's brace is the tremendous torque which its wide, 10- to 12-inch sweep can generate. Also used for drilling delicate holes is the *push drill*. It is much favored by professional carpenters and cabinet makers and is used primarily to drill small holes, with a maximum diameter of 11/64-inch. A hollow handle stores the bits. Pushing on the handle drives the bit into the work and a spring forces the handle back for the next stroke.

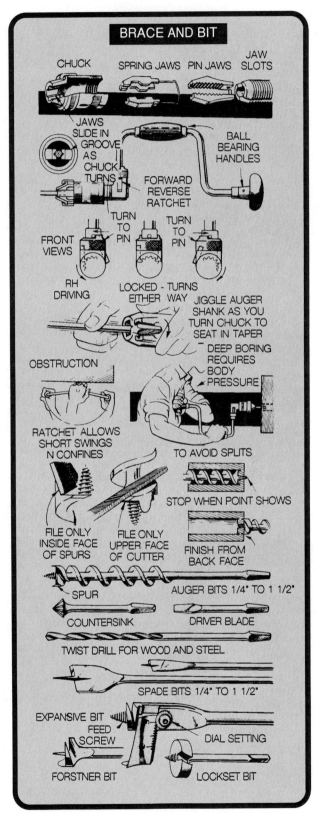

BRACE AND BIT

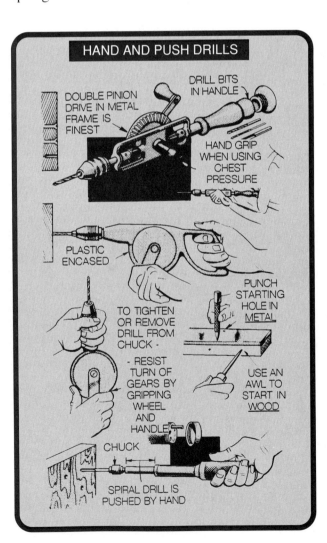

HAND AND PUSH DRILLS

TWELVE PRIMARY HAND TOOLS 10. MITER BOXES

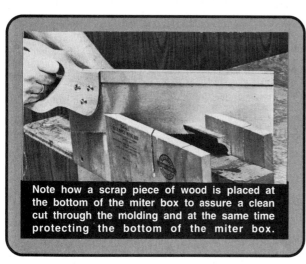

Note how a scrap piece of wood is placed at the bottom of the miter box to assure a clean cut through the molding and at the same time protecting the bottom of the miter box.

10. Miter Box. The *miter box*, always used with a *fine tooth backsaw* to keep chipping at a minimum, is primarily used for cutting trim or molding. Clamp the material firmly in place and start with a short, slow stroke. Once the cut is started you can make longer strokes until the saw blade hits the bottom of the box. If you need a 45° cut, slide the saw in the 45° slot all miter boxes have. The miter box is also ideal for holding rigid plastic tubing where a square cut is also necessary. Maple or molded plastic miter boxes are very inexpensive but you can also spend upwards of fifty dollars for a combination miter table and saw, as illustrated.

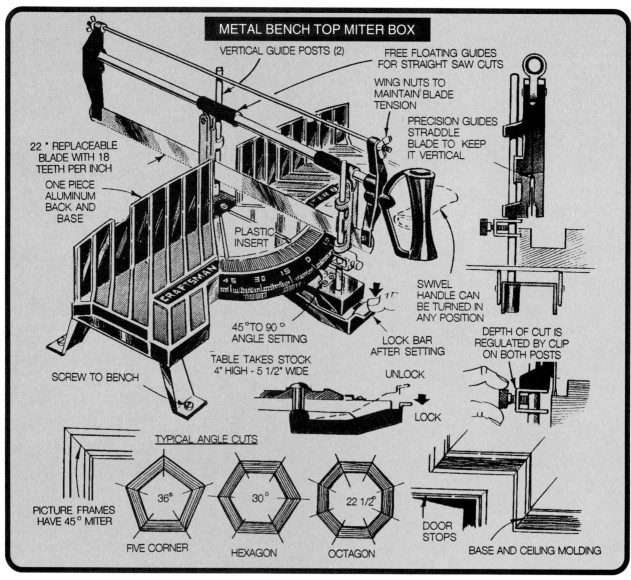

METAL BENCH TOP MITER BOX

VERTICAL GUIDE POSTS (2)

FREE FLOATING GUIDES FOR STRAIGHT SAW CUTS

WING NUTS TO MAINTAIN BLADE TENSION

PRECISION GUIDES STRADDLE BLADE TO KEEP IT VERTICAL

22" REPLACEABLE BLADE WITH 18 TEETH PER INCH

ONE PIECE ALUMINUM BACK AND BASE

PLASTIC INSERT

SWIVEL HANDLE CAN BE TURNED IN ANY POSITION

45° TO 90° ANGLE SETTING

TABLE TAKES STOCK 4" HIGH - 5 1/2" WIDE

LOCK BAR AFTER SETTING

DEPTH OF CUT IS REGULATED BY CLIP ON BOTH POSTS

SCREW TO BENCH

UNLOCK

LOCK

TYPICAL ANGLE CUTS

PICTURE FRAMES HAVE 45° MITER

36°

FIVE CORNER

30°

HEXAGON

22 1/2°

OCTAGON

DOOR STOPS

BASE AND CEILING MOLDING

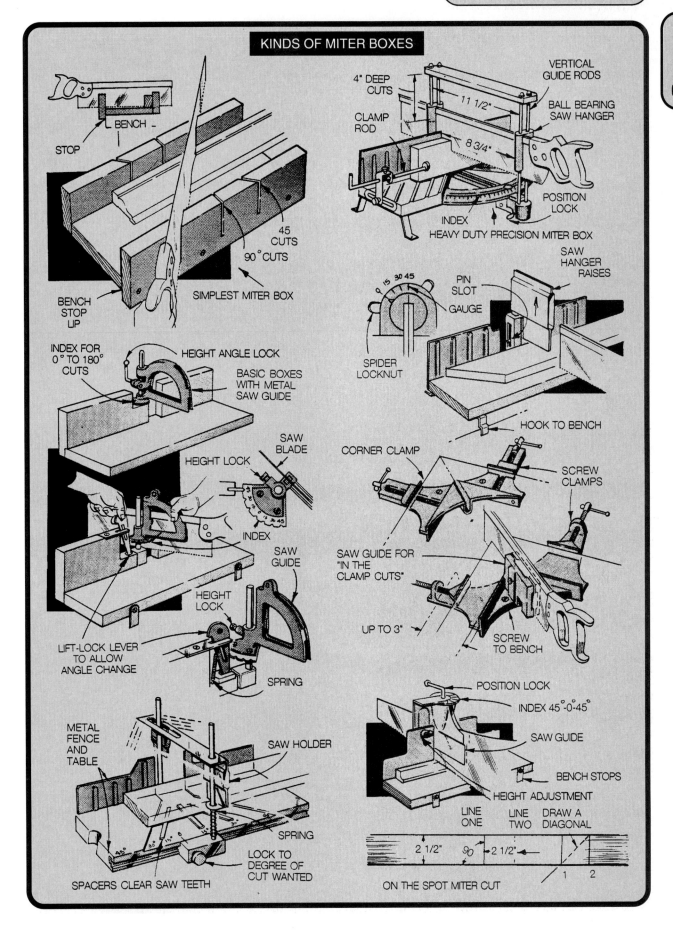

KINDS OF MITER BOXES

STOP

BENCH

45 CUTS

90° CUTS

BENCH STOP LIP

SIMPLEST MITER BOX

4" DEEP CUTS

VERTICAL GUIDE RODS

11 1/2"

CLAMP ROD

BALL BEARING SAW HANGER

8 3/4"

POSITION LOCK

INDEX

HEAVY DUTY PRECISION MITER BOX

INDEX FOR 0° TO 180° CUTS

HEIGHT ANGLE LOCK

BASIC BOXES WITH METAL SAW GUIDE

SAW BLADE

HEIGHT LOCK

INDEX

SAW GUIDE

HEIGHT LOCK

LIFT-LOCK LEVER TO ALLOW ANGLE CHANGE

SPRING

15 30 45

PIN SLOT

GAUGE

SAW HANGER RAISES

SPIDER LOCKNUT

HOOK TO BENCH

CORNER CLAMP

SCREW CLAMPS

SAW GUIDE FOR "IN THE CLAMP CUTS"

UP TO 3"

SCREW TO BENCH

METAL FENCE AND TABLE

SAW HOLDER

SPRING

LOCK TO DEGREE OF CUT WANTED

SPACERS CLEAR SAW TEETH

POSITION LOCK

INDEX 45°-0-45°

SAW GUIDE

BENCH STOPS

HEIGHT ADJUSTMENT

LINE ONE

LINE TWO

DRAW A DIAGONAL

2 1/2"

90

2 1/2"

1

2

ON THE SPOT MITER CUT

11. CLAMPS

11. Clamps. *Clamps* are a very necessary tool for holding work in position while sawing, drilling, sanding, etc. You have a large variety of clamps to choose from, each designed for a specific use. The *C-clamp*, appropriately named because it looks like the letter "C" (although the famous photographer, Simon Nathan, refers to it as a "U" clamp because he holds it in the horizontal position). Illustrated below are the major clamps use in a shop.

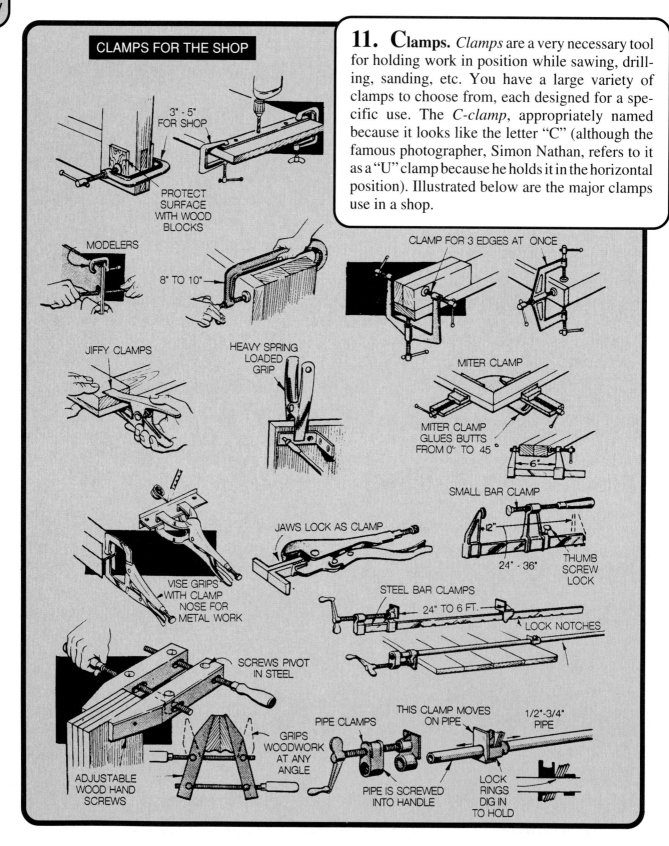

CLAMPS FOR THE SHOP

3" - 5" FOR SHOP

PROTECT SURFACE WITH WOOD BLOCKS

MODELERS

8" TO 10"

CLAMP FOR 3 EDGES AT ONCE

JIFFY CLAMPS

HEAVY SPRING LOADED GRIP

MITER CLAMP

MITER CLAMP GLUES BUTTS FROM 0° TO 45°

6"

SMALL BAR CLAMP

12"

24" - 36"

THUMB SCREW LOCK

JAWS LOCK AS CLAMP

VISE GRIPS WITH CLAMP NOSE FOR METAL WORK

STEEL BAR CLAMPS

24" TO 6 FT.

LOCK NOTCHES

SCREWS PIVOT IN STEEL

GRIPS WOODWORK AT ANY ANGLE

THIS CLAMP MOVES ON PIPE

1/2"-3/4" PIPE

ADJUSTABLE WOOD HAND SCREWS

PIPE CLAMPS

PIPE IS SCREWED INTO HANDLE

LOCK RINGS DIG IN TO HOLD

TWELVE PRIMARY HAND TOOLS **VISES**

12. Vises. One of the most important elements of a workbench is a *vise*, either one designed especially for holding wood or a metal one that can hold either metal or wood if you protect the jaws from denting the wood by inserting a piece of wood between the wood and the jaws of the vise. The vise that is permanently mounted on the corner of the workbench is best, although some clamp on vises do the job. The size of the vise is designated by its opening.

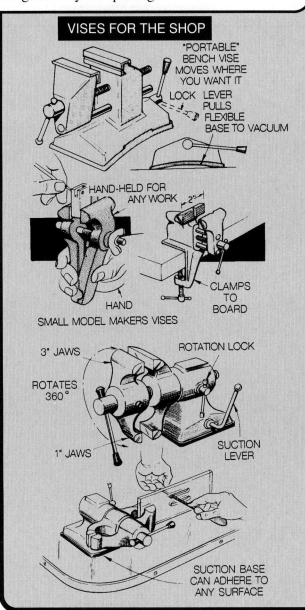

VISES FOR THE SHOP

"PORTABLE" BENCH VISE MOVES WHERE YOU WANT IT

LOCK LEVER PULLS FLEXIBLE BASE TO VACUUM

HAND-HELD FOR ANY WORK

CLAMPS TO BOARD

HAND

SMALL MODEL MAKERS VISES

3" JAWS

ROTATION LOCK

ROTATES 360°

1" JAWS

SUCTION LEVER

SUCTION BASE CAN ADHERE TO ANY SURFACE

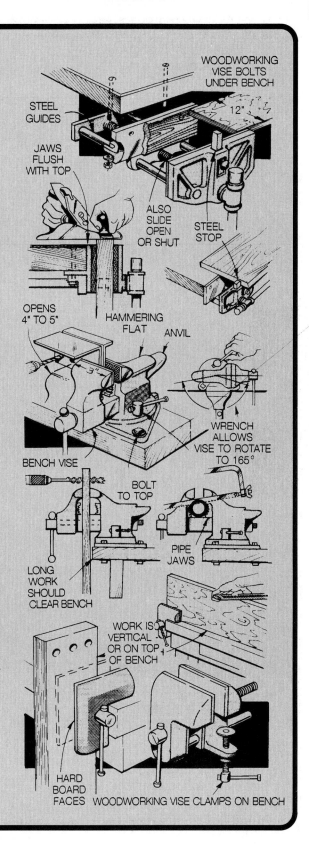

WOODWORKING VISE BOLTS UNDER BENCH

STEEL GUIDES

JAWS FLUSH WITH TOP

12"

ALSO SLIDE OPEN OR SHUT

STEEL STOP

OPENS 4" TO 5"

HAMMERING FLAT

ANVIL

BENCH VISE

WRENCH ALLOWS VISE TO ROTATE TO 165°

BOLT TO TOP

LONG WORK SHOULD CLEAR BENCH

PIPE JAWS

WORK IS VERTICAL OR ON TOP OF BENCH

HARD BOARD FACES

WOODWORKING VISE CLAMPS ON BENCH

MISCELLANEOUS HAND TOOLS

There are literally hundreds and hundreds of small hand tools, many of them designed expressly to do a specific job. Some are tremendous time-savers — and some do a specific job better than any other combination of tools. Browse through your local hardware store or home centers and also scan through the many specialty tool catalogues aimed at the various professions — electricians, plumbers, masons, carpenters, machinists, etc. You will be intrigued.

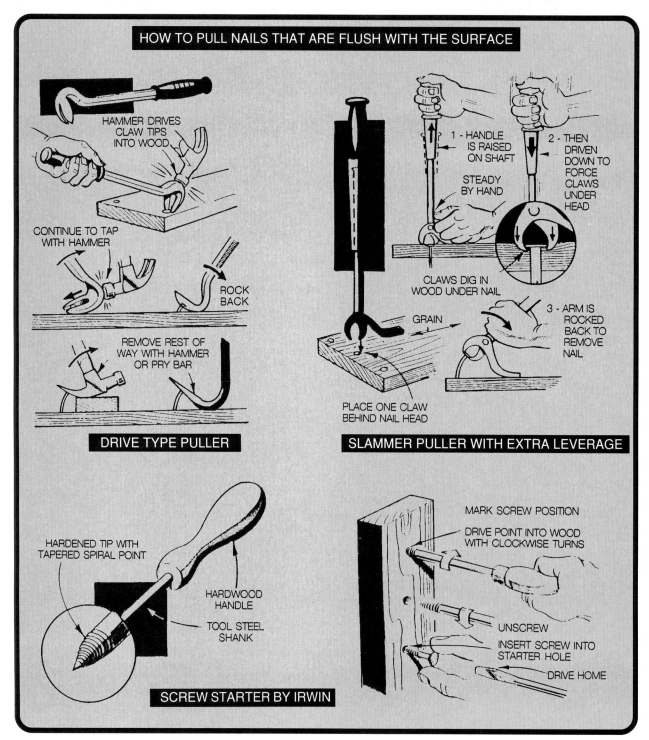

HOW TO PULL NAILS THAT ARE FLUSH WITH THE SURFACE

HAMMER DRIVES CLAW TIPS INTO WOOD

CONTINUE TO TAP WITH HAMMER

ROCK BACK

REMOVE REST OF WAY WITH HAMMER OR PRY BAR

DRIVE TYPE PULLER

1 - HANDLE IS RAISED ON SHAFT

STEADY BY HAND

2 - THEN DRIVEN DOWN TO FORCE CLAWS UNDER HEAD

CLAWS DIG IN WOOD UNDER NAIL

GRAIN

3 - ARM IS ROCKED BACK TO REMOVE NAIL

PLACE ONE CLAW BEHIND NAIL HEAD

SLAMMER PULLER WITH EXTRA LEVERAGE

HARDENED TIP WITH TAPERED SPIRAL POINT

HARDWOOD HANDLE

TOOL STEEL SHANK

SCREW STARTER BY IRWIN

MARK SCREW POSITION

DRIVE POINT INTO WOOD WITH CLOCKWISE TURNS

UNSCREW

INSERT SCREW INTO STARTER HOLE

DRIVE HOME

TYPES OF PLIERS AND CUTTERS

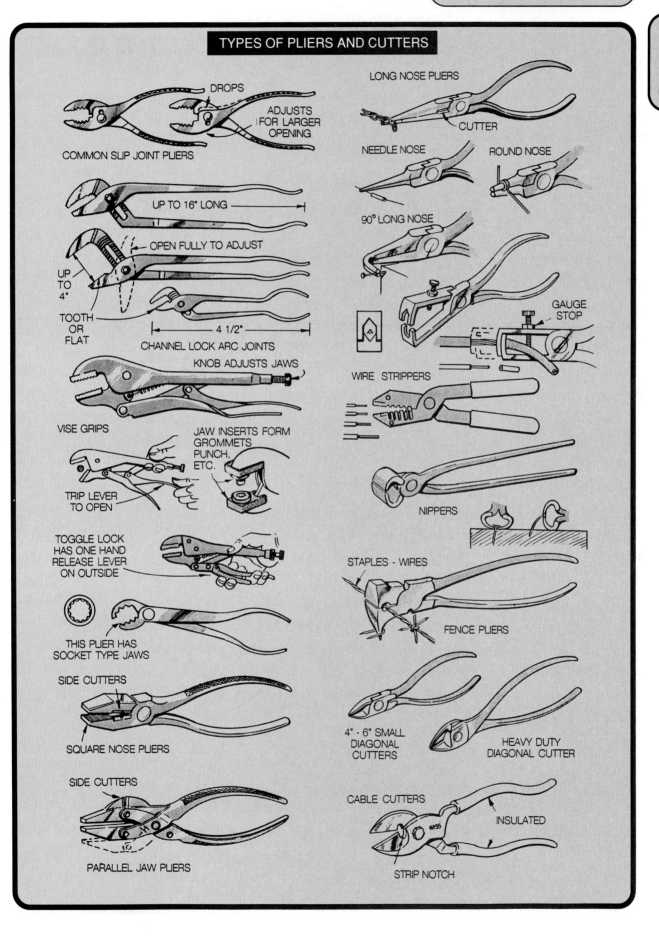

COMMON SLIP JOINT PLIERS

DROPS

ADJUSTS FOR LARGER OPENING

UP TO 16" LONG

OPEN FULLY TO ADJUST

UP TO 4"

TOOTH OR FLAT

4 1/2"

CHANNEL LOCK ARC JOINTS

KNOB ADJUSTS JAWS

VISE GRIPS

TRIP LEVER TO OPEN

JAW INSERTS FORM GROMMETS PUNCH, ETC.

TOGGLE LOCK HAS ONE HAND RELEASE LEVER ON OUTSIDE

THIS PLIER HAS SOCKET TYPE JAWS

SIDE CUTTERS

SQUARE NOSE PLIERS

SIDE CUTTERS

PARALLEL JAW PLIERS

LONG NOSE PLIERS

CUTTER

NEEDLE NOSE

ROUND NOSE

90° LONG NOSE

GAUGE STOP

WIRE STRIPPERS

NIPPERS

STAPLES - WIRES

FENCE PLIERS

4" - 6" SMALL DIAGONAL CUTTERS

HEAVY DUTY DIAGONAL CUTTER

CABLE CUTTERS

INSULATED

STRIP NOTCH

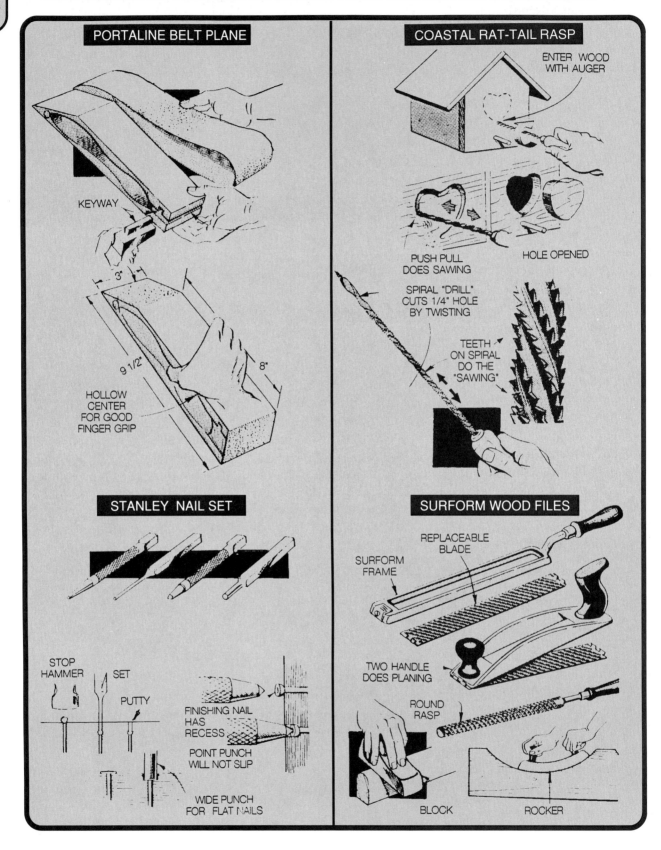

MORE MISCELLANEOUS HAND TOOLS

PORTALINE BELT PLANE

KEYWAY

3"

9 1/2"

8"

HOLLOW CENTER FOR GOOD FINGER GRIP

STANLEY NAIL SET

STOP HAMMER

SET

PUTTY

FINISHING NAIL HAS RECESS

POINT PUNCH WILL NOT SLIP

WIDE PUNCH FOR FLAT NAILS

COASTAL RAT-TAIL RASP

ENTER WOOD WITH AUGER

PUSH PULL DOES SAWING

HOLE OPENED

SPIRAL "DRILL" CUTS 1/4" HOLE BY TWISTING

TEETH ON SPIRAL DO THE "SAWING"

SURFORM WOOD FILES

REPLACEABLE BLADE

SURFORM FRAME

TWO HANDLE DOES PLANING

ROUND RASP

BLOCK

ROCKER

29

SCRAPERS AND PUTTY KNIVES

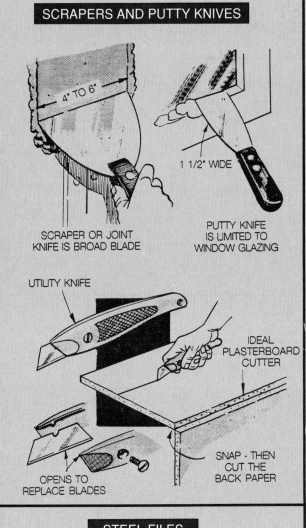

4" TO 6"

1 1/2" WIDE

SCRAPER OR JOINT KNIFE IS BROAD BLADE

PUTTY KNIFE IS LIMITED TO WINDOW GLAZING

UTILITY KNIFE

IDEAL PLASTERBOARD CUTTER

SNAP - THEN CUT THE BACK PAPER

OPENS TO REPLACE BLADES

WRECKING BARS

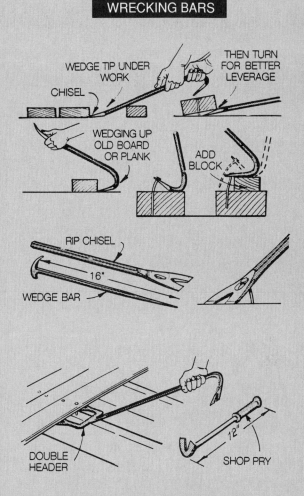

WEDGE TIP UNDER WORK

CHISEL

THEN TURN FOR BETTER LEVERAGE

WEDGING UP OLD BOARD OR PLANK

ADD BLOCK

RIP CHISEL

16"

WEDGE BAR

DOUBLE HEADER

12"

SHOP PRY

STEEL FILES

NEEDLE FILES

ROUND

FLAT

SEMI-ROUND

TRIANGULAR

SMOOTH END

WOOD RASP

FAST REMOVAL

MARKING GAUGE

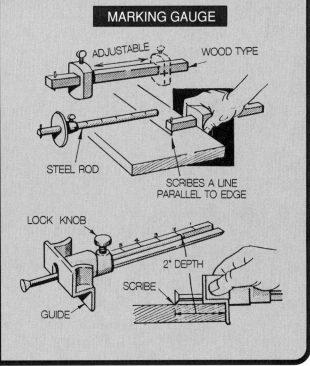

ADJUSTABLE

WOOD TYPE

STEEL ROD

SCRIBES A LINE PARALLEL TO EDGE

LOCK KNOB

2" DEPTH

SCRIBE

GUIDE

PORTABLE POWER TOOLS THE DRILL

The major portable power tools — drills, saws, sanders and planes — usually do a job better and faster than their hand counterparts.

Drills are constantly being improved. This 3/8"
B & D tool is variable speed, is reversible and has a
keyless chuck. The built-in level. in the top is very
handy when drilling vertical and horizontal holes.

The *portable electric drill* is still one of the tools most used by homeowners and professionals alike. Drills are usually classified by the diameter of the drill bit the chuck can hold. The quarter-inch drill can chuck this diameter drill and all smaller bits. The quarter-inch drill is still exceedingly popular and the lowest in cost, but the three-eighth inch drill is rapidly gaining in popularity. For example, a drill that draws 5 amps is more powerful than one which draws 3 amps. Now popular is a more descriptive designation of power, is to give the drill a *horsepower rating*, which some manufacturers do because the consumer can relate better to horsepower than to amperage.

The portable electrical drill produced years ago turned at the same revolutions per minute meaning they just had one speed. The *variable speed drill* is the drill of choice because you can regulate the speed and therefore do a better drilling job in that the material you are drilling and the drill bit size determine the speed you should select. For instance, drilling metal requires a slower speed than drilling wood. In fact, if you drill steel with

a one-speed drill the chances are the tremendous friction created by the drill will burn out your drill bit.

The ability to regulate speed by merely regulating the pressure of the trigger also gives you another very important capability — you can drive screws. Most variable speed drills are also reversible, which is an especially fine feature when removing screws. Incidentally, with the development of a wide selection of screws — some of which do not require a pilot hole — the screw is rapidly replacing the nail for many projects.

All portable electric drills used to have a *"keyed chuck"* to hold the drill bit in place. Now the *"keyless chuck"* is making its appearance. No longer must you hunt around for the chuck key; with the keyless chuck drill merely grasp the chuck, which usually has a rubberized exterior for better gripping and turning, and turn to securely hold the bit!

The popularity of the portable electric drill resulted in the development of a number of accessories to perform other jobs such as sanding, polishing, buffing, grinding and rotary filing; any function that calls for rotary action accessories, such as belt sanding are available as drill attachments.

Our recommendation for the homeowner: select a reversible three-eighth inch drill with variable speeds and a keyless chuck.

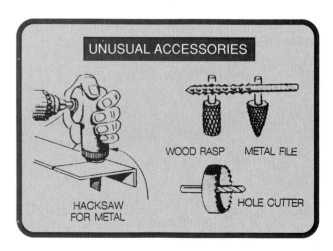

UNUSUAL ACCESSORIES

WOOD RASP   METAL FILE

HACKSAW
FOR METAL   HOLE CUTTER

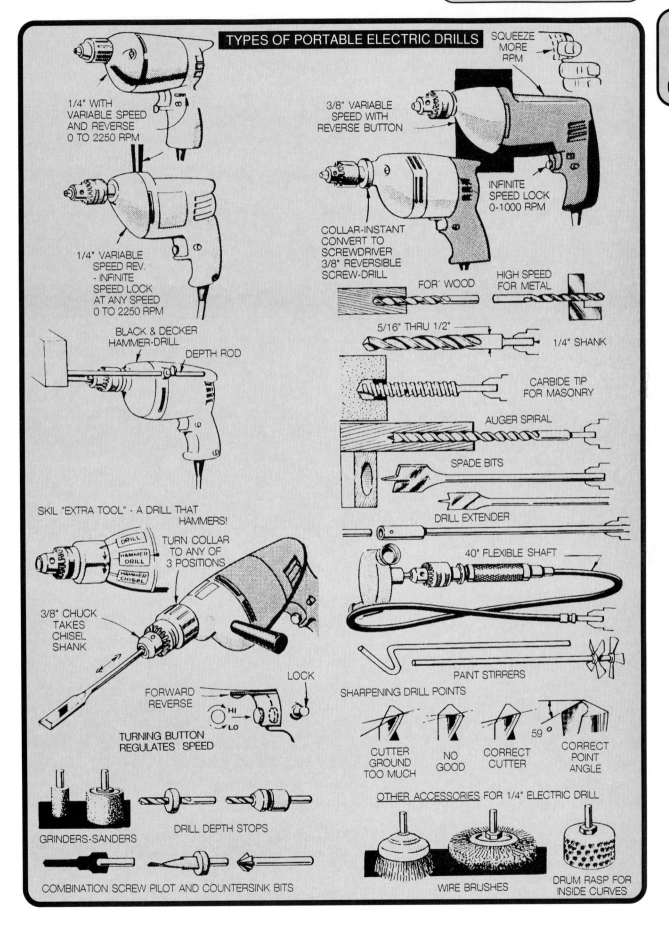

TYPES OF PORTABLE ELECTRIC DRILLS

1/4" WITH VARIABLE SPEED AND REVERSE 0 TO 2250 RPM

1/4" VARIABLE SPEED REV. - INFINITE SPEED LOCK AT ANY SPEED 0 TO 2250 RPM

BLACK & DECKER HAMMER-DRILL

DEPTH ROD

SKIL "EXTRA TOOL" - A DRILL THAT HAMMERS!

TURN COLLAR TO ANY OF 3 POSITIONS

DRILL
HAMMER DRILL
HAMMER CHISEL

3/8" CHUCK TAKES CHISEL SHANK

FORWARD REVERSE

LOCK

HI
LO

TURNING BUTTON REGULATES SPEED

GRINDERS-SANDERS

DRILL DEPTH STOPS

COMBINATION SCREW PILOT AND COUNTERSINK BITS

SQUEEZE MORE RPM

3/8" VARIABLE SPEED WITH REVERSE BUTTON

INFINITE SPEED LOCK 0-1000 RPM

COLLAR-INSTANT CONVERT TO SCREWDRIVER 3/8" REVERSIBLE SCREW-DRILL

FOR WOOD

HIGH SPEED FOR METAL

5/16" THRU 1/2"

1/4" SHANK

CARBIDE TIP FOR MASONRY

AUGER SPIRAL

SPADE BITS

DRILL EXTENDER

40" FLEXIBLE SHAFT

PAINT STIRRERS

SHARPENING DRILL POINTS

CUTTER GROUND TOO MUCH

NO GOOD

CORRECT CUTTER

59

CORRECT POINT ANGLE

OTHER ACCESSORIES FOR 1/4" ELECTRIC DRILL

WIRE BRUSHES

DRUM RASP FOR INSIDE CURVES

PORTABLE POWER TOOLS **THE CIRCULAR SAW**

This tool revolutionized the home building industry—and it can help you do jobs you never thought possible. Use it carefully.

Of all the portable electrical tools, no tool has made a greater contribution to lowering construction costs and making building easier and more precise for both professionals and homeowners than the portable electric saw. The portable electric saw is not new; the first one was invented in 1923 by Edmond Michel and it was this saw that led to the formation of the Skil Corporation. Now well over a dozen manufacturers produce a wide range of saws in many sizes with different engineering features but, because Skil was the first, many people still have the tendency to call all electric saws "Skilsaws!"

For homeowner use, the most popular saw has a 7 1/4 -inch diameter blade that can make a square cut 2 3/8 inches deep. If you have never used an electric saw before, here are a few very basic tips on safe use. Let the blade do the work and do not force the cut. A sharp blade will make your saw safer—which is why carbide-tipped blades are so highly regarded by professionals and amateurs alike. Carbide-tipped blades come in a variety of types designed for regular construction work, cutting plywood where you want to keep chipping to a minimum, and even special blades for cutting pressure-treated lumber. Different grades of carbide are used in the manufacturing process and the higher the grade the longer the blade will last. Even the most economical carbide blades will outlast a non-carbide blade by ten- or twentyfold. *Safety tips: wear clean safety glasses and make certain the retracting blade guard is in working order so that when you rest the saw on the floor or bench after a cut the guard is down.*

This is the original portable electric saw invented in 1923 by Edmond Michel, and manufactured by the Skil Corporation under the product label "Skilsaw." It featured a worm drive which is still used on many present day saws because of the high torque delivery. Worm drive saws are also more expensive to manufacture, which is why the helical gear drive saw made its appearance. While many other firms produce circular saws, to this day the name "Skilsaw" is often used when referring to a portable circular saw.

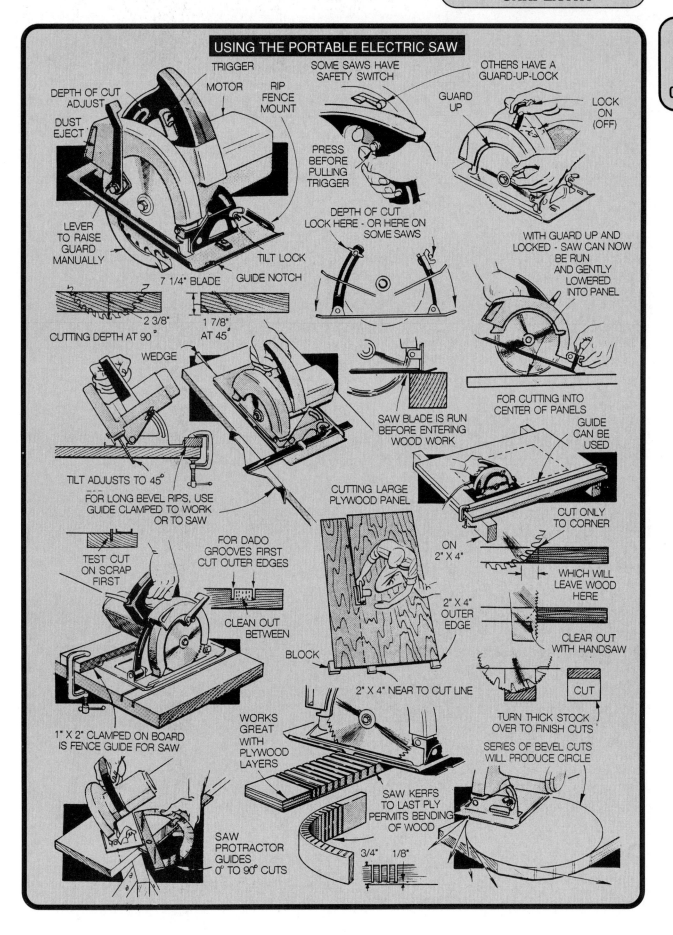

USING THE PORTABLE ELECTRIC SAW

TRIGGER

MOTOR

RIP FENCE MOUNT

DEPTH OF CUT ADJUST

DUST EJECT

LEVER TO RAISE GUARD MANUALLY

TILT LOCK

GUIDE NOTCH

7 1/4" BLADE

2 3/8"
CUTTING DEPTH AT 90°

1 7/8" AT 45°

SOME SAWS HAVE SAFETY SWITCH

PRESS BEFORE PULLING TRIGGER

DEPTH OF CUT LOCK HERE - OR HERE ON SOME SAWS

OTHERS HAVE A GUARD-UP-LOCK

GUARD UP

LOCK ON (OFF)

WITH GUARD UP AND LOCKED - SAW CAN NOW BE RUN AND GENTLY LOWERED INTO PANEL

FOR CUTTING INTO CENTER OF PANELS

GUIDE CAN BE USED

WEDGE

SAW BLADE IS RUN BEFORE ENTERING WOOD WORK

TILT ADJUSTS TO 45°

FOR LONG BEVEL RIPS, USE GUIDE CLAMPED TO WORK OR TO SAW

CUTTING LARGE PLYWOOD PANEL

ON 2" X 4"

CUT ONLY TO CORNER

WHICH WILL LEAVE WOOD HERE

TEST CUT ON SCRAP FIRST

FOR DADO GROOVES FIRST CUT OUTER EDGES

CLEAN OUT BETWEEN

2" X 4" OUTER EDGE

BLOCK

CLEAR OUT WITH HANDSAW

CUT

1" X 2" CLAMPED ON BOARD IS FENCE GUIDE FOR SAW

2" X 4" NEAR TO CUT LINE

TURN THICK STOCK OVER TO FINISH CUTS

WORKS GREAT WITH PLYWOOD LAYERS

SERIES OF BEVEL CUTS WILL PRODUCE CIRCLE

SAW PROTRACTOR GUIDES 0° TO 90° CUTS

SAW KERFS TO LAST PLY PERMITS BENDING OF WOOD

3/4" 1/8"

THE SANDER

WHEN WORKING WITH wood, how well the surfaces of a project are sanded will reflect on the overall finished look. Before the electric sander was developed, all surface sanding was done by hand; now only the final finishing sanding touch-up is done by hand, i.e., sanding in corners or around edges not accessible to the power sander.

For fine woodworking two major types of sanders are used: (1) *Belt sanders*, and (2) *Pad*, or *Finishing sanders*.

Belt sanders come in a variety of belt sizes, a 12 1/2" wide x 18" belt, 3" x 21", 3" x 24" belt, and the widest, a 4" x 24" belt. Some have a built-in dust collecting system with a bag, and some are variable speed, both features are very desirable. Cost, of course, varies with the tool size and the special features.

Finishing sanders for the shop include a pad sander that either orbits or sands straight and can accommodate either a half sheet, one third sheet or a quarter sheet of sandpaper. The quarter sheet pad sander is easily handled with one hand and is often referred to as a palm grip sander. As with belt sanders, horsepower can vary with 1/6 horsepower driving the palm sander, 1/4 horsepower driving the one third sheet and 3/8 to 1/2 horsepower handling the larger half sheet sanders. Like the belt sander, all are available with or without dust bags. Our recommendation for the serious craftsman: a 3 x 24 inch belt sander with variable speed and a dust bag, plus a one third sheet orbital and a quarter sheet palm grip sander.

Pad sanders (top) come with or without dust collecting systems and use half or one third sheets of paper. Palm grip finishing sander (right) use one quarter sheet.

Belt sanders come in various widths and sanding areas. A built in dust collecting system lets you see what you are sanding and also keeps the shop clean.

USING THE BELT AND PAD SANDER

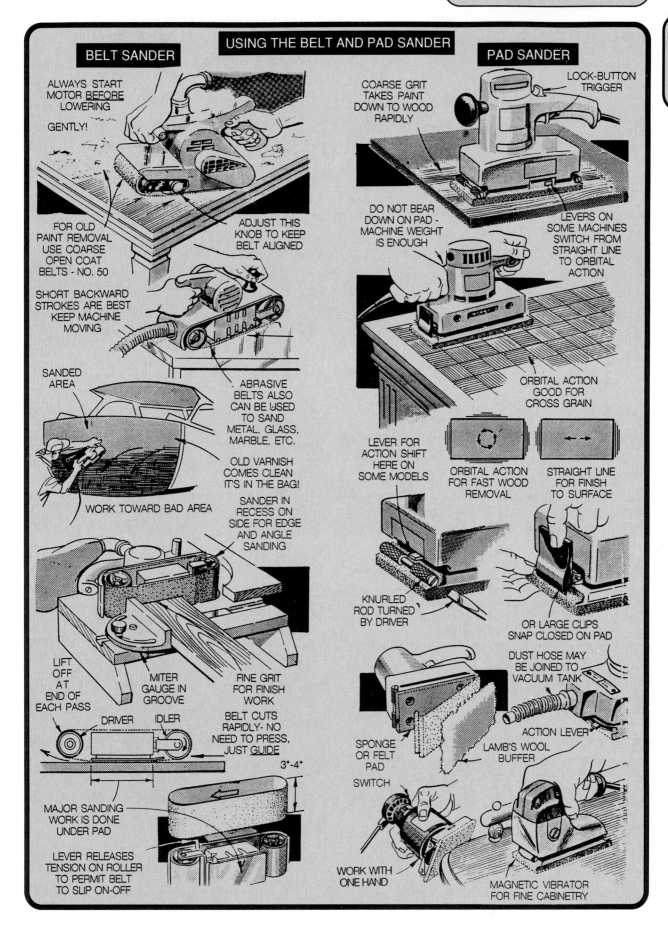

BELT SANDER

ALWAYS START MOTOR BEFORE LOWERING GENTLY!

FOR OLD PAINT REMOVAL USE COARSE OPEN COAT BELTS - NO. 50

SHORT BACKWARD STROKES ARE BEST KEEP MACHINE MOVING

ADJUST THIS KNOB TO KEEP BELT ALIGNED

SANDED AREA

ABRASIVE BELTS ALSO CAN BE USED TO SAND METAL, GLASS, MARBLE, ETC.

OLD VARNISH COMES CLEAN IT'S IN THE BAG!

WORK TOWARD BAD AREA

SANDER IN RECESS ON SIDE FOR EDGE AND ANGLE SANDING

LIFT OFF AT END OF EACH PASS

MITER GAUGE IN GROOVE

FINE GRIT FOR FINISH WORK

BELT CUTS RAPIDLY - NO NEED TO PRESS, JUST GUIDE

DRIVER   IDLER

3"-4"

MAJOR SANDING WORK IS DONE UNDER PAD

LEVER RELEASES TENSION ON ROLLER TO PERMIT BELT TO SLIP ON-OFF

PAD SANDER

LOCK-BUTTON TRIGGER

COARSE GRIT TAKES PAINT DOWN TO WOOD RAPIDLY

DO NOT BEAR DOWN ON PAD - MACHINE WEIGHT IS ENOUGH

LEVERS ON SOME MACHINES SWITCH FROM STRAIGHT LINE TO ORBITAL ACTION

ORBITAL ACTION GOOD FOR CROSS GRAIN

LEVER FOR ACTION SHIFT HERE ON SOME MODELS

ORBITAL ACTION FOR FAST WOOD REMOVAL

STRAIGHT LINE FOR FINISH TO SURFACE

KNURLED ROD TURNED BY DRIVER

OR LARGE CLIPS SNAP CLOSED ON PAD

DUST HOSE MAY BE JOINED TO VACUUM TANK

ACTION LEVER

SPONGE OR FELT PAD

LAMB'S WOOL BUFFER

SWITCH

WORK WITH ONE HAND

MAGNETIC VIBRATOR FOR FINE CABINETRY

PORTABLE POWER TOOLS
THE SABER SAW

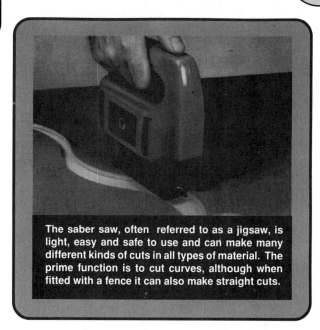

The saber saw, often referred to as a jigsaw, is light, easy and safe to use and can make many different kinds of cuts in all types of material. The prime function is to cut curves, although when fitted with a fence it can also make straight cuts.

The saber saw or jig saw as this tool is often called, is a very versatile saw that can make both straight and curved cuts. It is also extremely safe to use because of the manner in which it cuts wood, using up and down strokes. The most economical saws produce straight up and down movement of the blade while the slightly more expensive versions have either an automatic or hand-operated scrolling knob so the blade can be turned in any direction. Both types are very affordable and the wide range of blades available provide the capability of cutting all kinds of wood, plastic, plaster, aluminum and steel. When the saw is fitted with a carbide grit edge, you can easily cut ceramic tile.

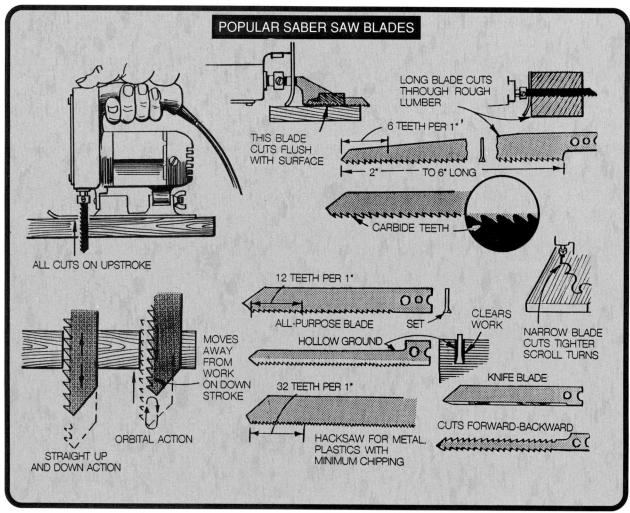

POPULAR SABER SAW BLADES

ALL CUTS ON UPSTROKE

THIS BLADE CUTS FLUSH WITH SURFACE

LONG BLADE CUTS THROUGH ROUGH LUMBER

6 TEETH PER 1"

2" TO 6" LONG

CARBIDE TEETH

STRAIGHT UP AND DOWN ACTION

ORBITAL ACTION

MOVES AWAY FROM WORK ON DOWN STROKE

12 TEETH PER 1"

ALL-PURPOSE BLADE   SET

HOLLOW GROUND

32 TEETH PER 1"

HACKSAW FOR METAL, PLASTICS WITH MINIMUM CHIPPING

CLEARS WORK

KNIFE BLADE

CUTS FORWARD-BACKWARD

NARROW BLADE CUTS TIGHTER SCROLL TURNS

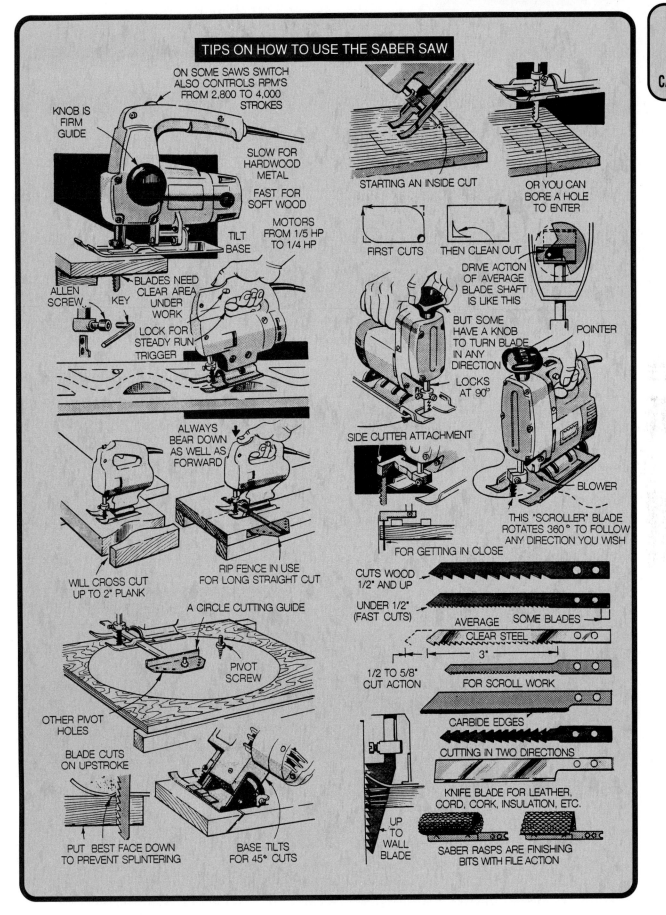

TIPS ON HOW TO USE THE SABER SAW

ON SOME SAWS SWITCH ALSO CONTROLS RPM'S FROM 2,800 TO 4,000 STROKES

KNOB IS FIRM GUIDE

SLOW FOR HARDWOOD METAL

FAST FOR SOFT WOOD

TILT BASE

MOTORS FROM 1/5 HP TO 1/4 HP

ALLEN SCREW

KEY

BLADES NEED CLEAR AREA UNDER WORK

LOCK FOR STEADY RUN TRIGGER

ALWAYS BEAR DOWN AS WELL AS FORWARD

WILL CROSS CUT UP TO 2" PLANK

RIP FENCE IN USE FOR LONG STRAIGHT CUT

A CIRCLE CUTTING GUIDE

PIVOT SCREW

OTHER PIVOT HOLES

BLADE CUTS ON UPSTROKE

PUT BEST FACE DOWN TO PREVENT SPLINTERING

BASE TILTS FOR 45° CUTS

STARTING AN INSIDE CUT

OR YOU CAN BORE A HOLE TO ENTER

FIRST CUTS

THEN CLEAN OUT

DRIVE ACTION OF AVERAGE BLADE SHAFT IS LIKE THIS

BUT SOME HAVE A KNOB TO TURN BLADE IN ANY DIRECTION

POINTER

LOCKS AT 90°

SIDE CUTTER ATTACHMENT

BLOWER

THIS "SCROLLER" BLADE ROTATES 360° TO FOLLOW ANY DIRECTION YOU WISH

FOR GETTING IN CLOSE

CUTS WOOD 1/2" AND UP

UNDER 1/2" (FAST CUTS)

AVERAGE

SOME BLADES

CLEAR STEEL

3"

1/2 TO 5/8" CUT ACTION

FOR SCROLL WORK

CARBIDE EDGES

CUTTING IN TWO DIRECTIONS

KNIFE BLADE FOR LEATHER, CORD, CORK, INSULATION, ETC.

UP TO WALL BLADE

SABER RASPS ARE FINISHING BITS WITH FILE ACTION

PORTABLE POWER TOOLS **THE UTILITY SAW**

For rough work, when equipped with the right blade, the reciprocating saw will cut anything from tree limbs, metal, plaster, plastic. A great tool for renovation work.

The reciprocating saw is a sort of large version of the saber saw. It is designed for heavy duty work and making rough cuts. The blades for the reciprocating saw are up to 12 inches long and can cut wood up to 6 inches thick. The blade is mounted parallel to the body of the saw, instead of at right angles as with the saber saw.

While the *chain saw* cannot really be considered a carpentry tool, it is extremely handy for removing trees, lopping off branches, cutting down large timbers and general demolition work. The introduction of chain saws weighing less than ten pounds has served to popularize this tool with many homeowners. A chain saw can cut through a 12-inch hardwood log in less than 12 seconds. A saw with a 12- to 16-inch bar is a good choice for most around-the-house work. Some are powered with a gasoline engine or electric motor for use with a long extension cord.

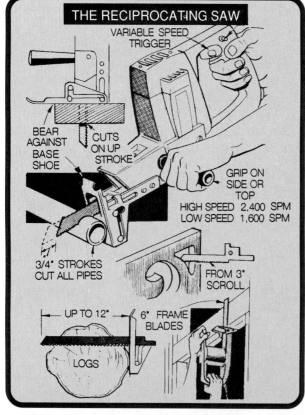

THE RECIPROCATING SAW

VARIABLE SPEED TRIGGER

BEAR AGAINST BASE SHOE

CUTS ON UP STROKE

GRIP ON SIDE OR TOP
HIGH SPEED 2,400 SPM
LOW SPEED 1,600 SPM

3/4" STROKES CUT ALL PIPES

FROM 3" SCROLL

UP TO 12"   6" FRAME BLADES

LOGS

For really rough work such as cutting timber, piling, etc., the chain saw does the job although it was designed primarily for cutting down trees.

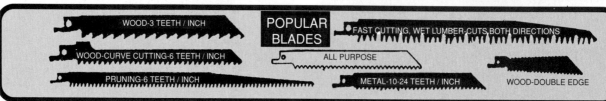

WOOD-3 TEETH / INCH

POPULAR BLADES

FAST CUTTING, WET LUMBER-CUTS BOTH DIRECTIONS

WOOD-CURVE CUTTING-6 TEETH / INCH

ALL PURPOSE

PRUNING-6 TEETH / INCH

METAL-10-24 TEETH / INCH   WOOD-DOUBLE EDGE

PORTABLE POWER TOOLS) # THE PLANE

Another portable power tool you may want to consider is the electric plane. There are two models available. One is a *block plane,* which like the conventional block plane is held in one hand. It can be used for planing the inside of windows and door jambs and for edge planing of sticking doors. Easing sticking drawers is a cinch with this handy tool. A larger version is the electric *jack plane.* This plane does the work of a hand plane but with much less effort and greater precision. It planes by means of a double edge revolving cutter, turning at a very high speed. Some planes can be fitted with a fence that projects downward from one side, perpendicular to the bottom surface of the plane. When planing the edge of a door or a board, this fence bears against the side of the work, assuring a perfectly square-edged cut. The fence can be removed for planing wide areas and it can be tilted for bevel planing.

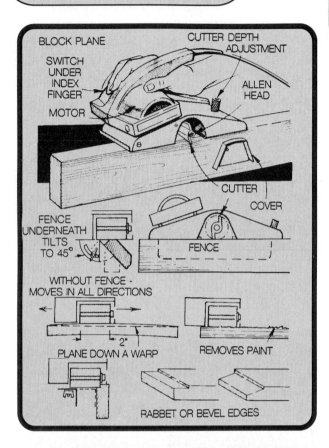

The electric plane is a great time-saver when it comes to the job of fitting a door. Some planes use a router as the power source. The router is fitted into a special holder—and presto—a plane.

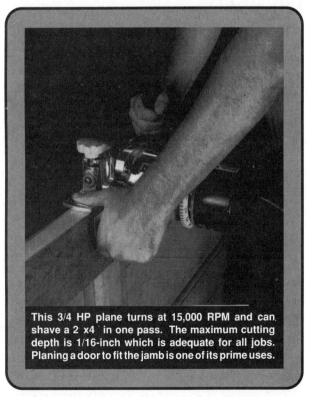

This 3/4 HP plane turns at 15,000 RPM and can shave a 2 x4 in one pass. The maximum cutting depth is 1/16-inch which is adequate for all jobs. Planing a door to fit the jamb is one of its prime uses.

PORTABLE POWER TOOLS

THE ROUTER

Routers turn at about 25,000 RPM with the pro models delivering up to three HP. Here a dovetail is being cut using a special jig.

ONE OF THE MOST sophisticated and important portable power tools is the router. Basically it consists of a high speed motor (about 25,000 rpm) mounted vertically on a horizontal base plate with a chuck at one end to accept various cutter bits. Once the bit has been mounted in the chuck—or collet—it can be moved up or down to cut deep or shallow grooves in the work. It is indispensable for mortising (recessing) hinges in door jambs and door edges. The router can also be used to make grooves and cut dados rabbets. Various accessories such as a dovetail template and a clamp-on base and cutter for biscuit joining make this tool even more versatile.

There are literally dozens of bits made for the router that will enable it to cut shapes suitable for moldings, making V-grooves, dovetails, beading, chamfering, ogee curves. concave and square cuts. The drawings illustrate some of the more common router bits and the cuts they make. A router guide is available for cutting a straight line at a set distance from the edge of the work.

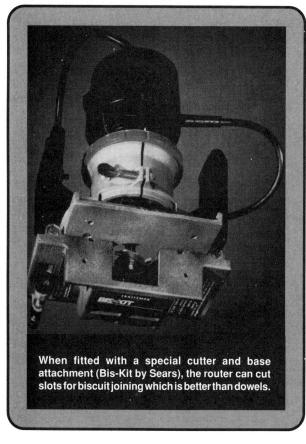

When fitted with a special cutter and base attachment (Bis-Kit by Sears), the router can cut slots for biscuit joining which is better than dowels.

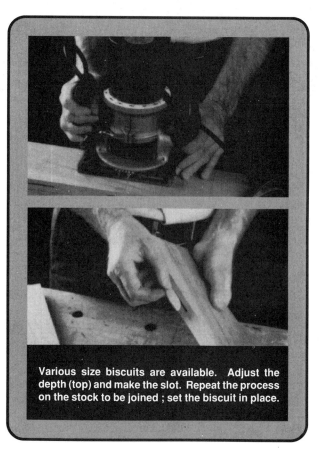

Various size biscuits are available. Adjust the depth (top) and make the slot. Repeat the process on the stock to be joined ; set the biscuit in place.

USING THE ROUTER

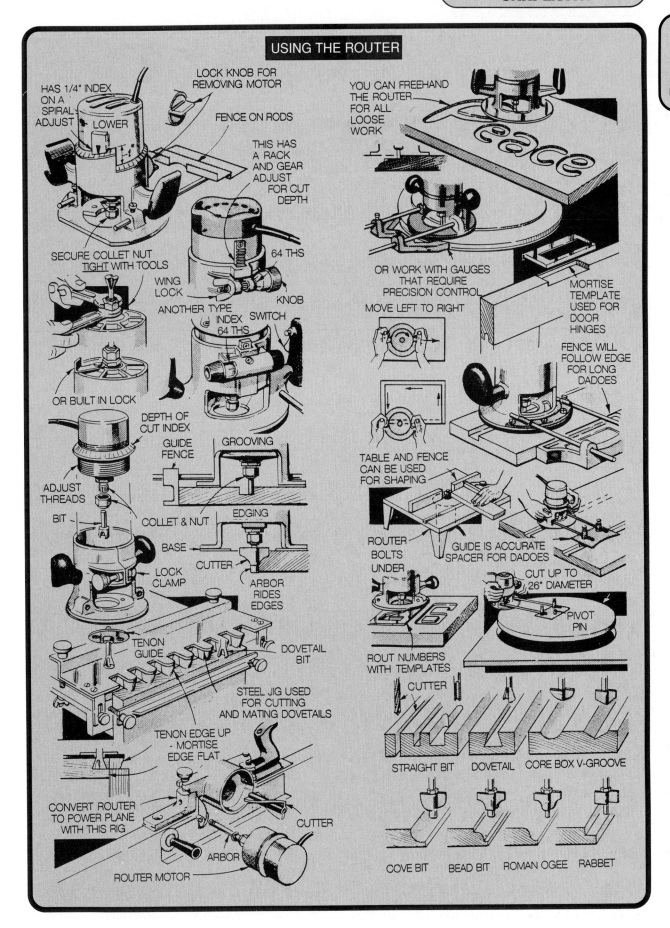

HAS 1/4" INDEX ON A SPIRAL ADJUST

LOWER

LOCK KNOB FOR REMOVING MOTOR

FENCE ON RODS

THIS HAS A RACK AND GEAR ADJUST FOR CUT DEPTH

SECURE COLLET NUT TIGHT WITH TOOLS

64 THS

WING LOCK

KNOB

ANOTHER TYPE

INDEX 64 THS

SWITCH

OR BUILT IN LOCK

DEPTH OF CUT INDEX

GUIDE FENCE

GROOVING

ADJUST THREADS

BIT

COLLET & NUT

EDGING

BASE

CUTTER

LOCK CLAMP

ARBOR RIDES EDGES

TENON GUIDE

DOVETAIL BIT

STEEL JIG USED FOR CUTTING AND MATING DOVETAILS

TENON EDGE UP - MORTISE EDGE FLAT

CONVERT ROUTER TO POWER PLANE WITH THIS RIG

CUTTER

ARBOR

ROUTER MOTOR

YOU CAN FREEHAND THE ROUTER FOR ALL LOOSE WORK

OR WORK WITH GAUGES THAT REQUIRE PRECISION CONTROL

MOVE LEFT TO RIGHT

MORTISE TEMPLATE USED FOR DOOR HINGES

FENCE WILL FOLLOW EDGE FOR LONG DADOES

TABLE AND FENCE CAN BE USED FOR SHAPING

ROUTER BOLTS UNDER

GUIDE IS ACCURATE SPACER FOR DADOES

CUT UP TO 26" DIAMETER

PIVOT PIN

ROUT NUMBERS WITH TEMPLATES

CUTTER

STRAIGHT BIT   DOVETAIL   CORE BOX V-GROOVE

COVE BIT   BEAD BIT   ROMAN OGEE   RABBET

PORTABLE POWER TOOLS # CORDLESS TOOLS

Of all the tools developed in the past decade the tremendous breakthrough in nickel-cadmium battery technology is responsible for a wide range of battery-powered tools ranging from the popular in-line and pistol grip screwdriver, combination drill/driver, stapling gun, glue gun, ratchet, and even a small-diameter circular saw.

Cordless tools are usually referred to by the voltage the batteries deliver, ranging from a 2.4 volt two-cell battery to a 12 volt ten-cell battery. The higher the voltage the more powerful the tool. All batteries are rechargeable and the rate of charging has a direct relationship to the number of battery cells and the price of the tool. The in-line screwdriver rests in a stand for automatic charging in as little as three hours, while the pistol grip screwdriver can be recharged in as little as one hour. The in-line single speed reversible driver is most popular because of the low cost but the more powerful pistol grip combination driver/drill with a removable battery pack is a preferred choice; if your battery wears down you can immediately replace it with a fully charged battery for use while the weak one is being recharged. The added cost is worth the difference!

Lowest in cost, the in-line screwdriver is also the handiest for most jobs calling for screws. Replaceable driver bits slip into the hex head chuck which can be removed for a hex-shanked pilot drill bit, Phillips head bit or a wide range of nut drivers.

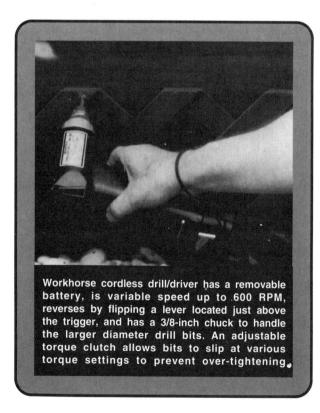

Workhorse cordless drill/driver has a removable battery, is variable speed up to 600 RPM, reverses by flipping a lever located just above the trigger, and has a 3/8-inch chuck to handle the larger diameter drill bits. An adjustable torque clutch allows bits to slip at various torque settings to prevent over-tightening.

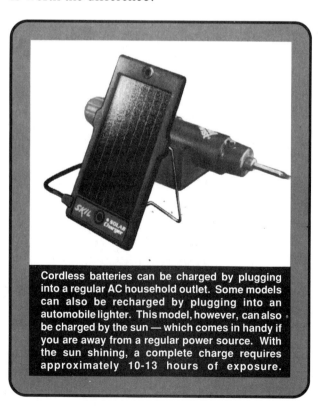

Cordless batteries can be charged by plugging into a regular AC household outlet. Some models can also be recharged by plugging into an automobile lighter. This model, however, can also be charged by the sun — which comes in handy if you are away from a regular power source. With the sun shining, a complete charge requires approximately 10-13 hours of exposure.

Information Security

An Integrated Collection of Essays

Edited by

Marshall D. Abrams
Sushil Jajodia
Harold J. Podell

IEEE Computer Society Press
Los Alamitos, California

Washington • Brussels • Tokyo

Library of Congress Cataloging-in-Publication Data

Information security: an integrated collection of essays / [edited by] Marshall D. Abrams, Sushil Jajodia,
   Harold J. Podell.
      p.   cm.
   Includes bibliographical references and index.
   ISBN 0-8186-3662-9. — ISBN 0-8186-3661-0 (fiche)
   1. Computer security.   I. Abrams, Marshall D.   II. Jajodia, Sushil.   III. Podell, Harold J.
   QA76.9.A25I5415   1995
   005.8—dc20   94-20899
                                                    CIP

Published by the
IEEE Computer Society Press
10662 Los Vaqueros Circle
P.O. Box 3014
Los Alamitos, CA 90720-1264

IEEE Computer Society Press Order Number 3662-01
IEEE Catalog Number EH0397-0
Library of Congress Number 94-20899
ISBN 0-8186-3662-9

Additional copies can be ordered from

IEEE Computer Society Press	IEEE Service Center	IEEE Computer Society	IEEE Computer Society
Customer Service Center	445 Hoes Lane	13, avenue de l'Aquilon	Ooshima Building
10662 Los Vaqueros Circle	P.O. Box 1331	B-1200 Brussels	2-19-1 Minami-Aoyama
P.O. Box 3014	Piscataway, NJ 08855-1331	BELGIUM	Minato-ku, Tokyo 107
Los Alamitos, CA 90720-1264	Tel: (908) 981-1393	Tel: +32-2-770-2198	JAPAN
Tel: (714) 821-8380	Fax: (908) 981-9667	Fax: +32-2-770-8505	Tel: +81-3-3408-3118
Fax: (714) 821-4641			Fax: +81-3-3408-3553
Email: cs.books@computer.org			

Technical Editor: Murali Varanasi
Production Editor: Lisa O'Conner
Copy Editor: Tom Culviner
Cover Artist: Alex Torres
Printed in the United States of America by Braun-Brumfield, Inc.

The Institute of Electrical and Electronics Engineers, Inc.

Contents

Introduction 1

Part 1. Motivation

Essay 1. What Is There to Worry About?
An Introduction to the Computer Security Problem 11
    Donald L. Brinkley and Roger R. Schell

Essay 2. Concepts and Terminology for Computer Security 40
    Donald L. Brinkley and Roger R. Schell

Essay 3. A Philosophy of Security Management 98
    David Bailey

Essay 4. Malicious Software 111
    Marshall D. Abrams and Harold J. Podell

Essay 5. Abstraction and Refinement
of Layered Security Policy 126
    Marshall D. Abrams and David Bailey

Part 2. Understanding and Working Security Issues

Essay 6. Evaluation Criteria for Trusted Systems 137
    Roger R. Schell and Donald L. Brinkley

Essay 7. Information Security Policy 160
    Ingrid M. Olson and Marshall D. Abrams

Essay 8. Formal Methods and Models 170
    James G. Williams and Marshall D. Abrams

Essay 9. Rule-Set Modeling of a Trusted Computer System 187
    Leonard J. LaPadula

Essay 10. Representative Organizations That Participate in Open Systems Security Standards Development........................ 242
Harold J. Podell

Essay 11. Penetration Testing 269
Clark Weissman

Essay 12. Evaluation Issues... 297
Marshall D. Abrams and Harold J. Podell

Essay 13. Supporting Policies and Functions............................... 318
Marshall D. Abrams and Harold J. Podell

Essay 14. Security Engineering 330
Marshall D. Abrams, Harold J. Podell, and Daniel W. Gambel

Essay 15. Cryptography 350
Marshall D. Abrams and Harold J. Podell

Essay 16. Local Area Networks 385
Marshall D. Abrams and Harold J. Podell

Essay 17. Internet Privacy Enhanced Mail 405
Stephen T. Kent

Essay 18. Electronic Data Interchange (EDI) Messaging Security 423
Ted Humphreys

Part 3. Database Security

Essay 19. Architectures for MLS Database Management Systems... 439
LouAnna Notargiacomo

Essay 20. Toward a Multilevel Secure Relational Data Model 460
Sushil Jajodia and Ravi S. Sandhu

Essay 21. Solutions to the Polyinstantiation Problem 493
Sushil Jajodia, Ravi S. Sandhu, and Barbara T. Blaustein

Essay 22. Integrity in Multilevel Secure Database Management Systems... 530
Catherine Meadows and Sushil Jajodia

**Essay 23. Multilevel Secure Database
Management Prototypes** 542
   Thomas H. Hinke

**Essay 24. Inference Problems in Multilevel
Secure Database Management Systems** 570
   Sushil Jajodia and Catherine Meadows

**Essay 25. Logical Design of Audit Information
in Relational Databases** 585
   Sushil Jajodia, Shashi K. Gadia, and Gautam Bhargava

Essay 26. A Multilevel Secure Object-Oriented Data Model 596
   Sushil Jajodia, Boris Kogan, and Ravi S. Sandhu

**Essay 27. Integrity Mechanisms in
Database Management Systems** 617
   Ravi S. Sandhu and Sushil Jajodia

References 635

Glossary 672

Index 733

About the Authors 742

Introduction

There is an increasing interest in research and development in information security. It is an area where active research is being conducted contemporaneously with application of the technology. For example, Internet and related information highway research and development are occurring while new applications are being added. Consequently, many research results are contained in technical reports that are available primarily within certain professional communities. The research results and applications reports that have appeared in the open literature (professional journals and conference proceedings) are scattered in several different sources. In spite of this, there aren't many new interdisciplinary books in this area. Those that are coming out focus primarily on application issues or address a narrow range of topics, such as computer viruses.

In assembling this collection of interdisciplinary essays, we have had a twofold objective: first, to provide a comprehensive summary of the results of the research, development, and application experience in information security up to this point, and second, to point toward directions for future work. We have attempted to obtain a balance among various viewpoints — some essays are research-oriented, some are from the producer's viewpoint, some from the consumer's perspective. We believe that this diversity of viewpoints provides a richness generally not available in one book. The diversity is evident in conflicts and contradictions among the essays. The opinions expressed are solely those of the individual authors and do not represent any organization. We have not tried to reconcile the differences. They reflect the dynamic nature of the subject matter.

To the greatest extent possible, we have tried to collect a coherent set of essays. The early essays provide background for those that follow. However, there is not a linear progression. Nor is there 100 percent uniformity in terminology. Concerning terminology, in some of the essays we have adopted a convention to identify words that are used in the context of information security in ways that differ from their common English usage. These "reserved words" are set in a different typeface. We hope that the change in typeface will remind you of the special usage without being too distracting.

Next we give brief summaries of all essays included in this collection. In Essay 1, "What Is There to Worry About? An Introduction to the Computer Security Problem," Don Brinkley and Roger Schell provide an overview of the vulnerabilities and threats to information security in computer systems. The essay begins with a historical presentation, contrasting the computer security problem with communication security problems. Next, it describes four broad areas of computer-related threats: theft of computational resources, disruption of computational services, unauthorized information disclosure, and unauthorized information modification. Classes of information-related threats are described, and examples of each are provided. These classes are *inadvertent human error, user irresponsibility, direct probing, probing with an artifice, direct penetration,* and *subversion of security mechanism.* The roles of Trojan horses, viruses, worms, bombs, and other kinds of malicious software are described and examples provided.

Essay 2, "Concepts and Terminology for Computer Security," also by Don Brinkley and Roger Schell, provides an introduction to many of the concepts and terms that are most important in gaining an understanding of information security. It focuses on techniques for achieving access control within computer systems and networks. The essay begins by defining what is meant by information security and describing why it is important to constrain the definition to protection that can be meaningfully provided with a significant degree of assurance within computer systems. The theory of information security — the reference monitor concept — is introduced next through an analogy with information security concepts from the world of people and sensitive documents. Next, the essay further develops the presentation of the theory by introducing concepts and terms related to the security policy. Distinctions between discretionary and nondiscretionary security policies are provided, and supporting policies are introduced. Techniques for building a secure system based on the principles of the theory are presented, along with methods for usefully verifying the security of a system. The security kernel is presented as a useful, high-assurance realization of the reference monitor concept, and the principles behind the process of designing and implementing one from scratch are discussed. Improvements to the security of an existing operating system that are feasible, as well as fundamental limitations on those improvements, are described next. Finally, the reference monitor concept is applied to networks, and cryptography and access control are shown to be useful partners.

Without appropriate management, it is impossible to maintain security in a system or network of more than minimum complexity. In Essay 3, "A Philosophy of Security Management," David Bailey discusses security management of complex systems, including the scope of the security manager's role and the conflicting pressures that must be balanced. Bailey ends by discussing a strategy for the security manager that has been used successfully on a large local network.

Essay 4, "Malicious Software," by Marshall Abrams and Harold Podell, discusses the threats, vulnerabilities, risk, effects, and countermeasures concerned with viruses, worms, and other forms of malicious software. It defines several common types of malicious software but avoids narrow semantic distinctions. The possible attacks include unauthorized modification of data and software (including the operating system) and unauthorized utilization of resources, often resulting in denial of service. The essay considers viruses in stand-alone computers as well as network vulnerabilities. Lessons learned from the study of various attacks are presented as general points for the future, including detection, reduction, recommendations, and legal remedies.

There are multiple views of corporate (enterprise) computing, each with its own metaphors and terms of reference. The different views incorporate different levels of abstraction, in which details are suppressed to concentrate attention on the issues important to the particular observer. Essay 5, "Abstraction and Refinement of Layered Security Policy," by Marshall Abrams and David Bailey, examines these different metaphors with respect to the enterprise security policy. The result is a layered policy in which each main layer relates to one of the system metaphors, and the policy described for a lower level of detail is an implementation of the policy at a higher level. The layered view of policy helps system designers, managers, and users understand the rationale for security policy at the lowest levels of abstraction, because the relationship of the low-level policy to the enterprise information policy is clear.

The Trusted Computer System Evaluation Criteria (TCSEC) provide the basis for evaluating the effectiveness of security controls built into computer systems. In Essay 6, "Evaluation Criteria for Trusted Systems," Roger Schell and Donald Brinkley summarize the definition and requirements of the TCSEC used to classify systems into seven hierarchical classes of enhanced security protection. This essay also summarizes the history, technical foundations, and basic security requirements of the TCSEC. These criteria have for a number of years been used in specifying security requirements during acquisition of products and systems, guiding the design and development of trusted systems, and evaluating systems used to process sensitive information.

In Essay 7, "Information Security Policy," Ingrid Olson and Marshall Abrams discuss information security policy for automated information systems (AISs), focusing on information control and dissemination. Information security policy addresses such issues as

- disclosure, integrity, and availability concerns;
- who may access what information in what manner;
- basis on which the access decision is made (for example, user characteristic such as nationality or group affinity, or some external condition such as time or status);
- maximized sharing versus least privilege;
- separation of duties;

- who controls and who owns the information; and
- authority issues.

This essay discusses some of the aspects that must be considered when developing an information security policy for a given organization.

In Essay 8, "Formal Methods and Models," James Williams and Marshall Abrams discuss how the motivation for using formal methods in the context of trusted system development stems primarily from their ability to provide precision, consistency, and added assurance during the elaboration of security requirements across different development stages. The subject matter of formal models and specifications can be illustrated by looking at the various kinds of security attributes and requirements that have turned up in published security models. Examples discussed in this essay relate to nondisclosure policies, data integrity policies, and user-controlled policies. This essay concludes with a discussion of technical and methodological issues relating to the effective use of formal methods.

Essay 9, "Rule-Set Modeling of a Trusted Computer System," by Leonard LaPadula, describes a new approach to formal modeling of a trusted computer system. A finite-state machine models the access operations of the trusted computer system, while a separate rule set expresses the system's trust policies. A powerful feature of this approach is its ability to fit several widely differing trust policies easily within the same model. LaPadula shows how this approach to modeling relates to general ideas of access control, and relates this approach to the implementation of real systems by connecting the rule set of the model to the operations of a Unix System V system. The trust policies demonstrated in the rule set of the model include the mandatory access control policy of Unix System V/MLS, a version of the Clark-Wilson integrity policy, and two supporting policies that implement roles.

Essay 10, "Representative Organizations That Participate in Open Systems Security Standards Development," by Harold Podell, presents an introduction to representative organizations that participate in open systems security standards development required for interoperability and security of business and government computer network communications. International agreements include a commitment of the standards organizations to support open systems security standards to achieve "brand-independent" network configurations and interfaces. Four interrelated issues provide a basis for interpretation of current trends in the development of selected open systems standards:

1. the importance of security standards as an economic issue to support international electronic commerce;
2. a conceptual view of open systems security standards relationships;

3. a brief overview of the committee structure of the International Organization for Standardization (ISO), the International Electrotechnical Commission (IEC), the International Telephone and Telegraph Consultative Committee (CCITT), and selected national and regional organizations; and

4. an overview of important security standards committees' activities.

Essay 11, "Penetration Testing," by Clark Weissman, introduces flawless penetration testing as a requirement for high-rated secure systems — those rated above B1 based on the Trusted Computer System Evaluation Criteria (TCSEC). Penetration testing is a form of stress testing, which exposes weaknesses — that is, flaws — in the trusted computing base (TCB). This essay describes the Flaw Hypothesis Methodology (FHM), the earliest comprehensive and widely used method for conducting penetration testing; reviews motivation for penetration testing and penetration test planning; defines a flaw as a demonstrated unspecified capability that can be exploited to violate security policy; and provides an overview of the FHM and its analogy to a heuristic-based strategy game. Ten most productive ways to generate hypothetical flaws are described as part of the method, as are ways to confirm them. A review of the results and representative generic flaws discovered over the past 20 years is presented. The essay concludes with speculations on future methods of penetration analysis using formal methods: mathematically specified design, theorems, and proofs of correctness of the design.

In Essay 12, "Evaluation Issues," Marshall Abrams and Harold Podell present an introduction to evaluation issues in the US and European Community (EC) to illustrate the two schools of thought. Following development of draft national and regional criteria, the US, Canada, and the EC are working on Common Criteria (CC). The authors compare the proposed evaluation approaches in the hope that, in the international process of developing the Common Criteria, there will be a convergence to assist the multinational producers of secure products and systems in evaluation by different national entities. Interoperability of information technology and IT security to support electronic commerce depends, in part, on an acceptance of evaluated products in different countries and regions. Therefore, an important aspect of evaluation is the development of international agreements for reciprocity of evaluations of secure products.

Essay 13, "Supporting Policies and Functions," by Marshall Abrams and Harold Podell, observes that the major policy objective — to protect information assets against specific harm — usually requires additional policies and functions for support and implementation. This essay discusses supporting policies and functions drawn from the TCSEC, the supporting "Rainbow" series, and the ITSEC.

Essay 14, "Security Engineering," by Marshall Abrams, Harold Podell, and Dan Gambel, is concerned with trusted system integration and/or development to meet multilevel security (MLS) and operational requirements. It addresses technical issues such as how to combine products securely, TCB alternatives, and typical security engineering phases. It also addresses the management concerns of certification and accreditation.

Essay 15, "Cryptography," which was written by Marshall Abrams and Harold Podell, discusses cryptographic protection of information confidentiality and integrity as that information passes from one point in space-time to another. More recent uses of cryptography, such as authentication and nonrepudiation, are also discussed.

The essay begins with an introduction of these ideas, including some basic examples, then proceeds to the definition of a cryptographic system, making the distinction between conventional key or symmetric key schemes and public key or asymmetric key schemes. The authors present some classical examples beginning with Julius Caesar. Both substitution and permutation ciphers are included, as well as a word about their weaknesses. The Data Encryption Standard (DES) serves as an example of a product cipher whose strength derives simply from repeated applications of both permutations and substitutions.

The essay then turns to public key schemes or systems. A public key system can be used by anyone to encrypt a message for a given recipient, but only that recipient can decrypt it. Although there are many proposed in the open literature and three have been widely implemented, the essay focuses on the most popular system — RSA. RSA (Rivest, Shamir, and Adleman) is a widely used public key system whose strength lies in the difficulty of factoring certain large numbers.

A discussion of public key management is followed by an introduction to public key and conventional key management issues. The authors also discuss authentication and integrity issues that are associated with conventional key systems. In addition, link encryption and end-to-end encryption are described and contrasted. The essay's final topic is the integration of computer and communications security.

Essay 16, "Local Area Networks," by Marshall Abrams and Harold Podell, addresses local area network (LAN) communications security. LANs are introduced as providing

1. a private communications facility,
2. services over a relatively limited geographic area,
3. a high data rate for computer communications, and
4. common access to a wide range of devices and services.

LANs share many security problems and approaches for their solutions with point-to-point conventional communications systems. In addition, LANs have some unique problems of their own:

1. universal data availability,
2. passive and active wiretap threats,
3. end-to-end access control, and
4. security group control.

Countermeasures include physical protection and separation by physical, logical, and encryption methods. Trusted Network Interface Units, encryption, and key distribution are also discussed. An example is discussed to illustrate different aspects of LAN security. The example is a composite of several existing product features, selected to demonstrate the use of encryption for confidentiality, and trusted system technology for local area networks.

Essay 17, "Internet Privacy Enhanced Mail," by Stephen Kent, presents Privacy Enhanced Mail (PEM) as consisting of extensions to existing message processing software plus a key management infrastructure. These combine to provide users with a facility in which message confidentiality, authenticity, and integrity can be effected. PEM is compatible with RFC-822 (Request for Comments[1]) message processing conventions and is transparent to SMTP (Simple Mail Transfer Protocol) mail relays. PEM uses symmetric cryptography — for example, the Data Encryption Standard (DES) — to provide (optional) encryption of messages. Although the RFCs permit the use of either symmetric or asymmetric (public key) cryptography (for example, the RSA cryptosystem) to distribute symmetric keys, the RFCs strongly recommend the use of asymmetric cryptography for this purpose and to generate and validate digital signatures for messages and certificates. Public key management in PEM is based on the use of certificates as defined by the CCITT Directory Authentication Framework [CCIT88c]. A public key certification hierarchy for PEM is being established by the Internet Society. This certification hierarchy supports universal authentication of PEM users, under various policies, without the need for prior, bilateral arrangements among users or organizations with which the users may be affiliated.

Essay 18, "Electronic Data Interchange (EDI) Messaging Security," by Ted Humphreys, observes that modern economy and the future wealth and prosperity of industry and commerce rely increasingly on the exchange of data and information, in electronic form, between business partners. In response to the need for effective and efficient solutions to handle this way of doing business, Electronic Data Interchange (EDI) of-

---

[1] The meaning of RFC has evolved. Today, most RFCs are effectively standards. Draft RFCs are used to solicit comments.

fers substantial advantages and opportunities. This essay looks at a particularly important aspect of EDI: the security of EDI messages. In particular, it focuses on the secure communications of EDI messages. To start with, some introductory material is presented that views security in the context of Open-EDI.

Essay 19, "Architectures for MLS Database Management Systems," by LouAnna Notargiacomo, presents an overview of the basic architectures that have been used in the development of trusted relational database management systems (DBMSs). While various approaches have been tried for special-purpose systems, the architectures presented are those that have been developed for general-purpose trusted DBMS products. The essay also reviews approaches that have been proposed in the research for new trusted DBMS architectures, although worked examples of these approaches may not exist in all cases. Each component of the architecture is defined and the relationships and flow of information among components presented. This presentation is followed by a discussion of how the architecture meets mandatory and discretionary security requirements and preserves data integrity.

Essay 20, "Toward a Multilevel Secure Relational Data Model," by Sushil Jajodia and Ravi Sandhu, observes that although there are several efforts under way to build multilevel secure relational database management systems, there is no clear consensus regarding what a multilevel secure relational data model exactly is. In part, this lack of consensus on fundamental issues reflects the subtleties involved in extending the classical (single-level) relational model to a multilevel environment. The authors' aim in this essay is to discuss the most fundamental aspects of the multilevel secure relational model. First, they identify four core integrity properties that should be required of all multilevel relations. Next, they give a formal operational semantics for the usual update operations (insert, update, and delete) on multilevel relations. Finally, they describe a decomposition algorithm that partitions the multilevel relations into collections of single-level relations, and a recovery algorithm that constructs the original multilevel relations from the decomposed single-level relations.

Essay 21, "Solutions to the Polyinstantiation Problem," by Sushil Jajodia, Ravi Sandhu, and Barbara Blaustein, addresses polyinstantiation, which has generated a great deal of controversy lately. Some have argued that polyinstantiation and integrity are fundamentally incompatible, and have proposed alternatives to polyinstantiation. Others have argued about the correct definition of polyinstantiation and its operational semantics. The purpose of this essay is to provide a tutorial on the subject. The authors begin by reviewing the concept of polyinstantiation; then they survey the various proposals to deal with it.

Essay 22, "Integrity in Multilevel Secure Database Management Systems," by Catherine Meadows and Sushil Jajodia, discusses the effects that satisfying security requirements in a multilevel database management system can have on the system's data integrity. The authors identify the conflicts between security and integrity in such databases, and show how the various components of integrity can be traded off both against each other and against security. They discuss recent work in maintaining integrity in multilevel relational database management systems and identify the emerging integrity issues in multilevel object-oriented systems.

In Essay 23, "Multilevel Secure Database Management Prototypes," Thomas Hinke describes, compares, and contrasts three of the most prominent research DBMS prototypes: SRI International's SeaView, TRW's Advanced Secure DBMS (ASD), and SCTC's Lock Data View (LDV). While each of these systems targets the A1 level of evaluation, they differ in the nature of the security policy enforced or in the architectural approach used to achieve their security. These systems represent a range of architectural approaches, with ASD taking a trusted process approach, and SeaView and LDV relying on the underlying trusted computing base (TCB) for mandatory security enforcement. These latter two systems thus provide an interesting contrast. LDV is also interesting because it enforces policies beyond those enforced in the other two systems.

In Essay 24, "Inference Problems in Multilevel Secure Database Management Systems," Sushil Jajodia and Catherine Meadows observe that inference is the process of deriving new information from known information. In multilevel database systems, the inference problem refers to the fact that the derived information can have higher sensitivity than the information provided to the user by the system. This essay surveys the state of the art in the study of inference problems. It defines and characterizes the inference problem as it relates to multilevel database systems and describes methods that have been developed for dealing with it.

Essay 25, "Logical Design of Audit Information in Relational Databases," by Sushil Jajodia, Shashi Gadia, and Gautam Bhargava, considers situations where the data is sufficiently sensitive that an audit trail becomes a necessity. Unfortunately, existing databases make a distinction between the current and past data. While they provide various types of support for dealing with the current data, the support for audit data is either nonexistent or very rudimentary. In this essay, the authors describe the database activity model that imposes a uniform logical structure on the past, present, and future data. There is never any loss of historical or current information in this model; thus the model provides a convenient mechanism for complete reconstruction of every action taken on the database.

Essay 26, "A Multilevel-Secure Object-Oriented Data Model," by Sushil Jajodia, Boris Kogan, and Ravi Sandhu, presents a new security model for mandatory access controls in object-oriented database systems. This model is a departure from the traditional security models based on the passive object, active subject paradigm. The authors' model is a flow model whose main elements are objects and messages. An object combines the properties of a passive information repository with those of an active agent. Messages and their replies are the basic instruments of information flow. The chief advantages of the proposed model are its compatibility with the object-oriented data model and the simplicity with which mandatory security policies can be stated and enforced.

The goal of Essay 27, "Integrity Mechanisms in Database Management Systems," by Ravi Sandhu and Sushil Jajodia, is to answer the following question: What mechanisms are required in a general-purpose multiuser database management system (DBMS) to facilitate the integrity objectives of information systems? Although existing commercial products fall short of providing the requisite mechanisms, in principle they can be easily extended to incorporate these mechanisms.

In addition to the essays, we provide an extensive glossary and an index. Biographies of the editors and authors follow.

What Is There to Worry About?
An Introduction to the
Computer Security Problem

Donald L. Brinkley and Roger R. Schell

This essay provides an overview of the vulnerabilities and threats to information security in computer systems. It begins with a historical presentation of past experiences with vulnerabilities in communication security along with present and future computer security experiences. The historical perspective demonstrates that misplaced confidence in the security of a system is worse than having no confidence at all in its security.

Next, the essay describes four broad areas of computer misuse: (1) theft of computational resources, (2) disruption of computational services, (3) unauthorized disclosure of information in a computer, and (4) unauthorized modification of information in a computer. Classes of techniques whereby computer misuse results in the unauthorized disclosure and modification of information are then described and examples are provided. These classes are (1) human error, (2) user abuse of authority, (3) direct probing, (4) probing with malicious software, (5) direct penetration, and (6) subversion of security mechanism. The roles of Trojan horses, viruses, worms, bombs, and other kinds of malicious software are described and examples provided.

In the past few decades, we have seen the implementation of myriads of computer systems of all sizes and their interconnection over computer networks. These systems handle and are required to protect credit data, justice information, computer vote tabulation, consumer billing, health data, insurance data, military and intelligence data, and computer and human communications, as well as countless other types of information. It is likely that readers of this essay have heard about some computer or network break-in at some time in the past few years. Such events have been the subjects of popular movies and books, and reports about them are appearing ever more frequently in the press. Even telephone service has been disrupted by what has been described as "electronic vandalism." Finding the source of such problems can amount to the electronic equivalent of looking for a needle in a haystack, so often the source of the problem is never discovered. Such is the nature of what we refer to in this essay as the computer security problem.

The first step in this introduction to the computer security problem will be a brief look at the historical parallels with a related subject — the communication security problem. The aspect of communication security addressed here is the protection of information while it is being communicated electronically from one place to another.

Historical lessons

The computer security problem has grown with the computer industry. For roughly the first two decades of the use of electronic digital computers, the problem of security really was not noticed. The early computers were used to process sensitive information, both in environments involving national security and in commercial applications. But the size of the computers and the nature of their applications allowed any security problems to be solved outside the computer. If the entire system was dedicated to a single user, protection consisted of the user simply picking up his tapes and cards and clearing CPU memory when the job was finished. If one had sensitive information on a computer, one locked the computer in a room. Basically the user had complete control over his processing environment, including his data and programs. The computer itself was not really part of the security problem or its solution.

In the 1960s, users began demanding better utilization of computing resources, and the security environment surrounding computer systems started to change. The response to the demand for more efficiency gave birth to multiplexing techniques, resource-sharing operating systems, multiprogramming, and various other techniques of the age. One could build a time-sharing computer system to serve many users simultaneously. Users suddenly found not only a lack of control over the processing environment but a lack of control over their data and programs as well. While some of the early time-sharing systems were used in so-called benign environments where there was no exposure to security problems, others were not.

Users of time-sharing computers — for example, in academic environments — rapidly found that there was a real threat of unauthorized disclosure or modification of any sensitive information processed on the early time-sharing systems. There arose the problem of defending independent software structures from each other, as these were often implemented on the same physical resources. Thus, multiprogramming operating systems began to enforce some sort of isolation of simultaneously executing processes. Since efficiency was the main consideration in computer systems, design criteria limited the "defending" and "isolation" primarily to the containment of accidents and errors.

Organizations desiring to utilize the increased capacities of resource-sharing systems demanded assurances that sensitive and nonsensitive information could be processed concurrently. Responding to customer pressure, computer systems manufacturers at first claimed that hardware and software mechanisms supporting resource sharing would also (with perhaps minor alterations) provide sufficient protection and isolation to permit multiprogramming of sensitive and nonsensitive programs and data.

This claim was soon discredited in the early 1970s with the introduction of several penetration tiger teams that were specifically tasked to test the protection offered by several major operating systems. Even those systems that underwent "retrofitting" to correct known implementation errors and design oversights were penetrated with only moderate amounts of energy. A Consensus Report published in the proceedings of the 1979 National Computer Conference [AFIP79] states:

> It is a fact, demonstrable by any of several studies, that no existing commercially-produced computer system can be counted upon to protect any of its moderately knowledgeable users from having complete and undetectable access to any information in the system, no matter what kinds of so-called security features or mechanisms have been built into the system.

Despite the fact that little substantive reduction in the basic vulnerabilities occurred throughout the 1970s and 1980s, vast numbers of computer systems serving every imaginable user population and processing information of every possible degree of sensitivity have been put in operation. These computer systems are connected together into communities via various types of networks. The connection to networks introduces a need for communication security (often utilizing cryptography) to counter the possibility of an attacker tapping into the communication lines used by the networks. Further, by providing more ways of accessing the systems (from other interconnected systems, from remote terminals, and so on), the connection to networks gives potential attackers greater accessibility to the computer systems, thus compounding the computer security problems. However, the fundamental computer security problems are little affected by the interconnection of systems via networks. That is, the networks themselves provide few fundamentally new computer security problems, other than enhanced accessibility of the interconnected systems to potential attackers. Thus, the primary computer security implication of connecting a computer system to a network is the increased exposure of the system to those individuals with the opportunity and the means to exploit the underlying computer security problems.

As noted in the preceding paragraph, however, communication security technology was developed to counter a different threat — that of an attacker tapping into communication lines. Communication security technology has a much longer history of development and use than that of computer security. Those concerned with computer security will be well served to learn from some of the errors made in using communication security. The remainder of this section briefly reviews some of the lessons from the history of communication security in an attempt to help those concerned with computer security avoid the mistakes encountered there.

Communication specialists, especially in the military, early recognized the vulnerability of electronic transmissions to interception (for example, through wiretaps or surreptitious listening to radio signals). The solutions were simple but drastic — restrict transmissions only to relatively unimportant (and nonsensitive) information or to transmission paths that were physically protected from intrusion. Obviously, these solutions limited use of the communications technology where it was most needed — in potentially hostile situations.

The communication security restrictions eventually gave rise to various cryptographic devices. These devices encode information into an unintelligible form so that protection of the entire transmission path is not required. But (of paramount importance) this dramatically changed the very nature of the security problem itself from a question of physical protection to a question of technical efficacy. Unfortunately, a problem arose with this new technology. When selecting a cryptographic device to use, rather than determining its effectiveness through careful technical analysis, selection was often based on the apparent absence of a known way to attack it.

Technically weak cryptographic devices found widespread military use because of misplaced confidence and the pressing operational need for electrical communications. One notable example was the Enigma machine used by the Germans during World War II. Their high-level national command and control network used it for communication security throughout the war. The Germans considered the Enigma completely safe. Yet before the war really got started, the British (perhaps aided by others) had in fact "solved the puzzle of Enigma" [WINT74].

The Enigma example also shows how the tendency to defend previous decisions (to accept and use techniques that were plausible but turn out to be insufficient) assures those so inclined of opportunities for exploitation. Ultra — what the broken Enigma signals were called — "not only gave the full strength and disposition of the enemy, it showed that the Allied (troops) could achieve tactical surprise." In fact, General Dwight Eisenhower stated that "Ultra was decisive" [WINT74].

To be sure, the Germans "must have been puzzled by our knowledge of their U-boat positions, but luckily they did not accept the fact that we had broken Enigma" [WINT74]. There was a similar misplaced trust by the Japanese. The Japanese "hypnotized themselves into the delusion that their codes were never seriously compromised" [KAHN67]. Both the Japanese and the Germans, it seems, would not acknowledge their security weaknesses without direct confirming counterintelligence — and this came only after they had lost the war.

Technical experts eventually provided a sound technical basis for countering these sorts of communication security problems. Today our military and the commercial sectors make widespread use of cryptographic devices with confidence. For computers, as for communications, the nub of the problem is the effectiveness of the security mechanism and the assurance of its implementation.

Applying this history further to computer security, important lessons become clear. Misplaced confidence in the security of a system is worse than having no confidence at all in its security. Each (formal or de facto) decision to use computer systems without proper computer security controls permits a technical weakness to become a vulnerability in the same way the broken codes were a vulnerability to the Germans and the Japanese. An implication for computer security in military systems is that the lack of hard counterintelligence on exploitation should not be offered as evidence of effective security, even though the absence of war against an enemy capable of exploiting such weaknesses in our military computer systems has precluded ultimate exploitation.

The thrust of this historical review is captured in the maxim, "Those who cannot remember the past are condemned to repeat it." The main lesson to be learned is this: Do not entrust security to technology unless that technology is demonstrably trustworthy, and the absence of demonstrated compromise is absolutely not a demonstration of security.

Computer misuse

As we observed earlier, today there are vast numbers of computer systems and networks serving every imaginable user population and processing information of every possible degree of sensitivity. There is also a large and growing threat to the security of much of this information and the resources that handle it. The threat stems from the potential for computer misuse.

With respect to the potential damage done, computer misuse can be categorized into four broad areas:

1. theft of computational resources,
2. disruption of computational services,
3. unauthorized information disclosure, and

4.   unauthorized information modification.

Within these areas of computer misuse, we are concerned about misuse effected by either authorized users of the computer or those not authorized to use the computer. However, the former is generally a much more difficult problem to counter. As we shall discuss further, countering unauthorized information disclosure and modification depends as heavily on preventing the illicit access of bona fide users as preventing illicit access of nonusers. On the other hand, countering theft of computational resources and disruption of computational services primarily requires keeping nonusers from using (and abusing) the resource.

Note that computer misuse may arise in situations where there are legal penalties for the attackers if they are caught and convicted of these acts (for example, in countries or states that have specific laws against them). However, misuse may also occur in situations in which there is not a reasonable chance that the attackers will be captured and punished (for example, in espionage or warfare between two countries). In the latter situations, of course, there will be more of a concern with protecting against the threat being carried out; in the former, determining the damage and identifying the attacker after the fact are important as well.

Theft of computational resources. The theft of computational resources is one area of computer misuse. Much as some people connect into electric utility lines and divert power for their use without payment, computer resources can be diverted. For example, the systematic use of computational resources on a large scale by unauthorized users can have both economic and production impacts. Likewise, the use of systems by authorized users for unauthorized purposes (game playing, office football pools, bowling league administration, and so on) is a theft of the computational resource, as it represents a drain upon the computer system. However, such theft by authorized users is usually on a limited scale and is much harder to control, since, in general, it is difficult to determine whether authorized users are using the computer for authorized purposes only. Hence, preventing theft of computational resources typically focuses on protecting against actions by unauthorized users. Not only is prevention easier than apprehension, but also it is the unauthorized users who most likely perpetrate a theft on a major scale with little evidence to permit apprehending the thief.

Unauthorized programs that extensively use the hardware and the operating system can consume many thousands of dollars of computer services and compete with authorized programs. In addition to lost time, hardware subsystems — memory, for example — may be filled by the unauthorized programs to the exclusion of valid data, causing failure or delay of authorized programs.

If measures are taken to exclude unauthorized users, say through passwords, the persons responsible may misrepresent themselves as valid users, for example, by using a valid password they guessed or observed. In this way, they can continue to run their programs and charge any expenses to some legitimate user. However, stronger measures than passwords can be used to make it harder for an unauthorized user to masquerade as a legitimate user. Furthermore, other technical controls (for example, what is known as a "trusted path," described in the next essay) can be used to substantially enhance the effectiveness of passwords and other measures.

Disruption of computational services. The second area of computer misuse is the disruption of computational services. Consider the situation of two companies competing for a contract. Company A has an automated cost/schedule system, while Company B does not. In the last several days before bidding closes, Company A's computer (upon which its management relies) is unavailable due to a series of failures. Company A is forced to develop its bid without benefit of its system and thus proposes a contract with a cost 5 percent higher than the more accurate, computerized figures would have suggested. Company A loses in its bid on the basis of cost. The computer failures were caused by saboteurs from Company B.

Such disruptions of service can be extremely expensive if the timing is correct. Interruptions can be caused by attacks on any of the computer system's components: hardware, software, or data. Physical damage to the hardware, confusion or modification of the operating system, subtle changes in the applications software, or modifications to the data or interface can all cause such problems. This form of attack does not necessarily use significant amounts of computer time, nor does it require either access to or modification of data. Nevertheless, access to the system by authorized users can be denied through these subtle attacks.

In such situations the misuse often goes undetected. The failures may be blamed on "bad luck" or on inadequate preventive maintenance. Since resources accessed may be minimal, few "tracks" may be left by the attackers, and proof of malicious acts or intent is often difficult to obtain. Identification of the perpetrators is even more difficult, since it is relatively easy to cover what "tracks" are left behind. Like preventing theft of computational resources, protecting against disruption of computational services typically focuses on protecting against actions by unauthorized users and on attempting to detect any misuse after the fact by authorized users by performing a "best effort" audit on their actions.

Unauthorized information disclosure. The third area of computer misuse is the unauthorized disclosure of data stored in the computer. This type of act, much akin to our popular view of espionage, is well understood when we speak of unauthorized access to conventional data files stored on paper in filing cabinets. Computers add a new dimension to this problem. The enormous storage capability and the fast access times make the stakes more costly. A criminal might normally have to search an office for hours to find the data he wants (if he finds it at all). The long periods required for such nefarious searches greatly increase the chances of being "caught in the act." Using a computer, the attacker can search databases equivalent to several offices' filing systems in a matter of seconds. The fact that computer data systems often store data used for critical decision-making processes (such as the hypothetical situation of Company A above) usually implies that the data is entered in a more timely manner than in paper-based systems. The complete and up-to-date information in a computer system makes it a tempting target. "Outsiders" with full access to "inside" information pose a significant threat to business and society.

Furthermore, a computer used to implement a cryptosystem to protect information from unauthorized disclosure (for example, by encrypting the files it stores) presents a particularly attractive target, since cryptosystems typically depend on the nondisclosure of the encryption or decryption keys for the protection of the data being encrypted. That makes the keys themselves a small but extremely valuable target. When such keys are included in the data processed by the computer, such a small target is far easier to "slip out" of the system than all of the data that the keys can be used to compromise. This presents a significant motivator to those bent on attempting to gain unauthorized access to such data to try to implant some malicious software in the system (for example, through a penetration of the system). The malicious software could covertly leak the keys once the system is operational. Perhaps even more so than other forms of computer misuse, unauthorized disclosures are difficult to detect, since there may be no apparent tracks left behind.

Unauthorized information modification. We have mentioned the advantage of knowing the facts upon which a competitor is basing his decisions, and of knowing the decisions as soon as they are made. Of far greater use is the ability to "feed" data (erroneous, misleading, or incomplete) into the competing system and thus control or influence the decisions to one's benefit. With such ability, one can virtually "change the facts" to suit the situation. Consider also the ability to "feed" keys into a cryptosystem such as that described in the preceding section (for example, where the keys are stored or manipulated by the computer that may be penetrated). If he had the ability to control the keys in a cryptosystem, an attacker could virtually control the cryptosystem. With this power to substitute his keys for the intended keys or to control the generation of the keys used, the attacker could not only read and write the data flowing through the cryptosystem as would be possible even if he only knew the key (see the preceding section), but he could also generally introduce new data and read and write any data of the sort protected by any of the keys in the system.

The classical cases of computer operators modifying their credit ratings or erasing the records of their outstanding debts are small examples of this area of misuse. Also included in this area are modifications made to programs. Modification of accounting routines to prevent charges to one's credit card from being billed to one's account is an example. In view of our ever-increasing dependence on computerized systems in banking and commerce, the potential for large-scale fraud is enormous.

Computer misuse techniques

The latter two areas of computer misuse discussed in the previous sections are threats to the information that computers handle rather than to the computers themselves. Threats to information (unauthorized information disclosure and modification) are fundamentally different from threats to resources (theft of computational resources and disruption of computational services). For one thing, countering information-oriented computer misuse depends as heavily on preventing the illicit access of bona fide users as preventing illicit access of nonusers, whereas countering resource-oriented computer misuse primarily requires keeping nonusers from using (and abusing) the resource. Further, resource-oriented computer misuse is countered using control mechanisms different from those necessary for countering information-oriented misuse. Generally, resource-oriented misuse is most effectively countered with measures such as maintaining separate rooms for computers, registering users of computers and networks, requiring use of passwords, and other physical and administrative security measures. Appropriate additional measures may include those that fall into the areas of computer system reliability and human engineering.

For the most part, this book in general and this essay in particular deal with information-oriented computer misuse. In thinking about how information-oriented computer misuse may be brought about, we have come to characterize "what there is to worry about" into six different classes. These classes are

1. human error,
2. user abuse of authority,
3. direct probing,
4. probing with malicious software,
5. direct penetration, and
6. subversion of security mechanism.

Common to all six of these classes are two elements:

1. A vulnerability: A quality or characteristic of the computer system (for example, a "flaw") that provides the opportunity or means of exploitation.
2. A threat: The possible existence of one who participates in the exploitation by gaining unauthorized disclosure or modification of information such as accompanies information-oriented computer misuse.

The product of threat and vulnerability is considered the risk one faces in operating a system. Each of these two elements may in theory be brought about either accidentally or deliberately. For example, a vulnerability may be introduced through either the accidental introduction of a "bug" into the system or the deliberate introduction of malicious software. However, although a threat of accidental exploitation of a vulnerability may exist, we are concerned in this essay only with deliberate exploitations of vulnerabilities (that is, intentional acts attempting unauthorized disclosure or modification of information), since these are the purview of computer security, as described in Essay 2.

Therefore, the remainder of this essay discusses the six classes of information-oriented computer misuse listed above, which we call "computer misuse techniques." We have used the rubric "computer misuse techniques" for all six classes, since what we are talking about with each is the threat of deliberate exploitation of an accidentally or deliberately introduced vulnerability. This distinction is clear in considering the first class — human error. The "error" allows the accidental introduction of a vulnerability, which may then be deliberately exploited, making it a "technique" for computer misuse.

We will now introduce the six classes of computer misuse techniques and provide examples for each class. Note that these classes of computer misuse are not mutually exclusive, as attackers may combine techniques to more effectively achieve their nefarious goals.

Human error. Human errors that lead to unauthorized disclosure or modification are basically probabilistic in nature. They may involve several human, hardware, and timing factors that when combined could allow an unauthorized disclosure or modification of information. Simple examples of this method are a computer operator inadvertently mounting the wrong tape, a user typing sensitive information into a file that is thought to be nonsensitive, or (assuming the computer has some sort of access controls for files) a user setting the authorized mode of access for a file to an inappropriate value. Users receiving information from this kind of disclosure or modifying information in this manner are often victims of circumstances and may not be malicious in their intent. However, even though the success of this method relies on probabilistic events that one cannot control, the method can be used by a determined attacker.

The basic approach used by an attacker in this method is to sit and wait for the proper set of circumstances to occur. Upon detection of a breach in the protection of information, the attacker acts to exploit the breach and make use of this accidentally introduced vulnerability.

This method could prove profitable to a malicious user, particularly if the system under attack has a history of human errors. Although this method is viable, other methods will be discussed that do not rely on these probabilistic circumstances and would thus be far more attractive to an attacker. Better human engineering reduces the probability of human error.

User abuse of authority. Al Capone's bookkeeper is reported to have said, "I can steal more with a pencil than ten men with machine guns." That was probably a conservative estimate. Regardless of the bookkeeper's actual capabilities, his chances of escaping detection and apprehension by law enforcement authorities would have been significantly better than those of a gang of gunslinging outlaws. If we can replace a hundred or a thousand crooked bookkeepers with a single vulnerable computer, consider the possibilities. The computer significantly increases the speed and possible scope of criminal acts.

Newspaper readers will occasionally encounter reports of "computer misuse" or "computer crime" at some financial institution that would probably be just as happy to avoid the publicity. The cases reported range from simple to fiendishly complex. In a simple case, perhaps a bank teller records, by a few keystrokes on a terminal, the receipt of a few thousand or hundred thousand dollars of money that "isn't there." An accomplice withdraws most or all of the money from another branch of the bank and both flee to some warmer and more hospitable clime. The daily audit of account balances and the real amount of cash on hand soon reveal the shortage, but by then the culprits are likely to be long gone.

More complex instances of this sort of computer misuse tax the imagination of the financial institution and the credulity of the reader. In one widely reported case, a bank officer is alleged to have submitted transactions with values in the millions over a period of more than a year. In this case, the strategy was allegedly to exploit the delay of funds or paperwork traveling from bank to bank or branch to branch, build up a large "float" of money in transit, and siphon off some of that float to the goals of personal enrichment and early retirement. The details of such a scheme are apparently intricate and difficult for the culprit as well as the reader. If the culprit slips up or there is some sort of accident, the float may sink, as it were, and the entire scheme could be discovered. In one case, the fatal flaw was apparently a computer outage that required a batch of bogus transactions to be processed by hand.

Computer crimes such as these make interesting reading, and it seems likely that they will become more common in the years to come, as computers become more common in every nook and cranny of life. There is already a vast literature on such incidents, and one might be tempted to conclude that these cases typify the computer security problem. In fact, however, a review of the cases shows that they have little to do with computers. Whether they are simple cases involving the entry of a fictitious transaction or complicated ones involving the management of vast "floats," these crimes could as well be carried out in a world of quill pens and green eyeshades as one that used the latest computer systems. The key common factor is the irresponsible action of an authorized individual who, in some manner, abuses a trust and abuses the authority granted to perform some task.

These essays have little to say about the problem of controlling authorized users of an application beyond confining the authorized users to their domains of authority and providing the capability to automatically audit the users' security-relevant actions. Computers cannot reach into users' minds and determine whether they are abusing the trust placed in them. We believe, in fact, that restricting the users to their domains of authority is a worthwhile goal for any system that processes valuable data, but the legitimacy of the authorized users' actions is better measured by auditors or experts in the area of action than controlled by computer systems.

Direct probing. If cases of user abuse of authority are as old as banks and ledger papers, the computer misuse technique that we have called "direct probing" is as old as shared computer systems. We use the term probing to distinguish those cases where an individual uses a computer system in ways that are certainly allowed, but not necessarily intended, by the system's operators or developers. It is important to realize that the individual who is attempting probing is deliberate in his attempts. This introduces a class of "user" that computer system designers may not have seriously considered. Often, designs reflect that the systems are expected to operate in a "benign environment" where violations of the system controls are presumed to be accidental. Because systems are presumed to be in a benign environment, the attacker may not have to exert much effort to succeed.

We present two examples because these cases are important. The second example bears many similarities to the story told by C. Stoll in *The Cuckoo's Egg* [STOL89], but it does describe a different event.

Students and sloppy security. The growth of computer literacy among high school (and younger) students has resulted in a large population interested in seeing "what systems are out there" and what information and programs are available. More frequently, there seems to be significant interest in gaining unauthorized access to other people's computers and information.

A widely reported incident involved students from a school in New York who learned a telephone number that would give them access to a time-sharing computer operated by a small business in another city. The students dialed the number and recognized the "banner" that the system displayed on their terminal as belonging to the same operating system used by their school's computer. They knew from experience with their school computer that copies of the operating system were distributed by the manufacturer with user accounts predefined for the system manager, who was expected to log in and create new accounts for his facility's users. The system manager account had privileges to access any information on the computer. It was always distributed with the same "secret password," and the documentation for the system directed the system manager to change the password as soon as he had installed the system.

The students tried the login sequence for the system manager's account and gave the "distributed" password. Although the small business system had been in place for a long time, the system manager's password had never been changed, and the students found themselves logged in with a fully privileged account. They read files, deleted files, and played games. They were able to create new accounts for themselves (they were, after all, the system manager for the computer) and made fairly general nuisances of themselves.

Eventually they asked for a "ransom" to stop playing on the system and leave its owners and users alone, and the ransom demand revealed enough information to allow the authorities to intervene. The students wound up the exercise with gently slapped hands, and the victims were not (very) much worse off for the experience.

The key aspect of this case is that the students did not use the computer or its software in any way that was unexpected by its developers or owners. They merely took advantage of sloppy administration by the system's operators and inserted themselves where they had no business being.

Network adventure. We expect that many of our readers will have playcd or hcard of some form of the computer game Adventure. In this game, one is presented with the computer's representation of a maze of interconnected chambers. Some contain treasures that the player can collect and bring back to a "home base" to gain points in the game. Other chambers contain various kinds of monsters, miscreants, and unfortunate circumstances. The topology of the maze is left to the player to infer. The object, of course, is to navigate the maze and collect the treasures without being destroyed by one of the unfortunate circumstances.

Some persons unknown played a form of real-life Adventure in the large computer network operated by a major manufacturer. They dialed an

"800" number that gave access to an account that was supposed to be used for reporting software problems. The account was improperly set up, and the "players" found that they could issue user commands to the operating system in question. In particular, they could try remote terminal logins to other systems in the manufacturer's network and could copy files from other machines.

In exploring the network, the adventurers discovered that it was easy to find the names of users on other machines by using the network file access facilities to list directory names, and by assuming that user names were the same as directory names. They tried guessing passwords for the user names they had found, and discovered that occasionally user name and password were the same. Then they could log in on a remote machine as one of its users.

As they wandered through the network, the adventurers discovered more user names and more passwords. Many files were unprotected (readable to any user on the network), and some gave clues to the names and passwords of yet more users. In addition, by logging into remote systems, the players were able to read files that were protected from "world" or general access — they now had legitimate local accounts that might belong to a group that had access to the files, or might own some files. Some of the files they found in this manner even contained stored passwords. In addition, some users had accounts on several machines. When those accounts all had the same password, it was a bonus to the now experienced adventurers.

Eventually the adventurers got access to some "privileged" accounts on a few machines. These accounts had the authority to bypass the normal system controls and read or write any information on the systems. In particular, the players could read lists of user names and passwords, and now had unrestricted access to many more "chambers" in the "maze." The adventurers were able to compromise numerous accounts and to read an "awesome" number of files during their explorations.

The only misfortune that the adventurers suffered was early discovery. They were logged into the machine that was their starting point using a user name and password that should not have been associated with that communication line at that time of day, and an alert user realized that fact. The user developed a program that could monitor all transactions from the "800" number, and the manufacturer was able to record all the adventurers' activities. Because they were apparently students on a low budget, the adventurers were unwilling to stop using the system through the all-important (and free) "800" number. Eventually, through a combination of telephone traces, rumors, and good luck, the management of the network got an idea of the identities of the players and the game was canceled.

This case is like the previous case in one key respect. The adventurers, like the student vandals, were using the computer roughly as it was intended. They were looking at files that were there for the reading, logging in through the normal paths with passwords that were legitimately installed in the systems, and issuing legitimate commands to operating systems and network software. Their ability to gain access to a huge quantity of information resulted from a combination of sloppiness on the part of system users and managers and the fact that most of the systems they were exploring had fairly "coarse" protection, so that files were frequently left accessible to the "world."

The results of this fairly unsophisticated game of Adventure are nonetheless frightening. Had the players had a sufficient budget to dial directly to a machine where they had gained access to an account (instead of reusing the "800" number and then exploring by use of the intercomputer network's communication), they need never have been discovered or stopped. They had access to a large volume of sensitive information, but were apparently more interested in seeing how far they could go than in making malicious use of the information they could find.

Probing with malicious software. This computer misuse technique is quite similar to the previous technique, in that it is a form of probing — it involves using a computer system in ways that are allowed, but not necessarily intended. With this technique, however, specially developed software is used by the attacker for the express purpose of carrying out the probing. The use of such malicious software in probing makes this technique unique and significant.

The Trojan horse. Ancient Greek mythology supplies us with the story of the Trojan horse, which when brought within the fortified walls of Troy, opened to reveal hostile Greek soldiers, who attacked the city's defenses from within. The term Trojan horse for software is widely attributed to Daniel Edwards [SALT75], an early computer security pioneer, and it has become standard in computer security. Like its mythological counterpart, it signifies a technique for attacking a system from within, rather than staging a frontal assault on well-maintained barriers. However, it does so without circumventing normal system controls (in the same manner in which the Trojans opened the doors of the city to bring in the horse). A Trojan horse is a program whose execution results in undesired side effects, generally unanticipated by the user. A Trojan horse will most often appear to provide some desired or "normal" function. In other words, a Trojan horse will generally have both an overt function (to serve as a lure to attract the program into use by an unsuspecting user) and a covert function (to perform clandestine activities).

The overt or "lure" function of a Trojan horse can, for example, be mathematical library routines, word processing programs, computer games, compilers, or any program that might be widely used at an installation. Because these programs are executing on behalf of the user, they assume all access privileges that the user has. This gives the covert function access to any information that is available to the user.

The covert function is exercised concurrently with the lure function. An example of this kind of malicious software might be a text editor program that legitimately performs editing functions for the unsuspecting user while browsing through his directories looking for interesting files to copy. Attackers have used seemingly harmless computer games (for example, backgammon) to set all of the player's files to "world read" so the game's author can copy the files without the knowledge of the files' owner.

This is a particularly effective option for the attacker due to the fact that as far as any internal protection mechanism of the computer system is concerned, there are no "illegal" actions in progress. The Trojan horse (for example, text editor) is simply a user program, executing in user address space, accessing user files, performing perfectly legitimate system service requests such as giving another user (for example, the attacker) copies of files.

An example comes from the security test of an Air Force system that was used to process sensitive information in the early 1970s. The installation in question was processing classified magnetic tapes using a computer and operating system that were widely known for the ease with which a hostile individual could access any information processed. The installation's solution was to use only a selected set of programs to process the classified tapes, while any user was allowed to submit any unclassified program that he or she wished. The programs used to process the classified tapes not only did the requisite processing, but also took special precautions to label the classified information that appeared on the line printers. They even erased the main memory areas that had been used to store the sensitive data before terminating processing and returning the memory areas to the operating system for reallocation.

A security test team (a tiger team) realized that the classified processing programs could be used to ease the attacker's job. By exploiting the operating system's weaknesses to access it, they modified the program used to print the contents of a classified magnetic tape to serve as a Trojan horse. The Trojan horse program completed the print job when requested, but also hid a copy of the classified data, lightly encrypted, in an "invisible" location on disk. A later unclassified job could be submitted to read the hidden data, print it out (still encrypted) for a member of the tiger team, and erase the hidden copy. In this case, a security solution actually made a security problem worse, since the use of the classified processing programs served to locate and save for the tiger team exactly those files and jobs that they wished to steal.

To reinforce the subtle nature of Trojan horses and the reality of the opportunities to plant them, the interested reader should read the story by Ken Thompson [THOM84], one of the codevelopers of Unix, of what he describes as "the cutest program [he] ever wrote." This program is a Trojan horse that he introduced into the C compiler. When the Trojan horse in the C compiler determined that it was compiling the "login" code for the Unix operating system, it would generate code to accept not only the valid password but also a fixed password that he had previously selected and built into the Trojan horse. He also planted another Trojan horse in the compiler. This Trojan horse added the code for the two Trojan horses to the object code each time it recompiled subsequent versions of the compiler, without the Trojan horse code having to be present in the compiler source code. In this way, he was able to cover his tracks for years, while his employer possibly continued to unknowingly crank out copies of the operating system and compiler containing his Trojan horses.

While our stable full of Trojan horses may seem quite different from the network Adventure or password exploitation cited above, there is a technical point that all three cases hold in common. That is, just as one can guess a password or read an unprotected file without doing violence to the mechanism of the underlying computer and operating system, one can install a Trojan horse in a program that will be used by an intended victim, and that Trojan horse can function within the normal rules and mechanisms of the computer and its operating system. By issuing operating system directives to reset the access controls on a file or make a new copy, the Trojan horse can take advantage of standard mechanisms to do its dirty work without detection.

Two things make Trojan horses particularly attractive to the hostile attacker. First, as a practical matter, there is no effective procedure for detecting whether a piece of software contains a Trojan horse, especially if the designer devoted a reasonable effort to hide it. Second, almost all computer users are compelled to use software (for example, operating systems and application programs) developed by persons completely unknown to them. The route this software takes to the user provides numerous opportunities for insertion of a Trojan horse.

Viruses, time bombs, logic bombs, and worms. These four eye-catching names have received some notoriety in the popular press in the past few years. Actually, these are four types of Trojan horses, with special characteristics.

A *virus* is a self-replicating Trojan horse that attaches itself to other programs in order to be executed. This method of self-replication by attaching to another program to be executed is the primary distinguishing feature of a virus. The primary covert function of some viruses may be simply to replicate and spread, performing no other harmful action. However, others may take such actions as to modify, copy, or destroy other files or entire disks. Viruses are carried from one personal computer to another by unsuspecting users sharing software that has already been infected. They spread among other computer systems in a similar manner via networks. Note that a virus's method of replication by attaching itself to another program is, in itself, an unauthorized modification of data (the program to which it is attached).

Since each copy of a virus may replicate itself, a virus's ability to spread quickly is one of its most distinctive qualities. For example, suppose one copy of a virus is introduced into a system through the execution of an infected text editor. If that virus is able to attach itself to a new program just once per day, and each of its copies does likewise, after a week there will be more than 50 copies. After about a month, there will be around a billion copies. Although this is not our serious prediction, it is interesting to note that at the rate currently identified viruses seem to be spreading, by 1995 every computer in existence could potentially have a virus. (Do not be overly frightened, however, as this book will describe the technology for arresting Trojan horses; it is only necessary to employ it.)

A *time bomb* is simply a Trojan horse set to trigger at a particular time. For example, time bombs have been set to trigger on Friday the 13th and on the anniversary of events that were significant to the attacker.

A *logic bomb* is a Trojan horse set to trigger upon the occurrence of a particular logical event. For example, the Trojan horse might be set to trigger at the worst possible time. An event such as the need to correct a temperature imbalance in a power plant might trigger a logic bomb that modifies data to make the imbalance worse. Another example of a logic bomb is a "letter bomb" — contained in electronic mail and triggered when the mail is read.

Another form of Trojan horse is known as a *worm*. A worm is a program that distributes multiple copies of itself within a system or across a distributed system either through the exercise of a flaw that permits it to spread or through normally permitted actions (for example, mailing copies of itself to other systems, compiling them on the remote systems, and initiating their execution). Once in place, the worm may attack in any number of ways, through the methods described above or in the paragraphs below. A good example of a worm in action is the "Internet worm" [SPAF89]; it invaded a large, nationwide network of computers called the Internet, spreading to thousands of machines and disrupting normal activities and connectivity of the machines for several days. Fortunately, the primary objective of this worm was simply to spread to more machines, rather than to do any particular damage once it was established on a new machine. Otherwise, the damage would have been far more significant.

Direct penetration. Probing relies on the fact that a computer's security controls are being used sloppily, or that the controls are so poorly designed that a user cannot control the sharing of information in a way that corresponds to his or her needs. Penetration, in contrast, involves the bypassing of intended security controls. In many cases, an attacker finds a single flaw in the implementation of an operating system or hardware, writes a program, and has the entire computer at his or her command.

Penetration typically involves the use of malicious software, such as a Trojan horse, to confirm and exploit the flaw. It is not necessarily difficult or costly. Three historical examples will illustrate the point.

The best is not good enough. Honeywell Information Systems and MIT conducted a cooperative research project during the late 1960s and early 1970s to develop the Multiplexed Information and Computing Service (Multics). This time-sharing system incorporated hardware and operating system software "designed with security in mind" and was widely touted as the most secure operating system of its time. An Air Force tiger team was evaluating Multics [KARG74] as a candidate for use in a Pentagon application where the computer itself would be required to protect sensitive information from authorized system users who were not "cleared" to see all the information in the computer. Only the Multics operating system would stand between classified information and users without the clearances to see it.

In examining the Multics operating system programs, the tiger team found one place where an ordinary user program could branch to any location in a supervisory (executive mode) program. Such instances were forbidden by the Multics design concepts, but the implementation had made this program directly accessible for reasons of efficiency. The tiger team examined the program listings and found two instructions that would store a word at any location they specified, then return to their program. The privileges of the supervisory program were such that the store instruction could operate even on the programs or data used by the operating system itself.

The tiger team also found a place where Multics first checked a user's authorization for access to a file and, when the request proved valid, executed the request. However, in this case, the user could change the request after the validity check and before the execution of the request. Again, the vulnerability could be exploited to operate on any information in the computer.

The tiger team tested the first apparent vulnerability on an Air Force laboratory computer, then tried it on the Multics development computer at MIT. They were able to use a small "hole" in the operating system to change the access privileges for a penetration job and gain complete and unrestricted access to any information on the computer. Specifically, they were able to change the "user ID" for their process from that of an ordinary user to that of the system manager who maintained the system programs and files. Given this level of access, the tiger team had effective ownership of the MIT Multics computer.

Once they had a way to penetrate Multics, the tiger team provided a number of additional demonstrations of the thoroughness of their work. (These will be described in a later section.)

When the hardware is soft. A major concern in computer security during the late 1960s and early 1970s dealt with security-related hardware flaws. There was a fear in that era that processor hardware might fail in such a way that the processor would keep running but security-related hardware checks would no longer be made. For example, the failed hardware might allow a privileged instruction to be executed from a user program. The people who hypothesized the problem also invented a form of solution: An unprivileged, interactive program they called "Subverter" would check periodically to see if any security-related hardware failures had occurred and, if they had, sound a suitable alarm.

The tiger team that penetrated Multics developed the Subverter program to check for flaws in the Multics processor. This program would awaken once every minute or so and try a few illegal operations, then go back to sleep. The illegal operations ranged from commonplace to obscure and were chosen to invoke the complexity of the Multics processor hardware. These tests included

1. trying to run privileged instructions,
2. attempting to violate read and write permission on segments,
3. testing of all instructions marked illegal, and
4. taking out-of-bounds faults on zero length segments.

During several hundred hours of execution while the tiger team's members were using Multics, Subverter never detected a security-related hardware failure. When the hardware broke, the system went down, and there was no opportunity for subtle security exploitation. The tiger team did, however, discover that Subverter would occasionally crash without apparent cause.

On investigation, it became clear that Subverter was crashing because its read-only program segment was being modified. The test case that Subverter used for illegal memory access was to try to write in itself, and in these cases it was succeeding. The cause was traced to a test that used a combination of register, indexed, and indirect addressing that spanned several of the segments that make up a Multics process's virtual memory. When the locations involved met certain requirements (one indirect address word had to be in location three of a specific segment in the address chain), the instruction that started the operation would succeed without regard to the process's access rights for the final target address. When the target address was in the read-only Subverter code segment, Subverter "clobbered itself."

The flaw that allowed Subverter to write in itself was not random. Every time the combination of addressing modes involved was used, the problem would occur. It could in fact be used to write anywhere in virtual memory on any Multics processor. Thus the hardware flaw was as exploitable from a security penetration standpoint as any of the flaws in the operating system. It was a speculation that there might be such a flaw that caused the tiger team to write Subverter so that it emphasized the testing of obscure and complex instructions and addressing modes. The flaw was found to have been introduced by a field change to the processor that had the side effect of removing a special-case security check.

The implications of the Multics hardware vulnerability are as frightening as those of the software flaws. The designer of a secure operating system usually assumes a known hardware base. In this case, the hardware was "almost" what was expected, but the difference was capable of rendering the system's controls ineffective.

Job security instead of computer security. An early instance of penetration illustrates the tremendous difficulties of penetration and security repair. Penetrate and patch, as this was called, was once thought to be an effective security method, but it is now known to be unreliable. In theory one could test all possible programs to find any that led to a security penetration. This method of exhaustion would be effective if it were possible, but it is far beyond the realm of feasibility. For any real computer, it would take so long that before the penetration and patch work was finished, the sun would literally have burned out! Essays 2 and 6 describe more productive schemes for designing and demonstrating the security of computer systems. See Essay 11 for additional information on penetration testing.

A large aerospace contractor operated a major computer center that was used to support both government contracts and a commercial service bureau. The government contracts required that the contractor process classified information, while the service bureau had a large population of customers who could access the computer center by telephone.

The contractor proposed to allow the service bureau users access to the computer that was processing classified information. It was well understood (by the contractor and government security officials) that the operating system used by the computer center could be penetrated by a hostile programmer, so the contractor proposed to fix the system's vulnerabilities. To that end, the contractor assigned a team of system programmers to review the operating system code, find the ways in which the controls could be subverted, and then repair the vulnerabilities. The team labored for several months and produced a system that they pronounced secure.

At this point the government brought in an independent tiger team to assess the contractor's work. The team found, in about two weeks, a set of ways to gain control of the computer in supervisor state and obtain access to any file stored or information processed in the system.

One would think that such an incident might be the end, but the contractor responded by mounting a new team that was directed to find all the remaining exposures and fix them as well. After a few more months, the tiger team was brought back with the same quick and successful results. The cycle may have been repeated once more — the history becomes vague around this point. However, the point that is not vague is that the contractor eventually gave up, bought a separate computer, and secured it by locking it up. The tiger team left the field victorious after the final "game."

Note, however, that this was a relatively happy ending only because the tiger team was fortunate enough to repeatedly find flaws with little effort. If they had not, it may well have been the case that the system would have been declared "secure," and the flaws would have been found and exploited only by malicious attackers, while the contractor and the government proudly used their "secure" computer.

Subversion of security mechanism. Subversion of a computer system's security mechanism involves the covert and methodical undermining of internal system controls to allow unauthorized and undetected access to information within the computer system. Such subversion is not limited to on-site operations, as in the case of deliberate penetration. It includes activities that spread over the entire life cycle of a computer system, including design, implementation, distribution, installation, and use.

The legitimate activities that are carried on during the various life-cycle phases offer ample opportunities for the subverter to undermine system components. The activities in the first four life-cycle phases identified above are basically not sensitive in nature and are carried out at relatively open facilities. Therefore, the subverter would have little difficulty in subverting the system components under development. Later in the use phase, these same components would be involved in the protection of information. By this phase the subverter would have an "environment" purposefully constructed for the unauthorized and undetected exploitation of a system and the information it contains.

The subverter is not an amateur. To be able to carry out subversive operations, the subverter must understand the activities that are performed during the various phases of a computer system's life cycle. But none of these activities is beyond the skill range of the average undergraduate computer science major. In fact, much of the activity involved with subversion can be carried out by individuals with much less technical knowledge. The subverter can utilize a diverse group of individuals who may or may not be aware of the subversive activities they are performing. One needs only to imagine the vast number of people who will have access to the various computer system components prior to their being installed at a site with sensitive information.

The subverter could, and undoubtedly would, use various methods to circumvent the control features of a computer system. But the subverter is concerned with the long-term return on his subversive efforts. To rely on a design oversight or an implementation flaw that might be eventually corrected would not be sound "business" practice. Rather, the subverter constructs his own clandestine mechanisms that are inserted into the controlling hardware or software during one of the various phases of a computer system's life cycle. Such clandestine mechanisms have historically been called artifices [LACK74]. These artifices can be implemented as either malicious hardware or malicious software. The most common forms of artifices used in subversion are known as trap doors [KARG74].

A key characteristic of a trap door is that, since it is installed in the controlling portion of the system (for example, operating system) and is therefore capable, it circumvents the system's normal control features. Another key characteristic is that a trap door is exercised under the direct control of an activation stimulus.

As the name implies, trap doors have a means of activation (like the latch on a door). This activation key is under the direct control of the attacker. A simple example of an activation key is a special sequence of characters typed into a terminal. A software trap door program embedded in the operating system code can recognize this key and allow the user of the terminal special privileges. This is done by the software circumventing the normal control features of the system. It is important to realize that the only purpose of a trap door is to "bypass" internal controls. It is up to the attacker to determine how this circumvention of controls can be utilized for his benefit.

Undetectable trap door. The attacker can construct the trap door in such a manner as to make it virtually undetectable to even suspecting investigators. The penetration of the MIT Multics computer by the tiger team that was described earlier led to further demonstrations of the significance of their work. Specifically, they installed a small trap door so undetectable that the manufacturer's personnel could not find the clandestine code, even when they were told it existed and how it worked.

The Multics system internally encrypted its password list so that even if the list was printed out, the passwords were not intelligible. When a user presented his or her password, it was encrypted and then compared with the user's entry in the encrypted list. The tiger team retrieved the encrypted password list, then broke the cipher at their leisure to obtain all of the passwords for MIT's Multics computer system. The MIT Multics computer was used as the development site for future versions of the Multics operating system.

The tiger team modified Honeywell's master copy of the Multics operating system by installing a trap door: a set of instructions to bypass the normal security checks and thus ensure penetration even after the initial flaw was fixed. The trap door was small (fewer than 10 instructions out of about 100,000) and required a coded password for use. As we said, the manufacturer's personnel could not find it, even when they knew it existed and how it worked. Furthermore, since the trap door was inserted in the master copy of the operating system, the manufacturer automatically distributed the trap door to all Multics installations. Multics kept an "audit trail" of accesses to files by users. The tiger team's activities were duly audited. However, the audit trail mechanism itself was subject to "repair" by an authorized system manager. Since the tiger team appeared to be the system manager, they merely had to modify the record to remove all traces of their actions, such as the insertion of the trap door.

The full effect of the tiger team's project was eventually demonstrated to Honeywell and Air Force management, and a series of projects was initiated to improve the system's security to allow it to be used in the Pentagon application. Of perhaps as much interest, though, are the depth and breadth of the impact that the tiger team's penetration and subversion had on the system's security.

The key point that distinguishes this subversion from the other forms of attacks described above is that the tiger team examined the mechanisms used to provide operating system security, then installed permanent artifices to bypass them all. Once the team had done that, they were able to access any information in the system repeatedly and undetectably, despite later efforts that might close the initial vulnerability they exploited.

A hardware trap door. The implications of the Multics hardware vulnerability described earlier are as frightening as those of the software flaws. The prospect for maliciously installed trap doors is presumably as great in hardware as in operating system software. It is arguable that, given the complexity of modern integrated circuits, such trap doors are even harder to find than their software brethren. While the tiger team's Subverter program described earlier was designed to find such an obscure case, all involved acknowledged that there was a certain amount of luck in the fact that the case of interest was one that Subverter tested in a finite amount of time.

Putting it all together. It is easy enough to imagine scenarios for attacks against the security of information in computer systems in which the use of techniques such as those described in the preceding paragraphs gives an attacker a decisive advantage. The number of avenues available for inducing security compromises in a typical computer system and the range of activities and capabilities that can be exercised once a flaw is located and exploited are frightening to consider.

Future attack scenario? To illustrate the range of subtlety and the indirect nature of such threats, we offer the following fictional scenario [SHOC88], which is at least technically realizable. The purpose of this scenario, it is emphasized, is to prompt a more careful consideration of the threat. For that reason, we deliberately present a "worst-case" scenario.

In 1995, the NATO nations undertook several technical initiatives in the area of command and control. Among these initiatives, a project was undertaken to interconnect many preexisting command and control systems located at various sites with high-speed, dedicated communications links. The preexisting systems were all thought to be "secure enough" and were accredited to process information of identical classification ranges. The systems nominally provided for the proper confinement of classified information. For that reason, the sponsors of the project assessed as minimal the additional risk to security induced by the new connectivity.

The successful completion of this project proved, in the ensuing conventional hostilities in the Middle East, to be one of the decisive factors leading to the losses suffered by the NATO alliance. Unknown to NATO engineers, technical saboteurs under the control of the enemy had managed to penetrate the system by installing a Trojan horse at one of the sites as early as 1989 to exploit a flaw in the command and control system. This obscure flaw provided a means to modify arbitrary system instructions, by sending a particular I/O device an undocumented sequence of control instructions, causing the device to modify an arbitrary memory location, bypassing the usual memory management access controls. The Trojan horse was introduced in a virus-infected graphics package distributed as "freeware" on a publicly accessible bulletin board system. An unsuspecting staff system programmer, who was a frequent contributor to the bulletin board, noticed the package, downloaded it into his personal home system, and transported it to the command and control system for evaluation, as it offered several features that were currently required for an application being developed at the site. Although the graphics package itself, after evaluation was completed, was rejected and removed from the system, the virus by this time had relocated itself and become a permanent resident of the command and control system.

The Trojan horse had been specifically designed to penetrate any command and control system site it should chance to find itself on. Its placement on the public bulletin board was a carefully targeted attack on the command and control system programming staff, who were known to be frequent contributors and subscribers. Because they placed the Trojan horse on a public bulletin board, there was little risk to the saboteurs of personal exposure even if the Trojan horse was eventually discovered. The Trojan horse had been carefully engineered in advance by the technical sabotage team, based on an exact understanding of the particular flaw exploited. This understanding was gained by lengthy experimentation on an identical computer system purchased off the shelf by the sabotage team in support of the penetration. Among the functions built into the Trojan horse was the ability to accept covert software "upgrades" to its own program once it had installed itself. In effect, the Trojan horse, once installed, gave its creators complete access to the system, provided a means of communication with the Trojan horse could be established.

When first executed at the command and control system site, the virus contained in the Trojan horse activated itself, confirmed that it indeed was now executing at one of the targeted sites, and relocated itself into the message processing subsystem, where it could monitor (without perceptible impact on ongoing operations) all incoming message traffic. By placing redundant "watchdog" processes in installed intelligent peripherals, the Trojan horse was able to ensure its continued existence past system maintenance and regeneration episodes.

The Trojan horse was designed to communicate with its creators via unclassified message traffic, such as that originated at (or addressed to) a remote diplomatic post to which the enemy had low-risk human access, at the unclassified level. In particular, the human agent had the ability to originate and receive routine unclassified messages of an administrative nature. The entire NATO communication system was available to ensure that such messages, once originated by either the human agent or the software Trojan horse, would be delivered unchanged to the recipient in the normal course of operations. The human operator could signal and control the Trojan horse by including a preselected string of code words in any unclassified message emanating from the post, followed by a "program" for the Trojan horse to execute, encoded as numeric table data. The enabling trigger and program code were carefully designed to mimic a routine report originating from this and similar posts, while ensuring that the risk of the "trigger" actually occurring in a genuine message was low. Signals from the Trojan horse to the operator could be sent using unclassified messages, similarly encoded, composed by the Trojan horse and transmitted from the command and control system site to the diplomatic post. The messages appeared, to superficial examination, to be routine logistics accounting messages containing tabular data. In fact, this data could be used to encode binary information (such as software upgrades for the Trojan horse itself).

The first action the Trojan horse took after installing itself was to announce its presence and location to its operator. It was decided to minimize the risk of detection by not further exercising the Trojan horse unless its operation would yield a decisive military or diplomatic advantage. Thus, for most of the years of its existence, the Trojan horse was inactive and remained undetected.

The interconnection of all of the command and control system sites increased the potential value of the Trojan horse to the enemy, as the means now existed to subvert the entire command and control system network. The enemy now felt prepared to commence hostilities, based, in part, on the successful (and undetected) exercise of the Trojan horse several weeks earlier, verifying that it still existed and was operable. It is probable that the Trojan horse was reprogrammed at this time so it could utilize the newly available remote access to other command and control system sites and could perform the precise intelligence and disinformation tasks needed for successful completion of the enemy mission.

The actual use of the Trojan horse during hostilities was carefully crafted to avoid detection. Prior to planned enemy thrusts, the Trojan horse transmitted selected allied order of battle information to the operator, who then passed the information to the enemy intelligence system. During enemy attack phases, the Trojan horse was used to introduce small distortions in enemy track and locating data. These modifications to system behavior were subtle enough to escape detection, but provided decisive intelligence and disinformation advantages, leading to the attainment of the enemy objectives during the hostilities.

The opportunity for exploitation exists. This scenario is, of course, intentionally alarming. (Similar scenarios have been described in articles [SCHE79, GRAN83] published in military professional journals, indicating that the tactical significance of computer security problems has not been lost on military professionals.)

Though this scenario was from the military context, the issues are equally relevant to any context where there are determined attackers. The credibility of such scenarios is based on the following factors.

Contemporary systems are vulnerable to attack by any individual with access to their hardware and/or software components at any point in their life cycle. The exposure of systems to attack has dramatically increased as systems are interconnected. The increasing use of preexisting and commercial off-the-shelf (COTS) software (for example, graphics packages), an increasingly attractive option, also significantly increases the exposure of systems, as the developers of such software must be regarded as having access to the system.

Potential attackers are capable of exploiting opportunities to penetrate mission-critical systems. No particular skills beyond those of normally competent computer professionals are required. In fact, such skills are now within the publicized repertoire of amateur "hackers." Trojan horses designed to penetrate particular systems can often be located "off the shelf" from underground bulletin board systems.

It must be assumed that potential attackers are motivated to exploit available opportunities. It would be imprudent to assume that potentially hostile interests will be restrained, particularly where decisive advantages are at stake.

We must assume that a serious penetration attempt will be indirect in nature, will not require direct physical access by the penetrator and/or operator to the penetrated target, and will not advertise its presence or cause easily observable disturbances to the system's behavior. In short, a serious penetration attempt will be quite unlike those of amateur penetrators (hackers) occasionally receiving media publicity.

This follows simply from the difference in goals assumed for the threats: Hackers generally have motivations related to the need for self-esteem and notoriety. A professional penetrator is motivated to remain undetected and effective for lengthy periods of time. What malicious software does after initial system penetration is influenced primarily by the goals of its author, not by technical difficulty. The nature of a professional threat may be assessed, even by computer nonprofessionals, by taking any of the recently publicized cases and estimating whether the penetration would have ever been detected if its author had wished it to remain indefinitely covert.

Perspective on the computer security problem

If we review the computer security "war stories" cited above, a number of facts become clear. The problems of human error are significant but not of substantial interest to the determined, hostile attacker. There are other, higher payoff methods of attacking the information in a computer system that render this problem less interesting. Proper training of users and good system administration are prerequisites to solving this problem. Further, protection against probing and penetration is necessary.

The computer is almost irrelevant to the issues of user abuse of authority. The problem is as old as the storage and manipulation of information. The solutions that applied in the era of ledger papers apply as well to equivalent records stored in a computer. To the extent that it can automate such methods as audits, cross-checks, and consistency checks, the computer can actually improve security against user abuse of authority.

User probing involves exploitation of computer security controls that have insufficient power, or controls that are improperly used. The user who probes the system is acting as a normal user and will be controlled by security measures that have adequate flexibility and are carefully applied.

Penetration depends on weakness in the implementation of a system's hardware or software security controls. Even if a system incorporates rich and flexible security features that are carefully used and conscientiously maintained, it may be vulnerable to penetration. To resist penetration, the controls themselves must be built "right." History has taught us that the challenge of building a penetration-proof system is very great indeed.

Finally, subversion of the security mechanism itself is most difficult to prevent. Not only must controls be built "right," as mentioned in the preceding paragraph, but they must also be built nonmaliciously and be simple and small enough for analysis to determine that they perform as expected (or at least do not perform as not expected). Essays 2 and 6 introduce measures that have been found effective against probing, penetration, and subversion of security mechanism. The reference monitor concept introduced in Essay 2 gives us a set of principles that can be applied to the design or selection of security features and to their implementation in ways that provide a high degree of resistance to penetration and a high degree of assurance that they are not subverted.

For further reading

More real examples of computer misuse can be found in the literature [BLOO90, HAFN91, SPAF89, STOL89]. In addition, Neumann and Parker [NEUM89] summarize and discuss classes of computer misuse techniques. These references, as well as the others cited in this essay, can help the reader gain a broader understanding of "what there is to worry about."

Acknowledgments

We would like to give a special acknowledgment to the contributions of Steven B. Lipner of Trusted Information Systems. Substantial portions of the text as well as several key insights for classifying threats are drawn from material he previously prepared and he has graciously permitted us to use in this essay.

Acknowledgment is also given to P.A. Myers, from whose work [MYER80] we have drawn excerpts for incorporation into this essay. Myers' fine thesis also contributed significant ideas to the discussion of malicious software and subversion presented here.

In addition, we acknowledge (and have excerpted) two early articles [COX79, SCHE79] that reached deeply into the cultures of their respective audiences to awaken them to the computer security problem.

We also gratefully acknowledge the substantial constructive comments and suggestions provided by James P. Anderson on an earlier version of this essay.

Essay 2

Concepts and Terminology for Computer Security

Donald L. Brinkley and Roger R. Schell

This essay introduces many of the concepts and terms most important in gaining an understanding of computer security. It focuses on techniques for achieving access control within computer systems and networks.

The essay begins by defining what is meant by computer security and describing why it is important to constrain the definition to protection that can be meaningfully provided with a significant degree of assurance within computer systems. The theory of computer security — the reference monitor concept — is introduced next through an analogy with security concepts from the world of people and sensitive documents.

Next, the essay develops the presentation of the theory by introducing concepts and terms related to the security policy. Distinctions between discretionary and nondiscretionary access control policies are provided, and supporting policies are introduced. Techniques used for building a secure system based on the principles of the theory are presented, along with methods of usefully verifying the security of a system. The security kernel is presented as a useful, high-assurance realization of the reference monitor concept, and the principles behind designing and implementing one from scratch are discussed. Feasible improvements to the security of an existing operating system, as well as fundamental limitations on those improvements, are described next.

Finally, the reference monitor concept is applied to networks, and cryptography and access control are shown to be useful partners.

This essay concerns concepts and terminology relevant to computer security. However, it is not a glossary. (A glossary typically does not make very interesting reading from beginning to end, and interesting reading is one of our goals for this essay.) This essay certainly does not define all concepts and terminology relevant to computer security; nor does it address concepts and terminology for communication security and related communication networking technology. It does address concepts and terms that we consider to be the most critical to gain a fundamental understanding of computer security technology — that is, the theory of this technology and something of its implementation.

Our approach in this essay is to focus primarily on explaining concepts critical to understanding computer security. For the basis of the communication about the concepts, we use a set of terms that have been consistently used over a period of time. Alternate terms have been used for some of the concepts we present, and in some cases, the alternate terms are being promulgated by other individuals and/or organizations. In contrast, in Essay 6, we have used terminology specific to a particular document [TCSE85] and to a specific organization (the US Department of Defense). However, in this essay, we have tried to remain clear of a specific set of organizational "utterances," instead preferring to use a set of widely and historically accepted terminology. Specific sources for some of the terms are given where the source is thought to be historically significant.

The next few sections focus on identifying the domain of discourse for the concepts and terminology discussed in the rest of the essay. They clarify what we mean by just one term — computer security.

Considerations for computer security

There are many characterizations of computer security. The one we use is related to the term information technology security. Information technology security is defined in a document [ITSE91] created by the European Community, which has gained some recent international acceptance. The document [ITSE91] defines information technology (IT) security to include the following:

- Confidentiality. Prevention of unauthorized disclosure of information.
- Integrity. Prevention of unauthorized modification of information.
- Availability. Prevention of unauthorized withholding of information or resources.

Essay 1 describes four broad areas of computer misuse: theft of computational resources, disruption of computational services, unauthorized information disclosure, and unauthorized information modification. These four areas correspond to threats to IT security. The first two categories correspond to threats to availability; the third corresponds to a threat to confidentiality; and the fourth to the integrity of the information. (Note that in this essay, theft of computational resources is considered a threat to availability of resources since it fundamentally results in the withholding of the stolen resources from those who are paying to use them.)

Integrity, which is also traditionally referred to as data integrity [TNI87], means that information is modified only by those who have the right to do so. However, integrity has meanings other than the meaning used here. These alternate meanings vary greatly from such a broad definition as "soundness" to the definition of system integrity, meaning that the hardware and software generally operate as expected. Program integrity means that programs can be invoked only by programs that are lower in integrity. This arrangement is intended to prevent corruption (that is, by unauthorized modification) of higher integrity programs [SHIR81] by lower integrity programs (for example, by viruses or other Trojan horses that might be in them). It has been shown [SCHE86] that program integrity is just a special case of the data integrity described here. Although in other contexts integrity may be used differently, throughout this essay, integrity is used with the first meaning given above — that of data integrity. Information is modified only by those who have the right to do so.

Distinctions among availability, confidentiality, and integrity

When considering the costs and benefits of protection against the list of threats to IT security given above, the distinctions among confidentiality and integrity and other system properties such as availability are important.

Availability differs in kind from the other two components of IT security. One difference acknowledged in the definition of IT security given in the EC document [ITSE91] is that availability pertains to both information and resources, such as computer systems themselves. On the other hand, confidentiality and integrity pertain only to information itself.

In a further distinction from availability, consider that confidentiality and integrity can be enforced by preventing illicit access to the information under protection (that is, access control in the computer context). In contrast, availability cannot be provided by access control within a computer system. Rather, the key objective of availability is that information or resources should not be withheld [ITSE91].

This distinction has very fundamental implications for the protection feasible against threats to availability, in contrast to the protection feasible against threats to confidentiality and integrity. This is easy to see, since, for example, a process may in general consume resources in a manner that may prevent other processes from accessing those resources when needed. The observation that a "runaway process" can waste resources, even in a system which implements access controls, was made by Butler Lampson as early as 1971 [LAMP71]. Twenty years later, Lampson [LAMP91] stated more flatly that access controls provide a foundation for confidentiality and integrity, but are less useful for availability.

We see then that there are very many things that can affect the availability of a system; in fact, it is not possible to identify all the factors that may affect availability. It is the unboundedness of the possible causes of a loss of availability that leads to the conclusion that it is not possible to verify to a high degree of assurance that a system possesses the quality of availability. However, it is possible to verify to a high degree of assurance that a system possesses qualities of confidentiality and integrity through the dependable enforcement of access controls.

Furthermore, consider the problem of malicious software. Essay 1 characterized the growth of malicious software. It is clear that as the use of commercial off-the-shelf software products or any other software of unknown pedigree grows, so do the opportunities for insertion of malicious software. This is because there are now many more points in the software life cycle, including during distribution as well as development, at which malicious software can be incorporated. However, even in the face of malicious software, we can obtain, for a reasonable cost, the benefit of meaningful assurance that a useful form of access control will continue to be enforced (as we see in a later section on mandatory access control policy). In contrast, current technology does not allow us to obtain at any cost, in the face of malicious software, this kind of assurance for other system properties such as availability. This is not because one cannot design a system that enhances availability, but rather because one cannot be sure the system will meet any particular level of availability in the face of malicious software. We shall see later that this means it is possible to provide a reference monitor for confidentiality and integrity, but not for availability.

The reason for this is the existence of a very basic distinction between confidentiality and integrity and other system properties, such as availability. The distinction is that confidentiality and integrity can be characterized in terms of properties that are precisely defined, global, and persistent. Confidentiality and integrity can be specified for a particular system in a way that allows one to know, beyond the shadow of a doubt, whether or not the system enforces those properties.

We understand that this is an incredibly strong statement which may be surprising to some. However, there is a set of mathematical tools in computer science that gives one the confidence to make such a statement. The characteristic ability to specify these properties for a particular system in a manner that allows one to positively know that they are enforced is known in the jargon of computer science as "being computable." It is not essential that a reader of this essay understand computability to understand the remainder of the essay. However, the next paragraph offers a very brief discussion of the implications of the computability of confidentiality and integrity for those readers who are interested. Others may wish to skip to the next section.

As implied by the above statements, confidentiality and integrity can be specified for a particular system such that whether or not that system enforces those properties is computable. Being computable means basically that one can specify an algorithm that can be used in a mechanical way to determine the result. This is particularly significant since computers can only execute algorithms and can therefore only dependably perform computable functions! This means that one can program a computer in such a way as to dependably determine whether it enforces confidentiality and integrity. On the other hand, whether a given system meets criteria of availability, reliability, safety, and other such properties is fundamentally "noncomputable," meaning that it is impossible to determine whether a computer's program enforces these properties, given their existing definitions. In fact, it is generally noncomputable to determine whether an arbitrary protection system enforces particular properties [HARR76]. It is fortunate that a particularly useful form of confidentiality and integrity (for example, mandatory access control) constitutes a special case whose enforcement within a protection system can be proven, as will be discussed subsequently in this essay.

Meaning of computer security

In the real world of information that people care about, it is highly beneficial to treat confidentiality and integrity separately from other system properties, including availability. Information can be very dependably protected from unauthorized modification or disclosure in the face of a large range of threats; that is, confidentiality and integrity can be provided with high assurance of enforcement. Availability cannot. If confidentiality and integrity were rolled into the same class as availability, an important and very sharp distinction between assurance that is feasible in the two cases would be lost. We feel that this would not serve well the readers of this essay who could benefit from the ability to provide access control to information with a high degree of assurance, despite the lesser assurance possible for other properties such as availability.

To clarify the importance of assurance, recall the danger described in Essay 1 that was associated with misplaced trust in a supposedly "secure" system — Enigma. The danger of misplaced trust in technology, of false assurance in the Enigma case, was a serious contributor to the loss of World War II by the Germans. False assurance is a danger that is avoidable by only trusting technology that is demonstrably trustworthy.

Because of these fundamental differences, we say that confidentiality and integrity are the two components of IT security in a computer system that make up computer security (that is, computer security is the subset of IT security that addresses security of information in a computer against threats to confidentiality and integrity, but which does not address availability). Therefore, computer security, as used in this essay, may be provided by the methods used for access control within a computer system.

The remainder of this essay is divided into major sections that present concepts and terminology related to

- the theory of computer security,
- an important aspect of that theory — the security policy,
- methods of building a secure system based on the principles of the theory, and
- application of the theory to networks.

Theory of computer security

As noted above, the threats to computer security can be countered by providing access control over information on a computer to ensure that only specifically authorized users are allowed access. What we desire is a set of methods that make it possible to build a relatively small part of the system in such a way that one can even allow a clever attacker who uses malicious software to build the rest of the system and its applications, and it will still be secure. The theory of computer security gives us this.

Understanding computer security involves understanding three fundamental notions:

1. a security policy, stating the laws, rules, and practices that regulate how an organization manages, protects, and distributes sensitive information;
2. the functionality of internal mechanisms to enforce that security policy; and
3. assurance that the mechanisms do enforce the security policy.

Now we introduce these three important notions and describe how they pertain to the reference monitor concept, which provides a set of principles that can be applied to the design or selection of security features and to their implementation in ways that afford a high degree of resistance to malicious software. We begin with an example from the world of people and sensitive documents to illustrate the requirements of any information security system. We then introduce the reference monitor concept as we apply it in designing secure computer systems.

An example: Protecting sensitive documents. If we had a collection of extremely sensitive documents — perhaps corporate plans and strategies or classified national security information — we might go to extreme lengths to protect that collection. Thinking about the measures that we might take to provide such protection will help us find an intuitive basis for the reference monitor concept.

Restricting access. Since we are talking about documents (presumably ink on paper), we can most naturally think about locking them up. So we buy something like a bank vault to hold our little library of priceless secrets. But the documents still have to be used, so we have to provide a way for authorized people to get at them and read them. Now we have to put a door in our vault and provide some set of controls over who can and who cannot go in.

We can place a guard post in front of our vault door and staff it with a team of extremely vigilant and trustworthy guards. These guards can surely exercise control over who goes in and who goes out, but they will need some set of criteria for determining who is authorized for such access. We can solve this problem by providing the guards with a list that specifies only those individuals we have authorized (in the national security case, those we have cleared) for access to the vault and its secrets. Now the guards know who may and who may not enter.

We are not finished, though. For when an individual shows up at the guard post and requests entry, the guards need some way to check that the person is not claiming a fake identity. We might simply rely on the guards' powers of recognition, or we can invent a variety of measures to provide the guards with the information they need. We can give each authorized individual a badge or pass and direct the guards to check the badge against the appearance of a valid badge. Perhaps we can store each individual's photograph, or even fingerprints, and associate them in the authorization list with individuals' names. This information is necessary to authenticate the identification of the individual in a reliable way. We can invent schemes of almost limitless cost and complexity to help the guards assure themselves that they are admitting only authorized people to the vault.

Finally, we might want to check up on the guards to make sure that only those users on the authorization list are being admitted to the vault to use the document collection — to ensure individual accountability for the guards' work. So we can add to our basic protection scheme a log that must be signed by both guard and visitor to give us a clear record of visits to our vault.

Of course, we must not only have a good security system; we must also implement it correctly. If a guard is subject to subversion or if our vault has walls of paper rather than steel, the security we provide will not be very effective. The extent to which we must worry about such matters will depend on the sensitivity of the information and on the threat we perceive. Perhaps we will put moderately sensitive documents in a locked room with an unarmed guard, and very sensitive ones in a real bank-style vault with armed guards.

The basic scheme outlined here is not too different from some that are actually used to protect very sensitive documents. If the users of the documents are at remote locations and too busy to come to our vault, perhaps we will send the guards to them. Then we have a system similar to that used to handle "Ultra" information before and during World War II [WINT74]. The point is that the basic scheme is simple, comprehensible, and secure.

When access rights vary. Our scenario of a vault full of sensitive documents differs from reality in (at least) one very important respect. When people or organizations go to such lengths to protect sensitive information, it is unlikely that they will simply put it in a room and give authorized visitors unrestricted access to the room. Rather, different people are likely to have access to different documents, and the document protection system will be required to recognize and enforce this sort of distinction. We may also want the document protection system to enforce some control over the use (or misuse) of the documents by authorized users. We will consider some of these issues in the paragraphs below.

In thinking about a document library in a vault that enforces "fine-grained" protection, we can at least start with the basic concepts that were introduced above. A would-be user will appear at the reading room, identify himself (or herself), and have his identity checked by the guards on duty. Now, however, the user will not simply be admitted to the library for unrestricted access. Instead, he will request access to a specific document or set of documents. The guard will check the user's access in some sort of list and, assuming all is in order, give the user both the documents requested and a place to work on them. Perhaps our library or reading room is divided into individual carrels to which authorized users take their documents. If several people must work together, they may be assigned a closed conference room in which they may work with documents that all are authorized to see.

This extension is a very crucial one. For now, instead of admitting one or more users for unconstrained access to the entire collection, our library grants individual users access to individual documents based on their authorization. Not only that, we also have a mechanism (the carrels or reading room) for ensuring that the access rights of individuals are enforced and that a user reading document A is prevented from gaining (inadvertently or deliberately) access to document B. The access rights are defined by the authorization list and enforced on a document-by-document basis. Some of the documents may have, associated with them on the authorization list, user access rights that are identical with those associated with other documents in the collection. These equivalence classes of document access rights define a notion called access class (also referred to outside this essay by other names, including "classification," "clearance," "security level," and "security class"). An access class is an equivalence class for the sensitivity of information and the authorization of people who share common access rights to the information in that class. An important observation about access classes is that the notion provides the basis for "fine-grained" protection, such as we are discussing. A document may have more or less sensitivity than another, or its sensitivity may differ from the other's in a noncomparable way, such as might be the case for unrelated documents in totally different fields.

In defining both our basic and enhanced scenarios, we have ignored the question, "Where does the authorization list come from?" We cannot yet deal fully with this question, but presumably the same authority that established the library also defined a mechanism by which some people can establish or change the list. To do so, they have to communicate the updated list to the guard force in some manner, and the mechanism that they use to identify themselves to the guards is probably similar to that used by the ordinary users of the library. It is even possible that some of the users of the library are themselves allowed to modify the authorization lists for some subset of the documents in the library and that the rules enforced by the guards handle this.

We have also ignored until now the practical question of what users of the library do with the information that they have access to. One possibility is that they leave their notes, extracts, and so on in the library. In this scheme, each user may be assigned a file folder for his or her notes, and the folder may be locked up by the guard force from one visit to the next. If a user takes information away from the library, the guards will probably attempt to check that the information can legitimately be removed, and perhaps that its access class is marked on the copy (so the user will assume due care in handling it). It is entirely possible that only a few people will be allowed to remove any written information from our library and then only under controlled circumstances.

If our library is to enforce access restriction at the level of the individual document, it can also collect a more detailed record of users' accesses to documents. The log that we mentioned above can be expanded to include documents accessed and individual users' actions.

The library scenario outlined here may sound unlikely. However, some government classified document libraries work almost exactly this way. The mode of operation outlined is not terribly inconvenient once the users and guards become accustomed to it. Such formal libraries typically do a good job of protecting the information entrusted to them, while making it available to the people who need to work with it. We shall see that these libraries also provide a fairly good model for the reference monitor that is implemented in a secure computer system.

The reference monitor. The reference monitor provides the underlying "security theory" for conceptualizing the idea of protection, thereby permitting one to focus attention only on those aspects of the system that are relevant to security. As we shall see, the reference monitor concept for the computer applies equally well to the design of a document library like the one we have just discussed.

The reference monitor [ANDE72] is an abstraction that allows active entities called subjects to make reference to passive entities called objects, based on a set of current access authorizations. The reference monitor is interposed between the subjects and objects. The reference monitor makes reference to an authorization database and reports information used to support an audit trail (similar to the "log" described above) that records operations which have been attempted or allowed.

At an abstract level, the reference monitor supports two classes of functions: reference functions and authorization functions [SCHE74]. Both are controlled by the current access authorization data in the authorization database. The authorization functions allow subjects to change the authorizations in the authorization database. The reference functions control the ability to access information. The utility of the reference monitor concept is independent of the specific rules that make up the access control policy. That is, the reference monitor is not defined by the access control policy, nor does the reference monitor define the access control policy.

The reference functions are defined in terms of only two generic access modes — observe and modify. The equivalents of these abstract access modes in a computer are read and write; therefore, we will use these terms. These are the only access modes for which one can be certain of the enforcement of access control; that is, these are the only access modes for which enforcement of access control policy can be verified. Read and write are fundamentally the only two types of access to computer memory, since, at the level of the hardware "chips" that implement the computer, even operations such as instruction execution begin as read and/or write operations. These two access modes provide the basis for describing the rules for access (that is, the access control policy or the access control aspects of the security policy).

With the following examples we try to clarify why other less primitive modes of access used in computers are not suitable for defining the access control policy. For an access mode to be suitable for this role, one must be able to verify that access control policy rules that are specified in terms of the particular access mode are enforced. For example, some computers support an append access mode. One might wish to build a system to enforce access control policy rules that allow a subject to append some objects but not to read or write them. One would like to be able to verify that the system enforces those rules. However, at the most primitive level in a computer, append relies on a read of some control information to determine where to write the information being appended. Thus, it would not be possible to build a system in such a way as to allow one to verify that access control policy rules that allow one to append but not to read or write will not result in undesired read or write accesses.

As another example, consider instruction execution as an access mode for defining access control policy. For execution to be suitable for this purpose, the following must be true: If an access control policy states that execution of an object (for example, a program file) is authorized for a particular subject, but read access to that object is not authorized for that subject, we must be able to verify that read access is not possible. However, it is easy to see a specific case in which the access control policy cannot be enforced — it is not generally possible to know that executing a program (which is desired to be "execute-only") will not "leak" information from the program and thus allow undesired read access. D.E. Denning [DENN76, DENN82] has described ways in which executing a program may result in information leaking out of the program. This means that it is not possible to specify that read access is not permitted for an object to which execute access is permitted. Therefore, execute access is not sufficiently primitive to define access control policy in a verifiable way.

It should now be clear how a reference monitor implementation in a computer is related to the document library that we described above. In the document library, the users are our subjects or active entities. They make access to passive documents that correspond to the objects of the reference monitor. The authorization list that defines access to the library itself governs what subjects are known to the library.

Note, as a detail, that the action taken by the guards in the library to authenticate the identification of the individual seeking entry to the library is not itself a function of the reference monitor. Rather, it is a trusted function which is implemented outside the reference monitor. Another trusted function that may be implemented outside the reference monitor is the construction of the audit trail (mentioned above) from information reported by the reference monitor. Recall that the reference monitor contains only reference functions and authorization functions. In a later section we give additional information about the roles of authentication and audit in supporting the reference monitor's functions.

The reference monitor's authorization database corresponds to the library's augmented authorization list that identifies which users may see each document. The reference monitor's reliance exclusively on the two access modes — read and write — corresponds to the library guards' exclusive reliance on controls for what documents users are allowed to read and what notes users may remove from the library. Fortunately, read and write mean the same thing in the computer that they do in the document library. In the library, as in the reference monitor, there is an authorization function that changes the authorization database, and there are reference functions for reading or writing documents. As noted, the library, like the reference monitor, can generate data for an audit trail that reflects those operations that have occurred or been attempted. The guards, walls, doors, and internal partitions (carrels, reading rooms, and so on) of the library are all reflected by the abstraction of the reference monitor.

The reference monitor implementation in a computer system must meet a set of requirements that are also met by components of our document library. These requirements were first identified by J.P. Anderson [ANDE72] and have been historically referred to as completeness, isolation, and verifiability:

- Completeness. The reference monitor must be invoked on every reference by a subject to an object.
- Isolation. The reference monitor and its database must be protected from unauthorized alteration.
- Verifiability. The reference monitor must be small, well-structured, simple, and understandable so that it can be completely analyzed, tested, and verified to perform its functions properly.

A review of the document library against these three requirements for a reference monitor will be instructive.

As to completeness, we presume that a user of the library cannot gain access to the collection by walking through a wall or around a guard. Note, however, that the guards do not necessarily have to watch the user directly through every moment of his or her use of a document. Our library is designed so that a user in a carrel with a document is still adequately restricted from gaining unauthorized access to other documents.

As to isolation, the library must be designed so that an interloper cannot replace a guard, drill though a wall, or replace the authorization database or other key reference monitor databases.

Finally, the procedures of the library must be simple enough so that they can be reviewed or inspected, thus meeting the requirement for verifiability. If the library system allows a user, for example, to check out a document at one desk and then carry it across a parking lot unobserved to get to a reading room, there is adequate opportunity for mischief, even though all the doors are locked and all the guards who are present are conscientious. The design of the security procedures themselves must be simple and sound, or the provision of more guards and thicker walls will be useless.

The reference monitor and the computer system. Before we leave this introduction of the reference monitor concept, we will tie it to the world of computer systems, and then to the classes of computer misuse techniques that we introduced in Essay 1.

The correspondence between reference monitor components and components of the computer system is reasonably clear: The subjects are the active entities in the computer system that operate on information on behalf of the system's users. The subjects are processes executing in a particular domain (see below for definition) in a computer system (that is, a <process, domain> pair). Most of the subjects are acting out the wishes of an individual whose identification has been authenticated by passing something like a password, using some means of reliable communication between the individual and the portion of the system performing the identification. The means of ensuring reliable communication between a human and the portion of the system performing identification (and certain other functions such as security administration) is called a trusted path. The topics of identification, authentication, and trusted path are explored more fully in a later section.

The objects hold the information that the subjects may access. A domain of a process is defined to be the set of objects that the process currently has the right to access according to each access mode. As noted above, two primitive access modes, read and write, are the basis for describing the access control policy. While we shall be concerned with many kinds of objects in general, we can think of objects as well-defined portions of memory within the computer, such as segments. Files, records, and other types of information repositories can be built from these primitive objects, but access control is provided by the reference monitor on the basis of the primitive objects over which it has total control. As mentioned earlier, the reference monitor controls access to them by controlling the primitive operations on them — the ability to read and write them.

There is another type of resource in the computer that needs to be tied to the reference monitor concept but that we have not yet mentioned — the device or communication channel. For clarity, we will include communication channel within the notion of device and use this term throughout. A device is the means whereby information is imported to or exported from the computer system — that is, it is the means for input/output. Note that by devices, we mean things that are actually under the control of and logically part of a computer system (for example, a controller connected to the computer's bus or a disk drive). We do not mean a separate "dumb" peripheral unit such as a dumb terminal or dumb printer, and not the actual storage media such as a tape or disk platter. Devices may be considered objects under certain circumstances, but they must be considered subjects under other circumstances. We will return to the topic of devices in a later section, when we discuss networks.

The authorization database specifies those circumstances under which a subject may or may not gain access to objects. There are many ways of specifying authorization in a computer system. We can think of authorization databases associated with each object in the computer system (called a "list-oriented" implementation [SALT75, WILK72]) or with each subject (called a "ticket-oriented" or "capabilities" implementation). Regardless of how authorization is represented, the reference monitor ensures that only authorized accesses occur.

The audit trail records what security-relevant operations have actually occurred in the computer system. These include introduction of objects into the domain of a process acting on behalf of a user (for example, file open), deletion of objects, and so on. For each security-relevant event captured in the audit trail, the audit record includes such information as the date and time of the event, the user who initiated the event, the type of event, and success or failure of the event. Note that while the reference monitor generates some of the information for the audit trail, it may not be the only source for audit trail information.

Finally, the reference monitor itself is that most primitive portion of the computer system that we rely on to control access. For the purposes of this essay, we shall think of implementing the reference monitor with a subset of a computer's operating system and hardware. We shall find that, to be efficient, the operating system software needs the assistance of computer hardware that is well suited to the task of providing security.

This last suggestion — that we can implement the reference monitor with a subset of a computer's operating system and hardware — will be especially important in our discussions of secure systems. A security kernel is defined as the hardware and software that implement the reference monitor. (In a specific context where the hardware is fixed, security kernel is sometimes used in reference to just the software.) The implication of the term security kernel is that we can design a hardware/software mechanism that meets exactly the requirements for a reference monitor. In particular, such a mechanism must be complete, isolated, and verifiable. While a computer operating system of the usual sort may attempt to meet the reference monitor requirements to some extent, it will normally fall short to some degree. Only by building a mechanism that is explicitly designed to meet the reference monitor requirements can we achieve a high degree of assurance in the security of a computer system. No alternative technical foundation has yet been identified.

Using the reference monitor. We can now turn, as promised, to the classes of computer misuse techniques introduced in Essay 1. The first class of computer misuse techniques resulting in unauthorized disclosure or modification is human error. This class can best be countered by a program of security consciousness; intensive user education; frequent training, retraining, and reminders; and conscientious system administration and operation. The reference monitor can prevent some forms of this class of misuse through the enforcement of access control using access classes. For example, an operator may be prevented from accidentally mounting the wrong tape if the access class of the tape does not meet the requirements specified in the access control policy enforced by the reference monitor. However, the reference monitor most often does not help or hinder this class of misuse.

If we are concerned about the second class, user abuse of authority, we must design a mechanism that meets our security requirements at the user interface and attempts to constrain the users or detect those times when they go astray. Implementing some of the reference monitor functions in an application program may be appropriate in these cases, though this would not give us a verifiable reference monitor. A functional implementation of some of the reference monitor may be sufficient in this case since, by the definition of this class of abuse given in Essay 1, our irresponsible user is not involved in probing (or else that user's actions would belong in a different class of computer misuse techniques). Therefore, we know that this irresponsible user we have hypothesized will not write a program to bypass the controls we have supplied.

If we are concerned about the threat of direct probing or probing with malicious software, we can probably implement our reference monitor functions in the operating system or within a subset of the operating system. Of course, we may have to pay more attention to security features than have most operating systems today, and we shall also have to use and manage the system with considerable attention to security. But an operating system that is designed with considerable attention to security and very well managed can be quite effective against probing.

If we are worried about penetration or subversion of security mechanisms, we had better go shopping for a security kernel. Not only does such a mechanism incorporate the security features we will need, it also provides (especially by its attention to compactness and verifiability) a high degree of assurance that the design and implementation are complete and that malicious software attacks will not succeed. Furthermore, its compactness and verifiability provide a significant degree of inspectability and assurance that its implementation has not been exposed to subversion. Other mechanisms, such as cryptography, can be used for detecting (after the fact) whether software or data has been modified (as discussed in a later section), but the security kernel is the only method proven effective at countering the threats of penetration and subversion of mechanism, and thus it is the only method effective at preventing illicit access to information under protection.

Computer security and security policy

In our discussion of a document library, we mentioned an authorization list or roster that determined which individuals could enter the library at all, and which documents they could see. External laws, rules, and regulations establish how, when, and what access by people is to be permitted. We do not expect the guards (or walls) of our library to determine who may and who may not enter. Instead, the organization that established the library in the first place also defined a security policy specifying who may enter and who may not. This section provides an introduction to the notion of a security policy and its enforcement in a computer system.

A useful security policy is quite general. It typically does not specify by name that certain people may or may not have access to certain information. Instead, it may state that the holders of certain positions have the authority to gain access to certain information. It may allow the holders of other positions to grant individuals access to information within some scope or set of checks and balances. A security policy may also state requirements that people must meet for access to information, as in the case of security clearances for access to classified national security information.

The Executive Branch of the US government (as well as branches of other governments) has a general security policy for the handling of sensitive information. This security policy involves giving an access class called a "security classification" to sensitive information and a clearance to individuals authorized to access it. No individual is granted access to information classified higher than that individual's clearance. (For example, since "Top Secret" is higher than "Secret," an individual with a "Secret" clearance is not permitted access to "Top Secret" information.) However, possession of a clearance at or higher than the classification of the information alone is not enough to gain access — that individual also must have a "need-to-know" the information, as judged by someone who already has access to the information.

To better understand how a general security policy such as this is enforced when computer systems are operating in different environments, consider three different modes of secure computing used in the Department of Defense: dedicated, system high, and multilevel.

In a simple computation environment, protection or security is enforced by physical means external to the computer (fences, guards, and so on) in a dedicated mode of operation. In this mode, all users allowed access to the system are cleared for the highest level of information contained in the system and have a need-to-know for all the information in the system (that is, it is dedicated to processing for users with a uniform need-to-know for this information at a given single security level). All users, equipment, and information reside within this protective boundary or security perimeter. Everything within the security perimeter is considered benign. The computer system is not expected to seriously "defend" information from any of its users because they are considered nonmalicious by virtue of their security clearances and need-to-know.

In another environment (called the system high mode), the computer not only provides computation but must internally provide mechanisms that separate information from users. This is because not all users of the system have a need-to-know for all the information it contains (but all are cleared for the highest level of information in the system).

In yet another environment (called the multilevel mode), the computer must internally provide mechanisms that distinguish levels of information and user authorization (that is, clearance and need-to-know). In this case, not all users of the system are cleared for the highest level of information contained in the system, nor do all users have a need-to-know for all the information contained in the system.

Here, the computer system must protect the information from the user who is not cleared for it and his possibly malicious software. In effect, the computer system must become part of the security perimeter. The internal protection mechanisms must "assume the roles" of the guards, fences, and so on, that are indicative of the external security perimeter. Anything outside the security perimeter (including software) should be considered suspicious, since it may be malicious.

Clearly, for a computer to operate in the system high or multilevel mode, in which it is responsible for enforcing a portion of the security policy, the security policy must be translated into rules for handling sensitive information on a computer. This translation is not always clear since the security policy is expressed in terms of persons accessing information and not in terms of computer processes (accessing files or segments or bytes). The security policy does not address how a computer may provide both computation and protection.

Thus, one of the first steps in building a secure computer system is to interpret the security policy to be enforced (for example, as described by Lunt et al. [LUNT88a]) in a way that allows it to apply to the internal entities of the computer system. A security policy is interpreted in terms of the permissible access modes (for example, read or write) between the active entities — subjects — and the passive entities — objects — to establish a technical security policy (or a "technical policy" [TDI91]) for the system. We therefore call the specific translation of a security policy into terms implemented on a computer the technical security policy, as distinct from the security policy stated in terms of people accessing information. To build a secure computer system, it is essential to have a technical security policy that is complete and precisely defined and interpreted.

It is adequate to characterize the access control requirements of a technical security policy in terms of the set of subjects to be controlled, the set of objects to be protected, and all the rules concerning the access of subjects to objects to be enforced by the system. The basic security-relevant operation available to subjects is a request to access a particular object in a particular access mode. In response to such a request, the secure system may either grant or deny access.

To decide whether a particular request for access is to be granted or denied, the system must make a decision as to whether the requested access is consistent with the access control policy to be enforced. Although actual mechanisms typically function on the basis of accesses that are to be permitted, it is useful to think of a policy abstractly as accesses that are to be prohibited. Therefore, consider an access control policy as a list of ordered triples $<s, o, m>$ of accesses that must be prohibited (where s is a particular subject, o is a particular object, and m is a particular access mode). This list of triples completely specifies the behavior of the access control policy's reference functions. For instance, if the triple $<x$, myfile, read> appears in the list, subject x may not be given read access to object myfile. The convention of representing the abstract access control policy as a list of prohibited accesses is useful because it enables the rules for verifying correct enforcement of the policy to be specified positively and completely. It is also particularly useful in composing access control policies belonging to different components in a network, as we show in a later section. (For access control policies expressed in this way, the composed access control policy is just the union of the access control policies of the components.)

A basic principle of computer security is that a given system can only be said to be "secure" with respect to some specific security policy, stated in terms of controlling access of persons to information. It is critical to understand the distinction between security policy (or technical security policy as defined above) and security mechanisms that enforce the security policy within a given computer system. For example, mechanisms might include type enforcement [BOEB85], segmentation, or protection rings [SCHR72]. These are all mechanisms that may be used within a computer system to help enforce a security policy that controls access of persons to information, but none of these is itself a security policy. Such mechanisms provide functionality that enables the implementation of access control within the computer system, but they do not directly represent rules in the security policy world of persons and information. It has been shown [HARR76, SHIR81] that in general for any given security mechanism, there are security policies that the mechanism is not sufficient to enforce. Thus the mechanism is molded by the security policy that it is designed to support. To understand the danger of mistaking security mechanisms for security policy, consider that some existing systems impose security mechanisms on users, but it is not at all clear what the security policy is that is being enforced. (Examples include the Unix "setuid" and "setgid" mechanisms [LEVI89].) This creates the illusion of security, without providing real security.

As we noted earlier, the reference monitor concept is not defined by the security policy, nor does it define the security policy. The reference monitor concept is compatible with a broad range of security policies that can be considered in two classes: access control policies and supporting policies. Access control policy is that portion of the security policy that specifies the rules for access control that are necessary for the security policy to be enforced (as will be described in later sections). Supporting policy is that part which specifies the rules for associating humans with the actions which subjects take as surrogates for them in computers to access controlled information (as will also be described later).

The access control policies in turn fall into two classes: discretionary and mandatory. These two classes were originally referred to as discretionary and nondiscretionary, and, as described in the following excerpt [SALT75], both have historically been considered necessary for commercial as well as military security:

We may characterize [one] control pattern as discretionary implying that a user may, at his own discretion, determine who is authorized to access the objects he creates. In a variety of situations, discretionary control may not be acceptable and must be limited or prohibited. For example, the manager of a new department developing a new product line may want to "compartmentalize" his department's use of the company computer system to ensure that only those employees with a need to know have access to information about the new product. The manager thus desires to apply the principle of least privilege. Similarly, the marketing manager may wish to compartmentalize all use of the company computer for calculating product prices, since pricing policy may be sensitive. Either manager may consider it not acceptable that any individual employee within his department can abridge the compartmentalization decision merely by changing an access control list on an object he creates. The manager has a need to limit the use of discretionary controls by his employees. Any limits he imposes on authorization are controls that are out of the hands of the employees, and are viewed by them as nondiscretionary. Similar constraints are imposed in military security applications, in which not only isolated compartments are required, but also nested sensitivity levels (for example, top secret, secret, and confidential) that must be modeled in the authorization mechanics of the computer system. Nondiscretionary controls may need to be imposed in addition to or instead of discretionary controls. For example, the department manager may be prepared to allow his employees to adjust their access control lists any way they wish, within the constraint that no one outside the department is ever given access. In that case, both nondiscretionary and discretionary controls apply.

More recently, nondiscretionary has been called mandatory [TCSE85], but the meaning has been retained: Mandatory is still the complement of discretionary. For reasons that will become clearer below, protection against malicious software is offered only by an implementation of the reference monitor concept enforcing mandatory access control policies, though the reference monitor paradigm of subjects, objects, authorization functions, and reference functions is also used for discretionary access control.

In general, one cannot a priori simply assert whether an arbitrary access control policy is mandatory or discretionary. However, it is clear that some access control policies cannot be mandatory (we will see why in the next section). The more appropriate question is whether the protection against malicious software that is uniquely possible with the high assurance enforcement of a mandatory access control policy is needed for a particular aspect of the security policy. The problem then becomes one of expressing that aspect of the security policy in a way that maintains the properties of a mandatory access control policy. This too is described in the next section.

As a practical matter, the choice between mandatory and discretionary access control policies to support a particular security policy is, in most cases, tied to the penalty for which one would be liable if one violated the policy in the "paper world" — if no computers were being used. If the person responsible for protecting the information could get into "real trouble" (for example, lose a job, get sued, be placed in jail, or even be severely reprimanded) for violating the policy in the paper world, then a mandatory access control policy should be used to protect the information in the computer.

Mandatory access control policy. A mandatory access control policy provides an overriding constraint on the access of subjects to objects, with high assurance of protection possible, even in the face of Trojan horses and other forms of malicious software, as described in Essay 1. In terms of the reference monitor concept, the idea is that we can affix a label to objects to reflect the access class of the information they hold. We can correspondingly affix a label to subjects to reflect the equivalence class of object sensitivity that the subject can access. The reference monitor compares the labels on subjects and objects, and grants a subject access, per the requested access mode, to an object only if the result of the comparison indicates that the access is proper.

Note that the preceding paragraph identifies the mapping between our two "worlds":

1. The world independent of computers, of people attempting to access information on paper.
2. The world of computers with objects that are repositories for information and subjects that act as surrogates for users in the attempt to access information in objects.

As noted above, the label associated with an object indicates the access class of the information that the object holds. The label associated with a subject that acts as a surrogate for a user indicates the authorization of the user — the access class of the information the user is authorized to access (for example, the user's clearance). Earlier we identified subjects as processes executing in a particular domain. In many systems, there is a single label associated with each process since, in these systems, there is a single domain per process. However, in some systems [SCHE85a, THOM90], each process may have a number of domains (and correspondingly, a number of subjects) simultaneously, each of which has a separate label. (Incidentally, these separate domains within a single process are typically implemented by a mechanism called protection rings [SCHR72].) Finally, the access modes used in the computer are the same as the fundamental access modes in the world independent of computers, of people attempting to access information on paper — read and write.

Mandatory access control policies can provide protection against unauthorized modification of information (integrity) as well as protection against unauthorized disclosure (confidentiality). The labels in a specific mandatory access control policy can be selected to accomplish many different purposes for integrity and confidentiality. For example, they can reflect the US government's security policy for confidentiality mentioned earlier, utilizing hierarchical classifications and security clearances (for example, Secret, Top Secret). They can reflect a corporate security policy [LIPN82, LEE88, SHOC88] (for example, Public, Proprietary for Confidentiality or Technical, Management for Integrity). They can also reflect a partitioning of activities into separate spheres or compartments, with different individuals authorized access to information in different areas (for example, Project A, Project B).

Abstractly, in the list of triples that specifies a particular mandatory access control policy, there is an entry for each subject, object, and access mode set (read or write) for which access should not be granted. In other words, if the mandatory access control policy requires that the label associated with the subject be "higher" than that associated with the object in order to grant read access, there are triples for each subject, object pair for which the third element in the triple is read and for which the subject's label is not "higher" than the object's. For a different mandatory access control policy, there would be a different list of triples.

Mandatory access control policies operate by partitioning the sensitivity of objects and the authorizations of subjects into access classes (which correspond to the labels mentioned above). The key to the power and effectiveness of mandatory access control policies is the verifiable restriction on the flow of information from one access class to another. Briefly, a mandatory access control policy reflects a set of rules for comparing access classes. Depending on the security policy being enforced, some flows are allowed and others forbidden. The distinguishing qualities of mandatory access control policies are that they are global and persistent within some universe of discourse; these qualities enable verifiability of the reference monitor implementations that enforce them.

In this context, "global" means that particular information has the same sensitivity wherever it is; "persistent" means that particular information has the same sensitivity at all times. In other words, the subject and object labels are "tranquil"; they do not change. For an access control policy to be global and persistent, the set of access classes (or labels) must form what is termed in mathematics a "partial order." This means that any members of the set can be compared by using a relation usually called dominate, written ">=" and meaning something like "greater than or equal to." For any two distinct members x and y of a partially ordered set, x dominates y, y dominates x, or x and y are noncomparable. (Most existing implementations of mandatory access control policies use a particular type of partially ordered set called a lattice. The distinctions between a partial order and a lattice are not particularly important for this essay, so we will not further discuss lattices.)

The partially ordered set of labels and the resulting restriction on the flow of information provide a tool of sufficient power to defend against even malicious software, described in Essay 1. The members of a set that forms a partial order can be compared by the dominate relation in a manner that satisfies three standard mathematical conditions:

1. reflexivity,
2. antisymmetry, and
3. transitivity.

We can say that for a particular set (for example, of labels) and the relation >=, these three conditions mean respectively that, for all x, y, and z in the set,

1. $x >= x$,
2. $x >= y$ and $y >= x$ implies $x = y$, and
3. $x >= y$ and $y >= z$ implies $x >= z$.

If any of these three conditions of a partially ordered set of labels is relaxed in an access control policy, either the global or persistent quality is destroyed, rendering the access control policy fundamentally vulnerable to Trojan horses. For that reason, arbitrary "tags" cannot be used as mandatory access control policy labels. For example, consider a violation of reflexivity — consider an access control policy in which all subjects and objects have either the label "Sensitive" or the label "Public" and which specifies that Public subjects can access Public objects except on odd Tuesdays. That is an example of the label Public not always dominating itself — a violation of reflexivity and of the "persistent" quality. For another example, if the access control policy specifies that Public subjects can access Sensitive objects only on weekends, the label Sensitive would dominate Public and on weekends Public would dominate Sensitive. But since Sensitive and Public are not equal, we lack antisymmetry, and the quality of persistence is again violated, leaving the opportunity for the access control policy to be circumvented. Similarly, if the access control policy uses the label "Proprietary" in addition to "Sensitive" and "Public," and if Proprietary subjects can access Sensitive objects, while Sensitive subjects can access Public objects, but if there are some Public objects that Proprietary subjects cannot access, then the access control policy lacks transitivity and the "global" quality is not met.

As we have noted, an access control policy which does not use labels that conform to the qualities of a partially ordered set for all its subjects and objects is not a mandatory access control policy — it is a discretionary access control policy. Each of the access control policies given as invalid mandatory access control policies in the preceding paragraph is a perfectly valid discretionary access control policy. The basic definitions themselves lead to an important, unavoidable conclusion. Any access control policy is either mandatory or discretionary; there is no gray area between. Furthermore, it is a mandatory access control policy if, and only if, it can be represented by a partially ordered set of access classes; otherwise, it is discretionary. Remember that the key distinction between these two forms of access control policy is the protection against malicious software that is possible with each.

We should note that if more than one mandatory access control policy must be enforced simultaneously within a system, then each subject and object may have a label associated with it for each mandatory access control policy. In this case, the labels may have no relationship with each other. Such is the case for the enforcement of mandatory access control policies for both confidentiality and integrity. For example, an object may have a "Secret" label for confidentiality but a "Junk" label for integrity. Another object may have a "Secret" label for confidentiality but a "High Integrity" label for integrity. The only requirement for these labels is that the set of labels for each mandatory access control policy must be partially ordered. Obviously, the overall decision of whether or not to grant access depends on the proper dominates relationship between the subject and object labels for each set of labels. However, this is easy, since the mathematics tells us that the product of partially ordered sets is another partially ordered set. In other words, since each set of labels is partially ordered, all the sets of labels can be combined into a single set, making the comparison of numerous labels a single operation. This technique has been used in practice in a commercial product to greatly simplify and improve the efficiency of the enforcement of mandatory access control policy [THOM90].

An example of a mandatory access control policy and its computer implementation with a partially ordered set of labels may make the discussion more comprehensible at this point. Let us divide an organization into two divisions — perhaps Marketing and Engineering. The employees in each division are allowed access to the information for their own division, but only top management is allowed access to both access classes. We might mark all the Marketing information in our computer with a label "M" and all the Engineering information "E." Employees of the Marketing and Engineering Divisions would be represented in the computer by processes labeled "M" and "E," respectively.

Our secure operating system would allow any process to read information with the same label it possessed or with no label at all. However, no process could remove or change the label on a file, and no process could write any information that did not have the same label as the process. Thus, when a Marketing person was using the computer, he or she could read "M" information or unlabeled information at will. But any information that the process wrote would be labeled "M." Neither the employee nor a Trojan horse could communicate information from one access class to the other.

A scenario that allows no communication at all sounds fairly useless. We shall later expand on this basic scenario to suggest ways in which users can share information and to discuss the access authorizations of our organization's top management. For this introduction, though, let it suffice to say that mandatory access control policies provide a powerful and flexible tool [BELL91] for controlling the flow of information among individuals, and a basic tool for the design of secure computer systems.

Discretionary access control policy. Discretionary access control policies are so named because they allow the subjects in a computer system to specify who shall have access to information at their own discretion. In a system that incorporates both mandatory and discretionary access control policies, the discretionary access control policy serves to provide a finer granularity within (but cannot substitute for) the mandatory access control policy. For example, the military need-to-know security policy in which each individual has a responsibility to determine that another has a valid requirement for information, even though the other has a clearance for the information, is a common discretionary access control policy. In other cases, allowability of access within a discretionary access control policy may be based on the content or context of the information to be accessed or on the role of the user at the time of the access request — or it may involve complex conditions for determining allowable access. In contrast to mandatory access control policies, it need not be global or persistent. Alternatively, a system may incorporate only a discretionary access control policy if the mandatory access control policy is degenerate so that all subjects and objects belong to just a single (implicit) access class. This is the case for the system high mode of operation discussed earlier.

A common example of a discretionary access control policy implementation is the ability of a computer user or a process which that user has executed to designate specific individuals as being authorized access to a given file. Many operating systems provide protection bit masks (for example, "owner," "group," and "world"), access control lists, or file passwords as mechanisms to support some form of discretionary access control policy.

As is the case with mandatory access control policies, we can talk about the abstract list of triples that specifies a particular discretionary access control policy. As with mandatory access control policies, for different discretionary access control policies, there are different lists of triples. With a particular discretionary access control policy, there is an entry for each subject, object, and access mode set for which access should not be granted. However, unlike the limitations on the access modes relevant to mandatory access control policies (that is, read and write), the access modes for a particular discretionary access control policy may be any set of functions. In other words, a particular discretionary access control policy may control not only static read and write access by subjects to objects but also, for example, read-on-every-other-Friday or read-only-if-another-object-has not-been-read, or any other content- or context-dependent rules. (The direct correspondence of security policy access modes to primitive controls — read and write — within a computer system is not important for discretionary access control policies as it is for mandatory access control policies because of the inherent limitations of discretionary access control policies, as is illustrated in the following paragraph.)

A discretionary access control policy is useful in some environments, but it will not defend against Trojan horses or other forms of malicious software such as may be used to perform probing, penetration, or subversion attacks, as described in Essay 1. This can be seen by considering a Trojan horse hidden in a useful program. The example Trojan horse is designed to make a copy, in a directory where the copy is not likely to be noticed right away, of all of the files that belong to a user who runs the program that are marked for reading only by that user. This copy is made readable by some other user who would not be intended to have access to the files. In contrast, consider a mandatory access control policy intended to provide confidentiality. Since the label is attached to any copy which is made and since the Trojan horse cannot change the label, the Trojan horse cannot give a user access to any file in a manner contrary to the mandatory access control policy. In other words, a mandatory access control policy does not prevent a copy from being made by a Trojan horse executing in a process with the same label (for example) as the file, but it does prevent the file's label from changing and prevents access to the file on a global and persistent basis. Discretionary access control policies offer no real protection against even such simply designed malicious software.

Supporting policy. In addition to the access control policies (mandatory and discretionary), there are additional security requirements relating to the accountability of individuals for their security-relevant actions in the computer system. These requirements make up supporting policy [TNI87]. Supporting policy fundamentally "supports" the tie of people in access control policies, about people accessing information, to subjects acting as surrogates for people in computers. Supporting policy provides an environment for ensuring individual accountability for the enforcement and monitoring of the access control policies. In contrast to access control policy, which associates directly with the "theory of computer security" — the reference monitor concept — there is no corresponding "theory" that helps one verify the implementation of supporting policy. Fortunately, it is possible to analyze and test software performing supporting policy functions to reasonably conclude that it functions properly. In contrast, as we have said, it is not possible to do this for an implementation of access control policy.

Supporting policy includes two subcategories: identification/authentication policy and audit policy. The former supports the access control policies by specifying the requirements for authenticating the identity of an individual prior to allowing subjects to act as surrogates for that individual in attempting access. Identification/authentication policy provides the basis for the labels that are used in enforcing the mandatory access control policy to be associated with subjects acting as surrogates in the computer for individuals. In other words, it determines whether subjects may act as surrogates for a particular individual and what label is associated with such subjects. It also provides the basis for the membership of individuals in a group and more generally for controls on subjects consistent with the discretionary access control policy. Further, it provides the basis for recording the identity of the individual causing an auditable action to be performed by a subject acting as the user's surrogate.

Audit policy provides the basis for the recording of those security-relevant events that can be uniquely associated with an individual. The objective is to provide accountability for the security-relevant actions of individual users. We do not have much more to say in this essay about audit policy. The following paragraphs expand a bit on identification and authentication and other aspects of accountability, as supporting policy considerations.

Identification and authentication overview. Identification is a rather straightforward notion. Our summary of identification is simply this: The secure computer system should associate subjects with the identities of individual users and have the option of making authorization decisions or recording an audit trail on the basis of those individual identities. This is in order to be able to trace back security-relevant actions on the computer to some individual. The question arises, "How do we know the identity is correct?" The answer to this question is the province of authentication.

When we discuss authentication, we are concerned with providing the system with some basis for confirming that the user's identity is as claimed. For example, authentication is commonly implemented with some sort of password scheme. The classic definition of authentication measures presents a taxonomy of something one has, something one is, or something one knows. In addition to password schemes (know), there are other methods, such as the use of badge readers (have), challenge/response calculator-like devices (have), smart cards (have), fingerprint readers (are), palm readers (are), and retinal scanners (are).

All of the authentication schemes attempt to provide a reason to believe that the individual who is claiming an identity is in fact the person claimed. All do so by provoking the occurrence of some event that would be much less likely if the person were not the one claimed, and all are probabilistic. The last point is critical. No matter how refined the password scheme or sophisticated the fingerprint reader, there is still a residual probability that one can "fool" it by luck or by cunning. Longer passwords and better fingerprint readers may reduce the probability of an error, but they cannot reduce it to zero. As with the guards in our document library, there is a chance that the authentication scheme will be fooled. For this reason, topics such as "password management" should be examined in greater detail by anyone implementing an authentication scheme based on passwords. However, such topics will not be discussed further in this essay.

There is another side to authentication in a secure computer system whose very existence may be a surprise to the reader. This side deals with the need to authenticate the system to the user.

Authenticating the system. To motivate the need to authenticate the computer system to its user [SALT75], we will again start with a "war story." Suppose we can write a program that will clear the screen of a display terminal and sit waiting for a user to type something. When the program detects a carriage return, it will respond with the string of characters that resembles the system's prompt for the login identifier (for example, "USERNAME:"). If a user types any string, the program will respond with the string the system uses to prompt for the password (for example, "PASSWORD:"), and, if appropriate, it will direct the terminal to cease printing the characters that the user types. After receiving the new string and a carriage return, the program will type some suitable error message and terminate, leaving the unsuspecting user with a real unassigned terminal. Of course, the program was a Trojan horse that just captured the user's authentication information and stored it some place where the attacker responsible for the Trojan horse can later retrieve it and use it to log in as the user who was the victim.

The scenario presented above is a simple way to capture an unsuspecting user's password. It can be executed more or less easily on almost any time-shared computer system that relies on passwords. This sort of attack is logically the same as one in which a separate computer intercepts communications between the user's terminal and computer and steals the password [SALT75]. The possibility of executing the scheme is directly traceable to the lack of an authentication mechanism that serves to authenticate the computer system to the user. As we have just shown, the lack of such a mechanism can have serious consequences.

If we wish to eliminate the possibility of writing a "password grabber" of the sort proposed, we must develop a sort of reverse authentication mechanism. Simply, what we would like to do is have some action that the secure system can take and a password grabber cannot. This can be accomplished by what is called a trusted path.

To implement a trusted path, we can provide a unique action that the user can take to communicate with the secure system. The user initiates the exchange, but is guaranteed that his or her action will result in a response from the trusted part of the secure system. For example, many current systems are guaranteed to respond when a terminal is powered off and then back on. This, or other hardware-supported measures such as pressing the break key, can be used when a terminal is directly connected to the system in a form of authentication of the system that is well suited to initiating the login dialogue.

Of course, this method violates the concept of "programming generality." For while the ideals of computer system design might direct that we always allow a program to intercept and interpret or filter the actions or responses of a user or another program, in the case of the secure system, we must have a class of action or response that cannot be filtered. In particular, it is important to the notion of a trusted path that no code outside the trusted part of the secure system may execute as part of the trusted path.

As mentioned, the password grabber is an instance of a Trojan horse. Once a valid <username, password> pair has been captured, the attacker can use it to establish a false identification as the victim. A trusted path can provide a means (for example, a reserved "secure attention key" on the terminal keyboard) whereby the user can ensure that communication is with the trusted part of the secure system before the username and password are typed. The trusted path is used at other times when a positive communication between a user and the secure system is needed, such as for performing security administration on the secure system (for example, entering user clearances, setting the access class label or range on devices) or downgrading a file (if such a capability is implemented).

Security policy in the document library. We might consider our document library once more and make the examples of authorization and partitioning a little more concrete. Suppose that the library contains documents classified "Secret" and "Top Secret." Individuals who have been granted access to the library have either a Secret or a Top Secret clearance, and the authorization list at the guard desk lists the clearance for each authorized individual.

The library is divided into a Secret area and a Top Secret area. While holders of a Secret clearance are restricted to the Secret area, those with a Top Secret clearance are allowed to enter either. Users of the library are normally forbidden to remove documents, and any notes they take are marked with the access class of the material they have been reading (and retained in the library for their later use). Secret notes may be carried to the Top Secret area. Documents may be removed or classification markings modified only under the control of elaborate procedures authorized by specially selected people. The partitioning of people and areas, and the restriction on removal and reclassification of documents, implement our library's mandatory access control policy.

Documents are stored in the two areas under the control of custodians who are part of the guard force. Each document has an access control list that identifies those cleared individuals who may have access to it. In addition, each document has designated "owners," typically library users who may add names of people to the access control list. The combination of access control lists, custodians, and owners implements a discretionary access control policy that operates within the constraints imposed by the mandatory access control policy.

An audit trail is kept to record the comings, goings, and accesses of individuals, as required by the audit policy.

Indirect access. Any discussion of security policy would be incomplete if it did not address the often-overlooked topic of indirect access. Indirect access is access that occurs outside the security perimeter of the secure computer system. Indirect access is particularly important precisely because it is often overlooked in establishing a security policy for a computer system. Often, the security policy of a so-called secure system may contribute to illicit indirect access; conversely, the security policy of a secure system can contribute to preventing illicit indirect access.

Of course, indirect access is not always overlooked. A description [TECH85] of what is meant by "clearances of system users" says,

> System users include not only those users with direct connections to the system but also those users without direct connections who might receive output or generate input that is not reliably reviewed for classification by a responsible individual.

This statement indicates a security concern not only with controlling the sensitivity of information that the system is processing but also with controlling the sensitivity of information the system is importing or exporting. Note that this illustrates the key to the techniques already partially described for defending against Trojan horses; the key lies not in stopping the Trojan horse from reading the information being protected, but rather in preventing that information from exfiltration.

Now we look at several examples of indirect access. Consider our document library and the security policy described in the preceding paragraphs. Recall that, in the library, documents are marked with their access class and that there are elaborate procedures for removal of documents from the library. Suppose that, for whatever reason, the procedures for removing materials from the library include changing their access class markings from Secret and Top Secret to Restricted and Very Restricted. (This is not as preposterous as it sounds; in some environments, the very names of the classification markings are sensitive, and code words are used outside of the "document library" instead of the real names.) If these documents are now taken to a different library in which the markings Restricted and Very Restricted do not mean the same things as in the original library, users of the new library may access them who would never have been granted access to them in the original library. In this manner, illicit indirect access might result.

There are many ways other than ambiguous security markings, as in the above example, in which illicit indirect access might occur. For example, there is a so-called secure system in use today that utilizes two types of access class markings. One is a label used by the system to implement its mandatory access control; the other is "advisory," not necessarily reflecting the full sensitivity of the information. The "advisory" marking's accuracy may be destroyed by malicious software that places into the object information more sensitive than that indicated by the "advisory" marking and yet, as enforced by the system, no more sensitive than the label used for the mandatory access control. Malicious software capable of performing this feat is quite simple to develop. In such a way, the "advisory" marking may no longer reflect the sensitivity of the information it marks.

The "advisory" marking may be printed on hard copy by the "secure system." Even though the specification for this system says that the "advisory" marking should not be used in determining whether to export information outside the system, in reality this practice is not always followed. In practice, the hard copy bearing the "advisory" marking is sometimes handled outside the computer in a manner consistent with the "advisory" marking but inconsistent with the mandatory access control label. Clearly, this marking is then the basis for decisions regarding the possession and access of this hard copy, quite possibly resulting in illicit indirect access. This illustrates again the "historical lesson" expounded in Essay 1 that misplaced confidence or false assurance of security is worse than if no security at all were provided.

Illicit indirect access may similarly be effected electronically if not carefully considered and prevented. This is trivially possible in the system just cited if, instead of generating hard copy, the system makes decisions about exporting information out of a communication port (for example, to a network or other computer). As a practical matter, it is impossible to detect all possible ways such electronic indirect access might occur. For example, consider a computer system operating in the system high mode described earlier, in which messages are created by users of the system. The sensitivity of these messages is recorded in the "header" of the message by the user who creates it, but, since the system is operating in the system high mode, the system does not enforce a mandatory access control policy based on the message sensitivity reflected in the header. Given that, as is the case for system high systems, each of the users on the system is cleared for all of the information on the system (but may not have the need-to-know for all of it), this design may operate with satisfactory security for quite some time. However, if this system is now connected to a network of other systems in a manner in which it is desired to enforce a mandatory access control policy over the messages, it would be a major mistake to trust the message sensitivity from the message header provided by the system high system to suffice as the mandatory access control policy label. This is true, of course, because of the ability of a Trojan horse on the system high system to modify the sensitivity in the header of potentially any message on that system — since that system implements only a discretionary access control policy.

As a final example of electronically effected illicit indirect access, consider a system that processes both sensitive and nonsensitive information. In this system, it is intended that no information will leave the system without undergoing review by a human reviewer to determine whether that information is sensitive or not. Of course, this security strategy can face a high risk of failure, since it pits the reviewer's skill and stamina against the cleverness of the designer of a Trojan horse. All the designer of the Trojan horse has to do to succeed is to find one way of "sneaking information past" the reviewer without detection. In practice, this is usually easy.

The specific method chosen by an attacker would vary based on the format for presenting the information to the reviewer and the media on which the information being reviewed is stored while being exported from the system. For example, if information is presented to the reviewer in a digital image, it is very simple to contaminate the digital image without detection by the reviewer. The interested reader is encouraged to read an insightful paper by Kurak and McHugh [KURA92]. It clearly shows that "image downgrading based on visual display of the image to be downgraded not be performed if there is any threat of image contamination by Trojan horse programs." As another example, if the information were being exported by the use of a magnetic tape, parts of the magnetic tape that are not easily humanly readable (perhaps "header" or unused bits of each byte) could be used to sneak information past the reviewer. Even if paper is used for exporting the information, sneaking information past the reviewer could be as simple as modulating the use of spaces that separate words in the information being exported.

The solution to the problems of indirect access lies in ensuring that the labels used to enforce a mandatory access control policy are reliable both inside and outside the system. This is possible only if the labels are maintained by an implementation of a trusted computing base, as described in the following section. For human interfaces, such as documents, deliberately and carefully choosing the human-readable access class markings for information exported from the secure system and used outside the system's security perimeter helps to guard against illicit indirect access by making such choices explicit during security policy development. Similarly, for electronic interfaces, a protocol is needed for unambiguously associating a label with all imported and exported information. Only through such explicit designs can the specter of false assurance be prevented.

Building a secure system

The primary focus of this section is the mechanization of security policies by a subset of an operating system called a trusted computing base (TCB) [TCSE85] and methods of achieving degrees of assurance that the mechanisms are correctly enforcing the security policy. (Note that this essay does not address specific evaluation criteria or evaluation classes [TCSE85], which are discussed in Essay 6.) These methods make it possible to build a relatively small part of the system (the TCB) in such a way that one can even allow a clever attacker to build the rest of the system and it will still be secure.

The TCB is defined to be the totality of protection mechanisms within a computer system — including hardware, firmware, and software — the combination of which is responsible for enforcing a security policy. Any software outside the TCB may be malicious software. If a security kernel is implemented in a TCB, then it is the most privileged part of the TCB, and it implements the reference monitor. The ability of a TCB to enforce a security policy depends solely on the mechanisms within the TCB and on the correct input by system administrators of parameters (for example, a user's clearance or the access class label for devices) related to the security policy. The input of these parameters is generally called security administration, and the specially privileged users responsible for the accuracy of this information are called security administrators. Entry of the parameters by the security administrators is an example of exercising the authorization functions.

The role of a security policy model. Once we have the reference monitor concept and a suitable security policy in hand, we are faced with the problem of building a secure system or TCB, as it is called. In other words, we have the problem of implementing the concept in a real hardware/software mechanism that enforces the security policy. In beginning this task of implementation, we shall find that a crucial role in the assurance of security policy enforcement is played by a model of the security policy of our TCB. The security policy model allows us to make the leap from security policy to real TCB by providing an intermediate step: a formal description of the functions that the TCB will perform. By "formal" we mean that the model must be a precise and complete mathematical statement which can be proven self-consistent — such statements are usually presented using predicate calculus.

This intermediate step offered by the security policy model bridges between two constrained universes of discourse — the computer-independent world of people attempting to access information, and the world of computers. We have already discussed the roles of subjects as surrogates for users and objects as containers of information. In a security policy model, we have a set of operations or rules that model the reference functions and the authorization functions that define the access of subjects to objects. The security policy model takes as a "given" (that is, does not model) certain initial state information — including certain information typically entered into a TCB by security administrators, as mentioned above. It also takes as a given the proper operation of the TCB to correctly implement the supporting policies, including the proper operation of the TCB to identify individuals authorized to perform as security administrators or as users of the system.

The security policy defines the behavior desired of the TCB but does not directly dictate the functions to be performed by the TCB. In fact, nothing in the security policy itself explicitly relates to the notion of a TCB or a computer system at all (remember that we just applied a "computer security" paradigm to a document library). We proceed by precisely (formally) defining the functions of the TCB. We must, of course, find functions such that the behavior exhibited by the security policy model complies with the security policy. The security policy model can be viewed as a formalization and particularization of the reference monitor, providing its reference and authorization functions. Note that current practice is for the security policy model to encompass only the access control policies of the TCB; it does not itself represent the supporting policies. As stated above, a security policy model takes as a given the proper operation of the TCB to correctly implement the supporting policies. History has shown that enforcement of the access control policy is one of the hardest things in a computer system to get right. It is fortunate that the technology has developed to allow this tool to be used to substantially increase the assurance of access control policy enforcement.

If the security policy model encompasses the discretionary access control policy, then it must represent authorization functions whereby a subject can, for some object, grant access to another specified subject. This function could, for example, correspond to adding a user's name to an access control list. If there is no explicit discretionary access control policy in the model, then the controls on access within the model reflect only the mandatory access control policy.

By the very definition of mandatory access control policy, in general, subjects cannot modify mandatory security authorizations. The access class labels for the initial objects are supplied from "outside" the TCB as part of its initial configuration, typically by security administrators. The security policy model may, however, include functions for creating and deleting objects, and for controlling the access class for new objects and subjects.

There is an exception, by the way, to the notion that in a mandatory access control policy, subjects cannot modify mandatory security authorizations. That exception is for trusted subjects. Trusted subjects are subjects outside the reference monitor, but within the TCB, that can read and write objects at different access classes, in a manner that would normally be prevented by the reference monitor. Trusted subjects are used, for example, in downgrading a file in TCBs, which permits sanitization of information, or they may be used simply in the course of implementing a TCB.

The use of trusted subjects is distinguished from the more general extension of privilege to read and write computer resources outside the reference monitor (for example, in "privileged" processes), as is implemented in some systems. In building a TCB, it is important to recognize the sharp distinctions that exist between privileged processes and trusted processes (that is, processes containing a trusted subject). Privileged processes are those that are capable of affecting access control decisions or other functions of the reference monitor. Since they can potentially affect any aspect of the reference monitor, the entire security of the system depends on the behavior of these privileged processes as much as any other part of the reference monitor. In other words, the reference monitor's security perimeter is extended to encompass privileged processes. This is in contrast to trusted processes that operate within a range of access classes but do not affect access control decisions. The difference in the level of system exposure that accompanies privileged processes from that which accompanies trusted processes is clearly considerable.

For example, in TCBs like Multics [SCHR72] and the Gemini Trusted Network Processor [THOM90], there are multiple protection rings where trusted processes can be placed, and therefore their actions can be constrained from affecting the rest of the TCB. However, there is no such thing in the typical Unix architecture. The usual choice for implementing trusted processes with Unix is to effectively modify the Unix kernel by implementing privileged code. However, this is a problem, since even if the Unix code is well-modularized and understandable, it is generally unreasonable to expect writers of privileged processes to understand the security implications of so fundamental a modification. Further, note that some implementations provide a "privilege bit" intended to allow one to build things like a trusted process, but this is the moral equivalent of extending the Unix kernel out into the trusted process. If one were to use this "privilege" mechanism, one would not be able to state any well-formed security properties about it. In contrast, building a trusted process on a base with protection rings, such as those mentioned above, allows one to make the trusted process somewhat independent from the rest of the TCB, thereby providing a valid basis for security in the system. Since trusted processes contain subjects that are outside the reference monitor and their behavior is constrained, their effects are not usually explicitly included in the security policy model for a mandatory access control policy. However, the effects of privileged processes must be included in the security policy model since their behavior is far less constrained.

While a number of security policy models have been developed, by far the most widely used has been the Bell-LaPadula security policy model [BELL73]. The Bell-LaPadula security policy model is an abstract model of the behavior of a TCB. It provides a framework within which a security policy can be formally represented as mandatory access control policy and discretionary access control policy. The Bell-LaPadula security policy model is security policy-independent. It has been used to represent a set of rules to enforce security policies whose primary objective is confidentiality, and it has also been used to represent a set of rules to enforce security policies whose primary objective is integrity. Each time it is used, it must be interpreted for a specific security policy and a specific system [BELL75, BIBA77, LUNT88a].

Each such interpretation of this model mathematically represents the state of a TCB and prescribes the criteria for a secure state with respect to the requirements of a mandatory access control policy and a discretionary access control policy. The TCB modeled is defined to be in a secure state only if no subject can access information that it is not authorized to access. Each interpretation of the Bell-LaPadula security policy model defines a set of functions or rules for changing the state of the TCB and for permitting subjects to reference objects. It is mathematically proven that the rules preserve the property that the new state of the TCB is still secure — no subject can access information that it is not authorized to access.

Bell and LaPadula presented an interpretation of their security policy model for the Multics system and for a security policy aimed at confidentiality [BELL75]. The key properties preserved in this interpretation for mandatory access control are the "simple security property" and the "*-property." The simple security property for confidentiality stipulates that the label of a subject must dominate the label of an object in order for that subject to get read access to that object. The *-property for confidentiality stipulates that the label of a subject must be dominated by the label of an object in order for that subject to get write access to that object. It is easy to see why these properties prevent information from flowing "downward" from an object labeled with a particular confidentiality access class (for example, Top Secret) to one lower (for example, Unclassified). In this way, confidentiality Trojan horses are rendered ineffective.

Biba's interpretation [BIBA77] of the Bell-LaPadula security policy model for the Multics system and for a security policy aimed at integrity is quite like Bell and LaPadula's [BELL75], except that the simple security property and *-property are changed in an interesting way. The equivalent of the simple security property stipulates that for integrity the label of a subject must be dominated by the label of an object in order for that subject to get read access to that object. The *-property for integrity stipulates that the label of a subject must dominate the label of an object in order for that subject to get write access to that object. It is easy to see why these properties prevent information from flowing "upward" from an object labeled with a particular integrity access class (for example, Junk) to one higher (for example, High Integrity). In this way, integrity Trojan horses are rendered ineffective.

Shockley [SHOC88] has pointed out that Biba's security policy model interpretation [BIBA77] is capable of satisfying commercial security requirements, as well as the more frequently seen military requirements. In particular, he said that the Clark/Wilson integrity policy that is claimed to be "an accurate representation of what the business and commercial data processing community means by the term 'integrity'...in commercial data processing" can be represented using Biba's techniques [BIBA77].

The power of the security policy model comes from the fact that a suitable set of rules has been developed. It has been inductively proven that if the initial state is secure, these rules can never produce a state that is not secure. That is, a set of sufficient (but not always necessary) conditions is assured by the rules. This power ensures that, if the security policy model indeed represents that behavior of a TCB, then no use of that TCB can cause a violation of the mandatory access control policy.

The security policy model dictates what must and what need not be included in the TCB of the secure system. Thus it has a strong impact on the design of any TCB that attempts to follow the security policy model's requirements rigorously.

Two key issues must be emphasized in closing this subject because they have been an occasional source of misunderstanding. First, the security policy model must be a valid representation of the behavior with respect to information protection of the entire system. Merely modeling distinct computer functions with respect to individual assertions about a protection mechanism provides little indication of overall system security and can even be misleading. Second, the security policy model must include a proven security theorem, which establishes that the security policy model's behavior always complies with the security requirements for the security policy of interest. As stated above, the security policy model takes as a given certain initial state information — including certain information typically entered into a TCB by security administrators. It also takes as a given the proper operation of the TCB to implement the supporting policies, and in particular that subjects faithfully represent the access classes of the individuals for which they are acting as surrogates. With this input, which it considers a satisfactory basis for establishing a secure initial state, the security theorem which is proven is that no matter which rule of the model is operated, all future states will also be secure. This proof of what is called the Basic Security Theorem is the key to the power and utility of this technique. We leave the topic of security policy models with one guiding principle: A security policy model without a proven security theorem is like a fire bucket with a large hole in its bottom — it is the sort of thing that can give you a warm feeling, but it is probably not what you really want. A false sense of assurance is a dangerous thing.

Design, specification, and implementation. The security policy model defines the functions the TCB must provide but does not specify the design for the TCB. The next step after the specification and interpretation of a security policy model is the specification of the interface to the TCB. The specification defines a set of subroutines (that is, TCB calls, similar to operating system calls) and hardware operations that implement the operations of the security policy model which provide access to the resources contained in the model's objects. The TCB contains internal databases that represent the security policy model's state. These internal databases are used by the TCB (in particular, by the reference monitor) to create the abstractions of subjects and objects that are entities outside the TCB.

When we reach the point of specifying the TCB's interface functions, we are at the point where our efforts reflect the level of system security, or assurance, that we are trying to attain. As we mentioned in the introduction to the reference monitor concept, if we are interested only in preventing probing we will probably elect to make a significant portion of or all of our operating system serve as the implementation of the reference monitor functions. On the other hand, if our system must also be resistant to penetration and subversion, we will need to have a much smaller subset which can be verified — a security kernel [AMES83, SCHE84a] that implements a true reference monitor. Gasser [GASS88] describes security kernel implementation strategies, noting that the security kernel is the single most often used technique for building a highly secure operating system.

While it might seem foolish to contemplate less than the best, and thus to build a system that would not resist malicious software attacks, there are reasons for electing to do so. Probably the best are cost and compatibility. Most existing operating systems can be modified to implement a portion of the reference monitor concept and get improved security at modest cost. Going further and actually modifying the system to incorporate a security kernel is, in general, as costly as reimplementing the system from scratch. If not engineered carefully, such modifications may have a noticeable impact on system performance (though it is quite possible to build an operating system with a security kernel in a way that has quite good performance [SCHE85a]). On the other hand, if a development is planned to build a new operating system "from scratch," one gains significant benefits from incorporating a security kernel, for in this case the incremental costs in development and performance are likely to be relatively modest. In addition, significant savings in life-cycle software maintenance costs are associated with the rigorous software engineering practices used in building a security kernel. Furthermore, the stable interface of a minimized security kernel appears from a software maintenance point of view to be an extension of the hardware interface, often resulting in a maintenance philosophy much more akin to hardware than to software.

For these reasons, we now consider the steps required to build a security kernel and a TCB *without* a security kernel. Because the latter approach represents a relaxation of requirements and a set of compromises, it is in some ways easier to deal with the security kernel case. We thus present the steps to a security kernel design first and then describe the compromises that one might make in developing a TCB that lacks a security kernel.

The security kernel. In the case of a security kernel, we will design a mechanism that performs a carefully selected subset of operating system functions to implement at least a mandatory access control policy. (Note that because a discretionary access control policy is fundamentally incapable of preventing Trojan horses, as described earlier, there is little need to strive for as high a level of assurance of enforcement as for a mandatory access control policy and therefore little need to include enforcement of a discretionary access control policy inside the security kernel.)

The reference monitor concept requires that every reference by a subject to an object be mediated and subject to the system's security policy and security policy model. To simplify a security kernel, we take steps to minimize its complexity, and we may minimize the number of different types of objects it supports.

The security kernel functions form its interface with the rest of the operating system. It turns out that, to meet the constraints of the security policy model for the mandatory access control policy, the security kernel interface will provide a pure virtual environment for the rest of the system. This requirement results from the need to eliminate (sometimes subtle) methods of circumventing the security policy model's restrictions on the flow of information from one access class to another. Frequently, specifications of the interface are expressed in a formal language capable of being analyzed by a computer program and of supporting a formal proof that the specifications conform to the requirements of the security policy model. Such specifications are termed formal top-level specifications (FTLSs). A system whose interface has been specified and proven in this manner is a system for which one has significantly increased assurance of its ability to enforce the security policy.

As with any design effort, preparing the specifications is a creative activity molded by the peculiar design goals (other than security) of the system. Typically, one proceeds iteratively, testing the design against such requirements as performance, functional richness, use of the underlying hardware, and compatibility with other software systems. Analytical tools supplement intuition in the effort to ensure that the resulting specification complies with the overriding security requirements of the security policy model.

Beneath the set of security kernel interface functions is a set of computer code, databases, and hardware structures. The selection of secure functions at the security kernel interface is of little benefit to assurance if, for example, the underlying software turns out to be a hundred thousand lines of incomprehensible assembly language "spaghetti code." The security kernel itself is structured in a series of layers (for example, SASS Kernel [SCHE83]), each performing a distinct set of services either for processes outside the security kernel or for other security kernel layers, and each depending only on the services of lower security kernel layers. A layered security kernel provides an opportunity to develop an informal proof sketch of each layer's sufficiency to meet the requirements of the next higher layer, based on an implementation specification for each layer. This proof sketch for succeedingly higher layers of the security kernel, if performed, would provide a clear correspondence of the layers in the design to the FTLS and hence to the security policy model. The correspondence of the layered implementation to the security policy model is also facilitated by breaking the implementation design into modules that have a clean, clear abstraction that allows for information hiding within modules in the manner described by Parnas [PARN72a, PARN72b]. The design of such a modular, layered security kernel is not an easy exercise, but it is by no means impossible. It pays rich dividends in providing assurance that the security kernel software in fact implements the primitives at the interface that were shown to be consistent with the security policy model.

The security kernel software will both control and be supported by the associated processor hardware. The requirements for hardware structures to support a security kernel derive from the basic requirements for a reference monitor: completeness, isolation, and verifiability. In addition, the need for well-defined subjects and objects is reflected in the choice of hardware to support a security kernel.

The key requirements are the following:

1. Hardware support for a notion of process and support for rapid change from process to process.
2. Hardware support for some sort of objects and for protection of those objects. In practice, this requirement is satisfied by a segmented virtual memory system and provisions for security kernel control over input/output operations.
3. Hardware support for the protection of the security kernel and its databases by some sort of protection domain or protection ring [SCHR72] mechanism.

The implementation of the security kernel programs typically involves the use of some form of structured coding and a higher level language. The choice of language and standards is influenced by efficiency as well as security since the security kernel is the heart of an operating system.

This brief summary of the security kernel design process has taken us from the high-level requirements of security policy and a security policy model to the implementation of the security kernel using a programming language. As the process of security kernel development proceeds, progressively more design detail is provided. At each step, though, there must be a correspondence between the detailed design produced and the requirements identified by the earlier steps. Layering, modularization, abstraction, and information hiding within the security kernel and documentation in the form of an implementation specification facilitate a demonstration of this correspondence. In this way, one can develop running code that corresponds to the requirements of a security policy model and security policy. There are formal tools available that support the demonstration of the correspondence between the FTLS and the security policy model, and there are informal techniques for demonstrating the correspondence between the code and the FTLS. However, even without mechanical tools, the discipline and structure of the security kernel design process provide a high degree of assurance about the security of the resulting system.

Improving an operating system. When we think about making an operating system or a subset of an operating system — a TCB — mimic the behavior of a reference monitor, we are frequently interested in making after-the-fact improvements to an existing system. For this reason, we often refer to such an effort as security enhancement and to the product as a security-enhanced system. The approach used to develop a security-enhanced system begins with identifying a security policy and security policy model, and specifying the interface of the security-enhanced system to the outside world (now an interface to the users and application programs). Instead of doing a layered design and structured implementation of the entire system "from the interface down to the hardware," we now modify the code of the operating system to implement the interface specification. However, in so doing, we accept that we will not be able to completely separate protection-critical components within the operating system from those that are not protection-critical. This places a fundamental limit on what one can know about the behavior of such a security-enhanced system and thus places a limit on the degree of assurance of security policy enforcement that is possible using one.

As noted in the previous section, to simplify a security kernel, we take steps to minimize its complexity, and we may minimize the number of types of objects it supports. However, in contrast to that approach, in developing the interface specification for the security-enhanced system we are talking about in this section, we may take additional short cuts.

For example, an existing operating system is likely to support a vast number of object types, and it may be impossible to apply controls to them all. We may leave some uncontrolled by the security policy model and, in doing so, leave in the system a much higher level of vulnerability to Trojan horse attack than a security kernel would suffer.

While the code of the security-enhanced system will be as clean and error-free as good practice can make it, it will not have the assurance advantages of the structured design and implementation that a security kernel has. It will be much more likely to contain residual errors in design and implementation (or even to contain malicious software), and it will be more likely to be subject to malicious software attacks from the outside.

The above is not to diminish the value of such security-enhanced systems. The primary value of these systems lies in their resistance to probing and in their improvement over a more conventional system against this threat. They typically provide a very robust environment and may have enhanced penetration resistance in addition to a rich set of security features. For that reason, and because of the feasibility of developing them with modest effort, security-enhanced systems offer an attractive option for those with limited needs for assured security.

TCB subsets. It is sometimes beneficial to develop a TCB and evaluate its security in parts, rather than as a monolith. A TCB subset [TDI91] is an extension of the reference monitor concept that enforces some access control policy on subjects that may attempt to gain access to a set of objects under the subset's control. The access control policy enforced by a TCB subset is a subset of the overall access control policy of the TCB. Access control policies of distinct TCB subsets are enforced by distinct domains within the TCB.

A TCB subset must meet the three requirements of a reference monitor: completeness, isolation, and verifiability. In fact, a reference monitor is a TCB subset. The primary difference is that a TCB subset may have an interface to a more primitive mechanism, which is also a TCB subset (enforcing a less restrictive access control policy). In the degenerate case of a single, monolithic TCB (for example, the sort of system described above as a security-enhanced system), there is a single TCB subset — which includes the portion of the system performing the reference monitor functions and the hardware. A TCB partition (more frequently called a network TCB partition or NTCB partition [TNI87]) that enforces an access control policy is a TCB subset which does not depend on another TCB subset. A TCB partition is thus in direct control of a particular, well-defined subset of subjects, objects, and hardware of a processing component of a particular networked system. NTCB partitions are discussed further in a later section.

As noted, the reference monitor implements the least restrictive mandatory access control policy in a TCB. Other TCB subsets within that TCB may implement other more restrictive access control policies, including more restrictive mandatory access control policies and discretionary access control policies. These TCB subsets are, like supporting policy implementations, within the TCB but outside the reference monitor.

The topic of TCB subsets is only briefly introduced here. Additional information about TCB subsets may be found in the paper [SHOC87] where the notion of TCB subsets was first formalized.

Demonstrating security. The discussions above have touched briefly on the tools that we can use to convince ourselves that a system is secure. We next give a little more of a feeling for the steps that we can take to achieve assurance of system security. The quest for system security is old enough to have a body of history. We mentioned in Essay 1 the iterative "fix and test" or "penetrate and patch" approach that some took at a time when computer security was in its infancy. We will begin this discussion with a few comments on how "not to do it" and then summarize the methods that can lead to effective assurance of system security.

Testing, penetration, and reading the code. In the early days of computer security, advocates of secure systems tried to follow a path of searching for ways to penetrate the systems' controls, often relying on malicious software in the same way a potential attacker could launch a probing, penetration, or subversion attack, as described in Essay 1. Their plan was that, failing to penetrate, they could plausibly argue that there was no way to penetrate since no way was known (to them). In this scenario, if a security hole is found, it can be patched before the argument for security is made. Obviously, this argument suffers from both theoretical and practical difficulties.

One presumes that one could test all possible programs to find any that led to a security penetration. If possible, this method of exhaustion would be effective, but it is far beyond the realm of feasibility. For any real computer it would take so long that before the evaluation was finished the sun would literally have burned out! Thus any evaluation conducted by exhaustion must be so incomplete as to be ludicrous.

Practically speaking, the effort spent in penetrate and patch techniques yields poor marginal return in terms of security. Experience has shown the following conclusions to be true:

1. New penetrators tend to find new holes — even after previous teams have found all that they could. It seems unlikely that a real, malicious attacker would fail to involve new people.

2. Holes do not generally result from rank stupidity but from human oversight in dealing with a difficult design problem. Thus the fixes themselves are likely to be flawed.

3. It does not take a highly specialized expert to penetrate system security. It is true that most computer professionals do not know ways to penetrate the systems they use; they want to do a job, not interfere with it. Yet when given the assignment, even junior and inexperienced professionals have consistently succeeded in penetration.

The real difficulty of achieving security by penetrate and patch techniques is precisely the difficulty of finding errors in a program by testing. A test can demonstrate the presence of an error but, short of exhaustion of every possible combination of inputs, it cannot demonstrate the absence of errors. Much of the weakness of security in existing systems results, in the first instance, from the fact that these systems were designed to perform a function and tested to assure that they did so correctly. The function to be performed had the nature of "the right answer" rather than secure operation.

A failure of system security results from the failure by a designer or implementer to anticipate a "functional" requirement for security, and to build and test a system to meet that requirement. Security is a fundamentally "negative" requirement stating that, for all possible applications, unauthorized access will not be granted. When examining the system, the penetrator tests a different function — namely, that there exists at least one way in which unauthorized access to information will be granted. There are many ways of succeeding with this function.

In the limit, the problem of security is that the designer must search out every way to penetrate security and correct all; the penetrator is really interested in finding and using only one. This is an unbalanced "game of wits" in which the attacker has a substantial advantage.

The key to successful functional testing lies in factoring the system's structure into the selection of test cases, and in designing the system to support testing. In a real sense, this is the approach we take with a security kernel: designing the system so that, by means of a proven security policy model, security becomes a positive requirement rather than the absence of errors, and structuring the system to support analysis and testing. Since testing security becomes testing for positive requirements, it is possible to test in the same manner as in the usual software testing scenario. In contrast to the strategy of testing for all possible penetration approaches, testing a security kernel is quite doable.

TCB design and security verification. When we discussed design and specification of a security kernel, we presented the process of system design, beginning with security policy and culminating in security kernel code.

We also indicated that formal security kernel verification tools could follow the same path. In the paragraphs below, we summarize the process of security kernel verification, then indicate how we might apply some of the same steps to the security evaluation of the TCB of a security-enhanced operating system.

The security policy model is the linchpin of verification. It translates the fundamentally negative requirements of security mentioned in the previous section into positive properties that can be verified. The security policy model bridges between the people-oriented world of security policy and the computer-oriented world of the reference monitor abstractions of subjects and objects. The step from security policy to security policy model is necessarily an informal one — at some point we must make the translation from English "legalese" to formal, mathematical language. By taking this step at the level of the security policy model, we reduce the complexity of the mechanism that we must review in an unstructured way. In the case of the Bell-LaPadula security policy model, while there is a fair amount of formalism to be dealt with, the basic objectives and approach are relatively simple. Numerous readers of the security policy model have convinced themselves that it is a formal statement of the objectives that it claims to support. It is easy to see that a security policy model that is simple and abstract is necessary to the verification process.

Once the security policy model is accepted, it provides a formal basis for the security evaluation of the rest of the TCB. We can state our TCB's interface specifications in a formal language and verify the correspondence between security policy model and interface specification. We can also specify the security kernel interface in the formal language and verify that the system implemented is the same as the security kernel whose interface has been specified. The specifications of the security kernel implementation are presented module by module for each layer and layer by layer in a structure corresponding to the security kernel software itself. This enables a proof sketch of each module's sufficiency to meet its specification and each layer's sufficiency to meet the requirements of succeedingly higher layers, all the way up to the interface, as described earlier.

The security kernel implementation specification supports the proof sketch of each corresponding module of security kernel code. The technology of program verification does not practically allow for formal code verification of large real programs. However, there are a few key factors that contribute to the success of this approach for providing a meaningful verification of the implementation. The decomposition of the implementation design into "Parnas modules" with a clean, clear abstraction that allows for information hiding, and strict layering of the modules, both make formal verification more thinkable and offer a structured way to read the code and review its correctness informally. In fact, it is information hiding and strict layering that provide the real basis for progressively developing a proof sketch of the code's sufficiency to meet the interface specification, module by module and layer by layer, as mentioned in the previous paragraph. Our experience shows that the difficulty of reviewing operating system code for correct and secure operation results from both the complexity of the code and the lack of any clear definition of what the code is supposed to be doing. The implementation specifications for a security kernel support the determination of what the code should be doing.

Beyond the higher level code are machine language and hardware implementation issues. Verification technology is not up to these issues yet. Again, however, the structure of the security kernel and its specifications at least offer meaningful support for a partially informal but effective assessment of security.

There is one more aspect of assessing security that we would like to address. It should also include a determination of whether the implementation of the reference monitor contains covert channels. Covert channels are flows of information between access classes in a manner that is counter to the mandatory access control policy portion of the security policy but allowed by the implementation. It is important to recognize that valid security policy models do not have covert channels; covert channels are an implementation phenomenon. A security policy model that allows information to flow in a manner counter to the security policy is a flawed security policy model [LEVI90].

Recall we observed earlier that the security policy model represents the state of the TCB. Covert channels operate because this state information is sometimes passed to subjects outside the reference monitor. The two types of covert channels — covert storage channels and covert timing channels — differ by the manner in which the state information is passed. In covert storage channels, information is passed out of the reference monitor through the value of an exception or error code. In covert timing channels, information is passed out of the reference monitor through a delay (that is, a measurable change in response time) observable by a subject. The only other way besides through covert channels in which information could flow through a reference monitor in a manner counter to the security policy would be through the use of a flawed security policy model, as described in the previous paragraph.

For an example of a covert storage channel, consider two subjects with Trojan horses operating at different access classes ("Marketing" and "Accounting") such that the security policy which the reference monitor is enforcing forbids any information to flow between the two. If, for example, one of the state variables in the reference monitor is used to indicate "disk_full," then information can easily flow between these two subjects. The Trojan horse in one of the subjects can signal a single bit of information to the other by filling the disk (or not filling it) at an agreed-upon time or after an agreed-upon condition, at which time the Trojan horse in the other subject checks to see whether the disk is full (for example, by trying to write to the disk). This signaling can be done repeatedly and rapidly. The maximum rate at which the signaling of a particular covert channel can be accomplished is called its bandwidth.

A similar exploitation scenario can be constructed to illustrate covert timing channels. Suppose that instead of the "disk_full" error condition, our Trojan horses were to use the amount of time required for a read from the disk to signal a bit. Suppose the Trojan horses in both subjects know how long a normal disk access takes. To signal a bit of information, the "writer" Trojan horse need only make sure the disk is busy enough to slow down the "reader" Trojan horse's disk access. Again, this can be done repeatedly and rapidly, and one can calculate or measure the bandwidth.

One might ask, "Doesn't the existence of covert channels destroy the assurance of enforcement of the mandatory access control policy we worked so hard to achieve?" Actually, while uncorrected, covert channel bandwidths can be quite high, though they may be difficult to exploit at the highest rates because of "noise." But there are many techniques available for reducing the bandwidths. In fact, security kernels are available today that can be configured to have no covert storage channels [THOM90]. The bandwidths of covert timing channels can be reduced in the most brute-force way by slowing down the functions that allow them to operate if it is detected that a particular bandwidth threshold is about to be exceeded. This can be mechanically accomplished by inserting delays wherever the functions are called. Of course, this can have an adverse impact on performance, but it permits stronger enforcement of the mandatory access control policy.

Finally, we promised to include in this discussion a comment about the problem of assessing the security of the TCB of a security-enhanced operating system. In such a system, we are concerned about features at the TCB interface as well as about having as "correct" an implementation as we can. The security policy model supports a review of the interface to the TCB in this case. We may prepare a formal or English specification of the TCB's interface, then review it for inappropriate ways that a subject can gain access to an object. We will probably supplement the interface analysis with a penetration test to help make sure that no obvious flaws remain. We may also look for covert channels and even work to reduce particular covert storage channels. However, experience tells us that the lack of a structured — layered and modular — implementation in a system which is not designed to be subjected to the level of analysis of a security kernel results in a system that is subject to penetration (as well as subversion of security mechanism), as defined in Essay 1. Such a system is of some value, though, since it can offer a relatively high degree of resistance to probing.

For further reading. More information on building a secure computer system can be found in a readable first book [GASS88] on this subject that presents difficult and subtle topics clearly, while achieving a good depth of coverage.

Special considerations for networks

As noted in Essay 1, networks present greater accessibility to potential penetrators by providing more ways of accessing the systems (through other interconnected systems, through dial-up terminals, through taps into the communication lines used by the networks themselves, and so on). Obviously, networks are strongly dependent on computer systems to provide the networks' services. The resources being shared within computer systems connected to or implementing the network provide numerous opportunities for sensitive information to "leak" out or be illicitly modified from within. The networks themselves provide no fundamentally new vulnerabilities, except through the enhanced accessibility to the computer systems that protect the information. The enhanced accessibility facilitates the exfiltration of information, which, as noted earlier, may aid the successful use of Trojan horses.

The reference monitor concept scales very nicely to networks that possess a coherent network security architecture and design — in other words, coherent security policies, security objectives, and protocols. In a network context, we speak of the trusted computing base or TCB as a network trusted computing base or NTCB. The computer systems that implement the switching and other processing within the network, as well as the client systems of the network, provide the opportunities for sensitive information to leak out or be illicitly modified, as described above. The NTCB prevents such leakage and illicit modification.

The enhanced accessibility of the connections between the computers or switching elements of the network system is countered most often through the use of cryptography, either alone or in combination with other security services (for example, physical protection of the wire) and security supporting protocols. The enhanced accessibility of one computer system from another is countered through applying the reference monitor concept to the computer systems that make up the network system.

The unique aspects of building secure networks are described in the following two sections. The first section applies the theory of computer security to networks with a coherent network security architecture, in the form of an NTCB [TNI87]. (The section contains some actual excerpts from the "Trusted Network Interpretation of the Trusted Computer System Evaluation Criteria" [TNI87] to explain the concepts.) The second section describes some of the fundamental access control problems that must be addressed in implementing cryptography within a computer system. We will not otherwise delve into the technology of cryptography or security supporting protocols in this essay.

Network trusted computing base. As stated previously, this section applies the theory of computer security — the reference monitor concept — to networks. In so doing, it also expands somewhat on the application of the reference monitor concept in stand-alone computing environments — specifically, in the area of input/output devices. So, note that the information presented here about devices also pertains to stand-alone computing environments; it is presented here as a convenience to the discussion of networks and the NTCB.

One of the first steps in the design of a secure network is the development of coherent network security architecture and design. The network security architecture addresses the security policies, objectives, and protocols of the network. The network security design specifies the interfaces and services that must be incorporated into the network for it to be secure, relative to its security policy.

The overall network security policy is the security policy of the NTCB. It may be decomposed into security policy elements that are allocated to appropriate components and used as the bases for the security policies for those components. This technique is referred to as partitioning a network's security policy into component security policies or NTCB partitions [SCHE85]. As used in this essay, a component is a collection of hardware, firmware, and software that performs a specific security function in a network and that contains an NTCB partition. A component is defined recursively, in that a component may consist of other components. The distinguishing quality of a component is that it has a security policy partition allocated to it — induced on it by the overall network security policy. The recursive definition of component is based on the fundamental concept that it contains an NTCB partition, a recursively defined concept based on the "partition" of mathematics. (As in mathematics, if a set is partitioned and if one of the partitions is further partitioned, the result is still partitions of the original set.) Such recursive definitions of component and NTCB partition are very useful in actual practice, since, once the security of a component is evaluated, the results of that evaluation may be directly reused in evaluating the security of a component which contains it. (See the section "Evaluation by parts" in Essay 6 for a further discussion of applying the strategy of "divide and conquer" by separately evaluating NTCB partitions and using the results to evaluate more complex components within which they may be contained.)

Therefore, one of the powerful design tools provided by this approach is the ability to compose a set of components, and then treat the result as a single component having a security policy made up of the set of allocated security policies and defined network interfaces. Once a composition is performed, the resulting component may be considered in a variety of network security architectures without having to reconsider the original components or the process of composition.

Much of the usefulness of this approach lies in its general applicability. For example, a host computer system that implements a full set of user services may be treated as a component for purposes of composing the computer system into the network system.

Components can include entire subnetworks within an overall network, encryption systems, local area networks, digital PABX systems, packet switched or circuit switched systems, and virtual machines running on a virtual machine monitor (VMM) on a single computer system, when analyzed as a network. The ability to view a set of virtual machines as distinct network components is a powerful tool that allows varied security policies to be implemented in virtual machine components on top of a VMM component. It is an efficient technique in that if the underlying VMM component has already been examined and found to enforce a security policy required for the network system, it does not have to be reexamined after the composition. In the case of network components implemented as virtual machines, the interface between the VMM component and the virtual machine components is the set of functions provided by the VMM component. An example of the use of this technique is described elsewhere [IRVI91].

Abstractly, the reference monitor for a partitioned NTCB is realized as a collection of security kernels for individual components. To obtain the required levels of assurance that each such security kernel enforces its security policy, a formal security policy model is formulated for each such component. However, it would be too restrictive to require that the formal security policy model for each security kernel be the same, or that an overall formal security policy model be formulated for the network. Instead, each formal security policy model is shown by convincing arguments to correctly represent the security policy allocated to the component. Since the overall security policy is stated informally, the convincing arguments are also stated informally, in the same manner as that described in the earlier section "TCB design and security verification."

The formal security policy models of components therefore provide the basis for the security policy exercised by the NTCB over subjects and objects in the entire network. The purpose of the formal security policy model for each component is to serve as a precise starting point in the chain of arguments leading to the sufficient levels of assurance required for each component in the network and ultimately for the whole network. These arguments are easier to make if the formal security policy model has an intuitively attractive resemblance to the abstractions of subject, object, and access properties of the computer system TCB on which the component is implemented.

Thus, the reference monitor subject and object definitions that pertain for a computer system TCB are sufficient also for an NTCB. The reference monitor represents the fundamental security policy enforcement at the individual component level but may not directly represent all of the overall network security policy issues such as the network's connection policy. In many networking environments, the overall network security policy includes controlling the establishment of authorized connections across the network. The access control mediation performed by the components of these networks enforces the establishment of connections between host computers on the network and provides the basis for a connection-oriented abstraction. Understanding the connection-oriented abstraction for a given network may be essential to understanding that network's overall security policy. The network security architecture describes the linkage between the connection-oriented abstraction and its realization in the individual components of the network.

Subjects in networks are therefore active entities outside the perimeter of the reference monitor in each component; that reference monitor's objects are passive entities that exist in the component which implements that reference monitor. Reference monitor support to ensure control over all the operations of each subject in the network is completely provided within the single NTCB partition on which that subject interfaces to the NTCB. This means that the entire portion of the formal security policy model's "secure state" that may undergo transitions because of the actions of this subject is likewise contained in the same component.

The level of abstraction of the formal security policy model and the set of subjects and objects that are explicitly represented in the formal security policy model are clearly affected by the NTCB partitioning. Subjects and objects are represented explicitly in the formal security policy model for a particular component whose NTCB partition exercises access control over them. Global network security policy elements that are allocated to a component must be represented by the formal security policy model for that component.

Each partition of the NTCB therefore enforces the security policy over all subjects and objects in its component. In a network, the responsibility of an NTCB partition encompasses all security policy functions in its component that would be required of a TCB in a stand-alone system. In particular, subjects and objects in a particular component that are used for communication with other components are under the control of the single component which contains them. Conceptual entities associated with communication between two components, such as sessions, connections, and virtual circuits, may be thought of as having two ends, one in each component, where each end is represented by a local object. Communication is viewed as an operation that copies information from an object at one end of a communication path to an object at the other end. Transient data-carrying entities, such as datagrams and packets, exist either as information within objects at one end of the communication path, or as a pair of objects, one at each end of the communication path.

Access by a subject in one component to information contained in an object in another component requires the creation of a subject in the remote component that acts as a surrogate for the first subject. The security policy must be enforced at the interface of the reference monitor (that is, the mechanism that controls physical processing resources) for each NTCB partition.

Recall the introduction of devices and communication channels and the roles they play in the reference monitor. The only links between NTCB partitions are the various communication channels provided by devices. Devices may import or export information only under the explicit control of the reference monitor in accordance with the security policy.

A basic choice must be made about each device of a TCB or of an NTCB partition allocated to a network component. That choice is

1. whether the information that will be imported or exported through the device at any particular point in time will have its label associated and flowing with it, or
2. whether the access class of the information will be established administratively (that is, whether the security administrator will "tell" the TCB or NTCB partition what the access class of the information is that can flow through that device).

If the access class of the information is associated with a label that flows with the information, that device may be used to import or export information whose access class varies within a range enforced by the reference monitor implementation, and it is called a multilevel device. On the other hand, if the access class of the information that may flow through the device is established administratively and thus cannot vary (until a different access class is administratively established), that device is called a single-level device. It should be explicitly recognized that a device or a communication channel that does not support the transmission of labeled information is, by definition, single-level. In a network component, therefore, the devices coupling the communication channel to the processing nodes may be single-level devices, administratively set to import or export information of the same access class, or they are multilevel devices, capable of handling information of some intersecting access class.

A single-level device may be regarded either as a subject or an object. A multilevel device is regarded as a subject that is within the TCB or NTCB partition (that is, it is a trusted subject — trusted to correctly associate information and labels within some range of access classes). However, as with all subjects, it is outside the reference monitor. For a multilevel device, the range of the subject is the minimum-maximum range of access classes of information that may be transmitted over the device.

To support single-level devices, the TCB or NTCB includes a trusted subject or a reliable communication mechanism by which the TCB or NTCB and a security administrator (via a trusted path) can designate the single access class of information imported or exported. A single-level device also has a range of access classes within which the access class set by the security administrator must fall, but it is important to note that single-level devices have only a single access class at one time.

The allocation of mandatory and discretionary access control policies to different components in a network may require communication between trusted subjects that are part of the NTCB partitions in different components. This communication is normally implemented with a protocol between the subjects as peer entities. The protocols and data which they carry between these subjects that associate the access class with exported information (for multilevel channels) or that designate the single access class of information imported or exported (for single-level channels) require special attention to ensure the NTCB's integrity. These protocols are actually being used to communicate internal NTCB data among NTCB subjects (that is, trusted subjects outside the reference monitor but inside the NTCB) belonging to different NTCB partitions. This data must be protected against external interference or tampering. For example, a cryptoseal (see the next section) or physical means may be used to protect such data exchanged between NTCB partitions.

The need to be concerned about the integrity of internal NTCB data is clear if one considers that labels are among the sort of information communicated between NTCB partitions. Since there is no standard representation for labels communicated between components, each component needs to be able to translate from the form in which the label is communicated to its own internal representation in a highly reliable way.

Subjects outside the NTCB but not direct surrogates for a user (human) are termed internal subjects. Protocol handlers are examples of services that are usually provided by internal subjects. It is important to understand that a key distinction of internal subjects from "regular" subjects is that since they are not acting for users, there is little or no need for a discretionary access control policy to be enforced over them. Similarly, since the purpose of supporting policy is to provide the tie between persons and access control policies, there is no need for supporting policy (for example, identification/authentication and audit policies) to be concerned with them.

Therefore, a crucial step in the design of a network is the allocation of the NTCB security policy to individual components within the network that share information using devices to provide communication channels. This partitioning into components must be done in such a way that all of the following conditions can be easily validated:

1. A subject is confined to a single component throughout its lifetime.
2. A subject may directly access only objects within its component.
3. Every component contains a component reference monitor (or, for security-enhanced systems, the functions of a reference monitor) that mediates all accesses made locally to enforce an overall access control policy for the whole network.

4. All communication channels linking components do not compromise the security of the information entrusted to them. This allows the conclusion that the total collection of components enforces the network's overall security policy.

Access control and cryptography in networks. Access control and cryptography interrelate in at least two fundamental ways. For one, cryptography may be useful in supporting access control decisions. As stated above, the reference monitor represents the fundamental security policy enforcement at the individual component level but may not directly satisfy all the overall network security policy requirements such as the network's connection policy. In many networking environments, the overall network security policy includes controlling the establishment of authorized connections across the network and protecting the information during transmission. The access control mediation performed by the components of these networks enforces the establishment of connections between host computers (including, for example, mainframes, workstations, and/or personal computers) on the network. Cryptography may be used (with specific security-enhancing communication protocols) to support the access control decisions (that is, to provide the mechanism to ensure that the host computers may communicate only as authorized by the overall network security policy). Of course, this is no different in principle from the use of cryptography in media encryption. All data on a medium such as a disk or transmission cable is encrypted to eliminate the risk of exposure in case the medium is stolen or tapped into — in other words, to prevent illicit access to the media.

That is all we are going to say specifically about the use of cryptography to enforce access control. Instead, this section focuses on access control issues involved in the implementation of cryptography on a computer system. Cryptography is, of course, in its simplest application, a way of protecting information from disclosure. However, the success of cryptographic techniques fundamentally depends on the protection of certain keys from disclosure and the assured application of the intended keys and algorithms. If the keys that require protection from disclosure are in any way disclosed, the information whose protection depends on those keys can no longer be assumed to be protected. If incorrect keys or algorithms (that is, those supplied by an attacker) are used, the protection is illusory.

It is because resource-sharing computer systems have difficulty with secure simultaneous processing of sensitive and nonsensitive information that computer security has arisen as an important discipline. For that same reason, systems have difficulty with secure simultaneous processing of plaintext, ciphertext, and keys. In a nutshell, this is why depending on cryptography to encrypt and keep separate individual files is usually not a good idea — because, to be secure, the system on which the cryptography is implemented must already have the capability of keeping separate the information of different sensitivities. That means that one can do no more for access control with cryptography than what a TCB enforcing a mandatory access control policy already supports. Providing individual file encryption is, therefore, quite susceptible to Trojan horses without the presence of a TCB that is enforcing a mandatory access control policy, rendering it also quite susceptible to false assurance. However, use of encryption under the control of a TCB enforcing a mandatory access control policy to protect information on a medium (for example, a disk or a transmission cable) is quite achievable, assuming one has such a TCB [FELL87, THOM90, WEIS92].

Up to this point in this section, we have only explicitly mentioned using cryptography in conjunction with a TCB to provide protection from disclosure. However, it should be noted that cryptography can also be used in conjunction with a TCB enforcing a mandatory access control policy to provide protection from illicit modification.

Most readers are probably familiar with techniques of using parity, a checksum, or some other checkfunction (that is, the result of some algorithmic function carried out on the data) to detect data errors, especially in communication. While such techniques are useful for detecting and sometimes even correcting random or burst errors on a communication line or in memory, they cannot protect against an intruder, with access to the data, illicitly modifying bits of the data. If an intruder can modify bits of the data, he can also recalculate the checkfunction (since the algorithm is typically well known) and insert this modified checkfunction.

The technique used to provide valid protection from illicit modification is called cryptosealing. Cryptoseals themselves are data that represent the result of a function involving cryptography being carried out over the data being protected. Cryptoseals are typically many fewer bits of data (64 to 128 bits) than the information they are protecting. They have the property that if any bit of data (or of the cryptoseal) is modified, the modification can be detected by carrying out the cryptographic function over the data again, using the same key. If the result is different from the cryptoseal, the data was modified. Cryptosealing is a useful technique when physical controls on access to the medium on which the data is held cannot be guaranteed. For example, bank (ATM) cards commonly use a form of cryptoseal to ensure that bank account numbers are not "forged." A number of techniques for generating and using cryptoseals in different applications have been standardized (for example, CCITT X.509 and ANSI X9.9).

The problems with trying to use cryptosealing on a resource-sharing computer system are the same as those noted above for cryptography in general. Similarly with the general case, the problem is secure simultaneous processing of data being cryptosealed, the cryptoseals themselves, and keys. That means that one is subject to the same security problems inherent to resource-sharing computer systems when using cryptography or specifically cryptosealing inside that computer system. In other words, cryptography and cryptosealing are not substitutes for a TCB enforcing a mandatory access control policy, and, if implemented in a computer system that is not enforcing a mandatory access control policy, there is a significant possibility of false assurance. Again, providing cryptosealing over individual files is susceptible to Trojan horses without the presence of a TCB enforcing a mandatory access control policy. However, use of cryptosealing under the control of a TCB enforcing a mandatory access control policy to protect information on a medium is a quite achievable task, assuming one has such a TCB. The application of this technique to database management systems has been addressed rather extensively [DENN84, DENN85], and the same basic techniques can be used for networks, as overviewed below.

With a TCB that enforces a mandatory access control policy to implement cryptosealing, an important class of NTCB extension can be built — commonly termed guards. The concept of a guard was first introduced in the early 1980s in a study by Roger Schell for the Korean Air Intelligence System or KAIS [DENN84]. Jim Anderson then used these ideas to develop the recon guard [ANDE81]. Guard is a term sometimes used (imprecisely and improperly) to indicate almost any form of application providing a security function in a network. We use the term precisely and consistently with the historical usage to refer to a technique for implementation of a specific function: communication of information of multiple sensitivities between secure computers by using a system high network, operating with the access class of the most sensitive information being communicated.

The guard method works in the following manner: For a particular transmission of information, two guards are involved. One is associated with the transmitting computer and has a secure communications path to the transmitting computer's TCB, and one is associated with the receiving computer and has a secure communications path to the receiving computer's TCB. The guard associated with the transmitting computer receives the data to be communicated and a label indicating its access class from the transmitting computer's TCB. (Note that the label is often implicit, say, at the single system high level of the transmitting computer.) The transmitting guard then cryptoseals the data to be transmitted, together with a representation of the label. This data may now be exported from the transmitting guard, since the network is at a single level which dominates that of the data, and it can be subsequently received by the receiving guard. The receiving guard now checks to see whether the cryptoseal is intact, indicating that no modification of the data or label has occurred. Assuming the cryptoseal checks out, the receiving guard hands off the data and its label to the receiving TCB for proper disposition based on the validated label. Note that the system high network can be carrying data of various sensitivities from one or more pairs of guards. The guards have now logically implemented a multilevel network out of a system high network, albeit a network providing transmission protection (that is, via cryptography) for up to the most sensitive information.

Some past efforts have used the terms guard and filter almost interchangeably. It is useful, however, to distinguish between these two. In a sense, both devices perform sanitization and/or downgrading from one access class to another in a manner normally counter to the access control policy. They perform this function against data sent to them, preventing unauthorized disclosure based on some policy, and then release the data. The nature of this policy allows us to distinguish between the relatively weak nature of filters and the more robust nature of guards. A policy for a filter may rely on virtually any content or context-dependent criteria for its decision to release the data. An example of a filter is a device performing "dirty word" sanitization, where data containing specific code words or combinations of code words will be deemed unreleasable. Thus, filters can be described as devices that determine the releasability of data by "figuring out" the sensitivity of the data.

The major distinction between filters and guards lies in the outcome of their correct operation. A filter examines data from a system high environment and attempts to downgrade this data to something other than its original system high access class. In the face of malicious software, no claim can be made about whether this downgrade is valid or not, since any number of tricks can be used by an attacker to "sneak information past" the filter, in a manner like that described earlier for illicit indirect access. A guard, on the other hand, bases its sanitization decision on the credible label, which is assigned and checked at a place where it is reliable and which is protected by a cryptoseal. Therefore, even though there are some problems that limit the protection against a determined attacker [DENN85], guards do offer some real protection against malicious software.

Conclusion

We have presented an introduction to the concepts and terminology of computer security and to the reference monitor concept that allows us to build secure systems in an orderly way. We have presented an introductory view of the role of a security policy in the development of a secure system and have outlined the processes of specifying, designing, implementing, and evaluating a TCB. We have also provided a summary of the application of computer security to networks. In all, we have addressed concepts and terms that we consider to be among the most critical to gaining a fundamental understanding of this technology.

The reference monitor concept, if applied properly, is a powerful tool for the control of computer misuse. While human error and user abuse of authority are largely external problems, a TCB is a vehicle for constraining users to their authorized domain and for obtaining data for an audit trail of the users' actions. Application of the reference monitor concept lets us enhance the security of an operating system and make it essentially immune to probing.

Finally, the consistent application of the reference monitor concept and the system implementation techniques that have grown up with it allows us to develop a security kernel for preventing penetration or subversion of security mechanism with a high degree of assurance. There is a firm technical foundation on which to build a security kernel for a specific system in a manner that yields good performance. The designs and implementations to date have empirically validated the principles needed to use the security kernel without degrading system capabilities [SCHE85a].

Epilogue

The statements above are strong ones. The reader may well ask, "Is all of this real?" In fact, the technology has been applied to real systems. Security-enhanced systems based on the reference monitor concept are in use today in commercial organizations, in the Defense Department, and in other places throughout the world. Several organizations have successfully developed security kernels, including the Gemini Trusted Network Processor (GTNP) from Gemini Computers [THOM90], the Honeywell SCOMP [FRAI83], the XTS-200/STOP from Honeywell Federal Systems, Inc., the Boeing Multilevel Secure Local Area Network Server System [SCHN85], the VAX VMM Security Kernel from Digital Equipment Corp. [KARG91], and Blacker [WEIS92]. The technology that we describe has sufficient credibility to be the basis of the National Computer Security Center's evaluation criteria for TCBs [TCSE85], trusted networks [TNI87], and trusted database management systems [TDI91] (presented in Essay 6), as well as the basis of multinational evaluation criteria [ITSE91].

We hope that this essay has given the reader a sense of the concepts and terminology of the technology that allows us to solve a significant portion of the computer security problem. The moral of this essay is perhaps summarized by the following quotation [SCHE79]: "Do not trust security to technology unless that technology is demonstrably trustworthy, and the absence of demonstrated compromise is absolutely *not* a demonstration of security."

Acknowledgments

We would like to give a special acknowledgment to the contributions of Steven B. Lipner of Trusted Information Systems. Substantial portions of the text as well as several key insights related to the reference monitor are drawn from material he previously prepared and he has graciously permitted us to use in this essay.

In addition, acknowledgment is given to "Trusted Network Interpretation of the Trusted Computer System Evaluation Criteria," National Computer Security Center [TNI87], from which excerpts have been drawn for incorporation into the discussion of NTCB-related concepts.

We also gratefully acknowledge the substantial constructive comments and suggestions provided by James P. Anderson on an earlier version of this essay.

Essay 3

A Philosophy of Security Management

David Bailey

It is not possible to maintain security in a system or network of more than minimum complexity unless appropriate management is possible. This essay discusses security management of complex systems, including the scope of the security manager's role and the conflicting pressures that must be balanced. It ends by discussing a strategy for the security manager that has been used successfully on a large local network.

The security manager's world

Security management is an important part of the whole secure system picture. A system whose security cannot be managed is not secure, no matter what evaluators may tell you about its internal controls. Today, the security of "secure systems" is difficult to manage, and the situation is rapidly getting worse for complex computer networks and systems. This requires the security manager to adopt a strategic point of view and to place more faith in architectural and environmental controls than in controls built into operating systems.

This essay is about developing a strategy for security management. It does not recommend specific controls, specific implementation techniques, or specific products. It does not even try to describe specific elements that should be included in every policy. None of this could be done without having a great deal of information about the system in which they were to be installed. Security management is a discipline in which making trade-offs is a continual activity: controls in the system versus controls in the environment, security control versus customer convenience and productivity, strong controls versus implementation and administrative costs, and so on. This essay is about how to make those trade-off decisions.

The reader should not expect to find a recipe for protecting a system or network in this essay. Instead, the essay describes an approach to the security management job that will allow the manager to avoid "falling behind," even if the system or network is large and complex. The observations below are based on a dozen years' security management experience with a large and complex network used for scientific computation and falling under US government rules for handling classified data. This may not be the type of network you are trying to manage. Nevertheless, whether your network is government, commercial, or military — or large or small — there are some commonalities in the pressures on the security manager. Elements of the strategy below may be helpful.

In the rest of this essay, we take a broad view of a security manager's responsibilities and develop a philosophy that can help one avoid the pitfalls produced by rapidly changing technology. There are a number of "rules of thumb" that apply to the world of computing in the 1990s and guide the security manager's strategy. We begin by discussing the security manager's role in an enterprise. Next we discuss some of the factors that affect how security management works, and finally we discuss a strategy for approaching the job.

For simplicity, only computer networks are discussed below. Every modern computing system can be thought of in network terms, so if we deal with network management issues, stand-alone systems will also have been addressed.

The basic job description

Security management is not simply watching over the computer and its operation after it has been installed (although this is an important activity). It also includes tasks that must be completed before installation, such as setting and articulating the security policy. It even includes tasks that are not started until after the system is removed from service, such as sanitization. These tasks can be summarized as two basic responsibilities:

- The security manager has an obligation to management to ensure that the security requirements imposed on the system will adequately protect the organization's resources and data.
- The security manager has an obligation to management to ensure that the system is operated in a manner that satisfies its security requirements and to report significant or continuing deviations in security.

Every system gets much of its security "direction" from the outside. Government and military systems must satisfy an agency security policy. Banking and insurance systems must satisfy various laws and rules imposed by regulators. Other commercial systems must satisfy a variety of laws and decisions imposed by upper management or the board of directors. However, external sources of direction, even if they are reasonably specific, do not directly apply to the computing system without local interpretation. Thus, creating a system-specific security policy is a task that the security manager cannot avoid. (See Essay 5 on multiple levels of policy for additional information.)

Unfortunately (for the security manager), long-term stability is not a property of computer systems. Every system breaks. Every system failure is ultimately repaired by the addition of hardware or software that makes the system different from how it was before the failure. Furthermore, every system is developed and changed over its lifetime. As new functionality is added, the system policy may have to change, and its detailed interpretation will certainly change. Thus, throughout the life of a system, the security manager must continually redevelop and extend the detailed security policy that it implements. Ideas that have been made obsolete by changes in the network have to be changed and redeveloped. The detailed policy also has to be expanded to cover new hardware, new software, new functionality, new connections, and sometimes new kinds of users.

System security evaluation is also part of security management. Evaluation is a continuous process beginning before the system is turned on and ending only after it is turned off to be removed. As development occurs, the policy may change, the protected assets may change, and the threat environment may change. All of these changes alter the security requirements, and they force reevaluation of the system against the new requirements. Even during normal operations in the periods between changes, the security manager must continually reevaluate the system. Unauthorized attempts to access the system also require the security manager to reevaluate the system. The judgment that continued operation will not harm the company is made anew every day. Most of the time, this is an analytic activity, but occasionally some system testing is required.

The scope of these activities is much broader than simply watching over the operation of the system and issuing a few passwords. The security manager must be prepared to be involved in policy development, threat and requirements analysis, configuration and usage management, hardware and software evaluation, and recovery management. All of these areas must be addressed to satisfy the basic job requirements.

A few of the facts of life

The life of a security manager is not as straightforward as deciding what should be done and then demanding that it happen. There are the normal constraints of lack of funds to do what should be done, lack of people to make it happen, and the desire of the users to do almost anything else. There are also constraints that arise from the current realities of computing, and these also have to be taken into account. A few of these constraints are described below.

The catch phrases used as headings are, of course, not literally true. They do, however, describe several facts about the current world that cannot be ignored. They are also suggestive of a useful attitude. The security manager should not become mired in the details of the operation but should always look at the bigger picture.

Software rots. A friend uses this phrase to describe the fragility of old software that has been enhanced and repaired many times. After a while the code becomes unmanageable, and new enhancements or repairs tend to result in more problems than they fix. Finally a time is reached when no one will touch the code anymore for fear of breaking it again.

The same phenomenon occurs in systems. It is largely a result of increases in internal complexity that occur when new functions are patched on top of old. As old pieces of the system are asked to do just a little bit more than they were originally designed to do, they necessarily become more complicated and harder to maintain. Over a decade or more this can happen to so many parts of the system that it can no longer be maintained at all.

The security manager cannot prevent this phenomenon from occurring, but strong security management can prolong the life of the system by resisting gratuitous increases in complexity. Systems break. This is usually bad for security. Complex systems break more often and are harder to fix. This is worse for security. Thus, it is in the organization's security interest to keep the system as simple as possible, and doing so is the responsibility of the security manager. Over the long term, complexity management is the security manager's most important function.

Everything is connected to everything else. The term "stand-alone computer" is an anachronism that has almost no place in the current environment. The security manager used to be responsible for watching the site's "Central Computing Facility" (CCF). This was all she or he had to worry about, but those days are gone. This is no longer a reasonable approach.

For many years at the Los Alamos National Laboratory, all of the computing capability was located in the CCF. This was true in 1950, and it was true when I arrived in the early 1970s. It changed rapidly in the 1980s. By 1990, when there were about 65 "Cray-1 equivalents" of raw computing power in the CCF, there were over 100 Cray-1 equivalents sitting on people's desks.

In terms of all the measures used by security managers — number of users, number of machines and sites to be protected, volume of audit data, number of network connections — the Los Alamos network exploded. All of these measures grew by three orders of magnitude between 1975 and 1985. For example, the number of network users grew from four in 1974 to over 4,000 a decade later.

Los Alamos was certainly not alone in experiencing explosive growth. It was a property of the whole world of computing in the 1980s. Explosive growth continues into the 1990s. The Internet had over 500,000 nodes in 1991. The number grew at about 10 percent per month during 1991 and 1992. By the end of 1992, the growth had slowed to only about 1,000 new hosts per day.

But the visible connections are not the only ones that have to be considered. Even if electronic links such as local area networks are absent, almost every small machine has a modem, and sharing of diskettes is pervasive. If data moves between machines, they must be considered connected, no matter how the data gets from one to the other. The components managed by a single security manager are a small portion of a vast network with no easily discernible boundaries. This means that security must be provided without the benefits of isolation.

Significant computing power is everywhere. An Intel-486-based machine running at 33 MHz with sufficient memory is roughly equivalent to a Cray-1, the supercomputer of 1980. Even small machines (that is, desktop machines) have enough computing capability to do significant damage to an organization's security. We used to depend for part of our security on the inability of a user to do much computing on his desk. Unfortunately, this simplification no longer works. Today, at some sites the computing power is fairly uniformly distributed, and the machines at the central facility are not much more powerful than those on people's desks.

If computing power is everywhere inside an enterprise, this will surely be true outside as well. This means that the system's adversaries have more capability, and more computationally intensive attacks can be expected in the future. Since it is no longer safe to hide behind complexity, stronger protective mechanisms will be required. Stronger mechanisms will sometimes include better controls within computer products. More often, however, needed isolation between functions — security-critical functions and user processing, for example — will be obtained architecturally.

Hardware is free. Some hardware — supercomputers, for example — appears to be very expensive. In an organization with a small budget, even a personal computer may appear expensive. But even the hardware costs of supercomputers are small when compared with the associated costs of buildings, installation, maintenance, software, and people. In a large enterprise, the cost of small machines is in the budget noise. Even in a small enterprise, where the budget arguments are more difficult, small machines are often on every desk. This means several things for the security manager.

First, since small machines are cheap, the growth of the network will be, to a first approximation, uninhibited by cost considerations. Cost may slow growth but does not prevent it. One should expect continuous growth. As long as the growth doesn't include structural change, however, it presents only mechanical problems (more users to service, more audit trails to process, and so on).

Second, it is easy for internal developers to obtain small machines. Thus, the pace of development is controlled more by the size of the staff than by the cost of hardware. Once again, if the development doesn't include structural change, it presents only minor problems. But if the network wasn't carefully planned in the first place, significant functional change can occur through the addition of small warts. Those development warts are the changes that eventually make the whole system too fragile to be maintained.

Third, it is also relatively easy for security people to get small systems. Often a security-critical process cannot be adequately protected if it has to share a processor with other activities. This is because needed isolation cannot be provided within a single machine. The right solution may be to provide it with its own processor. Often, this is much less expensive and more effective than trying to upgrade the security of the shared processor.

Developers are everywhere. The pace of development in the commercial hardware and software world is enormous, especially compared with the pace of security development. There are orders of magnitude more development people than there are security people. And it often seems that everything they do is specifically designed to make the security job harder. Worse yet, detailed security evaluation is expensive and slow. Detailed security evaluation of a new piece of software, when it is possible at all, takes approximately one software generation. That is, the evaluation will be finished at about the same time that the software is obsolete. Hardware is even more difficult and costly.

Change is nearly continuous in any large computing system, and the security officer must continually and rapidly evaluate proposed changes to determine if they should be rejected, be allowed to proceed, or be slowed to allow time for deeper evaluation.

Love is blind. When and how to evaluate are difficult problems. Developers have infinite confidence in their abilities and will always argue that evaluation is unnecessary. But, being absorbed in the beauty of their own creations, they will also propose outrageously dangerous ideas and fail to see obvious problems that should be repaired. Developers who normally are only marginally able to communicate in their native language can become passionately eloquent if the behavior of their creation is questioned. Evaluation is one area where a security manager should be rigid. All security-relevant code should be evaluated by someone other than the developer — no exceptions.

There are two important aspects to the evaluation problem: the initial baseline evaluation, and evaluation of development and maintenance changes. Both are important and difficult. Unfortunately, they are different, and one set of tools and techniques does not suffice for both problems.

The initial evaluation becomes increasingly difficult as the complexity of the system grows. A large system, such as the Los Alamos network or the network belonging to a large commercial organization, is not amenable to complete evaluation using the tools and techniques available today. It is simply too large and too complex. Even if it could be evaluated, however, it would undergo thousands or tens of thousands of changes during the evaluation period.

The rate of change in the Los Alamos network is tens to hundreds of changes per month. To install changes at this rate without evaluation is unacceptable. To incur the cost and delay of using presently available tools is also unacceptable. Thus, it is necessary to create new tools, speed up existing tools, and make the tools available to a less sophisticated class of users than the people who built them. In the interim, until the needed tools are developed (possibly a long time), it will be necessary for security managers to decide with almost no concrete information which changes have to be evaluated (and how carefully) and which can be installed without evaluation.

New tools are also needed to handle evaluation of maintenance changes. Most maintenance changes are minor and have no effect on system security. However, simply ignoring minor changes can be a big mistake — tiny changes can dramatically affect system security. A way must be found to evaluate the semantic effects of change rather than just the syntactic effects. We must be able to determine the importance of small changes to very large systems quickly and easily.

While we are waiting for better tools, much more effort needs to be spent on informal and semiformal evaluation techniques. Formal evaluation of large connection-rich networks will not be feasible for a long time, but large connection-rich networks are being built and used. Techniques must be available for analyzing them. Most of these networks do not need formal analysis, but they all require some protection and some analysis.

Formal, or even informal but detailed, security evaluation is not practical for any but the smallest or most critical networks today. There is no evidence that this will change anytime soon. A security manager with protection responsibilities today must find some way to do the job without detailed evaluation. Unfortunately, there are no systematic ways to do this. The result is usually a very conservative attitude about what can be allowed.

A strategy

The picture painted above is pretty bleak. Implementing and maintaining security are difficult and are getting more difficult rapidly. Data in large volumes is easily portable and easily changed, so simple isolation no longer works. The market for security products is still small and cannot keep up with the pace of change.

There is a strategy that will work. Interestingly, it relies on more distribution of computing rather than less. In fact, it requires distribution and decentralization of everything: computing power, security mechanism, and security management responsibility. The elements of the strategy are outlined below. The elements will be weighted differently, depending on the size and complexity of the system. Security managers of small systems may use some of these ideas very little, but even a large and complex system can be protected using this strategy.

Decentralize. We are at the end of a decade of massive decentralization of computing power. What used to be concentrated in one place is now spread out over the whole enterprise. Much of the decentralization occurred before we realized that security mechanism has to be distributed along with the computing power. Almost all of it occurred before we began to realize that security responsibility also has to be distributed with the computing power. One manager cannot be directly responsible for the activities of 1,000 workers, and, for the same reasons, one security manager cannot be directly responsible for the security of 1,000 workstations. The responsibility to protect must go with the power to compute.

Use the system architecture. Security mechanisms need isolation. If users can manipulate or change the security mechanisms, they lose their value because their properties are unknown. You can't depend on something you don't understand (massive application of faith is not generally considered a valid security strategy).

All security mechanisms are not equal. Some require better protection than others. If isolation is moderately important, improve the security in a shared processor. If isolation is really important, put the security process in its own processor. Remember that hardware is (close to) free.

It is generally true that putting a control process in its own processor improves security. Information hiding is recognized as an important means of managing complexity in the software world. The modern expression of this principle, object-oriented design and programming, is seen as a very exciting way to rapidly produce correct software.

The analog in the network world is to put an object in a processor. The benefits of information hiding accrue at this level of abstraction, just as they do in software applications. The "isolated" process is still subject to all of the tricks and manipulations through its interface that previously worked, but several avenues of attack have been removed. It is much less likely, for example, that the process's data structures can be manipulated directly than if it shared a processor with a potentially hostile user process.

Of course, in any specific situation, there are subtle manipulations that might be possible that would counter the claims made above. These are, however, second-order effects. Most security managers never have enough time, and little occasion, to consider second-order effects. This, like considering weaknesses in the gate when a fence has yet to be built, is a waste of time.

Write a threat statement. Threat can be analyzed in two ways: looking out and looking in. When one looks outward, one gathers information about what potential adversaries might try to do by looking at available intelligence information and at historical information about similar systems. This provides a sketchy picture of a threat environment that may be similar to the actual environment for the system in question. The picture, however, is necessarily incomplete — you cannot know exactly who all your adversaries are or what they might do. (Too bad — if the picture were complete, life would be simple.)

Looking inward, one asks which threats, if they were carried out, would be most damaging. Where possible, it is useful to validate the analysis with available historical or intelligence information. One then proceeds to install protective measures against the most damaging potential threats.

The threat statement should be a specific and detailed statement of what adversaries may try to do and how they might do it. Statements like "Espionage agents will try to obtain sensitive data" or "Criminals will try to steal money" are of no use in selecting controls to counter the threats.

Although it may seem difficult and perhaps unnecessary, the threat analysis must be much more specific. This is important when the implementers are designing specific security features. The threat statement is a road map for system designers. It is important because if you don't know where you are going, it is hard to tell whether you have arrived. The following can be used as tests to help decide when the threat statement is done:

- A test plan outline should be directly derivable from the threat statement. That is, a reader should be able to see exactly what threats the target is expected to counter and, therefore, should be able to see exactly what tests are needed to verify that the system does what is expected.

- The reader must be able to see the rationale for every required security feature. The reader must understand what threat or threats the feature counters and whether the feature does this alone or together with other features. These linkages should be exhibited explicitly by the authors.
- The described threat must still be clear in 10 years. See the first item above. This is partly a matter of language, partly a matter of presentation.
- Two completeness tests must be satisfied. These two forms of completeness are essential to the process of vetting the system design to determine if it should be implemented.
  - It must be possible to assess the completeness and reasonableness of the threat analysis. The reader must be able to look at the analysis and determine if any important threats have been left out or if threats that have been included are unimportant.
  - The reader must be able to examine the security features that have been specified to determine that all the threats the system is supposed to resist have been addressed adequately.

Avoid details. It is not always possible or desirable to avoid all details when managing a security program. Details are important. Yet a security manager is busy, and if all of her time is spent on details, the larger issues will escape attention. A security manager immersed in details has already lost. The following paragraphs give some hints about strategies that can be used to avoid this problem.

Structure the system as large components. The properties of a complex system cannot all be understood by a single person. But failure to understand how the system behaves can be fatal. Therefore, the security manager must always simplify. One simplification that helps is to structure the system so that many components contribute to a single kind of processing that can be thought of as a unit. For example, all of the components serving a particular kind of user might be grouped. If a group of components is implemented so that the group has a well-defined interface to the rest of the system, then it can be thought of as a single item — for example, as a single computer. This is just another application of object-oriented thinking. Details are hidden inside the object and can be thought of separately. The decoupling of different parts of the system that occurs when this technique is applied is an enormous simplification. It can be the difference between a system that is secure enough and one that is not.

For example, the Los Alamos network, which contains thousands of computers, supplies only four different kinds of computing (based on data sensitivity and user access). As a result, components can be grouped into a handful of computational structures, each of which can be thought of as an entity. Relative freedom of communication and functional development is allowed within an entity. But strong justification and detailed scrutiny are required for any new connections proposed between entities.

Use triage. "Every change to a system should be analyzed to determine that it has no adverse effect on security." This is a great idea, but it is impractical for any system larger than a few PCs. For a large system, it is impossible. Still, the security manager cannot delegate too much authority to the developers. I once discovered, at the last minute, that a critical security process was about to be changed without any independent testing. Even though the process had been reimplemented in a new language, and it was to run on a new machine with a different operating system, the developers didn't consider the change to be security relevant because no functionality was supposed to change.

The security manager should be aware of every change to the system but must learn to sort them quickly. Three categories are used: changes that are unlikely to affect security and should proceed without interference, those that have security implications and should be evaluated, and those that are outrageous and should be rejected without study. Although this takes experience, it becomes easier with time and is surprisingly effective.

Use the environment. Every system is different. Its purpose is different. Its users are different. And, its environment is different. The environment includes all of the context in which the system operates and must always be considered when the threat statement is written. No system can provide all of the controls that are necessary to protect the information processed in it. Some controls must always be placed in the environment.

Since the environment must contain some of the controls used to protect data, it is reasonable to consider using the environment whenever new or additional controls are needed. Often it will be cheaper and more effective to implement new controls in the environment instead of in the system. The point is that this option should always be considered. It is not necessary to tweak the system every time protection has to be improved.

Use deterrence. Security people like prevention. If something is not supposed to happen, don't let it happen. But prevention isn't always possible. Some undesirable actions are a result of an authorized person doing more than he or she was authorized to do, or doing something for the wrong reason. The computer system cannot be expected to tell the difference. The user can do what the user can do, and motivation cannot be assessed.

If prevention isn't possible, try for detection. Audit trails can be created for most actions and later processed by machines or by humans to detect actions that a user should not have taken. But detection sometimes isn't possible either. This might happen because the relevant event can't be captured, because it gets lost in a mass of detail, or because the volume of related events precludes inspection of each one. For example, the file storage system at Los Alamos holds several million files. While it is likely that a few of these contain unauthorized data, periodic inspection of them is out of the question. In a case like this, deterrence is the only solution. Warning notices, spot checks, and public hangings all serve to remind users that there are rules of conduct and that someone cares how they perform.

Guard the borders. The system being protected is probably connected to other systems, all outside the control of the local security manager. Data may flow regularly to and from outside systems in the performance of the company's business. The situation can easily become amorphous and highly fluid.

It is important for the security manager to establish a security perimeter outside of which control is not exercised. It is, of course, important to protect the perimeter well enough that control is not necessary on the outside. Three tools can be used to help accomplish this:

- Use strong authentication procedures for traffic crossing the perimeter. Authenticate everything if that is possible, even system-to-system transfers. Where the external connection is to the Internet, it is important to consider carefully which protocols should be passed through the perimeter, which should be buffered, and which should be stopped.
- Buffer critical decisions and critical transfers. Don't implement critical decisions about data movement across the perimeter in the processors that are on the perimeter. Instead, make them further inside the perimeter and validate their correctness redundantly in the processors on the perimeter.
- Audit more completely at the perimeter, and make it clear that auditing takes place. This will help to identify when something has failed. It will also help with the subsequent damage assessment, and it will serve as a deterrent to malicious activities in the first place.

Evaluate. I pointed out earlier that complete evaluation of complex systems is impossible. This means that it would not be possible to get the system to hold still long enough to apply any systematic technique to it in depth. It does not mean that evaluation cannot or should not be performed. In fact, evaluation must become a continuous activity of the security manager. The current state of the system is examined daily (a basic security responsibility), and changes are made as necessary.

The questions to be asked are:

- Has the threat environment changed in a way that calls for reassessment of the security controls in place?
- Has the system changed in a way that might create new vulnerabilities or exacerbate old ones?
- Has the erosion of security due to accumulated changes moved the system outside the parameters set by management?

If any of these questions is answered "Yes," action is required. The action could range from informing management to shutting down part or all of the system, but action cannot be avoided.

Summary

Computer users have gotten connected. They have computational capabilities on their desks that are electronically linked to everyone else's capabilities. This happened because the vast amounts of information available after connecting and the gains in productivity make the risks worth taking. A "trivial" consideration like security will not reverse, stop, or even slow the trend toward even greater connection.

Security must be provided even when complete isolation is no longer possible. This is difficult, but not impossible. Unfortunately, the security techniques of the 1970s and the early 1980s are either no longer applicable or no longer work. Isolation and centralization of processing no longer apply. Reliance on ever-stronger controls built into general-purpose operating systems no longer works because a large number of connected systems makes it impossible to understand how they should relate to each other.

Instead we can turn to object-oriented techniques. We encapsulate important processes in their own processors to create local isolation and take advantage of the benefits of information hiding. We build larger objects out of smaller objects and control the ways in which they can interact. And, finally, we control and monitor the interactions between the larger objects and the outside world.

Malicious Software

Marshall D. Abrams and Harold J. Podell

Risk — Possibility of system failure

Malicious software is one of the concerns of the contemporary computing environment. Malcontents, pranksters, vandals, and adversaries all have the potential ability to disrupt the conduct of our computing business. Prudence dictates that we analyze the situation and take appropriate countermeasures.

As with other concerns, the first responsive step is to perform a risk analysis. In the risk analysis we determine the threats and vulnerabilities, risk, effects, and countermeasures. That is, we conduct a study and make a managerial decision about what harm could occur to our computing environment, how likely it is that this harm will occur, what we could do to reduce the probability of this harm occurring, and what the impact would be if some harm did occur.

We must know what management's information technology (IT) and IT security policies are for the organization to establish the framework for assessing the results of a risk analysis. If we know the provisions of the applicable IT security policy, then we are in a better position to assess the relative importance of the countermeasures available to protect against the perceived threats. Money also plays an important part in our thinking. But there are also administrative and physical controls that could be implemented which have no direct cost, although they may have undesirable side effects in terms of convenience and productivity.

There are many terms for malicious software: Trojan horse, virus, worm, trap door, time/logic bomb, and so on. Some authors have spent considerable effort in developing precise taxonomies [EICH89, SPAF89, SPAF90a-c]. In this essay we use "virus" as a general term. If important, we will identify the particular malevolency by name or characteristic. Although interesting, we do not see much security value in overly precise semantics. Our focus is on identifying threats, vulnerabilities, and risk, and on providing countermeasures. We do not discuss in detail all types and varieties of malicious software or subtle differences and similarities between terms. Since the appearance of new malicious software is unpredictably dynamic, we refer the interested reader to bulletin boards or other publications of current threats.

Popular attention to viruses highlights a real problem. Computers are under attack. Malicious software has been released to work its harm. The damage worked by a virus can range from a gross denial-of-service attack to a subtle modification of stored data and programs that will result in future malfunction. Sometimes the attack is selectively targeted; more often it is undirected. Sometimes the attack results from a benign error or a misguided attempt to call attention to some cause or fact of importance to the originator. More often, the originator has an antisocial objective. Although at one time there may have been some ambivalence toward the creation of viruses, by now it is (or should be) well understood that such activity is in violation of most codes of computing ethics [FORC90].

The scope of an attack ranges from a single computer to international destinations, such as many computers connected to the well-known Internet. We are most concerned about the potential damage from future attacks that are more sophisticated than any seen to date. What would happen if virus attacks were a weapon of national or industrial warfare?

The possible impacts of a virus attack are limited by the imagination and competence (evil genius) of the perpetrator. Impacts can include destruction or modification of data, unavailability of computing resources, interruption of operations, fraud and other financial crime, embarrassment, or loss of life.

The writers of malicious programs are generally anonymous, but occasionally a virus writer is identified. Often the authors' desire for publicity leads them to self-identification. For example, the Macintosh virus "Universal Message of Peace" displays the name of Richard Brandow, the Montreal editor of *Macmag* who commissioned the virus [STEF90]. Drew Davidson, who wrote the virus, left his name in the code. In addition to its human interest value, knowledge about virus writers can help us improve our preventive measures.

We should clearly understand the limitations of reasoning by analogy. Infectious diseases spontaneously mutate. New strains that are resistant to previously effective countermeasures can be dangerously effective. Countering the attacks of malicious software much more closely follows the model of war against crime or a political enemy. It is the opposition of human intelligence and skill.

Case studies are instructive in dealing with an attack situation. They teach us how damage was done in the past and what countermeasures proved effective — and may even point to future attacks. When attacks follow a known pattern, we can mount effective defenses. We can use the power of the computer to (attempt to) search for, identify, block, and dis-able known attacks. We can apply similar techniques against generic types of attacks. But a truly innovative attack will probably surprise the defenders and be successful. Therefore, part of our defensive strategy must include damage assessment and recovery plans. In fact, we may decide to rely more on recovery than on prevention.

We study prior attacks as part of an engineering approach to learn from the past. It is easier to relate to an actual event than to abstractions. Case studies prove that the problem is real and provide psychological insight that may be helpful in constructing future defenses.

Publicity, especially in the press, focuses community attention on the problem. Managers need to understand that malicious software is a social phenomenon. It is not embarrassing to have been attacked, but it is a dereliction of duty to have been unprepared to deal with the situation. Taking no action in advance is itself evidence of having made a decision, albeit a questionable decision. Sticking one's head in the sand is not generally considered prudent management. The managerial response to malicious software attacks requires competent technical advice and support.

Definitions

The Trojan horse is a very common type of malicious software; it was probably the first. The *-property in the Bell-LaPadula policy model was designed to thwart the Trojan horse attack of illicit downgrading of classified information. The Trojan horse's modus operandi is that it appears to be an ordinary useful program which the user runs. Once in execution, the program runs with whatever privileges the user possesses. Most Trojan horses perform the desired function for the user. They often masquerade as legitimate programs or are malicious variants of legitimate programs. They often entice the user to execute them by promising some improvement over the legitimate program they replace. One-time-use Trojan horses only perform malicious activity; more sophisticated multi-use Trojan horses perform their advertised useful function while also surreptitiously performing malicious activity.

Protective countermeasures such as identification and authentication may have been used to keep out unauthorized people, but most systems have no means of identifying and authorizing trustworthy programs. There are research efforts that extend authorization to programs. Biba [BIBA77], Schell and Shirley [SHIR81], and Clark and Wilson [CLAR87] all have made contributions to this form of control. Strict configuration management practices are also useful in limiting the introduction of Trojan horses. The weak link is usually the human user, who is often unable to resist the temptation to run a faster, better, pirated, free, or test version of some game or useful software.

As mentioned, we do not offer overly precise semantics for definitions of malicious software types. For purposes of this discussion, we use generic definitions of a virus and a worm. A computer virus is usually constructed with two objectives. The first is to replicate. For example, a virus may copy itself into a useful program. A virus may invade system files and replicate itself. Second, a virus has a specific function (or functions) defined by the virus writer. This second objective could include displaying a message, erasing sectors on a hard disk, or expanding until it slows down other processes in the computer. A worm that is malicious may be considered a network extension of a virus that uses a network communication mechanism for propagation.

A virus can infect other programs by modifying them to include a copy of itself. The infected program in turn infects other programs. The infection spreads at a geometric rate. One symptom of a virus infection is a change in the length of a program. Some poorly designed viruses continue to install themselves in the same program, causing unlimited growth. This defect makes identification of such viruses a particularly easy job.

Time/logic bombs are malicious code that is executed when a certain event occurs, such as Friday the 13th. Trojan horses and viruses may contain time/logic bombs.

There is really no such thing as a harmless virus. Even if a virus was intended to cause no damage, it may do so in certain cases, often due to the incompetence of the virus writer. A virus may be modified, either by the original author or by someone else.

Threats — Possible attacks

A well-studied threat to information security is disclosure. The protection of secret information has always been part of diplomacy and warfare. Protection against unauthorized disclosure of information stored in computer systems was a direct generalization of manual methods used to protect similar information written on paper. In essence, when the computer replaced written records and communication, the protection policy was adapted to this new medium. Unauthorized disclosure can result from malicious software, such as a Trojan horse. Classical protection policy and mechanisms already exist to counter this threat.

In contrast, malicious software represents an attack on the computer itself. Existing policy is inadequate; the nature of the attack is understood but imperfectly. The theoretical models for protective mechanisms are still evolving.

An important threat to data integrity is unauthorized modification of information stored in computer memory. This information includes data, especially programs. The operating system and productivity programs are typical targets because of their ubiquitous potential to spread the harm.

Threats to resources include unauthorized utilization, destruction of information, and denial of service. Unauthorized utilization often results in theft of service. Time-sharing, information service, and electronic mail/bulletin board vendors all expect to be paid for the use of their services. Unauthorized unpaid use of such services is widely recognized as a crime. The damage caused by a virus may consist of the deletion of data or programs, maybe even reformatting of the hard disk, but more subtle damage is also possible. Some viruses may modify data; the amount and type of damage are limited only by the imagination, competence, and access of the perpetrator.

Destruction of information is an extreme case of unauthorized modification. It is probably easier for the malefactor to delete information than to change it, but the effect of subtly altered information can be much more devastating. The integrity of the system can be compromised, including databases and programs — especially system software and applications. If information is missing, it can be reloaded from backup media. But if it is maliciously altered, it could be used to produce erroneous results in far-ranging applications. For example, a change in the value of pi could cause operational errors. In severe cases, these errors could result in the crash of a satellite.

Denial of service can be a primary objective or an unintended by-product. For example, if a computer system is only performing operating system functions, there could be a denial of service to legitimate system users. This resource consumption can slow or stop information system operations. Communications networks are especially susceptible to such attacks. A flood of housekeeping messages, even maintenance messages or malfunction alarms, can make the network unavailable to perform its intended function. Such a flood of messages can be produced deliberately or can result from a design error in benign or malevolent software.

Virus vulnerabilities — Managerial responsibilities

Computer systems are often vulnerable to attack by malicious software because well-known protective measures are not implemented. For a privately owned personal computer, the responsibility is clearly on the owner. Since it is this owner who suffers the effect of an attack, one occurrence should be more than sufficient to induce self-protective behavior.

For organizational computing, there is a managerial responsibility to encourage, if not enforce, safe computing. The individual who has custody of an information asset may not be in a position to judge the value of that asset and may, therefore, not adequately protect the asset. Or the individual may make his or her own trade-off analysis of the risk, value of the asset, and effort required for protective measures. The individual's judgment may differ from management's. It is management's responsibility to specify the tools and procedures to be used to protect the organization's information assets and to provide the time and resources to enable employees to carry out the procedures.

Lack of management attention usually results in a lack of protection. Protective measures take time and effort to install and use. There are direct costs for purchase, storage, and labor. In contrast with centralized computer operations where security responsibility could be assigned to individuals and made an explicit part of their job subject to supervision and performance appraisal, distributed computing environments often place all responsibility on the individual who is the direct user of the computing equipment. These end users, be they members of the secretarial or professional staff, should be assigned specific responsibilities for protecting the information assets under their control.

In addition, open distributed processing (ODP) implies the existence of several sets of end users for business systems that support electronic commerce. For example, the enterprise viewpoint considers user interfaces that may be interpreted to include business requirements. ODP business requirements include electronic interfaces with end users outside the organization, such as customers and suppliers that have computer systems for EDI (Electronic Data Interchange).

When network communications are involved, management responsibility includes security operations. There is extensive connectivity in networks. Most networks also lack security control. Most came into existence with concern for functionality, not security. Small networks, especially local area networks (LANs), using homogeneous equipment and protocols and operating under the control of a single management scheme, can institute many security measures. In many ways LANs resemble individual computer systems. User programming and policy inadequacy are among the problems to be considered.

Large networks, or internets, created by connecting LANs with wide area networks (WANs), usually cannot be relied upon to provide adequate security services. The security must be provided by the LANs or the end systems — the computers used to provide user service. Management is responsible for determining the threat introduced by the network connection, the secure protocols and other measures that are available, and the extent to which these protocols and measures are used by other management domains accessible through the network. Given this information, management can then decide whether to connect to the WAN and which protective measures and protocols to use.

Malicious software threats

Stand-alone computers include single-user desktop computers and workstations. The minimum set of malicious software problems occurs in stand-alone computers: The use of corrupted programs and lax security are typical of open, trusting environments. Many users are unsophisticated about computers in general and unwilling to take precautions they consider too expensive, too technical, or too time-consuming or otherwise obtrusive into their work patterns.

Multiuser systems are also subject to irresponsible (or worse) activity by authorized users. In fact, protection of one user against malevolent or accidental damage by other users was the original thrust of computer security.

Computers connected directly or indirectly to WANs are susceptible to remote attack. Unfortunately, this evil potential makes an open sharing policy naive. Viruses work best when sharing in a network is inadequately controlled.

Network complexity offers considerable opportunity for errors, omissions, and exploitation beyond any one person's, or one organization's, control. There is continuing increasing investment in international networks. Major functions are being delegated to distributed processing systems in international commerce. Essays 17 and 18 discuss Privacy Enhanced Mail (PEM) and Electronic Data Interchange (EDI). These sophisticated applications require end-system/network security for user authentication, message authentication, and integrity. Encryption mechanisms are widely used as security countermeasures. (See Essays 15 and 17 on this point.)

Trojan horses need covert channels. Trojan horses can attempt to violate multilevel security by communicating classified information to a process below the classification level at which the Trojan horse is running. Remember that a Trojan horse operates with all the privileges of the process representing a user, so it is easy for the Trojan horse to obtain copies of information that the user processes. Multilevel security policies generally prevent a user from writing information at a lower level than the one at which it is read. In the Bell-LaPadula policy, this restriction is enforced by the *-property. In fact, the *-property was introduced more to block Trojan horses than to prevent user errors. When the Trojan horse is blocked by the *-property from illicitly downgrading classified information, it must use more sophisticated indirect methods to communicate information down to a less-classified accomplice process. One such method is the covert channel.

A covert channel is a means of signaling information from one user to another using a mechanism that was not designed as a communications channel. If one process can change the state of some system characteristic that another process can sense (in violation of the security policy), then a covert channel exists between the two processes. The system characteristic could be a shared variable, such as a register, or it could be the rate at which the receiver process was able to transfer information between primary and secondary storage. The former is an example of what is conventionally called a covert storage channel and the latter of a covert timing channel. Recent thinking is that all covert channels have both elements of timing and storage, reducing — if not eliminating — the distinction between types of covert channels.

Trap doors. Trap doors in software permit entry without detection. They are used by system designers for ease of entry; that is, the trap doors are inserted in the system by people in a position of trust to permit these people to bypass the system's protective mechanisms. Trap doors are often rationalized as necessary to permit access when the system has gone into an undesirable error state and all other means of access are blocked. Perhaps trap doors are necessary as a development tool, but when they are left in operational systems, it is relatively easy for penetrators to find and use them for unsanctioned entry.

Personal computer viruses. Two different types of viruses occur in PCs: boot sector viruses (BSV) and program viruses. A BSV infects the boot sector on a diskette. Normally the boot sector contains code to load the operating system files. The BSV replaces the original boot sector with itself and stores the original boot sector somewhere else on the diskette. When a computer is then later booted from this diskette, the virus takes control and hides in RAM. It will then load and execute the original boot sector, and from then on everything will be as usual. Except, of course, that every diskette inserted in the computer will be infected with the virus, unless it is write-protected. A BSV will usually hide at the top of memory, reducing the amount of memory that DOS sees. For example, a computer with 640K might appear to have only 639K. Some BSVs are also able to infect hard disks, where the process is similar to that described above.

Program viruses, the second type of computer viruses, infect executable programs. An infected program will contain a copy of the virus, usually at the end, but in some cases at the beginning of the original program. When an infected program is run, the virus may stay resident in memory and infect every program run. Viruses using this method to spread the infection are called "resident viruses." Other viruses may search for a new file to infect when an infected program is executed. The virus then transfers control to the original program. Viruses using this method to spread the infection are called "direct action viruses." It is possible for a virus to use both methods of infection.

In general, viruses are rather unusual programs — rather simple, but written just like any other program. It does not take a genius to write one — any average assembly language programmer can easily do it. Fortunately, few of them do.

Observations about network viruses

Network e-mail connectivity is important for reporting problems and getting bug fixes; disconnecting e-mail connectivity can cripple information flow. Networks that are loose confederations without central management find it difficult to respond to attacks. Even corporate networks may not have planned for attacks. When there are no plans for resisting an attack, personal contacts work well. Of course, there are problems at 3 a.m. in locating a responsible person at a remote site and authenticating yourself, especially if the normal mode of communication is e-mail and you are using the telephone.

Analyzing the attack and determining how to thwart it are difficult, intense intellectual activities. Misinformation and illusions run rampant. Source code availability is essential to understanding how the attack works. Vendors who do not release source code thereby take on full responsibility for fighting attacks. Marshaling the people with necessary skills is most easily done in an academic environment, which has such people available to be diverted from their regular tasks.

Lessons learned from fighting attacks are accumulated for future use [ROCH89]. Least privilege is one of the security approaches to reduce a computer system's exposure to attack. Users should be given all the privileges needed to do their work, but no more! Ignoring this fundamental principle frequently leads to disaster. Diversity is good; attacks are usually specific to an operating system and implementation of standard protocols. That is, malicious software exploits weakness in targeted design and code. The cure shouldn't be worse than the disease. The cost and inconvenience of countermeasures should be less than the effect of a successful attack. Denial-of-service attacks, in particular, are easy to launch but difficult to prevent. In the limit, it may be more expensive to prevent certain types of attack than to recover from them. In any case, local and remote backups, audit records, and archives are essential to recovery. Since preventive measures cannot be assumed to be 100 percent effective, the ability to recover system state prior to the attack is prudent. This recovery can often be facilitated by the use of redundant network and network security architectures.

Defenses must be at the host or end system level, not the network level. In terms of the OSI protocol layers, it is possible to implement some countermeasures in layer 3, but most are situated in higher layers. Any countermeasure that relies on least privilege and individual user identification must be implemented in the end system at layer 6 or 7. In other words, computers connected to networks must defend themselves from threats carried by the networks. It is not possible for the network to provide protection against each class of attack.

Logging of audit information is important. The more information that is specifically available about an attack, the easier it is to diagnose and neutralize. The audit trail can also make it possible to identify the source of an attack. However, too much information in an audit trail can make the resulting analysis very challenging. Electronic analysis of trends in the audit records can assist in the analysis.

A central repository of identified attacks and countermeasures is a good idea. But there are practical problems. Vendors must participate. When source code is proprietary, the vendors may be the only ones able to implement countermeasures. When a business relationship exits between the vendor and the customer, the vendor can provide security-related information to these customers, such as the existence of flaws and the appropriate fixes. But not all customers maintain a relationship with the vendors of their hardware and software. Equipment is resold or otherwise made untraceable. Even if the vendor's behavior is exemplary, the users may not be sufficiently security conscious. Fixes are often not installed because they are not identified as security related, or because the users have not experienced any problem, or because the installation is too difficult. Some users may even be malevolent; distributing information about security flaws could inspire further attacks.

Countermeasures

Our discussion of countermeasures is organized in order of detection, reduction, recommendations and observations, and legal remedies.

Procedural and administrative controls. One place to attack malicious code is at the source. Organizations need to guard against malfeasance on the part of their employees. Modern software development methods are quite useful for reducing the incidence of malicious code being inserted during the production cycle [AMOR91]. Division of labor specifies that programmers do not write their own program specifications. Code reuse assures that well-tested and debugged software is used in preference to writing new code. Of course, if reused code contains a virus, reuse assures its further dissemination. When software tools are prescribed, the programming environment is specified; this also reduces the freedom to introduce illicit code into production software. The formal team approach provides for peer review of software modules, independent testing, and configuration management.

Operational software, as well as software in development, is protected by the integrity controls of configuration management (CM). Configuration management includes a formal set of procedures to control all program modifications. The objectives of CM are to maintain program integrity, evaluate value and correctness of all proposed modifications, and exercise administrative control on test and installation procedures. It should be very difficult to insert malicious code into a system under CM.

Other administrative and physical integrity controls can be used to reduce vulnerability to attack. Management must decide which controls are applicable in their environment. One obvious step is to put all controlled software on read-only media. Note, however, that assurance of media write protection may not be as simple as it appears. Many forms of write protection use a hardware sensor to detect the presence of a physical marker, but the enforcement is left to software. Malicious code might be able to bypass this software protection. A physical switch that prevents write current from flowing is much more reliable.

Software engineering standards include life-cycle management functions. CM is one common control structure for life-cycle management, but it pertains almost exclusively to control of production code and documentation. The software life cycle also includes requirements definition, design, development, and testing. Security really needs to be considered in all of these phases. For example, policy decisions such as whether to permit program development, the use of software downloaded from bulletin boards and archives, or anonymous login and file transfer all have significant impact on the risk environment. These policy decisions are part of the administrative security measures.

Another name given to a class of countermeasures is internal controls. This term comes from the audit community, where it pertains to providing for financial and program integrity. There is an overlap of terminology; it is only necessary to note that internal controls are also countermeasures to malicious programs.

The principle of least privilege is simple in concept: Give people the privileges they need to do their jobs, but no more. In practice it may be difficult to determine what privileges are needed, or to dynamically change these privileges in coordination with changes in job assignments. Most observers agree, however, that the extreme of giving certain users unrestricted privileges is dangerously naive. The existence of an all-powerful "superuser" is dangerous unless benevolence and omnipotence can be guaranteed. Since this is unlikely, safe computing practice is to eliminate the "superuser" by such administrative techniques as separation of duties and rotating assignments.

PC virus protection programs. There are many programs available that offer some degree of protection against malicious code. In selecting a protective program, you should consider the type of detection. That is, upon what criteria does the antiviral program decide that a virus has been found? Antiviral programs are generally divided into three categories: filters, change checkers, and scanners.

A filter is a program that monitors the system for virus-like activity (that is, attempting to format a hard disk, write to a program file, and so forth). Filters have the advantage of being able to detect new viruses because they are not looking for specific viruses, but rather for suspicious activity. The disadvantage is that they can be prone to false alarms triggered by programs that perform potentially dangerous activities for legitimate reasons.

A change checker computes a checkfunction reference value for a protected file and is subsequently run to compare the current value against the reference. If the reference value and the just-computed value don't match, then the file has been modified and may be infected with a virus or otherwise subjected to unauthorized modification. Like the filters, change checkers will detect known and unknown malicious activity. They are not checking for specific pieces of code, but rather for changes to a computed value. This method works only if the change checker is installed in a virus-free machine. Otherwise, the reference values computed will reflect the installed malicious code.

A scanner works by checking the system for pieces of code unique to each virus. The scanner reads the files (boot sector, partition table, and so on) of a disk and does a match against a database of bytes that are segments of code unique to each virus. When a match occurs, a virus is reported. This is effective for finding known viruses, since a positive identification of the virus is made. Of course, a false alarm could also occur if a file had the same instructions in it. Scanners can also check for generic routines, like a series of program instructions to format a disk, but these could raise a false alarm concerning a program or routine for legitimate purposes. A scanner will detect only known viruses and must be updated frequently; as more viruses are added, the scanner gets slower. Scanners may also be ineffective against viruses hidden in compressed files, especially if multiple compression is used.

Technical integrity controls. Many malicious software attacks result in unauthorized modification, which is an integrity violation. Checksums provide an indication of unauthorized modification. A checksum is calculated by treating the source — program or data — as numerical. The numerical values are summed (over some modulus), the result being the checksum. When a function more complicated than simple addition is used, the result is known as a checkfunction or a hash sum. It is very difficult to modify software and preserve the value of the checksum. Cryptographic checkfunctions are among the strongest. A type of cryptographic checkfunction is called a digest of a message or a message digest. As discussed in Essay 15, cryptographic checkfunctions are formed by encrypting the variable-length source message, discarding all of the ciphertext except for a fixed-length residue, and using this residue as the checkfunction.

A variation of the cryptographic checkfunction is the use of a public key digital signature mechanism to securely sign a variable-length message or document. The resulting public key digital signature is fixed length and is appended to the unencrypted electronic image of the document.

Using this cryptographic method, a sender can assure a recipient of the document and digital signature that the source and integrity of the message are maintained.

For example, a hash function algorithm can be used to reduce the variable-length message to a fixed size, such as a message digest of 128 bits. The resulting mathematically unique hash value or message digest can be operated on by the sender's private key, such as the private key in RSA (Rivest, Shamir, and Adleman), to produce a digital signature. A digital signature provides integrity protection against viruses as well as other forms of unauthorized modification. A public key digital signature is the cryptographic result of the sender's private key operating on the message digest. With a public key algorithm, such as RSA, this process is called signing the message. The digital signature can be attached to the electronic image of the message and both encrypted using the recipient's public key. Only the recipient can decrypt the resulting message with his or her private key. After the recipient decrypts the digital signature with the sender's public key, the recipient has assurance that the signed message could only have come from the sender.

In the preceding example of a digital signature, authentication of the sender and message confidentiality can be provided together. The example discussed above is based on providing these combined security services by encrypting the message and its corresponding digital signature in the recipient's public key. In practice, high-volume encryption is generally achieved with more complex procedures that may involve one algorithm for key management or exchange and another for message confidentiality or privacy. Some of these issues are discussed in Essay 15.

Most malicious code operates by modifying other code or data. Modification controls are, therefore, appropriate countermeasures. Until the late 1980s, most attention in information security was focused on confidentiality. Some work was done on modification controls. Three approaches are discussed briefly below. These approaches are discussed in detail in Essay 8. Biba strict integrity provides protection by imposing hierarchical integrity levels and nonhierarchical integrity categories that govern which subjects may modify which objects. Biba strict integrity could be used to protect certain program and data files by marking them at the highest level or in a unique category. Clark-Wilson verified transactions can be used to control which programs, as well as which users, can modify which files. For example, only specified systems programs, using specified development tools, can modify operational programs. Type enforcement in lock extends the idea of verified transactions by specifying the types of programs that can modify files in specified domains.

Undesirable side effects of controls. Most of the countermeasures tend to limit information sharing. Systems that previously practiced open access are impacted.

Unfortunately, the misconduct of a few people can spoil the environment for the many who are well behaved. Some people believe that the imposition of controls can impair creativity.

Technical security, which primarily consists of confidentiality and integrity controls, generally has to be incorporated into life-cycle development of an information system. In any case, this is a fiscal and operational burden. It may be prohibitively difficult to add certain types of security measures to existing systems. Many countermeasures are considered as research topics. Operational overhead may be increased by technical countermeasures. Security operations may be user unfriendly.

However, when EDI is implemented for electronic commerce, there is generally an overall cost reduction to the purchaser of goods. Therefore, in those EDI cases where there are lower overall costs than with the predecessor information system and purchaser inventory maintenance operations, technical security costs are masked by the overall reduction in operational costs. For example, if an organization that manufactures automobiles uses EDI and related network operations with its paint suppliers to support just-in-time assembly of vehicles, the resulting information system and paint system inventory costs will drop considerably.

In this case, the EDI technical security costs may include the use of a MAC (message authentication code) for message integrity using DES (Data Encryption Standard) and a public key management system. However, the overall operational and paint inventory costs for the automobile manufacturer will tend to be less than for paper-based (first-class mail) purchase operations and larger on-site paint inventories.

Therefore, certain technical security methods to support electronic commerce may be associated with overall cost reductions. In addition, since EDI involves the development of new systems and security standards, there are opportunities to transfer much of the burden of access control and network security to cryptographic-based information-processing systems.

Legal remedies. Since malicious software has caused damage or at least inconvenience, it is natural to ask what protection is available under law. You may think of civil remedies, such as recovering damages by suing, or criminal punishment for the malefactor. The legal aspects are at least as dynamic as the technical ones. Enactment of legislation and its application have to lag technical changes in threats until the situation is well enough understood. Furthermore, the applicable law varies among jurisdictions. We can only generalize here.

Can hackers be sued for damages? There are legal theory problems. There may be no clearly applicable law. Extrapolation of existing law — such as trespass, conversion (recovery of damages caused by theft), and negligence — is possible but is subject to judicial restraint. New legislation is slow in coming, in part because it is difficult to write good laws. There are also practical problems. The cost of suing can exceed recovery from a hacker defendant. There are proof problems, such as a lack of paper records and witnesses. Cause and effect may be difficult to establish. For example, it may be difficult for the prosecutor to demonstrate that a hacker intentionally committed the act and without authorization [GEMI89].

A similar situation exists with respect to criminal law. Under British and US jurisprudence, a crime is an act declared to be illegal in a duly enacted statute. The law must be clear enough to give reasonable notice of the prohibited act. Ambiguity in drafting or error in specifying elements can preclude prosecution. The law must also specify the punishment. Even if there is an apparent violation of the law, a prosecutor may choose not to press charges. In the face of limited resources, prosecutors may exercise judgment concerning the cases which present the greatest danger to society. Lack of computer understanding on the part of prosecutors, judges, and jurors may also factor into the prosecutor's decision. There are also problems concerning the sophisticated circumstantial evidence usually required in computer crime prosecutions.

Notwithstanding these legal challenges, there are international trends to reconsider and strengthen a wide variety of laws pertaining to computer crime. Several European nations, such as Germany, France, and the United Kingdom, have already amended some of their laws pertaining to computer crime. In addition, the Netherlands recently reconsidered the need for legislation to restrict computer crime or "computer peace disturbance." One issue considered in the Netherlands proposals is the security of the attacked computer system. In other words, a conviction for a computer crime may be dependent on the existence of a "clear threshold" of security controls in the attacked system.

Essay 5

Abstraction and Refinement of Layered Security Policy

Marshall D. Abrams and David Bailey

There are multiple views of corporate (enterprise) computing, each with its own metaphors and terms of reference. The different views incorporate different levels of abstraction, in which details are suppressed to concentrate attention on the issues important to the particular observer. This essay examines these different metaphors with respect to the enterprise security policy, resulting in a layered policy where each main layer relates to one of the system metaphors and the policy described for a lower level of detail is an implementation of the policy at a higher level. The layered view of policy helps system designers, managers, and users understand the rationale for security policy at the lowest levels of abstraction, because the relationship of the low level policy to the enterprise information policy is clear.

Levels of abstraction and policy

There are multiple views of corporate (enterprise) computing, each with its own metaphors and terms of reference. The metaphors with which we view computing differ from level to level of abstraction. Abstraction serves the very useful purpose of suppressing details not of interest to the observer. Suppressing these details makes it possible to concentrate on the issues that the observer considers important. One observer may think of corporate information processing resources, another of the "operating system," and another of the "network." The terms of reference are different, the concerns are different, and the policy statements may appear different. But the policy and rules must be consistent at all levels of abstraction for the organization to achieve the protection desired.

This essay has two primary purposes. The first is to exhibit several different ways in which enterprise computing is viewed by different members of the enterprise. We observe that all of the enterprise members are talking about the same computing structure when they talk about computing, even though their interests and their language might suggest otherwise. Furthermore, each member of the enterprise has a view of the enterprise's policy for protecting information, and, once again, they are all talking about the same thing, even though their language might suggest otherwise.

The second purpose is to observe that when we choose the members of the enterprise appropriately, their views of computing can be seen as successive refinements of the high-level view taken by the CEO. Because the refinements cover a very broad range and use more than one metaphor, the nature of the layers as refinements is a little harder to see than it is in a decomposition that covers a narrow range. The structure of the policy is, again, parallel to the computing structure; the views of policy held by members of the enterprise constitute successive refinements of the policy expressed by the CEO.

Each of the many views of computing within an enterprise reflects its holder's responsibilities and relationship to the computing resource. What is important to workers at one level may be incomprehensible detail to those at another level. Conversely, a statement that is clear and complete at one level may appear vague and general to those at another level. While many views are possible, some are better suited than others to our primary purpose. The views or levels we will discuss include:

- Top management's view of computing as an information and resource management problem.
- The computer user's view of computing functions and data as resources available to support some task.
- The system builder's view of the computing system as physical components in specific locations delivering various services to users.

Both the complexity of modern computing and the different interests of various people in the enterprise warrant the use of different metaphors to provide a complete discussion of the computing system. This complexity will be reflected in the enterprise security policy, which must be discussed in terms of all metaphors. The result will be a layered policy where each main layer relates to one of the system metaphors. All views must fit together in the sense that the policy described for a lower level of detail must be shown to be an implementation of the policy at a higher level.

As one approaches a computing system from afar (that is, with progressively less abstract logical views), one sees a succession of different aspects of the same object. From great distance, one might see computing as an information management function of the enterprise. Moving closer, one might see a collection of services used by people in the enterprise and running on some sort of "computer." Still closer, the view might be of a network of computers providing different services in different physical locations, on different hardware, to different sets of users, connected in different ways. Even though the metaphors used to discuss the various layers differ, each can be seen as a refinement of the previous layer, including more detail and using a different language, but still discussing the same "computing system."

If the enterprise has any interest in protecting its information assets against undesirable events (and it is difficult to imagine one that doesn't), then it has (or should have) a policy for protecting those information assets, otherwise known as its information security policy. The policy should address the information assets of the organization, the threats to those assets, and the measures that management has decided are reasonable and proper to protect those assets. Management may base its decision on cost-benefit analysis by weighing the cost of expected (or experienced) losses against the cost of preventative measures. When cost analysis is not possible or believable, a policy basis may exist for protective measures. And in some cases management will have to make decisions based on insufficient information. Top management will usually be assisted by many other employees in reaching a decision. Policy statements will be prepared by subordinates for approval by top management. It is this approval that puts the policy into force.

We have one enterprise-wide computing system viewed from different perspectives with the aid of different metaphors or abstractions. The top management sees information and corporate functions. Some users and management see files and services on a computer; others see a network. For many organizations, computing is large and complicated, and we accept that different people with different interests have different views of it. We should not expect that a single view of security policy will suffice for all people. For example, the top management will probably not understand the terms of reference at the network level of abstraction and will not care about movement of bits from one network machine to another, as long as the information management policy is satisfied.

However, even though different people use different terminology, there is a need for a single unified policy (otherwise, someone has not been listening, and the top management has lost control). It is probably created by an iterative process of composition and decomposition. In the process, some of the policies at more detailed levels will have to be changed to conform with the highest level enterprise policy as it develops. Over the years the policies at various levels will have to be changed to accommodate new modes of operation, new insights, and new organizational concerns. Probably the various levels of policy will never be 100 percent synchronized at any instant of time.

Policies at different levels of abstraction must be connected. Policy is composable and decomposable in the same way as system design. At various levels of abstraction, the metaphors and terms of reference on which the policy is based change, but the levels remain connected. It must remain possible, even across changes in metaphor, to demonstrate that each lower level implements the level above it.

Three views of computing and security policy

Top management view. At the top level of abstraction, the interests of the CEO and the board of directors are in management and protection of corporate information. Computing may not even be an interest except to the extent that the computers themselves represent an asset and a cost, and the ability to compute represents a corporate resource. In a modern information-oriented corporation, the CEO may even have a view of the things that are done with information within the enterprise and the protection that must be afforded to various types of information. These views will be described in information terms, not in computing terms.

The policy for information management in the enterprise will similarly be expressed by (and for) the top management and the members of the board. It will cover the protection needs of the computing function viewed as a function within the enterprise, expressed as rules identifying information security objectives and delineating approved and unapproved behavior. At this high level of abstraction, all policies merge into something like "Protect the organization's information assets." While it is easy to understand the sentiment behind such a generalization, it does not provide much guidance on whether specific actions are permitted or not. Introducing such specificity at lower levels of abstraction requires interpretation of the high-level policy. Specifically, it requires an approval process (or delegation of approval authority) so that the implementation is scrutinized and approved by the upper level management.

Individual users' views. Moving to a lower level of detail, individual computer users using specific services become visible. The users have two different views of computing, depending somewhat on individual views of what they are doing. Some users think in terms of specific functions that they perform using a computer: "I process purchase requests using the computer." Others think in more machine-oriented terms: "I use the Dragon machine when I process purchase requests." We coalesce these two views into a single view in which users use "large" functions of the system, such as application programs.

At this level of detail, we see controls on the use and modification of data and on the way the services themselves are modified. These rules are imposed to satisfy the requirements created by the top management's policy. They may control who can view proprietary information. They may control who can modify high-integrity information and the circumstances under which it can be modified. They may be imposed in an attempt to maintain availability of data or services.

This collection of rules together constitutes a user access policy regulating the access of various users to various objects. This is only part of an information security policy; additional asset-protection information is necessary in such policy elements as physical and administrative security, backup procedures, disaster recovery, and so on.

The user access policy is an implementation of the top management's policy. The people concerned with the specification, design, and implementation of the user access policy have a different view of computing than the top management. Their interests and concerns are different based on a greater level of detailed knowledge of computing. These facts, however, do not permit them to create a new policy — they are expected to implement the policy adopted by management. And they will be expected to make a convincing argument that the policy regulating human user access to computer programs and files is an implementation of management's information policy. It must be an implementation in the sense that it does not permit computer users to take actions that violate the information policy.

Many organizations provide guidance on how to translate the top-level information security policy into a user access policy. This guidance is often called "implementing guidance," "implementing instructions," or something similar. Organizations with many hierarchical levels may provide implementing guidance at each level.

Process-level view. The next level of detail down from the user level can be described as the process level or the network level. At this level of detail we find the mechanisms that are invoked to satisfy user requests. Data units are messages or perhaps buffers full of bits rather than files residing on some disk. Here we see for the first time processing that is not directly associated with some human user. These processes are part of the management of the computing resource itself or are present to satisfy user requests for data.

The differences between the process level and the user level occur in several areas. The time scale is much shorter on the process level. At the user level, we talk in terms of requesting and obtaining services, items that are measured in seconds and larger units. At the process level, we talk about requests satisfied on scales of milliseconds or less. The units in which processes use data are much smaller at the process level. Processes deal with requests, messages, and buffers; human users deal with files or application programs.

When considering protection, however, the biggest difference is in the static character of the user level versus the dynamic nature of the process level. At the user level, access to information can be characterized using a finite-state machine in which a system state consists of a description of the access rights of every human user to every controlled object. A state transition is an atomic action changing the access relationship between one user and one object. At no time does a human subject "kind of" have access to any object.

At the process level, however, this clean state machine or "access matrix" model, as it is sometimes called, doesn't work very well. When a user is granted access to a file on a disk, the bits in the file have to be moved from the storage location into a buffer belonging to the user's surrogate process, where they can be used. At any given time after access is granted, some of the bits will be in the process buffer, some on the disk, and others in buffers in other locations. Depending on the complexity of the system, there could be many buffers in many locations. The undelivered bits will be delivered if requested, but this is not justification for asserting that the user has access to them any more than it was reasonable to claim the user had access to the file before the access was requested. At this level of detail, file access is not atomic — the user has partial access to the file.

Housekeeping and internal service processes introduce a complexity in the user access policy because access rights cannot be traced to an individual user. This dilemma is often resolved by identifying such processes as belonging to the system operator or security authority, as appropriate. This generally produces confusing and unsatisfactory results because thinking about what the human occupants of these roles should or should not do leads to inappropriate controls on the system. In the office analog of this situation, we carefully regulate who can use which information and what they can do with it, but we forget that the secretaries see everything. Declaring that the secretary is a security officer will not, by itself, improve our confidence that data is appropriately protected.

Technical policy models

Policy can be expressed in three different forms: natural language statements, mathematical or nonmathematical formal statements based on a model, and computer implementation mechanisms. Since natural language is prone to ambiguities and multiple interpretations, some means is necessary to determine whether a specific behavior constitutes a violation or attempted violation. In information security, there is an attempt to reduce the ambiguity by basing the policy on a policy model. If the policy model and the system-specific statement of policy are expressed in a mathematical form, the ambiguity will be reduced substantially. For more information about models, see Essay 8.

Expressing the policy models in a commonly understood notation may be helpful in many ways. Using this common notation to express the security policy models for each concern may make it easier for those people with mathematical intuition and experience to identify commonality among policies as well as issues within each policy. They may also compare alternative models to find the model(s) they consider best (according to some criteria not discussed here). Other people may find it easier to identify commonality in the mechanisms. Both sets of skills can contribute to the security of a real system.

Formal expression of policy

As we have said, formal expression of policy is used to reduce ambiguity. The expression can be either mathematical or nonmathematical. If it is done mathematically, the ambiguity inherent in natural language can be reduced to a minimum. Other advantages include a variety of tools that can be applied to find mistakes in the policy expression and to prove that the policy, if correctly implemented, will have certain desirable properties. The cost of specifying policy in this way is that far fewer people will be able to read the results. Generally, everything having to do with the policy will have to be done by specialists. In a practical sense, this may reduce the likelihood that the policy is correctly implemented, since the specialists will almost certainly not be the people writing the code.

A nonmathematical, but constrained and more precise form of natural language will inevitably be more ambiguous than a mathematical version. Such a policy expression is also less amenable to manipulation by supporting tools, so it will be harder to show that it is self-consistent and has the properties desired. On the other hand, more people can participate in its construction, and more people can read and understand the results. This means there is a higher likelihood that it expresses the desired policy and that it will be correctly used to implement the system. Which version to use depends on the degree of assurance of correctness that is required.

Each of the three policy levels we have discussed can be formalized. Formal models have been produced many times at the user access control level. There is less experience with formal models at the process or network level, but such models have been built as well. It is also possible to formalize a model for policy at the information handling level, although this is rarely done. For example, corporations keep various information about their employees. Consider just two categories of information — salary and health insurance — and the policy governing read access to the information by various people. An employee has access to all of his own information, but no information about other employees. A supervisor has access to salary information about all the people she supervises, but to health insurance information for none of them. A benefits counselor has access to all health insurance information, but no salary information. Notice also that all of the people with special roles are also employees — their status is governed by some combination of rules (see the section below on multiple policies).

The entire collection of rules in the example above could be written down in a precise form of English or could be specified using any specification language at least as rich as set theory. Either form would constitute a formal expression of a specific policy. The policy and many others that could be obtained by varying some of the rules are derived from a model based on people with specific roles accessing identified kinds of information.

Each of the policy levels seems to have a natural model. Not surprisingly, they are different. At the top level, a model can be built using people who are members of groups (probably based on the organizational roles the people play). Groups have information that they share internally, and they have some policy for sharing with other groups.

At the next level of detail, computer users with privileges access files with attributes. The policy is about (semi-) static relationships between users and collections of data. To maintain data integrity, the policy might make statements about which privileges are required to write or modify specific collections of data. The metaphor differs from that of people sharing information within groups, but it is not too difficult to see how to construct a mapping from one metaphor to the other. Such a mapping will be needed to demonstrate that the access controls provided for data files implement the policy of sharing information within groups.

At the process or network level of abstraction, packages of bits are moved about based on attributes of processes or storage containers for the bits. We can see two different kinds of process: those owned by users (that is, they didn't exist before the user took some action to directly or indirectly create them), and those that are part of the system (they pre-date any user sign-on and continue to exist after all users have signed off). The bits moved are generally only a part of something that has meaning to a user, and they have no meaning to the processes moving them. The natural expression for policy at this level of abstraction is to control the flow of bits between processes based on the type of the process (system or user), attributes of the bits (taken from a source process or container), and attributes of the medium over which the bits are to flow.

As is the case between the computer user level and the information management level, it is necessary to map from the abstraction of the lower level to those of the higher levels. This mapping is necessary to support the argument that the lower level is an implementation of the higher level.

Mapping between levels of policy. In general, the technical policy rules will not be an exact implementation of the high-level prose abstraction of the information policy. It may be impossible, or at least exceedingly difficult, to implement the natural language policy in rules within the computer. The conservative position is to make the rules more restrictive than the high-level policy statement. If the rules are too restrictive in the sense that they make it too difficult, or even impossible, to perform an operation that is necessary for the functioning of the enterprise, then special exemption rules are crafted to permit the desired operation(s).

The test of the connection between different levels of policy is that

1. every access allowed by the higher level policy should be supported by the lower level policy, and
2. no action allowed by the lower level policy should be forbidden by the higher level policy.

The conservative position is

1. that there may be an action allowed by the higher level policy that is forbidden by the lower level policy, but
2. no action or combination of actions allowed by the lower level policy can violate the higher level policy.

It is not necessarily easy to demonstrate the correspondence between the high-level and the low-level policies. The terms of reference are different, and the metaphors on which the policies are based are different. Controls will be implemented to maintain privacy or secrecy or to ensure integrity — whatever the top management told us we are supposed to do. These controls constitute a security policy that is expected to be an implementation of the top-level policy. We show this by showing that it implements the next higher level of policy.

Beginning at the network level, for example, we use the mapping between metaphors to map the policy controls at the lower level into controls at the user access level. If the policy has been constructed carefully, it will be possible to argue that it is exactly an implementation of the access policy in the sense given above. Otherwise, we need to show that it is more conservative than the higher level policy. To be less conservative means that some flow can be found that violates the access control rules, and this is not acceptable. In the same way, we show that the access control rules implement the corporate information management policy. By implication, the flows in the network also satisfy the information management policy.

Multiple policies. A single system may be required to satisfy several different policies covering different subject areas. For example, the system may be required to protect the confidentiality of its data. It may also attempt to protect correctness (usually called integrity) by, for example, limiting who can add to or modify some collections of data. In some situations, system behaviors may be limited because of safety concerns.

Other possible security concerns include completeness, accuracy, timeliness, and availability. Some authorities would include integrity; others would remove availability; most would not include safety. (See D.F. Sterne's paper [STER91] for one viewpoint.)

Every threat that management has decided to protect against must be addressed by a corresponding policy. Trying to produce a model that covers all of these subject areas could result in a policy that is very confusing. A mathematical expression of such a policy would be extremely complicated, and it would be very hard to claim that it actually captures the desired policy correctly. To avoid this, policy modelers typically make a simplifying assumption. They begin by assuming that the security concerns (for example, confidentiality, completeness, accuracy, timeliness, and availability) are independent. This is, of course, a simplification. There may be trade-offs or even conflicts. But it is convenient to assume independence as a first-order approximation. With this simplification, the policies can be modeled separately. The modeling can consider each policy as if it were the only policy in effect.

The effect of all the policies taken together is described by a metapolicy (a policy about policies) that describes how the applicable policies combine. Two simple metapolicies for combining two constituent policies will illustrate the concept. A metapolicy that requires approval of both constituent policies could be expressed "Access is permitted only if the user has the necessary clearance AND the need to access the resource in order to perform his/her job." A metapolicy that requires approval of either of the two constituent policies could be expressed "Access to salary information is granted to a supervisor OR to a member of the compensation administration."

Physical implementation

The implementation of a policy, defined as precisely as possible in a model, uses mechanisms within the computer system. Some mechanisms can be effective in implementing more than one policy. Identification of such mechanisms may be based on intuition, experience, or systematic analysis. There may be a cost savings in choosing to use such a mechanism in an application environment that includes these multiple policies. Selection of mechanisms involves many engineering analysis and design activities. Trade-off analysis among cost, performance, ease of use, storage requirements, and so on, is involved.

Conclusions

We have given examples to show that the single computing entity built by an organization to satisfy its information processing needs is viewed by different members of the organization in different ways. Some see information management, some see a computer used by users, and some see a network that moves bits around on behalf of users. Each of these collections of people uses different metaphors and different terminology to describe the same entity. We tolerate this diversity because the different collections of people have different needs and interests. Forcing them to speak the same language would interfere with their ability to perform their jobs and serve no useful purpose.

In the same way, there is one policy governing how the computing entity is used to process corporate information. The different collections of people have different metaphors and terminology for discussing the single policy for the same reasons that they have different metaphors and language for discussing the computer system. Again, for the same reasons, we must tolerate this diversity in language. There is one system. There is one policy governing it, and there are many ways to view both the system and the policy.

Evaluation Criteria for Trusted Systems

Roger R. Schell and Donald L. Brinkley

The Trusted Computer System Evaluation Criteria (TCSEC) provide the basis for evaluating the effectiveness of security controls built into computer systems. This essay summarizes the definition and requirements of the TCSEC used to classify systems into seven hierarchical levels of enhanced security protection. This essay also reviews the history, technical foundations, and basic security requirements of the TCSEC. For a number of years, these criteria have been used in specifying security requirements during acquisition of products and systems, guiding the design and development of trusted systems, and evaluating systems used to process sensitive information.

Most of us are aware that the problem of evaluating the security of computer systems has been with us for a long time. Essay 1 described the ever-growing need for building security into computer systems, wherever there is a need to share resources or information. Essay 2 described the technology that we now may bring to bear to counter threats to computer security. However, even though the available technology may be used to provide computer security, a critical question that builders, sponsors, users, and customers of a computer system must be able to answer is, "How good is its security?" In other words, "How can the security of the system be evaluated?" That is the question the techniques described in this essay are used to answer. These techniques are organized into the time-tested Trusted Computer System Evaluation Criteria (TCSEC) [DOD85], which, for those not familiar with them, this essay is intended to summarize.

Background

Penetration testing was among the first attempts at evaluating the security of a computer system, but the futility of substantially relying on that method for the evaluation became known relatively early. In the early days of computer security, advocates of secure systems tried to follow a path of searching for ways to penetrate the systems' controls, often using malicious software in the same way a potential attacker could launch a probing, penetration, or subversion attack, as described in Essay 1. Their plan was that, failing to penetrate, they could plausibly argue that there was no way to penetrate since no way was known (to them). In this scenario, if a security hole is found, it can first be patched before the argument for security is made.

Obviously, however, as described in Essay 2, this argument suffers from both theoretical and practical difficulties. One presumes that one could test all possible programs to find any that led to a security penetration. If possible, this method of exhaustion would be effective, but it is far beyond the realm of feasibility. For any real computer, it would take so long that before the evaluation was finished, the sun would literally have burned out! Thus, any evaluation conducted by exhaustion must be so incomplete as to be ludicrous.

The lesson that was learned is that a test can demonstrate the presence of an error but, short of exhaustion of every possible combination of inputs, it cannot demonstrate the absence of errors. Practically speaking, the effort spent in penetrate and patch techniques yields poor marginal return in terms of security [SCHE79].

In 1969 and 1970, a distinguished panel headed by Dr. Willis Ware of the Rand Corporation developed and published a seminal report [WARE70] concluding that it is very difficult to evaluate a system and determine whether it provides adequate security. Essay 2 described the major findings of a somewhat later Air Force panel headed by E.L. Glaser run under a contract with James P. Anderson (both members of the Ware panel). The Air Force panel published a report [ANDE72] that identified research aimed at solutions to some of the problems identified by the Ware panel.

In response to the recommendations of the Air Force panel, during the next few years there was substantial research and development in an attempt to devise a method of reliable security evaluation. In 1977, the Department of Defense (DoD) Computer Security Initiative began, and an effort was made to consolidate the R&D gains. In 1981, the DoD Computer Security Center was formed to expand DoD efforts to evaluate computer security. By 1983, the DoD had completed about six years of work with the National Bureau of Standards (NBS) (since renamed the National Institute of Standards and Technology, or NIST) specifically focused on building, evaluating, and auditing secure computer systems. In that year, the DoD Computer Security Center published the Trusted Computer System Evaluation Criteria (TCSEC) [DCSC83]. It was published only after worked examples of meeting each requirement existed and after being "subjected to much peer review and constructive technical criticism from the DoD, industrial research and development organizations, universities, and computer manufacturers" [DCSC83].

The center's charter was soon broadened, and the National Computer Security Center (NCSC) was established in 1985. The NCSC oversaw minor changes to the TCSEC, and it was established as a DoD standard in 1985 [DOD85]. The evaluation criteria presented in the TCSEC and overviewed in this essay deal with trusted computer systems, or computer systems that contain a trusted computing base (TCB), as introduced and described in Essay 2.

In the time since its publication, the TCSEC has been used by the DoD and other organizations in the US for security evaluations. However, some western European nations have in the meantime begun developing different criteria, the ITSEC [ITSE91]. In 1990, a group of four nations — France, Germany, the Netherlands, and the United Kingdom — published the first draft. These draft criteria, while substantially influenced by the TCSEC, were significantly different in a number of areas [BRAN91]. It is too early to tell how usable the new criteria will be for the purposes for which they are intended, since the development of successful security evaluation criteria takes many years.

Finally, in 1990 and 1991 a joint project to produce new "Federal Criteria" began within the US government at the National Institute of Standards and Technology (NIST) and the National Security Agency (NSA). The apparent goal of this multiyear criteria-development project is to eventually replace the TCSEC with a Federal Information Processing Standard (FIPS). The following paragraphs present some of the reasons why the development of practical and effective criteria is such a difficult task.

The criteria defined in the TCSEC have survived the test of time and have been used repeatedly and successfully. These criteria were devised to apply to evaluation of computer products and systems. They are applicable to general-purpose computer systems, as well as to special-purpose application systems. In characterizing the composition of the TCB, the Department of Defense standard [DOD85] says,

> For general-purpose systems, the TCB will include key elements of the operating system and may include all of the operating system. For embedded systems, the security policy may deal with objects in a way that is meaningful at the application level rather than at the operating system level. Thus, the protection policy may be enforced in the application software rather than in the underlying operating system.

The TCSEC is therefore based on a set of technical principles which are broadly applicable. Since the TCSEC was published, the NCSC has developed a number of interpretations and guidelines that assist in applying the principles of the TCSEC to networks [NCSC87a] and to database management systems and other applications [NCSC91].

The technically sound foundation of the TCSEC enables it to be used by a third party to accurately and objectively measure security trustworthiness of a system. It does this in a manner which does not require the highly skilled and experienced scientists who wrote the criteria to apply them, yet which allows those less experienced who apply the criteria to come to the same conclusion as would those who wrote them. This was a key goal in the development of the TCSEC — those who apply the criteria should not be simultaneously writing and interpreting them. That situation only leads to inequities in applying the criteria as interpretations differ between evaluations. Its practicality for objective use makes the TCSEC an important technological contribution.

Summarizing that contribution is the purpose of the remainder of this essay. Note that the requirements contained within the TCSEC are simply called the criteria in the remainder of this essay. Note also that this essay uses a number of terms of art from the TCSEC that are only briefly defined here and in the TCSEC. The reader is encouraged to refer to Essay 2 for a more detailed discussion of the important terms. For more information about any of the example or candidate evaluated trusted systems discussed in this essay, the reader is encouraged to contact the vendor — or the National Computer Security Center at Ft. Meade, Md., for more information about how to contact the vendor directly. For further reading, Gasser [GASS88] covers most of the technical concepts from the criteria in greater detail than presented here, though without much discussion of the evaluation ratings.

Technical foundations

The foundations for the criteria are the notions that revolve around the reference monitor concept, introduced in Essay 2. Recall from Essay 2 that the primary motivation for the development of the reference monitor concept was the potential presence of malicious software, as discussed in Essay 1. The following discussion summarizes some of the pertinent concepts from Essay 2, and, along with the next section, provides a framework for the discussion of the criteria themselves.

The notions fundamental to the criteria are as follows: One should know what it is one wants to protect (that is, one should have a security policy that defines what we mean by secure). Also, one should have some mechanism, called a reference monitor, for determining every time there is an attempt by some subject (some user or surrogate for that user) to reference an object (the information), and that mechanism should validate each reference. For this arrangement to be truly secure, we must have some model of our security policy. A system having a security policy that says a subject can access an object only on Thursdays may be secure with regard to that security policy, but not secure with regard to one that says the subject needs a Secret clearance. So we require some security policy model that defines what kind of system protection we want.

In addition, the idea of a reference monitor has with it three design requirements that are reflected in the criteria. The first of these is that if we are going to have a protection mechanism, that mechanism must be tamperproof and must be able to protect itself against invalidation. One technique that has been demonstrated in some of the penetration testing efforts is after penetrating a system, putting in some form of trap door — in other words, tampering with the mechanism itself so that later the attacker can regain control over the system. We termed this "subversion of security mechanism" in Essay 1.

Second, it is also necessary, of course, to ensure that the mechanism is always invoked. In efforts to provide security retrofits, a supposedly secure appliqué was put on top of a system, and the user was told that every time he was going to process sensitive information, he would use this appliqué. The problem was that there were many ways to get at the information without invoking the appliqué mechanism.

A final design requirement is that the mechanism should be subject to analysis and test. This turned out to be a rather difficult requirement and is one that led to the evolution culminating in the criteria. In implementation, this reference monitor mechanism will be some relatively small portion of the hardware and software. If this portion of the system meets these three design requirements, we refer to it as a security kernel.

Basic requirements

Why do we have this set of criteria? Why not some other set? The answer is that the criteria developers looked at the basic requirements that they were trying to address with a trusted computer system, and from these derived the criteria that would be sufficient to allow us to judge how well the system meets those requirements, even under the threat of malicious software. The following summarizes the requirements considered basic to the criteria. See Essay 2 for further discussion of these concepts.

The notion of controlled sharing in computer systems implies that it is possible to define what controls on the sharing of information are desired. This definition constitutes the security policy, as mentioned above. Fortunately, it is understood that all practical security policies for reading and/or modifying information (that is, for access control) can be grouped into two common classes: discretionary and nondiscretionary [SALT75] (also called mandatory). These provide a powerful and flexible tool for the design of secure computer systems [BELL91].

One type of security policy is a mandatory security policy, in the sense that an individual who, for example, has access to Secret information is (if he is going to follow the security policy) required to ascertain that somebody else has a Secret clearance before allowing him to have access to that information. Even if he may need the information to do his job, he is not to be granted access to it until he has a clearance. This mandatory restriction on the security must be similarly enforced in the computer system.

Another subtle problem in enforcing a mandatory security policy is uncontrolled downgrading. This perhaps is most easily illustrated with Trojan horses, a form of malicious software described in Essay 1. If, for example, a system has an editor that edits a Secret file, and in the course of editing that file, the Trojan horse in the editor can make a copy for an unauthorized individual in a new nominally Unclassified file, that individual can retrieve the new Unclassified file at a later time. The problem of uncontrolled downgrading really is unique to the nature of computers. Independently of computers, we trust individuals who have knowledge of classified information to exercise the good judgment not to communicate that information to unauthorized individuals, even though they may be communicating unclassified information to those same individuals. However, a computer is unable to exercise judgment; a computer only "does what it is told" by its software (which may be malicious). To prevent uncontrolled downgrading, we need assurance that the computer enforces the mandatory security policy.

One of the mandatory security policy requirements is marking the sensitivity of information. For example, corporations depend very heavily on such markings for protection of their proprietary information. Documents are commonly marked at the top and bottom of each page to reflect the sensitivity of the information contained in them. In computer systems, information is implicitly homogeneous with regard to markings. One cannot pick up a magnetic tape and tell what sensitivity the bits are. Some sort of sensitivity marking (or labeling) system is needed internal to the computer itself.

In addition to the mandatory security policy, we have a class of requirements that has been called the discretionary security policy. This class is discretionary in the sense that an individual who has control of sensitive information can exercise his discretion in determining if someone else has the need-to-know for that information (if he has a clearance). Then, and only then, is it released to him. The requirement to enforce need-to-know is closer to the historical notions of controls in a computer system where the users and the access that they have to the information are identified (for example, user/group/world, read/write/execute).

To implement these requirements, one needs to know who has access to the system; both in the world of documents and in the automated world, there is a need for individual accountability. There should be a record of what action an individual who processes or otherwise accesses sensitive information has taken with regard to that access. For example, if he exercises his authority to downgrade information after determining it is no longer classified, that should be recorded, so that if this judgment is called into question, it can be determined who in fact made that decision.

Finally, for the security controls to be effective, in a computer system or otherwise, there must be continuous protection of those things responsible for the security. In other words, we want to control changes to the protection mechanisms. Since we are depending on the hardware and software in the trusted system to assure the protection, we must have some way to be sure that what we have evaluated is in fact the same hardware and software that are actually executing at any point in time. The requirement for continuous protection provides increased assurance that the protection mechanisms are in place as expected and that they are not subverted through malicious software. This last point is particularly noteworthy, since even experts in the field of computer security sometimes apparently forget that increased assurance is primarily aimed at protection from malicious software. The TCB is not just "built using acceptable systems engineering practices (in order to minimize errors)" [CHOK92].

Criteria overview

In this section, the criteria defined in the TCSEC are overviewed. The criteria are structured into seven distinct "evaluation classes." These represent progressive increments in the confidence one may have in the security enforcement, and each increment is intended to reduce the risk taken by using that class of system to protect sensitive information. These increments are intended to be cumulative in the sense that each includes all the requirements of the previous. Between each distinct class and the next there is a significant jump in the capabilities provided (and in the difficulties in providing these capabilities). Furthermore, the classes form a natural evolution path such that, by choosing one of these classes, one is not precluded from going further. (A detailed discussion of and limitations on the extensibility of particular architectures in providing the basis for satisfying the requirements of progressively "higher" evaluation classes are presented elsewhere [SCHA84, SHOC87].)

The fact that the criteria scale upward in a manner that naturally extends the requirements of one class to the next higher class allows one to more fully understand the applicable principles by looking at the "highest" classes. Similarly, after understanding the principles applied in the highest classes, it is much easier to understand what is missing in the "lower" classes. If principles had not been applied in the formulation of this set of criteria, it would have been merely a hodgepodge of ad hoc requirements. The clear correspondence between the highest classes (closer to ideal) and the lowest classes allows easier judgment of whether a system meets any class of the criteria for satisfying the security requirements in a particular application environment.

The criteria are applied on a system basis. The seven classes are divided into four divisions, termed D, C, B, and A, that are independent of any specific applications. These divisions apply to general-purpose operating systems with their hardware, or to special-purpose operating systems and application combinations.

There are seven classes, ranging from class D to class A1, and we will address them individually. They are summarized below:

Overview of Evaluation Classes

Minimal: Division D

Class D: Minimal Protection

Discretionary: Division C

Class C1: Discretionary Security
Class C2: Controlled Access

Mandatory: Division B

Class B1: Labeled Security
Class B2: Structured
Class B3: Security Domains

Verified: Division A

Class A1: Verified Design

Division D. Division D has only one class. Evaluation class D, called Minimal Protection, is easy to address. It means that the system meeting this class fails to meet the requirements of any higher class and cannot even be expected to protect against human error.

Division C. Division C, the Discretionary Protection Division, has two classes. Systems meeting a class in this division provide some confidence that the hardware and software controls are enforcing a discretionary security policy. This means that one has some confidence that there is some protection against the class of computer misuse techniques described in Essay 1 as human error. A system meeting class C2 also provides some protection against and detection of user abuse of authority and direct probing — additional classes of computer misuse techniques described in Essay 1. This division is most generally intended to address protection against actions of users and nonusers who are not using malicious software.

Class C1. The lower class in this division is C1 (Discretionary Security Protection). This is the first point at which one may have some confidence that a system meeting this class is implementing a discretionary security policy. From the reference monitor concept, we note that there has to be isolation, that is, self-protection. User identification/authentication must be provided since there is sensitive information to be protected. There is some understandable definition of the controls provided so that at any point one can say that these are the people who will be allowed to access this information and no others.

The establishment of confidence that one has met this level (that is, assurance) is primarily based on functional testing. There is some nominal set of controls that has been advertised; one carefully tests these controls to demonstrate that they function as advertised.

Systems meeting this class therefore provide some protection against human error, but they are not much help in preventing or even detecting user abuse of authority and direct probing. This is because there is no required capability to audit user actions and there may be relatively weak access control over resources.

Examples of candidates for this class could be nearly any of the major commercial systems offered today. To date, product vendors have shown little interest in having their systems evaluated with this rating as the objective. This is probably because the class C1 rating is of little market advantage against an unrated or a class D rated system; it is perceived as offering only nominal security.

Class C2. The second class in this division, C2 (Controlled Access Protection), is one in which the resources are more heavily encapsulated, at least for a subset of the resources. The controls may not be applied to all the objects in the system; they may be principally applied to the ones that one is trying to protect and has a direct interest in. These would include objects like individual files or in some cases particular devices. In addition, in this class explicit auditing requirements are met. Not only has the individual identified and authenticated himself prior to using this system, but there can be a record of what that individual has done. There is probably an inverse relationship between the amount of audit information available and the amount of understanding people have about what is going on. So there has to be a selective way of recording the accesses that occur. In addition to having that selective recording, of course, there must be tools for examining the audit record.

Systems meeting this class therefore provide some protection against human error and some prevention and detection of user abuse of authority and direct probing.

Examples of systems that meet the requirements of this class are the operating systems for most of the major vendors' computers, including IBM, Digital Equipment Corp., Data General, Unisys, Control Data Corp., Prime Computer, Hewlett-Packard, Encore Computer Corp., and Wang Labs, as well as add-on systems for IBM computers by Computer Associates. Several of these are security-enhanced Unix look-alike operating systems. These provide the need-to-know controls that are required for a single-level mode of operation. Division C assumes that there is an implicit single mandatory sensitivity level for all the information.

Division B. Next, we move into the Mandatory Protection Division, division B, which has three classes. The hardware and software controls of systems meeting a class in this division enforce a mandatory as well as a discretionary security policy. This means that one has some confidence that there is some protection against the classes of computer misuse techniques addressed in class C2 (human error, user abuse of authority, and direct probing), as well as some protection against probing with malicious software. Systems meeting class B2 also offer some protection against direct penetration, while systems meeting class B3 provide some protection against subversion of security mechanism. This division is most generally intended to address protection against malicious software in the applications outside the TCB.

Class B1. The first class, B1, is called Labeled Security Protection. For this class, there is an explicit security policy model for the mandatory and discretionary security policies that are to be enforced. This class has been described as "C2 with labels," referring to the lack of real improvement over class C2 in assurance, coupled with the need for labels in order to enforce a mandatory security policy. For example, in the case of the usual classified processing in the Department of Defense, the security policy model for the mandatory security policy is quite straightforward. It says that if one is going to access information with a given sensitivity level, say Secret, one must have a Secret clearance. If one has access to Secret information, one is not allowed to downgrade that information unless one is explicitly authorized to downgrade.

The requirement is that the mandatory security policy be applied to a defined subset of the subjects and objects in the system, including some of the storage objects in the system (the things that actually store the information). It is also required that there be internal labels for the subjects and objects. This is not restricted to just DoD classified processing. Those labels are to be parametric, so that in one installation the printout might come out saying "Personnel Sensitive," whereas in another installation, identically the same system with a different set of parameters might print "Secret" or "Top Secret" at the top and bottom of the page. The parametric nature of the labels is quite important if the systems are to have broad application.

Because there has to be a security administrator with this class of system (to administer the labels, for example, on devices, and register user clearances), there must be a manual that describes how to use this system in a given installation. One of the emphases is on having suitable documentation, so the user can interface with requirements of the external controls (such as human-readable labels on output), as well as with the controls internal to the hardware and software.

By virtue of the application of a mandatory security policy on a subset of the subjects and objects in the system, one has some confidence that there is some additional protection against the classes of computer misuse techniques addressed by class C2, as well as some protection against subversion with malicious software. However, since there is really no more assurance than with class C2, there is no real protection against direct penetration or subversion of security mechanism.

Examples of systems that meet the requirements of this class are operating systems for a few of the major vendors' computers, including IBM, Unisys, and AT&T, as well as for the Apple Macintosh (by SecureWare).

Class B2. For the next class of the division, class B2 (called Structured Protection), the emphasis shifts more to support for actually evaluating a system's security. A system claimed to meet the requirements of this class must be built in a way that allows an objective assessment of whether it actually meets them. For this, the internal structure of the system must be evident. This is the first class where the TCB significantly implements the reference monitor concept.

In this class, there are identifiable security components in the system that are protected from the remainder of the system by what is called a security perimeter (that is, at least the portion of the system that contains the security-related components is inside the security perimeter). An attempt is made to show that the parts of the system inside the security perimeter are not harmful, even if they are not security-related. This represents a fairly distinct jump in capability from the previous classes. Thus, the tasks for the evaluators and the producers are to identify the security-related parts of the system and to show that the remainder of the system from which the security-related parts are not protected is not harmful. The importance of class B2 and higher classes, which also have a well-defined security perimeter, is particularly evident, even beyond security, when one considers the problem of system maintenance and support. If the evaluation is dependent on all the programs that are ever run on that processor for that system, any time there is a change in a program one must concern oneself with whether the evaluation is still valid. By limiting the portion of the system that is responsible for the security controls, one substantially eases that problem.

There should be distinct storage objects that can be identified. There should be, within the control mechanism itself, functionally distinct modules, designed so that the principle of least privilege is enforced, and one should be able to identify which module is providing which part of the protection. Hardware must separate the security-related modules from those that are not, and hardware mechanisms such as segmentation must be used to maintain the separation of objects on the basis of their different attributes (that is, whether they are readable or writable). The system may have components that are not security-related, but they must be separated through the use of hardware from those on which the security of the system depends. A descriptive top-level specification (DTLS) of the interface of the security-relevant portion of the system (the security perimeter) must be provided. The DTLS is not merely a set of manual pages, but rather it must be a complete and accurate specification that describes the TCB in terms of exceptions, error messages, and effects [PARN72a]. The DTLS must be provided along with a formal, proven representation of the security policy model.

In addition, this class introduces an emphasis on the problem of preventing unauthorized downgrading by covert channels through the mechanism itself leaking the information from one label to a lower label. At class B2, covert storage channels (covert channels involving the passing of information through a storage location, for example, through exceptions) should be identified. With this class, the focus is on identifying the covert channel problems that might be there and having the ability after the fact (after they may have been exploited) through audit to determine whether they may have been used for unauthorized downgrading.

The labels of the mandatory security policy are enforced for all the visible resources. These resources are not just the explicit storage objects, but also there should be labels for devices (for example, for communication lines). This includes single-level devices and multilevel devices. Whatever the resources are, if information is provided, there should be an explicit label for that information. For example, for multilevel communication lines over which packets are being communicated, labels for the packets are required. Control of unauthorized downgrading provides a substantially increased assurance that the system is in fact protecting the information, even from malicious software.

With this class, we also have increased assurance in the identification/authentication process. The need that this satisfies is illustrated by a well-known attack. The attacker will leave a terminal with a program that asks for a victim's password. The victim comes up to the terminal and logs in. The attacker's program will ask for the password, which will be provided. Thereupon, the attacker's program will simulate a crash of the system and save a copy of the victim's password for the attacker. This is a problem where there has not been a trusted path for providing the authentication. Class B2 requires a trusted path — a trusted way of making sure that when one is authenticating oneself, one is authenticating to the system and not just giving the password to some attacker.

Furthermore, there is increased concern for the continuous protection of the protection mechanism itself against illegal modification. For this class, there must be explicit tools provided for monitoring the configuration changes (that is, configuration management). The evaluators look at the builders' mechanisms for providing configuration management and also require tools for doing things like comparing this version of the system to a previous version.

In addition to the protection provided by systems meeting class B1, systems meeting this class also provide some protection against direct penetration but lack protection against subversion of security mechanism. Even with the increased assurance of class B2, penetration is still a distinct problem, and subversion is not really addressed. It is fortunate that we still have two classes to discuss.

Examples of systems that meet the requirements of this class are the Multics operating system developed by Honeywell, the trusted Xenix operating system developed by IBM and Trusted Information Systems, and VSLAN, a local area network developed by Verdix.

Class B3. Class B3, called Security Domains, is the final class in division B, and it addresses the remaining evaluation difficulty in this division. In class B2, there were still a lot of things to look at inside the security perimeter that really did not have anything to do with security. For example, linking mechanisms and file systems can be quite complex but for convenience may well have been put along with the basic security controls in the heart of the system. At the class B3 level, however, the intention is to have a simple, central encapsulation mechanism that separates those portions of the system that are security-related from those that may provide some necessary and common services to the users but really do not relate to security. This requires a layered set of abstract machines and an ability to separate those layers into distinct protection domains. The paradigm here is one of extending the hardware — a well-specified, stable, unchanging machine — upward to higher layers of the system.

In class B3, it should be possible to remove from inside the security perimeter all parts of the system that are not really security-relevant. This last point is the requirement for minimization of the complexity of the portion of the system inside the security perimeter. As a practical matter, minimization forces a general-purpose system to implement at least three protection domains: one for the portion of the system inside the security perimeter (the TCB), one for the operating system, and one for the application. However, some special-purpose or embedded systems may implement the application and the operating system in the same domain.

At the class B3 level, there is a highly structured implementation of the design. There is not just a set of functional capabilities that one can add, but at this point, one has to build the system in a way that is subject to the evaluation for class B3. This evaluation process is more akin to the notion of quality assurance — of looking at how the system is being developed — than it is to that of testing a black box after the fact. Class B3 requires an ongoing effort during development to make the design and implementation understandable and inspectable to later achieve a meaningful evaluation. The motivation for this is the third reference monitor design requirement described earlier — to ensure that the implementation of the reference monitor can be subjected to analysis and structured testing in a manner to assure completeness.

A system that meets the class B3 requirements contains a security kernel, which is the hardware and software that implement the reference monitor concept. It is this reference monitor implementation that realizes the abstractions of subjects and objects out of the physical hardware resources. Beneath the set of security kernel interface functions is a set of computer code, databases, and hardware structures. Above the security kernel, one can expect to find a set of additional security-relevant TCB code and databases that implement a discretionary security policy and support the identification/authentication and audit functions. The TCB is structured in a series of layers, each performing a distinct set of services either for processes outside the security-relevant portion of the system or for other security-relevant layers, and each depending only on the services of lower layers. A layered system provides an opportunity to develop an informal proof sketch of each layer's sufficiency to meet the requirements of the next higher layer, based on an implementation specification for each layer. The proof sketches for succeedingly higher layers of the system, if performed, would provide a clear correspondence of the layers in the design to the DTLS and hence to the formal security policy model. The correspondence of the layered implementation to the security policy model is also facilitated by breaking the implementation design into modules with a clean, clear abstraction that allows for information hiding within modules. Note that since module, layering, information hiding, and abstraction are all used in the TCSEC as terms of art, they are not fully defined there. However, these terms are well-described in the computer science literature (for example, in the early groundbreaking software engineering work of Parnas [PARN72a, b]).

Therefore, class B3 is the lowest class at which systems that meet it have at all addressed subversion of security mechanism. In a class B3 system, one can have some assurance in protection from subversion, in addition to significantly enhanced protection against direct penetration beyond that provided by a system meeting class B2.

A commercial class B3 system is the XTS-200/STOP from Honeywell Federal Systems, Inc. The XTS-200 is a multiprocessing superminicomputer, capable of supporting up to four independent processors. STOP is its multitasking system, which supports much of the Unix interface for application software.

Division A. Division A is distinguished by additional requirements substantially dealing with the problems of subversion of security mechanism. To gain increased assurance beyond division B, one needs more structured verification support tools. In division A, which includes only a single class, formal and informal analyses are required to support claims of the correspondence of the implementation to the interface specification and hence to the security policy model. This enhanced assurance means greater protection against subversion, as well as against direct penetration and the other classes of computer misuse techniques discussed in Essay 1.

Class A1. For class A1 (Verified Design), which is at the limit of the state of the art, mathematical tools are applied that use formal security policy models with explicit security theorems. A formal top-level specification (FTLS) of the TCB interface (the security perimeter) is required. This form of specification is expressed in a formal language capable of being analyzed by a computer program and of supporting a formal proof that the specifications conform to the requirements of the formal security policy model. The FTLS is analyzed in a systematic way, in order to gain a high degree of confidence that if that specification is correctly implemented, the security perimeter that is expected to have been provided will in fact have been provided. This FTLS is used for the analysis of covert storage channels that is required to use formal tools.

In addition to this analysis, it must be assured that the implementation corresponds to the specification. With the current state of the art, this will not be a wrapped-up mathematical proof that the system is secure since, in general, correctness proofs at the source code level are not practical. However, increased assurance over that of a class B3 system is afforded by an analysis showing the correspondence of the source code of the TCB to the FTLS, supplementing the layer-oriented analysis required for classes B3 and A1. The formal analysis is assisted by tools that can provide evidence in various degrees of formality, both at the specification level and at the level of the implementation correspondence.

In addition, configuration management becomes of increasing interest as these formal methods are introduced. Class A1 requires control not only of the hardware/software mechanism, but also of the specifications. Control must exist throughout the life cycle — during the system's design, development, production, and distribution. That says there is concern for the trusted distribution of the system. This trusted distribution requirement reflects that as we move to class A1, we expect to have increased dependence on the system. We expect a decrease in the risk from using it, and therefore we are more concerned about its vulnerability to subversion during the distribution process (for example, by replacement of part of the TCB with malicious software from an attacker).

The result of the enhanced assurance with class A1 is, as noted above, greater protection against subversion of security mechanism, as well as against direct penetration and the other classes of computer misuse techniques discussed in Essay 1.

An example of a system that was evaluated as meeting the class A1 requirements in 1985 is the Honeywell SCOMP minicomputer. We have already discussed its successor, the XTS-200, which is a class B3 system.

The Boeing Multilevel Secure Local Area Network Server System meets a subset of the class A1 requirements that are particularly applicable to networks. This subset, an evaluation of which is defined in the Trusted Network Interpretation (TNI) of the TCSEC [NCSC87a], includes support for enforcing a mandatory security policy between attached devices and identification/authentication of users of some of those devices. It supports devices such as terminals, host computers, serial devices, video devices, and stream devices.

The Gemini Trusted Network Processor (GTNP) from Gemini Computers is another candidate to meet the mandatory security policy requirements of class A1, as interpreted in the TNI. The GTNP product consists of security software that operates on a hardware base with up to eight processors (Intel iAPX 80286 or 80386) in hard-disk-based, floppy-disk-based, and RAM-based models. These systems include Gemini-specific device interfaces as necessary to support a particular configuration. The system takes an open-architecture approach in which applications and protocols may be developed to run on top of the base provided by the GTNP to support specific network requirements or network component compositions, without affecting the GTNP TCB. The GTNP provides device interfaces for several types of networks, a preallocated address (MULTIBUS I) interface, and a virtual machine monitor interface that can be used to implement applications such as guards and trusted database management systems [IRVI91] without requiring reevaluation of the underlying product. It also provides support for encryption and cryptographic sealing of critical system structures (including labels) and user data using the Data Encryption Standard (DES).

In modern communication systems, a dedicated, RAM-based GTNP configuration is well-suited as a secure front-end or interface processor. The flexible multiprocessor architecture provides low risk and at the same time meets demanding throughput requirements such as those encountered in high-speed packet switching or end-to-end encryption control [WEIS92]. The integral DES encryption hardware also makes it attractive for guard interfaces where encrypted checksums or digital signatures are used to establish the authenticity of received information. In workstation environments the disk-based configurations are well-suited for distributing the processing of sensitive information, especially when the workstation is part of a network. In addition, the high performance available from multiprocessor configurations offers unique opportunities for specialized systems such as high-capacity multiuser database management systems.

Beyond class A1. In considering the future, it is useful to note that the criteria have specifically provided for the addition of more evaluation classes in division A as the state of the art progresses. It is particularly important to note that the underlying technology provides the foundation for even higher assurance than what is realized by the current practices, that is, class A1 and lower. Thus, while class A1 provides truly outstanding security, it is reasonable to expect even greater security in the future for those applications facing extraordinarily intense and hostile threats, especially of penetration and subversion using malicious software.

For these classes, applications may have even greater dependence on the trusted system for security, so there is increased concern for the development environment (for the correctness of the tools used in the development). There is also increased concern for verifying the correctness of the TCB to a lower level (down to the source code level), including hardware and firmware. These are goals for future criteria.

Evaluation by parts. In dealing with any complex system, an attractive strategy is one of "divide and conquer." What is desired is an approach for dividing the trusted component of the system into simpler parts, evaluating each of the parts separately, and then validating the correctness of the way the parts are composed to form a single system enforcing a globally well-defined security policy. It is obviously desirable that the validation of the correct composition of evaluated parts be a relatively simple task. The simplicity of the reference monitor concept lends itself well to a divide-and-conquer evaluation strategy. In this section, two distinct strategies will be briefly overviewed. These ideas are an extension of the principles first described elsewhere [SCHA84], with the benefit of several additional years of experience and thought about how a complex TCB might be composed from a collection of simpler TCBs residing in individual protection domains.

The first strategy, the "partition evaluation" of a trusted distributed system or network, depends on the notion that a complex system may be decomposed into independent, loosely coupled, intercommunicating processing components. This strategy is most suitable for trusted systems that have a complex physical architecture (for example, distributed systems or networks). The partition evaluation strategy [SCHE85] is the basis for Appendixes A and B of the TNI [NCSC87a], which provides interpretations for the application of the TCSEC to networks.

The second strategy, the "incremental evaluation" or "subset evaluation" of a TCB, was used by Gemini Computers to internally structure the TCB of its GTNP and was first publicly presented by Shockley and Schell [SCHOC87]. It builds on the idea that a complex TCB may be divided into simpler TCB subsets, each of which enforces a subset of the global security policy. The effect of such a security policy decomposition, when allocated to the various TCB subsets, is to allow performance of a chain of simpler evaluations (each an evaluation of a subset), leading to an overall conclusion that the composite TCB is correct. Unlike a TCB consisting of multiple partitions, incrementally evaluated TCB subsets are thought of as residing in the same tightly coupled processing component. The subset strategy is particularly well-suited for TCBs that enforce relatively complex security policies over virtual objects which are very different from the physical storage objects provided by the processor hardware. For that reason, the TCB subset strategy is particularly appropriate for the application of the TCSEC to trusted database management systems. It is a key concept in the Trusted Database Interpretation (TDI) of the TCSEC [NCSC91], which provides interpretations for the application of the TCSEC to database management systems and other complex applications.

The partition and subset evaluation strategies are compatible and may be combined in various ways for TCBs that are complex in both architecture and security policy. This has been proposed, for example, for an embedded secure database management system [IRVI91].

As we have noted, there are fundamental differences between the degree of protection from malicious software offered by the enforcement of a mandatory security policy and that offered by a discretionary security policy. This difference has led to the development of a useful technique for enhancing assurance in parts of the TCB where it matters most. The technique is balanced assurance.

Using partitions or subsets, one of two positions for assurance in a TCB can be adopted. The more conservative approach holds that all assurance requirements for a particular evaluation class must be applied uniformly to the entire TCB. This is termed "uniform assurance." The less conservative position requires the application of assurances to partitions or subsets only where the assurances are relevant to the security policy enforced by the partition or subset and provide a genuine increase in the credibility of security policy enforcement. This approach is called balanced assurance [LUNT88a].

Balanced assurance is endorsed by the TNI's Appendix A (though not by name) through its stipulation of a maximum class of C2 (with respect to assurance) for those TCB subsets not enforcing or supporting the mandatory security policy. This means that, using the TNI, one can have a class A1 network that contains partitions (for example, enforcing discretionary access control and audit) that meet only the class C2 requirements for assurance. Balanced assurance is an important technique for achieving near-term high assurance where it counts in complex systems, but it is still controversial since it is a less conservative approach.

Conclusions

The criteria summarized in this essay give us the technology to build and objectively evaluate trusted computer systems. However, the techniques of applying the criteria are not the most difficult challenges that we face in maintaining a technology base on which secure systems can be efficiently developed and used. Managers of information systems must also meet their responsibilities to maintain a constant commitment to protect the information with which they have been entrusted. Moreover, trusted product developers must continue to provide the building blocks that enable trusted computer systems to be efficiently developed for specific applications.

Sound criteria. The practicality of applying the principles of the TCSEC and its interpretations, which were formulated based on both business and technical considerations, is demonstrated by the fact that TCSEC's development was based on worked examples. In fact, before there was a TCSEC, there were worked examples of the use of each of its principles. For example, TCB isolation in the first system to achieve a class A1 evaluation rating — the SCOMP, whose development was begun significantly prior to the completion of the TCSEC — was provided by a hardware implementation of a ring mechanism that was developed in the late 1960s and early 1970s for the Multics system [FRAI83, SCHR72]. The Blacker system, which was developed during the formulation of the TNI, confirmed the practicality of notions such as TCB partitions [WEIS92]. Similarly, the notion of TCB subsets [SHOC87] was incorporated into the TDI only after experience with it in the design of the SeaView multilevel database management system [LUNT88].

It was considered quite important during the formulation of the TCSEC to require, to the extent possible, only the minimum additional documentation for evaluation evidence beyond that produced already by a quality-conscious developer. The majority of the evidence is intended to be exactly that which the developer needed to design, build, and maintain the system. This goal of having most of the evaluation evidence produced as a by-product of the trusted system development is based on the principle that the evidence is produced for the developer — not for the evaluators. This goal is revealed in the fact that the TCSEC does not enumerate items to be "delivered" to the evaluators and does not impose requirements for "presentation" for the documents and evidence.

Another important goal in the formulation of the TCSEC was to support the procurement and approval processes by minimizing the number of discrete evaluation ratings — by providing only the ratings between which there was a clear difference in the protection offered by a system. Further, in the discrete evaluation classes, there is a coherence between features and assurance, so that they are combined in an intelligent fashion. The idea is that there is no need to encourage or even to have systems which possess higher assurance, without corresponding gains in the features. For example, there is no class C3 — offering higher assurance of a discretionary security policy. Since a discretionary security policy is fundamentally incapable of protecting against malicious software, there is no practical reason to have higher assurance of its enforcement beyond that offered by a class C2 system. For this reason, the TCSEC provides an enumeration of all evaluation classes; as stated above, there are only seven. The principle here is that the scientists who developed the criteria are in a much better position than are others, by virtue of their understanding of the principles, to determine the features and assurances that work together to counter specific threats.

As noted in the sections on technical foundations and basic requirements, the technical soundness of the TCSEC comes from its basis in valid scientific underpinnings. Fundamental to the TCSEC is the reference monitor concept, which implies the notion of having a security policy that possesses properties such that whether a given system enforces those properties is computable (see our statements about this in Essay 2). For this reason, the TCSEC provides criteria for the evaluation of a system with a definitive security perimeter that enforces access control policies. As stated in Essay 2, whether or not a given system meets the criteria of availability, reliability, safety, and other such properties is fundamentally noncomputable. The foundations of the reference monitor concept also imply (as described in the section on class B3) the minimization of the portion of the system inside the security perimeter, as well as the paradigm of verification of succeeding layers of the TCB by the development of an informal proof sketch for each layer. These reference monitor principles are key to attaining high levels of assurance and provide the basis for understanding what is lost by relaxation for the lower levels of assurance.

The practicality of applying alternate criteria that are just being placed into use (for example, the ITSEC [ITSE91]), as well as those under development (for example, the Federal Criteria), has yet to be significantly tested. However, these criteria are being developed based on considerations different from the business and technical considerations discussed above for the TCSEC. (In fact, the ITSEC differs from the TCSEC on each of the considerations described above in this section!) The results may affect both their usefulness (the degree to which product vendors and system procurers are willing to subscribe to them) and their soundness (the degree to which insecure implementations could be evaluated as secure and vice versa).

The criteria have a sound technology base, broad applicability, and several years of application experience in real evaluations. As it stands, the criteria are highly objective and effective as a measure of the appropriate confidence in the internal hardware and software controls. However, there have been reports of concerted opposition that would weaken the criteria's effectiveness ever since the TCSEC was first published [SCHE84]. For example, some have raised specious arguments for consciously limiting the criteria's use to just the DoD, implying that these criteria are applicable only to the DoD. Although there is a superficial appeal to this argument, it ignores the fact that both the underlying technology and the criteria themselves are not tied to DoD-unique characteristics. This argument also ignores the growing need for trusted systems that we have addressed in Essay 1. On the contrary, Shockley [SHOC88] demonstrates that this technology can satisfy a security policy claimed to be "an accurate representation of what the business and commercial data processing community means by the term 'integrity.'" Further, Bell [BELL91] shows how it is possible to support a number of non-DoD security policies with this technology.

In addition, both inside and outside the DoD, there have been efforts to make "plausible" but in fact devastating changes to the criteria that would seriously weaken the technical foundations. It is just these foundations that make it possible to clearly determine the effectiveness of the security. For example, eliminating the requirement for a proof of the security sufficiency of the rules of the formal security policy model would make the criteria much easier to meet, but correspondingly much less useful and in fact even seriously misleading.

In view of this sort of controversy, we must recognize that as an industry, it is an essential but elusive goal to have widely accepted, meaningful criteria. However, we must also recognize that technically weak criteria would deprive those with the critical need for trusted systems of what they need most — a tool for objectively determining the security of their systems in the face of practical attacks, including malicious software.

Responsibility for information protection. There is little in the way of laws, regulations, policy, and practice to mandate or even encourage meaningful hardware and software controls (especially at the higher assurance levels). Hence, some observe that there may be little incentive for management to buy the trusted products that are available or to implement trusted systems. It has been noted that many of the managers who are responsible for selecting the particular computer system an organization will use have little at stake in protecting the information they process. The serious potential damage is often not to their immediate group and may not even be to their parent organization — for example, where computers are used to provide service based on someone else's information. Even though an information service may be in a position to seriously damage individual privacy, the organization may feel it has little to risk itself.

To date, the response to the available trusted products has been less than overwhelming, even in the DoD, where use of a trusted system of sufficient assurance to meet the risk faced by each specific system is a part of DoD policy [DOD88b]. For example, the DoD, which sponsored the major security enhancements to the Honeywell Multics product, used this system in very few installations, even though various assessments highlighted the need for that type of security. (Perhaps as a consequence, Multics is no longer available as a standard product.) The DoD has more recently encouraged the broad use of lower assurance products (for example, through the "C2 by 92" initiative). However, it is essential that managers within the DoD begin to mandate use of trusted systems of sufficient assurance to meet the requirements of DoD Directive 5200.28 [DOD88b] (enclosure 4) if they want to prevent the moral equivalent of discussing classified information on open telephone lines.

If the appropriate trusted systems are not used in commercial as well as government installations, we are, in time, almost assured of a disastrous computer-security "Chernobyl"-like event of major proportion, in which serious damage will be done due to the continued negligence of those responsible for computerized information. Although this could well stimulate the use of trusted systems at that time, there is a high risk of overreaction in areas such as government regulation and restrictions on the use of automation. On the other hand, use of sound criteria to determine whether or not the security policy of a particular system is being enforced to an appropriate degree of assurance (that is, determining that the evaluation class met by the system satisfies the security requirements for the environment in which the system will operate) can go a long way to prevent a disaster.

Availability of trusted products. Trusted product availability at lower assurance classes is steadily improving. In addition, the criteria have been successfully used to support several assurance evaluations at class B2 or higher (including systems such as Blacker — which used "GEMSOS, an off-the-shelf kernel from Gemini Computers" [WEIS92] — and commercial products). Yet there are still only a small number of higher assurance product choices available. In addition, some of the products evaluated by the NCSC have not fared well in the marketplace. This is clearly related to the lack of overwhelming demand for those products that are available, as just addressed.

However, several vendors are seriously developing trusted systems. Also, the NCSC and NIST continue to respond to the growing need for computer security within the US. Among other things, as mentioned earlier, the NCSC manages evaluations of commercial products against the established criteria and publishes an "Evaluated Products List" so that customers can better determine what products are available.

On balance, we are persuaded that, as more trusted computer system products become available that are both practical and secure, managers will step up to their responsibility to use them to protect the information entrusted to their machines. We as computer professionals must accept our part of the responsibility for information security now and in the future. As we do, trusted systems will have an increasingly valuable place in our profession. Since it is not practical to individually evaluate the security of each system starting from basic science, the criteria are the primary tool that makes it possible for us to address our information security responsibilities effectively.

Essay 7

Information Security Policy

Ingrid M. Olson and Marshall D. Abrams

This essay discusses information *security* policy, focusing on information control and dissemination, for automated information systems (AISs). Most organizations have some sort of high-level information policy that addresses how and what information is to be handled by the organization. AISs have changed how information can be used. A further refinement of the high-level information policy is necessary to deal with this automation and establish what is considered acceptable behavior with respect to the information. This refinement process involves determining the appropriate set of policy-oriented limitations. It can take place at many levels, from a top-level corporate decision to a hardware implementation choice.

An information security policy addresses many issues such as the following: disclosure, integrity, and availability concerns; who may access what information in what manner; basis on which the access decision is made (for example, user characteristic such as nationality or group affinity, or some external condition such as time or status); maximized sharing versus least privilege; separation of duties; who controls and who owns the information; and authority issues. In the past, R&D has focused primarily on DoD policies based on user clearances and data classification, but many other access control policies are in use in the manual world, in other government agencies, and in the private sector. Policies such as a press release policy (sensitive until released at <time, date>), access based on roles (only vice presidents and above have access), and many others are real and useful policies with special characteristics not easily handled by most current systems. This essay discusses some of the aspects that must be considered when developing an information security policy for a given organization.

A policy is a plan or course of action, designed to influence and determine decisions, actions, and other matters [AMER82]. Organizations typically have many policies governing all aspects of their operations, security being one major consideration. The Information Technology Security Evaluation Criteria (ITSEC) define a corporate security policy as follows [COMM91]:

> The set of laws, rules, and practices that regulate how assets including sensitive information are managed, protected, and distributed within a user organization.

An organizational security policy has been defined as follows [STER91]:

> The set of laws, rules, and practices that regulate how an organization manages, protects, and distributes resources to achieve specified security policy objectives. These laws, rules, and practices must identify criteria for according individuals authority, and may specify conditions under which individuals are permitted to exercise their authority. To be meaningful, these laws, rules, and practices must provide individuals reasonable ability to determine whether their actions violate or comply with the policy.

This essay will focus on a subset of the organizational security policy: the information security policy governing the protection of *information*. Information is one of many resources an organization must protect. While the protection of information has always been a major concern for organizations, the computerized automation of information has vastly changed the threats to and vulnerabilities of the information, resulting in a need to further interpret and refine the information security policy for the automated information system (AIS) environment.

The ITSEC has defined a technical security policy as follows [COMM91]:

> The set of laws, rules, and practices regulating the processing of sensitive information and the use of resources by the hardware and software of an IT [information technology] system or product.

There are many aspects to a technical security policy or an information security policy. Areas such as the labeling of the information, accountability, information ownership, modification of the information, audit, and dissemination controls must all be addressed for the policy to be complete. This essay focuses primarily on the information dissemination/control aspects of the policy — that is, who can access information within the system and what they can do as a consequence of such access. In addition, the discussion focuses on the AIS-related aspects of the policy. Other implementations of the policy may be possible through personnel, physical security, or procedural controls.

Policy refinement

At a high level, the information protection objectives of many organizations look very similar. For example, the policy may state "sensitive information processed by the organization's resources shall be properly safeguarded against accidental or malicious disclosure, alteration, destruction, or delay" [OLSO90]. For different organizations, though, this statement can have very different implications. Within the government, this sensitive information may be designated sensitive unclassified and be subject to the Privacy Act and/or the Computer Security Act. National-security-related sensitive information is classified according to complex rules and is subject to Executive Order 12356 and numerous Department of Defense directives. Private organizations may identify sensitive information as proprietary, personnel confidential, source selection sensitive, and so on, each with its own implications of who may access the information and under what conditions.

The process of refining an organization's high-level policy into an implementable AIS security policy involves many choices and decisions, from top-level decisions concerning organization objectives to hardware implementation choices. Through this refinement process, there will be many representations of the policy. At the higher levels, the policy is likely to be written in a natural language, which is easy to understand in a general way but is also subject to ambiguity. At some point, a precise formal language restatement in a formal security policy model may be appropriate. The essay "Formal Methods and Models" (Essay 8), by Williams and Abrams, discusses these different representations in more detail.

National policy, other organization policy, international standards, particular project requirements, political issues, implementation platform limitations, or other factors may influence or determine some of the policy refinement decisions. Some of the choices may have legal, ethical, or privacy issues driving the decision. For example, should the stored record of a legal transaction be in its original form or is another format acceptable? Will the organization monitor the activities of its employees? Does the environment foster open exchange of information and allow access to everyone unless specifically denied, or is information closely held and access denied to anyone unless specifically authorized access?

At the implementation end, limitations of existing systems may not allow for precise implementations of the defined organization policy. In the past, research and development have focused primarily on Department of Defense (DoD) policies based on user clearances and data classification. Some security mechanisms developed to support these DoD policies may not be useful for supporting the many other information security policies in use in other government agencies and the private sector. Therefore, other nontechnical (for example, administrative) controls may need to be implemented around the AIS to support the policy objectives, or the organization may accept certain security compromises in exchange for the benefits of automation. So, while a high-level policy decision requires mechanisms available to support the decision, hardware limitations may also restrict some of the possible choices. The overall architecture of the system may drive some of the policy choices as well. Decisions made for a stand-alone system may be quite different from those made for a large central computer room facility supporting hundreds of users over a local area network, or a distributed system spread out over a campus of buildings, or a cross-country communication network.

The rest of this essay discusses some of these refinement decisions that must be made in developing an implementable information security policy and some of the implications of the decisions.

Information security objectives. Information security or information technology (IT) security has long been considered to consist of three main objectives: the preservation of the information's confidentiality, integrity, and availability [COMM91]. Donn Parker, a founding father in the field of information security, has also suggested adding to the list of objectives authenticity ("the valid representation of that which it is intended to represent") and utility ("the state of being useful or fit for some purpose and designed for use or performing a service") [PARK91].

One of the first decisions in the policy refinement process is the prioritization of these security objectives. In many cases, the written policy will emphasize only one objective; however, for most environments all objectives are of some concern.

Confidentiality, or the prevention of unauthorized disclosure of the information, has been the primary security objective of many of the DoD security efforts. The Trusted Computer Security Evaluation Criteria (TCSEC) have confidentiality as their primary concern. One normally thinks of the actual information as being the concern for protection. In a communication system, though, in some cases, knowing who is communicating can be as sensitive as what is being communicated. The frequency and volume of communication could also be very sensitive. For example, increased message traffic to a military base could indicate an upcoming activity, or increased traffic between two financial entities could imply a financial strategy [SIMP90]. Methods of disclosure may also vary, and further refinements of the policy should address all applicable areas. Unauthorized disclosure may be accomplished through

- wiretapping or eavesdropping,

- unauthorized access to the information in the AIS either by unauthorized users (for example, hackers) or by authorized users accessing information to which they are not authorized,
- printouts of sensitive information sent to unattended printers in public areas, or
- large amounts of information leaving the organization on a floppy disk.

Having a detailed policy about required technical controls to forestall hackers will not adequately protect the organization if other aspects of the policy do not prohibit authorized users from wrongdoing.

Integrity, another information security objective, is a current research topic. There is no accepted single definition of what integrity encompasses. A multipart definition of integrity has been formulated as follows [NCSC91a]:

1. A subgoal of computer security which pertains to ensuring that data continues to be a proper representation of information, and that information processes continue to perform correct processing operations.
2. A subgoal of computer security which pertains to ensuring that information retains its original level of accuracy.
3. Sound, unimpaired, or perfect condition [NCSC88].

Two examples of the areas to consider in the policy refinement process are (1) in a communication system, changing the order in which messages are received or when they are received, and (2) repudiation: the denial of either the receipt or the origin of a communication.

The availability objective is generally seen as ensuring that the system is available to authorized users when needed. In life-support systems, for example, the availability objective is paramount. The recent widely published incidents of the Internet worm and the large-scale telephone outages in major metropolitan areas demonstrate the implications of denial of service. To date, little research has been done on availability concerns. The Canadian government has recently issued some guidance in this area.

Granularity of controls. A policy may affect few or many users. Some policies are intended to apply to all users — for example, on a DoD system, the policy enforcing the concepts of users' clearances and data classifications. Other policies may apply only to a specific application or type of information. The coarsest granularity is concerned with access to the entire computer system. If there is access to the entire system, when users are authorized access to the system, they have access to everything on the system. For single-user systems or systems dedicated to a specific task, this granularity of control may be sufficient. However, for multiuser systems running several applications, a finer granularity of control is probably required. Performance and overhead considerations are key in determining the level of granularity. The flexibility of the policy and the ability of the supporting mechanism to be tailored as needed are also considerations.

Another aspect of granularity is the issue of centralized versus decentralized control. With centralized control, a single authority controls all security aspects of the system, reducing the complexity of the security controls and the administrative demands on other users, while creating a potential single point of failure and bottleneck. Decentralized control, on the other hand, while technically and administratively more complex, puts the responsibility for many security functions in the hands of individuals, users who are probably most familiar with the particular requirements of the information.

Authority. A vital part of defining the information security policy is defining the authority for the policies and providing for the delegation of authority. The strength, scope, and span of the AIS controls depend, at least in part, on the authority of the person or organization that makes the rules and maintains the information and rules used by the system.

At the highest level, for example, the country's president and national policy or the chairman of the board and corporate policy are the top levels of authority for the policy. The level of authority is delegated as the policy is refined, and at some point, we reach the boundary between the administrative controls among people and the technical controls within the computer. Defining this hierarchy of controls is part of determining authority, and even within the AIS there will be levels of authority. For example, a user may have authority over his own working files, the project manager has authority over the project group's files, and the system administrator has authority over system files. In addition, there may be a security officer who has authority over all files.

Another aspect of defining levels of authority in a system involves clearly defining the different types of users and the responsibilities and authority of each. Many systems support the concept of groups and roles. The policy should also address related issues such as who defines group membership, when the use of groups is appropriate, whether a user can belong to more than one group, what the individual accountability requirements are within the groups, and how to resolve conflicts between individual user and group privileges. As an example, a system may define four types of users:

1. *User.* One who has authorized access to information on a computer. Authorizations may include the ability to read, write, delete, append, execute, and grant/rescind permissions to some objects.

For example, the user may be granted all permissions for his own working files, read-only access to project files, and no access to system files. For some information, the user may be the owner or custodian.

2. *Owner.* That individual manager or representative of management who has the responsibility for making and communicating judgments and decisions on behalf of the organization with regard to the use, identification, classification, and protection of a specific information asset. For example, the owner of the information may be the only one authorized to grant/rescind user privileges to access the information.

3. *Custodian.* One having authorized possession of the information and entrusted by the owner to provide proper protection in an ongoing operational environment.

4. *Security administrator.* The person responsible for the security of a system. Functions that the security administrator is expected to perform include auditing, initializing, and maintaining the security parameters of the system.

Policy decision attributes. Another aspect of refining the information dissemination/control policy is determining what information needs to be maintained about the users and the information being accessed to make the access control decision. The inputs to access control decisions are attributes of the user (for example, identity or clearance level), attributes of the information being accessed (classification level, document number, source of information), or some attribute of the environment or context of the system (time of day, status). Each system must select the relevant information to make an access control decision. In general, a policy specifies a comparison of subject and object attributes and/or context, but some policies may involve only one of these sets. Some attributes may support many policies (for example, user identity), while others have a one-to-one relationship with the policy (for example, source of the document may be used to support an acquisition support system). The following paragraphs briefly describe some of the attributes more commonly used. They are divided into five main categories: user characteristics, object characteristics, external condition, data content versus context attributes, and others.

User characteristics. User characteristics are commonly used in an access control decision process. Conceivably any attribute of a user could be used (age, sex, residence, place of birth, and so on), as identified by the appropriate policy. The following are some attributes used in current policies:

- *User clearance level.* This attribute is based on national policy that requires the protection of sensitive national-security-related information based on a user clearance level and the information classification. Traditional mandatory access controls have been developed to handle access control based on this attribute. However, there is little consensus on the applicability of these types of controls outside of systems handling the hierarchical user clearance/information classification scheme.
- *Need-to-know.* An attribute may be associated with a user that indicates that the user has the "need-to-know" for a certain type of information. This type of attribute is commonly used in the intelligence community. It also may apply in other sensitive applications, such as payroll, where only the payroll clerk and an employee's supervisor have the "need-to-know" for an employee's salary information.
- *Role.* Associated with a user may be the role in which the user is currently acting. For example, there may be the role of "ordinary user," which does not allow for any special privileges. Other role examples include position title, place in the organization, or function, such as security officer, data entry clerk, or department manager.
- *Group affinity.* This attribute might include nationality, employer, or user organization. Within the Department of Defense, the designation NOFORN (not releasable to foreign nationals) uses the nationality attribute, as does the marking NATO (which implies individuals from certain countries may have access if they have the appropriate need-to-know). Exceptions to either of these policies may also be specified in the form Releasable to *X*. NOCONTRACT (no contractor) is a policy used in the federal government to indicate only government employees may have access. For this policy, the employer attribute could be used. Company Confidential is a similar policy used in the private sector to limit access to individuals within the organization. Today, most of these policies are handled administratively.

Object characteristics. Other common attributes used in the access control decision process are attributes associated with the information being accessed. Several examples of these attributes follow:

- *Sensitivity labels.* Within the Department of Defense, there is a well-defined structure for labeling information with a hierarchical classification level (Unclassified, Confidential, Secret, or Top Secret). In addition, within the DoD/intelligence community, there are numerous compartments, categories, handling restrictions, and other markings used to further restrict access to information, and well-defined policies stating the access rules — for example, LIMDIS (limited distribution), ORCON (originator controlled), and PROPIN (proprietary information).

- *Information identifiers.* Other identifying attributes of the information could also be used — for example, the source or originator of the information, the owner of the information, and the document number.
- *Access control list.* Associated with the information may be a list of who is authorized to access the information. The owner of the information might be allowed to specify the list according to whatever criteria he chooses — for example, "who do I like" or need-to-know.

External condition. Some policies might be based on attributes associated with some external condition (context), such as time, location, or status. In addition, most of the other attributes previously discussed were assumed to be relatively static. Some policy decisions may be based on data that is expected to change:

- *Location.* Access may be based on location (for example, only a user from the main office is allowed access to some information).
- *Time.* Access to the information may vary with time (a press release policy where the information is highly sensitive until 9:00 a.m. on Tuesday morning, when it is made public).
- *Status.* A status variable may be maintained that reflects some condition in the real world that affects the policy decision made (crisis or exercise status).

Data content versus context. Some access control policies may depend on the value of the data. For example, user *X* may not be allowed to see the personnel file of anyone earning more than $20,000. More complex policies may depend on context — that is, the identity of other data fields. The use of static labels is a carryover from manual methods of determining the sensitivity of information. The dynamic determination of access based on content and context has been recognized as a potential replacement for static labels and is currently a topic of research, particularly in the database area [SMIT88]. The rules for such dynamic real-time evaluation of content and context are very complex and probably not well understood in the manual world.

Others. Most automated computer security and access control today focus first on secrecy policies. As research continues and technology develops to support the integrity and availability concerns, other types of attributes will surely be needed to support those areas as well.

Summary

This essay has reviewed some of the policy decisions necessary to refine a high-level information dissemination/control policy into an implementable access control policy. Information security policy issues that were discussed with regard to policy refinement include information security objectives, granularity of controls, authority, and policy decision attributes.

Conclusions

Many types of information security policies are in use today in the private sector and the federal government, but technology still has a long way to go to adequately and efficiently support most of these policies. However, the process of refining an organization policy is critical to understanding the security requirements of the information, not only to adequately protect the resources of the organization, but also to guide the direction of technology to provide the automated support for these policies.

Essay 8

Formal Methods and Models

James G. Williams and Marshall D. Abrams

The motivation for using formal methods in the context of trusted development stems primarily from their ability to ensure precision, consistency, and added assurance during the elaboration of security requirements, across different stages in the development of a trusted computing system. The subject matter of formal models and specifications can be illustrated by the various kinds of security attributes and requirements that have turned up in published security models. Examples discussed in this essay relate to nondisclosure policies, data integrity policies, and user-controlled policies. This essay concludes with a discussion of technical and methodological issues relating to the effective use of formal methods.

While it is appealing to approach security intuitively, it is important to recognize that many "good ideas" turn out to be not so good upon close inspection. This essay is concerned with several ways to increase the probability that the trust placed in an automated information system (AIS) is justified. It discusses a set of approaches described as *formal*, including models written in a formal notation and the use of formal proofs.

In the context of information security, *formal* methods imply use of specialized language and reasoning techniques. *Informal* methods, by way of contrast, are couched in natural language and rely on common sense. The use of a formal notation, especially one with a well-understood semantics, can improve the precision with which a security policy is stated. The use of formal proofs can provide added assurance that specified policy-enforcement techniques succeed in satisfying a formal definition of security. Formal methods and proofs are required by the TCSEC for systems rated B2 and above.

By way of introduction, we first discuss the motivation for formal methods, and then we look at their application during the construction of secure systems.

Doing the "right thing"

How is one convinced that a system does the "right thing"? There could be many contributing factors, such as the reputations of the hardware and software vendors, some degree of testing, and prior experience. In the case of computer security, these factors are frequently not sufficient. The security features of a computing system are often considered to be *critical* system functions whose correctness must be assured to a high degree because the consequences of failure are unacceptable. Yet we know from experience that latent security flaws in operating system modules or in the system's underlying hardware can cause trouble after years of use.

In general, inadequacies in a system can result either from a failure to understand requirements or from flaws in their implementation. The former problem, defining what a system should do, is relatively difficult in the case of security, so the definition has to be unusually precise and well understood. Moreover, subtle flaws can show up at any spot where the system design has left a loophole, so the definition must be faithfully reflected down through all the various stages of requirements analysis, design, and implementation [GASS87, Sec. 9].

A primary strategy for assuring security is to provide a *security policy model* that simultaneously models both a security policy and an AIS. Such a model consists of two submodels: a *definition of security* that captures the security policy, and *rules of operation* that show how the AIS enforces the definition of security. In the case of a formal model, it is possible to be quite precise in stating the definition of security and to rigorously prove that the rules of operation guarantee that the definition of security will be satisfied. In some formalizations, initial-state assumptions and rules of operation are treated as axioms. In this case, the definition of security becomes a theorem of the resulting theory, in addition to defining the modeled portion of the security policy.

Stages of elaboration in the creation of a secure system. To gain a more detailed understanding of the role of formal methods, it is necessary to investigate the various stages in the development of a secure AIS, as pictured in Figure 1.

High-level policy objectives specify what is to be achieved by proper design and use of a computing system; they constrain the relationship between the system and its environment. Higher-level security objectives for the use of DoD computing systems have been given in DoD Directive 5200.28, "Security Requirements for Automated Information Systems (AISs)" [DOD88a]. Objectives relating to the disclosure of classified information stem from Executive Order 12356 [REAG82] and can be found in 5200.1-R [DOD86] and in the TCSEC "control objectives." Classified and other sensitive information needed for the conduct of federal programs is protected by the Computer Security Act of 1987 [CONG87], which requires safeguards against loss and unauthorized modification. The collection, maintenance, use, and dissemination of personal information are protected by DoD Directive 5400.11 [DOD82, § E.2], by the Privacy Act of 1974 [CONG74], and by the Computer Matching and Privacy Protection Act [CONG88, CONG90]. Security objectives for federal systems have been enumerated by the US Congress [CONG82], Government Accounting Office [GAO88], and Office of Management and Budget [OMB82, OMB84]. Security objectives for commercial systems have been articulated by Clark and Wilson [CLAR87, CLAR89b]. Finally, site-dependent organizational security policies may also contribute objectives for the design and use of a secure computing system.

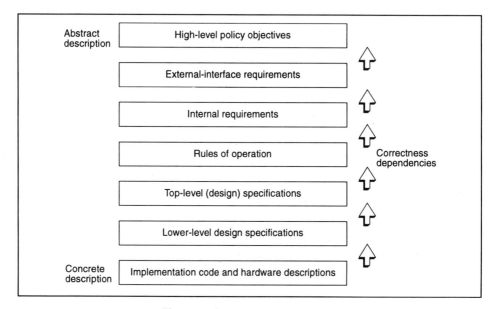

Figure 1. Stages of elaboration.

An *external-interface requirement* applies a higher-level objective to a computing system's external interface; it explains what can be expected from the system in support of the objective but does not unduly constrain internal system structure. The Goguen-Meseguer noninterference model is perhaps the best-known example of a formal external-interface requirement [GOGU82, GOGU84]. Various derivatives of this model have been advanced in support of DoD nondisclosure objectives. They say, essentially, that outputs from a system at a given nondisclosure level must not depend on inputs at a higher or incomparable level.

Internal requirements constrain relationships among system entities or components. The trusted computing base (TCB) emerges at this stage of elaboration; it contains those portions of the system which must be constrained to support the higher-level objectives and achieve the external-interface requirements. Bell and LaPadula's simple-security property is an example of an internal requirement; it says, essentially, that a subject may have read access to an object only if the security level of the subject dominates the security level of the object [BELL76]. Formal definitions of security usually contain a combination of internal and external-interface requirements. They are given as a formalization of a *system security policy* that specifies how an AIS helps prevent information and computing resources from being used to violate a corresponding organizational security policy [STER91].

Rules of operation explain how internal requirements are enforced by specifying access checks and related behaviors that guarantee satisfaction of the internal requirements. A top-level specification (TLS), like rules of operation, specifies the behavior of system components or controlled entities, but it is a more complete functional description of the TCB interface. There is no firm boundary between rules of operation and top-level specifications. Both explain how internal requirements are enforced by the TCB, but more detail is required in a TLS, including accurate descriptions of the error messages, exceptions, and effects of the TCB interface. In designing rules of operation, it may be convenient to separate access decisions from other kinds of system functionality, including the actual establishment or removal of access. This separation facilitates the exploration of new access control policies: Often, only the access-decision portion is affected by a change in policy because access enforcement depends only on the access decision, not on how it was made [LAPA90, ABRA90]. Isolation of the access-decision mechanism occurs in the LOCK system design [SAYD87] and in the security policy architecture of SecureWare's Compartmented Mode Workstation [NCSC91b, Sec. 2.2.1].

Finally, depending on the development methodology, there may be several lower levels of system description, ending at the level of executable code and hardware diagrams.

Correctness of elaboration. The appropriateness (as opposed to correctness) of higher-level objectives for the design of a computing system is determined by experience: Objectives are *appropriate* if they counter security threats and are achievable. Security objectives are seldom formalized. The adequacy of a system security policy is also a matter of judgment. Whether a system security policy is *adequate* plays a key role in the successful enforcement of an organizational security policy. In contrast to objectives, the adequacy of a system security policy can be supported through the use of engineering arguments showing how the system policy combines with constraints on the system's use and environment to achieve the identified objectives. Such an argument may be simpler and more persuasive if the system security policy is cast in terms of external-interface requirements. The formal definition of security must also be informally demonstrated to successfully codify the system security policy. For such a demonstration to be possible, it is necessary to assign real-world interpretations to the key constructs in the formal definition.

If the definition of security is cast at the system level, in terms of formal external-interface requirements, then the correctness of internal requirements can be formally proven. The TCB is largely determined by the elaboration of internal requirements. If the adequacy of the system security policy is based on external-interface requirements, then the trustworthiness of the TCB is established by requiring it to contain those portions of the system whose functionality must be constrained to prove the external-interface requirements. Notice that the TCB enforces only a system security policy. Enforcement of the corresponding organizational policy depends jointly on mechanisms within the TCB, on the correct input by system administrative personnel of parameters of the system security policy (for example, a user's clearance), and on the proper actions of users (proper labeling of input, password secrecy, and so on).

Rules of operation are normally verified by showing that they guarantee satisfaction of the internal requirements. This is a relatively straightforward mathematical effort. A formal top-level specification (FTLS) can be verified either by proving satisfaction of internal requirements or by proving that the FTLS is consistent with the rules of operation.

Formal assurance is not often applied to later stages of elaboration, due to cost constraints. Correctness of the implementation itself is established informally with the help of modern high-level languages, structured walk-throughs, and testing. During these later stages, it is essential to include in the TCB all code needed to support the TCB functionality identified at higher levels.[1] At whatever point formal assurance stops, there must be a transition from mathematics back to real-world concepts; the transition requires physical interpretations for all key concepts in the formal specification. These physical interpretations must be consistent with those used to establish the adequacy of the model's definition of security.

Formal security models

This section looks first at the basic concepts that turn up in security models, then at key distinctions among various kinds of security models, and finally at how these concepts and distinctions are reflected in well-known examples.

---

[1] The contents of the TCB might increase for other reasons as well [SCHA89, Sec. 2.2.1.2].

Basic concepts to be modeled. A secure computing system may decompose into data structures, processes, information about users, I/O devices, and security attributes for controlled entities. The following paragraphs discuss this decomposition in light of the need for accurate physical interpretations of model constructs.

As discussed earlier, the identification of controlled entities plays a crucial role in the development of a security policy model. For systems with a TCSEC evaluation of B2 or above, the controlled entities must include all system resources. An *explicitly controlled entity* is one that has explicitly associated security attributes. In addition to explicitly controlled entities, a system will have implicitly controlled entities: Such an entity might be contained in an explicitly controlled entity or might be a composite entity containing several explicitly controlled entities with differing security attributes.

A *data structure* is a repository for data with an internal state, or value, that can be written (changed) and/or read (observed) by processes (and possibly devices) using well-defined operations available to them. A data structure that is also a minimal, explicitly controlled entity is a *storage object.* Security attributes of storage objects may include security level and user access permissions (access permissions based on user identities, groups, and/or roles). In a model that includes security levels, a storage object has a unique security level, as a result of minimality. Storage objects may be combined to form multilevel data structures that are assigned their own security levels. Multilevel data structures called "containers" are used in the Secure Military Message System (SMMS) to address aggregation problems[2] [LAND84]; the level of a container is required to dominate the levels of any objects or containers inside it.

A *process* may create, destroy, and interact with storage objects and other processes, and it may interact with I/O devices. It has an associated runtime environment and is distinct from the program or code that defines it. An explicitly controlled process is a *subject.* It normally has a variety of associated security attributes, including perhaps a security level, hardware security attributes such as its process domain, the user and user group on whose behalf it is executing, indications of whether it belongs to the TCB, and, in this case, indications of whether it is exempt from certain access control checks. In general, the security-relevant attributes of a subject are part of its runtime environment.

User-related ideas often turn up in security models, despite the fact that users are not controlled entities and are not directly addressed in a system security policy. The users of a system may perform specific *user roles* by executing associated *role-support* programs. In general, a user may have a combination of several roles. As a matter of policy, a given

---

[2] An *aggregation problem* can occur when a user has access to individual pieces of data in a data set, but not to the entire data set.

user role may require system-mediated authorization and may provide specific system resources needed for performance of the role. The roles of administrative users are of particular interest in the construction of system security policies (for example, security administrator, system operator). Almost by definition, the corresponding role-support programs have security properties that are unacceptable without special constraints on the behavior of administrative users.

User interactions with the system may be modeled in terms of constraints on I/O devices if there is a convention for discussing the current user of a device. External policy on use of the system normally requires that devices pass information only to authorized users. An additional reason for interest in I/O devices is that I/O typically accounts for a large fraction of the TCB (in fact, upwards of 30 percent of an entire operating system [TANE87, Preface]). From the abstract perspective of a security model, I/O devices are encapsulated by TCB software and are typically seen as passive entities. In the TCSEC, devices may transport either unlabeled data or labeled data and are classified as *single-level* or *multilevel* devices accordingly. A significant aspect of multilevel devices is that they are not normally associated with a single security level; thus, they do not act like storage objects.

As already indicated, *security attributes* may be explicitly associated with explicitly controlled entities such as data structures, processes, and devices. Additionally, there may be security-relevant attributes of the system environment such as time of day, day of week, or whether the system or its environment is in a state of emergency.

Taxonomy of security models and attributes. Primary aspects of security policies that are usefully reflected in the security model include the policy objective, locus of policy enforcement, strength of policy enforcement, granularity of user designations, and locus of administrative authority. These policy aspects are normally reflected in the security attributes of controlled entities when the policies are formalized. Security attributes may be implicit; they need not be directly implemented in data structures.

AIS security objectives are traditionally classified as nondisclosure, integrity, or availability objectives [NCSC88a]. A draft Canadian standard has added accountability as a fourth, supporting objective [CSSC92]. *Nondisclosure* objectives guard against inappropriate disclosure of information. Associated system policies and attributes are used to prevent unauthorized release of information. There are two principal kinds of integrity objectives. *Source-integrity* objectives promote the correctness or appropriateness of information sources. Associated system policies guard against unauthorized creation or modification of information. *Content-correctness* objectives promote correctness of information. Associated system policies and attributes not only guard against unauthorized creation and modification of information but also actively assist in checking correctness of input and in ensuring correctness and appropriateness of software used for processing. *Availability* promotes the availability of information in a timely, useful fashion. Relatively little work has been done with availability policies per se. Availability is a broad topic that includes fault tolerance as well as the prevention of failures that can result from denial-of-service attacks, software errors, and/or design oversights. Finally, *accountability* promotes awareness of user actions. Associated accountability policies involve the collection, analysis, and use of audit data. There have been almost no formal models of accountability policies.

Informational policies maintain security attributes for use by the system and its users, whereas *access control* policies and attributes limit access to system resources and the information they contain. Access control policies are often described in terms of accesses by subjects or other active entities to objects or other passive entities. Access control is enforced by the *reference monitor* portion of the TCB. At lower levels of abstraction, the reference monitor is referred to as the TCB *kernel*.

Access control attributes may be classified according to what they control. A *loose* attribute is associated with a controlled entity, whereas a *tight* attribute is associated with both the entity and the information it contains. Access restrictions determined by tight access control attributes must propagate from one object to another when (or before) information is transferred, because control over the information must still be maintained after it is transferred. The *user granularity* of an attribute may be "coarse," controlling access on the basis of broadly defined classes of users, or it may be "per-user," controlling access by individual users and processes acting on their behalf. Finally, *centralized* authority implies that policy for use of attributes is predefined and takes place under the control of a system security administrator, whereas *distributed* authority implies that attributes are set by individual users for entities under their control. Most security policies use a mix of centralized and distributed authority.

A security attribute belonging to a partially ordered set may be referred to as a *level*. The use of partially ordered levels is usually associated with tight access control policies and constraints on information flow. Constraints on information flow can arise for several different reasons. As a result, a multifaceted policy might associate both *integrity levels* and *nondisclosure levels* with controlled entities to support both kinds of objectives. Within a computing system, the behavior of nondisclosure levels normally depends only on the abstract properties of the partial ordering, rather than on details of the internal structure of the levels (for example, hierarchical classifications and category sets). This fact can be exploited to enlarge the class of policies that a given system can enforce [BELL90].

Example definitions of security. Many if not most security models are deterministic state-machine models that formalize accesses of subjects to objects and are descendants of Lampson's access-matrix model [LAMP71]. In Lampson's model, objects are viewed as storage containers; the access control checks do not depend on the values stored in these containers. Security-critical aspects of the system state are summarized in an access matrix such as the one in Figure 2. In addition to state-machine models, other models of computation have been used successfully in formal definitions of security. Most of these are external-interface models based on event histories. The work of Andrew Moore is a good example [MOOR90].

Subjects	Objects		
	O_1	O_2	O_3
S_1	Read/Execute		
S_2		Write	
S_3	Execute		Read

Figure 2. An access matrix.

The following paragraphs discuss three classes of security models that have arisen in the literature, with emphasis on the taxonomic features mentioned above. All of these examples extend Lampson's access-matrix model by assigning security attributes to objects and adding definitions of security that constrain the possible forms that the access matrix can take.

Traditional mandatory access control (MAC)

- *Objective:* Nondisclosure
- *Locus of use:* Internal and external access control
- *Binding strength:* Tight
- *User granularity:* Coarse
- *Authority:* Centralized

MAC policies that meet TCSEC requirements must enforce nondisclosure constraints on information and may enforce integrity constraints as well. For systems evaluated at B2 and above, there are covert channel analysis requirements which imply that the controls are tight, controlling access to information as well as to individual objects and subjects. Although the TCSEC emphasizes labeling requirements at the user interface, this aspect of MAC has not received much formal attention. MAC policy identifies users only in terms of their associated maximum non-disclosure levels. Consequently, per-user granularity is not achieved because information available to a user at a given level is also available to other users at that or higher levels. In most systems, most users are not authorized to alter an object's nondisclosure level because decisions about availability of classified information are under centralized control.

A variety of external-interface models have been given for the nondisclosure objective, but not all succeed in providing tight controls on access to information. Noninterference is tight in the case of deterministic systems [GOGU82, GOGU84]. But the modeling problem is more difficult for nondeterministic systems whose behavior is not entirely predictable on the basis of system inputs [WITT90, GRAY91]. Internal requirements models are more common than external-interface models; they are "subject-point-of-view" models that describe constraints on the behavior of individual subject instructions. The best known of these internal constraints are the simple security property (a subject may read only at or below its level) and the *-property (a subject may write only at or above its level). But additional constraints on subject instructions are needed for tight policy enforcement, as are constraints on the scheduling of subjects [WILL91].

An interesting variant of traditional MAC is found in the floating-label policy of the Compartmented-Mode Workstation (CMW) [WOOD87, MILL90]. Each file has a floating "information" label and a fixed "sensitivity" label that dominates the floating label. The floating label is a potentially more accurate label that informs the user but is not used internally for access control. As implemented in the CMW, the floating-label mechanism is not tightly associated with information because of some unresolved covert channel issues.

Most MAC models require a subject that does not belong to the TCB to have a level that dominates the levels of its previous inputs and is dominated by those of its future outputs. This requirement fails to address the possibility that a subject may be able to produce information which is more highly classified than its inputs through some form of aggregation or inference. Definitions of security that accommodate aggregation have been given in the SMMS model [LAND84] and in the work of Meadows [MEAD90a]. Formal treatments of the inference problem are also available [HAIG90, DENN82, Ch. 6].

Traditional discretionary access control (DAC)

- *Objective:* Nondisclosure and integrity
- *Locus of use:* Internal access control
- *Binding strength:* Loose
- *User granularity:* Per user
- *Authority:* Distributed

The objectives behind DAC mechanisms are generally assumed to be user-dependent and have not been well articulated, for the most part. Typically, users are not automatically informed when they print out an object whose access is limited by another owner or, for that matter, when they copy it to another less-protected object. Authority to change discretionary attributes is usually distributed among all users on the basis of ownership, but this is not a TCSEC requirement. The primary distinguishing characteristic of the TCSEC DAC requirements is the ability to control access on a per-user basis.

Bell and LaPadula listed only one internal requirement for discretionary access: In each state, access to an object implied permission to access the information contained in that object [BELL76]. This and other internal requirements of their model were phrased as *state invariants*, properties that must hold in every "secure" state of the system. Unfortunately, their discretionary constraint is not actually satisfied in Unix-like systems because the following can happen: The owner of a file allows access to another user; a process acting on behalf of the other user opens the file; the owner revokes access; the process continues to access the file until it terminates. In Unix-like systems, the discretionary access constraint [BELL76] needs to be weakened to a *state-transition* constraint: If a process does not have a particular kind of access to a file in one state but does in the next state, then it must have had the necessary DAC permissions in the preceding state. The traditional weaknesses associated with DAC are not inherent. Methods for efficient revocation of access have also been devised [KARG89]. Moreover, tight access control mechanisms with per-user granularity and distributed control have been described and modeled by Millen and others [MILL84, ISRA87, GRAU89a, MCCO90].

Integrity à la Clark and Wilson

- *Objective:* Integrity
- *Locus of use:* External and internal consistency
- *Binding strength:* Loose
- *User granularity:* Per user and per procedure
- *Authority:* Centralized

The announced objective of Clark and Wilson's model [CLAR87] is to "ensure integrity of data to prevent fraud and errors." This objective implies some form of "external" consistency between data and real-world situations that the data refers to. External consistency, in turn, imposes recognizable structure on data, a form of "internal" consistency that can be automatically checked. Integrity is supported through various forms of external and internal redundancy. *Separation of duty* ensures that two or more users will independently be involved in key facts known to the computer, and *integrity-validation procedures* check the expected internal structure of data objects. Access control in the Clark-Wilson model is based on a set of triples of the form (user, program, object-list) used to control how and whether each user may access a given collection of objects. Manual methods are used to ensure that the triples adequately restrict user roles and enforce separation of duty. Clark and Wilson's original model was informal in the sense of this essay. Their access control mechanisms have since been formally modeled in the context of a Unix-based implementation [LAPA91]. But no formal definition of security is available for their work, and it is possible that their mechanisms do not fully address their objectives [MILL91].

Another access control mechanism that has been used to constrain user roles is type enforcement [BOEB85]. The type-enforcement mechanism itself assigns "types" to both subjects and objects. Subject types are referred to as "domains," and the accesses of each subject are constrained by a "type table" based on subject domain and object type. In the lock type-enforcement mechanism, each user has an associated set of domains that subjects running on his behalf may belong to, and these domains are used to define user roles [THOM90a]. In this way, the lock access control mechanisms can also enforce three-way constraints among users, subjects, and objects. Lock type enforcement lacks per-user granularity, but this may be an advantage, if role definitions change less frequently than users. Separation of duty itself has also turned up in role definitions for administrative users. Instructive examples include the Secure Military Message System model [LAND84] and the administrative roles for Secure Xenix [GLIG86], which is now referred to as Trusted Xenix.

Issues in the use of formal methods

Just how "formal" should formal methods be? What are the requirements for their use and what should they be? Is cost-effective use feasible within the current state of the art? The following paragraphs partially answer these questions.

Mathematical rigor and formal logical systems. There are three different common notions of "formal proof" that might be used with formal methods (and thus three somewhat different notions of what formal methods are):

1. *Mathematical proof.* A formal proof is a complete and convincing mathematical argument, presenting the full logical justification for each proof step, for the truth of a theorem or set of theorems [NCSC85].

2. *Machine-checked proof.* A formal proof is evidence accepted by a proof checker showing that a conjecture is a valid consequence of given axioms.

3. *Hilbert proof.* A formal proof in a theory T is a sequence of formulas, each of which is either an axiom of T or a direct consequence of preceding formulas in the sequence by virtue of a rule of inference associated with the underlying formal system [MEND79].

Mathematical proofs depend on the use of mathematical English for the formulation of a model or specification. They benefit from the basic flexibility of English, but they do not allow for automated assistance. Inaccuracies can result from the fact that there is no precise definition of mathematical English. In most contexts other than the TCSEC, mathematical proofs are regarded as *rigorous* but not *formal* — meaning that they conform to commonly accepted standards of mathematical reasoning but are not supported by a formal semantics in the sense mentioned below.

A machine-checked proof relies on the use of a mechanical *proof checker*, a tool with the following properties:

1. It accepts as input an assertion (called a conjecture), a set of assertions (called assumptions), and a proof.
2. It terminates and outputs either success or failure.
3. If it succeeds, then the conjecture is a valid consequence of the assumptions [NCSC89].

A proof checker has the potential of improving user efficiency. The need for such automated assistance is usually apparent in security policy models for operating systems. The definition of security typically contains dozens of requirements, possibly in the form of state invariants and state-transition constraints. There can easily be upwards of twenty rules of operation, each of which must be consistent with all of the requirements, and this amounts to hundreds of lemmas. Typically, a requirement deals with only a few state components, and any rule of operation that does not alter those components trivially fails to violate that requirement. Consequently, as many as 90 percent of the needed lemmas are likely to be essentially trivial.

A mechanical proof checker is unlikely to achieve a high level of assurance unless it is supported by a formal semantics that determines interpretations of formulas. In this case, a formula ϕ is a *valid consequence* of a set Ψ of formulas if and only if every interpretation that satisfies Ψ also satisfies ϕ. The problem is that, without a formal semantics, the proof checker might not be *sound* and might accept proofs of false conjectures. A *formal semantics* thus involves an interpretation function for formulas and an associated demonstration that a system's proof techniques are sound. Formal logical systems in the tradition of Hilbert, Tarsky, and others have excellent reputations for soundness, but they are not suitable for practical work because they fundamentally lack powerful semantic conventions [WILL90] needed for readable specifications and proofs [FARM86]. This conclusion has been independently arrived at in an unpublished "Review of Tools and Methods for System Assurance," by Andrews and MacEwen:

> Mathematical formalism has quite different goals for automated reasoning than for mathematical foundations. In the former context, the formalism exists primarily to aid human beings in the task of proving mathematical results. In the latter context, the goal is to clarify philosophical questions about basic mathematical questions: e.g., "What is a proof?", "What are the fundamental limitations of mathematical reasoning?", etc. The practical consequence is that mathematical formalism for automated reasoning ought to resemble quite closely the language of ordinary mathematics.

Fortunately, the goals of formal soundness and expressiveness are not fundamentally inconsistent. An Interactive Mathematical Proof System (IMPS) has been developed at MITRE [FARM91] that not only has an expressive semantics and convenient automated proof mechanism, but also is based on a rigorous, formal semantics whose soundness has been demonstrated relative to older, better known formal systems [FARM90].

Problems in the use of formal methods. Since the TCSEC was first published in 1983, there have been few successes in producing computing systems backed up by formal assurance. A lengthy investigation into the use of formal methods in trusted systems by Marvin Schaefer has the following conclusion:

> Hence, there is some reason to believe that there is value in the very analysis required to perform the exercise of producing a formal abstraction of the security-enforcing portion of a system design... However, it appears that the added value is much less than what is needed to conclude that a product with a verified FTLS is "secure" or even "more secure" than a comparable B3 product [SCHA89].

Schaefer identifies many of the underlying problems in the use of formal methods. The problems may be grouped into three main classes having to do with premature application of the methodology, holes in the chain of reasoning, and misapplication of the maxim "a chain is as strong as its weakest link."

Early efforts to develop trusted systems underestimated pragmatic difficulties involved in designing, building, and marketing them. Attempts to produce A1 systems without first developing and field testing B1, B2, or B3 systems led to expensive, poorly designed products with no established market. These efforts were accompanied by a belief that NCSC-endorsed verification tools were better than mathematical English. Until recently, the available tools have been unevaluated prototypes, and there has been little published experience in using them. The two existing systems are without a formal basis, for the most part, and they lag behind the current state of the art in automatic theorem proving. However, evaluations of the two currently supported tools have recently been performed, and relevant examples of their use are now available.

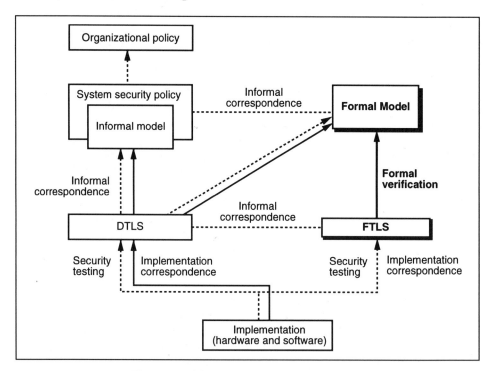

Figure 3. TCSEC assurance requirements.

Figure 3 summarizes TCSEC requirements for the use of formal methods in systems evaluated at B2 and above. Dotted lines indicate potential weaknesses found at B2, B3, and/or A1. To begin with, the TCSEC does not distinguish between the system security policy enforced by the AIS and organizational policies for use of the system. Consequently, there is no requirement for vendors to map their system security policy to higher-level objectives, including the "Control Objectives" of the TCSEC itself. In the case of nondisclosure objectives, some informal analysis is given in the TCSEC, and a vendor could voluntarily place additional information regarding higher-level objectives in the required "Philosophy of Protection."

The formal model is typically a subject-point-of-view model whose definition of security describes the reference monitor interface in terms of internal constraints on controlled entities. There is no requirement to model the system as a whole and thus no formal demonstration that the purported TCB has been correctly identified. Portions of the TCB not directly involved in access control are typically not modeled, and this tradition is affirmed in the *Trusted Network Interpretation* of the TCSEC [NCSC87a]. Devices are not explicitly modeled. TCB administrative software is not modeled. Typically, various subjects within the TCB are exempt from some part of the access mediation enforced by the TCB on non-TCB subjects, and the proper use of these exemptions is not modeled.

At B2 and above, there is no explicit requirement to make an English translation of the formal model available for nonspecialists, thereby reducing the likelihood of its consistency with the system security policy and descriptive top-level specification (DTLS).

Unmodeled portions of the TCB are constrained by the system security policy and the DTLS, but justification of the DTLS relative to the system security policy is required only at B3. At B2 there is also no requirement to justify the DTLS relative to either the formal model or the system security policy. The FTLS is required only at A1. The FTLS must be used in system testing, but there is no required correspondence between the FTLS and the DTLS, and unformalized portions of the DTLS no longer have to be tested. The implementation correspondence between the FTLS and the source code can take the form of a cheap syntactic comparison, and unresolved semantic discrepancies between the FTLS and the implementation are common. For example, the FTLS might use infinite storage buffers to avoid storage-allocation issues.

In summary, a strong link between an FTLS and a formal model need not be useful, if surrounding links above and below are weak or missing. The maxim that "a chain is only as strong as its weakest link" does not fully apply to the use of formal methods, however. The ideas and specifications associated with the development of a secure system tend to form an exponential hierarchy, with the vendor's definition of security at the top. Each succeeding layer (rules of operation, top-level description, pseudocode, TCB code, and hardware description) is several times the size of the previous layer, with perhaps a hundred lines in the definition of security and 100K lines of TCB source code. As a result, an error near the top of this hierarchy may affect a large portion of the finished code and is likely to be far more serious than an error farther down.

The proper use of formal methods. Formal methods are best suited to the study of relatively small, abstract issues. Researchers routinely provide formal security models, and the cost-effectiveness of formal methods for this purpose is generally accepted. Formal methods are especially important in those cases where traditional system testing is not effective. For example, one does not simply take down the Internet for system testing (at least not without getting a lot of attention). Thus, formal methods have their highest payoff at the early stages of product development and in studying global properties of large systems.

Formal methods can never fully replace informal development methods, and can never substitute for real experience. An A1 system makes much more sense as a follow-on to a series of B1 and B2 or B3 systems than as a new system developed from scratch.

NCSC-endorsed verification tools make sense as benchmarks that establish an expected level of rigor. They need not rule out the use of mathematical English or of newer, unendorsed verification tools, if the resulting evidence compares favorably with that of similar efforts based on the use of endorsed tools. The TCSEC wording already conveys this policy on the use of endorsed tools, and it would be counterproductive to strengthen the requirement beyond what is explicitly stated.

Rule-Set Modeling of a Trusted Computer System

Leonard J. LaPadula

This essay describes a new approach to formal modeling of a trusted computer system. A finite-state machine models the access operations of the trusted computer system while a separate rule set expresses the system's trust policies. A powerful feature of this approach is its ability to fit several widely differing trust policies easily within the same model. We will show how this approach to modeling relates to general ideas of access control, as you might expect. We will also relate this approach to the implementation of real systems by connecting the rule set of the model to the system operations of a Unix System V system. The trust policies we demonstrate in the rule set of the model include the mandatory access control policy of Unix System V/MLS, a version of the Clark-Wilson integrity policy, and two supporting policies that implement roles.

The modeling approach we will discuss grew out of several ideas developed in the Generalized Framework for Access Control project directed by Abrams [ABRA90]. The vision of that project was to gain greater utility in our trusted computer systems by creating a technology for putting a rich set of various access control policies into a single trusted computer system. Our modeling approach responds to the challenge of that vision, as expressed in these objectives:

- Make it easy to state, formalize, and analyze access control policies besides traditional mandatory access control (MAC) and discretionary access control (DAC), to increase the availability of diverse, assured security policies.
- Make it feasible to configure a system with security policies chosen from a vendor-provided set of options with confidence that the re-

sulting system's security policy makes sense and will be properly enforced.

- Construct the model in a manner that allows one to show that it satisfies an accepted definition of each security policy it represents.

The remainder of this essay has three parts:

- First we discuss the Generalized Framework for Access Control view of a trusted system. GFAC motivates the approach we have taken to modeling.
- Next we describe the modeling approach.
- Finally we illustrate elements[1] of the state-machine model and the rule-set model — the two components of the complete model.

Overview of the Generalized Framework for Access Control

The Generalized Framework for Access Control thesis asserts that all access control is based on a small set of fundamental concepts [ABRA90]. Borrowing some of its terminology and concepts from the ISO "Working Draft on Access Control Framework" [ISO90], GFAC starts with the premise that all access control policies can be viewed as rules expressed in terms of attributes by authorities. The three main elements of access control in a trusted computer system are:

>Authority: An authorized agent must define security policy, identify relevant security information, and assign values to certain attributes of controlled resources.

>Attributes: Attributes describe characteristics or properties of subjects and objects. The computer system will base its decisions about access control on the attributes of the subjects and objects it controls. Examples of attributes are:

>>security classification
>>type of object
>>domain of process
>>date and time of last modification
>>owner identification

---

[1] The reader will find additional analysis and a complete policy model in my report [LAPA91].

Rules: A set of formalized expressions defines the relationships among attributes and other security information
for access control decisions in the computer system, reflecting the security policies defined by authority.

The generalized framework explicitly recognizes two parts of access control — adjudication and enforcement. We use the term
access control decision facility (ADF) to denote the agent that adjudi-
cates access control requests, and the term access control enforcement facility (AEF) for the agent that enforces the ADF's decisions.
In a trusted computer system, the AEF corresponds to the system
functions of the trusted computing base (TCB) and the ADF corresponds to the access control rules that embody the system's security policy, also part of the TCB. Figure 1 depicts the generalized
framework in the terms just described.

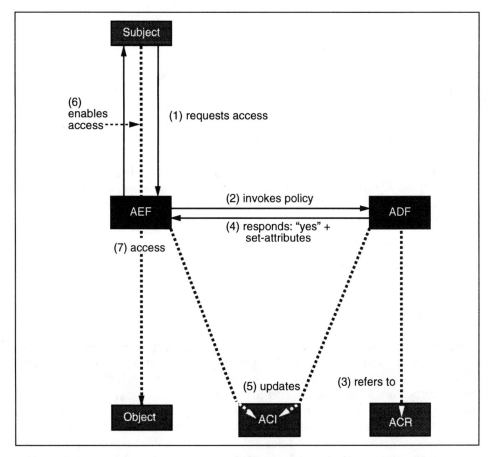

Figure 1. Overview of the Generalized Framework for Access Control.

Formal modeling approach

Background. The GFAC goals translate into these objectives for our formal model:

- Develop a modeling technology in which it is easy to express various policies besides traditional MAC and DAC.
- Fashion the modeling technology to enable the selection of a desired set of security policies from some preevaluated set without having to reevaluate the resulting collection of policies.
- Provide for showing that a model satisfies an accepted definition of each security policy enforced by the model.

Our rule-set modeling has much in common with traditional state-machine modeling. It differs significantly, though, in the way it sets up access rules. Models like the Bell-LaPadula model [BELL76] and the recent Compartmented Mode Workstation model [MILL90] include access control rules in their rules of operation. In these models, an Open File rule describes both access policy and system behavior. The rule uses built-in criteria to decide whether to permit the Open File request, and the rule describes the behavior of the modeled system as a state transition. A typical nondisclosure criterion is whether the security level of the subject making the Open File request dominates the security level of the object it wants to open. Information affected by the transition might include the set of objects currently held open by the subject that made the request.

Our approach separates the decision criteria from the state-transition descriptions. A rule set embodies the security policies of the modeled system, while a finite-state-machine model describes its behavior. Thus we have partitioned the system function (Open File) into two operations:

1. Decide if the request should be granted. (Is the subject allowed to open the referenced object?)
2. Grant the request (open the file) or not (return an error indication).

Figure 2 depicts this rule-set approach.

Structure of the model. A trusted computer system built according to our modeling plan has two major parts inside its trusted computing base (TCB). In the ISO terminology we mentioned earlier, our TCB has an access enforcement facility (AEF) and an access decision facility (ADF). In this scheme, the AEF owns and operates the system operations that are available to computer programs that it runs. The ADF keeps the rule set that expresses the access policies of the system. When a computer program attempts to execute some system operation, the AEF appeals to the

ADF for an access decision. As we pointed out earlier, the rule set of the ADF expresses the access policies of the system. Thus, the ADF will evaluate the rule set each time the AEF appeals to it for an access decision. Naturally, the AEF will provide some set of arguments to the ADF when it invokes the ADF. These arguments provide or define whatever access control information (ACI) the ADF needs for decision making.

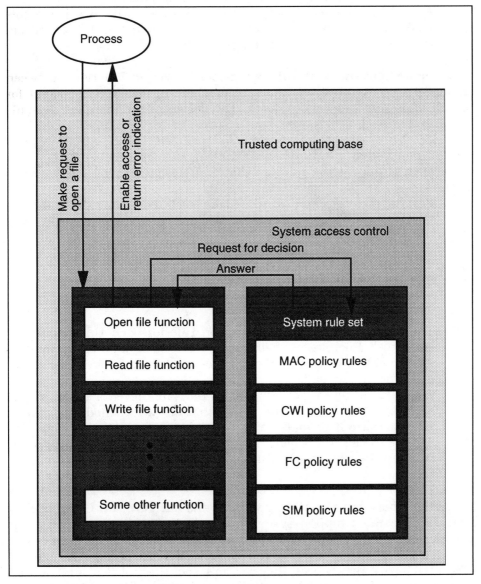

Figure 2. Rule-set modeling.

Applying an AEF-ADF partitioning to our modeling gives us:

- A model of the system operations, constituting an AEF. We treat this model as a state machine and call it the state-machine model. The state-machine model abstractly describes the interface of computer processes to the system's TCB and defines the relationship of the system operations to the system's trust policies.
- A model of the security policy, viewed as an ADF. We define this model as a rule set and call it the rule-set model. It defines the security policies of the trusted computer system.

The state-machine and rule-set models need an interface between them. This interface allows the state machine to invoke the rule set for adjudication of a process's request. The design of the interface depends on several critical factors:

- What system will the state-machine model describe?
- How detailed is the state machine's representation of the system to be?
- Will the rule set deal with the same level of detail as the state machine, or will it deal with abstractions of the system's elements and behavior?

We have decided these issues for this essay as follows:

- The state-machine model targets the class of Unix System V systems.
- The state machine has a transition rule for each Unix System V system call. Each transition rule is an abstraction of its corresponding system call, but the abstraction preserves the essential functionality of the system call.
- The rule set addresses essentially the same level of detail as the state machine. But, to the extent that our art of modeling allows, we generalize it to make it useful with other state machines. You will see the form this generalization has as we discuss the interface between the state machine and the rule set in the next section.

Interface between the state machine and the rule set. Our modeling mirrors a trusted computer system in which the TCB has two parts. The access control enforcement (AEF) part affords system services to processes and determines the behavior of the system. The access control decision facility (ADF) part remembers the system's security policies and decides whether processes' requests satisfy those policies. The AEF part communicates with the ADF part through some appropriate interface. Our modeling approach has the same structure:

- The state-machine model (enforcement agent) corresponds to the AEF part of the trusted computer system's TCB.
- The rule-set model (judicial agent) corresponds to the ADF part of the TCB.

The state-machine model has rules of operation. Each rule of operation abstractly describes some behavior of the modeled system. The rule-set model has rules of access. Each rule of access describes some security policy of the modeled system.

We relate the models to each other with an interface that permits communication between the state machine and the rule set. Briefly, the communication occurs through messages. We will see the formal structure of these messages later.

Let's consider an example, using a real system as an analog of our model's structure. The real system for this example is Unix System V. We imagine that its kernel has two parts — an AEF part, which we call the AEF-kernel, and an ADF part, which we call the ADF-kernel. Imagine that a process invokes the Open system call to open a file for reading. The AEF-kernel sends a message to the ADF-kernel to find out if the process's request is valid. The message must contain or reference the access control information (ACI) needed by the ADF-kernel to make its decision. The ACI could include many possible items of information. Some basic information items likely to be needed are identification of the requesting process, identification of the file to be opened, and attributes of the process and the file. The ADF-kernel may use other access control context (ACC) information, such as the time of day, to make its decision. The ADF-kernel returns the decision to the AEF-kernel. The AEF-kernel then completes the Open system call, enabling the requested access if the decision was favorable, or returning an error message if not.

Our model operates in much the same manner. The state-machine model corresponds to the AEF-kernel. Corresponding to each system call supported by the AEF-kernel we have a rule of operation in the state-machine model. The rule-set model corresponds to the ADF-kernel. The rule-set model expresses the security policies of the modeled system in its rules of access. Each rule of operation in the state-machine model "invokes" the rule-set model with a function we call "Access-Rules." The arguments of the function Access-Rules correspond to the messages exchanged between the AEF-kernel and ADF-kernel.

Again, let's consider a simple example based on the notion of an Open system call. A rule of operation for abstractly describing the Open operation might be the following:

Open (file_name, mode):
CONDITION
    Access-Rules (open, mode, current_process_aci, file_aci)
EFFECT
    Open_Set (current_process) = Open_Set (current_process) UNION (file_name,
mode)

The CONDITION means that if the function Access-Rules is true, then do the actions given in EFFECT. In this case, the EFFECT is to add the named file to the set of files accessible by the requesting process and to set its access mode.

We define the interface between the state machine and the rule set by specifying the valid arguments for Access-Rules. At each invocation of the rule-set model, the state-machine model identifies the desired action of the process and a set of relevant attributes (access control information). Hence, we can define the needed interface with a set of requests with appropriate access control information. We will use several terms for the needed information. We explain those terms now to show their specific meanings for the interface definition:

file	A set of attributes associated with a Unix file.
directory	A set of attributes associated with a Unix directory.
ipc	A set of attributes associated with a Unix storage object used for interprocess communication: These objects may be message queues or semaphores.
scd	A set of attributes associated with a Unix system object that stores system control data (hence the acronym "scd"). The inode is an example. When we use "scd" in the subsequent interface definition, we also show what the scd is referring to — either a file or a directory.

A final word is needed here before presenting the interface messages. The reader will see the requests CHANGE-ROLE and MODIFY-ATTRIBUTE in the interface. These requests have no counterparts in the set of Unix System V system calls. We include them to help exposition of various security policies later in this essay. Then their meaning and use should become clear.

Each element of the interface definition has the form "request (argument list)." The request usually identifies the action that a process wants to do, but it also may be used for communication of information from the state-machine model to the rule-set model. The argument list identifies a set of access control information (ACI). In the list that follows, terms like "process" or "object" are shorthand for "attributes associated with a process" or "attributes associated with an object." Modelers should choose whatever requests make sense for the system they wish to model. We describe requests here that seem appropriate for detailed modeling of systems like Unix System V. You should notice these features:

- For each system call of Unix System V, as defined by Bach [BACH86], there is at least one request that relates to its functionality. On the other hand, a single rule of operation that models a system call might use several requests. A Create File rule of operation, for example, might invoke Access-Rules twice. First it might need to know if the requesting process has permission to search the directory in which the file will be located. Then, if the search is valid, it again would appeal to the Access-Rules for a policy decision on creating the file.
- The set of requests we have defined here is not minimal. For example, we have several requests that represent variations of writing to an object; for these separate requests we could have substituted a single request with arguments. I believe my choice enhances the intuitive understanding of the modeler and affords greater flexibility in modeling the class of systems we have targeted.

Here is the list of requests:

- ALIAS (process, file). The process is attempting to create an alias for the file. A state-machine model of Unix would use this request in its rule of operation for linking to a file.
- ALTER (process, ipc). The process wishes to access the control information for an ipc-type object. This request relates to reading or modifying data about the ipc-type object. This is similar to the modify-permissions-data and get-permissions-data requests defined below for the access control information associated with files and directories. In a Unix environment this request would be used by the system calls that control message queues, semaphores, and shared memory.
- CHANGE-OWNER (process, scd(file/directory)). The process wants to change the owner of the indicated object. An scd object is one that contains system access control information. In Unix, this is the inode. The parenthetical remark "file/directory" means that the scd pertains to a file or directory. The attribute set passed to the

rule-set model will consist of attributes of the file or directory and an attribute that identifies the object to be modified.

- CHANGE-ROLE (process, role attribute, role value). The process wants to change the role of the owner of the process. The argument "role attribute" names the attribute to modify, and the argument "role value" gives the desired role.
- CLONE (process1, process2). Process1 wants to create a clone of itself: process2. In a Unix environment this corresponds to a fork system call.
- CREATE (process, file/directory/scd/ipc). The process wants to create a new file, directory, scd-type object, or ipc-type object.
- DELETE (process, file/directory/ipc). The process wants to delete the indicated object.
- DELETE-DATA (process, file). The process wants to truncate (remove all data from) the file.
- EXECUTE (process, file). The process wants to execute the file. This request compares to the Unix exec system call.
- GET-PERMISSIONS-DATA (process, scd(file/directory)). The process wants to read discretionary access permissions for the indicated file or directory.
- GET-STATUS-DATA (process, scd(file/directory)). The process wants to read status data about the file or directory. This corresponds to a Unix stat system call, which can return information such as file type, file owner, access permissions, and file size.
- MODIFY-ACCESS-DATA (process, scd(file/directory)). The process wants to modify access information about the object, such as the time of last modification. This compares to the Unix utime system call.
- MODIFY-ATTRIBUTE (process, user/process/object, attribute, value). The process wants to modify an attribute of the user, the process, or an object. The argument "attribute" names the attribute to change and the argument "value" gives the new value.
- MODIFY-PERMISSIONS-DATA (process, scd(file/directory)). The process wants to modify discretionary access permissions of the object. This request parallels the Unix chmod system call.
- READ (process, directory). The process wants to read data from the indicated directory.
- READ-ATTRIBUTE (process, user/process/object, attribute). The process wants to read an attribute of the user, the process, or an object. The argument "attribute" names the attribute to read.
- READ&WRITE-OPEN (process, file/ipc). The process wants to open the object for reading and writing. In Unix the object is either a file or a message queue.
- READ-OPEN (process, file). The process wants to open the file for reading.

- SEARCH (process, directory). The AEF part of the TCB needs to read the directory as part of some other operation requested by the process. This corresponds to searching a directory in Unix, so all rules of operation that model system calls using the Unix namei subroutine will invoke Access-Rules with this request.
- SEND-SIGNAL (process1, process2). process1 wants to send a signal to process2. This parallels the Unix kill system call.
- TERMINATE (process). The system has terminated the process. The state-machine model gives this request to the rule-set model for information only. This request enables the rule-set model to update its information base, if necessary.
- TRACE (process1, process2). process1 wants to trace process2. The rule set will interpret this to mean "read/write the memory of process2." This equates to the Unix ptrace system call.
- WRITE (process, directory). The process wants to write data to the directory. The Unix creat system call may have to search a directory before creating a file. Thus, in a Unix system built according to our modeling paradigm, the creat system call would use this request to check the process's permission to search the directory involved.
- WRITE-OPEN (process, file). The process wants to open the file.

Examples of the model components

State-machine model. The Unix System V system as described by Bach [BACH86] shapes the nature of our state-machine model. We will not develop a complete state-machine model in this essay since we want to explain the modeling approach, not build a trusted computer system. On the other hand, we have tried to achieve the breadth and depth of coverage needed to make obvious what a modeler should do. To this end, this section contains rules of operation that abstractly describe many of the key system calls of Unix System V. The selected rules adequately demonstrate the modeling approach we have described.

Introduction. The state-machine model is a state-transition machine. Its rules of operation define the valid transitions for the modeled system. Recall we said earlier that the state machine has a transition rule for each Unix System V system call. We validly could have chosen instead to make the model rules more primitive than system calls. Doing so gives the benefit of simpler rules of operation but has the undesirable effect of moving the model another level away from the real system. The additional level demands a one-to-many mapping of system call to rules of operation by the designer or evaluator of the system.

An example will show the difference between the two approaches. Taking the more abstract approach, we might define the Open rule of operation in the following form, as we saw earlier:

```
Open (file_name, mode):
CONDITION
    STATUS(file_name) = "active"
    AND
    Access-Rules (open, mode, current_process_aci, file_aci)
EFFECT
    Open_Set (current_process) = Open_Set (current_process) UNION (file_name,
mode)
```

The Unix open system call has an option to create the named file under certain circumstances. It also provides an option for the process to cause the file to be truncated (have all its data erased) during opening. The above form of the Open rule does not reflect these options. In the following form[2] we show not only these options but additional details of the system call such as directory searching.

Rules of operation. This section gives the state-machine model specification for the following rules of operation:

> Open
> Read
> Fork
> Create
> Execute
> Kill
> Unlink

• **Open** (file_name, mode, truncate_option, create_option[3]). The open system call is the first operation a process performs to access data in a file. When successful, the call returns a file descriptor that will be used by other file operations, such as reading, writing, determining status, and closing the file. If the file does not exist and the create_option argu-

---

[2] The reader with computer systems experience should have no trouble understanding the language that expresses the rules. The reader who may not be familiar with computer programming languages or who may want to verify the meaning of a language form should see Appendix A, which gives a description of the language as well as the modeling constructs used.

[3] The arguments used in this essay are similar to those defined by Bach [BACH86], but I have changed the names, invented some new ones, and sometimes rearranged them for clarity of the rules.

ment indicates that the process wishes to create the file in this case, then the call will create the file and open it in the mode specified. The mode argument indicates the type of open, such as reading or writing, and the truncate_option shows whether the process wants all the current data in the file cleared.

IF
    Access-Rules(search, directory_name[current directory or directory from
        specified pathname[4]]
THEN
  SELECT CASE STATUS(file_name)
    CASE STATUS(file_name) == "active" (* the directory search was valid
        and the file exists *)
      SELECT CASE truncate_option
        CASE ON
          IF
            NOT (Access-Rules(delete-data, current_process, file_name)));
          THEN
            error-exit;
          ELSE
            [* truncate the file *];
            [* open the file *];
            OPEN(current_process, file_name) =
              OPEN(current_process, file_name) SET-UNION {mode};
            set-attributes;
            normal-exit;

        CASE OFF
          IF
            (mode == "read" **AND**
            Access-Rules(read-open, current_process, file_name))
            OR
            (mode == "write" **AND**
            Access-Rules(write-open, current_process, file_name))
            OR
            (mode == "read&write" **AND**
            Access-Rules(read&write-open, current_process, file_name))
          THEN
            [* open the file *];
            set-attributes;

---

[4] I show the first argument to the open call (and others) as file_name. This may actually be a pathname involving one or more directories. When file_name is used as a parameter to the Access-Rules, the reader should understand that the name of the file itself, not the full pathname, is intended.

```
        OPEN(current_process, file_name) =
            OPEN(current_process, file_name) SET-UNION {mode};
        normal-exit;
    ELSE
        error-exit;


CASE STATUS(file_name) == "unused" (* the directory search was
    valid and the file does not exist *)
    SELECT CASE create_option
        CASE create_option == ON
            (* create the file and open it for the type of access
                specified by the mode argument *)
            [* create the attribute set for the file and set the basic
                values, such as object-identifier *]
            IF
                Access-Rules(create, current_process, file_name);
            THEN
                set-attributes;
                [* create the file *]
                (* check whether current_process may open the file *)
                IF
                    (mode == "read" AND
                    Access-Rules(read-open, current_process, file_name))
                    OR
                    (mode == "write" AND
                    Access-Rules(write-open, current_process, file_name))
                    OR
                    (mode == "read&write" AND
                    Access-Rules(read&write-open, current_process, file_name));
                THEN
                    set-attributes;
                    [* open the file *]
                    OPEN(current_process, file_name) =
                        OPEN(current_process, file_name) SET-UNION {mode};
                    normal-exit;
                ELSE
                    error-exit;
            ELSE
                error-exit;
        CASE create_option == OFF
            error-exit;
    CASE STATUS(file_name) == "inaccessible" (* the directory search
            failed — e.g., permission denied, directory nonexistent, etc. *)
        error-exit;
END-SELECT
```

ELSE
    error-exit;

• **Read** (file_descriptor, buffer, size). The read system call causes a specified number of bytes (size) to be moved from an open file (file_descriptor) to a data structure (buffer) in the requesting process. The read starts at the next byte after the last byte transferred by a read call so that successive reads of a file deliver the file data in sequence.

IF
    "read" is in OPEN(current_process, object[identified by file_descriptor])
    AND
    Access-Rules(read, current_process, object)
THEN
    set-attributes;
    [* read the file *];
    normal-exit;
ELSE
    error-exit;

• **Fork** ( ). The fork system call enables a process to create a new process. The created process, called the child process, is identical to the process that creates it, the parent process, except for their process identifiers. Also, some process-internal variable or variables of the child are set by the kernel so that the child process can recognize itself as the child when it runs, presumably so that it can do something different from its parent.

[* create the new process if resources are available *];
IF
    Access-Rules(clone, current_process, new_process);
THEN
    set-attributes;
    Open(new_process, object) = Open(current_process, object) for all objects
      in the system;
    (* the new process inherits access to all the objects the current process
      can access *)
    [* complete the fork operation *]
    normal-exit;
ELSE
    error-exit;

• **creat** (file_name, mode). The creat (create) system call creates a new file in the system. But if the file already exists, the kernel opens it and truncates it if permissible.

IF

Access-Rules(search, directory_name[current directory or directory from specified pathname]

THEN

SELECT CASE STATUS(file_name)

CASE STATUS(file_name) == "active" (* the directory search was valid and the file exists *)

(* check if it is permissible to delete the data in the file and write-open it *)

save (* attribute values of current_process and file_name *);

IF

Access-Rules (delete-data, current_process, file_name)

THEN

set-attributes;

IF

Access-Rules (write-open, current_process, file_name)

THEN

set-attributes;

(* clear the file and write-open it *);

OPEN(current_process, file_name) = OPEN(current_process, file_name) SET-UNION {mode};

normal-exit;

ELSE

restore (* restore the attribute values of current_process and file_name *);

error-exit;

ELSE

error-exit;

CASE STATUS(file_name) == "unused" (* the directory search was valid and the file does not exist *)

(* check if it is permissible to create the file, write the relevant directory, and write-open the file *)

save (* save the attribute values of current_process, file_name, and directory *);

IF

Access-Rules (create, current_process, file_name)

THEN

set-attributes;

IF

Access-Rules (write, current_process, directory (* directory is found by the namei kernel subroutine in Unix *))

THEN

set-attributes;

IF

Access-Rules (write-open, current_process, file_name)

THEN
    set-attributes;
    (* create the file, with appropriate directory entry, and
      write-open it *);
ELSE
    restore (* restore the attribute values of current_process,
      file_name, and directory *);
    error-exit;
ELSE
    restore (* attribute values of current_process, file_name,
      and directory *);
    error-exit;
ELSE
    error-exit;
ELSE
  error-exit;

• **exec** (file_name). The exec system call causes process execution to
continue with the code contained in the named file. This should not be
confused with creating a new process, which is the normal result of a
fork system call. The execution of the code specified by the exec system
call is part of the process that invoked the exec system call. Thus, the
open files of the process are still open after a successful exec.

IF
  Access-Rules(search, directory_name[current directory or directory from
    specified pathname]
THEN
  SELECT CASE STATUS(file_name)
    CASE STATUS(file_name) == "active" (* the directory search was valid
      and the file exists *)
    IF
    Access-Rules (execute, current_process, file_name)
    THEN
      set-attributes;
      (* carry out the "exec"ing of the filename *);
      normal-exit;
    ELSE
      error-exit;
    CASE STATUS(file_name) == "unused" (* the directory search was valid
      and the file does not exist *)
    error-exit;
ELSE
  error-exit;

• **kill** (process-identifier, signal). The kill system call enables a process to send one of a number of signals to another process. The SIGKILL signal causes the kernel to terminate the target process if appropriate authorizations are satisfied.[5] If the signal is any of the other valid signals, then the process(es) receiving the signal will process the signal in accordance with the specification established by its (their) signal system call(s) or with the default specification for the signal.

```
IF
    (* the process-identifier and signal arguments are valid *)
THEN
  SELECT CASE signal
    CASE signal is SIGKILL (* the sending process is attempting to kill a
          process or group of processes *)
      FOR-EACH process (* specified by the process-identifier argument *):
        (* terminate the process *)
        OPEN(process, file_name) = { }[6]  for every file_name;
        Access-Rules(terminate,[7] process);
      END-FOR-EACH;
      normal-exit;

    CASE ELSE
      FOR-EACH process (* specified by the process-identifier argument *):
        IF
          Access-Rules(send-signal, current_process, process) == YES
        THEN
          set-attributes;
        (* send the specified signal to the process *)
        ELSE
          error-exit;
      END-FOR-EACH;
      normal-exit;
ELSE
  error-exit;
```

---

[5] The real or effective user ID of the sending process must match the effective or saved effective user ID of the receiving process, unless the effective user ID of the sending process is superuser. Recall that we do not model superuser access controls or controls based on user IDs.

[6] { } denotes the empty set.

[7] Recall from the interface definition that the terminate message means that the system has terminated the process. The state-machine model gives this request to the policy model for information only. It enables the policy model to update its information base, if necessary.

- **unlink** (file_name). The unlink system call removes a directory entry for a file. In general, a number of directory entries may exist for a given file, created via the link system call. A file is not deleted until all its names (links) have been removed.

IF
  Access-Rules(search, directory_name[current directory or directory from specified pathname]
THEN
  SELECT CASE STATUS(file_name)
  CASE STATUS(file_name) == "active" (* the directory search was valid and the file exists *)
    IF
      (* unlinking the file will delete the file itself *)
    THEN
      IF
        Access-Rules (delete, current_process, file_name)
      THEN
        (* delete the file — remove directory entry and return file space to system pool *);
        STATUS(file_name) = "unused";
        normal-exit;
      ELSE
        error-exit;
    ELSE
      (* unlink the file — remove directory entry *);
      normal-exit;
  CASE STATUS(file_name) == "unused" (* the directory search was valid and the file does not exist *)
    error-exit;
ELSE
  error-exit;

Additional remarks. The modeler has choices to make. A fundamental decision is whether the rules of operation of the state-machine model will map one-to-one to system calls or not. Successful modeling can be done either way. The differences between the two approaches can be characterized as trade-offs, as you might expect. If the rules of operation are one-to-one with the system calls, they include a wealth of detail and make subsequent assurance efforts easier. If the rules of operation map many-to-one to the system calls, the rules can be simpler and the model will then be easier to understand and analyze. The modeler must decide how to approach this issue, based on an understanding of the modeled class of systems and the purposes of the modeling.

Having decided the basic approach, the modeler should examine each operation the system provides for processes. In Unix System V, these operations are system calls. The modeler should figure out what each system call does to the state of the system and whether it relates to the system's security policies. Every system call potentially has relevance to some policy. What we mean here are the policies defined by the rule-set model. Some system calls have no relevance to traditional mandatory access control policy but significant relevance to the Clark-Wilson integrity policy. Looking at the system calls in this way attracts attention to needed constraints in one or more policies that the modeler might otherwise overlook.

The modeler should decide if the rules of operation needed to model the system calls exist in the state-machine model. If not, they should, of course, be added to the model. The modeler also should define how each rule uses the interface definition to invoke the rule-set model.

This approach gives high confidence that a system's implementation could clearly derive from the elements of the formal model instead of additionally depending on many design and policy decisions not addressed in the model.

Rule-set model. This section describes a rule-set model for a trusted computer system that implements four policies:

- a mandatory access control (MAC) policy,
- a Clark-Wilson integrity (CWI) policy,
- a functional control (FC) policy, and
- a security information modification (SIM) policy.

The MAC policy represents the MAC policy of American Telephone and Telegraph's System V/MLS, Release 1.2.1. This system[8] received a B1 rating from the National Computer Security Center in 1989. The MAC policy shows the traditional security policy for a trusted computer system. Its inclusion shows that other policies can be integrated with the traditional nondisclosure security requirements. This policy uses a lattice of security levels as the basis for its access decisions. The CWI policy provides control over modification of information by regulating the transactions that users can apply to files of information. This policy uses roles and types and execute-control lists (the Clark-Wilson triples). Its inclu-

---

[8] The evaluated product was System V/MLS, Version 1.1.2, running with Unix System V, Release 3.1.1, on the AT&T 3B2/500 or 3B2/600 minicomputers. Through the rating maintenance program (RAMP) of the NCSC, the rating was extended in September 1990 to Systems V/MLS, Release 1.2.0, and 630/MLS, Release 1.2.0, running with Unix System V, Release 3.1.1, on the AT&T 3B2/500 and 3B2/600 minicomputers and the AT&T 630 MTG terminal.

sion shows how the commercial data processing requirements described by Clark and Wilson [CLAR87] can be modeled and integrated with the MAC policy for a Unix system. The functional control (FC) policy implements a general role and type policy in terms of system roles of users and categories of objects. This policy allows the roles system administrator, security officer, and user, and has the categories general, security, and system. The security information modification (SIM) policy is based on types of system data and system roles of users. This policy allows only the security officer to change the system's security information.

This essay focuses mainly on the MAC and CWI policies but includes the FC and SIM policies for completeness. A useful trusted computer system must provide the kinds of access control defined by FC and SIM, but formal models typically have not included such policies.

I will present the four policies of this model in detail in this section. But I will not give complete policies because the purpose is to describe the approach, not to provide a complete formal model. Before describing the policies modeled in this essay, we need to address the issue of why the rule-set model does not include the discretionary access control and identity-based access control of Unix System V.

System V DAC and IBAC. Unix System V controls access to resources through its discretionary access control (DAC) and identity-based access control (IBAC). DAC supports the ability of the system and its users to decide who may access the files they own and in what manner. It uses the familiar read, write, and execute privileges. What the kernel ensures is that the permissions defined by the users and the system will be enforced. But, in addition, the kernel incorporates a nondiscretionary policy based on superuser privileges and several types of user identifiers (real, effective, saved). This identity-based access control (IBAC) policy and the user-defined DAC policy are the access control of Unix System V.[9]

Our model includes neither of these policies. The IBAC policy of Unix is typically not modeled, although it is the kind of policy that should be of interest to the modeler. A more elaborate IBAC policy can replace the Unix superuser approach in trusted computer systems to provide better separation of duty. Instead of modeling the superuser-based IBAC of Unix, this rule-set model has a functional control policy that has better separation of duty and is also far less complicated than the IBAC of Unix.

Formal models often do include the DAC policy. This formal model does not because, in short, it is not an interesting policy. It should certainly be included in the state-machine representation of a Unix system, assuming its level of detail is appropriate to the model. But it really doesn't belong

---

[9] Note that the system in this context is System V, not System V/MLS. AT&T's System V/MLS additionally incorporates the mandatory access control (MAC) policy.

in the rule-set model because DAC is not a policy the system can enforce — DAC is a mechanism by which users attempt to impose their own sharing policy on the resources they own. But there's no assurance that they will succeed. For example, a Trojan horse can easily defeat a user's nondisclosure objectives since the DAC mechanism provides no way for a user to prohibit copying a file he has allowed to be read. Nor does the DAC mechanism adequately support integrity objectives, because it provides no way for a user to specify *how* others might modify objects that he owns. In summary, the DAC mechanism does not strongly support any known, well-conceived policy objective that users are likely to have an interest in.

In this formal model, we assume that a favorable DAC check, when appropriate, precedes each invocation of the rule-set model by the state-machine model. Any of the four policies we have included in the rule-set model can override a favorable DAC decision.

Access control information. To support the policies described herein, the following attributes in three groups of access control information (ACI) are needed. Each attribute shown here is explained in one of the policy descriptions that follow.

User-ACI	Values
user-identifier (CWI)	a user identifier
access-approvals (MAC)	a security level
system-role (FC & SIM)	user, security officer, or administrator
integrity-role (CWI)	NIL, TP-user, TP-manager, IVP-user,

Process-ACI	Values
owner (pointer to User-	—
security-level	a security level
process-identifier	a process identifier
process-type	NIL, TP, IVP, or TPICD

Object-ACI	Values
security-level (MAC)	a security level
object-identifier (CWI)	an object identifier
object-category (FC)	**general**, **security**, or **system**
object-type (MAC)	**file**, **directory**, **ipc**, or **scd**
program-type (CWI)	**NIL**, **TP**, **IVP**, or **TPICD**
data-type (SIM & CWI)	**NIL**, **CDI**, **CDIIC**, or **si**

Mandatory access control policy. Mandatory access control is based on security levels of the processes, users, and objects of the system and the request of the process. This policy affects:

- access of processes to objects — for example, reading, writing, and deleting files, directories, and message queues; and
- other aspects of processing — for example, spawning a child process and sending a signal to another process.

The policy described here represents the MAC policy of Unix System V/MLS, Release 1.2.1 [FLIN88], and uses the types of objects defined for that implementation. System V/MLS is a multiuser, multitasking operating system that maintains Unix System V application compatibility. In addition to using the traditional protection mechanisms of the Unix operating system to provide DAC, System V/MLS provides MAC to limit the distribution of information to authorized users. The MAC policy is consistent with the Bell-LaPadula model [NCSC85] and satisfies DoD policy.

Basically, the MAC policy depends on the security-level attribute of processes and objects and on the object-type attribute of objects.

The object-type values defined for this policy[10] are **file**, **directory**, **ipc**, and **scd**. **file** and **directory** have their obvious Unix meanings. **ipc** means "interprocess communication"; the message queue and shared memory in Unix map to this type. **scd** means "system control data"; the inode in Unix maps to this type. Generally, system control data refers to data the system uses to control its operations.

In the next several tables, the letter "P" stands for the security level of the process making the request for access, the letter "O" stands for the security level of the referenced object, ">=" indicates the usual dominates relation between levels, and "=" indicates equality between levels.

Tables 1 through 4 define, respectively, the policies for controlling access of a process to objects of types file, directory, ipc, and scd.

---

[10] We could model additional types as well. We might, for example, wish to include a type "communications-device," realized as a socket in some Unix systems, if we wanted to have intercomputer communications reflected in our model.

Table 1. MAC policy for objects of type file.

If the request is	then access is allowed if
create	O is set equal to P
delete	P = O
delete-data	P = O
execute	P >= O
read	no condition[11]
read-open	P >= O
read&write-open	P = O
write	no condition (see footnote for read above)
write-open	P = O

Table 2. MAC policy for objects of type directory.

If the request is	then access is allowed if
create	O is set equal to P
delete	P = O
read	P >= O
search	P >= O
write[12]	P = O

---

[11] A distinction is made between read and read-open and between write and write-open in this model. Read-open (write-open) enables the process to read (write) the object; read (write) actually transfers data from (to) the open object into (from) the memory space of the process. The MAC policy for controlling read (write) access applies at the read-open (write-open), and no MAC policy applies to the transfer of the data. Other models can be conceived in which a floating label policy for the security level of the object might be applied when a read or write (an actual transfer of data) occurs, similar to the floating information label policy of the CMW model [MILL90].

[12] "Write" to a directory includes addition, modification, and deletion of entries in the directory.

Table 3. MAC policy for objects of type ipc.

If the request is	then access is allowed if
alter	P = O
create	O is set equal to P
delete	P = O
read	no condition[13]
read&write-open	P = O
write	no condition

Table 4. MAC policy for objects of type scd.

If the request is	then access is allowed if
change-owner	P = O
create	O is set equal to P
delete	P = O
get-permissions-data	P >= O
get-status-data	P >= O
modify-access-data	P = O
modify-permissions-data	P = O

The requests get-permissions-data and get-status-data could be modeled as undistinguished reads of the system control data. Similarly, the change-owner, modify-access-data, and modify-permissions-data could be modeled as undistinguished writes. In this model, the separate requests have been used to illustrate the possibility of making access control decisions on the basis of the distinctions represented by these requests.

Table 5 defines the MAC policy governing process management.

Table 5. MAC policy for process management.

If the request is	then access is allowed if
clone	P2 is set equal to P1
send-signal	P1 = P2

---

[13] The distinction between read and read-open and between write and write-open for files applies also to ipc objects in this model.

Clark-Wilson integrity policy. The integrity policy comes directly from the Clark-Wilson integrity (CWI) policy [CLAR87]. I have attempted to model their policy in as straightforward a manner as possible, using their concepts, terminology, and point of view as literally as possible. In addition, I have included the ancillary policy that appears to me necessary to support their intentions. For the convenience of the reader, a summary of the Clark-Wilson model's certification and enforcement rules is given in Appendix B. But the reader is encouraged to read their paper [CLAR87] for an understanding of their motivation and a greater appreciation of their model.

The CWI policy provides for both external and internal consistency of data. Measures for external consistency, such as their integrity verification procedures (IVPs), ensure that the data stored in the computer system correctly models the state of the real-world systems it relates to. Measures for internal consistency ensure that modification of data results in a valid state. And some CWI rules deal with the relationship between the internal and external consistency of data. The integrity control policy in this model focuses on the rules for internal consistency and also supports the capability to ensure external consistency. Some of the CWI rules that deal with external consistency are, naturally, not reflected in this "internal" system model.

Integrity control in the model is based on:

- integrity-controlled programs called transformation procedures (TPs) and integrity verification procedures (IVPs),
- integrity-controlled objects called constrained data items (CDIs), and
- user permissions to apply certain TPs to specified CDIs and permission to apply an IVP to a CDI.

Users and objects in the computer system have the following attributes to support integrity control:

- The object attribute "program-type" may have the following values:

TP:	means that the object is a CWI TP.
IVP:	means that the object is a CWI IVP.
TPICD:	means that the object is a special TP that operates on CWI integrity control data.
NIL:[14]	means that the object is not an integrity-controlled object.

---

[14] NIL has its obvious meaning — nothing — which, in this context amounts to saying that the object is not any of the other types defined. The attribute

The use of these attribute values for controlling execution of integrity-related programs is discussed later.

- The object attribute "data-type" may have the following values:

CDI: means that the object is a CWI CDI.

CDIIC: means that the object is a CWI CDI that is used for integrity control.[15]

NIL: means that the data is not integrity-controlled; that is, in the terminology of Clark and Wilson, it is an unconstrained data item (UDI).

- The user attribute "integrity-role" may have the following values:

TP-user: means that the user is authorized to execute transformation procedures (TPs).

TP-manager: means that the user is authorized to manage (create, delete, and modify) certain integrity objects specified below.

IVP-user: means that the user is authorized to execute integrity verification procedures (IVPs).

IVP-manager: means that the user is authorized to manage IVPs, as specified below.

NIL: means that the user has no integrity role.

The authorizations of a user with an integrity role are described in Table 6.

"program-type" could be used for other policies as well, in which case other values might be defined for it. In this model, this attribute is used only for enforcing the integrity policy.

[15] An example is the user-transformation procedures associations (UTPA) table of this model, described subsequently.

Table 6. CWI policy for execute, create, delete, and modify.

User in integrity role	may execute	may create or delete	may modify
TP-user	TPs		
TP-manager	TPICD	TPs, TPICDs, CDIICs	CDIIC
IVP-user	IVPs		
IVP-manager		IVPs, CDIs	

Clark and Wilson require that the system "maintain a list of relations of the form: (UserID, TPi, (CDIa, CDIb, CDIc, ...)), which relates a user, a TP, and the data objects that TP may reference on behalf of that user." Further, the system "must ensure that only executions described in one of the relations are performed." This model uses a user-transformation procedures associations (UTPA) table to capture the Clark-Wilson triples. Each entry in the table is an ordered triple of the form

(user-identifier, TP, list of CDIs)

No constraint is put on modes or order of access since Clark and Wilson do not require it, although one can conceive a system in which such constraints would serve a useful purpose. Still, other policies in the system may constrain the TP with respect to mode of access. For example, when a TP attempts to open a CDI for writing, the TP must be allowed to write the CDI by the MAC policy of the system.

The UTPA satisfies the CWI requirement to maintain a list of relations. One can imagine many designs for ensuring that only executions described in the UTPA are performed. For example, we could define a new system call, say apply(TP,list_of_CDIs). Here "apply" would be like the exec system call, but having the additional second argument. This argument shows which CDIs the requesting process wishes the TP to operate on. The kernel would pass the arguments of this system call to the rule set. The rule set would check the UTPA to see if the list of CDIs was valid for the owner of the requesting process. The difficulty is that the "enforcement" provided by this approach is weak. Lacking any other access checks, the TP could access some CDI for which the user is not authorized. One may argue that the TP has been certified to operate correctly so that it should only carry out correct procedures. This would possibly be acceptable if all correct and authorized executions were built into the TP and certified. Clark and Wilson suggest, however, that "an important research goal must be to shift as much of the security burden as possible from certification to enforcement" since "the certification process is complex, prone to error, and must be repeated after each program change." Also, using "apply" effectively rules out interaction between the user and the TP. Ideally, the user should be able to provide input arguments specifying which CDIs to operate on.

Therefore, in this model of CWI, the initial request of the process is only a request to execute using the TP. In the Unix environment this is an exec system call in which the process names the object to execute. When the named object is a TP, its program-type attribute has the value **TP**. When the TP subsequently makes requests for access to CDIs, those requests are adjudicated by the rule set in the usual manner. In addition, the rule set keeps a record of the CDIs being accessed, ensuring at each request that the requested access is allowed by one of the triples defined in the UTPA. This idea needs further elaboration, provided in the following paragraphs.

When a process executes a TP, one of the rules for integrity control will add the process identifier of the process to all triples in the UTPA having the user identifier of the owner of the process and specifying the named TP. This marks all candidate executions of the named TP by this process. Note that the same user may already have other executions of this TP in progress. When the TP (now a process having the process identifier of the process that executed it) attempts to access an object that is a CDI22, one of the integrity control rules will remove the process identifier of the process from all triples in the UTPA currently marked with this process identifier but not having the named CDI listed. This reduces the set of candidate executions of the named TP by this process. If after taking this action there are no entries in the UTPA marked with this process identifier, then the attempted access by the TP on behalf of the user is not valid and the request will be denied. The next sequence of tables illustrates this method.

Suppose user A is allowed to apply TP1 in any of the following ways:

- to CDIs 1 and 2,
- to CDIs 1 and 3, or
- to CDIs 2 and 3.

This is illustrated in Table 7, the user-transformation procedures associations (UTPA) table.

Table 7. User-transformation procedures associations (UTPA).

user	TP	CDIs	processes
user A	TP1	CDI-1, CDI-2	
user A	TP1	CDI-1, CDI-3	
user A	TP1	CDI-2, CDI-3	
.	.	.	.
user Z	etc.	etc.	

Suppose a process having process identifier PID requests execution of TP1 on behalf of user A. Assuming the requested action is authorized, the UTPA table is marked as follows:

user A	TP1	CDI-1, CDI-2	PID
user A	TP1	CDI-1, CDI-3	PID
user A	TP1	CDI-2, CDI-3	PID

The process is now known as a TP-type process. If the process requests access to CDI-2, the table is modified, with the following result:

user A	TP1	CDI-1, CDI-2	PID
user A	TP1	CDI-1, CDI-3	
user A	TP1	CDI-2, CDI-3	PID

If the process now requests access to CDI-3, the table is modified, with the following result:

user A	TP1	CDI-1, CDI-2	
user A	TP1	CDI-1, CDI-3	
user A	TP1	CDI-2, CDI-3	PID

If the process now requests access to CDI-1, the request is invalid.

This approach to enforcing the Clark-Wilson triples has the advantage that it does not require a new system call or data structure in the Unix environment. The scheme just outlined describes the situation when a process executes just a single TP. The integrity policy must also cover the cases where a TP-type process attempts to execute another file (Unix exec) or attempts to clone itself (Unix fork).

If a TP-type process were to fork a child, the child would be identical to the parent with respect to executable code and open files (for example, the CDIs being worked on). However, it makes no sense for a TP-type child to continue processing with the executable code of its parent since to do so would require unwarranted complex coordination between parent and child to preserve integrity. It really only makes sense to consider the case that the child executes new code — that is, a new TP. Allowing a TP-type process to spawn another TP-type process in this way adds to the complexity of the certification of the original TP code but adds no functional capability. According to Clark and Wilson, the certification task should be kept as simple as possible by having the system enforce as much of the integrity policy as possible. The needed functionality, enforced by the system in the scheme above, is achieved by an ordinary process cloning a process that changes itself into a TP-type process by executing a TP-type object. In short, it is neither desirable nor necessary for a TP-type process to clone itself.

Thus, to carry out the intent of the Clark-Wilson integrity policy as I understand it, without significantly modifying the System V system calls, the abilities of a process to execute (exec system call) and clone (fork system call) must be constrained in the following ways:

- When an ordinary[16] process executes an object of type TP, IVP, or TPICD, the process executing the object becomes the type of the object. That is, its process-type attribute takes on the value of the program-type attribute of the object. When an ordinary process executes a TP-type object, the UTPA table is updated as described above. A TP-, IVP-, or TPICD-type process is allowed to execute only an object of its own type. When a TP-type process executes a TP-type object, no changes are made to the UTPA. Allowing the original TP to execute a TP-type object is a convenience related to how a TP is organized into units of executable code.
- A TP-, IVP-, or TPICD-type process is not allowed to clone (Unix fork).

The following additional constraints[17] are needed to support the intent of the CWI policy in the Unix System V/MLS environment:

- Changing ownership of TPs, IVPs, TPICDs, and CDIs is not allowed by CWI policy.
- Aliasing (via the link system call in Unix) of file names is not a good practice under the CWI policy. By aliasing, an ordinary user could defeat the attempt of an authorized user (that is, TP-manager) to

[16] In this context, an ordinary process is one whose process type equals NIL.

[17] Obviously, a certain amount of interpretation is involved here. The constraints I have specified seem reasonable to me, but I recognize that other interpretations of the intent of Clark-Wilson integrity are possible.

remove a TP from the system.[18] Our policy, then, is that only individuals with an appropriate role can give an integrity-controlled object an alias. Specifically, a user in the role TP-manager may alias TPs, TPICDs, and CDIs, while a user in the role IVP-manager may alias IVPs and CDIICs.

- Tracing (via the ptrace system call in Unix) of TPs, IVPs, or TPICDs should not be allowed under the CWI policy, since tracing would enable modification of a TP or IVP during its execution.

- Only authorized users may acquire or modify status information about integrity-controlled objects. Specifically, a user in the role TP-manager may read/modify status information about TPs, TPICDs, and CDIs. A user in the IVP-manager role may read/modify status information about IVPs and CDIICs.

- Our integrity policy allows a TP-type process to receive a signal (via the kill system call in Unix System V) from a non-TP-type process (presumably the parent process that spawned the TP-type process). The danger here is that the TP-process could be killed (terminated) at such a time that the CDIs on which it was operating would be left in an undefined state. A justification for allowing the signaling anyway is that it preserves functionality and the TP can be designed to take appropriate action on the CDIs before exiting. This preserves functionality but does put the burden on the certification of the TP to ensure that the TP handles signals appropriately.

Functional control policy. Functional control (FC) uses system roles of users and categories of objects. The system roles are **user**, **security officer**, and **administrator**. The categories are **general**, **security**, and **system**. When a process whose owner has system role R requests access to an object having object category C, the FC policy allows the access only if R *is compatible with* C. We define *is compatible with* as follows:

- **user** is compatible with **general**
- **administrator** is compatible with **general** and **system**
- **security officer** is compatible with **general** and **security**.

A functional control policy can and probably should be more elaborate than the one just described. It can, for example, specify who can change what attributes of what entities. And it's the logical place to have the policy that governs trusted subjects, such as daemons of the Unix system. But the simple policy just given satisfies the goals of this essay, so we develop it no further here.

---

[18] The Unix unlink operation actually deletes a file only when all links to it have been deleted.

Security information modification (SIM) policy. The policy for modification of security information uses types of data and system roles of users. The data type needed for this policy is **si**. The value **si** means the object contains security information. In Unix, for example, the /etc/password file would have this value for its data-type attribute. **NIL** means the object contains ordinary user or system data. The data attribute may have other values as well, such as those the CWI policy uses. But the SIM policy treats all values other than **si** the same as **NIL**.

When a process requests access to data of type **si** in a mode that enables modification of the information, the SIM policy allows the access only if the system role of the owner of the process (that is, the user) is **security officer**.

As with the FC policy, the SIM policy could encompass more elaborate rules of operation, but the simple form given here suffices for the purposes of this essay.

Rules of the rule-set model. Four groups of rules define the policies described above:

- mandatory access control (MAC) rules,
- Clark-Wilson integrity (CWI) rules,
- functional control (FC) rules, and
- security information modification (SIM) rules.

Each policy of the rule-set model is implemented as one or more rules. When combined as described below, the rules constitute the Access-Rules function.

Each rule is an expression having one of four values:

- **YES.** This value means that the request of the state-machine model has been evaluated by the rule and the result is that the request may be granted according to the rule's policy.
- **NO.** This value means that the request of the state-machine model has been evaluated by the rule and the result is that the request may not be granted according to the rule's policy.
- **DC.** This value means that the request of the state-machine model has been recognized by the rule but the rule's policy does not require any checks of attribute values and/or relations among attribute values. The rule's policy is tolerant of the request in the sense that the policy "doesn't care" (DC). DC is similar to YES but provides additional information useful for analysis of a rule set.
- **UNDEFINED.** This value means that the request of the state-machine model has not been recognized by the rule. UNDEFINED is different from NO and DC in that both NO and DC indicate that the rule-set model is cognizant of the request. UNDEFINED not

only provides useful information for analysis of a rule set, but in a system implementation might serve to detect improper configurations of the system.

In addition, a rule may specify an effect that should occur if the request of the process will ultimately be acted on by the state-machine model. Since all effects are changes to attribute values, an effect is specified in the form

set-attribute(attribute name, attribute value)

For example, when a file is to be created, the MAC rule specifies an effect that sets the sensitivity label of the file to the value of the sensitivity label of the process creating the file.

To define the Access-Rules function, we need the binary operator **(+)** (pronounced "and-plus") defined in Table 8.

Table 8. Definition of the binary operator (+).

A	B	A (+) B
YES	YES	YES
YES	NO	NO
YES	DC	YES
YES	UNDEFINED	UNDEFINED
NO	YES	NO
NO	NO	NO
NO	DC	NO
NO	UNDEFINED	UNDEFINED
DC	YES	YES
DC	NO	NO
DC	DC	DC
DC	UNDEFINED	UNDEFINED
UNDEFINED	YES	UNDEFINED
UNDEFINED	NO	UNDEFINED
UNDEFINED	DC	UNDEFINED
UNDEFINED	UNDEFINED	UNDEFINED

The Access-Rules function is defined as

Access-Rules(request(input argument), process/object(input argument), ..., process/object(input argument))):
  function-value = MAC (+) CWI (+) FC (+) SIM;

IF
  function-value is **UNDEFINED**;
THEN
  system-error;
ELSE
  return (**function-value**);

Each of the rules will be expressed in the following general form:

POLICY <- POLICY Rule

POLICY Rule:
SELECT CASE request
  CASE request, request, ... , request
    statement-block
  CASE request, request, ... , request
    statement-block
       *
       *
       *
  CASE request, request, ... , request
    statement-block
END SELECT

The notation "POLICY <- POLICY Rule" means that the variable POLICY should be set to the value of the expression in parentheses. For each POLICY (MAC, CWI, FC, and SIM), representative CASEs are given to illustrate the modeling approach. These representative CASEs come from a complete rule set, not reproduced here since, again, we are not trying to build a trusted computer system. However, to ensure that the CASEs given make sense, they were extracted from a complete rule set.

The MAC rules. The following logical operator is needed:

- <u>dominates</u>(level1, level2) has the value TRUE if level1 dominates level2, FALSE otherwise.

MAC <— (MAC Rule 1)

MAC Rule 1:

SELECT CASE request

  CASE alias
    return(DC);

```
CASE alter
  SELECT CASE object-type[object]
    CASE ipc
      IF
        security-level[process] equals security-level[object];
      THEN
        return(YES);
      ELSE
        return(NO);
      CASE ELSE
        return(UNDEFINED);

CASE clone
  return(set-attribute(security-level[process2], security-level[process1]);
        YES);

CASE create
return(set-attribute(security-level[object], security-level[process]); YES);

CASE execute
  SELECT CASE object-type[object]
    CASE file
      IF
        security-level[process] dominates security-level[object];
      THEN
        return(YES);
      ELSE
        return(NO);
      CASE ELSE
        return(UNDEFINED);

CASE modify-attribute (*arguments are process, qualifier, attribute,
value*)
  SELECT CASE qualifier[input argument]
    CASE user
      IF
        security-level[process] equals access-approvals[user pointed to
            by qualifier];
      THEN
        SELECT CASE attribute[input argument]
          CASE access-approvals
            IF
              system-role[user pointed to by owner[process]] equals
                  security officer;
            THEN
```

```
                    return(YES);
               ELSE
                    return(NO);
           CASE ELSE
                    return(YES);
       ELSE
            return(NO);
    CASE process
      SELECT CASE attribute[input argument]
        CASE security-level
            return(NO);
        CASE ELSE
           IF
               security-level[process] equals security-level[process pointed
                    to by qualifier];
           THEN
                return(YES);
           ELSE
                return(NO);
    CASE object
       IF
           security-level[process] equals security-level[object pointed to
                by qualifier];
       THEN
         SELECT CASE attribute[input argument]
            CASE access-approvals
               IF
                   system-role[user pointed to by owner[process]] equals
                        security officer;
               THEN
                    return(YES);
               ELSE
                    return(NO);
            CASE ELSE
                    return(YES);
       ELSE
            return(NO);
    CASE ELSE
            return(UNDEFINED);

CASE read
  SELECT CASE object-type[object]
    CASE directory
       IF
           security-level[process] dominates security-level[object];
```

```
            THEN
               return(YES);
            ELSE
               return(NO);
         CASE file, ipc
               return(DC);
         CASE ELSE
               return(UNDEFINED);

   CASE read-open
      SELECT CASE object-type[object]
         CASE file
            IF
               security-level[process] dominates security-level[object];
            THEN
               return(YES);
            ELSE
               return(NO);
         CASE ELSE
               return (UNDEFINED);

   CASE read&write-open
      SELECT CASE object-type[object]
         CASE file, ipc
            IF
               security-level[process] equals security-level[object];
            THEN
               return(YES);
            ELSE
               return(NO);
         CASE ELSE
               return(UNDEFINED);

   CASE write-open
      SELECT CASE object-type[object]
         CASE file
            IF
               (security-level[object] equals security-level[process]);
            THEN
               return(YES);
            ELSE
               return(NO);
         CASE ELSE
               return(UNDEFINED);
```

CASE change-owner, change-role, delete, delete-data, get-permissions-
data, get-status-data, modify-access-data, modify-permissions-
data, read-attribute, search, send-signal, terminate, trace,
write
<omitted: note that these cases would be grouped into several
cases or possibly even treated as separate cases if
specified in this model>
CASE ELSE
return(UNDEFINED);
END SELECT

The CWI rules. The rules for the Clark-Wilson integrity policy need the
following functions:

- The function Allowed-Access has the value TRUE or FALSE. It performs the search and modify of the UTPA as described earlier under integrity policy, returning TRUE if at least one triple remains in
  the UTPA as a candidate execution of the TP, FALSE otherwise.
- The function Allowed-Execute has the value TRUE or FALSE. It
  performs a search of the UTPA as described earlier under integrity
  policy, returning TRUE if there is some triple in the UTPA containing the ordered pair given as arguments to Allowed-Execute,
  FALSE otherwise.
- The function Mark-Candidates-in-UTPA places the process-
  identifier in each four-tuple of the UTPA containing the ordered
  pair (user-identifier, object-identifier) given as its first two arguments.

CWI <— (CWI Rule 1)

CWI Rule 1:

SELECT CASE request

  CASE alias, get-status-data, modify-access-data
    IF
      data-type[object] is not CDI AND data-type[object] is not CDIIC AND
      program-type[object] is not TP AND program-type[object] is not IVP
      AND program-type[object] is not TPICD
    THEN
      return(DC);
    ELSE
      IF

((data-type[object] is CDI OR program-type[object] is TP OR
program-type[object] is TPICD) AND integrity-role[user identified
by owner[process]] is TP-manager)
OR
((program-type[object] is IVP OR data-type[object] is CDIIC) AND
integrity-role[user identified by owner[process]] is IVP-manager)
THEN
    return(YES);
ELSE
    return(NO);

CASE alter, get-permissions-data, modify-permissions-data, read,
       write, search, send-signal, terminate
    return(DC);

CASE create, delete
  IF
    data-type[object] is not CDI AND data-type[object] is not CDIIC AND
    program-type[object] is not TP AND program-type[object] is not IVP
    AND program-type[object] is not TPICD
  THEN
    return(DC);
  ELSE
  IF
    ((data-type[object] is CDIIC OR program-type[object] is TP OR
    program-type[object] is TPICD) AND integrity-role[user identified
    by owner[process]] is TP-manager)
    OR
    ((program-type[object] is IVP OR data-type[object] is CDI) AND
    integrity-role[user identified by owner[process]] is IVP-manager)
  THEN
    return(YES);
  ELSE
    return(NO);

CASE execute
  SELECT CASE process-type[process]
    CASE NIL
      SELECT CASE program-type[object]
        CASE TP
          IF
            integrity-role[user identified by owner[process]] is TP-user
            AND
            Allowed-Execute

                         (user-identifier[user identified by
                         owner[process]],
                         object-identifier[object]);
THEN
    Mark-Candidates-in-UTPA
                         (user-identifier[user identified by
                         owner[process]],
                         object-identifier[object],
                         process-identifier[process]);
    return(set-attribute(process-type[process], program-
    type[object]);
         YES);
ELSE
    return(NO);

CASE IVP
  IF
    integrity-role[user identified by owner[process]] is IVP-user
  THEN
    return(set-attribute(process-type[process],program-
    type[object]);
         YES);
  ELSE
    return(NO);

CASE TPICD
  IF
    integrity-role[user identified by owner[process]] is TP-manager
  THEN
    return(set-attribute(process-type[process],program-
    type[object]);
         YES);
  ELSE
    return(NO);

CASE ELSE
    return(DC);

CASE ELSE
  IF
    process-type[process] is not TP AND program-type[object] is not
    TP AND
    process-type[process] is not IVP AND program-type[object] is not
    IVP AND

```
        process-type[process] is not TPICD AND program-type[object] is
        not TPICD;
    THEN
        return(DC);
    ELSE
        IF
            process-type[process] is TP AND program-type[object] is TP
            OR
            process-type[process] is IVP AND program-type[object] is IVP
            OR
            process-type[process] is TPICD AND program-type[object] is
            TPICD
        THEN
            return(YES);
        ELSE
            return(NO);

    CASE read-open, write-open
        SELECT CASE data-type[object]
            CASE CDI
                SELECT CASE object-type[object]
                    CASE file
                        IF
                            process-type[process] is TP AND
                            Allowed-Access(process-identifier[process], object-
                            identifier[object])
                            OR
                            process-type[process] is IVP
                        THEN
                            return(YES);
                        ELSE
                            return(NO);
                    CASE ELSE
                        return(UNDEFINED);
            CASE CDIIC
                SELECT CASE object-type[object]
                    CASE file
                        IF
                            process-type[process] is TPICD
                        THEN
                            return(YES);
                        ELSE
                            return(NO);
                    CASE ELSE
                        return(UNDEFINED);
```

CASE ELSE
    return(DC);
CASE change-owner, change-role, clone, delete-data, modify-attribute,
        read-attribute, read&write-open, trace
            <omitted: note that these cases would be grouped into several
                    cases or possibly even treated as separate cases if
                    specified in this model>
CASE ELSE
    return(UNDEFINED);

END SELECT

The FC rules

FC <— (FC Rule 1)

FC Rule 1:

SELECT CASE request
    CASE alias, alter, change-owner, create, delete, delete-data,
            execute, get-permissions-data, get-status-data, modify-access-
            data, modify-permissions-data, read, read&write-open, read-open,
            search, write, write-open
    IF
        (system-role[user pointed to by owner[process]] is user AND
        object-category[object] is general)
        OR
        (system-role[user pointed to by owner[process]] is administrator AND
        object-category[object] is system or general)
        OR
        (system-role[user pointed to by owner[process]] is security officer AND
        object-category[object] is security or general)
        OR
        (system-role[user pointed to by owner[process]] is daemon AND
        object-category[object] is system or general);
    THEN
        return(YES);
    ELSE
        return(NO);

    CASE clone, read-attribute, send-signal, terminate, trace
        return(YES);

    CASE change-role

<omitted>

CASE modify-attribute
    <omitted>

CASE ELSE
    return(UNDEFINED);

END SELECT

The SIM rules

SIM <— (SIM Rule 1)

SIM Rule 1:

SELECT CASE request

    CASE alias, alter, change-owner, create, delete, delete-data,
            modify-access-data, modify-permissions-data, write, write-open,
            read&write-open
      SELECT CASE system-data-type[object]:
        CASE system-data-type[object] is si:
          IF:
             system-role[user pointed to by owner[process]] is security officer;
          THEN:
             return(YES);
          ELSE:
             return(NO);
        CASE ELSE:
          return(DC);

    CASE change-role
          <omitted>

    CASE modify-attribute
          <omitted>

    CASE clone, execute, get-permissions-data, get-status-data, read,
            read-attribute, read-open, search, send-signal, terminate, trace
      return(DC);

```
    CASE ELSE
        return(UNDEFINED);

END SELECT
```

Additional remarks. The modeler interested in developing a complete rule set for the policies described in this essay should have little difficulty completing the rules just given. The next step in developing a useful model will be to analyze the rule set and convince oneself and others that it correctly and adequately reflects the desired policies. For these purposes, automated tools would help. Translating the language of the rules into specification, programming, or logic languages should be straightforward.

Conclusion

We can compare the rule-set model described in this essay to other formal models for secure computer systems, including the traditional Bell-LaPadula model (BLM) [BELL76]. Table 9, based on a taxonomy suggested by Williams [WILL90], shows several stages in the development of security requirements for a trusted system. Each succeeding stage has more detailed elaboration of a trust policy.

Table 9. Stages in development of security requirements.

Stage of Elaboration	Examples
1. Trust objective	• TCSEC mandatory security objective [NCSC85] • Clark-Wilson integrity objectives [CLAR87]
2. External model	• Noninterference [GOGU82] • SMMSM: User's view of SMMS operation and the security assumptions[19] [LAND84]
3. Internal model	• BLM *-property[20] [BELL76] • SMMSM: Security assertions[21] [LAND84] • CWI: Certification and enforcement rules[22] [CLAR87] • CMWM: Maccessible expression[23] [MILL90]
4. Rules of operation	• BLM: Open-file access checks [BELL76] • CMWM: Read-file label float [MILL90]
5. Functional designs	• Functional specification of Unix open system call [BACH86]

---

[19] The security assumptions part of the SMMSM reflects security constraints on the behavior of users.

[20] The BLM *-property specifies part of the mandatory access control policy of the model. It is defined as follows: The *-property places restrictions on current access triples (subject, object, attribute) based on the value of current-level(subject):

if attribute is *read*, current-level(subject) dominates level(object);

if *append*, current-level(subject) is dominated by level(object);

if *write*, current-level(subject) equals level(object);

if *execute*, current-level(subject) and level(object) have no required relation.

[21] The SMMSM has 10 security assertions. The *classification hierarchy* security assertion is: The classification of any container is always at least as high as the maximum of the classifications of the entities it contains.

[22] The CWI model has five certification rules and four enforcement rules. Enforcement rule 3 is: The system must authenticate the identity of each user attempting to execute a TP.

[23] The referenced expression specifies the mandatory access control policy for the Compartmented Mode Workstation. It is defined as follows: Maccessible(s: Subject, o: Object, m: Mode): Boolean = m = "read" **and** "mac_override_read" $\in$ Privs(s) **or** m = "write" **and** "mac_override_write" $\in$ Privs(s) **or** m = "read" **and** Sens_label(s) >= Sens_label(o) **or** m = "write" **and** Sens_label(o) >= Sens_label(s) **and** Max_level(Owner(s)) >= Sens_label(o).

- *Trust objective.* A trust objective specifies what to achieve by proper design and use of the computing system. It characterizes the desired conditions that the system should maintain for information. A nondisclosure objective, for example, states that there should be no unauthorized viewing of classified data. An integrity objective might state that there should be no unauthorized modification of sensitive data.

- *External model.* An external model describes the trust objectives for the system in a formal, abstract manner, in terms of real-world entities such as people, their roles, types and groupings of information, and operations on information. It may, for example, describe authorizations for people to access information of various kinds. (It should be understood that the authorizations are for the people who are potential users of the target system and that the information will become data managed by the target system.)

- *Internal model.* An internal model describes, in a formal, abstract manner, how the goals of the external model are met within the system. It may do this by specifying constraints on the relationships among system components and among controlled entities in the system.

- *Rules of operation.* Rules of operation explain how the system enforces the internal requirements developed in the internal model. They may do this by specifying access checks and related actions that guarantee satisfying the internal requirements.

- *Functional designs.* Like the rules of operation, functional designs specify behavior of system components and controlled entities, but they provide a complete functional description. A functional design may, for example, be a formal specification of the system calls or commands that will be available in the computer system.

The traditional Bell-LaPadula model (BLM) [BELL76] addresses the third and fourth stages of elaboration. The simple security property and the *-property are two axioms of the model that express the mandatory access control policy as constraints on a trusted computer system's operation. The BLM defines these properties as internal requirements at the third stage of elaboration. Its rules of operation elaborate the behavior of the system at the more detailed level 4. The proof of security in the BLM consists of showing that the rules of operation developed in stage 4 are a correct elaboration of the internal requirements developed in stage 3. The modeling approach makes no provision for demonstrating that the stage 3 requirements are a correct interpretation of a stage 2 model. This fact has been recognized in the past, notably by McLean [MCLE85]. Also, the BLM is quite general, even though some aspects are oriented toward the Multics system. This means it can have wide applicability to numerous different systems, but also that it provides no entrée to the development of detailed functional specifications, such as a descriptive top-level speci-fication as called for by the TCSEC[24] [NCSC85].

The more recent CMWM [MILL90], which essentially addresses the same stages as the BLM, is more heavily oriented toward a particular class of system, in this case Unix. Thus, the developer finds more guid-ance in the CMWM for the development of functional specifications. But, as with the BLM, the modeling approach does not take into account the desirability of being able to show correspondence with some external model.

The Clark-Wilson informal model [CLAR87] directly addresses external consistency issues. Although it does not explicitly articulate an external model, it describes an internal model (third stage) that appears capable of supporting a class of external models. The class is exemplified by an ac-counting enterprise in Clark and Wilson's paper [CLAR87].

The Secure Military Message System model (SMMSM) explicitly gives both an external model and an internal model. The external model is in-formal but is clearly reflected in the formal internal model. In the original formulation of the model, the Security Assertions were developed as an external model of the computer system, in that they define the properties that the computer hardware and software must ensure at the user (external) interface. In the terms defined here, however, the Security As-sertions can be viewed as an internal model. This internal model, in con-trast to the BLM and CMWM, defines a set of secure transforms rather than a set of secure rules of operation. The SMMSM's approach enhances the model's ability to avoid choosing implementation strategies, an avowed goal of the model's developers [LAND84].

The approach to modeling described in this essay particularly ad-dresses levels 3, 4, and 5. In addition, the use of a rule set provides a foundation for showing consistency of the model with some external model. Because the rule set is separate from the rules of operation, the task of proving assertions about the trust policies modeled should be easier than in the traditional approach. The separate rule set constitutes a specification of policy in a formal language. Thus, it can be analyzed with automated tools. The model described in this essay, although clearly similar to both the BLM and CMWM, has these significant differences:

---

[24] The TCSEC B2 design specification and verification criterion is: "A descrip-tive top-level specification (DTLS) of the TCB shall be maintained that completely and accurately describes the TCB in terms of exceptions, error messages, and effects. It shall be shown to be an accurate description of the TCB interface." At the B3 level this criterion is expanded, requiring that a convincing argument be made that the DTLS is consistent with the model. At the highest evaluation level, A1, a formal top-level specification (FTLS) also is required.

- The model draws heavily on the functional design of a Unix System V system for the specification of its rules of operation. A one-to-one correspondence exists between Unix system calls and rules of operation.
- The rules of operation include far more functional design than the BLM and CMWM, but they do not include the access checks and other actions that guarantee satisfaction of the internal requirements. Instead, the rules of operation appeal to the rule set that implements the internal requirements. The specification of the rules of operation shows the appropriate times in the behavior of the system for the rule set to be invoked.
- Internal requirements, the stage 3 elaboration, are implemented by a model in its own right, which we call the rule-set model. The rule-set model consists of a set of rules that express the security policies of the trusted computer system. The rules of this model play a role similar to that of the BLM *-property, but they are far more extensive and express policies in addition to mandatory access control.

Our approach includes far more detail than is usual in a formal security policy model. While recognizing that less detail has advantages like simplicity, easy comprehensibility, and manageability by existing automated tools, I believe we need detailed system models and that our collective knowledge base of ideas and techniques supports them. Moreover, a trusted computer system model must communicate its meaning easily to a wide audience, not just to mathematicians. For this reason, the formal language of the rule set takes the form of pseudocode.

Model building is a process of abstraction. Modelers suppress some details to focus on the issues they consider important. But what may seem unimportant to the model builder may be of great import during later definition of requirements, when more detail must be considered. Thus, model builders may err in their selection of the level of abstraction. They may abstract away important details. Having recognized this situation, the modeler should increase the level of detail sufficiently to include the details needing to be modeled. In traditional models, the access rules are built on the notion of access by an abstract subject to an abstract, undifferentiated object. The resulting models are then so abstract that they treat the opening of a file and the opening of an interprocess communication resource as the same thing. This is a convenience for the modeler, but may prove a burden for all who follow in the development, implementation, and evaluation of a trusted computer system. At these later stages of elaboration of requirements, there may be important policy differences between opening a file and opening a message queue.

The model builder of 20 years ago could not draw on experience with the technology of trusted computer systems to permit modeling at the level of concreteness I am advocating. There were many hard and important problems to solve at high levels of abstraction, where few details of any real system could be considered. Not all those problems have solutions today, but trust technology has matured enough to support modeling at a level of detail that can guide the detailed design of a trusted computer system. The detailed formal model of this essay is a step toward the goal of bringing formal methods closer to the final stages of implementation — complete functional design and coding.

Appendix A: Model language and constructs

Language for expressing rules. The method for expressing the model's rules departs from the traditional use of mathematical notation. A mixture of programming language statements and limited mathematical notation creates a specification language that is intuitively understandable to a broad audience.

Both rules of operation and rules of the rule set are defined in a language that looks like a programming language. Two basic language constructs are used to organize statements and show their interrelationships: **SELECT CASE** and **IF THEN ELSE**.

The **SELECT CASE** statement has the following syntax:

```
SELECT CASE attribute
   CASE attribute-value1
      statement-block-1
   CASE attribute-value2
      statement-block-2



      .
      .
      .



   CASE ELSE
      statement-block-n
END SELECT
```

A statement-block is one or more statements. Individual statements are terminated by a semicolon. The value of the **SELECT CASE** statement is the value of the statement-block following the **CASE** identified by the current value of the selected attribute. For example, the next **SELECT CASE** has the value of statement-block-2 when the "amount" is $200:

```
SELECT CASE amount
   CASE $100
```

```
        statement-block-1
    CASE $200
        statement-block-2
    CASE ELSE
        statement-block-n
END SELECT
```

If the current value of the selected attribute is not identified by one of the **CASE**s given, then the value of the **SELECT CASE** statement is the value of the **CASE ELSE** statement-block.

A final word on the **SELECT CASE** statement. The **END SELECT** part of the statement will be omitted when no ambiguity results — the use of indentation will make clear the scope of a **SELECT CASE**.

The **IF THEN ELSE** statement has the following syntax:

```
IF
    Boolean-expression
THEN
    statement-block
ELSE
    statement-block
```

The **IF THEN ELSE** statement has its usual meaning. A Boolean expression is an expression consisting of attributes and relational or logical operations and having a value of **TRUE** or **FALSE**.

A **FOR-EACH** statement is also useful. Its syntax is

```
FOR-EACH process:
statement-block
END-FOR-EACH
```

Because attributes may apply to more than one kind of entity, the language clarifies an ambiguous reference to an attribute by qualifying each attribute with the name of the entity the attribute belongs to. For example, the attribute "security-level" applies to processes and several kinds of objects. "security-level(process)" refers to the security level of the process.

Rules of operation use the form "[* . . . *]" to identify a system operation. For example, the Open rule uses the statement [* truncate the file *] to stand for the Unix operation that deletes the data in a file. Rules may use the form "(* . . . *)" to enclose a comment, such as (* the directory search was valid and the file exists *) appearing in the Open rule.

Boolean expressions and all statements except the **SELECT CASE** and the **IF THEN ELSE** end with a semicolon. Boolean expressions use the usual inequality operators "<" and ">" and use "==" for expressing equality. Logical operators such as **AND** and **OR** are used in obvious ways.

Rules use the specifications "set-attribute" and "set-attributes" to manage the values of attributes. The rules of the rule-set model use "set-attribute" to designate the value that an attribute should have if the current request is granted. The syntax for this use is

set-attribute(attribute_name, attribute_value)

The rules of the state-machine model use "set-attributes" to indicate that they are carrying out the set-attribute specifications given by the rules of the rule-set model. Suppose, for example, the state-machine model invokes the rule-set model with a create-file request. Suppose that the rules of the rule-set model approve the request and give two set-attribute specifications:

set-attribute(security-level(file), **SECRET**)
set-attribute(object-category(file), **general**)

Then, the portion of the create rule that carries out the create request will include a set-attribute statement. The meaning of the statement is that the security-level of the file is set to the value **SECRET** and the object-category of the file is set to the value **general**.

Constructs of the state-machine model

Types. A type is a class that is defined by the common attributes possessed by all its members. The name of each type suggests a useful interpretation for the class. The model uses the following types:

> request: {alias, alter, change-owner, change-role, clone, create, delete, delete-data, execute, get-permissions-data, get-status-data, modify-access-data, modify-attribute, modify-permissions-data, read, read-attribute, read&write-open, read-open, search, send-signal, terminate, trace, write, write-open}
>
> process
> file
> directory
> ipc
> scd
> signal
> object: [a file, directory, ipc, or scd]
> phase: {"active," "unused," "inaccessible"}
> flag: {ON, OFF}
> mode: {"read," "write," "read&write"}

Variables. A variable is an alterable entity. The variables of the state-machine model define the system states. We can think of variables as functions whose domains are types. Just as naturally, we can regard them as records of information containing one or more items of data. The model uses the following variables:

> current_process: process
> new_process: process
> file_name: file
> directory_name: directory
> truncate_option: flag
> create_option: flag
> STATUS(object): phase
> OPEN(process, object): set(mode)

Constants

> TRUE
> FALSE
> ON
> OFF

Expressions

> Access-Rules(request, process/object, process/object):
> Extended-Boolean

Effects. An effect is an action of the state machine. The model uses the following effects:

> normal-exit
> error-exit
> set-attributes
> save
> restore

Appendix B: Summary of the Clark-Wilson integrity model

Certification Rule 1: All IVPs must properly ensure that all CDIs are in a valid state at the time the IVP is run.

Certification Rule 2: All TPs must be certified to be valid. That is, they must take a CDI to a valid final state, given that it is in a valid state to begin with. For each TP, and each set of CDIs that it may manipulate, the security officer must specify a "relation" which defines that execution. A relation is thus of the form: (TPi, (CDIa, CDIb, CDIc, ...)), where the list of CDIs defines a particular set of arguments for which the TP has been certified.

Enforcement Rule 1: The system must maintain the list of relations specified in Certification Rule 2, and must ensure that the only manipulation of any CDI is by a TP, where the TP is operating on the CDI as specified in some relation.

Enforcement Rule 2: The system must maintain a list of relations of the form (UserID, TPi, (CDIa, CDIb, CDIc, ...)), which relates a user, a TP, and the data objects that TP may reference on behalf of that user. It must ensure that only executions described in one of the relations are performed.

Certification Rule 3: The list of relations in Enforcement Rule 2 must be certified to meet the separation of duty requirement.

Enforcement Rule 3: The system must authenticate the identity of each user attempting to execute a TP.

Certification Rule 4: All TPs must be certified to write to an append-only CDI (the log) all information necessary to permit the nature of the operation to be reconstructed.

Certification Rule 5: Any TP that takes a UDI as an input value must be certified to perform only valid transformations, or else no transformations, for any possible value of the UDI. The transformation should take the input from a UDI to a CDI, or the UDI is rejected. Typically, this is an edit program. [Note to the reader: My model of Clark-Wilson integrity allows a TP to access any UDI in the normal manner for access to an object by a process in this system, subject to the constraints of the other (than integrity) policies implemented by the ADF. It is up to the certification process to ensure that the TP accesses only those UDIs it should access for a particular execution. But this is not in keeping with the spirit of moving as much as possible from certification to enforcement, as suggested by Clark and Wilson. One possibility for changing this approach is to add the names of the allowed UDIs for a particular TP to the triples or, perhaps better, to the TP-CDIs relation, which would have to be added to the model since it is currently not included. Doing so would mean that the TP-CDI relation is no longer redundant with the triples.]

Enforcement Rule 4: Only the agent permitted to certify entities may change the list of such entities associated with other entities — specifically, those associated with a TP. An agent who can certify an entity may not (that is, must not) have any execute rights with respect to that entity.

Acknowledgments

I thank Marshall Abrams for his fundamental insights on access control that led to the modeling approach described in this essay and for his encouragement during the writing of this essay. I thank James Williams of the MITRE Corporation for sharing with me his views on the stages of elaboration of requirements for trusted systems and for many conversations about formal modeling. I thank Charles W. Flink II of AT&T Bell Laboratories for his patient and comprehensive explanations of many design aspects and system calls of System V/MLS, Release 1.2.1.

Essay 10

Representative Organizations That Participate in Open Systems Security Standards Development

Harold J. Podell

This essay presents an introduction to representative organizations that participate in open systems security standards development. The reason we focus on open systems security standards is the international need to support secure electronic commerce and trade. Open systems standards, including security standards, support interoperability and security of business and government computer network communications. International agreements include a commitment of the standards organizations to support open systems security standards to achieve "brand independent" network configurations and interfaces. These agreements mean, in part, that large organizations will be gradually phasing out proprietary network protocols. These protocols could be replaced during the next 10 to 20 years with open systems standards and implementable solutions. Included in these solutions could be the evolution of the mobile office and new international ways to extend the concepts of electronic commerce and trade. The long-term trends for the development of open systems standards and software systems include supporting more effective business processes and communications, and meeting the needs of secure electronic commerce and trade.

We develop four interrelated issues to interpret current trends in the development of selected open systems standards. First, we introduce security standards as important economic, political, and cultural issues to support international electronic commerce and trade. Second, we present a conceptual view of open systems security standards relationships. Third, we briefly overview the committee structure of the International Organization for Standardization (ISO), the International Electrotechnical Commission (IEC), the International Telecommunications Union — Telecommunications Standardization Sector (ITU-T) — formerly the International Telegraph and Telephone Consultative Committee (CCITT), and selected national and regional organizations. Our ISO/IEC and ITU-T focus is on the security standards responsibilities of the international committees and groups. Fourth, we overview ISO/IEC Joint Technical Committee 1 — Information Technology (JTC1) security standards activities. This overview highlights some of the security functions of three subcommittees doing security work: SC27 — Security Techniques; SC21 — Information Retrieval, Transfer, and Management for Open Systems Interconnection (OSI); and SC6 — Telecommunications and Information Exchange between Systems.

Open systems standards are necessary to support international commerce and trade and to assist computer and network companies in the process of marketing essentially the same secure product line in two or more countries. We anticipate that open systems security standards will eventually be more fully developed and products will be tested against the standards. There are important inputs to the development of these security standards. For example, questions remain regarding

- international commerce;
- architecture, which refers to the placement and relationships of certain functions, such as the required security services and mechanisms; and
- open systems.

The three leading organizations in the international standards community are the International Organization for Standardization, International Electrotechnical Commission, and International Telegraph and Telephone Consultative Committee (ISO, IEC, and ITU-T).

Open systems security standards may define the functionality and assurance necessary for a given set of security services. At the present time, functionality and assurance are the main focus of the security standards groups in ISO, IEC, and ITU-T, as well as national and regional organizations in the United States and Europe. Security criteria are examples of evolving international security standards activities that will consider assurance and functionality. National and regional contributions to the evolving international security criteria — Common Criteria (CC) — include the following:

- the draft US *Federal Criteria for Information Technology Security* (FC) [NIST92],
- the European *Information Technology Security Evaluation Criteria* (ITSEC) [ITSE91], and
- the Canadian *Trusted Computer Product Evaluation Criteria* (CTCPEC) [CANA92].

The CC is being developed under control of the Editorial Board (EB), which consists of members from North America and Europe. When the CC is ready, the EB will make it available to ISO Subcommittee (SC) 27, Working Group (WG) 3.

A wide variety of standards-promoting bodies interact in many ways with the international standards community. For example, the Open Software Foundation (OSF), which was formed in May 1988, develops core software technologies to support openness for the international Unix community. OSF has in excess of 200 international members that vary from commercial organizations to universities and government organizations. With respect to secure communications, OSF supports OSF/1. OSF/1 offers a variety of core (or "kernel") services derived from the Mach operating system. In addition, a vendor association — X/OPEN — is dedicated to the creation of an internationally supported, vendor-independent Common Application Environment (CAE) based on industry standards.

Another example of a standards-promoting body is the European Computer Manufacturers Organization (ECMA). ECMA furnishes input to the standards developers at ISO, IEC, and ITU-T. Two technical committees (TCs) in ECMA concerned with security issues are TC29 — Office Document Architecture (ODA) Security, and TC36 — Security Evaluation Criteria and Open Systems Security.

One of the first official open systems security standards for the international community was the OSI Security Architecture (ISO 7498-2), which was voted on and agreed to by members of ISO [ISO89]. Many of the terms in this essay, such as security services and mechanisms, are derived from this architecture. ISO is the international umbrella organization of voluntary national standards organizations, such as the American National Standards Institute (ANSI), the British Standards Institute (BSI), and the Deutsches Institut für Normung (DIN). IEC is a companion organization that now participates by means of a joint technical committee (JTC1) with ISO in the joint development of open systems standards.

Other examples of open systems standards evolution include the development of a compatible or harmonized suite of standards. For example, ISO has issued a Digital Signature standard (ISO 9796) [ISO91a], and ISO/ITU-T has issued standards for Directory Security (X.509) [CCIT88c]. X.509 Secure Directory can be used with ITU-T X.400 and related Message Handling System (MHS) standards to support secure electronic communications. Through an ISO/ITU-T collaboration agreement, a ITU-T recommendation has the international status of an ISO standard. In addition, there are many draft open systems security standards in process.

An important issue is the gradual expansion of the scope of open systems security standards. The long-term trend is to evolve from open systems interconnection (OSI) (for example, ISO 7498-2, ITU-T X.400 MHS, and X.509 Secure Directory) to open systems (for example, ISO/IEC draft open systems frameworks, databases, and Open Distributed Processing (ODP)). This evolution is occurring, in part, because of the international demand for secure electronic commerce and trade. The initial focus on OSI — the network building blocks of information systems — is being supplemented with consideration of applications in the end systems (for example, hosts, workstations, or PCs).

Standards evolve, and the international community strives to develop a comprehensive suite of open systems standards harmonized with the national and regional efforts. Such standards are targeted to provide both functional standards and assurance criteria for business and commerce.

The international trend toward open systems has been augmented with a trend to adopt internetworking standards, such as Transmission Control Protocol (TCP) and Internet Protocol (IP), which are Internet standards that approximately relate to OSI Layers 4 (Transport) and 3 (Network), respectively. Security standards are also being implemented in JTC1 and the Internet international communities. Examples include ITU-T X.509 for Secure Directory and Internet RFCs (Requests for Comments) 1421-4 for Privacy Enhanced Mail (PEM). Several nations, such as the United Kingdom and the United States, are updating their network guidance to reflect this trend to include open systems and internetworking standards.

At the time of writing, the international standards community has agreed to integrate the Internet standards process into JTC1. An agreement drafted between the Internet Architecture Board (IAB) and JTC1 appears to provide a high degree of standards autonomy to the Internet Engineering Task Force (IETF). IETF would be performing SC6 functions.

In addition, user- and market-led initiatives are being developed and coordinated by organizations such as X/OPEN, ECMA, and the World Federation of the Manufacturing Automation Protocol/Technical Office Protocol (MAP/TOP) Users Groups. MAP/TOP is an internationally accepted set of specifications for open communication based on ISO/OSI standards. MAP/TOP is produced by a standards consortium: the North American MAP/TOP Users Group. The secretariat for this group is the Corporation for Open Systems International (COS). International contributions are utilized in the development of each version of MAP/TOP, such as MAP/TOP 3.0. The systems security versions have been officially accepted by the Australian, European, and Japanese users groups.

Our discussions in this essay are limited in scope and currency because of the magnitude of the international security standards processes. For supplemental information, we refer you to the publications from the organizations that are discussed. In addition, security standards committee and group assignments are gradually evolving in the representative organizations, such as ISO, IEC, and ITU-T. We are only sampling representative security activities from certain standards organizations. There are many national and regional standards organizations doing important work that we do not mention.

In developing the ISO, IEC, ITU-T, national, and regional perspectives for this essay, considerable review effort was provided by two internationally respected authorities: Marshall D. Abrams (US) and E. (Ted) J. Humphreys (UK). Their comments and insights have contributed to the accuracy and balance of the presentation. If there are any omissions or misinterpretations, they are the author's responsibility.

Economic, political, and cultural issues to support international electronic commerce and trade

Open systems security standards may be considered as economic, political, and cultural issues. We need the standards to support the international sale of information technology (IT) equipment and to support international electronic commerce and trade. An example of a current issue is the international marketability of IT equipment and systems. Until there are international agreements on interoperability and functionality for reciprocity of security evaluations of IT equipment and systems, hardware and software vendors face difficult investment and marketing decisions.

Internationally agreed upon profiles — International Standardized Profiles (ISPs) — are aimed at helping procurement agencies and software developers focus on those options that will support global internetworking and functional selectivity. For example, an ISP may contain security features if one (or more) of the base standards to which it refers contains security features. However, with regard to certain functional and assurance aspects of a secure product, a hardware or software developer of a trusted or security enforcing operating system has to determine to submit the system for a security evaluation in one or more countries. This can become very costly if different nations use different security criteria and procedures for the evaluations.

Control of the security evaluation of products is also an economic, political, and cultural issue, because vendors and systems developers need creditability and marketability for their products and systems. Creditability is the need to have a product or system evaluated and "approved" by an independent third party as secure for certain applications. Marketability is the ability to meet national, regional, and eventually international security criteria and standards that are required by the using organizations. Marketability can be enhanced through the construction and implementation of standards.

GOSIP for a particular nation is based, in part, on international standards. For example, the US GOSIP Federal Information Processing Standard (FIPS) is based on a profiled subset of the ISO and ITU-T international open systems standards, implementers' agreements developed at the Open Systems Environment Implementors Workshop (OIW), and US federal government requirements. New versions of the GOSIP FIPS are produced as more open systems standards are agreed to. Open systems security standards can be considered for GOSIP as they are produced.

An international long-term goal is to develop an integrated set of open systems security standards for the interoperability of electronic commerce and trade. The open systems security standards development is occurring in parallel with and is related to the development of standards to support international commerce and trade, including marketability of IT equipment and systems. For example, substantial work is in process to fully develop open systems security standards that provide for peer-entity authentication, access control, and nonrepudiation. Business transactions supported by electronic commerce and trade require that the entities be securely identified at both ends — that is, they require authentication. Each business entity also requires that the data origin and receipt of electronic communications, such as business transactions, be verifiable — they require nonrepudiation.

Conceptual view of international open systems standards relationships

An overview of selected international open systems security standards relationships is presented to illustrate the complex interrelationships in open systems security standards development. In a sense, this discussion can serve as a "conceptual road map." The purpose of this road map is to assist in your understanding of the conceptual relationships of several of the interrelated open systems security standards activities in ISO, IEC, and ITU-T. We provide several figures to assist in visualizing this road map. Another way of viewing the road map is as a scorecard. There is a saying, "You cannot tell the players without a scorecard." More detailed taxonomies of open systems security standards are available elsewhere [HUMP92a, ITAE92b].

Open systems standards support international electronic commerce and trade as shown in Figure 1. Figure 1 shows that the Common Application Environment (CAE) for distributed processing applications depends on an evolving set of open systems standards, such as those that support Electronic Data Interchange (EDI). This figure presents a conceptual view of security standards at a high level of abstraction. Figures 2 and 3 present two more detailed views of selected aspects of Figure 1. To visualize the three figures, first you look at the entire picture (Figure 1), then you zoom in on the second level of detail for distributed applications (Figure 2), and finally you zoom in on the third level of detail for architectures, frameworks, Models/Guidelines, and techniques (Figure 3). The horizontal rectangles in Figure 1 suggest the importance of layers in viewing security standards. The five vertical bars represent operational requirements necessary for successful implementation of distributed applications, such as open systems management.

The three layers in Figure 1 show that distributed applications can be viewed as a higher-layer process that depends on protocols in an intermediate layer. The intermediate-layer protocols support functions such as EDI, file transfer, and interactive or transaction processing (TP).

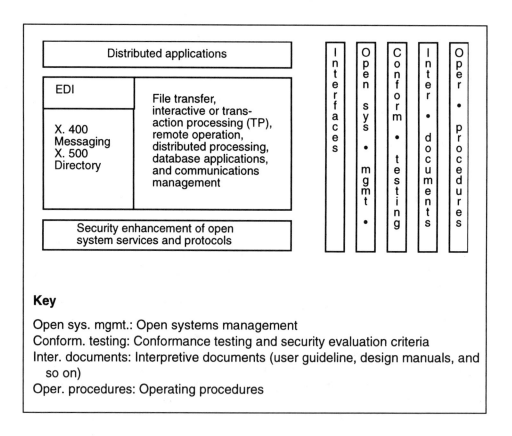

Figure 1. Conceptual overview of international computer and network security standards (source: E.J. Humphreys [HUMP90b]).

The example that we discuss is the evolving set of open systems standards, represented in Figure 1 as supporting EDI. These standards are ITU-T Recommendations X.400 Messaging and X.500 Directory. As mentioned, X.509 is the Recommendation for Secure Directory. X.400 is the Message Handling Service (MHS) series of standards that consists of

1. a user agent to enable users to create and read electronic mail;
2. a message transfer agent to furnish addressing, sending, and receiving services; and
3. a reliable transfer agent to provide routing and delivery services.

X.400 has been augmented to reflect the need for security. EDI security issues are presented in more detail in Essay 18.

Other distributed applications shown in Figure 1 include file transfer, interactive or transaction processing, remote operation, distributed processing, database applications, and communications management. Security enhancement of open system security services and protocols is necessary to support distributed applications.

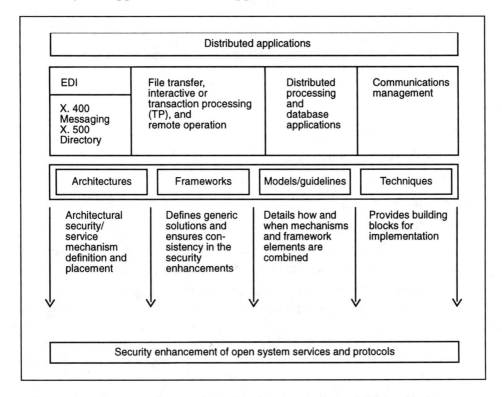

Figure 2. Intermediate-level conceptual view of international computer and network security standards (Source: E.J. Humphreys [HUMP90b]).

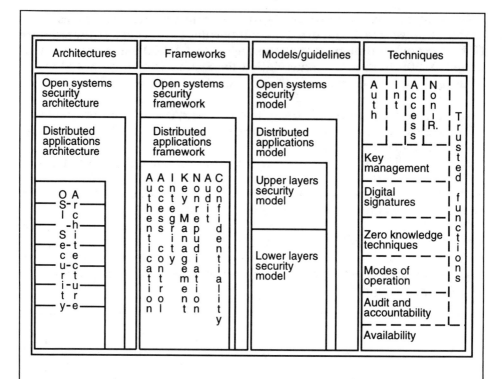

Key

Auth.: Authentication techniques

Int.: Integrity techniques

Access: Access control

Non-R.: Nonrepudiation techniques

——— : Nested (hierarchical) relationships within the hierarchical categories: architectures, frameworks, models/guidelines, and techniques

– – – : Interrelationships (nonhierarchical) within the hierarchical categories frameworks and techniques

Figure 3. Detailed conceptual view of international computer and network security standards (source: E.J. Humphreys [HUMP90b]).

In addition to the need for standards for distributed applications, there are five additional requirements, shown in Figure 1, which we referred to as vertical bars. These five additional requirements support the following operations:

1. interfaces;
2. open systems management;
3. conformance testing and security evaluation, certification, and accreditation;
4. interpretive documents (user guidelines, design manuals, and so on); and
5. operating procedures.

Conceptually, Figures 2 and 3 further illustrate the relationship of distributed processing applications to security architectures and supporting standards and draft standards. EDI and other distributed applications depend, in part, on an interrelated set of security architectures, frameworks, Models/Guidelines, and techniques. ISO, IEC, and ITU-T are working closely on developing the applicable open systems standards. See Essay 18 for further discussion of EDI message security.

We briefly define each of these terms, which represent a family of open systems standards and draft standards activities. First, as mentioned, security architectures refer to the placement and relationships of certain functions, such as the required security services and mechanisms. There are hierarchical relationships among the architectures. For example, the Open Systems Security Architecture could apply to database and/or other open systems architectures. The Open Systems Security Architecture covers the requirements for distributed applications and Open Distributed Processing (ODP). The Distributed Application Architecture is also supported by the OSI Security Architecture (ISO 7498-2) [ISO89]. This hierarchy has important implications. For example, as the original focus of OSI expands to include end systems, we need to supplement the OSI Security Architecture with an Open Systems Security Architecture.

In addition to the hierarchical relationships, there is a need for open systems management to integrate effective support for EDI processing. Open systems management interfaces with, relies on, and interacts with the set of architectures, frameworks, Guidelines, and techniques.

The architectures are supported by frameworks. Frameworks define generic solutions and ensure consistency in the security enhancements. As we have mentioned, a wide variety of frameworks is in process. These address or will address authentication, access control, audit, nonrepudiation, confidentiality, integrity, and key management. The international standards responsibility for developing frameworks is primarily in a joint technical committee operated by ISO and IEC in collaboration with ITU-T.

An example of a framework is the Authentication Framework, which defines the basic concepts for authentication, identifies the possible classes of authentication mechanisms, and defines the services for these classes of authentication mechanisms [ISO91d]. The Authentication Framework identifies functional requirements for protocols to support these classes of authentication mechanisms and identifies general management requirements for authentication.

Models/Guidelines detail how and when mechanism and framework elements are combined. We briefly introduce the Models/Guidelines under development. Models/Guidelines are being developed by ISO/IEC Joint Technical Committee 1 — Information Technology (JTC1). The three subcommittees (SCs) that are doing the work are SC27 — Security Techniques; SC21 — Information Retrieval, Transfer, and Management for Open Systems Interconnection; and SC6 — Telecommunications and Information Exchange between Systems. Below, the entries in parentheses are the subcommittee (SC) and work group (WG) doing the specific work. There are Security Models/Guidelines in process for:

1.   security mechanisms and techniques, for example, authentication (ISO/IEC 9798-1) and nonrepudiation (SC27);
2.   Transaction Processing (TP) Security Model (SC21/WG5);
3.   Generic Upper Layers Security (GULS) (SC21/WG8); and
4.   Lower Layers Model/Guideline (SC6/WG4).

Security in the application and presentation layers is addressed in GULS. Security in the transport and network layers is the focus of the Lower Layers Model/Guideline.

Techniques and mechanisms are necessary to support the provision of open systems services and protocols. Techniques are the responsibility of Subcommittee 27 — Security Techniques (JTC1/SC27). Mechanisms are the methods to implement security services. In addition to responsibilities for security techniques, SC27 (WG3 — Security Evaluation Criteria) is involved in the development of a harmonized set of international security evaluation criteria.

The development of the Common Criteria (CC), originally expected to be complete in the spring of 1994, will use the WG3 draft criteria documents (Parts 1 through 3) as an initial framework. Specific inputs will include the ITSEC, CTCPEC, draft FC, and the comments received on all these documents.

Examples of techniques include the methods necessary to support authentication, data integrity, access control, and nonrepudiation. Techniques are available in three broad categories: cryptographic, noncryptographic, and trusted or security enforcing functions. Important cryptographic techniques in addition to encipherment (encryption) are key management, digital signature, hash functions, zero knowledge techniques, and modes of operation. Digital signature is a mechanism that supports the business need for nonrepudiation and private communications. Public key cryptography is necessary for effective implementation of digital signature. Hash functions are used with digital signatures to reduce variable messages to unique fixed-length representations, such as a 128-bit message digest or "fingerprint." A message digest is encrypted by a public key algorithm using a key to develop a digital signature. See Essay 15 on cryptography for further discussion.

Zero knowledge techniques can be used for authentication, where any exchange authentication information cannot be used to produce valid exchange authentication information. Further, a single verification of authentication information may be sufficient to verify exchange authentication information produced by different claimants. One example of a zero knowledge technique is a process to select from a set of "problems," which the challenged entity must solve and combine together in such a way as to demonstrate ability to solve the problems without revealing exactly how.

Examples of noncryptographic techniques include the use of trusted third parties in networks to support nonrepudiation, audit, and accountability. In addition, availability can be considered as a noncryptographic technique (as well as one of the three aspects of IT security — protection against loss of confidentiality, integrity, and availability).

Another way of expressing the relationships necessary for successful standards development is to focus on the need for harmonization [HUMP89c]:

> Open systems: The harmonisation of communications between computer systems to allow internetworking independently of the nature of the systems involved.

There is no one international standards organization that has produced a set of integrated computer and network and related security standards that meets the needs of international electronic commerce and trade. We have introduced several organizations that are working separately and together to develop the required architectures, frameworks, Models/Guidelines, and techniques.

An introduction to ISO, IEC, ITU-T, and related liaison organizations

ISO, IEC, ITU-T, and related liaison organizations are introduced to illustrate their roles in the open systems standards process. ISO and IEC are major umbrella organizations for national voluntary standards organizations, and ITU-T is an influential treaty standards organization.

Our focus in this essay for ISO and IEC is on Joint Technical Committee 1 — Information Technology (JTC1). More formally, this committee is referred to as ISO/IEC JTC1 — Information Technology (ISO/IEC JTC1). As mentioned, ANSI is the secretariat for JTC1, and other nations serve as the secretariats for the various subcommittees (SCs) and work groups (WGs).

Again, the three major SCs concerned with security are SC27 — Security Techniques; SC21 — Information Retrieval, Transfer, and Management for OSI; and SC6 — Telecommunications and Information Exchange between Systems. SC21 is responsible for all of the frameworks except for key management, which is being developed by SC27. SC6 is responsible for the OSI Lower Layers. Coordination with ITU-T Study Group VII (Data Communications Networks) is also maintained on the development of frameworks.

Certain ISO technical committees (TCs) focus on security in addition to their sectorial focus. For example, TC68 — Banking and Related Financial Services coordinates with JTC1 subcommittees on a wide variety of security standards pertaining to conventional (symmetric) and public key (asymmetric) cryptographic algorithms, such as "Key Management by Means of Asymmetric Algorithms" (ISO CD [Committee Draft] 11166) [ISO91b].

ITU-T has four classes of members. Administrative or full members can be any of the International Telecommunications Union's approximately 160 member nations. A second class of full members consists of the Recognized Private Operating Agencies (RPOA), which are the international telecommunication services providers. Class three consists of the Scientific or Industrial Organizations (SIO). They provide a base of technical expertise but do not participate in the plenary sessions. The major international organizations constitute the fourth class of members. These organizations are invited to meetings to facilitate international coordination of standards development. ISO and IEC are examples of major international organizations. Not all standards organizations are included in this class.

ITU-T develops open systems recommendations or standards related to the OSI model. ITU-T also develops open systems and open systems security standards that will have a broader scope, such as applicability to EDI.

An important aspect of the trend toward open systems standards is that ITU-T has entered into formal agreements to harmonize its recommendations with the standards of ISO and IEC. A successful example is the ITU-T lead role in defining an approach to a Secure Directory (X.509) to support secure open systems communications [CCIT88c]. This directory can be conceptually viewed as a secure electronic telephone book to support computer communications.

ISO, IEC, and ITU-T, and Open Distributed Processing. An example of a long-term objective of the ISO, IEC, and ITU-T international cooperative efforts is their support of the development of Open Distributed Processing (ODP). ODP can be considered as including user requirements, conceptual design and specifications, software design and development, and infrastructure building blocks, as well as the realized components [CHAB90]. ODP systems will be developed as an aspect of open systems that pertains to distributed processing systems. Therefore, ODP systems will be users of communication data security services and distributed applications.

The planned ODP security architecture is considered by ISO/IEC JTC1/SC21 as a candidate for a set of security architectures to support open systems security [ISO91c]. This set has only one security architecture (ISO 7498-2) at present. Other possible security architectures could include a database security architecture.

JTC1 subcommittees. Many of the ISO/IEC JTC1 subcommittees and special working groups that focus on open systems issues are concerned, in varying degrees, with open systems security issues. The security and related activities of selected ISO/IEC JTC1 subcommittees are highlighted in this section.

Several ISO/IEC JTC1 subcommittees are briefly identified with some of their security responsibilities. SC6 — Telecommunications and Information Exchange between Systems has responsibilities for Open Systems Interconnection (OSI) security, such as the Lower Layers security guidelines, Network and Transport Layer security, and security protocols. SC17 — Identification and Credit Cards is responsible for integrated circuit (IC) card security. Examples include IC cards and IC-card communication protocols.

As mentioned, SC21 — Information Retrieval, Transfer, and Management for OSI is an active and well-known SC for security issues. Examples of responsibilities include OSI architecture (WG1) and management (WG4); specific application services, such as a preliminary TP security model (WG5); ODP (WG7); and Generic Upper Layer Security (GULS) (WG8).

Another SC is SC22 — Programming Languages, which focuses on the security interface for POSIX. POSIX is the Portable Operating System Interface for Computer Environments for Unix-like operating systems and is sponsored by the Institute of Electrical and Electronics Engineers (IEEE). The US federal government's FIPS 151-1 specifies POSIX and is based on IEEE Standard 1003.1-1988. FIPS 151-1 makes certain optional capabilities mandatory for US federal procurements. ANSI approved IEEE Standard 1003.1-1988 on November 10, 1989. IEEE Standard 1003.1-1990 has been proposed as an international standard, ISO 9945-1. A rapidly growing number of US vendors claim conformance for their products. POSIX products are being delivered as part of US federal procurements.

As mentioned, one of the newer SCs is SC27 — Security Techniques. SC27/WG1 — Security Requirements, Services and Security Guidelines is responsible for a variety of documents including:

1. Glossary of IT Security Definitions,
2. Entity Authentication Mechanisms — General Model,
3. Key Management Framework,
4. Guideline for the Management of IT Security, and
5. Security Information Objects.

WG2 — Security Techniques and Mechanisms is responsible for a wide variety of documents pertaining to topics such as integrity, authentication, digital signature, hash functions, nonrepudiation, and key management.

Other ISO technical committees. In addition to JTC1, there are other ISO technical committees (TCs) that can have an impact on security. For example, both banking and EDI TCs have activities that may pertain to security. TC68 — Banking and Related Financial Services addresses a wide variety of banking security issues, which interface with JTC1 activities. The example we have introduced is "Key Management by Means of Asymmetric Algorithms Part 2: Approved Algorithms Using RSA Cryptosystem — CD 11166" [ISO91b]. We introduced this example in the earlier section "Introduction to ISO, IEC, ITU-T, and Related Liaison Organizations." Our discussion pertained to the activities of TC68. The CD 11166 coordination is part of the responsibilities of SC2 — Operations and Procedures. Other security responsibilities of TC68 include SC6 — Financial Transaction Cards, Related Media and Operations. Two WGs that focus on security are WG6 — Security in Retail Banking and WG7 — Security Architecture of Banking Systems using the Integrated Circuit Card.

ITU-T study groups. There are several ITU-T study groups (SGs) that are actively concerned with security issues, such as those pertaining to ITU-T X.200, X.400, X.500, and distributed applications security. Examples of these SGs are presented. Security issues are included in parentheses after the study group name: (1) SG VII Q18 — Message Handling Systems (MHS framework and EDI security) and (2) SG VII Q19 — Framework for Support of Distributed Applications (OSI Security Architecture and frameworks, Generic Upper Layer Security (GULS), and security model for distributed applications). The frameworks and Security Models/Guidelines are coordinated as a joint work item with ISO/IEC.

Two other ITU-T SGs that work on security issues are (1) SG VII Q20 — Directory Systems (authentication-X.509 and access control) and (2) SG VIII

Q28 — Security in Telematic Services. SG VIII Q28 is working on a Proposed Security Framework for Telematic Services.

United Nations/Economic Commission for Europe (UN/ECE). In addition to ITU-T, there is a second treaty international organization concerned with open systems security standards. This organization is called the United Nations/Economic Commission for Europe (UN/ECE). There are approximately 34 UN/ECE member states located in North America and Europe.

The UN/ECE was created by the Economic and Social Council of the United Nations. The Electronic Data Interchange (EDI) standards work is performed by UN/ECE Working Party 4 on Facilitation of International Trade Procedures (UN/ECE WP4). An example of a national representative is the US Department of Transportation. UN/ECE performs a standards function for EDI, which has produced a standard that is becoming the international standard — EDI for Administration, Commerce and Transport (EDIFACT).

Examples of security-related standards-promoting bodies. One view of the open systems security community at a given point in time is a structural view. An overview of selected European, international, and United States security-related standards-promoting bodies working on open systems security standards issues is presented. We discuss these organizations to illustrate some of the sources for many of the security standards ideas that are considered by JTC1 and ITU-T.

Selected European organizations. European standardization of information systems security is performed by three organizations that broadly correspond to ISO, IEC, and ITU-T, respectively:

1. Comité European de Normalization (CEN),
2. Comité European de Normalization Electrotechnique (CENELEC), and
3. European Telecommunications Standards Institute (ETSI) [ITAE92b].

We use the term information systems security to include the security of IT systems, telecommunications, and other systems and services that handle information in electronic form.

Information systems security standardization in Europe is an evolving process that considers the experience of the European IT industry and users. The standardization process makes use of existing solutions and proposals, and is aimed at providing future solutions for new technical developments and market-driven requirements. Priority and preference are given to the adoption of international work items, with the intention of transposing the results into European Normen (ENs) (European Normal Standards) or European Norme Voransgaben (ENVs) (European Normal Prestandards) when appropriate. Provisions of two agreements are used — the Vienna Agreement and the ISO/CEN Cooperation Agreement. These standards may be supplemented by additional ENVs as necessary for European implementation.

The three official European organizations participating in the development of regional and international open systems security standards each represent important constituencies in the European Community (EC). CEN is concerned with the harmonization of standards for European ISO members. CENELEC is concerned with harmonization of standards for European IEC members. ETSI focuses on the harmonization of standards for the European ITU-T members. ETSI was created as a result of the activities of the European Conference of Postal and Telecommunications Administrations (CEPT) to produce standards for European telecommunications.

The CEN/CENELEC/ETSI Information Technology Steering Committee (ITSTC) established the Information Technology Advisory Expert Group on Information Systems Security (ITAEGV) in 1991. ITAEGV is developing a framework for future European IT security standards [ITAE92b] from a baseline document, *Taxonomy of Security Standardisation* [HUMP92a]. The baseline document was prepared by an earlier ad hoc group under the secretariat of CEN. The work of ITAEGV is to update this taxonomy, taking into account recent developments in the fast-changing world of information systems security.

A life-cycle orientation is used for the ITAEGV framework. Therefore, the classification scheme of information systems security standards reflects life-cycle phases. Briefly, the scheme covers:

1. S0, Architecture and Modeling;
2. S1, System Design;
3. S2, System Development and Implementation; and
4. S3, System Operational Aspects.

The framework includes a directory of standards that are placed in these classifications.

Our discussion of European security standards uses the ITAEGV work as of the time of writing. Since this process is ongoing, we suggest that the reader refer to the current version of ITAEGV work for the most up-to-date report on progress in European IT security standards. In addition, since ITAEGV makes extensive use of IT security standards prepared at the international level, current versions of JTC1 International Standards (ISs) and Draft International Standards (DISs) can be reviewed for additional up-to-date references.

We briefly discuss the three European standards bodies — CEN, CENELEC, and ETSI — and two standards-promoting bodies — the European Workshop for Open Systems (EWOS) and ECMA. Eighteen member countries of the European Community (EC) and the European Free Trade Association (EFTA) are the European countries that may participate in CEN and CENELEC. CEN and CENELEC are responsible for the drafting and ratification of harmonized European standards — ENs and ENVs. Further, there are proposed ENVs (prENVs).

Membership in ETSI is open to any organization that demonstrates an interest in European telecommunications standardization. At the time of writing, there were almost 300 members — manufacturers, telecommunications operators, administrations, and users. ETSI produces European Telecommunication Standards (ETSs) and Interim Telecommunication Standards (I-ETSs), corresponding to ENs and ENVs, respectively. ETSI also produces technical reports (ETRs) and performance specifications. For example, ETSI products pertain to certain aspects of the Special Mobile Services Group (GSM) pan-European digital cellular telephone system.

The European Workshop for Open Systems (EWOS) was established primarily to provide an open international forum to develop worldwide harmonized profiles and associated test specifications for open systems. EWOS is a standards-promoting body working in the forefront of standardization, building technical consensus, and directly contributing to CEN, CENELEC, ETSI, and ISO. EWOS was established by the main European IT supplier and user organizations with the support of CEN, CENELEC, ETSI, and the European Commission. Functional profiles are developed by EWOS to assist in utilizing OSI standards. In addition, EWOS works in collaboration with ETSI to develop profiles, such as X.400 [STRA92]. When these documents reach EN status, based on balloting, they can be considered stable.

EWOS participates in the development of International Standardized Profiles (ISPs) in collaboration with the North American regional workshop — the Open Systems Environment Implementors Workshop (OIW) — and the Pacific Rim-Asia Oceanic Workshop (AOW). AOW participation includes representatives from Japan, Korea, China, and Australia. As mentioned, ISPs are aimed at helping procurement agencies and software developers focus on those options that will support global internetworking and functional selectivity. In general, the specification of an ISP having security features has two distinct parts, one concerned with security-related functions and one concerned with other functions. A security subprofile specification is the specification of a distinct set of security-related functions in an ISP. An ISP may have one or more security subprofiles. ISPs are useful in effectively shortening the time it takes for certain standards to reach their final draft stage.

To assist in international collaboration, EWOS has established a Regional Workshop Coordinating Committee (RWS-CC) with OIW and AOW. The RWS-CC seeks to coordinate developments, acknowledging that worldwide interoperability requires worldwide harmonized implementation specifications. These specifications are to be approved at the ISO/IEC JTC1 level. Mechanisms are also being developed to ensure that only harmonized results are submitted for approval by JTC1 as International Standardized Profiles.

As mentioned, ECMA is also a standards-promoting body that furnishes input to the standards developers at ISO, IEC, and ITU-T. Two technical committees in ECMA that address security issues are TC29 — Office Document Architecture (ODA) Security and TC36. The latter includes the work of two technical groups: one for security evaluation criteria and one for open systems security (the former TC32 was merged into TC36).

Selected US-based organizations. In this section we introduce five US-based organizations. Our first organization is the American National Standards Institute (ANSI), which is a voluntary organization for developing industrial standards. Participation is open to interested and qualified parties, including government agencies. As mentioned, ANSI is the US member of ISO and the secretariat for ISO/IEC JTC1. ANSI coordinates with many organizations, such as the US National Institute of Standards and Technology (NIST). Many ANSI standards are also NIST Federal Information Processing Standards (FIPS). In certain cases, NIST and ANSI standards are also ISO standards.

Our second organization is one of the international regional organizations that promote the acceptance of standards-based open systems products. The organization is the Corporation for Open Systems International (COS) [WALT91]. COS is a US-based organization with approximately 55 international members from several countries, such as Canada, the United Kingdom, and Germany. COS has been active in contributing to the creation of ISPs. Another COS contribution has been in effecting the development of several OSI and ISDN standard test systems, such as those for electronic mail, file transfer access and management, network management, packet switching, and Ethernet. In addition, COS created the first certification process for open systems standards-based products and services — the COS Mark Program. COS also assisted in the development of the US GOSIP by sharing its COS Mark Program testing and registration process and procedures with NIST. As mentioned, COS also provides the secretariat for the North American MAP/TOP Users Group.

The Computer and Business Equipment Manufacturers Association (CBEMA) is our third organization. CBEMA is a US-based regional organization that provides technical assistance to ANSI. CBEMA is the US

Technical Advisory Group (TAG) to JTC1 and the secretariat to the ANSI Accredited Standards Committee X3 — Information Processing Systems.

Fourth, we mention a US-based international professional organization that has worked with ANSI on security-related draft standards. The Institute of Electrical and Electronic Engineers is an ANSI-accredited standards organization. For example, the IEEE developed a draft standard IEEE 802.10 SILS (Standard for Interoperable LAN [Local Area Network] Security).

Our last US-based organization is the Open Systems Environment Implementors Workshop (OIW), which is a regional organization that participates in various aspects of security profiles and implementers' agreements activities. The IEEE and NIST are the cosponsors of OIW. OIW is the US regional equivalent of EWOS and, as mentioned, works closely with EWOS and AOW in RWS-CC. An objective of this cooperation is to achieve consensus on proposed International Standardized Profiles.

Selected overview of ISO/IEC JTC1 security standards activities

We provide an overview of selected security-related work in ISO/IEC to illustrate the nature of several of the activities that pertain to open systems security standards. Our focus in this section is on the security standards activities of Joint Technical Committee 1 — Information Technology (JTC1) [ISO91c, ITAE92b]. We present selected aspects of the security activities of SC27, SC21, and SC6 to illustrate the type of activity. Although in subsequent sections we do not discuss the security activities of SC18 — Text and Office Systems, we should mention them here. SC18 is working on X.400 MHS, X.435 EDI, and Office Document Architecture (ODA). These standards are important components of interoperability necessary to support electronic trade and commerce.

Selected security activities of SC27. First, we discuss several security activities of SC27. The scope of SC27 is identification of generic requirements, development of standards for security services, development of security guidelines, development of security techniques and mechanisms, and the standardization of security evaluation criteria. This work supports a wide variety of security standardization needs reflecting a typical development cycle:

1. requirements and policy,
2. security services and applications,
3. security mechanisms and techniques,
4. security elements,
5. security management techniques,
6. guidelines, and

7. quality and evaluation of design.

For example, the following types of work are in process:

1. requirements and policy, for example, for medical and transport informatics security, and hyper/multimedia systems (in liaison with SC18);
2. services, for example, Open EDI;
3. mechanisms and techniques — digital signature, authentication, integrity, and so on;
4. data elements and objects; and
5. security management, for example, key management.

SC27 is also working on guidelines, for example, for the management of IT security. In addition, other guidelines work includes development of a Glossary of IT Security Technology and guidelines on the use and application of Trusted Third Party (TTP) services.

The SC27 work on evaluation criteria includes security evaluation methodologies. A European example of a contribution to the state of the art in evaluation methodologies is the *Information Technology Security Evaluation Manual* (ITSEM) [ITSE92]. Inputs to SC27 for evaluation criteria include European work on ITSEC, Canadian work on CTCPEC, and North American work on the *Federal Criteria for Information Technology Security* (FC). In addition, there is a variety of interregional coordination, such as close coordination among work on CTCPEC and FC and the ITSEC activity.

Recent SC27 work items for the development of security evaluation criteria include a multipart standard: Part 1, "Model"; Part 2, "Functionality Classes"; and Part 3, "Assurance." As mentioned, these three parts are used as an initial framework for the development of the Common Criteria (CC).

Selected security activities of SC21. Subcommittee 21 — Information Retrieval, Transfer and Management for OSI works on security standards, and in collaboration with ITU-T Study Group VII (SG VII) — Data Communications Networks, on architecture, frameworks, services and protocols. This work includes OSI Security Architecture, Open Systems Security Frameworks, and ODP. SC21 work on services and protocols includes:

1. Generic Upper Layer Security (GULS) (Layers 6 & 7, Abstract Syntax Notation 1 (ASN.1)),
2. Association Control Service Element (ACSE) authentication,
3. Remote Operations Service Element (ROSE),
4. TP, and

5. File Transfer and Access Management (FTAM) security.

In addition, SC21 work on applications/management and interfaces includes X.500 security and OSI management.

SC21 is perhaps best known for early work on OSI security. The result was the first SC21 security standard on security architecture (ISO 7498-2). While the earlier focus of SC21 was on OSI security, today much of its work addresses the needs of open systems security. The requirement for an open systems focus could result in consideration of more comprehensive security architectures, since the current security architecture concentrates on OSI issues.

Security architectures: SC21. As mentioned, the OSI Security Architecture developed by SC21 provides the fundamental description of security services and related mechanisms for the OSI Basic Reference Model. In addition, the security architecture presents tables that define the positions in the ISO seven-layer model where the security services and related mechanisms could be provided. Examples of our security definitions that we derive from the OSI Security Architecture include the following terms for security services: authentication, access control, nonrepudiation, integrity, and confidentiality.

Other architectures may be defined, as indicated in our conceptual discussion; however, to date there are no other architectures. SC21 is considering the need to develop broader architectures and their appropriate scopes.

Security frameworks: SC21, SC27. Each of the security frameworks documents in ISO/IEC is being developed or will be developed by SC21, except for key management, which is being addressed by SC27 — Security Techniques. Security frameworks are being developed to address the application of the security services in open systems. The term open systems is interpreted to include databases, distributed applications, Open Distributed Processing (ODP), and OSI. One reason for the frameworks is to provide a vehicle for defining the means of protection for systems and objects within systems as well as the interactions between systems. Frameworks use available information technology knowledge as a baseline. For example, the access control framework relies on object-oriented technology. The frameworks do not focus on methodology for constructing systems and mechanisms for implementing security services.

As mentioned, frameworks define generic solutions to ensure consistency in security enhancements. Frameworks do not provide protocol elements. Rather, they address data elements and sequences of operations used for specific security services. Security services may apply to the activities of the communicating systems and their representatives or entities. In addition, security services apply to the data managed and exchanged by systems. The access control scope of the frameworks may interface with but not include any data elements that are application specific or associated only with local internal access of a system.

As discussed, the security frameworks being developed are authentication, access control, nonrepudiation, integrity, confidentiality, audit, and key management (SC27). These frameworks are being developed for the five security services and audit and key management.

Security Models/Guidelines: SC21, SC6. As mentioned, Security Models/Guidelines define the details concerning how and when mechanism and framework elements are combined. Security Models/Guidelines provide architectural representations for the development of application-independent security services and protocols. In addition, Security Models/Guidelines provide for the utilization of security services and protocols to meet security requirements for many types of applications. At the time of writing, examples of Security Models/Guidelines being developed include the OSI Upper (SC21 — GULS) and Lower Layers (SC6) Security Models/Guidelines.

Generic Upper Layer Security (GULS) is concerned with providing details for the security aspects of communication in the upper layers of OSI. These aspects of communication pertain to the positioning and the interrelations between security services and the Presentation and Application Layers. This Model/Guideline also describes the way security transformation functions — such as encryption (encipherment) and security checkvalue functions — are processed for the Presentation and Application Layers. In addition, the Model/Guideline presents a concept of security exchange and provides for overview discussions of entity authentication, data origin authentication, association access control, resource access control, nonrepudiation, integrity, and confidentiality. GULS also discusses the concepts of a security policy and security state.

The Lower Layers Security Model/Guideline (SC6) is concerned with providing details for the security aspects of communication in the lower layers of OSI (for example, the Network and Transport Layers). SC6 (Telecommunications and Information Exchange between Systems) is focusing on security interactions within the lower layers and between the upper and lower layers. This Model/Guideline also describes the general security requirements for management across the lower layers to provide various types and levels of security.

Security in data management standards: SC21. A variety of data management standards is being developed to address many of the interrelated aspects of security in data management. For example, the Reference Model of Data Management (ISO DIS 10032) presents access control as a set of privileges. This reference model also provides an architectural Model/Guideline of access control, which considers access control data in a manner related to database data. The Model/Guideline presents a standardized approach to access control as a technical objective related to the standardization of data management. No other security service is supported within the scope of data management.

Another example is the Information Resource Dictionary System (IRDS), which is presented in IS (Information Standard) 10027. This document is a framework used to control and document the information resources in an enterprise. Control is provided for limiting access to data in the Information Resource Dictionary (IRD). The IRDS describes the type of data that could be used to control access.

Two other examples are the Remote Database Access (RDA) service and the Database Language SQL (Structured Query Language). The RDA (ISO CD [Committee Draft] 9579-1) provides for a terminal to have interactive access to a remote database. General-purpose support is presented in RDA. This support should be considered as a baseline when using "specialization" standards, such as SQL (ISO CD 9579-2).

In RDA, each user has to be identified as a valid user of the resource so the remote data resource can be opened and accessed. Important security attributes, such as user identity and authorization identity in the request/indication service primitives, are carried by RDA. A dialogue will be set up with a remote node if the user and authorization identities are valid. Certain functions are not performed by RDA, such as dictating the format or meaning of the security attributes.

The last example of a data management standard that we discuss is Database Language SQL (ISO 9075). Database Language SQL presents the logical structures and associated basic operations required for a SQL database. Users of SQL data or services are identified within SQL; however, the implementation specifics are defined outside the SQL environment. SQL "Catalogs" are used to group SQL data entities. These data entities are controlled by implementation specifics outside SQL.

SQL controls the user entities and "Catalogs." Other SQL entities are created and owned by SQL users. The access privileges for the other entities are under the control of the creating user. This control may be delegated to the entities of other SQL users. The ability to grant privileges on an object is included in the set of privileges that may be delegated.

Security in OSI management: SC21. A variety of ISO documents relate to OSI management standards. Three are highlighted in this section:

1. *OSI Systems Management* (ISO 10164), which has many parts in various stages of draft and approval;
2. *Common Management Information Service (CMIS) Access Control* (ISO 9595 and ISO 9595/PDAM); and
3. *Directory Authentication Framework* (ISO 9594-8; ITU-T X.509).

In the first example, *OSI Systems Management* (ISO 10164) presents an OSI security management overview that pertains to the security management functions. The relationships are given for the security management functions, the OSI Reference Model, and the Audit Framework. Other aspects of OSI security management are being developed: *Security Alarm Reporting Function* (ISO 10164-5), *Security Audit Trail Function* (ISO 10164-8), and *Objects and Attributes in Access Control* (ISO CD 10164-9).

The second example is *Common Management Information Service (CMIS) Access Control* (ISO 9595 and ISO 9595/PDAM). The access control parameters pertaining to ISO 9595/PDAM are A-associate, M-get, M-set, M-action, M-create, and M-delete.

We conclude with the third example, *Directory Authentication Framework* (ISO 9594-8, which is technically aligned with ITU-T X.509). The *Directory Authentication Framework* presents the basis for strong authentication essential for electronic commerce and trade. A certificate, which is described in this recommendation, may be conceptually considered as an "electronic envelope." The certificate is "sealed" cryptographically with a public key algorithm and the private key of a trusted third party in the network — the Certificate Authority. Conceptually, we can visualize that each certificate is a digital envelope that contains a digital "letter" with the identification of an authorized user in the network — the user's public key.

More formally, the certificate may be considered as a security token protected by integrity and data origin authentication security services. The mechanism that provides this protection uses public key cryptography, such as RSA (Rivest, Shamir, and Adleman).

There is also a Directory Access Control Model developed for general use for access control of directory information (ISO 9594-1,2,3,4/PDAM1). This provides hooks to facilitate control of directory access. Amendments to parts 3 and 4 of the Directory Access Control draft document enable the use of external access control to supplement the access control in part 2.

Security in OSI applications: SC21. There are many provisions for OSI in a variety of applications. We highlight seven examples:

1. File Transfer, Access, and Management (FTAM);
2. TP;
3. Terminal Management (TM);
4. Security Exchange Association Control Element (ASE);
5. Association Control Service Element (ACSE) authentication;
6. Presentation Layer confidentiality
7. Presentation Layer cryptographic techniques.

Examples of work in OSI applications include an amendment to ISO 8571 to evaluate the applicable authentication and access control requirements for FTAM. A similar development has occurred in TP security. There is work to develop amendments to OSI (DIS 10026, parts 1, 2, and 3) that will focus on evaluation of the appropriate mechanisms to provide security services. The security services that are being considered include authentication, access control, confidentiality, integrity, and nonrepudiation. Other considerations related to security services include auditing, "management," (access right) revocation, replay (protection), (prevention of the) denial of service, reliability, and traffic control confidentiality. The scope of these considerations includes TP resources and application entities.

There is a TM model (ISO CD 10184-1); however, there is no assessment of the security relevance of the TM model. Generic Upper Layers Security (GULS) is proposed as a multipart standard. Generic facilities are proposed to be defined to provide security services in OSI applications. Included in the proposal are a definition of the service and a protocol associated with the Security Exchange Service Element.

ACSE Authentication Service and Protocol is defined in an information standard addendum (ISO 8649/AMI, ISO 8650/AMI). An A-associate request and confirmation are defined in a field in the amendment. This field may contain arbitrary authentication information. Included in this example is work to determine conditions for ACSE authentication. The conditions are related to the applicable cryptographic mechanisms for use with ACSE authentication.

The Connection Oriented Presentation Service and Protocol (ISO 8822 and 8823) is being amended to provide confidentiality and integrity security services. Some of the security architecture (ISO 7498-2) connection-oriented security services are provided in Presentation Layer cryptographic techniques. The procedures and Presentation Layer protocol necessary to implement a set of security services are presented. The selected security services are peer entity authentication, connection confidentiality, selective field confidentiality, connection integrity, and selective field connection integrity.

Open Distributed Processing (ODP) security. The Reference Model of Open Distributed Processing (RM-ODP) contains six "aspects" of distributed systems (part II). Work is progressing on the RM-ODP (part I) to present the use and organization of security in distributed systems. The requirements to support security will be defined for specific systems (part II).

Summary

In this essay we have developed four interrelated issues concerning representative organizations that participate in open systems security standards development. Our discussions have included identification of the economic, political, and cultural needs for standards to support international electronic commerce and trade. We presented a conceptual view of open systems security standards relationships. Then we overviewed the committee structure of the International Organization for Standardization (ISO), the International Electrotechnical Commission (IEC), the International Telecommunications Union-Telecommunications Standardization Sector (ITU-T), and selected national and regional organizations.

Our ISO/IEC and ITU-T focus was on the security standards work responsibilities of the international committees and groups. We presented a selected overview of ISO/IEC Joint Technical Committee 1 — Information Technology (JTC1). This overview included highlights of the security functions of three subcommittees: SC27 — Security Techniques; SC21 — Information Retrieval, Transfer, and Management for Open Systems Interconnection; and SC6 — Telecommunications and Information Exchange between Systems.

Essay 11

Penetration Testing

Clark Weissman

The TCB shall be found resistant to penetration.

— Department of Defense, "Trusted Computer System Evaluation Criteria," DoD 5200.28-STD, December 1985 (The Orange Book).

Near flawless penetration testing is a requirement for high-rated secure systems — those rated above B1 based on the Trusted Computer System Evaluation Criteria (TCSEC) and its Trusted Network and Database Interpretations (TNI and TDI). Unlike security functional testing, which demonstrates correct behavior of the product's advertised security controls, penetration testing is a form of stress testing which exposes weaknesses — that is, flaws — in the *trusted computing base* (TCB). This essay describes the Flaw Hypothesis Methodology (FHM), the earliest comprehensive and widely used method for conducting penetrations testing. It reviews motivation for penetration testing and penetration test planning, which establishes the goals, ground rules, and resources available for testing. The TCSEC defines "flaw" as "an error of commission, omission, or oversight in a system that allows protection mechanisms to be bypassed." This essay amplifies the definition of a flaw as a demonstrated unspecified capability that can be exploited to violate security policy. The essay provides an overview of FHM and its analogy to a heuristic-based strategy game.

The 10 most productive ways to generate hypothetical flaws are described as part of the method, as are ways to confirm them. A review of the results and representative generic flaws discovered over the past 20 years is presented. The essay concludes with the assessment that FHM is applicable to the European ITSEC and with speculations about future methods of penetration analysis using formal methods, that is, mathematically specified design, theorems, and proofs of correctness of the design. One possible development could be a rigorous extension of FHM to be integrated into the development process. This approach has the potential of uncovering problems early in the design, enabling iterative redesign.

A security threat exists when there are the opportunity, motivation, and technical means to attack: the when, why, and how. FHM deals only with the "how" dimension of threats. It is a requirement for high-rated secure systems (for example, TCSEC ratings above B1) that penetration testing be completed without discovery of security flaws in the evaluated product, as part of a product or system evaluation [DOD85, NCSC88b, NCSC92]. Unlike security functional testing, which demonstrates correct behavior of the product's advertised security controls, penetration testing is a form of stress testing, which exposes weaknesses or flaws in the *trusted computing base* (TCB). It has been cynically noted that security functional testing demonstrates the security controls for the "good guys," while penetration testing demonstrates the security controls for the "bad guys." Also, unlike security functional testing by the product vendor, penetration testing is the responsibility of the product evaluators. However, product vendors would be ill advised to ignore their own penetration testing as part of the design, test, and preparation for a high-rated security product evaluation, for such vendors will surely be surprised by unanticipated debilitating vulnerabilities long after the development phase, when repairs are impractical.

Of all the security assurance methods — including layered design, proof of correctness, and software engineering environments (SEE) — only penetration testing is holistic in its flaw assessment. It finds flaws in all the TCB evidence: policy, specification, architecture, assumptions, initial conditions, implementation, software, hardware, human interfaces, configuration control, operation, product distribution, and documentation. It is a valued assurance assessment tool.

This essay is in 10 parts and describes a comprehensive method for conducting penetration analysis, of which penetration testing is but one aspect. The parts include background motivation, test planning, testing, and the analysis of the test results. The essay is largely based on the author's Flaw Hypothesis Methodology (FHM), the earliest and most widely used approach [WEIS73].

The "Background" section reviews the reference monitor concept of policy, mechanism, and assurance that forms the basis of the TCB. Penetration testing, a pseudo-enemy attack, is one method of evaluating the security strength of the reference monitor TCB. The section "Develop a penetration test plan" establishes the ground rules, limits, and scope of the testing. The test team identifies what is the "object" being tested and when the testing is complete. The section advances the idea that the tests seek to confirm security claims of the vendor and to support the evaluation class rating. Testing is not a challenge or invitation to the test team to "crack" the system and steal something of value.

The section "Flaw hypothesis methodology (FHM) overview" provides a technical foundation for penetration testing. It establishes the idea that a security flaw is an unspecified capability that can be exploited to violate security policy — for example, to penetrate the protection controls. Finding and assessing flaws is a four-phase process of flaw generation, flaw confirmation, flaw generalization, and flaw elimination. These phases are covered in separate sections. The section "FHM experience" provides examples of results of application of the method to dozens of systems. Some costs of penetration testing are also discussed. The final section, "Penetration analysis for the 1990s and beyond," examines the ITSEC and where FHM can be applied, and work in formal methods and promising future approaches to flaw detection.

Background

Per the TCSEC, a TCB is the amalgam of hardware, software, facilities, procedures, and human actions that collectively provide the security enforcement mechanism of the *reference monitor* [ANDE72]. A reference monitor mediates every access to sensitive programs and data (security *objects*) by users and their programs (security *subjects*). It is the security policy mechanism equivalent of abstract data-type managers in strongly typed programming languages such as Algol, Modula, and Ada. The reference monitor software is placed in its own execution domain, the privileged supervisor state of the hardware, to provide tamper resistance to untrusted code. The reference monitor software, often called the *security kernel*, is small and simple enough in its architecture to enable it to be evaluated for correctness with assurance that only the authorized security policy is enforced and never bypassed. The strength of this triad of policy, mechanism, and assurance of the reference monitor is the basis for the evaluation of the TCB. Penetration testing is but one method for assessing the strength of a TCB.

Traditional methods of testing and repair are poor strategies for securing TCBs. Such strategies lead to games biased in favor of the hacker, who possesses modern power tools to attack aging computer systems. The "hack-and-patch" approach to assure secure systems is a losing method because the hacker need find only one flaw, whereas the vendor must find and fix all the flaws [SCHE79]. Furthermore, there are many flaw opportunities with little risk of detection or punishment for the interloper. So why bother with penetration testing by FHM? Because FHM penetration testing is not hack-and-patch, but a comprehensive, holistic method to test the complete, integrated, operational TCB — hardware, software, and people. It is an empirical design review and a credible bridge between abstract design (theory) and concrete implementation and operation (practice). It is a peer review of all the TCB assurance evidence. It is one of many methods for satisfying assurance requirements. It works. It finds flaws. But we must not overstate its value. Penetration testing cannot prove or even demonstrate that a system is flawless. It can place a reasonable bound on the knowledge and work factor required for a penetrator to succeed. With that information, together with counter-measures, we can restrict the penetrator's access freedom below this bound, and therefore have a degree of assurance to operate the system securely in a specific threat environment [CSC85].

Develop a penetration test plan

Establishing the test ground rules is a particularly important part of penetration analysis. The rules are captured in the penetration test plan, which defines the test objective, the product configuration, the test environment, test resources, and schedule. It is important that penetration testing use ethical evaluators who are nonantagonistic toward the vendor to encourage cooperation, to protect proprietary information and vendor investment, and ultimately to yield an improved security product. Test results and flaws discovered during penetration testing must be kept strictly proprietary and not be made public by the test team.

Establish testing goal. There can be many goals for penetration testing, including security assurance [DOD85], system design research [KARG74], and systems training [HEBB80, WILK81]. For this essay, penetration testing will focus only on the goal of generating sufficient evidence of flawlessness to help obtain product certification to operate at a B2, B3, or A1 security assurance level.

The ground rules for the analysis define successful completion. The analysis is successfully concluded when

1. a defined number of flaws are found,
2. a set level of penetration time has transpired,
3. a dummy target object is accessed by unauthorized means,
4. the security policy is violated sufficiently and bypassed, or
5. the money and resources are exhausted.

Most often the last criterion ends the penetration test, after a defined level of effort is expended. For some systems, multiple independent penetration teams are used to provide different perspectives and increased confidence in the flawlessness of the product if few flaws are found. As a holistic assurance technology, penetration testing is best used to explore the broad capabilities of the object system for flaws rather than to create a gaming situation between the vendor and the penetration team of trying to acquire an identified protected object by unauthorized means. Dummy target acquisition penetration goals waste effort by forcing the test team to prepare and debug a break-in, rather than focusing their energy on proven methods of finding flaws.

The reference monitor defines a "security perimeter" between itself and untrusted user application code, and between different user processes. Flaws within the application code have no impact on the TCB and are of little interest to security or penetration testing. Flaws internal to the security kernel are of interest to security, but they cannot be exploited unless the security perimeter is breached. In international travel, it requires passports and visas to control border crossings. In banking, turning account balances into cash is a form of boundary crossing called "conversion." Control is imposed at the interface. Therefore, much of penetration testing focuses on the design, implementation, and operational integrity of the security perimeter, the control of the boundary crossings of this critical security interface.

Define the object system to be tested. FHM can be applied to most any system whose developers are interested in TCSEC evaluation. However, C1, C2, or B1 candidate systems are intended for benign environments, protected by physical, personnel, procedural, and facility security. Systems in these benign evaluation classes are not designed to resist hostile attack and penetration. Such attacks are always likely to uncover flaws. The TCSEC wisely does not require penetration analysis for these systems. FDM is most valuable for testing security resistance to attack of candidate systems for evaluation classes B2, B3, or A1, systems designed to operate in hostile environments.

A system intended for TCSEC evaluation at B2 or higher is delivered with a collection of material and documentation that supports the security claim, including a security policy model, a descriptive top level specification (DTLS), a formal top level specification (FTLS) for A1 evaluations, code correspondence matrices to the DTLS or FTLS, and security functional test results. All the source and object code, the design and test documentation, and the security evidence must be under configuration management control for B2, B3, or A1 evaluation classes. This controlled collection of security material will be referred to as the security "evidence," and defines the security system to be penetration tested. Not all the evidence will be complete if the penetration testing is performed by the vendor during the development phase. The evidence must be frozen and remain unmodified during the penetration testing period to avoid testing a moving target.

Experience has shown that probing for security flaws may require system halts and dumps by the penetration team. When tests succeed, they yield unpredictable results — for example, uncontrolled file modification or deletion, or system crash — which disrupt normal operation. Therefore, penetration testing should be performed in a controlled laboratory environment on a stand-alone copy of the target system to assure noninterference with real users of the system.

When the object system is a network, the TCB is distributed in various components, the whole collection of which is called the network TCB (NTCB). As noted in the TNI, penetration testing must be applied to

1. the components of the NTCB, that is, the partitions of the NTCB; and
2. the whole integrated network NTCB [NCSC87a].

Therefore, the TNI Mandatory (M), Audit (A), Identification & Authentication (I), and Discretionary (D) M-A-I-D network components must be penetration tested individually and collectively — individually during the component evaluation, and collectively during the network evaluation.

In a similar manner, a trusted application, for example, a DBMS, must be penetration tested individually as a component and collectively with the operating system TCB on which it depends, according to the "evaluation by parts" criteria of the TDI [NCSC91].

Posture the penetrator. When an actual test is required to confirm a flaw, a host of test conditions must be established, which derive directly from the test objectives and the test environment defined in the plan. These conditions derive from the security threats of interest and the posture of the "simulated" antagonist adopted by the evaluators. Will it be an "inside job" or a "break-and-entry" hacker? These assumptions demand different conditions for the test team. The test conditions are described as "open-box" or "closed-box" testing, corresponding to whether the test team can place arbitrary code in the product (open box) or not (closed box). In the latter case, the team is restricted to externally stimulated functional testing. Open-box penetration testing is analogous to computer software unit (CSU) testing, where internal code is accessible, and closed-box penetration testing is analogous to computer software configuration item (CSCI) integration testing, where code modules are an integrated closed whole. The TNI testing guideline calls these "white-box" (internal) and "black-box" (functional) testing, respectively [NCSC88b].

In open-box testing we assume the penetrator can exploit internal flaws within the security kernel and work backward to find flaws in the security perimeter that may allow access to the internal flaws. In the case of a general-purpose system such as Unix, open-box testing is the most appropriate posture. For special-purpose systems such as network NTCB components, which prohibit user code (for example, where code is in ROM), closed-box penetration testing by methods external to the product is analogous to electrical engineering "black-box" testing. In closed-box testing the penetrator is clearly seeking flaws in the security perimeter and exploiting flaws in the interface control document specifications (ICD). Open-box testing of the NTCB is still a test requirement to determine the vulnerability of the network to Trojan horse or viral attacks.

Fix penetration analysis resources. It was believed that finding flaws in OS VS2/R3 would be difficult [MCPH74]. However, another study claimed:

> The authors were able, using the SDC FHM, to discover over twenty such "exposures" in less than 10 man-hours, and have continued to generate "exposures" at the rate of one confirmed flaw hypothesis per hour per penetrator... Only the limitations of time available to the study governed the total number of flaws presented [GALI76].

Penetration analysis is an open-ended, labor-intensive methodology seeking flaws without limit. The testing must be bound in some manner, usually by limiting labor hours. Small teams of about four people are most productive. Interestingly, penetration testing is destructive testing. It is intense, detailed work that burns out team members if frequent rotation of the evaluators is not practiced. Experience shows the productivity of the test team falls off after about six months. Therefore, a penetration test by four people for no more than six months — 24 person-months — is optimal. The test team must include people knowledgeable in the target system, with security and penetration testing expertise. Much time is spent perusing the security evidence. However, there must be liberal access to the target system to prepare and run live tests. The team needs access to all the TCB creation tools — compilers, editors, configuration management system, word processors — and a database management system to inventory their database of potential flaws and to store their assessments of the flaws.

Flaw hypothesis methodology (FHM) overview

COMPUSEC's (computer security's) raison d'être is to automate many of the security functions traditionally enforced by fallible human oversight. In theory, a trusted system should perform as its security specifications define and do nothing more. In practice, most systems fail to perform as specified and/or do more than is specified. Penetration analysis is one method of discovering these discrepancies.

Evidence implication chain. For high-rated trusted systems, the trust evidence must show that theory and practice agree — that the "evidence implication chain" is correctly satisfied at each step. The implication chain of evidence shows:

1. the operation of the target system is compliant with hardware and software design, and human behavior;
2. those elements comply with the "correct" specifications;
3. the specifications satisfy the security policy exclusively; and
4. the policy meets operational requirements.

The TCSEC requires evidence that each step in the implication chain is correctly satisfied by various techniques, including human facility management and login procedures, audit trails, security officer oversight, automatic monitoring and alarms, code-to-specification correspondences, test results, peer review, mathematical proof, model-to-reality correspondence, and other methods. Penetration analysis is a disciplined method of examining weaknesses or failures in the implication chain.

Essentially, the method seeks counterarguments to the "truth" asserted by the evidence — that is, it seeks to establish the evidence is false or incomplete. A flaw is such a counterargument. A flaw is a demonstrated undocumented capability that can be exploited to violate some aspect of the security policy.

The emphasis of FHM is on finding these flaws. It is not on building demonstrations of their exploitation, though such examples may have merit in some cases. Exploitation demonstrations consume valuable resources that can better be applied to further flaw assessment of the implication chain.

The induction hypothesis. At the heart of the TCSEC is mathematical induction, sometimes called the *induction hypothesis*. It is the theoretical basis of TCSEC security and argues that

1. if the TCB starts operation in a secure state, and
2. the TCB changes state by execution from a closed set of transforms (that is, functions), and
3. each transform preserves defined security properties,
4. then, by mathematical induction, all states of the TCB are secure.

Finding flaws begins with finding weaknesses in implementation of this protection theory — policy, model, architecture, FTLS/DTLS, code, and operation. The evidence implication chain of the previous section forms the basis of the flaw search for violations of the induction hypothesis. As examples, false clearances and permissions void initial conditions (rule 1), bogus code (for example, a Trojan horse or virus) violates the closed set (rule 2), and a large covert channel does not preserve the information containment security properties of functions (rule 3).

Stages of the Flaw Hypothesis Methodology (FHM). FHM consists of four stages:

1. *Flaw generation* develops an inventory of suspected flaws.
2. *Flaw confirmation* assesses each flaw hypothesis as true, false, or untested.
3. *Flaw generalization* analyzes the generality of the underlying security weakness represented by each confirmed flaw.
4. *Flaw elimination* recommends flaw repair or the use of external controls to manage risks associated with residual flaws.

These stages are shown in Figure 1.

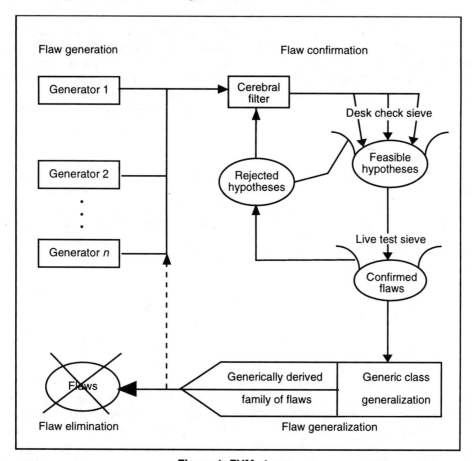

Figure 1. FHM stages.

FHM can be likened to a computer strategy game. In artificial intelligence (AI) game software, there is a body of logic that generates "plausible moves" which obey the legal constraints of the game — for example, it ensures a chess pawn never moves backward. In like fashion, penetration testing needs for *flaw generation* a "plausible flaw generator." Flaw finding begins with the evidence implication chain, our experience of security failures in the reasoning chain in other systems, and their potential for existence in the target system. The security evidence for the target system is the principal source for generating new flaw hypotheses.

Continuing our AI game analogy, there is a body of heuristic rules the game uses to distinguish good plausible moves from poor ones. Likewise, in penetration testing *flaw confirmation*, there is human judgment — a "cerebral filter" — that evaluates and rates each prospective flaw in terms of its existence and how significantly it violates the security policy. Filtering flaws for confirmation involves desk checking of code, specifications, and documentation evidence, as well as live testing.

The *flaw generalization* stage of penetration testing gives an assessment of our results in progress, the game analogy of "winning" or improving game position. Flaw generalization assesses confirmed flaws, seeking reasons why they exist. For example, in the penetration testing of OS VS2 [LIND75], a simple coding error was traced to a library macro and multiple instantiations of the flaw in the code. Inductive reasoning on the cause of confirmed flaws can lead to new flaws, generators for still more weaknesses.

The *flaw elimination* stage considers results of the generalization stage and recommends ways to repair flaws. Implementation flaws are generally easier to repair than design flaws. Some flaws may not be practical to repair; slow covert timing channel flaws may be tolerable, for example. These flaws remain in the system as residual flaws and place the operational environment at risk. However, external countermeasures can be recommended to the approving authority for managing these risks, by lowering the TCSEC Risk Index [CSC85], for example.

Flaw generation

Flaw generation begins with a period of study of the evidence to provide a basis for common understanding of the object system. Early in the effort there is an intensive "attack-the-system" session of team brainstorming. Target system expertise must be represented in the attack sessions. Each aspect of the system design is reviewed in sufficient depth during the session for a reasonable model of the system and protection mechanisms to be understood and challenged. The vendor's evaluation evidence is available for in-depth reference by the team. Flaws are hypothesized during these reviews. Critical security design considerations are the basis for the penetration team's probing of the target system's defenses. These design considerations become the "plausible move generators" of the flaw generation phase. The most productive "top 10" generators are the following:

1. Past experience with flaws in other similar systems.
2. Ambiguous, unclear architecture and design.

3. Circumvention/bypass of "omniscient" security controls.
4. Incomplete design of interfaces and implicit sharing.
5. Deviations from the protection policy and model.
6. Deviations from initial conditions and assumptions.
7. System anomalies and special precautions.
8. Operational practices, prohibitions, and spoofs.
9. Development environment, practices, and prohibitions.
10. Implementation errors.

Each candidate flaw is documented on a flaw hypothesis sheet (FHS), which contains a description of the flaw speculation. The total set of FHS becomes the flaw database that guides and documents the penetration analysis.

Past experience. The literature is filled with examples of successful penetration attacks on computer systems [ABBO76, ATTA76, BELA74, BISB78, BISH82, GALI75, GALI76, GARF91, KARG74, MCPH74, PARK75, SDC76]. There is also a body of penetration experience that is vendor proprietary or classified [BULL91, LIND76a, PHIL73, SDC75]. Although general access to this past experience is often restricted, such experience is among the best starting points for flaw generation.

Unclear design. The design must clearly define the security perimeter of the TCB. How are boundary crossings mediated? Where are the security attributes — permissions, classifications, IDs, labels, keys, and so on — obtained, stored, protected, accessed, and updated? What is the division of labor among hardware, software, and human elements of the TCB? And how are all the myriad other secure design issues described [GASS88]? If the secure design cannot be clearly described, it probably has holes. The team will rapidly arrive at consensus by their probing and uncover numerous flaws and areas for in-depth examination, particularly weaknesses in the evidence implication chain.

Circumvent control. What comes to mind is Atlas down on one knee holding up the world. The anthropomorphic view of TCB design gives the numerous protection control structures omniscience in their critical Atlantean role of supporting the secure design. If such control can be circumvented, the security can be breached. The security architecture evidence must show noncircumvention or bypass of security controls. The attack sessions will rapidly identify these omniscient objects, be they password checkers, label checkers, I/O drivers, or memory maps. A method of determining their vulnerability to attack is to build a "dependency graph" of subordinate control objects on which the omniscient ones depend. Each node in the graph is examined to understand its protection structure and vulnerability to being circumvented, spoofed, disabled, lied to, or modified. If the security design is weak or flawed, control can be bypassed. The penetration testing of OS VS2/R3 [SDC76] gives a detailed example of the use of dependency graphs to determine the vulnerability of VS2 to unauthorized access to job data sets, virtual memory, and password protection control objects.

Incomplete interface design. Interfaces are rife with flaw potential. Where two different elements of the architecture interface, there is a potential for incomplete design. This is often the case because human work assignments seldom give anyone responsibility for designing the interface. Although modern methodologies for system design stress interface control documents (ICD), these tend to be for interfaces among like elements — for example, hardware-hardware interfaces and software-software protocols. The discipline for specifying interfaces among unlike elements is less well established. Hardware-software, software-human, human-hardware, hardware-peripheral, and operating system-application interfaces can have incomplete case analyses. For example, the user-operator interface to the TCB must deal with all the combinations of human commands and data values to avoid operator spoofing by an unauthorized user request. Operating procedures may be hardware configuration dependent. For example, booting the system from the standard drive may change if the configuration of the standard drive is changed. All the various error states of these interfaces may not have been considered.

Implicit sharing is now a classical source of incomplete design flaws. Sharing flaws usually manifest themselves as flaws in shared memory or shared variables between the TCB and the user processes during parameter passing, state variables context storage, setting status variables, reading and writing semaphores, accessing buffers, controlling peripheral devices, and global system data access — for example, clock, date, and public announcements. Careful design of these interfaces is required to remove system data from user memory.

Policy and model deviations. For B2 and higher evaluation classes, the security evidence includes a formal security policy and a model of how the target system meets the policy. Subjects and objects are defined. The rules of access are specified. For lower evaluation classes, the policy and model are less well stated and, in the early years of penetration testing, required the penetration team to construct or define the policy and model during the attack sessions. However, penetration testing is not required for these classes today.

Consider the adequacy of the policy and the model for the target system. Is the model complete? Is the policy correct? Are there policies for mandatory and discretionary access control (MAC and DAC), identification and authentication (I&A), audit, trusted path, and communications security? Examine the security architecture and the TCB design to see if there are deviations from the stated policy or model. For example, are there user-visible objects that are not defined in the model, such as buffers and queues? Omniscient control objects, as described in the earlier section "Circumvent control," should certainly be represented. Are there deviations in the implementation of the policy and model? This consideration receives greater emphasis during flaw confirmation; however, there may be reasons to generate implementation flaws at this time.

Initial conditions. Assumptions abound in secure system design but are not documented well, except in evaluation class A1, where formal specifications require entry and exit assertions to condition the state-machine transforms. For all other evaluation classes the assumptions and initial conditions are often buried in thick design documentation, if they are documented at all. If these assumptions can be made invalid by the user, or if in the implementation reality the initial conditions are different from the design assumptions, the policy and model may be invalid and design flaws should exist. The induction hypothesis presented earlier begins with "starts operation in a secure state." Initial conditions determine the starting secure state. If the actual initial conditions are other than as assumed in the design, attacks will succeed.

The whole range of security profiles and administrative security data on user IDs, clearances, passwords, and permissions (MAC and DAC) defines the "current access" and "access matrix" of the Bell-LaPadula policy model [BELL76]. These data are initial conditions. Their correct initialization is a testable hypothesis. Other assumptions and initial conditions need to be established and tested by penetration analysis, including the computer hardware configuration, software configuration, facility operating mode (periods processing, compartmented, system high, MLS), operator roles, user I&A parameters, subject/object sensitivity labels, system security range, DAC permissions, audit formats, system readiness status, and more.

System anomalies. Every system is different. Differences that may have security ramifications are of particular interest. The IBM Program Status Word (PSW) implements status codes for testing by conditional instructions, unlike the Univac 1100, which has direct conditional branching instructions. The IBM approach allows conditional instructions to behave as nonconditional instructions if the programmer avoids checking the PSW [SDC76]. That is an anomaly. The Burroughs B5000-7000 computer series compiler software has privilege to set hardware tag bits that define "capabilities," many of which are security sensitive, such as write permission. The Master Control Program (MCP) checks the tag bit for permission validity. User code does not have this privilege. Code imports can circumvent such checks [WILK81]. That is an anomaly. The

IBM 370 I/O channel programs are user programs that can access real memory via the "Virtual = Real" command without a hardware memory protect fault [BELA74]. That's an anomaly. Nearly every software product has clearly stated limits and prohibitions on use of its features, but few define what occurs if a prohibition is ignored. What happens when an identifier greater than eight characters is used? Is the identifier truncated from the left, right, or middle, or is it just ignored? Anomalous behavior may not be security-preserving functionality per the induction hypothesis theory. This behavior can be exploited.

Operational practices. The complete system comes together during operation, when many flaws reveal themselves. Of particular interest are the man-machine relationship, the configuration assumptions, and error recovery. A well-designed TCB will have the system boot process progress in stages of increasing operating system capability. Each stage will check itself to ensure it begins and ends in a secure state. If there is need for human intervention to load security parameters, the human must be identified, authenticated, and authorized for known actions. The penetrator must see if the boot process progresses correctly. For example, how is the security officer/administrator authenticated? If via passwords, how did they get loaded or built into the initial boot load? Where does the operator obtain the master boot load? From a tape or disk library? Is the physical media protected from unauthorized access, product substitution, or label switching? If the security officer loads or enters on-line permissions to initialize the security parameters of the system, how does the security officer authenticate the data? If users send operator requests to mount tapes or disks, print files, or execute a myriad of other security-sensitive actions, how does the TCB protect the operator from spoofs to take unauthorized action? If the system crashes, does the system reboot follow a process similar to the initial "cold" boot? If there is a "warm" boot mode — a shortcut boot that salvages part of the system state — does the security officer have a role in the boot to ensure the system begins in a secure state? How is the assurance determined?

A common initialization flaw occurs when the system is shipped from the vendor with the "training wheels" still on [STOL89]. This class of flaw has been known to include training files that provide ID-password authorizations to users so they may train for jobs as security officers, system administrators, database controllers, and system operators. These files were not removed by good system operational practice per the Trusted Facility Manual (TFM) and can be used by unauthorized parties to circumvent security controls.

The development environment. Flaws may be introduced by bad practices in the security kernel/TCB development environment. A simple example is the conditional compilation, which generates special code for debugging. If the released code is not recompiled to remove the debugging "hooks," the operational system code violates the closed set (rule 2) and the secure transform (rule 3) of the induction hypothesis, similar to a trap-door bypass of security controls.

Large untrusted reuse and runtime libraries are properties of many programming environments. The TCB may be built using code from the library, which finds its way into operational use. All kinds of security flaws may obtain from such environments. If the libraries are not security sensitive, they can be searched for flaws that are exploitable in the operational TCB. If the penetration team can substitute its own code in the libraries, even more sophisticated flaws can be created. Runtime linkers and loaders have similar properties of appending unevaluated code to the trusted object code being loaded to enable code-operating system communication. If access to such tools is unprotected, similar code-substitution attacks are possible.

A classic way to attack an operational system is to attack its development environment, plant bogus code in the source files, and wait for the normal software update maintenance procedures to install your unauthorized code into the operational system object code. If the development and operational system are the same, then the penetration team must mount an attack on the development environment first, particularly the system configuration files. Flaws found there relate directly to the operational system, the source files of which are then accessible and modifiable by the penetrator without authorization. Substitute configuration files give the penetrator a high-probability attack and essential control of the TCB.

Implementation errors. In any system built by humans, there will be errors of omission and commission. This is not a promising class of flaws to explore, as there is no logic to them. Many are just typos. Implementation errors that can be analyzed are those of the IF-THEN-ELSE conditional form. Often a programmer fails to design or implement all the conditional cases. Incomplete case analysis may occur if the code logic assumes some of the predicates are performed earlier. Most often, implementation flaws are just coding errors.

Other areas for investigation are macros and other code generators. If the original macro is coded incorrectly, the error code will be propagated in many different parts of the system. Similarly, if data declarations are incorrect, they will affect different parts of the code. Incorrect code sequences should be traced back to automatic source code generators to see if the code error appears in multiple parts of the TCB.

Sometimes there are errors in the development tools that generate bad code. Few configuration management tools provide a trusted code pedigree or history of all the editor, compiler, and linker tools that touch the code. Therefore, an error in these tools, which becomes known late in the development cycle and is fixed, may persist in some earlier generated modules that are not regenerated. The penetration team may find it fruitful to interview the development team for such cases.

Flaw hypothesis sheets. FHM candidate flaws are documented on flaw hypothesis sheets (FHS), one page (record) per flaw. An FHS is intended to be concise and easy to use throughout the penetration testing. The FHS contains seven fields:

1. a flaw name for identification,
2. a brief description of the flaw vulnerability speculation,
3. a localization reference of the flaw to a part of the system or module,
4. an assessment of the probability of the flaw being confirmed,
5. an estimate of the damage impact of the flaw on the protection of the system if confirmed,
6. an estimate of the effort/work factor needed to confirm a flaw, and
7. a description of the attack and result.

Probabilities for fields 4, 5, and 6 are measured on a scale of high (H), medium (M), or low (L). The combined assessment of HH, HM, HL, MH, ..., LL yields an overall scale of nine for ranking FHS. The ranking is valuable in allocating resources during the flaw confirmation phase of penetration analysis. The FHS documents an estimate of the work required to demonstrate a flaw. High work-factor flaws — for example, cracking encryption codes — are given lower priority, even if the flaw is ranked HH. An FHS has a section for describing the results obtained from the flaw confirmation phase. The total set of FHS becomes the flaw database that guides and documents the penetration analysis. The FHS can be mechanized with tool support — for example, a word processor or a DBMS — to permit flexible sorts and searches based on key fields of an FHS database of hundreds of records.

Flaw confirmation

Conducting the actual penetration test is part of the testing procedure developed in the plan. The bulk of the testing should be by "Gedanken" experiments, thought experiments, that confirm hypothesized flaws in the product by examination of the product's documentation and code, that is, the security evidence. There are three steps to the flaw confirmation stage: flaw prioritization and assignment, desk checking, and live testing.

Flaw prioritization and assignment. The flaw hypothesis sheets represent a comprehensive inventory of potential flaws. Sorted by the probability of existence, payoff (damage impact, if confirmed), work factor to confirm, and area of the system design, they provide a ranking of potential flaws for each design area from high probability/high payoff (HH) to low probability/low payoff (LL). Usually, only high and medium ranks are studied. Team members divide the rank lists among themselves based on expertise in the different system design areas. They move out as individuals on their lists. At daily team meetings, they share one another's progress and findings. Management may reallocate staff and FHS to balance the work load. Often confirmed flaws raise the priority of other FHS or provide the analysts with insight to generate new FHS.

Desk checking. The penetrator analyst studies the FHS and the TCB evidence. Code, models, code correspondence maps, or dependency graphs are examined to see if the flaw exists. The analyst must be flexible in considering alternatives, but concentrate on what exists in the actual code and other evidence. Analysts use code walk-throughs, prior test results, their own insights, and conversations with other team members to reach conclusions about the likelihood of the flaw's existence.

Results are documented on the FHS. Confirmed flaws are flagged in the database for later examination. An analyst spends a few days, at most, on each flaw. The desk checking continues for weeks, and possibly a few months, yielding an FHS productivity rate of 10 to 20 FHS per person-month. The work is tedious and detailed, and requires destructive thinking. Occasionally an FHS is of sufficient complexity and interest to warrant a live test, but the investment in the testing process will lower productivity.

Live testing. Test case design, coding, and execution are expensive, so live testing is not the preferred FHS evaluation method. However, testing is often the fastest way to confirm complex or time-dependent flaws. In penetration testing, live tests are similar to computer software configuration item (CSCI) functional tests with the FHS acting as the (dis)functional specification for the test. There is little unique about these tests, except they may be destructive of the system. Avoid running them on the operational system since they can have unpredictable results. Also, the testing is to confirm the flaw, not to exploit it. Test code should be a narrowly focused (by the FHS) quick one-shot routine. This will be easier to write if there is a rich library of debug and diagnostic routines.

Flaw generalization

When the team assembles for the daily meeting, the confirmed flaws of the day are briefed and examined. Each team member considers the possibility that the flaw might exist in his area, and whether the test technique and code can be used on his FHS. Often a confirmed flaw has only medium payoff value but can be used with other confirmed flaws to yield a high payoff. This stringing of flaws together is called "beading" and has led to many unusual high-payoff penetrations.

Deductive thinking confirms a flaw. Inductive thinking takes a specific flaw to a more general class of flaws. The team examines the basic technology upon which each confirmed flaw is based to see if the flaw is a member of a larger class of flaws. By this generalization of the flaw, one may find other instances of the weakness or gain new insight on countermeasures. Inductive thinking proceeds simultaneously with deductive thinking of new instances of the flaw, so that the flaw becomes a new flaw hypothesis generator. Some classic flaws were discovered by this induction — for example, parameter passing by reference [LIND75, SDC76], piecewise decomposition of passwords [TANE87], puns in I/O channel programs [ATTA76, PHIL73], and time-of-check-to-time-of-use (TOCTTOU) windows [LIND75]. These are described in the upcoming section "FHM experience."

Flaw elimination

Experts have argued the futility of penetrate-and-patch and hack-and-patch methods of improving the trust of a TCB for substantial reasons that reduce to the traditional position that you must design security, quality, performance, and so on, into the system and not add it on [SCHE79]. However, most human progress is made in incremental forward steps. Products improve with new releases and new versions that fix flaws by patching, workarounds, and redesign.

The TCSEC requires that all known flaws be repaired. The evaluators can suggest to the vendor repair of simple implementation and coding errors, or recommend known generic design flaw countermeasures. After repair, the system must be reevaluated to confirm the flaws were fixed and to ensure no new flaws were introduced. Reevaluation is a complete repetition of the penetration testing process. However, application of the Ratings and Maintenance Process (RAMP) [NCSC89a] to B2 and better evaluations may be a possible method to avoid total repetition. This speculation has been tried on the B2 evaluation of trusted Xenix ported to new hardware platforms [MCAU92]. It is impractical for the vendor to fix some flaws. These residual flaws will result in a lower class rating. However, the using agency can prepare a risk analysis that shows the DAA (Designated Approving Authority) alternative security measures to counter the residual flaws.

FHM experience

FHM has been a cost-effective method of security system assurance assessment for over twenty years. Unlike other assurance methods, which focus on narrower objectives (for example, formal correctness proofs of design or risk assessment costs of failures), FHM seeks security flaws in the overall operation of a system due to policy, specification, design, implementation, and/or operational errors. It is a complete systems analysis method that uncovers flaws introduced into the system at any stage of the product life cycle.

FHM management experience. Management models and work breakdown structures (WBS) of tasks, schedules, and labor loadings to perform typical penetration testing are available in the literature [RUB86, WEIS92a]. For weak systems in the TCSEC C1 to B1 classes, experience predicts a typical penetration team of four people operating for six months will generate about 1,000 FHS and assess about 400 of the highest priority. Some 50 to 100 of these will be confirmed flaws. That yields a productivity rate of one flaw for every one to two person-weeks of effort. Stronger systems in the TCSEC B2 to A1 classes, by definition, must be flawless. However, even these systems have flaws — far fewer, of course, because of the greater attention to secure system development. Such flaws are repaired, audited, or considered an acceptable risk. Higher flaw rates may signal a lesser evaluation class than B2 is warranted for the target system.

Vulnerability classes of flaws. Confirmed flaws are sorted into vulnerability classes:

1. flaw gives total control of the TCB/system (TC),
2. security policy violation (PV),
3. denial of service (DS),
4. installation dependent (IN), and
5. harmless (H).

These vulnerability classes are based on the degree of unauthorized control of the system permitted by the flaw — that is, damage extent. The greatest vulnerability is TCB capture; the machine is under total control of the interloper (TC — total control — flaws). Flaws that permit lesser control are unintentional, undocumented capabilities that violate the policy model, but do not allow total control (PV — policy violation — flaws). Denial of service flaws permit the penetrator to degrade individual and system performance, but do not violate the confidentiality security policy (DS — denial of service — flaws). Installation-dependent flaws are weaknesses in the TCB that obtain from local initialization of the system, such as a poor password algorithm (IN — installation-dependent — flaws). Last, there are flaws that are harmless in the sense that they violate policy in a minor way, or are implementation bugs that cause no obvious damage (H — harmless — flaws). These codes will categorize flaws presented in subsequent sections.

Penetration results: Example generic attack methods. This section presents a representative collection of attack methods found effective in finding flaws by the innovative and skilled penetration teams using FHM. An extensive taxonomy of flaws is in preparation by NRL (Naval Research Laboratory) [BULL91].

Weak identification/authentication. Passwords are the cheapest form of authentication. Weak passwords, however, are quite expensive, allowing the penetrator to impersonate key security administrators to gain total control of the TCB (TC flaw). In one system, a weak password protected the password file itself. The password was a short English word that took but a few hours of trial and error to crack. A modern form of this attack on the Unix password file is embodied in a program called Crack, which runs for days as a background task generating popular candidate passwords and trying them for confirmation [MUFF4a]. Since most passwords are initialized by system administration, this is an example of an operational flaw and an initial-condition (IN) flaw.

On the DEC PDP-10 and many contemporary machines, there are powerful string compare instructions used to compare stored versus entered passwords. These array instructions work like DO-WHILE loops until the character-by-character compare fails or the password string ends. It was discovered in the Tenex operating system that the instruction also failed when a page fault occurred. This turned a neat binary password predicate — yes/no — into a trinary decision condition — yes/no/maybe — that enabled piecewise construction of any password in a matter of seconds. In this case the flaw was a weak password checking routine that permitted the user to position the candidate password across page boundaries [TANE87]. This is an example of a hardware anomaly and an implicit memory sharing (TC) flaw.

On the IBM OS/VS2 R3 and similar vintage operating systems, files or data sets are protected by password. When the user is absent during batch processing, surrendered passwords for the file are placed in the Job Control Language (JCL) load deck and queue file for command to the batch process. The JCL queue is an unprotected database, which is readable by any user process, thus permitting theft of passwords. This is an example of a badly designed user-system interface, where system data is placed in the user's address space [MCPH74, SDC75, SDC76]. It is also an example of bad security policy, a policy violation (PV) flaw.

In most systems the user logs into a well-designed password authentication mechanism. However, the system never authenticates itself to the user. This lack of mutual authentication permits users to be spoofed into surrendering their passwords to a bogus login simulation program left running on a vacant public terminal. This spoof has been around forever and is still effective. It is an example of a poor user-system interface that yields a policy violation (PV) flaw. Mutual authentication is a necessity in the modern world of distributed computing, where numerous network servers handle files, mail, printing, management, routing, gateways to other networks, and specialized services for users on the net. Without it, such services will surely be spoofed, modified, and/or falsified. New smart card I&A systems provide mutual authentication by use of public key cryptography [KRAJ92].

Security perimeter infiltration. Untrusted code must be confined and permitted to call the TCB only in a prescribed manner for secure access to needed system services [LAMP73]. These boundary crossings of the security perimeter are often poorly designed and result in "infiltration" flaws. A classic example of this is the uncontrolled channel program of the IBM 370. Since channel programs are allowed to be self-modifying to permit scatter reads and writes and the user can turn off memory mapping (for example, Virtual = Real), it is possible to write into protected system memory and modify code and/or process management data. Attempts to eliminate these problems by static analysis of the channel programs in VM/370 failed to prevent clever "puns" in the code from continued exploitation [ATTA76, BELA74, PHIL73].

Another example of poor confinement is the Honeywell HIS 6000 GCOS suspend feature. It allows a user to freeze an interactive session for a lunch break or longer suspension, and resume later by thawing the program. The design flaw stores the frozen image in the user's file space, including all the sensitive system context needed to restart the code. It is a simple process for a user to edit the frozen image file and modify the context data such that the restarted program runs in system state with total control of the TCB (TC flaw). This is yet another example of an implied memory sharing flaw.

Among the most sophisticated penetrations is the legendary breakpoint attack of Linde and Phillips [ATTA76, PHIL73]. It is an excellent example of a beading attack. When a user plants a breakpoint in his user code, the system replaces the user code at the breakpoint with a branch instruction to the system. The system's breakpoint routine saves the user code in a system save area. Later, when the breakpoint is removed, the user code is restored. The breakpoint feature helps the penetrator plant code in the system itself — that is, the replaced user code — an example of a harmless (H) flaw. It was observed that another existing harmless flaw, a move string error exit, left the address of the system memory map, rather than the address of the string, upon error return. It was possible to induce the string flaw by reference to an unavailable memory page — that is, a page fault. A third harmless flaw allowed control to return to the caller while the string move was in progress in the called program.

The penetrators set up the bead attack by planting a breakpoint at a carefully prepared instruction on the same page as a string move command. They carefully selected a string that crossed a page boundary. They executed the string move, and upon regaining control, released the page containing the end of the long string. That caused a page fault when the string move crossed the page boundary, at which time the breakpoint was removed. In restoring the prebreakpoint user code, the system retrieved the saved user code but erroneously wrote the user code into protected system memory, specifically, the system page map. This unauthorized system modification was possible because a hardware design flaw in the page fault error return left the page address of the system memory map, not the page address of the original user's string. The attack had successfully modified the system map, placing user data in the system interrupt vector table. The attack gave arbitrary control of the TCB — another subtle flaw in implicit memory sharing (a TC flaw).

Incomplete checking. Imports and exports that cross the security perimeter per the TCSEC are either label checked or use implicit labels for the I/O channel used. Lots of flaws occur when labels are not used or are used inconsistently. Another attack exploits interoperability between systems that use different label semantics. The Defense Data Network (DDN) employs the standard IP datagram Revised Internet Protocol Security Option (RIPSO) security sensitivity label [RFC1038]. It differs from emerging commercial standards. Here is a situation ripe for a future security (IN) flaw.

Array-bounds overflow is a particularly nasty flaw and quite pervasive and difficult to counter. The flaw manifests itself in system operation, but its cause is usually traced to the development compiler's failure to generate code for dynamic array-bounds checking. When the array bound is exceeded, the code or data parameters adjacent to the array are overwritten and modified. In one case the user-entered password was stored adjacent to the system-stored password, so the two strings (arrays) could be rapidly compared. However, there was no bounds checking. The user simply entered a maximum-size password twice so that it overflowed the user array into the system array, creating a password match [BISH82], a certain TC flaw.

Incomplete case analysis leads to flaws. Either the design specification has not considered all the conditions of an IF-THEN-ELSE form, or the programmer goofed. In either event, the penetrator creates the missing condition and forces the code to ignore the consequences, often creating an exploitable state, a PV flaw. The IBM PSW flaw mentioned in the earlier section "System anomalies" is an example.

The IBM 360 introduced the Program Status Word (PSW), which contained a status condition code for the machine instructions that have conditional execution modes. Many programmers ignore the PSW status code and assume the execution result of the instruction. This is poor coding practice but a surprisingly frequent occurrence [BULL91]. Often the programmer believes that prior checks filter the conditions before the instruction execution and that the data cannot cause the unanticipated condition, thus ignoring the condition code. The penetrator must find an opportunity to reset the parameters after the filter checks, but before the conditional code execution. time-of-check-to-time-of-use (TOCTTOU) attacks are exactly what's needed for penetration.

A TOCTTOU flaw is like a dangling participle grammatical flaw in English. The check code is distant from the using code, enabling intervening code to change the tested parameters and cause the use code to take incorrect, policy-violating actions (a PV flaw). The attack is a form of sleight of hand. The penetrator sets up a perfectly innocent and correct program, possibly an existing application program, and through multitasking or multiprocessing, has another program modify the parameters during the interval between check and use. The interval may be small, necessitating careful timing of the attack. The flaw is both an implicit memory sharing error and a process synchronization problem. The solution is not to place system parameters in user memory and/or prohibit interruptibility of "critical region" code [LIND75, MCPH74, PHIL73].

Read-before-write flaws are residue control flaws. Beginning with TCSEC C2 class systems, all reused objects must be cleaned before reuse. This is required as a countermeasure to the inadequate residue control in earlier systems. However, the flaw persists in modern dress. When disk files are deleted, only the name in the file catalog is erased. The data records are added to free storage for later allocation. To increase performance, these used records are cleared on reallocation (if at all), not on deallocation. That means the data records contain residue of possibly sensitive material. If the file memory is allocated and read before data is written, the residue is accessible. A policy of write-before-read counters this flaw, but such a policy may not exist or may be poorly implemented. This flaw also appears with main memory allocation and garbage collection schemes. In one example, the relevant alphabetical password records were read into memory from disk for the login password compare. After the compare, the memory was left unchanged. Using other attacks, such as the array-bounds overflow described above, that residue memory could be read and passwords scavenged. By carefully stepping through the alphabet, the complete password file could be recreated (a TC flaw) [LIND76a].

Planting bogus code. The most virulent flaws are created by the penetrator inserting bogus code into the TCB (a TC flaw). Bogus code includes all forms of unauthorized software: Trojan horses, trap doors, viruses, bombs, and worms. Fundamentally, flaws that admit bogus code are flaws in the configuration control of the TCB. The flaw may occur any time throughout the life cycle of the TCB. When development tools are uncontrolled, bogus code can be imbedded in the tools and then into the TCB. Ken Thompson's ACM Turing Lecture aptly documented such an attack [THOM84]. But there are easier methods — for example, planting bogus code in the runtime package of the most popular compiler and/or editor. Recent attacks on the Internet were exploitations of poor configuration control. Known flaws in Unix were not fixed with the free vendor patches. The hacker used the flaws to obtain unauthorized access [SPAF89a].

Among the more colorful attacks against human frailty in controlling bogus code is the Santa Claus attack. It is a classic example of an unauthorized code import, achieved by spoofing the human operator of a secure system. A penetrator prepared an attractive program for the computer operator, who always ran with system privileges. The program printed a picture on the high-speed printer of Santa and his reindeer — the kind you always see posted at Christmas in and about the computer facility. However, there was a Trojan horse mixed in with Dancer, Prancer, and friends that modified the operating system to allow undetected access for the interloper. Before you belittle the computer operator's folly, consider your own use of "freeware" programs downloaded from your favorite bulletin board. There are as many user and operator spoofs as there are gullible people looking for "gain without pain." Eternal vigilance is the price of freedom from spoof attacks. Also, improved role-authorization controls can limit the damage propagation of such flaws from human foibles.

Penetration analysis for the 1990s and beyond

This essay concludes with speculations on future directions of penetration analysis. The assumption is that the battle between the TCB developer or operator and the hacker will continue unabated. Better legal protection for users will always trail technology, and the technology will improve for both antagonists. It will be continuous digital electronic warfare among security measures, hacker attacks, user countermeasures, and security counter-countermeasures: perpetual offense against defense.

The defense, developers of TCBs, are using better methods of designing and implementing trusted systems. Lessons are being learned from past penetrations, both tests and real attacks. The generic flaws are leading to better understanding of security policy for confidentiality, integrity, and service availability, and of the confinement of overt and covert channels when sharing common mechanisms in trusted systems. This understanding is being captured in improved machine architectures with segregated privilege domains or protection rings to reinforce security perimeters and boundary crossings. Improved hardware supports safe and rapid context switching and object virtualization. Cryptography is playing a larger role in confidentiality, integrity, and authentication controls. Computers are getting faster and cheaper so that security mechanisms will be hardware-rich and not limit performance in secure solutions. Software is improving in quality, tools, development environments, testing standards, and formalism.

Applicability of FHM to ITSEC. It has been questioned whether penetration testing has meaning for a Target of Evaluation (TOE) of the European Information Technology Security Evaluation Criteria (ITSEC), since "penetration testing" or its equivalent never appear in the criteria [ITSE90]. For most of the reasons expressed earlier in this essay, penetration testing will be required for ITSEC high-assurance evaluations. However, the ITSEC is different from the TCSEC and the TCSEC interpretations. The applicability of FHM to ITSEC for the 1990s is discussed here.

A TOE is either a security product or a system to be evaluated. Penetration testing of a TOE is comparable in scope to penetration testing in accordance with the TCSEC. However, a TOE's evaluation criteria consist of two-tuples (Fi, Ej): Fi is one of 10 security functionality classes, and Ej is one of seven independent evaluation levels. To match the TCSEC classes of FHM interest, we have the two-tuples (F4, E4), (F5, E5), and (F5, E6), which correspond to B2, B3, and A1, respectively. The first five functional classes of the ITSEC, F1 through F5, match the six functional classes of the TCSEC, C1 through A1, with F5 functionality the same for B3 and A1.

The seven ITSEC evaluation classes are applied to the TOE Development Process (DP), Development Environment (DE), and Operational Environment (OE), each of which is further divided as follows:

- DP: Requirements, architectural design, detailed design, implementation.
- DE: Configuration control, programming languages and compilers, developer security.
- OE: Delivery and configuration, setup and operation.

The ITSEC is so new there is no practical experience to draw from in looking at the applicability of FHM, so we look more closely at the text. Although penetration testing is not mentioned, testing is widely referenced, particularly for the evaluator to perform "his own tests to check the comprehensiveness and accuracy of the sponsor testing, and also to address any points of apparent inconsistency or error found in the results of the sponsor's testing" [ITSE90]. Testing for errors and vulnerabilities is required even at evaluation class E1, retesting of corrected flaws is required at E3, independent vulnerability analysis is needed at E4, and all these requirements are cumulative with higher evaluation classes. These test requirements are quite similar to those addressed by the FHM described in this essay.

Assurance of a TOE is divided in the ITSEC between correctness and effectiveness. Correctness is based on the seven evaluation classes E0 to E6. Effectiveness of a TOE involves a number of considerations: the suitability of the security functionality for the proposed environment, analogous to the TCSEC environment guidelines [CSC85]; whether the functionality yields a sound security architecture; ease of use of security functions; assessment of the security vulnerabilities during development and operation; and the strength of the security mechanisms to resist attack. All these items are "generators" in FHM (see the earlier section "Flaw generation").

The FHM depends on discovering failures in the evidence implication chain, starting with a security policy (see the earlier section "Evidence implication chain"). The application of FHM to a TOE would require a similar procedure. A TOE has a hierarchy of security policies: a System Security Policy (SSP), a System Electronic Information Security Policy (SEISP), and a Security Policy Model (SPM), corresponding to security objectives, detailed security enforcement mechanisms, and a semiformal policy model, respectively. These policies are tied to the functional classes and form the basis for the correctness criteria for testing. Together with the evaluation classes, an evidence implication chain is formed for a specific TOE, and FHM can be successfully applied.

In conclusion, FHM should be equally as applicable to ITSEC as to TCSEC/TNI/TDI evaluations. Under both sets of criteria, the most significant open question is: How are evaluators to judge the security of a system composed of individually evaluated components? The composability controversy is beyond the scope of this essay. However, FHM is applicable to such composed systems and may be part of the controversy's resolution.

Formal methods of penetration testing. Formal methods use rigorous mathematical specifications of the TCB design (that is, FTLS), assumptions, initial conditions, and correctness criteria. Formal tools take these specifications and generate correctness theorems and proofs of the theorems and the design they portray. It is hoped that these formal methods can achieve similar success at the level of code proofs. A new form of penetration analysis is in progress with new TCB designs — rigorous formal models of the TCB. These models describe the TCB behavior as state machines, state-transition rules, security invariants, initial conditions, and theorems that must be proven. Penetration analysis is almost inseparable from the formal design process, producing conjectures of flaws with the model and trying to prove them as theorems. This is a rigorous extension of FHM. If successful, the correctness proof versus flaw conjecture proof becomes part of the design process and uncovers problems early in the design, enabling iterative redesign — unlike FHM, which often comes too late in the development cycle to permit more than hack-and-patch.

Recent work by Gupta and Gligor suggests a theory of penetration-resistant systems. They claim their method is "a systematic approach to penetration analysis" that "enables the verification of penetration-resistance properties, and is amenable to automation" [GUPTA91, GUPTA92]. They specify a formal set of design properties that characterize resistance to penetration in the same framework used to specify the security policy enforcement model — a set of design properties, a set of machine states, state invariants, and a set of rules for analysis of penetration vulnerability. Five penetration-resistance properties are described:

1. system isolation (tamperproofness),
2. system noncircumventability (no bypass),
3. consistency of system global variables and objects,
4. timing consistency of condition (validation) checks, and
5. elimination of undesirable system/user dependencies.

Gupta and Gligor contend system flaws "are caused by incorrect implementation of the penetration-resistance properties [that] can be identified in system (e.g., TCB) source code as patterns of incorrect/absent validation-check statements or integrated flows that violate the intended design or code specifications." They further illustrate how the model can be used to implement automated tools for penetration analysis. They describe an Automated Penetration Analysis (APA) tool and their experiments with it on Secure Xenix source code. Early results from this work indicate that penetration resistance depends on many properties beyond the reference monitor, including the development and programming environment, which is characterized as the evidence implication chain earlier in this essay. Although limited only to software analysis of attacks on the TCB from untrusted user code and leaving significant other system avenues for attack, the work may pave the way for new approaches to building and testing trusted systems and tip the balance in favor of the "good guys."

Automated aids. Earlier, in the infancy of penetration testing, it was believed that flaws would fall into recognizable patterns, and tools could be built to seek out these generic patterns during penetration testing [ABBO76, CARL75, HOLL74, TRAT76]. Unfortunately, the large number of different processors, operating systems, and programming languages used to build TCBs, with their different syntax and semantics, made it difficult and impractical to apply such pattern-matching tools to penetration testing. It is costly to port or reimplement the tools for each new environment and different programming language. Also, the flaw patterns tended to be system specific.

As modern secure systems focus on a few operating system standards (for example, Unix and MS-DOS) and fewer programming languages (Ada and C), and more mature expert systems become available, future penetration testing tool initiatives to capture flaw patterns may be more successful. A few specific examples of this trend are beginning to appear: antivirus tools for the popular workstations and PCs; Unix security test tools [FARM90a, MUFF4a]; intrusion detection monitors [DENN86, SMAH88, BAUE88, DIAS91, LUNT92, WINK92]; and formal specification proof tools [KEMM86], flow analyzers [ECKM87, KRAM83], and symbolic execution tools [ECKM85, WHEE92].

Evaluation Issues

Marshall D. Abrams and Harold J. Podell

In this essay we present an introduction to evaluation issues in the United States and European Community (EC) to illustrate the two schools of thought. Following development of draft national and regional criteria, the US, Canada, and EC are working on Common Criteria (CC). We compare the proposed evaluation approaches in the hope that in the international process of developing the Common Criteria there will be a convergence to assist the multinational producers of secure products and systems in evaluation by different national entities. Interoperability of IT and IT security to support electronic commerce depends, in part, on an acceptance of evaluated products in different countries and regions. Therefore, an important aspect of evaluation is the development of international agreements for reciprocity of evaluations of secure products.

Our focus is on the evolving importance of evaluation issues that pertain to IT security. These issues are national, regional, and international in scope. We consider evaluation to be the security evaluation of products and systems.

Terminology differs between the TCSEC and ITSEC. In some cases, the difference is superficial. We suspect that the varying cultures and, to some degree, the "not-invented-here" phenomenon may have had something to do with the differences. In other cases, there are fundamental differences in outlook and philosophy. Harmonization of criteria is desirable. Following development of draft national and regional criteria, the US, Canada, and European Community are working on Common Criteria. The current multilateral work on developing the CC could contribute to the convergence necessary for a harmonized standard. For this essay, we focus on what the TCSEC and ITSEC documents are saying. To that end, we present side-by-side discussion of related concepts.

In the EC, the term is target of evaluation (TOE), which includes products and systems. However, the US terms vary. For example, the National Security Agency (NSA) evaluates secure products and produces an Evaluated Products List (EPL). Secure systems are evaluated within US organizations in a phased process. For example, a system may first be certified to a level of IT security by a technical official or team. The final acceptance of the system can be referred to as accreditation, which is the managerial review and approval or rejection. If approval is granted, the implication is that management is accepting a degree of residual risk.

Evaluation of products and systems

There are two fundamental questions addressed in this essay: What is evaluated, and who does the evaluation? There are essentially two sets of answers considered in this essay: one represented by the practices of the United States National Computer Security Center and the other proposed for use by the EC in the Information Technology Security Evaluation Criteria (ITSEC) and its companion documents.

What are products? Products are developed by a company with the expectation that when they are offered for sale enough copies will be purchased to enable the developer to make a profit. In the computer and related industries, products are usually combinations of hardware, firmware, and software that can be purchased commercially. Some of the terms used to identify products are "commercial off the shelf," abbreviated COTS, and "nondevelopment item," abbreviated NDI.

There is also a class of trusted (security-enforcing) products designed specifically for networks, such as trusted network components. The Verdix VSLAN is an example of such a network product. In addition to "traditional" trusted system products, VSLAN provides an NTCB (network trusted computing base) that supports "trusted" interconnectivity between user systems. This interconnectivity should comply with a defined security policy. The VSLAN network component performs access control, identification, authentication, and audit. Other security-enforcing products can be used with VSLAN, such as the AT&T System V/MLS (Multilevel Security).

Products are developed for some generalized environment that the vendor selects based on market research, prior experience, and other business factors. With respect to security, products are designed to withstand generic threats. Standardization bodies or government agencies help formulate generic environments when they publish evaluation criteria such as the Trusted Computer System Evaluation Criteria (TCSEC) [DOD85] and the Information Technology Security Evaluation Criteria (ITSEC) [ITSE91].

The developer may have a general conceptual target, such as "a large insurance company." In general, the user (an individual person or an organization) who purchases a product must make sure that product is suitable for the actual environment in which it will be used. There are various ways for the user to increase the probability that the product is suitable for its intended purpose, but that is outside the scope of this discussion.

What are systems? In contrast to products, systems are designed and built for the needs of a specific user community. A system has a unique operational environment because the real-world environment can be defined and observed. The security threats are real-world threats. The user performs a risk analysis or takes some equivalent action to determine which threats are to be met with countermeasures. The strength and assurance of countermeasures are likewise selected by the user.

A system may consist of a single product, but more likely a system will be built by assembling products. The system integrator is responsible for making sure that the subsystems work together, from both functional and security viewpoints.

The integration of trusted products into systems is nontrivial. The security policies and mechanisms of the individual subsystems must be made compatible and consistent for the entire system to meet its security objectives. One way of expressing this requirement is to say a system must have a security architecture and design.

While the TCSEC introduced the distinction between products and systems, this distinction has not received much attention. When the TCSEC was used as the criteria for evaluating systems, such as SACDIN and Blacker, it was necessary to redefine the criteria for the system context. The TCSEC also anticipated issues such as identifying the TCB boundary when a trusted computer is embedded in a larger system.

Different practices and regulations have evolved in the US for the evaluation of products and systems. In contrast, the developers of the ITSEC saw a similarity that they attempted to take advantage of by introducing a generic term for both systems and products: target of evaluation (TOE). The intent was to apply the same evaluation criteria to both products and systems as far as possible. We will use the term TOE in our discussion.

Evaluation

Evaluation of the technical security capabilities of the TOE is performed to confirm the claims made about it. The function of independent evaluation is to assess the merit of the assertions about the TOE's security characteristics. These assertions may be stated in terms of conformance to published standards, criteria, or procurement specifications; or may simply be statements describing the TOE's security characteristics.

Security requirements are technically complex; they are not well or widely understood. Requirements and interpretations change. There are many requirements that are not susceptible to objective measurement so that repeated tests would yield the same result. Rather, these requirements call for subjective decisions by security subject area experts. Procedures are used to enhance consistency, but human variation cannot be eliminated.

Chronologically, the first independent evaluation function was provided by the National Computer Security Center (NCSC) at the National Security Agency (NSA). These evaluations focused on the NCSC objective of building up an Evaluated Products List (EPL). On a few occasions, NSA assisted in system evaluations in support of what is called certification and accreditation (C&A) in US usage.

NCSC product evaluations are performed primarily at government expense. There is no transfer of funds between the vendor and the NCSC. The NCSC and the vendor each pay the salaries and incidental expenses of their own employees.

At the time of writing, the European Community is developing the ITSEC and related evaluation policy and working with the US and Canada in the joint development of a draft CC. The UK has published an approach to evaluations that is probably applicable to the entire EC. Commercial licensed evaluation facilities (CLEFs) will be designated as approved organizations to confirm vendor security assertions and claims. CLEFs will be commercial organizations, operating on a fee-for-service basis. Although CLEFs may be independent business entities, it is more likely that they will be parts of larger organizations. There will be safeguards to enforce a CLEF's independence from influence from the parent organization. The CLEFs will evaluate both products and systems, their fees being paid by the sponsor of the evaluation, who is usually the manufacturer or vendor of a product or the user of a system. The results of an evaluation are reviewed and approved by a government certification body.

Note the difference in use of "certify" in US and EC usage. In the EC case, certification applies to the thoroughness and impartiality of the CLEF's evaluation process. In the US, certification generally is the technical evaluation of the IT security features for a system. After certification is complete, accreditation is the managerial approval or disapproval of the system. Table 1 illustrates the US and EC approaches to evaluation.

Some organizations may perform their own evaluations — at least until CLEFs get established and perhaps even after that, depending on the answers to the following questions: Will commercial fee-for-service evaluators have a conflict of interest? Some people are skeptical about whether CLEFs will be able to maintain their independence and protect the sponsor's and vendor's proprietary interests. There are also questions about the cost-benefit trade-offs of a user organization using a CLEF as compared with performing its own evaluations.

Table 1. Evaluation schemes compared.

Where	US	EC
Criteria	TCSEC, TNI, TDI	ITSEC
Product evaluation	NCSC, EPL (government)	Licensed laboratory
System evaluation	Purchaser	(Government review)
Direct cost	Government purchaser	Vendor
International evaluation acceptance	Canada, Australia, New Zealand	Not in EC

Key

TCSEC: Trusted Computer System Evaluation Criteria
TNI: Trusted Network Interpretation of TCSEC
TDI: Trusted Database Interpretation of TCSEC
ITSEC: Information Technology Security Evaluation Criteria
EC: European Community
NCSC: National Computer Security Center
EPL: Evaluated Products List

Scope: Type of system

Operating systems were the first concern of computer security. All of the research leading up to publication of the TCSEC was concerned with the technology of the 1970s, namely time-sharing operating systems. In fact, many of the mechanisms used to separate time-shared users are still in use today.

It is no longer sufficient to evaluate only operating systems. In the late 1980s and the early 1990s, the NCSC produced interpretations of the TCSEC for computer networks, the Trusted Network Interpretation (TNI), and for database management systems, the Trusted Database Interpretation (TDI). These interpretations recognized several advances in information technology (IT). Very few computer systems were sold without a communications capability. Point-to-point communications, the security of which was previously treated as communications security, were being replaced by computer networks.

The utility of computers continues to be enhanced by major applications and utilities, such as database management systems (DBMS). Networks and DBMS are considerably different from operating systems; they usually have their own security functionality in addition to the operating system. In producing the TNI and TDI, the NCSC took the position that the TCSEC contained the basic principles of information security and interpreted these principles for networks and DBMS.

US evaluation approach

In the US during the 1980s, the NCSC saw its primary mission as encouraging the commercial availability of trusted products. This is often expressed as "populating the Evaluated Products List (EPL)." NCSC conducted product evaluations that concentrated on commercial off-the-shelf products.

As mentioned, the evaluation of systems in the United States is termed system certification and accreditation. NSA occasionally participated in such system evaluations, but the responsibility typically rests with the organization procuring the system. Evaluations are conducted by the government at its expense. Vendors incur expenses, of course, in preparing for evaluations and providing training and evidence to the government evaluators.

The NCSC product evaluation process determines whether a commercial off-the-shelf product satisfies the TCSEC. The evaluation may be assisted by an interpretation such as the TNI. The primary goal is to encourage widespread availability of trusted computer systems. Evaluation is focused on technical evaluation of protection capabilities.

The NCSC product evaluation phases are evolving. These phases start with the *proposal phase*, during which the government checks for majority foreign ownership, performs market analysis to determine product viability, and issues a preliminary technical assessment (PTA). In the *vendor assistance phase* (VAP), two evaluators are assigned, with the major responsibility to make sure that the vendor understands the requirements. During the VAP, the *rating maintenance phase* (RAMP) is developed to provide for the continuation of the trust rating as product updates are released. RAMP is being expanded in scope to include the categories C2 through A1. The *design analysis phase* (DAP) begins one year before scheduled beta testing. Several evaluators are assigned, and an initial product assessment report (IPAR) is produced and reviewed by a technical review board (TRB). Product design is frozen and a beta test begins. The culmination is the *formal evaluation phase*, including formal testing, a final report drafted by the evaluation team and reviewed by the TRB, and the product rating on the EPL. If the vendor is unresponsive at any phase, the company returns to the proposal phase.

Technical system certification consists of a technical evaluation of a system's security features as part of the approval, acceptance, and accreditation process. This process is necessary to establish the extent to which system design and implementation meet a set of specified security requirements. Hardware, firmware, system software, applications software, communications equipment, and the operational facility must be configured, evaluated, and tested. To ensure objectivity, evaluations are performed by technical personnel independent of the development organization. Evaluation results in a statement identifying whether system security requirements are met. This statement lists problems and suggests solutions (if known), describes all known remaining vulnerabilities, and advises the Accreditor relative to the accreditation decision in a Certification Report of Findings submitted to the Accreditor.

The certification analysis includes the results of security test and evaluation. Certification is the technical evaluation of a system's security features — part of and in support of the approval/accreditation process to establish the extent to which a particular system's design and implementation meet a set of specified security requirements. Accreditation is the managerial authorization and approval granted to an ADP (automated data processing) or computer system or network to process sensitive data in an operational environment. Management needs to decide whether to operate a system or network using specific safeguards, against a defined threat, at an acceptable level of risk, under a stated operational concept, with stated interconnections, in a specific operational environment, with a specific security mode of operation.

Accrediting officials are agency officials or corporate management who have authority to accept or reject a system's security safeguards and issue an accreditation statement documenting their decision. They must also have authority to allocate resources to achieve acceptable security and to remedy security deficiencies. The ultimate responsibility for system security rests with the Accreditor. Systems must be accredited before they process or use sensitive or classified information unless a written waiver is granted by the Accreditor. The Accreditor must trade off technical shortcomings against operational necessity and may determine that it is preferable to accept a residual security risk rather than preclude mission-critical functions.

Considering all the responsibility and authority vested in the Accreditor, it is prudent for the Accreditor to be involved in system design decisions. The management practice of "no surprises" suggests that the Accreditor be at least informed and preferably allowed to participate in important decisions to be knowledgeable about the system when accreditation time arrives.

UK evaluation approach

At the time of writing, the EC is developing instructions for evaluation conducted against the ITSEC and, as mentioned, participating in the development of the CC. We believe that the UK information technology (IT) security evaluation scheme is a valid model for the EC scheme. The UK IT security evaluation and certification scheme establishes a UK Certification Body to

1. certify results of evaluations to common technical standards,
2. monitor all evaluations,
3. approve all proposed evaluations, and
4. deal with other nations on mutual recognition of certificates.

The objective is to offer evaluation services to industry and government so that vendors can demonstrate security claims of products, and users can be satisfied that security objectives are met by systems.

Government supervision is jointly provided by the Communications Electronics Security Group (CESG) of the Government Communications Headquarters (GCHQ) and the Department of Trade and Industry (DTI). Evaluations are conducted by commercial licensed evaluation facilities (CLEFs) and performed in accordance with the ITSEC against an explicit security target. A product target is a list of claims made by the vendor. These may be predefined targets included in the ITSEC or may be the capabilities of the product selected by the vendor as based on a marketing decision. A system target depends on the real-world applications environment. The Certification Body cannot assess completeness or accuracy of a system target; the fitness for purpose is determined by the sponsor of the evaluation, the user in this case. When the user is a UK government agency processing classified information, the CESG acts as the National Technical Security Authority advising government and contractors on national minimum standards for protection of classified information. This role is independent of the scheme.

Evaluations are conducted by an evaluation facility on behalf of the sponsor, who commissions and pays for the evaluation, and receives the evaluation and certification reports. The developer may be separate from the sponsor. For example, a contractor who is the developer normally must assist in the evaluation. The deliverables required for evaluation are normally the property of the developer. The deliverables include hardware, firmware, and software documentation, technical support, and access to the development facility. The developer may wish to limit the sponsor's access to proprietary information.

The sponsor determines the security target, which defines the security functions of the TOE, may describe threats or security mechanisms, and includes the evaluation level desired, specified in ITSEC terms. It is the sponsor's responsibility to determine the security target, which may derive from the sponsor's circumstances, may be a marketing decision, and/or may be required by law or corporate policy. The CLEF reviews the security target, prepares an evaluation work plan, and obtains the Certification Body approval. The development and evaluation process is illustrated in Figure 1.

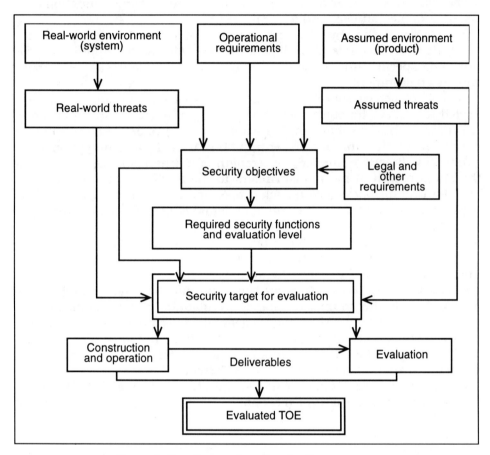

Figure 1. Development and evaluation process.

US and EC evaluations are based on factors that are both similar and different. Furthermore, the factors described in the ITSEC have yet to stand the test of use over time. It is reasonable to anticipate that the interpretation of the ITSEC factors will undergo further refinement and gradually move toward aspects of the evolving CC. The best we can do today is present the two sets of factors so that you can compare them.

US evaluation criteria factors

The NCSC "rainbow series" creates a set of common factors affecting the evaluation process, which differ, in part, from the ITSEC factors. In this section we will examine these sets of factors. Keep in mind that US practice will change as the draft FC is revised to move toward the evolving CC.

The US NCSC criteria are divided into three groups: functionality, strength of mechanism, and assurance.

Functionality is the objective and approach of a security service, including features, mechanism, and performance. Alternative approaches for providing specified functionality may be more suitable in different applications environments.

Strength of mechanism refers to how well a specific approach may be expected to achieve its objectives. Selection of parameters can significantly affect strength of mechanism. For example, the number of bits used in a checksum or the number of permutations used in an encryption algorithm may directly influence the strength of mechanism. For inadvertent threats, strength of mechanism refers to the ability to operate correctly after natural disasters, emergencies, operator errors, and accidents. This is particularly critical for prevention of denial of service as a consequence of inadvertent threats. For deliberate attack, strength of mechanism refers to the ability to resist that attack. Since a skillful attacker can make the attack look like an inadvertent threat, it is usually not useful to distinguish among the causes of threats.

Assurance refers to the basis for believing that the functionality will be achieved, including tamper resistance, verifiability, and resistance to circumvention or bypass. Assurance is generally based on analysis involving theory, testing, software engineering, and validation and verification. The analysis may be formal or informal, where formal implies mathematical techniques, such as those discussed in Essay 8.

When considering communications, the TNI provides additional definitions concerning strength of mechanism, which it considers a metric of how well a specific approach may be expected to achieve its objectives. The evaluating ratings available are none, minimum, fair, and good. Mechanisms that only protect against accident and malfunction are rated as minimum. Mechanisms must provide protection against deliberate attack to be rated as good. Criteria are specified for each security service. The TNI Environments Guideline (TNIEG) additionally recommends that inadvertent threats and malicious threats be analyzed separately; traditional risk management techniques are applicable only to inadvertent threats. The TNIEG suggests that malicious threats may dominate inadvertent threats and that malicious users can often duplicate circumstances of inadvertent threats.

In the TCSEC and all other "rainbow" documents and NCSC policy, the trusted computing base (TCB) is a very important concept. The network TCB (NTCB) is introduced in the TNI as a generalization of the TCB for a stand-alone computer. The NTCB reduces the risk of unauthorized modification to objects within a network system by maintaining the integrity of programs that provide security services. In the TCSEC, security services support confidentiality and accountability. In particular, the implementation of one security service can be prevented from degrading assurance of other services. This ensures that protection provided by one security service is not diluted by other security services.

The security services listed in Part II of the TNI are authentication, communications integrity, nonrepudiation, continuity of operations, protocol-based protection, network management, data confidentiality, traffic flow confidentiality, and selective routing. The assurance of these security services described in Part II of the TNI is related to the TCSEC operating system assurance included in Part I of the TNI. This is because a security service depends on the NTCB to protect it from unauthorized modification. It is very appealing, but wrong, to think that you can increase the assurance level of a network by adding security services. You can add functionality, but the assurance of this added functionality has an upper limit in the assurance of the NTCB. Even if the added security services are developed at a very high level of assurance, when installed in a real system the assurance can be no higher than that provided by the NTCB. This is analogous to saying that a chain is no stronger than its weakest link.

Some security services are strongly dependent on the computers in the network and can be directly evaluated under Part I and Appendix A of the TNI. Appendix A was written to support the evaluation of components and subsystems. Note that the TNI was a little imprecise in its definitions and has been corrected in the TNIEG as follows:

> A component is an individual physical unit that does not provide a complete set of end-user services. A system or subsystem is a collection of hardware, firmware, and software necessary [and] configured to collect, create, communicate, disseminate, process, store, and/or control data and information.

The recursive definition of the overall network security policy is discussed in Essays 2, 6, and 7.

The required strength of mechanism is determined using a risk index only slightly different from that used in the Yellow Book or DoD Directive (DODD) 5200.28 for stand-alone computer systems. The risk index computation takes the difference between the maximum data sensitivity, R_{max}, and the lowest clearance of a user who can gain physical access to some system device, R_{min}. Note that there is a difference from a Yellow Book risk index calculation, where the lowest cleared user is of concern; but that lowest cleared user includes indirect access, as discussed in Essay 2. This network risk index must also consider the most sensitive information in the network.

The general case is $R_{min} < R_{max}$, in which case

Risk Index = $R_{max} - R_{min}$

In the special case $R_{max} \geq R_{min}$, if there are any categories in the system to which some users are not authorized access

Risk Index = 1

otherwise

Risk Index = 0

The rating scale for maximum data sensitivity is given in Table 2.

Table 2. Rating scale for maximum data sensitivity. Risk Index = $R_{max} - R_{min}$.

R_{max} without Categories	Rating	R_{max} with Categories	Rating
U	0		
N	1		2
C	2		3
S	3	1 category in S	4
		>1 category in S	5
TS	5	1 category in S or TS	6
		>1 category in S or TS	7

Table 3. Rating scale for minimum user clearance.

Minimum User Clearance	Rating
U — Uncleared	0
N — Access to Sensitive Unclassified	1
C — Confidential	2
S — Secret	3
TS — Top Secret with Background Investigation (BI)	4
SBI — TS with Special Background Investigation	5
1 Category	6
>1 Category	7

The rating scale for minimum user clearance is given in Table 3. Note, however, that the two different background investigations have been recently abolished. No guidance has been issued on how this risk index calculation specified in DODD 5200.28 should be amended.

The operating modes are the same for networks and stand-alone operating systems; they indicate how much trust is placed in technical security by specifying who may use the network. Briefly, the modes are identified as follows: A dedicated network is exclusively used for one classification. In system high mode, the entire network is operated at, and all users are cleared to, the highest sensitivity level of information stored (historic definition). In a partitioned network, all personnel have clearance, but not necessarily formal access approval and need-to-know, for all information. A multilevel network has two or more classification levels, and not all users have clearance or formal access approval for all data.

The TNI/TNIEG security metrics include the security risk index, the evaluation structure for network security services, the minimum strength of mechanism requirement, the minimum assurance requirements, and the TNI Part II security service assurance rating. Table 4 shows the relationships among risk index, security mode, and minimum security class.

Table 4. Risk index, security mode, and minimum security class.

Risk Index	Security Mode	Minimum Security Class
0	Dedicated	No minimum class
0	System high	C2
1	Multilevel, partitioned	B1
2	Multilevel, partitioned	B2
3	Multilevel	B3
4	Multilevel	A1
5-7	Multilevel	*

* Beyond current state of computer security technology.

Table 5. Evaluation structure for network security services.

Network Security Service	Criterion	Evaluation Range
Communications integrity Authentication	Functionality Strength Assurance	None | present None-good None-good
Communications field integrity	Functionality Strength Assurance	None-good None-good None-good
Nonrepudiation	Functionality Strength Assurance	None | present None-good None-good
Denial of service Continuity of operations	Functionality Strength Assurance	None-good None-good None-good
Protocol-based protection	Functionality Strength Assurance	None-good None-good None-good
Network management	Functionality Strength Assurance	None-good None-good None-good
Compromise protection Data confidentiality	Functionality Strength Assurance	None | present Sensitivity level None-good
Traffic flow confidentiality	Functionality Strength Assurance	None | present Sensitivity level None-good
Selective routing	Functionality Strength Assurance	None | present None-good None-good

Table 5 shows the evaluation structure for network security services, Table 6 the TNI minimum strength of mechanism requirements and the assurance ratings for networks, and Table 7 the dependence of the TNI Part II assurance on the assurance of the NTCB.

Table 6. Minimum strength of mechanism and assurance requirements.

Risk Index	Strength of Mechanism	Part II Assurance Rating
0	None	None
1	Minimum	Minimum
2	Fair	Fair
>2	Good	Good

Table 7. Parts I and II assurance dependence.

Part II Assurance Rating	Minimum Part I Evaluation
Minimum	C1
Fair	C2
Good	C3

ITSEC evaluation factors

Under the ITSEC, the evaluation factors are functionality, correctness, and effectiveness. Functionality refers to the security functions (for example, access control, auditing, and error recovery), which may be individually specified or referenced by predefined functionality class. There are three levels of abstraction:

- Objectives. Why the functionality is wanted; the contribution to security.
- Enforcing functions. What functionality is actually provided; the features of the TOE that contribute to security.
- Mechanisms. How the functionality is provided; the logic or algorithm that implements a particular function.

The ITSEC requirements for functionality mandate the existence of a security target consisting of:

1. a system security policy or a product rationale,
2. a specification of the required security-enforcing functions,
3. an optional definition of required security mechanisms,
4. the claimed rating of the minimum strength of mechanism, and
5. the target evaluation level.

The following generic headings are recommended for specification of the security target:

1. identification and authentication,
2. access control,
3. accountability,
4. audit,
5. object reuse,
6. accuracy,
7. reliability of service, and
8. data exchange.

The ITSEC provides 10 predefined functionality classes that can be used as the basis for individual system and producer security targets, or can be used as guidelines to assist users in selecting appropriate security functionality for their environment or to help vendors configure their products. The first five predefined functionality classes are designed for close correspondence with the functionality requirements of the TCSEC classes. For easy reference, these classes are identified as F-C1, F-C2, F-B1, F-B2, and F-B3. Remember that the TCSEC classes B3 and A1 differ in assurance, not functionality.

The predefined functionality class F-IN is for targets with high integrity requirements for data and programs; databases are identified as a possible application. The predefined functionality class F-AV is for targets with high availability requirements, such as manufacturing process control computers. The predefined functionality class F-DI sets high requirements for safeguarding data integrity during communications. The predefined functionality class F-DC sets high requirements for data confidentiality during communication; this requirement might apply to cryptographic devices. The predefined functionality class F-DX is intended for networks with high demands for both confidentiality and integrity of communication. For example, public networks may require F-DX functionality for the transmission of sensitive information via insecure networks.

The ITSEC does not prescribe the particular methods or styles for the specification of security functions. Three styles are identified in the

ITSEC: informal, written in a natural language with the aim of minimizing ambiguity; semiformal, using a graphical or restricted natural language presentation; and formal, written in a formal notation according to mathematical concepts of syntax, semantics, notation, proof rules, and logical reasoning.

The ITSEC requirements for assurance of effectiveness are based on the proposed use of the TOE as described in its security target. The assessment of effectiveness involves consideration of:

- suitability of the TOE's security functionality to counter identified threats specified in its security target;
- whether individual security functions and mechanisms of the TOE bind together in a way that is mutually supportive and provides an integrated and effective whole;
- the ability of security mechanisms to withstand direct attack;
- whether known security vulnerabilities in construction and operation of the TOE could, in practice, compromise security; and
- whether the TOE can be configured or used in a manner that is insecure but which an administrator or end user of the TOE would reasonably believe to be secure.

The ITSEC strength of mechanism evaluation applies to all critical mechanisms whose failure would create a security weakness; these mechanisms are assessed for their ability to withstand direct attack. A basic rating means that all critical mechanisms provide protection against random accidental subversion, although knowledgeable attackers may be able to defeat them. A medium rating means that critical mechanisms provide protection against attackers with limited opportunities or resources. A high rating means that all critical mechanisms could be defeated only by attackers possessing a high level of expertise, opportunity, and resources, and successful attack is judged to be beyond normal practicality.

A TOE will fail evaluation only on effectiveness grounds and receive an overall evaluation level of E0, if an exploitable vulnerability found during evaluation is not eliminated before the end of evaluation.

The ITSEC requirements for assurance of correctness are expressed in seven hierarchical levels; E0 is the lowest and E6 the highest:

E0 Inadequate assurance.
E1 There is a security target and an informal description of the TOE security architecture, and functional testing indicates that the TOE satisfies its security target.
E2 (beyond E1 requirements) There is an informal description of the detailed design; evidence of functional testing is evaluated; there is

a configuration control system and approved distribution procedure.

E3 (beyond E2) The source code and/or hardware drawings for the security mechanisms are evaluated; evidence of testing these mechanisms is evaluated.

E4 (beyond E3) There is a formal model of the security policy; security-enforcing functions, architectural design, and detailed design are specified in a semiformal style.

E5 (beyond E4) Close correspondence exists between detailed design and source code and/or hardware drawings.

E6 (beyond E5) Security-enforcing functions and architectural design are specified in a formal style consistent with the formal model of policy.

The rating awarded to a TOE consists of a reference to the TOE security target, the assurance evaluation level for correctness and effectiveness, and the strength of mechanism rating. A TOE rated E0 is not rated on strength of mechanism.

Issues for consideration

This discussion of the US and EC approaches to criteria and evaluation raises certain issues that have been considered for the draft US FC and the evolving CC, including:

1. bundling of evaluation criteria factors,
2. ITSEC/TCSEC relationship and implications,
3. conceptual ITSEC issues,
4. implications of the ITSEC on the US computer industry,
5. whether criteria should prescribe policy,
6. evaluation by parts, and
7. a proposal for a US Information Security Foundation (ISF).

The TCSEC, TNI Part I, and TDI bundle (predetermine) functionality, strength of mechanism, and assurance; the TNI and ITSEC separately evaluate security factors. The claimed advantages of bundling are that fewer evaluation points simplify choices for vendors and users, and that these evaluation points provide government guidance. Having a limited number of security targets was quite important in the start-up phases of computer security in that the TCSEC provided indirect guidance to purchasers as well as vendors. However, the TCSEC was written by DoD for the defense sector; it is not necessarily applicable, without interpretation, to civil government and commercial applications. The draft FC introduced the Protection Profile, which specifies security aspects of an IT product.

The claimed advantages of unbundling are that there are fewer targets for vendors who are more free to offer products determined by market factors, and that it is easier for users to select systems. But many consumers are unsophisticated with regard to applying security evaluation criteria. These consumers do not know what they need, and they do not understand the IT security state of the art. Similarly, vendors may not understand the consumer's IT security needs. The flexible TOE claims structure permits an accurate representation of the TOE's capabilities, but excessive flexibility could lead to confusion.

The ITSEC is policy neutral; it is directed only at the evaluation of security targets. It leaves the policy to be defined externally. The TCSEC, in comparison, has US DoD confidentiality policy woven through it and has been interpreted to also apply to one form of integrity policy. Nevertheless, the ITSEC has included explicit measures for compatibility with the TCSEC by its definitions of the predefined functionality classes (F-C1, F-C2, F-B1, F-B2, and F-B3). The decision to make the ITSEC independent of a specific security policy leaves a void with respect to policy guidance. There is a need for supplementary guidance on the relationship between functionality and assurance requirements. Users could use guidance concerning the assurance required by each security mechanism.

Purchasers and users who are not experts need policy guidance from central policy-making government agencies, and from professional, legal, and ethical organizations and experts. A possible solution is to rely on the civil and defense establishments to make government security policy, and professional boards and societies to recommend commercial security policy. Perhaps the framers of the ITSEC intended such guidance to come into existence. The international CC developments may serve as a catalyst in this process.

The ITSEC effectiveness requirements, coupled with architectural and design constraints, correspond to the TCSEC concept of a trusted computing base. When combined with the appropriate effectiveness rating, a product meeting the ITSEC class should meet the corresponding TCSEC class. The reverse is not true, due to wider requirements in the ITSEC. Table 8 shows the intended correspondence.

The ability to configure products to satisfy TCSEC and ITSEC requirements does not solve all the problems. As long as the criteria are subject to separate interpretations by national bodies, there is no guarantee that evaluations in one country will be accepted in another country. Reciprocity is being tested by several vendors who are seeking multinational security evaluations for their products. This process could be facilitated as international agreements are developed that are based on the evolving CC.

Table 8. Intended correspondence between ITSEC and TCSEC classes.

ITSEC Classes	TCSEC Classes
E0	D
F-C1, E1	C1
F-C2, E2	C2
F-B1, E3	B1
F-B2, E4	B2
F-B3, E5	B3
F-B3, E6	A1

Compatibility of ITSEC predefined classes with the TCSEC is a "mixed blessing." The TCSEC has not been updated since its publication. The rewording of the TCSEC functional requirements is quite laudable. Unfortunately, well-known "defects" in the TCSEC are propagated. There is an opportunity to make improvements in the CC process. There is debate among security practitioners concerning some of these "defects." This healthy discussion of differences is reflected in this collection. Essay 2 takes a different position on some of these issues. Here are some TCSEC issues that could be addressed:

- The definition of DAC in the TCSEC is inadequate; it does not clearly explain what is discretionary. This is really a question of delegation of authority that could be explained much more clearly.
- The TCSEC DAC definition is so poorly worded that it permits the fundamental flaws identified in the DAC guideline [NCSC87b]. A more careful statement of transitivity and secondary delegation of authority could close or reduce these defects.
- The DAC statement concerning propagation of rights has proven to be unclear and ineffective. Here is an opportunity to be more effective and explicit.
- It is now understood that DAC is an example of an identity-based access control (IBAC). There are other stronger IBAC, such as ORCON (Organization Control), defined in DCID 1/7. In fact, these IBAC are nondiscretionary; there is disagreement among researchers about whether ORCON can be implemented using the TCSEC mandatory controls. These distinctions should be made much more clear.

- Addressing only human-readable labels onto printed output is obsolete; it is a gross oversight not to include all forms of human-readable output, especially video display.

There are potential implications for the international computer industry. For example, where do international computer companies submit their trusted products for evaluation? Will existing NCSC criteria and evaluations be changed to conform to the ITSEC, the draft FC, and/or the evolving CC? What role will the US National Institute of Standards and Technology (NIST) play in the security evaluation process? What will be the transition plans? Should US evaluations use the UK evaluation scheme?

Industry representatives have expressed a need for evaluation by parts, including parts sold by different vendors or parts previously evaluated but changed or rehosted. NCSC addresses part of the problem through the Rating Maintenance Phase (RAMP) Program, NCSC-TG-013 [NCSC89a], and another part of the problem through the concept of TCB subsets in the TDI.

While it is desirable that an entire assessment does not have to be redone for every software, hardware, or firmware upgrade or error correction, it is currently not possible to determine trust characteristics of an arbitrary collection of subsystems. The TDI may answer some of the evaluation requirements, if use of the TDI successfully provides: (1) a clear description of parts considered for separate evaluation, (2) a clear description of conditions for evaluation by parts, and (3) an interpretation of evaluation criteria for evaluation by parts.

Essay 13

Supporting Policies and Functions

Marshall D. Abrams and Harold J. Podell

The major policy objective, to protect information assets against specific harm, usually requires additional policies and functions for support and implementation. This essay discusses supporting policies and functions drawn from the TCSEC, the supporting "rainbow series," and the ITSEC.

The major security policies and functions are discussed in most of the other essays in this collection. This essay is concerned with the support necessary to enable the major security objectives to be achieved. The TCSEC and its "rainbow series" identify the supporting functions and often establish requirements for the presence of such functions in systems designated to protect specified levels and ranges of classified information. The ITSEC identifies similar functions but avoids establishing policy.

In this essay we first present the TCSEC and ITSEC approaches, and then provide detail on each individual policy or function. These supporting policies are sometimes considered part of the infrastructure. Sterne [STER91b], in his discussion of nontraditional security policy, observes that these supporting policies are likely to be applicable independent of policy objectives.

The TCSEC approach

The TCSEC identifies and sets requirements for six supporting policies:

- identification and authentication,
- accountability,
- assurance,
- continuous protection,
- object reuse, and
- covert channels.

The ITSEC approach

The ITSEC does not set policy; in fact, it very explicitly avoids doing so. It relies on external statements of policy, requirements, or security objectives. These external statements specify the security target. Once a security target is established, the ITSEC comes into play as the governing rules by which to determine whether the system or product meets the security target.

The ITSEC provides eight generic headings for groupings of security-enforcing functions. It recommends use of these generic headings to facilitate comparison of security targets and to simplify the work of the evaluators. The recommended headings are:

- identification and authentication,
- access control,
- accountability,
- audit,
- object reuse,
- accuracy,
- reliability of service, and
- data exchange.

The ITSEC recommended headings are a superset of the TCSEC supporting policies. The additions come from consideration of networks and database management systems, plus integrity objectives. While not establishing policy, the ITSEC headings are a good list of security-enforcing functions that should be considered for inclusion in any system or product.

Specific functions and policies

Identification and authentication. In the ITSEC, identification and authentication determine and control the users who are permitted access to controlled resources. This involves verifying the user's claimed identity. The user provides some information that is known by the target of evaluation (TOE) to be associated with the user in question. This heading also includes:

1. any functions to enable new user identities and the associated authentication information to be added, and old user identities to be removed or invalidated;
2. functions to generate, change, or allow authorized users to inspect the authentication information;

3. functions to assure the integrity of, or prevent the unauthorized use of, authentication information; and

4. functions to limit the opportunity for repeated attempts to establish a false identity.

The TCSEC identification and authentication policy requires that individual users be identified, and this claimed identification must be authenticated. Users must identify themselves before beginning to perform any other actions mediated by the TCB. For many users this login interaction is the only time they must explicitly deal with the TCB, so they mistakenly think that identification and authentication constitutes access control. It is somewhat ironic that the less obtrusive the TCB is, the higher the probability of this misunderstanding.

The TCB maintains authentication information for verifying the claimed identity. Authentication information is commonly divided into three groups:

1. something the user knows,
2. something the user has, and
3. something the user is.

Mechanisms and procedures are established to authenticate claimed identity by checking one or more of these groups. Using more than one piece of information, especially from different groups, increases the probability of valid authentication.

The most common form of "something the user knows" is a password. Although there are password guidelines published by both the Defense Department [CSCD85] and the National Institute for Standards and Technology [GUID85a], password protection is often the Achilles' heel of computer security.

For example, the Department of Defense Password Management Guideline [CSCD85] provides a set of good practices related to the use of password-based user authentication, including:

1. security management responsibilities for initial password assignment, password change authorization, and user ID revalidation;
2. user responsibilities for security awareness, and changing and remembering passwords; and
3. technical guidance on internal storage of passwords, transmission, login attempt rate, auditing, password distribution, password length, and the probability of guessing a password.

But well-known weaknesses [KLEI90] in the implementation and use of passwords have caused concerned security administrators to add password filters that reject weak passwords such as:

- passwords based on the user's identity;
- passwords that exactly match a word in a dictionary (with some or all letters capitalized);
- passwords that match a reversed word in a dictionary (with some or all letters capitalized);
- passwords that are simple modifications of a dictionary word (for example, words with added plural endings or added "-ing" or "-ed");
- passwords based on the user's initials or given name;
- passwords that match a dictionary word with the numerals 0 (zero) and 1 (one) substituted for the letters o (oh) and l (el);
- passwords that are patterns from the keyboard (for example, "aaaaa" or "qwerty");
- passwords that are shorter than a specified length (for example, six characters);
- passwords that do not contain a mixture of or at least two of the following: uppercase characters, lowercase characters, numerals, and punctuation; and
- passwords that look like a state-issued license plate.

Another form of information the user knows is maintained in a database of personal information, such as mother's maiden name, favorite flavor of ice cream, and so on. An inquiry about one or more of these items as part of the login sequence serves to authenticate identity.

"Something the user has" relies on a physical possession. Unlike "something the user knows," it may be difficult for two people to possess the physical item simultaneously. In contrast, "something the user knows" can be shared with other users without the first person giving up the information. A key to a locked terminal or workstation is a form of "something the user has," but technology has provided an electronic alternative. These electronic possessions can be incorporated into small calculators, or can be self-contained smart cards. Their general operating mode is to provide a number for the user to type into the computer as an authenticator. This number may be generated completely internally by the device, or may be derived from some input which the user enters. One form of the latter is a challenge-response system wherein the computer provides a multidigit number as a challenge; the user then enters this number into the calculator and receives a response to type into the computer. The variable user input is often coupled with a secret number the user knows to bind the device to the user.

"Something the user is" relies on a biometric characteristic, such as signature, hand geometry, fingerprint, or retina pattern. There has been considerable research into biometric input devices that would convert these physical characteristics into unique authentication data, but cost, speed, and reliability problems still remain.

Whatever the source of the authentication data, it is used by the TCB to authenticate the user's identity. The TCB must protect authentication data so that it cannot be accessed by any unauthorized user. At one time it was thought sufficient to protect authentication data by encryption, but this has proven inadequate.

Once identity has been authenticated, the user identity itself is the basis for identity-based access controls such as discretionary access control (DAC). Other security attributes can be associated with the user to be used by access control policies. Security clearance is used by mandatory access control (MAC). Other attributes may be used by other policies. For example, the employer attribute is used by proprietary and no contractor policies.

Authentication is also applicable to networks. The TNI specifies that the network should ensure that a data exchange is established with the addressed peer entity (and not with an entity attempting a masquerade or a replay of a previous establishment). The network should assure that the data source is the one claimed. When this service is provided in support of a connection-oriented association, it is known as *peer entity authentication*; when it supports a connectionless association, it is known as *data origin authentication.*

Attempts to create a session under a false identity or to play back a previous legitimate session initiation sequence are typical threats for which peer entity authentication is an appropriate countermeasure.

Authentication generally follows identification, establishing the validity of the claimed identity and providing protection against fraudulent transactions. Identification, authentication, and authorization information (for example, passwords) should be protected by the network.

In addition to the authentication methods used by people, network entities may be authenticated by cryptographic means and use of the characteristics and/or possessions of the entity. These mechanisms may be incorporated into the (N)-layer peer-to-peer protocol to provide peer entity authentication.

To tie data to a specific origin, implicit or explicit identification information must be derived and associated with data. Ad hoc methods for authentication may include verification through an alternate communications channel or a user-unique cryptographic authentication.

Encryption is discussed in Essay 15. To understand encryption used for authentication, it is sufficient to know that encryption acts as a function on a string of readable text to produce a string of unreadable symbols. These strings can be treated as numeric values for various purposes, such as authentication. A cryptographic checksum is similar to other checksums used for message authentication, with the difference that the algorithm that produces the checksum takes a secret quantity, the cryptographic key, as an input. As long as the key is kept secret, it is very difficult to create a valid checksum for an altered message.

When encryption is used for authentication service, it can be provided by encipherment or signature mechanisms. In conventional secret-key (symmetric) cryptosystems, the cryptographic checksum of a message that is produced with a secret key automatically implies data origin authenticity, because only the holder of that key can produce a cryptographic checksum form of a message. The kind of authentication provided by the conventional secret-key cryptosystem can protect both sender and receiver against third-party enemies, but it *cannot* protect one against fraud committed by the other. The reason is that the receiver, knowing the encryption key, could generate the cryptographic checksum of a message and forge messages appearing to come from the sender. In a case where disputes may arise from the dishonesty of either sender or receiver, a digital signature scheme is required.

In public-key (asymmetric) cryptosystems, message secrecy and message/sender authenticity are functionally independent. To achieve authenticity, the message digest (fixed-length representation of the message) is "decrypted" with the public key of the sender to provide proof of its origin, but that does not conceal the message. If both secrecy and authenticity are required, a public-key digital signature scheme must be used.

Access control. As used in the ITSEC, access control ensures that users and processes acting on their behalf are prevented from gaining access to information or resources that they are not authorized to access or have no need to access. There are similar restrictions concerning unauthorized creation, modification, or deletion of information. This heading includes functions intended to control the flow of information between, and the use of resources by, users, processes, and objects. This includes the administration (that is, the granting and revocation) of access rights and their verification. This heading also includes:

1. any function to set up and maintain any lists or rules governing the rights to perform different types of access;
2. functions concerned with temporarily restricting access to objects that are simultaneously accessible to several users or processes and are needed to maintain the consistency and accuracy of such objects;
3. functions to ensure that upon creation, default access lists or access rules apply to objects;
4. functions to control the propagation of access rights to objects; and
5. functions to control the inference of information by the aggregation of data obtained from otherwise legitimate accesses.

Accountability. In the ITSEC, accountability ensures that relevant information is recorded about actions performed by users or processes acting on their behalf so that the consequences of these actions can later be linked to the user in question, and the user held accountable for his actions. This heading also includes functions intended to record the exercising of rights that are relevant to security, and functions related to the collection, protection, and analysis of such information. Certain functions may satisfy requirements for both accountability and auditability; such functions may be included under either heading, but should be cross-referenced.

The TCSEC accountability policy requires that actions affecting security must be traced to the responsible party. The TCB must provide the capability of associating the user's identity with all auditable actions taken by that individual. Audit information must be selectively kept and protected. A trusted system must be able to record occurrences of security-relevant events in an audit log. Audit data must be protected from modification and unauthorized destruction to permit detection and after-the-fact investigations of security violations. The TCSEC requires that audit data be protected by the TCB so that read access to it is limited to those who are authorized for audit data.

Audit. In the ITSEC, audit ensures that sufficient information is recorded about both routine and exceptional events so that later investigations can determine if security violations have actually occurred, and if so what information or other resources were compromised. This heading covers any functions intended to detect and investigate events that might represent a threat to security. This heading also includes functions related to the collection, protection, and analysis of such information. Such analysis may also include trend analysis used to attempt to detect potential violations of the security target before a violation occurs.

A TCSEC audit system should be able to record the following types of events:

1. use of identification and authentication mechanisms,
2. introduction of objects into a user's address space (for example, file open, program initiation),
3. deletion of objects, and
4. actions taken by computer operators and system administrators and/or system security officers, and other security-relevant events.

Audit should also include any override of human-readable output markings. The TCSEC requires B2 and better systems to audit identified events that may be used in the exploitation of covert storage channels.

Audit records typically include date and time of the event, user identification, type of event, and success or failure of the event. For identification and authentication events, the origin of the request (for example, terminal ID) is also included in the audit record. For events that introduce an object into a user's address space and for object deletion events, the audit record includes the name of the object and the object's security level.

The capability to select audit events to be recorded is necessary to minimize the overhead of auditing and to allow efficient analysis. Collecting too much audit data can cause the important information to be hidden like the needle in the haystack. It can also cause the system to crash if there is no suitable place to store the audit data. Therefore, the security administrator must be able to selectively audit the actions of any one or more users based on individual identity and/or object security level. Flexibility in selecting audited events can be very helpful.

The TCSEC assigns the audit system of a B3 or better system the responsibility to monitor the occurrence or accumulation of security auditable events that may indicate an imminent violation of security policy and to immediately notify the security administrator when thresholds are exceeded. If the occurrence or accumulation of these security-relevant events continues, the system is to take the least disruptive action to terminate the event.

The TDI notes that the emphasis of the audit criterion is to provide individual accountability for actions by users. This goal is not the same as that for a backup and recovery log. There is no requirement in the TDI to integrate the audit log with the backup and recovery log, although such an integrated log is not prohibited. At the designer's discretion, there may be a selectable capability to reduce the number of audit records generated in response to queries that involve many access control decisions.

Object reuse. In the ITSEC, object reuse ensures that resources such as main memory and disk storage can be reused while observing security. This heading also covers any functions intended to control the reuse of data objects. This heading also includes functions to initialize or clear unallocated or reallocated data objects, to initialize or clear reusable media such as magnetic disks and tapes, or to clear output devices such as display screens when not in use.

According to the TCSEC object reuse requirement, introduced at C2 and unchanged thereafter:

> authorizations to the information contained within a storage object shall be revoked prior to initial assignment, allocation or reallocation to a subject from the TCB's pool of unused storage objects. No information, including encrypted representations of information, produced by a prior subject's actions is to be available to any subject that obtains access to an object that has been released back to the system.

The reference to encrypted information was added when the TCSEC was reissued as a DoD standard in 1985; it was not present in the 1983 version.

Accuracy. In the ITSEC, accuracy ensures that specific relationships between different pieces of data are maintained correctly and that data is passed between processes without alteration. This heading covers any function intended to ensure that data has not been modified in an unauthorized manner. This heading also includes functions to determine, establish, and maintain the accuracy of the relationships between related data; and functions to ensure that when data is passed between processes, users, and objects, it is possible to detect or prevent loss, addition, or alteration, and that it is not possible to change the claimed or actual source and destination of the data transfer.

Reliability of service. In the ITSEC, reliability of service ensures that time-critical tasks are performed when they are necessary, and not earlier or later; that non-time-critical tasks cannot be made time-critical; that access to resources is possible when it is needed; and that resources are not requested or retained unnecessarily. This heading covers any function intended to ensure that resources are accessible and usable on demand by an authorized user or process and to prevent or limit interference with time-critical operations. This heading also includes error detection and error recovery functions intended to restrict the impact of errors on operation and so minimize disruption or loss of service, and any scheduling functions that ensure response to external events and produce outputs within specified deadlines.

Data exchange. In the ITSEC, data exchange ensures the security of data during transmission over communications channels. The ITSEC recommends that the following subheadings from the OSI Security Architecture [ISO89] (also used in the TNI [NCSC87a]) be used to group functions:

- authentication,
- access control,
- data confidentiality,
- data integrity, and
- nonrepudiation.

Sterne et al. [STER91b] note that source authentication or nonrepudiation requirements appear to be widespread. Certain functions may satisfy requirements for both computer and communications security and so be relevant to other headings; such functions should be cross-referenced.

Assurance. In the TCSEC, assurance is concerned with guaranteeing or providing confidence that the security policy has been implemented correctly and that the protection-relevant elements of the system do indeed accurately enforce the intent of that policy. By extension, assurance must include a guarantee that the trusted portion of the system works only as intended. To accomplish these objectives, the TCSEC identifies two types of assurance: life-cycle assurance and operational assurance.

Life-cycle assurance refers to steps taken by an organization to ensure that the system is designed, developed, and maintained using appropriate controls and standards. Trusted computer systems depend on the hardware, firmware, and software to protect the information with which they are entrusted. It follows that the hardware, firmware, and software must be protected against unauthorized changes that could cause protection mechanisms to malfunction or be bypassed completely. For this reason, trusted computer systems must be carefully evaluated and tested during the design and development phases and reevaluated whenever changes are made that could affect the integrity of the protection mechanisms. Only in this way can confidence be provided that the hardware, firmware, and software interpretation of the security policy is maintained accurately and without distortion.

While life-cycle assurance is concerned with procedures for managing system design, development, and maintenance, operational assurance focuses on features and system architecture used to ensure that the security policy is uncircumventably enforced during system operation.

The TCSEC assurance policy requires the computer system to contain hardware, firmware, and software mechanisms that can be independently evaluated to provide sufficient assurance that the system enforces the major policy objectives and the supporting policies. Assurance refers to the basis for believing that the functionality will be achieved, including tamper resistance, verifiability, and resistance to circumvention or bypass. Assurance is generally based on analysis involving theory, testing, software engineering, and validation and verification. In the TCSEC, the assurance requirements parallel the evaluation classes, progressing from informal to formal, where formal implies mathematical techniques, such as those discussed in Essay 8. The basis for trusting system mechanisms in their operational setting must be clearly documented such that it is possible to independently examine evidence to evaluate the mechanisms' sufficiency.

The TCSEC provides requirements for operational assurance, including system architecture, system integrity (correct operation), covert channel analysis (starting at B2), trusted facility management, and trusted recovery. Security testing and design specification and verification are included under life-cycle assurance.

The ITSEC requirements for assurance of effectiveness are based on the proposed use of the TOE as described in its security target. The ITSEC requirements for assurance of correctness are expressed in seven hierarchical levels (see Essay 12).

Continuous protection. The TCSEC continuous protection policy requires that the trusted mechanisms that enforce these basic requirements must be continuously protected against tampering and/or unauthorized changes. No computer system can be considered truly secure if basic hardware, firmware, and software mechanisms that enforce security policy are themselves subject to unauthorized modification or subversion. The continuous protection requirement has direct implications throughout the computer system's life cycle.

The TCSEC introduces configuration management requirements at B2 and trusted distribution at A1. We suggest that both of these requirements should be effective at all levels, as they are in the ITSEC.

Covert channels. The TCSEC defines a covert channel as any communication channel that can be exploited by a process to transfer information in a manner that violates the system's security policy. The TCSEC also distinguishes two types of covert channels: storage channels and timing channels.

Current thinking refers to a covert channel as the use of some artifact not designed for communication to transfer information in a manner that violates the system's security policy. The misuse of a communications channel is simply a security violation.

Covert storage channels include all vehicles that would allow the direct or indirect writing of a storage location by one process and the direct or indirect reading of it by another. Covert timing channels include all vehicles that would allow one process to signal information to another process by modulating its own use of system resources in such a way that the change in response time observed by the second process would provide information.

Current thinking is that every covert channel involves elements of storage and timing. Information or state must exist long enough to be sensed in a storage channel. Timing involves the frequency of one event or state relative to another event or state. It is not necessary for one of these states to be related to the passage of time.

The TCSEC asserts that covert channels with low bandwidths represent a lower threat than those with high bandwidths. However, for many types of covert channels, techniques used to reduce the bandwidth below a certain rate (which depends on the specific channel mechanism and the system architecture) also have the effect of degrading the performance provided to legitimate system users. Hence, a trade-off between system performance and covert channel bandwidth must be made. Because of the threat of compromise that would be present in any multilevel computer system containing classified or sensitive information, such systems should not contain covert channels with high bandwidths.

The TCSEC covert channel guideline is intended to provide system developers with an idea of just how high a "high" covert channel bandwidth is. It considers a covert channel bandwidth that exceeds a rate of 100 bits per second to be "high." It also considers maximum bandwidths of less than 1 bit per second acceptable in most application environments. Finally, covert channels with bandwidths that exceed a rate of 1 bit in 10 seconds are to be audited. The rationale for these figures does not withstand close examination.

The TCSEC covert channel requirement begins at the B2 level, requiring a thorough search for covert storage channels and a determination (either by actual measurement or by engineering estimation) of the maximum bandwidth of each identified channel. At B3, timing channels are added, and at A1 it is required that formal methods be used in the analysis.

Essay 14

Security Engineering

Marshall D. Abrams, Harold J. Podell, and Daniel W. Gambel

This essay is concerned with trusted system integration and/or development to meet multilevel security (MLS) and operational requirements. It addresses technical issues such as how to combine products securely, TCB alternatives, and typical security engineering phases — as well as the management concerns of certification and accreditation.

This essay addresses the integration of multilevel security (MLS) technology into the concept definition, acquisition, design, product selection, and MLS integration phases of an operational system. Trade-off analysis is required among factors such as technical risk, security risk, cost, and satisfaction of operational requirements. The essay is divided into four phases:

1. In the requirements phase, we discuss policy determination, the need to identify trust requirements, application of user and mission requirements, use and development of the security Concept of Operations (ConOps), applications for scenarios, and selection of the correct version of security policy.
2. During the design phase, we discuss how to apply design guidance and regulations, and consider the advisability of including certification team participation in design.
3. Discussion of the integration phase surfaces issues from MLS integration policy needed, how to combine products securely, determination of whether to build or buy a TCB, use and considerations of trusted and untrusted processes, considerations for porting untrusted applications to a TCB, and approaching complex systems.
4. In closing, we discuss aspects of certification and accreditation, including the role of certification and accreditation (C&A) and establishing a C&A program.

Focusing on the end objective of getting the system accredited for operation, Bauer [BAUE91] identifies the key issues of the development process to be:

- consideration of mission requirements and security requirements prior to allocating requirements to trusted mechanisms,
- trade-offs between security disciplines and between overall security versus mission requirements, and
- structure of complex integrated systems using custom developed and commercial off-the-shelf (COTS) components.

However, a system integration normally involves a contract between the integration organization and a customer. Unlike a product evaluation, which has a primary goal of evaluating a vendor's secure system, the integration is based on the process of an integrator meeting a customer's operational mission. In many cases, the security features are secondary, while assurances are relegated to a distant secondary role.

It may be true that the system cannot be used if it is not adequately secure, but it is more true that if the operational requirements are not met, the system development either will not be funded or will not be accepted for contractor payment. This difference means that the requirement definition and interaction desired, and possibly achievable in a research environment, are not possible in a system integration. The system engineering trade-offs are not under the control of a single entity. Critical trade-offs occur prior to commencement of the system development by the prospective integrator and become determining factors in the system price. The structure of the final system is a result of the proposal preparation and evaluation process, and rarely represents an optimum set of answers.

Requirements phase

Policy determination. The system requirements phase includes determination of the applicable security policy. One of the first steps in security engineering is to identify the objective. As mentioned in Essay 13, there are varying statements of the security objectives in an organization, depending on an individual's responsibilities and job function. However, the TCSEC design and evaluation paradigm is predicated on the notion that "design and analysis of systems proceeds from policy to mechanisms" [TINT92].

At the general management level, the objectives of the system security policy have to be stated in generalities; while at the specific system implementation level, the objectives should be very concrete. The result will be a layered policy in which each main layer relates to a set of responsibilities. All layers must fit together in the sense that the policy described for a lower layer must be an implementation of the policy at a higher level.

The customer organization has an interest in protecting its information assets against undesirable events expressed in a high-level information security policy. This policy should address:

1. the information assets of the organization,
2. the damage that can occur to those assets, and
3. the measures that management has decided are reasonable, cost-effective, and proper to protect those assets.

Top management will probably not need to understand or care about the implementation details, as long as the information management policy is satisfied. At this high level, all policies merge into something like "Protect the organization's information assets." While it is easy to understand the sentiment behind such a generalization, it does not provide much guidance on whether specific actions are permitted or not. Introducing such specificity requires a significantly more detailed interpretation of the high-level policy. The specification, design, and implementation of a specific system require a different view of computing than that of the top management. But a greater knowledge of computing does not permit the creation of new policy. The AIS (Automated Information System) system policy is expected to be an implementation, at a lower level of detail, of the policy adopted by top management.

Many organizations provide very specific implementation guidance. This guidance should serve as a statement of policy that controls the solutions available to translate the top-level information security policy into a system. In general, the technical policy and solution available in a system implementation differ in substance and intent from the higher level prose abstraction. It may be impossible, or at least exceedingly difficult, to directly implement the natural language policy as rules within the computer. The security engineer is responsible for demonstrating the cost-effectiveness and correspondence between the high-level and implementation policies.

Since natural language is prone to ambiguities and multiple interpretations, information security policy is often expressed in a mathematical formalism. For more information about models, see Essay 8. Implementers should be able to rely on the formal model to resolve any ambiguities concerning the policy to be implemented.

Identify trust requirements. The TCSEC design philosophy is to separate trusted and untrusted code, relying on the trusted code to prevent policy violations. The trusted code constitutes the trusted computing base (TCB). But all TCBs are not created equal, and the customer's security engineer has to select the trustworthiness that provides sufficient countermeasures for the risk environment and simultaneously sustains the operational requirements set.

The TCSEC provides a set of countermeasures and associated assurances, as summarized in Table 1. This binding of functionality, strength of mechanism, and assurance is policy within the US DoD. Essay 7 discusses additional policy expressed in the Environments Guideline (Yellow Book) [CSC85] and DoD Directive 5200.28 [DOD88b] that relates TCSEC evaluation class to the risk environment. This foundation of policy applies only to the concepts and countermeasures associated with the confidentiality protection of classified information. In all other situations, including protecting information from unauthorized modification and assuring reliable service, the customer's security engineer must assist management in deciding what countermeasures and assurances are appropriate in terms of cost, feasibility, and inconvenience.

User and mission requirements. All security engineers must understand the security requirements as they relate to overall mission effectiveness. To achieve this understanding, the security engineer must develop a much broader outlook toward the system than simply security policy. Of particular concern are the constraints that can be placed in an unwelcome manner on information flow as necessitated by various combinations of countermeasures. It is rare that users see a need for sophisticated security technologies; they merely experience unwelcome constraints on their mission.

The engineering understanding of the system operation and its relationship to the operational requirements of the system are expressed in the system Concept of Operations (ConOps). This document communicates for the customer the integration of system requirements into a single view of how the resulting system will operate, given the total set of requirements. The document addresses all aspects of the operational environment, including communications, operations, data management, and applications of high-level security. However, a detailed examination of how the security mechanism operates is usually addressed in a subordinate security-specific document, the security ConOps. The development of a security ConOps and security scenarios to illustrate that unique security ConOps is important in gaining an understanding of user information security needs and the methods of addressing sensitivity of information.

Security Concept of Operations (ConOps). During the earliest phases of any project, mission needs are determined, alternatives explored, and cost and feasibility studies conducted to optimize the combination of requirements — and finally a high-level operational concept is explored and defined in the system-level Concept of Operations. Once this overview of the system is expressed, an extract and amplification of the security-relevant approach is documented in the security ConOps.

Table 1. TCSEC summary chart.

		C1	C2	B1	B2	B3	A1
Security policy	Discretionary access control	■	■	≡	≡	≡	≡
	Object reuse		■	≡	≡	≡	≡
	Labels			■	■	≡	≡
	Label integrity			■	≡	≡	≡
	Exportation of labeled info.			■	≡	≡	≡
	Multilevel export			■	≡	≡	≡
	Single-level export			■	≡	≡	≡
	Human-readable output			■	≡	≡	≡
	Mandatory access control			■	■	≡	≡
	Subject sensitivity labels				■	≡	≡
	Device labels				■	≡	≡
Account-ability	Identification & authentication	■	■	■	≡	≡	≡
	Audit		■	■	■	■	≡
	Trusted path				■	■	≡
Assur-ance	System architecture	■	■	■	■	■	≡
	System integrity	■	≡	≡	≡	≡	≡
	Security testing	■	■	■	■	■	■
	Design spec. & verification			■	■	■	■
	Covert channel analysis				■	■	■
	Trusted facility management				■	■	≡
	Configuration management				■	≡	■
	Trusted recovery					■	≡
	Trusted distribution						■
Documen-tation	Security users guide	■	≡	≡	≡	≡	≡
	Trusted facility manual	■	■	■	■	■	≡
	Test documentation	■	≡	≡	■	≡	■
	Design documentation	■	≡	■	■	■	■

Key

    No requirements for this class

≡ No additional requirements for this class

■ New or enhanced requirements for this class

The security ConOps emphasizes security over the other operational aspects to focus the technology on this constraint-prone aspect of a system design. Identification and agreement are required for security modes of operation, transitions between modes, and identification of

1. the sensitivity range of information,
2. the clearance range of users, and
3. security-relevant characteristics of external interfaces.

A key part of the security ConOps is a section that describes results from analysis of the anticipated flows of information:

1. where information originates,
2. where and how the information is anticipated to be received, and
3. the classification of that information.

The results of the analysis are used to identify cost-effective applications for MLS technology.

Requiring a security ConOps to be prepared and submitted by the prospective integrator during the competitive cycle of the system acquisition is an effective approach. Advantages of this approach include establishing a contract baseline, identifying applicable potential concepts for MLS technology insertion, and describing the security aspects of each competing design. If the security ConOps is to be delivered as part of the contractual deliverables, it should be initially delivered early in the design cycle in concert with preliminary design documentation.

The security ConOps should have a wide review audience, including customer and integrator management, software developers, end users, and the certification and accreditation team. Revisions to the security ConOps resulting from the design process (if procured) should present significant security issues. These issues are reviewed to provide validation and keep the review audience abreast of the evolution of the approach.

Scenarios. Scenarios are useful functions during several phases of the evolution of a system, particularly during:

1. the requirement definition phase,
2. the definition of demonstration or rapid prototype requirements,
3. the initial operational evaluation, and
4. technology insertion for a developed system.

One scenario composition strategy is to focus on areas likely to be affected in a substantial way by the introduction of MLS technology. By focusing on these areas, the customer's security engineers and end users could evaluate options and determine what specific MLS features and capabilities are required.

A second strategy is to use scenarios to evenly evaluate the proposed integrator's solutions when using commercial off-the-shelf technologies. Still later, scenarios are useful in developing test strategies and ensuring functional security support for all phases of the mission execution. Rapid prototyping can be a valuable method to introduce MLS concepts to the end users early in the acquisition using a site-specific application, especially as compared with abstract specification or criteria notations (for example, subjects, objects, read down, write up).

Another useful function for scenarios is to develop a range of flexibility for the User Interface Sets (UIS) [FERR91]. This conceptual approach to risk management provides the accreditor with significant insight into the real impact a user can have on the system security. Thus a rigidly controlled icon- or menu-driven interface can be used to restrict the operational user from access to capabilities (such as compilers) which may be used to explore or exploit the system security posture.

Security policy. A security policy specifies how to manage, protect, and distribute sensitive or critical information. Most of the time, the customer's security engineer supporting the acquisition will have to help select or identify the applicable security policy. In addition, the security engineer may be required to resolve conflicts between identified security policies from different layers of the organizational infrastructure. Most organizations are relatively hierarchical; therefore, it is logical to develop the information system security policy using a top-down hierarchical approach.

The results of the analysis can be represented using a structure that resembles a tree with corporate/national policy at the top of the tree and local policy and practices filling out the lower portions. This approach provides a "family tree" of security requirements. Some of the documents and their relationships are not necessarily common knowledge. For example, in some cases, they may have to be written. Identifying all of the documents and their relationships gives the customer's security engineering team a firm understanding of the overall security requirement. The family tree provides a common reference point for discussions with groups outside the security engineering team.

Once the customer's security engineering team has resolved the conflicts between policies and structured the system-unique policy, the customer's team should continue with the development of the eventual integrator's contractual requirement for the system undergoing acquisition. This approach is distinctly different from development of a product: With a product, the team defining the policy is normally the team developing the solution.

In acquired systems the customer's requirement team is defining the set of constraints or policies that will be considered or established as requirements during the acquisition. It is a rare situation where a revision to the security policy can be considered by an integrator subsequent to issuing the acquisition without significant impact on the cost and schedule of the system delivery.

Design phase

Design guidance and regulations. The DoD has separate sets of guidance governing the design and development of software systems and trusted systems. The system integrator is faced with the necessity to comply with the Contract Data Requirement List (CDRL) and the Statement-of-Work (SOW) for the contract. This does not necessarily result in the development of the standard TCSEC or system design documentation. In most cases, the TCSEC documentation for the products underlying the system architecture has historically been assumed to be adequate for the system itself. The result of this assumption is that the system adaptations to support the integration are poorly documented. In addition, there is little opportunity to develop documentation unique to the integrated system environment and remain within the cost and schedule originally conceived for the acquisition.

The general technical guidance for trusted systems design is contained in the TCSEC under the concept of a product evaluation; the DoD guidance for the design phase of a system development is contained in "Defense Systems Software Development," DOD-STD-2167A. [DOD88a]. Where the system integration has been structured to acquire both TCSEC-style and DOD-STD-2167A documentation, the two concepts can be reasonably synchronized. Figure 1 illustrates the time lines for the two sets of requirements and attempts to line them up one with the other.

However, an integration of commercial off-the-shelf (COTS) products cannot be guided by adherence to either set of documentation guidance. Strict adherence to the DOD-STD-2167A process would ultimately result in allocation decisions unmatched by any TCSEC-evaluated product. This approach invariably results in a custom system design rather than an integration. While DOD-STD-2167A can be subverted to use COTS products, there is significant risk of misunderstanding and conflict between the integrator and the customer organization. During the acquisition process, there is little opportunity for the customer to resolve at which point in the design process the integration may transition from the custom design philosophy to the COTS design philosophy. For competitive reasons, there is little incentive for the integrator to examine unspecified alternatives that would result in additional cost.

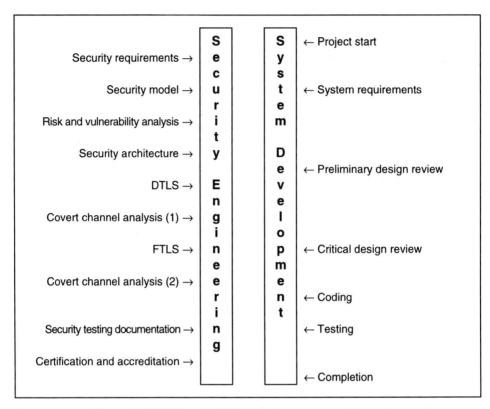

Figure 1. TCSEC and 2167A development requirements.

In a similar manner, vendor TCSEC documentation developed for a product has no relationship to the environmental and operational concerns that must be made a portion of the integrator's requirement set. This is not a fault of the documentation standard, the evaluation process, or the vendor. Rather, it is a situational fact. When the product vendor developed the TCSEC version of the document, the specific implementation being integrated was not foreseeable. Therefore, the documentation could not specifically address the environmental or operational needs of the specific system. In a like manner, the vendor was required to satisfy the documentation needs of the evaluation community in describing the generic application and use of the security features of the system. These requirements meant that the vendor developed the system documentation for the generic evaluation, not the operational system environment.

During system integration, it is normally necessary to modify existing products, develop "trusted processes," and intentionally violate product policy assumptions to meet system specifications. Each of these types of integration actions creates system changes that mandate modification of the vendor's product documentation. In most system integration environments, the TCSEC generic documentation is either invalidated or superseded. However, without adaptation for use in the customer environment, the resulting system integration would be unable to meet the customer's real purpose for the system.

Many customers have the misunderstanding that detailed application-specific, or environmentally specific, tailored documentation is automatically provided with a system. This type of customer misinterprets the requirement for TCSEC compliance as calling out TCSEC documentation, but tailored for the system. This belief that calling out the TCSEC, or even TCSEC documentation, as a requirement will result in usable system documentation has been repeatedly disproved.

The customer organization must establish the minimum set of reasonable documents that is cost-effective, while establishing the necessary discipline for the successful system. In many ways, it is the discipline mandated by requiring the documentation rather than the document itself that causes a gain in assurance. In other cases, it is critical to advise users and administrators on how to operate the selected set of features. In all cases, the need for a given document must be viewed in terms of cost-effectiveness and applicability. The integrator will be required to deliver only that documentation which the customer has specified for purchase.

Certification team participation in design. The TCSEC approach was formulated under the concept that the product evaluation team would be working in concert with the vendor development team to achieve and evaluate a secure product. This team effort was to be concerned with attaining the requisite level of adequacy of the security aspects of the system. There is little incentive for the evaluation team to consider operability or performance. These operational considerations are left to the vendor to address. The vendor evaluation team is thus frequently placed in the position of accepting trade-offs, reducing operational capability simply to satisfy security evaluation team desires.

In contrast, the certification team assigned to an integration cannot ignore the full set of requirements applicable to a system acquisition. This team will be faced with relaxing some levels of security functionality or assurance to meet operational requirements. This distinctly different trade-off environment makes it critical that the certification personnel be involved in all aspects of the system design, development, and integration.

During an integration and acceptance process, the impact of the security of the system is significantly influenced by the overwhelming set of operational customer requirements. The integrator team and the customer team are frequently placed in an adversarial position due to cost and performance constraints. A significant number of large integrations are additionally stressed by being fixed-price contracts with little room for optimizing or trade-offs. As a result, the focus of the normal integration effort is on meeting immediate operational needs. The integrator's program management is frequently unwilling to make further trade-offs that unfavorably affect the cost of the effort or that change the end-user perception of the system's operability.

The integration contractor does not have the authority to trade between different customer policy and requirement sets. This task falls to the customer certification and accreditation team, which should be composed of operational as well as security personnel. The certification team executing the certification and accreditation plan should be composed early in the project; it should include a representative of the Designated Approving Authority (DAA), whom we shall call the accreditor. Having the certification team participate in developing the security ConOps and system security architecture, or alternatively developing the set of security requirements to be tasked in the SOW for the intended operational environment, provides the accreditor with insight into the rationale for the security approach. It also allows trade-offs to be made by the customer early in the development cycle. The accreditor's agreement should always be documented.

A logical extension of the TCSEC design and evaluation paradigm as given by Tinto [TINT92] is that the product composition paradigm can be viewed as being initiated by decomposing the system policy, then by allocating the system policy and functional responsibilities across the selected system products.

Integration phase

MLS integration policy needed. There is no guidance for assessing the level of security in an integrated trusted system solution. Likewise, there is no nomenclature for even describing the level of technical security in such an integrated system. The efforts closest to a description are the product level descriptions (C1, C2, B1, B2, B3, A1) contained in the TCSEC and the modes (dedicated, system high, partitioned, compartmented, multilevel) of environmental description provided in the various DoD system policy documents. Security engineers need to know how to assess the level of trust of a system built from components. Lacking such a yardstick, the accreditor relies on instinct and experience in assessing the security of an integrated trusted system.

Much of this assessment is developed from the credibility of either the integrator's security organization or the customer's organization. Following Tinto again, the integration and assessment issue is to adapt the selected products and evaluate the adaptation of the system products in accordance with the specifications for each product in the context of the system policy.

Even when trusted components are used, the level of trust provided by the integrated system is unclear. The attributes of each component are affected by operation with other components. The unintended effects of their interaction are little understood. Trade-offs necessary to meet the customer's mission needs, and the revisions made in the respective components to achieve that result, further complicate the ability to accurately perceive the totality of security provided in a system. The various product security policies are, in many cases, different, resulting in even further difficulties. For example, products selected from different vendors by the integrator may have different approaches to labeling, auditing, and access control. Design decisions made by the independent vendor design teams are unconstrained by interoperability standards, resulting in invariable incompatibilities in format and policy enforcement. The result of the integration of these components may not provide adequate security controls for the system. Customer concepts requesting centralized authentication, audit, administration, and single-point (unitary) login each result in modifications to the various components that invalidate their individual evaluations. The impact of the adaptations or modifications on the integrated system solution is not defined and therefore cannot be reasonably assessed.

Combine products securely. Engineering a trusted system that meets requirements for functionality and trustworthiness is not simple or well defined. It involves identifying TCB alternatives such as:

1.   whether and how to modify the TCB,
2.   which trusted and untrusted processes can be modified and used,
3.   how to convert existing applications, and
4.   when to develop new applications [GAMB88].

In a custom solution to a secure system requirement, the first step is to decompose system requirements to the most detailed level possible, allocating software and hardware requirements into modules, components, or "boxes." The second step is to partition trusted and untrusted functionality for each requirement by determining which modules perform a security function in enforcement of security policy. Next come supplementary steps for trusted software, which include:

1.   minimization of trusted code by iteration until minimum trusted code remains,
2.   elimination of duplicate security functions,
3.   verification and validation of trusted software, and
4.   if new hardware is involved, code optimization for the new hardware platform.

The final step is then to recompose the policy to determine whether the intended policy is enforced by the combination of system products and adaptations.

For a COTS integration, the steps are somewhat different. The first step is to identify the functional "boxes" required in the operational system in a manner similar to a custom solution. The boxes likewise should not be constrained by the security requirement at this stage but reflect the best detail of the overall system requirements. Once the functional allocation is achieved, the information requirements for integration of those functional boxes need to be determined. These requirements may be expressed in the form of input, process, and output requirements, or in the form of a module interface definition.

Other approaches supported by formal security modeling may also be applied, such as information flow analysis. When these models are used, the policy enforced on that information flow between boxes can then also be described as either interface descriptions or input/output definitions. This description of information needs and information constraint should include elements essential to the security policy, such as security levels, access needs of users, and transmission across various media. Once this "architecture" has been validated, the security requirements should be overlaid to determine the functionality and level of product assurance needed to achieve that information transfer.

Integrating or composing two or more system components requires that an event in one component in some way causes a flow of information to an event in the target component. The method chosen to associate, or couple, events in the systems is the heart of TCB composition or trusted system integration. Possible levels of coupling range from completely disjoint to a completely coupled system in which all component policy elements are shared [FELL91]. Neither of these extremes is of practical use to the integrator. The real integration activity occurs in partially coupled cases. Partial coupling requires the precise definition of functionality and allocation of that functionality to the component.

Once the security functionality is established, the performance requirements need to be introduced into the solution. This late performance introduction ensures that the full set of operational requirements and security requirements is considered when calculating the hardware needs of the system. Invariably, the result will be a null set. This simply means that there is not available, as an evaluated solution, the precise combination of applications, trusted products, and hardware that meets the requirements defined by the customer. This fact results in a set of trade-offs that must be considered by the integrator to meet the customer needs.

Build or buy a TCB? The TCB integrator's basic alternative is whether to build or buy. You should, as an integrator, buy whenever you can, as

TCB development is very expensive, time consuming, and specialized. Basing the solution on a combination of NSA-evaluated TCB products listed in the evaluated products list (EPL) greatly simplifies certification, even though modification or addition will be required. A previously evaluated TCB can be modified, even though the modification destroys the EPL rating. Even with the EPL evaluation invalidated by adaptations, incorporating evaluated products into systems usually makes certification easier when the integrator is constrained by the contract in the formulation of the revisions. Building a new TCB is an integrator's last resort because of technical risk, expense, elapsed time, and certification difficulties.

The need to modify the product TCB occurs as a result of the trade-offs noted in the previous section in response to allocation decisions. In particular, the decisions regarding allocation of trusted features result in the need to modify the component TCB. The system-level security policy is used to ensure completeness of the functional security allocation. Once allocated to a component, the security function can then be compared with the component feature set. (This can be a recursive or reiterative process. The spiral approach has often been used to describe the allocation evolution.) Frequently, the component TCB contains features that are determined to be allocated to another component and not desired in this component. Additionally, the system may require a component to provide a function somewhat different from the product COTS capability. Note that if source code modification is necessary, it requires cooperation of the component TCB vendor. There are many business factors that might inhibit such cooperation.

You may elect to modify the component TCB by excising a feature of the component when that feature is to be provided in a different component. This is probably the more typical case of modification. You may amend the vendor software that provides a feature, when the system specification requires such a modification (for example, changing the password mechanism).

The third approach to modification may be to revise a vendor policy assumption used in the product evaluation (for example, identity based on TCB identity rather than user identity). This modification requires no revision to the TCB code but just as clearly invalidates the product evaluation.

Trusted and untrusted processes. Trusted processes are, by definition, part of the TCB. They are inside the TCB boundary because they enforce some customer security policy, or because they are exempt, in whole or in part, from mediation by other parts of the TCB. This exemption is necessary for the system to perform some element of the customer's intended mission. An "off-the-shelf" product's security policy often prevents necessary customer actions; this is circumvented by including selected "additional feature" modules within the TCB.

The concept of how a trusted process impacts on system integration requires some explanation. The common thought is that (a) because the processes violate the TCB policy, (b) they are trusted. However, these processes are not trusted because they violate the policy; rather they must be analyzed thoroughly to achieve a sufficient level of trust to be permitted to become part of the TCB. This means that the same level of assurance used for the product, or demanded by the system policy, must be applied to the design and development, evaluation, and configuration management of the "trusted processes" as defined for use in the system architecture.

Trusted processes are normally developed by the integrator as an adjunct to the COTS TCB. Trusted software must be analyzed extremely carefully for any undesirable interaction with other parts of the TCB. It is, therefore, highly desirable to minimize the amount of unique applications software with security relevance requiring insertion into the TCB. The process described in the section "Combine products securely" should be used to absolutely minimize the application requirement to that which is truly security relevant. Design review, redesign, and reanalysis should be iterated until you are satisfied that:

1. the amount of TCB code has been minimized,
2. the solution is necessary and sufficient to achieve only that minimum set of features required, and
3. the implementation is direct, concise, and easily assessable.

The untrusted processes are, by definition, outside of the TCB. These applications may have to be restructured to be integrated into a trusted system and continue to function correctly. This process is commonly called "porting the application," although normal portation is much simpler. You start by identifying all routines and software modules without security functions and continue by assessing compliance with system design objectives for all untrusted software.

Converting an existing application starts with selecting a TCB upon which to rehost it. Starting with a mature TCB is necessary to reduce the certification effort to permit the application to be installed as a single-level application in an overall trusted multilevel operation. After analyzing requirements to convert the existing software application to operate under the control of the selected TCB, you discard the code that performs features which will be performed by the underlying TCB. As a result of this process, it will normally be necessary to make modifications to the application because of partitioning between trusted and untrusted software. Certain functions will move from untrusted to trusted software.

Some existing applications may not work because of security violations caused by design or performance shortcuts, such as direct memory or screen access. These violations can be eliminated by rewriting, if you have the application source code. Other security violations, such as attempting to open files at multiple security levels at the same time, may require so much redesign as to be prohibitively difficult. This situation is especially critical if the integrator is not familiar with the detailed design of the application and its internal documentation is inadequate.

Porting untrusted applications to a TCB. Porting an application to a TCB involves understanding the needs of the application and the services offered by the target TCB. In this discussion, we concentrate on meeting security needs. Differences in operating systems are extremely important and may pose considerable difficulty, but these differences are well-known porting problems outside the scope of this discussion.

All TCBs will include a DAC mechanism that provides at least permission bits for read, write, and execute capabilities for owner, group, and others, and may also include an ACL (access control list) capability. This capability allows access control to the level of specific users or, at a more general level, multiple groups of users. For instance, an ACL can be composed that allows a specific user read and write access to a file or the members of several groups read access to a file. Since most operating systems provide some form of DAC, there should be little or no difficulty in adapting the application to the DAC on the target TCB. However, the interaction between permission bits and ACL may be complex and difficult to administer securely.

The creation and maintenance of DAC group membership vary among operating systems. Some permit any user to create a group; adding or removing members is under the control of the creator (the owner) of the group. Other operating systems centralize group administration under a role such as information system security officer. Such differences may affect the installation and operation of untrusted applications.

Mandatory access control (MAC) is one of the significant security features on the TCBs in the B and A classes. MAC enforces a security policy based on labels. MAC-based systems permit multilevel operation, but the MAC policy rules may not be compatible with some applications. Applications that internally manage temporary resources or cross-reference documents may fail when constrained by the MAC policy. Invariably, enabling an application to understand security labels necessitates placing some subset of that application inside the TCB boundary. Precluding the application from being either in the TCB or obstructed by the MAC policy generally requires conceptual reorganization in the application.

During the identification and authentication login dialogue, the user establishes an initial current sensitivity level at or below his or her clearance. Most operating systems allow a user to change the current sensitivity level without requiring the user to log off. However, there is a wide variation in restrictions applied to the initial login level, such as the initial level being constrained to a minimum or maximum level. Such variation between COTS TCBs may only be an inconvenience or may be a major problem, depending on the amount of flexibility the customer has allowed the integrator.

A multilevel directory capability is provided in most trusted operating systems, but some do not provide an interface that allows an application to use this capability. In certain situations, the multilevel directory capability is an effective means of buffering the application from the effects of MAC, thereby easing the installation of an untrusted application. However, there are quirks in the implementation of multilevel directories on TCBs that must be dealt with.

Some applications record events in an application audit file. Trusted systems enforce access policies to the audit file that may not be compatible with the untrusted application. Further, MAC can require an audit log at each sensitivity level if a "write equal" policy is enforced. When such a restriction is levied, unanticipated by the untrusted application, unexpected application errors will occur. User dictionaries may "disappear" as a result of being modified by a higher level application domain. In addition, logical views of separate database tables may malfunction due to similar modification difficulties.

The effects of multilevel security are generally transparent in a single-level mode of application operation, but can cause problems when the application attempts to dynamically create files and write to files, due to the "no write down" aspect of MAC policy. For example, temporary work files can be a problem due to a mismatch between the user's operating level and the directory in which the temporary file is written.

Complex systems. While developing trusted products is difficult, integrating evaluated trusted products (and some unevaluated products) into a real system to function in a real environment is even more challenging. If the system is sufficiently simple to permit implementation of a single security policy under a single security administration, the products possibly can be modified to meet the requirements for what the TNI calls a single trusted system. DODD 5200.28 uses the term unified system to refer to the same concept. In this concept, the integrator normally must demonstrate a single point of policy enforcement within the TCB which unambiguously performs each of the minimum functions of the TCSEC or TNI. This simplistic integration then could be evaluated under the concept of a network product. However, the network product rarely fully meets the needs of a secure system's integration.

The administration of a large integration necessarily requires multiple administration points. The geographical dispersion of a large integration requires multiple contingency recovery approaches.

The network-based alternative is to approach the integration as an interconnection of separately accredited AIS. In this approach, each of the partitioned components would be assessed on its own merits. In a typical system integration, there is also little likelihood that the system would meet the definition of the TNI for this product evaluation. However, each of these separately accredited AISs must fully support accreditation on its individual merits. The allocation of partitions of policy requirements for the system TCB to individual components removes features from the components necessary for the independent accreditation of those components. Even in the case of interconnection of separately accredited AISs, the collection of components within the integrated system cooperates to collectively meet the intent of, or the set of features required by, the security accreditation policy. As stated earlier, there is no guidance for evaluation of an integrated system. The available guidance focuses on merely the evaluation of the underlying computer or network components.

The salient feature of systems integration is that the community needs additional guidance. Although two integrated systems may be defined as requiring the same level of trust (either TCSEC or TNI), applicable security features and assurances associated with these systems can vary significantly [FERR91].

Certification and accreditation

In this section, we discuss the role of certification and accreditation (C&A) and establishing a C&A program.

Role of certification and accreditation (C&A). Certification is a formal extension of independent verification and validation (IV&V). That is, the organized process of quality control is separated from the process of system development and provided by independent persons. Certification provides a technical assessment of the security properties of a system relative to criteria selected at system inception. This process is actually the recomposition of the "system policy to determine that the intended policy is enforced by the combination of system elements" [TINT92]. The certification process then requires evaluation of the integrated system operating in its environment. The purpose of this process is to ensure that all of the criteria have been satisfied at some standard level. The technical certification report is a valuable input to accreditation.

Accreditation involves an assessment to determine if a system in its operational mode has minimized risks to a level that is secure enough to permit the system to process operational data. While certification is a technical assessment of the adequacy of the features of the system, accreditation is a management decision that balances operational mission criticality or need against the residual risk. This decision is made also considering:

1. the sensitivity of the data,

2. cost-effectiveness of additional enhancement of features or assurance,
3. definition and enforcement of administrative procedures, and
4. evaluation of the adequacy of the security administration and end-user training program.

The accreditor makes the case-by-case decision to permit the system to operate within a given set of operational constraints. These constraints are normally expressed as mode of operation. Only the dedicated mode processes a single level of information; system high, partitioned, and multilevel secure modes all simultaneously process multiple levels of information. Only the protection requirements or user/facility clearance environments are differently constrained.

The accreditor has other options, among which are:

1. reject the system for operational use,
2. modify the mode of operation to a mode having a lower risk,
3. redefine the operational environment by restricting potential users, or
4. accept the system for operational use, conditional upon progress being achieved on correcting the deficiency.

The ITSEC emphasizes that accepting a system for use in a particular environment requires consideration of multiple factors before the system can be considered as fit for its intended purpose. Considerations include:

- sensitivity of data processed,
- user trustworthiness,
- intended mode of operation (for example, dedicated, system high, multilevel),
- assurance in the technical security provided by the system,
- the owner of the information,
- confirmation of management responsibilities for security,
- compliance with relevant technical and legal/regulatory responsibilities for security,
- confidence in the adequacy of nontechnical security measures provided in the system environment, and
- the mission and operational concept.

The accreditor has the following options:

- permit operation as planned;
- require specified changes in system design or implementation, the way the system is operated, or the environment before operation is permitted;

- permit operation for a limited period on the condition that specified changes are made within that period;
- restrict the mode of operation (for example, deny multilevel operation but permit partitioned mode); or
- prohibit operation.

The available official guidance [GUID83, GUID84] is not current; some papers are available (see [BAUE91] and its references) that report on actual experience and lessons learned.

Summary

We have shown that the transition from product to workplace requires a set of ideals different from that of building a trusted or evaluated product. The dominance of security in the development of a product is replaced by the functional and performance requirements of a system statement of work or contract specification. The challenge is that of working in an environment which has no agreed on guidance or standards. This situation can be both frustrating and risky. The keys to achieving a successful system integration are the cooperation of the accreditor in establishing the requirements before contract solicitation, the skill of the integration teams in developing approaches that minimize risk, and the skill of the customer in choosing the winning approach.

Essay 15

Cryptography

Marshall D. Abrams and Harold J. Podell

This essay discusses cryptographic protection of information confidentiality and integrity as that information passes from one point in space-time to another. More recent uses of cryptography, such as authentication and nonrepudiation are also discussed.

The essay begins with an introduction of these ideas, including some basic examples, then proceeds to the definition of a cryptographic system, making the distinction between conventional key or symmetric key schemes and public key or asymmetric key schemes. We present some classical examples beginning with Julius Caesar. Both substitution and permutation ciphers are included, as well as a word about their weaknesses. The Data Encryption Standard (DES) serves as an example of a product cipher whose strength derives simply from repeated applications of both permutations and substitutions.

The essay then turns to public key schemes or systems. A public key system can be used by anyone to encrypt a message for a given recipient but only that recipient can decrypt it. Although there are many proposed in the open literature and three have been widely implemented, we focus on the most popular system, RSA. RSA (Rivest, Shamir, and Adleman) is a widely used public key system whose strength lies in the difficulty of factoring certain large numbers.

A discussion of public key management is followed by an introduction to public key and conventional key management issues. We also discuss authentication and integrity issues that are associated with conventional key systems. In addition, link and end-to-end encryption are described and contrasted. The essay's final topic is the integration of computer and communications security.

What is encryption?

Encryption is a fundamental tool for the protection of sensitive information. Its historical purpose is privacy (preventing disclosure) or confidentiality in communications. Encryption is a way of talking to someone while other people are listening, but such that the other people cannot understand what you are saying. It can also be used to protect data in storage as well as to detect active attacks, such as message or file modification.

We refer to encryption as a tool because it is a means for achieving an end; it is not an end in itself. Cryptography, hidden writing, is a method for transforming the representation (appearance) of information without changing its information content. Plaintext (cleartext) is one representation of the information expressed in natural language, intelligible to all. Ciphertext is a different representation, designed to conceal the information from unauthorized persons. Encryption (or encipherment) is the transformation from cleartext to ciphertext. Decryption (or decipherment) is the reverse transformation.

History. Since the time of Julius Caesar and even before, people have protected the privacy of their communications by cryptography. Things are still that way, and yet everything is quite different. People continue to use cryptography, though far more sophisticated than Caesar's, to protect their vital information as it passes through possibly hostile environments. Rather than crossing a few hills on its way to Rome, their data is moving from one point in the space-time continuum to another. Messages and documents created at one place are delivered at a later time at some distant place. When transmission of messages and documents is by electronic means, delivery is at essentially the same time but at a different place. A file created on a computer can be recovered at the same place but at a later time or, if it is copied onto a diskette, at some other place and at some later time.

Historically, cryptography has been used chiefly in communications. Its application in data retrieval is a far more recent occurrence. We shall tend to use the language of communications in describing cryptographic mechanisms, but the reader should keep the other examples in mind as well. The physical security and/or the access control mechanisms, whether they are on communications links, on network nodes and switches, on mainframes, file servers, and PCs, or on diskettes in transit, may not be sufficient to assure the confidentiality and the integrity of the data that passes through them. Cryptographic mechanisms are available that go far in establishing assurance in all these environments.

The word *cryptography* and the associated word *cryptology* have very similar etymological origins. They are derived from the Greek words *kriptos*, which means "hidden"; *graphos*, which translates to "writing"; and logos, which is "word" or "speech." In current usage, however, they have slightly different meanings. Cryptography is the science of hiding information. Encryption, sometimes called encipherment, is the act of concealing the meaning of a message. Decryption or decipherment is the inverse process of returning it to its original form. Any other, unauthorized method of recovering the original message is known as cryptanalysis or "breaking" the message. Cryptanalysis is the combination of science, art, and luck used to break messages or entire systems. The word cryptology nowadays refers to the study of both cryptography and cryptanalysis. When designing a strong cryptographic system, it is necessary to consider all possible attacks. In this essay, however, we discuss cryptography only. We include only such references to cryptanalysis that aid the reader in better understanding the strength of a particular cryptosystem.

Acknowledgments. In developing the perspectives for the history, types of attacks, encryption function standardization, and related topics for this essay, review assistance was provided by Shimshon Berkovits and H. William Neugent. Their comments and insights have been useful in balancing the presentation of cryptographic issues. If there are any omissions or misinterpretations in this essay, they are the authors' responsibility.

What is a cryptosystem?

A historical example. As a starting point for our description of what is cryptography, let us return to Julius Caesar. His scheme can encrypt any sequence of characters from the Roman or any other alphabet. His technique requires rotating the alphabet three positions to the right. Thus, each letter of the message is replaced by the one that occurs three places later in the alphabet. To decrypt, rotate the alphabet three positions to the left; that is, replace every letter in the encrypted message by the one that occurs three places to its left in the alphabet.

This is the basis for a class of ciphers known as Caesar ciphers. There is no great significance attached to the number three. Rotate the alphabet right k places to encrypt and k places left to decrypt. It is only necessary that both the sender and the receiver know the value of k. The k is called the key. For the single pair of encryption and decryption algorithms used in Caesar ciphers, different values of the key k will have different effects. The key can be changed once a month, once a day, or even for each message. There are even cipher systems that change the value of k for each character in the message. The sequence values for k can be randomly chosen, in which case the entire sequence is the key. The sequence can be generated by a pseudorandom number generator. If we incorporate the generator into the encryption and decryption algorithms, the generator's seed value becomes the key. Alternatively, the sequence can be derived from some preselected text, such as the jth line of the ith page of this book or the jth line of the ith column of today's *New York Times*. In this case, the key is the pair i, j and the name of the document to which they refer.

Any system of substituting an element of some ciphertext alphabet for each character in the plaintext alphabet yields an encryption algorithm. The key is the actual correspondence between the characters of the ciphertext alphabet and those of the plaintext alphabet. Actually, there is a slight difference between the encryption and decryption keys. The encryption key tells what cipher character to use in place of each plaintext character, much like an English-French dictionary indicates what French word to use in place of each English word. The decryption key indicates which plaintext character replaces each cipher character. That corresponds to a French-English dictionary. These two keys are not the same, but it is not difficult to derive one from the other.

These cipher systems are collectively called substitution ciphers. Given a long enough random key sequence or a pseudorandom number generator with a long enough cycle before it repeats its output sequence, such systems can encrypt long streams of plaintext characters. When used that way, they are examples of stream ciphers; they treat the plaintext as simply a long stream of characters.

Block ciphers have a different characteristic. Block ciphers subdivide the plaintext message into blocks of some fixed size. Each block is then encrypted as a whole. The simplest and oldest example of a block cipher is a permutation cipher. It shuffles the characters in a block. In fact, it shuffles each block in exactly the same way. One way is to break the plaintext into blocks of size $m \times n$. Write each block in m rows of n characters. Now read the characters by columns in some preselected order. To decrypt, write the ciphertext characters in columns in the same order and read the plaintext row by row. The key, which must be known to both sender and receiver, consists of the numbers m and n and the sequence of the columns. For the general permutation cipher, the encryption key is the size of the block and the permutation. The decryption key is the size of the block and the inverse permutation.

Product ciphers. Some very powerful encryption algorithms called product ciphers have been produced by using combinations of substitutions and permutations. In his information theory approach to cryptography, Claude Shannon spoke of two concepts for hiding information: "confusion" and "diffusion." Substitutions create confusion and permutations introduce diffusion.

For example, the Russian spy master Rudolf Abel used a cipher that followed a substitution cipher with two permutations. The cipher replaced the most frequently used letters of the Russian alphabet by single digits and all others by pairs of digits. It was done in such a way that there was no ambiguity on decryption how to divide the sequence of digits into single and double digit letters. The sequence of digits produced by the substitution was shuffled using a rectangular-array permutation cipher, as we have described.

The result was modified again by another rectangular-array permutation cipher. The dimensions of the second array were different from the first. The second cipher also featured triangular perturbations of the array. A letter written in this cipher was instrumental in the conviction of Abel. However, the cipher itself was so strong that it was never broken. Its workings were described to the authorities by Abel's assistant Reino Hayhanen when he defected.

The Data Encryption Standard (DES), about which we speak further on, is another example of a product cipher. We generally include product ciphers in a category referred to as conventional or symmetric key cryptography, because the sender and receiver share the same secret key.

A formal definition. Encryption functions take at least two inputs. The first is the plaintext, and the other is an encryption key that is sometimes referred to as keying material. It is useful to think of the algorithm as the way the tumbler action in a lock seals access to the information. The data is protected when the safe is locked by someone holding the key. In reality, the encryption key is information that affects the functioning of a given encryption transformation or algorithm, just as different tumbler settings affect the action of a single lock.

Similarly, decryption has two inputs also. They are the ciphertext and a decryption key. Again, think of the decryption algorithm as the way the tumblers work to open a physical lock. That lock cannot be opened without the key that corresponds to the tumbler settings. That key must correspond in some way to the encryption key. In fact, we are used to having a single key to lock and to unlock a door. But, when talking of cryptosystems, there can be a subtle difference.

Let us look at the Caesar cipher one more time. Let encryption be described as rotation of the alphabet E_k steps to the right, where E_k is the encryption key. Decryption can be described in one of two distinct (but related) ways. With decryption stated as rotation of D_k steps to the left, then $D_k = E_k$. But with decryption defined in the same way as encryption (and there is some benefit in having both algorithms the same), $D_k = -E_k$. The decryption key, while obviously tied to the encryption key, is nonetheless not identical to it. This possibility that the two associated keys are different leads to some interesting cryptosystems, as we shall see.

A generalized representation of the encryption and decryption processes is illustrated in Figure 1.

Let

A = Alice or the sender
B = Bob or the receiver
M = Plaintext message or message
C = Ciphertext
E_k = Encryption key
D_k = Decryption key
E = Encryption function or transformation
D = Decryption function or transformation

Then

$$C = E(E_k, M)$$

One way of reading this notation is as follows: The ciphertext (C) is produced by operating on the plaintext (M) with an encryption algorithm (E), using the encryption key (E_k). This notation is a variation of algebraic notation, where the parentheses indicate the operational relationships. For example, $C = E(E_k, M)$ uses parentheses to show that the encryption algorithm (E) is operating on the plaintext message (M) with a specific key (E_k).

For the cryptosystem to be of practical use, we must have

$$M = D(D_k, C) = D(D_k, E(E_k, M))$$

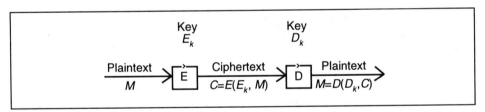

Figure 1. Generalized representation of encryption and decryption processes.

Conventional and public key systems. If it is easy to compute the decryption key D_k from the encryption key E_k, as is the case in all classical substitution and permutation examples, then both keys must be protected. Anyone who has access to either key can unlock the information protected by them. As introduced in our discussion of product ciphers, these cryptosystems are called symmetric key or conventional systems.

Unintuitive as it may seem at first reading, there are schemes in which it is computationally infeasible to derive the decryption key from the encryption key. Such cryptosystems are called asymmetric, and we present the most popular example, RSA (Rivest, Shamir, and Adleman), later in this essay. Asymmetric systems have a useful property. One can make the encryption key (E_k) public without fear of disclosing the decryption key (D_k). Then anyone can encrypt a message, but only the single holder of the decryption key can decrypt it. For this reason, asymmetric cryptosystems are also called public key systems. The published key is known as the public key, while the other is the private key. For certain public key digital signature systems, encryption and decryption are inverse functions. For these systems, it makes no difference which is performed first. However, this symmetry does not apply to other public key digital signature systems such as ElGamal, the associated Schnorr algorithm, and the proposed US Federal Digital Signature Standard (DSS). We use the notation of D_A for Alice's private key and E_A for her public key.

If the encryption and decryption functions of a public key cryptosystem commute, that is M (message) $= E(E_A, D(D_A, M))$, even though decrypting first seems to make no sense, we have another useful characteristic. Alice, who is the holder of her private key (D_A), can send information that is modified by applying her decryption algorithm using her private key. If the recipient, Bob, knows her corresponding public key (E_A), applying the encryption function to the modified information will give him assurance of the identity of Alice. In essence, Alice has "signed" the information by first using her secret or private key, which she alone possesses. This is an example of a digital signature, of which we speak again below. Figure 2 illustrates the process.

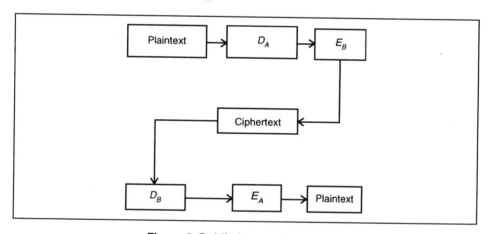

Figure 2. Public key cryptosystem.

The example in Figure 2 shows the plaintext or message (M) being signed by Alice with her secret or private key (D_A). After the plaintext is signed, it is now encrypted or "sealed" with Bob's public key (E_B). Only Bob can "open" or decrypt the ciphertext because he is the only entity in the network to possess the secret or private key (D_B) that corresponds to his public key used to "seal" the message (E_B). Once he has decrypted the message, he or anyone else possessing Alice's public key can verify her digital signature.

Encryption function confidentiality. The functions E (encryption) and D (decryption) may be kept secret or published, even as standards. The choice involves questions of work factor, open or closed network architecture, and user community. The cryptanalyst has a harder job in breaking the system if the functions E (encryption) and D (decryption) are kept secret. This is the approach taken for protecting national security related data. However, even in this highly sensitive arena, it is not the reliance on the confidentiality of the functions that protects the information. After all, there are too many known cases in which such information has been leaked or sold to "the enemy." It is the confidentiality of the decryption keys and the fact that they are changed on a regular basis that are the ultimate protection of the information.

Maintaining E (encryption) and D (decryption) as secret involves procedural and physical protection. If an intruder acquires a cryptographic device, secrets may be broken by reverse engineering. Physical protection can include denial of access to the cryptographic device and automatic destruction of the keys if unauthorized access is attempted. Advances in very large scale integration (VLSI) make it possible to implement the cryptographic function on a single chip that is highly resistant to reverse engineering, even to the extent of self-destruction or zeroization of the keys. Such chips can be put into service with considerably less physical protection than prior technology. In the final analysis, however, reverse engineering does not help recover the keys. If, at a minimum, the key registers zeroize on an intrusion attempt, the information they protect is still safe.

Types of attacks

Attacks and protection. Passive attacks consist of observation of information passing on a connection or residing in a file; release of message or file content is the fundamental compromise. Active attacks include modification, delay, reordering, duplication, and synthesis. Active attacks, resulting in message-stream modification (MSM) or file modification, offer three threats:

- *Authenticity attack.* Doubt of source and delivery to intended destination of a message; doubt of origin of the file or message.
- *Integrity attack.* Modifies information content.

- *Ordering attack.* Changes sequence of information arrival at destination; changes order of records in file.

Communication protocols and computer operating systems generally offer minimal protection against these threats, unless they are specifically to support secure communications. Masquerading, or spurious initiation, is an attack in which an intruder attempts to establish a communications session by falsifying his or her identity. Encryption is the fundamental tool for countering these attacks. Release of message or file content and traffic analysis can be prevented; MSM (message-stream modification), file modification, and masquerading can be detected.

There are several types of attacks that can be mounted against any cryptosystem. Some attacks attempt to recover the plaintext that corresponds to some stolen ciphertext or to discover the key in which one or more cryptograms are enciphered. Others seek to exploit weaknesses in the system so that plaintexts or keys can readily be recovered no matter what keys are used and how frequently they are changed. A cryptosystem designer must be wary of all these attacks.

Ciphertext only. The most difficult form of attack against a system is the ciphertext-only attack, which requires that someone has captured a segment of ciphertext. With no other information, except possibly a guess at the cryptogram's context, he or she attempts to determine the corresponding plaintext and, if possible, the key that was used. Many classical cryptosystems are vulnerable to ciphertext-only attacks which, given sufficient ciphertext, can be examined for evidence of the statistical properties inherent in the underlying plaintext language. Abel's product cipher, which combines one substitution and two permutations, successfully prevents these statistical characteristics from filtering through to the encrypted message.

It is always possible to begin a naive ciphertext-only attack. An intruder can expect that, if he or she begins exhaustively trying every possible decryption key from the space of all such keys, he or she will eventually try the correct one. Of course, if the key space is sufficiently large, that eventuality may not occur before the encrypted information no longer has any value, before the intruder losses interest, or before he or she dies of old age. Furthermore, there may be several different plaintexts that encrypt under different keys to the stolen ciphertext. The intruder has no way of knowing if an apparent decryption to some message that makes sense in the given context is, in fact, the correct decryption.

Alternatively, if the correct plaintext has no recognizable properties, the intruder cannot differentiate it from all the other trial decryptions he or she obtains. This situation occurs when the correct plaintext does not consist predominantly of real words or even of printable characters, but appears to be a random bit string such as the middle of a compressed ASCII file or some other cryptographic key.

These observations lead to several fundamental principles of system design. First and foremost, the key space must be large. The easier it is to recognize a correct decryption among all other possible decryptions the larger the key space should be. In the best of all worlds, the key space is so huge that an intruder would not even consider this attack, and the plaintext is so random that he or she could not recognize successful decryption if he or she stumbled onto it.

A known plaintext-ciphertext pair. Sometimes, through a lucky guess or other good fortune, an intruder has the plaintext that corresponds to a segment of ciphertext. He or she then tries to discover what key was used in the hope that other data is encrypted in the same key. This situation is similar to the 1799 discovery in Rosetta, Egypt, of the Rosetta stone. This basalt tablet has an inscription in Greek, Egyptian hieroglyphic, and Demotic. The stone provided known plaintext-ciphertext pairs that led to the decipherment of hieroglyphics.

A chosen plaintext-ciphertext pair. If an intruder can somehow obtain the ciphertext associated with one or more plaintexts possessing some special characteristics or the plaintext corresponding to ciphertexts with certain specific patterns, his or her chances of discovering the key may be enhanced. Consequently, the chosen plaintext-ciphertext attack has the potential to be more dangerous than either the ciphertext-only or the known plaintext-ciphertext attack.

Encryption function standardization

Interoperability, the ability for independently manufactured systems and subsystems to work together, is a major driving force for standardization. Market share competition is another driving force. Encryption standards can be used to protect information from intruders, yet permit mutually suspicious parties, such as competitive banks engaged in electronic funds transfer, to work with each other. The Data Encryption Standard (DES) is a well-know symmetric key encryption standard. The CCITT X.509 Secure Directory Service is a standard that includes the use of public key cryptography for certificates, which use a digital signature process. DES can be used for an encryption algorithm to provide for confidentiality in conjunction with a system based on CCITT X.509. For example, the Internet Privacy Enhanced Mail (PEM), which is discussed in Essay 17, uses two algorithms, RSA and DES, and a variation of CCITT X.509.

CCITT X.509 is one of several CCITT standards that pertain to secure international networking. For example, CCITT X.400 pertains to Message

Handling Services and does not assume the directory service. CCITT X.500 defines the use of certificates for Directory Service, and X.509 defines Secure Directory Service.

In addition to the standardization of encryption functions, there are international requirements for the registration of cryptographic algorithms. For example, the organizations that use nonpublic algorithms for secret messages may wish to identify these algorithms by neutral identifiers. Certain evolving protocols could be used to support this type of communication need. The Secure Protocol (SP) 4 at the Transport Layer is such a protocol, and it is being considered by ISO (International Organization for Standardization). ISO is also working to facilitate the registration of cryptographic algorithms.

The data encryption standard

Background. The United States National Institute of Standards and Technology (NIST, formerly National Bureau of Standards) established the Data Encryption Standard (DES) in 1977 as the federal standard encryption algorithm, following a public solicitation for suggested algorithms. The Data Encryption Algorithm (DEA), the algorithm in DES, was derived from a design submitted by IBM. DES is an example of conventional cryptography, because the sender (Alice) and the receiver (Bob) share the same secret key. The standards are:

- *Federal Information Processing Standards (FIPS).* Data Encryption Standard (DES), Publication (FIPS PUB) 46-1 (recertified until 1992, under review for recertification for another five years) and ISO standard IS 8372.
- *American National Standards Institute (ANSI).* Data Encryption Algorithm (DEA), X3.92-1981, and Model of Operation of the DEA, X3.106-1983.

DES is designated for non-national-security applications such as electronic funds transfer (EFT). In the late 1970s, several cryptographic authorities commented that DES may become inadequate in 10 years. However, DES has been reaffirmed over the years by NIST.

Recent information, however, has added new knowledge to the DES story. For example, the *New York Times* reported that DES is much stronger than people had thought. Adi Shamir and E. Biham had found an attack on DES that was initially reported as breaking DES, but that actually is only a "slight improvement over laboriously trying every key." Shamir said that DES is "the strongest possible code of its kind." He said that his attack method "devastates similar codes," while only slightly denting DES.

DES technology. The Data Encryption Standard (DES) is formed as a product of substitutions and permutations. It is a block cipher using a 64-bit block. The key consists of a 56-bit block, padded by eight parity bits, one for each byte. DES encryption begins with a 64-bit permutation. It ends with the inverse of that permutation. In between are 16 rounds of confusion and diffusion. The message block is split into two 32-bit halves. The old right half becomes the new left half. The right half is also replaced by using a number of small substitution ciphers. First, it is combined with 32 bits selected from the key and permuted. Then each group of four bits is replaced by a different four bits. For each group of four, there are four different substitution ciphers to be used. The choice for each group is determined by the first and last bit of the group, each combined with a different specified bit of the key. Decryption begins with the same initial permutation and ends with its inverse. In between, decryption goes through exactly the same rounds as encryption, with only one minor modification. The key bits are used in the reverse order.

Although each step in the Data Encryption Standard is a simple substitution, permutation, or exclusive OR operation, the total result is so complicated that an attempt to express a single ciphertext bit as a logical combination of the 64-bit block of plaintext and 56-bit key resulted in a computer printout that was several inches thick.

The strength of DES. The DES algorithm is well publicized and has withstood intensive attempts of many people the world over, who have tried and are trying to break it. Even though none of these efforts has yet succeeded, considerable insight into the inner workings of this and similar algorithms has been developed. At the time of writing, NIST has reaffirmed DES in hardware and certified software implementation of DES.

From the beginning, a major criticism of the DES has been the fact that each key has only 56 bits. That makes a key space of only 2^{56} or about 7.2×10^{16} different keys. The first attack ever suggested against DES was an exhaustive, known plaintext-ciphertext search. It exploited the size of the key space as well as the relation between EXCLUSIVE OR and bitwise complementation. Through a clever trade of time and memory, it searched for the key that encrypted a stolen DES cryptogram. At the time, it was estimated that within 10 years a special-purpose device could be built to do all the needed encryptions in a reasonable time and at a reasonable cost. No such machine has been announced, but it becomes more feasible with every improvement of microchip efficiency and price.

As mentioned, recent attacks on DES by Biham and Shamir [BIHA90] have shed new light on the inherent strength of DES. Their analysis is a variation on the chosen plaintext theme. Their approach, which they call Differential Cryptanalysis, collects many different plaintexts and their ciphertexts. It catalogs differences in the plaintexts and collects statistics on the differences in the corresponding ciphertexts. Then, given a known plaintext-ciphertext pair, they find the most likely key used in encrypting that pair. The known plaintext-ciphertext pair is conceptually similar to the pairs on the Rosetta stone. They have gradually developed their attack that now it threatens a full 16-round DES. However, the time currently required to complete a successful attack is, at this writing, no better than exhaustive search.

The volume of data that must first be collected and the time needed to complete an actual attack against a single DES key do not yet seem to justify the death knell that has been sounded for the standard in recent newspaper articles. Currently, Differential Cryptanalysis is an attack only against Electronic Code Book, the simplest mode of use included in the standard. It is possible that similar approaches are possible and will be developed for the other three modes (described below). It is also likely that the authors of this attack will push its development further in the hope of making it a meaningful threat.

Modes of operation

The Data Encryption Standard includes a set of standard modes of operation [NIST80]. These and one or two others are appropriate for use with any block cipher — that is, with any encryption algorithm that acts on a fixed-size plaintext block. Each mode possesses different characteristics that are important in different situations. We describe them briefly.

Electronic Code Book (ECB). The Electronic Code Book mode involves simple block encryption of a message or a file. The process is illustrated in Figure 3. The data is broken into blocks of a standard size. Each block in turn is the input to the encryption algorithm. The output blocks comprise the ciphertext message or file. For decryption, that message or file is again divided into blocks, and each block is decrypted individually. The resulting output blocks are concatenated to reconstruct the plaintext message or file. If an error occurs in a single ciphertext block, the decryption of only that block will be corrupted.

Electronic Code Book has a major disadvantage. A single block that appears several times in the plaintext stream will be encrypted in the same way each time. Suppose the plaintext is a file of sensitive information in a database system. If each field in some record forms a single block, an intruder can browse cryptographically. While he or she may not know what the individual entries in each field are, he or she can identify which records have the same value in any specific field. Any side information about the meaning of a single encrypted field entry may give him or her similar knowledge about many other similarly encrypted entries.

The remaining modes of operation use the context of each plaintext block to modify how it is encrypted. Therefore, ECB is generally used for low-volume operations, such as encrypting master keys for transmission.

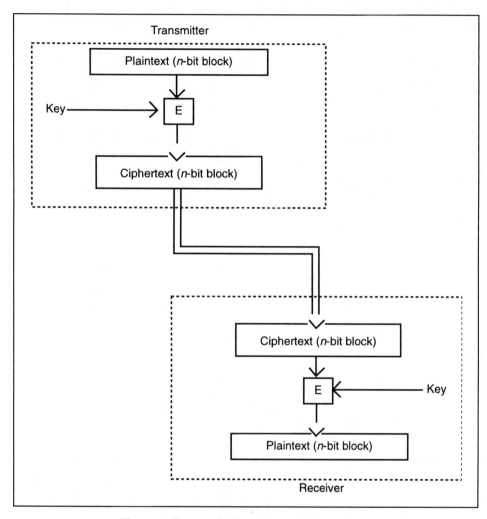

Figure 3. Electronic Code Book mode of DES.

Cipher Block Chaining (CBC). Cipher Block Chaining (CBC) is one way to change the encryption of plaintext blocks that repeat. CBC involves the EXCLUSIVE OR (XOR) of every plaintext block with the preceding cipher-text block. The first plaintext block must be treated differently. It is XORed with a publicly known initialization vector (IV) or with a secret initialization vector that is distributed with the key. For each block, the result of the XOR is the input to the encryption algorithm. The output of that algorithm becomes the next block in the ciphertext message or file. It is also XORed with the next plaintext block before that block is input to the algorithm. Figure 4 shows the process.

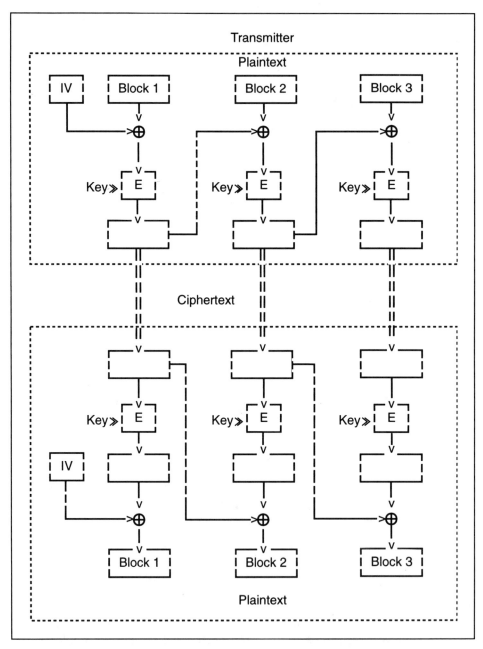

Figure 4. Cipher Block Chaining mode of DES.

The first ciphertext block is passed through the decryption algorithm, and the output is XORed with the initialization vector. The result is the first plaintext block. Thereafter, each ciphertext block is passed through the decryption algorithm. The output block is XORed with the preceding ciphertext block. The result is the next plaintext block. If a single ciphertext block contains an error, neither the corresponding plaintext block nor the next one will be recovered correctly. However, even in the face of errors, as soon as two ciphertext blocks are error free, the decryption is again successful. Such a scheme is called self-synchronizing.

It is apparent that Cipher Block Chaining does solve the cryptographic browsing problem. Records with the same plaintext value in a particular field will not be identifiable because each value will be encrypted using the presumably different ciphertext in the preceding field. Anyone with authorized read or write access to that field in those records can still decrypt correctly. He or she needs only the encrypted value in the preceding field. However, if he or she changes the value in that field, the entire file must be re-encrypted from that point on.

Cipher Block Chaining has another attraction. It can be readily used to create a message or file digest. Encrypt the data using this mode and save only the last ciphertext block as the digest. Then append the digest to the message or file. Anyone who reads it can, if he or she knows the correct key, recompute the digest. If it matches the one that came with the unencrypted message or file, he or she knows that, with very high probability, the data was not changed. He or she also knows that the message or file originated with the only other person who holds the same key. Thus, he or she has both message authentication and origin authentication. We shall see other cryptographic techniques that yield similar assurances.

Output and cipher feedback modes (OFB and CFB). Output and cipher feedback modes (OFB and CFB) can be illustrated by the US Department of Defense (DoD) Key Auto-Key or KAK and Ciphertext Auto-Key or CTAK, respectively. Before introducing these examples, we introduce applicable issues pertaining to stream ciphers, length of keys, and initialization vectors (IVs).

Stream ciphers all have the property that they attempt to integrate context into the encryption. The key is a long bit stream that is to be combined, through an XOR or some other operation, with the plaintext stream. What position a particular data segment takes in the plaintext stream determines with which segment of the key stream it will be combined. If the data segment repeats itself, its different occurrences will most likely be encrypted with different key stream segments. They will be encrypted differently.

The key can be either a long, completely random bit stream that must be delivered to both the encrypting and the decrypting stations, or a pseudorandom bit stream that is generated as needed. In the latter case, the authors prefer to reserve the word "key" for the pseudorandom seed and to refer to the pseudorandom bit stream that is generated as the "key stream." It should be noted that, if a pseudorandom generator is used, it must be cryptographically strong. That means it must not be possible predict the rest of the key stream even if some keys are discovered or guessed, as it might occur in a known plaintext-ciphertext attack.

One way to create cryptographically strong, pseudorandom bit streams is to use a block cipher like DES. Some fixed number of bits from the output block are added to the key stream on each iteration. The input to the block encryption algorithm is a shift register or a counter. In the latter case, the register is loaded with an initial value and incremented once after each encryption. The decryptor must start his or her counter at the same initial value. As long as he or she stays in synchronization, he or she will decrypt correctly.

If the input is a shift register, it must be loaded with an initialization vector. After each iteration, the register contents are shifted the same number of bits that are added to the key stream from the block encryptor output. The same number of bits are shifted in to fill the empty space in the register. They can be the same bits taken from block encryptor output. In that case, we have Output Feed Back (OFB) mode, which is used in the US DoD Key Auto-Key (KAK). Alternatively, they can be the last bits encrypted. This is Cipher Feed Back (CFB) mode, which is known in DoD as Ciphertext Auto-Key (CTAK). At the decryptor, exactly the same procedure is followed with the block algorithm used to encrypt. Now the key stream is combined with the ciphertext stream to recover the plaintext stream, and the ciphertext bits must be saved for use as feedback.

The reader is encouraged to consider what happens if errors occur in the ciphertext stream. Both OFB and CFB are self-synchronizing. There are, however, situations in which this property is undesirable. If it is most important to flag where a ciphertext stream has been tampered with, it is better to feed back plaintext bits. Then errors introduced into the ciphertext stream cause errors in the plaintext, which are shifted into the input register of the block encryptor. This causes an erroneous output which, in turn, yields an incorrect decryption. The wrong plaintext bits are again fed into the shift register and all decryption is incorrect from the point of the ciphertext error on. This is a very strong indication that the ciphertext has been modified, either accidentally or maliciously.

Perfect confidentiality

Perfect confidentiality can be achieved with a completely random key stream. For such an encryption mechanism, our distinction between key and key stream disappears. The key stream is the key. It must be as long as the message it is to encrypt. Although a courier with a large magnetic tape containing the random bit stream forms a communication channel with a large capacity, this encryption scheme seems somewhat unwieldy. Nonetheless, it does have a very important characteristic to recommend it for use in certain situations.

Because the keys are completely random, it is possible to find a candidate key stream that decrypts a given intercepted ciphertext message into any plaintext message of the same length. A cryptanalyst has no way of determining which is the right key and which is the right plaintext. Thus, there is one key that decrypts IPOOEHWLRCR as ILOVEMOTHER; another that yields IHATEMOTHER; a third that produces ATTACKATTWO; and one more that generates DONOTATTACK. The cryptanalyst has no way of determining which is the correct decryption. Stated another way, all decryptions are equally likely. In general, it is impossible for anyone who captures the ciphertext stream to determine statistically that one plaintext stream is more likely than any other. Even if he or she can guess a likely word in the plaintext, he or she cannot determine where to place it or what the remainder of the message might be. Perfect confidentiality occurs because no amount of analysis, and not even an exhaustive search were he or she to try it, will help the intruder guess the plaintext. This cryptosystem is unbreakable.

A stream cipher with a completely random key stream is called a one-time pad. It derives its name from the keypad that its users once employed and from the fact that any use of a key stream more than once can be disastrous. If the key stream is reused, the difference between the two ciphertext streams is the same as the difference between the two plaintext streams, the key stream canceling. Now an analyst who looks at the differences between the statistically most common letters in the alphabet will yield a breaking of both plaintexts. The one-time pad is the only kind of cryptosystem that exhibits perfect confidentiality. As such, it is often used for the most important of diplomatic correspondences. For everyday transmissions of lower priority between the many users of a communications network or the many files to be protected on sensitive databases, something less demanding in key handling is required. A block cipher, such as DES, in one of the feedback modes or a key stream with some other cryptographically strong pseudorandom bit stream generator is an approximation to a stream cipher with a completely random key stream.

All strive to achieve some form of computational security. This means that, given the computing resources available to a prospective intruder, it is very unlikely that he or she will be able to break a single cryptogram. In evaluating the computational security of a system, we must examine the computational time and resources required for each possible attack compared with legitimate decryption. This is the work factor associated with each attack.

Some estimate of the intruder's computing power and technology is also necessary. An intruder can compare his or her capability for attack with the potential value of the sensitive data he or she is trying to steal. That value can be measured in dollars, in time, or in intelligence. Unfortunately, the last metric is somewhat difficult to quantify. If, given the size of the work factor, the cost of the computational power needed to mount each attack exceeds the value of the information we are protecting, our system is computationally secure.

Public key cryptography[1]

Public key two-key cryptosystems may be considered to be supplementary to conventional cryptography, such as DES. Diffie and Hellman first envisioned a cryptosystem in which decryption keys cannot be derived from the corresponding encryption keys. Three public key systems that have been widely implemented are RSA (Rivest, Shamir and Adleman), ElGamal, and the Diffie-Hellman key exchange system. We use the RSA system as the main example for this discussion, because it is the most widely adopted by industry and the international standards community.

As mentioned, the important difference is that public key cryptography uses matched pairs of keys. For example, Alice has one for encryption (E_A) and one for decryption (D_A). The encryption key is called the public key and the decryption key is called the private key. One entity is responsible for each matched pair. The strength of the public key process is twofold. First, the public key (E_k) can be electronically published in a network directory for wide access. Second, anyone (for example, Alice) in a network system can send a secret message to the holder of the private key (for example, Bob) by using the public encryption key of the recipient (E_B).

Public key cryptography can provide secure key management or key exchange functions to transmit secret conventional keys to the receiver (Bob) or perform an equivalent operation. This process supports message privacy because the secret key, such a DES key, is transmitted with the protection of a public key algorithm. Message privacy is achieved using the conventional secret key to encrypt one or more messages between the sender (Alice) and the receiver (Bob). We discuss these and related issues in the subsequent sections.

RSA uses a pair of parameters consisting of a public exponent and an arithmetic modulus. Briefly, the plaintext M (message) is represented as a sequence of bits by using some encoding scheme. The sequence is then divided into blocks X of the largest length that can be interpreted as the

---

[1] The presentation on public key cryptography is adapted, in part, from [NECH91].

binary expansion of a number less than the modulus n. Encryption then produces numbers Y of the same binary length. The relationships are as follows:

n =   Arithmetic modulus
e =   Public exponent
d =   Secret exponent
Y = $X_e \bmod n \ (0 < X < n)$
X = $Y_d \bmod n \ (0 < Y < n)$
X, Y =   Data blocks that are arithmetically less than the modulus

The modulus n is chosen to be the product of two sufficiently large prime numbers p and q: $n = p \times q$. The value of n and e together form the public key; d and the two prime numbers — p and q — constitute the private key.

The exponents are chosen so that

$$e \times d = 1 \bmod (p - 1)(q - 1)$$

A key length of between 512 to 1,024 bits is generally recommended for RSA, as compared with 56 bits for DES (plus 8 parity bits). For approximation purposes, we can say that the strength of the RSA using a key length of 512 bits is generally comparable to a key length of 56 bits for DES. One reason for the general comparability of such different key lengths is that the computational processes differ substantially. An attack or cryptanalysis against RSA is considered, in part, to be a function of the difficulty to factor large numbers. Therefore, RSA is generally associated with large keys. The strength of DES is considered, in part, to be a function of the number of computational rounds in its algorithm (16 rounds). These 16 rounds, when coupled with a key length of 56 bits, are claimed to provide adequate resistance to attack.

Message confidentiality and authenticity. Message confidentiality can be supported by the transformations of public key systems that have the relationship $D(E(M)) = M$. The notation $D(E(M)) = M$ refers to the decryption of the ciphertext $C = E(M)$, which yields the plaintext message M. The ciphertext is created by $E(M)$ or encrypting the plaintext M. We designate the sender A as Alice and the receiver B as Bob.

For example, if Alice (A) wishes to send a secure or private message M to Bob (B), then Alice must have access to E_B (Bob's public key). We denote the common encryption algorithm using Bob's public key as E_B and the common decryption algorithm with his private key as D_B. The notation for this discussion of public key cryptography uses subscripts to refer to the sender (Alice) and the receiver (Bob) rather than keys. For example, we say that Alice encrypts the message M with Bob's public key (E_B). In other words, Alice encrypts M (the message) by creating ciphertext $C = EB(M)$ and sends C to Bob. Bob reverses the process when he receives C by using his private transformation D_B (Bob's private key) for decryption. This process requires that Bob computes $DB(C) = DB(EB(M)) = M$. We also generally refer to this process as Bob uses his private key (D_B) to "read" the encrypted message or ciphertext C.

If Alice's transmission is intercepted, the attacker or intruder cannot decrypt C (the ciphertext) since Bob's D_B (Bob's private key) is only known by Bob. This process provides for confidentiality. We assume that any entity in the network can access E_B (Bob's public key), because Bob has no means of identifying the sender. Also, Alice's transmission could have been changed. Therefore, authenticity and integrity are not assured in this example. However, authenticity and integrity can be provided.

Authentication of the sender (Alice) and integrity of the message (M) can readily be satisfied by using certain public key processes. The mathematical transformations in a public key system can be achieved in a variety of ways. In general, where Alice wishes to send an authenticated message M to Bob, he is able to verify that the message was sent by Alice and was not changed. Alice could use D_A (Alice's private key) to compute S (signature or signed text) $= D_A(M)$ and send S to Bob. We generally refer to this process as Alice signing her message. The signed message is also referred to as a digital signature. Bob can use E_A (Alice's public key) to find $E_A(S) = E_A(D_A(M)) = M$. Assuming M (message) is valid plaintext, Bob can verify that S was actually sent by Alice, and was not changed in transit. Verification follows from the one-way nature of E_A (Alice's public key). If a cryptanalyst or an intruder could start with a message M, he or she could find S' such that $E_A(S') = M$. The implication is that the intruder can invert or reverse E_A. However, inversion is not computationally feasible in this public key process.

Verifying the sender's (Alice's) identity could be difficult if M (the message) or any portion of M is a random string. For example, it may be difficult for Bob to determine that S is authentic and unchanged based only on review of $E_A(S)$.

In practice, a slightly more complex procedure is generally used. Variable-length long messages are uniquely reduced to fixed-length representations by an auxiliary public hash function or algorithm H. Therefore, Alice is actually "signing" ($H(M)$). This process yields a digital signature $S = D_A(H(M))$. Alice sends her digital signature S, which is unique to a given message M, to Bob along with M. If Alice encrypts her message M and digital signature $S = D_A(H(M))$ with Bob's public key (E_B), we can say the result is a digital envelope.

Bob can compute $H(M)$ directly when he receives a digital envelope. First, he "opens" the envelope by decrypting it with his private key (D_B). Second, $H(M)$ is found by using Alice's public key to operate on her signature S — that is, $E_A(D_A(H(M))) = H(M)$. Third, $H(M)$ may be checked against $E_A(S)$ to ensure authenticity and integrity of M. The ability of a cryptanalyst or intruder to find a valid S' (digital signature') for a given M (message) would violate the one-way nature of E. The hash function or algorithm (H) must also be one-way. A strong hash function has the property that it is computationally infeasible to find a message (M) which hashes to the same digest as a given message (M') with $H(M) = H(M')$. A security risk is that if Bob could find M' with $H(M') = H(M)$, then Bob could claim that Alice sent M'. A judge receiving M', $H(M)$ and S would reach a false conclusion.

Sending C (ciphertext) or S (digital signature) as shown above ensures authenticity and confidentiality. Confidentiality was provided because only Bob could "open" the digital envelope containing M and S. Bob used his private key (D_B) to open it.

If no digital envelope were used, M (the message) and S (the digital signature) would be transmitted in the clear. An attacker or intruder who intercepts C (ciphertext) = S = D_A (Alice's private key) (M) may have access to E_A (Alice's public key) and could therefore compute M (message) = $E_A(C)$. Therefore, confidentiality of M is denied.

International electronic commerce may require communication systems that provide confidentiality, authenticity, and integrity. However, in some cases it is possible to use the same public key system for these security services simultaneously. For example, RSA supports digital signature and confidentiality. In the authenticity/integrity-related process, D (decryption) is applied to M (message) or $H(M)$. This contrasts with applying E (encryption) to M (message) for confidentiality. If the same public key system is to be used in both cases, then $D(E(M)) = M$ and $E(D(M)) = M$ must both hold; that is, D (decryption) and E (encryption) are inverse functions. A requirement is that the plaintext space (the domain of E) must be the same as the ciphertext space (the domain of D).

In practice, there are no generally available systems versatile enough for the last usage without modification. There is only one major public key system (RSA) that satisfies $E(D(M)) = D(E(M)) = M$ (message). The absence of a common domain between two users creates a technical problem in using such a system for confidentiality and authenticity.

Figure 5 illustrates a method of achieving confidentiality and authenticity in a public key process. The message M is placed in a digital envelope which is sealed with Bob's public key (E_B).

The public key process in Figure 5 is a simplified version of a process for confidentiality and authenticity. Certain issues, such as the question of domains, are not considered in the figure. The illustrated public key system complies with a hash function H. This system works with any encryption and any signature. They need not be related. However, the verification for the DSS is slightly different.

Applicability and limitations. Public key algorithms are computationally intensive. Therefore, confidentiality of M (the message) can be achieved only for short Ms. The resulting slow encryption process may be referred to as a low-bandwidth secure transmission. In contrast, conventional key algorithms, such as DES, are must faster for encryption. Therefore, conventional key algorithms can produce wide-bandwidth secure transmissions.

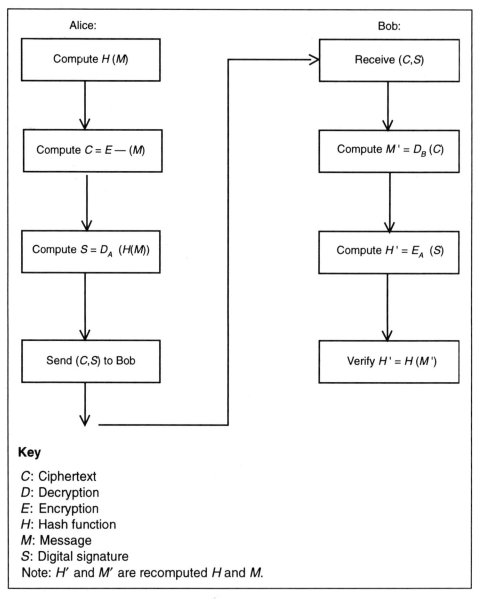

Figure 5. Using a public key process for confidentiality and authenticity.

Chip and algorithm breakthroughs will most likely continue to occur. Therefore, we do not rule out certain near-term and long-term uses of public key algorithms for message privacy. However, bulk encryption remains the domain of conventional cryptographic systems. These systems use fast encryption techniques such as permutations and substitutions.

The international electronic commerce process uses public key for two major applications:

- Secure distribution of secret conventional keys, such as DES keys, for bulk encryption.
- Digital signatures (Ss).

In electronic commerce, there is a need for confidentiality of conventional decryption keys and public key private keys. There is also a need for integrity of encryption keys, symmetric or asymmetric. For example, if Alice can trick Bob into believing that the encryption key she sent him (for which she has the corresponding decryption key) is that of the president of the XYZ Corporation, then she can read any secret that Bob is sending him. This case includes any conventional key system used by Bob to send the president of XYZ encrypted data.

Digital signature

Authentication, nonrepudiation, and integrity checks can be supported with a digital signature. A digital signature is similar to a written signature, however, it is stronger. For example, detection will result from any attempt to change the message content or to forge the signature. We note that a Message Authentication Code (MAC), as defined in ANSI X 9.9, provides integrity protection against alteration, but does not provide nonrepudiation because of the sharing of the conventional secret DES key. (Another term for a MAC is a manipulation detection code, or MDC.)

A digital signature must be a function of the entire document. Changing even a single bit should produce a different signature. A signed message cannot be changed without detection.

Public key digital signatures. The use of public key digital signatures and supporting hash functions can provide both authentication and verification of message integrity. Hash functions, which have been briefly introduced, will be discussed further. They can also serve as cryptographic checksums used for validating the contents of a message. Public key schemes supporting authentication permit generation of digital signatures algorithmically from the same key repeatedly, although the actual signatures are different. Digital signatures are a function of the message and a long-term key. Therefore, key material can be reused many times before replacement. Hash functions also reduce the impact of the computationally intensive nature of public key algorithms.

Public key digital signatures are generally preferred for electronic commerce because

1. private keys can be used repeatedly for generating digital signatures algorithmically, and
2. nonrepudiation of the sender (Alice) is inherently a part of the system design.

Therefore, public key implementation of digital signatures is effective and versatile.

Nonrepudiation. Nonrepudiation is the system capability that prevents a sender (Alice) from denying that she has sent a message. The integrity of nonrepudiation is a function of the degree of security maintained for the sender's (Alice's) private key (D_A) [NEED78, POPE79]. For example, Alice could repudiate or deny sending a message if D_A is compromised. Depending on the applicable legislation, Alice may still be held liable for messages signed before the compromise was reported to a central authority. Certain administrative approaches have been proposed for incorporation into protocols. Most of these involve use of some form of arbitrator [DEMI83]. However, certain disputes may require litigation, because nonrepudiation is a critical business issue.

One method of supporting nonrepudiation is to use a central authority. For example, the receiver of a message (Bob) sends a copy to the central authority. The central authority can verify sender's (Alice's) signature. This verification provides assurance that there is no report that Alice's private key (D_A) was compromised at the time of sending. In this case, Alice would have to rapidly report the compromise of her private key. We must also consider the impact of the increased workload of the central authority on the throughput of the network.

An alternate approach is to use time stamps [DENN81, MERK82]. Although a network of automated arbitrators may still be required, the system overhead is modest because the arbitrators only have time stamp messages. A receiver (Bob) may check the validity of the sender's (Alice's) private key by checking with a central authority. Bob has a degree of assurance of nonrepudiation if the received message is time stamped before the validity check. He still has to determine if a compromise is discovered and reported later.

Legal requirements for nonrepudiation may include a requirement that the sender (Alice) is responsible for signing until a compromise of her private key is reported to the central authority. Implementation of this approach could require an on-line central authority and real-time validity checks and time stamps. In addition to peak load concentrations that may occur at the central authority, certain requirements for a network-wide clock should be considered. A network-wide clock has other security vulnerabilities, such as vulnerability to forgery of time stamps [BOOT81].

If users, such as Alice, are permitted to change their private keys, a central authority should archive past keys to assist in resolving disputes. Each industry should have a set of legal and administrative safeguards to maintain continuity of operations in the event of a compromise or change of keys. For example, credit card systems have effective legal and administrative provisions for cases of lost or stolen credit cards.

Hash functions. Hash functions or algorithms (H) have been introduced as a method of producing a fixed-length representation of a variable-length message M. As mentioned, public key algorithms are generally computationally intensive and compute more slowly than conventional algorithms. Therefore, it is usually not desirable to apply a digital signature directly to a long message. Since we also want to sign the entire message, we need an algorithm to reduce the size of the message. Hash functions or algorithms meet this need for computation of digital signatures to supplement public key techniques. For example, MD (Message Digest) 4, from R. Rivest, produces a 128-bit representation or message digest of a variable-length message. RSA is used to encrypt this message digest with sender's (Alice's) private key (D_A). This becomes $S = D_A(H(M))$. Other hash functions that can be used include MD 5, from R. Rivest, which essentially adds an additional computational round to MD 4.

The encrypted message digest is a digital signature that can be attached to the message for secure transmission in a digital envelope (in this case, containing the digital signature and the message M). As mentioned, a digital envelope is sealed by the public key E_B of the receiver, Bob.

The receiver (Bob) may validate the signature on $H(M)$ and then apply the public function H (hash function) directly to M (message) and verify that it matched the received signed version of $H(M)$. Authenticity and integrity of M are validated simultaneously. Only integrity would be assured if $H(M)$ were unsigned.

Hash functions should produce unique message digests. However, it is theoretically possible that two distinct messages could be reduced to an identical same message digest and cause a collision. Collisions cannot be avoided completely because there are generally more potential messages than the number of possible message digests. In practice, the probability of collisions should be very low. For hash functions with random or near random output, the probability of collisions is a function of the size of the message digest and the number of bit sequences that are meaningful messages.

In public key cryptography, the minimum requirements for a hash function include the ability to adequately support the authentication process. For example, if we have a message M and a message digest MD, it must not be computationally feasible to find another message M' that also reduces to MD. Therefore, forgery can be avoided because appending the signed MD to M' would not verify as a valid signature.

Public key digital signature sequence. A public key digital signature process is briefly highlighted:

1. Compute a unique fixed-length message digest MD from the message M.
2. Use Alice's private key (D_A) to form the signature as encrypted hash, that is, $D_A(H(M)) = S$.
3. Attach Alice's signature S to her message M.
4. Seal in a digital envelope M and S with Bob's public key (E_B) for authenticity and confidentiality.
5. Bob opens the digital envelope on receipt using his private key (D_B).

Confidentiality is provided with the digital envelope, because only Bob can open the digital envelope with his private key (D_B). He validates Alice's signature S by computing $H(M) = E_A(S)$. As mentioned, Alice's public key (D_A) is a trapdoor one-way function. Therefore, an intruder should not be able to determine S' such that $H(M') = E_A(S')$ for a given forged message M'. As a result of this situation, Alice's signature cannot be forged. Also, if Alice attempts to repudiate the message sent to Bob above, Bob may present M (message) and S (digital signature) to a judge. The judge can use Alice's public key (E_A) to compute $H(M) = E_A(S)$. If Alice's private key has been kept private, then only Alice could have sent S. This is nonrepudiation.

To provide for nonrepudiation, Bob can use his private key to open DE (digital envelope) $= M, D_A(H(M)$. A judge can use E_A (Alice's public key) to operate on $D_A(H(M)$ and compare the results to $H(M)$.

Digital signatures and certificate-based systems. Electronic commerce requires sender authentication, data integrity, and nonrepudiation. These three security services are achieved with the use of digital signatures in distributed open systems. Certificate-based public key systems provide effective implementation.

For example, the Internet uses certificates to make public keys available to authorized entities. These issues are discussed in Essay 17 on Privacy Enhanced Mail (PEM). For example, PEM uses RSA and certificates derived from CCITT Recommendation X.509 for Secure Directory [CCIT88c]. Using RSA in X.509, Bob's (the receiver's) public key is cryptographically sealed (wrapped) in a certificate, along with other identification information. A trusted third party, called a Certification Authority (CA) in X.509, uses its private key (DCA) to seal the certificate. The use of PEM and

X.509 with DSS may not be exactly the same as for RSA. The PEM protocols may need to be extended to facilitate multiple algorithms.

Since X.509 provides for multiple CAs, a certification authority hierarchy or tree can be constructed. Authorized network entities (users) have the applicable CA's public key to decrypt or unseal the receiver's (Bob's) certificate in a directory. It may be necessary to repeat the process for nested certificates. The result is the receiver's (Bob's) public key, which can be used to send encrypted messages to Bob that only he can decrypt with his private key. Certificate-based key management is another way of describing this process. This process supports a zero knowledge technique that is being standardized as DIS 9979.

Public key management

In public key systems, the key management problem is inherently simple and relatively low risk (compared with conventional key management, for example, ANSI X9.17). For instance, the key information to be exchanged between users, or between a user and a central authority, is public. Also, a physical mail system might be satisfactory to communicate with the central authority, if redundant information is sent via an insecure (electronic) channel.

Management of public keys. We have briefly introduced the need for Alice and Bob to exchange their public keys. One reason is that public keys do not need privacy in storage or transit. For example, public keys can be managed by an on-line or off-line directory service, or they can also be exchanged directly by users.

Integrity has also been introduced. For example, if Alice thinks that the intruder's public key (E_I) is really Bob's public key (E_B), then Alice could possibly encrypt using E_I. The result would be that I could decrypt using D_I. Integrity should also be considered, because any error in transmission of a public key could eliminate its usefulness. Therefore, error detection is desirable.

A central authority, such as the Certification Authority (CA) that we introduced, is generally required for electronic commerce. However, there are situations where the CA may not have to be on-line. For example, Alice could retain Bob's public key for future use.

Use of certificate-based key management. We introduced certificate-based key management as a way of providing authenticity and integrity in the distribution of public keys [KOHN78]. A certificate-based system requires a central issuing authority CA (Certification Authority in CCITT X.509). For example, Alice will generally follow some form of identification and authentication procedure in registering with the CA. In addition, registration can be handled by a tree-structured system. In this case, the CA provides certificates to local CAs. The local CAs can register users at lower levels of the hierarchy.

In the general case, Alice receives a certificate signed by the CA (Certification Authority) and containing E_A (Alice's public key). The CA prepares a message M containing E_A, identification information for Alice, a validity period, and so on. Her certificate is computed by the CA as $CERT_A = D_{CA}(M)$. A certificate is a public document that contains E_A and authenticates it. The authentication occurs because the CA signs $CERT_A$. As we have mentioned, certificates can be distributed by the CA or by users. Our discussion of certificate validity can also be considered as a generalization of time stamping.

There are exceptions to the utility of time stamping. For example, a certificate may be compromised or withdrawn before its expiration date. Therefore, if certificates are retained by users (rather than being requested each time from the CA), the CA must periodically publish an invalidated certificate list.

Public key and conventional key management issues

We need public key management for confidentiality of private keys and integrity of public keys. In addition, we need secure delivery for conventional secret keys to assure confidentiality and integrity. In either case, if we have a hierarchy of keys with the confidentiality and/or integrity of each key guaranteed by some key one level up, we need the secure delivery of the key at the highest level in some secure channel. Public key standards that provide for these considerations include CCITT X.509 and the Internet Privacy Enhanced Mail (PEM).

Secure delivery of certain keys, such as public keys, may involve delivery in a nonelectronic channel at the highest level of trust. For example, some public keys may be delivered in person or by trusted courier to a Certification Authority (CA).

The applicable standards involve, in part, using public key systems for secure and authenticated exchange of verified identities and data-encrypting keys between two parties. Data-encrypting keys are secret shared keys connected with a conventional cryptographic system that may be used for bulk data encryption. The public key approach permits users to establish common keys for use with a system such as DES.

Conventional key systems often use a central authority for assistance in the key management and exchange processes. Use of a public key system permits users to establish a common secret key without the risk of a third party having the secret key. In other words, a public key system has a lower risk than a conventional key cryptosystem for key management and exchange. Therefore, international standards to support the evolving open distributed processing systems include public key management concepts.

Public key cryptography can be used to distribute conventional secret keys securely and effectively. The overhead is modest because keys are essentially short fixed-length messages. Also, digital signatures are generally applied only to outputs of hash functions, which are also the equivalent of short fixed-length messages. Therefore the bandwidth limitation of a public key cryptosystem is not a major factor for these applications.

Authentication, integrity, and key management issues for conventional key systems

We focus in this section on issues pertaining to MAC for authentication and integrity (X9.9) and a related standard for conventional key management (X9.17). Digital signature is discussed in the following section.

Certain financial systems use conventional cryptography to provide for authentication and integrity of financial messages. In this case, encryption is performed and used to generate a MAC, which is appended to the cleartext for transmission. The receiver (Bob) calculates the MAC and compares the calculated and received MAC. A match ensures that the sender (Alice) possessed the proper conventional encryption key and that the message was undamaged. The limitation of the MAC process is that Alice and Bob share the same secret key.

Historically, MACs have been used to provide message authentication in financial systems. The message remains in cleartext, which may be required in certain international banking communities. One of the difficulties of using MACs has been the complexity of conventional key management. However, a standard has evolved to assist in key management for well-defined communities.

We briefly introduce two representative ANSI (American National Institute of Standards Institute) standards for wholesale banking that have also been adopted internationally:

- ANSI X9.9-1982, 1986: Financial Institution Message Authentication (Wholesale).
- ANSI X9.17-1985, 1991 (Extension): Financial Institution Key Management (Wholesale).

It is important to note that in the interbank (wholesale) electronic funds transfer environment the primary goal is authentication rather than privacy. Privacy can be provided only by use of an additional key.

Message Authentication Code (MAC): Standard ANSI X9.9-1982, 1986. The Message Authentication Code (MAC) (ANSI X9.9), not to be confused with Mandatory Access Control (MAC), is a cryptographic checksum appended to a message. It seals the message against modification. All fields such as time, date, sources, and so on included in the checksum are rendered unalterable. Either the entire message or selected fields are processed through the algorithm using the Cipher Block Chaining Mode (CBC). As mentioned, the last block is the only output of the process that is used in the MAC. MAC requires a key management protocol, such as ANSI Standard X9.17.

Financial Institution Key Management: Standard ANSI X9.17-1985, 1991 (Extension). There are three environments in ANSI X9.17 for conventional key establishment:

- *Point-to-point environment.* Two parties share a master key, and the master key is used for distribution of working keys.
- *Key Distribution Center (KDC) environment.* Master keys are generated by a Key Distribution Center and are shared between each entity and the centralized server.
- *Key Translation Center environment.* One entity originates the working key. (This is a minor variation on Key Distribution Center.)

Two entities can share in the key management process in a point-to-point environment. Each entity has the same master key that is used to distribute working keys for individual messages. Working keys are generally changed periodically, depending on the risk associated with the application. For example, a high-risk environment could require a new working key for every transaction or every day.

The full implementation of this standard involves the second option, namely, the Key Distribution Center (KDC) environment. A trusted entity in the network is designated to perform the KDC functions for a defined community of users. Each entity in the user community has to establish a trusted relationship with the KDC, which has a duplicate of each of the user's master keys.

A Key Translation Center is used when one of the entities wishes to perform some of the KDC functions. This entity originates the working keys for the user community.

Risk and cost of conventional key management. The concentration of risk is a security disadvantage of conventional key management. Risk concentration may be considered a function of the need to have the secret keys for a network community concentrated in one node. Also, the cost or overhead of conventional key management is relatively high because of the need for the KDC to share all master keys. Substantial complexities may occur if a large number of KDCs wish to join together in ad hoc relationships to support international electronic commerce.

For example, if Alice and Bob wish to communicate securely, they must first securely establish a common key. As mentioned, one possibility is to employ a third party such as a courier. Historically, couriers have been used; however, electronic commerce requires electronic key management.

The most common approach for Alice and Bob to use in conventional key management would be to obtain a common key from a central issuing authority or a key distribution center [BRAN75]. The higher risk occurs because the key distribution center is at risk to attack from an intruder. Unfortunately, a single security breach by an intruder would compromise the entire system. For example, the intruder could passively eavesdrop without detection.

The higher overhead of a key distribution center occurs, in part, because of the bottleneck effect. Since each pair of users needing a key must access a key distribution center at least once, the volume of activity would increase rapidly. If the number of users is n, then the number of pairs of users wishing to communicate could potentially be as high as $n(n-1)/2$. In addition, each time a new secret key is needed, at least two communications are required for the user pair and the key distribution center. Furthermore, network availability could become a function of the key distribution system. Questions should also be asked concerning the capability for maintaining effective access control for the system containing the secret keys. Examples of systems that provide this type of access control are security-enforcing or trusted systems.

Other aspects of conventional key management are not unique to conventional cryptography. For example, life-cycle management is required over the life of conventional keys, which can include the need for archiving, for example, five to 30 years for business purposes. Life-cycle management procedures include distribution, storage, and destruction. Key maintenance is also required. For example, some keys may be lost or compromised. In addition, employee changes may make it necessary to cancel some keys and issue others.

Manual key distribution must occur at least once for conventional cryptographic key management, after which automated distribution can occur. Master keys or key-encrypting conventional keys (KEKs) are the manually distributed keys. These keys are used only to encrypt other conventional keys called "working keys." Other terms for "working key" include "data-encrypting keys" (DEKs).

An introduction to encryption in networks

We briefly discuss some network aspects of encryption. Our purpose is to introduce some of the common terms and concepts for link and network encryption. However, we do not address the encryption issues associated with communication protocols and internetworking. For some of these issues, see Essays 17 and 18.

Relating encryption to data network communications. The increased application of communication technology in international electronic commerce has accelerated the need for security in data network communications. These communications support global interconnectivity and distributed operations, thereby introducing security risks. New developments in communication protocols offer promise of providing solutions to reduce certain security risks. A protocol specification details the control functions that may be performed, the formats and control codes used to communicate those functions, and the procedures that the two entities must follow. We introduce some of the basic issues that are useful when evaluating security services that can be satisfied with encryption mechanisms.

Link encryption. The most straightforward application of encryption is to the communications link. Information is not processed as it passes on a link. There are no packet switches, no gateways or other intermediate systems. All of the information can be encrypted to prevent release of message contents. Traffic analysis can also be prevented by padding (adding null or blank characters so that all messages are the same length). Padding entails no additional cost if dedicated links are used; the converse is true on shared links. Link encryption provides protection only on the communications link. Information in an intermediate node reverts to plaintext. Protection of this plaintext involves physical protection of the node hardware and trust of the node software. Naturally, there are costs associated with physical protection as well as operation of the encrypted links, mostly in key management and distribution.

Link encryption is the oldest and most common form of encryption in computer networks. In a packet-switching network, link encryption can be used to encrypt the communication links between keys such as hosts and switches.

A simple view of data communications is to consider the system as composed of two pieces of equipment closely collocated. The communication path is protected and error-free, and possesses unlimited bandwidth. Equipment must be added to approximate this ideal in the real world.

Link encryption illustrated. Figure 6 shows a schematic representation of data circuit-terminating equipment (DCE) adapting a physical circuit to carry data communications. Figure 7 adds encryption equipment.

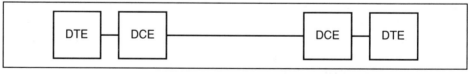

Figure 6. Data circuit without encryption (DTE: data terminal equipment; DCE: data circuit-terminating equipment).

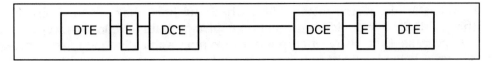

Figure 7. Data circuit with encryption (E: data encryption equipment).

Link encryption for point-to-point circuits. Link encryption is appropriate for point-to-point circuits. In addition, it can be easily placed in the OSI context. For example, the entire bit stream is encrypted when link encryption is present at the Physical Layer, layer 1. Encryption at the Data Link Layer, layer 2, results in some fields in plaintext and others encrypted.

End-to-end encryption. End-to-end encryption (E3 or E^3) is different from link encryption in that we no longer have to expose information in cleartext in packet switches — that is, at each node. The reason for this difference is that E3 refers to encryption above the Data Link Layer. Simple link encryption is inadequate when applied to ISO layered protocols for wide area networks (WANs) in layers 3 to 7, because commercial WANs generally do not provide link encryption capabilities among the switches.

When discussing E3 with respect to the ISO seven-layer model, we usually refer to encryption by layer. For example, encryption in layer 3 or 4 could be called Network or Transport encryption, respectively. Certain protocols that are being considered by ISO use more specific designations, such as encryption at the top of layer 3 (SP3, Secure Protocol 3) or the bottom of layer 4 (SP4).

Encryption must be generalized to protect the protocol data units (PDUs) at a given layer. Extending encryption into higher protocol layers increases the number of entities protected, at the cost of interfacing and the overhead associated with additional hardware and/or software. Higher layer encryption and the accompanying protocols can be intrusive. However, substantial hardware and software advances are being made. Therefore, there is a gradual international trend to higher layer encryption and encryption in commercial application software packages.

File encryption for storage protection. File encryption is the encryption of a file in a computer system and/or a distributed processing system. It gives protection in case someone breaks through electronic system defenses and accesses the file. File encryption also enables us to put the file on a floppy disk and mail it without any special protection. In other words, file encryption substitutes for physical protection. The main problem with file encryption is losing the key. Losing the key in file encryption is like losing all our data when our hard disk crashes, except that, with file encryption, our backup copies probably are lost as well.

A process that uses encryption to cryptographically "sign" or "seal" software before distribution has been introduced as digital signature. The digital signature is used to verify the integrity of the software in operation.

Integration of computer and communications security

In the past, computer security was used inside computers, and communications security was used outside on the transmission lines. Today this boundary is disappearing as file encryption, digital signatures, message integrity, E3 or E^3, password encryption, and other such applications are incorporated into computer systems. This change can strengthen functions such as identification, authentication, and access control. However, the integration of the two disciplines will require the interface of two cultures as two sets of rules are combined. This integration is complicated by the development of internetworking, which is bringing many technologies together, such as wired and wireless communications.

This interface of the two disciplines — computer and communications security — may require answers to systems questions. For example, should this integration of security-enforcing or trust technology in computer security (COMPUSEC) and cryptography in communications security (COMSEC) require that the information system provide both sets of security attributes — computer and communications security, that is, information security (INFOSEC)? Even as we bring the two disciplines together, we still may need well-defined interfaces and boundaries for reasons of modularity, certification, and international electronic commerce.

Local Area Networks

Marshall D. Abrams and Harold J. Podell

Local area network (LAN) communications security is addressed in this essay. LANs are introduced as providing: (1) a private communications facility, (2) services over a relatively limited geographic area, (3) a high data rate for computer communications, and (4) common access to a wide range of devices and services. Security issues pertinent to LANs are discussed. For example, LANs share many security problems and approaches for their solutions with point-to-point conventional communications systems. In addition, LANs have some unique problems of their own: (1) universal data availability, (2) passive and active wiretap threats, (3) end-to-end access control, and (4) security group control.

Countermeasures include physical protection, and separation by physical, logical, and encryption methods. Trusted Network Interface Units, encryption, and key distribution are also discussed.

Examples are discussed to illustrate the different approaches to LAN security. The examples in this essay are a composite of several existing product features, selected to demonstrate the use of encryption for confidentiality, and trusted system technology for a local area network.

Local area network technology/topology overview

This essay addresses LAN security from the viewpoint of open systems interconnection (OSI). That is, we focus on the seven-layer OSI protocols (illustrated in Figure 1); in fact, we concentrate on the lower layers. This focus follows the history of LANs; that is, the OSI communications problems had to be solved before open systems could be addressed.

It is usually not good form to start an essay by discussing what is not covered, but that is necessary in this case. Some people think of LANs in terms of the services they provide to users. This viewpoint is essentially looking at a LAN as a distributed system, with emphasis on the distributed operating system and the service it provides. This essay does not address this distributed processing within the terminals, workstations, and hosts connected to the LAN. That is another subject for another essay.

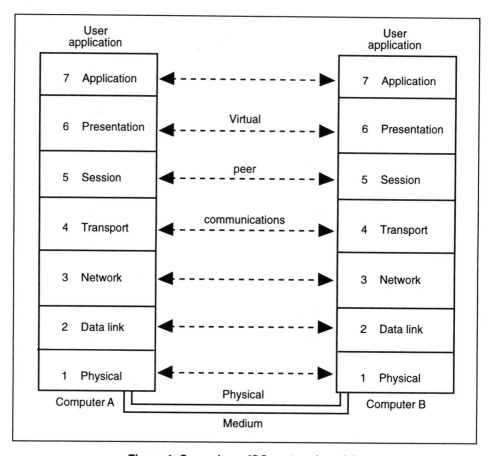

Figure 1. Seven-layer ISO protocol model.

Malicious software such as Trojan horses and worms can attack LANs. In fact, the physical distribution of any network increases the difficulty of protection. Malicious software is discussed in Essay 4.

LANs connect computers, terminals, workstations, and other *data terminal equipment* (DTE). In this essay we will use "DTE" to refer to whatever is connected to the LAN when it is not important what function it serves. The distinction between a personal computer and a workstation is not important for the purposes of this essay.

Let's start with a functional definition. A LAN is a private communications facility, usually owned by the organization that uses it. The cost of using the LAN is fixed, independent of level of usage. LANs provide an opportunity for the owning organization to customize its communications capabilities in many ways, such as carrying audio, video, and data traffic; providing multiple simultaneous connections; and providing security services. A LAN generally serves a limited geographic area, such as a single building or a campus, providing a high communications rate or bandwidth and common access to a wide range of devices and services. In general, LANs may be partitioned or zoned. The zones usually correspond to geographic or work units. Bridges or gateways between zones provide connectivity. Zones at physically separate locations can be connected, using wide area networks or private high-bandwidth circuits, to provide LAN services that attempt to be transparent to the physical separation.

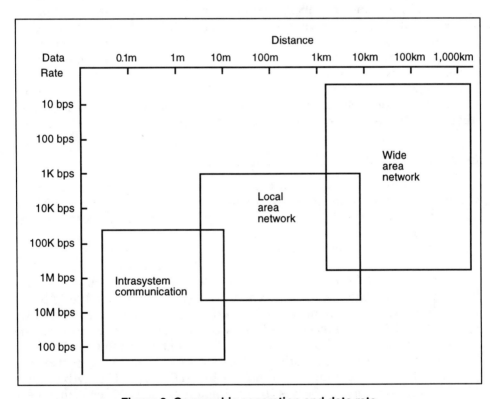

Figure 2. Geographic separation and data rate.

A more technical definition can be found in [PADL82], which we paraphrase as follows: A LAN is a communications mechanism using a transmission technology suitable for relatively short distances (typically a few kilometers) at relatively high bit-per-second rates (typically greater than a few hundred kilobits per second) with relatively low error rates, which exists primarily to support data communication among suitably attached computer systems and terminals (collectively, DTE). The DTE are, at least in principle, heterogeneous; that is, they are not merely multiple instances of the same product. The DTE are assumed to communicate by means of layered protocols.

Note that no assumptions are made about the particular transmission medium or the particular topology in play. LAN media can be twisted-pair wires, CATV or other coaxial-type cables, optical fibers, wireless, or whatever. LAN topologies can be "bus," "ring," or "star." For our purposes, the significant properties of a LAN are the high bit transmission capacity and the good error properties.

In Figure 2 we identify three network groups from a communications viewpoint. The exact numbers are not important and have changed as various technical breakthroughs have occurred. What are important are the concepts that physical characteristics such as data transmission and error rates can be related to distance and that protocols can be optimized for an assumed operational environment. Convenience, however, may dictate use of certain protocols over a wider distance range than is optimum. From the OSI perspective, most of the protocols used in a LAN should be the same as ones used in a WAN context.

Security-relevant LAN characteristics

All data traffic is available to every node in the LAN zone. There is no routing or switching in the conventional sense; rather there is selection. There is routing and filtering among zones, provided by devices such as bridges and gateways.

An adapter is required between the DTE and the LAN. This adapter goes by many names; in this essay, we shall call it the *network interface unit* (NIU). The NIU provides physical and logical conversions. For example, the voltages and ways of representing digital signals on the LAN are probably different from those used internal to the DTE. The first NIUs were external to the DTE. The NIU was connected to the DTE using the same standard that is used to connect to an external modem. External NIUs continue to be available. Efficiencies of space and power are achieved if the NIU is moved internal to the DTE. The NIU may be an internal board, whose interface is the backplane of the DTE, or it may be a chip on the main circuit board of the DTE.

Every NIU has an address. When messages are inserted on the network, the address of the destination NIU is part of the message header. As messages flow through an NIU, the destination address is examined. According to the protocol, if and only if the destination address matches the NIU doing the examining, the message is transmitted to the attached

DTE. By this very simple filtering mechanism, NIUs provide for pairwise communication between any two DTE attached to the network. It is also easy to provide broadcast communication to all NIUs by using a special address such as the binary value of all ones.

There are many reasons why LANs have become popular, the most salient being flexibility and cost. LAN flexibility derives from their inherent distributed control. That is, all of the active decision making takes place in individual NIUs. New NIUs may be added to the net or activated, or NIUs may be removed or deactivated without making a significant change to the overall intelligence controlling the network. This dynamic flexibility is quite valuable in environments where new DTE may be added to the network at any time or where DTE may be removed accidentally or purposefully without notification and coordination with a central authority. However, certain certification and accreditation processes for secure LANs may require notification to, and approval by, a central authority for all configuration changes.

A DTE may be either a terminal or a computer. Security vulnerabilities have been introduced by marketplace technology advances that have just about caused terminals to disappear. When computers emulate terminal protocols, it may not be possible to tell when the security assumptions about "dumb" terminals are valid. PC emulating terminals are qualitatively different, especially with regard to security. For example, a PC can record all the communications traffic. If the NIU is under program control, which might very well be the case for an internal NIU, address filtering can be turned off. The NIU can operate in "promiscuous" or "snooper" mode, passing all traffic to the PC, which in turn can record it for some future use.

The LAN provides universal access between and among devices. In particular, the LAN may be compared with the point-to-point wiring between terminals and computers that was prevalent in previous computer communications architectures. The lack of flexibility, the cost of installing point-to-point wiring, and the saturation of the physical space available for such wiring have all led to the replacement of this technology.

It is undoubtedly obvious that many of the operational advantages of LANs are also potential security liabilities. These liabilities will be discussed in some detail below.

LAN security problems

LANs share many security problems and approaches for their solutions with point-to-point conventional communications systems. In addition, they have some unique problems of their own. This section surveys these problems and leads into the section that discusses selected approaches for solution.

Universal data availability. The ready access to data anywhere along the LAN is one of its greatest security problems. Data is made available to any party whether it should have the data or not. LANs make all traffic available at or near every NIU. Covert activity is very difficult to detect. Every NIU has direct immediate access to all of the data on the network zone to which it is connected. A normal NIU is expected to ignore all data that is not addressed to itself. However, in some LANs malfunctioning or maliciously designed NIUs can be as acquisitive as they wish.

Passive and active wiretap threats. The interception of information transmission by an adversary has been traditionally referred to as wiretapping. We use the term "wiretap" when discussing LAN security even though it may not be strictly descriptive. Some network media are inherently more tap resistant, or at least may give indication when they are tapped. The media may also radiate information. Electromagnetic media, such as twisted-pair or coaxial cable, are notorious for this weakness. Optical media, such as fiber optics, are orders of magnitude better, but they still do radiate under certain conditions; this radiation can be detected if the adversary gets close enough.

Wiretapping is conventionally subdivided into passive and active categories. In passive wiretapping, the message traffic is observed but not modified. The most obvious objective of passive wiretapping is to learn the contents of messages; traffic analysis may provide the adversary with information when message content is not available. Traffic analysis could include steady-state and transient analysis of quantities of messages between parties and the lengths of these messages. A sudden change in traffic volume between national central banks, for example, might signal a change in the rate of exchange or some other financial activity that could be turned into a profit by someone.

In active wiretapping, there are a number of different ways in which the adversary can modify the communications stream. The generic name for this threat is message-stream modification (MSM). Messages can be completely deleted, they can be inserted, or their contents can be modified. Delay, reordering, duplication, and retransmission are also possible. Deliberate denial of service by temporary or permanent incapacitation of the LAN is yet another form of active wiretapping. Denial of service can also occur due to a variety of natural and accidental causes.

End-to-end access control

The term "end-to-end" is often used to (attempt to) describe the scope of control applied to a communications circuit. Unfortunately, end-to-end is one of the more overworked and less precise terms that one encounters in data communications. The problem is that one observer's end is another observer's midpoint. To communicate more precisely, we must identify exactly the endpoints being discussed. The communications engineer traditionally thinks of the endpoint as being the data circuit-terminating equipment (DCE) or at least the interface between the DCE and the DTE. In the LAN context, this means that the data communication end-to-end is from NIU to NIU. Figure 3 illustrates the scopes of NIU-to-NIU and DTE-to-DTE controls; these are also discussed below.

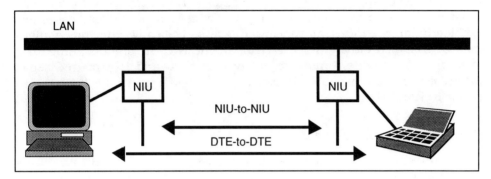

Figure 3. Different end-to-end scopes.

NIU-to-NIU access control. Access control encompasses a subset of correct operation of the LAN protocol. Access control, like flow control and error control, can occur at multiple levels in the OSI architecture. In fact, one of the criticisms of OSI implementations is the overhead of performing the same or similar functions more than once. But with LANs covering only the two or three lower layers of the OSI model, we must accept this duplication. Furthermore, access control can be useful within a LAN or set of compatible LANs, but the granularity of the access control is constrained by the nature of the identification provided by low layer addresses. Providing access control at high layers permits use of finer grained, globally meaningful identifiers, for example, directory distinguished names.

For the LAN to function, it must provide addressing and delivery services. These services require that data be delivered undamaged to its destination. For security considerations, misdelivery and nondelivery are problems associated with damage to the data communications, or at least to the address part thereof. The NIUs play an important part in the delivery mechanism. They must correctly place a destination address on each transmission and must likewise correctly identify the addresses of those messages, and only those messages, which they are to pass through to the attached DTE.

DTE-to-DTE access control. The first extension to end-to-end is to identify the person or process embodied in the DTE. This is the personnel identification problem.

External NIUs typically support two or more attached DTEs. For access control it would be simplest to restrict that number to one. Otherwise, we will have to increase our trust in the NIU, as discussed below. If the definition of end-to-end has been extended to include person or process, then a mechanism must be built to enforce this decision and the NIU must include protocols at higher layers, since people and processes are not identifiable entities at the lower layers. Logically, this mechanism may be installed either in the DTE or in the NIU. In practice, since the local area network is a more recent development and is procured separately, it is more reasonable to expect the access control mechanisms to reside in the NIU.

Security group control

In many communication systems, the users are subdivided into multiple security groups and levels. National defense classifications have coarse level granularities of confidential, secret, and top secret, and finer granularities based on a need-to-know. Groupings supporting unclassified protection might be based on membership in a particular organization, for example, work groups such as engineering, medical, and sales. It would be entirely reasonable for individuals to belong to more than one security group. Using NIUs to enforce rule-based access control is not based on user authorization, but on device authorization. The NIUs operate at protocol layers well below layer seven, where the individual user exists.

We can increase the workload being supported by the NIU and the convenience of its users if we make the NIU responsible for the enforcement of these security group rules. The most obvious function we would like the NIU to perform is to restrict communication to those people and processes that belong to the same security group.

Security approaches

LAN security can be provided by physical protection, separation, or both. The approaches are high-level design alternatives, not specific mechanisms. Physical protection and logical separation on the LAN are discussed. This section addresses alternative schemes for providing security groups. Logical protection of messages between pairs of communicants will be discussed under encryption in a subsequent section.

Physical protection. Physical protection is the most obvious form of security. It is applicable to almost any valuable resource. A local area network is only one example. A local area network can use attack-resistant enclosures or penetration detection and alarms.

Separation. There are a number of different schemes for separating the security groups using a LAN. The most obvious and straightforward is to provide physically separate LANs for each security group. Simply providing multiple cables may not be sufficient; some mechanism may be required to make sure that an unauthorized NIU does not get plugged into the wrong LAN.

On a single LAN, there are a number of ways of providing separate channels for each security group. One very common medium for local area networks is coaxial cable, which is modulated in frequency channels. These channels are very similar to and in many cases identical with the channels used for commercial television broadcast distribution. In addition to the broadcast channels, there are a large number of additional channels used by the cable television industry (CATV). Assigning separate channels to each security group is an obvious separation mechanism; in technical terms this is frequency division multiplexing (FDM).

Channel separation has been approved by some network security managers and rejected by others. This discrepancy is based, no doubt, on different threat scenarios. Before proceeding with channel separation, you should talk with the manager in charge.

An alternative is to provide separate logical channels by including a channel identification in the header of each data communication packet. The NIU would be required to enforce the channel separation in the same way that it enforces address filtering by recognizing the logical channel and passing messages from it only to authorized DTE. This is one form of time division multiplexing (TDM).

Another way to achieve logically separate channels is to use encryption. Cryptography is discussed in Essay 15; the application of cryptography to LANs is covered in a later section.

Implications and side effects

Security comes at a price. Part of this price is fiscal. There are additional components that must be implemented and paid for. Another part of the price is decreased convenience of usage. Introduction of security measures makes a LAN less convenient to use. Some of the burden may be borne by technology (implemented in the NIUs), but part of the burden must be borne by the parties attempting to communicate.

What happens if parties belonging to different security groups need to communicate? The devices that provide interconnection between LAN segments, between separate LANs, or between a LAN and a long distance network are variously known by a variety of terms, depending on the functions being performed. For example, repeaters are primarily associated with layer one functions; bridges, primarily with layer two functions; and routers and gateways, primarily with layer three functions. Therefore, this sequence of names generally reflects the amount of work that must be done in providing this interconnection. Outside of the security arena, there are problems of different protocols and address spaces, which have to be solved.

To a large extent, the solution to such problems is known; there are a large number of commercial devices available to provide such services. When security is an issue, we might add the name filter to the collection implying the function of enforcing security rules and allowing only some messages through. Filters may not be required where encryption is used for confidentiality. Confidential messages protected by encryption may be handled as nonsensitive information in a network. Alternatively, filters may be used in conjunction with secure protocols, such as the draft IEEE Standard for Interoperable Local Area Network Security (SILS), Part B — Secure Data Exchange (SDE) [IEEE90].

SDE is a Link Layer entity that provides services to permit the secure exchange of data. Within the Link Layer, SDE is part of the Logical Link Control Sublayer. SDE provides a connectionless service, which is located on top of the Medium Access Control Sublayer that is defined in IEEE 802 LANs and Metropolitan Area Networks.

Filters contribute to protection against denial of service by passing only properly addressed messages. Noise, "network storms," and messages addressed outside the range set for the filter are not passed through. As shown in Figure 4, the LAN segment behind the filter is protected from malfunction or attack, and has traffic reduced as well.

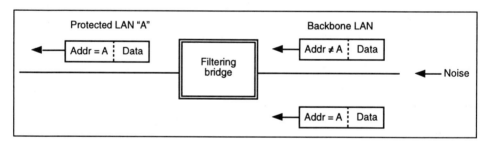

Figure 4. Filter protection.

Trusted NIU

In any local area network, the NIU must be relied on to perform properly. However, when security is a concern, the NIU must be trusted.

For an unevaluated LAN NIU, the trust is based on commercial practices. This should not make us exceptionally confident, for our experience probably indicates that many commercial products are released with the implicit decision that the customer will detect some latent errors. In the security environment, this approach is clearly unsatisfactory. The problem has been addressed in the Trusted Network Interpretation (TNI) [NCSC87a]. The TNI joined network technology with trusted system technology. Probably the major contribution was understanding how the protocol layer model could incorporate the concepts from the Trusted Computer System Evaluation Criteria (TCSEC) [DOD85].

NIUs evaluated under the TNI are trusted because their hardware and software have been demonstrated to properly implement a set of security rules.

We trust these NIUs to correctly implement the LAN protocols, in particular the affixing of destination addresses and the filtering of received messages according to these addresses. In the TCSEC B evaluation class, the NIU has the responsibility of associating security labels with messages, knowing the security level of the attached DTE, and enforcing the security rules for transferring messages.

NIU protocol support

The NIUs provide protocol support at the Link Layer (layer 2). Protocols supported could include IEEE Standard 802.3 Carrier Sense Multiple Access with Collision Detect (CSMA/CD) (Ethernet), 802.4 token bus, or 802.5 token ring. By definition, NIUs operate only at the lowest two layers. At higher layers the equipment to which the NIUs are interfaced could support one or more protocol suites.

MIL-STD-1777 [DOD83] defines one protocol suite known at TCP/IP (Transmission Control Protocol/Internet Protocol), or simply IP. Although originally developed for wide area network (WAN) applications, TCP/IP has achieved wide acceptance in LANs. The IP suite includes the following protocols that the NIUs may support: virtual terminal TELNET, DoD Transmission Control Protocol (TCP), User Datagram Protocol (UDP), Internet Protocol (IP), File Transfer Protocol (FTP), and Host to Front End Protocol (HFE).

The Internet community specifications for IP (RFC-791) and TCP (RFC-793) and the DoD MIL-STD specifications are intended to describe exactly the same protocols. The RFCs and the MIL-STDs for IP and TCP differ in style and level of detail.

Multilevel LAN using COMPUSEC technology

In this section we will address how a LAN could provide security services using COMPUSEC trust technology. LAN capabilities include:

1. communication among terminals and workstations,
2. terminal-to-host (end system) communications,
3. reliable host-to-host (end system-to-end system) communication,
4. host-to-host (end-system–to–end-system) datagram (connectionless) service, and
5. comprehensive network management for both performance and security.

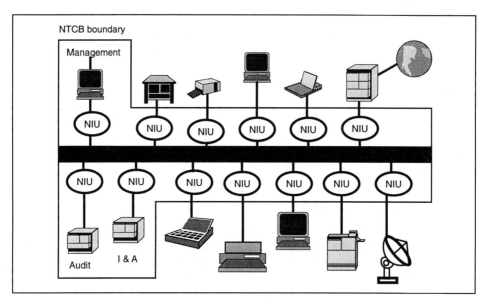

Figure 5. MLS LAN system diagram.

Access to network media is controlled by NIUs, as shown in Figure 5. Devices controlled include terminals, hosts (end systems), workstations, gateways, and various servers. The network management workstation provides centralized management of the network. DTE can operate within a range of security levels; end systems can support multiple concurrent sessions at different sensitivity levels.

The LAN NTCB (network trusted computing base) boundary shown in Figure 5 may be hard to identify in a physical implementation where the NIUs are implemented as integrated circuit cards that plug into expansion slots in other equipment, such as workstations. Essentially all major workstation vendors supply higher layer protocols as part of their product offerings.

The NIUs provide protocol processing and controlled access to the network for attached user devices at the lower layers, thereby providing complete isolation of user data streams. The NIU trusted software implements the local partition of the NTCB, which ensures that untrusted software supporting different user sessions is logically separated. To minimize the size of the NTCB, it should be designed so that untrusted software implements protocol services, including TELNET, most of TCP, most of host (end system)-to-SNS (Secure Network Server) protocol, and many data integrity features defined in TNI.

Protocol additions. To satisfy TNI evaluation requirements, it is presently necessary to develop protocols for end-to-end user identification and trusted path, since the DoD protocol suite does not support trusted path.

The NTCB partition in the NIU provides separation of all communications objects, complete logical isolation of user sessions, and all necessary support functions. Sensitivity labels may be applied to datagrams, connections, and sessions.

Applying TNI (Trusted Network Interpretation). The TNI allows a network, such as a LAN, to be evaluated as network components providing one or more of these functions:

- M: Mandatory access control (MAC)
- I: Identification and authentication (I&A)
- D: Discretionary access control (DAC)
- A: Audit

LAN subjects and objects. In developing a network security policy, it is necessary to identify the subjects and objects. The TNI emphasizes that it uses the same definition as the TCSEC, but it is still necessary to discuss the definitions. The part of the definition of subject that refers to a process-domain pair is unchanged, but the definition of "user" needs to be interpreted in the network context. There is no human user in any of the OSI protocol layers, just processes acting on behalf of the human user. In OSI terminology, this process is known as a protocol layer entity (for each protocol layer). It is the protocol layer entity that acts as the active agent, causing information to flow.

Discretionary access control in the LAN. DAC maps to the need for correct addressing and delivery. The fundamental address filtering function of the NIU implements DAC. The packet source and destination information constitutes the security attributes that support DAC. This protocol information is written and read by end system software in layer four and above. In the DoD protocol suite, source and destination addresses are part of IP. An NIU could enforce DAC based on these addresses without embodying any part of TCP. Both the address filtering functions in the NIU and IP have to be part of the NTCB.

If the DTE attached to the NIU is not capable of providing addressing information, this function must be provided by the NIU. DTE that require additional connection setup services from the LAN include terminals and terminal emulation programs in desktop computers, as well as computers that do not support the LAN protocols. NIUs typically provide dialogues or menus for loading addresses from terminal users and end system operators. Non-LAN network protocols or special host-to-front-end protocols may also be supported. In any case, the amount of trusted code in the NIU increases when the address specification function is added.

An end system address corresponds to two different DAC subject identifiers in the TCSEC operating system view. At layer three the address represents a single subject, the network service access point. The end system address also can be projected to include all the human users of the end system; in this view, the end system address is a group identifier for all of those users.

Identification and authentication. Every trusted system requires I&A. In the LAN, I&A applies to human users at terminals as well as trusted hosts. When a trusted host is connected to an NIU, it may take on the I&A responsibility.

Terminals or workstations are often the first point of contact between a human user and the automated information system. It is therefore necessary to provide trusted I&A supported by the NIU. The NIU does not provide the I&A service; it only provides the interface to that service. The following scenario is typical. The NIU is configured to make a connection to the authentication server, which is shown in Figure 5, whenever it senses a new user. Well-defined hardware and software signals from the terminal signal the presence of a new user. Security depends on the inability of the user to directly change addressing information. The authentication server provides the I&A security function for the LAN.

As a matter of improving the human interface to the automated information system, it is increasingly common to provide a single I&A function that propagates the authenticated identification to the end systems providing user services. This capability is known as unary login. Appropriate trusted protocols are required to transfer the authenticated identity to the end systems. Such a protocol may also instruct the NIU to change the destination address to the end system; this makes the network distribution of the I&A server and end system transparent to the user. Further discussion of authentication in distributed systems is available elsewhere [WOOD92].

I&A of end system hardware and software require physical protection and administrative controls, such as configuration management. For example, disconnection of end systems must be detected by the NTCB so that network operations personnel have assurance that they will be notified of configuration changes. Unauthorized configuration changes can signal an attack.

Trusted path. The TNI requires a trusted path from users to the NTCB at the TCSEC B2 level and higher. The trusted path between the user and the first NTCB partition encountered must be supported by the NIU for users at terminals that do not include such an NTCB partition. A trusted protocol is required to extend the trusted path to other NTCB partitions.

Audit. The TCSEC requirement to audit "introduction of objects into a user's address space" can be interpreted to require audit of individual packet delivery; this is clearly a high-overhead activity. A low-overhead alternative is to view the loading of a destination address as introducing a connection into the address space, thus drastically reducing the number of auditable events. Of course, exception events, such as all access control failures, have to be audited.

Figure 5 indicates the presence of an audit server. This server must operate in cooperation with the NIUs. The NIUs acquire the information to be placed in the audit trail and transmit it to the audit server using appropriate trusted protocols. These protocols must provide confidentiality and guaranteed delivery to satisfy the audit requirements.

Integrity. There are integrity requirements in both Part I and Part II of the TNI. The requirements for system integrity in Part I are focused on correct operation of the NTCB.

The LAN can satisfy this requirement by periodically validating the correct operation of the hardware and firmware elements of each NIU's NTCB partition. One time when such validation is required is when an NIU is added to the network. NIU protocols, implemented within the NTCB, must be designed to provide correct operation in the case of failures of network communications or individual components.

NTCB protocols should be robust enough so that they permit the system to operate correctly in the case of localized failure. The purpose of this protection is to preserve the integrity of the NTCB itself. It is not unusual for one or more NIUs to be inoperative at any time, so it is important to minimize the effects of such failures on the rest of the network.

Some integrity service features can reside outside the NTCB. Otherwise, all software in a network would be in the NTCB.

TNI Part II security services

The security services identified in Part II of the TNI are specified as being optional. LAN vendors decide whether to provide these services as part of product definition. LAN user management decides whether specific services are required in their environment to counter identified threats.

The TNI provides criteria for evaluating the functionality, strength of mechanism, and assurance of these security services. We discuss only functionality in this essay.

Authentication. The LAN should ensure that a data exchange is established with the addressed peer entity (and not with an entity attempting a masquerade or a replay of a previous establishment). The LAN should ensure that the data source is the one claimed.

Attempts to create a session under a false identity constitute a typical threat for which peer entity authentication is an appropriate countermeasure.

Communications field integrity. Communications field integrity refers to protection of any of the fields involved in communications from unauthorized modification. Integrity service counters active threats and protects data against unauthorized alteration. The LAN should ensure that information is accurately transmitted from source to destination. The LAN should be able to counter both equipment failure and actions by persons and processes not authorized to alter the data. The LAN should also have an automated capability of testing for, detecting, and reporting errors that exceed a given threshold.

Nonrepudiation. Nonrepudiation (NR) service provides unforgeable proof of shipment and/or receipt of data. This service prevents the sender from disavowing a legitimate message or the recipient from denying receipt. Since ISO 7498-2 makes it clear that NR is offered only at the Application Layer, it is out of scope for a LAN security device to provide this service.

Continuity of operations. The security features providing resistance against denial-of-service attacks may include the following:

1. Use of redundancy throughout the LAN components can enhance availability.
2. Reconfiguration can provide NIU software maintenance and program downloading to NIUs for software distribution. In addition, to provide initialization and reconfiguration after removing or replacing failed or faulty NIUs, reconfiguration can assist in isolating and/or confining LAN failures, accommodating the addition and deletion of LAN components, and circumventing a detected fault.
3. Distribution and flexibility of LAN control functions by replication of LAN management, both ordinary and security related, can reduce or eliminate the possibility of disabling the LAN. Flexible control capability able to respond promptly to emergency needs, such

as increase in traffic or quick restoration, can improve the capability to respond promptly to the changes in LAN topology and LAN throughput. Therefore, flexible control may enhance survivability and continuity of operation.

4. Fault tolerance mechanisms provide a capability to deal with LAN failures and to maintain continuity of operations. Such mechanisms may be single point, such as filtering gateways to partition the LAN to exclude erroneous traffic, or distributed, such as a maintenance channel among the NIUs and the LAN management center.

5. Measurement of noise and real-time statistical analysis of retransmission rates are typical LAN management services with availability implications.

LAN management. LAN management and maintenance deal with LAN viability, detecting failures and overt acts that result in denial of or reduced service. Simple throughput may not necessarily be a good measure of proper performance. Loading above capacity, flooding, replays, and protocol retry due to noise in the physical layer can reduce service below an acceptable level and/or cause selective outages. Management protocols, such as those which configure the LAN or monitor its performance, are current work items.

An availability problem may cause disruption of more than one peer entity association. The determination of a problem is an application management function, and the corrective action is a system management function.

Mechanisms for detecting denial of service are often protocol based and may involve testing or probing. A common technique is to sequentially poll all NIU addresses. Lack of response from known NIUs indicates an availability problem. Response from NIUs not configured as part of the LAN indicates another class of problem.

In addition to the LAN performance measurements mentioned above, a process may exist to measure the transmission rate between NIUs under conditions of input queuing. The measured transmission rate shall be compared with a predetermined minimum to detect an availability problem.

A request-response protocol such as "are-you-there" or "ping" message exchange may be used to detect availability problems when the connection is quiescent. The availability of entities at different protocol layers can be used to test remote NIUs, gateways, and end systems. Request-response protocols have been known to crash LANs when coupled with hardware failures and/or abnormal loading. Incompatibilities also sometimes show up when dissimilar LANs are interconnected. Any polling sequence should probably be metered to prevent creating the very condition it is designed to detect.

Note that denial of service is addressed only by detection. Methods for prevention of denial-of-service attacks have yet to be developed.

Confidentiality protection. Data confidentiality service protects data against unauthorized disclosure. Data confidentiality is mainly compromised by passive observation and cryptanalysis. Confidentiality protection is a collective term for a number of security services. These services, described below, are all concerned with the secrecy, or nondisclosure, of information transfer between peer entities through the LAN. COMPUSEC mechanisms do not provide protection against wiretapping or other physical attacks. Cryptographic protection, a COMSEC mechanism discussed in a later section, is often used to provide this protection.

The LAN must provide protection of data from unauthorized disclosure. Physical security, such as protected wireways, can also provide transmission security. The LAN manager must decide on the balance among physical, administrative, and technical security. This essay addresses only technical security.

Traffic flow confidentiality. Traffic analysis is a compromise in which analysis of message length, frequency, and protocol components (such as addresses) results in information disclosure through inference.

Traffic flow confidentiality is concerned with masking the frequency, length, and origin-destination patterns of communications between protocol entities. Encryption can effectively and efficiently restrict disclosure above the Transport Layer; that is, it can conceal the process and application but not the host computer node unless a red/black gateway is used in conjunction with a secure protocol that encrypts the end system address [DINK90].

Selective routing. Since LAN technology substitutes selection for routing, you may wonder why this security service is included in an essay on LAN security. Selective routing applies to gateways and bridges among LANs. Selective routing is the application of rules to choose or avoid specific LANs, gateways, or links between LANs. The selection may be based on static policy or on dynamic attack or error conditions.

Multilevel LAN using communications security technology

Communications security, COMSEC, provides confidentiality services by applying an encryption mechanism. Encryption is discussed in detail in Essay 15. We limit our discussion in this essay to several issues pertaining to LANs.

Channel separation. Encryption can be used in a rather straightforward way to establish logical channels. Each logical channel is assigned a symmetric encryption key or an asymmetric pair of keys. When an NIU is going to operate on a given logical channel, it need only load the appropriate key; thus it establishes a logical channel between NIUs.

If an NIU is to be trusted to operate on multiple logical channels, then it must apply a key for each of those channels to every message that passes through it. For certain symmetric key applications, this seems to be an unnecessarily complex procedure; it would not be unreasonable to restrict an NIU to operating on a single logical channel. If the attached person or process had access to multiple logical channels, then the appropriate encryption key could be changed appropriately under the control of that person or process.

Encryption can also be used to create separate channels. Assuming for the moment that the security group encompasses the NIU and that an NIU belongs to one and only one security group, then encryption between NIUs is analogous to link encryption in conventional communications systems.

There are two ways to achieve separate channels using encryption. Only those NIUs sharing the same symmetric encryption key or matched pairs of asymmetric keys would be able to communicate, thereby creating separate logical channels for their security groups.

A message may be encrypted more than once, if the encryption algorithms permit. This serial encryption is sometimes called superencryption. We shall assume multiple encryptions, thereby making it possible to form subgroups as many times as necessary and to encrypt specific messages between two parties, both of whom belong to the same security group.

Privacy between NIUs. Encryption between DTEs may require another pair of asymmetric keys or another symmetric key. Messages between DTEs would then be doubly encrypted. Without this second DTE-to-DTE key, any DTE attached to an NIU possessing the key for the logical channel could eavesdrop on all communication on that logical channel.

Key management. Key management is a necessary managerial function. The technology is the same for LANs and WANs. However, the logistics of a truly local area LAN may influence the selection of symmetric or asymmetric keying and the manual or automated methods used for key distribution. See the key management sections in the essay on cryptography (Essay 15) for further information.

If multilevel traffic messages of different sensitivity are required, different keying is required for each sensitivity level. This is the only way to achieve the cryptographic equivalent of labeling.

End-to-end symmetric key encryption example. Sometimes end-to-end symmetric key encryption may be used in a LAN to provide logical channel separation. Consider a LAN used by hosts operating at various security levels that send and receive encrypted messages. The NIUs connected to these hosts obtain symmetric encryption keys at the level of the appropriate information to be protected from a central key distribution center (KDC) supporting the various security levels of the network. The KDC is attached to the LAN in the same way as a host. A symmetric key is sent from the KDC to an NIU upon request, using an appropriately defined protocol that authenticates both the requester and the new symmetric key.

The purpose of key distribution is really to support a trusted local service within the LAN: the ability to transform classified or sensitive messages from the host into unclassified encrypted messages suitable for transmission over the LAN.

For symmetric key management, part of the trusted network service is implemented within the KDC, which must generate new symmetric keys for the level of information being communicated, and must also decide, on the basis of an access control policy, which NIUs may share keys. The granularity of key distribution is a trade-off between convenience and protection. Fine granularity would use a unique key for each sensitivity level for each session; coarse granularity would use the same key for all sessions during a time period.

Please see Essay 17 on Privacy Enhanced Mail (PEM) for an example of asymmetric key distribution and end-to-end encryption techniques.

Summary

This essay has reviewed local area networks with special attention paid to security issues. While the LAN offers many advantages in terms of data access and flexibility, the other side of the coin is increased vulnerability to wiretapping. The problems of end-to-end access control and security groups were also discussed. The mechanisms for providing security are physical protection and separation of security groups by physical, logical, or encryption methods — all of which may adversely affect interoperability. Most protection schemes require that the network interface units be trusted; the reasons and trusted functions were discussed. Encryption is used for creating logical channels as well as protecting sessions between two persons or processes; the distribution of symmetric encryption keys by a key distribution center was outlined.

Internet Privacy Enhanced Mail

Stephen T. Kent

Privacy Enhanced Mail (PEM) consists of extensions to existing message processing software plus a key management infrastructure. These combine to provide users with a facility in which message confidentiality, authenticity, and integrity can be effected. PEM is compatible with RFC 822 message processing conventions and is transparent to SMTP mail relays. PEM uses symmetric cryptography — for example, the Data Encryption Standard (DES) — to provide (optional) encryption of messages. Although the RFCs permit the use of either symmetric or asymmetric (public key) cryptography (for instance, the RSA cryptosystem) to distribute symmetric keys, the RFCs strongly recommend the use of asymmetric cryptography for this purpose and to generate and validate digital signatures for messages and certificates. Public key management in PEM is based on the use of certificates as defined by the CCITT Directory Authentication Framework [CCIT88c]. A public key certification hierarchy for PEM is being established by the Internet Society. This certification hierarchy supports universal authentication of PEM users, under various policies, without the need for prior bilateral agreements among users or organizations with which the users may be affiliated.

The primary focus of the effort to develop and deploy Privacy Enhanced Mail (PEM) is the provision of security services for e-mail users in the Internet community.[1] This effort began in 1985 as an activity [LINN86] of the Privacy and Security Research Group (PSRG)[2] of the Internet Re-

---

[1] The Internet e-mail community is interpreted here to include those users who use the protocols defined by RFC 821 and RCC 822 for e-mail.

[2] The PSRG was formed in 1985 and is one of several groups that pursue various research topics in the context of the Internet. Other groups have been constituted to explore topics such as end-to-end protocols, multimedia teleconferencing, information location services, and so on.

search Task Force, under the auspices of the Internet Architecture Board (IAB).[3] The effort has yielded a series of Requests for Comment (RFCs)[4] of which the most recent set, RFCs 1421 to 1424 [LINN93, KENT93, BALE93, KALA93], are Proposed Internet Standards. This essay describes the version of PEM defined by those RFCs. Ongoing work to integrate PEM with MIME [BORE92] is not detailed since, at the time at which this essay was prepared, that work was not yet stable.

Overview

PEM provides several security services for e-mail users: confidentiality, data origin authentication, and connectionless integrity, as defined by ISO [ISO89]. If appropriate algorithms are used, PEM also provides support for nonrepudiation with proof of origin. These services are bundled into two groups: All messages processed through PEM incorporate the authenticity, integrity, and nonrepudiation support facilities, whereas confidentiality is an optional security service.

The integrity and authenticity services ensure a message recipient that a message was sent by the indicated originator and that the message has not been modified en route. The nonrepudiation mechanisms allow a message to be forwarded to a third party, who can verify the identity of the originator (not just the identity of the forwarder) and verify that the message has not been altered, even by the original recipient. The optional confidentiality service ensures a message originator that the message text will be disclosed (decipherable) only to the designated recipients.

As noted above, PEM is intended for use with existing e-mail systems, primarily Internet e-mail as defined by RFC 822. Figure 1 illustrates how PEM can be integrated into existing mail system architectures. A variety of environments are illustrated here, including message preparation on a multiuser host incorporating a message transfer agent (MTA) and relay through an intermediate MTA.[5] In the figure, messages are retrieved

---

[3] The IAB oversees the development of the Internet architecture and the execution of the Internet standards process, under the auspices of the Internet Society.

[4] RFCs are the official, archival publications of the IAB. All protocol standards are published as RFCs, but not all RFCs are protocol standards. For example, some RFCs are merely informational, others describe experimental protocols, and still others constitute policy statements. RFCs are available on line from various sites and in hard-copy form from SRI International and the InterNIC.

[5] The concepts of UAs and MTAs are taken from X.400 [CCIT88a] but apply equally well to messaging in the TCP/IP environment. In the TCP/IP protocol suite, MTAs are represented by SMTP (defined in RFC 821) processes, which route and relay mail traffic. UAs are represented by processes that implement RFC 822 message processing.

from a mailbox on a computer that is separate from the recipient's workstation, for example, using the Post Office Protocol (POP) [ROSE91] (or P7 in an X.400 environment). To maximize compatibility with such systems, PEM is designed to be transparent to mail transfer systems, so that the existing transport infrastructure can be used for PEM. PEM also is designed to be minimally intrusive to mail system user agents, although transparency here seems to entail trade-offs in quality of the user interface.

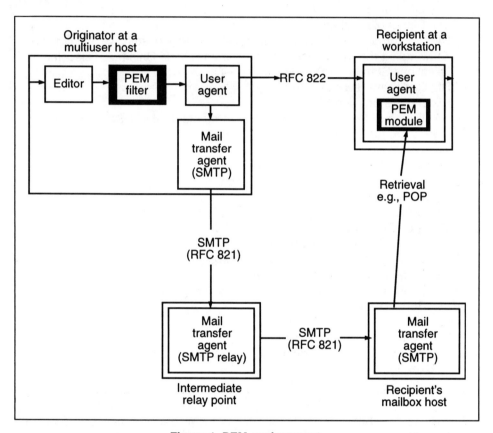

Figure 1. PEM environment.

One can implement PEM as a filter applied to a file created using an editor but prior to submission to a mail system user agent. However, this approach may provide a poor user interface unless a substantial amount of mechanism from the user agent is replicated in the PEM filter or the editor (for example, to deal with acquisition of recipient addresses). In contrast, if PEM processing is integrated into a user agent, the user agent must provide new user interface facilities to allow selection of security services, but the resulting interface can be especially "user friendly." Both approaches to PEM implementation are illustrated in Figure 1.

Acronyms used in this essay

ASCII: American Standard Code for Information Interchange
ASN: Abstract Syntax Notation
CA: Certification Authority
CBC: Cipher block chaining
CCITT: International Telegraph and Telephone Consultative Committee, now called the International Telecommunications Union — Telecommunications Standardization Sector (ITU-T)
CRL: Certificate revocation list
DES: Data Encryption Standard
DSA: Directory Services Agent (Note: In cryptography, DSA is the Digital Signature Algorithm.)
IAB: Internet Architecture Board
IPRA: Internet PCA Registration Authority
ISO: International Standards Organization
MIC: Message integrity code
MTA: Message transfer agent
OSI: Open Systems Interconnection
PCA: Policy Certification Authority
PSRG: Privacy and Security Research Group
PEM: Privacy Enhanced Mail
POP: Post Office Protocol
RFC: Request for Comments
RSA: Rivest, Shamir, and Adleman
SMTP: Simple Message Transfer Protocol
TCP/IP: Transmission Control Protocol/Internet Protocol
UA: User agent

In providing these security services, PEM uses a variety of cryptographic algorithms. These algorithms provide for message integrity, message encryption, digital signatures, and distribution of keys used to encipher messages. If public key algorithms are used in this latter context, then two additional algorithms must be specified: one for certificate hashing and one for certificate signatures. The base PEM standards do not require the use of specific algorithms for any of these purposes, but rather provide facilities to identify which algorithms are used on a per-message and per-recipient basis. A separate standard within the PEM series (initially, RFC 1115) provides specifications for the use of specific algorithms with PEM.

PEM is oriented primarily toward use in the Internet e-mail environment, as characterized by the use of two Internet standards: RFC 822 [CROC82] and SMTP [POST82]. The former defines the syntax and (header) semantics for messages, while the latter defines the protocol for transport of messages. Although designed expressly for use with these protocols, PEM can be used in a wider range of messaging environments; for example, the NIST Open Implementors Workshop has defined an X.400 body part to carry PEM messages. PEM-processed messages intentionally employ a 6-bit encoding that utilizes a subset of printable characters to maximize the likelihood that such messages can transit the mail gateways (many of which do not provide transparent forwarding of message contents) that link Internet e-mail to other e-mail systems — BITNET, UUNET, and so on.

In addition to the specification of message processing facilities, the PEM standards provide for a public key certification infrastructure. Although PEM allows for the use of either secret key (symmetric) or public key (asymmetric) cryptoalgorithms for key distribution, the standards encourage the use of public key cryptography because of its ability to support a very large, distributed user community. The specific approach to public key cryptography adopted for PEM is based on the use of certificates, as defined in CCITT Recommendation X.509.

The PEM standards establish a specific framework for a public key certification system for several reasons. Although PEM makes use of X.509 certificates, this CCITT recommendation does not provide a semantic context in which to interpret certificates. X.509 embodies a degree of generality that, if fully exploited, could result in rather complex certification relationships. The PEM certification system imposes conventions that make certification relationships straightforward and allow users to readily interpret each certificate associated with other PEM users. Another advantage of establishing this certification framework is that it can be used with other security protocols, for example, X.500 and X.400. The same certificates used for PEM could be employed with these other applications in support of security services.

PEM message submission: Message processing

The overall flow of data for PEM message submission processing is illustrated in Figure 2. There are two sources of data input to PEM for message submission: message header and message text. The message header information will be carried in the RFC 822 header of the final, processed PEM message. This data largely bypasses PEM processing, with the possible exception that the Subject field, if deemed sensitive, might be omitted or a benign Subject might be substituted (for example, "Encrypted Message"). This header is separated from the remainder of the data by a blank line, following the usual convention, and then an explicit boundary marker is inserted to identify this as a PEM message.

Some of the header data, namely recipient addresses, serve as input to PEM processing to control the (optional) message encryption function, which generates PEM encapsulated header data. Following this PEM message header data is another blank line. The message text itself, possibly augmented by header fields replicated so that they can be afforded protection, becomes the encapsulated text of the PEM-processed message, following the (second) blank line. Finally, a complementary PEM boundary message completes the PEM message.

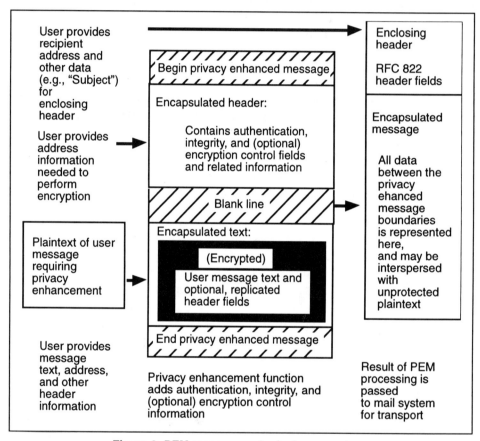

Figure 2. PEM message submission overview.

PEM message processing involves three major transformation steps: SMTP canonicalization, computation of the message integrity code, and optional message encryption followed by optional 6-bit encoding. These steps are illustrated in Figure 3.

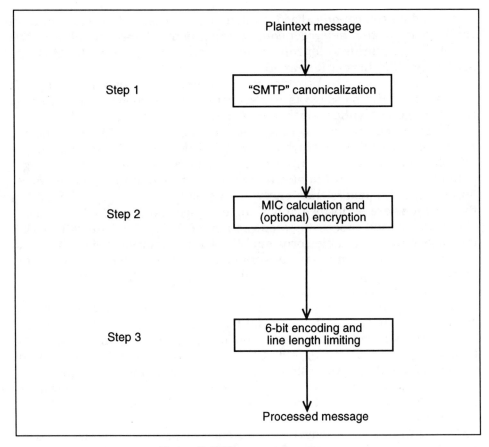

Plaintext message

Step 1   "SMTP" canonicalization

Step 2   MIC calculation and (optional) encryption

Step 3   6-bit encoding and line length limiting

Processed message

Figure 3. PEM processing steps.

The first step uses the canonicalization specified by SMTP to ensure a uniform presentation syntax among a heterogeneous collection of computer systems. A shortcoming of this particular choice of processing — as opposed to a more general presentation syntax such as the ASN.1 concrete encoding used in X.400 [CCIT88a] — is that it restricts the input to 7-bit ASCII. However, this specific canonicalization was selected because the primary application environment, that is, Internet e-mail, imposed the same restrictions.

The second step begins with the calculation of the message integrity code (MIC). PEM allows this function to be as simple as a DES message authentication code if the message is directed to only a single recipient. However, most messages will be addressed to multiple recipients, and in such circumstances a one-way hash function is required to prevent any one recipient from spoofing others. Moreover, support for nonrepudiation with proof of origin is provided only if a one-way hash is used. The MIC is calculated on the canonicalized version of the message to permit uniform verification in the heterogeneous environment alluded to above. The specific algorithm used for MIC computation is specified in the MIC-Info field of the PEM header (Figure 4).

The second step also provides message encryption (if selected by the originator). If the message is to be encrypted, any padding required by the message encryption algorithm is first applied. A message key, to be used exclusively to encrypt this message, is generated. The (symmetric) encryption algorithm employed is specified in the DEK-Info field in the PEM header (Figure 4), along with any parameters required by the algorithm (for example, an initialization vector). The canonical (padded as required) message text is then encrypted using the per-message key. All of these actions are performed only if the message is of type ENCRYPTED.

The third (final) processing step renders an ENCRYPTED or MIC-ONLY message into a printable form suitable for transmission via SMTP and across a variety of messaging system boundaries. This encoding step transforms the (optionally encrypted) message text into a restricted 6-bit alphabet (plus line length constraints that make the encoding compatible with SMTP canonicalization). If the message has been encrypted, this encoding serves to transform the resulting 8-bit ciphertext into a form that can be transmitted using SMTP and other message transfer protocols (which require 7-bit ASCII). MIC-CLEAR messages are not subject to any portion of the third processing step. A MIC-CLEAR message is a signed, but not encrypted, message that is not encoded, specifically so that it can be sent to a mixed set of recipients, some of whom use PEM and some who do not.

Even if the message has not been encrypted, this encoding ensures, with high probability, that the canonicalized version of the message (produced in step 1) will not be altered (benignly) in transit, for example, while passing through a mail gateway. A change in as little as one bit of the text would cause the MIC check to fail at a destination, hence the need to ensure that the transformed message text can be transmitted without modification. Because MIC-CLEAR messages are not encoded, they are susceptible to (benign) gateway manipulation and thus run an increased risk of failing the MIC check at recipients who perform PEM processing. The provision of the MIC-CLEAR message type in PEM thus represents an explicit trade-off between immunity to (benign) transport manipulation and flexibility in sending mail to mixed user communities.

PEM message submission: Header construction

After the processing steps described above have been accomplished, the PEM message header is constructed. The precise steps followed at this point depend on whether secret key or public key cryptography is used to distribute keys. Since the public key approach is expected to be most

```
To:        Linn@dec.com
From:      Kent@bbn.com
Subject:   Encrypted PEM Message
 -----BEGIN PRIVACY-ENHANCED MESSAGE-----
Proc-Type: 4,ENCRYPTED
Content-Domain: RFC822
DEK-Info: DES-CBC,BFF968AA74691AC1
Originator-Certificate:
 MIIBlTCCAScCAWUwDQYJKoZIhvcNAQECBQAwUTELMAkGA1UEBhMCVVMxIDAeBgNV
 BAoTF1JTQSBEYXRhIFNlY3VyaXR5LCBJbmMuMQ8wDQYDVQQLEwZCZXRhIDExDzAN
 BgNVBAsTBk5PVEFSWTAeFw05MTA5MDQxODM4MTdaFw05MzA5MDMxODM4MTZaMEUx
 CzAJBgNVBAYTAlVTMSAwHgYDVQQKExdSU0EgRGF0YSBTZWN1cml0eSwgSW5jLjEU
 MBIGA1UEAxMLVGVzdCBVc2VyIDEwWTAKBgRVCAEBAgICAANLADBIAkEAwHZHl7i+
 yJcqDtjJCowzTdBJrdAiLAnSC+CnnjOJELyuQiBgkGrgIh3j8/x0fM+YrsyF1u3F
 LZPVtzlndhYFJQIDAQABMA0GCSqGSIb3DQEBAgUAA1kACKr0PqphJYw1j+YPtcIq
 iWlFPuN5jJ79Khfg7ASFxskYkEMjRNZV/HZDZQEhtVaU7Jxfzs2wfX5byMp2X3U/
 5XUXGx7qusDgHQGs7Jk9W8CW1fuSWUgN4w==
Key-Info: RSA,
 I3rRIGXUGWAF8js5wCzRTkdhO34PTHdRZY9Tuvm03M+NM7fx6qc5udixps2Lng0+
 wGrtiUm/ovtKdinz6ZQ/aQ==
Issuer-Certificate:
 MIIB3DCCAUgCAQowDQYJKoZIhvcNAQECBQAwTzELMAkGA1UEBhMCVVMxIDAeBgNV
 BAoTF1JTQSBEYXRhIFNlY3VyaXR5LCBJbmMuMQ8wDQYDVQQLEwZCZXRhIDExDTAL
 BgNVBAsTBFRMQ0EwHhcNOTEwOTAxMDgwMDAwWhcNOTIwOTAxMDc1OTU5WjBRMQsw
 CQYDVQQGEwJVUzEgMB4GA1UEChMXUlNBIERhdGEgU2VjdXJpdHksIEluYy4xDzAN
 BgNVBAsTBkJldGEgMTEPMA0GA1UECxMGTk9UQVJZMHAwCgYEVQgBAQICArwDYgAw
 XwJYCsnp61QCxYykNlODwutF/jMJ3kL+3PjYyHOwk+/9rLg6X65B/LD4bJHtO5XW
 cqAz/7R7XhjYCm0PcqbdzoACZtIlETrKrcJiDYoP+DkZ8k1gCk7hQHpbIwIDAQAB
 MA0GCSqGSIb3DQEBAgUAA38AAICPv4f9Gx/tY4+p+4DB7MV+tKZnvBoy8zgoMGOx
 dD2jMZ/3HsyWKWgSF0eH/AJB3qr9zosG47pyMnTf3aSy2nBO7CMxpUWRBcXUpE+x
 EREZd9++32ofGBIXaialnOgVUn0OzSYgugiQ077nJLDUj0hQehCizEs5wUJ35a5h
MIC-Info: RSA-MD5,RSA,
 UdFJR8u/TIGhfH65ieewe2lOW4tooa3vZCvVNGBZirf/7nrgzWDABz8w9NsXSexv
 AjRFbHoNPzBuxwmOAFeA0HJszL4yBvhG
Recipient-ID-Asymmetric:
 MFExCzAJBgNVBAYTAlVTMSAwHgYDVQQKExdSU0EgRGF0YSBTZWN1cml0eSwgSW5j
 LjEPMA0GA1UECxMGQmV0YSAxMQ8wDQYDVQQLEwZOT1RBUlk=,
 66
Key-Info: RSA,
 O6BS1ww9CTyHPtS3bMLD+L0hejdvX6Qv1HK2ds2sQPEaXhX8EhvVphHYTjwekdWv
 7x0Z3Jx2vTAhOYHMcqqCjA==

 qeWlj/YJ2Uf5ng9yznPbtD0mYloSwIuV9FRYx+gzY+8iXd/NQrXHfi6/MhPfPF3d
 jIqCJAxvld2xgqQimUzoS1a4r7kQQ5c/Iua4LqKeq3ciFzEv/MbZhA==
 -----END PRIVACY-ENHANCED MESSAGE-----
```

Figure 4. Sample PEM message.

widely used and its use is strongly encouraged by the specifications, this essay focuses on that technique. Figure 4 displays a sample PEM message, with an RFC 822 header, and the following text is keyed to this example. The sample message makes use of version 4 of the protocol and is encrypted, as indicated by the Proc-Type field.

To provide data origin authentication and message integrity, and to support nonrepudiation with proof of origin, the MIC computed above in step 2 is padded and then encrypted using the private component of the originator's public key pair. This effects a digital signature on the message, which can be verified by any user employing the originator's public component. If the message is encrypted, this signature value is encrypted using the secret, per-message key, which was used to encrypt the message text itself. This last encryption step is used to protect against the disclosure of a (trivial) repetitive message content that could be discerned by observation of the signed hash value. The resulting value is 6-bit encoded and included in the MIC-Info field (Figure 4), along with the identifiers of the MIC algorithm and the digital signature algorithm. In this example, the MD5 hash function is used as the MIC algorithm, and the RSA algorithm is used as the digital signature algorithm.

If the message is encrypted, the algorithm used to encrypt the message and any parameters required by the (message) encryption algorithm are specified in the DEK-Info field, which appears once per message. In this example, the CBC mode of DES is used as the encryption algorithm, and the initialization vector used is represented as the second component of this field.

To provide confidentiality, one copy of the message key is encrypted using the public component of the public key pair for each recipient. In this way, each copy of the message key is protected in a fashion that makes it decipherable by exactly one recipient. The result of this encryption is placed in the Key-Info field, following an identifier for the public key algorithm used to encrypt the message key. Each Key-Info field is preceded by a Recipient-ID-Asymmetric field that identifies the recipient (by the X.500-distinguished name[6] of his certificate issuer and certificate serial number). Thus each pair of these PEM header fields together provides the information required for a recipient to decrypt a message. Here RSA is used as the public key encryption algorithm and is so identified in the Key-Info field.

The originator may, at his discretion, provide his certificate (using the Originator-Certificate field) and the certificate of the entity that issued his certificate, and so on (using multiple Issuer-Certificate fields as required).

---

[6] Each entry in an X.500 directory server has a unique name which identifies that entry, called the "distinguished name" of the entry. That name is composed of selected attributes from superior entries in the directory tree, all the way back to the root.

The inclusion of these certificates is intended to facilitate the certificate validation process by recipients, but is not required. This example illustrates the inclusion of the originator's certificate and one issuer certificate.

PEM message delivery processing

On receipt of a PEM-protected message, a recipient first scans the PEM header to identify the version of PEM that was used and the form of PEM processing that has been applied: ENCRYPTED, MIC-ONLY, or MIC-CLEAR. The message type determines the processing steps performed by the recipient.

If the message is ENCRYPTED or MIC-ONLY, the first step is the inversion of the encoding process applied by the originator, converting the 6-bit encoding back into the ciphertext or canonical plaintext form. If the message is ENCRYPTED, the recipient scans the PEM header to locate the Recipient-ID-Asymmetric field for this recipient. The recipient uses the private component of his public key pair to decrypt the associated Key-Info field, yielding the message key and extracting parameters associated with the message encryption algorithm. The recipient now uses the message key to decrypt the message text. After decryption, the message is now at the same processing status as a MIC-ONLY or MIC-CLEAR message, and the following text applies to those message types as well. (In fact, a MIC-CLEAR message requires a processing step unique to that message type. The step is the recanonicalization of the message insofar as lines are delimited by a carriage return and a line feed, versus a local representation of delimited lines.)

The recipient now processes the MIC-Info field, using the MIC algorithm and signature algorithm specified in this field. The recipient needs to acquire the public component of the originator to check the signature. In principle, this requires validating a chain of certificates that terminates with the certificate of the originator, although caching of certificates by user agents is expected to short-circuit this process in most instances. Using this public component, the recipient decrypts the signature, revealing the MIC value. The recipient computes the MIC on the canonical form of the message and compares the result with the decrypted value. If they match, the integrity and data origin authenticity of the message are verified. This verification step applies to all three message forms.

Finally, after verifying message integrity, the canonical form of the message is translated into the local representation apropos for the recipient's system and is displayed for the user. The recipient also should be informed of the cryptographically authenticated originator identity through some out-of-band means, that is, separate from the "From" field contained within the message. For example, in a graphical user interface system this notification could be effected using a window separate from that used to display the message text. Errors encountered in attempting to validate message integrity or decrypt the message may result in informative messages or may preclude display of the message for the recipient, depending on the severity of the error and on local security policy.

The PEM certification system

The PEM specifications recommend use of public key cryptography for message integrity and authentication, and key distribution for message encryption keys. As noted earlier, PEM makes use of public key certificates that conform to the CCITT X.509 recommendations. This recommendation defines an authentication framework in which certificates play a central role, which is quite general and places very few constraints on the resulting certification system. PEM "profiles" this framework, imposing conventions that result in a concrete realization of a certification system that is a conformant subset of that envisioned in X.509.

X.509 certificates. A (public key) certificate is a data structure used to securely bind a public key to a name and to specify who vouches for the binding. The structure as a whole is digitally signed in roughly the same fashion as a PEM message is signed (for example, the canonicalization rules are different). What follows is the certificate format specified by X.509, using ASN.1 notation to define the top-level fields in the structure:

```
Certificate ::=          SIGNED SEQUENCE{
version [0]                  Version DEFAULT v1988,
serialNumber                    CertificateSerialNumber,
signature                    AlgorithmIdentifier,
issuer                       Name,
validity                        Validity,
subject                         Name,
subjectPublicKeyInfo         SubjectPublicKeyInfo}
```

The *version* field is used to differentiate among successive versions of the certificate format. The *serialNumber* field uniquely identifies this certificate among those issued by the same entity. The *signature* field specifies the digital signature algorithm used to sign this certificate. The *issuer* field specifies the directory (distinguished) name of the entity that vouches for the binding between the *subject* directory (distinguished) name and the public key contained in the certificate. The *validity* field specifies the start and end times and dates that delimit the interval over which the certificate is valid. The key alluded to above is contained, along with an identifier to specify the algorithm and any parameters required by the algorithm, in the *subjectPublicKeyInfo* field.

As noted above, the *signature* field specifies the algorithms and any parameters required to verify the digital signature applied to the certificate. Typically, both a one-way hash algorithm and a public key signature algorithm will be specified. This signature is applied by the issuer (using his private component) and appended after these other certificate fields. Appended to the certificate is a data structure that reproduces the algorithm identifiers and parameters needed to verify this signature (using the public component of the issuer). Note that the algorithm used to sign the certificate may be different from the algorithm with which the subject's public key is employed.

One validates a certificate by verifying the signature applied by the issuer of the certificate. Specifically, one computes the one-way hash (specified in the *signature* field) over the certificate, uses the public component of the issuer to decrypt the value in the appended signature, and compares the two resulting values. The issues of how one acquires the public component of the issuer and how one determines whether to trust the issuer to vouch for this binding are the subject of the next section.

The Internet certification hierarchy. As noted above, the act of validating a certificate requires the user to possess the public key of the issuer of the certificate. This issuer also will have a certificate, and thus the process of certificate validation is recursive and implicitly defines a (directed) certification graph. However, the process must conclude at some point, implying that the user holds a public key that he obtained through some out-of-band channel. In X.509 the certification graph is largely unconstrained, and thus might be an arbitrary graph, for example, including loops.

Certification authorities. X.509 defines a Certification Authority (CA) as "an authority trusted by one or more users to create and assign certificates." X.509 also imposes no constraints on the relationship between a certificate issuer, such as a Certification Authority, and a subject — for example, with regard to distinguished names. Different CAs are expected to issue certificates under different policies, for example, varying degrees of assurance in vouching for name-public key bindings. However, X.509 makes no provisions for users to learn what policies each CA applies in issuing certificates. This makes it hard for a user to assign semantics to the bindings implied by certification.

The Internet community is adopting a certification graph that takes the form of a (singly) rooted tree, illustrated in Figure 5. The root of this tree is designated the Internet PCA Registration Authority (IPRA) and will be operated under the auspices of the Internet Society. The IPRA provides a reference point from which all certificates in the Internet certification hierarchy can be validated. The IPRA establishes a common policy that applies to all certificates issued under this hierarchy. The IPRA issues certificates to a second tier of entities designated Policy Certification Authorities (PCAs), which, in turn, issue certificates to CAs. CAs issue certificates to (subordinate) CAs or directly to users (including mailing lists).

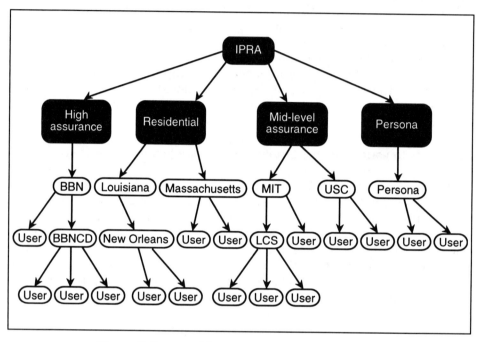

Figure 5. Proposed Internet certification hierarchy.

Typically, a CA will be certified by one PCA, and Figure 5 illustrates this common case. However, it is permissible for a single CA to be certified under multiple PCAs. In the latter case, the implication is that a single administrative entity is prepared to issue certificates under multiple disjoint policies. For each PCA under which a CA is certified, the CA certificate signed by the PCA must use a different public component. This ensures that the certificates issued by the CA under each policy are readily identifiable because each is signed using different private components. For example, in Figure 5, MIT is certified under both the mid-level and high assurance PCAs, and thus is capable of issuing certificates to faculty, staff, and students, based on either of the policies imposed by these PCAs.

In addition to the organizational CAs shown for MIT, BBN, and USC, residential CAs also are illustrated in Figure 5. These have been identified in more detail, using abbreviated forms of the distinguished name attributes for the geographic entities that they represent.[7] For example, two residential CAs are illustrated, one for Louisiana and another for Massachusetts, both within the United States. Below the Louisiana CA is a subordinate CA for the city (locality) of New Orleans.

IPRA common policy. The IPRA common policy is intended to encompass a minimum set of essential requirements that apply to all PCAs, CAs, and UAs. For example, this policy requires that each PCA file its statement of policy in accordance with a format that is also part of this policy. Each PCA policy must not contravene the IPRA common policy, but rather may specify additional policy aspects not addressed by the common policy. For example, a PCA policy statement will characterize the procedures used to authenticate CAs and users certified under this policy, plus any security requirements imposed on CAs for certificate management.

Each PCA policy statement must specify CRL management requirements, for example, upper and lower bounds on the frequency with which CAs must issue CRLs, provisions for archiving CRLs, and so on. The policy statement also must describe security measures used by the PCA in its management of certificates and to ensure the privacy of data held by the PCA in performing this task.

The IPRA policy also requires that all PCAs and CAs issue CRLs, although the policy does not constrain the frequency of issue of these CRLs. The IPRA also will establish and maintain a distributed database providing access to current CRLs for all PCAs and CAs within the community, at least until X.500 directory servers are sufficiently widely available to provide equivalent service.

The IPRA policy also requires PCAs and CAs to issue certificates in a fashion that ensures the uniqueness of distinguished names. To support PCAs in meeting this requirement, the IPRA will establish a registry of CA distinguished names, accessible by PCAs, which must be consulted before a PCA certifies a CA. An analogous but larger database will be established by the IPRA to record residential user distinguished names, to permit certification of such users by multiple PCAs. One approach to providing both of these databases involves having the IPRA operate an X.500 DSA, connected to other (extant) Internet DSAs. This would ensure that distinguished names associated with users and organizations registered in the existing X.500 system will not be infringed upon.

---

[7] The organizational CAs shown in Figure 5 do not contain their distinguished names due to space limitations. For example, the BBN CA might have a name of the form C=US, S=MA, O=BBN, where "O" is an abbreviation for the attribute "organization."

A critical aspect of the IPRA policy deals with UA processing of certificates, rather than PCA or CA issuance of certificates. The fundamental requirement is distinguished name subordination. Whenever a certificate is validated for use in PEM, it must have the characteristic that the subject distinguished name in the certificate is subordinate to the issuer distinguished name in that certificate, unless the certificate in question is issued by the IPRA or by a PCA. This rule provides the user with a "natural" certification path that can be inferred by examination of the final certificate in the path, plus display of the distinguished name of the PCA under whose policy the certificate was issued.

The following example illustrates this rule. The BBN CA certificate might contain the following subject distinguished name: C=US, S=MA, O=BBN. This name would appear as the issuer name in all certificates issued by this CA. A valid distinguished name that could appear as the subject in a certificate issued by this CA would be C=US, S=MA, O=BBN, CN=Steve Kent (where CN is an abbreviation for the "common name" attribute). However, BBN would not be allowed to issue a certificate in which the subject name was of the form C=US, S=MA, O=MITRE, CN=Richard Parker. The subject name would not be subordinate to the BBN CA name as issuer. However, there is no subordination restriction on the relationship between a PCA and the CAs it certifies. Thus the BBN CA can be certified by a PCA with any distinguished name.

This constraint prohibits "cross-certification." When two CAs issue certificates in which each is a subject of the other CA, the result is termed "cross-certification." Cross-certification would short-circuit the path back to the PCA layer of the hierarchy, and thus prevent a user from ascertaining the policy under which a certificate was issued. Hence UAs must reject certification paths that entail cross-certification. As noted above, these requirements on certification paths are imposed on PEM UAs rather than on CAs. The reason for this is that CAs may sign certificates for use with other applications where cross-certification might be appropriate; hence the enforcement requirement is levied on PEM UAs.

Sample PCA policies. Although none is yet in place at the time of writing, several PCA policies have been proposed and are being refined. One such policy would serve businesses or other organizations that require a high degree of security from their use of PEM: a "high-assurance" PCA. This PCA would execute a legal agreement with each CA and require high-quality credentials to authenticate the CA. The PCA would require that the CA grant certificates to its users (for example, employees) using the same level of authentication that it would use in issuing ID cards. The CA would be required to issue CRLs at least monthly and not more often than weekly.

There would also be a requirement that the CA use highly secure technology, approved by the PCA, to generate and protect the CA's component pair and to sign all certificates issued by the CA. The PCA would use the same technology in generating its own component pair and in signing CA certificates. The PCA would promise to protect the privacy of all information provided by the CA during registration. This level of service is expected to require that the CA pay a registration fee to the PCA.

Another candidate PCA policy that has been put forth might be termed that of a "mid-level assurance" PCA. Here the validation of CA credentials would be less stringent, for example, written registration using a company letterhead might suffice. The CA would execute a very simple agreement, which would require a "good faith effort" to authenticate users. There would be no requirement to issue CRLs with any specific periodicity. Here each CA would be free to use any technology it deems appropriate to generate the CA component pair and to sign certificates. However, the PCA itself expects to use strong security technology to generate and protect its own component pair. This PCA envisions no charge to certify CAs, but would level a charge if a CA certificate had to be placed on the PCA's CRL.

A third PCA is envisioned to support residential users, that is, users not claiming affiliation with any organization. Such users could be registered using distinguished names based on geographic attributes, for example, country, state, locality, and street address. (In the US, a nine-digit ZIP code might be used in lieu of locality and street address data.) The user would be required to submit a notarized registration form as proof of his identity claim. In this context, the PCA is expected to operate "virtual" CAs representing geographic areas in advance of civil authorities offering this service. The PCA, through its virtual CA, would issue CRLs biweekly. User registration under this PCA is expected to entail a fee.

Finally, in support of personal privacy, a PCA has been proposed which would issue certificates that do *not* purport to express real user identities. These "persona" certificates will allow anonymous use of PEM while providing continuity of authenticity. Thus, even though one might not know the true identity of the holder of a persona certificate, one could determine if a series of messages originated under that identity were all from the same user (assuming the persona user does not share his private component). A PCA supporting persona users would ensure that all certificates issued under it are globally unique. This requirement is easily enforced by establishing a persona CA under the PCA and following the name subordination rules cited earlier. These certificates should not be confused with certificates that do purport to convey true identities, since there is no overlap in the name space and because a persona PCA must publish a policy statement declaring the nature of certificates issued by the CA(s) under it. A candidate PCA has proposed to issue persona certificates without charge, although it would charge a fee to place one of these certificates on the CRL managed by the PCA.

Conclusions

PEM represents a major effort to provide security for an application that touches a vast number of users within the Internet and beyond. PEM has been designed to accommodate gradual deployment in the Internet, both because of the backward compatibility with existing message transfer services and through provision of features such as MIC-CLEAR processing. The ultimate success of PEM will depend not only on the widespread availability of implementations for the range of hardware and software platforms used throughout the Internet, but also on successful establishment of the certification hierarchy that underlies asymmetric key management for PEM.

PEM was envisioned not as a long-term goal technology for secure messaging, but as an interim step before widespread availability of secure OSI messaging (and directory) services. However, depending on the viability of X.400 in the marketplace, PEM may become a long-term secure messaging technology rather than an interim step. In either case, PEM (or a successor) has the opportunity to become a crucial component in the evolution of the Internet as it paves the way for various mail-based applications that would not be possible without the underlying security services provided by PEM.

Electronic Data Interchange (EDI) Messaging Security

Ted Humphreys

The modern economy and the future wealth and prosperity of industry and commerce rely increasingly on the exchange of data and information, in electronic form, between business partners. The speed and reliability of the information exchanged coupled with the spread in the distributed use and application of IT are increasingly affecting the competitiveness of businesses and international trade. Electronic information exchanged in this way is growing in volume because of the increasing number of business partners that may be involved (suppliers, customers, manufacturers, bankers, carriers, and so on) and the numerous documents that need to be exchanged.

The performance of the system handling these documents can significantly affect the economy and future prosperity of a business. The ability to process and exchange trade data as quickly as possible allows stocks to be reduced at a profitable rate, helps cut financial costs, and gives firms such as this an additional competitive edge by improving the service offered to their customers. In addition to the speed, the flexibility in responding to customers' changing needs and desires adds value to the service being offered and creates better commercial relationships.

In response to the need for effective and efficient solutions to handle this way of doing business, Electronic Data Interchange (EDI) offers substantial advantages and opportunities. The EDI approach has been identified as the most important user base of open networks and likely to create one of the most fundamental changes in the way that future business is carried out. EDI is starting to be used in a growing number of market sectors, in a wide range of user applications. The use of EDI trading systems is underpinned in many respects by the need for security, and it is the use of commercially reasonable security features for EDI that will bring about its long-term success.

This essay looks at a particularly important aspect of EDI — the security of EDI messages. In particular, it focuses on the secure communications of EDI messages. To start with, some introductory material is presented that views security in the context of Open-EDI.

Security and the Open-EDI conceptual model

There have been many attempts over the years to understand the security requirements for EDI. One of the most important efforts is described in the European report "Security in Open Networks" [SOGI89]. This report, commonly referred to as the SOGITS Report, confirmed the business need for EDI security. It identified EDI as the most important and demanding use of open networks, and, through an extensive survey covering 59 organizations in 12 countries in Europe, it reinforced the need for a range of solutions addressing several key areas of technical work. Since the publication of this report, several other European and international initiatives have contributed to the progression of work in a number of areas.

One particular important activity involved the JTC1 special working group, which was responsible for the Open-EDI Conceptual Model [JTC191], and its successor JTC1/WG3, which will take forward the Open-EDI work within JTC1. Figure 1 is a high-level view of security that might be used in the development of an Open-EDI Security Model, set beside the JTC1 Open-EDI Conceptual Model as a point of reference [HUMP92b].

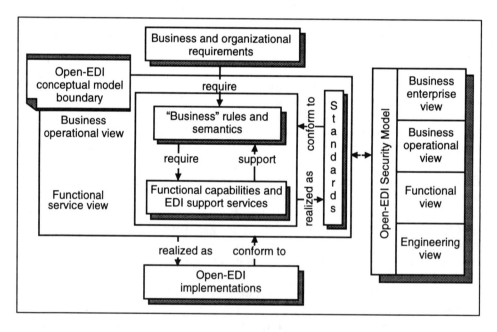

Figure 1. Security and Open-EDI.

The various views in the security model reflect a different aspect and definition of security. Figure 2 illustrates this security model in more detail, reflecting this progressive flow of security definition and specification of business requirements.

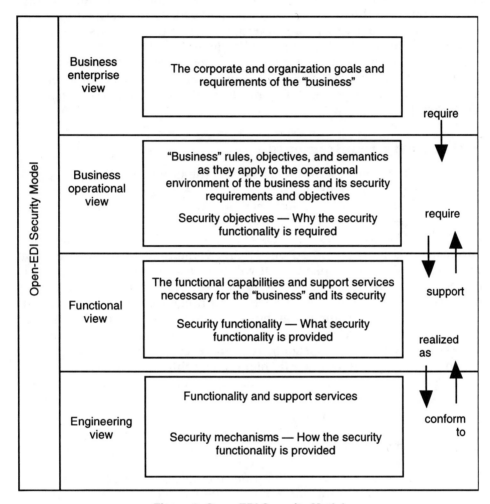

Figure 2. Open-EDI Security Model.

At the highest level, the enterprise view, security is expressed in terms of corporate policy and overall business strategy. At the next level down, such business policy and strategy are expressed in terms of specific security objectives as reflected in the operational environment in which the business is placed and operates.

At the functional level, the security objectives of the business are then specified in terms of a set of security functions to support the operational requirements for security. Finally, at the last level, the security functions are realized in terms of security mechanisms implemented in systems, products, and services. This model recognizes the need to be able to support a "complete" business activity and its security requirements — that is, a business activity involving several parties and numerous interlinked EDI transactions reflecting real-world activities.

Open-EDI is driven by electronic integration among enterprises and requires both simple and complex security solutions, depending on the nature of the business and the needs of different business scenarios [HUMP92b].

EDI security requirements

The SOGITS Report [SOGI89] considered the needs of users and suppliers of EDI-based systems across a wide range of applications, including corporate trading systems, financial systems, import/export systems, cargo handling systems, computer-aided acquisition and logistics (CALS), CAD/CAM (computer-aided design/computer-aided manufacturing), procurement and stores, and so on. IT and communications systems that are associated with the use of EDI will have a wide range of security requirements commensurate with the nature and value of the business using the system. These requirements can range from very broad, in the case of a sensitive commercial business exchange (where the integrity, confidentiality, and availability of the EDI information being exchanged are critical to the business mission), to a more basic form of requirement, which might be the data integrity of a regular shipment order.

Users of EDI trading systems include government departments (for example, Custom and Excise), manufacturing industries (including the car industry, aerospace industry, chemical industry, and electronics industry), finance, and insurance. In most areas of application, the three major risks to EDI messages are:

- loss of integrity (that is, alteration, modification, or destruction), for example, important for payment services; sensitive information (including medical records and personnel records); critical processes; commercial designs, specifications, and manufacturing processes (for example, in the case of CAD/CAM);
- loss of confidentiality (that is, copied, seen, or heard by unauthorized persons), for example, important for sensitive information (including medical records and personnel records) and for intellectual property, commercial designs, specifications, and manufacturing processes (for example, in CAD/CAM); and

- nonavailability (that is, not accessible when needed), for example, important for "just-in-time" situations and for 24-hour trading, production automation, critical processes, and so on.

There are many customer benefits and demands for EDI. As a result, there is a growing demand for a set of commercially reasonable security solutions. Priority must be given to a standardized approach to EDI security if the long-term benefits of EDI to the business environment are to be achieved.

The current trend to obtaining the more substantive business opportunities through the use of EDI will be through a standardized approach leading to a secure Open-EDI environment.

The essence of EDI messaging security

One must assume that EDI may be used across a wide-ranging messaging continuum covering different types of network services and various value-added application platforms. This range of communications provision will reflect a need for different levels and types of security to protect these EDI messages. The EDI components chain and the emerging EDI enabling technologies to support this chain are migrating the proprietary/direct-link type of offering to the Open-EDI approach based on international standards.

EDI security appears at several interrelated stages of system technology:

- the user/application interface,
- EDI applications and value-added services,
- the processing (both batch and interactive) and storage of EDI messages, and
- the communication of these messages in an open systems environment.

The basic security objectives that may need to be met at each stage are those of authentication and integrity, nonrepudiation, access control, availability, audit, and accountability. These objectives will need to be satisfied by both logical and legal controls and procedures, which are supported by a range of technologies, tools, and standards.

Current assertions about the security of EDI messages being handled at and between these various stages are often based on a level of "trust" in the increasingly complex systems that handle such messages, and the rules of engagement agreed to between messaging partners. It is therefore imperative that both the logical and legal aspects of EDI security are dealt with hand in hand. These two aspects of EDI security need to work with each other to provide the right levels of overall trust and protection to EDI messages and interchanges. The rest of this essay looks at secure messaging for EDI.

Secure messaging standards

The standards industry has tackled many aspects of EDI security. In particular, the most important work in this area concerns EDI messaging based on the use of International Message Handling Standards [CCIT88a], [CCIT90]. The scope of this work covers secure message transfer, which provides the benefits of secure messaging to a wide range of distributed applications such as EDI.

Protection in an EDI messaging environment is essentially concerned with the nonrepudiable submission, delivery, and receipt of messages in a way that preserves the integrity, confidentiality, and availability of the messages being communicated. The current messaging standards provide the means of applying security mechanisms to meet different types of security objectives and levels of security. A brief introduction to the most important standards in this area follows.

X.400 message handling systems (1988)

CCITT, in its 1988 version of the X.400 recommendations for message handling (and the corresponding ISO 10021 equivalent standard), has made major extensions to the Message Transfer System (MTS) to provide for secure messaging [CCIT88a].

The 1988 X.400 standard allows the provision of different types and levels of security service independent of the type of message being transferred. Applying security mechanisms to the MTS ensures that the benefits of secure messaging are obtained independent of the content type of the message. For some content types, additional security mechanisms may be defined in the content-type protocol. The security specified in this standard thus provides for secure message transfer services and distributed interworking in support of applications such as electronic mail and EDI, as illustrated in Figure 3.

The security model used to specify the security features of the 1988 standard is based on a threat assessment of an assumed messaging environment. This assessment considers the main threats to be associated with the unauthorized access to the messaging system, threats to the message itself, and intramessage threats. Table 1 shows an example threat/security service scenario that might be covered by this model.

This table of threats and services is an indicative example rather than a definitive list. The designer of a secure messaging system would need to determine which threats are actually present and applicable to the messaging environment under consideration and which of these can be countered by the X.400 security services available. In essence, the designer will need to develop a technical security policy for the messaging environment.

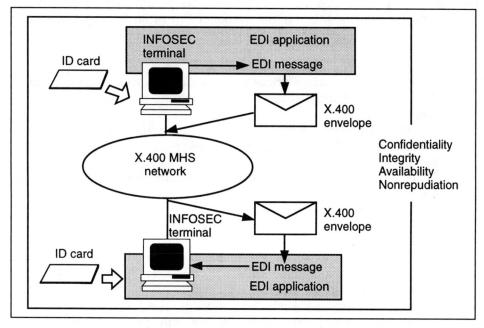

Figure 3. Secure EDI and X.400.

Table 1. Threats and services.

Threat	Examples	Security Services
Masquerade	Impersonation, false claims/acknowledgments	Authentication
Unauthorized message modification	Modify, delete, destroy messages	Integrity
Repudiation	Denial of origin, submission, or delivery of a message	Nonrepudiation
Leakage of information	Unauthorized release of message contents	Confidentiality

The security services defined in X.400 provide the link between the security requirements and objectives as described in a security policy, and the security mechanisms (for example, digital signatures) and management controls (for example, for the management of public keys) to satisfy these requirements. The 1988 X.400 recommendations specify the following security services:

- Authentication. Message origin authentication, peer entity authentication, probe/report origin authentication, proof of submission, and proof of delivery.
- Integrity. Connection, content, and message sequence integrity.
- Nonrepudiation. Nonrepudiation of delivery, of origin, and of submission.
- Confidentiality. Connection, content, and message flow confidentiality.
- Security content.
- Message security labeling.

Each of these security services can be implemented by one or more types of security mechanism, to satisfy the requirements of many different messaging applications needing different levels of security. In implementing these security measures and controls, the level of assurance at which these must be applied and maintained will need to be considered. In the case concerning the use of cryptographic mechanisms, it might be a question of the strength of mechanism and the mode of operation being used.

X.435 EDI messaging (1992)

Since the introduction of the 1988 X.400 standard, CCITT has been working on a series of recommendations, referred to as the X.435 series for secure EDI messaging. X.435 will use the X.400 security mechanisms in addition to some EDI-specific security measures not defined in the X.400 standard.

This standard will thus provide a security messaging capability for EDI applications, supporting the use of a range of EDI message formats currently being standardized, such as EDI for Administration, Commerce, and Trade (EDIFACT), American National Standards Institute ANSI/X12, and United Nations Trade Document 1 (UN/TD 1).

The basic security features being progressed by the X.435 EDI messaging standards work, in addition to the 1988 X.400 security features, include the following:

- *EDI Messaging (EDIM) responsibility authentication.* Proof of transfer, retrieval, and EDI notification.

- *Nonrepudiation of EDIM responsibility.* EDI notification, retrieval, transfer, and content.

In addition, work has started on:

- message store extensions (including control of delivery, user security management, and audit),
- message transfer audit, and
- other enhanced security management controls.

Figure 4 illustrates the concepts relating to the proof services offered by X.400 and X.435.

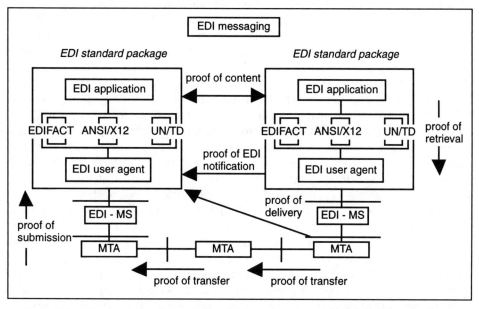

Figure 4. EDI security and proofs. The solid lines perpendicular to flow lines indicate EDIM responsibility transfer boundaries. MTA: message transfer agent; MS: message store.

The practical realization of this might typically be a standard EDI software package containing EDI application software, various format options (for example, EDIFACT), and an EDI user agent. The standard package could be modified to incorporate the necessary security controls to provide the capability of implementing a number of proof services, and possibly other services. In addition, security could be offered at the message transfer level via the message transfer agents to provide a secure transfer medium.

X.500 directory systems (1988)

CCITT and ISO/IEC incorporated into their 1988 X.500 series of directory system standards [CCIT88c] an "Authentication Framework" (X.509) that defines mechanisms and protocols for entity authentication. These mechanisms are based on the use of public key technology, digital signatures, and the introduction of various public key elements such as certificates and tokens. Other publications [ANSI92a, b] are applicable to the financial sector.

The X.509 standard also introduces the concept of a Certification Authority (CA) through which users are identified, registered, and then issued their public key certificate(s). The use and application of the X.509 certificates and the concept of Certification Authorities (CAs) are a natural complement to the distributed nature of the X.500 directory system approach and to the provision of publicly available information services. It can be shown that this natural duality also holds between the X.509 technology and the provision of a number of EDI security features. The X.509 standard when implemented will constitute a secure naming and routing process in a multidomain messaging environment. In addition, a number of the security services specified in X.400 can be implemented using the X.509 technology (certificate, token, and digital signature). These security services include user identification, content integrity, and various nonrepudiation/proof services, for example, proof of delivery.

X.509 technology can provide a distributed use of authentication, thus allowing secure distributed processing of EDI transactions and greater security of trading partner connectivity. Although the X.509 technology is not the only solution to the provision and implementation of X.400 and consequently EDI security, it is certainly one of the most effective and the most practical. The distributed nature of messaging and in particular EDI messaging makes the X.509 technology a natural partner for secure trading across distributed environments. Figure 5 shows the future EDI use of the X.500 directory system.

The X.509 technology is able to play a major part in the realization of a number of these services, in particular, the provision of nonrepudiation services, the responsibility authentication options, and the various authentication and integrity services. However, other methods for providing these services are also available; these include the use of symmetric encipherment techniques, message authentication codes (MACs), and manipulation detection codes (MDCs). The work of ISO/IEC JTC1/SC27 "Security Techniques" and ANSI X12 in this area provides some excellent examples.

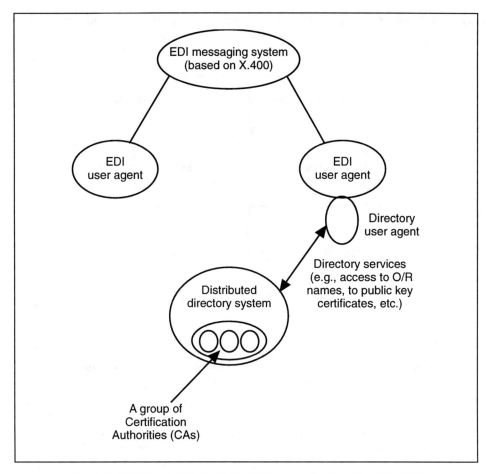

Figure 5. X.500 and EDI security (O/R: organizational/residential).

Nonrepudiation, responsibility, and proof

One of the important features of EDI messaging is that of nonrepudiation, which provides some level of proof or evidence that an EDI message has been sent or has been delivered. For example, nonrepudiation of delivery provides the originator of the message with proof that a message has been delivered, and this proof should hold up against any attempt by the recipient(s) to deny receiving the message or its content.

Both the X.400 and X.435 standards allow for a number of different elements of service to be available in order to provide a wide range of nonrepudiation services. Some of the important elements of nonrepudiation are shown in Figure 6.

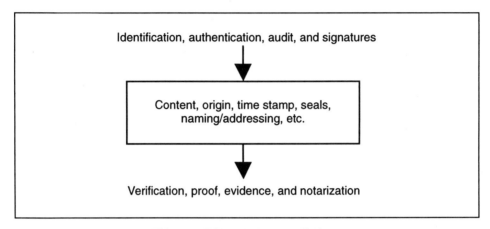

Figure 6. EDI and nonrepudiation.

Current standards [CCIT88a] introduce the concept of a "responsibility transfer boundary" and provide specification for the provision of several "responsibility" security services. The basic idea behind this concept is to transfer responsibility of certain aspects of a message, as it passes from one component of the EDI messaging systems to another component.

For example, after transferring an EDI message through the network of message transfer agents into the EDI message store (EDI-MS), the end system EDI user agent will at some point in time retrieve this message from the EDI-MS. By providing a proof of retrieval message, responsibility for that message now rests with the EDI user agent [SC2792].

Other security standards work

There are a number of other activities of relevance and support to the provision of secure EDI messaging [ITAE92b].

ISO/IEC JTC1/WG3 Open-EDI. WG3 is responsible for the coordination and development of Open-EDI standards. WG3 provides a coordination function across JTC1 and is also involved in liaison and collaboration with most of the major groups outside JTC1 that are also active in EDI work.

ISO/IEC JTC1/SC21 OSI Architecture, Management and Upper Layers. SC21 is involved in a number security projects related to OSI and open systems. In particular, with respect to EDI, it is involved in the development of a nonrepudiation framework and X.500 directory security.

ISO/IEC JTC1/SC27 Security Techniques. SC27 is responsible for the development of a wide range of security techniques for information processing systems. These techniques include digital signatures, data integrity techniques, authentication mechanisms, and nonrepudiation techniques. SC27/WG1 is particularly interested in the requirements and development of security services for Open-EDI based systems.

ANSI. ANSI X.12 has been considering several areas of EDI security, in particular, covering work on management of transaction sets, security structures, and key management.

This work includes:

- X12.58 "Draft Standard for the Trial Use for Managing EDI Security Structures,"
- X12.42 "Draft Standard for the Trial Use of Managing EDI Cryptographic Service Message Transaction Sets," and
- "Guideline for Implementing X12.42 and X12.58."

This work uses other ANSI standards, such as X.9.9 on MACs (Message Authentication Codes), X.3.92 (Data Encryption Algorithm), and X.9.17 (Key Management Using Symmetric Key Techniques).

ANSI is also working on the following two sets of signature standards for the financial services industry:

- X9.30-199X:
  Part 1: The Digital Signature Algorithm (DSA)
  Part 2: The Secure Hash Algorithm (SHA)
  Part 3: Certificate Management for DSA
  Part 4: Management of Symmetric Algorithm Keys Using
         Irreversible Cryptography

- X9.31-199X:
  Part 1: The RSA Signature Algorithm
  Part 2: Hash Algorithms
  Part 3: Certificate Management for RSA
  Part 4: Management of Symmetric Algorithm Keys Using RSA

Public domain standards. There are a number of de facto standards [RSAD91] for public key techniques, some of them based on X.509, which are applicable to the implementation of secure EDI messaging. These standards include the following:

- PKCS No. 1 "RSA Standard,"
- PKCS No. 6 "Extended-Certificate Syntax Standard,"
- PKCS No. 7 "Cryptographic Message Syntax Standard," and
- PKCS No. 8 "Private Key Information Syntax Standard."

EDIFACT Security Framework. The Western Europe EDIFACT Board (WE/EB) has a Security Group MD4.B that has developed a Security Framework for EDIFACT. This framework considers end-to-end security requirements for EDI systems for use in interchanges between corporations and banks.

The approach taken in this framework is one of combining existing standards and implementations specifically for EDIFACT interchanges, and is closely aligned with the ANSI X.12.58. It also uses some of the X.509 technology (the Directory Systems Authentication Framework), in particular, for key management.

TEDIS. The European initiative TEDIS (Trade EDI Systems) is a program of work sponsored by the European Commission. This program looks at three aspects of EDI systems: telecommunications, security, and legal. The aim of TEDIS security is to protect the EDI message itself and to stimulate the definition, development, and adoption of technical standards to ensure the security of EDI messages in a multicompany environment. A secondary aim of the TEDIS program is to coordinate the development of procedures and methods specific to the management auditing and control that are linked to the establishment and use of a secure EDI system.

The TEDIS program has been considering an EDI Agreement Model, which also includes security as a conditional feature. One of the results of TEDIS was the development of a report on Digital Signatures for EDIFACT, which is currently being considered by the UN/EDIFACT Working Group and by SC27. Another result is a report on Trusted Third Party Services [TEDI91].

Summary

This essay has mainly concentrated on X.400, X.435, and X.500 standards, and their use in EDI messaging. The X.400 technology provides a basis upon which secure trading systems can be developed which would satisfy a high percentage of the market requirements, in particular, for international trade and wide-area regional trade.

It is probably one of the most significant steps in achieving a secure Open-EDI environment. However, this is just part of the solution, albeit a very important part. There are still issues to be dealt with in providing secure distributed systems technology in such a way that all barriers (for example, technical, administrative, and international) are removed to allow the introduction of a fully integrated Open-EDI environment.

This standards-driven technology cuts across many multidisciplined areas: from work on CAEs (common application environments), open systems management, and distributed applications to work on techniques, services, and protocol building. It is a standards technology that is targeted toward the future integration of the current set of services and applications, together with the introduction of additional ones to meet the future needs of a wide range of distributed business environments.

This essay has considered some of the aspects of international security standards as they apply to the provision of secure EDI messaging. In particular, the use of the 1988 X.400 message handling system standards has been the basis for this overview.

The X.400 1988 standard, together with the X.500 directory systems standard and the X.435 EDI messaging standard, form an internationally agreed upon basis of future secure EDI technology and secure EDI messaging environments.

Other EDI-related security standards that are of relevance and support include:

1. the work of ANSI X.12 on EDI security structures [ANSI91a-c],
2. the WE/EB EDIFACT group on security,
3. the European TEDIS program, and
4. ISO/IEC JTC1/SC27 on security techniques, for example, digital signatures and authentication mechanisms, and the requirements for security.

Conclusions

There is no doubt that the growing trend toward open systems will see an ever-increasing requirement to achieve the right levels of business confidence and assurance in these systems [SOGI89, HUMP90a, BLAT90]. EDI is the growing business technology of the 1990s. It is a key change dynamic to business development. It is the baseline for improving business performance and efficiency, building new markets, and expanding old ones — and it allows the introduction of new business opportunities. It is a technology that has support from government, industry, finance, and commerce.

The SOGITS Report [SOGI89] confirmed the business need for EDI security. It identified EDI as the most important and demanding use of open networks and through an extensive survey reinforced the need for a standards program addressing several key areas of technical work.

This report provides valuable insight into the practical needs of users for trading system security. It identifies not only the need for technical and quality standards for EDI security but also the need for urgent consideration to be given to the legal aspects of these electronic solutions. It emphasizes the need for work on practical standards for EDI security, third-party services (directories, notaries, and so on), messaging gateways for multidomain communications, techniques for nonrepudiation, audit, and authentication — and the need for additional legislation.

There is a growing need for "interconnectivity platforms" using the concept of "one-stop shopping" to enable users to deal with only one business intermediary rather than a complex network of them.

The long-term EDI architecture will be based on international standards technology offered by X.400 (1988 and 1992) and X.500. It should provide a common messaging technology package to support different applications and future additional tailored services. It should also support a range of security policies and the provision of security for different application needs and at different levels of protection. In addition, it will need to aim to complement the X12 and EDIFACT work.

This architecture, based on internationally agreed upon standards, will provide the business platform and connectivity for future secure distributed trading.

Related work

There is also work going on considering APIs (application programming interfaces) for EDI messaging (for example, X/Open) and for generic security services (for example, Trusted Systems Interoperability Group TSIG). In addition, there is work going on in other areas of the open systems security standardization program that potentially supports the introduction of secure end-to-end EDI solutions (SC21 work, ECMA work, and so on).

There are also other groups in Europe considering other types of solutions for EDI security (for example, based on the use of FTAM) and mixed solutions (for example, the French ETEBAC 5 system, which uses ANSI and ISO/CCITT X.509 solutions). Some consideration is being given to the development of solutions for interactive EDI (for which there is a growing market).

Architectures for MLS Database Management Systems

LouAnna Notargiacomo

This essay presents a survey of the basic architectures that have been used in the research and development of trusted relational database management systems (DBMSs). While various approaches have been tried for special-purpose systems, the architectures presented here are those developed for general-purpose trusted DBMS products. In addition, this essay presents research approaches proposed for new trusted DBMS architectures, although worked examples of these approaches may not exist in all cases. While recent research has begun on the development of trusted DBMSs based on object-oriented models [JAJO90a, KEEF89, LUNT89], and a study was completed to design and prototype a trusted DBMS using the entity-relationship model [LEFK89], the majority of research and development efforts are based on the relational data model. This survey describes architectures that use the relational model. Although this survey attempts to include all documented architectures, the scope is limited to information in the public domain.

This survey presents architectures in their abstract form. This includes the definition of each component of the architecture, and a description of the relationships and flow of information between each component. The survey then presents a discussion of the benefits of the architecture in meeting mandatory and discretionary security requirements as well as preserving data integrity, followed by a presentation of known problems introduced by each approach.

Background

In the early 1970s, the Air Force sponsored two efforts that set the foundation for trusted relational DBMS research. In 1975, Hinke and Schaefer documented the design of a trusted DBMS for the Multics operating system [HINK75]. This work documented the design for a high-assurance DBMS where the operating system provided all the access control. This was followed by an effort at I.P. Sharp that also developed a model for a multilevel relational DBMS [GROH76, KIRK77]. This model is based on a layered internal DBMS architecture using the Parnas design method [PARN72a].

The Navy then sponsored two programs that have contributed to trusted DBMS progress. The Military Message System model addressed the information processing of multilevel messages [LAND84]. This work introduced the idea of a multilevel container that holds subobjects that the container's level dominates. Although this work influenced many trusted DBMS designs, it did not result in the development of a design for an MLS DBMS.

The Navy also sponsored MITRE to develop the Navy DBMS Security Model for the Naval Surveillance System [GRAU82]. This model addressed the specific requirements for Navy surveillance systems. A special feature of this model was its use of the container concept and nesting of database objects. Database objects could be databases, relations, tuples, attributes, and elements. Not all objects must be labeled. The sensitivity level of an unlabeled object defaults to the next higher object that contains it (for example, a tuple's level could default to the database level). The integrity-lock prototype that was built on the Mistress DBMS [GRAU84] used the requirements of this application and the Navy model. The Trudata DBMS also uses the Navy model as its basis [KNOD88]. This DBMS is currently being sold and is targeted for a B1-level evaluation.

The next landmark event in trusted DBMS development occurred when the Air Force sponsored a three-week study on trusted data management at Woods Hole, Massachusetts [SCHA83]. The participants at Woods Hole were divided into three groups. Group 1 concentrated on near-term architectures, Group 2 focused on multilevel document processing, and Group 3 investigated long-term research issues and approaches. Group 1 focused on architectures implementable in the three-to-five-year time frame. On the basis of a study of Air Force application needs, a majority of these applications required only a small set of sensitivity levels (that is, two to three). Group 1 recommended three approaches: the kernelized (or Hinke-Schaefer) approach, the integrity-lock approach, and the distributed or back-end approach. Group 3 concentrated on supporting access control to the data element level and on the problem of controlling inference and aggregation. Following this workshop, the government sponsored a number of studies and prototypes to investigate and prototype the Group 1 and 3 recommendations. The architectures described here are the results of these efforts.

Trusted DBMS abstract architectures

This survey divides trusted DBMS architectures into two main variations. The first set consists of architectures that use a trusted computing base (TCB) external to the DBMS (usually either a trusted operating system or network) for mandatory control of access to database objects. This approach is commonly referred to as a *kernelized, Hinke-Schaefer,* or *TCB subset DBMS architecture* (this essay uses the TCB subset terminology). These architectures are distinguished from architectures that delegate some or all responsibility for mandatory access control to the DBMS itself. Architectures that perform their own mandatory access control are referred to as *trusted subject DBMS architectures*. Within these two basic approaches, several major variations have developed.

At the conceptual level, a database that contains data labeled over a set of sensitivity levels has relations that may contain data labeled over this same set of sensitivity levels. In the TCB subsetting approach, these multilevel relations are, in some way, decomposed into single-level or system-high fragments. The multilevel secure (MLS) DBMS stores the fragments within physically separate single-level objects (for example, files, segments, or physically separate hardware devices). The MLS DBMS then enforces mandatory access control on requests to access these separate single-level or system-high objects.

The variations in the TCB subset architecture arise because of the different approaches used to separate the multilevel database into fragments and the different ways of managing the processes that access these data fragments. Dealing with process management, two variations to the TCB subsetting architecture have developed. The first approach uses multiple single-level DBMS processes running under a multilevel operating system. A multilevel database is then decomposed into a set of single-level database fragments (for example, single-level relations). These single-level database fragments are physically separated by being stored in single-level operating system storage segments. The Hinke-Schaefer Trusted DBMS [HINK75], one variation of the Trusted Oracle Version 7.0 DBMS [VETT89] (called *OS-MAC mode*), the Secure Distributed Data Views (SeaView) research prototype [LUNT88, LUNT90], and the Lock Data Views (LDV) architecture use this approach [DILL86, STAC90].

The second approach also uses separate instantiations of a DBMS process. This approach uses a trusted network for mandatory separation instead of relying on only a multilevel operating system. This variation also decomposes the multilevel database into multiple system-high fragments. However, in this case the DBMS replicates lower level data under the higher level fragments. The multiple DBMS processes used to access these fragments also operate at system-high levels, matching those of the database fragments. Relying on a multilevel network, the MLS DBMS separates the data by physically distributing them onto different interconnected system-high DBMS host processors. The Unisys Secure Distributed DBMS (SD-DBMS) research prototype [UNIS89] used this approach, and it is currently being used in the NRL Trusted DBMS (TDBMS) research project [FROS89].

In strong contrast to the TCB subset approach, the trusted subject DBMS stores the conceptual multilevel database in one or more operating system objects (for example, files). From the operating system's perspective, the database is a single-level object. For example, a multilevel database could be stored in one operating system file labeled at the highest level of any object in the database, referred to as *database high*, or each multilevel relation could be stored in a separate file labeled at *relation high*. While the object granularity for the operating system is the file, the object for the trusted DBMS is a database object stored within the file. The database object granularity could be a relation, view, tuple, or element. The MLS DBMS then associates a label with each database object. Since these database objects are invisible to the operating system, it cannot perform access mediation for database objects. The MLS DBMS is privileged to perform this access mediation and operates across a range of the operating system's sensitivity levels.

While various methods can be used to decrease the amount of trusted code within the DBMS itself, these architectures are generally referred to as *trusted subject* architectures. This indicates that some or all of the DBMS is a trusted process that is privileged to violate some or all of the underlying operating system's security policy, especially with respect to the privilege to write down in sensitivity level. This trust means that the DBMS process will write down data only to appropriately labeled operating system objects. For example, if the MLS DBMS is managing a database that contains data labeled up to the Top Secret level (stored in a Top Secret operating system object), it can write a database object labeled Secret into a Secret operating system object.

A major variation on the trusted subset architecture is the integrity-lock architecture. The name of this architecture stems from the fact that the sensitivity label associated with a database object is cryptographically sealed with the data to allow detection of modifications to the data or its label. With this approach, the multilevel database is stored under an untrusted DBMS with labels cryptographically attached to database objects.

While trusted DBMS architectures may be categorized into these two basic types, in reality, many architectures incorporate aspects of both approaches. This is because in most architectures that this essay surveys, techniques developed in the Hinke-Schaefer effort and Woods Hole study are used to minimize the amount of trusted code in the DBMS. Only the original Hinke-Schaefer architecture has the operating system perform all trusted functions, and that architecture has never been prototyped.

Now that the two basic approaches have been introduced, they will be presented in more detail with the variations of each approach that have developed.

TCB subset DBMS approach

TCB subset [SHOC87] architecture was first fully documented by Thomas Hinke and Marvin Schaefer at System Development Corporation [HINK75]. This DBMS was designed for the Multics operating system with the goal that the trusted operating system would provide all access control. The original design decomposed the multilevel database into single-level attributes or columns, with attributes of the same sensitivity stored together in single-level operating system segments. Tuples are recomposed through join operations. For example, to satisfy a select request, a DBMS process operating at the user's level is initiated. Through the operating system's enforcement of the mandatory access control (MAC) policy, the DBMS has access only to segments at or below its level. The DBMS then joins elements from the same relation to reconstruct multilevel tuples returned to the user.

Currently, all approaches that access the database files through a trusted mediator (for example, trusted operating system or trusted network) are referred to as Hinke-Schaefer approaches. This approach has two main characteristics:

1. the multilevel DBMS is in actuality multiple instantiations of single-level DBMSs, and
2. the multilevel database is decomposed into multiple single-level or system-high databases, each a fragment of the conceptual multilevel database.

There are two variations of this architecture: *centralized* and *distributed*. In the centralized approach, the single-level DBMSs are separate processes running under a trusted operating system, and the multilevel database is decomposed into single-level fragments that are each stored in a single-level operating system object (for example, files or segments). While the DBMS may be trusted to perform some access control functions, the trusted operating system enforces its full access control policy on all access by the DBMS to the DBMS objects. Figure 1 illustrates this approach.

In this architecture, the user is not operating in multilevel mode, but is operating at the session level established with the trusted operating system. Each user interacts with a DBMS operating at the user's session level, and multiple different DBMSs running at different sensitivity levels may be operating at the same time.

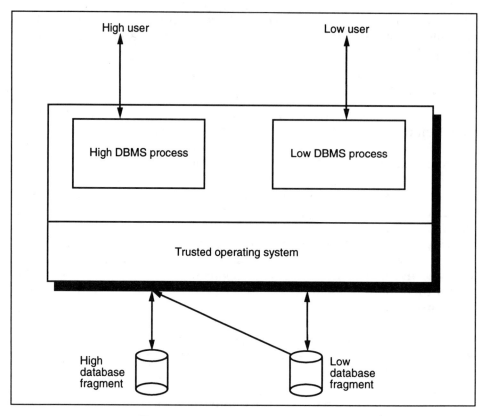

Figure 1. Hinke-Schaefer architecture.

Two research efforts aimed at the A1 evaluation level that use many of the Hinke-Schaefer concepts are the SeaView DBMS and LDV DBMS. Both of these approaches provide the user with a conceptual view of a multilevel database, with each element being labeled with its sensitivity.

Secure Distributed Data Views (SeaView) A1 DBMS. The SeaView program began as a research effort to design a trusted DBMS that could attain an A1 Trusted Computer System Evaluation Criteria (TCSEC) [DOD85] evaluation (based on an interpretation of the A1 requirements for a DBMS). The original agenda of this project was derived from the recommendations of Group 3 of the Woods Hole Summer Study. SeaView was not only designed to support element-level trusted access control and labeling, but was also supposed to address the difficult problems of inference and aggregation. These problems and discretionary access control were to be addressed by using viewlike mechanisms. In addition, the requirement to meet an A1 evaluation meant that the mechanisms to solve these problems had to be small and simple enough to be formally modeled and verified. These were very difficult requirements, and great advances toward solving these problems have been made in this project.

In the SeaView approach, a multilevel relation is decomposed into single-level relations, based on element-level labeling. Each tuple is then decomposed and stored within the appropriate single-level relation fragments. Fragments with the same relation type and level can then be stored in the same operating system segment, and it is unnecessary to store labels with the DBMS objects. To recompose multilevel tuples to satisfy a user select request, the DBMS joins single-level fragments at or below the user's session level and returns the resulting tuples matching the selection criteria. Since each user is interacting with a single-level DBMS process, the DBMS is not cognizant of any data above its level.

The SeaView architecture is based on an approach called *TCB subsets*. This approach hierarchically layers software components, where the underlying components provide the support needed by the high-level layers. Figure 2 shows the basic TCB layers for the SeaView architecture.

To illustrate the layering approach through an example, suppose an untrusted user application program establishes a session level. This application would interface with an instantiation of the multilevel relation manager at its level. This manager is specially developed software that translates between the user's multilevel conceptual view of relations and the single-level actual representation of the relation. It also performs content-independent discretionary access control (DAC) checks. The multilevel relation manager then issues requests to the single-level relation manager to both recompose the multilevel relations through joins and execute the user request. The single-level relation manager performs DAC on the single-level relation fragments. These single-level relation managers are instantiations of the Oracle Version 7.0 C2 DBMS. Oracle then interacts with the operating system kernel to access objects at or below its level. The operating system, currently Gemini's GEMSOS, is responsible for providing MAC and DAC to operating system objects (files or segments).

Since C2 DBMS processes execute the user's queries, the DBMS processes run as single-level GEMSOS processes. The GEMSOS operating system enforces the MAC policy and part of the DAC policy on each access to data stored in GEMSOS files or segments. Since the DBMS processes are single level, they are unable to enforce any integrity constraints that require knowledge of objects above the process level. For example, if a database relation is defined as having a unique primary key, the DBMS process would not know of the existence of any tuples that dominate the process' execution level. Therefore, on an insert request to enter a tuple with a primary key that matches a previously existing higher level tuple with the same key value, the DBMS would not reject the insert and would create a *polyinstantiated* version of the tuple. *Polyinstantiation* is a term first defined in the SeaView security model [DENN88a]. It is defined as multiple instantiations of tuples within a relation that have the same primary key, but different sensitivity labels. Within the SeaView effort, *primary key* is defined as including both the primary key attribute and the sensitivity label.

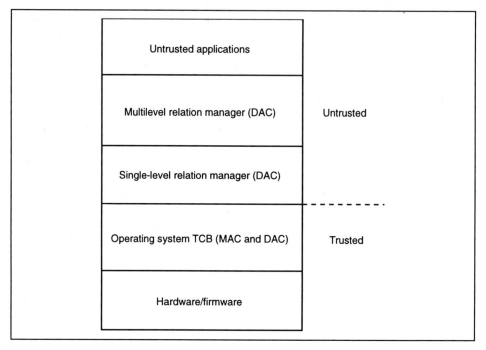

Figure 2. TCB subsetting architecture.

Two benefits arise from polyinstantiation. First, polyinstantiation on inserts and updates prevents lower level users from inferring the existence of higher sensitivity tuples with identical primary keys. The second benefit is that polyinstantiation allows for the simple implementation of cover stories. A cover story is the explicit input of untrue lower level data to hide the existence of higher level data.

Benefits. The most significant benefit of this approach is that the trusted operating system performs mandatory separation and access control. With this approach, a higher level of mandatory assurance is possible because an untrusted or lower assurance DBMS process can run as an untrusted process under a higher assurance operating system. This approach allows the system as a whole to meet the operating system's assurance level for MAC. This approach also allows the DBMS execution logic to be outside the MAC TCB boundary, thus reducing the size and complexity of the TCB. Assuming a previously existing operating system evaluation, this architecture should minimize the amount of time required to evaluate the DBMS.

Disadvantages. Several problems are introduced as side effects of this approach. Since this architecture uses multiple processes, it is not appropriate for applications requiring simultaneous operation of a large number of sensitivity levels. This limitation is due to constraints on the number of simultaneous processes an operating system can support and on its processing capacity. Therefore, this architecture is not appropriate for most intelligence applications. However, this architecture would be appropriate for applications requiring only a small number of sensitivity levels.

The use of view-based DAC requires some trust in the DBMS's capability to execute the view command and identify the subset of data defined by the view. Relying on a lower assurance DBMS with DAC capabilities (that is, a C2 DBMS) limits the assurance level the DAC enforcement can achieve, in most cases, to the DBMS's assurance level. An argument called *balanced assurance* has been used to counter this limitation [SHOC87]. Shockley and Schell argue that DAC mechanisms are inherently flawed and cannot achieve a high assurance level. This is due to the threat that would allow a Trojan horse in a user's process to take on all user DAC privileges and make copies of all user files. On the basis of the inherent flaw in the DAC policy, Shockley and Schell argue that attempting to attain a high-assurance DAC evaluation is futile and that systems which provide higher assurance MAC should not have their evaluation level limited.

A limitation of this architecture is the creation of polyinstantiated tuples. This is a problem because it violates the key uniqueness requirement of the relational model. To meet this requirement, the sensitivity level of the object is added to the logical key. As a result, when higher level users select tuples, they may receive multiple tuples with the same logical entity key, differentiated by the sensitivity level. However, the higher level users may not be able to discern which is the correct version for their application. In addition, the algorithm used to decompose and recompose multilevel relations introduces numerous extraneous polyinstantiated tuples to confuse end users further.

Lock Data Views (LDV) A1 DBMS (Assured Pipelines). The LDV DBMS is specifically designed to run on the Logical Coprocessing Kernel (LOCK) operating system being developed to meet the A1 evaluation criteria. While the LDV architecture also falls into the TCB subset category, its design uses object typing provided by the LOCK operating system and knowledge-based techniques for data classification that differentiate it from other efforts.

The LDV design is based on the special access control and type enforcement features of the LOCK operating system. In addition to mandatory access control based on sensitivity level and discretionary access control based on access control lists, LOCK also performs access control based on the domain (or role) in which a subject is acting and the type of object it is requesting to access. LOCK maintains a domain and type table, called the *Domain Definition Table* (DDT). In this table, the domains are intersected with data types. At the intersection, the access privileges are recorded (for example, read, write, execute). The DDT is the mechanism used to set up sequences of valid transitions of objects, called *pipelines*. These assured pipelines are used to isolate execution paths through the system in such a way that they can be independently verified. In essence, the LDV DBMS, rather than being considered a system, is a collection of related pipelines responsible for multilevel data manipulation. The three main pipelines in LDV are the response pipeline, the update pipeline, and the metadata pipeline. The response pipeline processes requests to retrieve data. The update pipeline manages all requests to modify the database, including insert, update, and delete operations. The metadata pipeline handles all administrator commands to manipulate the database metadata.

Another unique feature of the LDV design is its heavy reliance on classification rules to control data input and output labeling. The LDV security policy allows for the definition of rules for both discretionary access control on views and mandatory access control on storage objects to handle five types of classification: name dependent, content dependent, context dependent, aggregate, and inference. Name-dependent classification rules define an object's classification based on the object's identifier (for example, an attribute name). Content-dependent classification rules assign a level to an object dependent on the value of the object. Context-dependent classification rules assign a sensitivity level to a combination of data objects retrieved together, for example, enforcing the rule that a patient's name and illness retrieved together must be labeled Confidential. Aggregate classification rules assign a sensitivity to a collection of objects, for example, enforcing the rule that the result of retrieving the phone numbers of more than 10 employees of a company must be labeled Confidential. Finally, inference classification rules control the potential inferences that can be made from one or a sequence of requests over time. LDV enforces these rules such that the level of data may flow only to a more sensitive level.

Similar to the other TCB subset approaches, LDV is layered above the LOCK operating system, and the multilevel database is stored as a set of single-level objects protected by the LOCK operating system. Figure 3 illustrates the LDV architecture.

Benefits. The benefits of this architecture are the strong mandatory access control provided by the LOCK operating system, and the use of type enforcement in the LDV design. The isolation provided by domain and type enforcement allows for the separation of execution paths into pipelines. Pipelines facilitate the minimization of trusted code and isolate privileged software.

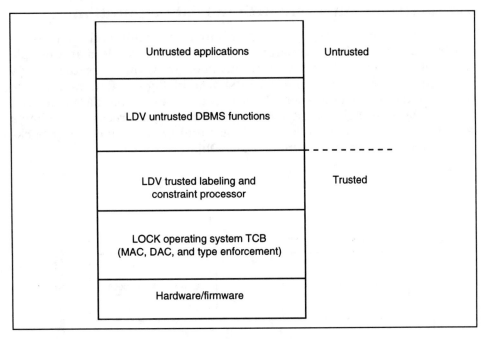

Figure 3. LDV architecture.

Disadvantages. This system is subject to problems with achieving high assurance in both its discretionary access control mechanism and its labeling enforcement based on classification constraints. The problems with discretionary access control are the same as discussed under the SeaView disadvantages. These are due to the complexity of view-based mechanisms and the difficulty in achieving a DAC enforcement capability that is both small enough and simple enough to verify.

The first problem with the labeling policy deals with the feasibility of capturing the complexity of inference and aggregation threats and expressing them as rules. In addition, this design proposes to use untrusted code for this function. Upgrading data above a user's level on inserts can result in integrity problems and additional inference threats. The LDV documentation discusses these problems and proposes several operational approaches to handle them. The approach proposed to handle inference and aggregation also includes the ability to include rules governing use by multiple users over time. In this case, LDV would lock objects from all further access when reaching certain stated limits (for example, a certain number of retrievals of a relation from all users within a specified length of time). While this technique does address a real threat, it creates an operational threat of denial of service.

Distributed architecture with full data replication

This architecture uses physical distribution of a multilevel database to achieve strong mandatory separation and access control. It is an example of the distributed architecture recommended by Group 1 of the Woods Hole study. The basic architecture, shown in Figure 4, uses multiple back-end database processors to separate a multilevel database into multiple, system-high fragments. A trusted front-end processor mediates all user access to the multilevel database and to each single-level back-end database processor [FROS89, JAJO90b].

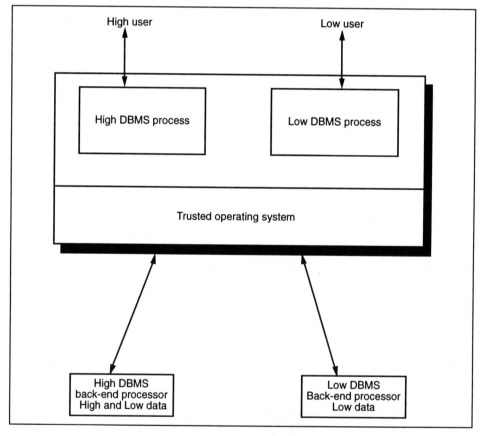

Figure 4. Fully replicated distributed architecture.

The database processor is untrusted in terms of MAC enforcement. Each back-end database processor manages the fragment of the multi-level database at that level and a replicated version of all lower level data.

The trusted front end is responsible for directing queries to the correct database processor, for ensuring that there is no illegal flow of information between the database processors, for maintaining data consistency between replicated database fragments, and for properly labeling query responses and sending them back to the appropriate user. In addition, the trusted front end is responsible for user identification and authentication, maintenance of the trusted path to the user, and auditing.

Each user interacts with the TDBMS through single-level sessions. A user's query is sent to the back-end DBMS running at the user's session level. Because all lower level data are replicated under the higher level processors, all data needed to satisfy a user's query are at that back end. Therefore, there is no need to modify the user's query.

This approach minimizes the need for trusted code in the front end, since a trusted front end can operate at the user's level. However, there is a need for trusted code to replicate tuples on updates to keep the versions consistent.

The Navy is currently pursuing the development of a trusted DBMS based on this approach [FROS89].

Benefits. This architecture has several benefits that promote achieving a high-assurance DBMS. First, the physical separation of the database into system-high fragments gives strong mandatory separation. Second, since the DBMS executes a user's query at the back end, which has all the needed data, there is no need to decompose the user query or perform additional DBMS functions in the front end. Third, the use of multiple DBMS physical processors should enhance the performance over methods using multiple software processes under a single trusted operating system.

Disadvantages. There are also several disadvantages to this architecture. First, the use of physically separate processors is hardware intensive. Therefore, this architecture is viable only for situations needing a small number of sensitivity levels and does not lend itself to use in intelligence applications, especially where there is a need for a large number of nonhierarchical sensitivity levels. For N nonhierarchical sensitivity levels, the number of back-end processors required is $2 ** (N - 1)$.

Similar to the single-processor TCB subset architecture, this architecture has problems in meeting high-assurance requirements for DAC. This is achievable if the DAC object is the entire back end. Since this is equivalent to no discretionary access, this is not an option. Therefore, the DAC objects must be a subset of the data stored under the back-end DBMS. Another option would be to store DAC access control information in the trusted front end. For any selected object, the back-end DBMS will still be responsible for retrieving the requested data objects. Therefore, using a back-end DBMS with its own DAC capability is a better option. Unfortunately, this approach does raise the cost of the system while still not achieving high-level DAC assurance.

For most applications, one reason for using an MLS DBMS is to have labels on smaller granularity objects. With current trusted workstation technology, the fact that workstations allow users to operate only within single-level windows negates the benefit of smaller granularity labels. The single-level window managers are not trusted to separate tuples or elements with different labels. In this architecture, having each user execute against a session-high version of the database means that the only trusted label the user will see is the session-high label. Use of a higher assurance DBMS back end that supports mandatory access control on DBMS objects will provide smaller granularity labels trusted at the DBMS's level, but that trust does not transfer to the workstation and, therefore, the labels are only advisory when presented to the end user. In addition, the use of a B1 or higher DBMS for each back end would increase the cost and degrade performance.

Distributed architecture with variable data replication

In contrast to the previous architecture, which used full replication of low data, the variable data replication architecture allows data to be distributed and replicated according to actual usage requirements. This approach was used in the Unisys Secure Distributed DBMS (SD-DBMS) project. This architecture is also based on the Woods Hole Group 1 recommendation for a distributed architecture.

The SD-DBMS acts as a single multilevel DBMS, providing trusted labeling at the tuple level. The architectural approach taken to achieve trusted operation is to distribute multilevel relations into single-level fragments and to store these single-level fragments under multiple commercial off-the-shelf DBMS processors. Figure 5 illustrates the SD-DBMS architecture, simplified to two security levels: high and low. This architecture consists of three types of components: user front end (UFE), trusted front end (TFE), and interconnection.

The UFE devices are either workstations operating in single-level mode or trusted workstations running in multilevel mode within a range of security levels. A UFE is intended to host applications that provide the interface between the end user and the TFE. With multilevel UFEs, these applications may be trusted to operate over a range of sensitivity levels.

The TFE component corresponds to the trusted front end found in the Woods Hole architectures. It controls the execution of all DBMS commands and serves as the reference monitor for database access. The TFE consists of trusted and untrusted functions built on a trusted, high-assurance operating system. Connected to the TFE are multiple untrusted back-end DBMS hosts, each operating in system-high mode at an access class within the TFE's access class range. These back-end DBMSs store data at the appropriate access class and respond to single-level requests generated by the TFE in carrying out end users' queries.

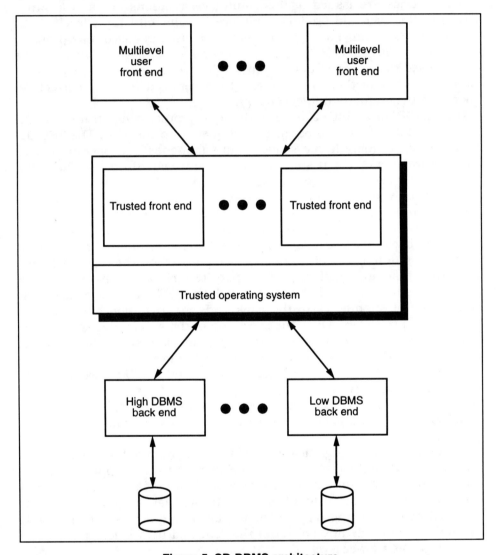

Figure 5. SD-DBMS architecture.

The interconnection component, potentially a multilevel local area network, supports isolation of the untrusted back ends and provides secure transmission of data between UFE devices and the TFE.

In the SD-DBMS, databases and relations are multilevel, each with a defined access class range. Each conceptual multilevel relation is physically decomposed into a set of single-level relation fragments. For a given multilevel relation, the relation schema is defined on each back-end DBMS operating at an access class within the relation's range.

User queries are issued against multilevel relations across the range visible to the user and produce multilevel results with tuple-level labels. The query processing strategy for this architecture is based on a property of relational algebra [OCON88]: Any query on a multilevel relation can be decomposed into a set of queries on single-level fragments, and the single-level results of these queries can be assembled into the correct response to the original multilevel query.

The SD-DBMS architecture uses this query processing strategy in the following manner. User programs send queries to the TFE. The TFE decomposes each query into a sequence of subqueries that operate on single-level fragments. Each subquery must be executed on the back end, whose access class is at the least upper bound of the access classes of all fragments on which the subquery operates. Since subqueries executed on the high back end may require access to low data (for example, to perform a join), the TFE may need to temporarily transfer fragments resident in the low back end to the high back end for the duration of a subquery, unless the required current fragment is replicated on the high back end. To assure that no data flow in the opposite direction, this architecture constrains all such transfers to go through the TFE. The TFE controls the submission of subqueries to the back ends for execution and performs any required transfers. Once the execution of the subqueries is complete, the TFE retrieves the individual results. The TFE labels the tuples in each result with the access class of the back end from which they were retrieved. These results are unioned together, and the TFE mediates their return to the user. (Volume 1, Appendix A, of the Unisys technical report "Secure Distributed Database Management System: Architecture" [UNIS89] discusses this query processing strategy in detail.)

Benefits. The most significant benefit of this approach is the ability to return trusted tuple-level labels to the user. All other approaches presented here return the results of a retrieval request labeled at the user's session level and with only advisory, untrusted labels attached to each returned object. Having only untrusted labels requires the end user to manually downgrade any subset of the returned data before releasing it or writing it at a lower level.

A secondary benefit of this approach is that it does not require full replication of data. The elimination of the requirement for full replication decreases the processing time for update replication and reduces storage overhead. In addition, the use of distributed data management techniques allows the subdivision of multilevel requests into multiple single-level requests that can be executed in parallel.

Disadvantages. The use of partial replication, while a benefit, is also the main deficiency of this architecture. The ability to transfer lower level data to a higher level back end to process a high request allows for a potential signaling channel. While this design uses various techniques to minimize the bandwidth of this channel, a small-bandwidth channel still exists and must be audited. Furthermore, the granularity of objects transferred between back ends during request processing is the entire single-level fragment. The requirement to transfer entire single-level fragments increases both the transmission overhead and the storage overhead to handle temporary fragments.

Integrity-lock DBMS

The integrity-lock architecture, shown in Figure 6, consists of three components: an untrusted front-end process, a trusted filter process, and an untrusted data manager process. The untrusted front-end process interacts with the end user. It is responsible for performing query parsing and for final processing of responses sent to the end user. This final output processing can include data management functions that operate at a single level — for example, summation functions that operate only at a single level. The trusted filter process is responsible for encrypting and decrypting objects and their labels, performing access mediation to identify the subset of data returned by the data management process, and downgrading the objects to be returned to the end user. Suppose that the database objects are tuples. In this case, the trusted filter would generate a cryptographic checksum by applying an encryption algorithm to each tuple and its sensitivity label, thus locking or sealing the tuple with its sensitivity label. The residue from the encryption process is associated with the tuple (either stored with the tuple or separately) as its checksum. The multilevel database is stored under the data management process that operates database high.

When the end user performs a selection operation against the database, the trusted filter will direct the data manager to retrieve all tuples matching the selection criteria. The data manager will not perform any operations that do not return entire unmodified tuples — for example, joins or projections. The tuples are then returned to the trusted filter. The trusted filter examines the sensitivity labels and discards tuples that do not pass the mandatory access policy check. The trusted process then reverifies that each tuple and its label have not been tampered with by reapplying the encryption algorithm and matching the residue from the algorithm with the tuple's cryptographic seal. The untrusted front-end process, running at the user's session level, then applies any additional functions required to satisfy the user request.

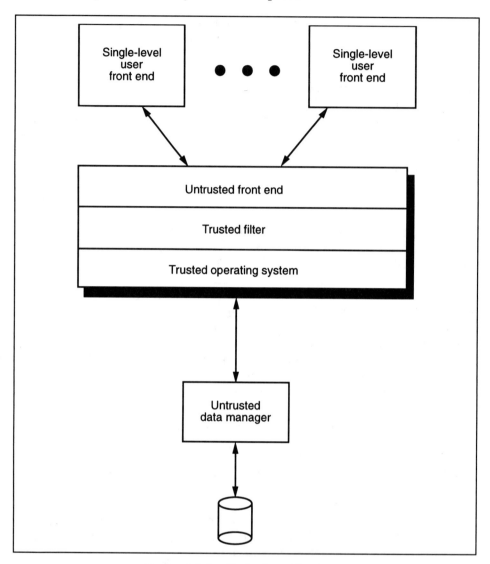

Figure 6. Integrity-lock architecture.

In the case of a user insert request, the trusted filter cryptographically seals the inserted tuple together with its label before directing the data manager to insert the tuple. For update commands, the tuples matching the selection criteria are retrieved and reverified, according to the technique described for a selection request. Each selected and verified tuple is then modified within the trusted process, resealed with a new crypto-graphic checksum, and stored under the DBMS.

Benefits. The main benefit of this architecture is the use of an un-trusted commercial DBMS to store the multilevel database as a database-high object. This approach decreases the number of DBMS functions re-quired in the trusted front end. Specifically, it alleviates the requirement for the trusted front end to support the functions related to indexed data storage and retrieval. In addition, the use of integrity locks enhances the assurance that modifications to the data, either accidental or malicious, can be detected.

Disadvantages. There are several deficiencies associated with this ar-chitecture. The use of cryptographic techniques adds complexity to the TCB by requiring key management. In addition, care must be taken in the selection of the object length and composition to ensure that patterns in the data do not occur that allow compromise of the encryption scheme.

This architecture is also subject to a large encoding channel. This channel occurs because the untrusted DBMS has access to all of the data and their labels that are stored in the clear. The DBMS can then return valid data that actually is an encoding of higher classified data.

The requirement to return entire objects to the trusted front end (for example, entire tuples) means that the DBMS cannot perform any func-tions that return parts of objects through use of the project function, combine portions of objects to form new objects through use of the join operation, or return only aggregates of database objects (for example, return an average). The trusted front end must perform these functions after verifying the checksum on each tuple. This process increases the complexity and size of the TCB.

The use of checksums does allow for the detection of modifications after they have occurred. It does not prevent modifications and cannot prevent deletion of objects.

Trusted subject-monolithic DBMS

Approaches relying on trusted operating system kernels for access control enforcement sacrifice some DBMS functionality for the higher mandatory assurance that can be achieved with these approaches. With the exception of one version of the Trusted Oracle Version 7.0 DBMS that uses the TCB subset approach, all of the DBMS products currently being sold or developed rely on the DBMS itself to enforce access control on database objects. These DBMSs aim at meeting the B1 level of TCSEC assurance, since this level does not constrain the DBMS to be small or simple. This level allows for the adaptation of an untrusted software product to operate on multilevel data. All of these products also use database tuples as labeled objects.

Figure 7 shows this type of architecture. With this approach, the DBMS software still runs above a trusted operating system. The operating system provides for isolation of the DBMS code and controls access to the database so that all access to the databases must be through the trusted DBMS. The DBMS stores the multilevel database in one or more files. For example, the DBMS could store the database in a single file labeled at the highest level of any data in the database. Or the DBMS could store each multilevel relation in a file labeled at the highest level of data within the relation. The DBMS associates a sensitivity label with each data tuple. The label is treated as an attribute within the relation, even though in reality it is a virtual attribute that need not actually be stored and managed as an attribute.

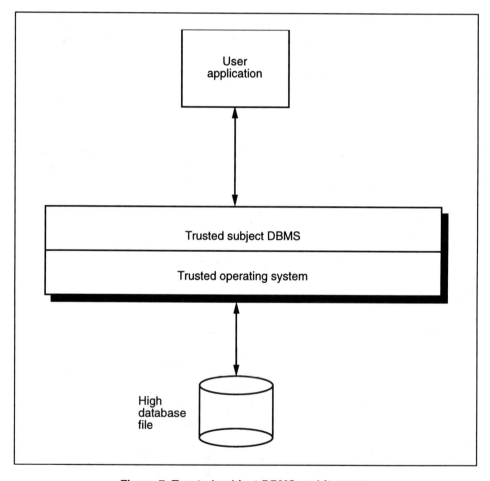

Figure 7. Trusted subject DBMS architecture.

Benefits. The benefits of this architecture lie in the ability of the DBMS to access all levels of data at the same time. This feature allows a single, multiuser process to service requests for all users, minimizing the operating system's processing load. It also allows for the handling of data labeled over a wide range of sensitivity levels.

This architecture can handle more complex forms of access control that involve data at multilevel access control levels. It also supports integrity constraints defined between data objects at different sensitivity levels, for example, referential integrity constraints.

Disadvantages. The main disadvantage of this architecture is its lack of potential to be evaluated to high TCSEC evaluation classes. Meeting higher assurance levels requires the ability to provide separation of mandatory objects by some form of hardware isolation. With the trusted subject approach, the physical object is the entire multilevel relation or multilevel database. Since the actual mandatory database objects are isolated by trusted software, it is more difficult to prove that this software operates correctly without allowing for the flow of high to low data.

Summary

While many different approaches have been pursued in the research community for high-assurance DBMSs, none of the approaches developed to date has been able to meet all of the high-assurance requirements and still provide the level of functionality provided by untrusted commercial DBMS products. The trusted subject approach has been predominantly used in trusted DBMS products, and only at the lower evaluation classes.

The critical research areas for the future are new architecture techniques to allow trusted subject architectures to minimize trusted code and meet high-assurance requirements. Advances are also needed in the workstation area to provide a flexible client-server environment that allows users to operate simultaneously over a range of sensitivity levels.

Essay 20

Toward a Multilevel Secure Relational Data Model

Sushil Jajodia and Ravi S. Sandhu

A large number of databases in the Department of Defense, the intelligence community, and civilian government agencies contain data that are classified to have different security levels. All database users are also assigned security clearances. It is the responsibility of a multilevel secure (MLS) database management system (DBMS) to assure that each user gains access — directly or indirectly — to only those data for which he has proper clearance. Some private corporations also use security levels and clearances to ensure secrecy of sensitive information, although their procedures for assigning these are much less formal than in the government.

Most commercial DBMSs provide some form of data security by controlling modes of access privileges of users to data [GRIF76, RABI88]. These discretionary access controls (DAC) do not provide adequate mechanisms for preventing unauthorized disclosure of information. Therefore, commercial DBMSs providing only DAC are not suitable for use in multilevel environments. Multilevel systems require additional mechanisms for enforcing mandatory (or nondiscretionary) access controls (MAC) [DENN82].

As a result, there are several efforts under way to build multilevel secure relational DBMSs. These efforts are following the same path taken by object-oriented databases. On one hand, several database vendors (Oracle, Sybase, and Trudata, to name a few) are busy building commercial products, and others (for example, SRI [DENN87, LUNT90] and SCTC [HAIG91a]) are building research prototypes. On the other hand, there is no clear consensus regarding what exactly an MLS relational data model is. This has led to continuing arguments about basic principles such as integrity requirements and update semantics. This lack of consensus on fundamental issues underscores the subtleties involved in extending the classical relational model to a multilevel environment. In the absence of a strong theoretical framework it is unfortunate, but inevitable, that much of the argument on basic issues is unduly influenced by implementation details of specific projects.

Our aim in this essay is to discuss the most fundamental aspects of the MLS relational model. It is our goal to be formal, analytical, and objective — in the sense of implementation independent. The contents of this essay are summarized in the following subsections.

Core integrity properties. It is important to specify precisely all constraints that relations must satisfy, since these constraints ensure that all instances in the database are meaningful. It is equally important to require only the minimal necessary constraints so as to allow as large a class of admissible instances as possible. In classical relational theory (see C.J. Date's work [DATE86], for example) the essential constraints have been identified as entity integrity and referential integrity. In a later section, we consider the multilevel analog of entity integrity. We identify four core integrity properties that should be required of all multilevel relations [JAJO91b]. One of these is a generalization of the usual entity integrity requirement to a multilevel context, while the other three are new to multilevel relations. For each property, we show why it is needed in multilevel relations. Our focus in this essay is on single relations, and we do not consider multilevel referential integrity here.

Relation updates. Somewhat paradoxically, the understanding of update operations is crucial to achieving secrecy of information in multilevel systems. We give a formal operational semantics for update operations on multilevel relations, that is, relations in which individual data elements are classified at different levels [JAJO90f]. For this purpose, the familiar INSERT, UPDATE, and DELETE operations of SQL [DATE86] are suitably generalized. Our goal here has been to preserve as much as possible the intuitive simplicity of these operations in classical relations without sacrificing security in the process. The main difference, with respect to the classical semantics of these operations, is that certain updates cannot be carried out by overwriting the data in place because doing so would result in leakage or destruction of secret information. This inescapable fact complicates the semantics of multilevel relations. These operations are consistent (or sound) in that all relations that can be constructed will satisfy the basic integrity properties required of multilevel relations. Additionally, these operations are complete in that every multilevel relation can be constructed by some sequence of these operations.

Decomposition and recovery of multilevel relations. We give a decomposition algorithm that breaks a multilevel relation into single-level relations and a new recovery algorithm that reconstructs the original multilevel relation from the decomposed single-level relations [JAJO91b]. There are several novel aspects to these decomposition and recovery algorithms, which provide substantial advantages over previous proposals [DENN87, JAJO90c, LUNT90]:

1. These algorithms are formulated in the context of an operational semantics for multilevel relations, defined here by generalizing the usual UPDATE operations of SQL to multilevel relations.
2. These algorithms, with minor modifications, can easily accommodate alternative update semantics that have been proposed in the literature.
3. These algorithms are efficient because recovery is based solely on unionlike operations without any use of joins.
4. The decomposition is intuitively and theoretically simple, giving us a sound basis for correctness.

Overview. The rest of this essay is organized as follows. The next section gives an overview of basic concepts of multilevel security. Then we review basic definitions for standard (single-level) relations; those for multilevel relations follow. We offer four core integrity requirements (together with their justification) that we feel must be met by all multilevel relations. Then we examine various UPDATE operations in a multilevel context, as outlined above. Before concluding, we give the decomposition and recovery algorithms that have been formulated in terms of UPDATE operations defined in the previous section.

Basic relational concepts and security requirements

The standard relational model is concerned with data without security classifications. Data are stored in tables, called *relations*. Each relation has a number of columns, called *attributes*. At any given time, a relation contains a number of rows, called *tuples*. The number of tuples in a relation varies with time. As an example, consider the relation SOD given in Figure 1, which contains for each starship its name, its objective, and its destination.

Starship	Objective	Destination
Enterprise	Exploration	Talos
Voyager	Spying	Mars

Figure 1. SOD.

There is a *relation scheme* corresponding to each relation, consisting of the relation name together with a list of its attribute names. The relation scheme for the relation SOD is denoted as follows:

SOD(Starship, Objective, Destination)

While the scheme for a relation is invariant over time, a relation is not static over time. Tuples are continuously being inserted, deleted, or updated in a relation to reflect changes in the real world. Not all possible relations are meaningful in an application; only those that satisfy certain integrity constraints are considered valid.

Let $R(A_1, A_2, ..., A_n)$ be a relation scheme, and let X and Y denote sets of one or more of the attributes A_i in R. We say Y is *functionally dependent* on X, written $X \rightarrow Y$, if any relation for R satisfies at all times the following property: It does not have two tuples with the same values for X but different values for Y.

A *candidate key* of a relation scheme R is a minimal set of attributes on which all other attributes of R are functionally dependent. The *primary key* of a relation scheme R is one of its candidate keys that has been specifically designated as such.

Moving on to a multilevel world, a major issue is how access classes are assigned to data stored in relations. Access classes can be assigned to relations, to individual tuples in a relation, to individual attributes of a relation, or to individual data elements of the tuples of a relation. In this essay, we will consider the general (and most difficult) case, and assign access classes to individual data elements of a relation.

As a consequence of Bell-LaPadula restrictions, subjects having different clearances see different versions of a multilevel relation: A user having a clearance at an access class c sees only that data which lies at class c or below. As an example, consider the relation scheme SOD(Starship, Objective, Destination), where Starship is the primary key and the security classifications are assigned at the granularity of individual data elements. A user with Secret clearance will see the entire multilevel relation SOD_S shown in Figure 2, while a user having Unclassified clearance will see only the filtered relation SOD_U shown in Figure 3.

Now, consider once again the multilevel relation given in Figure 2. Suppose that a U-user who sees the instance in Figure 3 wishes to replace the second tuple of SOD_U by the tuple (Voyager, Exploration, Talos). From a purely database perspective, this update by the U-user should be rejected because the attribute Starship constitutes the primary key of SOD_S. However, from the security viewpoint, this update cannot be rejected since doing so will be sufficient to establish a downward signaling channel. Since a Secret process can send one bit of information by either inserting or deleting a particular tuple at the Secret level, both Secret and Unclassified processes can cooperate to establish a covert channel.

Thus, both tuples (Voyager, Spying, Mars) and (Voyager, Exploration, Talos) must somehow coexist in SOD_S, as in Figure 4. This is called *polyinstantiation:* There are two or more tuples in a multilevel relation with the same primary key.

Starship		Objective		Destination		TC
Enterprise	U	Exploration	U	Talos	U	U
Voyager	U	Spying	S	Mars	S	S

Figure 2. SOD_S.

Starship		Objective		Destination		TC
Enterprise	U	Exploration	U	Talos	U	U
Voyager	U	Null	U	Null	U	U

Figure 3. SOD_U.

Starship		Objective		Destination		TC
Enterprise	U	Exploration	U	Talos	U	U
Voyager	U	Exploration	U	Talos	U	U
Voyager	U	Spying	S	Mars	S	S

Figure 4. SOD_S.

Thus, we see that even the basic relational notion of a key does not have a straightforward extension to multilevel relations. Polyinstantiation illustrates the intrinsic difficulty of extending the standard relational concepts to the multilevel world; therefore, we devote a separate essay (Essay 21) to this problem. In this essay, our position is that there is a need for polyinstantiation in multilevel systems. However, it must be carefully controlled to avoid confusion and ambiguity in the database. For example, the S-instance of Figure 5 should not be allowed because it gives ambiguous information about the Voyager's objective at the S level.

Throughout this essay, we use the terms *high* and *low* to refer to two access classes such that the former is strictly higher than the latter in the partial order. Also, if a user is logged on at an access class c, we refer to such a user as a c-user.

Starship		Objective		Destination		TC
Voyager	U	Exploration	S	Mars	S	S
Voyager	U	Spying	S	Mars	S	S

Figure 5. An illegal S-instance.

Multilevel relations

In this section, we review the basic concepts for the multilevel relations. In the next section, we will state four core integrity requirements that we feel must be satisfied by all multilevel relations. A *multilevel relation* consists of two parts: a relation scheme and relation instances.

Definition 1: Relation scheme. A state-invariant multilevel *relation scheme* is of the form

$$R(A_1, C_1, A_2, C_2, ..., A_n, C_n, TC)$$

where each A_i is a *data attribute* over domain D_i, each C_i is a *classification attribute* for A_i, and TC is the *tuple-class attribute*. The domain of C_i is specified by a set $\{L_i, ..., H_i\}$ which enumerates the allowed values for access classes, ranging from the greatest lower bound (glb) L_i to the least upper bound (lub) H_i. The domain of TC is the set $\{\text{lub}\{L_i: i = 1, ..., n\}, ..., \text{lub}\{H_i: i = 1, ..., n\}\}$.

Definition 2: Relation instances. For each relation scheme, there is a collection of state-dependent *relation instances*

$$R_c(A_1, C_1, A_2, C_2, ..., A_n, C_n, TC)$$

one for each access class c in the given lattice. Each relation instance is a set of distinct tuples of the form $(a_1, c_1, a_2, c_2, ..., a_n, c_n, tc)$, where each $a_i \in D_i$ or $a_i = $ null, $c \geq c_i$, and $tc = \{\text{lub}\{c_i: i = 1, ..., n\}$. Moreover, if a_i is not null, then $c_i \in \{L_i, ..., H_i\}$. We require that c_i be defined even if a_i is null — that is, a classification attribute cannot be null.

The multiple relation instances are, of course, related; each instance is intended to represent the version of reality appropriate for each access class. Roughly speaking, each element $t[A_i]$ in a tuple t is visible in instances at access class $t[C_i]$ or higher; $t[A_i]$ is replaced by a null value in an instance at a lower access class. We give a more formal description using the filter function in the next section.

Core integrity properties

In this section, we state four core integrity properties that must be satisfied by all multilevel relations. For each property, we justify why it is necessary.

Since a multilevel relation has different instances at different access classes, it is inherently more complex than a standard relation. In a standard relation, the definition of keys is based on functional dependencies. In a multilevel setting, the concept of functional dependencies is itself clouded because a relation instance is now a collection of sets of tuples rather than a single set of tuples.

We assume that there is a user-specified primary key AK consisting of a subset of the data attributes A_t. This is called the *apparent primary key* of the multilevel relation scheme. We will return to the issue of what constitutes the primary key of a multilevel relation after we define the polyinstantiation integrity property.

In general, AK will consist of multiple attributes. Entity integrity from the standard relational model prohibits null values for any of the attributes in AK. This property [DENN87] extends to multilevel relations, as shown in the following subsections.

Property 1: Entity integrity. Let AK be the apparent key of R. A multilevel relation R satisfies entity integrity if and only if for all instances R_c of R and $t \in R_c$:

1. $A_i \in AK \Rightarrow [A_i] \neq$ null;
2. $A_i, A_j \in AK \Rightarrow t[C_i] = t[C_j]$, that is, AK is uniformly classified; and
3. $A_i \notin AK \Rightarrow t[C_i] \geq t[C_{AK}]$ (where C_{AK} is defined to be the classification of the apparent key).

The first requirement is an obvious carryover from the standard relational model and ensures that no tuple in R_c has a null value for any attribute in AK. The second requirement says that all AK attributes have the same classification in a tuple, that is, they are either all U or all S, and so on. This will ensure that AK is either entirely visible or entirely null at a specific access class c. The third requirement states that in any tuple the class of the non-AK attributes must dominate C_{AK}. This rules out the possibility of associating nonnull attributes with a null primary key.

At this point it is important to clarify the semantics of null values. There are two major issues:

1. the classification of null values, and
2. the subsumption of null values by nonnull ones.

Our requirements are respectively that null values be classified at the level of the key in the tuple, and that a null value is subsumed by a non-null value independent of the latter's classification. These two requirements are formally stated in Property 2.

Property 2: Null integrity. A multilevel relation R satisfies null integrity if and only if for each instance R_c of R both of the following conditions are true:

1. For all $t \in R_c$, $t[A_i] = \text{null} \Rightarrow t[C_i] = t[C_{AK}]$; that is, nulls are classified at the level of the key.
2. Let us say that tuple t subsumes tuple s if for every attribute A_i, either (a) $t[A_i, C_i] = s[A_i, C_i]$ or (b) $t[A_i] \neq \text{null}$ and $s[A_i] = \text{null}$. Our second requirement is that R_c is subsumption free in the sense that it does not contain two distinct tuples such that one subsumes the other.

We will henceforth assume that all computed relations are made subsumption free by exhaustive elimination of subsumed tuples. The null integrity requirement was identified in an earlier work [JAJO90c].

Consider the relation instance for SOD given in Figure 6. The motivation behind the null integrity property is that if an S-user updates the destination of Enterprise to be Rigel, he or she will see the instance given in Figure 7 rather than the one given in Figure 8, since the first tuple in Figure 8 is subsumed by the second tuple.

The next property is concerned with consistency between the different relation instances. The need for such a property was identified earlier [DENN87], but the formulations were incorrect. The correct formulation [JAJO90c] was adopted by SeaView researchers [LUNT90].

Property 3: Interinstance integrity. R satisfies interinstance integrity if and only if for all $c' \leq c$ we have $R_{c'} = \sigma (R_c, c')$, where the *filter function* σ produces the c'-instance $R_{c'}$ from R_c as follows:

1. For every tuple $t \in R_c$ such that $t[C_{AK}] \leq c'$, there is a tuple $t' \in R_{c'}$ with $t'[AK, C_{AK}] = t[AK, C_{AK}]$ and for $A_i \notin AK$

$$t'[A_i, C_i] = \begin{cases} t[A_i, C_i] & \text{if } t[C_i] \leq c' \\ <\text{null}, t[C_{AK}]> & \text{otherwise} \end{cases}$$

2. There are no tuples in $R_{c'}$ other than those derived by the above rule.

3. The end result is made subsumption free by exhaustive elimination of subsumed tuples.

The filter function maps a multilevel relation to different instances, one for each descending access class in the security lattice. Filtering limits each user to that portion of the multilevel relation for which he or she is cleared. Thus, for example, an S-user will see the entire relation given in Figure 7, while a U-user will see the filtered instance given in Figure 6. It is evident that $\sigma(R_c, c) = R_c$, and $\sigma(\sigma(R_c, c'), c'') = \sigma(R_c, c'')$ for $c \geq c' \geq c''$, as one would expect from the intuitive notion of filtering.

Starship		Objective		Destination		TC
Enterprise	U	Exploration	U	Null	U	U

Figure 6. SOD$_U$.

Starship		Objective		Destination		TC
Enterprise	U	Exploration	U	Rigel	S	S

Figure 7. SOD$_S$.

Starship		Objective		Destination		TC
Entcrprise	U	Exploration	U	Null	U	U
Enterprise	U	Exploration	U	Rigel	S	S

Figure 8. Violation of null integrity.

We are now ready to state our fourth and final property. In a standard relation there cannot be two tuples with the same primary key. In a multilevel relation we will similarly expect that there cannot be two tuples with the same *apparent primary key*. However, as we observed earlier, secrecy considerations compel us to allow multiple tuples with the same apparent primary key. (See, however, Essay 21 on polyinstantiation.) We have the following property to control the manner in which this can be done.

Property 4: Polyinstantiation integrity. R satisfies polyinstantiation integrity (PI) if and only if for every R_c we have for all A_i: AK, C_{AK}, $C_i \to A_i$.

This property stipulates that the user-specified apparent key AK, in conjunction with the classification attributes C_{AK} and C_i, functionally determines the value of the A_i attribute. Thus, PI allows the instance in Figure 4 while ruling out the S-instance of Figure 5.

Property 4 implicitly defines what is meant by the primary key in a multilevel relation. The primary key of a multilevel relation is $AK \cup C_{AK} \cup C_R$ (where AK is the set of data attributes constituting the user-specified primary key, C_{AK} is the classification attribute for data attributes in AK, and C_R is the set of classification attributes for data attributes not in AK). This is because from PI it follows that the functional dependency $AK \cup C_{AK} \cup C_R \to A_R$ holds (where A_R denotes the set of all attributes that are not in AK). Note that for single-level relations, C_{AK} and C_R will be equal to the same constant value in all tuples. Therefore, in this case, PI amounts to saying that $AK \to A_R$, which is precisely the definition of the primary key in relational theory.

When Property 4 was originally proposed [DENN87], it was coupled with an additional multivalued dependency[1] (MVD) requirement AK, $C_{AK} \to\to A_i$, C_i to be satisfied by every instance. There are unpleasant consequences of this multivalued dependency [JAJO90c]. Hence, our position is that polyinstantiation integrity should require only the functional dependency stated in Property 4.

The UPDATE operations

In this section, we discuss in detail the three UPDATE operations (INSERT, UPDATE, and DELETE). We keep the syntax for these operations identical to the standard SQL.

Let $R(A_1, C_1, ..., A_n, C_n, TC)$ be a multilevel relation scheme. To simplify the notation, we use A_1 instead of AK to denote the apparent primary key.

Consider a user logged on at access class c. Now a c-user directly sees and interacts with the c-instance R_c. From the viewpoint of this user, the remaining instances of R can be categorized into three cases: Those strictly dominated by c, those that strictly dominate c, and those incomparable with c. The following notation is useful for ease of reference to these three cases:

1. $R_{c' < c} \equiv R_{c'}$, such that $c' < c$.
2. $R_{c' > c} \equiv R_{c'}$, such that $c' > c$.
3. $R_{c' \sim c} \equiv R_{c'}$, such that c' is incomparable with c.

---

[1] See [DATE86] for a definition of multivalued dependency.

Security considerations, and in particular the *-property, dictate that a c-user cannot insert, update, or delete a tuple, directly or indirectly (as a side effect) in any $R_{c'<c}$ or $R_{c'\sim c}$. Since actions of a c-user cannot have an impact on any $R_{c'<c}$, the effect of insertion, update, or deletion must be confined to those tuples in R_c with tuple class equal to c. Because of the interinstance property, these changes must be properly reflected in the instances $R_{c'>c}$. The latter effect is only partly determined by the core integrity properties presented earlier, leaving room for different interpretations [HAIG91a, JAJO90c, JAJO90f, LUNT91, SAND90a].

Strictly speaking, in all cases we should speak of operations being performed by a c-subject (or c-process) rather than a c-user. It is, however, easier to intuitively consider the semantics by visualizing a human being interactively carrying out these operations. The semantics do apply equally well to processes operating on behalf of a user, whether interactive or not.

The INSERT statement. The INSERT statement executed by a c-user has the following general form, where the c is implicitly determined by the user's login class:

```
INSERT
INTO      Rc[(Ai [, Aj]...)]
VALUES  (ai [, aj]...)
```

In this notation, the brackets denote optional items and the ellipsis (...) signifies repetition. If the list of attributes is omitted, it is assumed that all the data attributes in R_c are specified. Only data attributes A_i can be explicitly given values. The classification attributes C_i are all implicitly given the value c.

Let t be the tuple such that $t[A_k] = a_k$ if A_k is included in the attributes list in the INSERT statement, $t[A_k]$ = Null if A_k is not in the list, and $t[C_l]$ = c for $1 \le l \le n$. The insertion is permitted if and only if:

1. $t[A_1]$ does not contain any nulls, and
2.   for all $u \in R_c$: $u[A_1] \ne t[A_1]$.

If so, the tuple t is inserted into R_c and by side effect into all $R_{c'>c}$. This is, moreover, the only side effect visible in any $R_{c'>c}$.

To illustrate, suppose a U-user wishes to insert a second tuple into the SOD instance given in Figure 9. He or she does so by executing the following INSERT statement:

```
INSERT
INTO      SOD
VALUES  ('Voyager', 'Exploration', 'Mars')
```

As a result of the INSERT statement, the U-instance of SOD will become as shown in Figure 10. This insertion is straightforward and identical to what happens in single-level relations.

Starship		Objective		Destination		TC
Enterprise	U	Exploration	U	Talos	U	U

Figure 9. SOD$_U$ = SOD$_S$.

Starship		Objective		Destination		TC
Enterprise	U	Exploration	U	Talos	U	U
Voyager	U	Exploration	U	Mars	U	U

Figure 10. SOD$_U$.

On the other hand, suppose an S-user wishes to insert the following tuple into the SOD instance of Figure 9:

```
INSERT
INTO      SOD
VALUES    ('Enterprise', 'Spying', 'Rigel')
```

In this case, we can either reject the insert or accept it and allow two tuples with the same apparent key Enterprise to coexist, as shown in Figure 11. The two tuples in Figure 11 are regarded as pertaining to two distinct entities. We call such situations *optional polyinstantiations*. Insertion of the secret tuple is not required for closing signaling channels. It is secure to reject such insertions.

Finally, we illustrate the situation where polyinstantiation is required to close signaling channels. Consider the SOD$_S$ instance given in Figure 12. U-users see an empty instance SOD$_U$. Suppose a U-user executes the following INSERT statement:

```
INSERT
INTO      SOD
VALUES    ('Enterprise', 'Exploration', 'Talos')
```

This insertion cannot be rejected on the grounds that a tuple with apparent key Enterprise has previously been inserted by an S-user. Doing so would establish a signaling channel from S to U. Therefore, by security considerations we are compelled to allow insertion of this tuple. In such cases, we say we have *required polyinstantiation.* The effect of this insertion by a U-user is to change SOD$_S$ from Figure 12 to Figure 11.

Starship		Objective		Destination		TC
Enterprise	U	Exploration	U	Talos	U	U
Enterprise	S	Spying	S	Rigel	S	S

Figure 11. SOD$_S$.

Starship		Objective		Destination		TC
Enterprise	S	Spying	S	Rigel	S	S

Figure 12. SOD$_S$.

The UPDATE statement. Our interpretation of the semantics of an update command is close to the one in the standard relational model: An update command is used to change values in tuples that are already present in a relation. UPDATE is a set-level operator; that is, all tuples in the relation which satisfy the predicate in the UPDATE statement are to be updated (provided the resulting relation satisfies polyinstantiation integrity). Since we are dealing with multilevel relations, we may have to polyinstantiate some tuples. However, addition of tuples due to polyinstantiation is to be minimized to the extent possible.

The UPDATE statement executed by a *c*-user has the following general form:

```
UPDATE  R_c
SET     A_i = s_i [, A_j = s_j] ...
[WHERE  p]
```

Here s_k is a scalar expression, and p is a predicate expression which identifies those tuples in R_c that are to be modified. The predicate p may include conditions involving the classification attributes, in addition to the usual case of data attributes. The assignments in the SET clause, however, can involve only the data attributes. The corresponding classification attributes are implicitly determined to be c.

The intent of the UPDATE operation is to modify $t[A_k]$ to s_k in those tuples t in R_c that satisfy the given predicate p. In multilevel relations, however, we have to implement the intent slightly differently to prevent illegal information flows.

Examples of UPDATE operations. Consider the SOD instances given in Figures 13 and 14. Suppose the U-user makes the following update to SOD_U, shown in Figure 13:

```
UPDATE   SOD
SET       Destination = Talos
WHERE    Starship = 'Enterprise'
```

Starship		Objective		Destination		TC
Enterprise	U	Exploration	U	Null	U	U

Figure 13. SOD$_U$.

Starship		Objective		Destination		TC
Enterprise	U	Exploration	U	Rigel	S	S

Figure 14. SOD$_S$.

The changes to SOD_U in Figure 13 and SOD_S in Figure 14 are shown in Figures 15 and 16, respectively. Note that in SOD_S the Destination attribute for the Enterprise is now polyinstantiated. This is an example of required polyinstantiation that cannot be completely eliminated without introducing signaling channels or limiting the expressive capability of the database.

Starship		Objective		Destination		TC
Enterprise	U	Exploration	U	Talos	U	U

Figure 15. SOD$_U$.

Starship		Objective		Destination		TC
Enterprise	U	Exploration	U	Talos	U	U
Enterprise	U	Exploration	U	Rigel	S	S

Figure 16. SOD$_S$.

Next, suppose starting with the instance SOD$_S$ of Figure 16 an S-user invokes the following update:

```
UPDATE   SOD
SET      Objective = Spying
WHERE    Starship = 'Enterprise' AND
         Destination = 'Rigel'
```

In this case, SOD$_S$ will change to the instance given in Figure 17, not to the instance given in Figure 18. That is, the update is interpreted as applying only to the second tuple in Figure 16, not to the first tuple. The S-user can go from Figure 16 to Figure 18 by issuing the following update:

```
UPDATE   SOD
SET      Objective = Spying
WHERE    Starship = 'Enterprise'
```

This update is interpreted as applying to both tuples of Figure 16. The first two tuples of Figure 18 result from polyinstantiation of the first tuple of Figure 16. The third tuple of Figure 18 results from the normal replacement update of the second tuple of Figure 16.

Next, suppose a U-user makes the following update to the relation shown in Figure 15 (assume S-users see the instance given in Figure 16):

```
UPDATE   SOD
SET      Objective = Spying
WHERE    Starship = 'Enterprise'
```

As a consequence of the above update, not only SOD$_U$ will change from the relation in Figure 15 to the one in Figure 19, but SOD$_S$ will also change from the relation in Figure 16 to the one in Figure 20. Thus, polyinstantiation integrity is preserved in instances at different security levels. Note in particular how the secret tuple in Figure 16 has changed to the secret tuple in Figure 20 due to an update by a U-user.

Starship		Objective		Destination		TC
Enterprise	U	Exploration	U	Talos	U	U
Enterprise	U	Spying	S	Rigel	S	S

Figure 17. SOD$_S$.

Starship		Objective		Destination		TC
Enterprise	U	Exploration	U	Talos	U	U
Enterprise	U	Spying	S	Talos	U	S
Enterprise	U	Spying	S	Rigel	S	S

Figure 18. SOD$_S$.

Starship		Objective		Destination		TC
Enterprise	U	Spying	U	Talos	U	U

Figure 19. SOD$_U$.

Starship		Objective		Destination		TC
Enterprise	U	Spying	U	Talos	U	U
Enterprise	U	Spying	U	Rigel	S	S

Figure 20. SOD$_S$.

Effect at the user's access class. We now formalize and further develop the ideas sketched out above. First consider the effect of an UPDATE operation by a c-user on R_c. Let

$$S = \{t \in R_c: t \text{ satisfies the predicate } p\}$$

We describe the effect of the UPDATE operation by considering each tuple $t \in S$ in turn. The net effect is obtained as the cumulative effect of updating each tuple in turn. The UPDATE operation will succeed if and only if at every step in this process polyinstantiation integrity is maintained.

Otherwise, the entire UPDATE operation is rejected and no tuples are changed. In other words, UPDATE has an all-or-nothing integrity failure semantics.

It remains to consider the effect of UPDATE on each tuple $t \in S$. There are two components to this effect. First, tuple t is replaced by tuple t', which is identical to t except for those data attributes that are assigned new values in the SET clause. This is the familiar replacement semantics of UPDATE in a single-level world. In terms of our earlier examples, the update of SOD_U from Figure 13 to Figure 15 and then to Figure 19 illustrates this semantics. The formal definition of the tuple t' obtained by replacement semantics is straightforward, as follows:

$$t'[A_k, C_k] = \begin{cases} t[A_k, C_k] & A_k \notin \text{SET clause} \\ <s_k, c> & A_k \in \text{SET clause} \end{cases}$$

Second, to avoid signaling channels, we may need to introduce an additional tuple t'' to hide the effects of the replacement of t by t' from users at levels below c (c is the level of the user executing the UPDATE). This will occur whenever there is some attribute A_k in the SET clause with $t[C_k] < c$. The idea is that the original value of $t[A_k]$ with classification $t[C_k]$ is preserved in t''. At the same time, the core integrity properties presented earlier must be preserved.

To be concrete, consider our earlier example of the update of SOD_S from Figure 16 to Figure 17. The WHERE clause of the UPDATE statement picks up the second tuple in Figure 16, which by replacement semantics gives us the second tuple in Figure 17. In this case, the unclassified Exploration value of the Objective attribute continues to be available in the first tuple of Figure 17, and we need not introduce an additional tuple to hide the effect of this update from U-users. On the other hand, suppose the same UPDATE statement, that is,

```
UPDATE  SOD
SET     Objective = Spying
WHERE   Starship = 'Enterprise' AND
        Destination = 'Rigel'
```

was executed by an S-user in the context of Figure 14. Prior to the update, U-users see the instance in Figure 13 and therefore must continue to do so after the update. To achieve this, SOD_S changes from Figure 14 to Figure 21. The first tuple in Figure 21 is the tuple t' dictated by the usual replacement semantics. The second tuple is the t'' tuple introduced to hide the effect of the update from U-users and maintain interinstance integrity. It should be noted that Figure 22 also achieves these two goals.

However, it does so at the cost of a spurious association between Rigel and Exploration, which is avoided in Figure 21.

Starship		Objective		Destination		TC
Enterprise	U	Spying	S	Rigel	S	S
Enterprise	U	Exploration	U	Null	U	U

Figure 21. SOD$_S$.

Starship		Objective		Destination		TC
Enterprise	U	Spying	S	Rigel	S	S
Enterprise	U	Exploration	U	Rigel	S	S

Figure 22. SOD$_S$.

We now give a formal definition of the t'' tuple introduced to close the signaling channel:

$$t''[A_k, C_k] = \begin{cases} t[A_k, C_k] & t[C_k] < c \\ <\text{Null}, t[A_1]> & t[C_k] = c \end{cases}$$

To summarize, each tuple $t \in S$ is replaced by t' and possibly in addition by t'' (if t'' exists). The update is successful if the resulting relation satisfies polyinstantiation integrity. Otherwise, the update is rejected, and the original relation is left unchanged.

Effect above the user's access class. Next, consider the effect of the UPDATE operation on $R_{c'>c}$. This, of course, assumes that the UPDATE operation on R_c was successful. Unfortunately, the core integrity properties do not uniquely determine how an update by a c-user to R_c should be reflected in updates to $R_{c'>c}$. Several different options have been proposed [HAIG91a, JAJO90f, LUNT90, LUNT91]. In this section, we will adopt the *minimal propagation rule* [JAJO90f]. This rule introduces exactly those tuples in $R_{c'>c}$ needed to preserve the interinstance property — that is, put t' and t'' (if t'' exists and survives subsumption) in each $R_{c'>c}$ and nothing else.[2]

---

[2] The minimal propagation rule needs to be slightly extended to achieve completeness (that is, every multilevel relation can be constructed by some sequence of update operations).

Formally, the effect of the UPDATE operation is again best explained by focusing on a particular tuple t in S. Let A_k be an attribute in the SET clause such that:

1. $t[C_k] = c$ and
2. $t[A_k] = x$, where x is nonnull.

That is, the c-user is actually changing a nonnull value of $t[A_k]$ at his own level to s_k. Now consider $R_{c'>c}$. Due to polyinstantiation, there may be several tuples u in $R_{c'>c}$ which have the same apparent primary key as t (that is, $u[A_1, C_1] = t[A_1, C_1]$) and match t in the A_k and C_k attributes (that is, $u[A_k, C_k] = t[A_k, C_k]$). To maintain polyinstantiation integrity (that is, Property 4 presented earlier), we must therefore change the value of $u[A_k]$ from x to s_k. This requirement is formally stated as follows:

1. For every $A_k \in$ SET clause with $t[A_k] \neq$ Null, let

    $$U = \{u \in R_{c'>c} : u[A_1, C_1] = t[A_1, C_1] \wedge u[A_k, C_k] = t[A_k, C_k]\}$$

    Polyinstantiation integrity dictates that we replace every $u \in U$ by u' identical to u, except for

    $$u'[A_k, C_k] = <s_k, c>$$

    This rule applies cumulatively for different A_k's in the SET clause. This requirement is absolute and must be rigidly enforced by the DBMS.

2. The second requirement is imposed by the interinstance integrity property. To maintain interinstance integrity, we insert t' and t'' (if it exists and survives subsumption) in $R_{c'>c}$.

The second requirement is weaker than the first, in that interinstance integrity only stipulates what minimum action is required. We can insert a number of additional tuples v in $R_{c'>c}$ with $v[A_1, C_1] = t'[A_1, C_1]$, so long as the core integrity properties are not violated. In particular, if t' subsumes the tuple in $\sigma(\{v\}, c)$, interinstance integrity is still maintained. Minimal propagation makes the simplest assumption in this case; that is, only t' and t'' are inserted in $R_{c'>c}$, and nothing else is done.

The DELETE statement. The DELETE statement has the following general form:

DELETE
FROM R_c
[WHERE p]

Here, p is a predicate expression which helps identify those tuples in R_c that are to be deleted. The intent of the DELETE operation is to delete those tuples t in R_c that satisfy the given predicate. But in view of the *-property, only those tuples t that additionally satisfy $t[TC] = c$ are deleted from R_c. To maintain interinstance integrity, polyinstantiated tuples are also deleted from $R_{c'>c}$.

In particular, if $t[C_1] = c$, then any polyinstantiated tuples in $R_{c'>c}$ will be deleted from $R_{c'>c}$. Hence, the entity that t represents will completely disappear from the multilevel relation. On the other hand, with $t[C_1] < c$, the entity will continue to exist in $R_{t[C_1]}$ and in $R_{c'>t[C_1]}$.

Decomposition and recovery

In this section, we give the decomposition and recovery algorithms [JAJO91b] formulated in terms of UPDATE operations defined in the previous section. We give an abstract description and complete formal statement first and defer consideration of examples until later.

Background. In multilevel relational DBMSs, a major issue is how access classes are assigned to data stored in relations. The proposals have included assigning access classes to relations [GROH76], assigning access classes to individual tuples in a relation [GARV86], and assigning access classes to individual attributes of a relation [HINK75]. Unlike these proposals, in the Secure Data Views (SeaView) project, security classifications are assigned to individual data elements of the tuples of a relation [DENN87, DENN88a, LUNT90] (for example, see Figure 23).

SHIP		OBJ		DEST		TC
Ent	U	Exp	U	Talos	U	U
Ent	U	Mine	C	Sirius	C	C
Ent	U	Spy	S	Rigel	S	S
Ent	U	Coup	TS	Orion	TS	TS

Figure 23. A multilevel relation SOD.

Multilevel relations in SeaView exist only at the logical level. In reality, multilevel relations are decomposed into a collection of single-level base relations that are then physically stored in the database. Completely transparent to users, multilevel relations are reconstructed from these base relations on user demand. There are several practical advantages of being able to decompose and store a multilevel relation as a collection of single-level base relations. In particular, the underlying trusted computing base (TCB) can enforce mandatory controls with respect to the single-level base relations. This allows the DBMS to run mostly as an untrusted application with respect to the underlying TCB.

In SeaView, the decomposition of multilevel relations into single-level ones is performed by applying two different types of fragmentation: *horizontal* and *vertical*. Thus the multilevel relation in Figure 23 will be stored as *nine* single-level fragments (one primary key group relation and eight attribute group relations), shown in Figure 24. This leads to many problems with the SeaView decomposition and recovery algorithms:

1. *Repeated joins.* The vertical fragmentation used in SeaView results in single-level relations that consist of the key attribute, a single nonkey attribute, and their classification attributes. This means that nearly all queries involving multiple attributes necessitate repeated (left outer) joins of several single-level relations. It is well known that join is an expensive operation and should be avoided whenever possible [SCHK82].

2. *Spurious tuples.* Whenever a relation is stored as one or more fragments, it must be possible to reconstruct the original relation exactly from the fragments. This, however, is not the case with the SeaView decomposition. When the SeaView recovery algorithm is applied to the single-level relations in Figure 24, a Top Secret user will be shown the relation given in Figure 25. While the original Top Secret instance in Figure 23 describes four missions for the Enterprise, a Top Secret user will see the 16 missions of Figure 25 using the SeaView approach.

3. *Incompleteness.* The SeaView decomposition puts severe limitations on the expressive capability of the database. Several instances that have realistic and useful interpretations cannot be realized in SeaView [JAJO90c, JAJO91a].

4. *Left outer joins.* The SeaView recovery algorithm is based on the left outer join of relations. Many theoretical complications and pitfalls arise with outer joins [DATE86].

Elsewhere [JAJO90c] we have given a modified version of the SeaView decomposition and recovery algorithms. Our principal motivation was to give a lossless decomposition that avoids the spurious tuples introduced by SeaView. To achieve this, we store the relation in Figure 23 as a collection of 12 single-level relations. Figure 26 shows the four primary key group relations; the eight attribute group relations are identical to those given in Figure 24b. The recovery algorithm, when applied to these single-level base relations, yields exactly the original-instance SOD in Figure 23. While these algorithms eliminate the last three problems, the first problem remains: Satisfying queries involving multiple attributes requires taking repeated natural joins of several single-level relations.

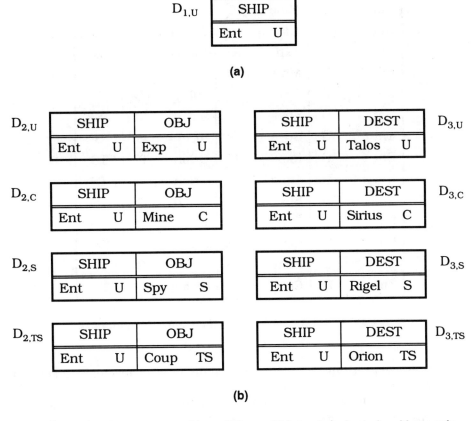

(a)

(b)

Figure 24. SeaView decomposition of Figure 23 into nine single-level base relations: (a) primary key group relation, (b) attribute group relations.

In this section, we give a decomposition algorithm and a recovery algorithm that have several advantages over the SeaView algorithms and our earlier algorithms discussed above [LUNT90, JAJO90c]:

1. The decomposition and recovery algorithms given below are based on operational semantics for the UPDATE operations on multilevel relations. The semantics of multilevel relations are defined here by generalizing the usual UPDATE operations of SQL.

SHIP		OBJ		DEST		TC
Ent	U	Exp	U	Talos	U	U
Ent	U	Exp	U	Sirius	C	C
Ent	U	Mine	C	Talos	U	C
Ent	U	Mine	C	Sirius	C	C
Ent	U	Exp	U	Rigel	S	S
Ent	U	Mine	C	Rigel	S	S
Ent	U	Spy	S	Talos	U	S
Ent	U	Spy	S	Sirius	C	S
Ent	U	Spy	S	Rigel	S	S
Ent	U	Exp	U	Orion	TS	TS
Ent	U	Mine	C	Orion	TS	TS
Ent	U	Spy	S	Orion	TS	TS
Ent	U	Coup	TS	Talos	U	TS
Ent	U	Coup	TS	Sirius	C	TS
Ent	U	Coup	TS	Rigel	S	TS
Ent	U	Coup	TS	Orion	TS	TS

Figure 25. SeaView recovery algorithm applied to Figure 24.

2. These algorithms, with minor modifications, can easily accommodate alternative update semantics that have been proposed in the literature. It is even possible to keep the decomposition fixed and vary the recovery algorithms to realize these alternate semantics.

3. These algorithms are computationally efficient because the decomposition uses only horizontal fragmentation to break multilevel relations into single-level ones. The decomposition for the relation in Figure 23 is shown in Figure 27. Since the decomposition does not require any vertical fragmentation, it is possible to reconstruct a multilevel relation from the underlying single-level base relations without having to perform any (left or natural) joins; only unions are required.

4. The recovery and decompositions are simple to state and prove correct.

$D_{1,U}$	SHIP		C_2	C_3
	Ent	U	U	U

$D_{1,C}$	SHIP		C_2	C_3
	Ent	U	C	C

$D_{1,S}$	SHIP		C_2	C_3
	Ent	U	S	S

$D_{1,TS}$	SHIP		C_2	C_3
	Ent	U	TS	TS

Figure 26. Primary key group relations after Jajodia-Sandhu decomposition of Figure 23 into 12 single-level base relations. The eight attribute group relations are identical to those in Figure 24b.

This section is organized as follows. First we give the decomposition and recovery algorithms that preserve the update semantics proposed earlier. Then we give several examples to illustrate the behavior of the update semantics, as well as the decomposition and recovery algorithms. We also show how these algorithms, with minor modifications, can easily accommodate alternative update semantics proposed in the literature.

Decomposition. The decomposition has for each multilevel relation scheme

$$R(A_1, C_1, ..., A_n, C_n, TC)$$

a collection of single-level base relations

$$D_c(A_1, C_1, ..., A_n, C_n)$$

one for each access class c in the security class lattice. This is in contrast to the SeaView decomposition [LUNT90] and the Jajodia-Sandhu decomposition [JAJO90c], both of which require several single-level relations at each access class (compare Figures 24 and 26 with Figure 27).

A c-user always sees and interacts with the c-instance R_c. Whenever a c-user issues an insert, update, or delete command against R_c, tuples are added, modified, or removed from the underlying base relation D_c. Any change in R_c must be properly reflected in $R_{c'>c}$ (and in $D_{c'>c}$), but this is accomplished during the recovery of a $R_{c'>c}$. Thus, when D_c is modified as the result of an update by a c-user, there are no changes made to any other $D_{c'}$, $c' \neq c$. Changes in $R_{c'>c}$ due to updates by c-users are accounted for by the recovery algorithm, which uses $\cup_{c' \leq c} D_{c'}$ to reconstruct an $R_{c'>c}$.

D_U

SHIP	OBJ	DEST
Ent U	Exp U	Talos U

D_C

SHIP	OBJ	DEST
Ent U	Mine C	Sirius C

D_S

SHIP	OBJ	DEST
Ent U	Spy S	Rigel S

D_{TS}

SHIP	OBJ	DEST
Ent U	Coup TS	Orion TS

Figure 27. New decomposition of Figure 23 into four single-level base relations.

The INSERT statement. Suppose as a result of the INSERT statement, a c-user successfully inserts the following tuple t in R_c: $t[A_k] = a_k$ if A_k is included in the attributes list in the INSERT statement, $t[A_k] = $ Null if A_k is not in the list, and $t[C_l] = c$ for $1 \leq l \leq n$. In this case, the decomposition will also insert the tuple t into D_c.

There are no other insertions. The recovery algorithm will use $\cup_{c' \leq c} D_{c'}$ to reconstruct an $R_{c'>c}$, and since t is in D_c, it will be in $R_{c'>c}$ as well.

The UPDATE statement. We next consider the effect of an UPDATE operation by a c-user on R_c. As we indicated earlier, only D_c will be modified by the decomposition algorithm.

Suppose that a c-user successfully executes the UPDATE statement presented earlier. Once again, let

$$S = \{t \in R_c: t \text{ satisfies the predicate } p\}$$

For each $t \in S$, there are two cases to consider:

1. $t[A_1, C_1] = c$. In this case, there can be no polyinstantiation of tuple t at the c level. There is exactly one tuple $u \in D_c$ with $u[A_1, C_1] = t[A_1, C_1]$. We replace u by the following tuple u': $u'[A_1, C_1] = u[A_1, C_1]$, and for $k \neq 1$,

$$u'[A_k, C_k] = \begin{cases} <s_k, c> & A_k \in \text{SET clause} \\ u[A_k, C_k] & A_k \notin \text{SET clause} \end{cases}$$

Note that in this case $u'[C_l] = c$ for $1 \leq l \leq n$.

2. $t[A_1, C_1] < c$. In this case, tuple t will be polyinstantiated at the c level. There are two separate subcases, depending on whether or not t has been polyinstantiated at level c prior to the update. These subcases are as follows:

(a) t is not polyinstantiated at level c prior to the update. In this case, there does not exist a tuple $u \in D_c$ with $u[A_1, C_1] = t[A_1, C_1]$. (Note that the tuple class of t must be strictly less than c.) We add a tuple u to D_c, where u is defined as follows: $u[A_1, C_1] = t[A_1, C_1]$, and for $k \neq 1$,

$$u[A_k, C_k] = \begin{cases} <s_k, c> & A_k \in \text{SET clause} \\ <?, t[C_k]> & A_k \notin \text{SET clause} \end{cases}$$

The symbol "?" is a special symbol that can never be an actual value for an attribute. It plays an important role during recovery, as we will see in a moment. Informally, a "?" means that this value is to be obtained from the corresponding tuple in

$$D_{t[C_k]}$$

(b) t is polyinstantiated at level c prior to the update. In this case, there will be one or more tuples $u \in D_c$ that satisfy the condition $u[A_1, C_1] = t[A_1, C_1]$, and for $k \neq 1$, (i) if $t[C_l] = c$, then $u[A_i, C_l] = t[A_i, C_l]$ and (ii) if $t[C_l] < c$, then $u[A_i, C_l] = <?, t[C_l]>$. For each tuple u that satisfies this condition, we replace u by the following tuple u': $u'[A_1, C_1] = u[A_1, C_1]$, and for $k \neq 1$,

$$u'[A_k, C_k] = \begin{cases} <s_k, c> & A_k \in \text{SET clause} \\ u[A_k, C_k] & A_k \notin \text{SET clause} \end{cases}$$

The DELETE statement. Finally, suppose a c-user executes the DELETE statement given earlier, and as a result all tuples t that satisfy the predicate p and $t[TC] = c$ are deleted from R_c. In terms of the decomposition, for each such t, we delete from D_c the tuple u that satisfies the following condition: $u[A_1, C_1] = t[A_1, C_1]$, and for $k \neq 1$, (i) if $t[C_i] = c$, then $u[A_i, C_i] = t[A_i, C_i]$ and (ii) if $t[C_i] < c$, then $u[A_i, C_i] = <?, t[C_i]>$.

Summary. To summarize, whenever a c-user updates the instance R_c, all changes are confined to the underlying base relation D_c. These changes leave ripple marks on $R_{c'>c}$, but this is accomplished when an $R_{c'>c}$ is constructed using the recovery algorithm described next.

Recovery algorithm. We are now prepared to give the recovery algorithm. To recover the instance R_c at an access class c, the following steps are taken:

1. Form the union $\bigcup_{c' \leq c} D_{c'}$. Extend each tuple t in the result by appending to it its tuple class computed as $t[TC] = \text{lub}\{t[C_i]: i = 1, ..., n\}$. Call the end result R_c.

2. Next, apply the following *key deletion rule* to R_c:

   Let $t_1 \in R_c$ be such that $t_1[C_1] < c$ and R_c does not contain a t_2 such that $t_2[A_1, C_1] = t_1[A_1, C_1]$ and $t_2[TC] = t_1[C_1]$. Then we delete t_1 from R_c. If $t_1[TC] = c$, then we delete t_1 from D_c as well.
   (Comment: The motivation for the key deletion rule is that a low user has deleted the tuple key. We therefore delete all higher tuples with that low key as well. Clearly t_1 is no longer needed, and its elimination amounts to garbage collection. We could alternately place tuples such as t_1 in a separate relation and have them examined by a suitably cleared subject before physically purging them from the database.)

3. Apply the following *?-replacement rule* to R_c:

   Let t be a tuple in R_c with $t[A_k] = $ "?." There are two cases:

   (a) There is a tuple $u \in R_c$ with $u[A_1, C_1] = t[A_1, C_1]$ and $TC[u] = t[C_k]$. In this case, we replace "?" in $t[A_k]$ by $u[A_k]$.

   (b) There does not exist a tuple $u \in R_c$ with $t[A_1, C_1] = u[A_1, C_1]$ and $TC[u] = t[C_k]$. In this case, we replace "?" by "Null" in $t[A_k]$.

4. Finally, make R_c subsumption free by removing all tuples s such that for some $t \in R_c$ and for all $i = 1, ..., n$ either (i) $t[A_i, s_i] = s[A_i, s_i]$ or (ii) $t[A_i] \neq$ Null and $s[A_i] =$ Null.

Examples. In this section, we give several examples to illustrate the update semantics as well as the decomposition and recovery algorithms.

The INSERT statement. To illustrate how the INSERT statement works, consider SOD_U and D_U as shown in Figure 28. Suppose a U-user wishes to insert a second tuple into SOD_U. He does so by executing the following INSERT statement:

```
INSERT
INTO      SOD
VALUES    ('Voy', 'Exp', 'Mars')
```

As a result of the above INSERT statement, SOD_U and D_U will change to the relations shown in Figure 29. If we wish to recover SOD_U, after step 1 of the recovery algorithm, SOD_U is identical to D_U of Figure 29. Since steps 2, 3, and 4 of the recovery algorithm make no changes to SOD_U, we have the desired result.

SHIP		OBJ		DEST		TC
Ent	U	Exp	U	Talos	U	U

SHIP		OBJ		DEST	
Ent	U	Exp	U	Talos	U

Figure 28. SOD_U and D_U.

SHIP		OBJ		DEST		TC
Ent	U	Exp	U	Talos	U	U
Voy	U	Exp	U	Mars	U	U

SHIP		OBJ		DEST	
Ent	U	Exp	U	Talos	U
Voy	U	Exp	U	Mars	U

Figure 29. SOD_U and D_U after INSERT.

The UPDATE statement. To illustrate the effect of an UPDATE statement, consider the instance SOD_U and the corresponding base relation D_U, given in Figure 30. Let the instance SOD_S be identical to SOD_U, in which case D_S is empty, as shown in Figure 31. Suppose an S-user makes the following update to SOD_S:

```
UPDATE SOD
SET      DEST = 'Rigel'
WHERE    SHIP = 'Ent'
```

Using the update semantics, SOD$_S$ will have one tuple, as shown in Figure 32, and by step 1 of the decomposition algorithm, D$_S$, which was empty prior to this update, will have a single tuple, call it u, as shown in Figure 32. Notice that u contains the pair <?, U>, which indicates that during the recovery "?" is to be replaced by the attribute value in the corresponding U-tuple. Specifically, let us use the recovery algorithm to reconstruct SOD$_S$. The first step of the algorithm forms the union of relations D$_U$ and D$_S$ in Figures 30 and 32. Since the key deletion rule does not apply, we move to step 3 (?-replacement rule) of the recovery algorithm, which will replace <?, U> in u by <Exp, U> (that is, the corresponding attribute values for 'Ent' in the lower level relation D$_U$ in Figure 30). After the union is made subsumption free (step 4), we end up with the instance SOD$_S$ in Figure 32, as desired.

SHIP		OBJ		DEST		TC
Ent	U	Exp	U	Null	U	U

SHIP		OBJ		DEST	
Ent	U	Exp	U	Null	U

Figure 30. SOD$_U$ and D$_U$.

SHIP		OBJ		DEST		TC
Ent	U	Exp	U	Null	U	U

SHIP	OBJ	DEST

Figure 31. SOD$_S$ and D$_S$.

SHIP		OBJ		DEST		TC
Ent	U	Exp	U	Rigel	S	S

SHIP		OBJ		DEST	
Ent	U	?	U	Rigel	S

Figure 32. SOD$_S$ and D$_S$ after UPDATE by S-user.

Next, suppose a U-user executes the following command against SOD$_U$, shown in Figure 30:

```
UPDATE   SOD
SET      DEST = 'Talos'
WHERE    SHIP = 'Ent'
```

As a result of this update, the decomposition algorithm only modifies D_U from the instance in Figure 30 to the one in Figure 33. Readers should verify that if we use the recovery to obtain SOD_S, we obtain the instance given in Figure 34, although no changes were made to the underlying D_S as a result of the above update. Of course, SOD_U will change to the relation shown in Figure 33.

SHIP		OBJ		DEST		TC
Ent	U	Exp	U	Talos	U	U

SHIP		OBJ		DEST	
Ent	U	Exp	U	Talos	U

Figure 33. SOD_U and D_U after UPDATE by U-user.

SHIP		OBJ		DEST		TC
Ent	U	Exp	U	Talos	U	U
Ent	U	Exp	U	Rigel	S	S

SHIP		OBJ		DEST	
Ent	U	?	U	Rigel	S

Figure 34. SOD_S and D_S after UPDATE by U-user.

SHIP		OBJ		DEST		TC
Ent	U	Exp	U	Talos	U	U
Ent	U	Spy	S	Rigel	S	S

SHIP		OBJ		DEST	
Ent	U	Spy	S	Rigel	S

Figure 35. SOD_S and D_S after UPDATE by S-user.

Finally, suppose starting with the instance SOD_S shown in Figure 34, an S-user invokes the following update:

```
UPDATE  SOD
SET     OBJ = 'Spy'
WHERE   SHIP = 'Ent' AND
        DEST = 'Rigel'
```

Using the update semantics, the SOD_S will change to the instance given in Figure 35, *not* to the instance given in Figure 36.

This follows from our underlying philosophy: We need to polyinstantiate either to close a signaling channel or to provide a cover story. In terms of the decomposition, D_S will change from the instance in Figure 34 to the one in Figure 35. We leave it to the reader to verify that the recovery algorithm operates correctly.

SHIP		OBJ		DEST		TC
Ent	U	Exp	U	Talos	U	U
Ent	U	Exp	U	Rigel	S	S
Ent	U	Spy	S	Rigel	S	S

Figure 36. A multilevel relation different from the one in Figure 35.

The DELETE statement. To illustrate how the DELETE statement works, suppose a U-user executes the following DELETE statement against the relation SOD_U shown in Figure 33 (assume S-users see the instance given in Figure 34, D_U is as in Figure 33, and D_S is as in Figure 34):

```
DELETE
FROM     SOD
WHERE    SHIP = 'Ent'
```

Following the delete semantics, not only will SOD_U become empty, but SOD_S will become empty as well. As a consequence of the above DELETE, the decomposition algorithm will make D_U in Figure 33 empty. The reader should verify that although D_S (shown in Figure 34) does not change, if we were to recover SOD_S at this point, the key deletion rule in the recovery algorithm will delete the tuple for the starship 'Ent.'

Options and extensions. As we indicated earlier, the core integrity properties do not uniquely determine how an update by a c-user to R_c should be propagated to $R_{c'>c}$, and several different options have been proposed. This section discusses the relationship between the algorithms and these options.

The algorithms can accommodate the SeaView MVD requirement [DENN87, DENN88a, LUNT90] most easily. No changes are required in the decomposition algorithm; only the recovery algorithm needs to be modified. Steps 1 and 2 of the recovery algorithm remain the same as before. Steps 3 and 4 are changed as follows:

3′. For each i, $2 \le i \le n$, repeat the following:

Whenever t_1 and t_2 are two tuples in R_c such that $t_1[A_1, C_1] = t_2[A_1, C_1]$, add to R_c tuples t_3 and t_4, defined as follows:

$$t_3[A_1, C_1] = t_1[A_1, C_1]$$
$$t_3[A_i, C_i] = t_1[A_i, C_i]$$
$$t_3[A_j, C_j] = t_2[A_j, C_j], \ 1 < j \le n, j \ne i$$
$$t_4[A_1, C_1] = t_1[A_1, C_1]$$
$$t_4[A_i, C_i] = t_2[A_i, C_i]$$
$$t_4[A_j, C_j] = t_1[A_j, C_j], \ 1 < j \le n, j \ne i$$

4'. Delete from R_c any tuple that has a "?" as a value.

5'. Step 5' is the same as step 4 of the original algorithm.

The decomposition and recovery algorithms will have to be modified to accommodate the single tuple per tuple class approach [SAND90a] or the closely related single maintenance level attribute approach adopted by the LDV model [HAIG91a, STAC90]. These modifications are straightforward.

This brings us to the dynamic MVD requirement [LUNT91]. It too will require modifications to both the decomposition and recovery algorithms along the lines discussed elsewhere [JAJO91a]. The major difference is that in the single-level relations D_c, we will sometimes require "?" for classification attributes (rather than just for data attributes, as shown earlier).

It is also possible to have a single decomposition algorithm for updates and realize the several alternate semantics discussed above (and others from the literature) by varying only the recovery algorithm.

Conclusion

In this essay, we have examined the entity integrity requirement and the semantics of various update operations in the context of multilevel relations. These concepts were suitably generalized to deal with polyinstantiation. We have also described a decomposition algorithm that breaks a multilevel relation into single-level relations and a recovery algorithm that reconstructs the original multilevel relation from the decomposed single-level relations.

We believe much interesting work remains to be done in this area [JAJO90e]. In particular, we would like to give a complete and formal set of principles that can help with design and implementation of multilevel secure relational DBMSs. Initial steps have been taken in this direction in the present essay, but more remains to be done.

Acknowledgments

This work was partially supported by the US Air Force, Rome Air Development, through subcontract #C/UB-49; D.O. No. 0042 of prime contract #F-30602-88-D-0026, Task B-O-3610, with CALSPAN-UB Research Center. We are indebted to Joe Giordano and RADC for making this work possible.

Solutions to the Polyinstantiation Problem

Sushil Jajodia, Ravi S. Sandhu, and Barbara T. Blaustein

What distinguishes a multilevel database from ordinary single-level ones? In a multilevel world, as we raise a user's clearance new facts emerge; conversely, as we lower a user's clearance some facts get hidden. Therefore, users with different clearances see different versions of reality. Moreover, these different versions must be kept coherent and consistent — both individually and relative to each other — without introducing any downward signaling channels.

The caveat of "no downward signaling channels" poses a major new problem in building multilevel secure database management systems (DBMSs) as compared with ordinary single-level DBMSs. Its considerations have led to the notion of *polyinstantiation* in multilevel relations. The need for polyinstantiation was first identified by T.H. Hinke and M. Schaefer [HINK75]; the term "polyinstantiation" was coined by the SeaView project [DENN87]. Polyinstantiation comes in several different flavors [DENN87; HAIG90a; JAJO90c, d, f; JAJO91a-c; LUNT90; LUNT90b; SAND90; SAND91; SAND92b, c]. There are significant differences among these approaches, and debate continues about the correct definition of polyinstantiation and its operational semantics. However, in each case polyinstantiation significantly complicates the semantics of multilevel relations (particularly for high users). As a result, recently some solutions have appeared that attempt to do away with polyinstantiation completely [BURN90, SAND91, WISE90]. In this essay, we carefully review how the need for polyinstantiation arises in multilevel relations, then survey methods that have been developed for dealing with it.

This essay is organized as follows. First we review the concept of polyinstantiation from an intuitive point of view, with the objective of identifying the sources of polyinstantiation. Next we present as a straw man a simple but unacceptable solution. After we introduce an example for comparison, we discuss different approaches to polyinstantiation and the architectural considerations that affect it.

What is polyinstantiation?

In this section we show by examples how polyinstantiation arises. We assume that readers are familiar with the basic concepts of the standard (single-level) as well as multilevel relations, as explained in Essay 20.

In multilevel relations, access classes can be assigned to data stored in relations in four different ways. One can assign access classes to relations, to individual tuples in a relation, to individual attributes (columns) of a relation, or to individual data elements of the tuples of a relation. Polyinstantiation does not arise explicitly when access classes are assigned to relations or individual attributes of a relation; therefore, we consider the cases when access classes are attached to tuples or the data elements themselves.

Types of polyinstantiation. A multilevel relation is said to be *polyinstantiated* when it contains two or more tuples with the same apparent primary key values [DENN87, JAJO91b]. There are two different types of polyinstantiation:

- entity polyinstantiation, and
- attribute polyinstantiation.

Entity polyinstantiation occurs when a relation contains multiple tuples with the same apparent primary key values, but having different access class values for the apparent primary key. As an example, consider the relation SOD given in Figure 1.

Starship		Objective		Destination	
Enterprise	U	Exploration	U	Talos	U
Enterprise	S	Spying	S	Rigel	S

Figure 1. A multilevel relation with entity polyinstantiation.

In Figure 1, as in most of our examples, each attribute in a tuple not only has a value but also a classification. We assume that the attribute Starship is the apparent primary key of SOD.

Now, the relation given in Figure 1 contains two tuples for the same starship Enterprise, resulting in entity polyinstantiation. These tuples can be regarded as pertaining to two different real-world entities or a single real-world entity. We cannot tell immediately by looking at the relation which is really the case.

The relation in Figure 2 illustrates attribute polyinstantiation. With attribute polyinstantiation, a relation contains two or more tuples with identical apparent primary key and the associated access class values, but having different values for one or more remaining attributes, as shown in Figure 2. In the figure, both tuples refer to a single starship Enterprise; an S-user sees different values for its objective and destination.

As we indicated, explicit polyinstantiation can occur with tuple-level labeling instead of element-level labeling. Let us consider the same example when access classes are associated with each tuple instead of each element. The S-user will see the multilevel relation shown in Figure 3.

Starship		Objective		Destination	
Enterprise	U	Exploration	U	Talos	U
Enterprise	U	Spying	S	Rigel	S

Figure 2. A multilevel relation with attribute polyinstantiation.

Starship	Objective	Destination	TC
Enterprise	Exploration	Talos	U
Enterprise	Spying	Rigel	S

Figure 3. A multilevel relation with tuple-level labeling.

Notice that with tuple-level labeling, we can no longer distinguish the entity polyinstantiation from attribute polyinstantiation. In our example relation, it is possible that both tuples relate to the same starship Enterprise; the U-tuple is merely the cover story. At the same time, it is also possible that there are two completely different starships; however, they have been given the same name, possibly by mistake.

How polyinstantiation occurs. Either type of polyinstantiation can occur in basically two different ways, which we call *visible* and *invisible* polyinstantiation for mnemonic convenience:

1. Visible polyinstantiation occurs when a high user[1] attempts to insert data in a field that already contains low data. Since overwriting the low data in place will result in a downward signaling channel, the high data is inserted by creating a new tuple to store it.

2. Invisible polyinstantiation occurs in the opposite situation, where a low user attempts to insert data in a field that already contains high data. Since rejecting the update is not a viable option because it establishes a downward signaling channel, the tuple is polyinstantiated to reflect the low update.

The next two subsections make visible and invisible polyinstantiation clearer by considering some examples. The examples illustrate attribute polyinstantiation only; examples illustrating entity polyinstantiation can be constructed similarly.

Visible polyinstantiation example. Let us now consider a concrete example to make visible and invisible polyinstantiation clearer. Consider the following relation SOD where Starship is the apparent primary key:

Starship		Objective		Destination	
Enterprise	U	Exploration	U	Null	U

Now consider the following scenario:

1. A U-user updates the destination of the Enterprise to be Talos. The relation is therefore modified as follows:

Starship		Objective		Destination	
Enterprise	U	Exploration	U	Talos	U

2. Next an S-user attempts to modify the destination of the Enterprise to be Rigel. Since we do not wish to deny entry of legitimate secret data, this update is not rejected. However, since we cannot over-

---

[1] Strictly speaking, we should be saying *subject* rather than *user*. For the most part, we will loosely use these terms interchangeably. Where the distinction is important, we will be appropriately precise.

write the destination in place because that would create a downward signaling channel, we polyinstantiate and modify the relation to appear as follows, respectively, for U- and S-users (note that U-users see no change):

Starship		Objective		Destination	
Enterprise	U	Exploration	U	Talos	U

Starship		Objective		Destination	
Enterprise	U	Exploration	U	Talos	U
Enterprise	U	Exploration	U	Rigel	S

What are we to make of the last relation above? There are at least two reasonable interpretations:

- *Cover story.* The destination of Talos may be a cover story for the real destination of Rigel. In this case, the database is accurately mimicking the duplicity of the real world. There are, however, other ways of incorporating cover stories besides polyinstantiation. For example, we may have two attributes, one for the cover-story destination and one for the real destination. Debate on the relative merits and demerits of these techniques is outside the scope of this essay.
- *Temporary inconsistency.* We may have a temporary inconsistency in the database that needs to be resolved. For instance, the inconsistency may be resolved as follows: The S-user who inserted the Rigel destination later logs in at the U level and nullifies the Talos value, so thereafter the relation appears respectively as follows to U- and S-users:

Starship		Objective		Destination	
Enterprise	U	Exploration	U	Null	U

Starship		Objective		Destination	
Enterprise	U	Exploration	U	Rigel	S

It is important to understand that this scheme does not create a downward signaling channel from one subject to another. The nullification of the destination at the U level is being done by a U-subject. One might argue that there is a downward signaling channel with a human in the loop. The human is, however, trusted not to let the channel be exercised without good cause. The real threat is to entity integrity: The U-user who executed step 1 of the scenario may again try to enter Talos as the destination, which brings us within the scope of invisible polyinstantiation.

Invisible polyinstantiation example. Our example for invisible poly-instantiation is similar to the visible polyinstantiation example, with the difference that the two update operations occur in the opposite order. So again consider the following relation SOD, where Starship is the apparent primary key:

Starship		Objective		Destination	
Enterprise	U	Exploration	U	Null	U

This time consider the following scenario:

1. An S-user modifies the destination of the Enterprise to be Rigel. The relation is modified to appear respectively as follows to U- and S-users (U-users see no change in the relation):

Starship		Objective		Destination	
Enterprise	U	Exploration	U	Null	U

Starship		Objective		Destination	
Enterprise	U	Exploration	U	Rigel	S

2. A U-user updates the destination of the Enterprise to be Talos. We cannot reject this update on the grounds that a secret destination for the Enterprise already exists, because that amounts to establishing a downward signaling channel. Thus we have only one of two options left. The first option is that we can overwrite the desti-

nation field in place at the cost of destroying secret data. This would give us the following relation for both U- and S-users:

Starship		Objective		Destination	
Enterprise	U	Exploration	U	Talos	U

For obvious reasons this alternative has not been seriously considered by most researchers. That leaves us the option of polyinstantiation, which will modify the relation at the end of step 1 to the following for U- and S-users respectively:

Starship		Objective		Destination	
Enterprise	U	Exploration	U	Talos	U

Starship		Objective		Destination	
Enterprise	U	Exploration	U	Talos	U
Enterprise	U	Exploration	U	Rigel	S

This is exactly the same relation as obtained at the end of step 2 in our visible polyinstantiation example. The possible interpretations are therefore similar — that is, we have either a temporary inconsistency or a cover story. The temporary inconsistency can be corrected by having a U-subject (possibly created by an S-user logged in at the U level) nullify the Talos destination. But the inconsistency may recur again and again.

A simple but unacceptable solution to polyinstantiation

There are two obvious "secure" alternatives to both visible and invisible polyinstantiations. These alternatives are secure in the sense of secrecy and information flow, and preserve primary key requirements in multi-level relations; but unfortunately, they suffer from denial-of-service and other integrity problems:

1. Whenever a high user makes an update that violates the uniqueness requirement, we simply refuse that update.

2. Whenever a low user makes a change that conflicts with the uniqueness requirement, the conflicting high data is overwritten in place by the low data.

It is not difficult to see that this simple solution preserves the uniqueness requirement in multilevel relations. This solution is secure in the sense of secrecy and information flow. It is our view that while this solution may be acceptable in some specific situations, it is clearly unacceptable as a general solution; it can lead to serious denial-of-service and integrity problems. Therefore, we now look for other alternatives that do not suffer from these problems.

An example

The next section will describe several solutions to the polyinstantiation dilemma. Some allow polyinstantiation in multilevel relations, while others seek to eliminate polyinstantiation completely. To help in appreciation of the differences among various solutions, this section develops an example in more detail. Consider once again the relation SOD, which has three attributes: Starship, Objective, and Destination, with Starship being the primary key.

If we were living in a single-level world, for each starship there would be at most one tuple in this relation giving us that starship's unique objective and unique destination. For example, the tuple <Enterprise, Exploration, Talos> would denote that the starship Enterprise has set out to explore Talos. We say that this entire tuple gives us the mission of the Enterprise.

Next consider a multilevel relation that attempts to represent the same information — that is, the objective and destination of a starship — but in a multilevel world where some facts are classified. Assume that there are just two levels, U for unclassified and S for secret. To further simplify the example, let us say the Starship attribute is always unclassified. Therefore, the classification range of the Starship attribute has lower and upper bounds of U. On the other hand, let the classification range of the Objective and Destination attributes have a lower bound of U and an upper bound of S. Let us call the resulting schema SOD, which is summarized in Figure 4. In this section, we will, for convenience, augment a relation scheme with a tuple class or TC attribute. This attribute is computed to be the least upper bound of the classifications of the individual data elements in the tuple. Thus, the value of TC gives the classification of the entire tuple.

The apparent primary key of SOD is specified as Starship. Intuitively this means that if only unclassified data is stored in SOD, then Starship would be the actual primary key of the relation. Similarly, if only secret data is stored in the Objective and Destination attributes, Starship would be the actual primary key. On the other hand, if a mix of secret and unclassified data is stored in these attributes, the actual primary key of SOD is Starship along with the attribute classifications. Instance 8 of Figure 5 contains four tuples for the starship Enterprise. What makes each tuple distinct is the classification of the Objective and Destination attributes.

Attribute	Classification Range
Starship	[U, U]
Objective	[U, S]
Destination	[U, S]
Tuple class (TC)	[U, S]

Figure 4. Schema for the multilevel relation SOD.

An instance of SOD is likely to contain different tuples at different levels. Therefore, it is important to distinguish between the U-instance of SOD, visible to Unclassified users, and the S-instance, visible to Secret users. As a user's clearance increases, it is reasonable to keep all previously visible information intact and perhaps add some new facts visible only at that level. To be concrete, consider the U-instance of SOD given in Figure 6. It contains exactly one tuple, telling us that, as far as Unclassified users are concerned, the starship Enterprise has set out to explore Talos. The eight different S-instances of SOD enumerated in Figure 5 are all consistent with the U-instance of Figure 6. Their common property is that the single tuple of the U-instance appears in all eight S-instances. We regard each tuple in an instance of SOD as defining a mission for the starship in question. A U-instance of SOD allows only one mission per starship. S-instances, on the other hand, allow up to four missions per starship, three of which are secret and one unclassified.

We now demonstrate there is a practically useful and intuitively reasonable interpretation for each of the eight S-instances of Figure 5. Consider each S-instance in turn, as follows:

1. *The S-instance is identical to the U-instance.* There is therefore no secret aspect to the Enterprise. This is the simplest case and needs little explanation.

No.	Starship		Objective		Destination		TC
1	Enterprise	U	Exploration	U	Talos	U	U
2	Enterprise	U	Exploration	U	Talos	U	U
	Enterprise	U	Spying	S	Talos	U	S
3	Enterprise	U	Exploration	U	Talos	U	U
	Enterprise	U	Exploration	U	Rigel	S	S
4	Enterprise	U	Exploration	U	Talos	U	U
	Enterprise	U	Spying	S	Rigel	S	S
5	Enterprise	U	Exploration	U	Talos	U	U
	Enterprise	U	Exploration	U	Rigel	S	S
	Enterprise	U	Spying	S	Rigel	S	S
6	Enterprise	U	Exploration	U	Talos	U	U
	Enterprise	U	Spying	S	Talos	U	S
	Enterprise	U	Spying	S	Rigel	S	S
7	Enterprise	U	Exploration	U	Talos	U	U
	Enterprise	U	Spying	S	Talos	U	S
	Enterprise	U	Exploration	U	Rigel	S	S
8	Enterprise	U	Exploration	U	Talos	U	U
	Enterprise	U	Spying	S	Talos	U	S
	Enterprise	U	Exploration	U	Rigel	S	S
	Enterprise	U	Spying	S	Rigel	S	S

Figure 5. Eight S-instances of SOD.

Starship		Objective		Destination		TC
Enterprise	U	Exploration	U	Talos	U	U

Figure 6. A U-instance of SOD.

In each of the next three cases there is a single tuple in the S-instance in addition to the tuple of the U-instance. This secret tuple defines a secret mission for the Enterprise in addition to its unclassified mission.

2. *The S-instance reveals the secret mission to be spying on Talos.* Presumably, the unclassified exploration mission to Talos is a cover story to hide the secret spying mission. To maintain the integrity of the cover story, the Enterprise will probably expend resources on exploring Talos. Conceivably, the bulk of its resources might be devoted to useful exploration of Talos, with the secret spying mission added on as a low-profile, low-marginal-cost, and opportunistic effort. We obviously cannot resolve this issue without further knowledge about the real situation, such as a competent user might have. The main point is that the Enterprise does have two distinct missions: the unclassified one of exploring Talos and the secret one of spying there.

3. *The S-instance reveals the secret mission to be exploration of Rigel.* This case is very similar to the previous one in that only one attribute has a secret value. Clearly the desire to explore Rigel under cover of exploring Talos is a realistic one, not only in the national security arena but also in a competitive commercial context.

4. *The S-instance reveals the secret mission to be spying on Rigel.* This case is similar to the previous two in that there is only one secret mission. It is different in that the objective and destination of the secret mission are now both classified.

Each of the three preceding cases presents a distinctly different secret mission — secretly spying on Talos, secretly exploring Rigel, and secretly spying on Rigel. These three secret missions do share the common property that exploring Talos is an acceptable unclassified cover story. The next three cases present situations where two of these three secret missions are concurrently in progress.

5. *The S-instance reveals two secret missions: to explore Rigel and to spy on Rigel.* Both secret missions are concerned with Rigel. Whether the principal one is to explore it or spy there, or the two missions are equally important, cannot be ascertained without further information. The secret exploration of Rigel may simply be a convenient damage-control story, should the secret destination of the Enterprise be leaked. Conversely, spying on Rigel may be an opportunistic and relatively unimportant add-on to its secret exploration.

6. *The S-instance reveals two secret missions: to spy on Talos and to spy on Rigel.* This is similar to the previous case, and once again we cannot a priori decide which, if any, is the principal secret mission.

7. *The S-instance reveals two secret missions: to spy on Talos and to explore Rigel.* This may appear strange at first, but it is perfectly proper. For instance, there may be no life-forms on Rigel worth

spying on, while there are indications of vast quantities of uranium. This S-instance does point out problems with simple rules such as "give the value with the highest classification for each attribute." Such a rule would manufacture the secret mission of spying on Rigel, which does not exist in the relation.

As the reader may have guessed by now, our final S-instance specifies that the three secret missions identified in instances 2, 3, and 4 are all concurrently in progress.

8. *The S-instance reveals three secret missions: to spy on Talos, to explore Rigel, and to spy on Rigel.* As before, without further information and knowledge, we cannot say very much about the relation of these three secret missions to one another. All we know is that they share the same cover story of exploring Talos.

To summarize, the eight S-instances of SOD can be partitioned into three classes as follows:

1. Instance 1 has no polyinstantiation and is therefore straightforward.
2. Instances 2, 3, and 4 are also relatively straightforward. Instance 2 has a cover story for the objective, but the U destination is correct. Instance 3, on the other hand, has a cover story for the destination, while the objective is correct. Instance 4 has a cover story for both the destination and the objective.
3. Instances 5, 6, 7, and 8 are confusing to interpret if it is assumed that the higher level data correctly represent the real world. Nonetheless, it is possible to give a meaningful and consistent interpretation and update semantics for both the objective and the destination.

Solutions to the polyinstantiation problem

There are a number of different approaches to implementing polyinstantiation in a database management system, reflecting divergent perspectives on the meaning and uses of polyinstantiation within an MLS environment. Each approach has its proponents and detractors, and each is suited to particular types of applications. It is not our intent to promote certain approaches or to dismiss others, but instead to discuss the perspective motivating each of them. It is our belief that different organizations and real-world enterprises will choose to model their understandings of multilevel data in distinct ways. Our goal here is to present multiple approaches and their rationales so that each organization can choose the most appropriate implementation for its requirements.

This section starts with approaches that view polyinstantiation (and the concomitant addition of tuples) as an integral part of an MLS database. Next, the section presents strategies that compose new tuples to answer queries based on the security levels of underlying tuples. Finally, it discusses approaches that include explicit restrictions on users' views of data.

Propagation of polyinstantiated tuples. One perspective on dealing with the tension between multilevel security and data semantics is to regard polyinstantiation as an inevitable and integral part of multilevel secure information. Users at different security levels may see different attribute values for the same real-world tuple (for example, secret versus unclassified objectives for the same starship), and the users must be allowed to update these values differently. This perspective leads to an approach to polyinstantiation in which new tuples are added to reflect the combinatorial explosion of attribute values. For simplicity, we will call this approach the *propagation approach* to polyinstantiation.

The propagation approach faces two key challenges:

1. ensuring that keys still function to identify distinct real-world entities, and
2. controlling the propagation of tuples to include only meaningful combinations of attribute values.

The first challenge is met by augmenting the apparent key with a security level and enforcing the standard key uniqueness property over this augmented key. The second challenge is more complex, and researchers are still debating which types of combinations are meaningful. In general, multivalued dependencies [DATE83] are used to define the particular combinations allowed by a specific solution. While many variants are possible, the SeaView project [DENN87; DENN88a, b; LUNT89c; LUNT90; LUNT90b] and the modifications proposed by Jajodia and Sandhu [JAJO90c] provide the basis of this approach. First we present the original SeaView approach, then Jajodia and Sandhu's proposed modification, and finally some new techniques proposed by the SeaView project.

The SeaView project began as a joint effort by SRI International and Gemini Computers with the goal of designing and prototyping an MLS relational database management system that satisfies the Trusted Computer System Evaluation Criteria for class A1 [DOD85]. Currently the project is in the final phase of a prototype implementation using GEMSOS as the underlying trusted computing base, along with the Oracle relational DBMS [LUNT90].

SeaView solves the problem of polyinstantiation of key attributes themselves by defining an entity integrity property. This property requires all attributes in a key to be uniformly classified. That is, for any instance R_c of a multilevel relation schema, for any tuple $t \in R_c$, and for any attributes A_i and A_j in the apparent primary key K_R of R, $t[C_i] = t[C_j]$. Notice that this means it is possible simply to define a single attribute C_K to represent the classification level of all attributes in the apparent primary key. Further, no tuples may have null values for key attributes. This restriction ensures that keys can be meaningfully specified and checked for uniqueness. In addition, all nonkey classification attributes must dominate C_K. This restriction guarantees that if a user can see any part of a tuple, then he or she can see the key.

To meet the first challenge, that of using keys to determine when tuples model distinct real-world entities, SeaView defines a polyinstantiation integrity property. The formulation of polyinstantiation integrity in SeaView consists of two distinct parts. The first part consists of a functional dependency component whose effect is to prohibit polyinstantiation within the same access class. The second part consists of a multivalued dependency requirement.

SeaView polyinstantiation integrity property. A multilevel relation R_c satisfies polyinstantiation integrity (PI) if and only if for every R_c there are for all $A_i \in K_R$

1. $K_R, C_K, C_i \rightarrow A_i$
2. $K_R, C_K \rightarrow\rightarrow A_i, C_i$

The PI property can be regarded as implicitly defining what is meant by the primary key in a multilevel relation. The primary key of a multilevel relation is $K_R \cup C_K \cup C_R$ (where C_R is the set of classification attributes for data attributes not in K_R), since from PI it follows that the functional dependency $K_R \rightarrow A_R$ holds (where A_R consists of all attributes that are not in K_R).

Of the eight instances defined in Figure 5, this definition of polyinstantiation integrity allows *only two* combinations of these eight instances within a single relation scheme [JAJO90c]. Specifically, a SeaView relation can accommodate either instances 1, 2, 3, and 8 or instances 1 and 4 within a single scheme in the absence of the uniform classification constraint. SeaView admits only instances 1 and 4 if the Objective and Destination attributes are uniformly classified (that is, either both are classified U or both S).

The inclusion of the multivalued dependency in the definition of polyinstantiation integrity means that one update may result in a number of tuples being added to the relation. To illustrate, consider the situation in which an S-user attempts to go from S-instance 1 to S-instance 4 in Figure 5 by inserting the secret tuple specifying the secret mission of spying on Rigel. SeaView will interpret this as a request to go from S-instance 1 to S-instance 8, thereby manufacturing two additional missions for the Enterprise. Unfortunately, this increases the potential for such additional information, which may not reflect true data, to be retrieved from the database by users with higher clearances.

It is easy to see that, in the worst case, the number of manufactured tuples grows at the rate of $|\text{security-lattice}|^k$, where k is the number of nonkey attributes in the relation. For example, Figure 7 shows a TS-instance of a relation similar to SOD, except that it has a range of four security levels for the Objective and Destination attributes. The particular TS instance shown describes four missions for the Enterprise, one each at the unclassified, confidential, secret, and top-secret levels. The definition of polyinstantiation integrity in SeaView requires that this information be represented by the 16 missions shown in Figure 8. Users with clearances U, C, S, and TS will respectively see 1, 4, 9, and 16 missions with the SeaView approach.

Starship		Objective		Destination		TC
Enterprise	U	Exploration	U	Talos	U	U
Enterprise	U	Mining	C	Sirius	C	C
Enterprise	U	Spying	S	Rigel	S	S
Enterprise	U	Coup	TS	Orion	TS	TS

Figure 7. A TS-instance of SOD with four missions.

Jajodia and Sandhu [JAJO90c] proposed dropping the multivalued dependency from the polyinstantiation integrity property defined in the SeaView model. They argued that the multivalued dependency prohibits the existence of relation instances desirable in practice. Specifically, it is possible to accommodate all eight instances of Figure 5. Jajodia and Sandhu also gave formal operational semantics for update operations in multilevel relations [JAJO91b, c].

Based on this proposal, the SeaView team began a reexamination of the SeaView definition of polyinstantiation integrity. Lunt and Hsieh [LUNT90b] developed a semantics for the basic database manipulation operations (insert, update, and delete). Based on these semantics, they proposed a different definition for polyinstantiation integrity consisting of two separate pieces: a state property containing the same functional dependency component and a transition property concerning a new dynamic multivalued dependency component. Although Lunt and Hsieh do not define the latter property precisely, the basic idea can be illustrated informally by way of an example from their work [LUNT90b].

Consider the multilevel relation scheme $R(A_1, C_1, A_2, C_2, A_3, C_3, TC)$, where each A_i is an attribute, each C_i is the classification attribute for A_i, and TC is the tuple class attribute. The attribute A_1 is the apparent primary key of R. An instance R_c at a classification level c is assumed to satisfy the two constraints of the PI property.

Starship		Objective		Destination		TC
Enterprise	U	Exploration	U	Talos	U	U
Enterprise	U	Exploration	U	Sirius	C	C
Enterprise	U	Mining	C	Talos	U	C
Enterprise	U	Mining	C	Sirius	C	C
Enterprise	U	Exploration	U	Rigel	S	S
Enterprise	U	Mining	C	Rigel	S	S
Enterprise	U	Spying	S	Talos	U	S
Enterprise	U	Spying	S	Sirius	C	S
Enterprise	U	Spying	S	Rigel	S	S
Enterprise	U	Exploration	U	Orion	TS	TS
Enterprise	U	Mining	C	Orion	TS	TS
Enterprise	U	Spying	S	Orion	TS	TS
Enterprise	U	Coup	TS	Talos	U	TS
Enterprise	U	Coup	TS	Sirius	C	TS
Enterprise	U	Coup	TS	Rigel	S	TS
Enterprise	U	Coup	TS	Orion	TS	TS

Figure 8. The SeaView materialization with 16 missions.

Now, consider the following relation instance R_U:

A_1	C_1	A_2	C_2	A_3	C_3	TC
a	U	b	U	x	U	U

Suppose a Confidential user changes the value of A_2 to d, as shown here:

A_1	C_1	A_2	C_2	A_3	C_3	TC
a	U	b	U	x	U	U
a	U	d	C	x	U	C

Under Lunt and Hsieh's update semantics, whenever an update involves some, but not all, of the nonkey attributes, certain dynamic multivalued dependencies are enforced in the multilevel relations. In the example, the dynamic multivalued dependencies are

$$A_1, C_1 \rightarrow\rightarrow A_2, C_2 \mid A_3, C_3$$

where the notation $X \rightarrow\rightarrow Y \mid Z$ denotes the multivalued dependencies $X \rightarrow\rightarrow Y$ and $X \rightarrow\rightarrow Z$.

Next, suppose a Top Secret user updates the value of A_3 to equal v. As before, since this update involves some (but not all) of the nonkey attributes, the dynamic multivalued dependency property causes two more tuples to be added to the relation:

A_1	C_1	A_2	C_2	A_3	C_3	TC
a	U	b	U	x	U	U
a	U	d	C	x	U	C
a	U	b	U	v	TS	TS
a	U	d	C	v	U	TS

At this point suppose a Secret user changes the value of the second attribute to q. The following relation instance results:

A_1	C_1	A_2	C_2	A_3	C_3	TC
a	U	b	U	x	U	U
a	U	d	C	x	U	C
a	U	b	U	v	TS	TS
a	U	d	C	v	U	TS
a	U	q	S	x	U	TS
a	U	d	C	v	U	TS

According to Lunt and Hsieh [LUNT90b], the way in which an update occurs determines whether or not the multivalued dependency should be enforced. Essentially, if two or more attributes were updated in a single update statement, the multivalued dependency would not be enforced. However, if the two attributes were updated in two independent operations, the multivalued dependency would be enforced.

This dynamic approach is not yet formalized, nor is it being incorporated in the SeaView prototype.

Derived values. A second perspective on polyinstantiation is that although a multilevel relation may have several tuples for the same real-world entity, there should be only one such tuple per classification level. Instead of a classification level C_i for each attribute A_i, the schema R_c includes a single classification level for each tuple, TC. When a user wants to update only certain attributes at a particular level, the values of the other attributes are derived from values at lower security levels.

Consider the following relation SOD where Starship is the key:

Starship	Objective	Destination	TC
Enterprise	Exploration	Talos	U

Now suppose an S-user wishes to modify the destination of the Enterprise to be Rigel. He or she can simply do so by inserting a new secret tuple to SOD, as follows:

$$(\text{Enterprise}, \hat{U}, \text{Rigel}, S)$$

The symbol $\hat{U}$ is to be interpreted as follows: For this S-tuple, the value of the Objective field is identical to the corresponding value in the U-tuple of SOD. As a consequence, when an S-user asks for the SOD relation to be materialized, he or she will see the following:

Starship	Objective	Destination	TC
Enterprise	Exploration	Talos	U
Enterprise	Exploration	Rigel	S

The relation will appear unchanged to the U-user.

The Lock Data Views (LDV) project [HAIG90a] follows this *derived data approach*. The derived data approach has been implemented for the US Transportation Command Air Mobility Command MLS Global Decision Support System (GDSS) [NELS91]. This implementation, the MLS GDSS, limits polyinstantiation in a multilevel relation to at most one tuple per security class. Information is labeled at one of two levels, U or S. The design is based on the organization's assumption that when S and U data are integrated into a single S response the S data takes precedence over the U data. This design can be extended to environments with more than two strictly ordered security levels. Organizations for which this strict hierarchical rule does not apply, such as those with many compartmented environments, would have to incorporate substantial changes into this design in order to use it.

In the MLS GDSS application, trusted application software functionally extends the commercial off-the-shelf (COTS) MLS DBMS to manage tuple-level polyinstantiation. Before inserting an S-tuple, the trusted software ensures that a U-tuple exists with the same key. If it does not exist, the insertion of an S-tuple is not permitted. If a U-tuple with the same apparent primary key does exist, the trusted application software examines each S-tuple attribute value, except the apparent key value, and determines if it replicates the attribute's value in the U-tuple. If so, the value is not replicated in the S-tuple but instead is set to null, minimizing data replication. The U-tuple thus serves as the foundation upon which the S-tuple is built. The MLS GDSS solution is best explained with several examples.

Consider the following relation:

Starship	Objective	Destination	TC
Enterprise	Exploration	Talos	U

Now suppose an S-user wishes to modify the destination of the Enterprise to Rigel. The S-user directs the system, through the trusted software, to insert an S-tuple into the SOD, as follows:

S-USER:

      Insert into
      (Starship, Objective, Destination)
      Values ('Enterprise', 'Exploration', 'Rigel')

The U- and S-tuples are now stored in the relation as:

Starship	Objective	Destination	TC
Enterprise	Exploration	Talos	U
Enterprise	Null	Rigel	S

Reducing the replication of data across polyinstantiated tuples improves the probability of maintaining the integrity of the database. Additionally, except for the key value, the sensitivity levels of all attribute values contained within the stored tuple are equivalent to the TC value. Given this equivalence to the TC value, trusted application software derives attribute value labels from the TC value. Users operating at the U level are presented with a display showing the derived attribute value labels, as follows:

Starship		Objective		Destination	
Enterprise	U	Exploration	U	Talos	U

Users operating at the S level are presented with a single composite display of a materialized tuple. This materialized tuple comprises S and U data, as follows:

Starship		Objective		Destination	
Enterprise	U	Exploration	U	Rigel	S

One of the major impacts of the polyinstantiation approach as implemented in the MLS GDSS involves the DBMS join operator at the S level. Figure 9 illustrates the simplest form of the problem. A typical join operation between two tables matches and retrieves rows based on the primary key Starship. To retrieve data residing at the same security level and thus permit proper collapsing of the rows into a materialized tuple, the join is further qualified by the row's security label attribute TC:

S-USER:

```
Select *
FROM Table1, Table2
where Table1.Starship = Table2.Starship
and Table1.TC = Table2.TC
```

Case 1:

Starship	Objective	Destination	TC
Enterprise	Exploration	Talos	U
Enterprise	Null	Rigel	S

Starship	Type	Propulsion	TC
Enterprise	Starship	Photon	U
Enterprise	Battlestar	Queller drive	S

Starship		Objective		Destination		Type		Propulsion	
Enterprise	U	Exploration	U	Rigel	S	Battlestar	S	Queller drive	S

Case 2:

Starship	Objective	Destination	TC
Enterprise	Exploration	Talos	U
Enterprise	Null	Rigel	S

Starship	Type	Propulsion	TC
Enterprise	Starship	Photon	U

Starship		Objective		Destination		Type		Propulsion	
Enterprise	U	Exploration	U	Talos	U	Starship	U	Photon	U

Figure 9. Joins in GDSS.

An important functional requirement in the MLS GDSS is that S-users expect to see S data as the end product of a retrieval, if S data exists; otherwise, U data is returned. Case 1 in Figure 9 shows a join between two tables that produces the correct materialized tuple for an S-user. Case 2 illustrates the anomaly associated with the join. In this case, the second table contains only U data. Since the query requires that the tuple labels match, the query does not return the S row of the first table joined with the U row of the second table. Thus, if data does not exist at the same security levels in each table, then S information may be lost during the join operation.

In this simplified example, one might argue that removing the qualification that the tables be joined by tuple labels would permit joins. Doing this would return two rows in Case 2, one containing only U information, the other containing S and U information. If this approach were taken, the tuple materialization process would become more complex and would need to extract multiple tuple labels and assign them to the appropriate columns in the row that was returned. Also, the join example shown in Case 1 would result in four rows of data returned from the server, instead of just two. The complexity of the problem and the work required of the DBMS server would increase significantly as more tables were joined. Database server performance would decrease accordingly, perhaps to unacceptable levels.

To ensure the correct materialization of a logical joined tuple, the MLS GDSS system does not currently use the join capabilities of the COTS MLS DBMS. Instead, tuples are selected from individual tables, and then joined outside the DBMS by trusted application software. While this operation does result in some processing overhead, it ensures that data are not accidentally excluded from the S-user.

Visible restrictions. The third perspective on polyinstantiation is that users are aware that data are restricted to certain levels. In practice, this means users know the levels of data that they can see and update. The goal is to provide a more "honest" database without compromising security. This perspective can lead to many different strategies; this section presents four different approaches.

The belief approach. One approach to polyinstantiation is motivated by the idea that data at each level reflects the "beliefs" of users at that level about the real world [KENS92]. For simplicity, we will call this work the *belief approach.* The belief approach differentiates between data that a user sees and data that a user believes. Updates reflect beliefs about the real world; they are regulated by the following property:

> *Update access property:* Data at a particular level can be inserted, modified, or deleted only by users at that level.

Thus, data at each level reflects the beliefs of the users who maintain it. Users can see the data that they believe as well as data believed by users at lower levels (that is, users see all data that they could read under the Bell-LaPadula model).

At the heart of this property is a model that takes a stand between entity- and attribute-level polyinstantiation. Keys may be classified at a different level than other attributes within the same tuple, but all nonkey attributes within a single tuple share a classification level.

Given a relation schema R, the multilevel relation R_c used in the belief model includes two additional classification attributes: a key classification level (K_c) and a tuple classification level (T_c). The model imposes two restrictions:

1. In any tuple, T_c must dominate K_c.
2. For the set of key attributes K and for all nonkey attributes A_i, ..., A_n in R_c,

$$K, K_c, T_c \rightarrow A_i, ..., A_n$$

Intuitively, then, tuples with the same values for key attributes but different key classification levels refer to different real-world entities. Tuples that are identical in key attributes and key classification levels but differ in tuple classification levels represent different beliefs about the same real-world entities. To maintain this distinction, users at a particular level are not allowed to reuse key attribute values for new entities.

Given the relation SOD in Figure 10, U-users believe the first and second tuples. C-users believe the third tuple, and S-users believe the fourth and fifth tuples. The second and third tuples in Figure 10 refer to the same real-world starship, but U- and C-users have different beliefs about its objective and destination. The first and fifth tuples refer to different starships.

Starship	K_c	Objective	Destination	T_c
Voyager	U	Shipping	Mars	U
Enterprise	U	Exploration	Vulcan	U
Enterprise	U	Diplomacy	Romulus	C
Zardor	S	Warfare	Romulus	S
Voyager	S	Spying	Rigel	S

Figure 10. Example of SOD in the belief model.

U-users can see only the first two tuples in Figure 10, C-users can see the first three tuples, and S-users can see all five tuples.

Although users are allowed to see all tuples at levels dominated by their belief levels, the query language includes the optional keyword BELIEVED BY to allow users to further restrict queries. Thus, S-users can ask to see all allowable tuples, or only those believed by C- and S-users, and so on.

The query "Display the destination of all starships named Enterprise" is expressed as

```
SELECT        Destination
FROM          SOD
WHERE         Starship = 'Enterprise'
BELIEVED BY   ANYONE
```

The result of this query when issued against the relation in Figure 10 is

Destination	TC
Vulcan	U

for a U-user, and

Destination	TC
Vulcan	U
Romulus	C

for all users at levels C or higher.

The query "Display the beliefs of U-users as to the destination of all starships named Enterprise" is expressed as

```
SELECT        Destination
FROM          SOD
WHERE         Starship = 'Enterprise'
BELIEVED BY   U
```

The result of this query when issued against the relation in Figure 10 is

Destination	TC
Vulcan	U

for all users.

The query "Display the classification level and destination of all starships named Voyager" is expressed as

```
SELECT        K_c, Destination
FROM          SOD
WHERE         Starship = "Voyager"
BELIEVED BY   ANYONE
```

The result of this query when issued against the relation in Figure 10 is

K_c	Destination	T_c
U	Mars	U

for U- and C-users, and

K_c	Destination	T_c
U	Mars	U
S	Rigel	S

for all users at levels S or higher.

The insert-low approach. Another variation of explicit restriction, the insert-low approach, has been adopted by the SWORD project at the Royal Signals and Radar Establishment in England [WISE90]. Briefly, this approach works as follows.

Each relation is assigned at the time of its creation a *table usage classification*, abbreviated as table class. Each attribute is assigned a *column classification* that must dominate the table class. The purpose of the table class is twofold: First, any insertion or deletion of tuples in a relation can be made by those users whose clearances equal the table class of the relation. Second, the table class controls exactly how the updates involving an access class that dominates the table class are made to the relation. This will be explained in greater detail below.

Consider once again the relation schema SOD. Say the table classification of SOD is U. A typical instance of SOD is given as follows:

Starship		Objective		Destination	
Enterprise	U	Exploration	U	Talos	U
Voyager	U	Spying	S	Rigel	TS

In this case, SWORD will show the entire relation to TS-users, while for those at lower levels SWORD will substitute <not cleared> whenever a user has insufficient clearance to view a value. Thus, for example, a C-user will see the following instance:

Starship		Objective		Destination	
Enterprise	U	Exploration	U	Talos	U
Voyager	U	<not cleared>	S	<not cleared>	TS

To see how SWORD avoids tuple polyinstantiation, consider once again the relation SOD with U as its table class. Suppose the initial database state is as follows:

Starship		Objective		Destination	
Enterprise	U	Exploration	U	Talos	U

Suppose some U-user inserts the tuple (Voyager, S, Spying, U, Talos, U) in SOD. SWORD allows lower level users to insert values at higher levels as long as the attribute value classifications are dominated by the appropriate column classification. In this example, the column classification for Starship would have to be S or higher. Furthermore, since the table classification of SOD is U, this constitutes a legal insertion, and as a result U-users and S-users will see the following states respectively:

Starship		Objective		Destination	
Enterprise	U	Exploration	U	Talos	U
<not cleared>	S	Spying	U	Talos	U

Starship		Objective		Destination	
Enterprise	U	Exploration	U	Talos	U
Voyager	S	Spying	U	Talos	U

At this point, suppose a U-user wants to make an insertion (Freedom, U, Mining, U, Mars, U) to SOD. Since the Starship attributes of all tuples in SOD are not visible to the U-user, there is always a possibility that the Starship value of the tuple to be inserted equals that of the existing high tuple, leading to attribute polyinstantiation (or tuple polyinstantiation, in the case of attributes constituting the primary key). SWORD avoids this by prohibiting U-users from inserting or modifying values in this attribute. In the case of key attributes, like Starship, this means that all further insertions by U-users are forbidden. However, since the table classification is U, only U-users can insert tuples into SOD. As a consequence, no further insertions can be made into SOD at all. In SWORD applications, then, the column classifications for all attributes constituting the primary key must equal the table class, or users may be able to prohibit future insertions.

The following instance illustrates in more detail how attribute polyinstantiation is avoided in SWORD:

Starship		Objective		Destination	
Enterprise	U	Exploration	U	Talos	U

Next, suppose a TS-user wishes to modify the destination of the Enterprise to be Rigel. This is accomplished in two steps. First, the TS-user must log in as a U-user and change the classification of Talos from U to TS. Having done so, the TS-user can log in at his level and then make the desired update. As a result, the U-instance and TS-instance will become as follows:

Starship		Objective		Destination	
Enterprise	U	Exploration	U	<not cleared>	TS

Starship		Objective		Destination	
Enterprise	U	Exploration	U	Rigel	TS

Given the database state shown immediately above, suppose an S-user wants to insert a secret destination for the Enterprise. He may do so by first logging in as a U-user, changing the classification of the attribute Destination from TS to S. As a result of this change, all users, including the TS-user, will see the following relation:

Starship		Objective		Destination	
Enterprise	U	Exploration	U	<not cleared>	S

Now, the S-user can log in at classification level S and make the appropriate change.

Prevention. The third variation of explicit restriction relies on preventing polyinstantiation completely. Jajodia and Sandhu [JAJO91d, SAND91, SAND92b] have described three basic techniques for eliminating entity polyinstantiation:

1. *Make all the keys visible.* In this method, the apparent primary key is required to be labeled at the lowest level at which a relation is visible. For example, suppose the designer requires that all keys be unclassified. Consequently, the relation

Starship		Objective		Destination		TC
Enterprise	U	Exploration	U	Talos	U	U
Enterprise	S	Spying	S	Rigel	S	S

   would be forbidden. Note that the two relations called USOD and SSOD in Figures 11 and 12 represent the same information. In other words, USOD and SSOD horizontally partition the original SOD relation, with all the U-Starships in USOD and all the S-Starships in SSOD.

2. *Partition the domain of the primary key.* Another way to eliminate entity polyinstantiation is to partition the domain of the primary key among the various access classes possible for the primary key. For our example, suppose that the application requires that starships whose names begin with A through E are unclassified, starships whose names begin with F through T are secret, and so on. Whenever a new tuple is inserted, the system enforces this requirement as an integrity constraint. In this case, the secret Enterprise must be renamed, perhaps as follows:

Starship		Objective		Destination		TC
Enterprise	U	Exploration	U	Talos	U	U
Freedom	S	Spying	S	Rigel	S	S

The DBMS can now reject any attempt by a U-user to insert a starship whose name begins with F through Z, without causing any information leakage or integrity violation.

3. *Limit insertions to be done by trusted subjects.* A third way to eliminate entity polyinstantiation is to require that all insertions are done by a system-high user, with a write-down occurring as part of the insert operation. (Strictly speaking, it is only necessary to have a relation-high user — that is, a user to whom all tuples are visible.) In the context of the example, this means that a U-user who wishes to insert the tuple (Enterprise, Exploration, Talos) must ask an S-user to do the insertion. The S-user does so by invoking a trusted subject that can check for key conflict and, if there is none, insert a U-tuple by writing down. If there is a conflict, the S-user informs the U-user about it, so the U-user can, for example, change the name of the starship to Voyager.

U-Starship		Objective		Destination		TC
Enterprise	U	Exploration	U	Talos	U	U

Figure 11. USOD.

S-Starship		Objective		Destination		TC
Enterprise	S	Spying	S	Rigel	S	S

Figure 12. SSOD.

The first approach is available in any MLS DBMS that allows a range of access classes for individual attributes (or attribute groups), by simply limiting the classification range of the apparent key to be a singleton set. The second approach is available to any DBMS that can enforce domain constraints with adequate generality. The third approach is always available but requires the use of trusted code. Note that although there is some leakage of information, it is with a human in the loop. This type of information flow cannot be completely eliminated [DOD85]. The best approach will depend on the characteristics of the MLS DBMS and the application, particularly concerning the frequency and source of insertions.

The prevention approach also proposes techniques to prevent attribute polyinstantiation without compromising on confidentiality, integrity, or denial-of-service requirements. The basic idea is to introduce a special symbol denoted by "Restricted" as the possible value of a data element. The value "Restricted" is distinct from any other value for that element and is also different from "Null." In other words, the domain of a data element is its natural domain extended with "Restricted" and "Null." Then we can define the semantics of "Restricted" so as to be able to eliminate both visible and invisible polyinstantiation [SAND91].

Consider again the visible polyinstantiation scenario presented earlier, beginning with the following relation:

Starship		Objective		Destination		TC
Enterprise	U	Exploration	U	Talos	U	U

Next, suppose an S-user attempts to modify the destination of the Enterprise to be Rigel. This update does not cause any security violation. But now suppose that the new destination is classified Secret. The prevention approach requires the S-user first to log in as a U-user[2] and to mark the destination of the Enterprise as "Restricted," giving the following relation:

Starship		Objective		Destination		TC
Enterprise	U	Exploration	U	Restricted	U	U

The meaning of <Restricted, U> is that this field can no longer be updated by an ordinary U-user.[3] U-users can therefore infer that the true value of Enterprise's destination is classified at some level not dominated by U. The S-user then logs in as an S-subject and enters the destination of the Enterprise as Rigel, giving us the following relations at the U- and S-levels respectively:

Starship		Objective		Destination		TC
Enterprise	U	Exploration	U	Restricted	U	U

---

[2] Alternately, the S-user logs in at the U level and asks some properly authorized U-user to carry out this step. Communication of this request from the S-user to U-user may also occur outside the computer system, say by direct personal communication or a secure telephone call.

[3] Only those U-users with the "unrestrict" privilege for this field can update it [SAND91].

Starship		Objective		Destination		TC
Enterprise	U	Exploration	U	Restricted	U	U
Enterprise	U	Exploration	U	Rigel	S	S

Note that this protocol does not introduce a signaling channel from an S-subject to a U-subject. There is an information flow, but from an S-user (logged in as a U-subject) to a U-subject. This is an important distinction. As mentioned in the Orange Book [DOD85], there is the possibility that subjects may themselves constitute Trojan horses. This type of information flow, which includes humans in the process, cannot be completely eliminated.

Next consider how the invisible polyinstantiation scenario presented earlier works with the restricted requirement. In this case, the Enterprise can have a secret destination only if the destination has been marked as being restricted at the unclassified level. Thus, one possibility is that the S- and U-users respectively see the following instances of SOD:

Starship		Objective		Destination		TC
Enterprise	U	Exploration	U	Restricted	U	U
Enterprise	U	Exploration	U	Rigel	S	S

Starship		Objective		Destination		TC
Enterprise	U	Exploration	U	Restricted	U	U

Alternatively, both S- and U-users may see the following instance:

Starship		Objective		Destination		TC
Enterprise	U	Exploration	U	Null	U	U

In the former event, an attempt by a U-user to update the destination of the Enterprise to Talos will be rejected, whereas in the latter event the update will be allowed (without causing polyinstantiation).

The concept of the "Restricted" mark is straightforward, so long as the classification lattice is totally ordered. In the general case of a partially ordered lattice, some subtleties arise. How to completely eliminate polyinstantiation using "Restricted" has been discussed at length elsewhere [SAND91]. In general, updating the value of an attribute to "Restricted" cannot cause polyinstantiation. On the other hand, updating the value of an attribute to a data value, say, at the C level, can be the cause of polyinstantiation. If polyinstantiation is to be completely prohibited, this update must require that the data element is restricted at all levels which do not dominate C. The fact that the data element is restricted at all levels below C can be verified by the usual integrity checking mechanisms in a DBMS [SAND91]. However, it is tricky to guarantee this at levels incomparable with C. In preparing to enter a data value at the C level, the system would need to start a system-low (really data-element-low) process, which could then write up. A protocol for this purpose has been described [SAND91].[4]

Explicit alternatives approach. The fourth approach described here allows the application developer to choose among explicit alternatives for polyinstantiation. Sandhu and Jajodia [SAND92c] brought together a number of their previously published ideas, along with some new ones, to define a particular semantics for polyinstantiation called *polyinstantiation for cover stories* (PCS). PCS allows two alternatives for each attribute (or attribute group) of a multilevel tuple:

1. no polyinstantiation, or
2. polyinstantiation at the explicit request of a user to whom the polyinstantiation is visible.

PCS strictly limits the extent of polyinstantiation by requiring that each real-world entity be modeled in a multilevel relation by at most one tuple per security class. The goal of PCS is to provide a natural, intuitive, and useful technique for implementing cover stories, with runtime flexibility regarding their use. A particular attribute may be used for cover stories for some tuples and not for others. Even for the same real-world entity, a particular attribute may be polyinstantiated at some time and not at other times.

PCS combines the "one tuple per tuple class" concept with the "Restricted" concept presented earlier. The basic motivation for PCS can be appreciated by considering the following instance of SOD:

Starship		Objective		Destination		TC
Enterprise	U	Restricted	U	Talos	U	U
Enterprise	U	Spying	S	Rigel	S	S

---

[4] It should be noted this protocol works for an arbitrary lattice, and does not require any trusted subjects. The use of trusted subjects will allow simpler protocols for this purpose.

In this case, the Destination attribute of the Enterprise is polyinstantiated so that <Talos, U> is a cover story for the real S destination of Rigel. The Objective is not polyinstantiated.

Consider the occurrence of polyinstantiation due to invisible polyinstantiation, as discussed by example earlier. This example begins with S- and U-users respectively having the following views of SOD:

Starship		Objective		Destination		TC
Enterprise	U	Exploration	U	Rigel	S	S

Starship		Objective		Destination		TC
Enterprise	U	Exploration	U	Null	U	U

So far, there is no polyinstantiation. Polyinstantiation occurs in the example when a U-user updates the destination of the Enterprise to be Talos.

PCS takes a slightly different approach to this example. According to the PCS approach, polyinstantiation does exist in the S-instance of SOD given above. PCS shows this instance as:

Starship		Objective		Destination		TC
Enterprise	U	Exploration	U	Null	U	U
Enterprise	U	Exploration	U	Rigel	S	S

In this approach, polyinstantiation already exists prior to the U-user updating the destination of the Enterprise to be Talos. This update merely modifies an already polyinstantiated relation instance to be:

Starship		Objective		Destination		TC
Enterprise	U	Exploration	U	Talos	U	U
Enterprise	U	Exploration	U	Rigel	S	S

With this approach, *element polyinstantiation* can occur *only due to visible polyinstantiation*. Invisible polyinstantiation simply cannot be the cause of element polyinstantiation. Consequently, polyinstantiation will occur only by the deliberate action of a user to whom the polyinstantiation is immediately available. In other words, polyinstantiation does not occur as a surprise.

The PCS approach treats null values like any other data value (except in the apparent key fields where "Null" should not occur). Previous work on the semantics of null in polyinstantiated databases has taken the view that nulls are subsumed by nonnull values independent of the access class [JAJO90c, SAND90]. In this case, the first tuple in the following relation available to S-users

Starship		Objective		Destination		TC
Enterprise	U	Exploration	U	Null	U	U
Enterprise	U	Exploration	U	Rigel	S	S

is subsumed by the second tuple, resulting in the following relation for S-users used in the earlier invisible polyinstantiation example:

Starship		Objective		Destination		TC
Enterprise	U	Exploration	U	Rigel	S	S

Under the explicit alternative approach, the former relation is completely acceptable. The latter can be acceptable, but only if the lower limit on the classification of the Destination attribute is S.

To further illustrate the semantics of null in PCS, consider the following relation:

Starship		Objective		Destination		TC
Enterprise	U	Exploration	U	Null	U	U
Enterprise	U	Exploration	U	Null	S	S

PCS considers this to be a polyinstantiated relation. The fact that there are nulls rather than data values in the polyinstantiated field has no bearing on the treatment of this relation. The semantics of null [JAJO90c, SAND90] require all null values to be classified at the level of the apparent key (U in this case), thereby deeming the second tuple illegal.

The PCS approach leaves many of the choices of whether or not to polyinstantiate to the application designer. It differentiates between updates that cannot cause polyinstantiation and those that can. The PCS design uses two different keywords (UPDATE and PUPDATE) to make the distinction explicit. The PCS approach also relies on the distinguished data value "Restricted." The meaning of this data value is that users at the associated classification level cannot modify the value of the restricted attribute. As in the prevention approach presented earlier, PCS includes special privileges for imposing and lifting such restrictions.

Architectural considerations

The architecture of an MLS DBMS affects the choices of polyinstantiation strategies available to the database administrator (DBA). There are two fundamentally different architectural alternatives available in building an MLS DBMS. The details of these architectures [SCHA83] are beyond the scope of this essay, but we present them briefly to point out their implications for polyinstantiation.

Figures 13 and 14 illustrate the two approaches (which are also dealt with in Essay 19). Figure 13 shows the trusted computing base (TCB) subset architecture. In this architecture, data at each classification level are stored in a separate database. Users at each level interact with a separate DBMS, and each DBMS has access to all databases at its level or lower.

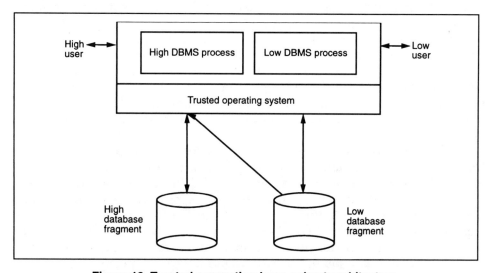

Figure 13. Trusted computing base subset architecture.

Figure 14 illustrates the trusted subject architecture. In this architecture, data at multiple levels are stored in the same database. Users at multiple levels interact with the same DBMS, and the DBMS is trusted to protect the data according to their classification levels.

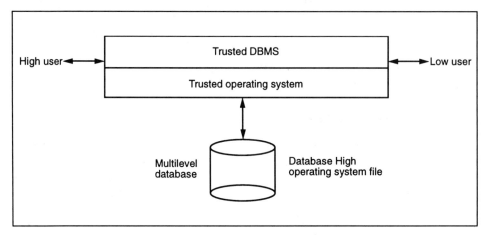

Figure 14. Trusted subject architecture.

The potential for polyinstantiation is inherent in the TCB subset architecture. The DBMS running at the lower level has no knowledge of data stored in higher level fragments, unless all keys are classified at the same (low) level. Unless specific measures are taken to cope with the problem (as, for example, in the approach described in the section "Visible restrictions"), polyinstantiation due to low users cannot be prevented. Attribute polyinstantiation may be allowed by defining logical relations that span multiple levels. The underlying databases would store single-level fragments of the relations. Restrictions on fragmentation are the first method to control the types of polyinstantiation semantics allowed within a system.

Various polyinstantiation strategies have been proposed to control the recomposition of relations at the time of data retrieval. The DBMS must determine how to combine the data received from the underlying databases into a single answer for the user. The approach may be to perform joins and return combinations of data (as in the SeaView approach, presented in the section entitled "Propagation of polyinstantiated tuples"), to choose the data with the highest classification level whenever there are polyinstantiated data (as in the MLS GDSS approach, in the section entitled "Derived values"), to return data at the classification levels explicitly requested by the user (as in the belief approach, in the section entitled "Visible restrictions"), or to use some other strategy.

Under the trusted subject architecture, a DBA has more flexibility to trade strict security enforcement for data integrity. If the DBA chooses to use polyinstantiation rather than to permit disclosure channels, then the trusted DBMS must enforce its own barriers between data at different levels. In effect, the barriers that were imposed by the TCB subset architecture are reinstated through software in the trusted DBMS. Under the trusted subject architecture, the DBA may also choose to allow lower level users to see some information about the existence of higher level data in order to enforce data integrity. Since the trusted DBMS has access to data at all levels, it is able to impose restrictions on lower level updates.

Conclusion

The design of an MLS DBMS must take into account the problem of polyinstantiation. When data items exist at multiple classification levels, there is the potential for inconsistent values for the same data item at different levels. Polyinstantiation may occur over tuples or attributes, and it may arise through updates at low or high classification levels. Researchers have developed a number of different approaches to polyinstantiation; no one solution is best for all applications. This essay outlined approaches in which the system:

- propagates polyinstantiated tuples to reflect valid combinations of values,
- shows users derived tuples based on underlying polyinstantiated tuples, or
- informs users explicitly of restrictions or inconsistencies present in the data so that polyinstantiation can be controlled.

Acknowledgment

The work of S. Jajodia and R.S. Sandhu was partially supported by the US Air Force, Rome Laboratory, under contract #F30602-92-C-0002. We are indebted to Joe Giordano for his support and encouragement, which made this work possible.

Essay 22

Integrity in Multilevel Secure Database Management Systems

Catherine Meadows and Sushil Jajodia

Integrity is usually considered to be at odds with security in multilevel databases. Integrity constraints enforce conditions on relations between data, while security constraints enforce separation between data. If an integrity constraint is defined over data at different security levels, a direct conflict results. However, the solution is not to sacrifice the integrity constraint altogether. Compromise solutions can often be found that guarantee some, although not all, of the desired results of the constraint. In this essay we will show that by dividing the desired goals of integrity into three areas — consistency, correctness, and availability — one can often find solutions to integrity problems that achieve some, if not all, of the goals without sacrificing security.

The rest of this essay is structured as follows. After a brief overview of security issues in multilevel databases, we discuss integrity and describe the three integrity properties: consistency, correctness, and availability. Then we discuss integrity in relational databases and integrity of transactions. We also discuss integrity of object-oriented databases.

Security issues in multilevel databases

Most security violations arising from the application of integrity constraints to multilevel secure databases do not result in the direct revelation of data. Instead, security violations arise from the fact that integrity constraints defined over data at more than one security class can provide channels by which information at a high security class can be passed down to users at a lower security class. These channels are of two kinds:

- *Inference channels.* A user at a low security class can use his knowledge of the low security class data and of the constraint (if it is made available to him) to infer information about high security class data also affected by the constraint.

- *Signaling channels.* Signaling channels are divided into storage channels and timing channels.

  In a *storage channel*, if satisfaction of an integrity constraint requires that changes to data at a high security class be reflected indirectly in the value of data at a lower security class, a Trojan horse program embedded in a process at a high security class could encode high data as low data by varying the high data involved in the integrity constraint so that it produces detectable changes in the low data. Such a channel could be used to pass on not only information directly affected by the constraint, but any other information the Trojan horse has access to.

  In a *timing channel*, if an integrity constraint depends on data at both high and low security classes, a Trojan horse program could encode high data by varying the time it takes to make the high data necessary for verification of the integrity constraint available. Again, such a channel could be used to pass on any information to which the Trojan horse has access.

Many of the conflicts between security and integrity in multilevel secure databases arise out of the fundamental incompatibility of what we will call the *basic security principle for databases* with the database integrity properties of consistency, correctness, and availability [MEAD88a]. The basic security principle is as follows: *The security class of a data item should dominate the security classes of all data affecting it.* The reason for the basic security principle is clear: If the value of a datum can be affected by data at levels not dominated by its own, information can flow into the item from those other levels.

The database integrity properties are defined as follows:

- *Consistency.* A database is consistent if, whenever two different methods exist for deriving a piece of information, a request for that information always yields the same response no matter what method is used.
- *Correctness.* A database is correct if all data satisfy all known constraints.
- *Availability.* A database is available if the data in it can be made available to any authorized user, and any user who is authorized to enter or update data may do so.

The three integrity properties are somewhat overlapping. However, since they often can be traded off against each other, we find it useful to distinguish between them.

In the remainder of this essay, we identify the various principles as they come into play. We also identify the trade-offs among them, and discuss techniques for optimizing multilevel secure databases with respect to the various properties.

Basic integrity

In this section, we consider three basic criteria for database correctness given by Date [DATE86], describe the conflicts that arise between these criteria and the basic security principle, and describe the solutions that have been recommended. This section is essentially a summary of the discussions in Hinke and Schaefer [HINK75] and Denning et al. [DENN87], with some comments of our own.

Key integrity. Every tuple in a relation must have a unique key. This constraint does not cause a problem when data is classified at the relational or column level, since in that case all keys in a relation are of the same security class. But consider a low security class user who wants to enter a tuple in a relation in which data are classified at either the tuple or the element level. If a tuple with the same key at a higher security class already exists, then to maintain key integrity, the DBMS must either delete the tuple or inform the user that a tuple with that key already exists. In the first case, data availability is reduced for the high user, possibly to an unacceptable degree. In the second case, the basic principle of database security is violated; the existence of high data is allowed to affect the existence of low data.

Similarly, if data is classified at the element level, the low user cannot be warned that a high-level element already exists when he attempts to insert a low-level element, nor can the high-level element be deleted. Thus two versions of the tuple will exist: one with a high-level value in the element, and one with a low-level value. If data is classified at the element level, the problem is potentially even worse. For then, not only can more than one tuple exist with the same key, but so can more than one element for each attribute of a given tuple.

The strategy of allowing more than one version of a tuple to exist to prevent security violations was first identified by Hinke and Schaefer [HINK75]. The name under which it is known today, *polyinstantiation*, was coined by the SeaView project [DENN87].

Polyinstantiation has been treated in depth in Essay 21, so we will not discuss it in detail here. However, we will briefly review the different approaches that have been taken to polyinstantiation and show how they trade off consistency, correctness, and availability.

It is generally agreed that the most serious threat to integrity comes from polyinstantiated elements. For example, consider the flights relation in Figure 1, in which the attributes are Flight Number, Destination, and Payload, and each element has its own classification.

Flight Number		Destination		Payload	
701	U	Persian Gulf	S	Nuclear weapons	TS
403	U	Newcastle	U	Coals	C

Figure 1. Flights relation.

Now consider Flight 701 in Figure 1. A low user will see that flight as having null entries in the Destination and Payload attributes. Thus that user, or two such users, could enter their own values for these elements. As Figure 2 shows, this could result in four possible tuples from the high user's point of view. In other words, the number of possible tuples grows exponentially with the number of polyinstantiated elements.

Flight Number		Destination		Payload	
701	U	Persian Gulf	S	Nuclear weapons	TS
701	U	Canada	U	Rugs	U
701	U	Persian Gulf	S	Rugs	U
701	U	Canada	U	Nuclear weapons	TS

Figure 2. Four tuples for Flight 701.

In the original SeaView approach to the problem, all possible tuples were allowed to exist: Thus correctness was sacrificed, since only one of the tuples could be the correct one. In later work, means have been developed for limiting the number of tuples displayed: Lunt and Hsieh [LUNT91] modify the original SeaView algorithm so that polyinstantiation can be limited to a certain extent when two or more fields in a tuple are updated in a single transaction. Jajodia and Sandhu [JAJO91b] give an algorithm that will implement any desired display policy on a per-relation basis. Haigh, O'Brien, and Thomsen [HAIG91a] present an algorithm that allows one to display no more than one tuple per security class.

All of the above techniques limit the display of polyinstantiated tuples. However, correctness is still sacrificed, since even with the most restrictive algorithm more than one tuple with the same key may exist. In some cases, we can take advantage of this feature by having the low-level tuples be *cover stories* designed to mislead users about the existence of classified data. However, this will not always be the case. As a matter of fact, in some cases the low-level information may be more accurate, if, for example, it is more recent.

These problems are solved by some recent algorithms that eliminate polyinstantiation altogether. In the SWORD database system [WOOD88] a user, before he can enter a high-level element, must log in at the lower level and upgrade that element. Sandhu and Jajodia [SAND91] present an algorithm with a similar effect that does not rely on trusted code, and is less restrictive in its handling of tuples at different security levels.

These algorithms assist one in achieving correctness: No more than one version of an element can exist at any time. However, they do this at the cost of availability. In both cases, restrictions are made on the way in which a user can enter high-level data. The SWORD algorithm is even more restrictive in that, once a high-level tuple has been created by upgrading the key of a low-level tuple, no more low-level tuples can be entered into the relation, since allowing this would either potentially violate key integrity or create a signaling channel. Since high-level tuples are created by upgrading the key of low-level tuples, this means that no new tuples at all can be entered once a high-level tuple has been created.

Entity integrity. Every tuple must have a nonnull key. When data is classified at the relational or tuple level, security considerations do not cause a problem with entity integrity. However, if data is classified at the column or element level, problems can arise if the security class of the key is higher than or incomparable with the security classes of other elements in the relation. Thus it is necessary to require that the security class of any field in the key be dominated by the security classes of all data in the relation, as is recommended by Hinke and Schaefer [HINK75]. (Note that this requirement means that all fields in the key must be of the same security class.) Depending on the way relations are defined, this approach may reduce data availability. For instance, consider the following example, similar to one discussed by Hinke and Schaefer [HINK75]: Let R be the relation $ABCD$ with key AB. Suppose that A and D are highly sensitive, that B and C are not, and that C functionally depends only on B. To maintain entity integrity, C must be classified at a level at least as high as A. This problem can be avoided by breaking R into two relations, ABD and BC.

The solution recommended by Hinke and Schaefer is to store data so that as little redundancy as possible exists in a relation; they suggest using third normal form.

Referential integrity. If an attribute in a relation is designated as a foreign key for another relation, then any tuple appearing in that relation either has a null value as its entry in that attribute or there is a tuple in that other relation with that entry as the key. In this case, database integrity can be violated when any of the four approaches to data classification is taken. For example, suppose that data are classified at the relational level, and that a foreign key in a relation with a low security class refers to a tuple in a relation with a higher security class. To the user with a lower clearance, the key would appear to be dangling. Similar problems can occur when data are classified at the tuple, column, or element level.

The obvious method for avoiding dangling keys is to require that, if an element A appearing in relation R is designated as a foreign key for relation R', then the security class of A in R must dominate the security class of A in R'. However, as has been pointed out [DENN87], if the security class of A in R strictly dominates the security class of A in R', this has the potential of creating signaling channels. Suppose that an element A appearing in tuple T in relation R is designated as a foreign key for R', and that T' is the tuple containing A in R'. There are two ways of enforcing referential integrity when a user attempts to delete T'. One way is to delete A from T automatically. The other is to prevent the user from deleting T' without first deleting A from T. If T is classified at a higher level than T', the second method opens a signaling channel, since, by repeatedly removing and inserting a tuple T, a Secret process could signal information to an Unclassified process that repeatedly attempts to remove and insert T'. The first method of automatically deleting A from T when T' is deleted does not open any signaling channel, since only data at the higher security level is affected when this approach is taken.

As Gajnak has pointed out [GAJN88], further problems can arise when referential integrity is enforced in the presence of polyinstantiation. When an element refers to a polyinstantiated tuple, which tuple does it refer to? Moreover, when referential integrity is enforced across several links (that is, if A is a foreign key for B, which contains C, which is a foreign key for D), the number of possible references grows exponentially.

The approach taken by SeaView was to enforce referential integrity only over the same security class. Thus correctness is sacrificed to security, but is still enforced in the cases in which security is not violated. Burns [BURN90] has suggested enforcing interclass referential integrity selectively in cases in which the signaling channel can be monitored or for some other reason is deemed not to cause a serious threat.

Referential integrity has not attracted the same degree of attention as key integrity. This is probably because until recently most commercial DBMSs did not enforce referential integrity either. Thus there was no point in providing a feature in multilevel DBMSs that was not even provided in single-level DBMSs. However, as Burns has pointed out [BURN90], this situation is now changing: Commercial DBMSs are now starting to offer referential integrity. Moreover, it is easy to imagine situations in which interclass referential integrity would be useful: Consider a specification for a classified computer system that will use some unclassified components. It is hoped that in the future researchers will start paying the same kind of attention to referential integrity that they have to polyinstantiation, and introduce new solutions in which correctness, consistency, and availability are traded off against each other to provide the best solution for individual database applications.

Atomicity of transactions

In recent years, more and more attention has been paid to concurrency control in multilevel databases. A number of algorithms have been developed that process multilevel transactions so that security and consistency are both preserved. However, there is one aspect of transaction management that has been pretty much ignored — that is, the preservation of failure atomicity, the property that transactions either succeed completely or fail completely. Consider a multilevel transaction that performs some reads and writes at a low security class and some at a high class. Suppose that the transaction has already performed some or all of the low writes, and one of the high reads or writes fails. If the transaction aborts, then the low writes must be undone to preserve failure atomicity. But this will result in a signaling channel. Nor can we delay the low writes until the high part of the transaction is done, since this will also result in a signaling channel.

There are several ways out of this dilemma. One is to allow a transaction to write only at a single security level. This will have the result of limiting availability; the kinds of transactions available to the user will be reduced. Another is to insist upon failure atomicity only at a single level. Transactions would be required to succeed or fail completely at each level, but could be allowed to succeed partially across levels. Thus correctness would be sacrificed for the sake of security. Another approach can be used when the database architecture is of the kind described by Froscher and Meadows [FROS89], in which the database is divided into single-level databases where each database contains all data classified at its level or below. In this architecture, an update to a data item at one level is propagated to all databases at its level and above. In this case, we can require failure atomicity at each database, and thus each database will be correct. However, since we cannot require failure atomicity among databases, it may be that after a while the databases will no longer be consistent with each other. Moreover, the lower the security class of a database, the more up to date it will be.

The effects of these various approaches to preserving atomicity are unknown and will probably depend on the application; they deserve further study.

Object-oriented databases

Unlike relational databases, object-oriented databases do not have a well-defined set of integrity rules. Each object is responsible for maintaining its own integrity policy. However, there is one general integrity principle that is widely agreed upon — that of the integrity of the object itself. An object should be a self-contained unit. In particular, permission to view or modify an object should imply permission to view or modify the entire object. Moreover, there are other integrity issues that arise in object-oriented DBMSs that must be addressed by the database designer. These include decisions as to whether to allow multiple inheritance and how it should be handled, how naming conflicts are handled in class hierarchies, and what should be inherited in a class hierarchy. Although the answers to these questions are implementation-dependent, we need to answer them in ways that will both satisfy the needs of the application and preserve security.

In this section, we look at both kinds of questions. In the first part, we discuss work that has been done in maintaining object integrity in multilevel object-oriented DBMSs. In the second part, we discuss implementation-dependent integrity issues and their relation to security.

Object integrity. Earlier attempts to develop models for secure object-oriented DBMSs [THUR89a, LUNT90d] modeled objects as multilevel entities, analogous to tuples in a multilevel relational database with element classification. Rules were developed for ensuring integrity in the sense that there should be no part of an object that was inaccessible to everybody. One such rule, for example, was a rule saying that the level of any component of an object should dominate the level of the object itself. However, more recently some researchers have come to believe that, in order to promote object integrity, objects should be single level [JAJO90a, MILL92]. In an object-oriented system, the objects should be self-contained entities. Allowing some users to deal with pieces of an object but not the entire object violates this principle.

Despite the need for integrity of objects, the existence of entities in the paper world that are both multilevel and have the characteristics of objects suggests that some way of representing multilevel objects is needed, although such objects should probably not be the basic components of the system. For example, a report or message will have a single classification, but each paragraph of the report will have its own label, dominated by the label of the report. If we modeled the report in an object-oriented system, then clearly it would be considered as an object. But if we made it single level, that would mean every time someone wanted to make a low-level paragraph of the report available, it would have to be downgraded to the appropriate level, with a resulting risk to security.

Thus, it would seem useful to have a way of modeling multilevel objects, perhaps as composite objects built out of single-level objects.

Probably the earliest attempt to model multilevel objects was that of the NRL Secure Military Message System [LAND84]. The SMMS did not use object-oriented concepts explicitly, but its security policy was formulated in terms of abstract data types, whose use of inheritance was a precursor of the notion of inheritance used in object-oriented systems. The SMMS has been interpreted as an object-oriented system [MEAD92]. In the SMMS, entities are either containers or objects. Each object has a single security label. Containers may contain other entities, while objects may not. Thus objects are the basic building blocks of the SMMS. Each container is given a container label that gives an upper bound on the labels of the entities (either containers or objects) that may be stored in it. If a container is marked Container Clearance Required (CCR), then only individuals cleared to the level of the container may access the entities stored in it via that container; otherwise, one may access any entity inside the container as long as one is cleared to see the entity. Thus, for example, an individual with a Top Secret mail file could still see the Unclassified mail in the file, even if he logged into the system from a nonsecure terminal. However, if a message was marked Container Clearance Required, one would need to be cleared to the level of the message even to read its unclassified paragraphs.

Containers give a natural interpretation of the paper world. However, it is difficult to construct a CCR container securely and conveniently if one uses the Bell-LaPadula paradigm on which most existing secure systems are based. To construct it without illegal write-downs, one would have to assemble each set of components at each security level separately and insert it into the container. This is acceptable if one is constructing and adding to a mail file, but it could be inconvenient if one is working on, say, a message. The other approach would be to construct the entire container at once at the level of the container. In such a case, one would have no assurance of the integrity of the labels of the components.

That these problems arise is not surprising, since the SMMS was designed as an alternative to the Bell-LaPadula model and was motivated largely by the fact that the Bell-LaPadula model failed to provide many of the features taken for granted in the paper world. However, we highlight them because they arise not when dealing with the SMMS; they are problems that one must confront in one form or another whenever one is dealing with multilevel entities in a Bell-LaPadula context.

Jajodia and Kogan [JAJO90a] have described a means of implementing multilevel objects using inheritance. A multilevel object is represented by a number of single-level objects. Each attribute of the object is defined at a single security level. Each single-level object inherits its lower level attributes from a lower level object. Thus, although a user at a given level will see the single-level object, he will also see the lower level attributes inherited from the lower level objects.

A method for constructing certain kinds of multilevel entities is presented by Lunt and Millen [MILL92]. This technique is used when the relation between two objects may be classified at a level higher than the objects themselves. In such a case, one creates a relationship object classified at the higher level that contains the information about the relation. No integrity constraints are enforced here. As a matter of fact, enforcing integrity constraints could result in inference and signaling channels, since if whenever one deleted an object the object to which it was related was automatically deleted, this might allow someone to deduce the existence of the relation. Thus, in this case correctness is sacrificed to preserve security; a description of the relationship is allowed to remain, but one or more of the related objects no longer exist.

Much remains to be done in the development of means to ensure the integrity of multilevel objects. It is still not clear what kind of integrity these objects should have, or how we should implement it. Moreover, as was shown in the SMMS example, there are certain security and integrity problems that arise when constructing multilevel objects that may prove intractable, unless we look for new points of view from which to approach the security problem.

Implementation-dependent integrity considerations. Although there are integrity principles that apply to object-oriented systems as a class, there are still a number of integrity considerations that must be taken into account when designing an object-oriented database that may vary with the application. These include questions such as the following:

1. Should multiple inheritance be allowed? If so, what restrictions should be put on it?
2. What should be done if there is a naming conflict in a class hierarchy?
3. What do objects inherit in a class hierarchy?
4. How is transaction processing managed?

Although these considerations may not be directly related to security, the choices one makes will perhaps require different notions of integrity that will have different effects on security. For example, consider the question of inheritance of instance variables, and the question of what should be inherited. Should one define a security class for an instance variable, and require that it be inherited as well? Spooner [SPOO89] discusses some of the problems that can arise in this case. If object class B inherits variable V from object class A, then its security class must dominate that of A. But what happens if B's security class strictly dominates A's security class, and a method of B (classified at B's level) attempts to alter a value of *V*? In such a case, we must either not allow inheritance of security classes of instance variables, or only allow methods inherited from *A* (or other object classes of the same security class as *A*) to alter the value of *V*.

Transaction processing is another thorny issue in multilevel object-oriented databases. Objects perform transactions by sending messages to each other. These messages execute methods. Thus, if object *O* wants to read object *U*, it sends a "read" message to object *U*, which executes a read method. If the security class of object *O* strictly dominates that of object *U*, then this causes a problem. In most multilevel systems, reading down is not considered a problem; indeed, in most cases a multilevel system that did not allow reading down would be pointless. But if the object that reads down needs to send a message to the object being read in order to do it, this opens an apparent signaling channel.

Two approaches have been taken to handling this problem. One, that followed by Jajodia and Sandhu, is to attempt to retain at least the appearance of the object-oriented paradigm, but to implement it in such a way that the signaling channel does not arise [SAND92a]. This has its risks, since it is done at the cost of greater system complexity, which makes errors more likely. The other approach, for example, that taken by Lunt and Millen, is to implement a straightforward Bell-LaPadula style version of read and write [MILL92]. This greatly simplifies the model, but at the risk of losing much of the advantage of the object-oriented paradigm.

As we see, although (or perhaps because) integrity issues for object-oriented systems are not as well-defined as they are for relational databases, the conflicts between security and integrity can have even greater impact and be harder to resolve. Moreover, since multilevel object-oriented databases (and object-oriented databases in general) are less well understood than relational databases, these conflicts have not been as thoroughly explored. It is hoped that as more work is done in this area, more of these conflicts will be brought to light and resolved.

Conclusion

In this essay, we have examined the various kinds of threats to integrity that arise in multilevel secure database systems, and the various ways there are to deal with them. In discussing the trade-offs between database integrity and security, we found it useful to think in terms of three database integrity properties — consistency, correctness, and availability — instead of a general notion of integrity. This was because it often turned out that, whenever a conflict arose between database integrity and security, it could be resolved more or less satisfactorily by introducing a trade-off among the three integrity properties instead of between integrity and security. For example, in the case of the key integrity property discussed in the section entitled "Basic integrity," it is possible to maximize availability and correctness at some cost to consistency, without any cost to security. Similarly, in the case of failure atomicity of transactions, it is possible to preserve security, correctness, and consistency by reducing availability, or to preserve security and availability by sacrificing either correctness or consistency, depending on the database architecture used.

In general, of all three database integrity properties, consistency is the easiest to sacrifice, perhaps because consistency is the most easily recoverable. When data availability is sacrificed, data may become irretrievably lost, and when data correctness is sacrificed, data may become irretrievably corrupted. However, it is always possible to recover database consistency, as long as well-defined rules exist for identifying the correct version of the data. That the definition of such rules is not always a trivial problem can be seen from the discussion of polyinstantiation. Thus, a goal of secure database research should be to identify cases in which rules for restoring database integrity can be defined in the context of multilevel database security, and to develop means of defining these rules.

Essay 23

Multilevel Secure Database Management Prototypes

Thomas H. Hinke

The three systems described in this essay each target the most stringent security standards embodied in the A1 requirements as defined by the US Department of Defense "Trusted Computer Systems Evaluation Criteria" [DOD85], which is commonly called the Orange Book. While the initial designs of all these systems — and in some cases the implementations — predate the "Trusted Database Management System Interpretation of the Trusted Computer System Evaluation Criteria" [NCSC91] (commonly called the TDI), they all had the Orange Book as a guide to the fundamental requirements that must be satisfied by a secure system at the A1 level. Also, in some cases, work on these prototypes provided the basis for comments on the evolving TDI.

In addition to their A1 target, these three systems share a similarity in that they were and are intended as research prototypes, not commercial products. This means that they are not held to the requirement of satisfying market conditions, but also that they may not have had the funding to include all of the capabilities that would be required of a commercial offering. Their intent was to push forward the frontier in the area of security, but not necessarily with all the "bells and whistles" of a complete product. This is not to detract from their contributions, which are many, but only to alert the reader to the fact that today's research prototype may lead tomorrow's commercial product by many years.

All of the systems enforce both a mandatory and a discretionary policy. The basis for mandatory enforcement is the *access class*, which includes a hierarchical, linearly ordered component called *levels* (for example, Top Secret > Secret > Confidential > Unclassified), and a nonhierarchical component called *categories*, which is not ordered. The set of access classes is partially ordered and forms a lattice. In this lattice, access class A is said to *dominate* access class B if the hierarchical component of A is greater than or equal to the hierarchical component of B, and the set of categories associated with A is a superset of the set of categories

542

Information Security

associated with B. Level A strictly dominates B if the access class of A dominates the access class of B, but is not equal to the access class of B.

While it is recognized that access class includes both a level and a category, this essay will sometimes use the terms access class and security level interchangeably. Also, to illustrate examples, the essay will sometimes describe activity in terms of a high level and a low level, where, depending on context, high will mean an access class that strictly dominates low, or an access class that is not comparable with low.

The access policies for the systems are stated in terms of active *subjects*, which represent users, and *objects* that are to be protected. All of the systems enforce a security policy that states that a subject can read an object only if the access class of the subject dominates the access class of the object. A subject can write into an object only if both have equivalent access classes. A subject is not permitted to write into an object that it strictly dominates, since this would be a write-down in security level and could provide an avenue for Trojan horse code to leak data to a less protected object (that is, one labeled with a lower access class label). This no-write-down policy is called the *-property [BELL75].

In this essay, we will call the access class at which a user is currently interacting with the system the user's current access class or current level. This current level must be dominated by the maximum security clearance held by the user.

The next three sections of this essay will describe each of the three prototype systems, first the SeaView project, then ASD, and finally LDV. Each of these three sections will begin with a discussion of the security model that each system is designed to enforce. The security model includes not only the security policy, but also the security operations that the system is designed to provide. In a sense, the model provides a high-level functional description of the system, with little concern for the details of how this will be accomplished in a secure manner. Following the description of the security model enforced by each system, the architecture of the system will be discussed. This architectural description will show how each of the systems is designed to satisfy the A1 requirements of a security reference monitor, while providing all of the security features called for in the model. In the case of ASD, which was designed for operation as a secure server, this section will show how the ASD architecture fits into the general network environment for which it was designed. The final section of this essay will compare and contrast the various systems, highlighting their fundamental differences.

SeaView

SRI International and Gemini Computers began the SeaView project in 1985 under the sponsorship of the US Air Force Rome Air Development Center. As this is being written, SRI International, Gemini Computers, and Oracle are currently in the final phase of a contract to implement the SeaView trusted DBMS.

The following SeaView discussion is divided into two major sections. The first section describes the security policy and features provided by the system, and the second describes the SeaView architecture. (Material presented here was taken from the work of T.F. Lunt et al. [LUNT88, LUNT90, LUNT90b].)

SeaView security policy and features. This section will describe the SeaView mandatory and discretionary access policies.

SeaView mandatory access policy. As a system targeting the A1 level, SeaView enforces a mandatory security policy. Its mandatory policy controls access to the granularity of an individual data element in a tuple. This means that within a single tuple, each data element representing a different attribute can have a distinct and possibly different access class. This also means that data elements for the same attributes in different tuples can have distinct and possibly different access classes. The access class of an element is indicated by associating an access-class label with each element of a tuple.

In addition to having an access-class label associated with each element of a tuple, SeaView also associates an access-class label with each individual tuple. This tuple access-class label represents the least upper bound of the access classes of all the information used to derive the data in the tuple. More will be said about this later.

SeaView represents the classification of each tuple and attribute as attributes in their own right. Thus, a relational query language can also make queries based on the classification of attributes.

An element-level granularity of control represents the most specific granularity of control that can be supported in a relational DBMS. It is more specific than attribute-level, tuple-level, or relation-level granularity of control. However, it should be noted that any type of relational granularity of control can be mapped into any other type. If, for example, the application requires element-level granularity of control, but only relation-, tuple-, or attribute-level protection can be provided by the multilevel relational DBMS, then the database can be decomposed by security level into objects with the granularity provided by the DBMS. The desired view of the database can then be reconstituted. As will be described shortly, although SeaView provides the user with an element-level granularity of control, at the storage level it uses a DBMS that provides only a relation-level granularity of control. While relation-level storage was selected for SeaView, a choice of tuple- or attribute-level control could also have been mapped into the element-level granularity that is provided to the user [HINK75].

Mandatory access control within SeaView is governed by the Bell-LaPadula security model [BELL75]. Subjects operating on behalf of a user operate at an access class that reflects the access class at which the user is currently interacting with the system. A subject can read a DBMS object only if the access class of the subject dominates the access class of the object. A subject can write into an object only if the access class of the object is equal to the access class of the subject.

To prevent the output of data that was derived by using data with a more dominant access class, SeaView (and any other system that purports to be secure) requires that the access class of the data output must dominate the access classes of all data used to derive the output data. SeaView handles this by assigning the tuple an access-class label that dominates all of the data contained in the tuple or that was used in deriving the tuple. The individual elements of that tuple will bear the original classifications of the elements stored in the database. In SeaView, element labels are advisory. This means that they are not provided via a path that contains only trusted code, and thus could have been modified by untrusted code in the path.

SeaView discretionary access policy. SeaView enforces a discretionary policy as required for A1 systems. However, under the current design, the discretionary policy-enforcement code would not be A1, in the sense that it is formally specified and verified. It would be considered to be at the C2 evaluation level. This concept of C2 assurance for discretionary and A1 assurance for mandatory has been called balanced assurance [LUNT88]. Although this concept is permitted by the "Trusted Network Interpretation" of the Orange Book for network applications [NCSC87a], it was unsuccessfully proposed by a number of database researchers as an effective method for meeting the A1 requirements for the "Trusted Database Interpretation" of the Orange Book [NCSC91].

The objects to which the SeaView discretionary access control is applied include the entire database or an entire relation. Thus, in contrast to the mandatory access control that is applied to a very fine granularity, the discretionary access control is applied to a much coarser granularity. The relations to which the discretionary controls can be applied include base relations, which are the actual relations in permanent storage; views, which are the data actually seen by a user; and snapshots, which are the relations that result from a relational query. The subjects to which discretionary access controls can be applied include both individual users and groups of users.

The nature of the discretionary access that can be granted is expressed in terms of access modes. A subject can be granted a particular access mode to a discretionary object. The access modes include the following: insert, delete, retrieval, update, reference, null, grant, and give-grant. While insert, delete, retrieval, and update have the usual meanings, the other access modes have SeaView-specific meanings that will be described in the following paragraphs.

The reference access mode is used to control access to views. A user (for example, user A) can define a view of a relation and provide another user (user B) access to the view, but not to the source relation(s) from which the view is derived. This has the effect of protecting sensitive data in the source relation(s) that user A does not want user B to see. However, as further security protection, SeaView requires that for a user to access a relation through a view, the user must have retrieval access to the view and reference access to the underlying source relations from which the view is derived.

SeaView has the null access mode to provide a means for denying access to a particular object for a user or group. If, for example, user B is to have no access to relation R, then user B is given null access to relation R.

As has been noted, users can be granted or denied access as individual users or as members of defined groups. This raises the possibility that there may be a conflict, in that a user may be granted access under one group and denied access under another group or as an individual. The SeaView discretionary access policy resolves this conflict with the following rules:

- The most specific access takes precedence. Thus, discretionary access permissions or denials specified for a specific user take precedence over any discretionary access permissions or denials specified for any group of which the user is a member.
- In the case of further conflict, denials take precedence over permissions.

To control the propagation of discretionary access modes to other users, SeaView uses the grant and give-grant access modes. The grant access mode allows the recipient to grant any of the accesses, except the grant access mode itself, for the object specified in the grant. The grant access mode itself can be propagated by the recipient only if he has been given the give-grant access mode.

Access modes previously granted can be revoked. The revocation of an access mode applies only to the specific user to which the revocation is applied. In SeaView, the revocation does not affect any subsequent grants that may have been performed by the user to whom access was granted. Thus, if user A gives both retrieval and grant access for relation R to user B, user B can then give retrieval access for relation R to user C. Now, if user A revokes user B's retrieval access to relation R, this affects only user B. User C's retrieval access to relation R is not affected.

SeaView relational integrity constraints. SeaView enforces a number of relational integrity constraints that must hold for data contained in the SeaView database. The first two are variations of the entity integrity and referential integrity constraints that are found in nonmultilevel databases, but that have been adapted to multilevel databases.

The entity integrity constraint requires that no primary key be null [ELMA89]. With SeaView this holds for multilevel relations as well. All of the elements that comprise the key for a relation must be visible at the lowest access class at which any part of the relation can be viewed. This means that the access class of the key elements must be dominated by the access classes of all other elements in the tuple. Thus, each nonkey tuple must possess a key for any access class at which the tuple is visible. This also means that all elements that comprise the key must have the same access class. Otherwise, there will exist some access class at which only a portion of the key will be visible, and this portion will no longer comprise a unique key, since by definition the key is the smallest set of elements that can uniquely identify a tuple.

Referential integrity requires that nonnull, nonprimary key elements of a tuple that references the primary key of another relation (these non-primary key elements are called foreign keys) must reference a primary key that currently exists as one of the tuples in the referenced relation [ELMA89]. In other words, a nonnull foreign key cannot refer to a currently nonexisting tuple. SeaView requires this to hold for multilevel relations as well. This means that if a foreign key is visible in a tuple at a particular access class, then the key portion of the tuple containing the referenced key must also be visible. The database cannot have foreign key references to primary keys that are not visible at the access class at which the foreign key is visible. Of course, if the foreign key value within the tuple is not visible (that is, null) at a particular level, then there is no requirement that the primary key be visible. SeaView further requires that both the foreign key and the referenced key have the same access class [LUNT90] to eliminate the possibility of referential ambiguity [GAJN88].

To understand the third constraint, the concept of polyinstantiation (the name originally coming out of the SeaView work) must be introduced. While a nonmultilevel relational database does not permit two tuples to have the same primary key, this is not necessarily the case in a multilevel database. This situation arises because the viewability of tuples or elements within tuples is a function of the access class of the user who is viewing the database. Users at lower access classes will not be able to see tuples of elements that strictly dominate the user's access class. From the perspective of this lower access class user, these tuples, or elements, do not exist; they are null. A problem arises if this low access class user attempts to enter a tuple with a key identical to that of a tuple with a strictly dominating or noncomparable access class. A problem will also arise if the user attempts to enter a value for what appears to be a null data element, when in reality a value already exists, but is invisible since its access class strictly dominates that of the user. A more complete description of polyinstantiation is contained in Essay 21.

There are three solutions to this problem. The first solution is to deny the data entry or update attempt. In effect, this informs the user that data exists whose access class does not permit the user to read it. If the low access class user can detect the existence of this data, this constitutes a covert channel and would be prohibited for systems at the B2 and above evaluation levels.

The second solution is to permit the entry or update. This destroys the dominant access class data, which means that less cleared users can potentially destroy the most classified data, a situation that is generally viewed as unacceptable.

The third solution avoids the covert channel problem by permitting the data entry or update attempt through polyinstantiation. If a user enters a tuple with a key identical to a more dominant tuple, this leads to polyinstantiated tuples. Both tuples will have identical primary keys, but will differ in access class and perhaps the access class of one or more nonkey elements, since the low access class user will have no knowledge of the contents of the dominant access class tuple.

If a user updates what appears to be a null element value with a new one (where an element value already exists at an access class that strictly dominates or is noncomparable with that of the user), this leads to a polyinstantiated element. This means that the particular element has multiple values, each entered at a different access class. In SeaView this is represented as multiple tuples, differing only in the value of the element that is polyinstantiated.

While it is clear that polyinstantiated tuples lead to multiple tuples, in SeaView this is also the result of polyinstantiated elements. SeaView handles polyinstantiated elements by polyinstantiating the tuple, with each of these tuples sharing the same primary key and the same classification of the primary key, but having different values and associated element classifications for the polyinstantiated element. This ensures that each tuple satisfies the requirements of the relational first normal form — that the value of each element is atomic [ELMA89].

SeaView enforces the polyinstantiation integrity rule, which states that tuples with duplicate keys are permitted only in the security-driven cases of tuple- or element-triggered polyinstantiation, as described previously.

The primary problem with polyinstantiation (both tuple and element) is that at higher access classes, users and their application programs will see multiple tuples with the same primary key, when only one is normally expected in a relational database. The user now has the problem of deciding which of the multiple values is to be used. At this stage of DBMS security with the relational model, the solution of this problem is left to the user or the application writer.

SeaView architecture. The SeaView architecture, shown in Figure 1, takes a strict TCB subset approach, in which layers of TCBs provide increasingly more restrictive controls over the protected data. The lowest TCB layer enforces the mandatory security policy, and the second TCB layer enforces the discretionary security policy. The highest layers are untrusted from both a mandatory and a discretionary perspective, but enforce the SeaView integrity controls and provide the multilevel view software.

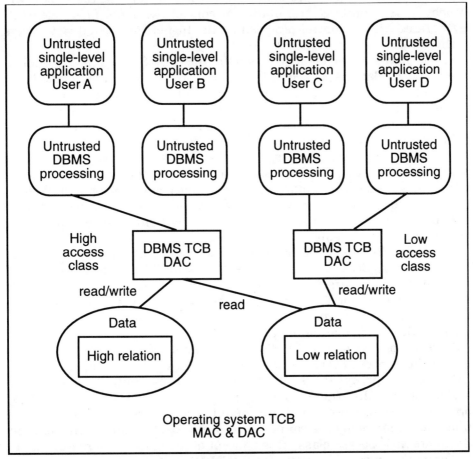

Figure 1. SeaView architecture.

To ensure that the SeaView processing is adequately encapsulated, subjects that support the discretionary controls of layer 2 must be single level, with each supporting only one of the access classes for which there is current activity. Since the highest layers are untrusted from both a mandatory and a discretionary perspective, there must exist one active subject for each active user.

With this basic outline of the SeaView architecture, the remainder of this section will describe the nature of the objects protected by the TCB layers, the software used by the TCB layers, and the nature of the processing supported by the higher layers.

SeaView object protection. As noted in the previous section, SeaView provides an element-level granularity of control. However, rather than having the lowest, mandatory TCB layer support element-sized objects, SeaView has taken the approach that at the lowest level, the DBMS will support a relation-level granularity of control, with the finer, element-level granularity of control provided by the higher, untrusted view layers of the DBMS.

At the lowest level of abstraction in the DBMS, data is partitioned among base relations by access class. Each base relation is "single level" for all of its nonkey data. The access class of all nonkey data contained within the relation is equal to that of the relation. The base relation also contains primary keys, whose access class may be dominated by the access class of the base relation. Within the base relation, only the primary key data has an explicit access-class label. The access class of all nonkey data is given by the access class associated with the base relation. The access-class labels are required for the primary key to support relational joins. During a join, the key value and the key's access class are used together to reconstitute the multilevel relations from what, except for the keys, are essentially single-level base relations.

The base relations are protected by the lowest, mandatory TCB layer. For this layer, SeaView uses the GEMSOS multilevel secure operating system, which is targeting the A1 evaluation level. Each of SeaView's base relations is stored in a GEMSOS segment of the appropriate access class. Under this approach, GEMSOS — rather than the DBMS code — enforces SeaView's mandatory access policy.

Since all of the higher DBMS layers execute as part of subjects restricted to processing for either a single access class or a single user, GEMSOS will permit these DBMS subjects to read only those operating system objects that they dominate in access class, and write into those operating system objects that are equal to their access class. This means that the DBMS subjects cannot access any base relations that strictly dominate their access class. This concept of using the underlying operating system to provide security for the DBMS was originally suggested in an earlier work [HINK75].

While GEMSOS is used to provide the mandatory controls, it does not provide the discretionary controls. This would require that the DBMS data be decomposed into objects that are homogeneous with respect to both mandatory and discretionary access permissions.

SeaView software. SeaView uses the Oracle mandatory prototype to provide both the discretionary access controls and the DBMS engine. Multiple instances of Oracle execute, each at a single access class. Thus, Oracle's access to the data is restricted by GEMSOS. Also, since there is an instance of Oracle for each access class, Oracle does not have the capability of compromising mandatory security — each executing instance of Oracle supports only a single access class of processing. Oracle provides its users with a secure DBMS that supports a relation-level granularity of control.

The software that maps the single-level relations provided by Oracle into the multilevel relations with element-level granularity of control that SeaView provides for the user is the multilevel SQL processor (MSQL). This software not only provides the multilevel relational view; it also enforces the various multilevel integrity rules previously described. An instance of MSQL executes for each SeaView subject.

The multilevel relations created by the user must be decomposed into the multiple, single-level base relations that are stored in the GEMSOS segments. Ideally, the decomposition of a user-provided multilevel relation or multilevel tuple into multilevel, single-level relations, and then the subsequent reconstitution of these multiple single-level relations into the multilevel relation originally entered, should be lossless. The data entered should be identical to the data that is viewable again after reconstitution. In addition, it is desirable to be able to enforce the various integrity constraints. As has been pointed out [JAJO90], there is a relationship between the objective of lossless decomposition/reconstitution and the polyinstantiation integrity constraint.

The original SeaView model was designed such that the decomposition and reconstitution of the multilevel relations automatically satisfied the SeaView polyinstantiation integrity constraint. The formalization of the SeaView polyinstantiation integrity rule requires both a functional dependency and a multivalued dependency, which preclude the existence of certain combinations of tuples. The SeaView designers argue that these are not relevant.

When the polyinstantiated tuples that have been created are stored, the polyinstantiated tuples and elements that exist in the relation viewable by the users are removed as the multilevel relation is decomposed into its single-level relation components. These polyinstantiated tuples and elements are then automatically restored when the multilevel relations are reconstituted from their single-level components. In the SeaView design, this is accomplished by using the outer join for performing the reconstitution. The use of the outer join results in the automatic enforcement of the SeaView polyinstantiation rule for the view that is reconstituted.

Had SeaView used another approach for reconstitution, then its polyinstantiation integrity would not necessarily have been automatically enforced. However, a different polyinstantiation integrity constraint would have been enforced. Jajodia and Sandhu [JAJO90] suggest the use of the natural join for reconstitution, with a polyinstantiation rule based only on functional dependency rather than the multivalued dependency of the SeaView polyinstantiation rule. Under their suggestion, any combination of polyinstantiated tuples entered by a user could be decomposed into base relations and reconstituted using the natural join.

An example taken from Jajodia and Sandhu's work [JAJO90] will illustrate this relationship and introduce one of the more challenging open research issues in multilevel DBMSs. The example uses the relation SOD, consisting of the attributes Starship, Objective, and Destination. It will be assumed that Starship is the primary key whose access class must be Unclassified, since it must be dominated by all of the other attributes in the relation. The access classes of Objective and Destination can range from Unclassified to Secret. Assume, after a series of updates, that the following tuples exist, reflecting Objective and Destination:

Starship		Objective		Destination	
Enterprise	U	Exploration	U	Rigel	S
Enterprise	U	Spying	S	Talos	U
Enterprise	U	Exploration	U	Talos	U

As noted by Jajodia and Sandhu [JAJO90], these tuples could represent two secret missions: one to explore Rigel, a secret destination, and the other to spy on Talos, a secret objective. The totally unclassified tuple could represent an unclassified cover story for both the missions.

The original SeaView decomposition/reconstitution approach enforced the SeaView polyinstantiation integrity constraint. This integrity constraint consists of two parts. The first requires that there be a functional dependency from the primary key, the access class of the primary key, and the access class of the ith element and the value of the ith element. This means that there can be only a single value associated with a particular tuple key and nonkey element class.

The second requires that there be a multivalued dependency from the primary key to the ith element access class and value. It is this part of the polyinstantiation integrity constraint that leads to the loss during reconstitution. In the above example, this would require that, when reconstituted, the data included in the three previously presented tuples actually be reconstituted as the four following tuples:

Starship		Objective		Destination	
Enterprise	U	Spying	S	Rigel	S
Enterprise	U	Exploration	U	Rigel	S
Enterprise	U	Spying	S	Talos	U
Enterprise	U	Exploration	U	Talos	U

As can be noted, there exists a tuple instance that was not intended, but the multivalued part of the polyinstantiation integrity constraint is satisfied. What is lost is the fact that the users had entered three tuples, and now there are four tuples, thus losing the intent of the users. To rectify this problem, Jajodia and Sandhu [JAJO90] suggest that the multivalued dependency portion of the polyinstantiation integrity constraint be dropped, and the SeaView use of the outer join to reconstitute the multilevel relations from the single-level base relations be dropped in favor of the natural join.

The SeaView designers argue that the focus should not be on the decomposition/reconstitution approach taken, but rather on the update semantics desired for database operations, including those involving polyinstantiation [LUNT90]. They propose a first cut at a desired set of update semantics and identify the development of a decomposition/reconstitution algorithm as an open research question.

It is beyond the scope of this essay to provide an in-depth discussion of the issues inherent in polyinstantiation integrity constraints, decomposition/reconstitution algorithms, or desired update semantics. However, it is important to alert the reader to the fact that there are deep issues buried in these areas. The interested reader is referred to the cited papers and Essay 21 on polyinstantiation for more information on this area.

Advanced Secure DBMS

The TRW Advanced Secure DBMS (ASD) was developed under an internal TRW research and development project. The goal of ASD was to investigate the technology required to design and implement a trusted DBMS targeting the A1 evaluation class as defined by the Orange Book (DoD 5200.28-STD). The Orange Book, rather than the Trusted Database Interpretation, was the target guidance, since the work on ASD predated the Trusted Database Interpretation. In addition, it should be noted that ASD was simply a research prototype; it was never intended to be a product. ASD was written in Ada to run on the ASOS operating system.

The following ASD discussion is divided into two major sections. The first section describes the security policy and features provided by the system, and the second describes the ASD architecture. (Material presented here was taken from earlier work [HINK88, HINK89].)

ASD security policy and features. This section will describe the ASD mandatory and discretionary access policies.

ASD mandatory access policy. ASD supports a tuple-level granularity of control for its mandatory access. All of the data within a single tuple are considered to have the same access class. Thus a tuple is single level. However, each tuple in a relation can bear a distinct access class; thus the ASD relation is multilevel.

ASD enforces the Bell-LaPadula security policy, which requires that subjects must have a dominant access class to read data. All data that is written will have an access class equal to the access class of the subject that is performing the write [BELL75].

As has been described in detail under the SeaView discussion, tuples within ASD can be polyinstantiated. However, since ASD supports a tuple-level granularity of control, polyinstantiated elements are not possible.

ASD discretionary access policy. While ASD enforces its mandatory access policy for the individual tuples of the relation, it enforces discretionary access controls on the entire relation. All of the tuples within the relation are subjected to the discretionary controls imposed on it.

The discretionary controls are associated with the DBMS relational operations of select, insert, delete, and update. For each relation, discretionary access can be specified as a permission or a prohibition for a subject to perform the specified relational operation on the designated relation. The subjects for which the permissions or prohibitions can be specified include individual users, groups of users, or the public as a whole.

If there is a conflict between discretionary access permissions and prohibitions, the following two rules are used:

- The most specific access constraint takes precedence over the least specific access constraint.
- If the permission and the prohibition have the same specificity, the prohibition takes precedence over the permission.

The primary justification for associating the discretionary access controls with the relation rather than with the tuple is to conserve storage space. The amount of data required to represent the discretionary access permissions or prohibitions is considerably greater than the data required to represent the mandatory access labels. For example, each of the discretionary access permissions could have a long list of users associated with each type of access. Thus, the decision was made to associate the greater volume of discretionary access control data with the entire relation — where it could apply to all of the tuples within the relation — rather than with each individual tuple.

ASD architecture. This section will first describe the internal ASD architecture, then the network architecture that permits ASD to operate as a trusted server. The ASD architecture is shown in Figure 2.

Internal architecture. The ASD architecture will be described in terms of its process structure, storage structure, and network architecture.

In contrast to SeaView and LDV, ASD takes a trusted process approach to its internal security architecture. What this means is that trusted ASD code, called the ASD TCB, enforces both the discretionary and the mandatory DBMS security policies. This contrasts with both SeaView and LDV, which rely on the operating system TCB to enforce the mandatory policy, with the DBMS TCB enforcing only the discretionary policy.

While the ASD TCB runs as a trusted process under the control of the operating system TCB, this is not to say the ASD TCB is coresident with it. The trusted ASD code does not share the protection domain of the underlying operating system.

Like the other secure DBMSs, ASD consists of both trusted and untrusted code. The untrusted ASD code performs those DBMS operations that are not security relevant. Multiple instantiations of this untrusted code run, one for each user. This code runs at the access class of the user on whose behalf it is processing.

The operating system TCB ensures that the ASD TCB is a security reference monitor. It protects the DBMS TCB from tampering by other processes operating on the system. It also ensures that no process can access the DBMS data except through the ASD TCB. The details of this will be described shortly.

Conceptually, all of the ASD tuples are placed in a single operating system file. The file must be classified at the least upper bound of the tuples it contains. Each of the tuples stored in this file bears a classification assigned by the ASD TCB, based on the security level of the subject that initiated storage of the tuple.

In addition, since the ASD data file contains tuples labeled with different classifications, this file must be protected from modification by untrusted processes that may have a classification equal to the ASD data file. There are a number of ways that this could be accomplished. One of the least desirable would be to use the discretionary access features of the underlying operating system to ensure that only the DBMS TCB could have write access to the ASD data file. This has the unfortunate consequence of allowing a mandatory access mechanism to rely on a discretionary access mechanism for its tamper-resistant property.

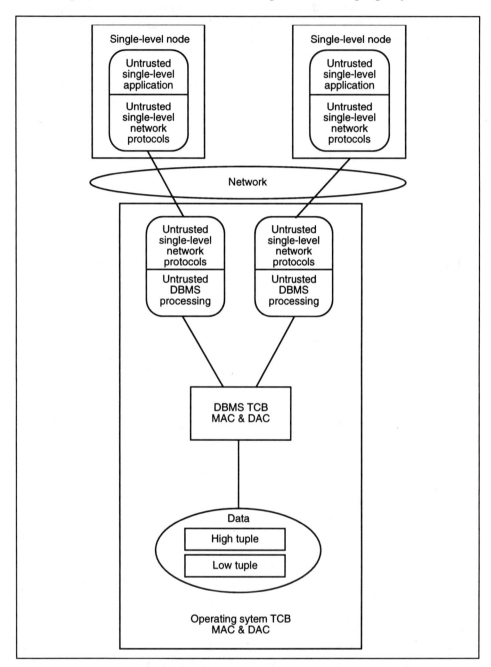

Figure 2. ASD trusted server architecture.

A better approach — and the one used for ASD — is provided by the fact that the underlying ASD operating system supports the Biba integrity policy [BIBA77]. This policy assigns integrity labels to subjects and objects. These labels are analogous to the security labels associated with classification. Under the Biba integrity policy, a subject can write into a protected object only if the integrity level of the subject dominates the integrity level of the object. To protect the ASD data, the operating system object that contains that data is assigned a DBMS integrity compartment label. This label restricts write access to the object to only those subjects that have a dominant DBMS compartment. Since the ASD TCB is the only subject that has this integrity compartment, no other subject can write directly into the operating system object that contains the ASD data. Of course, other subjects can use the facilities of the ASD TCB to store data tuples in the object, but only under the control of the ASD TCB.

Network architecture. ASD is implemented as a trusted server, as shown in Figure 2. Under the trusted server approach, the basic ASD processing engine operates on its own node of the network. It serves other nodes that are likely to be single level, but that operate at different security classifications. ASD provides the multilevel engine that facilitates sharing among levels. A top secret node could retrieve data from the ASD trusted server, where the data was entered from an unclassified node.

To provide network access means that the required network protocols must be supported in a secure manner. The network protocols supported on the ASD server are TCP, IP, and SLIP (Serial Line IP). SLIP permits the TCP/IP protocols to be used over serial lines, such as phone lines. This allows ASD to be used in a tactical environment.

Since the network protocol software actually handles the data, this software will become security relevant if it concurrently or sequentially handles data that is classified at multiple access classes. If, for example, a top secret message is sent to a top secret node, followed by an unclassified message sent to an unclassified node, the potential exists for the software to leak some of the top secret data from the top secret message into the unclassified message. This would lead to a write-down of information, in violation of the mandatory security policy.

One solution to this problem is to make the network protocol software trusted. This solution was rejected, since it would increase the size of the TCB and its complexity, due to the high complexity of network protocol software.

The solution adopted was to use a separate network protocol instance for each security level. Conceptually, a separate stack of network protocol software was associated with each of the two serial ports of the Sun, and each of these ports was connected to a node operating at a different access class.

LDV

Lock Data Views (LDV) is a design for a trusted DBMS that is to run under the control of LOCK (Logical Coprocessor Kernel). LOCK represents a hardware and software approach to providing a secure operating system. LDV is being developed by the Secure Computing Technology Corporation (formerly Honeywell Secure Computing Technology Center), under the sponsorship of the Rome Air Development Center (now Rome Laboratory).

The following LDV discussion is divided into two major sections. The first section describes the security policy and features provided by the system, and the second describes the LDV architecture. (Material presented here was taken from work by J.T. Haigh et al. [HAIG88, HAIG90, HAIG90a, HAIG91].)

LDV security policy and features. This section will describe the LDV mandatory and discretionary access policies.

LDV mandatory access policy. LDV, like SeaView, provides an element-level granularity of control. This means that each element of a tuple can have a distinct and possibly different security classification. The LDV security model includes not only the security policy that is enforced by LDV, but also a description, at an abstract level, of how LDV will enforce the policy.

The first requirement of any secure system is to label the objects. In contrast to the two DBMS systems previously considered in this essay, LDV labels data based on three different criteria: name-based, content-based, and context-based.

Using *name-based object labeling*, the name of the database object determines its security label. For example, an entire relation or all of the data of one attribute of a relation could be uniformly labeled with an access-class label. This is the basic type of labeling provided by the other two systems. For this type of labeling, neither the value of the data nor its context must be considered in determining its access class.

Under *content-based* (or *value-based*) *object labeling*, the value of the contents of a particular data item determines the access-class label of the item. Thus, salaries greater than $50,000 might have an access-class label of Secret, while salaries less than or equal to $50,000 might have an access-class label of Confidential.

With *context-based object labeling*, the label associated with the data is a function of the other data that can be associated with it. Thus, while a salary alone or a name alone might be considered Unclassified, the combination of a salary with a name might be considered Secret.

The object labels are used to label both data stored and data retrieved from the database. In the case of name-based labeling, all data entered into a named object will inherit the security level of the object. Likewise, all data retrieved from an object will bear its security label. If data is retrieved from multiple objects, then the security label associated with the response will be the least upper bound of the security labels associated with all of the data accessed to make the retrieval.

Data cannot be entered into an object labeled with name-based labels unless the current access class of the user is identical to the access class of the object. Thus, with name-based labeling a user cannot enter data that the system considers more sensitive than the user's current access class. The DBMS will prevent the user from writing data into any DBMS object whose access class is not equal to the user's current access class. However, such is not the case with the other forms of data labeling.

Since LDV supports value- and context-based security labeling, the potential exists for a user to enter data whose access class strictly dominates the access class at which the user is currently interacting with the system. When the data is entered, the system may detect that the value of the data requires an access-class label that strictly dominates the user's current access class. This is not possible under the current designs of the other two systems, since the access class of the data entered is taken to be identical to the user's current access class.

To address this possibility, the LDV design uses a maintenance level and a storage level. The maintenance access level is the level at which the data was originally entered and at which any updates or deletions of the data must occur. The storage access level reflects the actual access class of the data based on the value and context classification rules. The data will actually be stored by the system at the storage level.

It should be recognized that while the maintenance level is the level at which data can be updated or deleted, this does not mean that data so entered can be viewed at this level. Viewing the data, once entered, must be by a subject whose current access class dominates the storage access level of the data. Ultimately, what will be required is a multilevel workstation with which a user can view data through two windows. One window would have an access class that dominates the storage level, providing the ability to view data. The other window would have an access class equal to the maintenance level, providing the ability to update data whose maintenance level is equal to the access class of the window.

To support the element-level granularity of control, an access-class label is associated with each element. A maintenance-level label is associated with each tuple of the relation. Thus, the tuple is the finest granularity at which database maintenance can occur.

The maintenance-level label plus the attributes that comprise the key for the tuple form the enhanced key that uniquely identifies each tuple in the relation. All elements that comprise the enhanced key are stored at the maintenance level of the tuple.

Since all of the data within a tuple is entered from the same access class (the access class of the maintenance level), polyinstantiated elements do not occur. There will not be any null fields that the user will unwittingly attempt to fill, thus leading to a polyinstantiated element.

LDV provides the capability for users to create a new tuple that is substantially the same as an existing one, differing only in one or more element values. To form this new tuple, the user can specify which values of the new tuple are to be derived from the original tuple. For those elements of the new tuple that are to be identical to elements in the previously existing tuple, pointers are used for the element values, rather than the actual element values. This means that any change to these fields in the previously existing tuple will be reflected in the new tuple. For those elements of the new tuple that are to have values distinct from the previously existing tuple, the user can store new values in the appropriate elements of the new tuple.

With this capability, the same effects that are provided by SeaView's polyinstantiated elements can be obtained. While the polyinstantiated elements due to lower access class users updating null values are avoided, as has been noted, the LDV pointers provide the means to create lower access class cover stories, and then create higher access class tuples that reflect some classified operation. However, since the combination of key attributes and storage class must uniquely identify the tuple, any additional tuples that have the same key attribute values must be created with different storage levels.

Access to an LDV object is governed by the Bell-LaPadula security model. Subjects operating on behalf of a user bear an access-class label. A subject can read an LDV object if the access class of the subject dominates the access class of the object. A subject can write only those objects that have an access class equal to the access class of the subject.

The access-class label of the data accessed by the user is based on three security considerations: the access-class label associated with the named DBMS object, the access-class label associated with the value that is being retrieved, and the access-class label associated with the context in which the data is being retrieved. A subject will be able to retrieve the data only if the access class of the subject dominates the most dominant access-class label associated with the data retrieved.

To support the context retrieval constraints, LDV stores a history of the retrievals that have been performed for a particular subject. Each additional retrieval is considered in the context of all previous retrievals maintained by the LDV history mechanism.

As an example, assume that salary data taken alone is Unclassified and name data alone is Unclassified. However, the combination of name and salary data is considered to be Secret. This means that a user could retrieve a list of names, but once these names are retrieved, the user will not be able to retrieve a list of salaries. Or the user could retrieve a list of salaries, but once these salaries are retrieved, he would not be able to retrieve a list of names. In this case, it is assumed that both the name list and the salary list include a unique identifier that the user could use to associate the names with the salaries.

The problem with a history mechanism is that it can grow without bounds, eventually exceeding the size of the original database. To address this concern, the LDV design allows the history file to be purged when desired by appropriate authorities. Of course, this means that it is possible for a user to record the salary data off line and then wait until the time period maintained by the history mechanism has been exceeded, and then request the associated name data. This is a problem generic to context-based access control, which considers the total temporal context.

LDV relational integrity constraints. LDV enforces entity integrity, which requires the following:

1. The enhanced key, which consists of the key attributes and the maintenance level, uniquely identifies a tuple in the database. This means that no two tuples can have the same enhanced key.
2. No attribute that is part of the enhanced key can be null.
3. The attributes that comprise the enhanced key are uniformly classified at the maintenance level.

The first of these entity integrity rules eliminates the need for multivalued dependencies. which is found in SeaView. The reason is that there is only a single tuple associated with each key and maintenance level combination.

LDV architecture. Internally at the lowest level of abstraction, LDV maintains a relation-level granularity of control, with each relation having a uniform access class. The actual protection of each LDV relation is provided by LOCK, the underlying operating system with its associated hardware support. Each relation is stored in an operating system object with the same classification as the relation.

For data whose access class is derived from name-based labeling or value-based labeling, the data is stored in operating system objects whose access class is that of the data label. However, for data whose context-derived access-class label is higher than the access class of the data components taken separately, the components will be stored at the access class that applies to the component alone, not at the access class of the context-based label. The LDV design ensures that users accessing one of the components will not have any access to the other component, based on the current state of the access history. This is called a store-low-and-upgrade approach.

The alternative is to store such relationships high and then downgrade the individual components. The problem with this approach is that the data to be downgraded could have become contaminated by other data whose access class is high. There is the potential that this other high-level data could then be downgraded when one of the components of the context-relevant object is downgraded. The LDV designers argue that the store-low-and-upgrade approach avoids this vulnerability. Of course, the upgrade software must work correctly; otherwise, sensitive data will be compromised. In reality, if the DBMS TCB is the only software that is allowed access to the data, it probably makes little difference which approach is used.

While all of the DBMS systems presented can be described in terms of their functional decomposition and the partitioning of the various functions into different privilege domains, LDV provides the most extensive privilege partitioning of any of the systems discussed. This partitioning is provided by the type enforcement of the underlying LOCK trusted operating system. Type enforcement is somewhat analogous to strong typing in a programming language such as Pascal. One of the services provided by type enforcement is used to ensure that only LDV subjects can access LDV objects. However, the LDV type enforcement mechanism goes further than this by providing a means to implement a relatively fine granularity least privilege within the LDV software.

Through type enforcement, only subjects of a particular type can perform the operations associated with an object of the specified type. This represents a finer control than is found in ASD, in which all trusted DBMS code is, in effect, part of a single DBMS trusted process. It also represents a finer granularity of control within the DBMS code than is found in SeaView, in which all of the trusted code is part of the operating system trusted computing base.

In LDV, least privilege is carried even further, in that all LDV processes, whether trusted or not, run at a particular security level. In some cases, because of the need for these processes to see data that could have been entered at any security level, they operate at system high. However, those trusted processes that do not require the global viewability provided by system high can operate at a level that is less than system high.

In addition to providing type enforcement, LDV partitions the supported DBMS operations into what are called "pipelines." Pipelines are sequences of domains that perform operations. Domains provide a set of object types and associated operations that can be used by processes operating within the domain.

LDV supports three pipelines: query/response, data input/update, and database definition/metadata. While ASD and SeaView also support these operations, the code that implements them is not explicitly partitioned into pipelines. In a sense, the pipeline represents a clustering of subjects and data that can interact with each other to perform particular types of database operations. The type enforcement is the glue that binds these various processes and data together to form a pipeline.

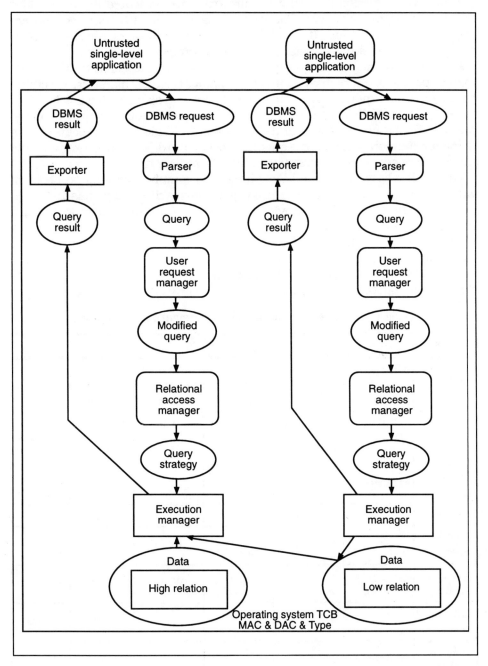

Figure 3. LDV architecture: Query/response pipeline.

The LDV architecture for the query/response pipeline is shown in Figure 3. Within LDV, trust is defined as the ability to override the *-property. Those domains that require trust are indicated by rectangular boxes with square corners. The rectangular boxes with rounded corners are untrusted domains. It can be observed that most of the domains in each of these pipelines consist of untrusted processes.

As shown in the figure, the query/response pipeline consists of five domains: parser, user request manager, relational access manager, execution manager, and exporter. The data in the query/response pipeline is partitioned into the following six types: DBMS request, query, modified query, query strategy, query result, and DBMS result. Table 1 is an example of a domain definition table for the query/response pipeline. In this example, the write-type of access is not partitioned into its various types.

The table shows that the LDV pipeline is simply a joining together of various domains by the access privileges that each domain has to its input and export data. This provides a finer level of granularity in the implementation of the DBMS code than is possible with either ASD or SeaView. Within ASD, the DBMS software is either trusted to enforce mandatory and discretionary policy or untrusted. Within SeaView, the various GEMSOS rings could be used to provide some additional partitioning, similar to Multics, but not at as fine granularity as in LDV.

Table 1. LDV query/response pipeline domain definition table.

Types	Subjects					
	Client	Parser	User request manager	Relational access manager	Execution manager	Exporter
	Untrusted	Untrusted	Untrusted	Untrusted	Some trusted code	Some trusted code
DBMS request	Write	Read				
Query		Write	Read			
Modified query			Write	Read		
Query strategy				Write	Read	
Query result					Write	Read
DBMS result	Read					Write

As will be noted, while most of the LDV pipeline consists of untrusted domains and associated untrusted code, even this untrusted code is partitioned through the LOCK type mechanism. To allow this code to be untrusted, each of these domains operates at the level of the user that submitted the query and will receive the response. Thus, there will be multiple instances of this code, one for each level at which users are interacting with the system.

In the query/response pipeline, the only trusted processes exist in the execution manager and the exporter. The execution manager addresses context-dependent access policy and inference. The acceptability of data to be released to a user is determined by the access class of the user, the access class at which the data is stored, and the context in which the data is released. This context is not limited to just the data that is requested as part of the same query, but also includes data that has been released in the past. Information about what has been previously released is contained in a history database, which keeps track of accesses by users or groups. In addition, the execution manager is intended to prevent the release of data into a group where the new data, combined with that accessed in the past, would permit inference of unauthorized data. The history manager runs in the execution manager domain at database high. Database-high operation is required so that the history manager will be able to see all of the history. It must be trusted to properly interpret the history and not to downgrade classified information when it reports the result of its history consultation to the level at which the query response is to be provided.

Trust in the exporter is required if the response needs to be reclassified to a higher level, due to aggregation constraints based on the cardinality of the response. Cardinality limits might, for example, permit the release of up to 10 names and phone numbers from a classified agency, but not the release of greater than 10 names and numbers. The release of too many names and phone numbers could reveal sensitive information about the capabilities of the agency. If the release of data must be prevented due to such cardinality concerns, LDV proposes to release a message to the user indicating that such information cannot be provided, rather than releasing the results of the query.

The input/output pipeline consists of the following four domains that are a subset of the domains in the query/response pipeline: parser, user request manager, relational access manager, and execution manager. The data in the input/output pipeline is partitioned into the following five types: DBMS request, which feeds into the parser; update, which joins the parser to the user request manager; updates and levels, which joins the user request manager and the relational access manager; update strategy, which joins the relational access manager to the execution manager; and the DBMS results, which provides the output to the user from the execution manager.

The only trusted code in the input/update pipeline is contained in the user request manager and the execution manager. The user request manager contains an upgrader that raises the level of data input, based on content or context constraints. The upgrader determines the level at which data entered into the database should be stored. The upgrader is a database-high process, since it must be able to see all appropriate constraints. These constraints may themselves be classified at a level that dominates the level at which the data is entered, or even the level at which the data should be stored after applying the appropriate classification constraints. The execution manager is trusted to insert the data into the proper files.

LDV decomposes each relation into multiple relations, each representing a single attribute. These decomposed relations are then stored at the level of the attribute. However, LDV stores data that may be subject to cardinality-based aggregation constraints or context constraints at the lowest level at which this data could be accessed (ignoring these types of constraints), rather than at the highest level that could apply, based on the constraints. While the data is stored at a low level of classification, it is accessible only by appropriate LDV subjects. As further protection, all data stored on disk is encrypted.

The final pipeline is the database definition/metadata pipeline. This pipeline is used to define new relations and the associated security data required to enforce access to these relations.

SeaView, ASD, and LDV comparison

The three systems described in this essay can be compared in terms of their granularity of control, the nature of the security policy that they enforce, and the nature of their internal architecture.

Granularity of control. This section will compare two aspects of granularity of control. First, the stored and exported granularity of control of the DBMSs will be compared. Then, the match between operating system object and DBMS object will be compared.

Stored and exported granularity of control. Table 2 shows the relationship between the security granularity of the DBMS storage object and the security granularity of the view that is provided to the user. For SeaView and LDV, there is a difference in granularity of view and storage. This means that software — in this case, untrusted software — must be provided to translate the storage granularity into the view granularity. To support this translation, there must be decomposition and reconstitution algorithms and software with the goal that this process be lossless. As noted in the polyinstantiation discussion for SeaView, there are open research questions in this area.

ASD, on the other hand, does not have this problem since no translation is required between what the user views and what is stored. Also, since the granularity of control is the tuple, there will not be any polyinstantiated elements. While ASD could impose polyinstantiation integrity rules, those rules would not be connected with the decomposition/reconstitution algorithms as they are in SeaView, since decomposition and reconstitution are not required.

DBMS/operating system granularity match. Both SeaView and LDV store their objects in operating system objects that have the same classification as the DBMS objects stored. This results in an operating system object that contains DBMS objects uniformly classified with respect to access class. As will be noted in the next section, this is why neither SeaView nor LDV enforces mandatory security. However, the operating system objects do not contain DBMS objects that are uniform in their discretionary access. Thus, the DBMSs must provide the discretionary enforcement.

Table 2. Relationship between the security granularity of the DBMS storage object and the security granularity of the view provided to the user.

View Object	Storage Object			
	Element	Tuple or row	Attribute or column	Relation or table
Element				SeaView LDV
Tuple or row		ASD		
Attribute or column				
Relation or table				

In contrast, the underlying operating system object which supports ASD does not contain DBMS objects that are uniform in access class. The operating system object contains DBMS objects that are classified at multiple access classes. Thus, the operating system cannot provide either mandatory or discretionary controls to these DBMS objects. All the operating system can do is ensure that only the DBMS TCB has access to those operating system objects that contain DBMS objects.

Security policy enforced. Both SeaView and ASD enforce a name-based access policy. This means that the name of the object is adequate to determine its security. For ASD, the access-class label is associated with each tuple, so in a sense it is associated with the tuple identifier or name.

While LDV enforces a name-based access policy, its design also calls for the enforcement of both a context-based and value-based policy. In addition, the initial LDV design calls for the system to address the inference problem, including the problem of restricting the release of data based on its cardinality.

Internal architecture. Relying on an extension of the taxonomy presented elsewhere [HINK90], this section will classify the various systems in terms of the nature of the security policy enforced by each of the major components of the DBMS, and in terms of the way the internal architecture is constrained by least privilege.

In Table 3, the horizontal axis indicates the nature of the DBMS policy enforcement provided by the DBMS code. The vertical axis indicates the nature of the partitioning inherent in the trusted code (both operating system and DBMS).

Table 3. Policy enforcement provided by the DBMS code and the partitioning inherent in the trusted code (OS: operating system).

	Null DBMS TCB: No trusted code	DBMS TCB enforces discretionary policy	DBMS TCB enforces mandatory and discretionary policies
DBMS TCB and untrusted code partitioned into multiple domains		LDV	
DBMS TCB partitioned into multiple domains			
DBMS and OS TCB in different domains	Hinke-Schaefer	SeaView	ASD
DBMS and OS TCB share same domain			Coresident DBMS

As noted, both the SeaView and LDV systems enforce only discretionary access policy. They are thus members of the class of trusted DBMSs in which the DBMS TCB can only subset the privileges provided by the underlying operating system. Since in both cases the DBMS contains trusted code that provides additional discretionary controls, these are classified as subset privilege systems in which the DBMS trusted component is nonnull.

LDV provides a greater degree of partitioning of the privileges of its DBMS software, both trusted and untrusted, than does either ASD or SeaView. ASD, on the other hand, represents a trusted subject approach, in that both the DBMS TCB and the underlying operating system TCB have responsibility for enforcing mandatory and discretionary security. The DBMS TCB performs this enforcement on the finer granularity DBMS objects (for example, tuples) that are contained within the operating system object, which is classified at the least upper bound of the DBMS data stored in the object.

Table 3 also contains two other generic DBMS architectures that provide a point of contrast to the research prototypes discussed in this essay. The Hinke-Schaefer approach relied totally on the underlying operating system for its security [HINK75]. Thus it has a null DBMS TCB. Nevertheless, it is shown in the row "DBMS and OS TCB in different domains": Even though the DBMS TCB is null, the untrusted DBMS code executes in a domain distinct from the operating system.

The second generic system shown is the coresident DBMS. Under this architecture, both the DBMS TCB and the operating system TCB share the same protection domain. In a sense, the DBMS TCB is just an extension of the operating system TCB.

Essay 24

Inference Problems in Multilevel Secure Database Management Systems

Sushil Jajodia and Catherine Meadows

An inference channel in a database is a means by which one can infer data classified at a high level from data classified at a low level. The inference problem is the problem of detecting and removing inference channels. It is clear that inference problems are of vital interest to the designers and users of secure databases. Database management systems are intended to provide the means for efficient storage and retrieval of information. Their very power means that if they are not properly designed to prevent illegal inferences, they not only will not prevent such inferences, but will greatly assist users in forming them. Yet so far inference problems in multilevel databases have not been studied very deeply. This is partly due to the difficulty of the problem, and probably also due to the fact that one cannot implement any means of controlling inferences until one has solved the more fundamental problem of determining how one stores and retrieves multilevel data.

This essay surveys the state of the art of the study of inference problems in multilevel databases. We describe particular strategies that have been developed for certain inference problems, as well as more general models of the inference problems and the tools that have been developed for handling them. We do not describe work on preventing inferences in statistical databases, which we consider a specialized problem not necessarily relevant to the inference problem in multilevel databases. However, we do note that the work on statistical databases shows that one can be successful in preventing inferences if one carefully limits the scope of the problem one is studying.

Before beginning our survey, we should point out that all the models and techniques discussed here, and indeed all attempts to deal with inference control in database systems, have one limitation in common. An inference of sensitive data from nonsensitive data can only be represented within a database if the nonsensitive data itself is stored in the database. We have no way of controlling what data is learned outside of the database, and our abilities to predict it will be limited. Thus even the best model can give us only an approximate idea of how safe a database is from illegal inferences. This fact should always be kept in mind when dealing with inference problems.

The remainder of this essay is structured as follows. We begin with a description of some specific inference channels that have been discovered in the design of multilevel databases, and some techniques that have been developed to close them. Then we move to a more general consideration of the inference problem, and we describe some of the formal models and characterizations of the general inference problem that have been developed. We also describe some of the tools that have been proposed and developed for dealing with inference problems in databases. We discuss aggregation problems, which constitute a special kind of inference problem that is usually mentioned in connection with inference problems in databases.

Specific inference problems

In this section we describe a number of inference channels that have been discovered in the course of database security research, and some techniques that have been developed to deal with them. These channels by no means constitute an exhaustive list of all the possible channels that can arise in a multilevel database; however, they are often easy to recognize and avoid. In some cases, specialized techniques have been developed to handle them. Thus, they deserve special mention.

Inference from queries based on sensitive data. In this section, we assume that a user makes a sequence of queries q_1, q_2, ..., q_n against the database. The user then utilizes the responses to these queries to derive an inference which has a higher classification than that of the retrieved data. We illustrate this situation by giving an example.

Example 1 [MEAD88a]. Suppose that data is classified at the relation level. We have two relations, an Unclassified relation called EP, with attributes EMPLOYEE-NAME and PROJECT-NAME, and a Secret relation called PT, with attributes PROJECT-NAME and PROJECT-TYPE, where EMPLOYEE-NAME is the key of the first relation and PROJECT-NAME is the key of the second. (The existence of the relation scheme PT is Unclassified.) Suppose an uncleared user makes the following SQL query:

```
SELECT   EP.EMPLOYEE-NAME
FROM     EP, PT
WHERE    EP.PROJECT-NAME = PT.PROJECT-NAME
```

If this query is evaluated by taking the natural join of the two relations EP and PT along PROJECT-NAME, and then projecting along EMPLOYEE-NAME, we have an inference channel, even though only the Unclassified data (employee names) is being returned to the user. Although the output of this query is Unclassified, it reveals Secret information.

The following SQL query posed by an uncleared user represents a similar problem:

```
SELECT   EP.EMPLOYEE-NAME
FROM     EP, PT
WHERE    EP.PROJECT-NAME = PT.PROJECT-NAME
AND      PT.PROJECT-TYPE = 'SDI'
```

If we examine the above SQL queries carefully, we quickly observe that even though the data returned to the user has a low classification, the data that is required to evaluate the query has a higher classification. Thus, the inference channels arise from the fact that these queries are conditioned on data that are supposed to be invisible to the user [DENN86a].

Inferences of this type are easy to eliminate. The system can either modify the user query such that the query involves only the authorized data or simply abort the query. If the user is cleared to see all data involved in the query, then the result can be returned to him, but it must be labeled at the least upper bound of all labels involved in the query.

Statistical databases. The problem of statistical database security is the problem of answering queries about statistics on data, such as mean, median, standard deviation, and so on, without releasing the data itself. A typical application of statistical database security would be that used by the US Census Bureau, in which aggregate statistics on groups of individuals are made public (for example, the average income of people in a particular geographic area), but in which information about particular individuals is kept secret. The threat against statistical database security is that an attacker may be able to find out statistical information about individuals by posing queries on aggregate statistics over a period of time and performing arithmetic operations on the answers received, using his own information about the size and nature of the sets of individuals involved. For example, suppose that an attacker wishes to find out the salary of A1. He can do this by asking for the average salaries of A1, A2, and A3; of A2, A3, A4, and A5; and of A4 and A5. Or he can ask for the average salary of some set of individuals of which he knows that A1 is the only member.

The security of statistical databases is an area that has received much study and really deserves an essay of its own. Rather than attempt to cover the subject here, we refer the reader to several of the survey papers that already exist [ADAM89, DENN83].

Inference from data combined with metadata. Many of the inference channels that arise in multilevel secure DBMSs are due to combining data retrieved from the database with the metadata used for its storage and management. This is particularly true for integrity constraints. A user at a low security class can use his or her knowledge of the low security class data and of the constraint (if it is made available to the user) to infer information about high security class data also affected by the constraint. In this section we will consider some kinds of metadata used in databases, and show how it can be used to assist in making inferences. We will concentrate on the relational model, since this is the one that has been most closely studied from the point of view of security. However, we note that many of these issues arise when other models are used, although in somewhat different form.

Key integrity. One of the basic integrity requirements of the relational model is key integrity, which requires that every tuple in a relation must have a unique key. This constraint does not cause a problem when data is classified at the relation or column level, since in that case all keys in a relation are at the same security class. But consider a low security class user who wants to enter a tuple in a relation in which data is classified at either the tuple or the element level. If a tuple with the same key at a higher security class already exists, then to maintain key integrity, the DBMS must either delete the existing tuple or inform the user that a tuple with that key already exists. In either case, we have a problem. In the first case, the actions of a low user can cause data inserted by a high user to be deleted, which is unacceptable.[1] In the second case, we have an inference channel: The existence of high data is allowed to affect the existence of low data.

To illustrate, consider the following instance (where "Name" is the key for the relation):

Label	Name	Destination	Engine
S	Wombat	Persian Gulf	Nuclear

---

[1] Although it is not a secrecy violation, it could lead to serious integrity problems and also cause denial of service.

Suppose an unclassified user wants to insert the tuple (Wombat, Norfolk, Nuclear). If we choose to preserve key integrity, we must either delete the secret tuple or reject this insertion. We have an integrity problem if we delete the secret tuple (since it is possible that the entry "Norfolk" in the unclassified tuple is merely a cover story for the real, classified entry "Persian Gulf"). If we reject the insertion, then the low user can derive an inference.

It turns out that this problem can be eliminated using polyinstantiation, in which case both tuples are allowed to exist. Polyinstantiation and its effects are discussed in more detail in Essay 21.

Functional and multivalued dependencies. A more general situation than the one discussed in the previous section has been considered by Su and Ozsoyoglu [SU86, SU87, SU90]. They study inference channels that arise because of the functional and multivalued dependencies that are constraints over the attributes of a relation. The following example illustrates how inference channels can arise if certain functional dependencies are known to low users.

Example 2 [SU87]. Assume that a company database consists of the relation scheme EMP-SAL, which has three attributes: NAME, RANK, and SALARY. The attributes NAME and RANK are considered nonsensitive in the database, while the attribute SALARY is considered sensitive. (Thus, the labeling is at the column level.) Suppose every employee is aware of the constraint that all employees having identical ranks have the same salaries. Given this scenario, an employee who is not permitted to have access to sensitive data can easily determine employee salaries, which are sensitive.

If we examine the above example carefully, we see that it contains an inference channel because the functional dependency RANK $\rightarrow$ SALARY is not properly reflected in the classification levels of attributes RANK and SALARY. If the rank of an employee is known to a user, then the employee's salary is also known to that user. The way to avoid the problem in cases such as this is to raise the classification of the attribute RANK from nonsensitive to sensitive. If attributes are assigned security labels in a manner consistent with the functional dependencies, then these inference threats can be eliminated. This process is formalized by Su and Ozsoyoglu [SU86, SU87, SU90].

Su and Ozsoyoglu give several algorithms for raising the classification labels of attributes based on functional and multivalued dependencies among them. One of their algorithms takes as input a list of attributes, the proposed classification labels of the attributes, and a set of functional dependencies that cause inferences. The algorithm produces as output another list of attributes together with their classification labels (which may be different from the assignment that was input), such that the list is free of inference channels arising from functional dependencies.

Value constraints. A value constraint is a constraint on data values that can involve one or more items of data. If a constraint is defined over data at different security levels, availability of the constraint may lead to inference channels.

Example 3 [MEAD88a]. Suppose that an attribute A is Unclassified while attribute B is Secret. Suppose the database enforces the constraint $A + B \leq 20$, which is made available to Unclassified users. The value of B does not affect the value of A directly, but it does determine the set of possible values A can take. Thus we have an inference channel. The usual solution to this problem is to allow such constraints to be defined only over a single security level. If a constraint is defined over several levels, then it is necessary to partition it into several single-level constraints. Thus, for example, the constraint $A + B \leq 20$ can be partitioned into $A \leq 10$ and $B \leq 10$.

Classification constraints. A classification constraint is a rule describing the criteria according to which data is classified. It is also possible to infer sensitive data from the classification constraints themselves, if they are known. Consider the following example.

Example 4 [SICH83]. Suppose the following integrity constraints apply to a database containing the fact that Mediocrates is an Athenian:

Every man is an Athenian, a Boeotian, a Corinthian, or a Dorian.
All Athenians and Corinthians are peaceable.
All Boeotians and Dorians are violent.

Mediocrates does not wish it to be known that he is peaceable. Rhinologus, a public nuisance, tries to find out about Mediocrates from a system that refuses to answer whenever the answer, together with the integrity constraints, would imply the secret:

Rhinologus: Is Mediocrates an Athenian?
System: I will not tell you.
Rhinologus: Is he a Boeotian?
System: No.
Rhinologus: Is he a Corinthian?
System: No.
Rhinologus: Is he a Dorian, then?
System: I will not tell you.

Rhinologus, knowing that it is his disposition that Mediocrates is trying to conceal, notes that if he were not an Athenian, then the system could have answered "no" to the first question without revealing the secret. Thus Mediocrates must be a peaceable Athenian.

Sicherman, de Jonge, and van de Riet [SICH83] consider the problem of protecting secrets in cases when classification constraints are known and when they are not known. They define a number of conditions for refusing to answer a query, and describe a set of strategies based on these conditions. They then develop a formal model of a secure database with inference rules and prove theorems that show what are the safe responses, depending on whether or not the classification constraints are known.

The results Sicherman, de Jonge, and van de Riet present are rather pessimistic. In particular, they show that, if the classification constraints are known, then the only one of their strategies that is safe requires that no queries about a value in a tuple be answered if that value is secret. This is a result of the rigidity of their strategies: Each of their strategies applies a set of criteria consistently over time. Thus it is not possible to adopt a more liberal policy initially and switch to a more restrictive one as the number of options for the secret value decreases, as is done for some statistical databases. However, their result is important because of its extreme generality: It applies to all databases and all inference systems, and thus can be used as a basis for further study of this problem.

General characterizations of the inference problem

In the previous section, we discussed some specific inference channels that could be easily characterized and had relatively straightforward solutions. But pinning down inference channels in general is not always so easy. As a case in point, consider the following two stories from Stanislaw Ulam's *Adventures of a Mathematician* [ULAM76]. The stories concern the US government's attempt to keep the existence and the location of the Manhattan Project secret during World War II:

> Finally I learned that we were going to New Mexico, to a place not far from Santa Fe. Never having heard about New Mexico, I went to the library and borrowed the Federal Writers' Project Guide to New Mexico. At the back of the book, on the slip of paper on which borrowers signed their names, I read the names of Joan Hinton, David Frisch, Joseph McKibben, and all the other people who had been mysteriously disappearing to hush-hush war jobs without saying where. I had uncovered their destination in a simple and unexpected fashion. It is next to impossible to maintain absolute secrecy and security in war time.

This reminds me of another story. Since I knew Stebbins well, about a month after arriving at Los Alamos, I wrote to him. I did not say where I was but I mentioned that in January or February I had seen the star Canopus on the horizon. Later it occurred to me that as an astronomer he could easily have deduced my latitude since this star of the Southern skies is not visible above the 38th parallel.

There are several important things to note about these stories. First of all, in figuring out the destination of his mysteriously vanishing colleagues, Ulam did not use standard logical deduction. Instead, he looked for the best explanation for the fact that they had all checked out a guidebook for the same place. Second, although Ulam was able to deduce the destination of his friends from the guidebook, he did not know enough to look for the guidebook until he already knew some sensitive information: the location of the project he himself would be working on. If he hadn't known that information, he might have had to look at every guidebook in the library to find out the location of the Manhattan Project. Third, Ulam also needed some relatively nonsensitive information to make his deduction: namely, the fact that some of his colleagues had been leaving to work on what were apparently secret government projects. Finally, it is not always possible to predict what information an individual will know that can be used to deduce facts from other, apparently nonsensitive facts; this is the point of the story about Canopus and the 38th parallel.

Probably the earliest formal characterization of the inference problem in databases is that of Goguen and Meseguer [GOGU84]. Consider a database in which each data item is given an access class, and suppose that the set of access classes is partially ordered. Define the relation $\rightarrow$ as follows: Given data items x and y, we say $x \rightarrow y$ if it is possible to infer y from x. The relation $\rightarrow$ is reflexive and transitive. A set S is said to be inferentially closed if whenever x is in S and $x \rightarrow y$ holds, then y belongs to S as well. Now, for an access class L, let $E(L)$ denote the set consisting of all possible responses that are classified at access class less than or equal to L. There is an inference channel if $E(L)$ is not inferentially closed.

Goguen and Meseguer do not set forth any one candidate for the relation $\rightarrow$. They merely require that it be reflexive and transitive, and say that it will probably be generated according to some set of rules of inference: for example, first-order logic, statistical inference, nonmonotonic logic, knowledge-based inference, and so on. They do note, however, that for most inference systems of interest, determining that $A \rightarrow b$ (where A is a set of facts and b is a fact) is at best semidecidable — that is, there is an algorithm that will give the answer in a finite amount of time if $A \rightarrow b$, but otherwise may never halt. Complexity-theoretic properties of inference relations in multilevel databases are considered further by Thuraisingham [THUR90].

Goguen and Meseguer, besides not fixing on any inference system or set of inference systems, leave several other questions unexplored. For example, they do not consider the effect on the inference problem of information that may exist outside the database (as in the Canopus example cited above). Nor do they attempt to include any measure of the difficulty of computing an inference. Some of these problems, however, have been discussed in the work that has followed.

In a refinement of Goguen and Meseguer's definition, Denning and Morgenstern [DENN86] derive the inference relation from classical information theory. Given two data items x and y, let $H(y)$ denote the uncertainty of y, and let $H_x(y)$ denote the uncertainty of y given x (where uncertainty is defined in the usual information-theoretic way). Then, the reduction in uncertainty of y given x is defined as follows:

$$INFER(x \rightarrow y) = \frac{H(y) - H_x(y)}{H(y)}$$

The value of $INFER(x \rightarrow y)$ is between 0 and 1. If the value is 0, then it is impossible to infer any information about y from x. If the value is between 0 and 1, then y becomes somewhat more likely given x. If the value is 1, then y can be inferred given x.

The INFER relation can be used in the following way, as is done by Morgenstern [MORG88]. Choose an $\varepsilon > 0$ and define the *sphere of influence* of a set (or core) of data to be the set of all data items y such that there exists an x in the core such that $INFER(x \rightarrow y) > \varepsilon$. A system is safe from inference if, for each security class C, the sphere of influence of all data items with security level $\leq C$ does not contain any data elements of a higher or incomparable class.

Note that, unlike the inference relations discussed by Goguen and Meseguer, the sphere of influence relation is nontransitive. For example, knowing the street on which someone lives may reduce our uncertainty about that person, knowing that an individual works on a project may reduce our uncertainty about the nature of the project, but knowing the name of a street inhabited by someone working on a project reduces our uncertainty about the project somewhat less.

This formulation is especially nice since it shows that inference is not an absolute problem, but a relative one. It gives us a way to quantify the bandwidth of the illegal information flow. On the other hand, Denning and Morgenstern [DENN86, p. 5] point out its serious drawbacks:

1. In most cases it is difficult, if not impossible, to determine the value of $H_x(y)$.

2. It does not take into account the computational complexity that is required to draw the inference.

To illustrate the second point, they give the following example from cryptography: With few exceptions, the original text can be inferred from the encrypted text by trying all possible keys (so $H_x(y) = 1$ in this case). However, it is hardly practical to do so.

A discussion of the kinds of inference functions that would be appropriate for determining the security of a multilevel database is given by Garvey, Lunt, and Stickel [GARV91]. The authors discuss three kinds of inference channels:

- deductive channels, in which high data may be formally derived from low data;
- abductive channels, in which a deductive proof could be completed if certain low-level axioms were assumed; and
- probabilistic channels, which occur when there is low data that can be used to decrease the uncertainty about the nature of high data, and it is likely that the low data will be known by a low user.

Ulam's second story, about the sighting of Canopus, is an example of abductive reasoning applied in the manner proposed by Garvey et al. (although a little too late). Ulam wrote his friend that he had seen Canopus on the horizon and then realized that, not only could the low-level fact, together with another low-level fact, be used to deduce the high-level fact, but that the second low-level fact was likely to be known to the low-level recipient of his letter.

Techniques and tools that make use of abductive reasoning and probabilistic reasoning provide a good way of characterizing cases in which high-level information can be derived using low-level information from both inside and outside a database. Garvey et al. [GARV91] discuss how these techniques might be used to make sure that a database is free from inference channels. For each high-level fact in the database, one attempts to discover what low-level facts could be used either to derive the high-level fact or to make it more likely to be derived. One also measures the likelihood that these low-level facts are known. Garvey et al. also point out that automated tools used for abductive proofs have features that measure the difficulty of a proof, and that such a feature can provide a guide to the difficulty a low-level user would have in performing the inference.

Tools and techniques for dealing with inference channels

In this section, we discuss the various techniques and tools that have been proposed for locating inference channels and preventing their exploitation once they have been found. Basically two kinds of techniques have been proposed for locating and eliminating inference channels. One is to use semantic data modeling techniques to detect inference channels in the database design, and then to redesign the database so that these channels no longer exist. The other is to evaluate database transactions (involving either reads or updates, or both) to determine whether they lead to illegal inferences. If they do, the query is either disallowed or re-classified at the higher level.

One of the earliest examples of the semantic data modeling approach is found in Hinke's work on the ASD Views project [HINK88a]. This work describes the construction of a semantic relationship graph to express the possible inferences in a database. Data items are represented as nodes connected by edges that represent the relationships between them. A relationship may or may not be classified. A possible inference channel is said to exist if there are two paths from node A to node B such that it is possible to be cleared to see all edges in one path and not all edges in another. If such an inference channel is found, one analyzes to see whether it is a genuine channel. If it is, one raises the classification of one or more edges, if possible. This process continues until all inference channels are closed.

This technique is very simple. No assumptions are made about the nature of the relationships between data items except that they either exist or they do not. For example, if A implies B, then an inference path is assumed to exist, not only from A to B, but from B to A. Applying this technique is relatively straightforward. The main danger appears to be that, if data is very highly interrelated, then so many false channels will be discovered that the database designer wastes most of his or her time trying to eliminate them.

An implementation of a model similar to Morgenstern's is described by Buczkowski [BUCZ90]. In Buczkowski's system, a PINFER function is developed that is similar to the INFER function described by Denning and Morgenstern. For certain pairs of facts x and y, one asks an expert to determine $PINFER(x, y)$, the probability that one can infer y from x. One then uses fuzzy logic to estimate other probabilities — for example, the probability that one can infer z from x — where these probabilities have not been explicitly provided by the expert. These probabilities are computed using knowledge about the degree of dependency between various facts.

Smith [SMIT90, SMIT90a] proposed a scheme using a semantic data model that refines Hinke's by allowing the user to express different kinds of relationships. In Smith's system a number of possible types of data items and relationships between them are identified. These include abstract class, attribute, identificate (an identificate is something that can serve to identify a data item, or nearly so), association, external identifier, generalization, and disjoint subclasses. Any of these can be classified.

Thus, if one wishes to hide the relationship between employee and salary, one merely classifies that relationship, and leaves both employee and salary unclassified.

This technique also has its dangers, although it is less likely to give false inference channels than Hinke's tool. Since types of relationships are enumerated and explicitly identified in the database, there is the danger that not all possible types of relationships have been identified. Moreover, it is not necessarily the case that classifying a relationship will make it impossible to infer by some other means. This is especially true if the database is dynamic. For example, Lunt [LUNT89a] points out that, even if one classifies the association between employees and salaries, it is still possible that it can be deduced for some cases whenever employee-salary pairs are entered into or deleted from the system, or if both employees and salaries are presented in the same order. Thus, this approach should be thought of more as a tool for developing and describing a security policy than as a way of telling the database designer exactly what data should be classified.

All of the tools described above are used to assist in database design and classification. Other researchers have considered tools to evaluate queries. Mazumdar, Stemple, and Sheard [MAZU88] propose a system that evaluates the security of transactions by using a theorem prover to determine whether one of a set of predefined secrets can be derived from the integrity constraints of the database, the precondition of the transaction, and the type of data input into the transaction. Since their techniques do not depend on any specific data that is stored in the database, they can be applied to a transaction when it is compiled. Thus they can be used to determine, for example, what the level of a certain type of canned transaction should be. Mazumdar et al. also point out that their techniques can be used to test the security of the database and point out ways in which it can be redesigned to make it more secure.

A somewhat different approach is followed by the Lock Data Views (LDV) project [STAC90]. Classification constraints are defined on sets of data according to the level of the information that may be inferred from the data. When a query is presented to the system, the result is upgraded to the appropriate level according to the classification constraints and then released. It is possible to include an inference control mechanism in this system so that the classification constraints will be based on the results of its analysis of a query. It is also possible to use a history mechanism to guard against gathering together information that can be used to infer sensitive information over time. Thus if A and B together imply C where C is sensitive and A and B by themselves are not, and a low-level user has already seen A, one can prevent that user from seeing B, or prevent any low-level user from seeing B, according to the security policy.

Another approach, described by Thuraisingham [THUR87], uses a version of query modification [STON74]. A query is first evaluated to determine whether it will lead to illegal inferences, and then, if it will, is transformed into a query that will not lead to such inferences. Such an approach can be helpful to a user since, not only does the system prevent the user from making illegal queries, it also assists him or her in making legal queries. However, such a system must be carefully implemented, since there is the danger that a user may be able to form inferences from the ways in which legal queries differ from illegal queries.

Searching for inferences at query processing time has some obvious potential drawbacks. As has been pointed out [HAIG90], it may be necessary to keep some kind of history of past accesses and to use that history when evaluating the security level of a query, so that low-level users cannot infer high-level information by building up a store of low-level information through repeated queries. In certain circumstances, this can make the system vulnerable to a denial-of-service attack: A low-level user could prevent other low-level users from accessing data they need by accessing other data, that, together with the needed data, would lead to an inference channel.

Nonetheless, such an approach may have its use in certain applications. For one thing, in many cases it may be prohibitively expensive to search an entire database for illegal information flows, but somewhat easier to evaluate a particular query. Moreover, the addition of new data in updates may cause new illegal inferences that are best checked for at the time of the update; a query-time inference checker might be useful in detecting such inferences. But it is clear that more work needs to be done to understand the relative advantages and disadvantages of the two approaches.

Aggregation problems

Inference and aggregation are usually discussed together. Many of the tools discussed in the previous section are described by their builders not as inference detecting tools, but as inference and aggregation tools. But aggregation problems, although they are motivated by inference problems, are actually somewhat different in nature, and thus we devote a separate section to them.

We say that an aggregation problem or aggregation policy exists when the aggregate of two or more data items is classified at a level higher than the least upper bound of the classification of the individual items. The most commonly cited example is the SGA (Secretive Government Agency) phone book [SCHA83]: The entire phone book is classified but individual numbers are not.

Aggregation policies are usually assumed to arise because sensitive information can be deduced from the aggregate that cannot be deduced from any individual member. Thus, they are generally discussed in connection with inference problems. However, they differ in that in the case of an aggregation problem, a particular labeling policy has been recommended. Even so, once such an aggregation problem has been identified, there is still a wide variation in how it can be handled, depending on the situation. Some examples include [MEAD90]:

1. Use the aggregation policy as a guide for downgrading. That is, begin by classifying all members of the aggregate at the level of the aggregate, and then downgrade as many as is consistent with the aggregation policy.

2. Use the aggregation policy as a guide for relaxing security requirements. In one example, the members of the aggregate were made available only to individuals who were cleared to the level of the aggregate, but they were allowed to follow less strict policies for handling individual aggregate members. Thus, an Unclassified member of a Confidential aggregate could be stored on an Unclassified PC.

3. Release individual members of an aggregate to individuals cleared at the lower level, but do not release more than a certain fixed number to any one individual. This was the policy followed in the SGA phone book example. Any individual could be given as many as N phone numbers, where N was some fixed number, but no more.

Another possible way of handling an aggregation problem can be used when inferences may be formed by watching the ways in which data changes over time. In this case, one could prevent inferences by limiting not the amount of data an individual sees, but the amount of time during which he has access to the data. This is essentially the "snapshot" approach discussed by Meadows and Jajodia [MEAD88a].

Aggregation policies are generally the result of an uneasy compromise between the need to protect sensitive data and the need to release useful data. This makes them difficult to account for in a formal security model and difficult to implement in a secure database without violating the general security policy. Moreover, the fact that different aggregation problems are dealt with using different security policies means that it is hard to come up with a mechanism that can be used to deal with all cases.

Nevertheless, a number of researchers have proposed various mechanisms to implement aggregation policies. These usually involve keeping some sort of history of each user's access, and granting or denying access to a member of the aggregate based on that history:

- In the SeaView system [LUNT89a], data is stored high and selectively downgraded according to the requester's past access history.

- In the LDV system [STAC90], data is stored low and access to it is selectively restricted based on its access by low users.
- In the Brewer-Nash model [BREW89] and its generalization by Meadows [MEAD90a], data is stored at different levels and access is granted to levels based on the past access history of the user or of a set of users. In Meadows' model, histories may also be kept of devices and other environments to which the data may be exported.

A problem closely related to aggregation and often confused with it is one commonly known as the "data association problem." This occurs when two data items may not be sensitive, but their association is. The most commonly cited example is the one in which names and salaries are considered non-sensitive, but the association between a name and a salary is. One way of dealing with this problem is to treat it as an aggregation problem; that is, to give a user access to names or to salaries, but not to both. However, as Lunt has pointed out [LUNT89a], what is really sensitive in this case is not the combination of a list of names and a list of salaries, but the association between individual names and individual salaries. If there is a way of keeping the association hidden, then there is no reason to prevent a user from learning names and salaries. Of course, as Lunt also points out, hiding such an association is by no means trivial. As a matter of fact, much of the work that has been done in statistical database security has been devoted to preventing inferences about such associations. However, the recognition that a particular aggregation problem is really a data association problem in disguise allows us to explore other techniques for dealing with it that may be more convenient to implement.

Conclusion

In this essay, we have identified various approaches to inference problems in databases. We have described some of the specific inference channels that can arise, and have outlined the various approaches to eliminating them. We have also described some general models of the inference problem in databases, as well as some tools and methodologies that implement these models. We have also presented some of the various approaches to aggregation problems, which are related to but not identical to inference problems.

Inference problems are an important but still relatively unexplored aspect of database security. However, the works surveyed in this essay show a number of promising ways of attacking these problems and a number of interesting angles from which they can be approached. A complete and general solution to the inference problem is impossible. However, in the future, given a good understanding of one's problem area and the ways in which inferences are made, it should be possible to construct a database that is both usable and reasonably secure against inference.

Logical Design of Audit Information in Relational Databases

Sushil Jajodia, Shashi K. Gadia, and Gautam Bhargava

In the "Trusted Computer System Evaluation Criteria" [DOD85], the accountability control objective is stated as follows:

> Systems that are used to process or handle classified or sensitive information must assure individual accountability whenever either a mandatory or discretionary security policy is invoked. Furthermore, to assure accountability the capability must exist for an authorized and competent agent to access and evaluate accountability information by a secure means, within a reasonable amount of time and without undue difficulty.

Existing databases clearly fail to meet this objective. They treat only the current data in a systematic manner; the old information is either deleted or stored on an ad hoc basis. If we wish to meet the above requirements in a database, we need to treat the audit data in a systematic way as well, not just the current data. Once this is done, we can then begin to address other issues related to audit.

A similar situation existed in the early 1960s. An application program used its own specially designed files. As a consequence, it was very difficult for a user to know what files already existed in the system. Knowing about the existence of a file was not sufficient; the user needed to know the actual file structure as well. If a file maintained by some program was reorganized, there was no assurance that other programs wishing to access the reorganized file would still work. Thus, much information was stored redundantly; however, there were problems when users started to look for mutual consistency of replicated data.

The database approach in the early 1970s overcame many of these problems. An important tool called a *data model* was developed, which imposed a logical structure on all the (current) data in the system. This allowed users to see data not as an arbitrary collection of files, but in more understandable terms. Database researchers developed another key concept called *independence:* The logical structure of the data became independent of the details of physical storage of data. Since now users could reorganize the physical scheme without changing the logic of existing programs, duplication of data could be avoided.

We assert that we must take a similar approach when it comes to audit data. First we must carefully list the audit objectives, then provide mechanisms to achieve these objectives. In addition to the actual recording of all events that take place in the database, a logical structure needs to be imposed on audit data. An audit trail requires mechanisms for a complete reconstruction of every action taken against the database [BJOR75, BONY88, FERN81]. Finally, an audit trail must also provide the capability (a query language) to easily access and tools to evaluate the audit information.

The organization of this essay is as follows. First we give the audit requirements and argue the need for two time dimensions to logically organize audit data. Then we present some notation and definitions. We devote a section to the database activity model and another to showing how we can restrict access to the database.

Audit requirements

A detailed discussion of audit requirements in trusted systems has been published by the National Computer Security Center [NCSC88] and other discussions are available in the literature [BJOR75, BONY88, FERN81]. An audit trail is a mechanism for a complete reconstruction of every action taken against the database: *who* has been accessing *what* data, *when,* and in what *order.* Thus, it has three basic objects of interest:

- The user. Who initiated a transaction, from what terminal, and when?
- The transaction. What was the exact transaction that was initiated?
- The data. What was the result of the transaction? What were the database states before and after the transaction initiation?

In addition to the actual recording of all events that take place in the database, an audit trail must also provide query support for auditing. The central point of this essay is to describe the data model called the *database activity model* [JAJO90g], which meets these objectives by providing a convenient mechanism for recording and querying accesses to the database.

Need for two time dimensions

In an auditable system, there must be a way to examine an old value of an attribute and to allow correction to this old value. At the same time, the database should retain the old value for future query and reexamination. This requires at least two time dimensions: one time dimension to order every operation against an object and a second time dimension to time stamp values of objects with their periods of validity in the real world [BJOR75, JAJO90g, LUM87, SNOD86, SNOD87]. This second time dimension is different from the first time dimension since an earlier value of an object may be corrected later in time.

As an example, suppose we have a relation called EMPLOYEE having two attributes NAME and SALARY. Suppose we inserted the tuple (Smith, 25K) on 1/11/85. On 3/2/86, we discovered an error in Smith's salary and made a retroactive change to 30K. Now, in an auditable system such as we discuss here, it is possible to overwrite errors, but records will be kept of any errors that are corrected. Thus, we need to retain both facts in the database:

1. Smith's salary was known to be 25K from 1/11/85 to 3/2/86.
2. On 3/2/86, a change was made to the salary from 25K to 30K, and this change was retroactive.

If we simply change the salary from 25K to 30K, we lose the second fact that an error was discovered in Smith's salary on 3/2/86, a change was made, and this change was retroactive. On the other hand, if we just change the value of the first time parameter from 1/11/85 to 3/2/86, we lose the first fact that the salary was considered to be 25K from 1/11/85 to 3/2/86.

Therefore, we need two different time parameters to describe this situation. We call the first time dimension the *transaction time*, the time at which the information is stored in the database. The second time dimension is the *valid time*, the time when the information in the database is valid in the real world. A relation that incorporates both transaction and valid times is called a *bitemporal relation*.

Preliminaries

We work in the context of the relational model of data. We presume the reader is familiar with relational database theory. A *relation scheme* R is a collection of attributes. K is said to be a *key* of R if the functional dependency $K \to R$ holds and if K does not contain a proper subset K' such that $K' \to R$ holds. A *relational scheme* R is a collection $\{R_1, ..., R_n\}$ of relation schemes, and a database $\mathbf{r}$ over $\mathbf{R}$ is a set of relations $\{r_1, ..., r_n\}$ such that each r_i is a relation over R_i.

We assume that users access the database by executing procedures, called *transactions*. A transaction is a sequence of operations viewed as an atomic unit of integrity, consistency, and recovery. We allow the usual operations in any transaction:

- Insert. Add a tuple in a relation.
- Delete. Remove a collection of tuples from a relation.
- Modify. Change values of a tuple in a relation.
- Retrieve. Access all tuples satisfying a given condition.

The database activity model

In this section, we describe the database activity model [JAJO90g]. A formal treatment of the temporal aspects of our model is given elsewhere [BHAR90, BHAR93].

Let **R** be a relational scheme. The *database activity scheme* over **R** is a triple <**D**, **Update-Store**, *Query-Store*> where

- For every relation scheme R in **R**, there is a two-dimensional temporal relation D (as illustrated in Figure 1) in **D**. It encapsulates the complete history of each and every modification made to a value of an attribute in R.
- For every D in **D**, there is a relation *Update-Store(D)* in **Update-Store**. *Update-Store(D)* records the circumstances surrounding the updates made to D.
- *Query-Store* is a single relation. It is essentially a log of all queries.

We describe each of these in detail next.

The bitemporal relations. We will describe a temporal relation that incorporates the concept of time at the logical level of design and use it to represent the two time dimensions. The resulting relation is called a *two-dimensional temporal relation*. An example of a bitemporal relation is shown in Figure 1. Although time typically consists of times or dates of events (as shown in Figure 3 later), for simplicity we will use integers as time values.

In a bitemporal relation, two different time parameters are associated with each value:

- *Transaction time.* The first time value, called the transaction time, is used to capture the complete history of all operations on an object. The domain for the transaction time is the time interval [0, *now*), where *now* is a special symbol that denotes the changing value of the present time.

- *Valid time.* The second time value, called the valid time, is used to time stamp a value with its period of validity in the real world, giving rise to a historical relation. The domain for the valid time is the time interval $[0, \infty)$. We augment $[0, \infty)$ with a new symbol *uc*, which stands for "until changed" [WIED91]. When we associate the valid time $[l, uc)$ with a value, the value is interpreted to be valid until it is changed.

NAME	SALARY	DEPT
$[8, now) \times [11, uc)$ John	$[8, 53) \times [11, uc)$ 15K $[53, now) \times [11, 50)$ 15K $[53, now) \times [50, uc)$ 20K	$[8, 40) \times [11, uc)$ Toys $[40, now) \times [11, 45)$ Toys $[40, now) \times [45, uc)$ Shoes
$[48, now) \times [48, uc)$ Doug	$[48, now) \times [48, \infty)$ 20K	$[48, now) \times [48, uc)$ Auto

Figure 1. A bitemporal relation.

Thus, our changing knowledge of the real world is modeled by associating two-dimensional time stamps with each value, and $[0, now) \times [0, \infty)$ serves as the universe of time. It should be pointed out that while the transaction time is always monotonically increasing, the valid time is not, since our knowledge of a history may change with time, requiring updates to the historical database.

Figure 2 illustrates how the two-dimensional time stamps should be interpreted. It shows the values taken by the attribute SALARY for the employee John in Figure 1.

$[8, 53) \times [11, uc)$ 15K
$[53, now) \times [11, 50)$ 15K
$[53, now) \times [50, uc)$ 20K

**Figure 2. John's salary in the
bitemporal relation.**

The semantics of the values is that "there was a transaction posted at time 8 declaring John's salary to be 15K from time 11 onward, but another transaction that was posted at time 53 updated John's salary to be 15K from time 11 to 50 and 20K from time 50 onward." Thus, we can think of salary as consisting of many versions, and the transaction time reflects the sequence of changes made to the salary over time. The valid time associated with each version provides the period of validity of that version.

Figure 3 gives the bitemporal relation for our earlier example with Smith. It is easy to verify that the temporal relation given in Figure 3 cleanly and accurately models the situation we described. It shows that Smith's salary is 30K from 1/11/85 onward; however, Smith's salary was known to be 25K during the time period 1/11/85 to 3/2/86, and a correction was made to the salary on 3/2/86.

NAME	SALARY
[1/11/85, *now*) × [1/11/85, *uc*) Smith	[1/11/85, 3/2/86) × [1/11/85, *uc*) 25K
	[3/2/86, *now*) × [1/11/85, *uc*) 30K

Figure 3. The bitemporal relation for the Smith example.

Thus, we see that the reexamination of historical data is possible in a bitemporal relation, and this allows corrections to be made as necessary (but still retains for future query and examination the fact of and data associated with the original "estimate" or "observation"). Moreover, the database may carry predictions of future operations or values. For example, the data may contain the required list of actions for the following weeks, such as times and places of any meetings, personnel actions to be taken, and so on [WIED91].

Update-Store and Query-Store relations. For each bitemporal relation, the database activity model maintains a relation called an *Update-Store* relation, which records information about all updates to the relation, and a relation called a *Query-Store* relation, which is essentially a log of all queries concerning the relation.

More formally, let R be a relation scheme in **R**, and let K be the key for R. Then the attributes of *Update-Store*(R) are the key K, the transaction time (TT), the authorizer of the transaction (AUTHORIZER), the user of the transaction (USER), and the reason for executing the transaction (REASON). (See Figure 4 below.)

The Query-Store relation contains a log of all the queries. It has the following attributes: the query (QUERY), the query time (TT), and the user posing the query (USER). (See Figure 5.)

One interesting property is that once we supplement the bitemporal relations with the Update-Store and Query-Store relations, the transaction log can be restored from these three relations. There is never any loss of information, and therefore we have the complete audit trail concept. We illustrate this next by way of an example.

Suppose our database consists of a single relation scheme EMP with attributes NAME, SALARY, and DEPT such that the attribute NAME is the key. Suppose for each transaction, we wish to keep track of the following audit information: transaction time (TT), who authorized the update (AUTHORIZER), the user making the update (USER), and the reason for the update (REASON). For each query, we store the query (Query-id), time of the query (TT), and user making the query (USER). Consider the following sequence of transactions:

T_1. TT = 8; User = Mark.
insert (NAME: [11, uc) JOHN; SALARY: [11, uc) 15K; DEPT: [11, uc) Toys)
with (Authorizer = Don; Reason = New Employee);

T_2. TT = 40; User = Ryne.
modify (NAME: [11, uc) JOHN) to (DEPT: [11, 45) Toys, [45, uc) shoes)
with (Authorizer = Don; Reason = Reassignment);

T_3. TT = 42; User = Vance.
Q1: What is John's salary?

T_4. TT = 48; User = Rick.
insert (NAME: [48, uc) Doug; SALARY: [48, uc) 20K; DEPT: [48, uc) Auto)
with (Authorizer = Joe; Reason = New Employee);

T_5. TT = 53; User = Dameon.
modify (NAME: [11, uc) JOHN) to (SALARY: [11, 50) 15K, [50, uc) 20K)
with (Authorizer = Don; Reason = Promotion);

T_6. TT = 54; User = Andre.
Q1: What is John's salary?

T_7. TT = 55; User = Mitch.
Q2: What is John's department?

T_8. TT = 56; User = Don.
Q3: Who made inquiries about John's salary?

T_9. TT = 58; User = Paul.
Q2: What is John's department?

Figure 1 gives the two-dimensional temporal relation corresponding to these transactions. Figures 4 and 5 give the resulting Update-Store and Query-Store relations, respectively.

Logical Design of Audit Information in Relational Databases   **591**

NAME	TT	AUTHORIZER	USER	REASON
John	8	Don	Mark	New Employee
John	40	Don	Ryne	Reassignment
Doug	48	Joe	Rick	New Employee
John	53	Don	Dameon	Promotion

Figure 4. The Update-Store relation.

QUERY	TT	USER
Q1: John's SALARY	42	Vance
Q1: John's SALARY	54	Andre
Q2: John's DEPT	55	Mitch
Q3: USER ID of Q1	56	Don
Q2: John's DEPT	58	Paul

Figure 5. The Query-Store relation.

It is easy to verify that all the transactions can be completely restored using the three relations in our database activity model: The values of the key NAME in the bitemporal relation (Figure 1) and in the Update-Store relation (Figure 4) set up a logical correspondence between the tuples in the two relations. By including the transaction time, the logical correspondence can be refined to a one-to-one correspondence between all the updates to the temporal relation and the tuples in the Update-Store relation. As a result, the transactions T_1, T_2, T_4, and T_5 can be completely restored from the relations in Figures 1 and 4. The transactions T_3 and T_6 through T_9 can be completely restored from the relations in Figures 1 and 5. Finally, using the transaction time TT, we can order all nine transactions to obtain the original sequence of transactions.

Support for auditing. Another nice feature of the database activity model is that it has a simple yet powerful relational algebra to express audit and other queries about relations. We refer the reader elsewhere for a brief description [JAJO90g] of the relational algebra and more complete descriptions [BHAR90, BHAR93].

Restricting access to the database

Since our database activity model contains information about the complete activity in the database system, we next consider how we can restrict user access to the database.

Assigning security level to transactions. It is possible to assign a security level to each transaction, which allows the incorporation of still further concepts of tagging the data with its security level at the object level [JAJO90g]. The data takes on the security level of the transaction because of the level of authority implied by the transaction creating or modifying the elements of the object. Thus, an object is itself not classified, but its parts carry different (possibly time-variant) security constraints. As a consequence, the response to a query or update transaction depends on the security level of the system user or the level at which the user is operating, in conjunction with the security policy that applies at the time of the operation.

The user hierarchy. A second way we limit access of a user is by filtering the database through a user hierarchy defined as follows. We use the symbol *now* to denote the changing value of the current time.

The master user. The master user has access to the whole database (for example, Figure 1) and enjoys the power to query errors and updates in the database.

The history user. This user sees only information filtered through the time domain $now \times [0, uc)$, and thus has access to only the most up-to-date knowledge of the history of objects (for example, the relation in Figure 6). Errors that have been corrected are not available to the history user. Such a user can ask questions of a historical nature such as "When did Tom's salary increase?"

NAME	SALARY	DEPT
[11, *uc*) John	[11, 50) 15K [50, *uc*) 20K	[11, 45) Toys [45, *uc*) Shoes
[48, *uc*) Doug	[48, *uc*) 20K	[48, *uc*) Auto

Figure 6. The bitemporal relation as seen by a history user.

The snapshot user. The filter in this case is the time domain $now \times now$, and this user sees precisely what is available to a traditional user in databases (for example, Figure 7). In our framework such a user lies at the lowest level of the user hierarchy.

NAME	SALARY	DEPT
John	20K	Shoes
Doug	20K	Auto

Figure 7. The bitemporal relation as seen by a snapshot user.

The audit user. This user sees the data filtered through the time domain $\{(t,\ t'):\ t' \leq t\}$, does not have the concept of future (since $t \leq now$), and sees only the actions taken by the organization. Since the rest of the world is affected only by the organization's actions, this user can deal with the public relations and legal aspects of the enterprise.

The rollback snapshot user. This user sees the data filtered through the time domain $t \times t'$ for fixed values of t and t'. Like the snapshot user, this user sees a snapshot relation, with the difference that this user can see a snapshot at any point in the past, present, or future. For example, a rollback snapshot user will be given the snapshot in Figure 8 for the time domain 8 × 11, and the snapshot in Figure 9 for the time domain 48 × 50.

NAME	SALARY	DEPT
John	15K	Toys

Figure 8. The bitemporal relation filtered through the time domain 8 × 11.

NAME	SALARY	DEPT
John	15K	Shoes
Doug	20K	Auto

Figure 9. The bitemporal relation filtered through the time domain 48 × 50.

Conclusion

In an audit trail, it should be possible to audit every event in a database; we call this *zero-information loss*. What events are actually audited depends on the sensitivity of the events in question and the results of a careful risk analysis.

Our new model seems to be a building block for a general-purpose database system that holds the promise for a perfect logical organization of past, present, and future data. This aspect of our model can be exploited further to allow automatic regeneration and review of events that occur in the database system to detect and discourage security violations. As an example, Meadows and Jajodia [MEAD88b, Section 3] describe a situation with several instances where security requirements are in conflict with the data availability requirements, and they recommend auditing as a means of controlling information leaks. Our model can help identify such attempts to bypass security controls.

Essay 26

A Multilevel Secure Object-Oriented Data Model

Sushil Jajodia, Boris Kogan, and Ravi S. Sandhu

Recently, several security models have appeared in the literature dealing with mandatory access controls in object-oriented databases. While some of them are of considerable interest and merit (see the later section "Review of relevant research" for a discussion), they seem to lack intuitive appeal because they do not appear to model security in a way that takes full advantage of the object-oriented paradigm. Our goal in this essay is to construct a database security model for mandatory access controls that dovetails with the object-oriented data model in a natural way. The result, we hope, is a set of principles to help design and implement security policies in object-oriented database management systems in a clear and concise fashion.

The object-subject paradigm of Bell and LaPadula [BELL76, DENN82] is widely used in work on mandatory access controls. An object is understood to be a data file or, at an abstract level, a data item. A subject is an active process that can request access to objects. Every object is assigned a classification, and every subject a clearance. Classifications and clearances are collectively referred to as security levels (or classes). Security levels are partially ordered. A subject is allowed a read access to an object only if the former's clearance is equivalent to or higher (in the partial order) than the latter's classification. A subject is allowed a write access to an object only if the former's clearance is equivalent to or lower than the latter's classification. Since a system may not be secure even if it always enforces the two Bell-LaPadula restrictions correctly, a secure system must guard against not only the direct revelation of data but also violations that produce illegal information flows through indirect means, including *covert* channels [DENN82]. The above restrictions are intended to ensure that there is no flow of information from high objects to low subjects. For otherwise, since subjects can represent users, a breach of security occurs wherein users get access to information for which they have not been cleared.

Most security models for mandatory access controls are based on the traditional Bell-LaPadula paradigm. While this paradigm has proven to be quite effective for modeling security in operating systems as well as relational databases, it appears somewhat forced when applied to object-oriented systems. The problem is that the notion of object in the object-oriented data model does not correspond to the Bell-LaPadula notion of object. The former combines the properties of a passive information repository, represented by attributes and their values, with the properties of an active agent, represented by methods and their invocations. Thus, the object of the object-oriented data model can be thought of as the object and the subject of the Bell-LaPadula paradigm fused into one.

Continuing the examination of the object-oriented model from the security perspective, one arrives at the realization that information flow in this context has a very concrete and natural embodiment in the form of messages and their replies. Moreover, taking into account encapsulation, a cardinal property of object-oriented systems, messages can be considered the only instrument of information flow.

The main elements of our model can be sketched out as follows. The system consists of objects (in the object-oriented sense rather than the Bell-LaPadula sense). Every object is assigned a unique classification. Objects can communicate — and thereby exchange information — only by sending messages and replies among themselves. However, messages are not allowed to flow directly from one object to another. Instead, every message or reply is intercepted by the message filter, a system element charged with implementing security policies. The message filter decides, upon examining a given message (or reply) and the classifications of the sender and receiver, what action is appropriate. It may

- let the message go through unaltered,
- completely reject the message (for example, when a low object sends a message to a high object requesting the value of one of the latter's attributes), or
- take some other action (such as restricting the method invocation which processes the message to be "memoryless," as will be discussed later).

The principal advantages of the proposed model are its compatibility with the object-oriented data model and the simplicity and conceptual clarity with which mandatory security policies are stated and enforced.

One comment is in order at this point. Even though all objects are single-level (in the sense of having a unique classification assigned to the entire object and not assigning any classifications to individual attributes or methods), this does not preclude the possibility of modeling multilevel entities by means of multiple single-level objects, as will be demonstrated later.

The organization of this essay is as follows. We begin by introducing our basic object-oriented data model and then enhance this basic model by adding to it the elements needed for security. We discuss how our security model handles information flow due to inheritance in a class hierarchy. Then we show how we can represent multilevel entities in a security model in which all objects are single-level. After a brief review of related research, we give our conclusions and discuss our future work.

Object-oriented data model

An object-oriented database is a collection of *objects* communicating via *messages* and their *replies*. Objects are of two types: primitive and nonprimitive. We postulate a finite set of domains D_1, D_2, ..., D_n. Let D be the union of the domains augmented with a special element *nil* (whose purpose we explain later). Every element of D is referred to as a *primitive object*.

A *nonprimitive object o* is defined by its unique identifier i, an ordered set $a = (a_1, ..., a_k)$ of attribute names, an ordered set $v = (v_1, ..., v_k)$ of corresponding values, and a set μ of methods. A value is either a primitive object or an identifier. (A more general object model would also permit a value to be a set of identifiers and/or primitive values. However, for simplicity of exposition, we forego this generalization in this essay. The results developed here do not depend on this simplification.)

We will use the following notation in the rest of the essay. For an object o, $i(o)$ denotes its unique identifier, $a(o)$ denotes its attributes, $v(o)$ denotes the corresponding values, and $\mu(o)$ denotes its methods.

A *message g* consists of a *message name h*, an ordered set $p = (p_1, ..., p_k)$, $k \geq 0$, of primitive objects or object identifiers called the *message parameters*, and a *reply r*. Similar to the notation used for objects, we let $h(g)$, $p(g)$, and $r(g)$ denote the name, the parameter list, and the reply for message g, respectively.

Each object o has an interface f_o that determines which messages o responds to. Moreover, the interface determines which particular method, out of the set of methods $\mu(o)$ defined for object o, is to be invoked, depending on the name of the given message.

An object will invoke one of its methods in response to a message received from another object.[1] A method invocation can, in turn, carry out one or more of the following actions:

1. directly access an attribute belonging to the object (read or change its value),
2. invoke other methods belonging to the object,

---

[1] If an object cannot find a method to process this particular message, we assume there is a default failure method that returns an appropriate reply.

3. send a message to another object, or
4. create a new object, eventually returning a reply to the source of the message.

An object sends a message g by invoking a system primitive $SEND(g, i)$, where i is the identifier of the receiver object. The reply $r(g)$ is computed by the method activated in the receiver upon the arrival of g there and returned to the sender. As we shall see in the next section, sometimes the security component of the system will have to interfere in the matter of computing $r(g)$ (particularly to ensure that this computation is "memoryless" if so required by security considerations).

There is a special type of object, called *user* object. A user object represents a user session with the system. User objects can be created only by the system, at login time. User objects differ from regular objects in that, in addition to being able to invoke methods in response to messages, they can also invoke methods spontaneously. The notion of spontaneous method invocation may seem rather arbitrary at first. It is, however, necessary to avoid running into a version of the chicken-or-the-egg paradox: Namely, if a message can be sent only through a method invocation (see property 3 of method invocations) and if a method can be activated only by a message received from another object, then how does any processing in such a system ever get initiated? (One has to insist that either the egg or the chicken comes first.) In reality, we want a user to be able to initiate a system activity, for example, by typing a string of characters on the keyboard. This would serve as a signal for the corresponding user object to initiate a method. We choose to think of this as a "spontaneous" initiation, because the keyboard and any signals that it sends are external to our model.

Objects are used to model real-world entities. This is done by associating properties, or facets, of an entity with attributes of the corresponding object.[2] The attribute values are, then, instantiations of those properties. For instance, a country can be represented in a geographic object-oriented database by an object o where $a(o)$ = (COUNTRY_NAME, POPULATION, CAPITAL, NATIONAL_FLAG, FORM_OF_GOVERNMENT) and $v(o)$ = ("Albania", 117, $i(o_1)$, $i(o_2)$, $i(o_3)$). The values of the first and second attributes are a string and an integer, respectively. The values of the rest of the attributes are references to other objects that, in turn, describe the capital, the national flag, and the form of government of the nation Albania.

Note that an object's methods, unlike its attributes, do not have counterparts in the real-world entity modeled by the object. The purpose of methods is quite different. It is to provide support for manipulation of

---

[2] More generally, as we will see later, a single entity may be modeled by more than one object.

objects, including the basic database functions of querying and updating objects.

A realistic object-oriented model should also contain the notion of constraints. For instance, an attribute of an object may be allowed to assume values only from a restricted subset of domains or object identifiers. To simplify the exposition, we choose to disregard the issue of constraints in this essay. However, it is a conceptually simple matter to incorporate this notion in our secure data model.

Object-oriented security model

We gave our earlier informal exposition of our security model in terms of objects with unique security-level assignments exchanging messages subject to some security constraints. This section is devoted to developing a formal model of object-oriented security, in accordance with this general idea.

Security levels and information flow. The system consists of a set O of objects and a partially ordered set S of security levels with ordering relation $<$. A level $S_i \in S$ is said to be dominated by another level $S_j \in S$, this being denoted by $S_i \leq S_j$, if $i = j$ or $S_i < S_j$. For two levels S_i and S_j that are unordered by $<$, we write $S_i <> S_j$.

There is a total function $L: O \rightarrow S$, called the *security classification* function. In other words, every object o has a unique security level $L(o)$ associated with it.

Characterization of information flows. The main goal of a security policy concerned with confidentiality is to control the flow of information among objects. More specifically, information can *legally* flow from an object o_j to an object o_k if and only if $L(o_j) \leq L(o_k)$. All other information flows are considered *illegal*.

In the Bell-LaPadula model this objective is achieved by prohibiting read-ups and write-downs. That is, a subject is allowed to read an object only if the security level of the subject dominates the security level of the object. Similarly, a subject is allowed to update an object only if the security level of the former is dominated by that of the latter.

In our model, due to the property of encapsulation, information transfer between objects can take place either

1. when a message is passed from one object to another, or
2. when a new object is created.

In the first case, information can flow in both directions: from the sender to the receiver and back. The *forward* flow is carried through the list of parameters contained in the message, and the *backward* flow through the reply. In the second case, information flows only in the forward direction: from the creating object to the created one — for example, by means of supplying attribute values for the new object.

A transfer of information does not necessarily occur every time a message is passed. An object acquires information by changing its internal state, that is, by changing the values of some of its attributes. Thus, if no such changes occur as a result of a method invocation in response to a message, then no information has been transferred. In such cases we can say that the forward flow has been *ineffective*. This situation is analogous to taking pictures with an unloaded camera. The information in the form of light is flowing into the camera but not being retained there.

Similarly, if the reply of a message is *nil*, the backward flow has been ineffective. To eliminate the information channel associated with the receiver object's security level being dynamically changed (in which case the sender can get back a sequence of *nil* and non-*nil* replies if it repeatedly sends messages to the same object), we have to require that all security-level assignments be static. That is, the level associated with an object at creation time cannot be changed.[3] If, however, the security level of the real-world entity that the object models must be changed, then a new object has to be created. The new object will be exactly like the one that it replaced, except for the new security level to reflect the desired change.

We say that a *transitive* flow from an object o_1 to an object o_2 occurs when there is a flow from o_1 to a third object o_3 and from o_3 to o_2.

All types of flows discussed until now can be termed *direct* flows. Now, consider what happens when an object o_1 sends a message g_1 to another object o_2, and o_2 does not change its internal state as a result of receiving g_1, but instead sends a message g_2 to a third object o_3. Further, suppose that $p(g_2)$ contains information derived from message g_1 (for example, by copying some parameters of g_1 to g_2). If, then, the invocation of $f_{o_3}(h(g_2))$ results in updating o_3's state, a transfer of information has taken place from o_1 to o_3. There is no message exchange between o_1 and o_3, nor was o_3 created by o_1; therefore, this flow cannot be considered direct. Moreover, there may or may not be a flow from o_1 to o_2; therefore, this is not necessarily a transitive flow either. This is an instance of what we call an *indirect* flow of information. Note that an indirect flow can involve more than three objects. For example, instead of updating its state, o_3 could send a message to a fourth object that would result in updating the latter's state.

---

[3] This is similar to the tranquillity requirement in the Bell-LaPadula model, whereby the security labels on subjects and objects cannot change [DENN82].

Both direct and indirect illegal flows of information should be prevented (this will also account for all transitive flows) if the system is to be secure.

Primitive messages. We assume that access to internal attributes, object creation (creation by an object of an instance of itself), and invocation of internal methods are all effected by having an object send a message to itself.[4] We now define three built-in messages for that purpose. First, however, it is necessary to modify the definition of a message as follows. A message g consists of a message name h, an ordered set $p = (p_1, ..., p_k)$, $k \geq 0$, of message parameters where a p_i can be a primitive object or an object identifier or a security level, and a reply r. (The difference, with respect to our earlier definition, is that now a parameter can be a method, an attribute name, or a security level in addition to the previous cases of a primitive value or an object identifier.)

The three primitive messages can now be defined as follows:[5]

- A *read* message is a message sent by an object o to itself defined as $g = (READ, (a_j), r)$ where $a_j \in a(o)$. A read message results in binding r to the value of attribute a_j. If this cannot be done, say, because there is no attribute a_j, r is returned as FAILURE (which is a reserved symbol with obvious significance).
- A *write* message is a message sent by an object o to itself defined as $g = (WRITE, (a_j, v_j), r)$ where $a_j \in a(o)$. The effect of sending a write message is an update of attribute a_j with value v_j. The reply r is either SUCCESS or FAILURE (SUCCESS, like FAILURE, is a reserved symbol with obvious significance).
- Finally, a *create* message is defined as $g = (CREATE, (v_1, ..., v_k, S_j), r)$ where p is a list of attribute values, $v_1, ..., v_k$, appended with a security level S_j. When sent by an object o to itself, a create message results in a new object being created. This new object is assigned an identifier i by the system. The object inherits attributes

---

[4] There are existing object-oriented database systems (for example, GemStone) that, in fact, actually use this kind of implementation. At the same time it is important to note that our model is a conceptual one telling us *what* needs to be done, rather than *how* it will actually be implemented. A correct implementation must demonstrate that it satisfies the model's requirements, even though it may do so without mimicking each aspect of the model action for action.

[5] In reality, we would need additional primitive messages in a practical system. The three primitives identified here suffice to illustrate the main ideas. Additional primitive messages would be handled in much the same way. In particular, we have not included a delete primitive operation. Delete can be regarded as an extreme form of write, and essentially requires the same kind of security mediation as write.

and methods from o. The attributes are initialized with the values $v_1, ..., v_k$. The new object is assigned security level S_j, as specified in g. If the creation is successful, the identifier i is returned to o as r. Otherwise, FAILURE is returned.

Message-filtering algorithm. The *message filter* is a security element of the system whose goal is to recognize and prevent illegal information flows. The message filter intercepts every message sent by any object in the system and, based on the security levels of the sender and receiver, as well as some auxiliary information, decides how to handle the message. In other words, the message filter is the reference monitor of the system.

The message-filtering algorithm is presented in Figure 1. We assume that o_1 and o_2 are sender and receiver objects respectively. Also, let t_1 be the method invocation in o_1 that sent the message g_1, and t_2 the method invocation in o_2 on receipt of g_1. The two major cases of the algorithm correspond to whether or not g_1 is a primitive message.

Cases 1 through 4 in Figure 1 deal with nonprimitive messages sent between two objects, say o_1 and o_2. In case 1, the sender and the receiver are at the same level. The message and the reply are allowed to pass. The *rlevel* of t_2 will be the same as that of t_1. Note that *rlevel* is a property of a method invocation. We will explain its significance shortly, but for the moment let us ignore it. In case 2, the levels of o_1 and o_2 are incomparable, and thus the message is blocked and a *nil* reply returned to method t_1. In case 3, the receiver is at a higher level than the sender. The message is passed through. However, a *nil* reply is returned to t_1, while the actual reply from t_2 is discarded, thus effectively cutting off the backward flow. (Note that the delivery of this *nil* reply to t_1 cannot be synchronized with the attempted reply from t_2 to t_1; otherwise, there will be information leakage associated with the timing of the reply.) For case 4, the receiver is at a lower level than the sender. The message and the reply are allowed to pass. However, the *rlevel* of t_2 (in the receiver object) is set in such a manner as to prevent illegal flows. In other words, although a message is allowed to pass from a high-level sender to a low-level receiver, it cannot cause a "write-down" violation because the method invocation in the receiver is restricted from modifying the state of the object or creating a new object (that is, the method invocation is "memoryless"). Moreover, this restriction is propagated along with further messages sent out by this method invocation to other objects, as far as is needed for security purposes.

% let $g_1 = (h_1, (p_1, ..., p_k), r)$ be the message sent from o_1 to o_2

if $o_1 \neq o_3 \vee h_1 \notin$ {READ, WRITE, CREATE} then case
% i.e., g_1 is a nonprimitive message

(1) $L(o_1) = L(o_2)$:   % let g_1 pass, let reply pass
         invoke t_2 with $rlevel(t_2) \leftarrow rlevel(t_1)$;
         $r \leftarrow$ reply from t_2; return r to t_1;

(2) $L(o_1) <> L(o_2)$: % block g_1, inject NIL reply
         $r \leftarrow$ NIL; return r to t_1;

(3) $L(o_1) < L(o_2)$:   % let g_1 pass, inject NIL reply, ignore actual reply
         $r \leftarrow$ NIL; return r to t_1;
         invoke t_2 with $rlevel(t_2) \leftarrow lub[L(o_2), rlevel(t_1)]$;
         % where lub denotes least upper bound
         discard reply from t_2;

(4) $L(o_1) > L(o_2)$:   % let g_1 pass, let reply pass
         invoke t_2 with $rlevel(t_2) \leftarrow rlevel(t_1)$;
         $r \leftarrow$ reply from t_2; return r to t_1;

end case;

if $o_1 = o_2 \wedge h_1 \in$ {READ, WRITE, CREATE} then case
% i.e., g_1 is a primitive message

(5) $g_1 = $ (READ, (a_j), r): % allow unconditionally
         $r \leftarrow$ value of a_j; return r to t_1;

(6) $g_1 = $ (WRITE, (a_j, v_j), r): % allow if status of t_1 is unrestricted
         if $rlevel(t_1) = L(o_1)$
            then $[a_j \leftarrow v_j; r \leftarrow$ SUCCESS$]$
            else $r \leftarrow$ FAILURE;
         return r to t_1;

(7) $g_1 = $ (CREATE, $(v_1, ..., v_k, S_j)$, r): % allow if status of t_1 is unrestricted
                               relative to S_j
         if $rlevel(t_1) \leq S_j$
            then [CREATE i with values $v_1, ..., v_k$ and
                    $L(i) \leftarrow S_j; r \leftarrow i]$
            else $r \leftarrow$ FAILURE;
         return r to t_1;

end case

Figure 1. Message-filtering algorithm.

The intuitive significance of $rlevel$ is that it keeps track of the least upper bound of all objects encountered in a chain of method invocations, going back to the user object at the root of the chain. We can show this by induction on the length of the method invocation chain. To do so, it is also useful to show the related property that $rlevel(t_i) \geq L(o_i)$. For the basis case, we assume that the spontaneous method invocation in the root user object has its $rlevel$ set to the level of the user object. The induction step follows by inspection of cases 1, 2, and 3 of Figure 1. The use of least upper bound is explicit in case 3.[6] In cases 2 and 4, because of the induction hypothesis and the relative levels of o_1 and o_2, the assignment of $rlevel$ can be equivalently written as in case 3.

We say that a method invocation t_i has restricted status if $rlevel(t_i) > L(o_i)$. In such cases, t_i is not allowed to write to o_i (case 6 of Figure 1) or to create an object (case 7). A key element of the message filter algorithm is that the restricted status is propagated along with further messages sent out by a method invocation to other objects (exactly so far as is needed for security purposes). This is critical in preventing indirect information flows.

To understand how the message filter algorithm propagates the restricted status on method invocations, it is useful to visualize the generation of a tree of method invocations, as shown in Figure 2. The root t_0 is a "spontaneous" method invocation by a user. The restricted method invocations are shown within shaded regions. Suppose t_k is a method for object o_k and t_n a method for object o_n, which resulted from a message sent from t_k to o_n. The method t_n has a restricted status because $L(o_n) < L(o_k)$. The children and descendants of t_n will continue to have a restricted status until t_s is reached. The method t_s is no longer restricted because $L(o_s) \geq L(o_k)$ and a write by t_s to the state of o_s no longer constitutes a write-down. This is accounted for in the assignment to $rlevel(t_2)$ in case 3 of Figure 1.

The variable $rlevel$ clearly plays a critical role in determining whether the child of a restricted method should itself be restricted. A method invocation potentially obtains information from security levels at or below its own $rlevel$. It follows that a method invocation should only be allowed to record information labeled at levels which dominate its own $rlevel$. For example, consider a message sent from a Secret object to a Confidential one (where Secret > Confidential). The $rlevel$ derived for the method invocation at the receiver object will be Secret.

---

[6] We need to use the least upper bound for computing $rlevel$ in case 3 rather than the maximum, because the security levels are partially ordered. It is possible for a chain of method invocations to descend in security levels along one branch of the partial order, and then turn around and start ascending along a different branch.

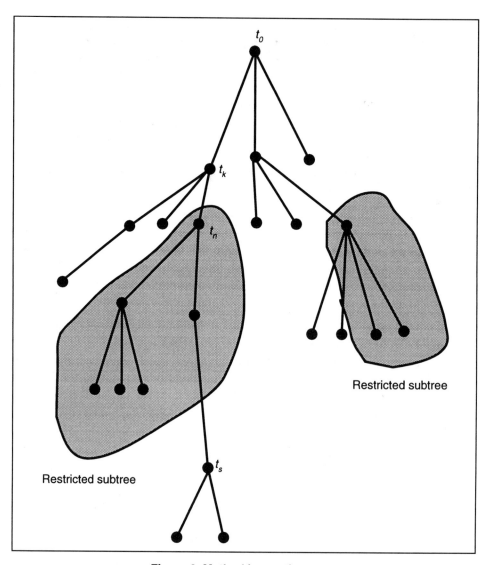

Figure 2. Method invocation tree.

We now discuss the security mediation of primitive messages. Read operations (case 5) never fail due to security reasons because read-up operations cannot occur. This is because read operations are confined to an object's methods, and their results can only be exported by messages or replies which are filtered by the message filter. The write and create operations invoked on receiving the write and create messages (cases 6 and 7) will succeed only if the status of the method invoking the operations is unrestricted. If a write or create operation fails, a failure message is sent to the sender. This failure message does not violate security since information is flowing upward in level.

The general idea of the message filter is similar to that of the law filter introduced by Minsky and Rozenshtein [MINS87], although their work has no direct relation to security. The message filter can be implemented on top of the object layer. Since its purpose is to enforce security, the message filter has to be trusted (that is, it has to be part of the trusted computing base).

An example of message filtering. We now present a brief example to illustrate the message-filtering algorithm of Figure 1 with the help of a payroll database. Our simple object-oriented database consists of three classes of objects: (1) EMPLOYEE (Unclassified), (2) PAY-INFO (Secret), and (3) WORK-INFO (Unclassified) with the corresponding attributes as shown in Figure 3. Objects EMPLOYEE and WORK-INFO are Unclassified as their attributes (such as name, address, hours worked) represent information about an employee that can be made readily available. The object PAY-INFO is Secret because its attributes contain sensitive information such as hourly rate and weekly pay.

Let us see how cases 1, 3, and 4 in the filtering algorithm apply to the payroll database. Case 1 occurs when the sender and receiver are at the same level and applies to the message exchange between objects EMPLOYEE and WORK-INFO. The message RESET-WEEKLY-HOURS and reply DONE are both allowed to pass by the message filter. Case 3 applies to the message exchange between objects EMPLOYEE and PAY-INFO. As the latter is classified higher, a NIL reply is returned in response to the PAY message and the actual reply is discarded. Case 4 involves the objects PAY-INFO and WORK-INFO. As the object WORK-INFO is classified lower than PAY-INFO, the message GET-HOURS and reply HOURS-WORKED are allowed to pass. However, the method invocation in WORK-INFO is given the restricted status (due to its *rlevel* being Secret). This prevents the method from updating the state of object WORK-INFO (which, if allowed, would cause a write-down violation).

Class hierarchy and security

The notion of *classes* is usually considered very important for object-oriented databases, if not for object-oriented systems in general. Most existing object-oriented databases support classes. In this section, we discuss how our security model deals with information flow due to inheritance in a class hierarchy.

The notion of classes is akin to that of relations in relational databases. Objects of similar structure (types and names of attributes) and similar behavior (methods) are grouped into classes, just like tuples of the same structure, in relational databases, are grouped into relations. The parallel to relational systems does not go very far, however. First, in relational databases, there is no notion analogous to that of object behavior. Second, classes in object-oriented databases are represented by objects that contain information on the names and types of attributes of the constituent *instance* objects of the class as well as the methods common to them. Objects of this kind are called *class-defining* objects, or simply class objects. Thus, there is essentially no distinction between representations of data and metadata in object-oriented systems.

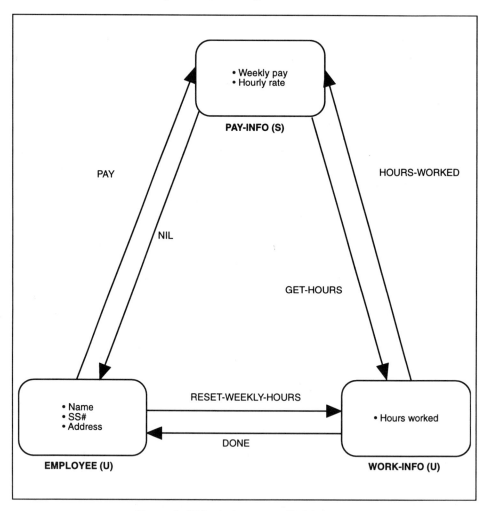

Figure 3. Objects in a payroll database.

We assume that the reader has a basic familiarity with the notions of inheritance and class hierarchy [KIM89, ZDON90]. A typical class hierarchy has a class OBJECT at its root. It also includes a special class CLASS such that every object defining a class is an instance of CLASS.

Earlier we discussed ways by which objects can transfer information to one another. Message sending and object creation were mentioned in this connection. We then went on to define several types of information flow. With the introduction of classes and inheritance, two more (implicit) ways to transfer information are added.

Since a class object (that is, a class-defining object) contains structure and behavior information for all its instance objects, the latter have an implicit read access to the former. Thus, an information flow exists from a class object to an instance object. We refer to this type of flow as a *class-instance flow*.

Since classes inherit attributes and methods from their ancestors in the class hierarchy, a class object has an implicit read access to all its ancestors. Therefore, there is an information flow down along all hierarchy links. This type of flow is designated *inheritance flow*.

It is easy to see that an inheritance flow is illegal unless the level of a class object dominates the level of each of its ancestors. Similarly, a class-instance flow is illegal unless the level of an instance object dominates that of its class.

Our approach to dealing with illegal inheritance and class-instance flows is to implement the classification and inheritance features by means of message passing. (The details of such an implementation are available elsewhere [MINS87].) The purpose of this approach is to make the *implicit* flows discussed above *explicit*, that is, realized by messages. As a consequence, class-instance and inheritance flows can be checked by the message filter, just as forward, backward, and indirect flows are.[7]

It is still a good idea, though, to place the following constraints on the way the security levels of instance objects and subclass objects relate to those of the corresponding class objects:

- *Security-level constraint 1.* If o_j is an object of class c_j (c_j also denotes the corresponding class object), then $L(c_j) \leq L(o_j)$.
- *Security-level constraint 2.* If c_i and c_j are classes such that c_j is a child of c_i in the class hierarchy, then $L(c_i) \leq L(c_j)$.

It is important to understand that these two constraints are not introduced for security reasons — security is still handled by the message-

---

[7] It should be noted that there is a great deal of disagreement with respect to the exact scope of inheritance in a class hierarchy (for example, see [NIER89]). Since we have chosen to define our security model in terms of information flow among objects, any illegal information flow due to inheritance, regardless of its specific inheritance features, will be prevented as long as these features are implemented by message passing.

filtering algorithm because all flows, including the class-instance and inheritance flows, are explicitly cast in the form of messages. Therefore, a violation of these constraints will not lead to a violation of security. Instead, a violation of security-level constraint 2, for example, will result in breakdown of the inheritance mechanism. It will create a situation wherein a class object is prevented by the message filter from gaining access to a method it inherits from its parent class (because the security level of the child does not dominate that of the parent, as required by the constraint).

Note that security-level constraint 1 is automatically satisfied by the message-filtering algorithm (see case 7 of Figure 1) at the instance-creation time. It is interesting to note, though, that this feature was originally included in the algorithm to prevent the illegal direct flow to the newly created object at the creation time, rather than the illegal class-instance flow, which can take place at any time after the instance is created. However, the provision works equally well in both cases.

Constraint 2 is not automatically satisfied by the message-filtering algorithm, but the algorithm could be modified for that purpose. Alternatively, the constraint could be enforced by supplying the object CLASS with a method for creation of new classes that would check that the security levels of the new classes are in the prescribed relationship to the levels of their parents. The second possibility is, perhaps, preferable because we want to keep the message filter — a trusted piece of software — as small as possible.

Modeling multilevel entities with single-level objects

In an object-oriented data model, objects are used to model real-world entities. Therefore, it may seem somewhat discouraging that our security model insists that all objects be "flat," that is, at a single security level. Much modeling flexibility would be lost if multilevel entities could not be represented in our database.

In this section, we will demonstrate that restricting objects to be single-level does not have to imply that the same type of restriction exists for entities that we are trying to model. We will do this by means of a few simple examples.

Suppose that there are two security levels: U (Unclassified) and S (Secret), the latter dominating the former. Consider an entity e characterized by attributes A, B, and C such that A and B are at level U and C is at level S (e could be a collection of information pertaining to an employee, where A is the employee's name, B is the home address, and C is the salary). The intention is to allow access to C only for users with Secret clearance. All other users can access only A and B. Entity e can be represented by objects o_1 and o_2 such that $a(o_1) = (A, B)$, $a(o_2) = (A, B, C)$, $L(o_1) = U$, and $L(o_2) = S$. Object o_2 is the internal representation of entity *e* for users with the Secret clearance, while o_1 is the representation of *e* for all other users. The example is illustrated in Figure 4. Attributes of entity *e* have individual security labels (shown in parentheses). This is in contrast to objects o_1 and o_2, which have labels only at the object level.

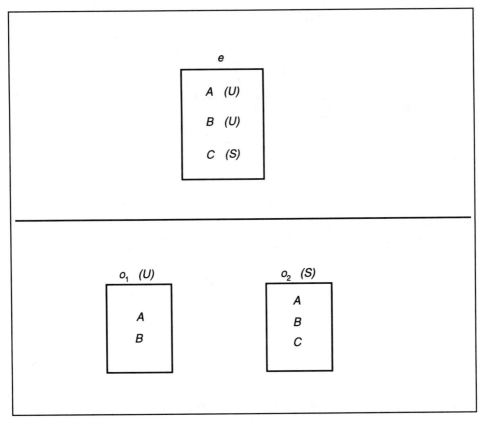

Figure 4. Representing a multilevel entity by multiple single-level objects.

Suppose now that we have an entire collection of entities of the same type as *e* (a set of entities with Unclassified attributes *A* and *B* and a Secret attribute *C*). Let us call this type of entity *X*. In our model, each entity of this type will be represented by two objects: one for users with the Secret clearance and one for all others. Thus, we end up with two classes of objects for one type of entity. The distinction between the two classes is based on security, not semantics, as would normally be the case in object-oriented databases. Let *XU* be the class of the Unclassified objects and *XS* the class of the Secret objects representing entities of type *X*.

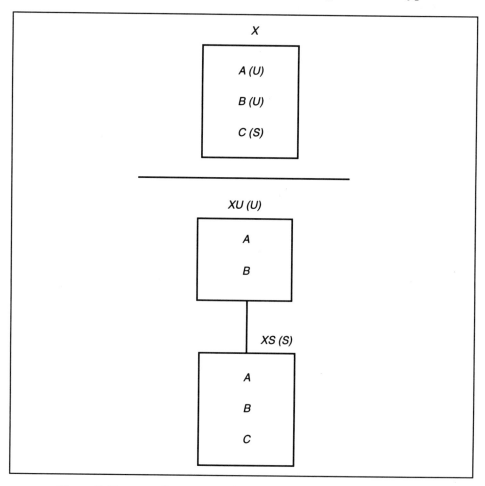

Figure 5. Representing a type of multilevel entity by a hierarchy of classes of single-level objects.

It is convenient, for modeling purposes, to relate classes *XU* and *XS* in the class hierarchy. Namely, if *XS* is made a child of *XU*, then it can inherit from *XU* attributes *A* and *B* and add to them a locally defined attribute *C*. Figure 5 shows the relevant segment of the hierarchy. Note that the class object *XU* is placed at security level *U*, and *XS* at level *S*. The effect of this is that not only do the Unclassified users have no access to the values of attribute *C* in entities of type *X*, but also they are not even aware of the existence of this Secret attribute because *e* access to the class object *XS* is prohibited to them. It is possible to place the class object *XS* at level *U*, while keeping instances of *XS* at level *S*. In that case, the Unclassified users will be aware of the existence of attribute *C* but not of any values of it in instance objects. Note that such a dichotomy between the class-object level and the level of its instances is in conformity with security-level constraint 1. The choice of label for *XS* depends on the policy decision.

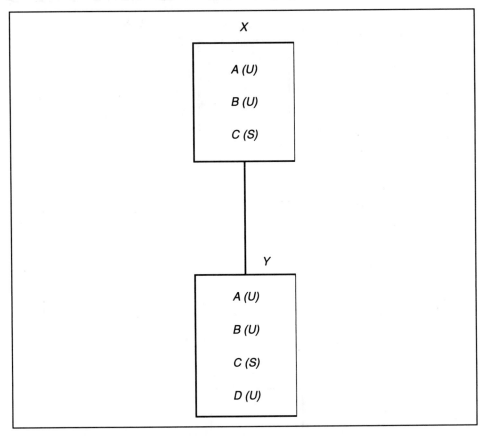

Figure 6. Conceptual schema for types *X* and *Y*.

To carry our example a little further, suppose that there is a second type of entity that we have to model, type *Y*. Type *Y* consists of the same attributes at the same security levels as *X*, plus a new attribute *D* at level *U*. The *conceptual* class hierarchy (or schema) is shown in Figure 6. In that schema, *Y* is a child of *X*.

Let us now address the question of how this schema can be implemented in our model. Using the idea of Figure 5, we arrive at the *implementation* schema for our database, shown in Figure 7. The implementation schema takes into account security-level assignments to attributes in the conceptual schema and transforms the latter into the form ready for actual implementation in a system that uses our security paradigm. In particular, we have four classes in our implementation schema: *XU*, *XS*, *YU*, and *YS*. Class *XU* represents the view of *X* for Unclassified users; *XS*, the view of *X* for users with the Secret clearance; *YU*, the view of *Y* for Unclassified users; and *YS*, the view of *Y* for users with the Secret clearance.

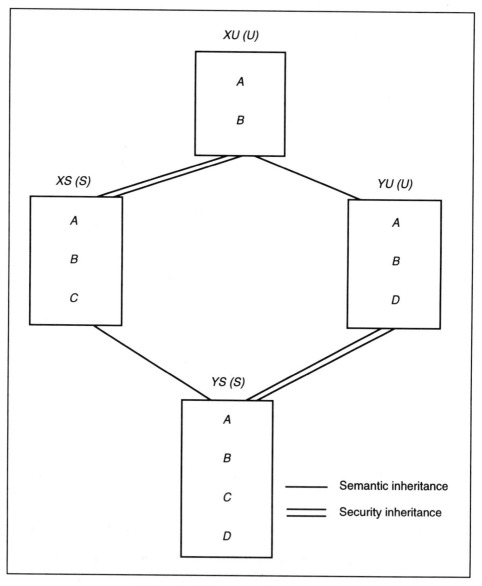

Figure 7. Implementation schema.

In Figure 7, links between classes represent inheritance relationships among classes. It is helpful to distinguish between two kinds of inheritance in the implementation schema: *semantic* inheritance and *security* inheritance. The actual inheritance mechanism is identical in both cases, but the motivation is different. Semantic inheritance corresponds to the usual notion of inheritance in object-oriented databases. It is intended to represent the semantic relationships among data types found in the conceptual schema. The notion of security inheritance, on the other hand, is introduced solely for representing multilevel entities in our security paradigm. Thus, for instance, YU is a subclass of XU in the semantic sense because this relationship reflects the specialization of the entity type X into Y by adding to the former a new attribute D. On the other hand, XS is a subclass of XU in the security sense because XS reveals a new attribute of entities of type X that is not visible to Unclassified users. Note that the notion of security inheritance is in agreement with security-level constraint 2, which requires that the security level of a class dominate that of its ancestors.

Instance objects, as was discussed earlier in this section, do not have to be at the same security level as their class object. By the same token, instance objects may sometimes be placed at different levels with one another, just as it may be required that real-world entities of the same type have different security classifications. Our model allows for this flexibility.

Review of relevant research

The object-oriented approach has been a major area of research in the context of programming languages, knowledge representation, and databases for some years now [KIM89, ZDON90]. In spite of this, there has been relatively little work on security-related issues in object-oriented databases, although some work does exist. Initial efforts [DITT89, FERN89, RABI88] handle only the discretionary access controls. Meadows and Landwehr [MEAD92] were the first to model mandatory access controls using the object-oriented approach; however, their effort is limited to considering the Military Message System. Spooner [SPOO89] takes a preliminary look at mandatory access control and raises several important concerns.

In other approaches [KEEF88a, THUR89b], objects can be multilevel. This means, for example, that an object's attributes can belong to different security levels, which in turn means that the security system must monitor all methods within an object. As we have argued in the introduction, we consider this to be contrary to the spirit of the object-oriented paradigm. Lunt and Millen [LUNT89b] mention some problems associated with having multilevel objects. In their model, only single-level objects are permitted. However, the notion of subjects is still retained, and subjects are assigned security levels.

Conclusions and future work

An examination of the object-oriented data model leads one to believe that there is much in it, particularly in the notion of encapsulation, that makes this model naturally compatible with the notion of security. However, until now, relatively little use has been made of this apparent compatibility.

This essay is part of an effort to develop a better understanding of the interactions between multilevel security and the object-oriented data model. This interaction, in our opinion, can be very subtle, and for that reason, we chose a formal approach. We wanted to state precisely all critical assumptions, which is necessary if we hope to use this essay as a departure point for further research.

We believe that there is much more interesting work to be done in the area of object-oriented multilevel security. In particular, we presented in this essay some ideas for representing multilevel entities using multiple objects at different security levels and illustrated these ideas with examples. The subject clearly merits further study, and perhaps one should address the issue of designing an algorithm for multiobject representation of multilevel entities.

Implementing the class and inheritance mechanisms by message passing is essential to our approach to enforcing security. In a system that follows such an implementation, all information flows are rendered explicit, and therefore controllable uniformly by the message filter. Consequently, our future work should address this issue of implementation, as it relates to modeling security, at a more detailed level.

Acknowledgment

The work of Sushil Jajodia and Boris Kogan was partially supported by the US Air Force, Rome Air Development Center, through the subcontract #RI-64155X of prime contract #F30602-88-D-0028, Task B-9-3622 with the University of Dayton. We are indebted to Joe Giordano for his support and encouragement, which made this work possible.

Integrity Mechanisms in Database Management Systems

Ravi S. Sandhu and Sushil Jajodia

Information integrity means different things to different people, and will probably continue to do so for some time. The 1989 NIST workshop, which set out to establish a consensus definition, instead arrived at the following conclusion [NIST89, page 2.6]:

> The most important conclusion to be drawn from this compilation of papers and working group reports: don't draw too many conclusions about the appropriate definition for data integrity just yet.... In the mean time, papers addressing integrity issues should present or reference a definition of integrity applicable to that paper.

So the first order of business is to define integrity. Our approach to this question is pragmatic and utilitarian. The objective is to settle on a definition within which we can achieve practically useful results, rather than search for some absolute and airtight formulation.

We define integrity[1] as being concerned with the *improper modification* of information (much as confidentiality is concerned with improper disclosure). We understand modification to include insertion of new information and deletion of existing information, as well as changes to existing information.

---

[1] Our definition of integrity is considerably broader than the traditional use of this term in the database literature. For instance, Date [DATE86] says, "Security refers to the protection of data against unauthorized disclosure, alteration, or destruction; integrity refers to the accuracy or validity of data." The consensus view among security researchers is that integrity is one component of security and accuracy/validity is one component of integrity [FERN81, NIST89].

The reader has probably seen similar definitions using "unauthorized" instead of "improper." Our use of the latter term is quite deliberate and significant. First, it acknowledges that security breaches can and do occur without authorization violations — that is, authorization is only one piece of the solution. Second, it adheres to the well-established and useful notion that information security has three components: integrity, confidentiality, and availability. We see no need to discard this standard viewpoint in the absence of some compelling demonstration of a superior one. Finally, our definition brings to the front the very important question: What do we mean by improper? It is obvious that this question intrinsically cannot have a universal answer. So it is futile to try to answer it outside of a given context.

We are specifically interested in information systems used to control and account for an organization's assets. In such systems, the primary goal is prevention of fraud and errors. The meaning of improper modification in this context has been given by Clark and Wilson [CLAR87] as follows:

> No user of the system, even if authorized, may be permitted to modify data items in such a way that assets or accounting records of the company are lost or corrupted.

Note their express qualification: "even if authorized." The word "company" in this quotation reveals the authors' commercial bias but, as they have clarified [CLAR89a], these concepts apply equally well to any information system that controls assets — be it in the military, government, or commercial sectors.

Our goal in this essay is to answer the following question: What mechanisms are required in a general-purpose multiuser DBMS to help achieve the integrity objectives of information systems? There are many compelling reasons to focus on DBMSs for this purpose. The most important has been succinctly stated by Burns [BURN89] as follows:

> A database management system (DBMS) provides the appropriate level of abstraction for the implementation of integrity controls as presented in the Clark and Wilson paper [CLAR87].... It is clear that the domain of applicability of the Clark and Wilson model is not an operating system or a network or even an application system, it is fundamentally a DBMS.

This is particularly true when we focus on mechanisms. Moreover, DBMSs have the wonderful ability to express and manipulate complex relationships. This comes in very handy when dealing with sophisticated integrity policies.

The operating system must clearly provide some core integrity and security mechanisms. In terms of the Orange Book [DOD85], one would need at least a B1 system to enforce encapsulation of the DBMS — that is, to ensure that all manipulation of the database can only be through the DBMS. The question of what minimal features are required in the operating system is important, but outside the scope of this essay. For now, let us assume that operating systems with the requisite features are available.

The bulk of integrity mechanisms belong in the DBMS. Integrity policies are intrinsically application specific, and the operating system simply cannot provide the means to state application-specific concerns. One might then argue: Why not put all the mechanism in the application code? There are several persuasive reasons not to do this. First, it is not very conducive to reuse of common mechanisms. Second, any assurance that integrity mechanisms interspersed within application code will be correct or even comprehensible is rather dubious. Third, the whole point of a database is to support multiple applications. A particular application may well be in a position to handle all its integrity requirements. Yet it is only the DBMS which can prevent other applications from corrupting the database.

The rest of the essay is organized as follows. First we discuss principles for achieving integrity in information systems. Then we describe the mechanisms required in a DBMS to support these high-level principles. In some of the more detailed considerations, we will limit ourselves specifically to relational DBMSs. As we will see, traditional DBMS mechanisms provide the foundations for this purpose, but by themselves do not go far enough.

Integrity principles

We begin by describing basic principles for achieving information integrity. These can be viewed as high-level objectives that are made more concrete when specific mechanisms are proposed to support them. In other words, these principles lay down broad goals without specifying how to achieve them. We will subsequently map these principles to DBMS mechanisms. We emphasize that the principles themselves are independent of the DBMS context. They apply equally well to any information system, be it a manual paper-based system, a centralized batch system, an interactive and highly distributed system, and so on.

The nine integrity principles enumerated below are abstracted from the Clark and Wilson papers [CLAR87, CLAR89a, CLAR89b], the NIST workshops [NIST87, NIST89], and the broader security and database literature.[2] These principles express what needs to be done rather than how it is going to be accomplished (the latter question is addressed in the next section):

1. *Well-formed transactions.* Clark and Wilson [CLAR87] have defined this principle as follows: "The concept of the well-formed transaction is that a user should not manipulate data arbitrarily, but only in constrained ways that preserve or ensure the integrity of the data." This principle has also been called *constrained change* [CLAR89b] — that is, data can be modified only by well-formed transactions rather than by arbitrary procedures. Moreover, the well-formed transactions are known ("certified") to be individually correct with some (mostly qualitative) degree of assurance.

2. *Authenticated users.* This principle stipulates that modifications should be carried out only by users whose identities have been authenticated to be appropriate for the task.

3. *Least privilege.* The notion of least privilege was one of the earliest to emerge in security research. It has classically been stated in terms of processes (executing programs) [SALT75]: A process should have exactly those privileges needed to accomplish its assigned task, and none extra. The principle applies equally well to users, except that it is more difficult to precisely delimit the scope of a user's "task." A process is typically created to accomplish some very specific task and terminates on completion. A user, on the other hand, is a relatively long-lived entity and will be involved in varied activities during his life span. His authorized privileges will therefore exceed those strictly required at any given instant. In the realm of confidentiality, least privilege is often called *need-to-know.* In the integrity context, it is appropriately called *need-to-do.* Another appropriate term for this principle is *least temptation* — that is, do not tempt people to commit fraud by giving them greater power than they need.

4. *Separation of duties.* Separation of duties is a time-honored principle for prevention of fraud and errors, going back to the very beginning of commerce. Simply stated, no single individual should be in a position to misappropriate assets on his own. Operationally, this means that a chain of events that affects the balance of assets must require different individuals to be involved at key points, so that without their collusion the overall chain cannot take effect.

5. *Reconstruction of events.* This principle seeks to deter improper behavior by threatening its discovery. It is a necessary adjunct to

---

[2] The literature is too numerous to cite works individually. For those unfamiliar with the "older" literature, there are some useful starting points [DENN79, FERN81, GRAY78, LIND76, SALT75].

least privilege for two reasons. First, least privilege, even taken to its theoretical limit, will leave some scope for fraud. Second, a zealous application of least privilege is not a terribly efficient way to run an organization. It conveys an impression of an enterprise enmeshed in red tape.[3] So practically, users must be granted more privileges than are strictly required. We therefore should be able to accurately reconstruct essential elements of a system's history, so as to detect misuse of privileges.

6. *Delegation of authority.* This principle fills in a piece missing from the Clark and Wilson papers and much of the discussion they have generated.[4] It concerns the critical question of how privileges are acquired and distributed in an organization. Clearly, the procedures to do so must reflect the structure of the organization and allow for effective devolution of authority. Individual managers should have maximum flexibility regarding information resources within their domains, tempered by constraints imposed by their superiors. Without this flexibility at the end-user level, the authorization will most likely be inappropriate to the actual needs. This can only result in security being perceived as a drag on productivity and something to be bypassed whenever possible.

7. *Reality checks.* This principle has been well motivated by Clark and Wilson [CLAR89b] as follows: "A cross-check with the external reality is a central part of integrity control. …integrity is meaningful only in terms of the relation of the data to the external world." Or in more concrete terms: "If an internal inventory record does not correctly reflect the number of items in stock, it makes little difference if the value of the recorded inventory has been reflected correctly in the company balance sheet."

8. *Continuity of operation.* This principle states that system operations should be maintained to some appropriate degree in the face of potentially devastating events beyond the organization's control. This catchall description is intended to include natural disasters, power outages, disk crashes, and the like.[5]

---

[3] This comment is made in the context of users rather than processes (transactions). Least privilege with respect to processes is more of an internal issue within the computer system, and its zealous application is most desirable (modulo the performance and cost penalties it imposes).

[4] The closest concept that Clark and Wilson have to this principle is their Rule E4, which they summarize as follows [CLAR87, Figure 1]: "Authorization lists changed only by the security officer." This notion of a central security officer as an authorization czar is inappropriate and unworkable. Rational security policies can be put in place only if appropriate authority is vested in end users.

[5] One might argue that we are stepping into the scope of availability here. If so, so be it.

9. *Ease of safe use.*[6] In a nutshell, this principle requires that the easiest way to operate a system should also be the safest. There is ample evidence that security measures are all too often incorrectly applied or simply bypassed by the system managers. This happens due to one or a combination of the following: (1) poorly designed defaults (such as indefinite retention of vendor-supplied passwords for privileged accounts), (2) awkward and cumbersome interfaces (such as requiring many keystrokes to effect simple changes in authorization), (3) lack of tools for authorization review, and (4) mismatched policy and mechanism ("...to the extent that the user's mental image of his protection goals matches the mechanism he must use, mistakes will be minimized" [SALT75]).

It is inevitable that these principles are fuzzy, abstract, and high level. In developing an organization's security policy, one would elaborate on each of these principles and make precise the meaning of terms such as "appropriate" and "proper." How to do so systematically is perhaps the most important question in successful application of these principles. In other words, how does one articulate a comprehensive policy based on these high-level objectives? This question is beyond the scope of this essay. Our present focus is on this question: How do these principles translate into concrete mechanisms in a DBMS?

The goals encompassed by these principles may appear overwhelming. After all, in the extreme these principles amount to solving the total system correctness problem, which we know is well beyond the state of the art. Fortunately, in our context, the degree to which one would seek to enforce these objectives and the assurance of this enforcement are matters of risk management and cost-benefit analysis. Laying out these principles explicitly does give us the following major benefits:

- The overall problem is partitioned into smaller components for which solutions can be developed independently of each other (that is, divide and conquer).
- The principles suggest common mechanisms that belong in the DBMS and can be reused across multiple applications.
- The principles provide a set against which the mechanisms of specific DBMSs can be evaluated (in an informal sense).
- The principles similarly provide a set on the basis of which the requirements of specific information systems can be articulated.
- Last, but not least, the principles invite criticism from the security community, particularly regarding what may have been left out.

---

[6] Thanks to Stanley Kurzban and William Murray for coining this term.

Integrity mechanisms

In this section, we consider DBMS mechanisms to facilitate application of the principles defined in the previous section. The principles have been applied in practice [MURR87a, WIMB71], but with most of the mechanisms built into application code. Providing these mechanisms in the DBMS is a prerequisite for their widespread use.

Our mapping of principles to mechanisms is summarized in Table 1. Some of these mechanisms are available in commercial products. Others are well established in the database literature. There are also some newer, recently proposed mechanisms, for example, transaction controls for separation of duties [SAND88b], the temporal model for audit data [JAJO90g], and propagation constraints for dynamic authorization [SAND88a, SAND89]. Finally, there are places where existing mechanisms and proposals need to be extended in novel ways. Overall, the required mechanisms are quite practical and well within the reach of today's technology.

Table 1. Summary.

Integrity Principle	DBMS Mechanisms
Well-formed transactions	Encapsulated updates Atomic transactions Consistency constraints
Continuity of operation	Redundancy Recovery
Authenticated users	Authentication
Least privilege	Fine-grained access control
Separation of duties	Transaction controls Layered updates
Reconstruction of events	Audit trail
Delegation of authority	Dynamic authorization Propagation constraints
Reality checks	Consistent snapshots
Ease of safe use	Fail-safe defaults Human factors

Well-formed transactions. The concept of a well-formed transaction corresponds very well to the standard DBMS concept of a transaction [GRAY78, GRAY86]. A transaction is defined as a sequence of primitive actions that satisfies the following properties:

1. *Failure atomicity.* Either all or none of the updates of a transaction take effect. We understand update to mean modification; that is, it includes insertion of new data, deletion of existing data, and changes to existing data.
2. *Serializability.* The net effect of executing a set of transactions is equivalent to executing them in some sequential order, even though they may actually be executed concurrently (that is, their actions are interleaved or simultaneous).
3. *Progress.* Every transaction will eventually complete; that is, there is no indefinite blocking due to deadlock and no indefinite restarts due to livelock.
4. *Correct state transform.* Each transaction if run by itself in isolation and given a consistent state to begin with will leave the database in a consistent state.

We will elaborate on these properties in a moment. First let us note the basic requirement that the DBMS must ensure that updates are restricted to transactions. Clearly, if users are allowed to bypass transactions and directly manipulate relations in a database, we have no foundation to build upon. We represent this requirement with the diagram in Figure 1 — updates are encapsulated within transactions. At this point it is worth recalling that the database itself must be encapsulated within the DBMS by the operating system.

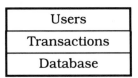

Figure 1. Encapsulated updates.

It is clear that the set of database transactions is itself going to change during the system life cycle. Now the same nine principles of the previous section apply with respect to maintaining the integrity of the transactions. In particular, transactions should be installed, modified, and supplanted only by the use of well-formed "transaction-maintenance transactions." One can apply this argument once again to say that the transaction-maintenance transactions themselves need to be maintained by another set of transactions, and so on indefinitely. We believe there is little to be gained by having more than two steps in this potentially unbounded sequence of transaction-maintenance transactions. The rate of change in the transaction set will be significantly slower than the rate of change in the database proper. Going one step further, the rate of change in the transaction-maintenance transactions will be yet slower to the point where, for all practical purposes, these can be viewed as static over the life span of typical systems. With this perspective, the database administrator is responsible for installing and maintaining transaction-maintenance transactions, which in turn maintain actual database transactions.

We now return to considering the four properties of DBMS transactions enumerated earlier. The first three properties — failure atomicity, serializability, and progress — can be achieved in a purely "syntactic" manner — that is, completely independent of the application. These three requirements for a transaction are recognized in the database literature as appropriate for the DBMS to implement. Mechanisms to achieve these objectives have been extensively researched in the last 15 years or so, and our understanding of this area can certainly be described as mature. The basic mechanisms — two-phase locking, time stamps, multiversion databases, two-phase commit, undo-redo logs, shadow pages, deadlock detection and prevention — have been known for a long time and have made their way into numerous products. In developing integrity guidelines and/or evaluation criteria, one might consider some progressive measure of the extent to which a particular DBMS meets these objectives. For instance, with failure atomicity, is there a guarantee that we will know which of the two possibilities occurred? Similarly, with serializability, does the DBMS enforce the concurrency control protocol or does it rely on transactions to execute explicit commands for this purpose? And, with the issue of progress, do we have a probabilistic or absolute guarantee? Such questions must be systematically addressed.

The fourth property, correct state transforms, is the ultimate bottleneck in realizing well-formed transactions. It is also an objective that cannot be achieved without considering the semantics of the application. The correctness issue is, of course, undecidable in general. In practice, we can assure correctness only to some limited degree of confidence by a mix of software engineering techniques such as formal verification, testing, quality assurance, and so on. Responsibility for implementing transactions as correct state transforms has traditionally been assigned to the application programmer. Even in theory, DBMS mechanisms can never fully take over this responsibility.

DBMS mechanisms can help in assuring the correctness of a state by enforcing *consistency constraints* on the data. Consistency constraints are also often called integrity constraints or integrity rules in the database literature. Since we are using integrity in a wider sense, we prefer the term consistency constraint.

The relational data model in particular imposes two consistency constraints [CODD79, DATE86]:

- *Entity integrity* stipulates that attributes in the primary key of a base relation cannot have null values. This amounts to requiring that each entity represented in the database must be uniquely identifiable.
- *Referential integrity* is concerned with references from one entity to another. A foreign key is a set of attributes in one relation whose values are required to match those of the primary key of some specific relation. Referential integrity requires that either a foreign key be all null[7] or a matching tuple exist in the latter relation. This amounts to ruling out dangling references to nonexistent entities.

Entity integrity is easily enforced. Referential integrity, on the other hand, requires more effort and has seen limited support in commercial products. The precise manner in which to achieve it is also very dependent on the semantics of the application. This is particularly so when the referenced tuple is deleted. There are several choices:

1. prohibit this delete operation,
2. delete the referencing tuple (with a possibility of further cascading deletes), or
3. set the foreign key attributes in the referencing tuple to null.

There are proposals for extending SQL so that these choices can be specified for each foreign key.

The relational model in addition encourages the use of *domain constraints*, whereby the values in a particular attribute (column) are constrained to come from some given set. These constraints are particularly easy to state and enforce, at least so long as the domains are defined in terms of primitive types such as integers, decimal numbers, and character strings. A variety of *dependency constraints* [DATE86] that constrain the tuples in a given relation have been extensively studied in the database literature.

In the limit, a consistency constraint can be viewed as an arbitrary predicate that all correct states of the database must satisfy. The predicate may involve any number of relations. Although this concept is theoretically appealing and flexible in its expressive power, in practice the overhead in checking the predicates for every transaction has been pro-

---

[7] Often the notion of a null foreign key is semantically incorrect. In such cases, an additional consistency constraint can disallow null values.

hibitive. As a result, relational DBMSs typically confine their enforcement of consistency constraints to domain constraints and entity integrity.

Continuity of operation. The problem of maintaining continuity of operation in the face of natural disasters, hardware failures, and other disruptive events has received considerable attention in both theory and practice [GRAY78]. The basic technique to deal with such situations is redundancy in various forms. Recovery mechanisms in DBMSs must also ensure that we arrive at a consistent state. In many respects, these mechanisms are "syntactic" in the sense of being application independent, much as mechanisms for the first three properties presented in the section "Well-formed transactions" were.

Authenticated users. Authentication is primarily the responsibility of the operating system. If the operating system is lacking in its authentication mechanism, it would be very difficult to ensure the integrity of the DBMS itself. The integrity of the database would thereby be that much more suspect. It therefore makes sense not to duplicate authentication mechanisms in the DBMS.

Authentication underlies some of the other principles, particularly least privilege, separation of duties, reconstruction of events, and delegation of authority. In all of these, the end objective can be achieved to the fullest extent only if authentication is possible at the level of individual users.

Least privilege. The principle of least privilege translates into a requirement for fine-grained access control. Earlier we noted that least privilege must be tempered with practicality in avoiding excessive red tape. Nevertheless, a high-end DBMS should provide for access control at very fine granularity, leaving it to the database designers to apply these controls as they see fit.

It is clear from the Clark and Wilson papers, if not evident from earlier work, that modification of data must be controlled in terms of transactions rather than blanket permission to write. We have already put forth the concept of encapsulated updates for this purpose. In terms of the relational model, it is not immediately obvious at what granularity of data this should be enforced.

To control read access, DBMSs have used mechanisms based on views (as in System R) or query modification (as in INGRES). These mechanisms are extremely flexible and can be as fine grained as desired. However, neither one provides the same potential for flexible control of updates. The fundamental reason for this is our theoretical inability to translate updates on views unambiguously into updates of base relations. As a result, authorization to control updates is often less sophisticated than authorization for read access.

In relational systems, it is natural for obvious reasons to represent the access matrix by one or more relations [SELI80]. At a coarse level, we might control access by tuples of the following form:

user, transaction, relation

This means that the specified user can execute the specified transaction on the specified relation. Tuples of the form shown below would give greater selectivity:

user, transaction, relation, attribute

This would allow us to control the execution of transactions such as "give everyone a 5 percent raise," without giving the same transaction permission to change employee addresses. The following authorization tuple accomplishes this:

Joe, Give-5%-raise, Employees, Salary

A transaction that gives a raise to a specific employee needs a further dimension of authorization to specify which employee it pertains to. Thus, if Joe is authorized to give a 5 percent raise to John, the authorization tuple would look as follows:

Joe, Give-5%-raise, John, Employees, Salary

We are assuming here that John uniquely identifies the employee receiving the raise. The update is restricted to the Salary attribute of a specific tuple with key equal to "John" in the Employees relation. So it takes a key, relation, and attribute to specify the actual parameter of such a transaction.

Now consider a transaction which moves money from account A to account B; that is, there are two actual parameters of the transaction. In terms of least privilege, we need the ability to bind this transaction to updating the two specific accounts A and B. More generally, we will have transactions with N parameters identified in an actual parameter list. So we need authorization tuples of the following form:

user, transaction, actual parameter list

Here each parameter in the actual parameter list specifies the item authorized for update by specifying one of the following identifiers:

- relation,
- relation, attribute,

- key, relation, attribute.

These three cases respectively give us relation-level, "column"-level, and element-level granularity of update control.

It is also important to realize that element-level update authorizations should properly be treated as consumable items. For example, once money has been moved from account A to account B, the user should not be able to move it again, without fresh authorization to do so.

Separation of duties. Separation of duties finds little support in existing products. Although it is possible to use existing mechanisms for this purpose, these mechanisms have not been designed with this end in mind. As a result, their use is awkward at best. This fact was noted by the DBMS group at the 1989 NIST data integrity workshop, who concluded their report with the following recommendation [NIST89, section 4.3]:

> While the group was able to use existing DBMS features to implement separation of roles controls, we were, however, unable to use existing features in a way that would support easy maintenance and certification. We recommend that data definition and/or consistency check features be enhanced to provide operators that lend themselves to the expression of integrity controls and to allow separation of integrity controls and traditional data.

Separation of duties is inherently concerned with sequences of transactions, rather than individual transactions in isolation. For example, consider a situation in which payment in the form of a check is prepared and issued by the following sequence of events:

1. A clerk prepares a voucher and assigns an account.
2. The voucher and account are approved by a supervisor.
3. The check is issued by a clerk who must be different from the clerk in step 1. Issuing the check also debits the assigned account. (Strictly speaking, we should debit one account and credit another in equal amounts. The important point for our purpose is that issuing a check modifies account balances.)

This sequence embodies separation of duties since the three steps must be executed by different people. The policy, moreover, has a dynamic flavor in that a particular clerk can prepare vouchers as well as, on different occasions, issue checks. However, he cannot issue a check for a voucher prepared by himself.

Implementation of this policy in a paper-based system follows quite directly from its statement:

- The voucher is realized as a form with blanks for the amount and account, as well as for signatures of the people involved. As the above sequence gets executed, these blanks are filled in. On its completion, copies of the voucher are filed in various archives for audit purposes.
- The account is represented by, say, a ledger card, where debit and credit entries are posted, along with references to the forms that authorized these entries.

By their very nature, paper-based controls rely on employee vigilance and internal/external audits for their effectiveness. Computerization brings with it the potential to enforce the required controls by means of an infallible, ever-vigilant, and omniscient automaton — the computer itself.

The crucial question is, how do we specify and implement similar controls for separation of duties in a computerized environment? A mechanism for this purpose called *transaction-control expressions* [SAND88b] is based on the following difference between vouchers and accounts:

- The voucher is *transient* in that it comes into existence, has a relatively small sequence of steps applied to it, and then disappears from the system (possibly leaving a record in some archive). The history of a voucher can be prescribed as a finite sequence of steps with an a priori maximum length.
- The account, on the other hand, is *persistent* in the sense that it has a long-lived — and essentially unbounded — existence in the system. During its life there may be a very large number of credit and debit entries for it. Of course, at some point the account may be closed and archived. The key point is that we can only prescribe its history as a variable-length sequence of steps with no a priori maximum length.

Both kinds of objects are essential to the logic and correct operation of an information system. Transient objects embody a logically complete history of transactions corresponding to units of service provided to the external world by the organization. Persistent objects embody the internal records required to keep the organization functioning with an accurate correspondence to its interactions with the external world.

Separation of duties is achieved by enforcing controls on transient objects, for the most part. The crucial idea that makes this possible is that transactions can be executed on persistent objects only as side effects of executing transactions on transient objects. This thesis is actually simply borrowed from the paper-based world, where it has been routinely applied ever since bookkeeping became an integral part of business operations.

With this perspective, we arrive at the diagram shown in Figure 2. The idea is that a sequence of transactions is viewed as transient data in the database. In this picture, there is a double encapsulation of the database, first by transactions on persistent data and then by transactions on transient data. Users can directly execute only the latter. The former are triggered indirectly as a result, when the transient data is in the proper state for doing so. In other words, transient data is singly encapsulated and has direct application of separation of duties. Persistent data is doubly encapsulated and has indirect application of separation of duties by means of transient data.

Users	
Transactions on transient data	
Transactions on persistent data	Database of transient data
Database of persistent data	

Figure 2. Layered updates.

Reconstruction of events. The ability to reconstruct events in a system serves as a deterrent to improper behavior. In the DBMS context, the mechanism to record the history of the system is traditionally called an audit trail. As with the principle of least privilege, a high-end DBMS should be capable of reconstructing events to the finest detail. It should also structure the audit trail logically so that it is easy to query. For instance, logging every keystroke does give us the ability to reconstruct the system history accurately. However, with this primitive logical structure, it takes substantial effort to reconstruct a particular transaction. In addition to actually recording all events that take place in the database, an audit trail must also provide support for auditing. In other words, an audit trail must allow "an authorized and competent agent to access and evaluate accountability information by a secure means, within a reasonable amount of time and without undue difficulty" [DOD85]. In this respect, DBMSs have a significant advantage, since their powerful querying abilities can be used.

The ability to reconstruct events means different things to different people. At one end of the spectrum, we have the requirements of Clark and Wilson [CLAR89b]. They require only two things:

1. A complete history of each and every modification made to the value of an item.
2. With each change in value of an item, storage of the identity of the person making the change.

Of course, the system must be reliable in that it makes exactly those changes that are requested by users and the binding of a value with its author is also exact. Clark and Wilson call this "attribution of change."

This can be easily accomplished if we are willing to extend slightly the standard logging techniques for recovery purposes. For each transaction, a recovery log contains the transaction identifier, some *before-images*, and the corresponding *after-images*. If we augment this by recording the user for each transaction, we have the desired binding of each value to its author. There is one other change that needs to be made. To support recovery, there is a need to keep a log only up to a point from which a complete database backup is available. Of course, now there is a need to archive the logs so they remain available.

Others have argued that this simple "attribution of change" is not sufficient. We need an audit trail, a mechanism for a complete reconstruction of every action taken against the database: *who* has been accessing *what* data, *when*, and in what *order*. Thus, it has three basic objects of interest:

1. *The user.* Who initiated a transaction, from what terminal, when, and in what order?
2. *The transaction.* What was the exact transaction that was initiated?
3. *The data.* What was the result of the transaction? What were the database states before and after the transaction initiation?

For this purpose, a *database activity model* has been recently proposed [JAJO90g] that imposes a uniform logical structure upon the past, present, and future data. There is never any loss of historical or current information in this model; thus the model provides a mechanism for complete reconstruction of every action taken on the database. It also logically structures the audit data to facilitate its querying.

Delegation of authority. The capability to delegate authority and responsibility within an organization is essential to its smooth functioning. It appears in its most developed form with respect to monetary budgets. However, the concept applies equally well to the control of other assets and resources of the organization.

In most organizations, the ability to grant authorization is never completely unconstrained. For example, a department manager may be able to delegate substantial authority over departmental resources to project managers within his department and yet be prohibited to delegate this authority to project managers outside the department. These situations cloud the classic distinction between discretionary and mandatory policies [MURR87b, SAND90]. The traditional concept of ownership as the basis for delegating authority also becomes less applicable in this context [MOFF88]. Finally, we need the ability to delegate privileges without having the ability to exercise these privileges. Some mechanisms for this purpose have been recently proposed [MOFF88, SAND89].

The complexity introduced by dynamic authorization has been recognized ever since researchers considered this problem, for example, as stated by Saltzer and Schroeder [SALT75]:

> ...it is relatively easy to envision (and design) systems that statically express a particular protection intent. But the need to change access authorizations dynamically...introduces much complexity into protection systems.

This continues to be true, despite substantial theoretical advances in the interim [SAND88a]. Existing products provide few facilities in this respect, and their mechanisms tend to have an ad hoc flavor.

Reality checks. This principle inherently requires activity outside of the DBMS. The DBMS does have the obligation to provide an internally consistent view of that portion of the database which is being externally verified. This is particularly so if the external inspection is conducted on an ad hoc on-demand basis.

Ease of safe use. Ease of safe use is more an evaluation of the DBMS mechanisms than something to be enforced by the mechanisms themselves. The mechanisms should, of course, have fail-safe defaults [SALT75] — for example, access is not available unless explicitly granted or this default rule is explicitly changed to grant it automatically. DBMSs do offer a significant advantage in providing user-friendly interfaces intrinsically, for their main objective of data manipulation. These interface mechanisms can be leveraged to make the authorization mechanisms easy to use. For instance, having the power of SQL queries to review the current authorizations is a tangible benefit.

Conclusion

In a nutshell, our conclusion is that realistic DBMS mechanisms do exist to support the integrity objective of information systems. Some are well established in the literature, while others have been proposed more recently and are not so well known.

In terms of what DBMS mechanisms can do for us, we can group the nine principles enumerated in this essay as follows:

Group I	Group II	Group III
Well-formed transactions	Least privilege	Authenticated users
Continuity of operation	Separation of duties	Reality checks
	Reconstruction of events	Ease of safe use
	Delegation of authority	

Group I principles are adequately treated by current DBMS mechanisms and have been extensively studied by database researchers. With the single exception of assuring correctness of state transformations, these principles can be achieved by DBMS mechanisms. Techniques for implementing well-formed transactions and maintaining continuity of operation across failures have been studied extensively. Their practical feasibility has been amply demonstrated in actual systems. Assuring that well-formed transactions are correct state transformations remains a formidable problem, but there is little that the DBMS can do to alleviate it. As such, it is a problem outside the scope of DBMS mechanisms. The DBMS can

1. enforce encapsulation of updates by restricting their occurrence to be within transactions, and
2. provide controls for installing and maintaining these transactions.

Group II principles need newer mechanisms and conceptual foundations. Several promising approaches have emerged in the literature. Practical demonstration of their feasibility remains to be done, but in concept they do not present prohibitive implementation problems. They do require that current DBMSs be extended in significant ways. Group II principles are the ones for which additional DBMS mechanisms hold the promise of greatest benefit.

Group III principles are important, but there is little that DBMS mechanisms can do to achieve them. Authentication is principally an operating system problem. Reality checks necessarily involve external procedures. Ease of safe use is more an evaluation of the DBMS mechanisms than something to be enforced by the mechanisms themselves. It is facilitated in the DBMS context by the intrinsic DBMS requirement of user-friendly query languages.

In conclusion, for group I principles we need little more than has currently been demonstrated in actual products. For group II principles, current systems do something for each one but do not go far enough. There are several promising proposals but no "worked examples." Group III principles are important but are not fully achievable by DBMS mechanisms alone.

References

[ABBO76] Abbott, R.P., et al., "Security Analysis and Enhancement of Computer Operating Systems," NBSIR 76-1041, Nat'l Bureau of Standards, ICST, Gaithersburg, Md., Apr. 1976.

[ABRA87] Abrams, M.D., and H.J. Podell, *Tutorial: Computer and Network Security*, IEEE Computer Society Press, Los Alamitos, Calif., 1987.

[ABRA90] Abrams, M.D., et al., "A Generalized Framework for Access Control: An Informal Description," *Proc. 13th Nat'l Computer Security Conf.*, 1990, pp. 135–143.

[ADAM89] Adam, N.R., and J.C. Wortmann, "Security-Control Methods for Statistical Databases: A Comparative Study," *ACM Computing Surveys*, Vol. 21, No. 4, Dec. 1989, pp. 515–556.

[AFIP79] "Consensus Report, Processors, Operating Systems and Nearby Peripherals," *AFIPS Conf. Proc.*, T.M.P. Lee (chairman), Nat'l Computer Conf., 1979.

[AMER82] *The American Heritage Dictionary*, Second College Edition, Houghton Mifflin, Boston, 1982.

[AMES83] Ames, S.R., Jr., M. Gasser, and R.R. Schell, "Security Kernel Design and Implementation: An Introduction," *Computer*, Vol. 16, No. 7, July 1983, pp. 14–22.

[AMOR91] Amoroso, E., et al., "Toward an Approach to Measuring Software Trust," *Proc. IEEE Symp. Research in Security and Privacy*, IEEE Computer Society Press, Los Alamitos, Calif., 1991, pp. 198–218.

[ANDE72] Anderson, J.P., "Computer Security Technology Planning Study," ESD-TR-73-51, Vol. 1, Hanscom AFB, Mass., 1972 (also available as DTICAD-758206).

[ANDE81] Anderson, J.P., "On the Feasibility of Connecting RECON to an External Network," Tech. Report, James P. Anderson Co., Mar. 1981.

[ANSI91a] X12.58, "Draft Standard for the Trial Use of Managing EDI Security Structures," 1991.

[ANSI91b] X12.42, "Draft Standard for the Trial Use of Managing EDI Cryptographic Service Message Transaction Sets," 1991.

[ANSI91c] "Guideline for Implementing X12.42 & X12.58," 1991.

[ANSI92a] X9.30-199X, "Public Key Cryptography Using Irreversible Algorithms for the Financial Services Industry," 1992.

[ANSI92b] X9.31-199X, "Public Key Cryptography Using Reversible Algorithms for the Financial Services Industry," 1992.

[ATTA76] Attanasio, C.R., P.W. Markstein, and R.J. Phillips, "Penetrating an Operating System: A Study of VM/370 Integrity," *IBM Systems J.*, Vol. 15, No. 1, 1976, pp. 102–106.

[BACH86] Bach, M.J., *The Design of the Unix Operating System*, Prentice-Hall, Englewood Cliffs, N.J., 1986.

[BALE93] Balenson, D., "Privacy Enhancement for Internet Electronic Mail: Part III — Algorithms, Modes, and Identifiers," RFC 1423, Feb. 1993.

[BAUE88] Bauer, D.S., and M.E. Koblentz, "NIDX — A Real-Time Intrusion Detection Expert System," *Proc. Summer 1988 USENIX Conf.*, 1988.

[BAUE91] Bauer, R.K., et al., "A Framework for Developing Accreditable MLS AIS," *Proc. 14th Nat'l Computer Security Conf.*, 1991.

[BELA74] Belady, L.A., and C. Weissman, "Experiments with Secure Resource Sharing for Virtual Machines," *Proc. Int'l Workshop Protection in Operating Systems*, IRIA/LABORIA, Rocquencourt, Le Chesnay, France, 1974.

[BELL73] Bell, D.E., and L.J. LaPadula, "Secure Computer Systems: Mathematical Foundations and Model," M74-244, MITRE Corp., Bedford, Mass., 1973 (also available as DTIC AD-771543).

[BELL75] Bell, D.E., and L.J. LaPadula, "Secure Computer Systems: Unified Exposition and Multics Interpretation," MTR-2997, MITRE Corp., Bedford, Mass., July 1975.

[BELL75a] Bell, D.E., and L.J. LaPadula, "Computer Security Model: Unified Exposition and Multics Interpretation," ESD-TR-75-306, Hanscom AFB, Mass., 1975 (also available as DTIC AD-A023588).

[BELL76] Bell, D.E., and L.J. LaPadula, "Secure Computer Systems: Unified Exposition and Multics Interpretation," MITRE Corp. ESD-TR-75-306, NTIS #AD-A023588, Electronic Systems Division, Air Force Systems Command, Mar. 1976.

[BELL90] Bell, D.E., "Lattices, Policies, and Implementations," *Proc. 13th Nat'l Computer Security Conf.*, NIST/NCSC, 1990, pp. 165–171.

[BELL91] Bell, D.E., "Putting Policy Commonalities to Work," *Proc. 14th Nat'l Computer Security Conf.*, 1991, pp. 456–471.

[BHAR90] Bhargava, G., and S.K. Gadia, "The Concept of Error in a Database: An Application of Temporal Database," in *Data Management: Current Trends*, McGraw-Hill, ed., New Delhi, India, Dec. 1990, pp. 106–121.

[BHAR93] Bhargava, G., and S.K. Gadia, "Relational Database Systems with Zero Information Loss," *IEEE Trans. Knowledge and Data Eng.*, Vol. 5, No. 1, Feb. 1993, pp. 76–87.

[BIBA77] Biba, K.J., "Integrity Considerations for Secure Computer Systems," ESD-TR-76-372, USAF Electronic Systems Division (also MTR3153, MITRE Corp.), Bedford, Mass., Apr. 1977.

[BIHA90] Biham, E., and A. Shamir, "Differential Cryptanalysis of DES-like Cryptosystems," Tech. Report CS90-16, Weizmann Inst. of Science, Dept. of Applied Mathematics and Computer Science, Rehovot, Israel, July 1990.

[BISB78] Bisbey, R., and D. Hollingworth, "Protection Analysis Project Final Report," ISI/RR-78-13, DTIC AD A056816, USC Information Sciences Inst., Marina del Rey, Calif., May 1978.

[BISH82] Bishop, M., "Security Problems with the UNIX Operating System," Computer Science Dept., Purdue Univ., West Lafayette, Ind., Mar. 1982.

[BJOR75] Bjork, L.A., "Generalized Audit Trail Requirements and Concepts for Database Applications," *IBM Systems J.*, Vol. 14, No. 3, 1975, pp. 229–245.

[BLAT90] Blatchford, C.W, "Information Security — The European Perspective," CEN/CENELEC document, CSecG/13/90.

[BLOO90] Bloombecker, B., *Spectacular Computer Crimes*, Dow-Jones-Irwin, Homewood, Ill., 1990.

[BOEB85] Boebert, W.R., and R.Y. Kain, "A Practical Alternative to Integrity Policies," *Proc. 8th Nat'l Computer Security Conf.*, 1985, pp. 18–27.

[BONY88] Bonyun, D.A., "Logging and Accountability in Database Management Systems," in *Database Security: Status and Prospects*, C.E. Landwehr, ed., North-Holland, Amsterdam, The Netherlands, 1988, pp. 223–227.

[BOOT81] Booth, K.S., "Authentication of Signatures Using Public Key Encryption," *Comm. ACM*, Vol. 24, No. 11, Nov. 1981, pp. 772–774.

[BORE92] Borenstein, N., and N. Freed, "Multipurpose Internet Mail Extensions," RFC 1341, May 1992.

[BRAN75] Branstad, D.K., "Encryption Protection in Computer Data Communications," *Proc. 4th Data Comm. Symp.*, IEEE Press, New York, N.Y., 1975, pp. 8.1–8.7.

[BRAN91] Branstad, M.A., et al., "Apparent Differences Between the US TCSEC and the European ITSEC," *Proc. 14th Nat'l Computer Security Conf.*, 1991, pp. 45–58.

[BREW89] Brewer, D.F.C., and M.J. Nash, "The Chinese Wall Security Policy," *Proc. IEEE Symp. Security and Privacy*, IEEE Computer Society Press, Los Alamitos, Calif., 1989, pp. 206–214.

[BUCZ90] Buczkowski, L.J., "Database Inference Controller," in *Database Security III: Status and Prospects*, D.L. Spooner and C. Landwehr, eds., North-Holland, Amsterdam, The Netherlands, 1990, pp. 311–322.

[BULL91] Bull, A., et al., "A Taxonomy of Computer Program Security Flaws," Center for Secure Information Technology, Naval Research Laboratory, draft in preparation, 1991.

[BURN89] Burns, R.K., "DBMS Integrity and Secrecy Control," in [NIST89], sec. A.7, pp. 1–4 (1989).

[BURN90] Burns, R.K., "Referential Secrecy," *Proc. IEEE Symp. Research in Security and Privacy*, IEEE Computer Society Press, Los Alamitos, Calif., 1990, pp. 133–142.

[CANA92] Canadian System Security Centre, Communication Security Establishment, *The Canadian Trusted Computer Product Evaluation Criteria*, Version 3.0e, Government of Canada, 1992 draft. Note: Version 3.0e was published in Jan. 1993.

[CARL75] Carlstedt, J., R. Bisbey, and G. Popek, "Pattern-Directed Protection Evaluation," ISI/RR-75-31, USC Information Sciences Inst., Marina del Rey, Calif., June 1975.

[CCIT88a] "Data Communications Networks: Message Handling System and Service Overview," CCITT Recommendation X.400, Nov. 1988.

[CCIT88b] "Message Handling Systems: Message Transfer System; Abstract Service Definition and Procedures," CCITT Recommendation X.411, 1988.

[CCIT88c] "The Directory-Authentication Framework," CCITT Recommendation X.509, Nov. 1988.

[CCIT88d] "Specification of Abstract Syntax Notation One (ASN.1)," CCITT Recommendation X.208, Nov. 1988.

[CCIT90] CCITT 1990 X.400 Series of Recommendations, "Message Handling System."

[CCITT92] CCITT X.435 (1991) EDI Messaging SC27/WG1/N131.

[CHAB90] Chabernaud, C., and B. Vilain, "Telecommunications Services and Distributed Applications," *IEEE Network Magazine*, Nov. 1990, pp. 10–13.

[CHOK92] Chokhani, Santosh, "Trusted Products Evaluations," *Comm. ACM*, Vol. 35, No. 7, July 1992, pp. 64–76.

[CLAR87] Clark, D.D., and D.R. Wilson, "A Comparison of Commercial and Military Computer Security Policies," *Proc. IEEE Symp. Security and Privacy*, IEEE Computer Society Press, Los Alamitos, Calif., 1987, pp. 184–194.

[CLAR89a] Clark, D.D., and D.R. Wilson, "Comments on the Integrity Model," in [NIST89], sec. 9, pp. 1–6 (1989).

[CLAR89b] Clark, D.D., and D.R. Wilson, "Evolution of a Model for Computer Integrity," in [NIST89], sec. A.2, pp. 1–13 (1989).

[CODD79] Codd, E.F., "Extending the Relational Database Model to Capture More Meaning," *ACM Trans. Database Systems*, Vol. 4, No. 4, 1979.

[CONG74] Congress, US, Privacy Act of 1974, Public Law 92-579, 1974.

[CONG82] Congress, US, Federal Managers' Financial Integrity Act of 1982, Public Law 97-255, Sept. 1982.

[CONG87] Congress, US, Computer Security Act of 1987, Public Law 100-235, Jan. 1988.

[CONG88] Congress, US, Computer Matching and Privacy Protection Act of 1988, Public Law 100-503, Oct. 1988.

[CONG90] Congress, US, Computer Matching and Privacy Protection Amendments of 1990, Public Law 101-508, Nov. 1990.

[COX79] Cox, L.A., and R.R. Schell, "Understanding Computer Related Crime," *Crime Prevention Rev.*, June 1979, pp. 1–10.

[CROC82] Crocker, D., "Standard for the Format of ARPA Internet Text Messages," [Internet] RFC 822, Aug. 1982.

[CSC85] Computer Security Center, "Computer Security Requirements: Guidance for Applying the Department of Defense Trusted Computer System Evaluation Criteria in Specific Environments" (The Yellow Book), CSC-STD-003-85, June 25, 1985.

[CSCD85] *Department of Defense Password Management Guideline*, Dept. of Defense Computer Security Center, CSC-STD-002-85, Apr. 12, 1985.

[CSSC92] Canadian System Security Centre, Communications Security Establishment, *The Canadian Trusted Computer Product Evaluation Criteria*, Government of Canada, Apr. 1992.

[DATE83] Date, C.J., *An Introduction to Database Systems*, Vol. 2, Addison-Wesley, Reading, Mass., 1983.

[DATE86] Date, C.J., *An Introduction to Database Systems*, Vol. 1, fourth edition, Addison-Wesley, Reading, Mass., 1986.

[DCSC83] DoD Computer Security Center, Trusted Computer Security Evaluation Criteria, CSC-STD-001-83, Aug. 15, 1983.

[DENN76] Denning, D.E., "A Lattice Model of Secure Information Flow," *Comm. ACM*, Vol. 19, No. 5, May 1976, pp. 236–243.

[DENN79] Denning, D.E., and P.J. Denning, "Data Security," *ACM Computing Surveys*, Vol. 11, No. 3, 1979, pp. 227–249.

[DENN81] Denning, D.E., and G.M. Sacco, "Time Stamps in Key Distribution Protocols," *Comm. ACM*, Vol. 24, No. 8, Aug. 1981, pp. 533–536.

[DENN82] Denning, D.E., *Cryptography and Data Security*, Addison-Wesley, Reading, Mass., 1982.

[DENN83] Denning, D.E., and J. Schlorer, "Inference Controls for Statistical Databases," *Computer*, Vol. 16, No. 7, July 1983, pp. 69–82.

[DENN84] Denning, D.E., "Cryptographic Checksums for Multilevel Database Security," *Proc. IEEE Symp. Security and Privacy*, IEEE Computer Society Press, Los Alamitos, Calif., 1984, pp. 52–61.

[DENN85] Denning, D.E., "Commutative Filters for Reducing Inference Threats in Multilevel Database Systems," *Proc. IEEE Symp. Security and Privacy*, IEEE Computer Society Press, Los Alamitos, Calif., 1985, pp. 134–146.

[DENN86] Denning, D.E., and M. Morgenstern, "Military Database Technology Study: AI Techniques for Security and Reliability," SRI tech. report, Aug. 1986.

[DENN86a] Denning, D.E., "A Preliminary Note on the Inference Problem in Multilevel Database Management Systems," *Proc. Nat'l Computer Security Center Invitational Workshop on Database Security*, 1986.

[DENN86b] Denning, D.E., "An Intrusion-Detection Model," *Proc. IEEE Symp. Security and Privacy*, IEEE Computer Society Press, Los Alamitos, Calif., 1986, pp. 118–131.

[DENN87] Denning, D.E., et al., "A Multilevel Relational Data Model," *Proc. IEEE Symp. Security and Privacy*, IEEE Computer Society Press, Los Alamitos, Calif., 1987, pp. 220–234.

[DENN88a] Denning, D.E., et al., "The SeaView Security Model," *Proc. IEEE Symp. Security and Privacy*, IEEE Computer Society Press, Los Alamitos, Calif., 1988, pp. 218–233.

[DENN88b] Denning, D.E., "Lessons Learned from Modeling a Secure Multilevel Relational Database System," in *Database Security: Status and Prospects*, C.E. Landwehr, ed., North-Holland, Amsterdam, The Netherlands, 1988, pp. 35–43.

[DIA87] Defense Intelligence Agency (DIA), "Security Requirements for System High and Compartmented Mode Workstations," DDS-2600-5502-87, Nov. 1987.

[DIAS91] Dias, G.V., et al., "DIDS (Distributed Intrusion Detection System) — Motivation, Architecture, and an Early Prototype," *Proc. 14th Nat'l Computer Conf.*, 1991, pp. 167–176.

[DILL86] Dillaway, B.B., and J.T. Haigh, "A Practical Design for a Multilevel Secure Database Management System," *Proc. 2nd Aerospace Computer Security Conf.*, 1986, pp. 44–57.

[DINK90] Dinkel, C., ed., *Secure Data Network System (SDNS) Network, Transport, and Message Security Protocols*, Nat'l Inst. of Standards and Technology, US Dept. of Commerce, NISTIR 90-4250, Feb. 1990.

[DITT89] Dittrich, K.R., M. Hartig, and H. Pfefferle, "Discretionary Access Control in Structurally Object-Oriented Database Systems," in *Database Security II: Status and Prospects*, C.E. Landwehr, ed., North-Holland, Amsterdam, The Netherlands, 1989, pp. 105–121.

[DOD82] Dept. of Defense, *Department of Defense Privacy Program*, DOD Directive 5400.11, June 1982.

[DOD83] Dept. of Defense, *Military Standard Internet Protocol*, MIL-STD-1777, Aug. 12, 1983.

[DOD85] Dept. of Defense Standard, *Department of Defense Trusted Computer System Evaluation Criteria*, DOD 5200.28-STD, GPO 1986-623–963, 643 0, Dec. 26, 1985.

[DOD86] Dept. of Defense Standard, *Department of Defense Trusted Computer System Evaluation Criteria, Information Security Program Regulation*, DOD Regulation 5200.1, May 1986.

[DOD88a] Dept. of Defense, *Military Standard: Defense Systems Software Development*, DOD-STD-2167A, Feb. 29, 1988.

[DOD88b] Dept. of Defense, *Security Requirements for Automated Information Systems*, DOD Directive 5200.28, Mar. 21, 1988.

[DTI92] Dept. of Trade and Industry (DTI), "The UK IT Security Evaluation and Certification Scheme: UKSP 01," "Description of the Scheme; UKSP 06," "UK Certified Product List: Issue 1.4," UKSP01 06, DTI, Mar. 1, 1991; reprinted for the 15th Nat'l Computer Security Conf., Oct. 1, 1992. Note: These publications are updated periodically. For example, "The UK IT Security Evaluation and Certification Scheme" and "Certified Product List" were published together in Oct. 1994.

[ECKM85] Eckmann, S., and R.A. Kemmerer, "INATEST: An Interactive Environment for Testing Formal Specifications," *Software Eng. Notes*, Vol. 10, No. 4, Aug. 1985, pp. 17–18.

[ECKM87] Eckmann, S., "In a Flo: The FDM Flow Tool," *Proc. 10th Nat'l Computer Conf.*, 1987, pp. 175–182.

[EDIF91a] Recommendation for UN/EDIFACT Security Joint WG, 1991.

[EDIF91b] Security Framework for EDIFACT (SC27/WG1/N135), 1991.

[EICH89] Eichen, M.W., and J.A. Rochlis, "With Microscope and Tweezers: An Analysis of the Internet Virus of November 1988," *Proc. IEEE Symp. Security and Privacy*, IEEE Computer Society Press, Los Alamitos, Calif., 1989, pp. 326–343.

[ELMA89] Elmasri, R., and S.B. Navathe, *Fundamentals of Database Systems*, Benjamin/Cummings, 1989.

[FARM86] Farmer, W.M., D.M. Johnson, and F.J. Thayer, "Towards a Discipline for Developing Verified Software," *Proc. 9th Nat'l Computer Security Conf.*, 1986, pp. 91–98.

[FARM90] Farmer, W.M., "A Partial Functions Version of Church's Simple Theory of Types," *J. Symbolic Logic*, Vol. 55, 1990, pp. 1269–1291.

[FARM90a] Farmer, D., and E.H. Spafford, "The COPS Security Checker System," CSD-TR-993, Dept. of Computer Sciences, Purdue Univ., West Lafayette, Ind., 1990 (software available by anonymous ftp from cert@sei.cmu.edu).

[FARM91] Farmer, W.M., J.D. Guttman, and F.J. Thayer, "IMPS: An Interactive Mathematical Proof System," M90-19, MITRE Corp., July 1991.

[FELL87] Fellows, J., et al., "The Architecture of a Distributed Trusted Computing Base," *Proc. 10th Nat'l Computer Security Conf.*, 1987, pp. 68–77.

[FELL91] Fellows, J., "Federated Trustworthy Systems," NATO Workshop on Composite Trustworthy Systems, Naval Research Laboratory, Oct. 1991.

[FERN81] Fernandez, E.B., R.C. Summers, and C. Wood, "Database Security and Integrity," Addison-Wesley, Reading, Mass., 1981.

[FERN89] Fernandez, E.B., E. Gudes, and H. Song, "A Security Model for Object-Oriented Databases," *Proc. IEEE Symp. Security and Privacy*, IEEE Computer Society Press, Los Alamitos, Calif., 1989, pp. 110–115.

[FERR91] Ferraiolo, D., and K. Ferraiolo, "Another Factor in Determining Security Requirements for Trusted Computer Applications," *Proc. 14th Nat'l Computer Security Conf.*, Nat'l Computer Security Center, 1991.

[FLIN88] Flink, Charles W., and J.D. Weiss, "System V/MLS Labeling and Mandatory Policy Alternatives," *AT&T Technical J.*, May/June 1988.

[FORC90] Forcht, K.A., "Ethical Use of Computers," in *Rogue Programs: Viruses, Worms, and Trojan Horses*, L.J. Hoffman, ed., 1990, pp. 117–120.

[FRAI83] Fraim, L., "SCOMP: A Solution to the Multilevel Security Problem," *Computer*, Vol. 16, No. 7, July 1983, pp. 26–34.

[FROS89] Froscher, J.N., and C. Meadows, "Achieving a Trusted Database Management System Using Parallelism," in *Database Security II: Status and Prospects*, C.E. Landwehr, ed., North-Holland, Amsterdam, The Netherlands, 1989.

[GAJN88] Gajnak, G., "Some Results from the Entity/Relationship Multilevel Secure DBMS Project," *Proc. 4th Aerospace Computer Security Applications Conf.*, IEEE Computer Society Press, Los Alamitos, Calif., 1988, pp. 66–71.

[GALI75] Galie, L.M., R.R. Linde, and K.R. Wilson, "Security Analysis of the Texas Instruments Inc. Advanced Scientific Computer," TM-WD-6505/000/00, System Development Corp., Washington, D.C., June 1975.

[GALI76] Galie, L.M., and R.R. Linde, "Security Analysis of the IBM VS2/R3 Operating System," TM-WD-7203/000/00, System Development Corp., Washington, D.C., Jan. 1976.

[GAMB88] Gambel, D., and S. Walter, "Retrofitting and Developing Applications for a Trusted Computing Base," *Proc. 11th Nat'l Computer Security Conf.*, Nat'l Computer Security Center, 1988.

[GAO88] US General Accounting Office, "GAO Policy and Procedures Manual for Guidance of Federal Agencies # Title 2, Accounting," Aug. 1987, revised May 1988.

[GARF91] Garfinkel, S., and G. Spafford, *Practical Unix Security*, O'Reilly and Assoc., Sebastopol, Calif., 1991.

[GARV86] C. Garvey, "Multilevel Data Storage Design," TRW Defense Systems Group, 1986.

[GARV88] Garvey, C., and A. Wu, "ASD-Views," *Proc. IEEE Symp. Security and Privacy*, IEEE Computer Society Press, Los Alamitos, Calif., 1988, pp. 85–95.

[GARV90] Garvey, C., et al., "A Layered TCB Implementation Versus the Hinke-Schaefer Approach," in *Database Security III: Status and Prospects*, D.L. Spooner and C.E. Landwehr, eds., North-Holland, Amsterdam, The Netherlands, 1990, pp. 151–165.

[GARV91] Garvey, T.D., T.F. Lunt, and M.E. Stickel, "Abductive and Approximate Reasoning Models for Characterizing Inference Channels," *Proc. Computer Security Foundations Workshop IV*, IEEE Computer Society Press, Los Alamitos, Calif., 1991, pp. 118–126.

[GASS87] Gasser, M., *Building a Secure Computer System*, Van Nostrand Reinhold, New York, N.Y., 1987.

[GASS88] Gasser, M., *Building a Secure Computer System*, Van Nostrand Reinhold, New York, N.Y., 1988.

[GEMI89] Gemignani, M., "Viruses and Criminal Law," *Rogue Programs: Viruses, Worms, and Trojan Horses*, L.J. Hoffman, ed., 1990, pp. 99–103.

[GLIG86] Gligor, V.D., et al., "On the Design and the Implementation of Secure Xenix Workstations," *Proc. IEEE Symp. Security and Privacy*, IEEE Computer Society Press, Los Alamitos, Calif., 1986, pp. 102–117.

[GOGU82] Goguen, J.A., and J. Meseguer, "Security Policies and Security Models," *Proc. IEEE Symp. Security and Privacy*, IEEE Computer Society Press, Los Alamitos, Calif., 1982, pp. 11–20.

[GOGU84] Goguen, J.A., and J. Meseguer, "Unwinding and Inference Control," *Proc. IEEE Symp. Security and Privacy*, IEEE Computer Society Press, Los Alamitos, Calif., 1984, pp. 75–86.

[GRAN83] Grant, P., and R. Riche, "The Eagle's Own Plume," *US Naval Inst. Proc.*, July 1983.

[GRAU82] Graubart, R.D., and J.P.L. Woodward, "A Preliminary Naval Surveillance DBMS Security Model," *Proc. IEEE Symp. Security and Privacy*, IEEE Computer Society Press, Los Alamitos, Calif., 1982, pp. 21–37.

[GRAU84] Graubart, R.D., "The Integrity-Lock Approach to Secure Database Management," *Proc. IEEE Symp. Security and Privacy*, IEEE Computer Society Press, Los Alamitos, Calif., 1984, pp. 62–74.

[GRAU89] Graubart, R.D., "A Comparison of Three Secure DBMS Architectures," *Proc. IFIP WG 11.3 Workshop on Database Security*, 1989.

[GRAU89a] Graubart, R., "On the Need for a Third Form of Access Control," *Proc. 12th Nat'l Computer Security Conf.*, NIST/NCSC, 1989, pp. 296–304.

[GRAU90] Graubart, R., "A Comparison of Three Secure DBMS Architectures," in *Database Security III: Status and Prospects*, D.L. Spooner and C.E. Landwehr, eds., North-Holland, Amsterdam, The Netherlands, 1990, pp. 109–114.

[GRAY78] Gray, J., "Notes on Data Base Operating Systems," in *Operating Systems — An Advanced Course*, R. Bayer et al., eds., Springer-Verlag, Berlin, 1978, pp. 393–481.

[GRAY86] Gray, J., "Why Do Computers Stop and What Can Be Done About It?" *Proc. IEEE Symp. Reliability in Distributed Software and Database Systems*, IEEE Computer Society Press, Los Alamitos, Calif., 1986, pp. 3–12.

[GRAY89] Gray, J.W., et al., "Secure Distributed Database Management System: Architecture," final tech. report, Vols. 1–5, RADC-TR-89-314, Unisys Corp., McLean, Va., Dec. 1989.

[GRAY91] Gray, J.W., "Toward a Mathematical Foundation for Information Flow Security," *Proc. IEEE Symp. Research in Security and Privacy*, IEEE Computer Society Press, Los Alamitos, Calif., 1991, pp. 21–34.

[GRIF76] Griffiths, P.P., and B.W. Wade, "An Authorization Mechanism for a Relational Database System," *ACM Trans. Database Systems*, Vol. 1, No. 3, Sept. 1976, pp. 242–255.

[GROH76] Grohn, M.J., "A Model of a Protected Data Management System," ESD-TR-76-289, I.P. Sharp Associates, June 1976.

[GUID83] *Guidelines for Computer Security Certification and Accreditation*, US Dept. of Commerce, Nat'l Bureau of Standards, FIPS PUB 102, Sept. 27, 1983.

[GUID84] Ruthberg, Z.G., and W. Neugent, *Overview of Computer Security Certification and Accreditation*, US Dept. of Commerce, Nat'l Bureau of Standards, NBS Special Publication 500-109, Apr. 1984.

[GUID85a] *Password Usage Standard*, US Dept. of Commerce, Nat'l Bureau of Standards, FIPS PUB 112, May 30, 1985.

[GUPTA91] Gupta, S., and V.D. Gligor, "Towards a Theory of Penetration-Resistant Systems and Its Application," *Proc. 4th IEEE Workshop Computer Security Foundations IV*, IEEE Computer Society Press, Los Alamitos, Calif., 1991, pp. 62–78.

[GUPTA92] Gupta, S., and V.D. Gligor, "Experience with a Penetration Analysis Method and Tool," *Proc. 15th Nat'l Computer Security Conf.*, 1992, pp. 165–183.

[HAFN91] Hafner, K., and J. Markoff, *Cyberpunk: Outlaws and Hackers on the Computer Frontier*, Simon and Schuster, New York, N.Y., 1991.

[HAIG88] Haigh, J.T., "Modeling Database Security Requirements," in *Database Security: Status and Prospects*, North-Holland, Amsterdam, The Netherlands, 1988.

[HAIG90] Haigh, J.T., et al., "The LDV Approach to Database Security," in *Database Security III: Status and Prospects*, D.I. Spooner and C. Landwehr, eds., North-Holland, Amsterdam, The Netherlands, 1990.

[HAIG90a] Haigh, J.T., R.C. O'Brien, and D.J. Thomsen, "The LDV Secure Relational DBMS Model," *Proc. IFIP W.G. 11.3 Workshop on Database Security*, 1990.

[HAIG91] Haigh, J.T., "LOCK Data Views (LDV)," *Lecture Notes for the Short Course Trusted Database Management Systems*, C. Garvey, coordinator, Univ. Extension, Univ. of California, Los Angeles, Apr. 2–5, 1991.

[HAIG91a] Haigh, J.T., R.C. O'Brien, and D.J. Thomsen, "The LDV Secure Relational DBMS Model," in *Database Security IV: Status and Prospects*, S. Jajodia and C. Landwehr, eds., North-Holland, Amsterdam, The Netherlands, 1991, pp. 265–280.

[HARR76] Harrison, M.A., W.L. Ruzzo, and J.D. Ullman, "Protection in Operating Systems," *Comm. ACM*, Vol. 19, No. 8, Aug. 1976, pp. 461–471.

[HEBB80] Hebbard, B., et al., "A Penetration Analysis of the Michigan Terminal System," *ACM SIGOPS Operating System Rev.*, Vol. 14, No. 1, Jan. 1980, pp. 7–20.

[HINK75] Hinke, T.H., and M. Schaefer, "Secure Data Management System," Tech. Report RADC-TR-75-266, System Development Corp., Nov. 1975.

[HINK85] Hinke, T.H., and M. Schaefer, "Secure Data Management System," CARADC-TR-266 (AD-A019201), System Development Corp., Santa Monica, Calif., Nov. 1985.

[HINK88] Hinke, T.H., et al., "A1 Secure DBMS Design," *Proc. 11th Nat'l Computer Security Conf.: A Postscript*, 1988, pp. 1–13.

[HINK88a] Hinke, T.H., "Inference Aggregation Detection in Database Management Systems," *Proc. IEEE Symp. Security and Privacy*, IEEE Computer Society Press, Los Alamitos, Calif., 1988, pp. 96–106.

[HINK89] Hinke, T.H., "The Trusted Server Approach to Multilevel Security," *Proc. 5th Ann. Computer Security Applications Conf.*, IEEE Computer Society Press, Los Alamitos, Calif., 1989, pp. 335–341.

[HINK90] Hinke, T.H., "DBMS Trusted Computing Base Taxonomy," originally presented at Workshop on Database Security, IFIP Working Group 11.3, Monterey, Calif., Sept. 1989; published in *Database Security III: Status and Prospects*, D.L. Spooner and C.E. Landwehr, eds., North-Holland, Amsterdam, The Netherlands, 1990.

[HOLL74] Hollingworth, D., S. Glaseman, and M. Hopwood, "Security Test and Evaluation Tools: An Approach to Operating System Security Analysis," P-5298, Rand Corp., Santa Monica, Calif., Sept. 1974.

[HUMP89a] Humphreys, E.J., "Towards a Secure Messaging Environment," *Proc. European Seminar on Security in Comm. Networks*, London, 1989.

[HUMP89b] Humphreys, E.J., "Open Systems Security and the Impact on Business in Europe," *IT Security in the '90s — Threats and Countermeasures Conf.*, London, Nov. 1989.

[HUMP89c] Humphreys, E.J., "Security Standards for Open Systems," *Proc. 5th Ann. Computer Security Applications Conf.*, IEEE Computer Society Press, Los Alamitos, Calif., 1989, p. 64 (and graphs used in a presentation).

[HUMP90a] Humphreys, E.J., "Overview of ISO/CCITT Security Standards for Open Systems," Danish Data Society 3rd EDP Conf., Feb. 1990.

[HUMP90b] Humphreys, E.J., "Open Systems Security, Paperless Trading and the Single European Market," *EDI: Letters of the Law Conf.*, Dallas, Feb. 1990.

[HUMP92a] Humphreys, Ted, ed., *Taxonomy of Security Standardisation: Version 2.0*, ITAEGV N69, XISEC Consultants Ltd., Apr. 30, 1992.

[HUMP92b] Open-EDI Security, SC27/WG1/N153, 1992.

[IEEE90] IEEE 802.10 (Editor at the LAN Security Working Group), Standard for Interoperable Local Area Network (LAN) Security (SILS), Part B — Secure Data Exchange, P802.10B/D2, Jan. 23, 1990.

[IRVI91] Irvine, C.E., R.R. Schell, and M.T. Thompson, "Using TNI Concepts for the Near Term Use of High Assurance Database Management Systems," *Proc. 4th RADC Multilevel Database Security Workshop* 1991, pp. 107–121.

[ISO89] "Information Processing Systems — Open Systems Interconnection — Basic Reference Model — Part 2: Security Architecture," ISO 7498-2, Feb. 1989.

[ISO90] Int'l Standards Organization (ISO), Working Draft on Access Control Framework, ISO/IEC JTC 1/SC 21 N5045, July 1990.

[ISO91a] ISO/IEC JTC 1/SC 27 (Int'l Organization for Standardization/Int'l Electrotechnical Commission, Joint Technical Committee 1 — Information Technology/Subcommittee 27 — Security Techniques), final text of ISO/IEC 9796, "Information Technology — Security Techniques — Digital Signature Scheme Giving Message Recovery," N289, July 7, 1991.

[ISO91b] ISO/IEC JTC 1/SC 27/WG2 (Int'l Organization for Standardization/Int'l Electrotechnical Commission, Joint Technical Committee 1 — Information Technology/Subcommittee 27 — Security Techniques; Working Group 2 — Techniques and Mechanisms), "CD 11166-2 — Banking Key Management by Means of Asymmetric Algorithms Part 2: Approved Algorithms Using the RSA," N102, Nov. 20, 1991.

[ISO91c] ISO/IEC JTC 1/SC 21 (Int'l Organization for Standardization/Int'l Electrotechnical Commission, Joint Technical Committee 1 — Information Technology/Subcommittee 21 — Information Retrieval, Transfer and Management for OSI), "Guide to Open Systems Security," N Project 97.21.9 Q53, Nov. 1991.

[ISO91d] ISO/IEC JTC 1/SC 21 (Int'l Organization for Standardization/Int'l Electrotechnical Commission, Joint Technical Committee 1 — Information Technology/Subcommittee 21 — Information Retrieval, Transfer and Management for OSI), Revised Text of CD 10181-2.2, "Information Technology — Open Systems Interconnection — Security Frameworks in Open Systems — Part 2: Authentication Framework," N5727 (DIS 10181-2), May 13, 1991.

[ISRA87] Israel, H., "Design of Originator Controls in a Computer System: A Trusted Discretionary Access Control Mechanism," *Proc. 3rd Symp. Physical/Electronic Security*, Armed Forces Communications and Electronics Assoc., 1987, pp. 3#1–3#6.

[ITAE92a] "Taxonomy of Security Standardisation," Version 2.0, E.J. Humphreys, ed., Apr. 1992.

[ITAE92b] Information Technology Advisory Expert Group on Information Systems Security (ITAEGV), Memorandum M-IT-06 (Draft 2.0) on Taxonomy and Directory of European Standardisation Requirements for Information Systems Security, Oct. 12, 1992.

[ITSE90] "Information Technology Security Evaluation Criteria," Version 1, Der Bundesminister des Innern, Bonn, Germany, May 2, 1990.

[ITSE91] Commission of the European Communities, *Information Technology Security Evaluation Criteria* (ITSEC), Provisional Harmonized Criteria: Version 1.2, Office for Official Publications of the European Communities, Luxembourg, June 1991.

[ITSE92] Commission of the European Communities, *Information Technology Security Evaluation Manual* (ITSEM), Draft V0.2, Directorate — General XIII Telecommunications, Information Industries and Innovation, Directorate F — RACE [Research and Development in Advanced Communications Technology for Europe (for coordination of different systems and advanced communications technologies)] Programme and Development of Advanced Telematic Services, Brussels, Apr. 2, 1992.

[JAJO90] Jajodia, S., and R. Sandhu, "Polyinstantiation Integrity in Multilevel Relations," *Proc. IEEE Symp. Research in Security and Privacy*, IEEE Computer Society Press, Los Alamitos, Calif., 1990, pp. 104–115.

[JAJO90a] Jajodia, S., and B. Kogan, "Integrating an Object-Oriented Data Model with Multilevel Security," *Proc. IEEE Symp. Research in Security and Privacy*, IEEE Computer Society Press, Los Alamitos, Calif., 1990, pp. 76–85.

[JAJO90b] Jajodia, S., and B. Kogan, "Transaction Processing in Multilevel-Secure Databases Using Replicated Architecture," *Proc. IEEE Symp. Research in Security and Privacy*, IEEE Computer Society Press, Los Alamitos, Calif., 1990, pp. 360–368.

[JAJO90c] Jajodia, S., and R. Sandhu, "Polyinstantiation Integrity in Multilevel Relations," *Proc. IEEE Symp. Security and Privacy*, IEEE Computer Society Press, Los Alamitos, Calif., 1990, pp. 104–115.

[JAJO90d] Jajodia, S., and R. Sandhu, "A Formal Framework for Single Level Decomposition of Multilevel Relations," *Proc. IEEE Workshop Computer Security Foundations*, IEEE Computer Society Press, Los Alamitos, Calif.,1990, pp. 152–158.

[JAJO90e] Jajodia, S., and R. Sandhu, "Database Security: Current Status and Key Issues," *ACM SIGMOD Record*, Vol. 19, No. 4, Dec. 1990, pp. 123–126.

[JAJO90f] Jajodia, S., R. Sandhu, and E. Sibley, "Update Semantics of Multilevel Relations," *Proc. 6th Ann. Computer Security Applications Conf.*, IEEE Computer Society Press, Los Alamitos, Calif., 1990, pp. 103–112.

[JAJO90g] Jajodia, S., et al., "Audit Trail Organization in Relational Databases," in *Database Security III: Status and Prospects*, D.L. Spooner and C. Landwehr, eds., North-Holland, Amsterdam, The Netherlands, 1990, pp. 269–281.

[JAJO91a] Jajodia, S., and R. Sandhu, "Polyinstantiation Integrity in Multilevel Relations Revisited," *Database Security IV: Status and Prospects*, S. Jajodia and C.E. Landwehr, eds., North-Holland, Amsterdam, The Netherlands, 1991, pp. 297–307.

[JAJO91b] Jajodia, S., and R. Sandhu, "A Novel Decomposition of Multilevel Relations into Single-Level Relations," *Proc. IEEE Symp. Research in Security and Privacy*, IEEE Computer Society Press, Los Alamitos, Calif., 1991, pp. 300–313.

[JAJO91c] Jajodia, S., and R. Sandhu, "Toward a Multilevel Secure Relational Data Model," *Proc. ACM SIGMOD Int'l Conf. Management of Data*, ACM Press, New York, N.Y., 1991, pp. 50–59.

[JAJO91d] Jajodia, S., and R.S. Sandhu, "Enforcing Primary Key Requirements in Multilevel Relations," *Proc. 4th RADC Workshop on Multilevel Database Security*, 1991.

[JTC191] "Report on the Open-EDI Conceptual Model JTC1/N1384" (SC27/WG1/N130), 1991.

[KAHN67] Kahn, D., *The Codebreakers*, Macmillan, New York, N.Y., 1967, pp. 67, 591.

[KALA93] Kalaski, B., "Privacy Enhancement for Internet Electronic Mail: Part IV: Key Certification and Related Services," RFC 1424, Feb. 1993.

[KARG74] Karger, P.A., and R.R. Schell, *Multics Security Evaluation: Vulnerability Analysis*, ESD-TR-74-193, Vol. 2, Hanscom AFB, Mass., 1974 (also available as NTIS AD-A001120).

[KARG89] Karger, P.A., "New Methods for Immediate Revocation," *Proc. Symp. Security and Privacy*, IEEE Computer Society Press, Los Alamitos, Calif.,, 1989, pp. 48–55.

[KARG91] Karger, P.A., et al., "A Retrospective of the VAX VMM Security Kernel," *IEEE Trans. Software Eng.*, Vol. 17, No. 11, Nov. 1991, pp. 1147–1165.

[KEEF88] Keefe, T.F., and W.T. Tsai, "Prototyping the SODA Security Model," *Database Security III: Status and Prospects*, David L. Spooner and Carl Landwehr, eds., North-Holland, Amsterdam, The Netherlands, 1990, pp. 211–235.

[KEEF88a] Keefe, T.F., W.T. Tsai, and M.B. Thuraisingham, "A Multilevel Security Model for Object-Oriented System," *Proc. 11th Nat'l Computer Security Conf.*, 1988, pp. 1–9.

[KEEF89] Keefe, T., W. Tsai, and B. Thuraisingham, "SODA: A Secure Object-Oriented Database System," *Computers and Security*, Vol. 8, Oct. 1990.

[KEMM86] Kemmerer, R.A., "Verification Assessment Study Final Report, Vol. I, Overview, Conclusions, and Future Directions," C3-R01-86, Library No. SW-228, 204, Dept. of Computer Science, Univ. of California, Santa Barbara, Mar. 27, 1986.

[KENS92] Smith, K., and M. Winslett, "Entity Modeling in the MLS Relational Model," *Proc. 18th Int'l Conf. Very Large Data Bases*, 1992, pp. 199–210.

[KENT89] Kent, S., and J. Linn, "Privacy Enhancement for Internet Electronic Mail: Part II — Certificate-Based Key Management," [Internet] RFC 1114, Aug. 1989.

[KENT90] Kent, S., and K. Rossen, "E-Mail Privacy for the Internet," *Business Comm. Rev.*, Vol. 20, No. 1, Jan. 1990.

[KENT93] Kent, S., "Privacy Enhancement for Internet Electronic Mail: Part II — Certificate-Based Key Management," RFC 1422, Feb. 1993.

[KIM89] Kim, W., and F.H. Lochovsky, eds., *Object-Oriented Concepts, Databases, and Applications*, Addison-Wesley, Reading, Mass., 1989.

[KIRK77] Kirkby, G., and M.J. Grohn, "On Specifying the Functional Design of a Protected DMS Tool," I.P. Sharp Associates, Mar. 1977.

[KLEI90] Klein, D.V., "'Foiling the Cracker': A Survey of, and Improvements to, Password Security," *Proc. UNIX Security Workshop II*, USENIX Assoc., 1990.

[KNOD88] Knode, R.B., and R.A. Hunt, "Making Databases Secure with TRUDATA Technology," *Proc. 4th Aerospace Computer Security Applications Conf.*, IEEE Computer Society Press, Los Alamitos, Calif., 1988, pp. 82–90.

[KOHN78] Kohnfelder, L.M., "A Method for Certification," MIT Laboratory for Computer Science, Cambridge, Mass., May 1978.

[KRAJ92] Krajewski, M., "Concept for a Smart Card Kerberos," *Proc. 15th Nat'l Computer Security Conf.*, 1992, pp. 76–83.

[KRAM83] Kramer, S., "The MITRE Flow Table Generator — Vol. I," M83-31, Vol. 1, MITRE Corp., Bedford, Mass., Jan. 1983.

[KURA92] Kurak, C., and J. McHugh, "A Cautionary Note on Image Downgrading," *Proc. 8th Ann. Computer Security Applications Conf.*, IEEE Computer Society Press, Los Alamitos, Calif., 1992, pp. 153–159.

[LACK74] Lackey, R.D., "Penetration of Computer Systems, an Overview," *Honeywell Computer J.*, Vol. 8, No. 2, 1974.

[LAMP71] Lampson, B.W., "Protection," *Proc. 5th Princeton Symp. Information Sciences and Systems*, Princeton Univ., Princeton, N.J., 1971, pp. 437–443, reprinted in *Operating Systems Rev.*, Vol. 8, No. 1, Jan. 1974, pp. 18–24.

[LAMP73] Lampson, B.W., "A Note on the Confinement Problem," *Comm. ACM*, Vol. 16, No. 10, Oct. 1973, pp. 613–615.

[LAMP91] Lampson, B.W., et al., "Authentication in Distributed Systems: Theory and Practice," *Operating Systems Rev.*, Vol. 25, No. 5, Oct. 1991, pp. 165–182.

[LAND81] Landwehr, C.E., "Formal Models for Computer Security," *ACM Computing Surveys*, Vol. 13, No. 3, Sept. 1981, pp. 247–278.

[LAND84] Landwehr, C.E., C.L. Heitmeyer, and J. McLean, "A Security Model for Military Message Systems," *ACM Trans. Computer Systems*, Vol. 2, No. 3, Aug. 1984, pp. 198–222.

[LAPA90] LaPadula, L.J., "Formal Modeling in a Generalized Framework for Access Control," *Proc. IEEE Computer Security Foundations Workshop III*, IEEE Computer Society Press, Los Alamitos, Calif., 1990, pp. 100–109.

[LAPA91] LaPadula, L.J., "A Rule-Base Approach to Formal Modeling of a Trusted Computer System," M91-021, MITRE Corp., Aug. 1991.

[LEE88] Lee, T.M.P., "Using Mandatory Integrity to Enforce 'Commercial' Security," *Proc. IEEE Symp. Security and Privacy*, IEEE Computer Society Press, Los Alamitos, Calif., 1988, pp. 140–146.

[LEFK89] Lefkovits, Henry C., et al., "Multilevel Secure Entity-Relationship DBMS, Final Technical Report," RADC-TR-88-310, Jan. 1989.

[LEVI89] Levin, T.E., S.J. Padilla, and C.E. Irvine, "A Formal Model for UNIX Setuid," *Proc. IEEE Symp. Security and Privacy*, IEEE Computer Society Press, Los Alamitos, Calif., 1989, pp. 73–83.

[LEVI90] Levin, T.E., A. Tao, and S.J. Padilla, "Covert Storage Channel Analysis: A Worked Example," *Proc. 13th Nat'l Computer Security Conf.*, 1990, pp. 10–19.

[LIND75] Linde, R.R., "Operating System Penetration," *Proc. Nat'l Computer Conf.*, Vol. 44, AFIPS Press, Montvale, N.J., 1975.

[LIND76] Linden, T.A., "Operating System Structures to Support Security and Reliable Software," *ACM Computing Surveys*, Vol. 8, No. 4, 1976, pp. 409–445.

[LIND76a] Linde, R.R., and R.F. von Buelow, "EXEC-8 Security Analysis," Memo. Report 3205, Naval Research Laboratory, Jan. 1976.

[LINN86] Linn, J., and S. Kent, "Electronic Mail Privacy Enhancement," *Proc. 2nd Aerospace Computer Security Conf.*, 1986.

[LINN89a] Linn, J., "Privacy Enhancement for Internet Electronic Mail: Part I — Message Encipherment and Authentication Procedures," [Internet] RFC 1113, Aug. 1989.

[LINN89b] Linn, J., "Privacy Enhancement for Internet Electronic Mail: Part III — Algorithms, Modes, and Identifiers," [Internet] RFC 1115, Aug. 1989.

[LINN93] Linn, J., "Privacy Enhancement for Internet Electronic Mail: Part I — Message Encipherment and Authentication Procedures," RFC 1421, Feb. 1993.

[LIPN82] Lipner, S.B., "Non-Discretionary Controls for Commercial Applications," *Proc. IEEE Symp. Security and Privacy*, IEEE Computer Society Press, Los Alamitos, Calif., 1982, pp. 2–10.

[LUM87] Lum, V., et al., "Designing DBMS Support for the Temporal Dimension," *Proc. ACM SIGMOD Int'l Conf. Management of Data*, ACM Press, New York, N.Y., 1987, pp. 115–130.

[LUNT88] Lunt, T.F., et al., "A Near-Term Design for the SeaView Multi-level Database System," *Proc. IEEE Symp. Security and Privacy*, IEEE Computer Society Press, Los Alamitos, Calif., 1988, pp. 234–244.

[LUNT88a] Lunt, T.F., et al., "Secure Distributed Data Views: Security Policy and Interpretation for Database Management System for a Class A1 DBMS," RADC-TR-89-313, Vol. 1 of 5, Rome Labs, Griffiss AFB, Rome, N.Y., 1988.

[LUNT88b] Lunt, T.F., et al., "Element-Level Classification with A1 Assurance," *Computers and Security*, Vol. 7, 1988, pp. 73–82.

[LUNT89] Lunt, T.F., "Multilevel Security for Object-Oriented Database Systems," *Proc. IFIP WG 11.3 Workshop on Database Security*, 1989.

[LUNT89a] Lunt, T.F., "Aggregation and Inference: Facts and Fallacies," *Proc. IEEE Symp. Security and Privacy*, IEEE Computer Society Press, Los Alamitos, Calif., 1989, pp. 102–109.

[LUNT89b] Lunt, T.F., and J.K. Millen, "Secure Knowledge-Based Systems," Interim Tech. Report, Computer Science Laboratory, SRI Int'l, Aug. 1989.

[LUNT89c] Lunt, T.F., et al., *Secure Distributed Data Views*, Vols. 1–4, SRI Project 1143, SRI Int'l, 1988–1989.

[LUNT90] Lunt, T.F., et al., , "The SeaView Security Model," *IEEE Trans. Software Eng.*, Vol. 16, No. 6, June 1990, pp. 593–607.

[LUNT90a] Lunt, T.F., et al., "The SeaView Security Model," *IEEE Trans. Software Eng.*, Vol. 15, No. 6, June 1990.

[LUNT90b] Lunt, T.F., and D. Hsieh, "Update Semantics for a Multilevel Relational Database System," *Proc. 4th IFIP Working Group: 11.3 Workshop on Database Security*, Halifax, U.K., 1990.

[LUNT90c] Lunt, T.F., and D. Hsieh, "The SeaView Secure Database System: A Progress Report," *Proc. European Symp. Research on Computer Security (ESORICS 90)*, Toulouse, France, 1990.

[LUNT90d] Lunt, T.F., "Multilevel Security for Object-Oriented Database Systems," in *Database Security III: Status and Prospects*, D.L. Spooner and C. Landwehr, eds., North-Holland, Amsterdam, The Netherlands, 1990, pp. 199–210.

[LUNT91] Lunt, T.F., and D. Hsieh, "Update Semantics for a Multilevel Relational Database System," in *Database Security IV: Status and Prospects*, S. Jajodia and C. Landwehr, eds., North-Holland, Amsterdam, The Netherlands, 1991, pp. 281–296.

[LUNT92] Lunt, T.E., et al., "A Real-Time Intrusion Detection Expert System (IDES) — Final Tech. Report," SRI Int'l, Menlo Park, Calif., Feb. 1992.

[MAZU88] Mazumdar, S., D. Stemple, and T. Sheard, "Resolving the Tension between Integrity and Security Using a Theorem Prover," *Proc. ACM Int'l Conf. Management of Data*, ACM Press, New York, N.Y., 1988, pp. 233–242.

[MCAU92] McAuliffe, N., "Extending Our Hardware Base: A Worked Example," *Proc. 15th Nat'l Computer Security Conf.*, 1992, pp. 184–193.

[MCCO90] McCollum, C.J., J.R. Messing, and L. Notargiacomo, "Beyond the Pale of MAC and DAC: Defining New Forms of Access Control," *Proc. IEEE Symp. Research in Security and Privacy*, IEEE Computer Society Press, Los Alamitos, Calif., 1990, pp. 190–200.

[MCCO91] McCollum, C.J., and L. Notargiacomo, "Distributed Concurrency Control with Optional Data Replication," *Proc. IFIP WG 11.3 Workshop on Database Security*, Shepardstown, W.Va., Nov. 1991.

[MCLE85] McLean, J., "A Comment on the 'Basic Security Theorem' of Bell and LaPadula," *Information Processing Letters*, Vol. 20, Feb. 1985, pp. 67–70.

[MCPH74] McPhee, W.S., "Operating System Integrity in OS/VS2," *IBM Systems J.*, No. 3, 1974, pp. 231–252.

[MEAD88a] Meadows, C., and S. Jajodia, "Integrity versus Security in Multi-Level Secure Databases," in *Database Security: Status and Prospects*, C. Landwehr, ed., North-Holland, Amsterdam, The Netherlands, 1988, pp. 89–101.

[MEAD88b] Meadows, C., and S. Jajodia, "Maintaining Correctness, Availability, and Unambiguity in Trusted Database Management Systems," *Proc. 4th Aerospace Computer Security Applications Conf.*, IEEE Computer Society Press, Los Alamitos, Calif., 1988, pp. 106–110.

[MEAD90] Meadows, C., "Aggregation Problems: A Position Paper," *Proc. 3rd RADC Workshop in Multilevel Security*, June 1990.

[MEAD90a] Meadows, C.A., "Extending the Brewer-Nash Model to a Multilevel Context," *Proc. IEEE Symp. Research in Security and Privacy*, IEEE Computer Society Press, Los Alamitos, Calif., 1990, pp. 95–102.

[MEAD92] Meadows, C., and C. Landwehr, "Designing a Trusted Application in an Object-Oriented Data Model," in *Directions in Database Security*, T. Lunt, ed., Springer-Verlag, Berlin, 1992.

[MEND79] Mendleson, E., *Introduction to Mathematical Logic*, D. Van Nostrand, 1979.

[MERK82] Merkle, R.C., *Secrecy, Authentication, and Public Key Systems*, UMI Research Press, Ann Arbor, Mich., 1982.

[MILL84] Millen, J.K., "A1 Policy Modeling," *7th DoD/NBS Computer Security Conf.*, Sept. 1984, pp. 137–145.

[MILL90] Millen, J.K., and D.J. Bodeau, "A Dual-Label Model for the Compartmented Mode Workstation," M90-51, MITRE Corp., Bedford, Mass., Aug. 1990.

[MILL91] Millen, J.K., and D.J. Bodeau, "Report on Computer Security Foundations Workshop IV," *Cipher*, 1991.

[MILL92] Millen, J.K., and T.F. Lunt, "Security for Object-Oriented Database Systems," *Proc. IEEE Symp. Research in Security and Privacy*, IEEE Computer Society Press, Los Alamitos, Calif., 1992, pp. 260–272.

[MINS87] Minsky, N.H., and D. Rozenshtein, "A Law-Based Approach to Object-Oriented Programming," *Proc. Conf. Object-Oriented Programming: Systems, Languages, Applications*, ACM Press, New York, N.Y., 1987, pp. 482–493.

[MOFF88] Moffett, J.D., and M.S. Sloman, "The Source of Authority for Commercial Access Control," *Computer*, Vol. 21, No. 2, 1988, pp. 59–69.

[MOOR90] Moore, A.P., "The Specification and Verified Decomposition of System Requirements Using CSP," *IEEE Trans. Software Eng.*, Vol. 16, No. 9, Sept. 1990, pp. 932–948.

[MORG88] Morgenstern, M., "Controlling Logical Inference in Multilevel Database Systems," *Proc. IEEE Symp. Security and Privacy*, IEEE Computer Society Press, Los Alamitos, Calif., 1988, pp. 245–255.

[MUFF4a] Muffett, A.D.E., "Crack Version 4.0a, A Sensible Password Checker for Unix," Computer Unit, Univ. College of Wales, Aberwystwyth, Wales (software available by anonymous ftp from cert@sei.cmu.edu).

[MURR87a] Murray, W.H., "Data Integrity in a Business Data Processing System," in [NIST87].

[MURR87b] Murray, W.H., "On the Use of Mandatory," in [NIST87].

[MYER80] Myers, P.A., *Subversion: The Neglected Aspect of Computer Security*, master's thesis, Naval Postgraduate School, Monterey, Calif., 1980.

[NCSC85] Nat'l Computer Security Center, *Dept. of Defense Trusted Computer Security Evaluation Criteria*, DOD 5200.28-STD, Dec. 1985.

[NCSC87a] Nat'l Computer Security Center, *Trusted Network Interpretation of the Trusted Computer System Evaluation Criteria*, NCSC-TG-005, July 31, 1987.

[NCSC87b] Nat'l Computer Security Center, *A Guide to Understanding Discretionary Access Control in Trusted Systems*, NCSC-TG-003, Version 1, 1987.

[NCSC88] Nat'l Computer Security Center, *A Guide to Understanding Audit in Trusted Systems*, June 1, 1988.

[NCSC88a] Nat'l Computer Security Center, *Trusted Network, Glossary of Computer Security Terms*, NCSC-TG-004, Oct. 1988.

[NCSC88b] Nat'l Computer Security Center, "Trusted Product Evaluations — A Guide for Vendors," draft, Mar. 1, 1988.

[NCSC88c] Nat'l Computer Security Center, "Trusted Network Testing Guideline," NCSC-TG-010, Version 1, draft, Aug. 1988.

[NCSC89] Nat'l Computer Security Center, *Guidelines for Formal Verification Systems*, Version 1, NCSC-TG-014, Apr. 1989.

[NCSC89a] Nat'l Computer Security Center, *Rating Maintenance Phase — Program Document*, NCSC-TG-013, Version 1, June 23, 1989.

[NCSC91] Nat'l Computer Security Center, *Trusted Database Management System Interpretation of the Trusted Computer System Evaluation Criteria*, NCSC-TG-021, Apr. 1991.

[NCSC91a] Nat'l Computer Security Center, "Integrity in Automated Information Systems," C Tech. Report 79-91, Sept. 1991.

[NCSC91b] Nat'l Computer Security Center, *Final Evaluation Report, SecureWare Incorporated, Compartmented Mode Workstation Plus*, Jan. 1991.

[NCSC92] Nat'l Computer Security Center, *Trusted Product Evaluation Questionnaire*, NCSC-TG-019, Version 2, May 2, 1992.

[NECH91] Nechvatal, J., "Public-Key Cryptography," Special Publication 800-2, Nat'l Inst. of Standards and Technology, US Dept. of Commerce, Apr. 1991.

[NEED78] Needham, R.M., and M.D. Schroeder, "Using Encryption for Authentication in Large Networks of Computers," *Comm. ACM*, Vol. 21, No. 12, Dec. 1978, pp. 993–999.

[NELS91] Nelson, D., and C. Paradise, "Using Polyinstantiation to Develop an MLS Application," *Proc. IEEE 7th Ann. Computer Security Applications Conf.*, IEEE Computer Society Press, Los Alamitos, Calif., 1991, pp. 12–22.

[NEUM89] Neumann, P.G., and D.B. Parker, "A Summary of Computer Misuse Techniques," *Proc. 12th Nat'l Computer Security Conf.*, 1989, pp. 396–407.

[NIER89] Nierstrasz, O., "A Survey of Object-Oriented Concepts," in *Object-Oriented Concepts, Databases, and Applications*, W. Kim and F.H. Lochovsky, eds., Addison-Wesley, Reading, Mass., 1989, pp. 3–21.

[NIST80] Nat'l Inst. of Standards and Technology, "DES Modes of Operation," Dec. 1980. A companion ISO standard is IS8372.

[NIST87] *Report of the Invitational Workshop on Integrity Policy in Computer Information Systems (WIPCIS)*, S.W. Katzke and Z.G. Ruthberg, eds., Special Publication 500-160, NIST, Jan. 1989.

[NIST89] *Report of the Invitational Workshop on Data Integrity*, Z.G. Ruthberg and W.T. Polk, eds., Special Publication 500-168, NIST, Sept. 1989.

[NIST91] Burr, W.E., *Security in ISDN*, Special Publication 500-189, NIST, Sept. 1991.

[NIST92] Nat'l Inst. of Standards and Technology (NIST) and Nat'l Security Agency (NSA), *Federal Criteria for Information Technology Security: Vol. I, Protection Profile Development; Vol. II, Registry of Protection Profiles*, Version 1.0, Dec. 1992.

[OCON88] O'Connor, J.P., and J.W. Gray, "A Distributed Architecture for Multilevel Database Security," *Proc. 11th Nat'l Computer Security Conf.*, 1988, pp. 179–187.

[OLSO90] Olson, I.M., and M.D. Abrams, "Computer Access Control Policy Choices," *Computers and Security*, Vol. 9, No. 8, Dec. 1990, pp. 699–714.

[OMB82] Office of Management and Budget, "Internal Control Guidelines: Guidelines for the Evaluation and Improvement of and Reporting on Internal Control Systems in the Federal Government," Dec. 1982.

[OMB84] Office of Management and Budget, "Financial Management Systems," OMB Circular No. A-127, Dec. 1984.

[PADL82] Padlipsky, M.A., TCP-on-a-LAN, RFC 872, M82-48, Sept. 1982.

[PAGE89] Page, J., et al., "Evaluation of Security Model Rule Bases," *Proc. Nat'l Computer Security Conf.*, 1989.

[PARK75] Parker, D.B., "Computer Abuse Perpetrators and Vulnerabilities of Computer Systems," Stanford Research Inst., Menlo Park, Calif., Dec. 1975.

[PARK91] Parker, D.B., "An Essay: Restating the Foundation of Information Security," *ISP News*, May/June 1991, pp. 23–27.

[PARN72a] Parnas, D.L., "A Technique for Software Module Specification with Examples," *Comm. ACM*, Vol. 15, No. 5, May 1972, pp. 330–336.

[PARN72b] Parnas, D.L., "On the Criteria to Be Used in Decomposing Systems into Modules," *Comm. ACM*, Vol. 15, No. 12, Dec. 1972, pp. 1053–1058.

[PHIL73] Phillips, R., "VM/370 Penetration Study Final Report," TM(L)-5196/006/00, System Development Corp., Santa Monica, Calif., Oct. 1973.

[POPE79] Popek, G.L., and C.S. Kline, "Encryption and Secure Networks," *ACM Computing Surveys*, Vol. 11, No. 4, Dec. 1979, pp. 331–356.

[POST82] Postel, J., "Simple Mail Transfer Protocol," [Internet] RFC 821, Aug. 1982.

[RABI88] Rabitti, F., D. Woelk, and W. Kim, "A Model of Authorization for Object-Oriented and Semantic Databases," *Proc. Conf. Extending Database Technology*, 1988, pp. 231–250.

[REAG82] Reagan, R.L., Executive Order 12356, US Government Printing Office, Apr. 1982.

[RFC1038] "Revised Internet Protocol Security Options, RIPSO," RFC 1038, Network Information Center. See also RFC 791 and RFC 1108.

[ROCH89] Rochlis, J., and M. Eichin, "With Microscope and Tweezers: The Worm from MIT's Perspective," *Comm. ACM*, June 1989, pp. 689–698.

[ROSE91] Rose, M., "Post Office Protocol: Version 3," [Internet] RFC 1225, May 1991.

[ROUG87] Rougeau, P.A., and E.D. Sturms, "The Sybase Secure Dataserver: A Solution to the Multilevel Secure DBMS Problem," *Proc. 10th Nat'l Computer Security Conf.*, 1987, pp. 211–215.

[RSAD91] "Public-Key Cryptography Standards," RSA Data Security Inc., June 1991.

[RUB86] Rub, J.W., "Penetration Handbook," Aerospace Corp., El Segundo, Calif., Jan. 1986.

[SALT75] Saltzer, J.H., and M.D. Schroeder, "The Protection of Information in Computer Systems," *Proc. IEEE*, Vol. 63, No. 9, Sept. 1975, pp. 1278–1308.

[SAND88a] Sandhu, R.S., "The Schematic Protection Model: Its Definition and Analysis for Acyclic Attenuating Schemes," *J. ACM*, Vol. 35, No. 2, 1988, pp. 404–432.

[SAND88b] Sandhu, R.S., "Transaction Control Expressions for Separation of Duties," *4th Aerospace Computer Security Applications Conf.*, IEEE Computer Society Press, Los Alamitos, Calif., 1988, pp. 282–286.

[SAND89] Sandhu, R.S., "Transformation of Access Rights," *Proc. IEEE Symp. Security and Privacy*, IEEE Computer Society Press, Los Alamitos, Calif., 1989, pp. 259–268.

[SAND90] Sandhu, R.S., "Mandatory Controls for Database Integrity," in *Database Security III: Status and Prospects*, D.L. Spooner and C.E. Landwehr, eds., North-Holland, Amsterdam, The Netherlands, 1990, pp. 143–150.

[SAND90a] Sandhu, R., S. Jajodia, and T. Lunt, "A New Polyinstantiation Integrity Constraint for Multilevel Relations," *Proc. IEEE Computer Security Foundations Workshop*, IEEE Computer Society Press, Los Alamitos, Calif., 1990, pp. 159–165.

[SAND90b] Sandhu, R., and S. Jajodia, "Integrity Mechanisms in Database Management Systems," *Proc. 13th NIST-NCSC Nat'l Computer Security Conf.*, 1990, pp. 526–540.

[SAND91] Sandhu, R., and S. Jajodia, "Honest Databases That Can Keep Secrets," *Proc. 14th NIST-NCSC Nat'l Computer Security Conf.*, 1991, pp. 267–282.

[SAND92a] Sandhu, R., R. Thomas, and S. Jajodia, "Supporting Timing Channel Free Computations in Multilevel Secure Object-Oriented Databases," in *Database Security V: Status and Prospects*, C.E. Landwehr and S. Jajodia, eds., North-Holland, Amsterdam, The Netherlands, 1992, pp. 297–314.

[SAND92b] Sandhu, R.S., and S. Jajodia, "Eliminating Polyinstantiation Securely," *Computers and Security*, Vol. 11, 1992, pp. 547–562.

[SAND92c] Sandhu, R.S., and S. Jajodia, "Polyinstantiation for Cover Stories," *Proc. European Symp. Research in Computer Security*, Lecture Notes in Computer Science, Vol. 648, Springer-Verlag, Berlin, 1992, pp. 307–328.

[SAYD87] Saydjari, O.S., and J.M. Beckman, "Locking Computers Securely," *10th Nat'l Computer Security Conf.*, NCSC/ICST, 1987, pp. 129–141.

[SC2792] "Guidelines on the Use and Management of Trusted Third Party Services," study document (SC27/WG1/N331), 1992.

[SCHA83] Schaefer, M., ed., *Multilevel Data Management Security*, Air Force Studies Board, Committee on Multilevel Data Management Security, Nat'l Academy Press, Washington, D.C., 1983.

[SCHA84] Schaefer, M., and R.R. Schell, "Toward an Understanding of Extensible Architectures for Evaluated Trusted Computer System Products," *Proc. IEEE Symp. Security and Privacy*, IEEE Computer Society Press, Los Alamitos, Calif., 1984, pp. 41–49.

[SCHA89] Schaefer, M., "Symbol Security Condition Considered Harmful," *Proc. IEEE Symp. Security and Privacy*, IEEE Computer Society Press, Los Alamitos, Calif., 1989, pp. 20–46.

[SCHA90] Schaefer, M., "Reflections on Current Issues in Trusted DBMS," in *Database Security IV: Status and Prospects*, S. Jajodia and C.E. Landwehr, eds., North-Holland, Amsterdam, The Netherlands, 1991.

[SCHE74] Schell, R.R., "Effectiveness — The Reason for a Security Kernel," *Proc. Nat'l Computer Conf.*, 1974, pp. 975–976.

[SCHE79] Schell, R.R., "Computer Security: The Achilles' Heel of the Electronic Air Force," *Air Univ. Rev.*, Jan.-Feb. 1979, pp. 16–33.

[SCHE83] Schell, R.R., "A Security Kernel for a Multiprocessor Microcomputer," *Computer*, Vol. 16, No. 7, July 1983, pp. 47–53.

[SCHE84] Schell, R.R., "The Future of Trusted Computer Systems," *Computer Security: A Global Challenge, Proc. 2nd IFIP Int'l Conf. Computer Security*, J.H. Finch and E.G. Dougall, eds., 1984, pp. 55–67.

[SCHE84a] Schell, R.R., "Security Kernel Design Principles," Auerbach 84-02-07, 1984.

[SCHE85] Schell, R.R., "Position Statement on Network Security Policy and Models," *Proc. Dept. of Defense Computer Security Center Invitational Workshop on Network Security*, 1985, pp. 2-61–2-70.

[SCHE85a] Schell, R.R., T.F. Tao, and M. Heckman, "Designing the GEMSOS Security Kernel for Security and Performance," *Proc. 8th Nat'l Computer Security Conf.*, 1985, pp. 108–119.

[SCHE86] Schell, R.R., and D.E. Denning, "Integrity in Trusted Database Systems," *Proc. 9th Nat'l Computer Security Conf.*, 1986, pp. 30–36.

[SCHK82] Schkolnick, M., and P. Sorenson, "The Effects of Denormalization on Database Performance," *Australian Computer J.*, Vol. 14, No. 1, Feb. 1982, pp. 12–18.

[SCHN85] Schnackenberg, D.D., "Development of a Multilevel Secure Local Area Network," *Proc. 8th Nat'l Computer Security Conf.*, 1985, pp. 97–101.

[SCHO87] Shockley, W.D., and R.R. Schell, "TCB Subsets for Incremental Evaluation," *Proc. 3rd Aerospace Computer Security Conf.*, 1987, pp. 131–139.

[SCHR72] Schroeder, M.D., and J.H. Saltzer, "A Hardware Architecture for Implementing Protection Rings," *Comm. ACM*, Vol. 15, No. 3, Sept. 1981, pp. 157–170.

[SDC75] "Fujitsu, Ltd., Security/Privacy Report," TM(L)-5593/000/00, System Development Corp., Santa Monica, Calif., Oct. 1975.

[SDC76] "A Security and Integrity Analysis of OS/VS2 Release 3," TM-5662/000/00, System Development Corp., Santa Monica, Calif., Apr. 1976.

[SELI80] Selinger, P.G., "Authorization and Views," in *Distributed Data Bases*, I.W. Draffan and F. Poole, eds., Cambridge Univ. Press, Cambridge, UK, 1980, pp. 233–246.

[SHIR81] Shirley, L.J., and R. Schell, "Mechanism Sufficiency Validation by Assignment," *Proc. IEEE Symp. Security and Privacy*, IEEE Computer Society Press, Los Alamitos, Calif., 1981, pp. 26–32.

[SHOC87] Shockley, W.D., and R.R. Schell, "TCB Subsets for Incremental Evaluation," *Proc. AIAA/ASIS/IEEE 3rd Aerospace Computer Security Conf.*, 1987, pp. 131–139.

[SHOC88] Shockley, W.R., "Implementing the Clark/Wilson Integrity Policy Using Current Technology," *Proc. 11th Nat'l Computer Security Conf.*, 1988, pp. 29–37.

[SHOC88a] Shockley, W.R., T.F. Tao, and M.F. Thompson, "An Overview of the GEMSOS Class A1 Technology and Application Experience," *Proc. 11th Nat'l Computer Security Conf.*, 1988, pp. 238–245.

[SHOC88b] Shockley, W.R., R.R. Schell, and M.F. Thompson, "The Importance of High Assurance Computers for Command, Control, Communications, and Intelligence Systems," *Proc. 4th Aerospace Computer Security Applications Conf.*, IEEE Computer Society Press, Los Alamitos, Calif., 1988, pp. 331–342.

[SICH83] Sicherman, G.L., W. de Jonge, and R.P. van de Riet, "Answering Queries without Revealing Secrets," *ACM Trans. Database Systems*, Vol. 8, No. 1, Mar. 1983, pp. 41–59.

[SIMP90] Simpact Associates, Inc., "Security in Electronic Messaging: Things You Should Know," 1990.

[SMAH88] Smaha, S.E., "Haystack: An Intrusion Detection System," *Proc. IEEE 4th Aerospace Computer Security Applications Conf.*, IEEE Computer Society Press, Los Alamitos, Calif., 1988, pp. 37–44.

[SMIT88] Smith, G.W., "Identifying and Representing the Security Semantics of an Application," *Proc. IEEE 4th Aerospace Computer Security Applications Conf.*, IEEE Computer Society Press, Los Alamitos, Calif., 1988, pp. 125–130.

[SMIT90] Smith, G.W., "Modeling Security-Relevant Data Semantics," *Proc. IEEE Symp. Research in Security and Privacy*, IEEE Computer Society Press, Los Alamitos, Calif., 1990, pp. 384–391.

[SMIT90a] Smith, G.W., *The Modeling and Representation of Security Semantics for Database Applications*, doctoral dissertation, George Mason Univ., Fairfax, Va., 1990.

[SNOD86] Snodgrass, R., and I. Ahn, "Temporal Databases," *Computer*, Vol. 19, No. 3, Sept. 1986, pp. 35–42.

[SNOD87] Snodgrass, R., "The Temporal Query Language TQuel," *ACM Trans. Database Systems*, Vol. 12, No. 2, June 1987, pp. 247–298.

[SNYD81] Snyder, L., "Formal Models of Capability-Based Protection Systems," *IEEE Trans. Computers*, Vol. C-30, No. 3, 1981, pp. 172–181.

[SOGI89] Senior Official Group for IT Standards, "Security in Open Networks (SOGITS) Report," Jan. 1989.

[SPAF89] Spafford, E.H., "The Internet Worm: Crisis and Aftermath," *Comm. ACM*, Vol. 32, No. 6, June 1989, pp. 678–688.

[SPAF89a] See [SPAF89].

[SPAF90a] Spafford, E.H., K.A. Heaphy, and D.J. Ferbrache, "What Is a Computer Virus?" in *Rogue Programs: Viruses, Worms, and Trojan Horses*, L.J. Hoffman, ed., 1990, pp. 29–42.

[SPAF90b] Spafford, E.H., K.A. Heaphy, and D.J. Ferbrache, "Further Information on Viruses," in *Rogue Programs: Viruses, Worms, and Trojan Horses*, L.J. Hoffman, ed., 1990, pp. 173–179.

[SPAF90c] Spafford, E.H., "The Internet Worm Incident," in *Rogue Programs: Viruses, Worms, and Trojan Horses*, L.J. Hoffman, ed., 1990, pp. 203–227.

[SPOO89] Spooner, D.L., "The Impact of Inheritance on Security in Object-Oriented Database Systems," *Database Security II: Status and Prospects*, C.E. Landwehr, ed., North-Holland, Amsterdam, The Netherlands, 1989, pp. 141–160.

[SSSC91] System Security Study Committee; Computer Science and Telecommunications Board; Commission on Physical Sciences, Mathematics, and Applications; National Research Council, *Computers at Risk: Safe Computing in the Information Age*, Nat'l Academy Press, 1991.

[STAC90] Stachour, P.D., and B. Thuraisingham, "Design of LDV: A Multilevel Secure Relational Database Management System," *IEEE Trans. Knowledge and Data Eng.*, Vol. 2, No. 2, June 1990, pp. 190–209.

[STEF90] Stefanac, S., "Mad Macs," in *Rogue Programs: Viruses, Worms, and Trojan Horses*, Lance J. Hoffman, ed., 1990, pp. 180–193.

[STER91] Sterne, D.F., "On the Buzzword 'Security Policy,'" *Proc. IEEE Symp. Research in Security and Privacy*, IEEE Computer Society Press, Los Alamitos, Calif., 1991, pp. 219–230.

[STER91b] Sterne, D.F., et al., "An Analysis of Application Specific Security Policies," *Proc. 14th Nat'l Computer Security Conf.*, Nat'l Computer Security Center, 1991.

[STOL89] Stoll, C., *The Cuckoo's Egg*, Doubleday, New York, N.Y., 1989.

[STON74] Stonebraker, M., "Implementation of Integrity Constraints and Views by Query Modification," *ACM Nat'l Conf. Proc.*, ACM Press, New York, N.Y., 1974, pp. 180–186.

[STRA92] Stranger, J., "EWOS/ETSI Report," Minutes of Mar. 9–12, 1992, X.400 SIG Meeting, Nat'l Inst. of Standards and Technology OSI Implementers Workshop (NIST OIW), X.400 SIG (Special Interest Group), Mar. 19, 1992.

[SU86] Su, T.-A., *Inferences in Databases*, doctoral dissertation, Case Western Reserve Univ., Cleveland, Ohio, 1986.

[SU87] Su, T.-A., and G. Ozsoyoglu, "Data Dependencies and Inference Control in Multilevel Relational Database Systems," *Proc. IEEE Symp. Se-*

curity and Privacy, IEEE Computer Society Press, Los Alamitos, Calif., 1987, pp. 202–211.

[SU90] Su, T.-A., and Gultekin Ozsoyoglu, "Multivalued Dependency Inferences in Multilevel Relational Database Systems," *Database Security III: Status and Prospects*, D.L. Spooner and C. Landwehr, eds., North-Holland, Amsterdam, The Netherlands, 1990, pp. 293–300.

[TANE87] Tanenbaum, A.S., *Operating Systems: Design and Implementation*, Prentice-Hall, Englewood Cliffs, N.J., 1987.

[TCSE85] *Trusted Computer System Evaluation Criteria*, DOD 5200.28-STD, US Dept. of Defense, Dec. 1985.

[TDI91] *Trusted Database Management System Interpretation of the Trusted Computer System Evaluation Criteria*, NCSC-TG-021, Nat'l Computer Security Center, Apr. 1991.

[TECH85] *Technical Rationale Behind CSC-STD-003-85: Computer Security Requirements — Guidance for Applying the Department of Defense Trusted Computer System Evaluation Criteria in Specific Environments*, CSC-STD-004-85, June 1985, p. 27.

[TEDI91] "Trusted Third Parties and Similar Services" (CEC TEDIS Document), TEDIS Project Report (SC27/WG1/N214), 1991.

[THOM84] Thompson, K., "Reflections on Trusting Trust," *Comm. ACM*, Vol. 27, No. 8, Aug. 1984, pp. 761–763.

[THOM90] Thompson, M.F., et al., "Introduction to the Gemini Trusted Network Processor," *Proc. 13th Nat'l Computer Security Conf.*, 1990, pp. 211–217.

[THOM90a] Thompson, D.J., "Role-Based Application Design and Enforcement," *Proc. 4th IFIP WG 11.3 Workshop on Database Security*, Halifax, UK, 1990.

[THOM90b] Thomas, R., L.R. Rogers, and J.L. Yates, *Advanced Programmer's Guide to UNIX\254 System V*, Berkeley, Calif., Osborne McGraw-Hill, 1986.

[THUR87] Thuraisingham, B.M., "Security Checking in Relational Database Management Systems Augmented with Inference Engines," *Computers and Security*, Vol. 6, 1987, pp. 479–492.

[THUR89a] Thuraisingham, B.M., "A Multilevel Secure Object-Oriented Data Model," *Proc. 12th Nat'l Computer Security Conf.*, 1989, pp. 579–590.

[THUR89b] Thuraisingham, B.M., "Mandatory Security in Object-Oriented Database System," *Proc. Conf. Object-Oriented Programming: Systems, Languages, and Applications*, ACM Press, New York, N.Y., 1989, pp. 203–210.

[THUR90] Thuraisingham, B., "Recursion Theoretic Properties of the Inference Problem in Database Security," MTP 291, MITRE Corp., Bedford, Mass., May 1990.

[TINT92] Tinto, M., "The Design and Evaluation of INFOSEC Systems: The Computer Security Contribution to the Composition Discussion," C Tech. Report 32-92, Nat'l Security Agency, June 1992.

[TNI87] *Trusted Network Interpretation of the Trusted Computer System Evaluation Criteria*, NCSC-TG-005, National Computer Security Center, July 1987.

[TRAT76] Trattner, S., "Tools for Analysis of Software Security," ATR-77(2780)-1, Aerospace Corp., El Segundo, Calif., Oct. 1976.

[TSIC82] Tsichritzis, D.C., and F.H. Lochovsky, *Data Models*, Prentice-Hall, Englewood Cliffs, N.J., 1982.

[ULAM76] Ulam, S.M., *Adventures of a Mathematician*, Charles Scribner's Sons, New York, N.Y., 1976.

[UNIS89] See [GRAY89].

[VETT89] Vetter, L., and G. Smith, "TCB Subsets: The Next Step," *Proc. 5th Aerospace Conf.*, 1989.

[WALT91] Walter, Michael J., "Getting What You Want," *OPtiv: The Business J. for Open Systems* (Corp. for Open Systems Int'l), Vol. 1, No. 1, Fall 1991, pp. 44–45.

[WARE70] Ware, W.H., ed., "Security Controls for Computer Systems: Report of Defense Science Board Task Force on Computer Security," DTIC AD-A076-617/0, Rand Corp., Santa Monica, Calif., Feb. 1970, reissued Oct. 1979.

[WEIS73] Weissman, C., "System Security Analysis/Certification Methodology and Results," SP-3728, System Development Corp., Santa Monica, Calif., Oct. 1973.

[WEIS92] Weissman, C., "Blacker: Security for the DDN, Examples of A1 Security Engineering Trades," *Proc. 1992 IEEE Symp. Research in Security and Privacy*, IEEE Computer Society Press, Los Alamitos, Calif., 1992, pp. 286–292.

[WEIS92a] Weissman, C., "Security Penetration Testing Guideline, Navy Handbook on Security Certification," TM-8889/000/00 (draft), Paramax Systems Corp., Camarillo, Calif., Dec. 1992.

[WHEE92] Wheeler, T., S. Holtsberg, and S. Eckmann, *Ina Go User's Guide*, TM-8613/003, Paramax Systems Corp., Reston, Va., 1992.

[WIED91] Wiederhold, G., S. Jajodia, and W. Litwin, "Dealing with Granularity of Time in Temporal Databases," *Lecture Notes in Computer Science*, Vol. 498, R. Anderson et al., eds., Springer-Verlag, New York, N.Y., 1991, pp. 124–140.

[WILK72] Wilkes, M., *Time-Sharing Computer Systems*, 2nd ed., American-Elsevier, New York, N.Y., 1972.

[WILK81] Wilkinson, A.L., et al., "A Penetration Analysis of the Burroughs Large System," *ACM SIGOPS Operating Systems Rev.*, Vol. 15, No. 1, Jan. 1981, pp. 14–25.

[WILL90] Williams, J.G., "On the Formalization of Semantic Conventions," *J. Symbolic Logic*, Vol. 55, No. 1, Mar. 1990, pp. 220–243.

[WILL90a] Williams, J., "Stages of Elaboration of Security Requirements for a Trusted Computer System," private communication, Dec. 1990.

[WILL91] Williams, J.G., "Modeling Nondisclosure in Terms of the Subject-Instruction Stream," *Proc. IEEE Symp. Research in Security and Privacy*, IEEE Computer Society Press, Los Alamitos, Calif., 1991, pp. 64–77.

[WILS88] Wilson, J., "Views as the Security Objects in a Multilevel Secure Relational Database Management System," *Proc. IEEE Symp. Security and Privacy*, IEEE Computer Society Press, Los Alamitos, Calif., 1988, pp. 70–84.

[WILS89] Wilson, J., "A Security Policy for an A1 DBMS (a Trusted Subject)," *Proc. IEEE Symp. Security and Privacy*, IEEE Computer Society Press, Los Alamitos, Calif., 1989, pp. 116–125.

[WIMB71] Wimbrow, J.H., "A Large-Scale Interactive Administrative System," *IBM Systems J.*, Vol. 10, No. 4, 1971, pp. 260–282.

[WINT74] Winterbotham, F.W., *The Ultra Secret*, Harper and Row, New York, N.Y., 1974.

[WINK92] Winkler, J.R., and J.C. Landry, "Intrusion and Anomaly Detection: ISOA Update," *Proc. 15th Nat'l Computer Security Conf.*, 1992, pp. 272–281.

[WISE90] Wiseman, S.R., "On the Problem of Security in Data Bases," in *Database Security III: Status and Prospects*, D.L. Spooner and C.E. Landwehr, eds., North-Holland, Amsterdam, The Netherlands, 1990, pp. 143–150.

[WITT90] Wittbold, J.T., and D.M. Johnson, "Information Flow in Nondeterministic Systems," *Proc. IEEE Symp. Research in Security and Privacy*, IEEE Computer Society Press, Los Alamitos, Calif., 1990, pp. 144–161.

[WOOD87] Woodward, J.P.L., "Exploiting the Dual Nature of Sensitivity Labels," *Proc. IEEE Symp. Security and Privacy*, IEEE Computer Society Press, Los Alamitos, Calif., 1987, pp. 23–30.

[WOOD88] Wood, A., "The SWORD Model of Multi-Level Secure Databases," RSRE Report 4247, RSRE, Nov. 1988.

[WOOD92] Woodfield, N.K., "An Approach for Evaluating the Security of an Air Force Type Network," *5th Ann. Computer Security Applications Conf.*, IEEE Computer Society Press, Los Alamitos, Calif., 1989, pp. 53–62.

[ZDON90] Zdonik, S.B., and D. Maier, eds., *Readings in Object-Oriented Database Systems*, Morgan Kaufmann, San Mateo, Calif., 1990.

Glossary

*-property (star property): A Bell-LaPadula security model rule allowing a subject write access to an object only if the security level of the subject is dominated by the security level of the object. Also known as the confinement property.

A

acceptance inspection: The final inspection to determine whether a facility or system meets the specified technical and performance standards. Note: This inspection is held immediately after facility and software testing and is the basis for commissioning or accepting the information system.

acceptance procedure: A procedure which takes objects produced during the development, production, and maintenance processes for a target of evaluation and, as a positive act, places them under the controls of a configuration control system.

access: (1) The ability and means to communicate with (that is, input to or receive output from) or otherwise make use of any information, resource, or component in an information technology (IT) product. (2) A specific type of interaction between a subject and an object that results in the flow of information from one to the other. Note: An individual does not have "access" if the proper authority or a physical, technical, or procedural measure prevents him or her from obtaining knowledge or having an opportunity to alter information, material, resources, or components.

access control: (1) The process of limiting access to the resources of an information technology (IT) product only to authorized users, programs, processes, systems (in a network), or other IT products. (Synonymous with controlled access and limited access.) (2) The limiting of rights or capabilities of a subject to communicate with other subjects, or to use functions or services in a computer system or network. (3) Restrictions controlling a subject's access to an object.

access control list: (1) A mechanism implementing discretionary access control in an IT (information technology) product that identifies the users who may access an object and the type of access to the object that a user is permitted. (2) A list of subjects authorized for specific access to an object. (3) A list of entities, together with their access rights, which are authorized to have access to a resource.

access control mechanism: (1) Security safeguards designed to detect and prevent unauthorized access, and to permit authorized access in an IT (information technology) product. (2) Hardware or software features, operating procedures, management procedures, and various combinations of these designed to detect and prevent unauthorized access and to permit authorized access in an automated system.

access level: The hierarchical portion of the security level used to identify the sensitivity of data and the clearance or authorization of users. Note: The access level, in conjunction with the nonhierarchical categories, forms the sensitivity label of an object. (See category, security level, and sensitivity label.)

access list: Synonymous with access control list.

access mediation: Process of monitoring and controlling access to the resources of an IT (information technology) product, including but not limited to the monitoring and updating of policy attributes during accesses as well as the protection of unauthorized or inappropriate accesses (see access control).

access period: A segment of time, generally expressed on a daily or weekly basis, during which access rights prevail.

access port: A logical or physical identifier that a computer uses to distinguish different terminal input/output data streams.

access type: The nature of an access right to a particular device, program, or file (for example, read, write, execute, append, modify, delete, or create).

accountability: (1) Means of linking individuals to their interactions with an IT (information technology) product, thereby supporting identification of and recovery from unexpected or unavoidable failures of the control objectives. (2) The quality or state that enables actions on an ADP (automated data processing) system to be traced to individuals who may then be held responsible. These actions include violations and attempted violations of the security policy, as well as allowed actions. (3) The property that enables activities on a system to be traced to individuals who may then be held responsible for their actions.

accreditation: (1) The procedure for accepting an IT (information technology) system to process sensitive information within a particular operational environment. (2) The formal procedure for recognizing both the technical competence and the impartiality of an IT test laboratory (evaluation body) to carry out its associated tasks. (3) Formal declaration by a designated approving authority that an automated information system (AIS) is approved to operate in a particular security configuration using a prescribed set of safeguards. (4) The managerial authorization and approval granted to an ADP (automated data processing) system or network to process sensitive data in an operational environment, made on the basis of a certification by designated technical personnel of the extent to which design and implementation of the system meet pre-specified technical requirements, for example, TCSEC (Trusted Computer System Evaluation Criteria), for achieving adequate data security. Management can accredit a system to operate at a higher or lower level than the risk level recommended (for example, by the requirements guideline) for the certification level of the system. If management accredits the system to operate at a higher level than is appropriate for the certification level, management is accepting the additional risk incurred. (5) A formal declaration by the DAA (designated approving authority) that the AIS (automated information system) is approved to operate in a particular security mode using a prescribed set of safeguards. Accreditation is the official management authorization for operation of an AIS and is based on the certification process as well as other management considerations. The accreditation statement affixes security responsibility with the DAA and shows that due care has been taken for security.

accreditation authority: Synonymous with designated approving authority.

accreditation range: The accreditation range of a host with respect to a particular network is a set of mandatory access control levels (according to "Computer Security Requirements: Guidance for Applying the Department of Defense Trusted Computer System Evaluation Criteria in Specific Environments," CSC-STD-003-85) for data storage, processing, and transmission. The accreditation range will generally reflect the sensitivity levels of data that the accreditation authority believes the host can reliably keep segregated with an acceptable level of risk in the context of the particular network for which the accreditation range is given. Thus, although a host system might be accredited to use the mandatory access control levels Confidential, Secret, and Top Secret in stand-alone operation, it might have an accreditation range consisting of the single value Top Secret for attachment to some network.

add-on security: The retrofitting of protection mechanisms, implemented by hardware or software.

administration documentation: The information about a target of evaluation supplied by the developer for use by an administrator.

administrative security: The management constraints and supplemental controls established to provide an acceptable level of protection for data. (Synonymous with procedural security.)

administrator: A person in contact with the target of evaluation who is responsible for maintaining its operational capability.

algorithm: A mathematical procedure that can usually be explicitly encoded in a set of computer language instructions that manipulate data. Cryptographic algorithms are mathematical procedures used for such purposes as encrypting and decrypting messages and signing documents digitally.

application program interface: System access point or library function that has a well-defined syntax and is accessible from application programs or user code to provide well-defined functionality.

approval/accreditation: The official authorization that is granted to an ADP (automated data processing) system to process sensitive information in its operational environment, based upon comprehensive security evaluation of the system's hardware, firmware, and software security design, configuration, and implementation, and of the other system procedural, administrative, physical, TEMPEST, personnel, and communications security controls.

architectural design: A phase of the development process wherein the top-level definition and design of a target of evaluation are specified.

assignment: Requirement in a protection profile taken directly as stated, without change, from the list of components or derived by placing a bound on a threshold definition. Note: The assignment of environment-specific requirements to generic component requirements is performed when a component requirement corresponds to an environment-specific requirement.

assurance: See profile assurance and development and evaluation assurance. (1) The degree of confidence that a target of evaluation adequately fulfills the security requirements. (2) A measure of confidence that the security features and architecture of an AIS accurately mediate and enforce the security policy. Note: The two main aspects of assurance are *effectiveness* and *correctness* (ITSEC — Information Technology Security Evaluation Criteria) or *development* and *evaluation* assurance (Federal Criteria).

assurance level: In evaluation criteria, a specific level on a hierarchical scale representing successively increased confidence that a target of evaluation adequately fulfills the security requirements.

assurance profile: An assurance requirement for a TOE (target of evaluation) whereby different levels of confidence are required in different security-enforcing functions.

attack: The act of trying to bypass security controls on a system. An attack may be active, resulting in the alteration of data; or passive, resulting in the release of data. Note: The fact that an attack is made does not necessarily mean that it will succeed. The degree of success depends on the vulnerability of the system or activity and the effectiveness of existing countermeasures.

audit: Independent review and examination of records and activities to determine compliance with established usage policies and to detect possible inadequacies in product technical security policies of their enforcement.

audit trail: (1) A set of records that collectively provide documentary evidence of processing used to aid in tracing from original transactions forward to related records and reports, and/or backward from records and reports to their component source transactions. (2) A chronological record of system activities that is sufficient to enable the reconstruction, reviewing, and examination of the sequence of environments and activities surrounding or leading to an operation, a procedure, or an event in a transaction from its inception to final results. (3) Information collected or used to facilitate a security audit. Note: Audit trail may apply to information in an IT (information technology) product or an AIS (automated information system) or to the transfer of COMSEC (communications security) material.

authenticate: (1) To verify the identity of a user, user device, or other entity, or the integrity of data stored, transmitted, or otherwise exposed to unauthorized modification in an IT (information technology) product. (2) To verify the validity of a claimed identity of a user, device, or other entity in a computer system, often as a prerequisite to allowing access to resources in a system. (3) To verify the integrity of data that have been stored, transmitted, or otherwise exposed to possible unauthorized modification.

authentication: (1) To establish the validity of a claimed identity. (2) To provide protection against fraudulent transactions by establishing the validity of a message, station, individual, or originator. (3) Means of verifying an entity's (for example, individual user's, machine's, or software component's) eligibility to receive specific categories of information.

authenticator: The means used to confirm the identity or to verify the eligibility of a station, originator, or individual.

authorization: Access rights granted to a user, program, or process.

authorized: Entitled to a specific mode of access.

automated data processing (ADP) security: Synonymous with automated information systems security.

automated data processing (ADP) system: An assembly of computer hardware, firmware, and software configured for the purpose of classifying, sorting, calculating, computing, summarizing, transmitting and receiving, storing, and retrieving data, with a minimum of human intervention.

automated information system (AIS): (1) Any equipment or interconnected systems or subsystems of equipment that are used in the automatic acquisition, storage, manipulation, management, movement, control, display, switching, interchange, transmission, or reception of data and include computer software, firmware, and hardware. (2) An assembly of computer hardware, software, and/or automated information system (AIS) firmware configured to collect, create, communicate, compute, disseminate, process, store, and/or control data or information. Note: Included are computers, word processing systems, networks or other electronic information handling systems, and associated equipment.

automated information systems (AIS) security: Measures and controls that protect an AIS against denial of service and unauthorized (accidental or intentional) disclosure, modification, or destruction of AISs and data. AIS security includes consideration of all hardware and/or software functions, characteristics, and/or features; operational procedures, accountability procedures, and access controls at the central computer, remote computer, and terminal facilities; management constraints; physical structures and devices; and personnel and communication controls needed to provide an acceptable level of risk for the AIS and for the data and information contained in the AIS. It includes the totality of security safeguards needed to provide an acceptable protection level for an AIS and for data handled by an AIS.

automated security monitoring: The use of automated procedures to ensure that security controls are not circumvented.

availability: (1) The ability to access a specific resource within a specific time frame as defined within the IT (information technology) product specification. (2) The ability to use or access objects and resources as required. The property relates to the concern that information objects and other system resources are accessible when needed and without undue delay. (3) The prevention of the unauthorized withholding of information or resources.

B

back door: Synonymous with trap door.

backup plan: Synonymous with contingency plan.

bandwidth: (1) A characteristic of a communication channel that is the amount of information that can be passed through it in a given amount of time, usually expressed in bits per second. (2) Rate at which information is transmitted through a channel. (See channel capacity.) Note: Bandwidth was originally a term used in analog communication, measured in hertz, and related to the information rate by the "sampling theorem" (generally attributed to H. Nyquist, although the theorem was in fact known before Nyquist used it in communication theory). Nyquist's sampling theorem says that the information rate in bits (samples) per second is at most twice the bandwidth in hertz of an analog signal created from a square wave. In a covert-channel context, "bandwidth" is given in bits per second rather than hertz and is commonly used, in a nonstandard use of terminology, as a synonym for information rate.

basic component: A component that is identifiable at the lowest hierarchical level of a specification produced during detailed design.

Bell-LaPadula model: (1) A formal state-transition model of computer security policy that describes a set of access control rules. In this formal model, the entities in a computer system are divided into abstract sets of subjects and objects. The notion of a secure state is defined, and it is proven that each state transition preserves security by moving from secure state to secure state, thereby inductively proving that the system is secure. A system state is defined to be "secure" if the only permitted access modes of subjects to objects are in accordance with a specific security policy. To determine whether a specific access mode is allowed, the clearance of a subject is compared with the classification of the object, and a determination is made as to whether the subject is authorized for the specific access mode. The clearance/classifications scheme is expressed in terms of a lattice. (See *-property (star property), simple security property, and lattice). (2) A formal state-transition model of a technical security policy for an AIS (automated information system) that presents: (a) access constraints (including initial-state constraints and variants or the simple security and star properties), (b) allowed state transitions (called "rules of operation"), and (c) a proof that the allowed state transitions guarantee satisfaction of the constraints.

benign environment: A nonhostile environment that may be protected from external hostile elements by physical, personnel, and procedural security countermeasures.

between-the-lines entry: Unauthorized access obtained by tapping the temporarily inactive terminal of a legitimate user. (See piggyback.)

beyond A1: A level of trust defined by the US DoD (Department of Defense) Trusted Computer System Evaluation Criteria (TCSEC) that is beyond the state-of-the-art technology available at the time the criteria were developed. It includes all the A1-level features plus additional ones not required at the A1 level.

binding of security functionality: The ability of security-enforcing functions and mechanisms to work together in a way that is mutually supportive and provides an integrated and effective whole.

bit: Short for binary digit — 0 or 1. Keys are strings of bits.

browsing: The act of searching through storage to locate or acquire information without necessarily knowing of the existence or the format of the information being sought.

C

call back: A procedure for identifying a remote terminal. In a call back, the host system disconnects the caller and then dials the authorized telephone number of the remote terminal to reestablish the connection. (Synonymous with dial back.)

Canadian Trusted Computer Product Evaluation Criteria (CTCPEC): Canadian secure products criteria.

candidate TCB (trusted computing base) subset: The identification of the hardware, firmware, and software that make up the proposed TCB subset, along with the identification of its subjects and objects — one of the conditions for evaluation by parts.

capability: A protected identifier that both identifies the object and specifies the access rights to be allowed to the accessor who possesses the capability. In a capability-based system, access to protected objects such as files is granted if the would-be accessor possesses a capability for the object.

category: (1) A grouping of objects to which a nonhierarchical restrictive label is applied (for example, proprietary, compartmented information). Subjects must be privileged to access a category. (2) Restrictive label that has been applied to both classified and unclassified data, thereby increasing the requirement for protection of, and restricting the access to, the data. Note: Examples include sensitive compartmented information and proprietary information. Individuals are granted access to a special category of information only after being granted formal access authorization.

cellular transmission: Data transmission via interchangeable wireless (radio) communications in a network of numerous small geographic cells. Most current technology is analog — represented as electrical levels, not bits. However, the trend is toward digital cellular data transmission.

certification: (1) Comprehensive evaluation of the technical and nontechnical security features of an AIS (automated information system) and other safeguards, made in support of the approval/accreditation process, to establish the extent to which a particular design and implementation meet a set of specified security requirements. Note: There remain two other definitions in active common usage that differ according to circumstances. (See IT (information technology) security certification and site certification.) (2) The issue of a formal statement confirming the results of an evaluation, and that the evaluation criteria used were correctly applied. Synonym for IT (information technology) security certification.

certification body: An independent and impartial national organization that performs certification. Also referred to as an evaluation body or entity.

channel: An information transfer path within a system — may also refer to the mechanism by which the path is effected.

channel capacity: Maximum possible error-free rate, measured in bits per second, at which information can be sent along a communications path.

cleartext: Intelligible data, the semantic content of which is available. Also referred to as plaintext.

closed security environment: An environment in which both of the following conditions hold true: (1) Application developers (including maintainers) have sufficient clearances and authorizations to provide an acceptable presumption that they have not introduced malicious logic and (2) configuration control provides sufficient assurance that applications and the equipment are protected against the introduction of malicious logic prior to and during the operation of system applications.

closed user group: A closed user group permits users belonging to a group to communicate with each other, but precludes communications with other users who are not members of the group.

Common Criteria for Information Technology Security (CC): Evolving international security evaluation criteria being developed by the US, Canada, the UK, Germany, and France.

communication channel: The physical media and devices that provide the means for transmitting information from one component of a network to (one or more) other components.

communication link: The physical means of connecting one location to another for the purpose of transmitting and/or receiving data.

communications security (COMSEC): Measures taken to deny unauthorized persons information derived from telecommunications of an entity concerning national or organizational security, and to ensure the authenticity of such telecommunications. Communications security includes cryptosecurity, transmission security, emission security, and physical security of communications security material and information.

compartment: (1) A designation applied to a type of sensitive information, indicating the special handling procedures to be used for the information and the general class of people who may have access to the information. It can refer to the designation of information belonging to one or more categories. (2) A class of information in the US government that has need-to-know access controls beyond those normally provided for access to Confidential, Secret, or Top Secret information.

compartmented mode or compartmented security mode: See modes of operation.

component: (1) A device or set of devices consisting of hardware, along with its firmware and/or software, that performs a specific function on a computer communications network. A component is a part of the larger system and may itself consist of other components. Examples include modems, telecommunications controllers, message switches, technical control devices, host computers, gateways, communications subnets, and so on. (2) An identifiable and self-contained portion of a target of evaluation which is subjected to security evaluation. (3) An organization that is part of a larger organization, for example, a US Defense Component. (4) A requirement that is part of a larger set of requirements that may be called a package. For example, protection profiles are assembled from components. Groups of components can be assembled into predefined packages.

component reference monitor: An access control concept that refers to an abstract machine that mediates all access to objects within a component by subjects within the component.

compromise: A violation of the security system such that an unauthorized disclosure of sensitive information may have occurred.

compromising emanations: Unintentional data-related or intelligence-bearing signals that, if intercepted and analyzed, disclose the information transmission received, handled, or otherwise processed by any information processing equipment. (See TEMPEST.)

computer abuse: The misuse, alteration, disruption, or destruction of data processing resources. The key aspect is that it is intentional and improper.

computer architecture: The set of layers and protocols (including formats and standards that different hardware/software must comply with to achieve stated objectives) which define a computer system. Computer architecture features can be available to application programs and system programmers in several modes, including a protected mode. For example, the system-level features of computer architecture may include: (1) memory management, (2) protection, (3) multitasking, (4) input/output, (5) exceptions and multiprocessing, (6) initialization, (7) coprocessing and multiprocessing, (8) debugging, and (9) cache management.

computer cryptography: The use of a cryptoalgorithm in a computer, microprocessor, or microcomputer to perform encryption or decryption in order to protect information or to authenticate users, sources, or information.

computer fraud: Computer-related crimes involving deliberate misrepresentation, alteration, or disclosure of data to obtain something of value (usually for monetary gain). A computer system must have been involved in the perpetration or cover-up of the act or series of acts. A computer system might have been involved through improper manipulation of input data, output or results, applications programs, data files, computer operations, communications, or computer hardware, systems software, or firmware.

computer security (COMPUSEC) : Synonymous with automated information systems (AIS) security.

computer security subsystem: A device designed to provide limited computer security features in a larger system environment.

Computer Security Technical Vulnerability Reporting Program (CSTVRP): A program that focuses on technical vulnerabilities in commercially available hardware, firmware, and software products acquired by the US Department of Defense. CSTVRP provides for the reporting, cataloging, and discreet dissemination of technical vulnerability and corrective measure information to Defense Components on a need-to-know basis.

concealment system: A method of achieving confidentiality in which sensitive information is hidden by embedding it in irrelevant data.

confidentiality: (1) The assurance that information is not disclosed to inappropriate entities or processes. (2) The property that information is not made available or disclosed to unauthorized entities. (3) The prevention of the unauthorized disclosure of information. (4) The concept of holding sensitive data in confidence, limited to an appropriate set of individuals or organizations.

configuration: Selection of one of the sets of possible combinations of features of a system or target of evaluation.

configuration control: (1) A system of controls imposed on changing controlled objects produced during the development, production and maintenance processes for a target of evaluation. (2) Management of changes made to a system's hardware, software, firmware, and documentation throughout the development and operational life of the system. (3) The process of controlling modifications to the system's hardware, firmware, software, and documentation that provides sufficient assurance that the system is protected against the introduction of improper modifications prior to, during, and after system implementation. (Compare configuration management.)

configuration management: The management of security features and assurances through control of changes made to a system's hardware, software, firmware, documentation, test, test fixtures, and test documentation throughout the development and operational life of the system. (Compare configuration control.)

confinement: The prevention of the leaking of sensitive data from a program.

confinement channel: Synonymous with covert channel.

confinement property: Synonymous with *-property (star property).

connection: A liaison, in the sense of a network interrelationship, between two hosts for a period of time. The liaison is established (by an initiating host) for the purpose of information transfer (with the associated host). The period of time is the time required to carry out the intent of the liaison (for example, transfer of a file, a chatter session, or delivery of mail). In many cases, a connection (in the sense of this glossary) will coincide with a host-host connection (in a special technical sense) that is established via TCP (Transmission Control Protocol) or an equivalent protocol. However, a connection (liaison) can also exist when only a protocol such as IP (Internet Protocol) is in use. (IP has no concept of a connection that persists for a period of time.) Hence, the notion of connection can be independent of the particular protocols in use during a liaison of two hosts.

construction: The process of creating a target of evaluation.

consumers: Individuals or groups responsible for specifying requirements for IT (information technology) product security (for example, policy makers and regulatory officials, system architects, integrators, acquisition managers, product purchasers, and end users).

contamination: The intermixing of data at different sensitivity and need-to-know levels. The lower level data is said to be contaminated by the higher level data; thus, the contaminating (higher level) data may not receive the required level of protection.

content-dependent access control: Access control in which access is determined by the value of the data to be accessed.

context-dependent access control: Access control in which access is determined by the specific circumstances under which the data is being accessed.

contingency plan: A plan for emergency response, backup operations, and postdisaster recovery maintained by an activity as a part of its security program that will ensure the availability of critical resources and facilitate the continuity of operations in an emergency situation. Synonymous with disaster plan and emergency plan.

control objective: Required result of protecting information within an IT (information technology) product and its immediate environment.

control zone: The space, expressed in feet of radius, surrounding equipment processing sensitive information, that is under sufficient physical and technical control to preclude an unauthorized entry or compromise.

controlled access: See access control.

controlled sharing: The condition that exists when access control is applied to all users and components of a system.

corporate security policy: The set of laws, rules, and practices that regulate how assets including sensitive information are managed, protected, and distributed within a user organization.

correctness: (1) A property of a representation of a target of evaluation such that it accurately reflects the stated security target for that system or product. Correctness consists of determining if the description and implementation are consistent. There are levels of correctness that depend on the evidence requirements and the intensity of verification and analysis. (2) In security evaluation, the preservation of relevant properties between successive levels of representations. Examples of representations could be top-level functional specification, detailed design specification, and actual implementation. This is an aspect of assurance. (3) Correctness in the draft Federal Criteria equates to assurance in the Information Technology Security Evaluation Criteria. Development and evaluation assurance constitute correctness criteria. Effectiveness is addressed in vetting of protection profiles. (4) The extent to which a program satisfies its specifications.

cost-risk analysis: The assessment of the costs of providing data protection for a system versus the cost of losing or compromising the data.

countermeasure: Action, device, procedure, technique, or other measure that reduces the vulnerability of a system, such as an AIS (automated information system).

covert channel: (1) A communication channel that allows a process to transfer information in a manner that violates the system's security policy. A covert channel typically communicates by exploiting a mechanism not intended to be used for communication. (See covert storage channel and covert timing channel.) (2) The use of a mechanism not intended for communication to transfer information in a way that violates security. (3) Unintended and/or unauthorized communications path that can be used to transfer information in a manner that violates an AIS (automated information system) security policy. (See overt channel and exploitable channel.)

covert storage channel: A covert channel that involves the direct or indirect writing of a storage location by one process and the direct or indirect reading of the storage location by another process. Covert storage channels typically involve a finite resource (for example, sectors on a disk) that is shared by two subjects at different security levels.

covert timing channel: (1) A covert channel by which a process signals information to another process by modulating its own use of system resources (for example, CPU time) in such a way that this manipulation affects the real response time observed by the second process. (2) A communications channel that allows two cooperating processes to transfer information in a manner that violates the system's security policy. Synonymous with confinement channel.

criteria: See DoD Trusted Computer System Evaluation Criteria. Examples of other criteria are the Information Technology Security Evaluation Criteria (Europe), Canadian Trusted Computer Product Evaluation Criteria, Federal Criteria for Information Technology Security: Draft (US), and the forthcoming Common Criteria for Information Technology Security (international).

critical mechanism: A mechanism within a target of evaluation whose failure would create a security weakness.

cryptoalgorithm: A well-defined procedure or sequence of rules or steps used to produce a key stream or ciphertext from plaintext and vice versa.

cryptography: (1) The principles, means, and methods for rendering information unintelligible, and for restoring encrypted information to intelligible form. (2) The transformation of ordinary text, or "plaintext," into coded form by encryption and the transformation of coded text into plaintext by decryption. Cryptography can be used to support digital signature, key management or exchange, and communications privacy.

cryptosecurity: The security or protection resulting from the proper use of technically sound cryptosystems.

D

data: Information with a specific physical representation.

data confidentiality: The state that exists when data is held in confidence and is protected from unauthorized disclosure.

Data Encryption Standard (DES): (1) A cryptographic algorithm for the protection of unclassified data, published in US Federal Information Processing Standard (FIPS) 46. The DES, which was approved by the US National Institute of Standards and Technology (NIST), is intended for public and government use. (2) A NIST Federal Information Processing Standard and commonly used secret key cryptographic algorithm for encrypting and decrypting data and performing other functions. For example, DES can be used to check message integrity. DES specifies a key length of 56 bits.

data flow control: Synonymous with information flow control.

data integrity: (1) The property that data has not been altered or destroyed in an unauthorized manner. (2) The state that exists when computerized data is the same as that in the source documents and has not been exposed to accidental or malicious alteration or destruction.

data security: The protection of data from unauthorized (accidental or intentional) modification, destruction, or disclosure.

database management system: A computer system whose main function is to facilitate the sharing of a common set of data among many different users. It may or may not maintain semantic relationships among the data items.

DBMS: Abbreviation for database management system.

declassification of AIS storage media: An administrative decision or procedure to remove or reduce the security classification of the subject media.

decomposition: Requirement in a protection profile that spans several components. Note: The decomposition of a specific requirement becomes necessary when that requirement must be assigned to multiple components of the generic product requirements during the interpretation process.

dedicated security mode: See modes of operation.

default classification: A temporary classification reflecting the highest classification being processed in a system. The default classification is included in the caution statement affixed to the object.

degauss: To reduce magnetic flux density to zero by applying a reverse magnetizing field.

degausser: An electrical device that can generate a magnetic field for the purpose of degaussing magnetic storage media.

Degausser Products List (DPL): A list of commercially produced degaussers that meet US National Security Agency (NSA) specifications. This list is included in NSA's "Information Systems Security Products and Services Catalogue," available through the US Government Printing Office.

delivery: The process whereby a copy of the target of evaluation is transferred from the developer to a customer.

denial of service: (1) The prevention of authorized access to system assets or services or the delaying of time-critical operations. (2) Any action or series of actions that prevents any part of a system from functioning in accordance with its intended purpose. This includes any action that causes unauthorized destruction, modification, or delay of service. (Synonymous with interdiction.)

dependency: Condition in which the correctness of one TCB (trusted computing base) subset is contingent (depends for its correctness) on the correctness of another TCB subset. Note: A TCB subset A depends for its correctness on TCB subset B if and only if the (engineering) arguments of the correct implementation of A with respect to its specification assume, wholly or in part, that the specification of B has been implemented correctly.

descriptive top level specification (DTLS): A top-level specification that is written in a natural language (for example, English), an informal design notation, or a combination of the two.

designated approving authority (DAA): (1) Official with the authority to formally assume responsibility for operating an IT (information technology) product, an AIS (automated information system), or network at an acceptable level of risk. (2) The official who has the authority to decide on accepting the security safeguards prescribed for an AIS or that official who may be responsible for issuing an accreditation statement that records the decision to accept those safeguards.

detailed design: A phase of the development process wherein the top-level definition and design of a target of evaluation are refined and expanded to a level of detail that can be used as a basis for implementation.

developer: The person or organization that manufactures a target of evaluation.

developer security: The physical, procedural, and personnel security controls imposed by a developer on its development environment.

development assurance: (1) Establishes specific requirements to document appropriate aspects of the development process, the development environment, and operational support of the product. Development assurance specifies the manner in which products should be developed and/or details the amount and kind of evidence to be produced and retained during development. (2) Sources of IT (information technology) product assurance ranging from how a product was designed and implemented to how it is tested, operated, and maintained.

development assurance component: Fundamental building block, specifying how an IT (information technology) product is developed, from which development assurance requirements are assembled.

development assurance package: Grouping of development assurance components assembled to ease specification and common understanding of how an IT (information technology) product is developed.

development assurance requirements: Requirements in a protection profile that address how each conforming IT (information technology) product is developed, including the production of appropriate supporting developmental process evidence and how that product will be maintained.

development environment: The organizational measures, procedures, and standards used while constructing a target of evaluation.

development process: The set of phases and tasks whereby a target of evaluation is constructed, translating requirements into actual hardware and software.

dial back: Synonymous with call back.

dial-up: The service whereby a computer terminal can use the telephone to initiate and effect communication with a computer.

digital signature: A cryptographic method, provided by public key cryptography, used by a message's recipient and any third party to verify the identity of the message's sender. It can also be used to verify the authenticity of the message. A sender creates a digital signature or a message by transforming the message with his or her private key. A recipient, using the sender's public key, verifies the digital signature by applying a corresponding transformation to the message and the signature.

Digital Signature Standard (DSS): A US Federal Information Processing Standard proposed by NIST (National Institute of Standards and Technology) to support digital signature.

digital telephony: Telephone systems that use digital communications technology.

disaster plan: Synonymous with contingency plan.

discretionary access control (DAC): (1) A means of restricting access to objects based on the identity of subjects and/or groups to which they belong. The controls are discretionary in the sense that a subject with a certain access permission is capable of passing that permission (perhaps indirectly) on to any other subject (unless restrained by mandatory access control). (2) Methods of restricting access to objects or other resources based primarily on the instructions of arbitrary unprivileged users. Note: DAC is often used to enforce need-to-know.

documentation: The written (or otherwise recorded) information about a target of evaluation required for an evaluation. This information may, but need not, be contained within a single document produced for the specified purpose.

DoD Trusted Computer System Evaluation Criteria (TCSEC): A document published by the US National Computer Security Center containing a uniform set of basic requirements and evaluation classes for assessing degrees of assurance in the effectiveness of hardware and software security controls built into systems. These criteria are intended for use in the design and evaluation of systems that will process and/or store sensitive or classified data. This document is government standard DoD 5200.28-STD and is frequently referred to as "The Criteria" or "The Orange Book."

domain: The unique context (for example, access control parameters) in which a program is operating — in effect, the set of objects that a subject has the ability to access. Note: A subject's domain determines which access control attributes an object must have for a subject operating in that domain to have a designated form of access. (See process and subject.)

dominate: Security level S1 is said to dominate security level S2 if the hierarchical classification of S1 is greater than or equal to that of S2 and the nonhierarchical categories of S1 include all those of S2 as a subset.

dominated by (the relation): (1) A security level A is dominated by security level B if the clearance/classification in A is less than or equal to the clearance/classification in B and the set of access approvals (for example, compartment designators) in A is contained in (the set relation) the set of access approvals in B (that is, each access approval appearing in A also appears in B). Depending on the policy enforced (for example, nondisclosure or integrity), the definition of "less than or equal to" and "contained in" may vary. For example, the level of an object of high integrity (that is, an object which should be modifiable only by very trustworthy individuals) may be defined to be "less than" the level of an object of low integrity (that is, an object which is modifiable by everyone). (2) Security level A is dominated by security level B if (a) the clearance/classification in A is less than or equal to the clearance/classification in B, and (b) the set of access approvals (for example, compartment designators) in A is contained in the set of access approvals in B (that is, each access approval appearing in A also appears in B). This dominance relation is a special case of a partial order.

dominates (the relation): "Security level B dominates security level A" is synonymous with "security level A is dominated by security level B." (See dominated by.)

E

ease of use: An aspect of the assessment of the effectiveness of a target of evaluation, namely, that it cannot be configured or used in a manner which is insecure but which an administrator or end user would reasonably believe to be secure. Note: This term can be used as a reference for each type of item to be evaluated or under evaluation.

effectiveness: (1) A property of a target of evaluation representing how well it provides security in the context of its actual or proposed operational use. (2) In security evaluations, an aspect of assurance assessing how well the applied security functions and mechanisms working together will actually satisfy the security requirements. (3) Effectiveness is established by evaluation (vetting) of a protection profile (or security target, if there is no protection profile) description of anticipated threats, intended method of use, and residual risk. Effectiveness includes establishing suitability for use in the specified environment.

emanations: See compromising emanations.

embedded system: A system that performs or controls a function, either in whole or in part, as an integral element of a larger system or subsystem.

emergency plan: Synonymous with contingency plan.

emission security: The protection resulting from all measures taken to deny unauthorized persons information of value that might be derived from interception and from an analysis of compromising emanations from systems.

encryption: The process of making information indecipherable to protect it from unauthorized viewing or use, especially during transmission or storage. Encryption is based on an algorithm and at least one key. Even if the algorithm is known, the information cannot be decrypted without the key(s).

end-to-end encryption: The protection of information passed in a telecommunications system by cryptographic means, from point of origin to point of destination.

end user: A person in contact with a target of evaluation who makes use only of its operational capability.

Endorsed Tools List (ETL): The list of formal verification tools endorsed by the US NCSC (National Computer Security Center) for the development of systems with high levels of trust.

enhanced hierarchical development methodology: An integrated set of tools designed to aid in creating, analyzing, modifying, managing, and documenting program specifications and proofs. This methodology includes a specification parser and type checker, a theorem prover, and a multilevel security checker. Note: This methodology is not based on the hierarchical development methodology.

entrapment: The deliberate planting of apparent flaws in a system for the purpose of detecting attempted penetrations.

environment: (1) All entities — users, procedures, conditions, objects, AISs (automated information systems), and other IT (information technology) products — that interact with (affect the development, operation, and maintenance of) an IT product. (2) The aggregate of external procedures, conditions, and objects that affect the development, operation, and maintenance of a system.

erasure: A process by which a signal recorded on magnetic media is removed. Erasure is accomplished in two ways: (1) by alternating-current erasure, by which the information is destroyed by applying an alternating high and low magnetic field to the media; or (2) by direct-current erasure, by which the media are saturated by applying a unidirectional magnetic field.

Evaluated Products List (EPL): A list of equipment, hardware, software, and firmware that have been evaluated against, and found to be technically compliant, at a particular level of trust, with the DoD (US Department of Defense) TCSEC (Trusted Computer System Security Evaluation Criteria) by the NCSC (National Computer Security Center). The EPL is included in NSA's "Information Systems Security Products and Services Catalogue," which is available through the Government Printing Office.

evaluation: (1) Technical assessment of a component's, product's, subsystem's, or system's security properties that establishes whether the component, product, subsystem, or system meets a specific set of requirements, for example, defined evaluation criteria. Note: Evaluation is a term that causes much confusion in the security community, because it is used in many different ways. It is sometimes used in the general English sense (judgment or determination of worth or quality). Based on common usage of the term in the security community, one can distinguish between two types of evaluation: (a) evaluations that exclude the environment, and (b) evaluations that include the environment. This second type of evaluation, an assessment of a system's security properties with respect to a specific operational mission, is termed certification. Evaluations that exclude the environment are assessments of the security properties against a defined criterion. (2) The process — given a security policy, a consistent description of required security functions, and a targeted assurance level — of achieving assurance. Evaluation also includes the checking for security vulnerabilities (in relation to the security policy). (3) The assessment of an IT (information technology) system or product against defined evaluation criteria.

evaluation assurance: (1) Source of IT (information technology) product assurance based on the kind and intensity of the evaluation analysis performed on the product. (2) Specifies the nature and intensity of evaluation activities to be performed on a TOE (target of evaluation), based on the expected threat and the intended environments.

evaluation assurance component: Fundamental building block, specifying the type and the rigor of required evaluation activities, from which evaluation assurance requirements are assembled.

evaluation assurance package: Grouping of evaluation assurance components assembled to ease specification and common understanding of the type and the rigor of required evaluation activities.

evaluation assurance requirements: Requirements in a protection profile which address both the type and the rigor of activities that must occur during product evaluation.

evaluation body or **entity:** See certification body.

evaluation criteria: A set of requirements defining the conditions under which an evaluation is performed. These requirements can also be used in specification and development of systems and products.

evaluator: (1) The independent person or organization that performs an evaluation. (2) Individual or group responsible for the independent assessment of IT (information technology) product security (for example, product evaluators, system security officers, system certifiers, and system accreditors).

evaluator actions: A component of the evaluation criteria for a particular phase or aspect of evaluation, identifying what the evaluator must do to check the information supplied by the sponsor of the evaluator, and the additional activities he must perform.

executive state: (1) One of several states in which a system may operate and the only one in which certain privileged instructions may be executed. Such instructions cannot be executed when the system is operating in other (for example, user) states. Synonymous with supervisor state. (2) A privileged state that can be used by supervisory software for multitasking operations. Reliable multitasking requires protection, such as segment-level protection. For example, segment-level protection can have the following protection checks: (a) type check, (b) limit check, (c) restriction of addressable domain, (d) restriction of procedure entry points, and (e) restriction of instruction set.

explain: Give required information and show that it satisfies all relevant requirements.

exploitable channel: (1) Any channel that is usable or detectable by subjects external to the trusted computing base. (2) A covert channel that is usable or detectable by subjects external to the AIS's (automated information system's) trusted computing base and can be used to violate the AIS's technical security policy. (See covert channel.) (3) Any information channel that is usable or detectable by subjects external to the trusted computing base whose purpose is to violate the security policy of the system. (See covert channel.)

external security controls: Measures that include physical, personnel, procedural, and administrative security requirements and a separate certification and accreditation process which govern physical access to an IT (information technology) product. Note: These measures constitute assumptions and boundary conditions that are part of the environment described in a protection profile.

F

fail safe: Pertaining to the automatic protection of programs and/or processing systems to maintain safety when a hardware or software failure is detected in a system.

fail soft: Pertaining to the selective termination of affected nonessential processing when a hardware or software failure is detected in a system.

failure access: An unauthorized and usually inadvertent access to data resulting from a hardware or software failure in the system.

failure control: The methodology used to detect failures and provide fail-safe or fail-soft recovery from hardware and software failures in a system.

fault: A condition that causes a device or system component to fail to perform in a required manner.

Federal Criteria for Information Technology Security (FC) (draft): US draft security criteria for trusted systems.

fetch protection: (1) A system-provided restriction to prevent a program from accessing data in another user's segment of storage. (2) The aggregate of all processes and procedures in a system designed to inhibit unauthorized access, contamination, or elimination of a file.

file security: The means by which access to computer files is limited to authorized users only.

flaw: An error of commission, omission, or oversight in a system that allows protection mechanisms to be bypassed.

flaw hypothesis methodology: A system analysis and penetration technique where specifications and documentation for the system are analyzed and then flaws in the system are hypothesized. The list of hypothesized flaws is then prioritized on the basis of the estimated probability that a flaw actually exists and, assuming a flaw does exist, on the ease of exploiting it and on the extent of control or compromise it would provide. The prioritized list is used to direct the actual testing of and/or penetration attack against the system.

flow control: See information flow control.

formal access approval: Documented approval by a data owner to allow access to a particular category of information.

formal development methodology: A collection of languages and tools that enforces a rigorous method of verification. This methodology uses the Ina Jo specification language for successive stages of system development, including identification and modeling of requirements, high-level design, and program design.

formal model of security policy: An underlying model of security policy expressed in a formal style, that is, an abstract statement of the important principles of security that a TOE (target of evaluation) will enforce.

formal proof: A complete and convincing mathematical argument, presenting the full logical justification for each proof step, for the truth of a theorem or set of theorems. The formal verification process uses formal proofs to show the truth of certain properties of formal specification and to show that computer programs satisfy their specifications. Automated tools may (but need not) be used to formulate and/or check the proof.

formal security policy model: (1) A mathematically precise statement of a security policy. To be adequately precise, such a model must represent the initial state of a system, the way in which the system progresses from one state to another, and a definition of a "secure" state of the system. To be acceptable as a basis for a TCB (trusted computing base), the model must be supported by a formal proof that if the initial state of the system satisfies the definition of a "secure" state and if all assumptions required by the model hold, then all future states of the system will be secure. Some formal modeling techniques include state-transition models, denotational semantics models, and algebraic specification models. (See Bell-LaPadula model and security policy model.) (2) Mathematically precise statement consisting of (a) a formal technical security policy (given by constraints on a product's external interface and/or constraints on the handling of controlled entities internal to the product), (b) rules of operation that show how the definition of security is to be enforced, and (c) a formal proof showing that the rules of operation guarantee satisfaction of the definition of security.

formal specification: Statement about a product made using the restricted syntax and grammar of a formal reasoning system and a set of terms that have been precisely and uniquely defined or specified. Note: The formal statement should be augmented by an informal explanation of the conventions used and the ideas being expressed. A well-formed syntax and semantics with complete specification of all constructs used must be referenced.

formal top level specification (FTLS): A top-level specification that is written in a formal mathematical language to allow theorems showing the correspondence of the system specification to its formal requirements to be hypothesized and formally proven.

formal verification: The process of using formal proofs to demonstrate the consistency (design verification) between a formal specification of a system and a formal security policy model or (implementation verification) between the formal specification and its program implementation.

front-end security filter: (1) A process that is invoked to process data according to a specified security policy prior to releasing the data outside the processing environment or upon receiving data from an external source. (2) A process implemented in hardware or software that is logically separated from the remainder of the system to protect the system's integrity.

functional component: Fundamental building block, specifying what an IT (information technology) product must be capable of doing, from which functional protection requirements are assembled.

functional package: Grouping of functional components assembled to ease specification and common understanding of what an IT (information technology) product is capable of doing.

functional protection requirements: Requirements in a protection profile that address what conforming IT (information technology) products must be capable of doing.

functional testing: The portion of security testing in which the advertised features of a system are tested, under operational conditions, for correct operation.

functional unit: A functionally distinct part of a basic component.

functionality: (1) Set of functional protection requirements to be implemented in IT (information technology) products. (2) The totality of functional properties of a TOE (target of evaluation) that contributes to security.

functionality class: A defined set of security functions in a system or product, designed to meet a security policy.

G

general-purpose system: A computer system that is designed to aid in solving a wide variety of problems.

generic threat: Class of threats with common characteristics pertaining to vulnerabilities, agents, event sequences, and resulting misfortunes.

global requirements: Those which require analysis of the entire system and for which separate analysis of the individual TCB (trusted computing base) subsets does not suffice.

granularity: (1) Relative fineness or coarseness to which an access control mechanism or other IT (information technology) product aspect can be adjusted. (2) An expression of the relative size of a data object. Note: Protection at the file level is considered course granularity, whereas protection at the field level is considered to be finer granularity. The phrase "the granularity of a single user" means the access control mechanism can be adjusted to include or exclude any single user.

granularity of a requirement: Determination of whether a requirement applies to all the attributes of users, subjects, or objects, and all TCB (trusted computing base) functional components.

group: Named collection of user identifiers.

guard: A processor that provides a filter between two disparate systems operating at different security levels or between a user terminal and a database to filter out data that the user is not authorized to access.

Gypsy verification environment: An integrated set of tools for specifying, coding, and verifying programs written in the Gypsy language, a language similar to Pascal which has both specification and programming features. This methodology includes an editor, a specification processor, a verification condition generator, a user-directed theorem prover, and an information flow tool.

H

handshaking procedure: A dialogue between two entities (for example, a user and a computer, a computer and another computer, or a program and another program) for the purpose of identifying and authenticating the entities to one another.

hierarchical decomposition: The ordered, structured reduction of a system or a component to primitives.

hierarchical development methodology: A methodology for specifying and verifying the design programs written in the Special specification language. The tools for this methodology include the Special specification processor, the Boyer-Moore theorem prover, and the Feiertag information flow tool.

host: Any computer-based system connected to the network and containing the necessary protocol interpreter software to initiate network access and carry out information exchange across the communications network. This definition encompasses typical "mainframe" hosts, generic terminal support machines (for example, ARPAnet TAC, DoDIIS NTC), and workstations connected directly to the communications subnetwork and executing the intercomputer networking protocols. A terminal is not a host because it does not contain the protocol software needed to perform information exchange; a workstation (by definition) is a host because it does have such capability.

host to front-end protocol: A set of conventions governing the format and control of data that are passed from a host to a front-end machine.

I

identification: Process that enables recognition of an entity by an IT (information technology) product/system that may be by the use of unique machine-readable user names.

impersonating: Synonymous with spoofing.

implementation: A phase of the development process wherein the detailed specification of a target of evaluation is translated into actual hardware and software.

incomplete parameter checking: A system design flaw that results when all parameters have not been fully anticipated for accuracy and consistency, thus making the system vulnerable to penetration.

individual accountability: The ability to associate positively the identity of a user with the time, method, and degree of access to a system.

informal specification: Statement about (the properties of) a product made using the grammar, syntax, and common definitions of a natural language (for example, English). Note: While no notational restrictions apply, the informal specification is also required to provide defined meanings for terms which are used in a context other than that accepted by normal usage.

information flow control: A procedure to ensure that information transfers within a system are not made from a higher security level object to an object of a lower security level. (See covert channel, simple security property, and *-property (star property). Synonymous with data flow control and flow control.)

information processing standard: A set of detailed technical guidelines used to establish uniformity to support specific functions and/or interoperability in hardware, software, or telecommunications development, testing, and/or operation.

information protection policy: Set of laws, rules, and practices that regulate how an IT (information technology) product will, within specified limits, counter threats expected in the product's assumed operational environment.

information system security officer (ISSO): The person responsible to the DAA (designated approving authority) for ensuring that security is provided for and implemented throughout the life cycle of an AIS (automated information system) from the beginning of the concept development plan through its design, development, operation, maintenance, and secure disposal.

Information Systems Security Products and Services Catalogue: A catalogue issued quarterly by the National Security Agency that incorporates the DPL (Degausser Products List), EPL (Evaluated Products List), ETL (Endorsed Tools List), PPL (Preferred Products List), and other security product and service lists. This catalogue is available through the US Government Printing Office, Washington, DC 20402, (202) 783-3238.

Information Technology Security Evaluation Criteria (ITSEC): European security evaluation criteria for targets of evaluation (TOE).

information technology (IT) system: An international term for an information system, which consists of one or more automated information systems (AISs) or computer systems and communications systems.

Integrated Services Digital Network: An emerging communications system enabling the simultaneous transmission of data, facsimile, video, and voice over a single communications link.

integrity: (1) Correctness and appropriateness of the content and/or source of a piece of information. (See data integrity and system integrity.) (2) The prevention of the unauthorized modification of information. (3) Sound, unimpaired, or perfect condition.

integrity policy: A security policy to prevent unauthorized users from modifying — that is, writing — sensitive information. (See security policy.)

interdiction: See denial of service.

internal security controls: (1) Hardware, firmware, and software features within a system that restrict access to resources (hardware, software, and data) to authorized subjects only (persons, programs, or devices). (2) Mechanisms implemented in the hardware, firmware, and software of an IT (information technology) product which provide protection for the IT product.

internal subject: A subject that is not acting as a direct surrogate for a user. A process that is not associated with any user but performs system-wide functions such as packet switching, line printer spooling, and so on. (Also known as a daemon or a service machine.)

interoperability: The ability of computers to act upon information received from one another.

isolation: The containment of subjects and objects in a system in such a way that they are separated from one another, as well as from the protection controls of the operating system.

IT (information technology) security: The state of security in an IT system.

IT (information technology) security certification: The issue, by an independent body, of a formal statement or certificate confirming the results of an evaluation of a TOE (target of evaluation) and the fact that the evaluation criteria used were correctly applied. Note: This term could also be called "TOE certification" to make its application clearer.

IT (information technology) system: A specific IT installation, with a particular purpose and operational environment.

K

key: A long string of seemingly random bits used with cryptographic algorithms to create or verify digital signatures and encrypt or decrypt messages and conversations. The keys must be known or guessed to forge a digital signature or decrypt an encrypted message.

key-escrow system: An electronic means of reconstructing a secret key (for secret key encryption) or a private key (for public key encryption). The reconstructed key can then be used in a process to decrypt a communication.

key management/exchange: A method of electronically transmitting, in a secure fashion, a secret key for use with a secret key cryptographic system. Key management can be used to support communications privacy. This method can be accomplished most securely with public key cryptographic systems, which do not require the sharing of secret keys with third parties. Instead, a secret key is encrypted with a recipient's public key, and the recipient decrypts the result with his or her private key to receive the secret key. A variation of key management that is based on key exchange does not require encrypting the secret key.

L

label: See sensitivity label.

lattice: A partially ordered set for which every pair of elements has a greatest lower bound and a least upper bound.

least privilege: A principle that requires that each subject be granted the most restrictive set of privileges needed for the performance of authorized tasks. For certain applications, the most restrictive set of privileges could pertain to the lowest clearance. The application of this principle limits the damage that can result from accident, error, or unauthorized use of an AIS (automated information system).

limited access: Synonymous with access control.

list-oriented: A computer protection system in which each protected object has a list of all subjects authorized to access it. (Compare ticket-oriented.)

local requirements: Those for which separate analysis of the individual TCB (trusted computing base) subsets suffices to determine compliance for the composite TCB. (See the trusted database interpretation of the Trusted Computer System Evaluation Criteria for further information.)

lock-and-key protection system: A protection system that involves matching a key or password with a specific access requirement.

logic bomb: A resident computer program that triggers the perpetration of an unauthorized act when particular states of the system are realized.

loophole: An error of omission or oversight in software or hardware that permits circumvention of the system security policy.

M

magnetic remanence: A measure of the magnetic flux density remaining after removal of the applied magnetic force. Refers to any data remaining on magnetic storage media after removal of the power.

maintenance hook: Special instructions in software to allow easy maintenance and additional feature development. These are not clearly defined during access for design specification. Hooks frequently allow entry into the code at unusual points or without the usual checks, so they are a serious security risk if they are not removed prior to live implementation. Maintenance hooks are special types of trap doors.

malicious logic: Hardware, software, or firmware that is intentionally included in a system for an unauthorized purpose — for example, a Trojan horse.

mandatory access control: A means of restricting access to objects based on the sensitivity (as represented by a label) of the information contained in the objects and the formal authorization (that is, clearance) of subjects to access information of such sensitivity. (See nondiscretionary access control. Compare discretionary access control.)

masquerading: Synonymous with spoofing.

mass-market software: Software that is (1) generally available to the public by sale, without restriction, from stock at retail selling points through over-the-counter, telephone, and mail transactions and (2) designed for user installation without substantial supplier support.

mechanism: Operating system entry point or separate operating system support program that performs a specific action or related group of actions.

metadata: (1) Data referring to other data; data (such as data structures, indices, and pointers) that are used to instantiate an abstraction (such as "process," "task," "segment," "file," or "pipe"). (2) A special database, also referred to as a data dictionary, containing descriptions of the elements (for example, relations, domains, entities, or relationships) of a database.

mimicking: Synonymous with spoofing.

modes of operation: A description of the conditions under which an AIS (automated information system) functions, based on the sensitivity of data processed and the clearance levels and authorizations of the users. Four modes of operation are authorized:

(1a) An AIS is operating in the *dedicated mode* when the system is specifically and exclusively dedicated to and controlled for the processing of one particular type or classification of information, either for full-time operation or for a specific period of time. (1b) An AIS is operating in the *dedicated mode* when each user with direct or indirect individual access to the AIS, its peripherals, its remote terminals, or its remote hosts has all of the following: (a) a valid personnel clearance for all information on the system, (b) formal access approval for, and signed nondisclosure agreements for, all the information stored and/or processed (including all compartments, subcompartments, and/or special access programs), and (c) a valid need-to-know for all information contained within the system.

(2a) An AIS is operating in the *system-high mode* when each user with direct or indirect access to the AIS, its peripherals, remote terminals, or remote hosts has all of the following: (a) a valid personnel clearance for all information on the AIS, (b) formal access approval for, and signed nondisclosure agreements for, all the information stored and/or processed (including all compartments, subcompartments, and/or special access programs), and (c) a valid need-to-know for some of the information contained within the AIS. (2b) An AIS is operating in the *system-high mode* when the system hardware and software are trusted only to provide discretionary protection between users. In this mode, the entire system, to include all components electrically and/or physically connected, must operate with security measures commensurate with the highest classification and sensitivity of the information being processed and/or stored.

All system users in this environment must possess clearances and authorization for all information contained in the system. All system output must be clearly marked with the highest classification and all system caveats until the information has been reviewed manually by an authorized individual to ensure appropriate classifications and that caveats have been affixed.

(3) An AIS is operating in the *compartmented mode* when each user with direct or indirect access to the AIS, its peripherals, remote terminals, or remote hosts has all of the following: (a) a valid personnel clearance for the most restricted information processed in the AIS, (b) formal access approval for, and signed nondisclosure agreements for, that information to which he or she is to have access, and (c) a valid need-to-know for that information to which he or she is to have access.

(4) An AIS is operating in the *multilevel mode* when all the following statements are satisfied concerning users with direct or indirect access to the AIS, its peripherals, remote terminals, or remote hosts: (a) some do not have a valid personnel clearance for all the information processed in the AIS, (b) all have the proper clearance and have the appropriate formal access approval for that information to which they are to have access, and (c) all have a valid need-to-know for that information to which they are to have access.

monolithic TCB (trusted computing base): A TCB that consists of a single TCB subset.

multilevel device: A device that is used in a manner that permits it to simultaneously process data of two or more security levels without risk of compromise. To accomplish this, sensitivity labels are normally stored on the same physical medium and in the same form (that is, machine-readable or human-readable) as the data being processed.

multilevel mode: See modes of operation.

multilevel secure: A class of system containing information with different sensitivities that simultaneously permits access by users with different security clearances and needs-to-know, but prevents users from obtaining access to information for which they lack authorization.

multilevel security mode: See modes of operation.

multiple access rights terminal: A terminal that may be used by more than one class of users — for example, users with different access rights to data.

multiuser mode of operation: A mode of operation designed for systems that process sensitive unclassified information in which users may not have a need-to-know for all information processed in the system. This mode is also for microcomputers processing sensitive unclassified information that cannot meet the requirements of the stand-alone mode of operation.

mutually suspicious: The state that exists between interacting processes (subsystems or programs) in which neither process can expect the other process to function securely with respect to some property.

N

National Computer Security Assessment Program: A program designed to evaluate the interrelationship of empirical data of computer security infractions and critical systems profiles, while comprehensively incorporating information from the CSTVRP (Computer Security Technical Vulnerability Reporting Program). The assessment will build threat and vulnerability scenarios that are based on a collection of facts from relevant reported cases. Such scenarios are a powerful, dramatic, and concise form of representing the value of loss experience analysis.

National Computer Security Center (NCSC): Originally named the DoD Computer Security Center, the NCSC is responsible for encouraging the widespread availability of trusted computer systems throughout the US Department of Defense.

National Security Decision Directive 145 (NSDD 145): Signed by US President Reagan on September 17, 1984, this directive is entitled "National Policy on Telecommunications and Automated Information Systems Security." It provides initial objectives, policies, and an organizational structure to guide the conduct of national activities toward safeguarding systems that process, store, or communicate sensitive information; establishes a mechanism for policy development; and assigns implementation responsibilities. In 1990, National Security Directive 42 replaced NSDD 145, except for ongoing telecommunications protection activities mandated by NSDD 145 and Presidential Directive 24.

National Telecommunications and Information Systems Security Advisory Memoranda/Instructions (NTISSAM, NTISSI): Under NSDD (National Security Decision Directive) 145, NTISS Advisory Memoranda and Instructions provided advice, assistance, or information of general interest on telecommunications and systems security to all applicable US federal departments and agencies. NTISSAMs/NTISSIs were promulgated by the

National Manager for Telecommunications and Automated Information Systems Security. (See National Security Decision Directive 145.)

National Telecommunications and Information System Security Directives (NTISSD): Under NSDD 145, NTISS Directives established national-level decisions relating to NTISS policies, plans, programs, systems, or organizational delegations of authority. NTISSDs were promulgated by the Executive Agent of the US Government for Telecommunications and Information Systems Security, or by the chairman of the NTISSC when so delegated by the executive agent. NTISSDs were binding upon all federal departments and agencies. (See National Security Decision Directive 145.)

need-to-know: (1) Access to, or knowledge or possession of, specific information required to carry out official duties. (2) The necessity for access to, knowledge of, or possession of specific information required to carry out official duties.

network architecture: The set of layers and protocols (including formats and standards that different hardware and software must comply with to achieve stated objectives) which define a network.

network component: (1) A physical unit that does *not* provide a complete set of end-user services. A network component may support all or part of MDIA (mandatory access control, identification and authentication, and audit). This definition is used with the Trusted Network Interpretation of the Trusted Computer System Evaluation Criteria Environments Guideline (TNIEG). (2) A network subsystem which is evaluatable for compliance with the trusted network interpretations, relative to that policy induced on the component by the overall network policy. Note: This definition is used with the Trusted Network Interpretation of the Trusted Computer System Evaluation Criteria (TNI).

network connection: A network connection is any logical or physical path from one host to another that makes possible the transmission of information from one host to the other. An example is a TCP (Transmission Control Protocol) connection. But also, when a host transmits an IP (Internet Protocol) datagram using only the services of its "connectionless" Internet Protocol interpreter, there is considered to be a connection between the source and the destination hosts for this transaction.

network front end: A device that implements the necessary network protocols, including security-related protocols, to allow a computer system to be attached to a network.

network reference monitor: An access control concept that refers to an abstract machine that mediates all access to objects within the network by subjects within the network.

network security: The protection of networks and their services from unauthorized modification, destruction, or disclosure — providing an assurance that the network performs its critical functions correctly and there are no harmful side effects. Includes providing for information accuracy.

network security architecture: A subset of network architecture specifically addressing security-relevant issues.

network sponsor: The individual or organization that is responsible for stating the security policy enforced by the network, for designing the network security architecture to properly enforce that policy, and for ensuring that the network is implemented in such a way that the policy is enforced. For commercial off-the-shelf systems, the network sponsor will normally be the vendor. For a fielded network system, the sponsor will normally be the project manager or system administrator.

network system: A system that is implemented with a collection of interconnected network components. A network system is based on a coherent security architecture and design.

network trusted computing base (NTCB): The totality of protection mechanisms within a network system — including hardware, firmware, and software — the combination of which is responsible for enforcing a security policy. (See trusted computing base.)

nondiscretionary access control: Means of restricting access to objects based largely on administrative actions. (See mandatory access control.)

normal operation: Process of using a system.

NSDD 145: See National Security Decision Directive 145.

NTCB (network trusted computing base) partition: The totality of mechanisms within a single network component for enforcing the network policy, as allocated to that component; the part of the NTCB within a single network component.

O

object: (1) A passive entity that contains or receives information. Access to an object potentially implies access to the information it contains. Examples of objects are records, blocks, pages, segments, files, directories, directory trees, and programs, as well as bits, bytes, words, fields, processors, video displays, keyboards, clocks, printers, and network nodes. (See passive.) (2) A controlled entity that precisely gives or receives information in response to access attempts by another (active) entity.

object reuse: The reassignment and reuse of a storage medium (for example, page frame, disk sector, or magnetic tape) that once contained one or more objects. To be securely reused and assigned to a new subject, storage media must contain no residual data (magnetic remanence) from the object(s) previously contained in the media.

open security environment: An environment that includes those systems in which at least one of the following conditions holds true: (1) Application developers (including maintainers) do not have sufficient clearance or authorization to provide an acceptable presumption that they have not introduced malicious logic. (2) Configuration control does not provide sufficient assurance that applications are protected against the introduction of malicious logic prior to and during the operation of system applications.

operating procedure: A set of rules defining correct use of a target of evaluation.

operation: The process of using a target of evaluation.

operational documentation: The information produced by the developer of a target of evaluation to specify and explain how customers should use it.

operational environment: The organizational measures, procedures, and standards to be used while operating a target of evaluation.

operations security (OPSEC): An analytical process by which the US government and its supporting contractors can deny to potential adversaries information about capabilities and intentions by identifying, controlling, and protecting evidence of the planning and execution of sensitive activities and operations.

Orange Book: Alternate name for DoD (US Department of Defense) Trusted Computer Security Evaluation Criteria.

organizational security policy: Set of laws, rules, and practices that regulate how an organization manages, protects, and distributes sensitive information.

OSI architecture: The International Organization for Standardization (ISO) provides a framework for defining the communications process between systems. This framework includes a network architecture, consisting of seven layers. The architecture is referred to as the Open Systems Interconnection (OSI) Model or Reference Model. Services and the protocols to implement it for the different layers of the model are defined by international standards. From a systems viewpoint, the bottom three layers support the components of the network necessary to transmit a message, the next three layers generally pertain to the characteristics of the communicating end systems, and the top layer supports the end users. The seven layers are: (1) Physical Layer, (2) Link Layer, (3) Network Layer, (4) Transport Layer, (5) Session Layer, (6) Presentation Layer, and (7) Application Layer.

output: Information that has been exported by a TCB (trusted computing base).

overt channel: Communications path within a computer system or network that is designed for the authorized transfer of data. (See covert channel.)

overwrite procedure: A stimulation to change the state of a bit followed by a known pattern. (See magnetic remanence.)

owner: User-granted privileges with respect to security attributes and privileges affecting specific subjects and objects.

P

partial order: A relation that is symmetric (a is related to a), transitive (if a is related to b and b is related to c, then a is related to c), and antisymmetric (if a is related to b and b is related to a, then a and b are identical).

partitioned security mode: A mode of operation wherein all personnel have the clearance but not necessarily formal access approval and need-to-know for all information contained in the system. Not to be confused with compartmented security mode.

passive: (1) A property of an object or network object that it lacks logical or computational capability and is unable to change the information it contains. (2) Those threats to the confidentiality of data which, if realized, would not result in any unauthorized change in the state of the intercommunicating systems (for example, monitoring and/or recording of data).

password: Protected/private character string used to authenticate an identity or to authorize access to data.

penetration: The successful act of bypassing the security mechanisms of a system.

penetration study: A study to determine the feasibility and methods for defeating controls of a system.

penetration testing: (1) Security testing in which evaluators attempt to circumvent the security features of an AIS (automated information system) based on their understanding of the system design and implementation. (2) Tests performed by an evaluator on the target of evaluation to confirm whether known vulnerabilities are actually exploitable in practice. (3) The portion of security testing in which the evaluators or penetrators attempt to circumvent the security features of a system. The evaluators or penetrators may be assumed to use all system design and implementation documentation, which may include listings of system source code, manuals, and circuit diagrams. The evaluators or penetrators work under no constraints other than those that would be applied to ordinary users or implementers of untrusted portions of the component.

periods processing: The processing of various levels of sensitive information at distinctly different times. Under periods processing, the system must be purged of all information from one processing period before transitioning to the next, when there are different users with differing authorizations.

permissions: A description of the type of authorized interactions a subject can have with an object. Examples include read, write, execute, add, modify, and delete.

personal communications network: Advanced cellular telephone communications and the interworking of both wired and wireless networks that will offer new communications services via very small, portable handsets. The network will rely on microcellular technology — many low-power, small-coverage cells — and a common channel-signaling technology, such as that used in the telephone system, to provide a wide variety of features in addition to the basic two-way calling service.

personnel security: The procedures established to ensure that all personnel who have access to sensitive information have the required authority as well as appropriate clearances.

physical security: The application of physical barriers and control procedures as preventive measures or countermeasures against threats to resources and sensitive information.

piggyback: Gaining unauthorized access to a system via another user's legitimate connection. (See between-the-lines entry.)

plaintext: See cleartext.

Preferred Products List (PPL): A list of commercially produced equipment that meets TEMPEST and other requirements prescribed by the US National Security Agency (NSA). This list is included in NSA's "Information Systems Security Products and Services Catalogue," issued quarterly and available through the Government Printing Office.

primitive: Orderly relation between TCB (trusted computing base) subsets based on dependency. Note: A TCB subset B is more primitive than a second TCB subset A (and A is less primitive than B) if A directly depends on B or a chain of TCB subsets from A to B exists such that each element of the chain directly depends on its successor in the chain.

print suppression: Eliminating the display of characters to preserve their secrecy — for example, not displaying the characters of a password as it is keyed at the input terminal.

privacy: (1) The ability of an individual or organization to control the collection, storage, sharing, and dissemination of personal and organizational information. (2) The right to insist on adequate security of, and to define authorized users of, information or systems. Note: The concept of privacy cannot be very precise, and its use should be avoided in specifications except as a means to require security, because privacy relates to "rights" that depend on legislation.

private key: The undisclosed key in a matched key pair — private key and public key — that each party safeguards for public key cryptography.

privilege: Special authorization that is granted to particular users to perform security-relevant operations.

privileged instructions: A set of instructions (for example, interrupt handling or special computer instructions) to control features (such as storage protection features) that are generally executable only when the automated system is operating in the executive state.

procedural security: Synonymous with administrative security.

process: A program in execution. It is completely characterized by a single current execution point (represented by the machine state) and address space. (See domain and subject.)

producers: Providers of IT (information technology) product security (for example, product vendors, product developers, security analysts, and value-added resellers).

product: (1) A package of IT (information technology) software and/or hardware, providing functionality designed for use or incorporation within a multiplicity of systems. (2) A package of IT software and/or hardware designed to perform a specific function either stand alone or once incorporated into an IT system.

product rationale: (1) A description of the security capabilities of a product, giving the necessary information for a prospective purchaser to decide whether it will help to satisfy his system security objectives. (2) Overall justification — including anticipated threats, objectives for product functionality and assurance, technical security policy, and assumptions about the environments and uses of conforming products — for the protection profile and its resulting IT (information technology) product.

production: The process whereby copies of the target of evaluation are generated for distribution to customers.

profile: Detailed security description of the physical structure, equipment component, location, relationships, and general operating environment of an IT (information technology) product or AIS (automated information system). (See protection profile.)

profile assurance: Measure of confidence in the technical soundness of a protection profile.

programming languages and compilers: The tools used within the development environment in the construction of the software and/or firmware of a target of evaluation.

proprietary information: Information that is owned by a private enterprise and whose use and/or distribution is restricted by that enterprise. Note: Proprietary information may be related to the company's products, business, or activities, including but not limited to financial information, data, or statements; trade secrets; product research and development information; existing and future product designs and performance specifications; marketing plans or techniques; schematics; client lists; computer programs; processes; and trade secrets or other company confidential information.

protection-critical portions of the TCB (trusted computing base): Those portions of the TCB whose normal function is to deal with the control of access between subjects and objects. Their correct operation is essential to the protection of the data on the system. (See subject, object, and trusted computing base.)

protection philosophy: (1) An informal description of the overall design of a system that delineates each of the protection mechanisms used. A combination (appropriate to the evaluation class) of formal and informal techniques is used to show that the mechanisms are adequate to enforce the security policy. (2) Informal description of the overall design of an IT (information technology) product that shows how each of the supported control objectives is dealt with.

protection profile: (1) An implementation-independent specification of the security requirements to be met by any of a set of possible products or systems. It is a high-level abstraction of the security target, and principally includes rationale, functional requirements, and assurance requirements. (2) Statement of security criteria shared by IT (information technology) product producers, consumers, and evaluators — built from functional, development assurance, and evaluation assurance requirements to meet identified security needs through the development of conforming IT products.

protection profile family: Two or more protection profiles with similar functional requirements and rationale sections but with different assurance requirements.

protection ring: One of a hierarchy of privileged modes of a system that gives certain access rights to user programs and processes authorized to operate in a given mode.

protocols: A set of rules and formats, semantic and syntactic, that permits entities to exchange information.

prove a correspondence: Provide a formal correspondence, using a formal reasoning system (for example, typed lambda calculus), between the levels of abstraction. Note: This involves proving that required properties continue to hold under the interpretation given in the formal correspondence.

pseudoflaw: An apparent loophole deliberately implanted in an operating system program as a trap for intruders.

public key: The key in a matched key pair — private key and public key — that may be published, for example, posted in a directory, for public key cryptography.

public key cryptography: Cryptography using two matched keys (or asymmetric cryptography) in which a single private key is not shared by a pair of users. Instead, users have their own key pairs. Each key pair consists of a matched private and public key. Public key cryptography can perform (1) digital signature, (2) secure transmission or exchange of secret keys, and/or (3) encryption and decryption. Examples of public key cryptography are DSS (Digital Signature Standard) and RSA (Rivest, Shamir, and Adleman).

Public Law 100-235 (P.L. 100-235): Also known as the Computer Security Act of 1987. This US law creates a means for establishing minimum acceptable security practices for improving the security and privacy of sensitive information in federal computer systems. The law assigns to the National Institute of Standards and Technology responsibility for developing standards and guidelines for federal computer systems processing unclassified data. The law also requires establishment of security plans by all operators of federal computer systems that contain sensitive information.

purge: The removal of sensitive data from an AIS (automated information system), AIS storage device, or peripheral device with storage capacity, at the end of a processing period. This action is performed in such a way that there is assurance proportional to the sensitivity of the data that the data may not be reconstructed. An AIS must be disconnected from any external network before a purge. After a purge, the medium can be declassified by observing the review procedures of the respective agency.

R

rating: A measure for the assurance that may be held in a target of evaluation, consisting of a reference to its security target, an evaluation level established by assessment of the correctness of its implementation and consideration of its effectiveness in the context of actual or proposed operational use, and a confirmed rating of the minimum strength of its security mechanisms.

RC2, RC4 (Rivest Cipher 2 and Rivest Cipher 4): Two secret key encryption systems that are implemented in mass-market software. These systems are proprietary and are marketed by RSA Data Security, Inc. RC2 and RC4 can be used with various key lengths, such as 40 bits or 56 bits.

read: A fundamental operation that results only in the flow of information from an object to a subject.

read access: (1) Permission to read information. (2) A fundamental operation that results only in the flow of information from an object to a subject.

read-only memory (ROM): A storage area in which the contents can be read but not altered during normal computer processing.

real time: The actual time in which something, such as the communication of information, takes place.

recovery procedures: The actions necessary to restore a system's computational capability and data files after a system failure.

reference monitor: An access control/mediation concept that refers to an abstract machine that mediates all accesses to objects by subjects.

reference monitor concept: See reference monitor and security kernel.

reference validation mechanism: (1) Portion of a trusted computing base, the normal function of which is to mediate access between subjects and objects, and the correct operation of which is essential to the protection of data in the system. Note: This is the implementation of the reference monitor. (2) An implementation of the reference monitor concept. A security kernel is a type of reference validation mechanism. (3) An implementation of the reference monitor concept that validates each reference to data or programs by any user (program) against a list of authorized types of reference for that user. It must be tamperproof, must always be invoked, and must be small enough to be subject to analysis and tests, the completeness of which can be assured.

refinements: Requirement in a protection profile taken to a lower level of abstraction than the component on which it is based. Note: The refinement of a component requirement is necessary when multiple environment-specific requirements must be assigned to a single component requirement.

reliability: (1) The extent to which a system can be expected to perform its intended function with required precision. (2) The probability of a given system performing its mission adequately for a specified period of time under the expected operating conditions.

requirements: (1) A phase of the development process wherein the security target of a target of evaluation is produced. (2) Phase of the development process wherein the top-level definition of the functionality of the system is produced.

requirements for content and presentation: A component of the evaluation criteria for a particular phase or aspect of evaluation identifying what each item of documentation identified as relevant to that phase or aspect of evaluation shall contain and how its information is to be presented.

requirements for evidence: A component of the evaluation criteria for a particular phase or aspect of evaluation defining the nature of the evidence to show that the criteria for that phase or aspect have been satisfied.

requirements for procedures and standards: A component of the evaluation criteria for a particular phase or aspect of evaluation identifying the nature and/or content of procedures or standard approaches that shall be adopted or utilized when the TOE (target of evaluation) is placed into live operation.

residual risk: Portion of risk that remains after security measures have been applied.

residue: Data left in storage after processing operations are complete, but before degaussing or rewriting has taken place.

resource: Anything used or consumed while performing a function. Note: The categories of resources include time, information, objects (information containers), or processors (the ability to use information). Specific examples include CPU (central processing unit) time, terminal connect time, amount of directly addressable memory, disk space, and number of I/O (input/output) requests per minute.

resource encapsulation: The process of ensuring that a resource is not directly accessible by a subject, but that it is protected so that the reference monitor can properly mediate accesses to it.

restricted area: Any area to which access is subject to special restrictions or controls for reasons of security or safeguarding of property or material.

risk: (1) The expected loss due to, or impact of, anticipated threats in light of system vulnerabilities and strength or determination of relevant threat agents. (2) The probability that a particular threat will exploit a particular vulnerability of the system.

risk analysis: The process of identifying security risks, determining their magnitude, and identifying areas needing safeguards. Risk analysis is a part of risk management. (Synonymous with risk assessment.)

risk assessment: Synonymous with risk analysis.

risk index: The disparity between the minimum clearance or authorization of system users and the maximum sensitivity (for example, classification and categories) of data processed by a system. (A complete explanation of this term is provided in CSC-STD-003-85 and CSC-STD-004-85 — US government publications.)

risk management: The total process of identifying, controlling, and eliminating or minimizing uncertain events that may affect system resources. It includes risk analysis, cost-benefit analysis, selection, implementation and test, security evaluation of safeguards, and overall security review.

RSA: A public key algorithm invented by Ronald L. Rivest, Adi Shamir, and Leonard M. Adleman (RSA). RSA can be used to generate digital signatures, encrypt messages, and provide key management for DES (Data Encryption Standard), RC2 (Rivest Cipher 2), RC4 (Rivest Cipher 4), and other secret key algorithms. RSA performs the key management process, in part, by encrypting a secret key for an algorithm such as DES, RC2, or RC4 with the recipient's public key for secure transmission to the recipient. This secret key can then be used to support private communications.

S

safeguards: See security safeguards.

scavenging: Searching through object residue to acquire unauthorized data.

scope of a requirement: Determination of whether a requirement applies to: all users, subjects, and objects of the TCB (trusted computing base); all the TCB commands and application programming interfaces; all TCB elements; all configurations; or only a defined subset of configurations.

secrecy policy: A security policy to prevent unauthorized users from reading sensitive information. (See security policy.)

secret key: The key that two parties share and keep secret for secret key cryptography. Given secret key algorithms of equal strength, the approximate difficulty of decrypting encrypted messages by brute force search can be measured by the number of possible keys. For example, a key length of 56 bits is over 65,000 times stronger or more resistant to attack than a key length of 40 bits.

secret key cryptography: Cryptography based on a single key (or symmetric cryptography). It uses the same secret key for encryption and decryption. Messages are encrypted using a secret key and a secret key cryptographic algorithm, such as Skipjack, DES (Data Encryption Standard), RC2 (Rivest Cipher 2), or RC4 (Rivest Cipher 4).

secure configuration management: The set of procedures appropriate for controlling changes to a system's hardware and software structure for the purpose of ensuring that changes will not lead to violations of the system's security policy.

secure state: A condition in which no subject can access any object in an unauthorized manner.

secure subsystem: A subsystem that contains its own implementation of the reference monitor concept for those resources it controls. However, the secure subsystem must depend on other controls and the base operating system for the control of subjects and the more primitive system objects.

security: (1) The combination of confidentiality, integrity, and availability. (2) The quality or state of being protected from uncontrolled losses or effects. Note: Absolute security may in practice be impossible to reach; thus the security "quality" could be relative. Within state models of security systems, security is a specific "state" that is to be preserved under various operations.

security architecture: The subset of computer architecture dealing with the security of the computer or network system. (See computer architecture and network architecture.)

security audit trail: The set of records that collectively provide documentary evidence of processing used to aid in tracing from original transactions forward to related records and reports, and/or backward from records and reports to their component source transactions.

security-compliant channel: A channel is security compliant if the enforcement of the network policy depends only upon characteristics of the channel either (1) included in the evaluation or (2) assumed as an installation constraint and clearly documented in the trusted facility manual.

security-critical mechanisms: Those security mechanisms whose correct operation is necessary to ensure that the security policy is enforced.

security enforcing: That which directly contributes to satisfying the security objectives of the target of evaluation.

security evaluation: An evaluation done to assess the degree of trust that can be placed in systems for the secure handling of sensitive information. One type, a product evaluation, is an evaluation performed on the hardware and software features and assurances of a computer product from a perspective that excludes the application environment. The other type, a system evaluation, is done for the purpose of assessing a system's security safeguards with respect to a specific operational mission and is a major step in the certification and accreditation process.

security fault analysis: A security analysis, usually performed on hardware at gate level, to determine the security properties of a device when a hardware fault is encountered.

security features: The security-relevant functions, mechanisms, and characteristics of system hardware and software. Security features are a subset of system security safeguards.

security filter: A trusted subsystem that enforces a security policy on the data that pass through it.

security flaw: An error of commission or omission in a system that may allow protection mechanisms to be bypassed.

security flow analysis: A security analysis performed on a formal system specification that locates potential flows of information within the system.

security kernel: The hardware, firmware, and software elements of a trusted computing base (or network trusted computing base partition) that implement the reference monitor concept. It must mediate all accesses, be protected from modification, and be verifiable as correct.

security label: See sensitivity label.

security level: The combination of a hierarchical classification and a set of nonhierarchical categories that represents the sensitivity of information.

security measures: Elements of software, firmware, hardware, or procedures that are included in a system for the satisfaction of security specifications.

security mechanism: (1) That which implements a security function. (2) The logic or algorithm that implements a particular security-enforcing or security-relevant function in hardware and software.

security objectives: The contribution to security that a system or product is intended to achieve.

security perimeter: The boundary where security controls are in effect to protect assets.

security policy: (1) A set of rules and procedures regulating the use of information, including its processing, storage, distribution, and presentation. (See corporate security policy, system security policy, and technical security policy.) (2) The set of laws, rules, and practices that regulate how an organization manages, protects, and distributes sensitive information.

security policy model: (1) A formal presentation of the security policy enforced by the system. It must identify the set of rules and practices that regulate how a system manages, protects, and distributes sensitive information. (See Bell-LaPadula model and formal security policy model.) (2) An informal presentation of a formal security policy model. Note: This is the original definition from the US Trusted Computer System Evaluation Criteria.

security range: The highest and lowest security levels that are permitted in or on a system, system component, subsystem, or network.

security relevant: That which is not security enforcing, but must function correctly for the target of evaluation to enforce security.

security-relevant event: Any event that attempts to change the security state of the system (for example, change access controls, change the security level of a user, change a user password). Also, any event that attempts to violate the security policy of the system (for example, too many attempts to log in, attempts to violate the mandatory access control limits of a device, attempts to downgrade a file, and so on).

security requirements: The types and levels of protection necessary for equipment, data, information, applications, and facilities to meet security policy.

security requirements baseline: A description of minimum requirements necessary for a system to maintain an acceptable level of security.

security safeguards: The protective measures and controls that are prescribed to meet the security requirements specified for a system. Those safeguards may include but are not necessarily limited to hardware and software security features, operating procedures, accountability procedures, access and distribution controls, management constraints, personnel security, and physical structures, areas, and devices. Also called safeguards.

security specifications: A detailed description of the safeguards required to protect a system.

security target: (1) A specification of the security required of a target of evaluation, used as a baseline for evaluation. The security target will specify the security-enforcing functions of the target of evaluation. It will also specify the security objectives, the threats to those objectives, and any specific security mechanisms that will be used. (2) Product-specific description, elaborating the more general requirements in a protection profile and including all evidence generated by the producers, of how a specific IT (information technology) product meets the security requirements of a given protection profile.

security test and evaluation: An examination and analysis of the security safeguards of a system as they have been applied in an operational environment to determine the security posture of the system.

security testing: A process used to determine that the security features of a system are implemented as designed and that they are adequate for a proposed application environment. This process includes hands-on functional testing, penetration testing, and verification. (See functional testing, penetration testing, and verification.)

sensitive information: (1) Information that, as determined by a competent authority, must be protected because its unauthorized disclosure, alteration, loss, or destruction will at least cause perceivable damage to someone or something. (2) Any information, the loss, misuse, modification of, or unauthorized access to, could affect the national interest or the conduct of federal programs, or the privacy to which individuals are entitled under Section 552a of Title 5, US Code, but that has not been specifically authorized under criteria established by an executive order or an act of Congress to be kept classified in the interest of national defense or foreign policy.

sensitivity label: A piece of information that represents the security level of an object and that describes the sensitivity (for example, classification) of the data in the object. Sensitivity labels are used by the TCB (trusted computing base)/NTCB (network trusted computing base) as the basis for mandatory access control decisions.

sensitivity level: See security level.

shall: Indication that a requirement must be met unless a justification of why it cannot be met is given and accepted.

should: Indication of an objective requirement that requires less justification for nonconformance and should be more readily approved. Note: "Should" is often used when a specific requirement is not feasible in some situations or with common current technology.

simple security condition: See simple security property.

simple security property: A Bell-LaPadula security model rule allowing a subject read access to an object only if the security level of the subject dominates the security level of the object. Synonymous with simple security condition.

single-level device: A device that is used to process data of a single security level at any one time. Since the device need not be trusted to separate data of different security levels, sensitivity labels do not have to be stored with the data being processed.

site certification: The comprehensive assessment of the technical and nontechnical security functions of an IT (information technology) system in its operational environment to establish the extent to which the system meets a set of specified security requirements, performed to support operational system accreditation.

Skipjack: A classified 64-bit block encryption, or secret key encryption, algorithm. The algorithm uses 80-bit keys (compared with 56 for DES) and has 32 computational rounds or iterations (compared with 16 for DES). Skipjack supports all DES modes of operation. Skipjack provides high-speed encryption when implemented in a key-escrow chip.

software development methodologies: Methodologies for specifying and verifying design programs for system development. Each methodology is written for a specific computer language. (See enhanced hierarchical development methodology, formal development methodology, Gypsy verification environment, and hierarchical development methodology.)

software security: General-purpose (executive, utility, or software development tools) and applications programs or routines that protect data handled by a system.

software system test and evaluation process: A process that plans, develops, and documents the quantitative demonstration of the fulfillment of all baseline functional performance, operational, and interface requirements.

sponsor: The person or organization that requests an evaluation.

spoofing: An attempt to gain access to a system by posing as an authorized user. (Synonymous with impersonating, masquerading, and mimicking.)

stand-alone, shared system: A system that is physically and electrically isolated from all other systems, and is intended to be used by more than one person, either simultaneously (for example, a system with multiple terminals) or serially, with data belonging to one user remaining available to the system while another user is using the system (for example, a personal computer with nonremovable storage media such as a hard disk).

stand-alone, single-user system: A system that is physically and electrically isolated from all other systems, and is intended to be used by one person at a time, with no data belonging to other users remaining in the system (for example, a personal computer with removable storage media such as a floppy disk).

star (*) property: See *-property (at the beginning of the Glossary).

state: Give required information with no attempted or implied requirement, to justify the information presented.

state delta verification system: A system designed to give high confidence regarding microcode performance by using formulas that represent isolated states of a computation to check proofs concerning the course of that computation.

state variable: A variable that represents either the state of the system or the state of some system resource.

storage object: An object that supports both read and write accesses.

strength of a requirement: Definition of the conditions under which a functional component withstands a defined attack or tolerates failures.

strength of mechanism: A rating of the ability of a security mechanism to withstand a direct attack.

strength of mechanisms: An aspect of the assessment of the effectiveness of a target of evaluation, namely, the ability of its security mechanisms to withstand direct attack against deficiencies in their underlying algorithms, principles, and properties.

Subcommittee on Automated Information Systems Security (SAISS): NSDD (National Security Decision Directive) 145 authorized and directed the establishment, under the NTISSC (National Telecommunications and Information Systems Security Committee), of a permanent Subcommittee on Automated Information Systems Security (SAISS). The SAISS is composed of one voting member from each US federal organization represented on the NTISSC. In 1990, the NTISSC was replaced with the NSTISSC (National Security Telecommunications and Information Systems Security Committee) pursuant to NSD-42.

Subcommittee on Telecommunications Security (STS): NSDD (National Security Decision Directive) 145 authorized and directed the establishment, under the NTISSC (National Telecommunications and Information Systems Security Committee), of a permanent Subcommittee on Telecommunications Security (STS). The STS is composed of one voting member from each US federal organization represented on the NTISSC. In 1990, the NTISSC was replaced with the NSTISSC (National Security Telecommunications and Information Systems Security Committee) pursuant to NSD-42.

subject: Active entity in an IT (information technology) product or AIS (automated information system), generally in the form of a process or device, that causes information to flow among objects or changes the system state.

subject security level: A subject's security level is equal to the security level of the objects to which it has both read and write access. A subject's security level must always be dominated by the clearance of the user the subject is associated with.

subset domain: A set of system domains. For evaluation by parts, each candidate TCB (trusted computing base) subset must occupy a distinct subset domain such that modify-access to a domain within a TCB subset's subset domain is permitted only to that TCB subset and (possibly) to more primitive TCB subsets.

suitability of functionality: An aspect of the assessment of the effectiveness of a target of evaluation, namely, the suitability of its security-enforcing functions and mechanisms to in fact counter the threats to the security of the target of evaluation identified in its security target.

supervisor state: Synonymous with executive state.

system: (1) A specific IT (information technology) installation, with a particular purpose and operational environment. (2) An assembly of computer and/or communications hardware, software, and firmware configured for the purpose of classifying, sorting, calculating, computing, summarizing, transmitting, receiving, storing, and retrieving data with the purpose of supporting users. (3) IT products assembled together — either directly or with additional computer hardware, software, and/or firmware — configured to perform a particular function within a particular operational environment.

system development methodologies: Methodologies developed through software engineering to manage the complexity of system development. Development methodologies include software engineering aids and high-level design analysis tools.

system entry: Mechanism by which an identified and authenticated user is provided access into the system.

system high: The highest security level supported by a system at a particular time or in a particular environment.

system-high security mode: See modes of operation.

system integrity: (1) The quality of a system fulfilling its operational purpose while (a) preventing unauthorized users from making modifications to resources or using resources, and (b) preventing authorized users from making improper modifications to resources or making improper use of resources. (2) The quality that a system has when it performs its intended function in an unimpaired manner, free from deliberate or inadvertent unauthorized manipulation of the system.

system low: The lowest security level supported by a system at a particular time or in a particular environment.

system security officer (SSO): See information system security officer.

system security policy: The set of laws, rules, and practices that regulate how sensitive information and other resources are managed, protected, and distributed within a specific system.

Systems Security Steering Group: The senior US government body established by NSDD (National Security Decision Directive) 145 to provide top-level review and policy guidance for the telecommunications security and automated information systems security activities of the US government. This group is chaired by the Assistant to the President for National Security Affairs and consists of the Secretary of State, Secretary of Treasury, Secretary of Defense, Attorney General, Director of the Office of Management and Budget, and Director of Central Intelligence. In 1990, NSDD 145 was partially replaced by NSD-42.

T

tampering: An unauthorized modification that alters the proper functioning of equipment or a system in a manner that degrades the security or functionality it provides.

target of evaluation (TOE): An IT (information technology) system, product, or component that is identified/subjected as requiring security evaluation.

TCB (trusted computing base) subset: A set of software, firmware, and hardware (where any of these three could be absent) that mediates the access of a set S of subjects to a set O of objects on the basis of a stated access control policy P and satisfies the properties:

1. M mediates every access to objects O by subjects in S,
2. M is tamper resistant, and
3. M is small enough to be subject to analysis and tests, the completeness of which can be assured.

technical attack: An attack that can be perpetrated by circumventing or nullifying hardware and software protection mechanisms, rather than by subverting system personnel or other users.

technical policy: (1) The set of rules regulating access of subjects to objects enforced by a TCB (trusted computing base) subset. (2) The set of rules regulating access of subjects to objects enforced by a computer system.

technical security policy: (1) Specific protection conditions and/or protection philosophy that expresses the boundaries and responsibilities of the IT (information technology) product in supporting the information protection policy control objectives and countering expected threats. (2) The set of laws, rules, and practices regulating the processing of sensitive information and the use of resources by the hardware and software of an IT system or product.

technical vulnerability: A hardware, firmware, communication, or software flaw that leaves a computer processing system open for potential exploitation, either externally or internally, thereby resulting in risk for the owner, user, or manager of the system.

TEMPEST: The study and control of spurious electronic signals emitted by electrical equipment, such as computer equipment.

terminal identification: The means used to uniquely identify a terminal to a system.

threat: (1) An action or event that might prejudice security. (2) Sequence of circumstances and events that allows a human or other agent to cause an information-related misfortune by exploiting a vulnerability in an IT (information technology) product. (3) Any circumstance or event with the potential to cause harm to a system in the form of destruction, disclosure, modification of data, or denial of service.

threat agent: A method used to exploit a vulnerability in a system, operation, or facility.

threat analysis: The examination of all actions and events that might adversely affect a system or operation.

threat monitoring: The analysis, assessment, and review of audit trails and other data collected for the purpose of searching out system events that may constitute violations or attempted violations of system security.

ticket-oriented: A computer protection system in which each subject maintains a list of unforgeable bit patterns, called tickets, one for each object the subject is authorized to access. (Compare list-oriented.)

time-dependent password: A password that is valid only at a certain time of day or during a specified interval of time.

tool: A product used in the construction and/or documentation of a target of evaluation.

top-level specification (TLS): A nonprocedural description of system behavior at the most abstract level — typically, a functional specification that omits all implementation details.

trace a correspondence: Explain a correspondence, using natural language prose, between levels of abstraction.

tranquillity: A security model rule stating that the security level of an object cannot change while the object is being processed by an AIS (automated information system).

transaction: Set of subject actions and their associated data storage accesses.

transmission security: Maintaining confidentiality of information in a telecommunications network.

trap door (or trapdoor): (1) Hidden software or hardware mechanism that can be triggered to permit protection mechanisms in an automated information system to be circumvented. Note: A trap door is usually activated in some innocent-appearing manner (for example, a special random key sequence at a terminal). Software developers often write trap doors in their code that enable them to reenter the system to perform certain functions. (2) A secret entry point to a cryptographic algorithm through which the developer or another entity can bypass security controls and decrypt messages.

Trojan horse: A computer program with an apparently or actually useful function that contains additional (hidden) functions that surreptitiously exploit the legitimate authorizations of the invoking process to the detriment of security — for example, making a "blind copy" of a sensitive file for the creator of the Trojan horse.

trusted channel: A mechanism by which two NTCB (network trusted computing base) partitions can communicate directly. This mechanism can be activated by either of the NTCB partitions, cannot be imitated by untrusted software, and maintains the integrity of information that is sent over it. A trusted channel may be needed for the correct operation of other security mechanisms.

trusted computer system: A system that uses sufficient hardware and software assurance/integrity measures to allow its use for processing simultaneously a range of sensitive or classified information.

trusted computing base (TCB): The totality of protection mechanisms within a computer system, including hardware, firmware, and software, the combination of which is responsible for enforcing a security policy. A TCB consists of one or more components that enforce a unified security policy over a product or system. The ability of a TCB to correctly enforce a security policy depends solely on the mechanisms within the TCB and on the correct input by system administrative personnel of parameters (for example, a user's clearance) related to the security policy.

trusted distribution: A trusted method for distributing the TCB (trusted computing base) hardware, software, and firmware components, both originals and updates, that provides methods for protecting the TCB from modification during distribution and for detection of any changes to the TCB that may occur.

trusted functionality: That which is determined to be correct with respect to some criteria, for example, as established by a security policy. The functionality shall neither fall short of nor exceed the criteria.

trusted identification forwarding: An identification method used in networks whereby the sending host can verify that an authorized user on its system is attempting a connection to another host. The sending host transmits the required user authentication information to the receiving host. The receiving host can then verify that the user is validated for access to its system. This operation may be transparent to the user.

trusted path: A mechanism by which a person at a terminal can communicate directly with the trusted computing base. This mechanism can be activated only by the person or by the trusted computing base and cannot be imitated by untrusted software.

trusted process: A process whose incorrect or malicious execution is capable of violating system security policy.

trusted software: The software portion of a trusted computing base.

trusted subject: (1) A subject that is part of the TCB (trusted computing base). It has the ability to violate the security policy, but is trusted not to actually do so. For example, in the Bell-LaPadula model, a trusted subject is not constrained by the *-property and thus has the ability to write sensitive information into an object whose level is not dominated by the (maximum) level of the subject, but it is trusted to only write information into objects with a label appropriate for the actual level of the information. (2) A subject that is permitted to have simultaneous view and alter-access to objects of more than one sensitivity level.

U

untrusted process: A process that has not been evaluated or examined for adherence to the security policy. It may include incorrect or malicious code that attempts to circumvent the security mechanisms.

usage security policy: Assumptions regarding the expected environment and intended method of IT (information technology) product use.

user: (1) Any person who interacts directly with a computer system. (2) Any person who interacts directly with a network system. This includes both those persons who are authorized to interact with the system and those people who interact without authorization (for example, active or passive wiretappers). Note that "users" do not include "operators," "system programmers," "technical control officers," "system security officers," and other system support personnel. They are distinct from users and are subject to the trusted facility manual and the system architecture requirements. Such individuals may change the system parameters of the network system, for example, by defining membership of a group. These individuals may also have the separate role of users. (3) Any person or process accessing an IT (information technology) product by direct connections (for example, via terminals) or indirect connections. Note: Indirect connection relates to persons who prepare input data or receive output that is not reviewed for content or classification by a responsible individual.

user documentation: The information about a target of evaluation supplied by the developer for use by its end users.

user identifier (user ID): Unique symbol or character string that is used by an IT (information technology) system or product to uniquely identify a specific user.

user profile: Patterns of a user's activity that can be used to detect changes in normal routines.

V

validation: The process of assessing the usefulness of a system in relation to its intended use or purpose.

verification: (1) The process of ensuring correctness. (2) The process of comparing two levels of system specification for proper correspondence (for example, security policy model with top-level specification (TLS), TLS with source code, or source code with object code). This process may or may not be automated.

view: That portion of the database that satisfies the conditions specified in a query.

view definition: A stored query, sometimes loosely referred to as a "view."

virus: (1) Malicious software, a form of Trojan horse, which reproduces itself in other executable code. (2) A self-propagating Trojan horse, composed of a mission component, a trigger component, and a self-propagating component. (3) Self-replicating malicious program segment that attaches itself to an application or other executable system component and leaves no external signs of its presence.

vulnerability: (1) A security weakness in a target of evaluation (for example, due to failures in analysis, design, implementation, or operation). (2) Weakness in an information system or components (for example, system security procedures, hardware design, or internal controls) that could be exploited to produce an information-related misfortune. (3) A weakness in system security procedures, system design, implementation, internal controls, and so on, that could be exploited to violate system security policy.

vulnerability analysis: The systematic examination of systems to determine the adequacy of security measures, identify security deficiencies, and provide data from which to predict the effectiveness of proposed security measures.

vulnerability assessment: (1) An aspect of the assessment of the effectiveness of a target of evaluation, namely, whether known vulnerabilities in that target of evaluation could in practice compromise its security as specified in the security target. (2) A measurement of vulnerability which includes the susceptibility of a particular system to a specific attack and the opportunities available to a threat agent to mount that attack.

W

wiretapping: The real-time collection of transmitted data, such as dialed digits, and the sending of that data in real time to a listening device.

work factor: An estimate of the effort or time needed by a potential penetrator with specified expertise and resources to overcome a protective measure.

write: A fundamental operation that results only in the flow of information from a subject to an object.

write access: Permission to write an object.

Index

*

*-property • 74

A

A1 (Verified Design) • 151
abstraction • 311
  level of • 126–33
access control • 45–93, 187–89, **323**
  decision facility • *See* ADF
  enforcement facility • *See* AEF
  granularity • 627
  list • 63, **168**
  policy • 49–95, **49**
access matrix • 178
access mode • 50, 52–64
accountability • 64, 142, 165, 177,
  324
accreditation • 298–303, 347
accreditor • 348
accuracy • **326**
ACL • *See* access control list
active attack • 357
ADF • 188–94
adjudication • 188
administration • 67
administrator • 165, 166
Advanced Secure DBMS • *See* ASD
advisory marking • 69
AEF • 188–89
American National Standards Institute • *See* ANSI
ANSI • 244–61, **260**
architecture • 263
artifices • 33

ASD • 553–57, 580
assurance • **143**–58, 145, 270, 306,
  313, **327**
  balanced • 154
  uniform • 154
assured pipelines • *See* LDV
asymmetric cryptosystem • *See*
  public key
atomicity • 536
attack
  active • 357
  authenticity • 357
  integrity • 357
  masquerade • 358
  ordering • 358
  passive • 357
  scenario • 35
attribute • 188–92, 419
  policy decision • 166–69
  polyinstantiation • 495
  propagation • 177
audit • **324**, 585–95
  policy • 65
  record • 34, 49, **52**, 120
  requirements • **586**
authentication • 65, 145–52, 288,
  319
authenticity attack • 357
authority • 165, 177
availability • 42, **164**, 177, 312,
  401, 422

B

B1 (Labeled Security Protection) •
  146
B2 (Structured Protection) • 147

B3 (Security Domains) • 149
balanced assurance • 154
Bell-LaPadula • 74, 173
Biba • 74
block
    cipher • 353
    encryption • 362
bridge • 394
bundling • 314
bus interface unit • *See* NIU
business activity • 426

C

C1 (Discretionary Security Protection) • 145
C2 (Controlled Access Protection) • 145
CA • 377, 417–21, 432
CAE • 244–47
Canadian Trusted Computer Product Evaluation Criteria • See CTCPEC
CBEMA • 261
CC • 243–62, 297–317
CCITT • *See* ITU-T
CEN • 257
CENELEC • 257
centralized authority • 177
certificate • 408–22
certificate-based key management • 377
certification • 300–304, **302**, 339, 347
Certification Authority • *See* CA
certification body • 304
CESG • 304
checkfunction • 122, 323
cipher
    block • 353
    product • 353
    substitution • 353
ciphertext • 92, 351–83, 351. *Compare* plaintext
Clark-Wilson • 75, 180, 189–94

class • *See* evaluation class
clearance • 167
cleartext • *See* plaintext
CLEF • 300–304
CMW • 179
Comité European de Normalization • *See* CEN
Comité European de Normalization Electrotechnique • *See* CENELEC
commercial licensed evaluation facility • *See* CLEF
commercial off the shelf • *See* COTS
Common Application Environment • *See* CAE
Common Criteria • *See* CC
communication channel • 52
Communications Electronics Security Group • *See* CESG
Compartmented-Mode Workstation • *See* CMW
completeness • 51
component • 307
computable • 44
Computer and Business Equipment Manufacturers Association • *See* CBEMA
COMSEC • 402
Concept of Operations • *See* ConOps
concurrency control • 536
confidentiality • 43, 370, 406
    perfect • 366
    traffic flow • 402
connection-oriented abstraction • 89
connectivity • 101
ConOps • 333
consistency • 180
container • 178
content-correctness • 176
continuous protection • 143, **328**
Corporation for Open Systems • *See* COS
correctness • 173, 176, 311
COS • 260

COTS • 298, 331
  integration • 342
countermeasures • 120
cover story • 497
covert channel • **84**, **117**, 148, **328**, 531
cryptography • 92, 350–84, 393
cryptoseal • *See* digital signature
CTCPEC • 244–62

D

DAC • *See* discretionary security policy
DAP • 302
data
  exchange • **326**
  integrity • 42, 114, 312, 397, 435
  management standards • 264
  origin authentication • 406
  replication • 450–52

                                        See DTE
                              • *See*
                              • *See*

    problems • 582
    association problem • 584
    inference
      channels • 571
        abductive • 579
        deductive • 579

  problems • 570–84
  integrity • 617–34
  multilevel relational • 460–91
  object-oriented • 537, 595–617
  prototypes • 542–69
  relational • 462
DEA • 360
decipherment • *See* decryption
decomposition • 483–86

dedicated mode • 55
delete operation • 478–79
Department of Trade and Industry • *See* DTI
DES • 354–78, 360, 411–14
design • 337
deterministic • 178
deterrence • 109
development process • 331
device • 52, 176, 400
Diffie-Hellman • 368
digital signature • 93, 356–84, **373**
disclosure • *See* unauthorized disclosure
discretionary security policy • 58, **63**, 142–56, 179, 316
disruption • 17
distributed authority • 177
distributed DBMS • 450–52
domain • 52, 371
dominate • 60
DTE • 386–403
DTI • 304

E

ECMA • 244–60
EDI • 247–62, 424–38
EDIFACT • 430–38
electronic code book • 362
Electronic Data Interchange • *See* EDI. *See* EDI
ElGamal • 368
e-mail • 406–22
encipherment • *See* encryption
encryption • 351–84
  block • 362
  cipher block chaining • 363
  cipher feedback • 365
  end-to-end • 383
  initialization vector • 363
  key auto-key • 365
  one-time pad • 367
enforcement • 188
engineering, security • 330–49

enterprise • 99–105, 126–34
entity integrity • 534
entity polyinstantiation • 494
EPL • 298–302
espionage • *See* unauthorized disclosure
European Computer Manufacturers
Organization • *See* ECMA
Evaluated Products List • *See* EPL
evaluation • 297–317
  by parts • 153, 317
  class • 143–58, **144**
  design analysis phase • *See* DAP
  incremental • 154
  initial product assessment report
    • *See* IPAR
  partition • 153
  rating maintenance phase • *See*
    RAMP
  subset • 154
  target • *See* TOE
  technical review board • *See* TRB
  vendor assistance phase • *See*
    VAP
export • 90
external consistency • 180
external-interface requirement • 172

F

FC • 244–62
Federal Criteria for Information
Technology Security • See FC
Federal Information Processing
Standard • *See* FIPS
FHM • 269–95, **276**
file encryption • 383
filter • 95
FIPS PUB 46-1 • 360
flaw • 120, 270, 287
Flaw Hypothesis Methodology • *See*
FHM
floating label • 179
formal
  description • 71

methods • 170–86, **181**
model • 190–95
semantics • 182
top-level specification • *See* FTLS
FTLS • 77, 151, 174, 185
functionality • 306, 311
functionality class • 312

G

GCHQ • 304
Generalized Framework for Access
Control • *See* GFAC
Generic Upper Layers Security • *See*
GULS
GFAC • 187–89
global and persistent • **60**
Government Communications
Headquarters • *See* GCHQ
granularity of control • 165
guard • 94
GULS • 252–67

H

hardware
  flaw • 30
  trap door • 34
hash function • 375
Hinke-Schaefer • 439–44
human error • 20

I

I.P. Sharp • 440
IBAC • 316
identification • 65, 145–52, 194,
288, 318–25, **319**
identity-based access control • *See*
IBAC
IEC • 243–68
IETF • 245
import • 90
incremental evaluation • 154
indirect access • 68

individual accountability • 64, 142, 165
inference channel • 530
information
   assets • 332
   dissemination • 166
   hiding • 78
Information Technology Security Evaluation Criteria • *See* ITSEC
inheritance • 539
insert operation • 470–72
integration • 299, 330–49, 331, 342
integrity • 43, 157, **164**, 312
   attack • 357
   authenticated users • 627
   Biba • 74
   Clark-Wilson • 75, 180, 189–94
   continuity of operation • 627
   data • 42, 114, 435
   DBMS • 530–41, 617–34
   ease of safe use • 633
   entity • 534
   implementation-dependent • 539
   key • 532, 573
   least privilege • 627
   message integrity code • *See* MIC
   object • 537
   polyinstantiation • 469, 506
   program • 42, 120
   reality checks • 633
   reconstruction of events • 631–32
   referential • 535
   separation of duties • 629–31
   source • 176
   system • 42
   well-formed transaction • 624–27
integrity-lock • 440–55
interface • 280
internal controls • 121
internal requirement • 172
International Electrotechnical Commission • *See* IEC
International Organization for Standardization • *See* ISO

International Telecommunications Union • *See* ITU-T
Internet Engineering Task Force • *See* IETF
Internet Protocol • *See* IP
interpretation • 301
invisible polyinstantiation • 498–99
IP • 245
IPAR • 302
ISO • 243–68
isolation • 51, 102–11, 145
ITSEC • 139–56, 244–62, 293, 297–317
ITU-T • 243–68

J

Joint Technical Committee 1 • *See* JTC1
JTC1 • 243–68

K

kernel • **53**, 77, 141, 150
kernelized DBMS • 439–44
key • 352–83
   distribution center • 380
   integrity • 532
   management • 368–82
   public • 355–79
   symmetric • 355
   translation center • 380
key-encrypting key • 381
keying material • 354

L

label • 59, 167
   floating • 179
LAN • 385–404
lattice • 61
LDV • 447–49, **558–66**
least privilege • **121**, 627
legal remedies • 124
link encryption • 382

LOCK • 447
Lock Data Views • *See* LDV
logic bomb • 28

M

MAC • *See* mandatory security policy, message authentication code
malicious software • 18–37, 111–24
manager • 97–110
mandatory security policy • 58, 73,
  141–55, **141**, 178–79, 187
MAP/TOP • 245
marking • 142, 167
masquerade • 358
master key • 380
mathematical formalism • 183
mechanical proof checker • 182
mechanism • 32, 105, 313
message authentication code • 379,
  411
message digest • 375
message integrity code • *See* MIC
message-stream modification • 357,
  390
messaging • 427
MIC • 411–22
MIME • 406
mission • 333
misuse • 15–38
model
  database activity • 588
  formal • 170–86, 190–95
  object-oriented • 598–603
  rule-set • 192
  security policy • 171
  state-machine • 178, 192
multilevel • 55, 330–49
  relational DBMS • 460–91

N

National Computer Security Center
  • *See* NCSC
NCSC • 300–317

NDI • 298
need-to-know • 167
network • 86, 89, 301
network interface unit • *See* NIU
network TCB partition • *See* NTCB
NIU • 388–404
nondevelopment item • *See* NDI
nonrepudiation • 374, 400, 406,
  433
NTCB • 86

O

object
  integrity • 537
  reuse • **325**
objectives • 163, 176
object-oriented
  data model • 598–600
  databases • 537
  security model • 600–603
ODA • 244–61
Office Document Architecture • *See*
  ODA
OIW • 261
Open Software Foundation • *See*
  OSF
open systems • 243–68, **253**
Open Systems Environment Imple-
  mentors Workshop • *See* OIW
Open Systems Interconnection • *See*
  OSI
operating systems • 301
ordering attack • 358
OSF • 244
OSI • 244, 385–97
OSI management • 265

P

partially ordered set • 61
partition evaluation • 153
passive attack • 357
password • 320
PCA • 418–22

PEM • 406–22
penetration • 28, 37, 81, 138
  testing • 13–29, 269–95
perimeter • 109, 147–56
plaintext • 92, 351–83. *Compare*
  ciphertext
policy • **45**, 127–34, 160–69, 187–
  89, 318–28
policy certification authority • *See*
  PCA
policy model • 71, 72, 171
polyinstantiation • 446, **494–99**,
  547
  entity • 494
  integrity • 469, 506
  invisible • 498
  problem
    belief approach • 514–17
    derived data approach • 511
    derived values approach • 510
    explicit alternatives approach •
      524–27
    insert-low approach • 517–20
    prevention • 520–27
    propagation approach • 505
  visible • 496
porting • 345
prevention • 16, 109, 306
privacy enhanced mail • *See* PEM
probing • 22–28, **22**, 81
product • 297–317, **298**
product cipher • 353
program integrity • 42, 120
proof • 181
protection bit mask • 63
protection rings • 57
protocol • 395
pseudorandom bit stream • 366
public key • 355–79, 408–17

R

rainbow documents • 306
RAMP • 302
reciprocity • 315

recovery • 486–91
reference monitor • 48–95, **49**, 140–
  56
referential integrity • 535
relation
  multilevel • 465
relational DBMS • 462
reliability • **326**
repudiation • 164
requirements • 330–49
  interface • 172
rigor • 181
risk • **20**, 143, 158, 371
  analysis • 111
  index • 307
role • 167
RSA • 368–77
rule-set model • 192

S

scenario • 335
SeaView • 444–49, **544–53**
secure distributed data views • *See*
  SeaView
security kernel • *See* kernel
security-enforcing • 319
segmentation • 57
selective routing • 402
self-protection • *See* isolation
sensitive information • 12
sensitivity label • 167
separately accredited • 346
separation • 393
  of duties • 180, 629–31
service • 243–67, 307
signaling channel • 531
signature • *See* digital signature
simple mail-transfer protocol • *See*
  SMTP
simple security property • 74
single trusted system • 346
SMTP • 409–12
software, malicious • 111–24
SOGITS Report • 424

source-integrity • 176
sponsor • 304
standards • 242–68
star-property • *See* *-property
state invariant • 182
state-machine model • 178, 192
state-transition • 182
storage channel • *See* covert channel
storage container • 178
storage object • 175
strength of mechanism • 306
subset evaluation • 154
substitution cipher • 353
subversion of security mechanism • 19–39, 141–53
supporting policy • 64
symmetric key • 355
system • 297–317, **299**
   high • 55
   integration • 330–49
   integrity • 42, 114–24

T

target • 304
target of evaluation • *See* TOE
TCB • **71**, 139–56, 172, 330–47
   design • 82
   partition • 80
   subset • 80, 154, 317
   subset DBMS • 441–57, **443**
TCP • 245
TCSEC • 138–57, 297–317
TDI • 154–55, 301–17, 542
technical security policy • 56, **161**
test plan • 107, 272
theft • 16
threat • **20**, 111–24, 270, 303, 306
tiger team • *See* penetration testing
time bomb • 28
timing channel • *See* covert channel
TLS • 173
TNI • 152–55, 301–14
TNI Environments Guideline • *See* TNIEG

TNIEG • 306
TOE • 297–315
top-level specification • *See* TLS, FTLS
trade-off • 330
trading systems • 424–38
traffic flow confidentiality • 402
transaction atomicity • 536
transaction processing • 539
Transmission Control Protocol • *See* TCP
trap door • 33, **118**
TRB • 302
triage • 108
Trojan horse • 25–37
trust requirements • 332
trusted
   computer system • 327
   computing base • *See* TCB
   distribution • 152, 328
   path • 67, **149**
   process • 344
   product • 298
   subject DBMS • 441–59, **457**
   subjects • 73
Trusted Computer System Evaluation Criteria • *See* TCSEC
Trusted Database Interpretation • *See* TDI
Trusted Network Interpretation • *See* TNI
type enforcement • 57, 181, 447

U

unauthorized disclosure • 17, 114
unauthorized modification • 18
unbundling • 315
unified system • 346
uniform assurance • 154
Unix • 187–91
update operations • 469–79
user abuse • 21
user agent • 407–15

V

VAP • 302
verification • 51, 82
virus • 27, 118
visible polyinstantiation • 496–97
vulnerability • **20**–29, 121

W

wiretap • 390
working key • 380
worm • 28

X

X.400 • 244–61, **249**, 428–38
X.435 • 430
X.500 • 249–63, 432–38
X.509 • 244–66, 416
X12 • 430–38
X9.17 • 379
X9.9 • 379

About the Authors

Marshall D. Abrams is a principal scientist in the Information Systems Security Division at the MITRE Corp. in McLean, Va. His research interests focus on access control in trusted systems. He has led and managed a group supporting the National Security Agency (NSA) in the extension of computer security concepts to computer networks and open distributed systems, and participated on a similar team addressing database security. He is currently a member of the working group developing new Federal Criteria for information security under the joint sponsorship of NSA and the National Institute of Standards and Technology (NIST). He has served as technical consultant and/or project leader on tasks involving local networks, office automation, requirements analysis, and system design.

Abrams was previously the principal participant at the (then) National Bureau of Standards in projects concerned with computer networks. In this capacity, he was the project manager for computer network performance measurement, distributed processing, and general studies of performance criteria and data analysis procedures for evaluating the quality of computer network service. He was honored with the National Bureau of Standards Applied Research Award and the Department of Commerce Silver Medal Award. He also held the position of associate professor of electrical engineering at the University of Maryland.

He holds a BSEE from the (then) Carnegie Institute of Technology, and an MSEE and a PhD from the University of Pittsburgh. He has been instrumental in establishing the Computer Security Applications Conference, is a senior member of the IEEE, and a member of the ACM. Abrams teaches professional development continuing education seminars in information security.

Sushil Jajodia is professor of information and software systems engineering and director of the Center for Secure Information Systems at George Mason University, Fairfax, Va. He joined GMU after serving as the director of the Database and Expert Systems Program within the Division of Information, Robotics, and Intelligent Systems at the National Science Foundation. Before that, he was the head of the Database and Distributed Systems Section in the Computer Science and Systems Branch at the Naval Research Laboratory, Washington, and associate professor of computer science and director of graduate studies at the University of Missouri, Columbia.

Jajodia received his PhD from the University of Oregon, Eugene. His research interests include information systems security, database management and distributed systems, and parallel computing. He has published more than 100 technical papers in the refereed journals and conference proceedings, and has coedited eight books.

Jajodia has served in different capacities for various journals and conferences. He is the founding coeditor-in-chief of the *Journal of Computer Security* and serves as an associate editor of the *International Journal of Intelligent and Cooperative Information Systems*. He was on the program committees for the 1993 International Conference on Very Large Data Bases, IEEE Symposium on Research in Security and Privacy, and First ACM Conference on Computer and Communications Security. He is a senior member of the IEEE Computer Society and a member of the Association for Computing Machinery.

Harold J. Podell has attained international recognition as a lecturer on computing and communications security. Marshall Abrams and Harold Podell's book *Computer and Network Security: Tutorial* (IEEE Computer Society Press) is acknowledged as a definitive text in this field. He has been influential in the review of system controls for information technology (IT) applications in distributed environments. His analysis interests also focus on network security standards developed by the US National Computer Security Center, the US National Institute of Standards and Technology, and the International Organization for Standardization.

His experience includes DBMS benchmark testing for the US National Flight Data Center, architectural development of an Internal Revenue Service on-line processing system, and DBMS analyses supporting the World Wide Military Command and Control System (WWMCCS). He was previously with the MITRE Corp. and is currently assistant director, Accounting and Information Management Division, US General Accounting Office.

Podell is a former faculty member of the University of Maryland and a member of the IEEE Computer and Communications Societies. He is a past session chairman of the Aerospace Computer Security Conference and has given presentations on network security at similar events sponsored by the Computer Security Institute and the Institute for International Research. Podell has taught courses internationally on computer and network security for many organizations, including educational programs in the United States, Canada, Europe, and Australia.

Dave Bailey is a senior analyst with Galaxy Computer Services, where he works on a wide variety of computer and network security subjects. In the recent past, these have included development of new Federal Criteria intended to extend and replace the Orange Book, development and deployment of a network surveillance system, development of a network alarm system, and support of law enforcement in active investigations. He started the computer security program at the Los Alamos National Laboratory and ran it from 1974 to 1986. He founded the DOE Center for Computer Security and was its director twice. He was trained in physics and mathematics, and holds a master's degree from UCLA. His interests include system specification and verification, security policy, networking, running, music, and digital typography. He is a member of the IEEE.

Gautam Bhargava received his BTech in computer science from the Indian Institute of Technology, Kanpur, in 1983, and his MS and PhD in computer science from Iowa State University in 1986 and 1989, respectively. He is currently with the IBM Santa Teresa Laboratory, San Jose, Calif. His interests include relational and deductive databases and transaction processing systems. Bhargava is a member of ACM.

Barbara T. Blaustein received a BS in computer science from the University of Maryland, College Park, in 1975 and an SM and a PhD in computer science from Harvard University, Cambridge, Mass., in 1977 and 1981, respectively.

From 1980 to 1992 she worked for Xerox Advanced Information Technology (formerly the Research and Systems Division of the Computer Corp. of America). She is now a lead scientist in the Information Security Division of the MITRE Corp., McLean, Va. Her main research interests are distributed transaction management, semantic integrity, and database security.

Donald L. Brinkley joined Sybase, Inc., in April 1993 as the product manager for secure products in the Server Products Group. He manages the efforts necessary to ensure the success of the secure products from functional, commercial, and security evaluation perspectives. Current products include the commercially available Secure Server, which is under evaluation as a TDI class B1 database management system. Formerly, he was the product manager at Gemini Computers, Inc. There he managed the development and evaluation activities for Gemini's two trusted products: (1) the flagship Gemini Trusted Network Processor (GTNP), which is commercially available and is in formal evaluation as a TNI class A1 mandatory access control component, and (2) the Gemini Multiprocessor Secure Operating System (GEMSOS) trusted computing base (TCB), an early prototype of which is commercially available. His major contributions included establishing the organization, standards, and practices within which the engineering activities that are critical to developing high-assurance products can be performed in a manner that simultaneously meets requirements for cost-effectiveness, product quality, and evaluatable security.

Brinkley has been working in the information security field since 1984, when he joined the McLean Research Center of the System Development Corp. as a staff research scientist. He went on to establish and manage the Internet Security Branch, which developed security solutions, guidelines, and recommendations for further R&D in distributed systems security as part of a number of US government programs. Prior to that, he worked in real-time process control with Logicon and in networking and communications with Magnavox. He received an MS in electrical engineering and computer science and a BS in computer science and engineering, both from the Massachusetts Institute of Technology.

Shashi K. Gadia received his BS and MS in mathematics from the Birla Institute of Technology and Science, Pilani, in 1970 and 1971, respectively, his PhD in mathematics from the University of Illinois at Urbana-Champaign in 1978, and his MS in computer science from Ohio State University in 1980. He is currently an associate professor at Iowa State University in Ames.

His interests include temporal, spatial, and security databases, and access methods. Gadia is a member of ACM and the Association for Symbolic Logic.

Daniel W. (Dan) Gambel is the deputy director of engineering, systems integrity, and manager of the Trusted Systems Engineering Group at Grumman Data Systems. He is a member of the board of directors for Paige International and an independent consultant in information security. Mr. Gambel's work in information security includes development of the security solution for the Headquarters System Replacement Program, an Air Force certified B2-level integrated system located in the Pentagon. He provides the system integration perspective to a number of national and international forums, including the National Computer Security Center guideline development process and the National Institute of Standards and Technology acquisition standards and guidelines. He has worked as a security engineer on a large number of government systems. He guided the recent development of an integrated multilevel secure network demonstration effort at Grumman.

Gambel was previously with the US government at the Defense Intelligence Agency as a senior accreditor of sensitive government and contractor systems. In that role he was responsible for evaluating the security of over 100 computer and communications systems, and he has extensive experience in the application of information security policy to a practical operational environment. Prior to being assigned to DIA, he was an engineer on the first Navy Compartmented Mode system and a project engineer on one of the early multilevel secure intelligence systems.

Thomas H. Hinke received a BS in electrical engineering from the University of California, Berkeley; an MBA in industrial management from Oklahoma City University; an MS in computer science from the University of California at Los Angeles, and a PhD in computer science from the University of Southern California.

From 1974 to 1987 he was with System Development Corp. (which ultimately became part of Unisys) in Santa Monica, Calif., where he led research projects in computer security as manager of SDC's System Security Branch within the Research and Development Division. He also served as the technical area manager for all of SDC's internal research and development projects in computer security. From 1987 until 1990, he was with TRW in Redondo Beach, Calif., where he managed the TRW Advanced Secure DBMS project during its final phase of development. He is currently an associate professor in the Computer Science Department at the University of Alabama in Huntsville, where he is leading research in database security.

Hinke is a member of the IEEE Computer Society, where he served as chairman of its Technical Committee on Security and Privacy. He is also a member of the ACM and the American Association for Artificial Intelligence.

E. (Ted) J. Humphreys is a director of XiSEC Consultants, Ltd., a company involved in providing international consultancy services in the field of IT and telecommunications security. Ted is directing XiSEC activities in the provision of expertise and advice on a wide range of security issues, including security policy and strategy, research, products, standards, evaluation, and training. Among the many key roles played by Ted Humphreys in this field is his current role as senior consultant to the European Commission on its INFOSEC initiative.

Before establishing XiSEC, Humphreys worked for British Telecom, where he played a major role in developing the company's position as an international player in IT security. While at British Telecom, he undertook many key assignments in the research and development of secure IT systems, as consultant and adviser to its operational divisions and their major customers, and to the UK government.

Among his many talents in the INFOSEC world, he is a leading expert on X.400 message handling security, X.500 directory systems security, the security of EDI-based trading systems, and many other aspects of open systems security.

On the standardization front, he is chair of the European Advisory Group (ITAEGV) on information systems security standards, convener of SC27/WG1 on Security Requirements, Services and Guidelines, and chair of the UK/BSI equivalent of SC27.

Humphreys is the author of countless publications, articles, and conference presentations on INFOSEC topics.

 **Stephen Kent** is the chief scientist of BBN Communications, a division of Bolt Beranek and Newman, Inc., where he has been engaged in network security research and development activities for 15 years. His work has included the design and development of user authentication and access control systems, network layer encryption and access control systems for packet networks, secure transport layer and electronic messaging protocols, and a multilevel secure directory system.

Kent has served as the chair of the Privacy and Security Research Group of the Internet Research Task Force and as a member of the Internet Architecture Board since 1985. He served on the Secure Systems Study Committee of the National Research Council and on the NRC technical assessment panel for the NIST Computer Systems Laboratory. He was a charter member of the board of directors of the International Association for Cryptologic Research.

Kent is the author of two book chapters and numerous technical papers on network security, and has served as a referee, panelist, and session chair for a number of security conferences. He has lectured on the topic of network security on behalf of government agencies, universities, and private companies throughout the United States, Europe, and Australia. Kent received his BS in mathematics from Loyola University of New Orleans, and his SM, EE, and PhD degrees in computer science from the Massachusetts Institute of Technology. He is a member of the Internet Society, ACM, and Sigma Xi, and appears in *Who's Who in the Northeast* and *Who's Who of Emerging Leaders*.

Boris Kogan received his BS in computer science from Columbia University, New York, in 1983, and his MSE, MA, and PhD, all in computer science, from Princeton University, Princeton, N.J., in 1985, 1986, and 1988, respectively. He is currently with MicroMax Computer Intelligence as the vice president of technology.

Leonard J. LaPadula is a principal engineer in the Information Systems Security Division of the MITRE Corp., Bedford, Mass. He has maintained an interest in computer security since his and D. Elliott Bell's foundational work in 1973 that produced the Bell-LaPadula model of computer security. His current professional interests also include intercomputer networking security, from both policy and implementation points of view.

LaPadula received his BS in mathematics in 1959 from St. Peter's College, his MA in mathematics from Fordham University, and his EE degree in computer science from Northeastern University.

Catherine Meadows works in the Formal Methods Section in the Center for High Assurance Computer Systems at the Naval Research Laboratory. Prior to joining NRL, she was an assistant professor of mathematics at Texas A&M University.

Meadows received a PhD in mathematics from the University of Illinois. Her research interests include database security, the application of formal methods to the analysis of security protocols, and formal models of secure computer systems. She has published more than 40 papers in refereed journals and conference proceedings. She has served as program chair of the Computer Security Foundations Workshop, and is currently program cochair of the IEEE Symposium on Research in Security and Privacy, editor of *ACM SIGSAC Review*, and a member of the editorial board of the *Journal of Computer Security*.

Louanna Notargiacomo has been involved in DBMS security for the last eight years. She currently manages a group performing research in DBMS security for the MITRE Corp. Her research areas include data integrity, MLS distributed and federated data management, and benchmarking MLS DBMSs. Prior to employment at MITRE, Ms. Notargiacomo managed the Secure DBMS Branch at the Unisys McLean Research Center. She was project manager of the Secure Distributed DBMS Project to develop a B3 DBMS. Ms. Notargiacomo was also involved with research in heterogeneous distributed data management while with Unisys and with DBMS product development while at Data General Corp. Ms. Notargiacomo holds a BSE in computer engineering from the University of Michigan, Ann Arbor.

Ingrid M. Olson is a member of the technical staff at the MITRE Corp. in McLean, Va. As part of the Secure Information Technology Department, she is currently involved in developing a concept of operations and architecture for a system that will provide for worldwide collection of open source information, through processing and analysis, to production and dissemination services. She was also involved in supporting the National Security Agency in developing INFOSEC standards and guidelines. Ms. Olson was previously involved in an internal research project developing a generalized framework for access controls. Ms. Olson has a BA in mathematics and music from Hood College, and an MS in computer science from George Washington University.

Ravi Sandhu is associate chairman of the Information and Software Systems Engineering Department at George Mason University, Fairfax, Va. He is also affiliated with the Center for Secure Information Systems at GMU. His principal research and teaching interests are in information systems security, particularly in database management systems, distributed systems, and computer security models. Prior to joining GMU he served on the Computer and Information Science faculty at Ohio State University, Columbus. He has published over 60 refereed technical papers on computer security in journals, books, and conference proceedings, and teaches several graduate-level security courses at GMU. He has served as program cochairman of the First ACM Conference on Computer and Communications Security (1993) and as general chairman of the Seventh IEEE Computer Security Foundations Workshop (1994). He is an editor of the *Journal of Computer Security*. He has been a computer security consultant to several organizations.

Sandhu received his BTech and MTech in electrical engineering from the Indian Institutes of Technology in Bombay and New Delhi respectively, and his MS and PhD in computer science from Rutgers University in New Brunswick, N.J.

Roger R. Schell is a senior development manager in Network Products Engineering at Novell. Previously, he was vice president for engineering at Gemini Computers, Inc., in Monterey, Calif. He brought Gemini from a handful of young engineers in a garage to an engineering organization that is internationally recognized for its excellence in secure computer systems. Under his leadership, they developed a family of commercial off-the-shelf trusted multiprocessing computer hardware and software products used operationally in systems in the US and overseas. Currently, the trusted computing base (TCB) for these products is under formal evaluation for class A1 under the TCSEC and its interpretations.

Before retiring as a colonel in the USAF, Schell was the original deputy director of the DoD (now National) Computer Security Center. Prior to that, he was an associate professor of computer science at the Naval Postgraduate School. His technical contributions include design and full implementation of dynamic reconfiguration for a commercial operating system and origination of several key modern security design and evaluation techniques, including the concepts for security kernels, TCB partitions, and TCB subsets. He received a BSEE from Montana State College, an MSEE from Washington State University, and a PhD in computer science from the Massachusetts Institute of Technology.

Clark Weissman is an independent INFOSEC consultant to industry and government. He has worked in the aerospace industry for 38 years as an aeronautical, electronics, and computer engineer, mostly in software systems. He has pioneered in the fields of list processing languages (Lisp), operating systems, time-sharing, networking, database systems, and computer and network security (INFOSEC), and has won numerous honors, including three "best paper" awards in time-sharing, computer, and network security from the ACM, AFIPS, and IEEE professional societies. He received a BS in aeronautical engineering from MIT in 1956. He was chief technologist and division manager for 35 years with System Development Corp. (SDC), Burroughs, and Unisys. He is married to Elaine Weissman, executive director of a nonprofit music society. They have six children and two grandchildren, and live in Tarzana, Calif., a suburb of Los Angeles.

James Williams is a lead scientist in the Security Technology and Engineering Department at the MITRE Corp. He is currently working on security profiles for networks and on new, more cost-effective approaches to trusted product evaluation. Williams is principal author of the NSA-sponsored Security Modeling Guideline and has participated in the development of formal security models of integrity and confidentiality. He has extensive experience with automated deduction and its use in the formal verification of high-assurance computing systems. Williams joined MITRE in June 1979 after postgraduate study in computer science at the University of Texas, after becoming an associate professor of mathematics at Bowling Green State University. He received his PhD in topology from the University of California at Berkeley in 1971 and his BA from Carleton College in 1966.

CARPENTRY

CARPENTRY

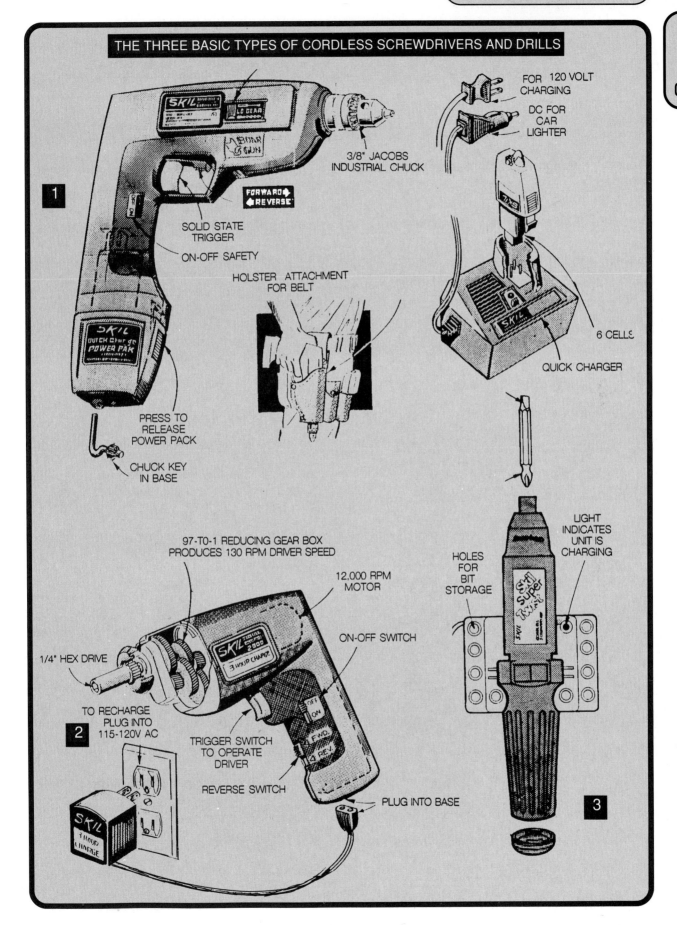

THE THREE BASIC TYPES OF CORDLESS SCREWDRIVERS AND DRILLS

STATIONARY POWER TOOLS
THE TABLE SAW

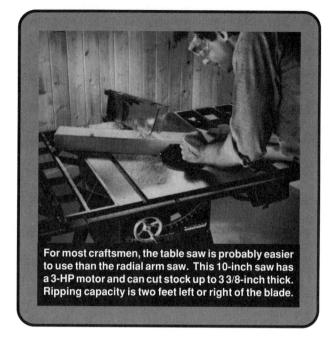

For most craftsmen, the table saw is probably easier to use than the radial arm saw. This 10-inch saw has a 3-HP motor and can cut stock up to 3 3/8-inch thick. Ripping capacity is two feet left or right of the blade.

The *table* saw, interchangeably referred to as a *bench* saw because it can be mounted on a bench, is usually designated by the diameter of the blade, with the most widely used saws for the homeowner being the 8-inch and 10-inch. Horsepower can vary, with the most powerful 10-inch saws developing 3 HP.

Some saws have a direct motor drive—meaning the motor shaft is extended to accommodate the blade. Both types do the job, but a 10-inch belt drive with the most powerful motor can make the quickest and deepest cuts which are important when the blade is tilted at 45 degrees.

One of the key elements of a good table saw is the size of the table and how it is machined to accommodate both the rip fence which, as the name implies, is used when ripping lumber and plywood and the miter gauge which is always used when making crosscuts. All saws, of course, have a safety guard which slips over the blade as the wood is being cut.

When using the table saw, adjust the height of the blade so it will clear the work being cut about 1/4-inch. At regular intervals before ripping, to make certain the blade is parallel to the fence, raise the blade as high as it will go and move the fence flat against the blade surface. If you note the slightest angle between the blade and the fence adjust the fence with the adjusting screws which are provided for this purpose.

Always use a sharp blade with the correct

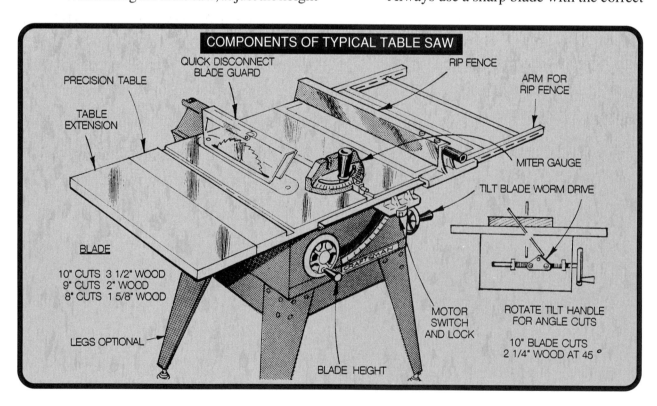

COMPONENTS OF TYPICAL TABLE SAW

PRECISION TABLE
TABLE EXTENSION
QUICK DISCONNECT BLADE GUARD
RIP FENCE
ARM FOR RIP FENCE
MITER GAUGE
TILT BLADE WORM DRIVE
BLADE
10" CUTS 3 1/2" WOOD
9" CUTS 2" WOOD
8" CUTS 1 5/8" WOOD
LEGS OPTIONAL
MOTOR SWITCH AND LOCK
BLADE HEIGHT
ROTATE TILT HANDLE FOR ANGLE CUTS
10" BLADE CUTS 2 1/4" WOOD AT 45°

number of teeth for the wood you are cutting. Carbide tipped blades will outlast regular steel blades by ten or twenty times and they will produce smooth, relatively chip-free cuts. Naturally, a blade with many teeth will make a smoother cut.

Many accessories are available for the table saw, ranging from a dado head, which will cut dadoes, to a table extension, which comes in handy when you are cutting large pieces of stock. Know your tool and keep your fingers away from the blade. Wear safety glasses and do not rush the cut. Let the blade do the work!

Also important is a strong base, preferably fitted with casters so the tool can be moved around when necessary. Investigate other attachments available for cutting and holding wood in place to make using this saw safe, thus ensuring a better cut.

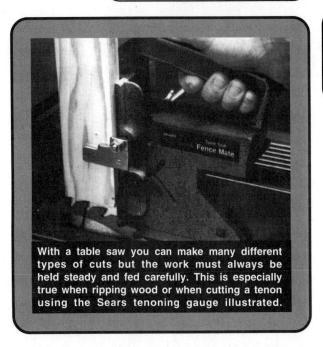

With a table saw you can make many different types of cuts but the work must always be held steady and fed carefully. This is especially true when ripping wood or when cutting a tenon using the Sears tenoning gauge illustrated.

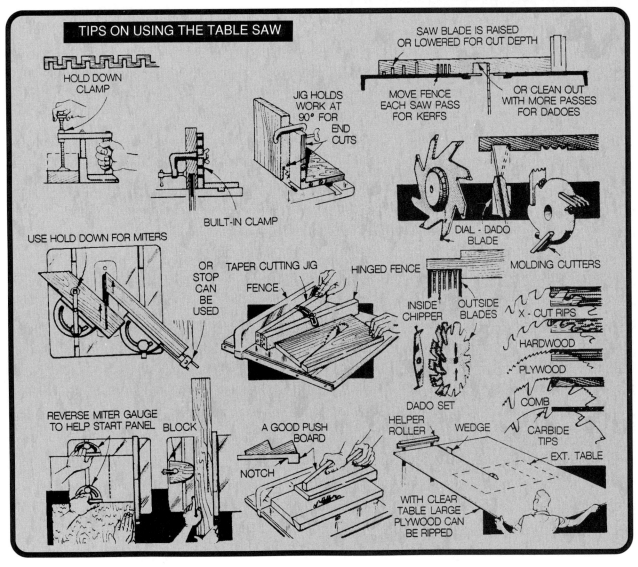

TIPS ON USING THE TABLE SAW

STATIONARY POWER TOOLS: THE RADIAL ARM SAW

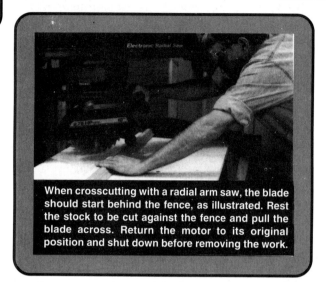

When crosscutting with a radial arm saw, the blade should start behind the fence, as illustrated. Rest the stock to be cut against the fence and pull the blade across. Return the motor to its original position and shut down before removing the work.

Originally developed for industrial use to cut lumber by moving the saw and motor across the work rather than feeding the lumber into the blade (as is the case with a table saw), many manufacturers have improved the the working principle and developed *radial arm* saws with additional features for the home craftsman and builder. For home use the two most popular sizes are the 8-inch and 10-inch versions. With it you can rip lumber and plywood by turning the motor so the blade is parallel with the fence but the prime use is for crosscutting, mitering, dadoing and angle cutting. Some manufacturers produce accessories that can be added for grinding and shap-

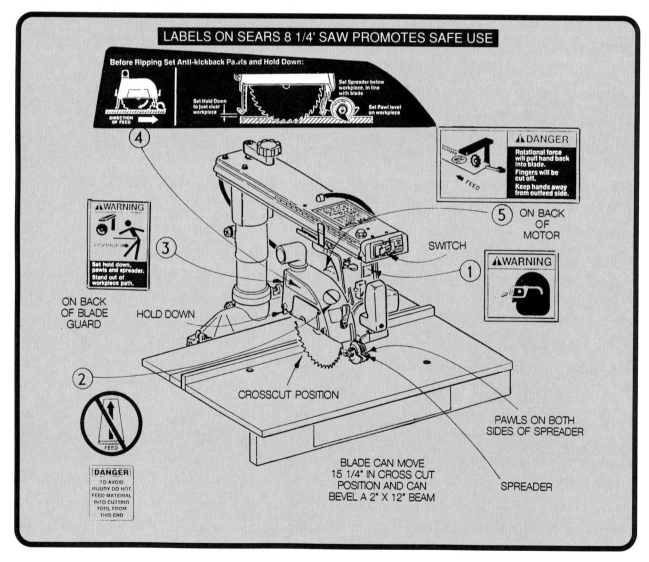

LABELS ON SEARS 8 1/4' SAW PROMOTES SAFE USE

ing; however, these functions are better performed by tools designed especially for the purpose and by portable tools.

Most manufacturers provide excellent manuals that go into great detail on how the tool should be used safely. For instance, when cross-cutting, push the motor as far back of the fence as possible so the work can be rested against the fence. Then make the cut by pulling the handle attached to the motor to draw the blade over the work. After the cut is made, push the motor so the blade is in the original position over the fence. *Then, and only then, remove the work from the table after the blade has stopped turning.*

For ripping, make certain the blade is ab-

solutely parallel with the fence, which is done when the table is first set up to make regular crosscuts. If the blade is not parallel you will not be able to rip accurately. Once the motor is turned and locked in place, and the crank used to lower and raise the blade turned so the blade teeth cut into the table about 1/8-inch, feed the work into the revolving blade from the direction marked on the guard — into the cut, *never* in the same direction as the cut. To prevent kick back, the hold down at the rear of the guard and the spreader that has pawls on either side should be adjusted; the hold down should just clear the work and the spreader should be in line with the cut, while the pawls also just clear the surface.

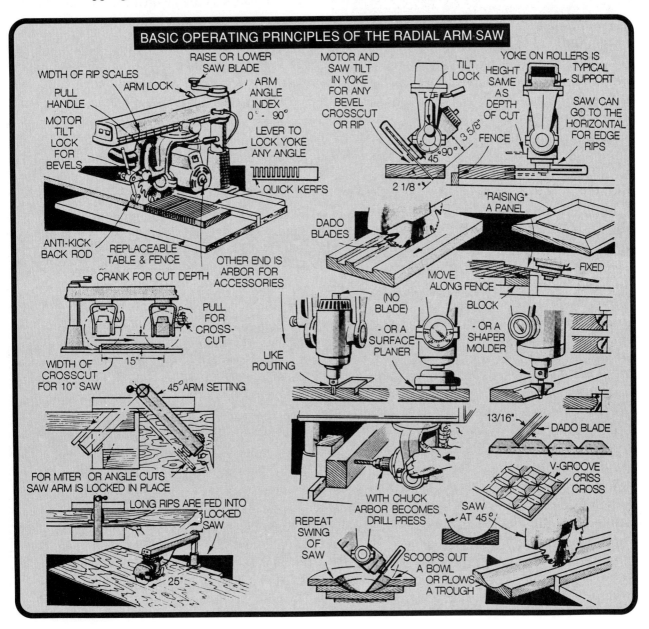

BASIC OPERATING PRINCIPLES OF THE RADIAL ARM SAW

STATIONARY POWER TOOLS) THE MITER SAW

Just as accurate as a miter box, the miter saw can make accurate cuts on all kinds of molding. Baseboard molding should be clamped to a table top and the work held firmly against the fence.

The miter saw — often called a "chop saw" if it cannot be tilted to cut miters — is a relatively new addition to the home workshop, although the principle of a blade driven by a direct drive motor and pulled down to cut lumber first made its appearance in the metal working field as a cut-off saw. The building boom created a contractor market for accurately cutting molding, rather than the "old fashioned" way of using a miter box. The surge of deck building in recent years made it even more popular. It is easier than the radial arm saw to carry to a job site and is less expensive than a radial arm saw. The 8 1/4-inch saw can crosscut stock up to 2x6 inches and the 10-inch model can also cut the popular 2x6 inch decking and bevel it at 45 degrees. Chop saws with a large blade are also available for cutting metal studs.

A newer compound miter saw has a unique sliding carriage arrangement that makes possible cutting 2x12 inch stock.

This 10-inch miter saw is driven by a 3-HP motor and easily cuts 2x6 inch lumber. Work should always be held tight against the rear fence, the motor started & the saw pulled down into the work

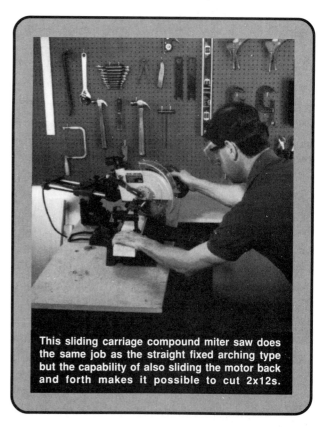

This sliding carriage compound miter saw does the same job as the straight fixed arching type but the capability of also sliding the motor back and forth makes it possible to cut 2x12s.

STATIONARY POWER TOOLS — THE BAND SAW

The band saw is one of the safest power tools in the workshop. It consists of a flexible steel blade resting over large pulleys, and is an ideal tool for cutting curves in wood or plastic, for ripping long boards and for crosscutting, though crosscutting is limited by the distance between the post and the blade. Most band saws can cut wood up to six inches thick and can also cut at an angle by tilting the table to the desired degree. Band saw blades come in various widths. Use a narrow 1/4-inch blade for cutting sharp curves, and wide blades for straight-line cutting. When the blade becomes dull, discard it. New blades are relatively inexpensive.

The band saw is the ideal tool for cutting curves; it can make cuts in wood that are as much as six inches thick. Mark the cut in pencil before starting; cut on waste side.

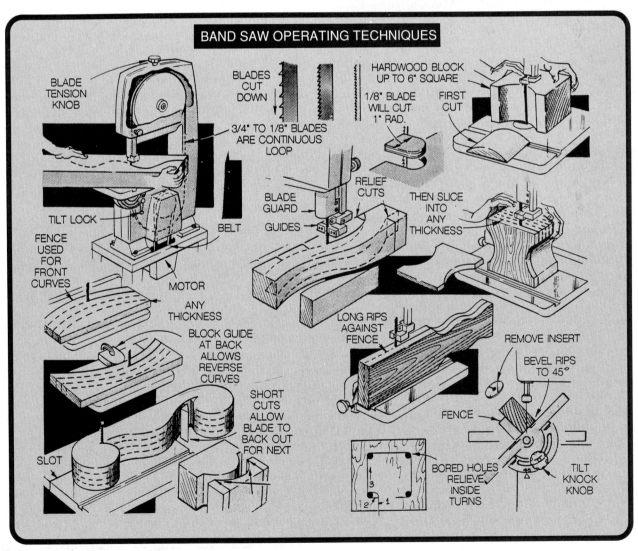

BAND SAW OPERATING TECHNIQUES

BLADE TENSION KNOB

TILT LOCK

FENCE USED FOR FRONT CURVES

BELT

MOTOR

ANY THICKNESS

BLOCK GUIDE AT BACK ALLOWS REVERSE CURVES

SLOT

SHORT CUTS ALLOW BLADE TO BACK OUT FOR NEXT

BLADES CUT DOWN

3/4" TO 1/8" BLADES ARE CONTINUOUS LOOP

BLADE GUARD

GUIDES

RELIEF CUTS

HARDWOOD BLOCK UP TO 6" SQUARE

1/8" BLADE WILL CUT 1" RAD.

FIRST CUT

THEN SLICE INTO ANY THICKNESS

LONG RIPS AGAINST FENCE

BORED HOLES RELIEVE INSIDE TURNS

REMOVE INSERT

BEVEL RIPS TO 45°

FENCE

TILT KNOCK KNOB

THE DRILL PRESS

While the drill press is ideal for accurately drilling holes in wood, it is a must tool if you work with metal. Drill speed is regulated by rearranging the drive belt housed in the cover at the extreme top.

The drill press is used for drilling round holes, but it can also drill square holes with a special mortising attachment consisting of a hollow chisel and drill bit. The drill press can also drill holes at an angle by tilting and locking the drill press table. When using the drill press, always place a block of wood under the work to be drilled. The block of wood will prevent the drill bit from splintering the work as it emerges at the bottom and will also protect the drill press table. Always raise the drill press table as close as you can to the work piece to utilize the full length of the drill bit.

There are many attachments for the drill press: a countersink; a hole saw for large holes; a fly cutter for cutting out discs; a drum sander, files and rasps. Speed can be adjusted to drill at low speed when drilling large holes or holes in thick metal and at higher speeds when drilling small holes in wood and soft metals. Safety tip: *always wear goggles!*

USING THE DRILL PRESS

STATIONARY POWER TOOLS THE SANDER

The combination belt and disc sander performs many sanding functions. The disc part of the sander is usually used for fast stock removal while the belt is employed for fine sanding. Fine to extra coarse grades are available for the belt as well as for the disc but, because the disc cuts across the grain, final finishing should always be done on the belt, with the grain. The table adjacent to the disk can be tilted for sanding miters to an exact 45-degree angle. It also has a miter-gauge slot for trimming work to fit. For sanding awkward or large pieces, the belt assembly can be raised to a vertical position, or to any position in-between. The rounded ends of the belt assembly are especially suitable for sanding interior curves. When sanding with the disc, hold the work so that the action of the disc forces the work against the table—*downward*. When sanding flat on the belt, hold the work at a slight angle.

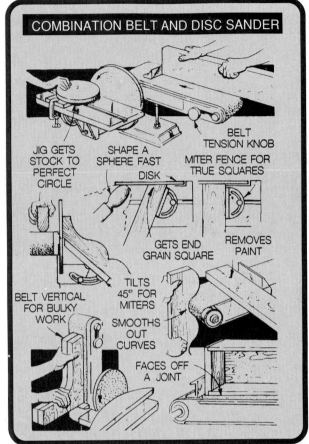

COMBINATION BELT AND DISC SANDER

STATIONARY POWER TOOLS
THE GRINDER

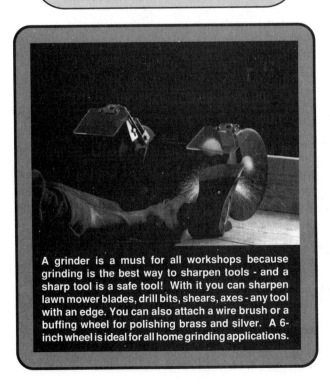

A grinder is a must for all workshops because grinding is the best way to sharpen tools - and a sharp tool is a safe tool! With it you can sharpen lawn mower blades, drill bits, shears, axes - any tool with an edge. You can also attach a wire brush or a buffing wheel for polishing brass and silver. A 6-inch wheel is ideal for all home grinding applications.

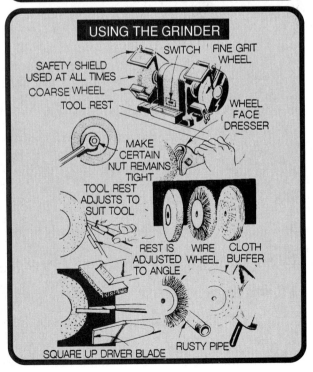

USING THE GRINDER

STATIONARY POWER TOOLS THE JIG SAW

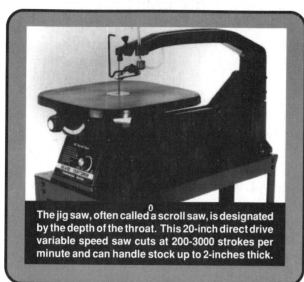

The jig saw, often called a scroll saw, is designated by the depth of the throat. This 20-inch direct drive variable speed saw cuts at 200-3000 strokes per minute and can handle stock up to 2-inches thick.

The jig saw, sometimes called the *scroll saw*, has a blade that moves up and down and is used to cut intricate curves in wood and light metal. Its capacity is determined by the distance from the post to the blade. An important feature of the jig saw is its ability to make internal cuts. This is done by first drilling a pilot hole in the work and then inserting the blade through the hole. The jig saw table can be tilted to make angle cuts in work up to about 2 inches thick. There are many blades available; the narrower the blade the smaller the radius it can cut. The blades are held at top and bottom, secured in a chuck by means of a setscrew. Heavy blades (called saber blades) are secured only at the bottom, as their stiffness does not require a support at the top.

HOW TO USE THE JIG SAW

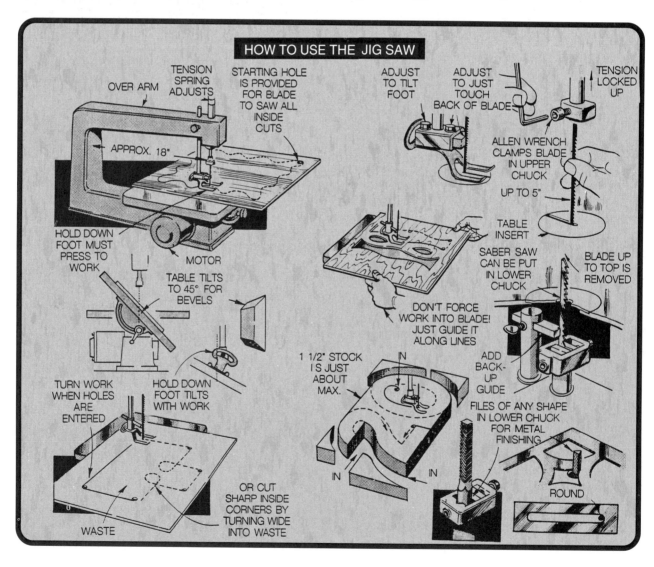

OVER ARM

TENSION SPRING ADJUSTS

STARTING HOLE IS PROVIDED FOR BLADE TO SAW ALL INSIDE CUTS

ADJUST TO TILT FOOT

ADJUST TO JUST TOUCH BACK OF BLADE

TENSION LOCKED UP

APPROX. 18"

ALLEN WRENCH CLAMPS BLADE IN UPPER CHUCK

UP TO 5"

HOLD DOWN FOOT MUST PRESS TO WORK

MOTOR

TABLE TILTS TO 45° FOR BEVELS

TABLE INSERT

SABER SAW CAN BE PUT IN LOWER CHUCK

BLADE UP TO TOP IS REMOVED

DON'T FORCE WORK INTO BLADE! JUST GUIDE IT ALONG LINES

TURN WORK WHEN HOLES ARE ENTERED

HOLD DOWN FOOT TILTS WITH WORK

1 1/2" STOCK IS JUST ABOUT MAX.

IN

IN

IN

ADD BACK-UP GUIDE

FILES OF ANY SHAPE IN LOWER CHUCK FOR METAL FINISHING

ROUND

WASTE

OR CUT SHARP INSIDE CORNERS BY TURNING WIDE INTO WASTE

STATIONARY POWER TOOLS
THE SHAPER

The shaper is a tool used primarily for shaping the edges of wood—scalloping, rabbetting molding—in much the same manner as the router. The major difference is that with the shaper you bring the work to the table and slide it along a fence to make the cut. Like the router, many different shape bits are available for making the most intricate shapes. A specialty tool for the serious woodworker.

Shapers should be mounted on a bench or fitted with wide-tread legs so the tool will not move while the work is being fed into the cutter which revolves anywhere from 9,000 - 20,000 RPM!

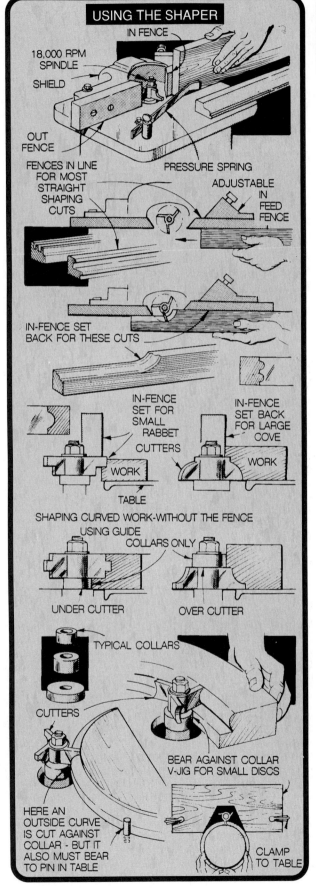

USING THE SHAPER

18,000 RPM SPINDLE

SHIELD

IN FENCE

PRESSURE SPRING

OUT FENCE

FENCES IN LINE FOR MOST STRAIGHT SHAPING CUTS

ADJUSTABLE IN FEED FENCE

IN-FENCE SET BACK FOR THESE CUTS

IN-FENCE SET FOR SMALL RABBET

CUTTERS

IN-FENCE SET BACK FOR LARGE COVE

WORK

WORK

TABLE

SHAPING CURVED WORK-WITHOUT THE FENCE

USING GUIDE COLLARS ONLY

UNDER CUTTER

OVER CUTTER

TYPICAL COLLARS

CUTTERS

BEAR AGAINST COLLAR V-JIG FOR SMALL DISCS

HERE AN OUTSIDE CURVE IS CUT AGAINST COLLAR - BUT IT ALSO MUST BEAR TO PIN IN TABLE

CLAMP TO TABLE

STATIONARY POWER TOOLS THE JOINTER-PLANER

Another specialty tool is the *jointer-planer* which is used primarily to edge lumber so the surface is perfectly flat, although you can also cut a tenon or taper a leg as illustrated in the drawing below. The fence is adjustable for planing at an angle. Jointer-planers are referred to by the width of the cutter which can be either four or six inches. Larger industrial models are also available.

This six inch Sears jointer planer is driven by a 2 HP motor which is necessary for making wide cuts. Like the shaper, mount the tool on a sturdy base

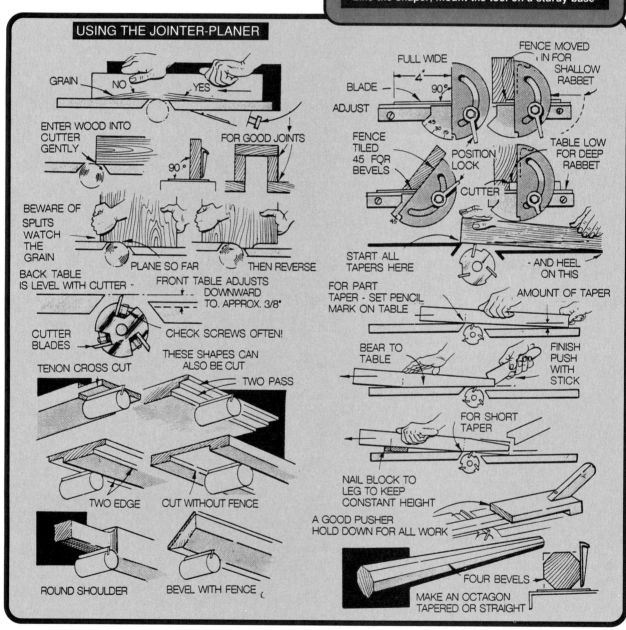

USING THE JOINTER-PLANER

STATIONARY POWER TOOLS) THE LATHE

The *lathe* is certainly one of the most fascinating tools you can own because with it you can transform blocks of wood into candle sticks, circular legs, bowls — any item that is circular.

This is a true craftsman's tool that requires extreme expertise, which can only be developed by working with the tool. Imagination and time are the two major ingredients you will need!

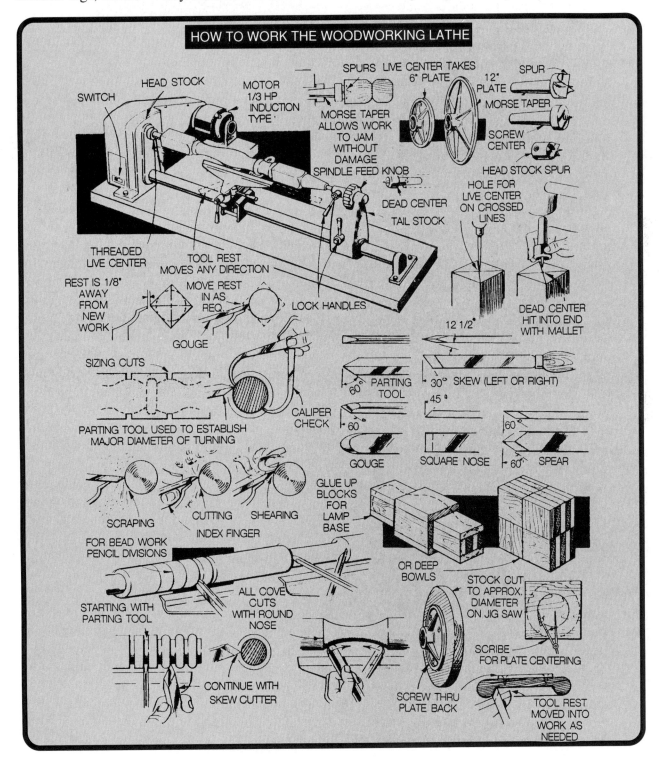

HOW TO WORK THE WOODWORKING LATHE

Automatic machinery, conveyor belts and skilled operators — plus a nearby log site — are the key ingredients to producing lumber and plywood. At this western pine sawmill boards are sorted by length. Most mills run 24 hours a day and nothing is wasted; even the sawdust is used for either heating or to make other products.

LUMBER AND PLYWOOD

Lumber and plywood are the prime building materials for houses and furniture. Here is data on how both are milled and how they are graded.

The wood you buy from a lumber yard or home center is usually available in two broad classifications: *select* and *common*. *Select* is used when appearance and finish are important and this category is in turn divided into four grades. The best is *B grade*, sometimes called *No. 1 clear*; next is *Better grade,* or *No. 2 clear*. Both grades are devoid of imperfections, except for minute ones which are scarcely visible in No. 1 clear. *C select grade* has minor imperfections such as small knots; *D select grade* may have larger knots and imperfections which can be concealed by painting. Idaho white pine bears the classifications: *Supreme, Choice* and *Quality*.

Common lumber has five classifications: *No. 1* contains tight knots, few blemishes, can be stained or painted; *No. 2* has somewhat larger knots and blemishes and is often used for flooring and paneling; *No. 3* has some loose knots and may have some pitch blemishes, though it is still suitable for shelving; *No. 4* is of low quality, used for crating, bracing, etc. *No. 5* is akin to firewood in quality, with large holes, cracks and rough surfaces and sides.

When you buy wood, you pay for it by the *board foot*. A board foot is the amount of wood in a piece of lumber that is one foot long, one foot wide, and one inch thick. As an example, if you

This is a sawmill planer machining a decorative edge on a length of sanded stock. The same machine had already cut the tongue and groove along the opposite edge.

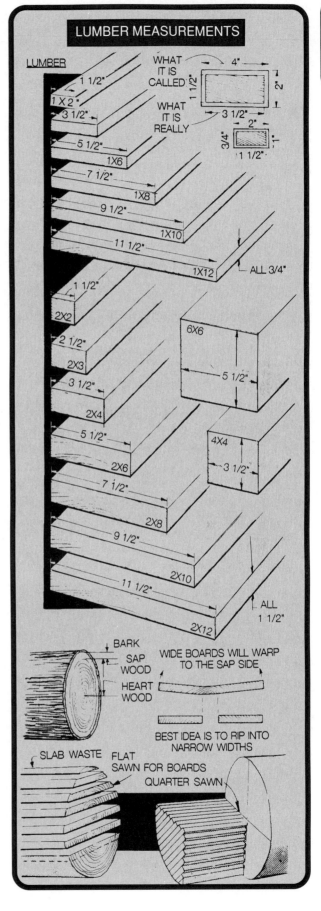

LUMBER MEASUREMENTS

buy a piece of lumber that is ten feet long, two inches thick, and one foot wide, you pay for 20 board feet. To calculate the number of board feet in a piece of lumber, multiply the length in feet by the nominal thickness and the width in inches and divide by 12 as follows:

$$\frac{10 \text{ feet } \times 2" \times 12"}{12} = 20 \text{ board feet}$$

We must caution about lumber sizes. You are no doubt aware that a 2x4 does not measure an exact two by four inches. A ruler will tell you that it really is 1 1/2 x 3 1/2 inches, sometimes a bit more and sometimes a bit less, depending upon the mill that supplied the lumber yard. The illustration at the right shows how the actual size of the lumber you buy differs from the nominal size. The length of a board is always as stated, it is not reduced by the cutting and sanding operation.

Lumber, of course, is further classified into *hardwoods* and *softwoods*. The hardwoods,

Plywood starts with a log that moves along a conveyor belt where it is cut to length. Then the length is placed in a lathe where the bark is trimmed.

Logs are sliced much like peeling an apple. The continuous strip is a few inches wider than 8 feet so the panel can be later trimmed to size.

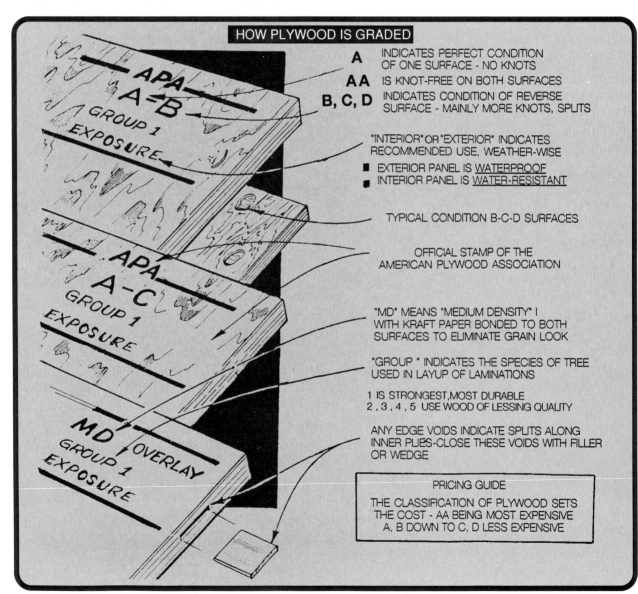

HOW PLYWOOD IS GRADED

A INDICATES PERFECT CONDITION OF ONE SURFACE - NO KNOTS

AA IS KNOT-FREE ON BOTH SURFACES

B, C, D INDICATES CONDITION OF REVERSE SURFACE - MAINLY MORE KNOTS, SPLITS

"INTERIOR" OR "EXTERIOR" INDICATES RECOMMENDED USE, WEATHER-WISE

■ EXTERIOR PANEL IS <u>WATERPROOF</u>
■ INTERIOR PANEL IS <u>WATER-RESISTANT</u>

TYPICAL CONDITION B-C-D SURFACES

OFFICIAL STAMP OF THE AMERICAN PLYWOOD ASSOCIATION

"MD" MEANS "MEDIUM DENSITY" I WITH KRAFT PAPER BONDED TO BOTH SURFACES TO ELIMINATE GRAIN LOOK

"GROUP " INDICATES THE SPECIES OF TREE USED IN LAYUP OF LAMINATIONS

1 IS STRONGEST, MOST DURABLE
2 , 3 , 4 , 5 USE WOOD OF LESSING QUALITY

ANY EDGE VOIDS INDICATE SPLITS ALONG INNER PLIES-CLOSE THESE VOIDS WITH FILLER OR WEDGE

PRICING GUIDE

THE CLASSIFICATION OF PLYWOOD SETS THE COST - AA BEING MOST EXPENSIVE A, B DOWN TO C, D LESS EXPENSIVE

Once cut to length the sheets of veneer are baked in an oven to remove water and bring the moisture down to the desired level. Gluing is next.

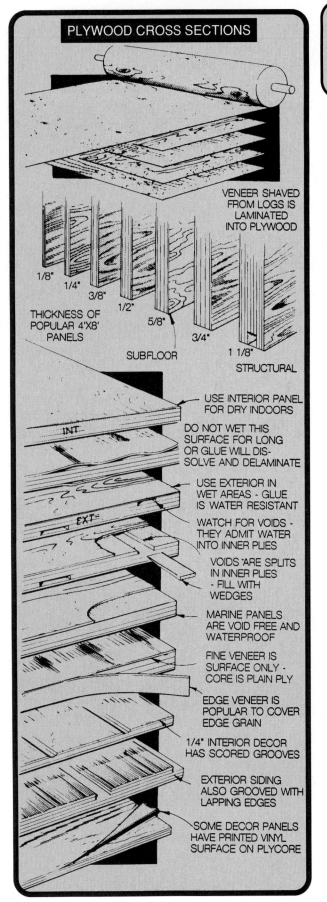

PLYWOOD CROSS SECTIONS

VENEER SHAVED FROM LOGS IS LAMINATED INTO PLYWOOD

1/8" 1/4" 3/8" 1/2" 5/8" 3/4" 1 1/8"

THICKNESS OF POPULAR 4'X8' PANELS

SUBFLOOR

STRUCTURAL

INT

EXT

USE INTERIOR PANEL FOR DRY INDOORS

DO NOT WET THIS SURFACE FOR LONG OR GLUE WILL DIS-SOLVE AND DELAMINATE

USE EXTERIOR IN WET AREAS - GLUE IS WATER RESISTANT

WATCH FOR VOIDS - THEY ADMIT WATER INTO INNER PLIES

VOIDS ARE SPLITS IN INNER PLIES - FILL WITH WEDGES

MARINE PANELS ARE VOID FREE AND WATERPROOF

FINE VENEER IS SURFACE ONLY - CORE IS PLAIN PLY

EDGE VENEER IS POPULAR TO COVER EDGE GRAIN

1/4" INTERIOR DECOR HAS SCORED GROOVES

EXTERIOR SIDING ALSO GROOVED WITH LAPPING EDGES

SOME DECOR PANELS HAVE PRINTED VINYL SURFACE ON PLYCORE

chiefly used for making fine furniture, are walnut, mahogany, oak, maple, cherry, rosewood and teak. The softwoods are pine, spruce, fir, hemlock and redwood.

Don't be afraid of working with hardwoods. Treat them the same as softwoods. As long as your tools are sharp, the technique is the same.

PLYWOOD

Plywood is another matter. The nominal thickness of a sheet of plywood is also its actual thickness. Plywood is made from an odd number of sheets of veneer glued together with the grain of adjacent layers running at right angles. *Lumber core plywood,* used in furniture construction, has a single thick core of solid wood instead of several laminations. The most commonly available plywoods are the softwoods made from pine, fir, and spruce and graded according to the quality of the outside veneers.

Most plywood is graded and stamped by the American Plywood Association. Reproduced is their inspection stamp from which you can determine the type panel. The two large capital letters refer to the grade of the veneer on front and back. *A-A* means that both sides are smooth, suitable for painting or for a less exacting natural finish. *B* would mean that small repair plugs and tight knots are present, while *C* is for a face that has limited splits and somewhat larger knots: *D* indicates similar flaws, but larger than those permitted in the preceding grade.

The *veneer designation Group Number* is listed right below the grade. This indicates the species group and relative strength. *Group 1,* the strongest, includes plywood made of sugar maple, birch, Western larch, loblolly pine, long- and short-leaf pine, and Douglas fir from Washington, California, Oregon, British Columbia and Alberta. *Group 2* plywood is made of Douglas fir from Nevada, Utah and New Mexico, as well as cedar, Western hemlock, black maple, red pine and Sitka spruce. *Group 3* plywood includes Alaska cedar, red alder, jack pine, lodgepole pine, Ponderosa pine, and red, white and black spruce. Aspen, paper birch, Western red cedar, Eastern hemlock, sugar

pine and Engelmann spruce comprise *Group 4.* The last group, *No. 5,* consists of plywood made from balsam and poplar—the weakest of all the woods listed.

The waterproof or water resistant quality of a panel is indicated by the Exposure number. A panel labeled as Exposure 1 is waterproof; a panel with an Exposure 2 number is considered a interior panel.

Soon after the technique of slicing logs to produce *plies (*thin sheets of wood which in turn are glued at right angles to make plywood) was perfected, manufacturers devised a method of utilizing waste wood by grinding it up into uniform pieces, mixing it with a specific resin and then under heat and pressure forming it into a

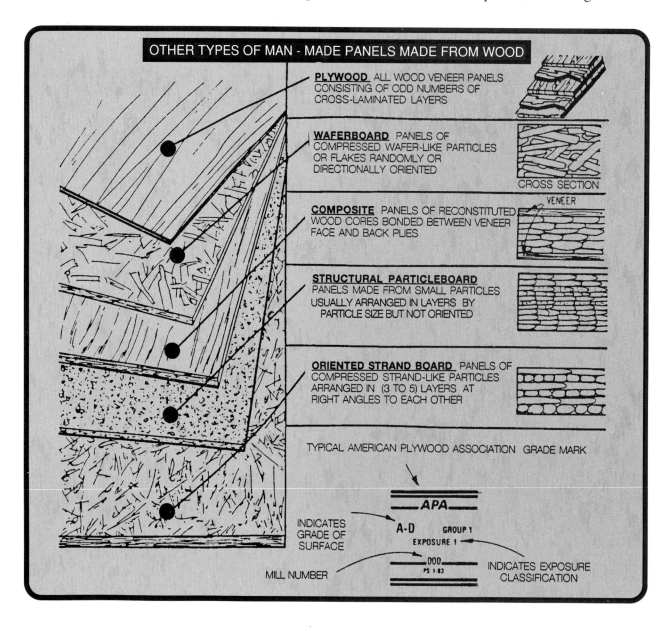

Laying up the plies requires skill because the operator must select the correct ply. Spreading glue is automatic but laying up is by hand.

A batch of glued-up plywood is pressed together and the adhesive allowed to cure. The next step is to trim the edges and sand, if necessary.

standard 4x8 foot or larger sheet in various thicknesses. Here are the manufactured wood panels that are used in both home construction, remodeling and furniture building. These have a price advantage over regular plywood.

Waferboard. Panels are made from compressed waferlike particles randomly oriented, mixed with a resin and made under heat and pressure in special molds. It is widely used for subflooring and sheathing.

Structural Particleboard. Panels are created in a manufacturing process similar to that of producing waferboard except that the layers in the panel are arranged by size but not direction.

Oriented Strand Board. Consists of compressed elongated particles arranged in layers of three to five and set at right angles to each other.

Composite. Panels consist of reconstituted wood core bonded between a veneer or face plies. Composite looks just like regular panels.

MDO Plywood. Regular plywood with both faces covered with a kraft paper which makes finishing easier. The MDO stands for *Medium Density Overlay*.

Manufactured wood panels not only take the place of regular plywood but the fact that they are made from wood particles means many lumber species that grow rapidly, but not to a diameter where they can be sliced for making plywood, can now be made into a panel that is substantially lower in cost.

The trend toward manufactured specialty wood products has also extended toward making certain framing such as floor and ceiling joists, from a combination of plywood and regular 2x4s, or larger stock, to form a wooden I-beam. These are lighter, easier to handle, available in various sizes, and engineered for specific spans. What's more, they are absolutely straight and are the key to building a "squeak-proof" floor.

Lumber yards generally carry plywood in 4x8-foot sheets from 1/4 inch to 3/4 inches thick. Large yards may carry, or can order for you, non-standard sheets 10 feet long and 1 1/4 inches thick. Plywood can be cut, mortised, mitered and finished the same as solid stock wood. Always use a fine-tooth saw to cut plywood and, when using a hand saw, cut with the good side *up* to avoid splintering. When using a portable power saw, have the good side facing down. Pilot holes should always be made in plywood before using screws. Screws do not hold as well in the ends or edges of plywood as they do in the face. Before applying glue to plywood, roughen the edges to give the glue an extra "purchase." Exposed edges of plywood should be covered with molding or a filler strip, or packed with filler to hide the end grain. This does not apply to some imported plywood, made with 11 and 13 layers, that is actually so decorative it is often left exposed.

ALL ABOUT WALL PANELING

Paneling a room is not as easy as painting or applying paper or vinyl wall covering but the advantages of low maintenance and impressive appearance are worth the effort.

PREFINISHED PANELS of wood or wood by-products represent a quick way to produce a beautiful and maintenance-free wall. Panels are available to fit any budget, and the factory-made surfaces do not stop at wood grain patterns; simulated marble, brick, basket weave, tile and even stucco, are just a few of the other surfaces available.

Plywood: The most popular size measures 4x8 feet, although 4x7 and 4x10 footers are available on special order. These panels are laminated from three or more layers of wood, the total thickness of which can range anywhere from 1/8 inch up to 3/4 inch. The more economical panels are 5/32 inch thick and require studs at least 16 inches on center.

Chip or particleboard: This type of panel is made by reducing wood to fine chips, adding a synthetic resin, and then curing under heat and pressure.

The final surface is usually finished with a simulated wood grain and grooved to give the appearance of narrow-width boards. The grooves also make it convenient to conceal nailheads.

Hardboard: This type of panel is factory made from wood pulp and is often referred to as Masonite, the firm that first created the process. In fact, this firm is the leader in the industry and one of the most creative innovators of new patterns. Hardboard is exceedingly tough because of the manner in which it is manufactured and stands up to abuse better than wood.

Solid Panels: Before the development of machines to prefinish paneling, the solid tongue and groove board was the only route to a beautiful and maintenance-free wood-covered wall. While some homeowners still panel with solid boards, this type of wall covering is more expensive than prefinished panels, take longer to install and, once installed, requires finishing.

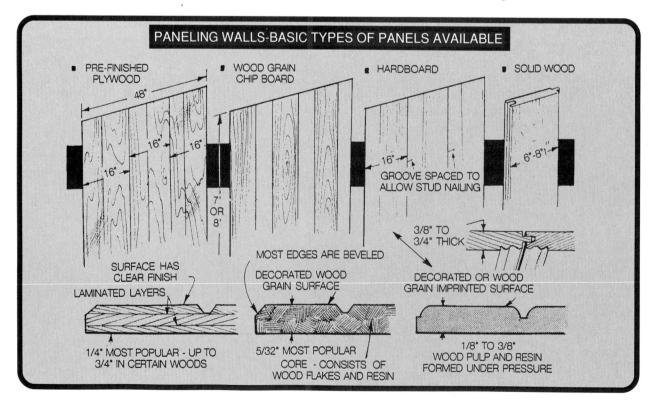

PANELING WALLS-BASIC TYPES OF PANELS AVAILABLE

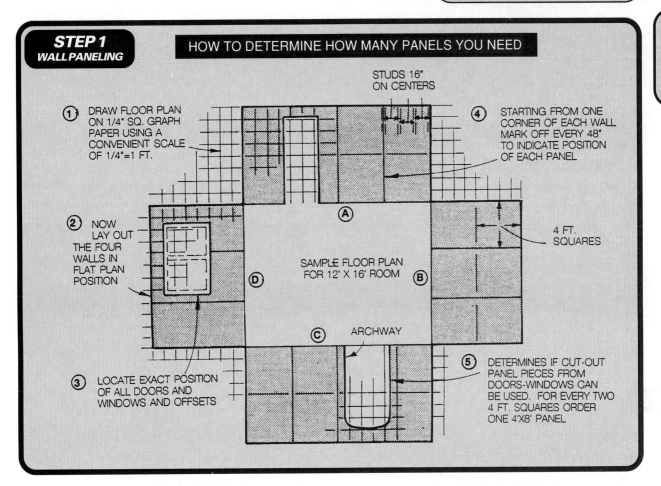

STEP 1
WALL PANELING

HOW TO DETERMINE HOW MANY PANELS YOU NEED

STUDS 16"
ON CENTERS

① DRAW FLOOR PLAN ON 1/4" SQ. GRAPH PAPER USING A CONVENIENT SCALE OF 1/4"=1 FT.

④ STARTING FROM ONE CORNER OF EACH WALL MARK OFF EVERY 48" TO INDICATE POSITION OF EACH PANEL

② NOW LAY OUT THE FOUR WALLS IN FLAT PLAN POSITION

4 FT. SQUARES

Ⓐ

SAMPLE FLOOR PLAN FOR 12' X 16' ROOM

Ⓓ   Ⓑ

Ⓒ   ARCHWAY

③ LOCATE EXACT POSITION OF ALL DOORS AND WINDOWS AND OFFSETS

⑤ DETERMINES IF CUT-OUT PANEL PIECES FROM DOORS-WINDOWS CAN BE USED. FOR EVERY TWO 4 FT. SQUARES ORDER ONE 4'X8' PANEL

CALCULATING just how much prefinished paneling you need for a room can be either simple or complex, depending upon the shape of the room and how you feel about ordering an extra sheet or two "just to be safe." Since 99 percent of all paneling is 48 inches wide, measuring the perimeter of the room and dividing by four will give you the maximum number of sheets required. As an example, if this simple exercise in math calls for, say, 10 1/2 panels, you round it off to 11. Unless, of course, you can utilize some of the "waste" that is left over when paneling around a window or door and get by with 10 sheets.

The best way to accurately determine just how many panels your job requires is to make a floor plan to scale on regular 1/4-inch-square graph paper, or else you can rule your own. Start with your floor plan outline first, and then lay out the wall plan along each of the four sides as shown in the drawing. Measure all your window and door openings and carefully outline them on the wall plan.

Now, starting from one corner, draw a

vertical line every four feet to indicate the coverage of each panel. Since all doors and windows are framed by studs on both sides, in most instances it is possible to cut a piece of "scrap" left over from a window and fit it above the door, rather than run a panel around the top. By working with an exact plan you can literally pinpoint the location of each panel and the various "scraps" so you can keep track of what goes where!

Some paneling scrap requires ingenuity to find a use, especially a narrow strip that runs the full length of the panel. But if your room requires a ceiling molding (most do, unless you have a suspended ceiling), 2-inch-wide strips ripped down from such leftover paneling make a good molding. The panel must be at least 1/4-inch thick. With a radial arm or bench saw, bevel the strips at 45 degrees and nail them at this 45-degree angle between the top of the panels and the ceiling.

If you also plan to install a new ceiling, either suspended or with individual tiles stapled to furring strips, the floor plan will come in handy when ordering your material.

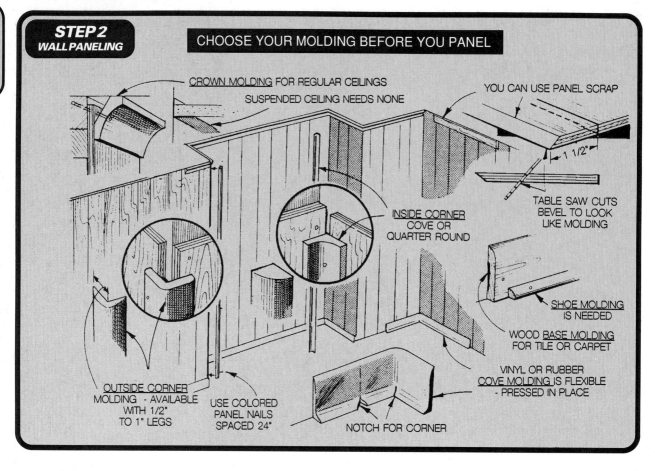

STEP 2
WALL PANELING

CHOOSE YOUR MOLDING BEFORE YOU PANEL

CROWN MOLDING FOR REGULAR CEILINGS
SUSPENDED CEILING NEEDS NONE

YOU CAN USE PANEL SCRAP

1 1/2"

TABLE SAW CUTS
BEVEL TO LOOK
LIKE MOLDING

INSIDE CORNER
COVE OR
QUARTER ROUND

SHOE MOLDING
IS NEEDED

WOOD BASE MOLDING
FOR TILE OR CARPET

VINYL OR RUBBER
COVE MOLDING IS FLEXIBLE
- PRESSED IN PLACE

OUTSIDE CORNER
MOLDING - AVAILABLE
WITH 1/2"
TO 1" LEGS

USE COLORED
PANEL NAILS
SPACED 24"

NOTCH FOR CORNER

IF YOU ARE PANELING a single wall or a complete room, before you cut your first panel examine the various types and sizes of molding available for ceiling, base, outside or inside corner use. Molding is used to cover the unsightly gaps, so the trick in paneling a room is to keep these gaps within the dimension of the molding.

Molding comes in various sizes, with the rule of thumb being the larger the molding the higher the cost. Since you obviously are interested in saving money, calculate how many feet of ceiling baseboard and corner molding you need and then compare the total cost of the smaller sections vs. the larger cross sections. Compare the total cost of wide baseboard molding against narrow baseboard molding and you will note the narrow strips can save up to 50 percent!

With a wood-paneled wall and a regular gypsum ceiling, the easiest way to blend the wall into the ceiling is to span the crack with a piece of 1 1/2-inch ceiling or crown molding. Another way to achieve the same effect and save quite a few dollars is to cut your own molding by ripping

down a piece of flat paneling, as shown, nailing it at a 45 degree angle. A bench or radial arm saw is an absolute necessity for cutting your strips if you are to maintain that exact 45-degree angle on both edges. Incidentally, 1/4-inch plywood is just about the thinnest you can use for ripping your own molding. Like crown molding, baseboard molding is essentially priced by the foot (or length) and is available in longer lengths to eliminate butt joints along a wall. Two-inch-wide base molding costs a third less than 3-inch — the two most widely used of the stock prefinished sizes — although an unfinished pine molding comes in numerous widths and shapes. And for a room with a tile floor, consider using rubber or vinyl cove molding that is glued to the wall and forms a curved joint that makes mopping easy. Inside and outside corner molding, plus a divider cap that is used to cover an unsightly butt joint, rounds out the selection of molding that adds that touch of perfection to all paneling jobs. Remember, even the pros rely on molding to hide those glaring corner, base or ceiling gaps.

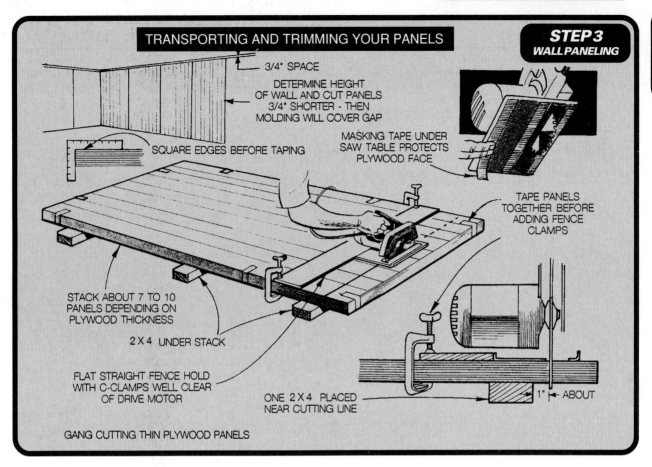

TRANSPORTING AND TRIMMING YOUR PANELS

STEP 3
WALL PANELING

3/4" SPACE

DETERMINE HEIGHT
OF WALL AND CUT PANELS
3/4" SHORTER - THEN
MOLDING WILL COVER GAP

SQUARE EDGES BEFORE TAPING

MASKING TAPE UNDER
SAW TABLE PROTECTS
PLYWOOD FACE

TAPE PANELS
TOGETHER BEFORE
ADDING FENCE
CLAMPS

STACK ABOUT 7 TO 10
PANELS DEPENDING ON
PLYWOOD THICKNESS

2 X 4 UNDER STACK

FLAT STRAIGHT FENCE HOLD
WITH C-CLAMPS WELL CLEAR
OF DRIVE MOTOR

ONE 2 X 4 PLACED
NEAR CUTTING LINE

1" ABOUT

GANG CUTTING THIN PLYWOOD PANELS

Most PREFINISHED panels sold today are picked up at the lumber yard or home center on either car top carriers or roped to the car roof. We have found the best way to transport up to 10 panels is to first tape them together at the corners with masking tape. This makes it easier to tie down and prevents shifting .

The majority of the prefinished—and most economical— wall panels are only 5/32-inch thick, making them quite flexible to handle and cut. If you must trim your panels, rather than cut each panel to length separately, the best way is to decide on an average length for all panels, allowing space at the top and the bottom of the framing, and cut them all at one time. The top gap will be covered by your ceiling wall angle (if you plan to use a hung ceiling) and the bottom gap by the usual baseboard. It is always better to work with a slightly shorter panel because the top and bottom spaces are covered eventually by molding. If your base and top frame is 2" x 4", you can be as short as l inch from the top and the bottom and still find enough framing lumber to nail and glue the paneling. A 3/4-inch gap is ideal.

Unless you can use the standard 4x7 or 4x8 foot panels, once you have decided on how much you must trim off, rest the stack of panels on three 2x4's with the face down and clamp a straight piece of plywood at least 1/2-inch thick to the end to act as a ripping fence. Apply pressure against the fence and push the saw slowly along. When gang cutting in this manner always make certain you use a sharp blade, preferably a plywood blade with small teeth. If you detect the slightest bit of smoke when cutting, you know that either the blade is not sharp or you are forcing the cut.

Also, since the base of a portable saw is metal, in the course of regular use the bottom surface plate may become nicked and burred. Burrs are acceptable when cutting framing lumber, but with prefinished surfaces they can produce deep permanent scratches. One way to prevent this from happening is to apply three strips of masking tape to the bottom of the saw base, as shown. The tape can be built up so it is higher than the burr and since it is also softer than the paneling face it will not scratch the surface! Of course, if you cut the panel with its face down this will not happen.

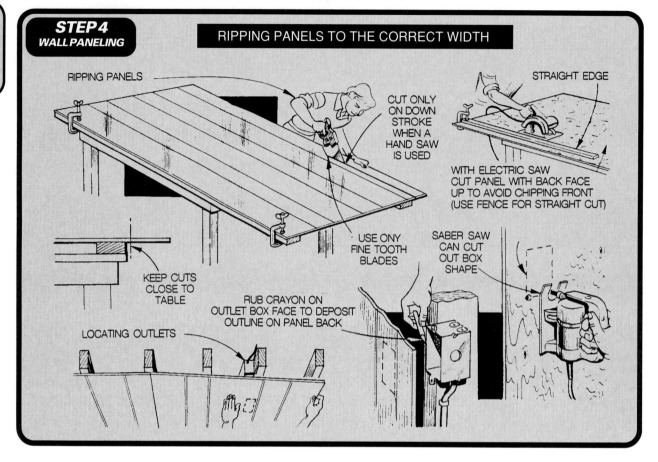

STEP 4
WALL PANELING

RIPPING PANELS TO THE CORRECT WIDTH

RIPPING PANELS

CUT ONLY ON DOWN STROKE WHEN A HAND SAW IS USED

STRAIGHT EDGE

WITH ELECTRIC SAW CUT PANEL WITH BACK FACE UP TO AVOID CHIPPING FRONT (USE FENCE FOR STRAIGHT CUT)

KEEP CUTS CLOSE TO TABLE

USE ONY FINE TOOTH BLADES

SABER SAW CAN CUT OUT BOX SHAPE

RUB CRAYON ON OUTLET BOX FACE TO DEPOSIT OUTLINE ON PANEL BACK

LOCATING OUTLETS

THE MOST DIFFICULT chore in paneling is accurately cutting out holes for outlets and switches. Panels should be about 3/4-inch shorter than the ceiling height, and if you must trim a sheet at the bottom, the cut need not be absolutely straight. A variation of 1/4 inch or so will not make any difference because the base or the top is usually covered with trim. Also, a section of paneling that must be cut vertically to fit a corner can have such a variation because corner molding will cover up the gap and produce a finished look. Mark off a pencil line (or snap a chalk line) and follow it freehand with an electric saw or even a hand saw. In fact, the latter is often easier to use because most panels are very flexible, which makes cutting difficult.

However, ripping a panel to an exact width, or cutting out holes to accommodate electric or duct outlets, requires some finesse because a mistake of l/4-inch can easily ruin the panel. A bench or radial arm saw set up for ripping will produce a smooth parallel cut, but in many instances the flexible panel requires two people to hold and feed it into the saw. Feed the panel into the saw slowly and keep constant pressure against the fence, or else the cut will be ragged and uneven.

Clamping a fence to the wood and using a portable electric saw is a much better way to rip a panel, providing the fence is straight and remains flat against the surface. Rest the paneling on a flat surface with only an inch or so extending beyond the cutting line and use a sharp fine-tooth plywood blade to ensure a splinter-free cut. Since the cut of a portable saw starts from the underside, the top usually splinters; therefore, as mentioned previously, transfer the cutting mark to the back side and lay the panel face down while making the cut.

When cutting holes for outlets, the best way is to transfer the outline of the electrical box or register by smearing the edge of the box with crayon or chalk, placing the panel in position against the adjacent panel, and pressing over the outlet so the outlet box outline is accurately transferred to the back. Make these cutouts with a saber saw from either the front or the back because the outlet trim plate of the outlet permits a variation of l/4-inch. A rough edge or any splintering will be concealed by the wall plate.

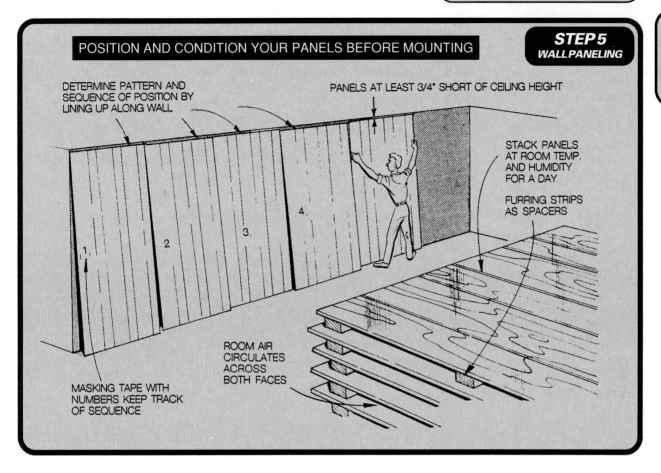

POSITION AND CONDITION YOUR PANELS BEFORE MOUNTING

STEP 5
WALL PANELING

DETERMINE PATTERN AND SEQUENCE OF POSITION BY LINING UP ALONG WALL

PANELS AT LEAST 3/4" SHORT OF CEILING HEIGHT

STACK PANELS AT ROOM TEMP. AND HUMIDITY FOR A DAY

FURRING STRIPS AS SPACERS

ROOM AIR CIRCULATES ACROSS BOTH FACES

MASKING TAPE WITH NUMBERS KEEP TRACK OF SEQUENCE

BEFORE YOU permanently mount a prefinished wall panel you should rest each panel against the wall to note any variation in color or grain, and then stack them in the room to be paneled, with furring strips or other pieces of lumber separating each panel. Exposure to the room temperature and relative humidity for 24 to 48 hours will condition them so the finished wall will show neither signs of buckling caused by expansion nor a noticeable crack between panels because of shrinkage.

Panels faced with real wood (most panels have printed variations in tone and grain) are particularly prone to tone and grain variations because of the natural qualities of wood. If the panels are longer than the floor-to-ceiling height, cut them about 3/4 inch shorter than this measurement and rest them against one wall so you can compare the tone and grain. Move them around so the adjacent panels blend into each other and, once satisfied with tone and grain, mark their sequence with a piece of numbered masking tape.

You may think that most particle and hardboard panels with printed wood grain surfaces are identical because of the quality control in the manufacturing process, but ink densities change; therefore it is a good idea to also prop these panels against the wall to determine the best order of installation.

Solid lumber can have an exceedingly wide range of grain and color fluctuation, and since the boards are only 6 or 8 inches wide, a wild grain or contrasting tone between boards can often prove unattractive. Solid lumber paneling is rarely prefinished (finishing is usually done after all boards are erected), so sand the surface of each board before erecting *and* give it a base coat of sealer. Colors and grain patterns not visible on the unfinished board will literally pop out after the sealer is dry, permitting you to place each board in the most decorative sequence. Also, the sealer will protect the surface from hand smudges during installation. When you do get a smudge, which is usually oil from your hands mixed with dirt, you can sand it out on the finished wall and touch up the spot again before finally finishing the entire wall with shellac, lacquer or one of the everlasting clear urethane coatings.

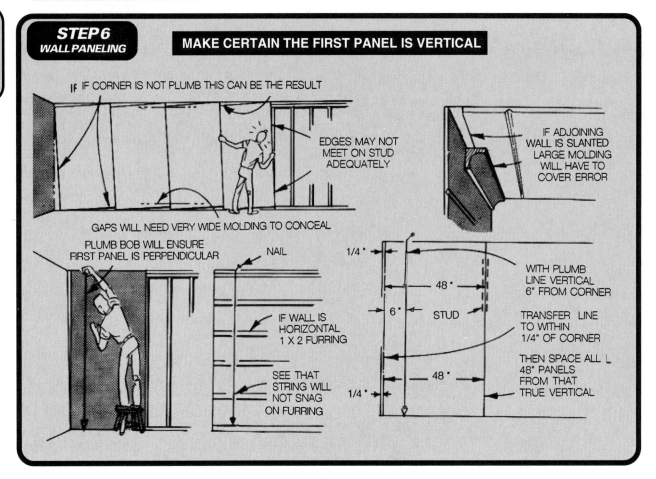

STEP 6
WALL PANELING

MAKE CERTAIN THE FIRST PANEL IS VERTICAL

IF IF CORNER IS NOT PLUMB THIS CAN BE THE RESULT

EDGES MAY NOT MEET ON STUD ADEQUATELY

IF ADJOINING WALL IS SLANTED LARGE MOLDING WILL HAVE TO COVER ERROR

GAPS WILL NEED VERY WIDE MOLDING TO CONCEAL

PLUMB BOB WILL ENSURE FIRST PANEL IS PERPENDICULAR

NAIL

IF WALL IS HORIZONTAL 1 X 2 FURRING

SEE THAT STRING WILL NOT SNAG ON FURRING

1/4"

48"

6" STUD

1/4"

48"

WITH PLUMB LINE VERTICAL 6" FROM CORNER

TRANSFER LINE TO WITHIN 1/4" OF CORNER

THEN SPACE ALL L 48" PANELS FROM THAT TRUE VERTICAL

LAST YEAR MILLIONS of do-it-yourself homeowners paneled either a wall or a complete room, and this popular form of remodeling shows no sign of letting up. The reasons are obvious: a beautiful, nearly maintenance-free wall surface that will last for years and complement just about any type of decorating scheme . . . no painting . . . no mess . . . no fuss! Panels can be a low cost alternative, depending upon the type used.

You need not be an expert craftsman to do a professional paneling job; some care, a few tools, the ability to follow instructions and enthusiasm are all that is required. Aside from a fairly straight (but absolutely plumb) frame, the most important point that will make your job easier is to make certain your first panel is mounted absolutely vertical. A 2 x 4 inch stud or 1 x 2 inch furring strip wall provides only 1 1/2 inches of space for the panels to butt; each panel edge must rest on a 3/4 inch base. If you are 1/2 inch off in 8 feet on your perpendicular line you run the risk of too little nailing or gluing surface!

Most new do-it-yourselfers are inclined to use a level to check that important vertical line, but often the level is inaccurate or is not read accurately. The foolproof way is to use a plumb bob.

Work about 6 inches away from the corner and drive a nail at the top frame. Drop the plumb bob so it barely touches the bottom frame and, when it is absolutely still, mark this point. Transfer both the top nail hole mark and bottom pencil mark to your corner, allowing about 1/4 inch from the adjacent wall. It is equally important that the other edge of the panel be centered on the vertical frame member. The gap in the corner can be hidden by prefinished corner molding to match your paneling.

Once the first panel is straight and secure, the remaining panels will automatically be vertical. You will have a sound wall and a minimum gap at the ceiling and floor, which will be covered with molding. Incidentally, this plumb bob technique is even more important when you are hanging patterned wallpaper. You can be off 1/8 inch with wall paneling, but with patterned wallpaper such an error is easily noticed.

MOUNTING PANELS TO STUDS WITH NAILS AND ADHESIVES

STEP 7
WALL PANELING

ONCE PANEL POSITION IS KNOWN - DRIVE TWO NAILS PART WAY IN TO FIX LOCATION

SPACE BUTT JOINTS WITH DIME FOR EXPANSION

DRIVE IN PILOT NAILS

PRESS PANEL TO STUDS TO CONTACT ADHESIVE BEADS

INTERMITTENT BEAD SAVES ADHESIVE

AFTER PREFIT REMOVE PANEL WITH PILOT NAILS STILL IN PLACE

APPLY ADHESIVE BEADS TO STUDS ONLY

WALLBOARD NAILS AT TOP AND BOTTOM ARE COVERED WITH MOLDING

THE DEVELOPMENT of adhesives now makes it possible to panel a wall without the fear of future nail popping, which was quite common before good adhesives and special nails were available. Annular nails to match the color of your panel grooves have excellent holding power, but a combination of adhesive and nailing produces the best job. This is especially true when the paneling is less than 1/4 inch thick. In such instances the panel thickness in the groove is only about 1/32 inch, which is just not enough to prevent small nail heads from pulling through.

Paneling adhesive is actually a cousin to contact cement; it has a convenient open working time and, more importantly, when the panels are finally positioned, they can be shifted slightly to produce a good joint. The adhesive is gooey to the touch, so the trick is to first prefit each panel on your frame wall; when the panel is in the exact position, drive two locating nails in the corner groove at the top and then remove the panel. Leave the locating nails in the panel so you can find the same holes to reposition the panel after the adhe-

sive has been applied to the studs. Run an intermittent bead of adhesive at 4-inch spurts on the vertical studs; it is not necessary to cover either the base or the ceiling 2x4 with adhesive if you are hanging a ceiling that will cover the top one inch, or if you plan on a baseboard. Regular gypsum board nails placed every four inches at the bottom and top will keep the paneling flat at these nailing points. Once the adhesive is on the surface of the studs, relocate the panel and press it against the stud so some of the adhesive sticks to the back of the panel. Pull the panel slightly away from the wall, using the two top locating nails as a hinge. Allow the adhesive to air dry as recommended by the adhesive manufacturer, and then push the panel in place against the studs. The adhesive will immediately grab but will still be flexible enough to permit whatever shifting that may be necessary to produce a good joint. If you find an area with a slight bulge, tack it down with regular paneling nails that can later be removed after the adhesive has set. Or you can drive the nail flush with the surface in the groove. It will be hardly visible.

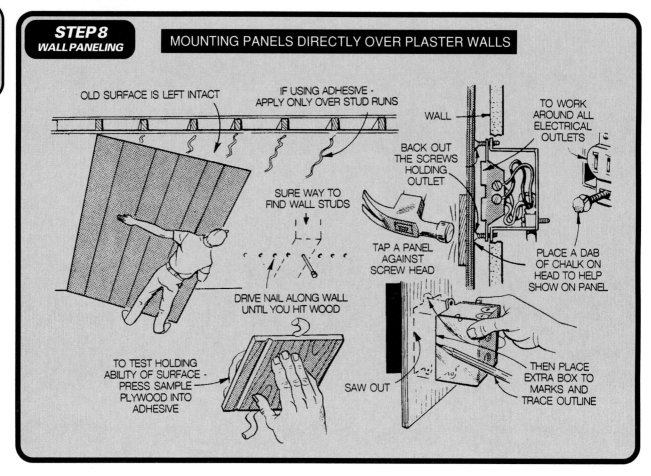

STEP 8
WALL PANELING

MOUNTING PANELS DIRECTLY OVER PLASTER WALLS

OLD SURFACE IS LEFT INTACT

IF USING ADHESIVE - APPLY ONLY OVER STUD RUNS

WALL

TO WORK AROUND ALL ELECTRICAL OUTLETS

BACK OUT THE SCREWS HOLDING OUTLET

SURE WAY TO FIND WALL STUDS

TAP A PANEL AGAINST SCREW HEAD

PLACE A DAB OF CHALK ON HEAD TO HELP SHOW ON PANEL

DRIVE NAIL ALONG WALL UNTIL YOU HIT WOOD

TO TEST HOLDING ABILITY OF SURFACE - PRESS SAMPLE PLYWOOD INTO ADHESIVE

SAW OUT

THEN PLACE EXTRA BOX TO MARKS AND TRACE OUTLINE

CAN YOU PANEL a plaster wall without using furring strips? Of course you can—apply the panels directly to the wall.

Some wall surfaces just won't take adhesive, so it is best to make a test with a small piece of paneling. If it doesn't hold too well after a few days, you may find it necessary to use the regular colored 1 1/4 inch paneling nails exclusively.

For nailing or adhesive mounting you must locate the position of the studs and, while there are simple stud finders on the market, the easiest way is to drive a series of nail holes at either 16 or 24 inches from the corner of the room. Bracket the stud when you hit wood and then repeat the process to see just how far apart your studs are mounted. Many older homes have studs 24 inches on centers, but most dwellings built during the past 35 years have studs every 16 inches.

Remove the base molding, which usually can be reused later. Cut your panels 3/4 inch shorter than the floor-to-ceiling height and work from the corner out. As is the case with all paneling projects, the first panel must be absolutely perpendicular.

When you come to an electrical outlet, transfer the outline of the box to the back of your panel; back off the two screws that hold the receptacle in place and dab the tip of each screw with chalk or anything that will smear. With one edge of the panel resting against the adjacent panel, swing it over the backed-off screws and tap the surface above to get an impression of the screws on the panel back. Using an actual box (or cardboard template), trace the box outline and then cut out the opening with a saber saw. When the panel is finally mounted, tighten the screws so that the heads are just slightly below the surface of the panel; the screw will pull the receptacle tight.

This same procedure can be used to transfer the outline of boxes with push button switches; with toggle switches one must remove the switch completely and replace only the screws for the transfer process. Reconnect the switch after the panel is in place. Naturally, kill the power when doing any electrical work!

MEASURING THE LAST CORNER PANEL FOR A PERFECT FIT

STEP 9
WALL PANELING

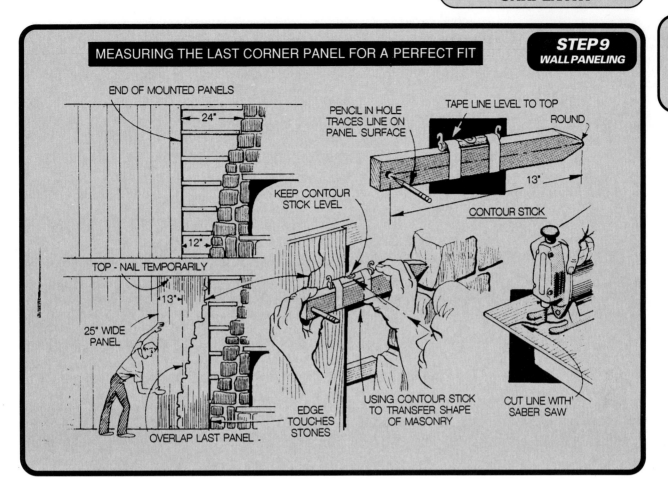

END OF MOUNTED PANELS

24"

12"

TOP - NAIL TEMPORARILY

13"

25" WIDE PANEL

OVERLAP LAST PANEL

EDGE TOUCHES STONES

KEEP CONTOUR STICK LEVEL

PENCIL IN HOLE TRACES LINE ON PANEL SURFACE

USING CONTOUR STICK TO TRANSFER SHAPE OF MASONRY

TAPE LINE LEVEL TO TOP

ROUND

13"

CONTOUR STICK

CUT LINE WITH SABER SAW

WHEN PANELING a room the job progresses very rapidly after the studs or furring strips are in place to accommodate the paneling, However, when you come to butting a panel against an irregular surface—such as a stone or brick wall—you must resort to a simple yet time-consuming technique to transfer the irregular wall contour to the plywood.

To illustrate the basic principle of marking a line for a perfect fit, the drawing shows a stone fireplace that is tapered so the bottom measurement is 12 inches from the center of the nearest vertical stud and 24 inches at the top. We want to cut a panel that will fit this area so this panel will hug the masonry wall with no more than 1/16-inch clearance.

First, rip panel about one inch wider than the 24-inch dimension and nail it temporarily at top and bottom over the area to be paneled so the bottom touches the masonry. The panel must be exactly parallel with the panels that already are in place. In this case, the best way is to mark both top and bottom of the adjacent panel 13 inches from the center of the stud, as shown. In fact, drive a nail at the top and bottom where marked and butt the panel against the nails.

Next, make a contour transfer stick by drilling a hole in a piece of 1/2 x 1-inch plywood so that the center of the hole is an exact 13 inches from the rounded end. Tape a line level to the top because the transfer stick must be absolutely level when the rounded tip is drawn against the masonry wall while the pencil or felt tip draws a line down the panel. The line drawn will be perfectly parallel with the masonry only if the stick is held horizontally—so keep the bubble centered while marking. After you have drawn the line from top to bottom, remove the panel and cut along the line. You may encounter a little chipping, but to keep this to a minimum use a fine-tooth saber saw blade. We have found a metal-cutting blade does the best job because the teeth are fine. Of course, this technique can also be used to mark corner panels so the joint will be small enough to be covered by a 3/4-inch length of corner molding. The panel will fit the area perfectly!

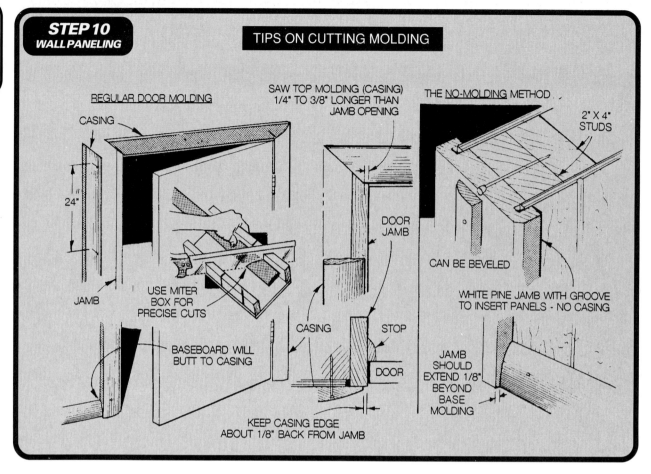

STEP 10
WALL PANELING

TIPS ON CUTTING MOLDING

REGULAR DOOR MOLDING

SAW TOP MOLDING (CASING) 1/4" TO 3/8" LONGER THAN JAMB OPENING

THE NO-MOLDING METHOD

CASING

24"

2" X 4" STUDS

USE MITER BOX FOR PRECISE CUTS

DOOR JAMB

CAN BE BEVELED

JAMB

WHITE PINE JAMB WITH GROOVE TO INSERT PANELS - NO CASING

BASEBOARD WILL BUTT TO CASING

CASING   STOP

DOOR

JAMB SHOULD EXTEND 1/8" BEYOND BASE MOLDING

KEEP CASING EDGE ABOUT 1/8" BACK FROM JAMB

TRIMMING DOORWAYS adds the finishing touch to a paneling project because the molding covers the gaps that always exist where a piece of paneling or gypsum ends. The most common method of trimming a doorway is to use regular casing; miter the top piece first and then fill in the side members. Casing always is slightly thicker than the baseboard molding and is never nailed flush to the door jamb. As shown in the drawing, the edge is kept about 1/8 inch away from the corner; just be sure it is the same on both sides and the top. If the door casing is mounted exactly flush with the edge of the jamb, the top miter must also be perfect—which is not as easy to do as it may appear. So the pros keep that casing edge away from the jamb!

Also, casing is subjected to some hard knocks, so nail it in place with 6- or 8-penny finishing nails driven every 24 inches. Make sure you hit the framing stud and set each nail below the surface. Fill the hole with spackle or wood dough if the trim is to be painted; use a matching color putty stick, if your walls are paneled. Vibration and wood shrinkage can often dislodge casing from the jamb, so it is a good idea to run a bead of white glue along the jamb in addition to nailing.

Some homeowners prefer to use as little molding as possible. One way to trim a door without molding is shown above. Rather than have the door jamb the thickness of the wall, the jamb extends so the baseboard can butt against the projecting lip. One-half inch is usually sufficient. Since it is impractical to butt the adjacent panels to the jamb, cut a groove in the jamb to accommodate the thickness of your paneling. The edge of the panel fits into the groove and provides an adequate margin of error for squaring the doorway or cutting the panels. Door jamb stock is usually 3/4-inch thick, so the groove can be at least 3/8 inch deep. Set up your door jamb first and fit the paneling in place. The extra depth of the groove will compensate for any expansion or contraction. Of course, this type of trimming technique requires more skill and also a bench or radial arm saw. One or two passes with a saw will produce a groove wide enough for the panel.

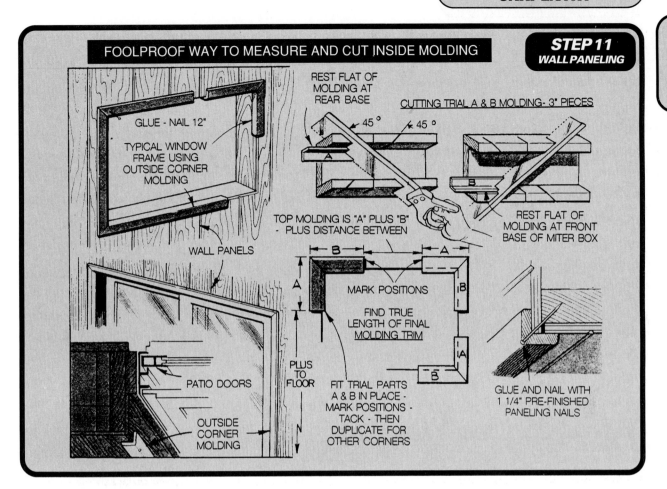

FOOLPROOF WAY TO MEASURE AND CUT INSIDE MOLDING

STEP 11
WALL PANELING

GLUE - NAIL 12"

TYPICAL WINDOW FRAME USING OUTSIDE CORNER MOLDING

WALL PANELS

PATIO DOORS

OUTSIDE CORNER MOLDING

REST FLAT OF MOLDING AT REAR BASE

CUTTING TRIAL A & B MOLDING- 3" PIECES

45°   45°

TOP MOLDING IS "A" PLUS "B" - PLUS DISTANCE BETWEEN

REST FLAT OF MOLDING AT FRONT BASE OF MITER BOX

MARK POSITIONS

FIND TRUE LENGTH OF FINAL MOLDING TRIM

PLUS TO FLOOR

FIT TRIAL PARTS A & B IN PLACE - MARK POSITIONS - TACK - THEN DUPLICATE FOR OTHER CORNERS

GLUE AND NAIL WITH 1 1/4" PRE-FINISHED PANELING NAILS

MOLDING SERVES two very basic and necessary purposes. (A) It permits up to a 1/2 inch working tolerance with the panels to compensate for uneven walls and minor cutting or measuring errors on your part, and (B) it produces a professional touch.

Of the many different types of molding you will use the most difficult to cut and position is the inside corner that frames an opening on three or four sides. For example, when you are trimming the opening for a patio door or interior passageway the mitering sequence can be most confusing. Therefore, here is a foolproof way to produce a perfect fit on the first attempt without the risk of wasting a single length of molding.

A miter box is an absolute necessity, although a radial arm or bench saw can also be used. A back saw is most desirable but with care you can even use a regular crosscut saw. The best way to do the job is to first cut two 3-inch sections of the molding as shown in the drawing. Lay a length of molding flat on the bottom of the miter box with one leg resting against the rear wall, then cut as shown using soft short strokes to prevent the edge from splintering. Once the angle cut is made, make a crosscut so the piece is about 3" long. Label this piece "A." Next reset the length of molding on the front of the miter box and cut the 45 degree angle opposite in direction to the cut made on piece "A." Crosscut this piece 3" from the miter and label it "B." Now fit both pieces in one corner, tacking them in position with a 1 1/4" prefinished paneling nail. Mark off with a sharp pencil where the edges rest and then rearrange the pieces in the opposite corner. Then cut the entire length of your top molding: the miter and length of piece "B", plus the distance between the two pencil marks, plus the length and miter of piece "A." This technique will produce an exact length with the correct miters. The left side molding has the miter and length of piece "A" to which you add the distance from the pencil mark to the floor. The right side has the miter and length of piece "B" to which the distance between the pencil mark and the floor is also added.

This five foot bench is a handy two feet wide. Made from 2x4s and a sheet of 3/4-inch plywood, the top is covered with tempered hardboard smooth side up .

BUILDING A WORKBENCH

Tools are necessary to make repairs and build projects. But a good workbench is also a must.

A good deal of the preparatory work for do-it-yourself projects around the house is done on the workbench. Here is a bench that is easy to build, using standard 2x4s, 3/4-inch plywood and a 1/4-inch hardboard top.

First cut the four 2x4 legs, each 34 inches long. Next cut 2x4s for the upper and lower framework to the lengths indicated in the drawing. Notch each of the four long lengths to accept the crosspieces. The notches, or dadoes, should be about 1/2-inch deep and just wide enough to fit the 2x4 crosspiece. The notch should be about three inches from each end. Next apply some white glue to the inside of the notch and drive the two cross-pieces in the notches. They should fit snugly. Drill pilot holes for 1/4-inch lag screws. Inasmuch as you will be driving the screws into the end grain of the crosspieces, use lag screws at least four inches long to assure a good purchase. Assemble both frameworks. You will now have two oblong frames, 60 inches long and 20 inches wide.

With the upper framework resting on the floor, clamp the legs (using C-clamps) in each corner, then drill clearance holes through legs and frame for 5/16 x 4-inch carriage bolts. Apply white glue where the surfaces will meet, insert the bolts in the holes, add a washer and nut to the end of each and tighten securely. Remove the clamps and gently ease the second frame over the legs so that it is about six inches from the ends of the legs. Clamp it in place, drill clearance holes as before and insert carriage bolts, washers and nuts to finish the lower part of the workbench.

The top is made of two layers of 3/4- inch plywood, glued together and faced with a sheet of 1/4-inch tempered hardboard. Buy a single 4x8 foot panel of B-C grade 3/4-inch plywood. Rip the sheet in half the long way, then cut each piece so that it is 60 inches long. You will now have two 24 x 60-inch pieces of plywood. Coat the top of one piece with a layer of white glue or construction adhesive. Pay special attention to applying the adhesive around the corners and the edges. Carefully place the second panel over the glued panel, line up the edges, and nail the two panels together. Use annular ring nails—they hold better. The nailheads will be hidden by the hardboard top.

Cut a sheet of 1/4-inch hardboard to 24 x 60 inches. Apply white glue to the top side of the glued-up plywood—the side with the nailheads showing. Set the hardboard in place with the good side facing up. This time you will have to use

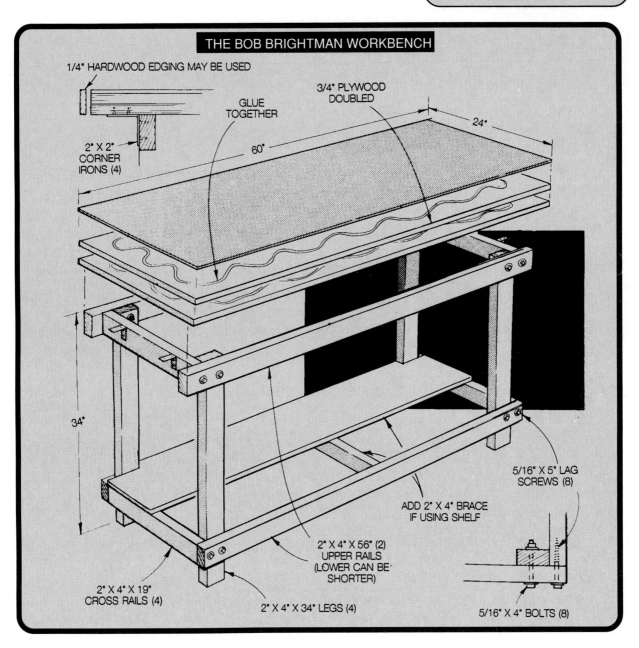

THE BOB BRIGHTMAN WORKBENCH

1/4" HARDWOOD EDGING MAY BE USED

3/4" PLYWOOD DOUBLED

GLUE TOGETHER

24"

60"

2" X 2" CORNER IRONS (4)

34"

5/16" X 5" LAG SCREWS (8)

ADD 2" X 4" BRACE IF USING SHELF

2" X 4" X 56" (2) UPPER RAILS (LOWER CAN BE SHORTER)

2" X 4" X 19" CROSS RAILS (4)

2" X 4" X 34" LEGS (4)

5/16" X 4" BOLTS (8)

clamps or weights to apply pressure if you are using white glue; with construction adhesive it may not be necessary. Do not clamp directly to the hardboard; use scrap wood to spread the pressure and to avoid marking the surface. You won't be able to clamp the center of the workbench top so use weight pressure. A few buckets filled with sand or even water will do. Allow the entire assembly to dry overnight. Remove the clamps and weights and install the laminated top to the workbench framework. Its own weight will help to hold it in place. To prevent shifting, use an angle iron at each leg to secure the top.

MATERIALS REQUIRED

Two	3/4"x24"x60"	plywood (for top)
One	1/4"x24"x60"	tempered hardboard
Four	2"x4"x34"	legs
Four	2"x4"x20"	crosspieces
Four	2"x4"x56"	frame members
Eight	5/16"x4"	lag screws
Eight	5/16"x4"	carriage bolts, nuts
Sixteen	3/8-inch	washers

White glue or construction adhesive

FOUR WAYS TO INSTALL CEILING TILE

Ceiling tile is available in many patterns, but the installation can be broken down into four basic categories. You can (1) staple 12 x 12-inch tiles to furring strips nailed to the ceiling, (2) cement these same tiles directly to existing plaster or gypsum board, (3) hang large 24x48- or 24x24-inch tiles in an exposed metal grid-work, or (4) use a grid system that is concealed with 12x48-inch tile.

Each type method has certain advantages. Cementing individual tile is a good choice if your ceiling is smooth and level. A few cracks do not matter in that they are easily spanned. Adding furring strips (1x2-inch) over an existing plaster ceiling, or directly to ceiling joists if they are exposed, and then stapling the individual tiles in place is even more popular, especially in basement or attic remodeling projects.

If you do not mind cutting down the ceiling height 2-5 inches, suspending a ceiling on metal grids—often referred to as a "hung" ceiling—is the recommended choice from the standpoint of installation ease.

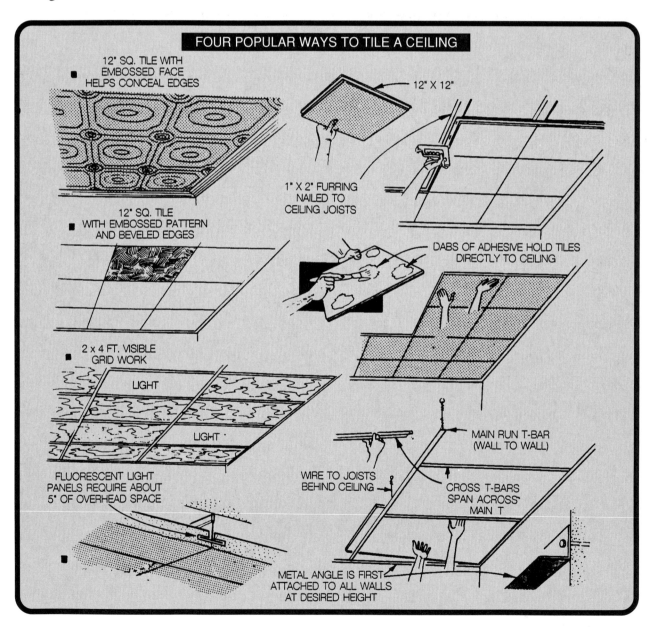

FOUR POPULAR WAYS TO TILE A CEILING

12" SQ. TILE WITH EMBOSSED FACE HELPS CONCEAL EDGES

12" X 12"

1" X 2" FURRING NAILED TO CEILING JOISTS

12" SQ. TILE WITH EMBOSSED PATTERN AND BEVELED EDGES

DABS OF ADHESIVE HOLD TILES DIRECTLY TO CEILING

2 x 4 FT. VISIBLE GRID WORK

LIGHT

LIGHT

FLUORESCENT LIGHT PANELS REQUIRE ABOUT 5" OF OVERHEAD SPACE

WIRE TO JOISTS BEHIND CEILING

MAIN RUN T-BAR (WALL TO WALL)

CROSS T-BARS SPAN ACROSS MAIN T

METAL ANGLE IS FIRST ATTACHED TO ALL WALLS AT DESIRED HEIGHT

3 WAYS TO ARRANGE CEILING TILE

Despite the fact that suspended ceilings are extremely easy to install, are low in cost and give the homeowner the ability to easily add fluorescent fixtures, tile stapled or glued in place is still widely used for certain rooms, especially if you do not wish to lose any ceiling height.

Tile can be installed as either straight, staggered or diagonal squares. The choice is yours, but you should know that, of the three, the staggered square arrangement is easiest to install because any error that creeps in along one edge is not noticeable. If you have straight squares you must be extremely careful to make certain the corners always meet. With all types of tile arrangement, the furring strips must be an exact 12 inches between centers. Remember, you have only 3/4-inches for stapling when lx2s are used.

Diagonal squares may have certain appeal, but they complicate the furring problem and also result in waste along the edge. If you have a smooth ceiling use adhesive for setting diagonal squares in place.

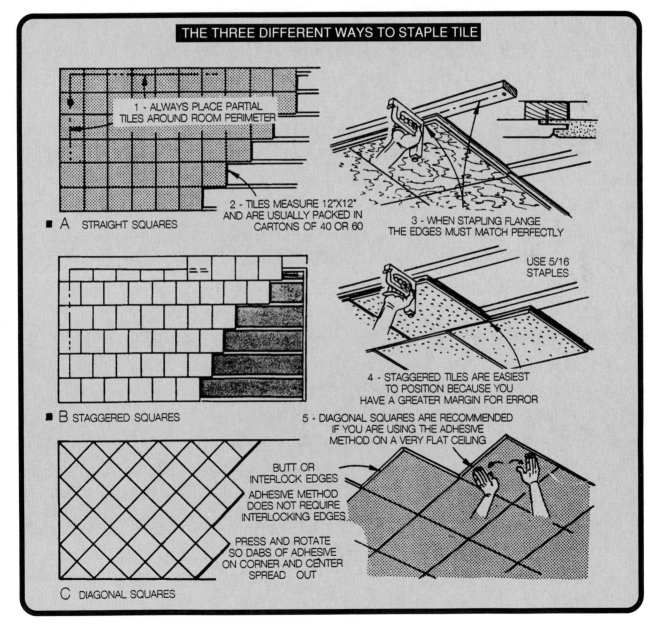

THE THREE DIFFERENT WAYS TO STAPLE TILE

1 - ALWAYS PLACE PARTIAL TILES AROUND ROOM PERIMETER

2 - TILES MEASURE 12"X12" AND ARE USUALLY PACKED IN CARTONS OF 40 OR 60

A STRAIGHT SQUARES

3 - WHEN STAPLING FLANGE THE EDGES MUST MATCH PERFECTLY

USE 5/16 STAPLES

4 - STAGGERED TILES ARE EASIEST TO POSITION BECAUSE YOU HAVE A GREATER MARGIN FOR ERROR

B STAGGERED SQUARES

5 - DIAGONAL SQUARES ARE RECOMMENDED IF YOU ARE USING THE ADHESIVE METHOD ON A VERY FLAT CEILING

BUTT OR INTERLOCK EDGES

ADHESIVE METHOD DOES NOT REQUIRE INTERLOCKING EDGES

PRESS AND ROTATE SO DABS OF ADHESIVE ON CORNER AND CENTER SPREAD OUT

C DIAGONAL SQUARES

HOW TO WORK WITH WALLBOARD

Gypsum wallboard — often referred to as "Sheetrock", the name United States Gypsum (USG) bestowed upon the product when they invented the manufacturing process over 70 years ago, is the most widely used wall and ceiling covering material in home building and remodeling. It is a factory fabricated panel composed of a fireproof gypsum core, encased in a heavy manila paper on the face side, and a strong liner paper on the back side. It is provides a smooth unbroken surface, is relatively easy to work with and is by far more economical than the wet plaster system it replaced.

Many different types of gypsum panels are available, some with beautiful wood grained paper faces and others with wallpaper designs. Some panels have an aluminum foil backing which serves as an excellent vapor barrier when attached to wall or ceiling framing Even exterior grade panels are available for use as sheathing in home building.

Before adhesives were developed all ceramic tile was set in a bed of mortar, which requires a great deal of experience. However, when ceramic tile adhesive was invented over 50 years ago and tile became available to the homeowner (before that time tile was distributed strictly through contractors) often when the tile was glued to the regular wallboard water seeped through the grouting and the gypsum board would soon collapse. This in turn created the "green" or "blue" tile board which had a water resistant paper coating instead of the regular coating. But even this water-resistant panel did not perform too well—all of which gave way to the Portland cement base panel that is now the product of choice when working with ceramic tile. Many manufacturers produce a tile board; USG calls theirs Duroc.

Gypsum panels come in many thicknesses, with the 4x8 foot, 1/2-inch panel, being the most popular, although some builders use 3/8-inch thick panels on the ceiling. Other builders use a 3/8-inch double layer, the first layer screwed to the studs and the second layer mounted over the first with adhesive. Wallboard cuts easily with a utility knife and is best mounted on walls and ceilings with drywall screws, rather than annular nails. Screws — 1 1/4 inch long for half-inch boards — do a much better job than nails, especially when driven by a drywall screw gun. When drywall was first introduced you had to mix your joint compound; now the ready mixed gypsum compound is not only better but easier to use. The illustrations show various working techniques which anyone can easily master.

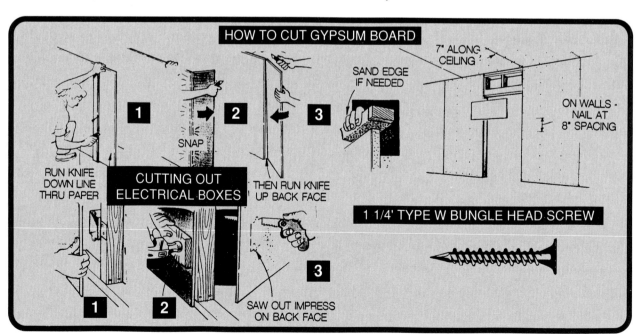

DRYWALLS TOOLS AND TECHNIQUES

DRYWALLS TOOLS

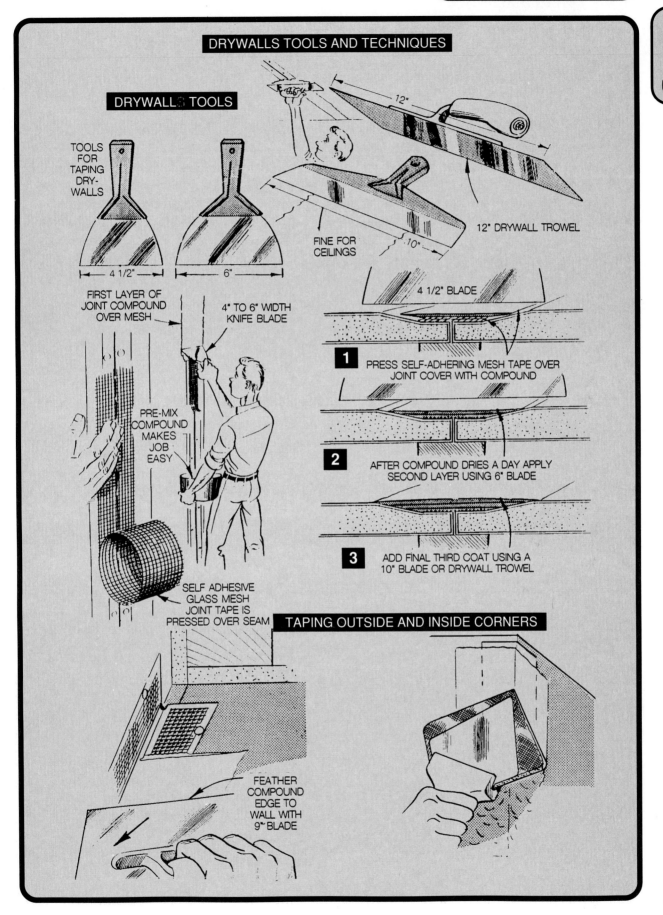

TOOLS FOR TAPING DRYWALLS

4 1/2"

6"

12"

FINE FOR CEILINGS

10"

12" DRYWALL TROWEL

FIRST LAYER OF JOINT COMPOUND OVER MESH

4" TO 6" WIDTH KNIFE BLADE

PRE-MIX COMPOUND MAKES JOB EASY

SELF ADHESIVE GLASS MESH JOINT TAPE IS PRESSED OVER SEAM

4 1/2" BLADE

1 PRESS SELF-ADHERING MESH TAPE OVER JOINT COVER WITH COMPOUND

2 AFTER COMPOUND DRIES A DAY APPLY SECOND LAYER USING 6" BLADE

3 ADD FINAL THIRD COAT USING A 10" BLADE OR DRYWALL TROWEL

TAPING OUTSIDE AND INSIDE CORNERS

FEATHER COMPOUND EDGE TO WALL WITH 9" BLADE

NAILS AND SCREWS

THERE ARE literally thousand of different types of nails, but the homeowner only need be aware of a dozen or so types to tackle the usual around-the-house repairs and remodeling projects. Most widely used in framing is the "common" nail, the length of which is designated by the term "penny"(d). The illustration shows the relative length of common nails with a penny designation and the size in inches. Finishing nails and casing nails differ primarily in the shape of the head and are used on trim and cabinet work where the head is sunk and then filled. Brads are smaller finishing nails and are referred to by length in inches, plus a gauge number which indicates the diameter. Upholstery nails come in a few sizes but with a wide selection of decorative head shapes, while *tacks* also used in some upholstery work have flat heads and tapered shanks. *Masonry* nails are made from hardened steel and use the inch rather than the penny designation. *Roofing* nails come in many sizes and their head diameters are galvanized. Nails are also used for attaching fiberglass or corrugated metal panels, and these are usually fitted with a special rubber or lead seal to prevent possible leakage around the head. *Flooring* nails have spiraled shanks and small heads,

The aforementioned are the most widely used types of nails you will find at your home center, hardware store or lumber yard.

THE DRY WALL SCREW

The *drywall* screw is rapidly being substituted for the nail; it does a better job and often is easier to drive than nailing. Years ago it was not uncommon for nails to pop from the surface of drywall panels. In fact, even if you use the special drywall annular ring nails today (which were created to replace the old cement-coated nails) you can still experience an occasional popped nail within a few years of application. However, if you use the newer special *hardened steel drywall* screws with the Phillips head you can use fewer screws than nails, less compound to fill the screw heads and be assured of a surface with no head popping. Preventing head popping was only one problem

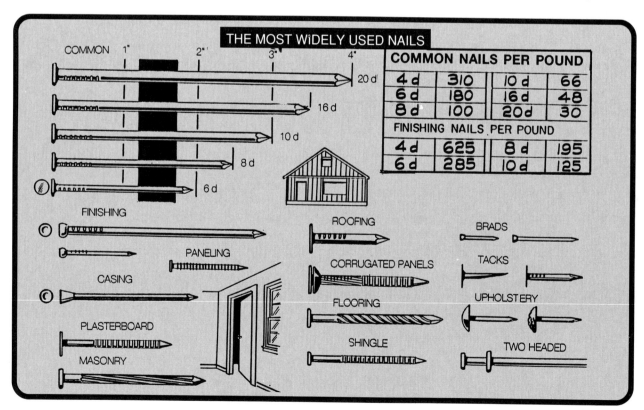

THE MOST WIDELY USED NAILS

COMMON NAILS PER POUND			
4 d	310	10 d	66
6 d	180	16 d	48
8 d	100	20 d	30

FINISHING NAILS PER POUND			
4 d	625	8 d	195
6 d	285	10 d	125

these screws solved; perhaps even more important was the fact that the screws could also be used with metal studs which are widely used in fireproof wall construction. The sharp hardened tip will self-tap right through steel studs.

USG developed these unique screws well over 20 years ago. Now they are available to consumers in either package or loose form and with the popularization of the regular and 3/8-inch drywall screwdriver, plus cordless screwdrivers, you will find a screw size that does a better job than a nail for many areas.

THE SELF-DRILLING SCREW

Automatic screw manufacturing has reached the point where another breed of screws - the *self-drilling* screw - is replacing the nail.

For instance, if you are building a deck the self-drilling screw is ideal for anchoring the floor planks in place. The ability to drill a hole while the screw is being driven is the result of the slotted tip which cuts the wood while the threads pull the screw deeper. These screws drive fast and the bungle style head (originally conceived for drywall screws) will produce a clean countersink. Also, these screws do not have the usual slotted head; an extra deep Phillips head (No. 2 bit), combined with the fact that the screw is case hardened, virtually eliminates stripping the head.

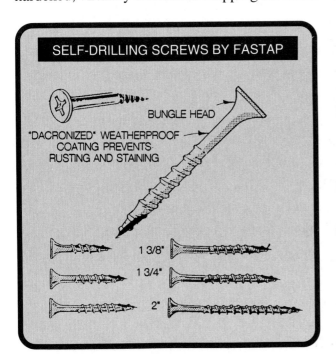

SELF-DRILLING SCREWS BY FASTAP

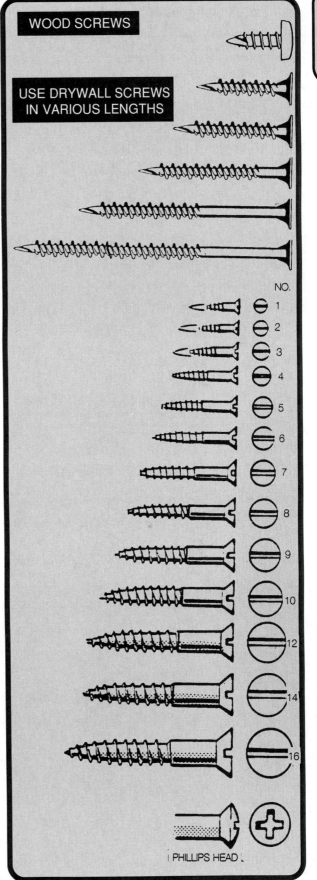

WOOD SCREWS

USE DRYWALL SCREWS IN VARIOUS LENGTHS

PHILLIPS HEAD

SPLICES AND JOINTS

If you are building furniture or installing trim, making accurate joints is a must. Here are some tips.

A miter box is a must when cutting molding. Once you have the line marked on your stock, hold it in place and make the cut just outside the mark.

When cutting baseboard or ceiling molding, or trimming windows and doors, always use a square to mark off where you want the cut made.

When you have familiarized yourself with the tools described earlier in this book, you will want to take a look at some of the many splices and joints every home carpenter should know, and know when and how to use them.

A *splice* is a means of connecting two lengths of wood, end to end, to run in the same line. A splice can be made with a *"fishplate"* nailed to one or both sides of the connecting members; with a half-lap joint; a *splayed lap*; a *scarf joint*; a *bolted joint*; or with a *V-splice joint*.

Joints are used to connect wood at an angle.

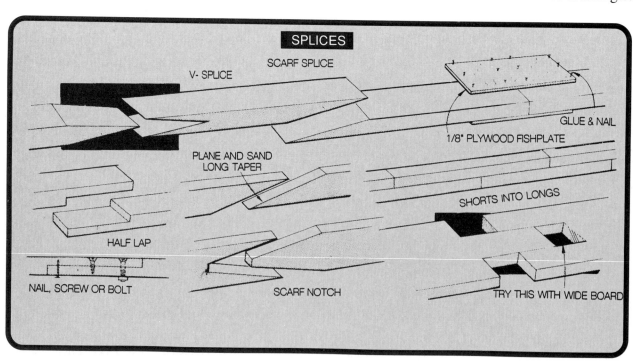

SPLICES

SCARF SPLICE

V- SPLICE

GLUE & NAIL

1/8" PLYWOOD FISHPLATE

PLANE AND SAND
LONG TAPER

SHORTS INTO LONGS

HALF LAP

NAIL, SCREW OR BOLT

SCARF NOTCH

TRY THIS WITH WIDE BOARD

Hardware can be used to make a joint. For example, a corner brace, a T-plate or a corrugated fastener may be used to make corner joints, such as in wooden window screens.

Full- and half-lap *joints* are used for fitting cross rails flush to their meeting members; both are simple to make. Use a back saw and sharp

chisel to make the required cuts.

The plain and stopped dado are more sophisticated methods of joint making. In the plain dado, the cut-out area extends across the complete width of the work; in the stopped dado, the cut stops short of the end of the work. This results in a clean-looking joint and is used quite often when

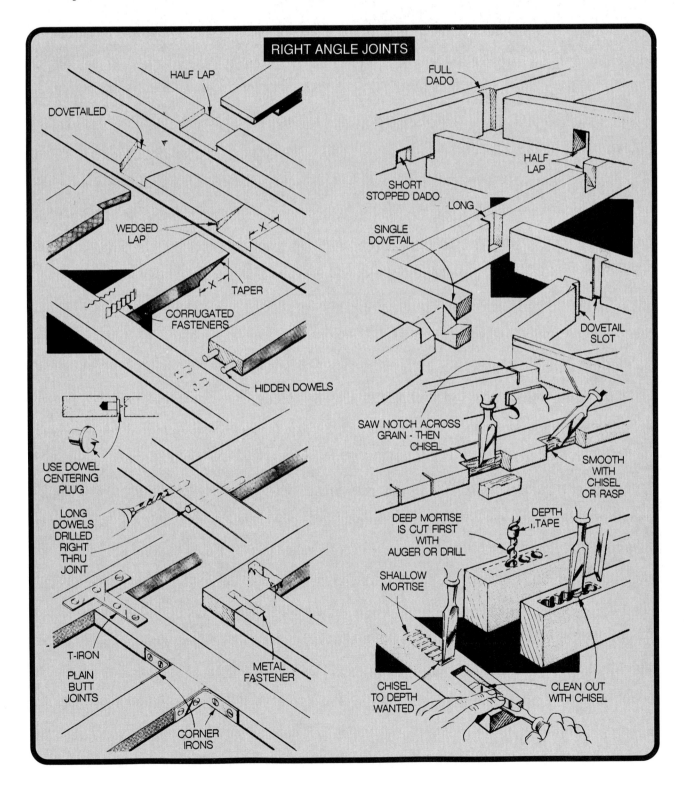

RIGHT ANGLE JOINTS

appearance is a factor. The work that is to fit into the stopped dado is cut away, as shown in the drawing.

The *mortise* and *tenon* is a still more sophisticated joint. It is the strongest of the T-joints and is generally used in heavy framing work. The thickness of the tenon (the tongue) should never be less than one-third the thickness of the stock from which it is cut. A variation of the mortise and tenon joint is the *stub tenon* where the tenon goes only part way into the mortise. A *double tenon* shown in the drawing is just what its name implies.

The *dovetail joint* is the strongest of all corner joints. Careful marking and sharp tools are important requisites for its construction. Dovetail joints fall into several categories. The most common—and simplest—is the *through dovetail*. A bit more complicated is the *lap dovetail*, often used in bookcase and drawer construction. The *double lap dovetail* shows very little end grain but demands great care in its construction. The *secret*, or *miter*

dovetail, is often used for high-quality cabinet work. The knife-edge miter requires great care in its execution. Prior to the invention of the router, making a dovetail was an exacting and tedious job. Now, thanks to the router with special bits and a dovetail attachment, anyone can make this strong, impressive looking joint.

The *box joint* is a sort of simplified dovetail joint and is used quite often in light furniture work and drawer construction. It is of fairly simple construction and, if you have access to a bench saw, the required cuts can be made in minutes.

A *miter joint* is assembled by one of four methods. The simplest—and weakest—is by nailing the two meeting members together. The second method is to cut two or more slots in the top for reinforcing splines. A third method is to cut along the width of each piece to accept a single long spline as shown. The last method is to reinforce the miter joint by means of dowels. To assure accuracy in the placement of the dowels, tempo-

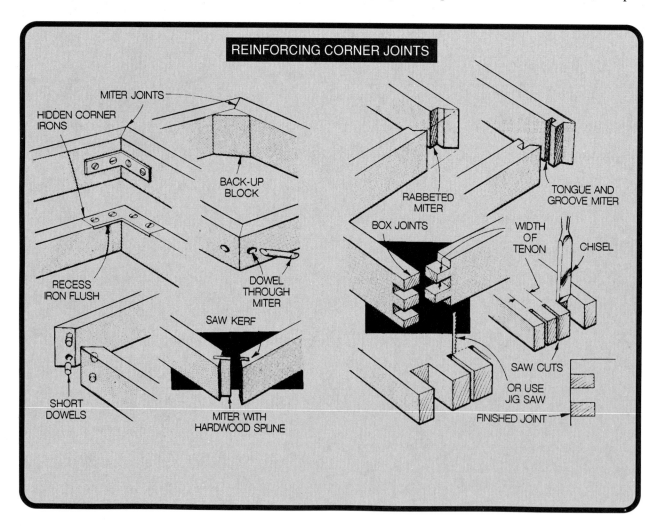

REINFORCING CORNER JOINTS

MITER JOINTS

HIDDEN CORNER IRONS

BACK-UP BLOCK

RECESS IRON FLUSH

DOWEL THROUGH MITER

SAW KERF

SHORT DOWELS

MITER WITH HARDWOOD SPLINE

RABBETED MITER

BOX JOINTS

TONGUE AND GROOVE MITER

WIDTH OF TENON

CHISEL

SAW CUTS

OR USE JIG SAW

FINISHED JOINT

rarily drive a couple of brads into one face. Cut them off, not quite flush, and press the two pieces together so that the brads will leave their marks on the other face. Remove the brads and drill holes for the dowels.

    Cross-over joints. The simplest cross-over or X-joint is the plain overlap. Glue, nails or screws secure the joint. A neater version is the *cross-lap joint* made by cutting a half-lap in each piece of wood. A third way of making a cross joint is by means of two or three dowels as shown in the drawing. A *mitered bridle joint* takes a bit more care in its construction, but it is strong and somewhat decorative. A fifth way of making a cross

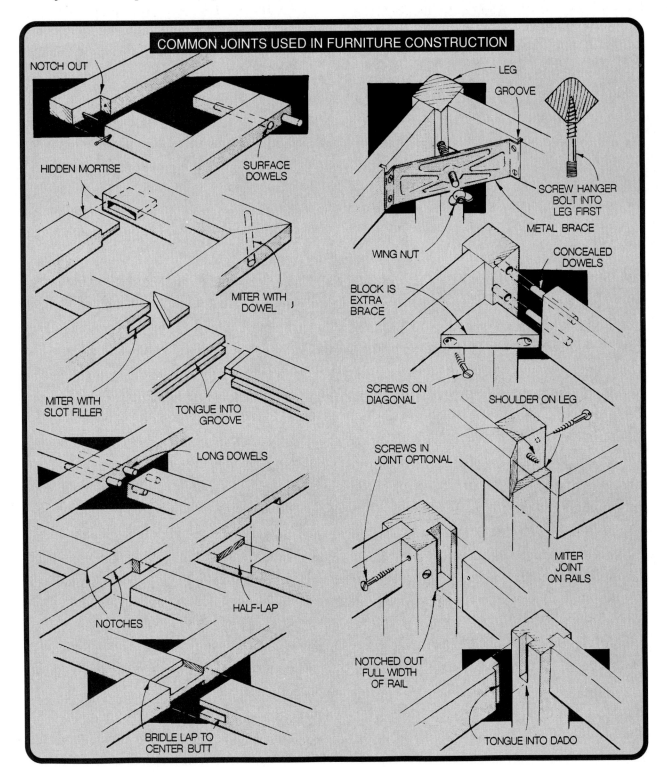

COMMON JOINTS USED IN FURNITURE CONSTRUCTION

NOTCH OUT

HIDDEN MORTISE

SURFACE DOWELS

MITER WITH DOWEL

MITER WITH SLOT FILLER

TONGUE INTO GROOVE

LONG DOWELS

NOTCHES

HALF-LAP

BRIDLE LAP TO CENTER BUTT

LEG

GROOVE

SCREW HANGER BOLT INTO LEG FIRST

METAL BRACE

WING NUT

BLOCK IS EXTRA BRACE

CONCEALED DOWELS

SCREWS ON DIAGONAL

SHOULDER ON LEG

SCREWS IN JOINT OPTIONAL

MITER JOINT ON RAILS

NOTCHED OUT FULL WIDTH OF RAIL

TONGUE INTO DADO

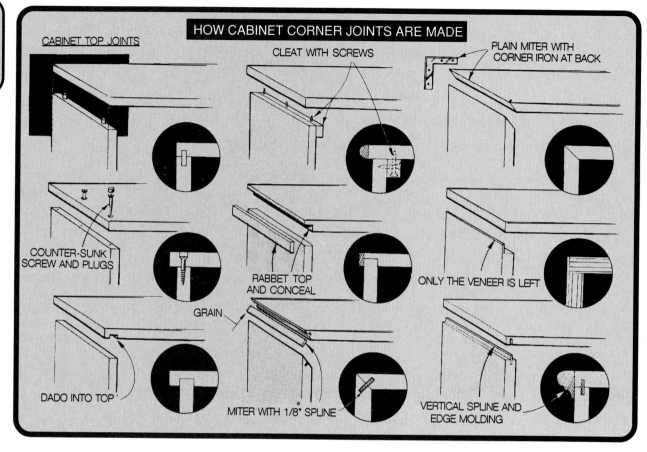

HOW CABINET CORNER JOINTS ARE MADE

CABINET TOP JOINTS

CLEAT WITH SCREWS

PLAIN MITER WITH CORNER IRON AT BACK

COUNTER-SUNK SCREW AND PLUGS

RABBET TOP AND CONCEAL

ONLY THE VENEER IS LEFT

GRAIN

DADO INTO TOP

MITER WITH 1/8" SPLINE

VERTICAL SPLINE AND EDGE MOLDING

joint is by means of a mortise and tenon. Use white glue to secure the joint.

Edge-to-edge joints can be made in several ways. The easiest and the least strong is by gluing the work together using bar or pipe clamps as shown. Dowels make a stronger joint, but require accuracy in preparation. A splined joint is the strongest joint of all for edge-to-edge work; however, it does require a power saw to cut the required grooves accurately. The grooves should be slightly deeper than the spline to allow for glue "expansion."

Lengthening joints. There are six common methods of making a long piece of wood out of two short pieces. They are the *lapped joint*, the *splayed lap*, the *scarf joint*, the *V splice*, and the *bolted joint* using fishplates or joining plates as they are sometimes called.

Three-way joints. Attaching legs (for example, in the construction of a workbench) calls for three-way joints. The drawings show five ways to attach legs. No. 1 is by means of a metal corner brace, a wing nut and a hanger bolt. These corner braces are made commercially; you can buy them in any hardware store. Note the slots cut in the side members to accept the curved edges of the metal brace. No. 2 shows construction and assembly by means of dowels. Dowel placement should be staggered to prevent their meeting in the middle of the leg. Use two or more dowels for each leg. Numbers 3 and 4 are very similar in construction, except for the placement of the leg. No. 3 has the leg on the inside, while No. 4 has the leg on the outside. No. 5 is a haunched and mitered mortise and tenon joint; it is the strongest of the leg joints. When making this joint, leave a quarter-inch or so of waste at the top of the leg and trim it off with a plane and rasp after the glue has dried.

Coped joints. This joint is used in combination with a miter joint when installing ceiling and floor molding. It is not necessary to miter all four corners of this molding. The professional will first put up two lengths of molding, at *opposite* sides of the room, butting them snug against the wall (see drawing). The other two pieces of molding are then mitered and coped to fit. The advantage of a coped joint is that it will hide any irregularities due to walls not meeting at an exact right angle. If the molding is flat on the back, you can use a short piece of scrap molding as a pattern. Trace the contour as shown in the drawing on the flat side. Tape the front (to avoid splintering) and cut through the molding with a coping saw. If the molding is irregular on the back, which is usually the case with crown molding used at the ceiling, you will have to use another technique. First cut the mold-

ing at a 45° miter. Make sure you have measured carefully. Then cut away excess wood following the outline of the miter. As you cut, tilt the coping saw slightly to the long side of the molding instead of cutting straight across at a 90° angle. This way you will gain a bit of extra clearance.

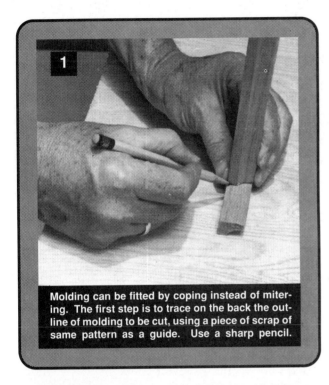

Molding can be fitted by coping instead of mitering. The first step is to trace on the back the outline of molding to be cut, using a piece of scrap of same pattern as a guide. Use a sharp pencil.

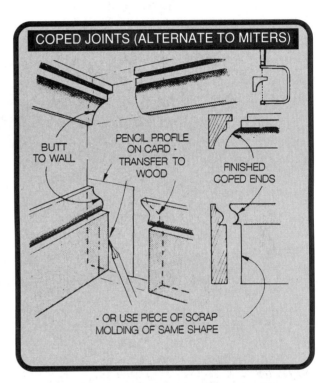

COPED JOINTS (ALTERNATE TO MITERS)

BUTT TO WALL

PENCIL PROFILE ON CARD - TRANSFER TO WOOD

FINISHED COPED ENDS

- OR USE PIECE OF SCRAP MOLDING OF SAME SHAPE

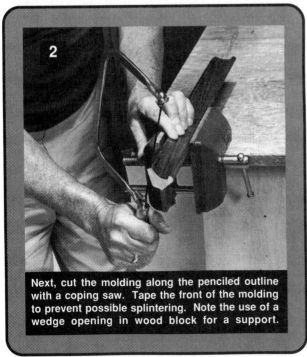

Next, cut the molding along the penciled outline with a coping saw. Tape the front of the molding to prevent possible splintering. Note the use of a wedge opening in wood block for a support.

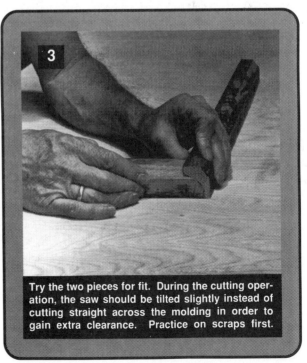

Try the two pieces for fit. During the cutting operation, the saw should be tilted slightly instead of cutting straight across the molding in order to gain extra clearance. Practice on scraps first.

THREE MAJOR IDENTIFICATION LABELS OF PRESSURE TREATED LUMBER

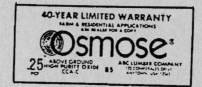

| RED AND BLACK LABEL .40 MINIMUM CCA RETENTION | YELLOW TAG ON EACH PIECE OF LUMBER | BLUE AND BLACK TAG STAPLED TO END |

These three leading pressure treated lumber labels identify each plank with a colorful paper label stapled to the end grain and a plain stamp on the surface of each board.

PRESSURE TREATED LUMBER

Although *pressure treated lumber* has been around for many decades only in recent years has this decay resistant lumber been available to homeowners building decks, fences and other outdoor structures. What is pressure treated lumber? It is regular lumber that is usually impregnated with chromated copper arsenate (CCA). A stack of lumber is wheeled into a special cylindrical chamber, often eight feet in diameter and as long as forty feet, the chamber sealed and the air sucked out. Water mixed with the chemical CCA is pumped into the chamber and allowed to permeate the cells of the wood for a few hours under pressure, depending upon the treatment desired. Eventually, the water is pumped out leaving traces of the CCA in the cells of the wood — which makes the wood decay resistant. Not absolutely rot-proof; just decay resistant.

Retail outlets are supplied either direct from a lumber mill (such as Weyerhaeuser who market their product under their LifeWood label) or from smaller mills and even local yards who ship dimensional stock to treatment centers who in turn pressure treat the lumber. The most popular treatment plant operator is Osmose with well over one hundred plants located nationally. Koppers, the marketing arm for Wolmanized lumber, is also a major chemical supplier.

So how does the consumer know the lumber purchased contains the prescribed amount of chemicals for above grade outdoor exposure, on-grade, below grade or even in-water use? An industry standard has been established for all such conditions.

Each piece of treated lumber should display the label of the American Wood Preservers Bureau, with the trademark illustrated identifying the recommended use.

Unfortunately some retail outlets sell green tinted lumber that may have been pressure treated but does not comply with the industry standards — so buy only lumber that has a stamp indicating the recommended use.

How much does pressure treated lumber cost? It varies depending upon your location, the type of lumber and from where it was shipped. Pressure treated lumber costs about 15 to 20 percent more than regular lumber. In those parts of the country nearest our redwood forests, pressure treated lumber is not widely used for decks as redwood contains a natural anti-decay ingredient. However, in the eastern, southern and central markets, redwood is substantially more expensive than pressure treated lumber; in fact, many lumber yards do not even stock the popular sizes because of low consumer demand.

Most consumers seem to like a reddish color for their deck to a point where a few manufacturers market a line of stains intended to cover the greenish tint of pressure treated lumber. And only a few years ago the Osmose people logically concluded that if lumber is treated chemically to make it decay resistant, why not concoct a formula that will also tint the wood! And so the product

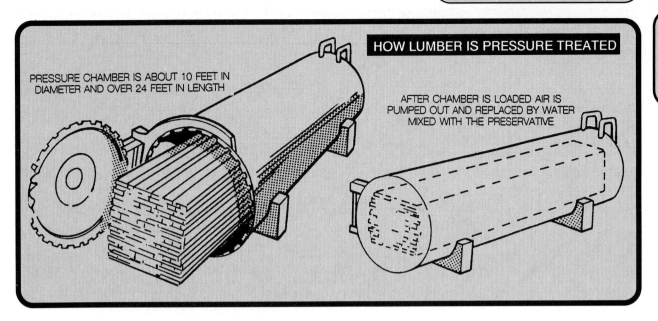

HOW LUMBER IS PRESSURE TREATED

PRESSURE CHAMBER IS ABOUT 10 FEET IN DIAMETER AND OVER 24 FEET IN LENGTH

AFTER CHAMBER IS LOADED AIR IS PUMPED OUT AND REPLACED BY WATER MIXED WITH THE PRESERVATIVE

Sunwood made its appearance. It is about 10 or 15 percent more expensive than regular pressure treated lumber but it represents a real competitor to redwood, even in some of the areas where heretofore redwood was king.

If you are building a deck or another outdoor project, and want it to last at least a few decades, make sure the pressure treated lumber you use carries the label that indicates the industry standard.

RECOMMENDED WOOD PRESERVATIVE CCA RETENTION		
	CCA RETENTION*	
ABOVE GROUND USES	.25 L-2	DECKING, RAILING, SILLS, JOISTS
GROUND, FRESH WATER CONTACT (NON-STRUCTURAL)	.40 L-22	POSTS, LANDSCAPE TIMBERS RETAINING WALLS, STAKES
GROUND, FRESH WATER CONTACT (STRUCTURAL)	.60 FDN	WOOD FOUNDATIONS, BUILDING POLES
SALT WATER CONTACT	2.50	DOCK PILINGS, BULKHEADS

*PCF--POUNDS OF CAA PER CUBIC FOOT OF LUMBER

LUMBER MAY ALSO HAVE THIS LABEL STAMPED ON EACH PIECE OF LUMBER

B   F A C H   E

A
W P
B
GROUND
CONTACT
LP-22
ABC WOOD PRESERVING

D

G

KEY TO AMERICAN WOOD PRESERVERS BUREAU OR AGENCY

A YEAR OF TREATMENT
B AMERICAN WOOD PRESERVERS BUREAU TRADEMARK OR TRADEMARK OF THE AWPB CERTIFIED AGENCY
C THE PRESERVATIVE USED FOR TREATMENT
D THE APPLICABLE AMERICAN WOOD PRESERVERS BUREAU QUALITY STANDARD
E TRADEMARK OF THE AWPB CERTIFIED AGENCY
F PROPER EXPOSURE CONDITIONS
G TREATING COMPANY AND PLANT LOCATION
H DRY OR KDAT IF APPLICABLE

DECK CONSTRUCTION TECHNIQUES

Millions of homeowners each year gain additional outdoor living space by adding a deck to their home. With pressure treated lumber a deck can easily last for decades.

Adding a deck to your home is one of the most rewarding remodeling projects because it represents a relatively low cost method of obtaining additional living space and utilizing yard space which otherwise would be confined to a lawn or garden. Often a deck is merely a patio constructed from wood, and while such a structure provides additional leisure living space, the deck that is attached to the home with access to the interior is more functional. Depending upon your particular layout and desires, you have many options when planning and building a deck. In fact, home centers and lumber yards stock complete deck kits with a set of instructions and all parts labeled.

If you feel such a project is beyond your capability then professionals are available to do the job. However, whether you do it yourself or have a pro do the job you should know how decks are constructed. On the following pages you will find time-tested construction techniques utilizing the latest materials and building techniques for a 10' x 14' deck.

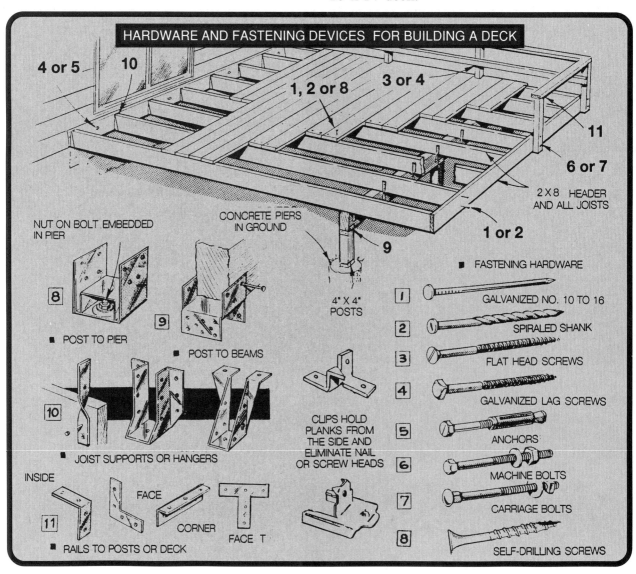

HARDWARE AND FASTENING DEVICES FOR BUILDING A DECK

4 or 5   10

1, 2 or 8   3 or 4

11

6 or 7

2 X 8 HEADER AND ALL JOISTS

1 or 2

NUT ON BOLT EMBEDDED IN PIER

CONCRETE PIERS IN GROUND

9

■ FASTENING HARDWARE

8 — POST TO PIER

9 — POST TO BEAMS

4" X 4" POSTS

1   GALVANIZED NO. 10 TO 16

2   SPIRALED SHANK

3   FLAT HEAD SCREWS

4   GALVANIZED LAG SCREWS

10 — JOIST SUPPORTS OR HANGERS

CLIPS HOLD PLANKS FROM THE SIDE AND ELIMINATE NAIL OR SCREW HEADS

5   ANCHORS

6   MACHINE BOLTS

7   CARRIAGE BOLTS

INSIDE   FACE   CORNER   FACE T

11 — RAILS TO POSTS OR DECK

8   SELF-DRILLING SCREWS

Most decks are attached to the house and a doorway cut in the wall (usually at a window location) so access is from either the inside or the outside via steps. Attaching the ledger to the side of your home is critical in that it must be level and capable of holding up half the weight of the deck. Many deck builders use lag screws to attach the ledger but the better way is to use carriage bolts that run completely through the ledger, the siding, the sheathing and the band joist on the inside of the house. If you have a brick home, mounting the ledger with lead expansion anchors is often done but, since a hole must be drilled for the anchors, you might as well drill completely through the interior sheathing and band joist and use long bolts. Once you have temporarily positioned the ledger by nailing so it is about 3 inches below the inside floor and also level, drill 9/16 inch diameter holes for 1/2-inch diameter bolts and slip the bolts through from the inside; tighten from the outside. Bolts at about 4 foot intervals are sufficient. One important point: if the ledger rests directly against the siding it is a good idea to slide aluminum flashing underneath the clapboard and extend it over the top of the ledger. Incidentally, it is always easier to nail the joist hangers on the ledger before attaching it to the wall. Lay the ledger flat on the ground or on two horses, mark off the position of each hanger working from the center. Use a tri square and nail each hanger in place with 1 1/2 inch galvanized nails.

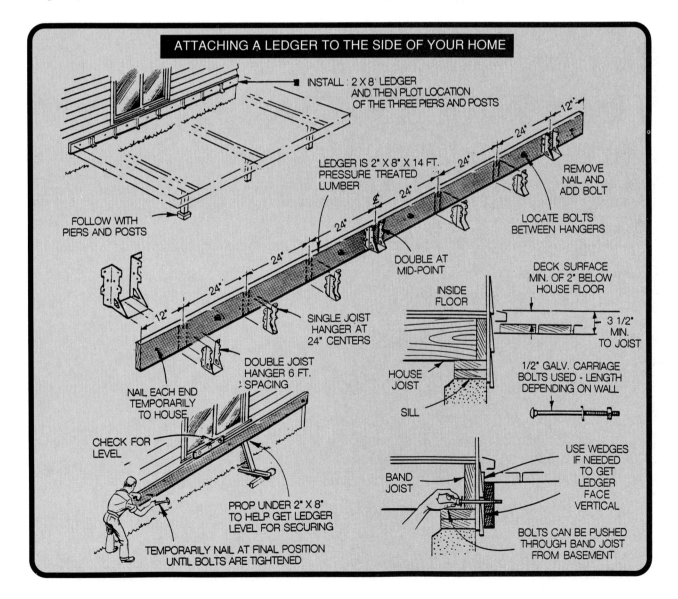

ATTACHING A LEDGER TO THE SIDE OF YOUR HOME

INSTALL 2 X 8 LEDGER AND THEN PLOT LOCATION OF THE THREE PIERS AND POSTS

LEDGER IS 2" X 8" X 14 FT. PRESSURE TREATED LUMBER

REMOVE NAIL AND ADD BOLT

LOCATE BOLTS BETWEEN HANGERS

FOLLOW WITH PIERS AND POSTS

DOUBLE AT MID-POINT

DECK SURFACE MIN. OF 2" BELOW HOUSE FLOOR

INSIDE FLOOR

3 1/2" MIN. TO JOIST

SINGLE JOIST HANGER AT 24" CENTERS

HOUSE JOIST

SILL

1/2" GALV. CARRIAGE BOLTS USED - LENGTH DEPENDING ON WALL

DOUBLE JOIST HANGER 6 FT. SPACING

NAIL EACH END TEMPORARILY TO HOUSE

CHECK FOR LEVEL

BAND JOIST

USE WEDGES IF NEEDED TO GET LEDGER FACE VERTICAL

PROP UNDER 2" X 8" TO HELP GET LEDGER LEVEL FOR SECURING

TEMPORARILY NAIL AT FINAL POSITION UNTIL BOLTS ARE TIGHTENED

BOLTS CAN BE PUSHED THROUGH BAND JOIST FROM BASEMENT

CARPENTRY

STEP 2
DECK BUILDING

One major — and very important — decision in building a deck is to determine if the posts that hold up the outer half should be (A) resting on a concrete pier, or (B) resting in a hole in the ground like a fence post.

The in-ground post method is widely used in most parts of the country, and if you go this route your posts should rest on a bed of gravel in a hole that has been thoroughly tamped and, even more important, the 4 X 4-inch posts (or 6 x 6s) must be pressure treated to the tune of .40 CCA (chromated copper arsenate). However, our preferred method in deck construction is to have the posts resting directly on a concrete pier that projects a few inches above the ground. In the 10-by-14-foot-deck example that is illustrated, three posts are required, and these are located directly opposite the double hangers on the ledger that is attached to the house. In this type of deck design, the deck extends a foot beyond the posts which means the holes for the piers should be an exact 9 feet from the wall.

Using the age-old 3-by-4-by-5-foot triangle method, locate the first hole and then string a line to position the second and third pier (or post) holes. Dig each hole to a depth slightly below the frost line in your area; tamp, form and pour, as illustrated. Make the top of all forms level with each other and, after the pour is made, insert an anchor bolt in the wet mix to hold the post anchor base which is positioned after the forms are removed.

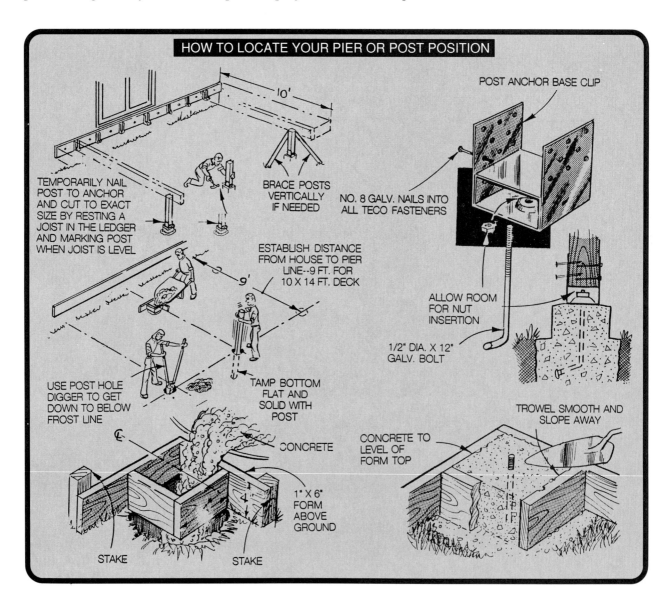

HOW TO LOCATE YOUR PIER OR POST POSITION

STEP 3
DECK BUILDING

To span the ten feet depth of this deck, pressure treated 2 x 8 inch lumber with the crown up spaced 24 inches on centers is adequate. Check to make absolutely certain the top of the three footings are level and then cut the 4 x 4 inch posts so when a double joist rests in the hardware the top of the joists will be at the same level as the ledger. Set the posts on top of the pier in the hardware and tack each post *temporarily* in place because after all three are vertical you will want to make one last check to make certain they are all even. To do this, run a taut string from the two outside posts to check the center post height and if any post is short trim the others so the line is straight. Trimming a post may result in a floor that is slightly slanted away from the ledger but this does not matter; in fact some builders purposely tilt their decks away from the home. What you are trying to achieve is absolutely level floor joists so all floor planks touch all joists.

Nail in place the joist hangers to the double end header in much the same manner as the hangers were added to the ledger, then slip the header over the three double joists. Finally, insert the remaining single joists in place making certain the crown is always up. Since the next step is to lay down the flooring - either 2 x 6s or five quarters - you will have easy access to all the joists and the post hardware. Drive 11/2 inch galvanized nails in the side of the joist and the post hardware. Do not skip a nail hole!

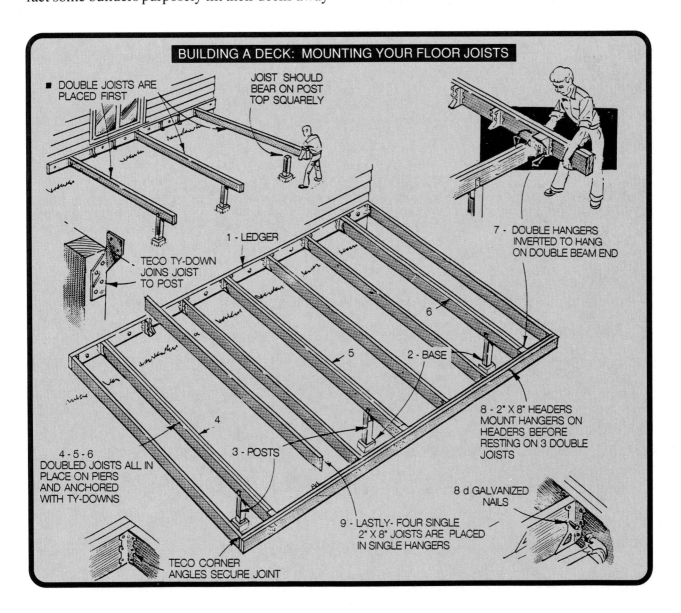

BUILDING A DECK: MOUNTING YOUR FLOOR JOISTS

- DOUBLE JOISTS ARE PLACED FIRST

JOIST SHOULD BEAR ON POST TOP SQUARELY

TECO TY-DOWN JOINS JOIST TO POST

1 - LEDGER

4-5-6 DOUBLED JOISTS ALL IN PLACE ON PIERS AND ANCHORED WITH TY-DOWNS

3 - POSTS

4

5

2 - BASE

6

7 - DOUBLE HANGERS INVERTED TO HANG ON DOUBLE BEAM END

8 - 2" X 8" HEADERS MOUNT HANGERS ON HEADERS BEFORE RESTING ON 3 DOUBLE JOISTS

8 d GALVANIZED NAILS

9 - LASTLY- FOUR SINGLE 2" X 8" JOISTS ARE PLACED IN SINGLE HANGERS

TECO CORNER ANGLES SECURE JOINT

STEP 4
DECK BUILDING

The kind of deck planks you use and the manner in which they are attached is one of the most important construction decisions you can make. Decks built more than ten years ago had planks - usually 2 x 6s — but now five quarter inch thick decking with slightly rounded corners is popular, probably because of the lower cost.   In some instances the ten penny nails had a tendency to work themselves above the surface and often the wood split around the nailhead after a few years of being exposed to the elements. Many deck builders resorted to using self-drilling screws along with a bead of outdoor construction adhesive on the joists. This technique is still excellent because the fewer nail or screw heads exposed the better. However, you also have available clips that grasp the planks from the side which eliminates surface nail or screw heads. Our recommendation? The clip route is great if you have straight kiln dried planking but we prefer the deck adhesive method in combination with a polymer-coated deck screw that is impervious to weather. If for some reason a plank loosens or cracks, all you need do is to add another screw or, if a new plank is required, back off the screws and add the plank.   Whatever material you use, select long lengths of decking because it is best not to have joints butting each other. Start with the first plank near the ledger and use either silicone sealer or flashing - or both -to make certain water will not collect behind the plank.

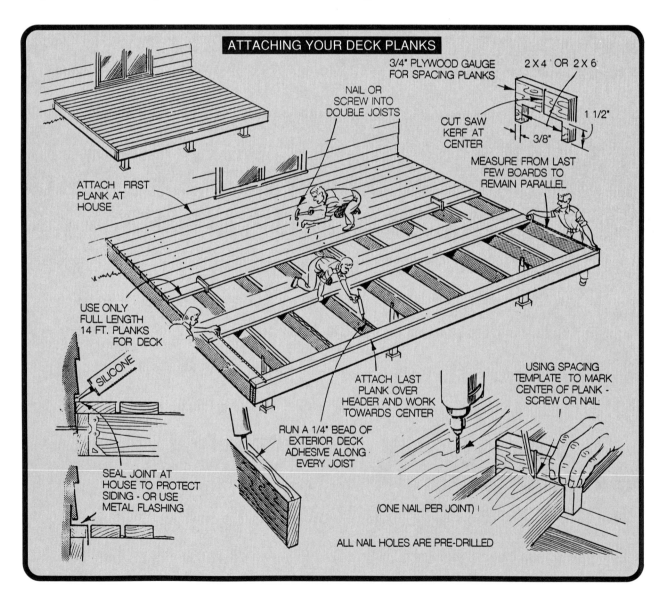

ATTACHING YOUR DECK PLANKS

3/4" PLYWOOD GAUGE FOR SPACING PLANKS

2 X 4 OR 2 X 6

NAIL OR SCREW INTO DOUBLE JOISTS

CUT SAW KERF AT CENTER

1 1/2"

3/8"

MEASURE FROM LAST FEW BOARDS TO REMAIN PARALLEL

ATTACH FIRST PLANK AT HOUSE

USE ONLY FULL LENGTH 14 FT. PLANKS FOR DECK

SILICONE

SEAL JOINT AT HOUSE TO PROTECT SIDING - OR USE METAL FLASHING

ATTACH LAST PLANK OVER HEADER AND WORK TOWARDS CENTER

RUN A 1/4" BEAD OF EXTERIOR DECK ADHESIVE ALONG EVERY JOIST

USING SPACING TEMPLATE TO MARK CENTER OF PLANK - SCREW OR NAIL

(ONE NAIL PER JOINT)

ALL NAIL HOLES ARE PRE-DRILLED

All decks, even those built a foot off the ground, should have a railing. Many different designs are available ranging from lattice panels to 1 1/2 inch square balusters mounted vertically at six inch intervals; the type illustrated (made from 2 x 4s) is not only strong but is very easy and economical to make.

The railing height should be between 32 and 36 inches, with the vertical uprights 3 1/2 feet on centers. Once you have decided upon the desired height, cut your vertical members slightly longer and clamp them to the side joist and header, as illustrated. Then drill through both the 2 x 4 uprights and the joist (or header) for the two 3/8-inch diameter carriage bolts that hold the uprights to the three sides. With all in place, run a string from the side to the end post to determine the exact height and mark and cut each post down. Now either screw or nail the top horizontal 2 x 4 in place on the side and glue a flat 2 x 4 on top. In deck construction, especially with horizontal surfaces, i.e., the top of a railing, table top, benches, planters. Try not to have any exposed nail heads or indentations made by driving a head beneath the surface. Water will usually collect after a rain or snow and in a short time you will note splinters developing around the head. That is why we like the adhesive route and adding an occasional screw where necessary. Finally, add the center 2 x 4 as illustrated.

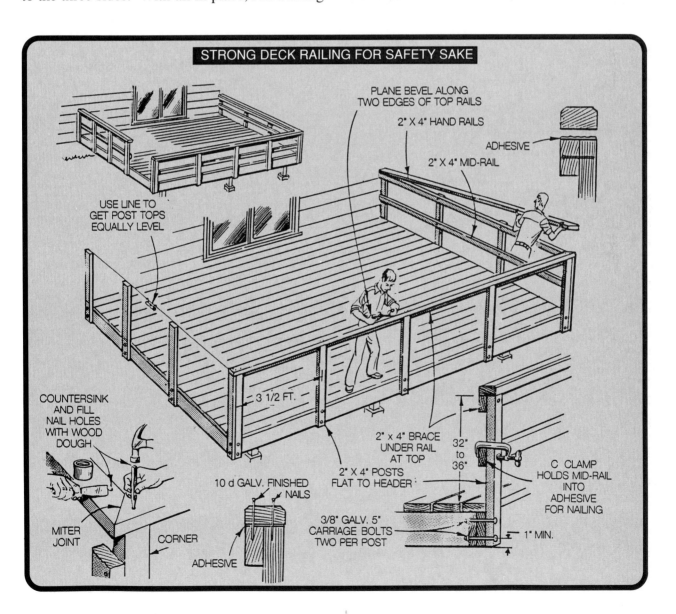

STRONG DECK RAILING FOR SAFETY SAKE

CARPENTRY

STEP 6
DECK BUILDING

Decks will usually have a table in addition to other furniture. And if you have a table a bench is always more functional than individual chairs. The idea of building a bench as part of the railing not only saves lumber but results in a bench that actually reinforces the railing. The bench illustrated is seven feet long, but if you care to make it longer merely continue the construction technique. In fact, many decks have a complete perimeter of benches.

Tool up to cut as many base pieces as per the measurements and then mount the leg sections to both the flooring and the center deck rail.

Again, to cut down on exposed nail or screw heads use an exterior construction adhesive and screws. Once the base long sections are in place, add two 2 x 6s plus a 2 x 4 that make up the seat. With all legs in place, cut your seating from the same width planking used on your floor and round the corners slightly. Then attach the seating planks to the leg sections by driving two screws per plank from the underside rather than from the top.

Remember, you want to keep the seating plank as free from splinters as possible and one way to do that is to eliminate nails or screw heads that tend to crack all surfaces because the rate of expansion of metal is different than that of wood. If necessary, you can add an additional horizontal member between the bench on the top railing.

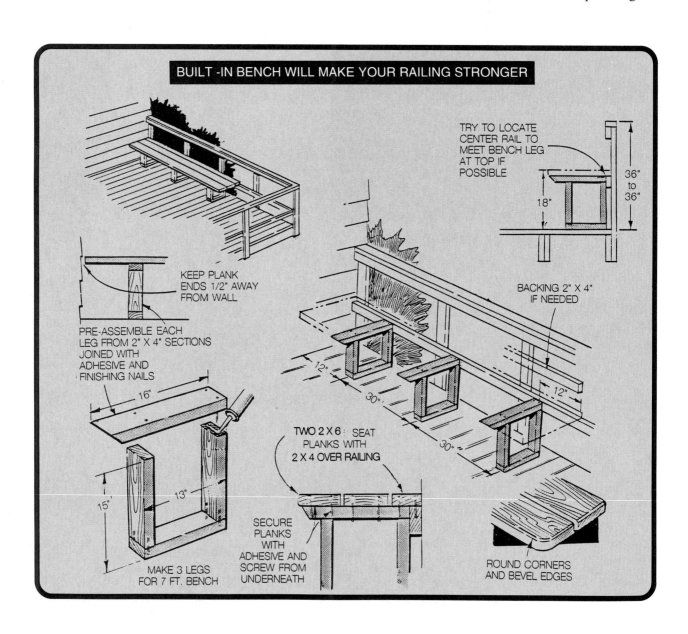

BUILT -IN BENCH WILL MAKE YOUR RAILING STRONGER

TRY TO LOCATE CENTER RAIL TO MEET BENCH LEG AT TOP IF POSSIBLE

36" to 36"

18"

KEEP PLANK ENDS 1/2" AWAY FROM WALL

BACKING 2" X 4" IF NEEDED

PRE-ASSEMBLE EACH LEG FROM 2" X 4" SECTIONS JOINED WITH ADHESIVE AND FINISHING NAILS

16"

15"

13"

12"

30"

30"

12"

TWO 2 X 6 SEAT PLANKS WITH 2 X 4 OVER RAILING

SECURE PLANKS WITH ADHESIVE AND SCREW FROM UNDERNEATH

MAKE 3 LEGS FOR 7 FT. BENCH

ROUND CORNERS AND BEVEL EDGES

BOOK 2 PLUMBING

Prime Author: RICHARD DAY

CONTENTS

98 Basics of Your Plumbing System
104 Pipe and Fittings
106 Galvanized Steel Pipe
108 Black Iron Pipe
109 Threaded Brass Pipe
110 Copper Tubing
114 Plastic Water Supply Pipe
118 Plastic Drain-Waste-Vent Pipe
120 Other Types of Pipe

WORKING WITH PIPE

122 Cast Iron Pipe
126 Copper Tubing
128 How to Sweat Solder
130 Working with Flare Fittings
132 Working with Threaded Pipe
136 Working with Plastic Tubing

PROJECTS

142 Installing a Water Heater
144 Replacing a Kitchen or Bathroom
       Sink
150 Changing a Toilet
154 Changing Faucets
160 Private Water Supply
166 Plumbing Tips for an Add-On Room
174 Fixing Faucets
178 Fixing Toilets
184 Washing Machine Plumbing
186 Stopping Leaks
188 Tips on Unclogging

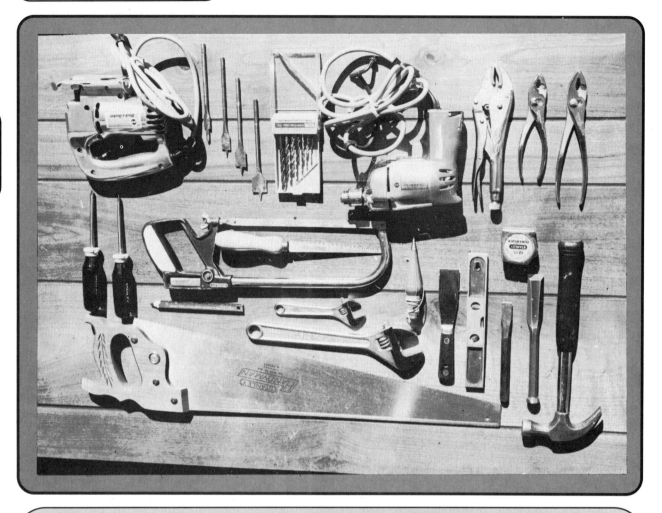

BASICS OF YOUR PLUMBING SYSTEM

Plumbing problems develop at the most inopportune time. But before you can even attempt to correct a condition you should know how your system works.

To DO SIMPLE HOME PLUMBING, you need not be a plumber, any more than you have to be a musician to hum a tune. Much home plumbing lends itself to do-it-yourself work. In all instances you will save substantially by making the repair yourself you will not be inconvenienced by waiting hours for a professional during which time you could do the job yourself. Yet, there are some things you should not tackle, so once you know the basics you can determine just what you can—or cannot—do.

When you understand the piping system in your home, you will find it easy to do things with it and to it. Basically, there are three separate areas to study: water-supply system, drain-waste-vent system, and fixtures to which these are connected.

The water supply system is easy to identify. It uses small pipes, usually no bigger than 1-inch, and often half that diameter. As you know, they bring potable water under pressure into the house and route it to the various fixtures. They also lead to hose and sprinkler outlets, to the water heater and to the water softener, if there is one, and to the boiler, if you have a wet-heating system.

If you have a municipal water system, your water supply starts at the street. Leading from the street connection and underground shutoff, next in line comes the main shutoff valve. It is a gate valve so, when open, it will not restrict the

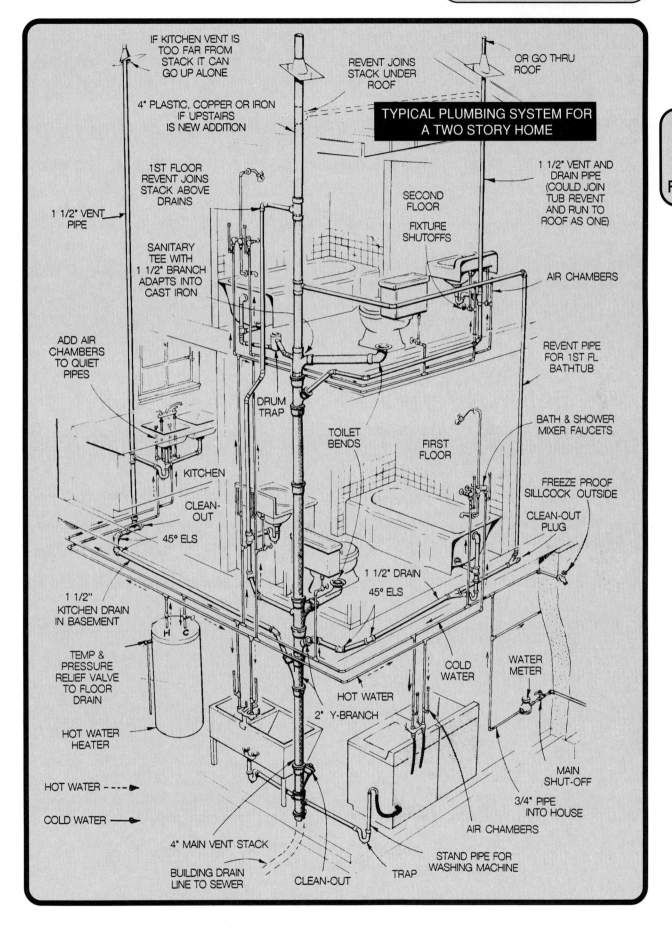

IF KITCHEN VENT IS TOO FAR FROM STACK IT CAN GO UP ALONE

REVENT JOINS STACK UNDER ROOF

OR GO THRU ROOF

4" PLASTIC, COPPER OR IRON IF UPSTAIRS IS NEW ADDITION

TYPICAL PLUMBING SYSTEM FOR A TWO STORY HOME

1 1/2" VENT AND DRAIN PIPE (COULD JOIN TUB REVENT AND RUN TO ROOF AS ONE)

1ST FLOOR REVENT JOINS STACK ABOVE DRAINS

SECOND FLOOR

1 1/2" VENT PIPE

FIXTURE SHUTOFFS

AIR CHAMBERS

SANITARY TEE WITH 1 1/2" BRANCH ADAPTS INTO CAST IRON

REVENT PIPE FOR 1ST FL BATHTUB

ADD AIR CHAMBERS TO QUIET PIPES

DRUM TRAP

BATH & SHOWER MIXER FAUCETS

TOILET BENDS

FIRST FLOOR

KITCHEN

FREEZE PROOF SILLCOCK OUTSIDE

CLEAN-OUT

CLEAN-OUT PLUG

45° ELS

1 1/2" DRAIN

45° ELS

1 1/2" KITCHEN DRAIN IN BASEMENT

TEMP & PRESSURE RELIEF VALVE TO FLOOR DRAIN

COLD WATER

WATER METER

H   C

HOT WATER

HOT WATER HEATER

2" Y-BRANCH

HOT WATER - - - ▶

MAIN SHUT-OFF

COLD WATER ▬▶

3/4" PIPE INTO HOUSE

4" MAIN VENT STACK

AIR CHAMBERS

STAND PIPE FOR WASHING MACHINE

BUILDING DRAIN LINE TO SEWER

CLEAN-OUT

TRAP

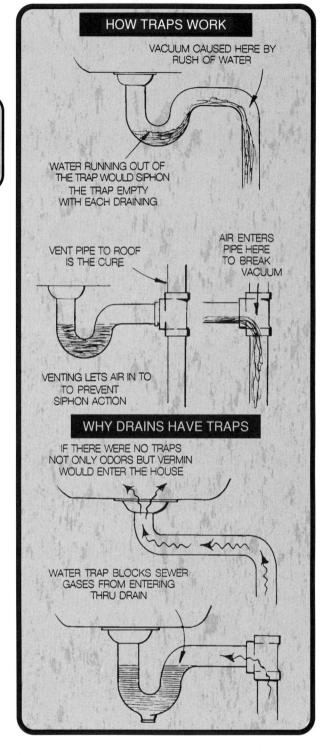

HOW TRAPS WORK

VACUUM CAUSED HERE BY RUSH OF WATER

WATER RUNNING OUT OF THE TRAP WOULD SIPHON THE TRAP EMPTY WITH EACH DRAINING

VENT PIPE TO ROOF IS THE CURE

AIR ENTERS PIPE HERE TO BREAK VACUUM

VENTING LETS AIR IN TO TO PREVENT SIPHON ACTION

WHY DRAINS HAVE TRAPS

IF THERE WERE NO TRAPS NOT ONLY ODORS BUT VERMIN WOULD ENTER THE HOUSE

WATER TRAP BLOCKS SEWER GASES FROM ENTERING THRU DRAIN

second parallel run called the hot-water main. These mains are usually of pipe, 3/4-inch in diameter.

At each fixture, or group of fixtures, 3/8-inch or 1/2-inch pipes branch off to the fixture. Cold water connects to the right side of the fixture, hot to the left side. Except in special cases, a toilet gets cold water only. A dishwasher hot only.

Behind the wall at each fixture location (except toilets) are foot-long air-filled vertical pipes called air chambers that trap a column of air to cushion onrushing water when the faucet is turned off. Without an air chamber, an abrupt turn-off could create several hundred pounds per square inch of pressure within the water-supply system. This effect, called water hammer, has been known to burst a system.

The best plumbing systems station a fixture shut-off valve where the hot and cold pipes come out of the wall or floor. Water then reaches the fixture through a controlled supply tube.

FIXTURES

The most visible part of the home plumbing system, fixtures let you use the water, as desired, then drain it away. Sinks, tubs, lavatories and showers combine faucets and a receptacle. The faucets connect to the water-supply system and the receptacle connects to the drain-waste-vent system.

Toilets are different from other plumbing fixtures. They use only cold water and, while you control the discharge of water, you do not control the incoming supply. That is done by a float valve inside the toilet tank.

DRAIN-WASTE-VENT

The drain-waste-vent (DWV) system carries water away from the fixtures. Between it and each fixture (except a toilet) is a trap. The trap keeps gases, odors, and vermin in the DWV system from getting into the house through fixture waste openings. A trap is a water-filled "P", S ", or a drum with its inlet at the bottom and its outlet at the top. Toilets have their own built-in traps, which serve the same purpose.

The pipe leading out of the trap is called its waste arm and leads directly into the first portion of the DWV system, the fixture waste pipe. Usu-

flow. Closing it involves quite a few turns. After the main shutoff valve usually comes the water meter which can be located either outside or inside the house, depending upon your climate.

From the meter, the water-supply system becomes the cold-water main. Cold-water-only uses, such as outdoor spigots, branch off the main. One branch leads to the water heater and begins a

ally 1 1/4- to 2-inch diameter pipe, the fixture waste pipe slopes so that waste water will flow away from the fixture. All parts of the DWV system that are not vertical have a downward slope, about 1/4 inch per foot.

Most waste pipes lead directly into a larger vertical 3- or 4-inch pipe called a vent stack, soil stack, or main stack (if it serves a toilet). Most of those that do not join with other fixture waste pipes, then dump into a vent stack. The vent stack reaches up through the roof where its open top vents into the air. The reason for this is two-fold: to let air in and keep the traps from being siphoned dry by the downrushing waste water, and to let sewer gases out without pressure past the trap

seals. Every trap is vented.

Traps that cannot vent into a stack directly have vent pipes that run horizontally to the soil stack and connect to it above the highest fixture. These are called branch vents or revents. Whether separate vent or revent, the system that costs less and meets code is usually used.

Any part of a fixture's waste pipe that also serves as a vent for it or another fixture is called a *wet vent*. Wet vent length is limited by code. The larger the pipe diameter, the longer the wet vent may be and still not siphon the trap seals.

Waste water is collected into one large horizontal pipe called the building drain. This drain eventually flows to the street sewer (if you

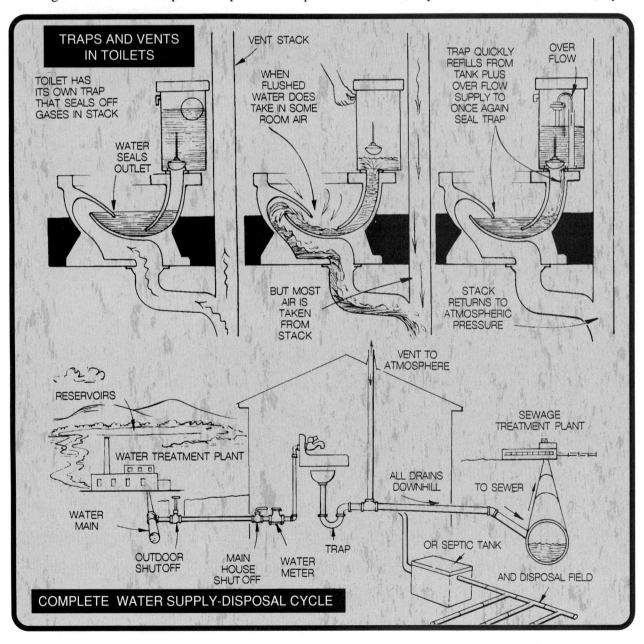

TRAPS AND VENTS IN TOILETS

TOILET HAS ITS OWN TRAP THAT SEALS OFF GASES IN STACK

WATER SEALS OUTLET

VENT STACK

WHEN FLUSHED WATER DOES TAKE IN SOME ROOM AIR

BUT MOST AIR IS TAKEN FROM STACK

TRAP QUICKLY REFILLS FROM TANK PLUS OVER FLOW SUPPLY TO ONCE AGAIN SEAL TRAP

OVER FLOW

STACK RETURNS TO ATMOSPHERIC PRESSURE

VENT TO ATMOSPHERE

RESERVOIRS

WATER TREATMENT PLANT

WATER MAIN

OUTDOOR SHUTOFF

MAIN HOUSE SHUT OFF

WATER METER

TRAP

ALL DRAINS DOWNHILL

OR SEPTIC TANK

TO SEWER

SEWAGE TREATMENT PLANT

AND DISPOSAL FIELD

COMPLETE WATER SUPPLY-DISPOSAL CYCLE

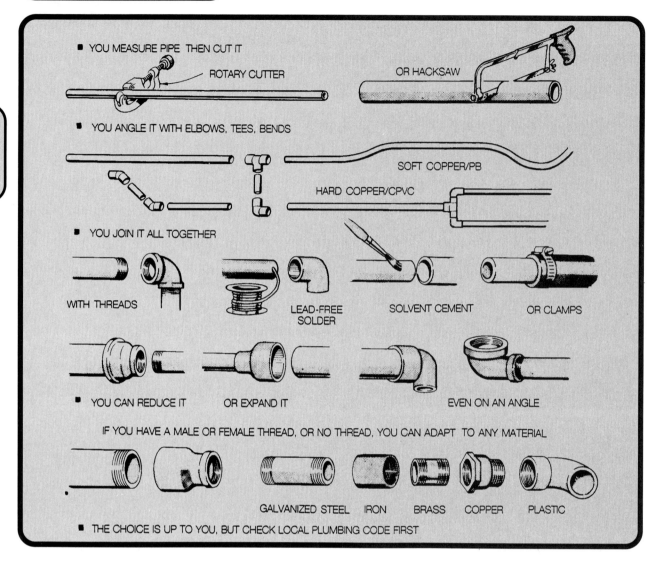

- YOU MEASURE PIPE THEN CUT IT — ROTARY CUTTER — OR HACKSAW
- YOU ANGLE IT WITH ELBOWS, TEES, BENDS — SOFT COPPER/PB — HARD COPPER/CPVC
- YOU JOIN IT ALL TOGETHER — WITH THREADS — LEAD-FREE SOLDER — SOLVENT CEMENT — OR CLAMPS
- YOU CAN REDUCE IT — OR EXPAND IT — EVEN ON AN ANGLE

IF YOU HAVE A MALE OR FEMALE THREAD, OR NO THREAD, YOU CAN ADAPT TO ANY MATERIAL

GALVANIZED STEEL — IRON — BRASS — COPPER — PLASTIC

- THE CHOICE IS UP TO YOU, BUT CHECK LOCAL PLUMBING CODE FIRST

are fortunate enough to have a community sewer system) or your septic tank.

Because of gravity flow and the sluggish-flowing nature of household wastes, horizontal DWV pipes may clog up. For this reason every horizontal drain run should be fitted with a clean out opening. It is installed in the higher end of the run and has a removable cover for access into the pipe. Some houses have a main trap located in the house just before the pipe runs to the street sewer or septic tank. Every main trap with its cleanout must be accessible in the house, crawl space, basement or outdoors. Trap arms and fixture waste pipes can be cleaned from the fixture drain, so they do not need separate cleanouts. In the case of cast iron main traps, the clean out plug may be brass and, after some years, it will tend to weld itself to the fitting. Unscrewing is impossible, so you must cut out the plug with a cold chisel and replace it with a lead or plastic plug that will never freeze up.

When you have a clogged line you want to get it cleared out in a hurry.

PLUMBING REGULATIONS

Whatever plumbing you install must meet local regulations, called codes, which vary depending upon where you live. Some can be highly restrictive, even stating that no one but a licensed plumber may install plumbing. The best codes keep abreast of new developments in the plumbing field. These pertain to the safety and health oriented provisions of design, materials and workmanship.

You must obey your local code or your job may be condemned. The first step is to find out what your code says. You can often get a copy from your city or county building department. If you live in a city, your plumbing comes under its

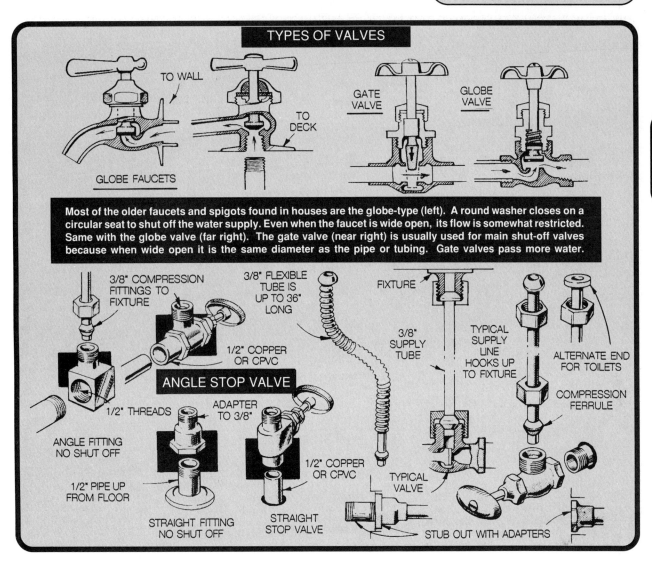

TYPES OF VALVES

GLOBE FAUCETS

TO WALL

TO DECK

GATE VALVE

GLOBE VALVE

Most of the older faucets and spigots found in houses are the globe-type (left). A round washer closes on a circular seat to shut off the water supply. Even when the faucet is wide open, its flow is somewhat restricted. Same with the globe valve (far right). The gate valve (near right) is usually used for main shut-off valves because when wide open it is the same diameter as the pipe or tubing. Gate valves pass more water.

3/8" COMPRESSION FITTINGS TO FIXTURE

3/8" FLEXIBLE TUBE IS UP TO 36" LONG

FIXTURE

1/2" COPPER OR CPVC

ANGLE STOP VALVE

3/8" SUPPLY TUBE

TYPICAL SUPPLY LINE HOOKS UP TO FIXTURE

ALTERNATE END FOR TOILETS

COMPRESSION FERRULE

1/2" THREADS

ADAPTER TO 3/8"

ANGLE FITTING NO SHUT OFF

1/2" PIPE UP FROM FLOOR

STRAIGHT FITTING NO SHUT OFF

1/2" COPPER OR CPVC

STRAIGHT STOP VALVE

TYPICAL VALVE

STUB OUT WITH ADAPTERS

regulations. If you live outside an incorporated area, your work usually comes under county or parish supervision. While you are at it, find out whether the work you plan requires a building permit. Most plumbing remodeling does.

Also, find out what inspections of your work are required before it can be finally approved. Most codes call for a pressure-test of new water supply piping and a static-fill test of new DWV piping to make sure there are no leaks.

No plumbing system should contain cross-connections. A cross-connection is any linkage between the house water-supply system and water that could possibly be contaminated. If your plumbing is very old, it may have some cross-connections built in. Look for them. A water faucet that discharges below the flood rim of its fixture basin is a cross-connection. Should the fixture bowl back up and fill with water, the submerged inlet of the faucet could, under a back-siphonage, draw dirty bowl water into the fresh-water pipes. A back-siphonage—water being drawn backwards into pipes—can be caused by a drop in water pressure when a fire hydrant down the street is opened for cleaning. Or it can come when a faucet somewhere else in the house is opened wide. The best way to stop the danger from cross-connections is to eliminate them entirely. Any submerged inlet is a cross-connection waiting for back-siphonage. This can even come through a closed faucet. A hose on the laundry tub spigot is a common cross-connection. So is a garden hose used to fill a pool and left submerged in the water. A fertilizer sprayer left connected to a garden hose is deadly in its potential.

To avoid cross-connections, vacuum breaker valves should be installed on all outdoor hose spigots and at the laundry tub.

Adapters let you connect from one pipe type to another: (top row) copper sweat elbows to threads; (bottom row) fixture angle-stop, solvent plastic to threads and polyethylene pipe to female

MATERIALS:
ABOUT PIPE & FITTINGS

Lots of times, doing it easily is knowing what is available to help.

PLUMBING IS PIPE. Small pipe is used for the water-supply system, large pipe for the drain-waste-vent system, and still larger pipe for the sewer.

FITTINGS

Along with each type of pipe comes an array of fittings designed to help you use that pipe. Fittings enable the pipe to branch out around turns, connect to different sizes of pipe and connect to other kinds of pipe. Branches are called tees and wyes. Water supply turns are called *elbows,* while some DWV turns are called *bends*—such as *1/4 bends.* Fittings from one of the same pipe to another are called *reducers* or *bushings.* Reducers do the job along a pipe run; bushings do it within another fitting.

Fittings from one kind of pipe to another are called *adapters.* Adapters are available straight, elbowed or branching. Using elbows, tees, wyes, adapters and reducers you can make pipe do just about anything you want it to do.

Other fittings make pipe even more useful. Couplings let you connect one length of pipe to another in a straight line. Unions do the same thing, but let the connection be taken apart easily at any time. Dielectric couplings connect threaded pipes of dissimilar metals, such as copper adapters and galvanized steel pipe. They are designed to prevent bimetallic action between the two in prob-

lem-water areas. A union that does the same thing is available

Fittings, you will find, come in two styles: standard and drainage. Standard fittings are used for water-supply systems and vent runs in DWV systems. They are simpler and less costly, but have inner shoulders that can trap solids. For that reason, drainage-type fittings must be used in drain-waste runs to provide for smooth flow. Either standard or drainage fittings may be used for vent runs in DWV work.

Specialized fittings handle specific purposes such as a toilet flange, a fitting that lets a toilet be joined to the DWV system. DWV fittings that serve vent runs are used upside down.

"READING" A TEE

When you describe a wye or tee fitting, always state the "run" or "through" size first. Then state the branch size. A tee to tap in a 3/4-inch pipe and branch off with a 1/2-inch would be a 3/4 x 3/4 x 1/2 tee.

Pipe diameters are based mostly on inside diameter. For example, a standard 3/4-inch galvanized steel pipe, rarely used these days but still found in many old homes, measures somewhat larger than 3/4 inches on the inside and a full inch outside. Copper and plastic water supply tubing is sized by nominal inside diameter. So watch pipe sizes. They can fool you.

PIPE FITTING IDENTIFICATION CHART

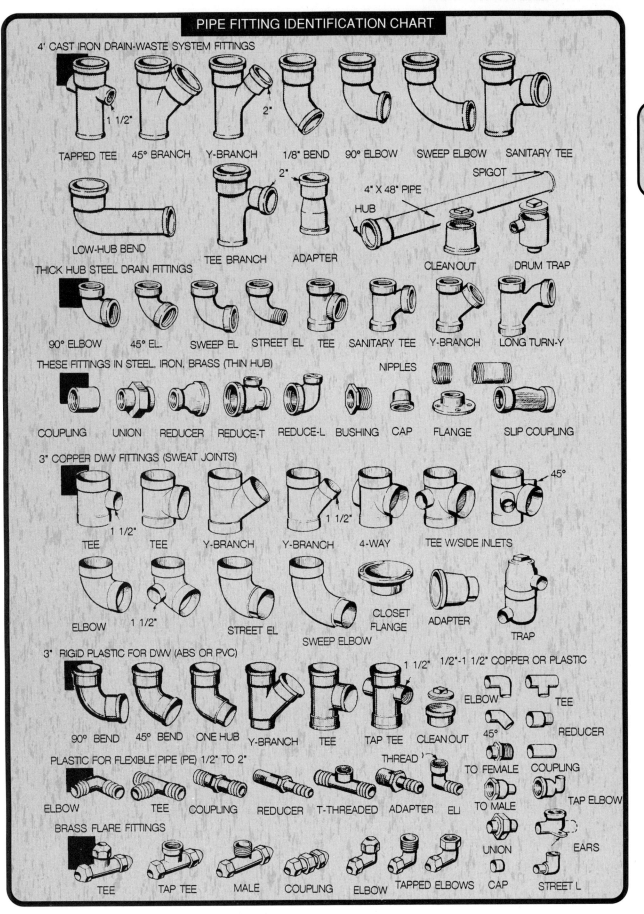

4' CAST IRON DRAIN-WASTE SYSTEM FITTINGS

TAPPED TEE · 45° BRANCH · Y-BRANCH · 1/8" BEND · 90° ELBOW · SWEEP ELBOW · SANITARY TEE

LOW-HUB BEND · TEE BRANCH · ADAPTER · SPIGOT · 4" X 48" PIPE · HUB · CLEAN OUT · DRUM TRAP

THICK HUB STEEL DRAIN FITTINGS

90° ELBOW · 45° EL. · SWEEP EL · STREET EL · TEE · SANITARY TEE · Y-BRANCH · LONG TURN-Y

THESE FITTINGS IN STEEL, IRON, BRASS (THIN HUB)

NIPPLES

COUPLING · UNION · REDUCER · REDUCE-T · REDUCE-L · BUSHING · CAP · FLANGE · SLIP COUPLING

3" COPPER DWV FITTINGS (SWEAT JOINTS)

TEE · TEE · Y-BRANCH · Y-BRANCH · 4-WAY · TEE W/SIDE INLETS · 45°

ELBOW · STREET EL · SWEEP ELBOW · CLOSET FLANGE · ADAPTER · TRAP

3" RIGID PLASTIC FOR DWV (ABS OR PVC)

1/2"-1 1/2" COPPER OR PLASTIC

90° BEND · 45° BEND · ONE HUB · Y-BRANCH · TEE · TAP TEE · CLEAN OUT

ELBOW · TEE · 45° · REDUCER · COUPLING · TAP ELBOW

PLASTIC FOR FLEXIBLE PIPE (PE) 1/2" TO 2"

THREAD

ELBOW · TEE · COUPLING · REDUCER · T-THREADED · ADAPTER · ELL

TO FEMALE · TO MALE · UNION · EARS

BRASS FLARE FITTINGS

TEE · TAP TEE · MALE · COUPLING · ELBOW · TAPPED ELBOWS · CAP · STREET L

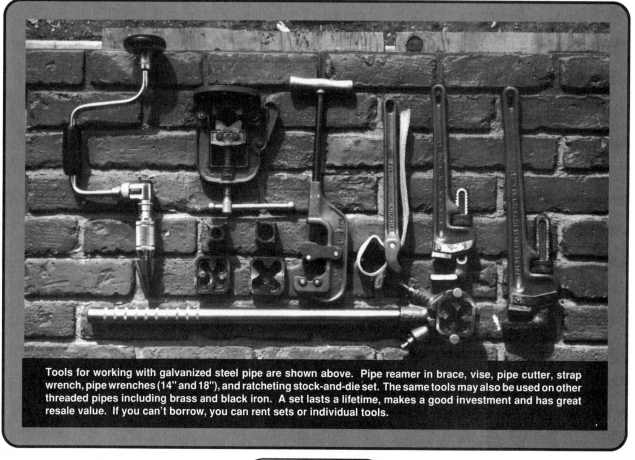

Tools for working with galvanized steel pipe are shown above. Pipe reamer in brace, vise, pipe cutter, strap wrench, pipe wrenches (14" and 18"), and ratcheting stock-and-die set. The same tools may also be used on other threaded pipes including brass and black iron. A set lasts a lifetime, makes a good investment and has great resale value. If you can't borrow, you can rent sets or individual tools.

MATERIALS:
GALVANIZED STEEL PIPE

While galvanized steel pipe went out of style along with tub butter, here are a few things you should know.

Galvanized pipe was the major water supply pipe before brass pipe, copper and plastic tubing were invented. It has steel's high strength and low cost. High pressures and water hammer have less effect on it. Leakage is rare because the threaded joints between galvanized steel pipe and its fittings tend to seal themselves. Nails driven into framing after the plumbing has been put in cannot possibly penetrate galvanized pipe and fittings.

As threads must be provided at each joint, galvanized pipe, like other threaded pipes, is tough to install. Cutting threads, even with proper tools, is hard work.

But because galvanized pipe is so widely used, fixtures and all appliances are designed to be adapted to it. Water heaters come with threaded tappings for direct connections. The same applies to water softeners, many appliances and fixtures.

Galvanized pipe is also available, though not very popular in many parts of the country, for drain-waste-vent systems. For this, 1 1/2-, 2- and 3-inch diameters are used along with drainage-type fittings. Galvanized steel pipe may be used above ground, but may not be buried under buildings or embedded in concrete. Outdoor burial is permitted if backfill is not composed of cinders. A big disadvantage of galvanized steel or any threaded pipe is that tap-in of new lines is difficult. Anytime you want to cut into the system to add a branch, the mechanics of threading require that a union be installed alongside the fitting to let everything be threaded. Unions are costly fittings. A way out is provided by saddle tees, if your code permits, but these greatly reduce flow. Another way out: for a full flow tee connection you can use a slipnut tee (Dresser tee). This allows teeing off from a galvanized steel pipe run without rethreading the cut-off pipe ends. Slip couplings rather than threads are used.

NIPPLES AVAILABLE

The tools for working with galvanized steel (as well as threaded brass) pipe are costly. On small jobs you can do without buying them, by using ready-made short lengths of pipes called nipples. Nipples are threaded on both ends. A "close" nipple is the shortest, containing threads along its entire length. A "short" nipple is a little longer, leaving a small gap between fittings. Other nipples are made 1 1/2, 2, 2 1/2, 3, 4, 6, 8, 10, and 12 inches long, end to end. Some dealers carry 2-, 3- and 4-foot nipples, ready made.

Pipe threads are called *male* or outside threads. Fitting threads are called *female* or inside threads.

Galvanized pipes are available in 21-foot lengths and diameters of 3/8, 1/2, 3/4, 1-inch and larger and smaller. These always refer to nominal inside diameter. Outside diameter measures about l/4 inch more, allowing for wall thickness. Full lengths are threaded on both ends and come with one coupling loosely screwed on.

Three sizes of galvanized steel pipe: 3/8", 1/2", and 3/4". All have threaded ends to connect to threaded galvanized-steel fittings. A wide range of sizes is available. Note how threads taper.

Slip-coupling with rubber O-ring seals at each end lets you fasten two galvanized steel pipes together without the need for threading the ends of the pipe or using a union. A great labor saver.

These are the three popular sizes you will find in a home. The 1/2" line (left) usually serves the hot water heater or range. The 3/4" line (center) feeds the furnace. Main lines are usually 1" or larger.

Note that this regular galvanized 3/4" T fitting at the left is identical to the black iron T. The working techniques of both pipe are the same; you need plenty of muscle and cutting oil.

This is the typical bronze gas valve you have in your home if, of course, you use gas. Each appliance should have a separate valve, clearly labeled. A quarter turn shuts off the supply.

MATERIALS:
BLACK IRON PIPE

Unless you run your own gas lines, you will probably never use black iron pipe. It is cheaper than galvanized but just as tough to handle.

BLACK IRON PIPE is used primarily for gas piping. Galvanized pipe is usually not permitted for piping gas because flakes of the galvanizing can drop off into the gas stream and find their way to small burner orifices where they may put out the burner flame and, if safety cutoff devices fail, let gas escape into the house.

Black iron pipe comes in the same sizes as galvanized pipe and the fittings are interchangeable. But don't mix them, because you can be made by a building inspector to tear out a whole run of black pipe to remove one galvanized fitting and replace it with a black one.

SIZE IS DIFFERENT

Choosing pipe sizes for gas runs is not as simple as for water-supply piping. The smallest gas pipe permitted in a system is usually 1/2 inch, where it supplies only a stove or a water heater. The pipe size coming from the gas meter is determined by how many and what size appliances must be served. Figuring this is a job for your gas utility. Ask them to help plan. They'll need to know the BTU (British Thermal Unit) input rating of each gas appliance along with the distance the appliance is located from your meter. If any extra-long piping runs are required, or you have too many gas appliances, you may find you should not attempt to add another gas eater. Such may be the case with a swimming pool heater or an outdoor barbecue. Incidentally, pipe sizes for natural gas are larger than for more concentrated LP gas.

Once you have determined exactly what is required, you should be able to make the pipe installation yourself. Black pipe to be buried should be the coated kind; otherwise it has no protection against corrosion. The coating may be a factory-applied vinyl covering or a factory finish. Joints and openings in this coating should be wrapped with plastic tape.

MATERIALS:
THREADED BRASS PIPE

Brass pipe is still used in the more expensive homes. It works like galvanized and will not rust. It will outlast the home.

WHERE WATER IS CORROSIVE to galvanized steel or tends to build up scale, threaded brass pipe is used. This may even be a code requirement. Brass pipe is expensive compared to other pipe types. If your house has it, it has the finest water-supply system available. Brass has the strength benefits of galvanized steel. Nails won't puncture it; high pressure won't harm it. Unlike steel, its inner walls are so smooth they present little resistance to water flow. The only damage it may suffer is when connected to galvanized steel pipe without a dielectric coupling or union in a corrosive-water area. If you extend a brass water system with galvanized steel, you should use such a connector between the two kinds of pipe. Copper and plastic extensions from a brass system require no special protection, because they do not create harmful bimetallic action with brass.

Like galvanized steel, brass has threaded fitting drawbacks because costly threading tools are otherwise necessary. However, one advantage brass has over galvanized threaded pipe is that when threads are cut, a protective oxide coating quickly forms again.

STRAP WRENCH

Brass, being the Rolls Royce of pipes, calls for extra care in pipe assembly. Whereas on steel pipe you would screw the joints together with serrated-jaw pipe wrenches and think nothing of it, the use of these tools mars the fine appearance of brass pipe. For a workmanlike job it should be tightened with a strap wrench, so as not to deface the surface.

VALVES

Most valves are made of brass. They may be installed in a run of galvanized steel pipe without dielectric fittings, provided the water is not highly corrosive and a good joint material is used on the pipe threads. More on that later.

That gleam you see is not gold but you might think it is after purchasing a 20' length. The 3/8" feeds lavatories and toilets; the 1/2" kitchen sinks and water heaters. Main branch is 3/4".

Compared to steel, brass is soft so some pros use a strap wrench on the pipe and a regular wrench on the fittings. If you will accept a few nicks and burrs you can use a regular pipe wrench.

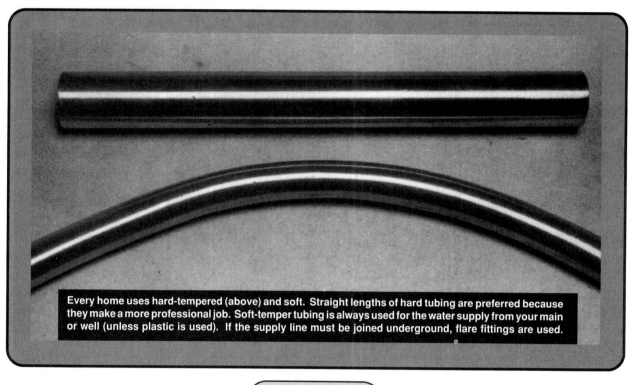

Every home uses hard-tempered (above) and soft. Straight lengths of hard tubing are preferred because they make a more professional job. Soft-temper tubing is always used for the water supply from your main or well (unless plastic is used). If the supply line must be joined underground, flare fittings are used.

MATERIALS:

COPPER TUBING

Copper tubing and pipe have long been a favorite in plumbing, heating and cooling. It works easily and will last many lifetimes.

COPPER IS NO LONGER the most versatile pipe for plumbing. It is reasonably easy to install, resists corrosion and scale build up, and serves both water-supply and drain-waste-vent systems. While sweat-type solder fittings are most commonly used, copper tubing may be joined with flare and compression fittings if desired. Copper tubing is light in weight compared to like-diameter steel pipe. Copper sweated joints can be made with everyday shop tools. Copper builds what is considered a permanent plumbing system. The material resists corrosion and scale build-up. Additions to a copper system are simple; one need only saw through the tube and install a tee or whatever style of branch is needed.

Copper can be punctured when nailing wall materials, so care should be taken to protect piping from such damage. Straps installed wherever copper tubes pass through wood frame-ing members will prevent nailing in those locations. Copper costs more than steel or plastic pipe but is less expensive than brass. A minor copper disadvantage of which you should be aware is the fire danger when using a flame to solder the joints.

HARD vs. SOFT

Copper tube comes in two types: hard-tempered and soft-tempered. Hard-tempered tubing is straight and rigid, while soft-tempered is flexible and bendable. The smooth bends of a copper system made with soft-tempered copper water tubing present very little resistance to flow. Moreover, it is easier to thread into walls in remodeling work. Usually a pipe one size smaller than galvanized steel pipe will provide a good rate of flow. Copper water-supply tubing is designated by nominal inside diameter sizes with the

Three sizes of copper water tubing most often used in home plumbing are (top to bottom) 3/8", 1/2" and 3/4". Copper's smooth inner walls deliver more water than comparable sizes of galvanized steel pipe, less than plastic pipe.

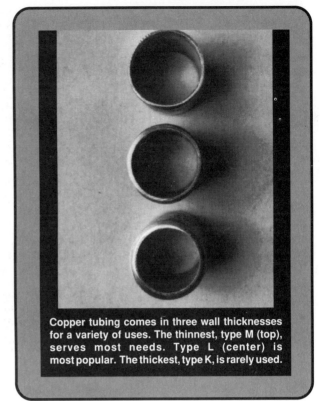

Copper tubing comes in three wall thicknesses for a variety of uses. The thinnest, type M (top), serves most needs. Type L (center) is most popular. The thickest, type K, is rarely used.

outside diameter always 1/8-inch larger than the nominal size. Inside diameters are close to, but not always equal to, the nominal size. Air-conditioning/refrigeration tubing goes by outside diameter. Wall thickness of copper tubing can vary without changing the outside diameter. You can get copper tubing in three wall thicknesses: Type K, which has thick walls; Type L, which is the most commonly used wall thickness for home plumbing; and Type M, which is low-cost, thin-wall tubing. All fit the same sweat-type fittings because the outside diameter is the same in each. Naturally, Type K tubing is slightly smaller in inside diameter than Types L and M.

When buying copper tube, you can get into a lot of trouble over the size question. You may end up with a fitting too large or a pipe too small. For this reason, you are safest to spell it out: ''I want 60 feet of 1/2-inch Type L flexible copper water tubing, 1/2-inch inside diameter.'' For fittings say, ''I want four 90° copper sweat elbows for 1/2-inch *ID* tubing.'' You will eliminate mistakes by being specific.

Types K, L, and M copper tube are available in hard-tempered straight lengths, 20 feet long. Types K and L may also be had in soft-

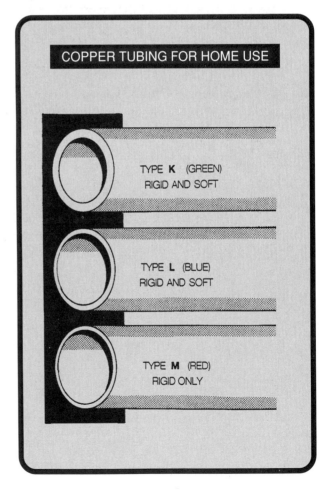

COPPER TUBING FOR HOME USE

TYPE **K** (GREEN)
RIGID AND SOFT

TYPE **L** (BLUE)
RIGID AND SOFT

TYPE **M** (RED)
RIGID ONLY

Joining copper tubing without solder, you have two choices: compression fittings (above) or flare fittings. Compression uses nuts and brass ferrules; flare uses nuts and flared ends.

tempered flexible tubing, usually 30 or 60 feet long. You can often get cut-to-length copper tubing from a dealer by paying a somewhat higher price per foot for exactly the length you need. Hard-tempered tubing may be joined only by sweat-soldering or by annealing the end and using a flare fitting. Soft-tempered tubing may be joined with solder, flare or compression fittings.

FLARE AND COMPRESSION

Flare and compression fittings cost more than sweat-soldered fittings, but they have several advantages fore creating a water-supply piping system using copper tubing. They're mechanical couplings: therefore, no sweat-soldering is needed. They are thus lead-free. What's more, every flare and compression fitting is like a union, letting it be taken apart and put back together as often as necessary without leaking.

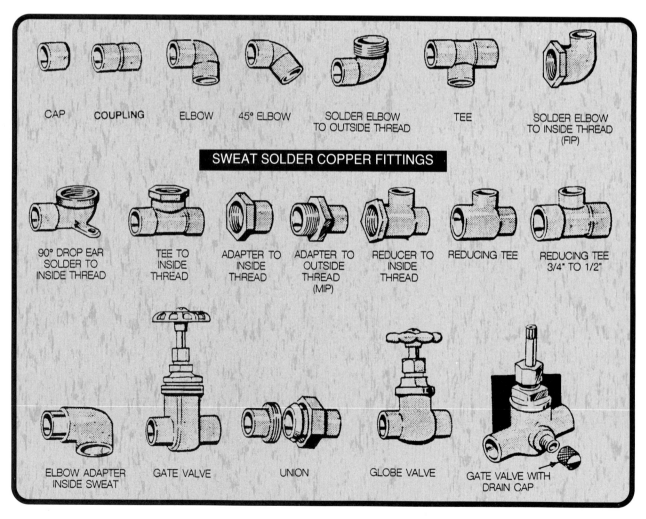

CAP COUPLING ELBOW 45° ELBOW SOLDER ELBOW TO OUTSIDE THREAD TEE SOLDER ELBOW TO INSIDE THREAD (FIP)

SWEAT SOLDER COPPER FITTINGS

90° DROP EAR SOLDER TO INSIDE THREAD TEE TO INSIDE THREAD ADAPTER TO INSIDE THREAD ADAPTER TO OUTSIDE THREAD (MIP) REDUCER TO INSIDE THREAD REDUCING TEE REDUCING TEE 3/4" TO 1/2"

ELBOW ADAPTER INSIDE SWEAT GATE VALVE UNION GLOBE VALVE GATE VALVE WITH DRAIN CAP

Flared fittings need the ends of the tube flared before joining (see page 132). This is done with a flaring tool—two types are available, drive-in and clamp down. Then the fitting is wrench-tightened. Compression fittings need only be assembled and wrenched up watertight. In both cases, the flare or compression nuts must be properly installed on the tube and before anything else is done. Otherwise, they won't go on.

Flare and compression fittings are available in all water-supply sizes from 1/4-inch to 3/4-inch nominal sizes. Flare fittings work with soft-tempered copper tube only: compression fittings will work with both soft- and hard-tempered copper tube.

Soft-tempered copper pipe or tubing has the advantage that in it water can freeze several times without bursting the pipe. But remember, with each freeze the diameter gets larger—and the walls get thinner.

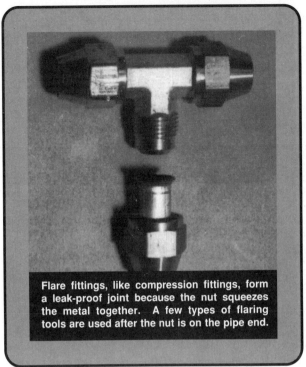

Flare fittings, like compression fittings, form a leak-proof joint because the nut squeezes the metal together. A few types of flaring tools are used after the nut is on the pipe end.

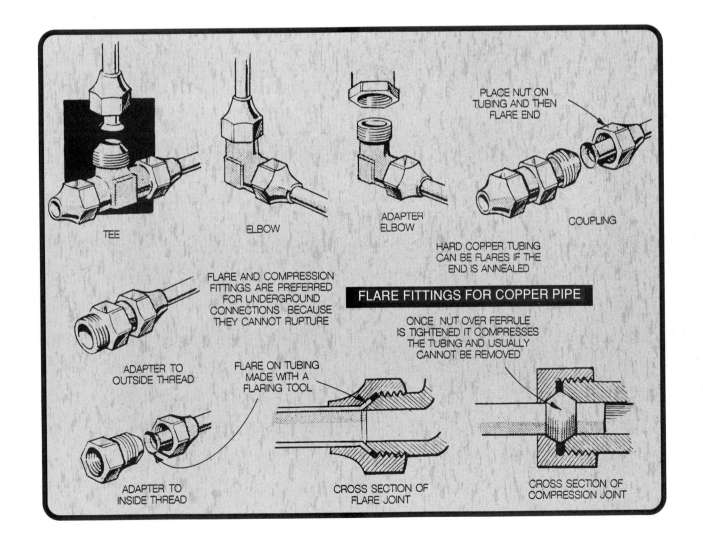

TEE

ELBOW

ADAPTER ELBOW

PLACE NUT ON TUBING AND THEN FLARE END

COUPLING

HARD COPPER TUBING CAN BE FLARES IF THE END IS ANNEALED

FLARE AND COMPRESSION FITTINGS ARE PREFERRED FOR UNDERGROUND CONNECTIONS BECAUSE THEY CANNOT RUPTURE

ADAPTER TO OUTSIDE THREAD

FLARE ON TUBING MADE WITH A FLARING TOOL

ADAPTER TO INSIDE THREAD

FLARE FITTINGS FOR COPPER PIPE

ONCE NUT OVER FERRULE IS TIGHTENED IT COMPRESSES THE TUBING AND USUALLY CANNOT BE REMOVED

CROSS SECTION OF FLARE JOINT

CROSS SECTION OF COMPRESSION JOINT

CPVC fittings come as elbows, tees, valves, unions, various adapters, street elbows, reducing fittings and wing fittings. CPVC costs more than PVC but CPVC is heat-resistant.

MATERIALS:
PLASTIC WATER SUPPLY PIPE

Plastic pipe is truly do-it-yourself pipe. All major plumbing codes approve. Equally important—you will like working with plastic pipe.

THE EASIEST-TO-USE PIPE for do-it-yourself water-supply installation is plastic. Like copper, it comes in sizes and fittings for both water-supply and drain-waste-vent use. There are also two other kinds of plastic pipe for cold-water-only use.

If there is no old-fashioned local code preventing it, we recommend the use of plastic piping. Besides being easy to cut and join, it is low in cost. It's lightweight, too. The inner walls of plastic pipe are so smooth that water passes easily through. A smaller size can do the same job as a size larger metal pipe. Normally, though, the same size is used.

For cold and hot-water lines, plastic pipe is naturally insulating and eliminates sweating in cold-water lines. For hot-water lines, the plastic cuts heat loss, which can be considerable with metal piping. Plastic pipes may be installed above or below ground.

Drawbacks are few. Two types of plastic pipe may be used with hot water: CPVC (Chlorinated Poly Vinyl Chloride) and PB (Polybutylene). The others are intended for cold-water lines only. Plastic pipe is easily punctured by nailing and so must be protected the same as with copper tubing. Over-temperatures and over-pressures must be avoided. With any other kind of pipe, a misjudged fitting, once assembled, can be taken apart and refitted. Not so if the joints are welded. If you make a mistake, you have to saw the fitting out of the run and install a new one with suitable couplings to join it to the cut-off ends. To be sure everything fits correctly the first time, thought must be given before making up each joint. Otherwise, the useless pile of sawed-out parts left over after a job can cancel out any savings in material or time over some other type of pipe.

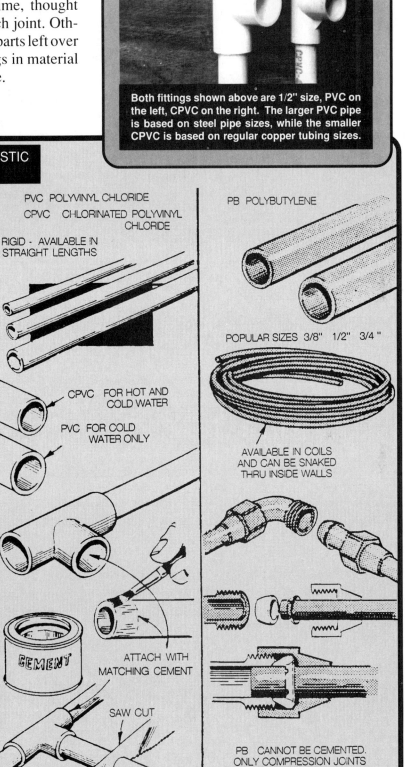

Both fittings shown above are 1/2" size, PVC on the left, CPVC on the right. The larger PVC pipe is based on steel pipe sizes, while the smaller CPVC is based on regular copper tubing sizes.

THE THREE TYPES OF PLASTIC WATER SUPPLY PIPE

PE   POLYETHYLENE

POPULAR SIZES ARE 3/4", 1", 1 1/2" SMALLER SIZES FOR DRIP WATERING SYSTEMS

FLEXIBLE COILS OF WALL THICKNESS FOR 80, 100, 125, 160 PSI

MAJOR USES - COLD WATER FROM WELLS, WATER MAIN TO HOME, UNDERGROUND SPRINKLERS, POOL LINES

ATTACH WITH STAINLESS STEEL CLAMPS

ADAPTERS TO STEEL AND COPPER

PVC POLYVINYL CHLORIDE
CPVC   CHLORINATED POLYVINYL CHLORIDE

RIGID - AVAILABLE IN STRAIGHT LENGTHS

CPVC FOR HOT AND COLD WATER
PVC FOR COLD WATER ONLY

CEMENT

ATTACH WITH MATCHING CEMENT

SAW CUT

PB POLYBUTYLENE

POPULAR SIZES 3/8" 1/2" 3/4"

AVAILABLE IN COILS AND CAN BE SNAKED THRU INSIDE WALLS

PB CANNOT BE CEMENTED. ONLY COMPRESSION JOINTS ARE USED

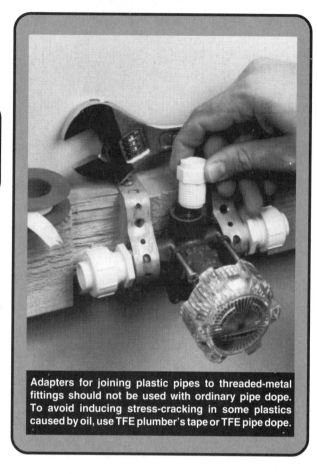

Adapters for joining plastic pipes to threaded-metal fittings should not be used with ordinary pipe dope. To avoid inducing stress-cracking in some plastics caused by oil, use TFE plumber's tape or TFE pipe dope.

CPVC PLASTIC

For water-supply systems, the pipe to use is CPVC (chlorinated polyvinyl chloride). The trouble with most plastic pipes is that they soften when hot. CPVC does only slightly, as it is chemically toughened against heat by putting an extra chlorine atom into the composition. CPVC pipe is rated to withstand 100 psi (pounds per square inch) at 180°F.

CPVC pipe is widely available; the most popular sizes being 3/4- and 1/2-inch. It is sold in 10-foot lengths. Transition adapters connect CPVC to threaded-metal piping without leaks.

Fittings for CPVC are just as expensive as those for galvanized steel pipe. Use CPVC solvent cement for joining; it takes a quarter pint to do 63 1/2-inch joints.

PB PLASTIC

The other material of choice for creating a hot/cold water-supply system is PB (poly-butylene). PB plays "soft copper" to CPVC's "hard

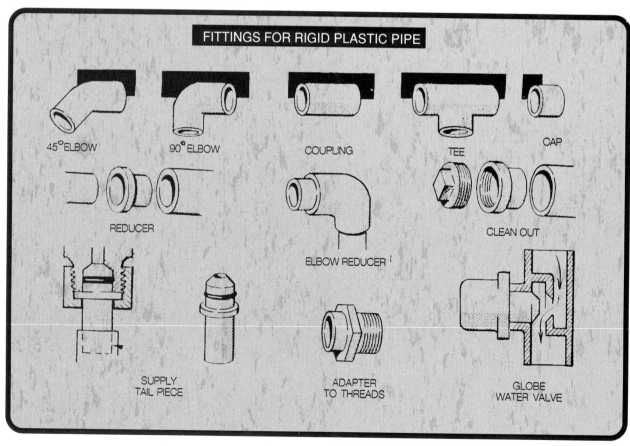

FITTINGS FOR RIGID PLASTIC PIPE

45°ELBOW   90° ELBOW   COUPLING   TEE   CAP

REDUCER   ELBOW REDUCER   CLEAN OUT

SUPPLY TAIL PIECE   ADAPTER TO THREADS   GLOBE WATER VALVE

copper," giving you the same flexible/rigid selection in easy-working plastic water-supply tubing that you have in copper. PB is available in 1/4-, 1/2- and 3/4-inch nominal sizes based on inside diameter in straight lengths and coils. PB cannot be solvent welded; joining is by push-on, hand-tightening mechanical fittings. PB is ideal for remodeling work where the tubing can be snaked into walls, floors and ceilings and for making long, joint-free runs.

COLD WATER ONLY

CPVC pipe's lower-temperature cousin PVC pipe (polyvinyl chloride), is fine for cold-water lines anywhere inside or outside the house. Maximum working temperature is 150°F. PVC pipe is made in both light-duty solvent-welded pipe and fittings or in heavy-duty Schedule 40 and 80 pipe. The latter is used mostly for irrigation work. PVC water-supply sizes are less costly than CPVC and sizes go along steel-pipe diameters, thus giving a larger pipe passageway. Fittings are almost unlimited to adapt, reduce, couple, bend and connect. Use only PVC solvent cement for making the solvent-welded joints.

POLYETHYLENE PIPE

Still another useful plastic pipe is PE (polyethylene). Being flexible and furnished in long coils, it is especially useful for underground water-supply lines from water main to house. Size is based on inside diameter; it comes 1/2-, 3/4-, and 1-inch and larger. Fittings consist of adapters to inside and outside threads, couplings, elbows and tees. Fittings are either of plastic or galvanized steel. The pipe slips over serrated fittings and is clamped with stainless steel band screw clamps. PE pipe is available in wall thickness for 80 psi, 100 psi, 125 psi, and 160 psi. If it is to be used for your water supply, it should be rated by the National Sanitation Foundation. (The same is true of any pipe and fittings you use for that purpose.) All PE pipes so rated are stamped with the letters NSF.

A prime use for PE pipe is to bring the water up from a well. The 125 psi pipe will withstand 150 safely. It is also an excellent choice for an underground service line for the well or water main to the house.

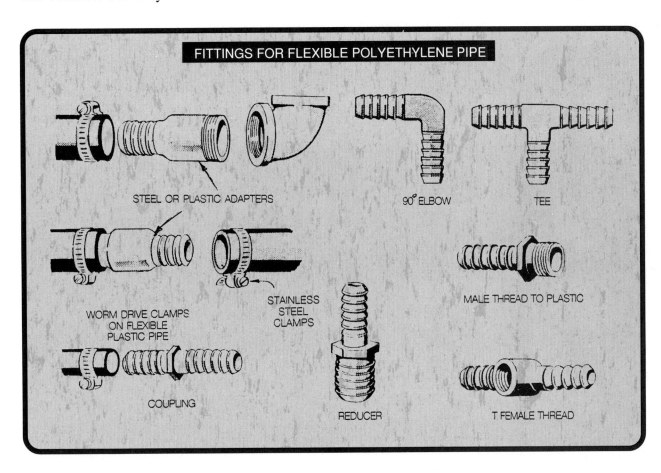

FITTINGS FOR FLEXIBLE POLYETHYLENE PIPE

STEEL OR PLASTIC ADAPTERS

90° ELBOW

TEE

WORM DRIVE CLAMPS ON FLEXIBLE PLASTIC PIPE

STAINLESS STEEL CLAMPS

MALE THREAD TO PLASTIC

COUPLING

REDUCER

T FEMALE THREAD

Plastic DWV pipe is a natural for prefabrication of components on the floor. Its quick-drying, solvent-welded joints let an entire section of the DWV system be assembled in just a few minutes.

MATERIALS:
PLASTIC DRAIN-WASTE-VENT PIPE

If your code permits, plastic is the easiest to use and the most economical DWV pipe you can buy. It is efficient, too.

PLASTIC PIPE IN DWV sizes comes in either of two materials: PVC and ABS (Acrylonitrile-Butadiene-Styrene). PVC drain-waste-vent pipe, like PVC water-supply pipe, is light in color; ABS is black. PVC solvent welding cement is used to join PVC DWV pipe and fittings. ABS calls for

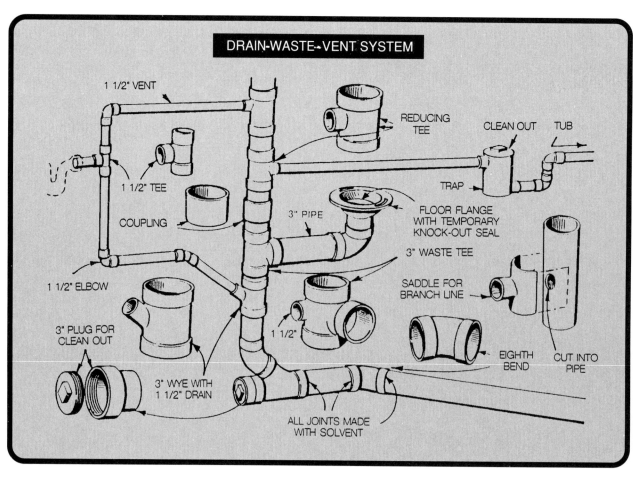

DRAIN-WASTE-VENT SYSTEM

1 1/2" VENT
REDUCING TEE
CLEAN OUT
TUB
1 1/2" TEE
TRAP
COUPLING
3" PIPE
FLOOR FLANGE WITH TEMPORARY KNOCK-OUT SEAL
3" WASTE TEE
1 1/2" ELBOW
SADDLE FOR BRANCH LINE
3" PLUG FOR CLEAN OUT
1 1/2"
EIGHTH BEND
CUT INTO PIPE
3" WYE WITH 1 1/2" DRAIN
ALL JOINTS MADE WITH SOLVENT

the use of ABS cement, which is black like the pipe. PVC and ABS pipes, their fittings and their solvent cements are not interchangeable unless a special all-purpose solvent cement is used. Incidentally one pint of solvent will do about 30 3-inch joints or more than 65 1 1/2- inch joints.

PVC pipe has been widely used in this country and Europe for years. ABS pipe is also popular, probably because it costs slightly less than PVC. However, PVC DWV pipe and fittings in the 3-inch Schedule 30 size have a big advantage over ABS because they fit perfectly within a standard 3 l/2-inch stud wall. ABS pipe and fittings, though their nominal size is also 3 inches, are larger on the outside than PVC. To use them requires furring the wall out an extra inch.

Plastic DWV pipes and fittings have the benefit of being lightweight and thus need less support from the house framing. One minor drawback is they can be penetrated by nails. The plastic also may be affected by certain chemical solvents, but how often do you pour methyl-ethyl-ketone down your drains? Most chemical drain cleaners, soaps, detergents sold for home use have no harmful effect on plastic.

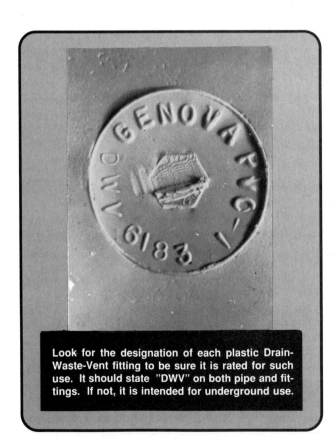

Look for the designation of each plastic Drain-Waste-Vent fitting to be sure it is rated for such use. It should state "DWV" on both pipe and fittings. If not, it is intended for underground use.

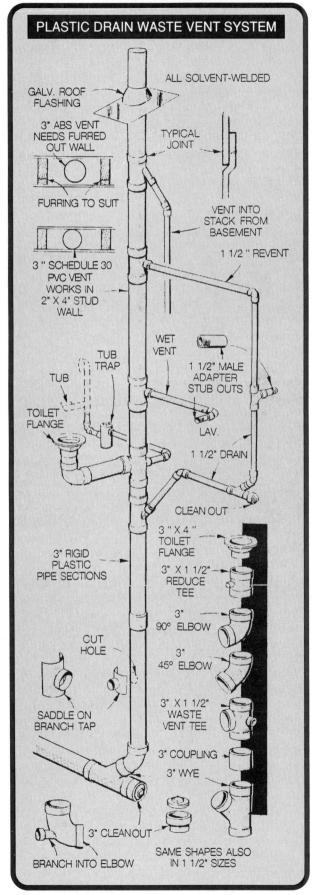

PLASTIC DRAIN WASTE VENT SYSTEM

Corrugated lightweight underground pipes come in rolls and 10-foot lengths that can be carried even in your sub-compact or your trunk. No need for tying red flags behind.

MATERIALS:

OTHER TYPES OF PIPE

This "catch-all" section deals with other kinds of pipe you may need in or around your home.

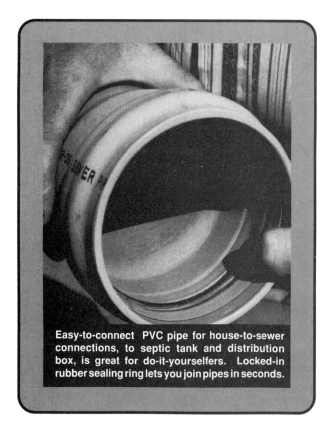

Easy-to-connect PVC pipe for house-to-sewer connections, to septic tank and distribution box, is great for do-it-yourselfers. Locked-in rubber sealing ring lets you join pipes in seconds.

WE'VE SAVED THIS SPOT for a description of the other kinds of pipe you can purchase. Clear vinyl tubing is good for serving humidifiers and water coolers. It uses standard compression fittings except that a plastic ferrule, instead of a brass one, is installed over the tube end, as with copper tubing. Vinyl tubing is so light and flexible it can run anywhere and be free from physical damage. It is also cheaper than copper tubing of the same diameter.

UNDERGROUND DRAINAGE

A number of different pipe types are used for underground outside-the-home drainage of sewage, roof runoff water, and ground water. While DWV pipes and fittings could be used, lower-cost underground pipes may be substituted. Sizes are 3- and 4-inch ID; lengths are typically 10 feet. Underground plastic pipe does not bear the DWV or Schedule 40 designation, and therefore should

Seepage pipe for fields is available in either the usual perforated pipes or in slotted pipes as here. Saw cuts spaced like perforations let water out as it flows along pipe.

Flexible plastic 1/4 bend snaps onto the end of a length of pipe. Corrugations permit the pipe to be made of very light gauge plastic yet still withstand backfill pressures. Pipe is not for sewers.

never be used indoors, except perhaps for under floor basement drainage into a sump pit.

Here are the kinds of underground pipe you should know about:

PVC /ABS—made of the same materials as the DWV piping, are light in weight and easy to join with solvent-welded couplings. Perforated pipe is available for seepage-trench use.

RS—Rubber-styrene pipe works pretty much the same as the above pipes. Use ABS cement to join RS pipes and fittings. Diameter is 4 inches. Perforated RS pipe is available.

PITCH-FIBER—Old and reliable, pitch-fiber, or bituminous pipe, goes together with tapered couplings. The joints are tapped together to hold. Diameter is 3 or 4 inches, and perforated as well as solid-wall pipe is available. For less than full lengths, a taper-jointing field lathe is needed. Try renting it where you buy the pipe.

VITRIFIED-CLAY—More expensive than plastic; if you use vitrified-clay pipe, get the kind with self-joints using either neoprene rubber gaskets or asphalt solvent-welded joints. It comes in 4-inch and larger diameters, 2-foot and 5-foot lengths.

ADS SYSTEM—This patented corrugated plastic pipe is so light in weight that you can carry an entire septic field installation in one coil. Pipe and fittings snap together through their formed corrugations. It is available solid-wall or slotted for seepage. If your dealer doesn't have it, write Advanced Drainage Systems, Inc., Box 489, Pomona, California, 91769, for information on where to buy it.

Before perforated plastic, foundation perimeter and sewage disposal fields used short clay or concrete pipe, allowing about a half-inch for drainage. Top of pipe over the crack is covered with tar paper.

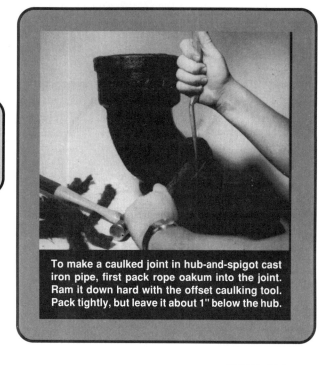

To make a caulked joint in hub-and-spigot cast iron pipe, first pack rope oakum into the joint. Ram it down hard with the offset caulking tool. Pack tightly, but leave it about 1" below the hub.

Melt one pound of lead per inch of joint in a ladle. While still hot, pour the molten lead in to fill joint. A joint-running tool and clamp hold the lead in joints on horizontal runs.

WORKING WITH PIPE:
CAST IRON

Like brass pipe in water lines, cast iron has been time-tested as the most permanent Drain-Waste-Vent system. Now lead–and-oakum joints are out, No-Hub joints are in.

CAST IRON is widely recognized as the best drain-waste-vent piping. Until recently, the common joining method required for cast iron pipe involved stuffing rope oakum around the joint, packing it in place, then pouring in lead. This was hard and troublesome work, not well suited to

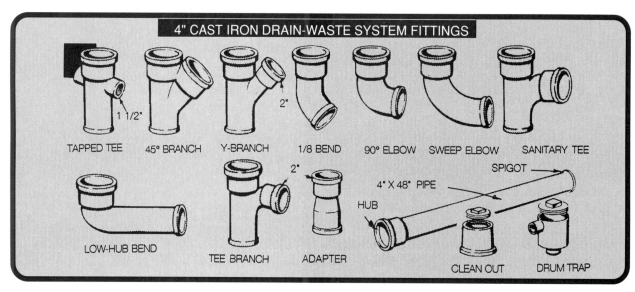

4" CAST IRON DRAIN-WASTE SYSTEM FITTINGS

TAPPED TEE   45° BRANCH   Y-BRANCH   1/8 BEND   90° ELBOW   SWEEP ELBOW   SANITARY TEE

1 1/2"

2"

LOW-HUB BEND   TEE BRANCH   ADAPTER

2"

SPIGOT

4" X 48" PIPE

HUB

CLEAN OUT   DRUM TRAP

Pack the cooled lead against the hub and pipe with the caulking tool. If you get a dual-purpose flattened tool, it can do both jobs. Angled-end tools require one for hub, another for the pipe.

cut out the necessary amount of old pipe, leaving plain ends on the pipe at either end and installing a new hubless fitting. A tee or wye, or whatever is wanted, can be installed in this way. But you will find the hardest part is cutting out the old pipe.

USE ANYWHERE

Hubless pipe comes in 2-, 3-, and 4-inch diameters and 5-foot and 10-foot lengths. Diameters are ID. All can be adapted to fixture traps, toilets, sewer pipes with available adapters, and couplings. Branch drains of less than 2 inches are made with 1 1/2-inch galvanized steel pipe and drainage-type threaded fittings used in the No-Hub tappings.

do-it-yourself. Now, however, the use of No-Hub pipe has simplified matters for the professional and nonprofessional alike. It is such a great method for joining these heavy pipes that the pros use it widely.

Instead of having a bell-and-spigot design built into the pipe ends and fittings, No-Hub pipes and fittings are plain-ended. To make a joint, the ends are slipped into a neoprene rubber sleeve and a stainless steel shield is slipped over the sleeve and tightened at both ends with screw clamps. The resulting joint is both flexible and leakproof. Only one tool is needed: a 60-inch-pound torque wrench for tightening. Unless you have a lot of work to do, tightening can be handled with a 5/16-inch socket wrench.

A WAY OUT

In practical application, there is no space between the joints and none need be allowed for. This simplifies pipe assembly and minimizes errors. If an error is made with No-Hub, the joint can be taken apart in seconds and the error corrected by cutting or by installing a longer pipe.

Just as easily, the system can be opened up for adding onto the DWV system. When adding onto an old cast iron DWV system, the best way is to

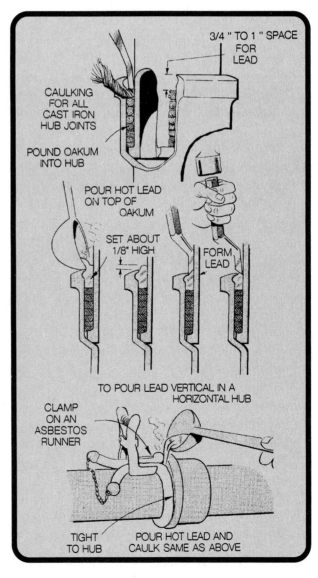

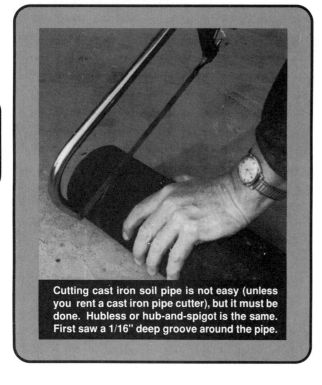

Cutting cast iron soil pipe is not easy (unless you rent a cast iron pipe cutter), but it must be done. Hubless or hub-and-spigot is the same. First saw a 1/16" deep groove around the pipe.

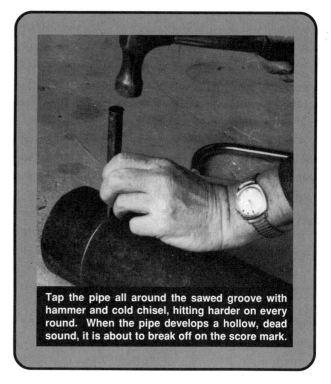

Tap the pipe all around the sawed groove with hammer and cold chisel, hitting harder on every round. When the pipe develops a hollow, dead sound, it is about to break off on the score mark.

No-Hub pipe and fittings may be used above or below ground. You can run it all the way to the sewer, if you wish. Like all cast iron pipe, it is crushproof and resistant to acids and most solvents. Cast iron pipe needs no protection from careless nailing. The 3-inch size with fittings can go into a standard stud wall with an inch of furring added. As is the case with conventional cast iron,

the No-Hub system is designed to outlast your house. It is ideal for remodeling because of its compatibility with existing cast iron pipe used in many older homes.

Because hubless pipe is cast iron and must be cut with hacksaw and chisel, working with it is not as easy as working with plastic pipe. Still, if

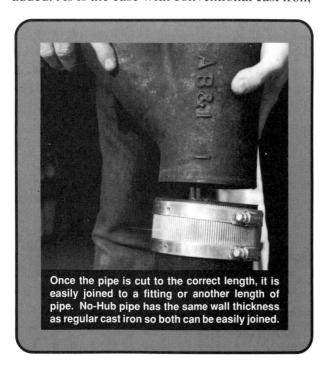

Once the pipe is cut to the correct length, it is easily joined to a fitting or another length of pipe. No-Hub pipe has the same wall thickness as regular cast iron so both can be easily joined.

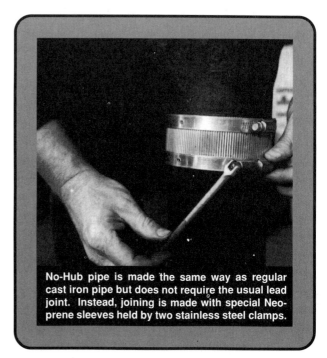

No-Hub pipe is made the same way as regular cast iron pipe but does not require the usual lead joint. Instead, joining is made with special Neoprene sleeves held by two stainless steel clamps.

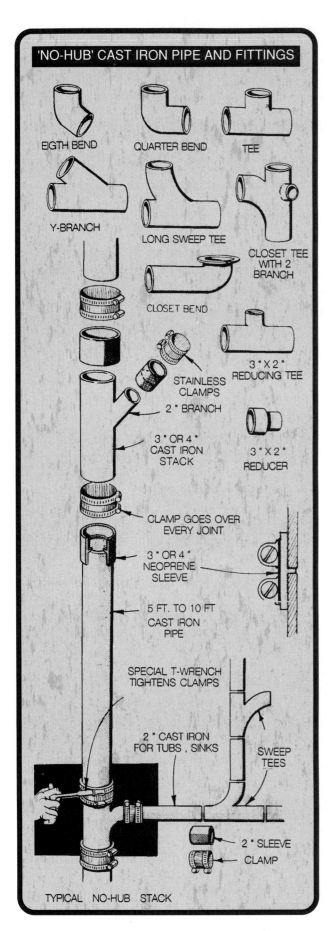

'NO-HUB' CAST IRON PIPE AND FITTINGS

EIGTH BEND
QUARTER BEND
TEE
Y-BRANCH
LONG SWEEP TEE
CLOSET TEE WITH 2 BRANCH
CLOSET BEND
STAINLESS CLAMPS
3"X2" REDUCING TEE
2" BRANCH
3" OR 4" CAST IRON STACK
3"X2" REDUCER
CLAMP GOES OVER EVERY JOINT
3" OR 4" NEOPRENE SLEEVE
5 FT. TO 10 FT CAST IRON PIPE
SPECIAL T-WRENCH TIGHTENS CLAMPS
2" CAST IRON FOR TUBS, SINKS
SWEEP TEES
2" SLEEVE
CLAMP
TYPICAL NO-HUB STACK

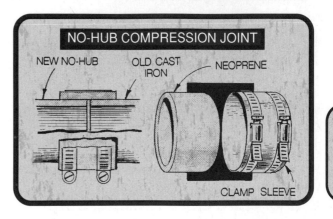

NO-HUB COMPRESSION JOINT

NEW NO-HUB   OLD CAST IRON   NEOPRENE   CLAMP SLEEVE

you want the very best and most flexible system, and are willing to do the cutting, No-Hub is for you.

If you go the hubless route with cast iron DWV pipe, cutting the pipe (unless you can rent a cast iron pipe cutter), is the hardest part of the installation. First, figure out how long the pipe should be. If you prop the end fittings in place, you can take a direct measurement. Nothing need be added for makeup, the distance the pipe reaches into the fitting. With No-Hub, pipe ends almost butt together and no makeup allowance is needed.

Mark a line squarely around the pipe with a chalkline. Wrapped around the pipe, it not only gets the line square, but is self-marking.

Next, saw a groove 1/16- to 1/8-inch deep all the way around the pipe. Then take a cold chisel and hammer and work around the groove several times, hitting harder with each round. When you hear a hollow sound, the pipe is about to break. Don't hit too hard at first or you are apt to break the pipe away from the line.

NO-HUB JOINT

To join two pipes with the hubless method, place the rubber sleeve on the end of one pipe and the stainless steel shield on the end of the other pipe or on the fitting. Insert the pipe or fitting into the sleeve until the ends butt against the separator ring inside the sleeve. Tighten first one screwclamp then the other, alternating until you tighten to 60-inch pounds torque.

Provide support for horizontal runs of hubless pipe at every joint if the length between hangers is more than 4 feet. Suspensions more than 18 inches below the supports need bracing to keep them from swinging.

Tools for easy working with copper pipe are simple and basic. You will need hacksaw, steel wool (for cleaning ends of pipe and fittings), tubing cutter, propane torch, striker, flaring set.

WORKING WITH PIPE:
COPPER TUBING

Next to plastic, copper tubing is the easiest material to work. Join by sweat-soldering, flare or compression fittings.

HOW YOU INSTALL COPPER tubing depends on what type of joints you plan to use. For DWV copper, which is rare these days because plastic and No-Hub cast iron are more economical, there is only one kind of joint—sweat-soldered. For water supply tubing you have a choice of sweat-soldered joints, flare or compression fittings. A flare or compression joined copper water-supply system is easy to work on but the cost of the fittings is substantial. So soldered fittings are usually used.

Start by measuring the tubing, the length of the tubing the run requires, allowing extra makeup at each end that is equal to the diameter of the tubing. Thus, add 1/2 inch at each end when using 1/2-inch tubing, etc. However, because different fitting manufacturers may have different socket depths, it is best to check the socket depth of the fitting you use and adjust your makeup accordingly.

When cutting the tubing, make certain the cut is square and all burrs are removed. Clean the surface of both the tubing and the inside of the fitting with emery cloth, flux all surfaces and join together. Wearing safety goggles, heat the joint with your torch and feed in lead-free plumbers solder. If you get the

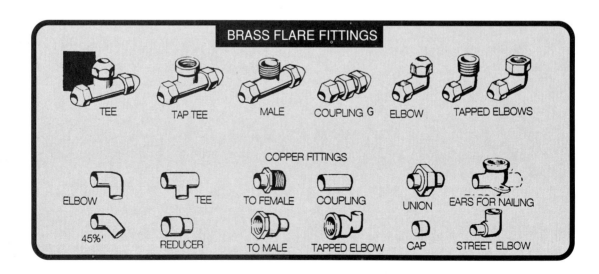

BRASS FLARE FITTINGS

TEE   TAP TEE   MALE   COUPLING G   ELBOW   TAPPED ELBOWS

COPPER FITTINGS

ELBOW   TEE   TO FEMALE   COUPLING   UNION   EARS FOR NAILING

45%'   REDUCER   TO MALE   TAPPED ELBOW   CAP   STREET ELBOW

PHYSICAL CHARACTERISTICS OF COPPER TUBING

Size Inches	Outside Diameter	Inside Diameter	Weight Pounds Per Lin.Ft.		Size Inches	Outside Diameter	Inside Diameter	Weight Pounds Per Lin.Ft.
TYPE K					**TYPE L**			
1/4	.375	.305	0.145		1 1/4	1.375	1.265	0.884
3/4	.500	.402	0.269		1 1/2	1.625	1.505	1.14
1/2	.625	.527	0.344		**TYPE M**			
5/8	.750	.652	0.418		3/8	.500	.450	0.145
3/4	.875	.745	0.641		1/2	.625	.569	0.204
1	1.125	.995	0.839		3/4	.875	.811	0.328
1 1/4	1.375	1.245	1.04		1	1.125	1.055	0.465
TYPE L					1 1/4	1.375	1.291	0.682
1/4	.375	.315	0.126		**TYPE DWV**			
3/8	.500	.430	0.198		1 1/4	1.375	1.295	.65
1/2	.625	.545	0.285		1 1/2	1.625	1.541	.81
5/8	.750	.666	0.362		2	2.125	2.041	1.07
3/4	.875	.785	0.455		3	3.125	3.030	1.69
1	1.125	1.025	0.655		4	4.125	4.009	2.87

joint too hot, it will oxidize and cannot be soldered successfully. Pull it apart while still hot, reclean, flux and try again. If the joint is too cold the solder won't flow either. But with a little practice you will know just when you have the correct amount of heat to produce a perfect joint.

The time to fix a poor joint is before you get water in the system. Once you have water in the system, even getting the fitting hot enough to pull apart is difficult because water and steam inside the pipe keep it too cool for the solder to melt. Sometimes the pipe must be sawed apart to let the water and steam out so the fitting can be resoldered. In any case, it is okay to reuse the fitting if you clean it carefully until both the copper and the tinned portions are bright.

A good way to work with copper is to clean, flux and pre-assemble several joints then solder them in production line fashion. This way an entire tee fitting, for instance, can be soldered with one heat-up. Also, when soldering valves, remove the stem to protect the delicate washer from being damaged by heat.

FLARING

Flared joints in soft-tempered copper water supply tubing are easy to make with a flaring tool. Two types of flaring tools are available, the knock-in kind or the clamping kind. With either one, be sure to install the flare nut on the tube facing out *before* you make the flare.

To use the knock-in type, insert the right-sized tool in the end of the tube and tap it in until the flare is made. With the clamp-type tool, fasten the tube into the clamp with no more than 1/16-inch protruding from the tapered-seat side of the tool. Then screw the cone clamped down into the end of the tube until it seats hard. Unclamp everything and the flare is ready for use.

Compression fittings need no tools other than a pair of wrenches to tighten them. To make one up, slip on the compression nut facing out, then install the brass ferrule onto the end of the tube, allowing about 1/8 inch of tubing to extend beyond the ferrule. Slip the tube into the compression fitting, tighten with one wrench while holding the fitting with another and the job is done. The

1

Here, step-by-step, is how to make successful sweat-soldered joints in copper tubing. First measure the length of tubing needed, allowing for fitting makeup. Also measure the fitting.

2

Tubing can be cut hand-held if your cutter works easily and you tighten the handle a little at a time. Start the roller right on its mark. Tubing cutters are much better than using hacksaw.

HOW TO SWEAT SOLDER

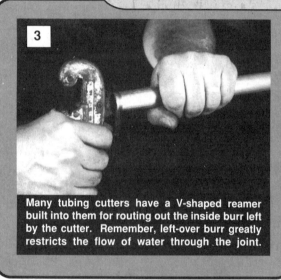

3

Many tubing cutters have a V-shaped reamer built into them for routing out the inside burr left by the cutter. Remember, left-over burr greatly restricts the flow of water through the joint.

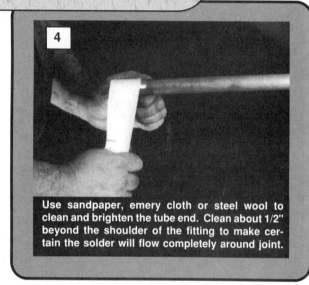

4

Use sandpaper, emery cloth or steel wool to clean and brighten the tube end. Clean about 1/2" beyond the shoulder of the fitting to make certain the solder will flow completely around joint.

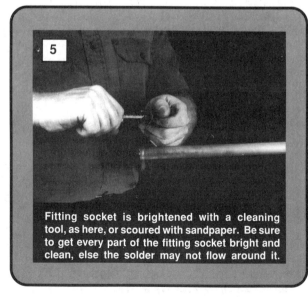

5

Fitting socket is brightened with a cleaning tool, as here, or scoured with sandpaper. Be sure to get every part of the fitting socket bright and clean, else the solder may not flow around it.

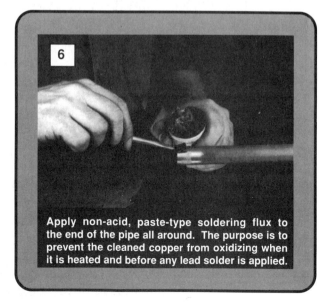

6

Apply non-acid, paste-type soldering flux to the end of the pipe all around. The purpose is to prevent the cleaned copper from oxidizing when it is heated and before any lead solder is applied.

129
PLUMBING

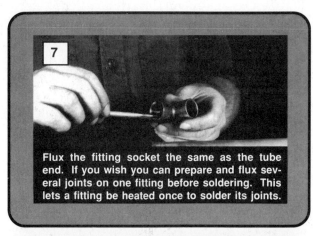

7 Flux the fitting socket the same as the tube end. If you wish you can prepare and flux several joints on one fitting before soldering. This lets a fitting be heated once to solder its joints.

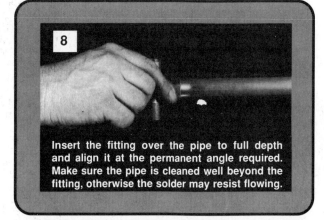

8 Insert the fitting over the pipe to full depth and align it at the permanent angle required. Make sure the pipe is cleaned well beyond the fitting, otherwise the solder may resist flowing.

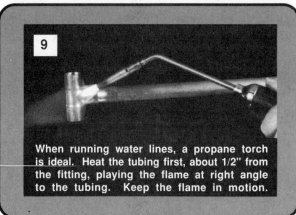

9 When running water lines, a propane torch is ideal. Heat the tubing first, about 1/2" from the fitting, playing the flame at right angle to the tubing. Keep the flame in motion.

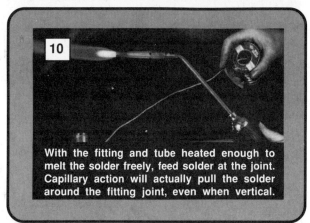

10 With the fitting and tube heated enough to melt the solder freely, feed solder at the joint. Capillary action will actually pull the solder around the fitting joint, even when vertical.

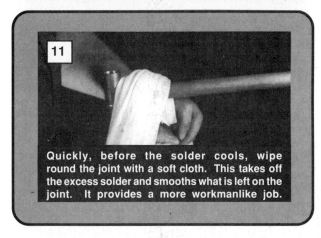

11 Quickly, before the solder cools, wipe round the joint with a soft cloth. This takes off the excess solder and smooths what is left on the joint. It provides a more workmanlike job.

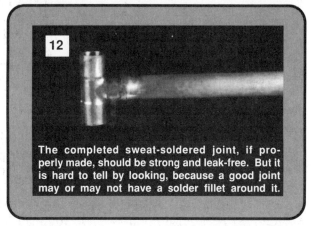

12 The completed sweat-soldered joint, if properly made, should be strong and leak-free. But it is hard to tell by looking, because a good joint may or may not have a solder fillet around it.

ferrule is squeezed down around the tube to form a tight take-apart seal.

HANGING COPPER RUNS

Support horizontal runs of copper water tubes and DWV lines from every other joist. Supports should be made of copper or copper-plated steel to prevent bimetallic action. Or copper pipe clamps can be used.

BENDING COPPER

You can bend flexible copper tubing most easily around a form. Even your knee will do but be careful not to make the bends too sharp else the tubing will kink. Kinks restrict water flow and may even close the tube off entirely. If you want smooth, tight bends, fit a bending spring over the tube then bend. Filling the tube with sand works, too, though it is more trouble.

Impact and screw-type flaring tools are used for flaring soft tubing. The impact tool, machined from steel, is most economical. Remove all burrs and then slip the coupling nut on tube.

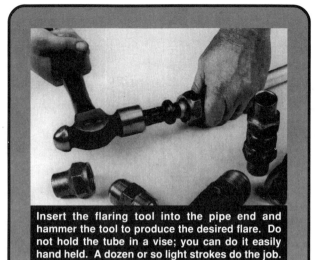

Insert the flaring tool into the pipe end and hammer the tool to produce the desired flare. Do not hold the tube in a vise; you can do it easily hand held. A dozen or so light strokes do the job.

WORKING WITH FLARE FITTINGS

Assemble the joint by placing the fitting squarely against the flare. Engage the coupling nut with the fitting threads. Tighten with two wrenches, one on the nut and one on the fitting.

Screw-type flaring tools are more expensive but can handle different size tubing. With coupling nut on, clamp the tube in the flaring block so the end extends slightly past the face of block.

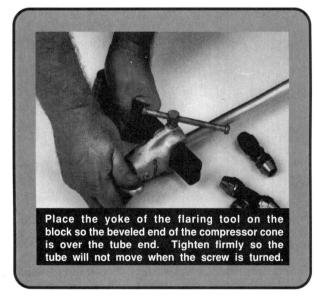

Place the yoke of the flaring tool on the block so the beveled end of the compressor cone is over the tube end. Tighten firmly so the tube will not move when the screw is turned.

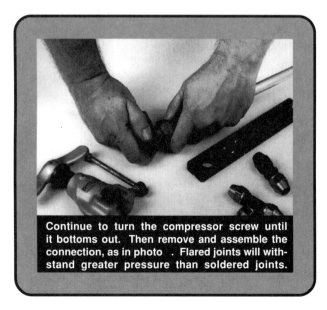

Continue to turn the compressor screw until it bottoms out. Then remove and assemble the connection, as in photo . Flared joints will withstand greater pressure than soldered joints.

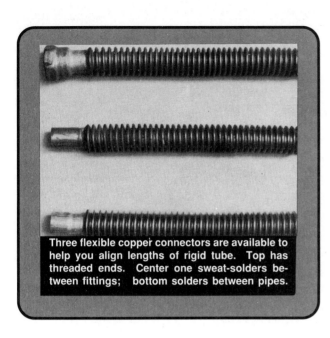

Three flexible copper connectors are available to help you align lengths of rigid tube. Top has threaded ends. Center one sweat-solders between fittings; bottom solders between pipes.

GET SMOOTH BENDS EVERY TIME

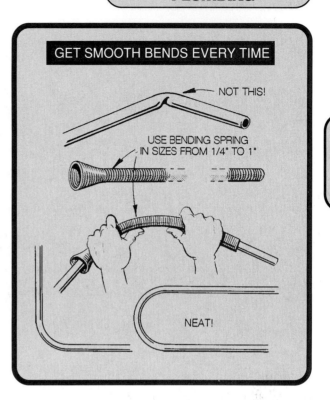

NOT THIS!

USE BENDING SPRING IN SIZES FROM 1/4" TO 1"

NEAT!

THE THREE WAYS TO JOIN COPPER TUBING

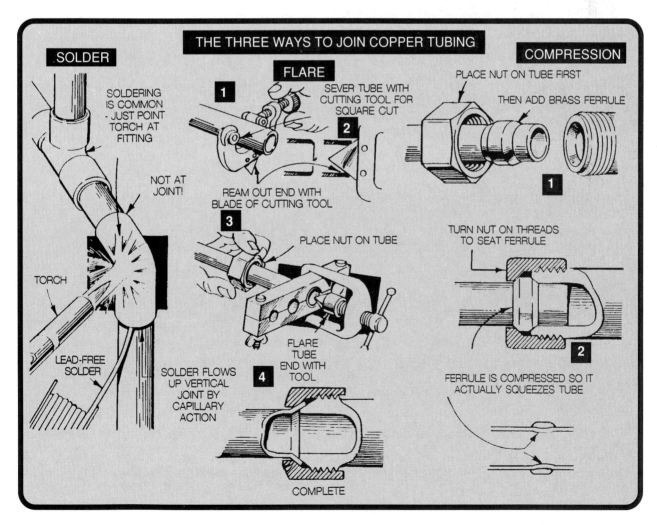

SOLDER

SOLDERING IS COMMON - JUST POINT TORCH AT FITTING

NOT AT JOINT!

TORCH

LEAD-FREE SOLDER

SOLDER FLOWS UP VERTICAL JOINT BY CAPILLARY ACTION

FLARE

1 SEVER TUBE WITH CUTTING TOOL FOR SQUARE CUT

2 REAM OUT END WITH BLADE OF CUTTING TOOL

3 PLACE NUT ON TUBE

FLARE TUBE END WITH TOOL

4 COMPLETE

COMPRESSION

PLACE NUT ON TUBE FIRST

THEN ADD BRASS FERRULE

1

TURN NUT ON THREADS TO SEAT FERRULE

2

FERRULE IS COMPRESSED SO IT ACTUALLY SQUEEZES TUBE

1

To cut and thread galvanized steel pipe to length, clamp it in a pipe vise and start the pipe cutter with its wheel on the cut mark. Rotate the cutter, and keep tightening handle until pipe severs.

WORKING WITH PIPE:
THREADED PIPE

If you like working with galvanized steel, black iron or brass pipe, you will need some special tools and a little know-how.

WORKING WITH THREADED pipe calls for a few specialized tools. If you plan to do much with threaded metal piping, buy a set of tools. If not, you can rent what you need, including a large, portable pipe vise for holding the pipe.

FITTING MAKEUP

Before you cut, be sure the length is right. The makeup distance, which is the distance the pipe screws into the fitting, varies with pipe size.

If you measure face-to-face of the fittings, only these makeup measurements need be added to the result. If the measurement is from center-to-center of two pipes and must include the fitting, then you must subtract for the distance covered by the fittings. The best way to do this is to lay the fitting out and actually measure.

Here are the usual threaded-pipe makeup allowances:

1/2-inch pipe— 1/2 inch
3/4-inch pipe—1/2 inch
1-inch pipe——— 9/16 inch
1 1/2-inch pipe- 5/8 inch
2-inch pipe——— 1 1/16 inch

TYPICAL PROCEDURE

Clamp the pipe in a vise. Do not use a metal-working vise because it tends to squeeze the pipe out of shape. Some, however, have separate

Run a tapered pipe reamer into the end of the previously cut pipe to remove the burr left by the cutter. Keep reaming until surface is smooth; otherwise the burr will restrict the flow of water.

Now you are ready to cut threads in the pipe. Start the right-sized pipe guide and die on the pipe, placing guide end first. Guide it straight on by hand and turn gently until the die takes hold.

After every turn of the die, stop and squirt some thread-cutting oil on the pipe through openings in the die. If you try to cut without oil, you may tear the threads or break the die.

Now release the pipe from the vise. Pipe vises are especially good for cutting and threading because they are designed to keep from crushing pipe. They also open out for easy assembly.

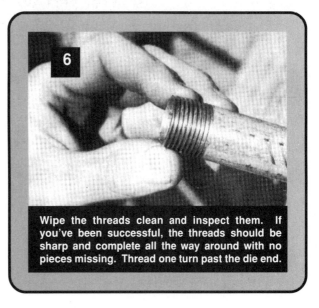

Wipe the threads clean and inspect them. If you've been successful, the threads should be sharp and complete all the way around with no pieces missing. Thread one turn past the die end.

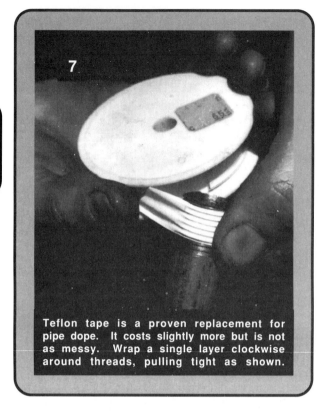

Teflon tape is a proven replacement for pipe dope. It costs slightly more but is not as messy. Wrap a single layer clockwise around threads, pulling tight as shown.

Where possible, hold the pipe and then screw on the fitting. Start the fitting on the threads slowly; if it does not catch check the edge for burrs.

jaws for clamping pipes and may be used. Cut with a pipe cutter and then remove the burr inside the pipe with a pipe reamer or round file. If you leave

Makeup, in any pipe, is the distance the pipe goes into the fitting. In this case the 3" nipple will extend 1/2" into fitting. Check the face-to-face and face-to-center line measurements before you cut and thread.

a burr, it will restrict the flow of water through the pipe. If you use a ratchet type pipe-threading stock, put the appropriately sized pipe die into one side of the pipe stock. The printing should face out, not in. Install the matching pipe guide in the other side. The size is stamped on each. Tighten the hold-in bolts.

Start the guide onto the pipe and set the stock's ratchet for clockwise rotation. Push the die onto the pipe and ratchet several times around until the threads are well started. Squirt cutting oil generously onto the end of the pipe. Rotate the die, oiling more with every turn. If the die binds, back it off a quarter turn to clear chips.

Keep going one full turn past the point where the end of the pipe emerges from the die. Stop, reverse the ratchet and back the cutter off. The threads should be clean, sharp and continuous with no broken ones along the way. Broken threads indicate a lack of cutting oil or a worn-out die. Wipe the threads free of excess cutting oil and chips.

INSTALLING FITTINGS

If a fitting is to be installed on the pipe, it

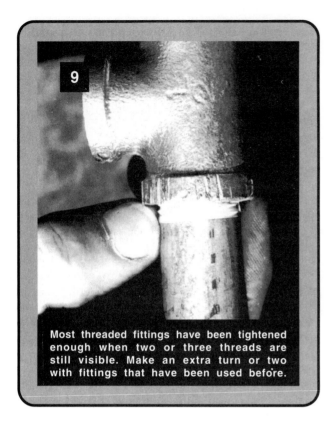

Most threaded fittings have been tightened enough when two or three threads are still visible. Make an extra turn or two with fittings that have been used before.

When adding to an existing run, hold the pipe in place with one wrench while you tighten the fitting with a second wrench. It is not necessary to tighten the fitting as far as it will go.

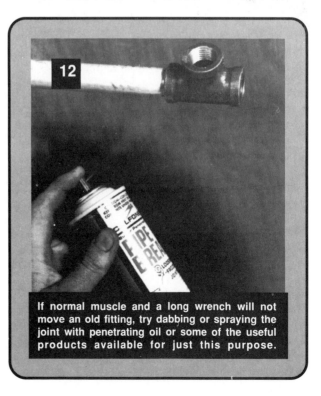

If normal muscle and a long wrench will not move an old fitting, try dabbing or spraying the joint with penetrating oil or some of the useful products available for just this purpose.

can be done most easily with the pipe still in the vise.

Some joint material should be used between pipe threads and fitting threads. It not only enables them to be screwed more tightly but, if necessary, it lets them be removed easily. Plumber's pipe dope is commonly used. It comes in stick or putty form. Apply it to the male pipe threads, never to the fitting. Teflon pipe tape is easy and clean to use. Wrap a single layer of tape around the pipe threads in a clockwise direction, stretching the tape so that the thread pattern shows through. Install the fitting over the tape.

Tighten the fitting with a pipe wrench, pulling the handle toward the open jaws so that the teeth bite and hold. If the handle is pulled away from the open jaws, the wrench only slips. If the pipe is not held in a vise, keep it from turning by holding it with another pipe wrench facing in the opposite direction. You may turn either the pipe or the fitting, whichever is free to move. Keep going until the fitting is tight. Usually this occurs when only two or three threads are left exposed beyond the fitting. Since pipe threads are tapered, you can split the fitting if you go too far.

Two-part solvent-welding joint system comprises a cleaner/primer that is applied first followed by a solvent cement. Applied according to instructions, the system produces a joint stronger than the tubing.

WORKING WITH PIPE:
PLASTIC TUBING

Plastic is the easiest of all types of pipe to work with. Don't rush, because once a joint is cemented it is permanent. If you make a mistake you must cut out the fitting and start again!

PLASTIC PIPE with solvent-welded joints goes together so easily that it is hard to make mistakes. Count one-two-three before you start the put-together process and you should come out okay.

Measuring for plastic pipe, make allowance for pipe-into-fitting makeup. Measure the fittings you are using, because socket depth varies.

Cutting plastic pipe is best done with a fine-toothed saw in a miter box to make certain the edge is square. The burr left inside the pipe after sawing can be shaved away quickly with a knife; the one outside the pipe can be taken off by sanding.

Test-fit the pipe dry into its fitting; it should enter and slip on tight enough so the fitting won't fall off when held facing down.

SOLVENT-WELDING

Take apart and wipe the pipe and fitting clean. If you use a two-part joint cement , cleaner (primer) and solvent, first apply the cleaner with the brush provided. This step prepares the surfaces for

bonding. Then apply a heavy coat of CPVC solvent-welding cement to the pipe end, and a light coat to the inside of the fitting. Don't leave any of the mating surfaces uncoated. Do just one joint at a time. That is all anyone can handle. Also close the solvent can afterward to prevent any thickening.

Now comes the critical part of the job. Be quick. You have less than a minute. Immediately after coating the fitting, slide it onto the end of the pipe with a twist until it bottoms. Adjust the direction exactly as it should face, then hold it there for ten seconds. That's it.

CHECK INSIDE

If properly made, the joint should show a fillet of dissolved plastic all around the edge. The solvent should not be so thickly applied that it blocks the pipe passage. Reach a finger in through the fitting and check. If there is any excess cement, pull it out of the pipe and use less solvent next time. If there is no fillet all around, use more solvent next time.

Within 30 seconds a joint is pretty well set. After an hour it is ready to take water pressure.

Never try to move the fitting after a few seconds. If it is in the wrong position, cut it off and start over with another fitting. If you move it, you will destroy the rapidly developing bond.

Brush size is important in solvent welding. The brushes and daubers that come with cans of solvent are fine for doping water-supply pipes. But for doping larger DWV pipes you need

WORKING WITH RIGID PLASTIC PIPE

TO CUT ANY RIGID PIPE

USE HACKSAW WITH 24-TOOTH PER-INCH BLADE

REGULAR MITER BOX

1 ALL CUTS MUST BE SQUARE

90°

HOLD PIPE FIRMLY IN CORNER TO CUT PIPE REALLY SQUARE

2 REMOVE BURRS INSIDE WITH UTILITY KNIFE

THEN FILE OR SAND OUTER RIM

FIT JOINTS DRY FIRST

3 AND MARK WHEN FITTING IS IN THE DESIRED POSITION

4 DAB PRIMER ON OUTSIDE END OF PIPE

5 THEN TO INSIDE OF FITTING

APPLY PROPER CEMENT TO OUTSIDE OF PIPE

AND INSIDE OF FITTING

SOLVENT CEMENT

PRESS PIPE INTO FITTING UNTIL IT BOTTOMS

6 TWIST 1/8 TURN ALIGN AND HOLD FOR 10 SECONDS

a larger brush. Ideal brush width is half the pipe diameter. Either use a paint brush (an inexpensive one that you can discard) or buy one of the special can-top brushes made for this purpose. They take the place of the dauber supplied with the larger cans of solvent cement.

THREADED FITTINGS

Threaded adapter fittings should be tightened with a smooth-jawed open-end wrench or a strap wrench, never a pipe wrench. Use Teflon pipe tape or special plastic-thread dope on the male threader. Never use ordinary pipe dope, as it can weaken plastic. TFE pipe is also excellent for use on plastic pipe threads.

Install the threaded fitting hand-tight, then give it one full turn (360°) more with a smooth-jawed wrench.

Plastic pipes need good support or else they will sag. Use plastic or metal hangers to attach them to framing. Horizontal DWV runs need a support every 48 inches, maximum; water-supply runs should be supported on 32-inch centers. Unlike metal pipes, long runs of plastic must not be so tightly fastened to the framing that they cannot slide back and forth with pipe expansion and contraction. In addition, the ends of runs should be free to move. Special hangers made for CPVC pipe permit bind-free movement. Vertical runs of DWV may be supported by resting the lowest fitting on a wooden cross-

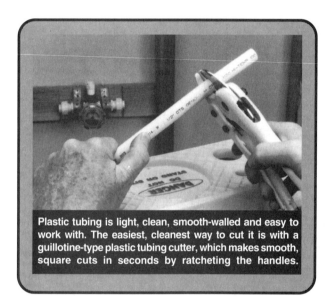

Plastic tubing is light, clean, smooth-walled and easy to work with. The easiest, cleanest way to cut it is with a guillotine-type plastic tubing cutter, which makes smooth, square cuts in seconds by ratcheting the handles.

Then the tube is beveled inside and out with a chamfering tool. Lacking that, a knife or file will do the job. Do not use sandpaper on the tube end, as that may remove too much material for successful solvent welding.

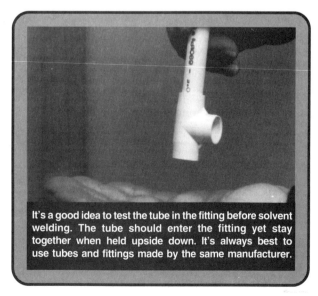

It's a good idea to test the tube in the fitting before solvent welding. The tube should enter the fitting yet stay together when held upside down. It's always best to use tubes and fittings made by the same manufacturer.

Start the solvent-welding process by applying cleaner/primer to the tube end. This can be done with a furnished dauber or with a clean cloth. Cleaning and priming prepares the tube end for successful solvent welding.

member or letting one fitting within the run rest on a header in the wall. Two-story installations need a similar support in each floor.

TRANSITION FITTINGS

Whenever plastic hot-water tubing and metal pipe or fittings are joined, a fitting called a *transition* is needed. This is designed to allow for the difference in expansion between metal and plastic piping. Simple male-threads adapters will not do the job. They will eventually leak around the threads. Transitions come as transition adapters and transition unions.

Using a transition fitting is the only way to prevent leaks at threaded-metal-to-plastic joints.

Transition fittings are called for at the hot-water heater and at other such connections between plastic and threaded-metal hot-water pipes and fittings. Transitions are not required at cold-water-only locations, such as at the water meter, or at nonpressurized locations, such as at a sillcock or the joint between a shower valve and the run up to a showerhead.

Transition fittings are made to fit both male and female threads. One design mates two flat faces—metal and plastic—with a thick elastomeric gasket between the two. The metal and plastic faces are clamped tightly together by a threaded hand-collar. Copper-to-plastic transitions are made with slip-on, hand-tightened mechanical couplings, which need no sweat soldering.

Next apply solvent cement generously to the tube end — apply to fitting depth, no more. The solvent cement should match the tube/fitting, or else be an all-purpose cement. Don't try to solvent-weld CPVC with PVC cement.

It's tough to use too much cement on the tube end. In fact, you can even give the tube a second application, but not the fitting. To keep volatile solvents from evaporating, replace the dauber in the can between uses.

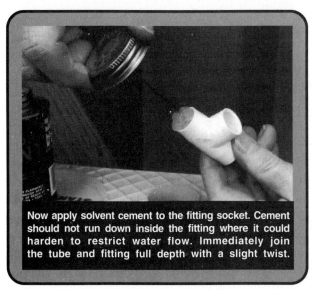

Now apply solvent cement to the fitting socket. Cement should not run down inside the fitting where it could harden to restrict water flow. Immediately join the tube and fitting full depth with a slight twist.

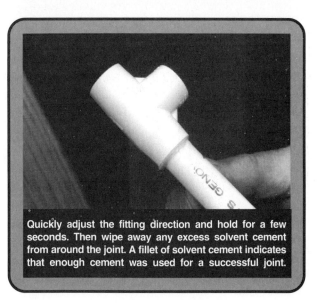

Quickly adjust the fitting direction and hold for a few seconds. Then wipe away any excess solvent cement from around the joint. A fillet of solvent cement indicates that enough cement was used for a successful joint.

WING FITTINGS

Plastic water-supply tees and elbows with wing-like extensions are called "drop-ear" or wing elbow and tees. The extensions are secured to framing with screws. Wing fittings are especially useful in anchoring fixture drops—the water-supply piping serving sinks, lavatories and toilets. Wing tees—a pair—are used behind the stubouts reaching through the wall toward a sink or washbasin. Fastened to a wood support, wing fittings make a solid stubout that won't move when the fixture shutoff valve is turned. A single wing elbow is used for the toilet's cold-water drop, which needs no water-hammer protection. Another version of wing elbow with transition capabilities anchors a shower arm to the framing.

Wing tees (lower center) hold a sink's water-supply piping to headers. The tees take feed water from the house water supply and route it to the fixture and the arresters.

CUTTING PLASTIC PIPING

Any fine-tooth saw may be used to cut plastic pipe or tubing. PB tubing may be cut with a knife. However, the quickest and best way to make clean, square, burr-free cuts is with a guillotine-type plastic tubing cutter. Plastic tubing cutters are available for sizes up to and including DWV pipe.

SPECIAL CARE

CPVC tube needs special care to prevent pressures above its limits. Install a water-hammer arrester or an extra-long 18-inch air chamber at each fixture. Washing machines need additional protection because their solenoid control valves shut off so quickly. Your washing machine supply should have an air chamber made of 3/4 x 18-inch pipe, a size larger than the water-supply branch to the washer. Do it by using 3/4-inch tees at that point and reducing the branches to 1/2 inch with bushings. Or install a water-hammer arrester.

Three types of transition unions for joining CPVC to threaded-metal piping are (l. to r.): male (MIP), female (FIP) and Special Female Adapter. All prevent metal-to-plastic leaks.

CODES

CPVC, PB, PVC-DWV and ABS-DWV pipes and fittings are accepted for use in home plumbing by the six major regional plumbing codes (there is no nationally accepted code). If you have doubts, you can check with your local building department.

Cross section of a CPVC transition union shows the metal and plastic sides separated by a thick elastomeric gasket that permits thermal movements without leaking.

WORKING WITH UNCOPPER MECHANICAL COUPLINGS

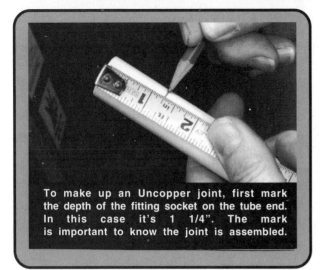

To make up an Uncopper joint, first mark the depth of the fitting socket on the tube end. In this case it's 1 1/4". The mark is important to know the joint is assembled.

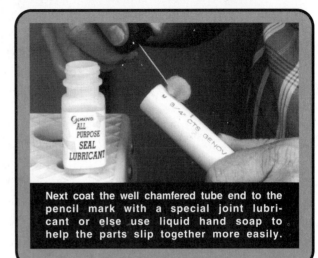

Next coat the well chamfered tube end to the pencil mark with a special joint lubricant or else use liquid hand soap to help the parts slip together more easily.

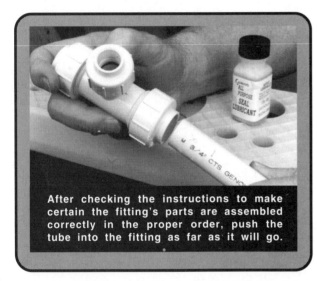

After checking the instructions to make certain the fitting's parts are assembled correctly in the proper order, push the tube into the fitting as far as it will go.

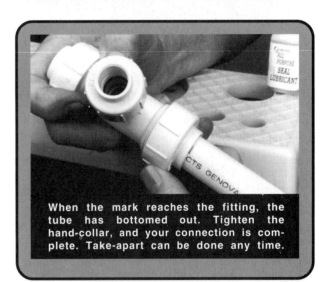

When the mark reaches the fitting, the tube has bottomed out. Tighten the hand-collar, and your connection is complete. Take-apart can be done any time.

Called Uncopper, these fittings let CPVC, PB, and copper tubing be joined mechanically without solvent welding or sweat soldering. They include valves, tees, etc.

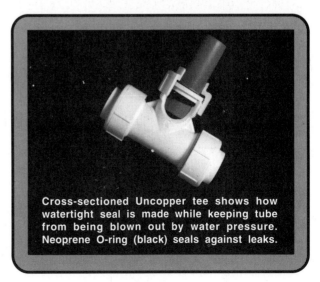

Cross-sectioned Uncopper tee shows how watertight seal is made while keeping tube from being blown out by water pressure. Neoprene O-ring (black) seals against leaks.

Four kinds of connections are needed by most water heaters: flue (as above), water, fuel and safety relief. An electric water heater needs no flue. Double-insulated vent can pass near framing.

INSTALL A NEW WATER HEATER

The average hot water heater should last about 7 to 10 years, with a 15-year-life maximum. Here are the replacement techniques.

WHEN YOU NOTICE a puddle of water underneath the water heater, it is time to replace it because it seldom pays to try to patch up an old water heater. The majority of heaters are glass lined and a leak starts when the glass ruptures ever so slightly in one area, permitting water to come into direct contact with the steel tank. Rust starts to develop and in a relatively short time the tank rusts through and a leak develops. Attempting to repair the heater is a lost cause because by the time you rip off the metal covering, peel away the tank insulation, find and fix the leak, then replace everything again, you have done more than the work of installing a new heater.

WHAT SIZE WATER HEATER?

Heater size is always a big question. Remember, the actual amount of hot water you can draw in an hour equals 70 per cent of the heater's storage capacity plus its recovery rate. Recovery rate is the number of gallons of water the heater will raise 100° in temperature per hour.

To find your family's hot-water requirements, check the following table.

FIRST-HOUR HOT WATER DELIVERY (Recovery rate plus 70% of storage capacity)	
People in Family	Gas Heater Size
2	45 gal.
3-4	50 gal.
5	60 gal.

The following heaters would do for a family of five with a two-bedroom home and automatic washer and dishwasher: A 30-gallon natural gas heater with a rapid recovery 63 gallon per hour recovery rate; a 50 gallon, LP-gas model with a 38-gph recovery; a 30-gallon oil-fired heater with a 130-gph recovery (oil-fired water heaters have fantastic recovery rates); or a 66-gal. electric heater with dual 4500-watt elements for a 28-gph recovery rate.

HEATER QUALITY

A good water heater with proper care should give 15 years of service. Length of the guarantee is an indication of quality. The best heaters are covered in full —not pro-rated— for ten years.

Of course, your water's corrosive and scale formation properties will affect the tank life. For most waters, a glass-lined steel tank is the best choice. It's the industry standard. If you have hard or corrosive water, consider installing water-treatment equipment right along with your new heater.

INSTALLATION

To install a new gas heater, turn off the supply line to the heater and the cold water supply. Empty the old heater through its drain tap and by opening a hot-water faucet upstairs. Disconnect the pipes leading to the heater while it drains. You are fortunate if unions were provided. Otherwise, cut through the pipes and install unions when replacing them.

Heaters of the same gallon capacity by different manufacturers have different piping measurements so if you install an exact replacement of the unit the old pipe connections should fit perfectly. If they do not, consider using the flexible pipe water connectors that make installation a cinch.

The most important thing to remember about installing any water heater is to see that it is fitted with a temperature-pressure relief (T & P) valve. No water heater is safe without one. New heaters have top tappings for easy installation of T & P valves. All you have to do is thread the valve in and run 3/4-inch pipe from it to a convenient drain. The T & P valve prevents your water heater from literally exploding should all of its energy cut-off features fail.

Every burner-fired heater installation should include a flue check. Hold a lighted match in the draft diverter or draft regulator opening with the heater's burner operating. The flame should be drawn into the opening. Incidentally, some of the newer heaters do not require connection to a chimney if your fuel is gas or oil; a small diameter PVC pipe leads to the outside to vent combustion gases.

HEATER CARE

Once a month, after your heater is installed, you should test the T & P valve by lifting up the test lever. If some water is valved off, it is working satisfactorily. Open the heater's drain valve and run off a pail of water to flush any accumulated sediment from the tank. If left, it can harden into an insulating crust that hastens tank burnout.

If your tank has a magnesium anode, it may be used up after some 3 to 10 years of service. Check on it occasionally by screwing it out of the top of the tank; if it has deteriorated it should be replaced.

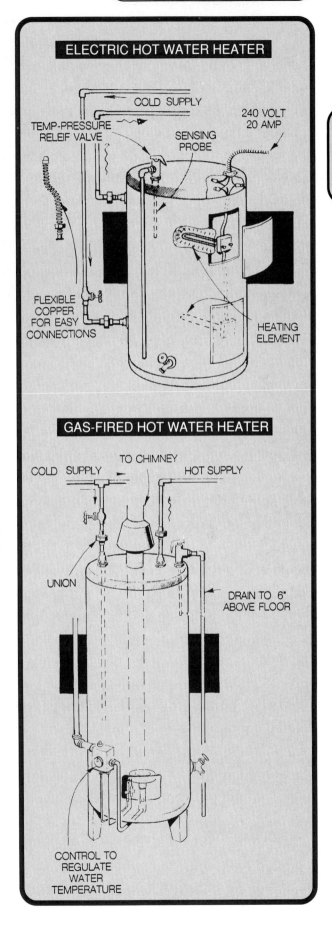

ELECTRIC HOT WATER HEATER

COLD SUPPLY

240 VOLT 20 AMP

TEMP-PRESSURE RELEIF VALVE

SENSING PROBE

FLEXIBLE COPPER FOR EASY CONNECTIONS

HEATING ELEMENT

GAS-FIRED HOT WATER HEATER

TO CHIMNEY

COLD SUPPLY

HOT SUPPLY

UNION

DRAIN TO 6" ABOVE FLOOR

CONTROL TO REGULATE WATER TEMPERATURE

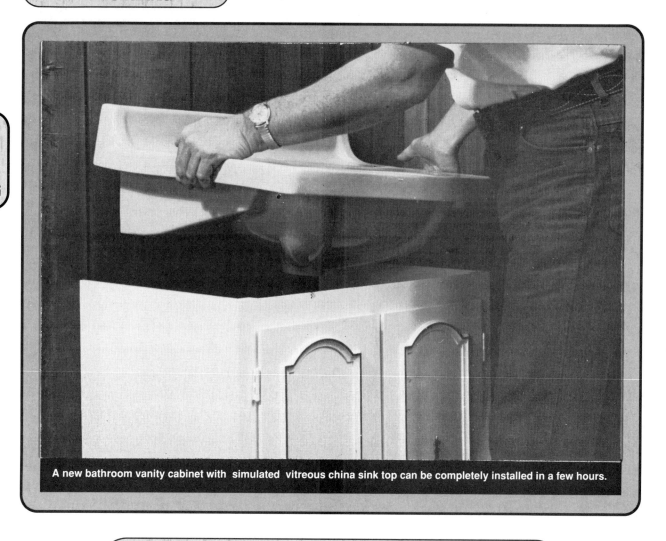

A new bathroom vanity cabinet with simulated vitreous china sink top can be completely installed in a few hours.

REPLACING A KITCHEN OR BATHROOM SINK

New sinks come in all sizes, shapes and colors. If you are remodeling your bath or kitchen you will want new fixtures. Here is how to install them.

STAINED, CHIPPED, OR DENTED kitchen and bathroom sinks can make your house look old before its time. The best way to fix them is by replacement. In the bathroom in addition to replacing the sink, you may also want to install one of the attractive wood lavatory vanity cabinets that both hide piping and provide storage space. If you are replacing the kitchen sink it probably is time to consider a new countertop, especially if the sink was attached from beneath and is not of the self-rimmed type.

The new fixture should be centered as nearly as practical on the existing pipes. Drain placement is most critical. If extended too far, a trap arm poses the dangers of trap siphonage and grease-clogging of the waste pipe. Fortunately, now we have swinging waste pipes and traps. They can be twisted to connect a drain that may be an inch or more out of alignment. The fixture supply lines of old installations were usually rigid threaded pipe; now the supply tubes are made of copper tubing that is soft enough to bend slightly to make the connection, polybutylene, which also bends easily, or the exceedingly flexible plastic with a nylon or stainless steel braided exterior. These can be twisted in loops if necessary to make the connection.

The older sinks, like the original bathtub, were cast iron with a porcelain finish. While some replacement cast iron sinks are still available, they are heavy and expensive. Most bathroom sinks are ceramic or simulated marble that is molded but the most popular kitchen sinks are either ceramic or stainless steel. Stainless steel sinks come in a variety of bowl configurations and finishes, ranging from satin to a mirror finish. Even the most economical will gleam for years and, unlike ceramic sinks, they will not chip or stain. The top-of-the-line stainless sinks have a mirror finish and all have a self rim so the sink can easily drop into the countertop opening and fasten permanently in place from underneath.

Years ago, kitchen sinks had 1 1/2-inch waste pipes and bathroom sinks had 1 1/4-inch pipes. Now most are installed with 1 1/2-inch piping. The 1 1/4-inch lavatory trap adapts to the larger waste pipe with a 1 1/4 x 1 1/2-inch slipnut and washer. If you are working with what is already there, simply use the same waste arm slipnut that you remove.

Countertop sinks and lavatories can be removed without damage to the countertop by taking off the screw clamps from beneath. Then turn off the water to both hot and cold fixture supply pipes and disconnect the hot and cold water connections. Since the wall (or floor) outlets are more accessible than the lower end of the faucet, you may find it easier to do the removal at this point. Save the fixture supply pipes unless you intend to replace them along with the faucet.

Using a trap wrench or an adjustable pipe or monkey wrench, loosen and remove all the slipnuts on the trap. If they are corroded or resist being taken apart, discard them and replace. Save the dual drain connectors for a two-compartment kitchen sink. These usually can be reused. The sink basket drains and lavatory pop-up drain should be discarded along with the old fixture.

The bowl should lift out of the countertop with ease. If not, try prying underneath the trim ring atop the counter.

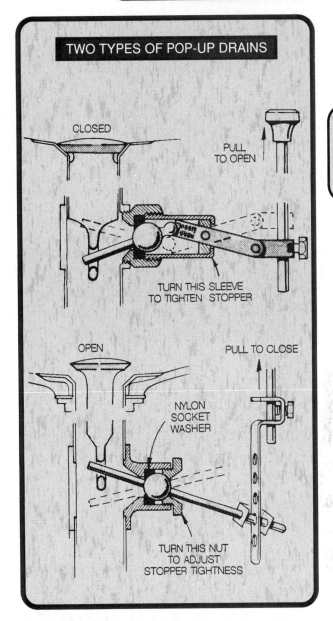

TWO TYPES OF POP-UP DRAINS

CLOSED

PULL TO OPEN

TURN THIS SLEEVE TO TIGHTEN STOPPER

OPEN

PULL TO CLOSE

NYLON SOCKET WASHER

TURN THIS NUT TO ADJUST STOPPER TIGHTNESS

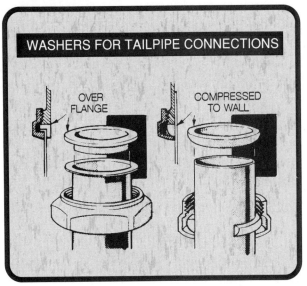

WASHERS FOR TAILPIPE CONNECTIONS

OVER FLANGE

COMPRESSED TO WALL

A wall-hung bathroom sink merely lifts off of its bracket on the wall. The new one, if the same style, hangs from the same bracket. If you are replacing a wall-hung lavatory with a cabinet-style model, remove and dispose of the screws in the old bracket.

SINK INSTALLATION

If the new countertop sink or lavatory is the same shape and size as the old one, nothing need be done about remodeling the old countertop opening. If the new countertop sink is larger than the old, the opening should be revised, using the new trim ring as a cutting guide. If the new bowl is smaller, you will have to build a whole new countertop, cutting the opening according to the

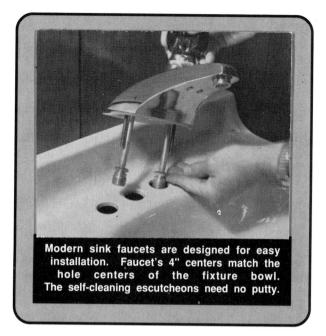

Modern sink faucets are designed for easy installation. Faucet's 4" centers match the hole centers of the fixture bowl. The self-cleaning escutcheons need no putty.

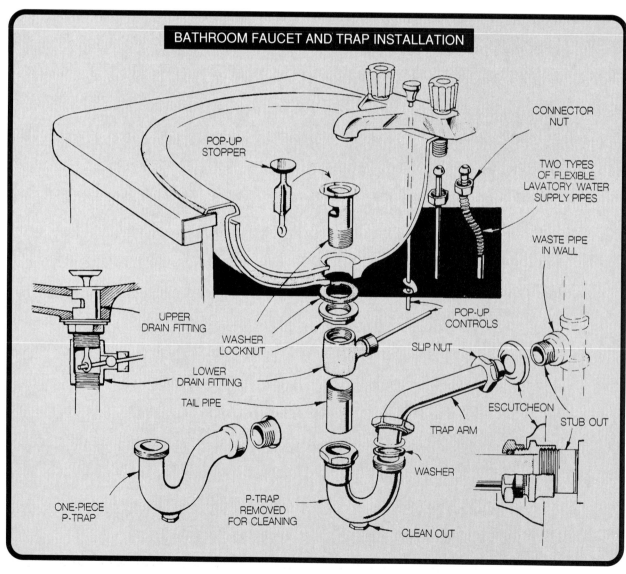

BATHROOM FAUCET AND TRAP INSTALLATION

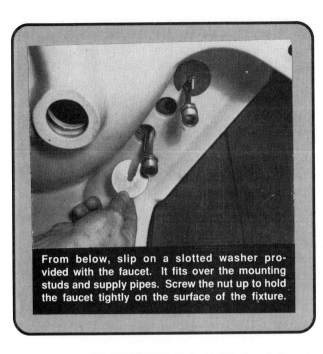

From below, slip on a slotted washer provided with the faucet. It fits over the mounting studs and supply pipes. Screw the nut up to hold the faucet tightly on the surface of the fixture.

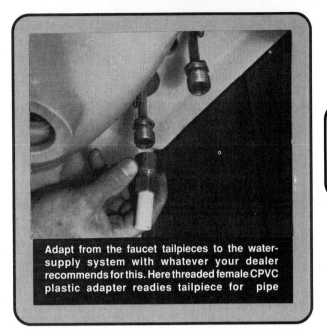

Adapt from the faucet tailpieces to the water-supply system with whatever your dealer recommends for this. Here threaded female CPVC plastic adapter readies tailpiece for pipe

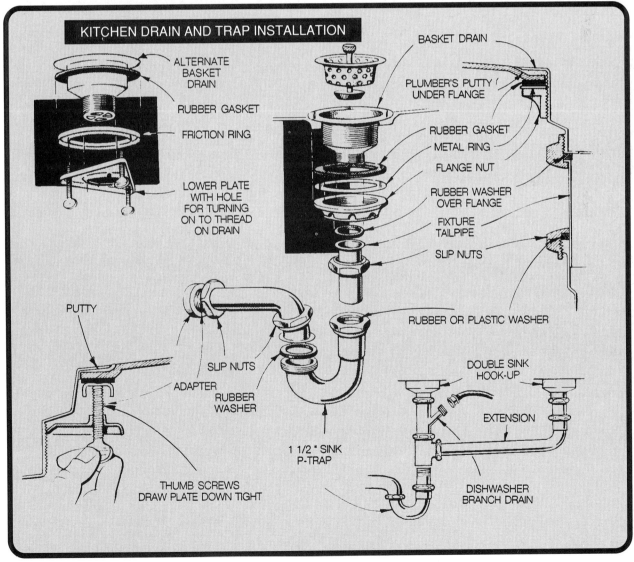

KITCHEN DRAIN AND TRAP INSTALLATION

ALTERNATE BASKET DRAIN
RUBBER GASKET
FRICTION RING
LOWER PLATE WITH HOLE FOR TURNING ON TO THREAD ON DRAIN

BASKET DRAIN
PLUMBER'S PUTTY UNDER FLANGE
RUBBER GASKET
METAL RING
FLANGE NUT
RUBBER WASHER OVER FLANGE
FIXTURE TAILPIPE
SLIP NUTS
RUBBER OR PLASTIC WASHER

PUTTY
SLIP NUTS
ADAPTER
RUBBER WASHER
THUMB SCREWS DRAW PLATE DOWN TIGHT
1 1/2 " SINK P-TRAP
DOUBLE SINK HOOK-UP
EXTENSION
DISHWASHER BRANCH DRAIN

new bowl's trim ring.

A cabinet-style unit can be fastened right up to the wall. Attach it to the floor with four steel angle-brackets and screws, and to the wall with four wall anchors. Mount the bowl and secure it, using the hardware provided with the cabinet-bowl assembly.

A countertop sink or lavatory mounts the same way as the old one. Have a helper hold the bowl and trim ring in position in the countertop while you reach underneath and insert several screw clamps at intervals around the ring. Install the rest of the screw clamps and tighten them snugly without distorting the trim ring or damaging the bowl. When installing stainless steel kitchen sinks, be especially careful that the screws do not dimple the sink top. For a leak-free installation, lay a thin bead of plumber's putty around the top of the bowl where the trim ring will compress it into a watertight gasket. The excess that oozes out can be cleaned up later with a toothpick without scratching the bowl.

Before you install the lavatory pop-up drain parts, remove the pop-up lever and fittings from the lower half of the drain. Then unscrew the lower and upper halves and insert in the bowl.

Install the pop-up drain in the lavatory bowl using plumber's putty under the upper half. Next, screw the tailpiece into the lower half of the drain, as tight as it will go by hand-turning.

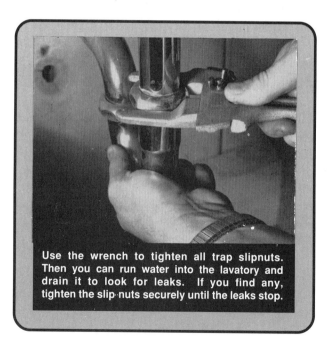

Assemble pop-up drain parts and tighten the drain into the bowl using a fixture trap wrench, as shown, or a monkey wrench. The pop-up rods can be adjusted for the desired height and action.

Use the wrench to tighten all trap slipnuts. Then you can run water into the lavatory and drain it to look for leaks. If you find any, tighten the slip-nuts securely until the leaks stop.

FAUCET

The new faucet must match the spacing of openings in the bowl. Most bathroom sink faucets use 4-inch openings. Most kitchen sinks, either three-hole or four-hole, are made to take faucets with 8-inch centers. Two and three-hole sink bowls are standard for sinks without spray attachments. Four-hole sink bowls are intended for use with faucets having spray attachments, for dishwasher venting or for an instant hot water heater. If you combine a four-holer and a faucet without sprayer, you will need a chrome plug snapped in to cover the exposed fourth hole. Put plumber's putty around it and install it in the right-hand opening.

Faucets on modern sinks are designed for deck-mounting. Some require the use of plumber's putty between the faucet body and the deck; others come with a rubber gasket that takes the place of putty. In any case, follow the directions with the faucet unit.

TRAP CONNECTION

Don't turn on the water until you have installed the drain system. Plumber's putty is used between the drain and the bowl to prevent leaking. Tighten the large ring nuts beneath each basket drain with a trap wrench or by pushing on the lugs with a screwdriver. Hold the drain so it does not turn with the nut.

Screw the short chrome tailpiece into the bottom of the lavatory drain. Put pipe dope around the threads to prevent leaks. Fasten a rubber ring gasket, tailpiece, and slipnut to the lower end of each sink basket drain. The gasket goes between the tailpiece and the drain.

Put a slipnut over the tailpiece facing down, slip on a rubber gasket and install the first trap section loosely to the slipnut. Install the horizontal trap arm to the vertical one with a gasket between and a slipnut to draw the connection tight. The trap arm slips into the waste pipe in the wall. (A floor hookup is slightly different, using an S-trap. Some codes do not permit S-traps). Be sure to put a rubber gasket and slipnut over the trap arm before inserting it in the pipe. Align all the trap parts so they slope toward the waste pipe, then tighten all slipnuts without disturbing the alignment. Use a monkey wrench or a pipe wrench with adhesive bandages over its serrated jaws to protect the soft brass slipnuts. Turn on the fixture shutoff valves and watch the supply pipe for leaks.

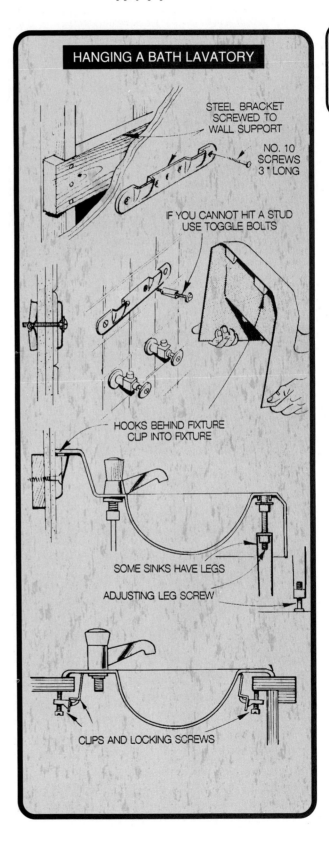

HANGING A BATH LAVATORY

STEEL BRACKET SCREWED TO WALL SUPPORT

NO. 10 SCREWS 3" LONG

IF YOU CANNOT HIT A STUD USE TOGGLE BOLTS

HOOKS BEHIND FIXTURE CLIP INTO FIXTURE

SOME SINKS HAVE LEGS

ADJUSTING LEG SCREW

CLIPS AND LOCKING SCREWS

The newer water closets have many features worthy of consideration. They are styled better and work more efficiently. You can install a new one°in an hour!

CHANGING A TOILET

A "John" need not be a permanent fixture. If yours is noisy, slow and hard to clean, turn it in for a new model, especially if it is a "water waster" that uses 5–7 gallons per flush.

MODERNIZING THE BATHROOM sooner or later calls for adding a modern toilet. Many low-cost houses have been built with low-cost washdown-type toilets. These use lots of water, are noisy, and provide only a minimum of bowl-protecting fill water. They are also frequently subject to clogging because their action is so sluggish. You can tell this type of toilet because its outlet is at the front of the bowl.

The replacement toilet you get can be one of the new single-piece tank-bowl models or a two-piece unit. Both will flush more quietly than a washdown, and will use less water. Statistics show that the average family of four will flush about 20 times a day, and if you have a toilet that uses 5 to 7 gallons of water per-flush this in itself is sufficient reason to replace your existing unit. The new ones are engineered more efficently and will flush using as little as one-and-a-half-gallons per flush.

We recommend getting either a siphon-jet or a siphon-vortex unit. They cost more, but they work so much better that they are worth the difference. In the siphon-jet, a built-in jet of water

In renovation or new construction, it is always a good idea to cover the waste hole to prevent tools and debris from falling in. This plastic bend has a knock-out cover that is knocked out last.

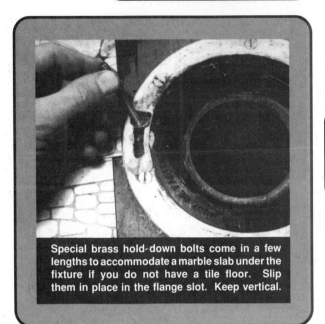

Special brass hold-down bolts come in a few lengths to accommodate a marble slab under the fixture if you do not have a tile floor. Slip them in place in the flange slot. Keep vertical.

REPLACING A TOILET

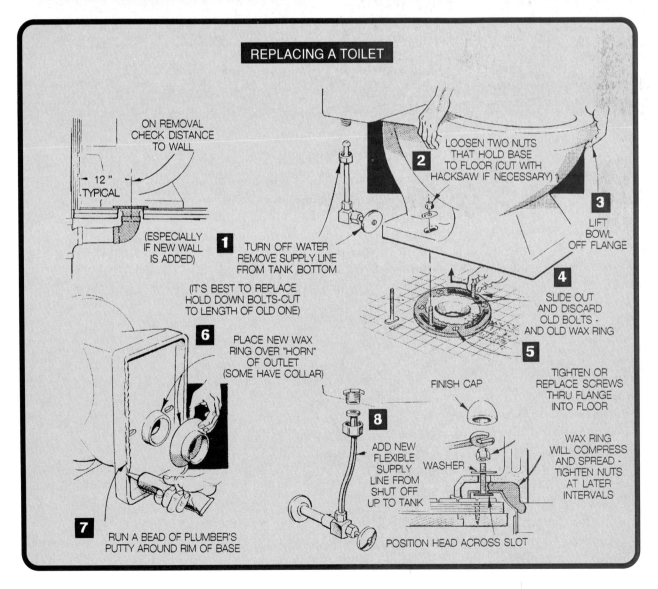

ON REMOVAL CHECK DISTANCE TO WALL

12" TYPICAL

(ESPECIALLY IF NEW WALL IS ADDED)

1 TURN OFF WATER REMOVE SUPPLY LINE FROM TANK BOTTOM

(IT'S BEST TO REPLACE HOLD DOWN BOLTS-CUT TO LENGTH OF OLD ONE)

2 LOOSEN TWO NUTS THAT HOLD BASE TO FLOOR (CUT WITH HACKSAW IF NECESSARY)

3 LIFT BOWL OFF FLANGE

4 SLIDE OUT AND DISCARD OLD BOLTS - AND OLD WAX RING

5 TIGHTEN OR REPLACE SCREWS THRU FLANGE INTO FLOOR

6 PLACE NEW WAX RING OVER "HORN" OF OUTLET (SOME HAVE COLLAR)

FINISH CAP

8 ADD NEW FLEXIBLE SUPPLY LINE FROM SHUT OFF UP TO TANK

WASHER

WAX RING WILL COMPRESS AND SPREAD - TIGHTEN NUTS AT LATER INTERVALS

7 RUN A BEAD OF PLUMBER'S PUTTY AROUND RIM OF BASE

POSITION HEAD ACROSS SLOT

Inserting the wax seal on the fixture horn and making certain it will form an airtight seal is the most important part of installing a bowl. All seals are the same size and fit all horns.

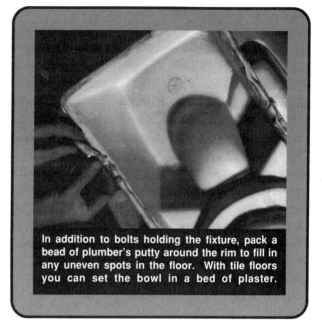

In addition to bolts holding the fixture, pack a bead of plumber's putty around the rim to fill in any uneven spots in the floor. With tile floors you can set the bowl in a bed of plaster.

starts the flushing action as soon as the trip lever is depressed. The siphon-vortex gets the action going with a tornado-like whirlpool. The very least toilet you should get is a reverse-trap type. While this lacks an improved flushing action, it offers a large bowl seal and comes in a modern elongated bowl design.

One thing to watch when buying a new toilet is to make certain the new unit's *rough-in* dimension — the distance from the wall back of the tank to the center of the outlet horn on the bottom — matches the rough-in of your existing toilet; if it does not, you will have to make the toilet's waste pipe shorter or longer to suit. This doubles the work. Fortunately, practically all toilets use a 12-inch rough-in. To check yours, measure from side bolts at the rear of the toilet base back to the wall. That distance is the toilet's rough-in, and it should be 12 inches. If it is more, a 12-inch rough-in toilet can still be used, however, it will leave a space between the toilet tank and the wall. If it is less, you will have to buy a special toilet having a shorter rough-in.

REMOVAL

To get the old toilet out, first turn off the water. If it does not have a shutoff valve at the wall or floor, consider installing one as part of your changeover. An angle-stop or straight-stop valve screwed onto the pipe stub-out will enable easy shutoff when needed in the future.

Flush the toilet, holding the trip handle depressed until most of the water drains out of the tank. Get rid of the rest of the tank water by sopping it up with a sponge; if you have a wet-dry vac you can vacuum out the remaining water. Disconnect the supply pipe underneath the left side of the toilet tank. Removal of the flange nut from the ball cock valve base will do the job.

Take the two tank-to-bowl bolts out from inside the tank. If they are badly corroded, you may have to hold them with locking pliers while you apply enough force to break them. Now the tank can be lifted from the toilet bowl. If the tank is wall-mounted, disconnect the flush pipe between it and the bowl and lift it off its wall bracket and remove the bracket, too.

To get the toilet bowl out, pry the covers from the base bolts, and remove the nuts thus exposed. Stand straddling the bowl, twist it, rock it, and lift. This should break the seal with the floor flange and let the bowl be lifted free. Be careful not to tilt it backward or some bowl water may come out the discharge opening.

Now scrape out any putty or wax left in the toilet flange cavity, leaving it clean. Install two new flange bolts in the slots of the closet flange,

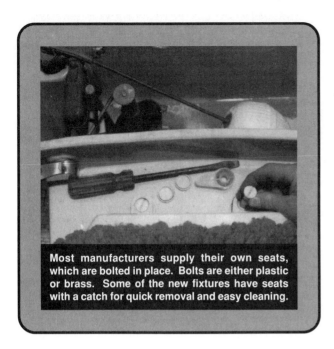

Most manufacturers supply their own seats, which are bolted in place. Bolts are either plastic or brass. Some of the new fixtures have seats with a catch for quick removal and easy cleaning.

One of the most difficult jobs is to fit the bowl on the flange hold-down bolts and have the wax seal set perfectly around the opening. Press down firmly until both the wax and putty settles.

holding them vertical with plumber's putty.

Unpack the new toilet carefully and read the instruction sheet. Follow the specific directions given for the installation. In general, it goes like this:

Invert the bowl on newspapers to prevent scratching and lay a ring of plumber's putty around the base flange. Slip a new wax toilet gasket down over the outlet horn on the bottom of the toilet bowl. Pick up the toilet, invert it and carry it over to the closet flange. Lower it gently and squarely, mating the outlet horn with the closet flange and getting the two bolts through the holes provided in the toilet base. Press down and rock the bowl gently to compress the wax gasket into the closet flange. This should bring the bowl square with the back wall and level on the floor. Install the base nuts over washers and tighten them snugly but gently. Scrape up excess putty squeezed out from the base. The base nuts are intended to be covered with plastic or ceramic caps. Stuff some putty inside the caps and stick them on over the bolts. Scrape up the excess. Some toilets have four base bolts.

TANK INSTALLATION

Two-piece tank/bowl toilets come with the parts separated for easier handling. Set the tank over the bowl's water inlet, using the rubber gasket supplied. Install the bolts and their gaskets,

tightening them snugly. Make sure that the tank is aligned with the wall.

Don't even think about using the same supply piping or tubing from your old toilet. Most of the oldies were either threaded pipe or short, rather stiff, copper tubing. The new flexible supply line with either a nylon or stainless steel exterior, can be bent into just about any position, including a full loop! The use of O-rings as seals, instead of washers, can really take the work out of making a leakproof connection. Connect the water-supply tube, put on the tank top and install a new toilet seat. The toilet seat hardware fits through two holes in the top of the toilet bowl. Modern elongated bowls need elongated toilet seats. Use the rubber washers against the bowl to protect it from damage when the nuts are tightened. Get them tight enough to hold the seat in proper alignment but not so tight that they might crack the bowl.

Turn on the water and check your installation for leaks during filling and flushing.

Kitchen sink faucets are usually 8'"on centers. This four-hole Carrollton stainless steel double-bowl sink takes Peerless single-lever self-sealing faucet with spray attachment using all four holes.

CHANGING FAUCETS

If your sink is readily accessible, you can easily replace any faucet. And you will save a considerable sum if you do it yourself.

FAUCETS SOMETIMES reach the point where they cannot be successfully repaired. These "oldies" can easily be replaced. Modern, high quality faucets are designed to last for years without problems.

Faucet replacement begins with selection of the new unit. You must first decide whether you want separate faucets or a single-unit mixing faucet. You must then decide on quality and relative cost. Quality in function pays for itself in longer life and

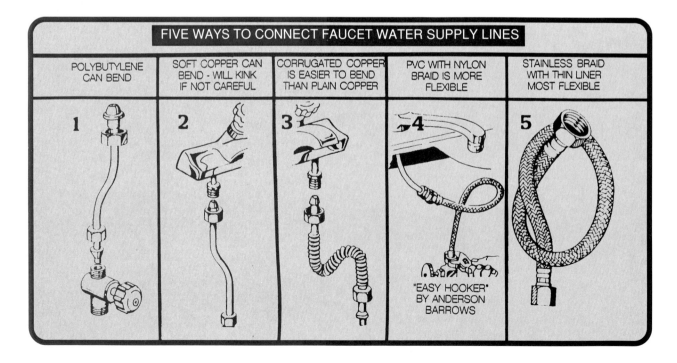

FIVE WAYS TO CONNECT FAUCET WATER SUPPLY LINES

POLYBUTYLENE CAN BEND	SOFT COPPER CAN BEND - WILL KINK IF NOT CAREFUL	CORRUGATED COPPER IS EASIER TO BEND THAN PLAIN COPPER	PVC WITH NYLON BRAID IS MORE FLEXIBLE	STAINLESS BRAID WITH THIN LINER MOST FLEXIBLE
1	2	3	4	5
			"EASY HOOKER" BY ANDERSON BARROWS	

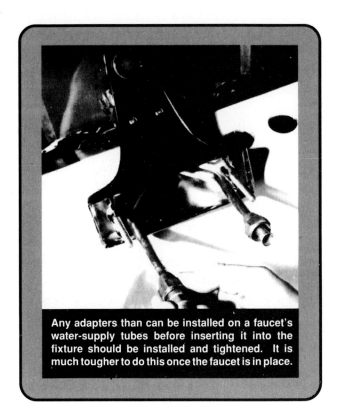

Any adapters than can be installed on a faucet's water-supply tubes before inserting it into the fixture should be installed and tightened. It is much tougher to do this once the faucet is in place.

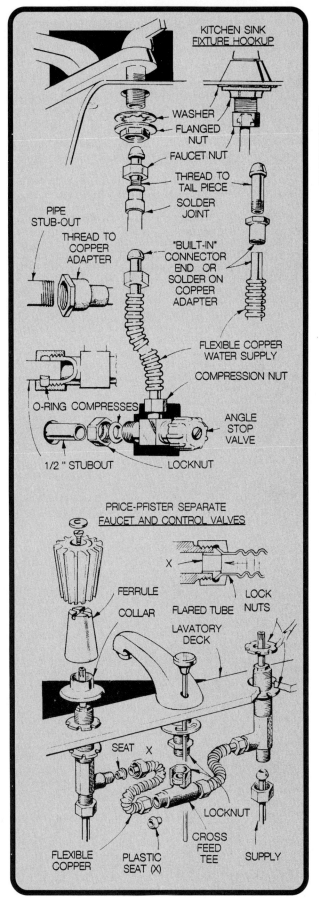

less trouble.

When selecting a bathroom sink faucet, you must also decide if want one with a pop-up drain or one with a stopper. If the old unit had a pop-up drain, you will want to retain that feature.

Order a mixing faucet to match the bowl's hole centers. Most bathroom sinks use holes with four-inch centers, whereas other sinks and built-in laundry tubs use eight or more inch centers.

TAKE-APART

On a bathroom sink, start with the drain. Using a trap wrench, or monkey wrench, loosen all the slipnuts. Take apart the old pop-up drain parts, removing the pop-lever from the drain. If possible, unscrew the tailpiece from the drain; otherwise leave it. Remove the drain plug. Sometimes a counter-clockwise twist is needed to get it free.

FAUCET REMOVAL

To take off the old faucet, turn off the water to the fixture. Plan on replacing the supply tubes, too. When you remove the upper end of the supply tubes, you will probably need a tool called a basin wrench. This tool is the only practical way of turning the flange nuts in the limited space behind the bowl. A basin wrench costs little and makes a lifetime addition to your plumbing tools. The basin wrench also works on the fixture hold-down nuts, which must also be removed. Revolve the serrated basin wrench grabber bar one way to remove, the other way later to tighten.

When the water-supply tubes are disconnected and the hold-down nuts are removed, the old faucet can then be lifted out of the bowl.

INSTALLING THE NEW

Unpack the new faucet unit and follow the specific directions prepared by the manufacturer.

Here are a few points we would like to add. Faucets without built-in gaskets should be installed on a ring of plumber's putty. Lay the putty out on the bowl-top and lower the faucet in place. Install the hold-down nuts over the faucet stubs below the bowl, being sure to use the washers provided.

You will find many combinations of water-supply outlets and faucet requirements at your home center, mass merchandiser or hardware dealer. You will find a good assortment of fixture supply pipe and the fittings for each end available. Most houses today have angle-stop valves at the wall for both hot and cold water. The supply lines can be polybutylene, chrome-plated soft copper

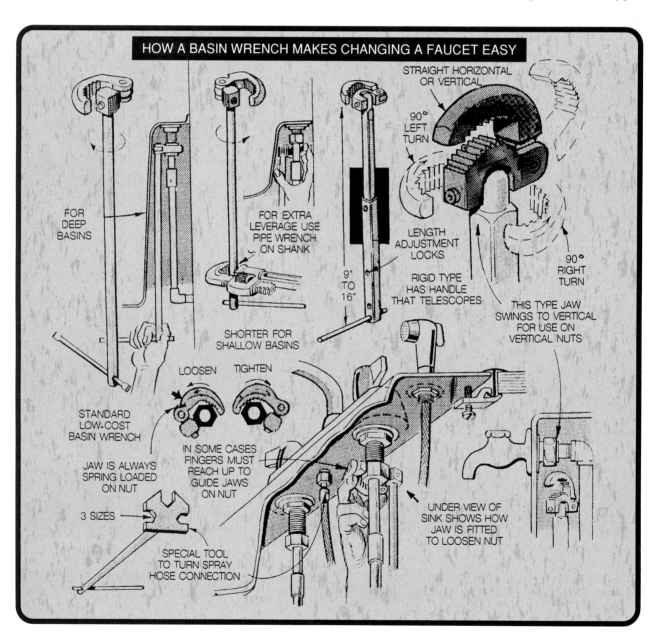

HOW A BASIN WRENCH MAKES CHANGING A FAUCET EASY

FOR DEEP BASINS

FOR EXTRA LEVERAGE USE PIPE WRENCH ON SHANK

SHORTER FOR SHALLOW BASINS

STANDARD LOW-COST BASIN WRENCH

JAW IS ALWAYS SPRING LOADED ON NUT

LOOSEN   TIGHTEN

IN SOME CASES FINGERS MUST REACH UP TO GUIDE JAWS ON NUT

3 SIZES

SPECIAL TOOL TO TURN SPRAY HOSE CONNECTION

9" TO 16"

LENGTH ADJUSTMENT LOCKS

RIGID TYPE HAS HANDLE THAT TELESCOPES

STRAIGHT HORIZONTAL OR VERTICAL

90° LEFT TURN

90° RIGHT TURN

THIS TYPE JAW SWINGS TO VERTICAL FOR USE ON VERTICAL NUTS

UNDER VIEW OF SINK SHOWS HOW JAW IS FITTED TO LOOSEN NUT

tubing or the stainless steel braided lines; the latter have an inside wall which consists of a non toxic synthetic polymer suitable for water temperatures ranging from 32 to 212 degrees Farenheit. The braided covering not only is attractive but easily withstands the highest household water pressure. No washers are used. Instead, O-rings are used to make a drip-proof connection. Some faucets have no threaded fitting on the end of the tailpiece and instead just have a plain tubing end. This hookup can be made with a flare or compression fitting. Hook in the pop-up drain parts in the opposite way

described for taking them out. Remember to put plumber's putty between the upper drain and the bowl, and use the furnished rubber washer between the lower one and the bowl. Connect the trap and drain-control lever to the control rod and adjust it for free action.

Remove the faucet aerator. Turn on both hot and cold water and let them run for a minute to clear any debris from the pipes. Install the aerator and run in a bowl full of water. Drain the bowl and check for leaks in the trap system. Leaks are usually stopped by further tightening of nuts.

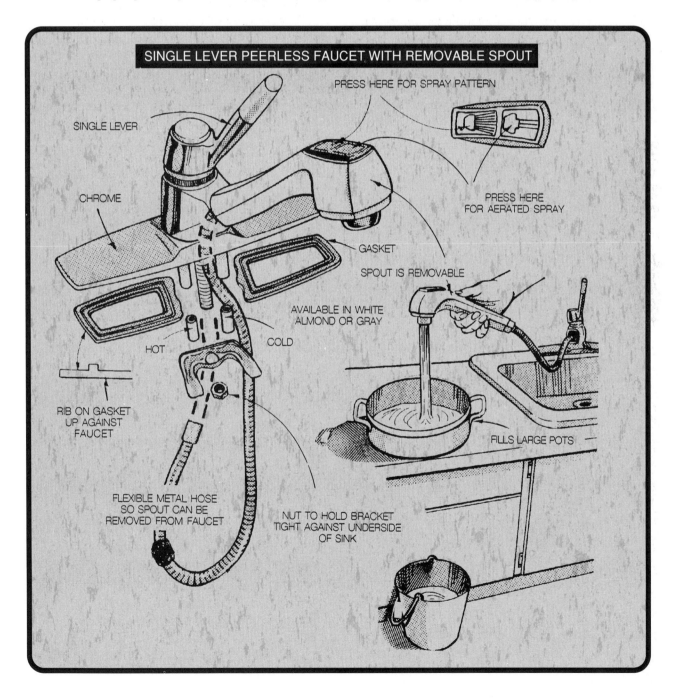

SINGLE LEVER PEERLESS FAUCET WITH REMOVABLE SPOUT

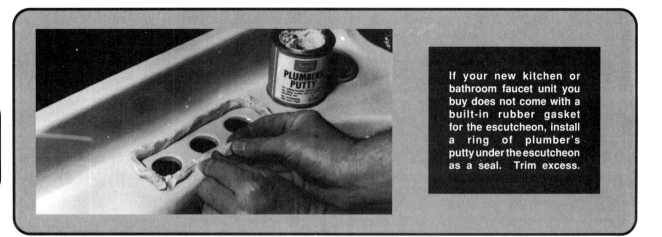

If your new kitchen or bathroom faucet unit you buy does not come with a built-in rubber gasket for the escutcheon, install a ring of plumber's putty under the escutcheon as a seal. Trim excess.

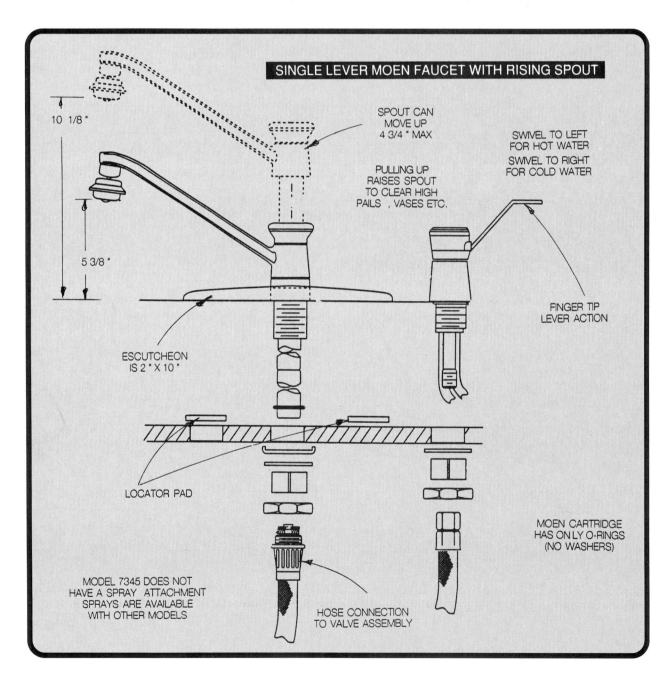

SINGLE LEVER MOEN FAUCET WITH RISING SPOUT

10 1/8 "

SPOUT CAN MOVE UP 4 3/4 " MAX

PULLING UP RAISES SPOUT TO CLEAR HIGH PAILS , VASES ETC.

SWIVEL TO LEFT FOR HOT WATER
SWIVEL TO RIGHT FOR COLD WATER

5 3/8 "

FINGER TIP LEVER ACTION

ESCUTCHEON IS 2 " X 10 "

LOCATOR PAD

MOEN CARTRIDGE HAS ONLY O-RINGS (NO WASHERS)

MODEL 7345 DOES NOT HAVE A SPRAY ATTACHMENT SPRAYS ARE AVAILABLE WITH OTHER MODELS

HOSE CONNECTION TO VALVE ASSEMBLY

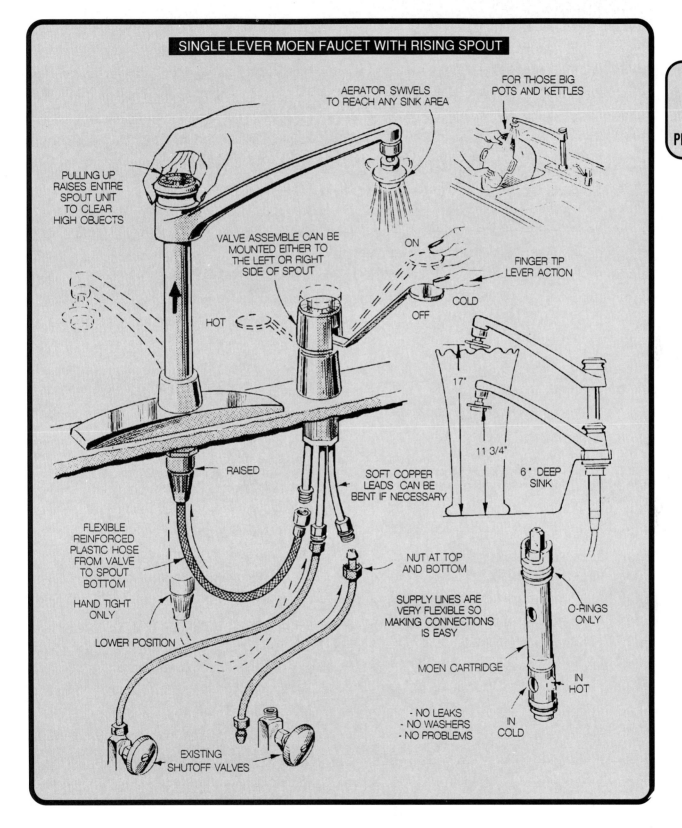

SINGLE LEVER MOEN FAUCET WITH RISING SPOUT

AERATOR SWIVELS
TO REACH ANY SINK AREA

FOR THOSE BIG
POTS AND KETTLES

PULLING UP
RAISES ENTIRE
SPOUT UNIT
TO CLEAR
HIGH OBJECTS

VALVE ASSEMBLE CAN BE
MOUNTED EITHER TO
THE LEFT OR RIGHT
SIDE OF SPOUT

ON

FINGER TIP
LEVER ACTION

COLD

HOT

OFF

17"

11 3/4"

6 " DEEP
SINK

RAISED

SOFT COPPER
LEADS CAN BE
BENT IF NECESSARY

FLEXIBLE
REINFORCED
PLASTIC HOSE
FROM VALVE
TO SPOUT
BOTTOM

NUT AT TOP
AND BOTTOM

HAND TIGHT
ONLY

SUPPLY LINES ARE
VERY FLEXIBLE SO
MAKING CONNECTIONS
IS EASY

O-RINGS
ONLY

LOWER POSITION

MOEN CARTRIDGE

IN
HOT

- NO LEAKS
- NO WASHERS
- NO PROBLEMS

IN
COLD

EXISTING
SHUTOFF VALVES

The most satisfactory source of plentiful water is usually a deep drilled well. Professional equipment and a crew is needed for drilling. The cost of the well is usually determined by its depth.

PRIVATE WATER SUPPLY

Water storage that you develop yourself, on your own land, can taste wonderful if kept free of pollutants.

IF YOU BUILD A HOUSE away from a municipal water supply, you will have to develop your own water supply. In fact, your health department may even require a source of potable house water before granting you a building permit. That source may be a shallow well, a deep well, a spring or a source of surface water such as a lake or stream. Surface water sources will require treatment, usually chlorination, before they can be considered pure enough to drink.

Look for the easiest-to-develop sources of water first. Later, after you're settled, you can develop better ones. If there are any year-round springs on the property, this is your first consideration. Be careful, however, when using surface water. It can become contaminated by wildlife, even though no people are in the area.

A continuously wet spot in the ground or on the side of a hill may be developed to provide ample water for vacation living. Actually, with adequate storage, not much water flow is needed. A half-gallon-a-minute rate of flow, is more than adequate to supply the needs for an average household.

DEVELOPING A SPRING

Water from a flowing spring is tapped via enclosure. You have got to get the water, contain it, and control it without exposing it to surface pollution. The water can flow over rocks or sand, but not over soil containing living organisms. Dig away all such soil from the spring to get down to the source, which is often a crack or fault in underlying rocks.

A hillside spring's water can be tapped by digging a trench across the hill just below the spring. Lay a perforated pipe in gravel in the trench and backfill it to keep surface water out. Slope the connection pipe and connect a plastic pipe to its lower end. This should lead into a closed collection tank of at least 500 gallons. The collection tank may be constructed of steel or concrete. It stores an average day's supply of water for the family and provides an overflow for excess water.

If you can get at the spring's source, clean it and build a concrete or masonry box to collect the water. The box need not be large. Fit it with a bug-tight plywood cover to prevent contamination. If the spring area is not accessible to materials, but stones are plentiful, build the spring box out of stone and a mortar mix.

A tunnel can be dug back into a hillside to collect spring water in porous material. If a spring's water comes out containing much silt, build a series of in-the-box dams to catch the silt before the water enters your collection pipe. Clean out behind the dams at intervals to keep the spring free of silt .

A plastic pipe can lead from the collection box (or boxes if there are several springs) to the storage tank. No pump is necessary if your springs are high enough above the house to allow the water to flow from the storage bank. One hundred feet of elevation yields approximately 45 psi water pressure.

WELL WATER

The simplest well is a driven well, in which pointed pipe is sledge-hammered into soft, loose ground. Pointed pipe cannot penetrate rocky ground; nor can it reach to great depth. For these reasons, driven wells are both relatively inexpensive and easily contaminated.

The lower end of the pointed pipe is perforated and screened so that, when it reaches the water, it can fill. If the well is horizontal, water will flow out without pumping. Otherwise, a suction pipe is used.

A drilled deep well is the best; however, it

Lowering a submersible pump and down-pipe into a drilled well can be a do-it-yourself job, but you need a heavy tripod, a hoist, and a reliable clamp. The pros do it with power equipment.

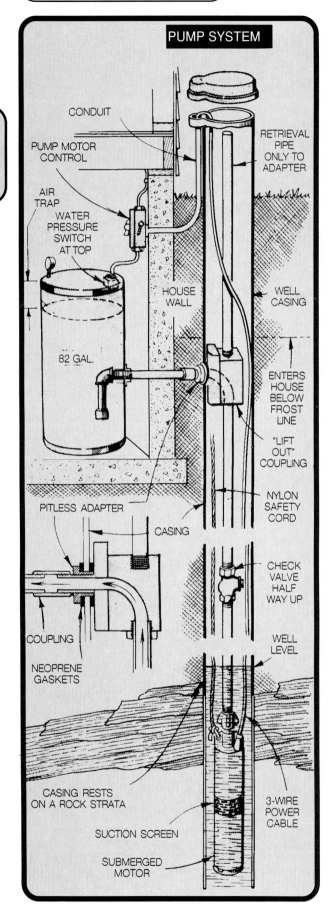

PUMP SYSTEM

CONDUIT

PUMP MOTOR
CONTROL

RETRIEVAL
PIPE
ONLY TO
ADAPTER

AIR
TRAP

WATER
PRESSURE
SWITCH
AT TOP

HOUSE
WALL

WELL
CASING

82 GAL.

ENTERS
HOUSE
BELOW
FROST
LINE

"LIFT
OUT"
COUPLING

NYLON
SAFETY
CORD

PITLESS ADAPTER

CASING

CHECK
VALVE
HALF
WAY UP

COUPLING

WELL
LEVEL

NEOPRENE
GASKETS

CASING RESTS
ON A ROCK STRATA

SUCTION SCREEN

SUBMERGED
MOTOR

3-WIRE
POWER
CABLE

Sections of well down-pipe are joined with doped couplings. The pipe clamp is critical to keep the pipes from falling into the well while you make up all of the connections.

is no do-it-yourself job. Hire a reputable drilling contractor. The depth necessary depends on the location of the water-bearing strata and how much water you need. One gallon a minute is enough for the household with adequate water storage, but 5 gallons a minute will handle most households without providing any storage. Greater flows can provide enough water for irrigation. Drilled wells usually go straight down, but may go laterally into a hillside. If successful, water from laterally drilled wells flows out in artesian fashion. Most vertical wells must be pumped. Drillers install 4- to 6-inch well casing pipes down to solid rock.

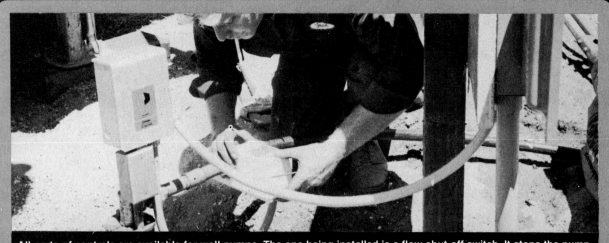

All sorts of controls are available for well pumps. The one being installed is a flow-shut-off switch. It stops the pump should it run out of water. A timer restarts it 15 minutes later. The control prevents possible pump motor burnout.

WHERE'S THE WATER?

You can choose from among three methods to determine where to drill: proximity to the house, geology and dowsing. To locate the well using the geological method, you will need a science background or a friend with one. Water-dowsing takes a talent that not everyone has, plus a certain amount of faith on your part. I didn't believe it until I saw it work. You most likely won't either.

PUMPS

Water is moved out of a well or storage tank and pressurized with an electric pump. A shallow well pump will handle huge quantities of water from depths up to 25 feet. For depths beyond 25 feet you need a deep-well rig, either jet or submersible.

The submersible pump is superb for a deep well, but cannot be used for sandy wells. The

More than 500 gallons a day of pressurized, flowing water is enough for household needs and successful irrigation.

Installing the sanitary well seal caps off the well and prevents surface infiltration. The seal's valves expand against the well casing. The single pipe to a submersible pump extends through the sanitary seal.

pump and electric wires serving it are lowered into the well casing. The pump discharges into a sealed 42- or 80-gallon air tank, compressing air in the top of the tank until the desired pressure of 40 to 60 psi is reached. Then a pressure switch shuts off the pump. To prevent water from running down through the pump and back into the well, a check valve is located in the bottom of the pump.

Jet pumps are lower in cost. The motor and turbine pump are above the well, with a suction pipe extending down into the water. If the water depth is more than 22 feet, the jet must also be lowered into the well. Two pipes lead between pump and jet. One, a pressure pipe, is smaller than the other, a suction pipe. Water is pumped down the pressure pipe, through the jet and upward into the suction pipe. The jetted water draws some well water along with it up to the intake side of the pump. Excess water is diverted from the pump to the pressure tank. A jet should be located no more than 20 feet above the lowest water level in the well. Water delivery of any pump depends on the lift and delivery head or pressure. The higher the head, the fewer gallons per minute delivery. Each person uses about 40 gallons of water a day, but water delivery must be much faster because use is periodic. Therefore, minimum pump capacity rec-

Ugly but workable, this set-up gets spring water out of a canyon and 300 feet up to a house. The storage tank (rear) collects the spring's flow. A submersible pump in foreground tank pumps it.

ommended for a house is 550 gallons per hour.

You can buy submersible or jet pumps and their controls and install them yourself. They come with on/off pressure switches and with or without pressure tanks.

PE PIPE

If the well is more than about 150 feet deep it is best to have the installation done by the well-driller. If you do it, use polyethylene pipe for the down pipe in the well. Size depends on pump capacity. Read the instructions with your pump. Same for wiring it. You can handle about 150 feet of pipe and submersible pump or about 100 feet of double jet pipes without a hoist. In any case, you should provide some means of stopping the pipe's descent into the well so you can make connections or rest. This is a job for two people.

Use a sanitary well seal in the well casing at the upper end to keep out contaminants. The top of the well may be above ground or installed in a completely drained pit. If you prefer, you can bury the well underground and run the water pipes directly into a pressure tank inside the house. For this, use what is called a pitless adapter. You can also consider rigging up a windmill to pump water, using one of the few available texts on the subject. A solar pump works well, too.

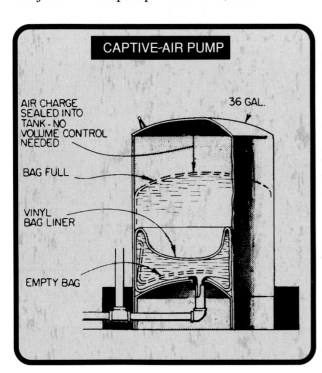

CAPTIVE-AIR PUMP

AIR CHARGE SEALED INTO TANK - NO VOLUME CONTROL NEEDED

36 GAL.

BAG FULL

VINYL BAG LINER

EMPTY BAG

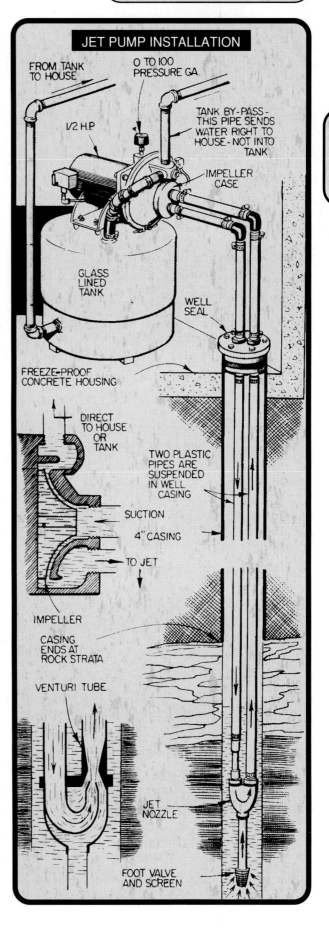

JET PUMP INSTALLATION

FROM TANK TO HOUSE

0 TO 100 PRESSURE GA.

1/2 H.P.

TANK BY-PASS - THIS PIPE SENDS WATER RIGHT TO HOUSE - NOT INTO TANK

IMPELLER CASE

GLASS LINED TANK

WELL SEAL

FREEZE-PROOF CONCRETE HOUSING

DIRECT TO HOUSE OR TANK

TWO PLASTIC PIPES ARE SUSPENDED IN WELL CASING

SUCTION

4" CASING

TO JET

IMPELLER

CASING ENDS AT ROCK STRATA

VENTURI TUBE

JET NOZZLE

FOOT VALVE AND SCREEN

Here is one way to raise the roof and add on to your living space. In this case the exterior walls were finished and made weather-tight. Then the stacks were extended and rooms partitioned.

PLUMBING TIPS FOR AN ADD-ON ROOM

Solving plumbing problems is a lot easier than solving structural problems. Here are some answers to your questions.

Plumbing for an extra bathroom involves running hot and cold water supply lines and waste lines for each fixture. This involves tapping into the existing hot- and cold-water mains and extending them to the new bathroom and then to each toilet, lavatory and tub or shower. The supply pipes are small and may go up or down as needed, so this is easy. Much tougher is finding a route for the add-on 1 1/2, 2 or 3-inch drain lines to handle the waste, and perhaps running a new vent stack up through the roof to provide necessary venting for the new fixture traps.

The first step is to draw a plan. It need not be fancy, just a sketch showing what is already there and what you plan to add. Then plan how you will run the Drain-Waste-Vent (DWV) pipes. Walls will have to be opened up. Floors, ceilings, and roof will have to be drilled to provide a passage for the new stack.

If you are lucky enough to have an existing 3- or 4-inch vent stack in one wall of the added bath, it could be tapped to save putting in a new stack. However, a new stack may be easier to install. Whatever stack is used must be at least 3 inches in diameter to serve a toilet. The toilet should be located as close as possible to the vent stack. Seldom is more than 10 feet separation permitted.

DRAIN AND VENT RUNS

Other fixtures should be located so their waste pipes can run to the stack without need for reventing. Maximum trap-arm lengths (trap to vent) under many codes are:

1 1/2-inch pipe	— 5 feet
2-inch pipe	— 8 feet
3-inch pipe	— 10 feet

* check local code

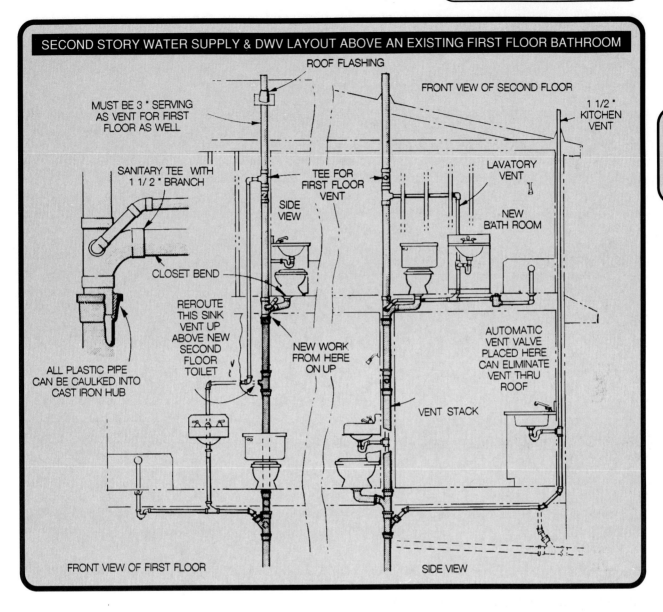

SECOND STORY WATER SUPPLY & DWV LAYOUT ABOVE AN EXISTING FIRST FLOOR BATHROOM

If this proves impractical, one fixture can be placed across the room where it is revented. Thus, its drain would run down from the fixture then across and into the vent stack. Its vent would run up from the fixture across the ceiling and join the vent stack above where the highest fixture drains.

A drainage tee in the wall behind the fixture is placed with its smooth, curved passage going down to act as starter for both drain and vent. A stub-out enters the room and a trap adapter is connected to it.

Next give some thought to routing of water-supply pipes, especially the hot-water line. Hot piping runs from the water heater should be kept short and direct. All runs should contain as few elbows and bends as possible. The whole new bath can be served by 1/2-inch hot-and-cold-water pipes. They should connect to the existing mains with full-flow fittings, not with restricting saddle tees.

Finally, consider how the new room's drain pipe will reach the existing house drain or sewer. The easiest method is to connect outdoors underground to the existing sewer or septic tank line. Some codes won't permit this. An indoor hookup depends on how close the add-on room is to the existing building drain. Remember that the new drain must slope 1/4-inch per foot toward the drain. Install the sloped portion at proper pitch, then elbow straight down if it needs to go lower to reach the building drain. Avoid 90° bends in horizontal drain runs; use two 45° quarter bends

When adding a new stack, always cut through the roof after the inside pipe is in place and you can transfer the measurement. Cut a small hole, peek down at the pipe and then enlarge the hole.

Horizontal runs of DWV piping should slope about 1/4" per foot. The fittings, if properly installed, are designed to set up the right slope; drain runs slope toward stack, vent slopes away

instead.

Drains entering other drain pipes—except vertical ones—should do so at a 45° angle through tee-wyes instead of at right angles through tees. (Some codes say that drains may only enter a stack.) A drain emptying into a vertical pipe may do so at a right angle. However, if there is space, the connection should be made at a 45° angle. Toilets should enter directly into the stack behind the toilet. Two toilets may be connected back to back on one vent stack by using a double sanitary tee fitting.

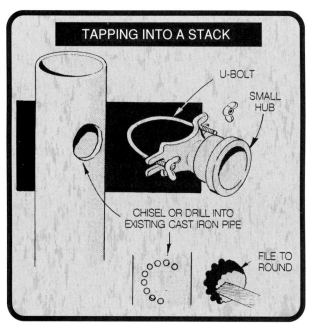

TAPPING INTO A STACK

U-BOLT

SMALL HUB

CHISEL OR DRILL INTO EXISTING CAST IRON PIPE

FILE TO ROUND

MORE RULES OF GOOD DWV WORK

Every horizontal drainage run (except short drain-and-vents that can be reached for cleaning through the fixture trap) should have a cleanout fitting installed at the higher end. The cleanout must be accessible inside or outside the house or in the basement or crawl space. It should be no closer than 18 inches to a wall to allow room to get a cleanout tool into the pipe run. If it comes too close, the cleanout should be extended through the wall with pipe and the cleanout cover installed on the other side of the wall. Sometimes cleanouts are installed outside of buildings, so they'll be accessible. Most, however, can be reached through the basement or crawl space.

All vent piping must connect to drain lines from the top. From there the vent must rise vertically at no less than a 45-degree angle until it is 6 inches higher than the flood rim of the fixture it serves. This keeps drain water from backing up in vent piping and possibly clogging it.

If there are fixtures on both stories of two-story construction and there is a toilet on the second story, all first-floor revents will probably have to tie into the vent stack above the highest fixture drain on the second floor. Usually this means reventing them above the second-story ceiling.

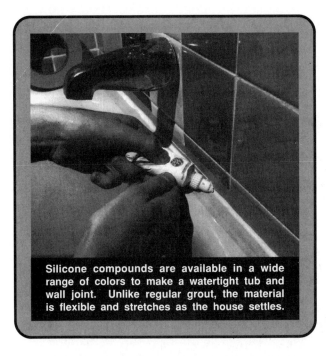

Silicone compounds are available in a wide range of colors to make a watertight tub and wall joint. Unlike regular grout, the material is flexible and stretches as the house settles.

The no-mess way to use this material is to stick masking tape about 1/4" from both the wall and the tub. Then cut the nozzle to the correct width and squeeze a bead. Pull tape off.

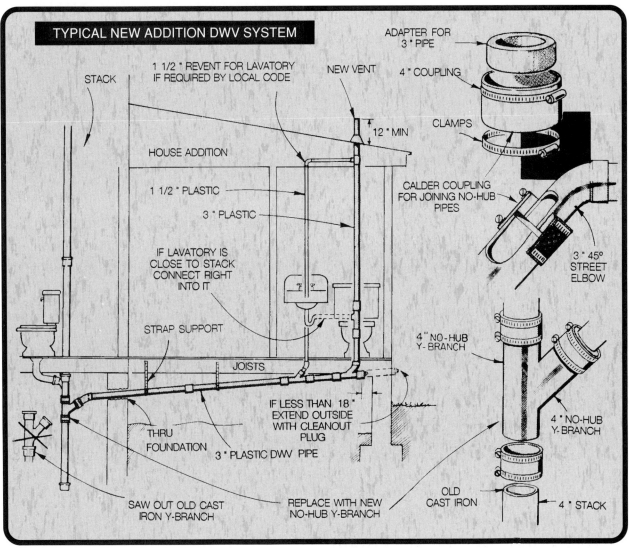

TYPICAL NEW ADDITION DWV SYSTEM

STACK

1 1/2 " REVENT FOR LAVATORY IF REQUIRED BY LOCAL CODE

NEW VENT

12 " MIN

HOUSE ADDITION

1 1/2 " PLASTIC

3 " PLASTIC

IF LAVATORY IS CLOSE TO STACK CONNECT RIGHT INTO IT

STRAP SUPPORT

JOISTS

IF LESS THAN 18 " EXTEND OUTSIDE WITH CLEANOUT PLUG

THRU FOUNDATION

3 " PLASTIC DWV PIPE

SAW OUT OLD CAST IRON Y-BRANCH

REPLACE WITH NEW NO-HUB Y-BRANCH

ADAPTER FOR 3 " PIPE

4 " COUPLING

CLAMPS

CALDER COUPLING FOR JOINING NO-HUB PIPES

3 " 45° STREET ELBOW

4 " NO-HUB Y-BRANCH

4 " NO-HUB Y-BRANCH

OLD CAST IRON

4 " STACK

RUNNING DWV AROUND JOISTS

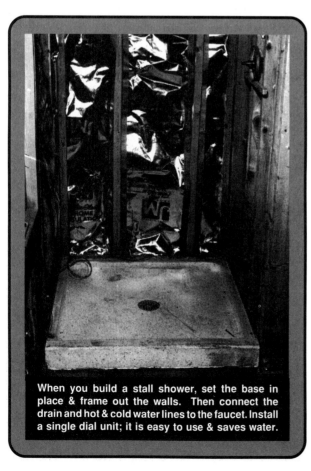

45°

STRUCTURE
AT ALL
LEVELS

TWO
45° STREET ELBOWS

LONG-SWEEP ELBOW

Under some plumbing codes, sinks and lavatories may drain into a stack above the toilet. In others, these drain runs must be carried down through the floor and enter the soil stack below the toilet's entrance. Then reventing of each is necessary to prevent trap siphonage. Check your code.

RUNNING PIPES

Start your installation at the toilet's sanitary tee. Put a large nail through the floor centered on the toilet and 12 inches out from the finished wall. Go below and check to see if any framing is in the way. If not, proceed. Open the wall behind the toilet and cut openings for the toilet's sanitary tee and soil stack. If you use a 3-inch copper, No-Hub cast iron, or PVC or ABS plastic DWV system, the wall need not be furred out. A 3-inch ABS system needs a 4 1/2-inch wall. Use a 2 x 8 wall for a 4-inch leaded cast iron system. Start assembling the system with the sanitary tee behind the toilet. Its smoothly rounded slope should follow the direction the water will take. Install the toilet waste pipe, toilet bend, and toilet flange, cutting out for the toilet flange around the large nail in the floor on which it should be centered. Set the toilet flange so its side slots are square with the rear wall.

Next, work up from the sanitary tee, installing a 3 x 3 x 1 1/2 inch tee for the lavatory, with

When you build a stall shower, set the base in place & frame out the walls. Then connect the drain and hot & cold water lines to the faucet. Install a single dial unit; it is easy to use & saves water.

Holes for new pipe runs are cut where needed in floors, ceilings and walls. Do it by drilling a series of holes or just saw them. A 3" copper DWV vent pipe fits snugly within a 2 x 4 stud wall.

its branch opening centered 16 inches above the finished floor and aimed to connect to the lavatory waste pipe. If revents are being used, be sure to incorporate tees for them as you go up. These are installed upside down, with the smooth curve heading upward. Finally, go out through the roof 6 inches above or more. A flashing should be worked under the shingles for a leak-free joint. Some codes call for a vent increaser through the roof, perhaps to 6 inches in diameter. Check.

Notches for piping should follow the notching rules. Now work down from the sanitary tee. Put in a 3 x 3 x 1 1/2 inch tee for the bathtub drain or a 3 x 3 x 2 inch tee for a shower drain. If the lavatory drains below the toilet, put in a 3 x 3 x 1 1/2 inch tee. Then turn the soil stack horizontally, providing a cleanout opening at the turn, and carry it to its connection with the building drain. A good place to make an easy connection to the building drain is at an existing cleanout.

Next install the various waste lines and their revents, if used. The bathtub or shower trap should be installed as a part of its waste line. Later, the lavatory gets a separate trap. The toilet contains its own bowl trap.

WATER-SUPPLY LINES

Connecting water pipes to your add-on bath is much like adding washing machine supply lines. Use 12-inch long air chambers at every fixture except the toilet. Stub-out pipes entering the room from the wall should be 1/2-inch. Install temporary caps on them.

The completed plumbing system should be water-tested and inspected before closing in the walls. Make sure everything is capped, then turn on the water and check for leaks immediately and after four hours. To test DWV piping, plug all fixture waste pipe openings. Ready-made solvent-welded plugs can be used in a plastic system. Later they are cut out. Otherwise, use concrete or mortar-packed plugs on top of newspapers. The lower end must also be plugged off from draining into the existing drain. Later, after the plugs have set, run water from a garden hose into the roof vent, filling the new DWV system with water. Check every joint for leakage. Leave the hose in, but turned off. When the inspector comes, he will turn on the water. If he sees an immediate cascade of water

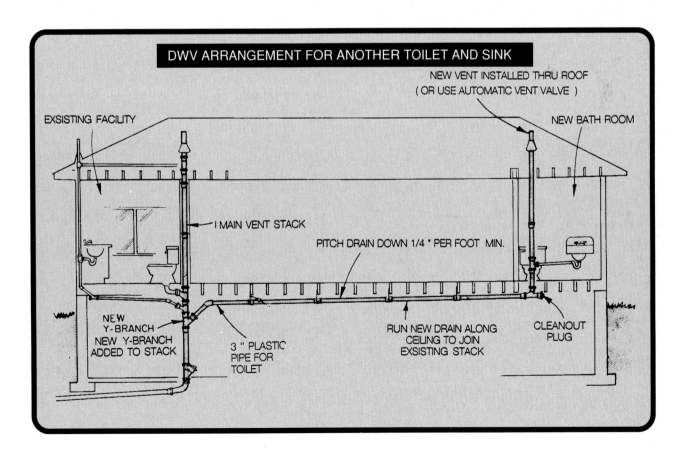

DWV ARRANGEMENT FOR ANOTHER TOILET AND SINK

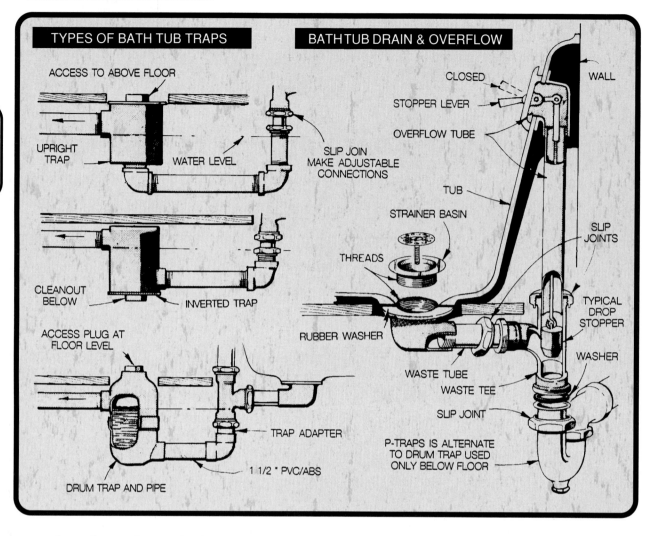

come from the roof vent, he knows there is no DWV leakage.

FIXTURES

Once the rough plumbing is completed, you can close in the walls with whatever material you wish and install the fixtures. When installing a tub, you'll need to provide a 12 x 14-inch-wide access at the head end of the tub through the floor for installing the overflow and waste fittings to the trap. The use of front-access tub/shower faucet hardware eliminates the need for providing for access behind them. The large escutcheon gives all the room you need for servicing and replacement. The tub waste uses a slipnut connection, just like a lavatory but 1 1/2-inch, not 1 1/4-inch.

A shower consists of a floor pan and walls to surround the pan. The pan is usually molded PVC with a high lip surround so shower water

splashing from the walls will drain into the pan. Years ago the pans were formed on the job from sheet lead, but molded plastic is much easier to install In some areas precast concrete pans are available, but these are heavy and not as easy as plastic to install. Once you have set your pan install its drain fitting and lower it over the 2-inch waste riser coming up from the floor. The riser should be cut off below shower floor level. Caulk the joint between the drain and waste pipe with oakum and lead or a plastic and lead seal. A shower control valve centered 48 inches high reaches through a hole cut in the shower wall. Set the shower head outlet at eye level or higher and install the chromed shower pipe and head.

RULES FOR NOTCHING

(l) Notch joists only in their end quarters, never in the center half. Then notch no more than one quarter of the joist depth.

(2) Drill joists to a maximum diameter of one quarter of the joist depth. Locate along the span, preferably centered but no closer than 2 inches to an edge.

(3) Notch studs no larger than 2 1/2 inches square. Nail steel strap reinforcement over each notch after installing the pipe. Notches to 1 1/4-inches square need not be reinforced.

(4) Larger cutouts in framing members require an additional 2 x 4 or heavier bracing be nailed on both sides of the affected member.

TIPS ON RUNNING PIPES

FIXING FAUCETS

Leaky faucets are responsible for more wasted water than anything else. Your plumbing supply house, home center or hardware store has parts for many brands.

A FAUCET THAT LEAKS a 1/16-inch stream of water wastes 100 gallons a day. With critical water shortages in many areas, and the cost of water escalating each year, every drip we fix saves water and dollars.

Faucets are made so many different ways that fixing a leaky one is no rigid procedure. First you must get the faucet apart, then effect the repair. Most faucets, especially old ones, are the washer-type which use flat washers. Most of the better, newer faucets are washerless. They have O-rings and discs instead of washers, and are superior in many ways.

Identification comes first. To do this take the handle off. Handle screws may be exposed, but more likely they are hidden underneath caps. Screw or pry the cap off and you can remove the screw, then the handle by pulling or prying up. Sometimes you must remove a decorative cover to expose the faucet's works. If the faucet has a packing nut, you are likely looking at a washer-type faucet.

With the water turned off, unscrew the packing nut. Then slip the faucet handle back on and twist out the spindle by turning the faucet toward "on" position. Some spindles come out along with a threaded sleeve as soon as the packing nut sleeve is unscrewed.

At the lower end of the spindle is the washer. If it is flat, or deeply grooved and hard, replace it. As a temporary cure, an old washer can sometimes be installed backwards.

Modern faucet spindles use rubber O-rings to keep water from leaking out around the stem. Older ones used packing. A stem-leaker can be cured by replacing the O-ring (available in many sizes) or installing new packing. If the spindle is partially eaten away by corrosion, it can be replaced with a new one.

If the faucet still leaks, its seat may need attention. Some seats can be screwed out and

Repairing a modern single-lever Delta faucet is easy, should one ever drip. First turn off the hot and cold water supplies to the faucet. 1) Remove the handle and unscrew the cap nut. Pull out the works. 2) Insert a small screwdriver into each of the rubber seats inside the faucet body, pull out and discard them. 3) Slip new springs and seats into their openings in the faucet, springs down. Push them all the way down into their recesses. 4.) Now the reconditioned valve assembly can be installed into the faucet and pushed down the way it was before it came out. The rest of the job is simply reinstalling the chrome cap nut and running it down finger-tight. If you get any leakage around the top of the faucet, loosen the cap nut again and tighten its adjusting ring slightly before snugging it down. 5) Parts needed come in kit form.

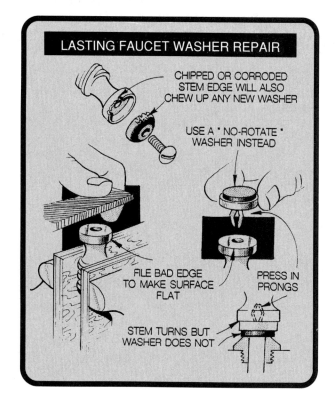

LASTING FAUCET WASHER REPAIR

CHIPPED OR CORRODED STEM EDGE WILL ALSO CHEW UP ANY NEW WASHER

USE A "NO-ROTATE" WASHER INSTEAD

FILE BAD EDGE TO MAKE SURFACE FLAT

PRESS IN PRONGS

STEM TURNS BUT WASHER DOES NOT

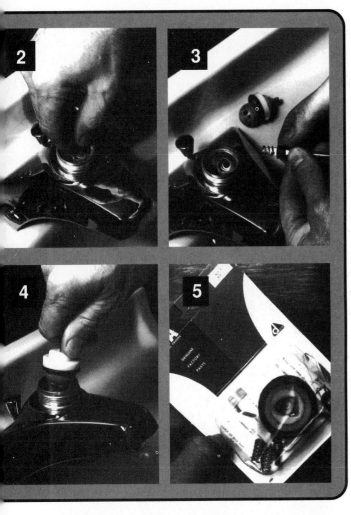

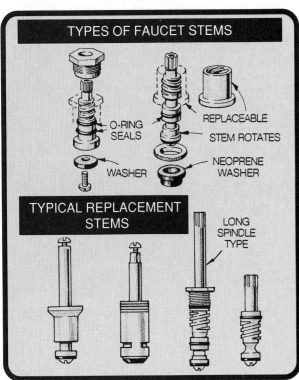

TYPES OF FAUCET STEMS

O-RING SEALS

REPLACEABLE

STEM ROTATES

WASHER

NEOPRENE WASHER

TYPICAL REPLACEMENT STEMS

LONG SPINDLE TYPE

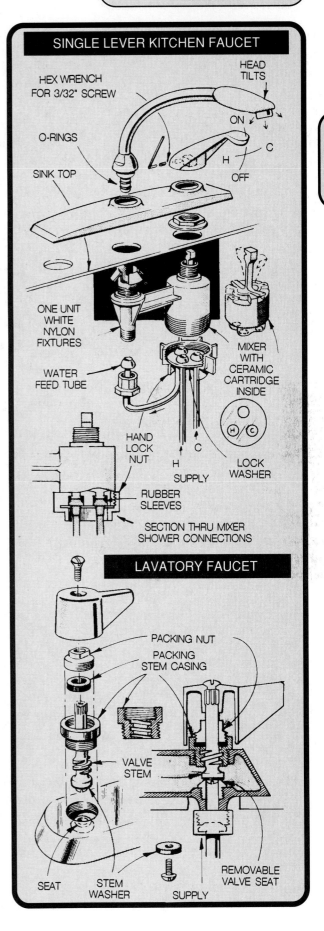

SINGLE LEVER KITCHEN FAUCET

HEX WRENCH FOR 3/32" SCREW

HEAD TILTS

O-RINGS

SINK TOP

ON
OFF
H
C

ONE UNIT WHITE NYLON FIXTURES

WATER FEED TUBE

MIXER WITH CERAMIC CARTRIDGE INSIDE

H C

HAND LOCK NUT

H C

SUPPLY

LOCK WASHER

RUBBER SLEEVES

SECTION THRU MIXER SHOWER CONNECTIONS

LAVATORY FAUCET

PACKING NUT

PACKING
STEM CASING

VALVE STEM

REMOVABLE VALVE SEAT

SEAT

STEM WASHER

SUPPLY

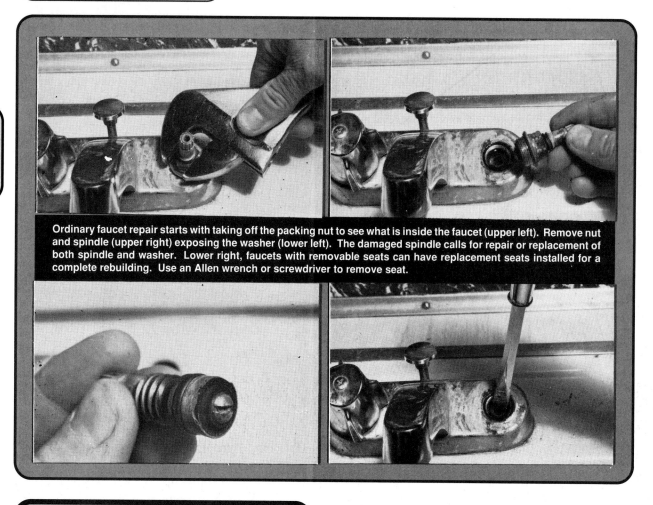

Ordinary faucet repair starts with taking off the packing nut to see what is inside the faucet (upper left). Remove nut and spindle (upper right) exposing the washer (lower left). The damaged spindle calls for repair or replacement of both spindle and washer. Lower right, faucets with removable seats can have replacement seats installed for a complete rebuilding. Use an Allen wrench or screwdriver to remove seat.

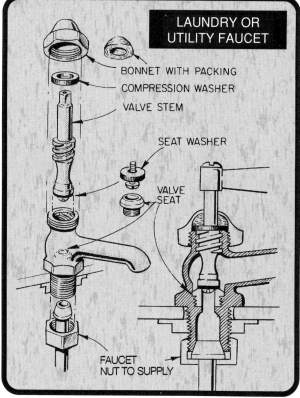

LAUNDRY OR UTILITY FAUCET

BONNET WITH PACKING

COMPRESSION WASHER

VALVE STEM

SEAT WASHER

VALVE SEAT

FAUCET NUT TO SUPPLY

replaced. Others are refaced in the faucet.

Washerless faucets are less prone to leak and easier to fix than washer-type ones. A rubber diaphragm or a pair of ceramic or metal discs hold back water flow. The washerless spindle unit is held in by a nut. Remove it and the whole works just lifts out. Sometimes a knurled cap holds the spindle in place. In this case, no wrench is needed. Your plumbing supply dealer can probably sell you a replacement spindle unit or else get the parts necessary to rebuild the old one.

A wide variety of single-lever faucets are available and if you can get the manufacturer's leaflet on service for that faucet, you are ahead of the game. Usually some manufacturer identification is stamped on the faucet; find the name and your plumbing supply dealer may have the exploded parts drawing and parts list.

The newer single-lever faucets with top control, including tub and shower units, are repaired from the front with the handle off. Leakage around the control is a simple matter of tension adjustment. Other leakage calls for easy replacement of the rubber valves from a kit.

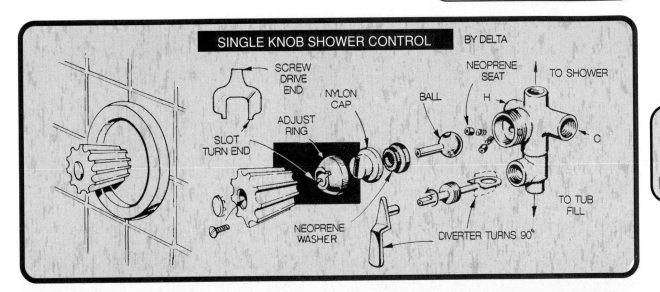

SINGLE KNOB SHOWER CONTROL   BY DELTA

SCREW DRIVE END

NYLON CAP

NEOPRENE SEAT

TO SHOWER

BALL

H

C

ADJUST RING

SLOT TURN END

NEOPRENE WASHER

DIVERTER TURNS 90°

TO TUB FILL

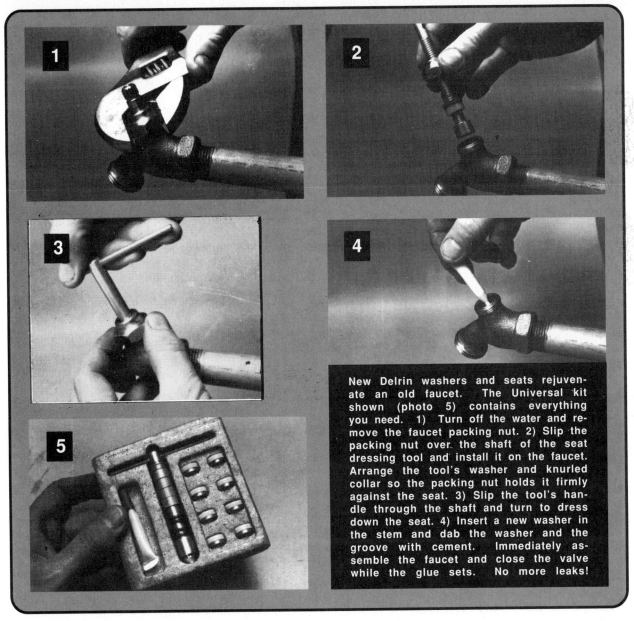

New Delrin washers and seats rejuven-ate an old faucet. The Universal kit shown (photo 5) contains everything you need. 1) Turn off the water and re-move the faucet packing nut. 2) Slip the packing nut over the shaft of the seat dressing tool and install it on the faucet. Arrange the tool's washer and knurled collar so the packing nut holds it firmly against the seat. 3) Slip the tool's han-dle through the shaft and turn to dress down the seat. 4) Insert a new washer in the stem and dab the washer and the groove with cement.   Immediately as-semble the faucet and close the valve while the glue sets.   No more leaks!

This may look complex, but it works the same way as most toilets with one exception. It features a Vent-Away system that removes odors before they permeate the room. Pulling the handle permits a small amount of water to flow through a jet aspirator; this causes a vacuum in the bowl which draws air (and odors) back through holes in the toilet rim.

FIXING TOILETS

If your toilet wastes water or makes unusual noises, try fixing it yourself. It is really easy.

DESPITE THE EFFORT of manufacturers all around the world, the home toilet flush tank is probably the most troublesome piece of plumbing equipment in the house. One reason is that it gets so much use. The second is that it has so many automatic functions. All you do to start the flush is trip the lever once. The toilet tank then (1) continues the flush until it empties the tank; (2) stops the flush when the tank water is almost gone; (3) turns on the water supply to refill the tank; (4) diverts some of the refill water to replace trap-sealing water siphoned from the toilet bowl; and (5) shuts off the water supply when tank water level reaches the correct height. Up-to-date toilet tanks also contain vacuum-breaker inlet valves that admit only air to the supply pipes should there be a back-siphonage in the water-supply system.

WATER KEEPS RUNNING

Most toilet tank troubles can be spotted by the sounds they make. The most common one, failure of the tank to shut off a minute or two after a flush, shows itself as the noise of water running. The cure depends on whether the tank refills or whether it stays empty after the flush. If it stays empty, the flush valve is not closing as it should. This problem is so common that toilet manufacturers have produced all kinds of flush valve designs trying to prevent it. They have partially succeeded.

The new designs give less trouble than the old flush ball valve. As the lever is tripped to start the flush, the rubber flush ball is lifted by wires, then it is held up by the outflow of water until the tank is almost empty. The flush ball is supposed to lower and reseat itself on the valve seat. Trouble is the lift wire hangs up on the guide arm, or if the trip lever fails to release properly, the ball stays up. Refill water keeps coming into the toilet tank but it flows right on out again. You have to jiggle the trip lever or reach into the tank and lower the flush ball manually.

One cure is to dispose of the whole flush ball system, removing the guide arm, and install a more reliable rubber flapper valve, costing only a little more than a new flush ball. Slide the flapper down on the overflow pipe until it seats on the flush valve. Rig the furnished stainless steel chain up to the end of the trip lever arm with 1/2-inch slack and your problems should be over for a long time. Some adjustment of flapper height may be needed to get a complete flush.

If you prefer to stick with the flush ball system, check the lift wires for hang-ups, or else install new one. The good thing about toilet tank repairs is that lots of parts are available.

WATER RUNS, TANK FULL

If the tank fills but a water-running noise can still be heard several minutes after a flush, look closely at the float and float arm to see if they are touching any other parts of the tank. If so, bend the float arm to give clearance. If that is not the problem, see whether the flush ball or rubber flapper is encrusted with hard-water scale. Do the same with the flush valve seat. Scale prevents a tight seal. You can either clean or replace; new valve seats are available in brass or plastic.

You can get a new seal kit (by Fluidmaster) that consists of a stainless steel rim and a ring of epoxy. Press the epoxy over the existing seat and then add the ring. Beats trying to replace the original valve seat!

If water is running over the top of the overflow pipe, bend the float arm down to lower the water level.

A leaking ballcock inlet valve can be the cause of water-running sounds. Remove the screws from the lever mechanism, take it apart and pull out the ballcock valve with pliers. Check the valve's washer and seat. Bad washer? Install a new one or a new ballcock valve. the washer pulls out with pliers. Damaged or scale-encrusted seat? Replace the whole float valve assembly in the tank hole. It is an easy task.

Look at the toilet bowl-refill tube, the one coming out the top of the float valve and entering the top of the overflow pipe. It should not reach below tank water level or it will siphon water out of the tank. Bend it upward to correct.

If all else fails, you can replace everything in the tank.

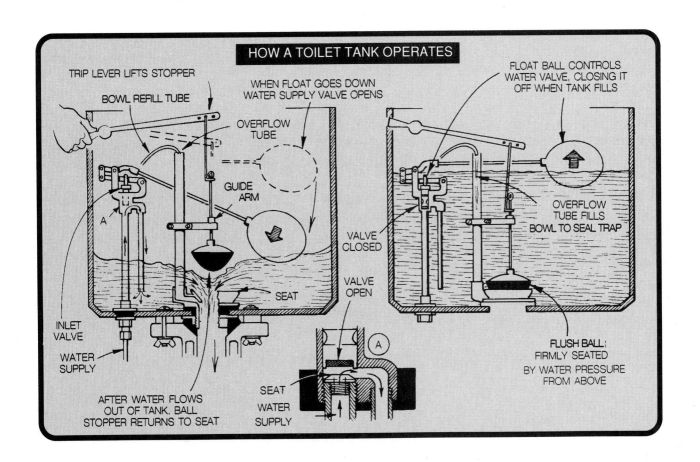

HOW A TOILET TANK OPERATES

PLUMBING

Small tank leaks are hard to detect. One way to find them is to press a piece of paper to the back of the bowl several hours after a flush; it should be dry. Another way is to add a few drops of food coloring to the tank and note if it seeps into the bowl after a few hours.

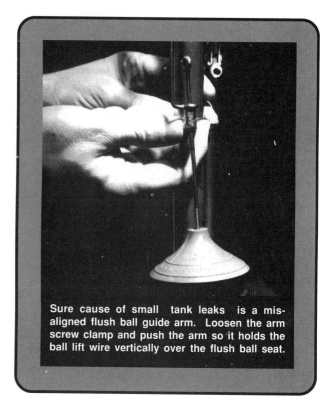

Sure cause of small tank leaks is a mis-aligned flush ball guide arm. Loosen the arm screw clamp and push the arm so it holds the ball lift wire vertically over the flush ball seat.

OTHER FLOAT VALVES BEING USED

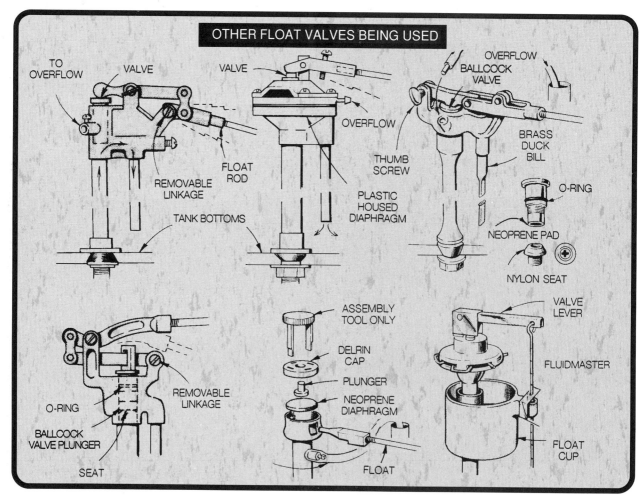

TO OVERFLOW — VALVE — REMOVABLE LINKAGE — FLOAT ROD — TANK BOTTOMS

VALVE — OVERFLOW — THUMB SCREW — PLASTIC HOUSED DIAPHRAGM

OVERFLOW — BALLCOCK VALVE — BRASS DUCK BILL — O-RING — NEOPRENE PAD — NYLON SEAT

O-RING — BALLCOCK VALVE PLUNGER — SEAT — REMOVABLE LINKAGE

ASSEMBLY TOOL ONLY — DELRIN CAP — PLUNGER — NEOPRENE DIAPHRAGM — FLOAT

VALVE LEVER — FLUIDMASTER — FLOAT CUP

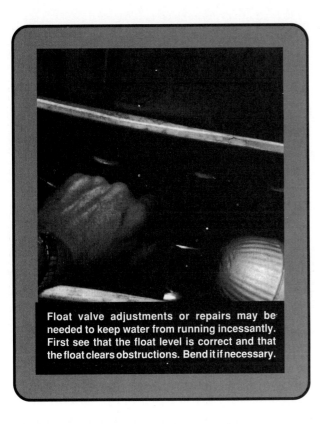

Float valve adjustments or repairs may be needed to keep water from running incessantly. First see that the float level is correct and that the float clears obstructions. Bend it if necessary.

Scouring lime encrustations off the flush valve seat with steel wool may be preferable to replacing the valve. These buildups prevent a tight seal between flush ball and seat, letting water leak.

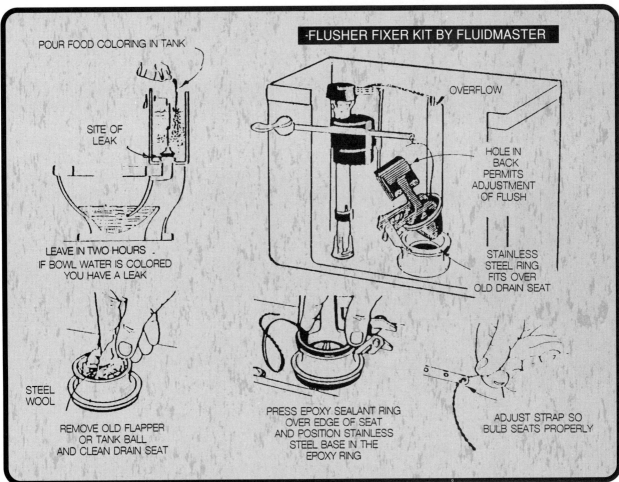

POUR FOOD COLORING IN TANK

FLUSHER FIXER KIT BY FLUIDMASTER

SITE OF LEAK

OVERFLOW

HOLE IN BACK PERMITS ADJUSTMENT OF FLUSH

STAINLESS STEEL RING FITS OVER OLD DRAIN SEAT

LEAVE IN TWO HOURS
IF BOWL WATER IS COLORED YOU HAVE A LEAK

STEEL WOOL

REMOVE OLD FLAPPER OR TANK BALL AND CLEAN DRAIN SEAT

PRESS EPOXY SEALANT RING OVER EDGE OF SEAT AND POSITION STAINLESS STEEL BASE IN THE EPOXY RING

ADJUST STRAP SO BULB SEATS PROPERLY

"FUTURE FLUSH" BY CON-TECH INDUSTRIES BOX 160 CRESWELL OR 97426 — 5-7 GALLON TANK — PUSH SHORT HANDLE FOR SHORT FLUSH — NORMAL WATER LINE

FULL FLUSH — FLAPPER FULLY OPEN — LIQUID AND TISSUE WASTE REQUIRES LESS THAN 2 GALLONS PER FLUSH — SHORT FLUSH — FLAPPER PARTIALLY OPEN

WATER LEVEL

The tank water level after refill should be 3/4-inch below the top of the overflow tube. If different from this, a water level will be marked on the side of the tank. To lower the level, bend the float arm down. Bend up to raise the level. Check for float and arm binding before replacing the tank cover.

PARTIAL FLUSH

An incomplete flush is caused by the rubber flush ball or rubber flapper not getting a high enough lift to stay up. Bend the lift wires, or shorten the chain as necessary to get a higher lift.

SPLASHING SOUND

If, during refill, you hear splashing noises coming from the tank, see if the refill tube has slipped out of the overflow pipe; its water will then be running directly into the tank. This prevents the bowl's trap-sealing water from being replaced after a flush. The cure is to replace the refill tube in the overflow pipe.

TILTING BUCKET

The newer tilting bucket flush valves are pretty reliable. If they give problems, it's probably because of binding against the float arm, trip lever, or hinge. Check and bend the parts out of the way. The float arm and trip lever can be bent to get

them out of the way. Cleaning should cure any hinge-binding problems. A no flush with any type of flush valve makes for a self-guiding repair. Usually when you remove the tank cover, you will find a broken tripstrap, wire, or chain. You can fix it temporarily with cord.

Besides the standard ballcock float valves, you can get a floating-cup inlet valve. Made of plastic, it eliminates the float entirely. Water level is controlled by pressure within the unit. It also does away with gurgling sounds during tank refill. Most dealers have them as replacements that fit in your present toilet tank. Any replacement inlet valve should be of the antisiphon type.

SAVING WATER

Water is one of our most precious resources and as our population increases, regional droughts develop, and sewage-treatment plant operating costs zoom. Most of us are finding this resource harder to come by, and also more expensive. Yet many of us are still not too concerned if a faucet drips constantly, ten-minute or longer showers are taken, or if the yard is watered in excess. These are a few of the many major water wasting habits that exist.

The household toilet is responsible for about 35 percent of the water usage in the home — so this has always been a good area to start conservation. Brick and glass jars are often put into the tank to take up cubic inches that would otherwise be filled by water. Dams are created within the tank so when the flush handle is turned not all of the tank water would go down the drain. These work to a degree, but do so with minimal efficiency.

Another commonly used method to save water is to bend the float arm down and lower the tank water level. Try lowering it half an inch a week until you begin experiencing incomplete flushes. Then raise it back to the last successful position and leave it. This way you will be getting the most efficient use of flush water.

Of course, the newer toilets are designed to flush effectively with as little as one-and-a-half-gallons a flush, but for those who currently have the old 5-to-7 gallons-a-flush tank and are watching their water bills soar, short of replacing the fixture you can install an ingenious device in your present tank called the "Future Flusher."

Over 80 percent of the flushes are for liquid and tissue; the remainder are for solids. "Future Flusher" gives you the option to select a short one-and-a-half gallon flush for liquids and the regular full tank flush for solids. A dual handle that replaces the existing handle is connected to the unusual float and lever arrangement illustrated, giving you the two options. Since the average household of four flushes 7,500 times a year, this product could save more than 24,000 gallons a year! The drawing on page 182 shows how the unit works and how it is installed.

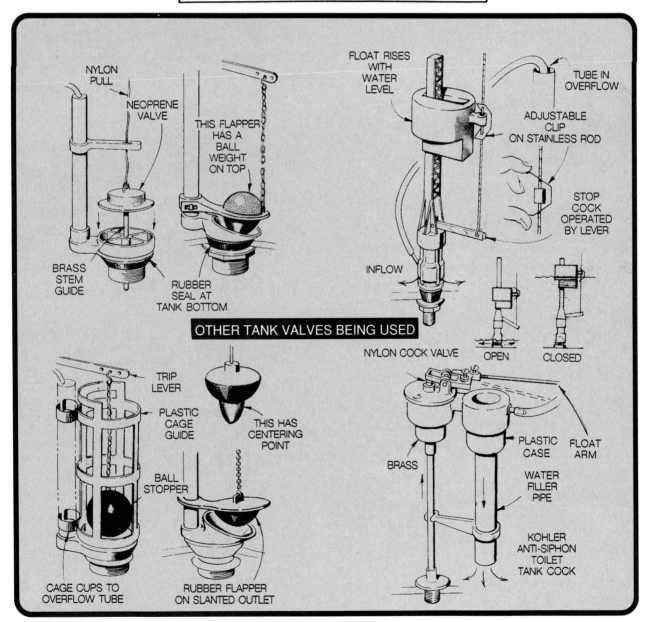

WASHING MACHINE PLUMBING

Shut-off valves should be readily accessible so the machine can be removed for service. Install a single-lever valve (illustrated in drawing) that permits you to turn off the hot and cold line in one flick.

The installation of a normal washing machine requires very little plumbing. All you need is access to a hot and cold water line plus a nearby drain.

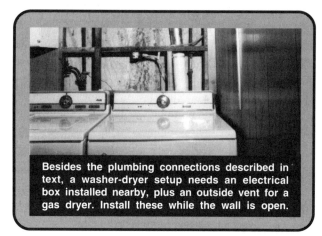

Besides the plumbing connections described in text, a washer-dryer setup needs an electrical box installed nearby, plus an outside vent for a gas dryer. Install these while the wall is open.

YOU CAN HAVE the convenience of an upstairs laundry with automatic washer by putting in the necessary drain and water-supply pipes. Running the supply pipes is much the same as adding an outdoor hose outlet. The difference is that both hot-water and cold-water lines are run parallel to each other about 6 inches apart. Once you have water to the washer location, the next job is to connect the hot-water line from the washer to the hot-water supply line, and the cold-water line from the washer to the cold-water supply line. Many homeowners use regular globe valves for each line but a more convenient and safer connection is made with the single lever on-off valve to which the hot- and cold-water supply lines are connected. A few manufacturers produce a valve that does the same job. This permits you to turn off the hot- and cold-water lines simultaneously by the flip of a lever. Theoretically, you should turn off the water after each wash because as time takes its toll the flexible hoses leading from the machine deteriorate and may eventually leak and burst because of constant water pressure. If your machine is in the basement or an area not frequented regularly, you might be greeted with a few inches of water on the basement floor caused by a broken hose. So make it a point to connect to a dual faucet valve and pull the lever after each wash. Beats trying to turn two globe valves on and off every time you wash.

CLOSE TO STACK

For the easiest job, locate the washer within a few feet of a vent stack. This lets you avoid installing new vent runs for the washer drain. The 1 1/2-inch diameter washer waste pipe may run 5 feet total horizontal length to the point where it enters the vent stack. If the run is longer, you may have to use a large waste pipe or provide separate venting. (A 2-inch pipe may run 8 feet.) Instead of draining into a vent stack, you may connect into the main building drain. Then, no matter how short the run, separate venting must always be provided for the washer drain.

DRAIN CONNECTIONS

Start at the vent stack or building drain. Cut out enough of it to let you install a tee-wye

The finished installation looks as though it belongs. Done this way, no pipes need show outside the wall. Drains and water supply pipes all connect up or go down behind tthe easily removed panel.

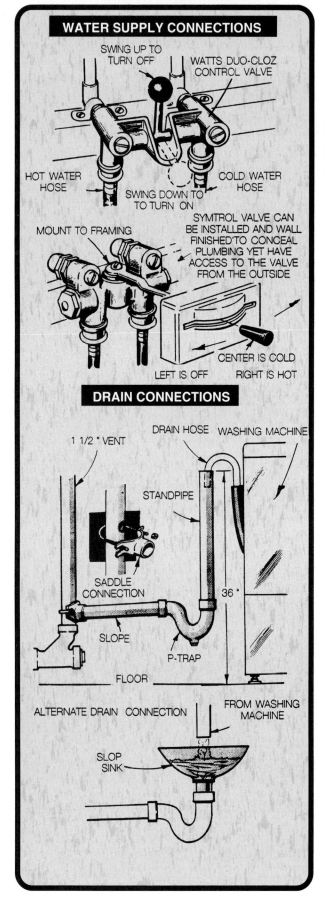

WATER SUPPLY CONNECTIONS

SWING UP TO TURN OFF

WATTS DUO-CLOZ CONTROL VALVE

HOT WATER HOSE

COLD WATER HOSE

SWING DOWN TO TO TURN ON

MOUNT TO FRAMING

SYMTROL VALVE CAN BE INSTALLED AND WALL FINISHED TO CONCEAL PLUMBING YET HAVE ACCESS TO THE VALVE FROM THE OUTSIDE

CENTER IS COLD

LEFT IS OFF   RIGHT IS HOT

DRAIN CONNECTIONS

1 1/2 " VENT

DRAIN HOSE WASHING MACHINE

STANDPIPE

SADDLE CONNECTION

36 "

SLOPE

P-TRAP

FLOOR

ALTERNATE DRAIN CONNECTION

FROM WASHING MACHINE

SLOP SINK

fitting below the floor, aimed in the direction of the flow. If your DWV house system is plastic, and code permits, you can cut a hole in the vent stack and install a solvent-welded saddle tee over it. Wire it temporarily to hold while the solvent cement sets. On a cast-iron system, use a 3 x 3 x 1 l/2-inch No-Hub tee-wye. On a copper or plastic system you can install a 3 x 3 x 1 1/2-inch tee-wye in the cut 3-inch vent. Aim the tee centered on the point where the washer drain will pass through the floor. Run the pipe, sloping it up and away from the stack 1/4 inch per foot. Install a P-trap so that it faces upward through a hole in the floor behind the washer. These are available in plastic, copper and threaded-steel in the 1 1/2-inch size. They make the right-angle bend without other fittings. If the horizontal distance is more than the maximum trap-arm distance, a cleanout should be provided. Use a 1 1/2-inch tee-wye fitting at the outlet end of the P-trap, with a removable plug in the branch end. The 1 l/2-inch vertical washer standpipe extends up from the trap. Cut it off about 36 inches above the floor. After the water lines are connected, slip in the washer drain hose and you are ready to wash.

STOPPING LEAKS

No pipe or plumbing system is leakproof. Until you can make a permanent repair, here are some stop-gap measures.

THE REAL CURE for a leaking pipe, fitting, or tank is to remove and replace the faulty part. This may eventually be what you will do. However, it might be convenient to get months or years of additional service by patching the leak. Most exposed leaks lend themselves to this treatment with a variety of commercial and homemade leak-stopping methods.

Leaks are caused by expansion of water during freezing or by corrosion. Leaking at fittings may be due to incorrect assembly. In any case, replacement can be hard, while patching is easy. It is usually worth a try.

PIPE LEAKS

A homespun patch using a piece of tire inner tube clamped tightly around a small leak in a pipe will usually work. A crack caused by freezing needs the more extensive coverage of a commercial pipe-clamp patcher or a build-up of epoxy material over the leak. Either method will last until corrosion enlarges the opening beyond

Commonly available half-diameter clamp-type pipe patch comprises a metal shield that is tightened over a soft rubber gasket to seal off leaks in pipes. Get the right size to suit the leaky pipe.

what the patch covers. But this could take years.

If the leak is in a portion of the drain-waste-vent system which has no water pressure, a tight wrapping with plastic tape when the pipe is dry can stop the leak temporarily. One tape made especially for garden hose repair withstands water better than others. Otherwise, electrical tape may be used. For health reasons a permanent repair should be made without delay.

Of course, the real cure for a leaky pipe is to cut out the damaged area and install a new piece.

Several types of patches for leaking water tanks use soft washers that are tightened over leaks to seal them: (left to right) toggle-type uses a drilled hole; rubber and lead washer types.

A self-tapping leak-stopper needs no drilled hole. Just screw it into the leak and let it make its own threads. The leak should stop when the rubber gasket is squeezed against the tank wall.

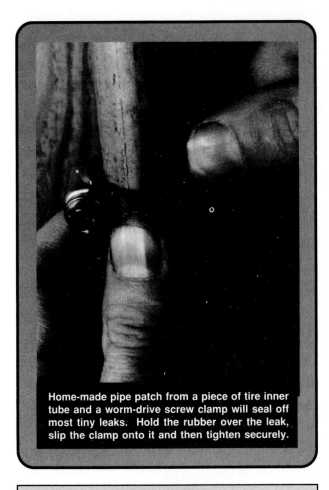

Home-made pipe patch from a piece of tire inner tube and a worm-drive screw clamp will seal off most tiny leaks. Hold the rubber over the leak, slip the clamp onto it and then tighten securely.

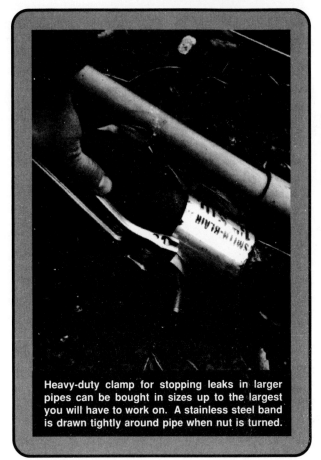

Heavy-duty clamp for stopping leaks in larger pipes can be bought in sizes up to the largest you will have to work on. A stainless steel band is drawn tightly around pipe when nut is turned.

LEAKY FITTINGS

Two-part epoxy glue makes a good lasting patch for a leaking fitting. The area of the leak should be dry and clean. Turn the water off before you mix the epoxy. Apply it liberally, working it onto the metal around the leak. Get it as thick as possible over the leak to hold against water pressure. Plastic pipe should be scuff-sanded before patching. Allow overnight curing at room temperature before turning the water on. The use of 5-minute epoxy glue will speed things considerably, but its pot-life is short and its water-resistance low.

HOLES

Water storage tanks with accessible leaks — not water heaters with their insulated jacketing — can be saved temporarily with self-tapping repair plugs. Several types are available. Screw one of them into the rusted-out opening and it seats against a gasket. One type uses a toggle system and is inserted after drilling out the hole to accept the toggle.

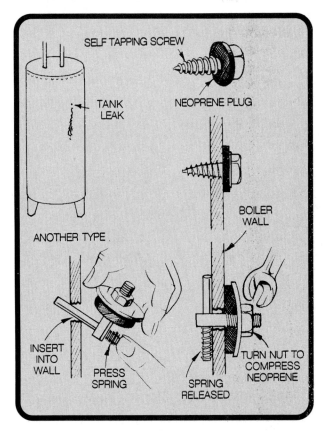

A complete set of plumbing maintenance tools is no big thing. Here are tools you will find handy for unclogging drains, as well as changing fixtures and repairing faucets. (You will also need the basic tools). At top is a curved toilet auger. Familiar plumber's force cup is below that. Also, (l. to r.) are self-storing drain auger, basin wrench, seat dressing tool and combination fixture wrench. These tools are a must for all homeowners.

TIPS ON UNCLOGGING

If chemical drain cleaners do not work, you must resort to mechanical methods plus some ingenuity.

THE CLOGGED DRAIN is such a common occurrence that chemical firms make millions selling drain-opening potions. Some work, some don't. It would be wonderful if there were a chemical that would solve all clogged-drain problems. However, some clogs involve more than pouring a bottle of liquid down the drain. You'll do best if you tackle a clogged drain in easy steps. Start with the least troublesome method and work toward the most effective method.

Most clogs are caused by a mixture of soap residue, hair, grease, and hard-water scale. Favorite places for blockage build-ups are inside fixture traps and at sharp turns in waste and drain pipes. A clog can even develop as far away as in the house-to-street sewer pipe. In this case, all house plumbing backs up, with upstairs waste water coming out of first-floor fixtures and spilling out onto the floor.

It is a mess, but usually not beyond an owner's ability to find and fix it.

MOP UP

The first step is to mop up the overflow water before it seeps down through floors and ceiling, doing damage to the house. If more keeps coming, head for the house main shutoff valve and cut off the water to all fixtures. Now sit down and think about what happened. Did one fixture drain back up? Or are other fixtures involved?

What you are trying to do is deduce where to look for the clog. Here is a checklist:

One fixture — clog probably is in fixture's trap or waste pipe.

Lavatory and tub or shower — clog is probably farther down in the bathroom branch drain leading to the soil stack.

All fixtures — clog is in building drain or house sewer.

PLUMBER'S FRIEND

Most often, only a single fixture is involved and the problem is close to the fixture. Get out a rubber force cup — also called a plumber's friend. It is the quickest, easiest, and cheapest drain-unblocker made. If you get the kind with a fold-down rim, it can be used to best advantage on both fixtures and toilets. Fold the rim down for toilets, up for fixtures.

Force cups work best with several inches of hot water in the fixture bowl to serve as a seal and help melt grease. If the drain has a stopper, take it out to get full force through the drain and onto the clog. Lavatory and bathtub drains with overflow openings require plugging of the overflows with a wet washcloth; otherwise the pressure of your plunging will escape ineffectively through the overflow. Tilt the force cup to one side to fill it with water and hold it squarely over the drain. Push the handle down and pull it up about ten times in succession. Work with the rhythm of

Through-the-roof-vent drain cleaning is pleasant because you work neat and dry. It is most effective for reaching stoppages below where the waste pipe enters slack. 50' units are best rented.

BREAKING UP A CLOG IN A PIPE

A HAND AUGER

REACHES FAR INTO LONG DRAIN TO CLEAR CLOG

PAIL

IF OLD DRAIN PIPES CORRODE TO A FULL BLOCKAGE - AT DISTANT LOCATIONS IN PIPE "X"

CUT THRU THE CLOGGED SECTION WITH A HACKSAW

PAIL

MOVE PIPE APART AND CLEAN OUT WITH A "SNAKE"

REJOIN PIPE WITH NO-HUB CONNECTOR

OR SLIP ON A "DRESSER COUPLING"

AND WRENCH IT UP TIGHT

Drain snake that fits an electric drill rotates as it reaches into the drain to grind out clogs. Be sure to use a well-grounded or double-insulated drill around plumbing. Use a variable speed drill.

put the force cup away and get out the drain-opening chemical. Many are available but whatever you use, follow the directions on the container. Powerful chemicals are involved. They can burn eyes, skin, and some can harm fixture materials. It is best to pour the chemical directly down the drain. Some claim to work even though water is still in the bowl but application directly to the drain is more effective.

If the required time goes by and the clog remains, get out the drain auger or "snake." A long flexible cable or tape, it should be pushed in past the trap, through the waste pipe and on in until you can hear it hitting against the back of the soil stack. Rotating will help clear turns and get rid of the clog. Some snakes are slim steel tapes that are pushed into the drain and pounded against the clog. This type cannot be rotated.

An auger, built just for toilets, contains a sharp bend at the lower end of the handle to get the auger started up the toilet trap. One costs very little and makes a worthwhile addition to the home plumbing tool line-up. A toilet auger can save toilet bowl removal by snagging and pulling back things like teddy bears, wash cloths and paper towels that are accidentally flushed down but do not go all the way. The auger is long enough to reach the toilet's outlet horn, but no farther. Most toilet troubles are in the first bend of the trap.

the water flowing down and back into the drain to add extra push against the clog. On the final stroke, pull up hard, lifting the plunger sharply off the drain. This may send a column of water gushing up from the drain. It also exerts great back pressure on the clog and does more to loosen it than the hardest downward push could.

If several sessions at plunging do not work,

Unclogging a drain mechanically—snake, auger, etc.—is usually more effective than trying to dissolve the blockage chemically. In addition to the variety of wire snakes, two water-assist devices that slip into the pipe are worth considering. One called Drain King, with a combination balloon and nozzle, which attaches to the end of a garden hose. Push the hose into the pipe as far as it will go and then turn on the water. The balloon on the end will inflate and press tightly against the walls of the pipe, thereby preventing water jetting from the nozzle from returning. The force of the jet stream and the build-up of water pressure will usually dislodge the clog and break it into small particles which will easily flow into the sewer or septic system. This clever device is available in sizes for 1 1/2-inch pipe up to 6-inch pipe. The fact that it has been around for years and the principle is used by other manufacturers proves it works.

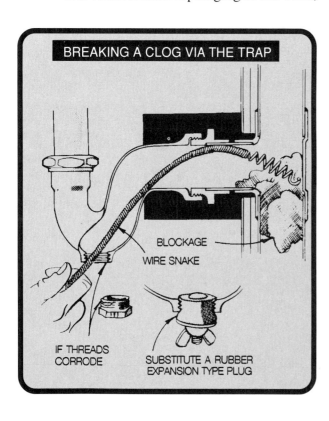

BREAKING A CLOG VIA THE TRAP

BLOCKAGE

WIRE SNAKE

IF THREADS CORRODE

SUBSTITUTE A RUBBER EXPANSION TYPE PLUG

Another snake-like drain unclogger uses a rotating jet stream of water to break up a clog. Unlike the expanding balloon type product, this one — appropriately called Drain Blaster — consists of eight feet of flexible plastic tubing; one end has a fitting so it can be screwed onto the faucet after the aerator has been removed and the opposite end is fitted with a brass nozzle which revolves as it is pushed along and into the clog. The tubing can negotiate a trap and when the nozzle hits the blockage the jet stream and the revolving jets usually do the job. The plastic washes off easier and it will never rust so using this device is not as messy as the steel snake.

If you still find the drain blocked, things are getting serious. It may open up, but block again within a few weeks. This problem is often due to pipe scale. The scale gets so thick that perhaps only a very narrow passageway is left through the trap and waste pipes. To fix this kind of clogging, take off the trap and discard it. Be sure to put a pail under it to catch the surplus water from the bowl. Remove the waste pipe from the wall using a pipe wrench and scrape the scale out with a screwdriver before replacing it. Install a new trap. Try to rod the pipes inside the wall with your drain auger. A garden hose can be used for flushing.

When a toilet keeps clogging, and it is not a cheapie washdown type, suspect a restriction in the bowl seal at the closet flange. You will have to remove the toilet bowl to check.

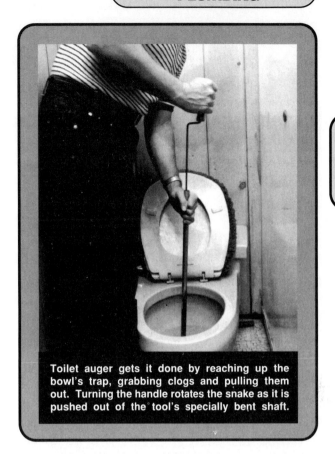

Toilet auger gets it done by reaching up the bowl's trap, grabbing clogs and pulling them out. Turning the handle rotates the snake as it is pushed out of the tool's specially bent shaft.

BLOCKED BRANCH DRAIN

When several fixtures are involved, the clog is farther down than any single fixture's trap or waste pipe. Clogs nearly always catch in horizontal pipes where the flow is slowest or most restricted. Look in the basement or crawl space

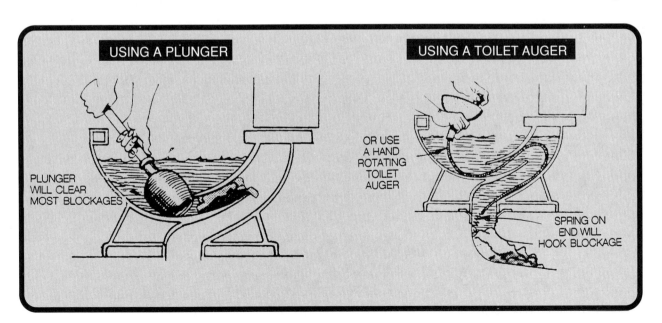

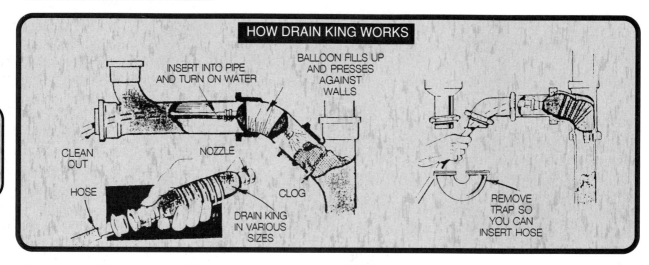

HOW DRAIN KING WORKS

INSERT INTO PIPE AND TURN ON WATER

BALLOON FILLS UP AND PRESSES AGAINST WALLS

CLEAN OUT

NOZZLE

HOSE

CLOG

DRAIN KING IN VARIOUS SIZES

REMOVE TRAP SO YOU CAN INSERT HOSE

and see what horizontal pipe serves the affected fixtures but does not serve any unaffected ones. Then trace this pipe to its upper end.

A cleanout opening should be located at the high end. Place a pail under it and take off the cleanout cover. You may have to tap it with a cold chisel to loosen it. If no water comes out and the drains are still backed up, the clog is above the cleanout. Replace the cleanout cover and move back upstairs, working in through the nearest fixture waste pipe with trap removed.

BLOCKED SEWER

If the blockage turns out to be even farther along, rod out the building drain. Your drain auger may be too short so a good substitute is a garden hose or better yet, a sewer tape. These come in 25- and 50-foot lengths and can be obtained from a tool rental firm. They are coiled-up strips of steel, inserted in the pipe to break up clogs.

If tree roots have grown into a sewer pipe joint and blocked it, you will have to rent an electrical auger with a root-cutting attachment. This is fed into the drain like a sewer tape. As it moves along, its cutter slices off roots inside the sewer pipe. Of course, you can also hire a professional to do this for you, but at what cost? Once cut, the roots can be washed along the sewer by several flushes of the toilet.

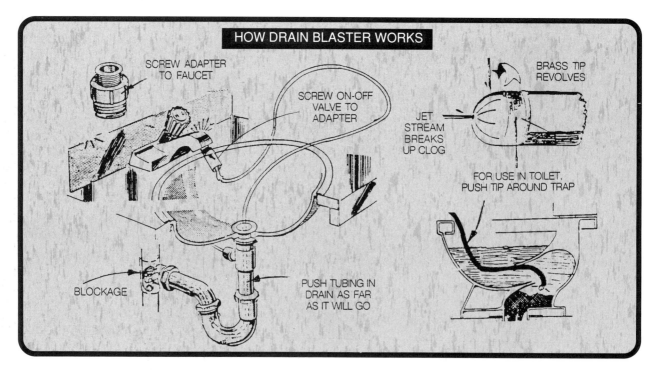

HOW DRAIN BLASTER WORKS

SCREW ADAPTER TO FAUCET

SCREW ON-OFF VALVE TO ADAPTER

BRASS TIP REVOLVES

JET STREAM BREAKS UP CLOG

FOR USE IN TOILET, PUSH TIP AROUND TRAP

BLOCKAGE

PUSH TUBING IN DRAIN AS FAR AS IT WILL GO

BOOK 3 ELECTRICAL

Prime Author: ROBERT HERTZBERG

CONTENTS

194 Basic Facts About Electricity
198 Electrical Safety
206 How to Read a Meter
208 Fuses vs. Circuit Breakers
212 Tools and Testers
218 Successful Soldering
220 Making Wire Nut Connections
222 GFCI Ground-Fault Circuit Interrupter
226 Installing Outlets and Switches
230 Wiring Techniques
238 Wiring Tricks You Can Use
242 Amperage Requirements
244 ENT: The Do-It-Yourself Conduit
248 All About Fluorescent Lamps
254 Door Chimes, Bells and Buzzers
258 Dramatic Lighting
262 Landscape Lighting Ideas
268 Lighting for Security and Safety

272 What to do Before a Storm
274 Lamp Repair
275 Hanging a Swag Lamp

TELEPHONE INSTALLATION

276 Installing Your Telephones
277 Your Telephone Company
278 The Point of Demarcation
280 Pulse and Tone Dialing Telephones
281 Safety Tips when Running Your Lines
282 Apartment Telephone Layout
283 Two-Story Telephone Layout
284 Major Accessories for Running Telephone Lines
286 Converting Hard Wired to Modular
287 Tapping into a Junction Box
288 The Ringer Equivalence Number

This turbine at the Con Edison generating plant in New York City produces 971 megawatts of electricity and is the largest unit in the Con Ed system. The unit uses #6 residual oil as its primary fuel but can also use gas. Originally a coal-fired plant it still retains a coal burning capacity in case of a fuel emergency. The use of coal is not presently permitted in New York City. Incidentally, all Con Ed units must use .3 percent sulphur oil which must be imported.

BASIC FACTS ABOUT ELECTRICITY

Even if you do not make any elaborate electrical repairs, you should know about *WATTS, AMPERES and VOLTS* or the newer international term *HERTZ (Hz)*.

You do not have to know a thing about electricity to enjoy the conveniences of electrical appliances—press the switches and the power company does the rest. But it helps.

Let's start where the "juice" starts, in the power station of the local utility company. Here, huge rotating machines generate current that changes its direction of flow rapidly. It goes one way for 1/120th of a second then the other way for another 1/120th, and keeps repeating itself. Each of these movements is called an "alternation," hence the common term "alternating current," or "AC."

Two complete alternations comprise a "cycle," or, to use the newer international term, a "hertz." The number of hertz per second (Hz) is called the frequency. In the United States all the current furnished to homes is 60 Hz.

AC generators are run by engines using a variety of fuels. In most big stations, a water boiler heated by burning coal or oil makes steam at high pressure. This is directed against the blades of a turbine, which turns at high speed. The turbine itself is coupled to or is part of the alternator proper. So-called "atomic powered" electric plants use the same boiler-turbine-alternator combination just described, but the water is turned to steam by heat from a nuclear reactor instead of from conventional fossil fuel.

Medium-sized stations use automobile-type internal combustion engines of either the diesel or spark-ignition type, fueled by oil or

This is a typical pole transformer in a residentlal area that reduces the overhead line of possibly 2,200 volts to 120-240 volts. This single transformer will usually feed six to ten residences.

Sometimes two or three transformers may be mounted on a single pole to feed several square blocks of houses. And sometimes a single transformer will only serve a solitary farm.

gasoline. Some even use jet engines or turbines borrowed from the aviation industry.

The really big power stations of the world depend on a fuel that is clean and quiet, doesn't burn at all, and costs virtually nothing—water. From natural falls such as those at Niagara, in New York, and man-made falls at Hoover Dam, on the Arizona-Nevada border, the water merely drops by gravity through paddle wheels connected to the alternators, and runs out downstream to irrigate thousands of acres of farm land.

THE ELECTRICAL UNITS

Let's talk about volts, amperes, ohms and watts. "Voltage" is the pushing action of electricity in the wires of a circuit or appliance. "Ohms" is their tendency to resist the pressure. Thin wire has a relatively high resistance; thick wire has lower resistance. "Amperes" is a measure of the electricity pushed through the resistance by the voltage. One ampere is defined as the current that flows for one second through a resistance of one ohm with a pressure of one volt. Note that this is a *rate of flow*, not an *amount of current*. There is no way of storing electricity for future use, as

you can with water from a pipe, because nothing tangible comes out of an electric circuit. What we think of as an electric "current" is a movement of electrons within and between the atoms of the conducting wires. Only when they are in motion do the electrons produce the thermal, magnetic, chemical and various other effects that constitute useful work.

In the technical sense, the term "power" is the *rate* of doing work. The concept of "horsepower," is credited to James Watt, the Scotsman who made the steam engine. One horsepower is the force required to raise 33,000 pounds at the speed of one foot a minute. The electrical power unit is the "volt-ampere, or watt," substantially equal to volts multiplied by amperes. The practical unit, for figuring the cost of electrical energy, is the "kilowatt-hour," meaning 1,000 watts consumed during 60 minutes. Kilowatt hours are what the electric meter in your house registers.

HEATING EFFECTS OF ELECTRICITY

In rushing around electrical circuits at the speed of light, electrons create heat through friction. This can perform valuable tasks. The higher the resistance of the wires and the more current pushed through them, the higher the heat. If bare wire is allowed enough amperes to make it glow red, we can toast bread over it, grill meat, cook soup, etc. If the current is increased a little too much, the wire becomes white hot, it combines with the oxygen in the air, and it simply burns up. This is precisely the action of a fuse in protecting a circuit from an overload of current.

If we want the wire to stay white hot, so that we can illuminate a room with it, we put it in a glass bulb from which the air has been removed, and presto, we have electric light.

The watt rating and the line voltage of most appliances is marked somewhere on their cases, but the ampere draw is not usually included. Nevertheless, it is easy to figure this from the other two values; divide watts by volts and you have amperes. For example, a typical household iron marked "1,110 watts, 120 volts" draws a little more than 9 amperes. (The word amperes is often shortened to amps.)

There is a common misconception that high voltage means high power. This isn't so; power is any combination of voltage and amperes. A 12-volt automobile headlamp that draws 5 amperes is equivalent to a 120-volt house lamp that takes 1/2 ampere; both are 60-watt lamps.

All the wiring beyond the meter is the responsibility of the home owner. It is sealed by the utility company to discourage tampering and to let you know that there are no fuses inside, only wire connections.

THE VERSATILE TRANSFORMER

One of the important features of AC is the ease of transforming it from any voltage to a higher or lower voltage, with great efficiency. The transformers that do this are of simple construction.

By the time a power line gets to a residential area, it might be running at some 2,000 volts. The job of the final transformer is to bring this 2,000 volts down to household use. There are often two or three transformers in sight on a single utility pole. These feed different groups of houses, depending on what type and size of electrical service is wanted in them. An average pole-mounted transformer is about the size of a 36-gallon garbage can. Larger models are usually installed in underground vaults in the street or on the ground in fenced enclosures.

CONDUCTORS VS. NON-CONDUCTORS

All common metals conduct electricity, some better than others. Silver has the lowest resistance, but because of its cost is used generally only to coat the contact surfaces of switches that carry heavy currents. Copper is very close behind, and because it is relatively cheap, highly ductile, and easy to solder, it is used for probably 95 per cent of all electrical wiring. Aluminum is about 50 percent more resistant than copper, but with its weight advantage—and lower cost—it is useful for many purposes.

Metals are generally good conductors because the electrons in them can be set into motion readily by outside influences.

Materials having so much resistance that they are absolute nonconductors of electricity are

If there is a box next to the meter, you can be pretty sure that it holds either a circuit breaker or a switch. The circuit breaker, or switch, is used to turn off all the current from entire house.

A hinged plate covering the box can be swung up revealing a large black handle. Pushing it down, will cut off all the current to the house. Always turn off current before doing any electrical work.

called "insulators" and are used to protect live wires from "short-circuiting" against each other, and also to prevent live people from touching live wires. In this category is a large variety of substances: paper, cotton, wool, glass, ceramics, plastics, silk, nylon and most other man-made fabrics, and air, or no air at all—a vacuum.

HOW LONG IS A "SHORT CIRCUIT?"

At this point you're probably asking, "Just what is a short circuit?" It is a temporary, accidental and altogether unwelcome connection between exposed wires or other parts of an electrical system. For instance, suppose that the insulation on the line cord of a vacuum cleaner is damaged by careless treatment; the machine is pulled over it, it is stepped on, or a dog chews on it. Eventually the bare wires show and are squeezed together the

next time the wheels of the cleaner roll over the cord. These touching wires constitute a short circuit. Because the resistance here is low, the current jumps to a high rate of flow, a lot of heat is generated, and then three events occur at the same time: the joint flares up, the line fuse or circuit breaker kicks open, and the person using the machine gets a bad scare.

A really solid short-circuit like this one is not usually dangerous in the sense that it might start a fire, because the instantaneous current is probably 100 amperes or more, a load that no fuse or circuit breaker can resist. The sneaky shorts are those whose connections are a bit loose and have enough resistance to heat up appreciably and ignite nearby materials without disengaging the fuse or circuit breaker. Finding and repairing worn wires and similar faults is a vital part of good electrical maintenance and safety in any home.

ELECTRICAL SAFETY

To prevent shocks and fires, electrical wiring must be done properly and safely.

ELECTRICAL WIRING is the most pleasant around-the-house work you could think of. Nevertheless, if not done properly, there's a danger of shock or fire. To minimize these risks, work carefully, take recommended safety precautions and use recognized safe materials and methods.

Electricity is a flow of pressurized electrons that are constantly seeking to complete their circuit to ground. In addition to the earth, good electrical grounds are everywhere—metal water faucets, plumbing pipes and fixtures, the metal parts of heating systems and more. Undesired electrical flow to ground is prevented by insulating the live portions of electrical circuits with nonconductors. For example, the plastic insulation on current-carrying wires keeps the electrons from flowing to ground, even though the wires may be buried in the ground.

Because the human body is a fairly decent

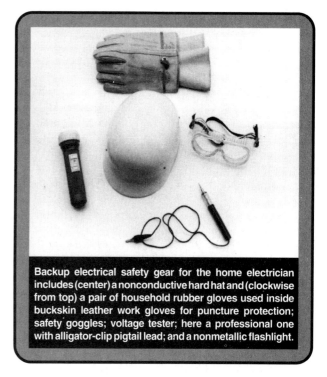

Backup electrical safety gear for the home electrician includes (center) a nonconductive hard hat and (clockwise from top) a pair of household rubber gloves used inside buckskin leather work gloves for puncture protection; safety goggles; voltage tester; here a professional one with alligator-clip pigtail lead; and a nonmetallic flashlight.

conductor of electricity, the danger of getting an electric shock comes when part of the body gets between the pressurized electrons and a ground. If it flows through the heart, just the tiny electric current that lights a Christmas tree bulb can be lethal. Therefore, you should avoid getting between an energized circuit and a ground.

1. For this reason, always turn off the power before working on anything electrical. Turning off a branch circuit or power to the entire house can be done at the service panel or at the house main

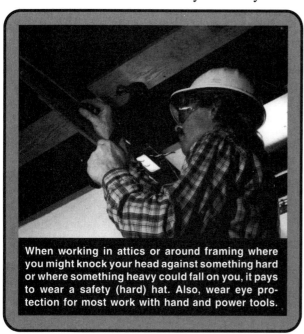

When working in attics or around framing where you might knock your head against something hard or where something heavy could fall on you, it pays to wear a safety (hard) hat. Also, wear eye protection for most work with hand and power tools.

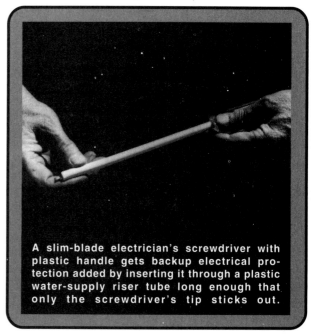

A slim-blade electrician's screwdriver with plastic handle gets backup electrical protection added by inserting it through a plastic water-supply riser tube long enough that only the screwdriver's tip sticks out.

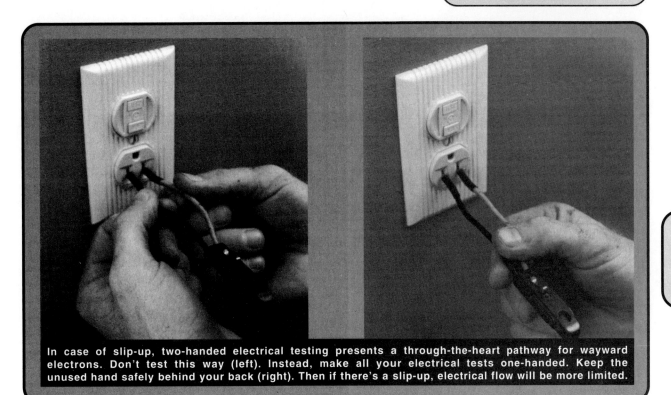

In case of slip-up, two-handed electrical testing presents a through-the-heart pathway for wayward electrons. Don't test this way (left). Instead, make all your electrical tests one-handed. Keep the unused hand safely behind your back (right). Then if there's a slip-up, electrical flow will be more limited.

disconnect by removing a fuse or switching a circuit breaker to the off position. Never depend on a wall switch. Leave a prominent note on the panel letting others know that the power shouldn't be restored while you're working.

If you don't know how to turn off the power or if it fails to turn off, do not proceed. Consult a qualified electrician.

Working inside a service panel is not recommended because it contains wires and terminals that cannot be turned off except by the power company. For this reason, new branch circuits in your home should be connected by an electrician.

2. More than one branch circuit may be supplying power to an outlet. To be safe, always follow power shutoff by testing to make certain that what you are working on is no longer live.

3. Even though it tests dead, avoid touching a bare wire end with your fingers or with metal tools. Instead, handle it by the insulation.

4. Always unplug electrical tools and equipment before working on them.

Because water is a good electrical conductor, wetness or dampness compromises a circuit's insulation and encourages those eager electrons out where they can flow to ground through the next person touching them.

5. Therefore, stay away from any combination of water (or dampness) and electricity. Don't work with electrical tools under damp or wet conditions. Keep hair dryers, radios, etc., well away from bathtubs, showers, pools and spas—anywhere it's wet or damp. Stand on a dry board while changing fuses and switching circuit breakers.

6. Never work with wet or damp wiring.

7. Even though it's dry, avoid becoming grounded around electricity, for example, keep from touching a water pipe while working with electrical equipment.

8. Because of the risks, children and pets should be kept away from the work area. Remove metal jewelry and watches. Light your work area well, even if you have to bring in an extension cord from another part of the house. Don't work when tired or under the influence of alcohol or drugs.

EQUIPMENT GROUNDING

If there should be an insulation breakdown, electrical tools and appliances with metal housings can present a shock danger. Called a *ground fault*, an insulation breakdown can occur when a live portion of the equipment's circuit comes into contact with the metal body. A wire breaking loose inside an electric

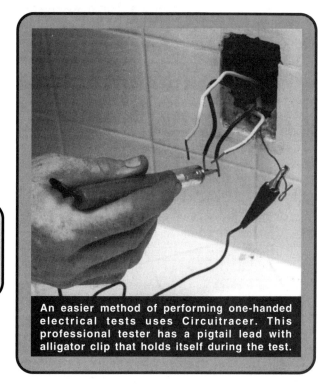

An easier method of performing one-handed electrical tests uses Circuitracer. This professional tester has a pigtail lead with alligator clip that holds itself during the test.

metal body of the equipment, keeping it at ground potential.

Should a ground fault develop, current flow through the tool and back through equipment-grounding wires would be so great that the fuse or circuit breaker would be tripped immediately, removing the shock danger.

9. This is why you should never cut off a plug's grounding prong. Use grounding plugs only in three-slot grounding outlets. Avoid using 3-by-2 grounding adapters. (These are not permitted in Canada.) And use a three-wire extension cord with remote electrical equipment that requires grounding.

Many portable power tools today are double insulated. These bear the familiar square-within-a-square double-insulated insignia. Fitted with two-prong plugs, they have nonmetallic housings and may be used without grounding.

Still another method of protecting the user from electric shock is the ground-fault circuit-interrupter.

10. Make full use of GFCI protection by installing GFCI outlets at all code-recommended locations: bathroom, kitchen countertop within 6 feet of the sink, laundry, garage, basement, workshop and outdoor outlets. Also, buy a GFCI extension cord and use it whenever you work with power tools and other portable electrical equipment outdoors, on concrete surfaces or near other good grounds. If the GFCI extension isn't long enough to reach, an ordinary three-wire extension cord may be plugged in to extend the GFCI-cord's shock-protection.

drill, for example, could create ground fault.

For this reason, electric tools and appliances are further protected by what's called *equipment-grounding*. Equipment grounding makes use of three-pronged grounding-type cords and plugs in three-slot grounding-type receptacles. A receptacle's D-shaped grounding hole connects to an equipment-grounding wire that extends unswitched and unfused back to the main service panel and from there all the way back to the power-company transformer. The round grounding prong of the plug is wired to the

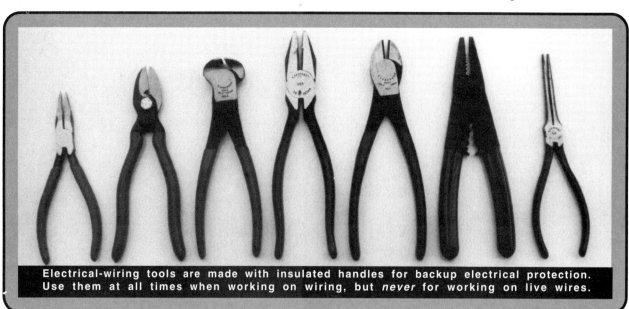

Electrical-wiring tools are made with insulated handles for backup electrical protection. Use them at all times when working on wiring, but *never* for working on live wires.

BACKUP ELECTRICAL PROTECTION

Electrical safety is so important that multiple layers of protection are necessary. These are called *backup electrical protection.* The idea is: don't rely on a single layer of shock-protection. Backup electrical protection is the reason that electrical tools come with insulated handles.

For further backup electrical protection, wear household rubber gloves while changing fuses, working with circuit breakers and when testing live circuits. Don't count on household gloves, however, for basic shock-protection. They're for backup only.

Other good backup electrical protection involves taking such previously described measures and using a nonconducting stepladder for electrical work (wood or fiberglass).

WHAT TO DO IN CASE OF SHOCK

Fortunately, the reflexes of many shock victims throw them back away from the source of electricity. However, some lock onto a tool or wire. If you encounter someone in contact with electricity who cannot let go, avoid touching the person or the source of electricity. Instead, quickly turn off the power at the main service panel. Or unplug the tool or appliance. If you go for the plug, safeguard yourself from getting shocked by wrapping it with a dry rag or towel.

When working with electric tools and appliances outdoors and near grounds like these LP-gas tanks, plug into a GFCI-protected outlet or GFCI extension cord.

Another method is to try to break the victim's contact with electricity using a chair or a dry broomstick.

Once the shock danger is over, have someone call 911 (most areas) for medical aid. Check the victim for breathing and a pulse. If there is no breathing, administer artificial respiration. If there is no breathing *and* no pulse, and you are qualified, administer cardiopulmonary resuscitation (CPR). While waiting for medical help, keep the victim calm

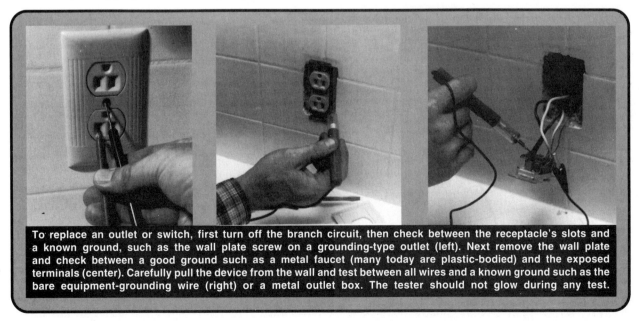

To replace an outlet or switch, first turn off the branch circuit, then check between the receptacle's slots and a known ground, such as the wall plate screw on a grounding-type outlet (left). Next remove the wall plate and check between a good ground such as a metal faucet (many today are plastic-bodied) and the exposed terminals (center). Carefully pull the device from the wall and test between all wires and a known ground such as the bare equipment-grounding wire (right) or a metal outlet box. The tester should not glow during any test.

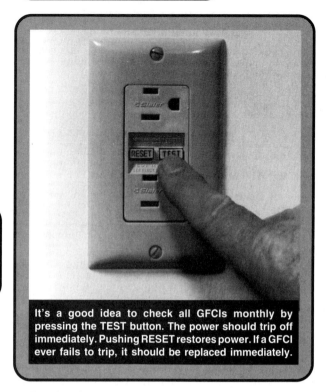

It's a good idea to check all GFCIs monthly by pressing the TEST button. The power should trip off immediately. Pushing RESET restores power. If a GFCI ever fails to trip, it should be replaced immediately.

and maintain an open airway.

TESTING FOR POWER

A prime electrical safety tool is the voltage tester, used to make certain that circuits and wires are dead before working on them. It can be a simple, low-cost neon test light or the professional kind with an

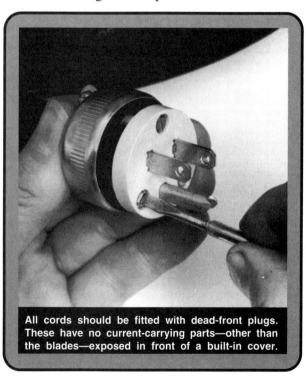

All cords should be fitted with dead-front plugs. These have no current-carrying parts—other than the blades—exposed in front of a built-in cover.

alligator-clip pigtail lead. The lead attaches to a ground (see photos). Before using any tester, try it out in a live outlet. The light should glow, indicating that it is working.

To keep from offering a through-the heart pathway for electricity, all electrical testing should be done single-handed. With a simple neon voltage tester, hold both test prods by their insulated handles in one hand, and keep from touching the metal part of the prods. A tester with alligator-clip pigtail lead makes one-handed testing easy. First attach the lead to a good ground or push it into the D-shaped equipment-grounding hole of a three-slot receptacle. Then make your test using the insulated prod. In either case, keep the unused hand behind your back.

On a receptacle, the initial test is made before removing the wall plate from the device. Test between the two rectangular slots, then between each rectangular slot and the D-shaped grounding hole or the wall plate attachment screw.

Then remove the wall plate and make another test directly on the device terminals. Check from the brass-colored hot terminal, then from each of these terminals to the green-colored equipment-grounding terminal.

After that, you can remove the mounting screws and pull the receptacle carefully away from its box in the wall. Take off the wires, handling them by the insulation without touching the bare ends or screw terminals with your fingers or with metal tools. Then make a third voltage check, testing between all wires and from every wire to the metal outlet box. (With a plastic box, this last check cannot be made.) The light shouldn't glow on any test. If it does, the power is not off.

With a switch, the first test comes when the wall plate has been removed to expose the switch terminals. With a lighting fixture, the first test is made inside the socket, bulb removed. Test between the center bulb contact and the metal screw shell. Make a second test with the fixture removed and the wire nuts off to expose the bare splices. Test between all wires and from every wire to the metal fixture box. If the tester doesn't glow in any test, you can proceed.

ELECTRICAL CODES

Unlike plumbing, electrical work in the United States is regulated by a single code, the

National Electrical Code (NEC). The Canadian Electric Code covers Canada. The NEC is updated every three years and concerns itself with wiring materials and the methods used to install them. The codes establish things like the number of outlets in a room; wire size, wire type and current-carrying capacity; outlet box size; wiring methods; grounding; overcurrent protection; ground-fault protection; and more. All new wiring must conform to the latest edition of the code. A copy can often be found at the local public library.

Most jurisdictions call for getting an electrical-wiring permit before doing any new wiring, plus having an official inspection made of the wiring. An inspection helps make sure your wiring is safe. When applying for an electrical-wiring permit, ask at what stage the work must be inspected. This usually comes before closing in walls and before powering up. Unlike new wiring, electrical repairs usually don't call for getting a permit or inspections.

In the United States, electrical supplies and equipment are tested and listed by Underwriters

When everything checks out electrically dead, you can begin changing the device. Even then, be careful not to touch any bare wires or terminals.

Laboratories (UL) and in Canada by the Canadian Standards Association (CSA). The familiar UL and CSA designations should appear on every wire, cable, wiring device, etc.

FIRE DANGER

The second concern of safe electrical wiring is fire. As electrical current flows through a circuit, it heats the wires. While only a large electrical flow could produce enough heat to start a house fire, it can occur if a live wire comes into direct contact with something that's grounded. This is one reason the house main service panel and all branch circuits are fitted with overcurrent protection, taking the form of fuses or circuit breakers. Fuses and circuit breakers will cut off heavy current flow before it can make enough heat to cause a fire.

On the other hand, if the insulation on an extension cord that is run beneath a carpet should fray, letting the wires touch, enough current could flow to start a fire without triggering the overcurrent protection. This is a reason that extension cords are prohibited, except on a temporary basis. In any case, cords should not be run beneath rugs or carpets.

Circuit overloading is another fire-causing problem. House wiring is designed to serve the loads expected of it. Trouble is, these loads have increased significantly over the years, and old-house wiring may no longer be adequate. Fuses or circuit breakers

A circuit-breaker service panel should have each breaker cycled off and on periodically to keep its contacts bright and clean and help prevent overheating.

that trip off frequently are a tipoff to overloading. So are lights that dim when electrical loads hit.

If the main electrical service has additional unused capacity, adding new branch circuits can help alleviate an electrical overload. Otherwise the house service entrance must be enlarged to handle the added circuits. It's a job for a professional electrician. He will calculate what's needed, then install it. What you can do is:

1. Avoid replacing fuses with heavier-rated ones than originally intended.

2. If an electric appliance continues to trip its branch-circuit overcurrent protection, either have the appliance repaired or, if it is dry, use it in a circuit that isn't overloaded.

ALUMINUM WIRING

While aluminum wiring is accepted by the codes, it suffers considerably more from corrosion than copper wire does. Not installed properly, aluminum wiring connections and splices can overheat and cause a fire. Soft, aluminum wire also tends to work loose from binding-screw terminals. For these reasons, additional precautions should be taken with aluminum wires.

Outlets, switches, wire nuts and other devices used with aluminum wire must bear the CO/ALR stamp, indicating that they are listed for use with aluminum as well as copper wire. Older wiring devices marked AL/CU are not acceptable. Likewise, aluminum wire shouldn't be used with devices having back-wired push-in terminals. Wire nuts may be used for making splices, even when aluminum is combined with copper in the same splice, provided the wire nuts are marked AL/CU. Even then, wire nuts are suited for splicing aluminum wire in dry locations only—meaning indoor wiring above ground.

Aluminum wire's terminal loops should be made extra carefully, and the binding screws should be given half a turn beyond making full contact with the wire. This flattens the wire slightly for a better connection.

Switches and outlets that aren't UL/CSA-listed for use with aluminum wire may still be used by splicing short copper jumper wires to the aluminum wires inside the outlet box. Then the device can be connected with the copper jumpers.

Corrosion of aluminum is reduced by applying antioxidant paste to all terminals and splices. It's sold by many electrical supplies dealers.

Because aluminum wires offer more resistance to electrical flow than copper, they need to be larger by two AWG wire sizes. (The smaller the AWG number, the larger the wire size.) For example, a 15-ampere branch circuit needing No. 14 copper wire would call for No. 12 aluminum wire.

ELECTRICAL SAFETY CHECK

Every once in a while it pays to make a walk-around electrical safety check of your home. Start by inspecting all lamp and appliance cords. These should be routed where they cannot get stepped on. Any frayed cords should be replaced immediately. Cords should never be nailed or stapled in place, wrapped around furniture or coiled up.

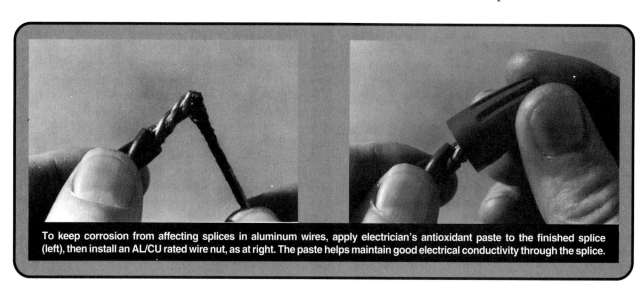

To keep corrosion from affecting splices in aluminum wires, apply electrician's antioxidant paste to the finished splice (left), then install an AL/CU rated wire nut, as at right. The paste helps maintain good electrical conductivity through the splice.

Extension cords are only for temporary use and should not be permanently installed. Add more outlets instead. Compare an extension cord's wire size to the required wire size for any equipment plugged into it to make sure an extension isn't carrying more current than it's rated for.

See that all cords have modern dead-front plugs.

Check behind beds, sofas, etc. for wall plugs that stick out where they could rub against furniture. Plugs that stick out can be replaced with angled plugs. Or a replacement outlet that keeps plugs close to the wall can be installed.

Check fixtures to see that a bulb no larger than the fixture's power rating is used. If no watt (volt-ampere) rating appears on the fixture, a 60-watt bulb is the largest that should be used in it.

See that appliances such as refrigerators, ranges, ovens, washing machines and dryers, are grounded. Those that plug in should have three-prong grounding-type plugs used in three-slot outlets. See that all such plugs have the third grounding prong intact.

Any outlets and switches that feel warm to the touch or that fail to work properly are suspect, especially with aluminum wiring. Every outlet and switch should have a wall plate so that no wiring is exposed. Outdoor outlets need waterproof covers. Plugs should fit tightly into the outlets and the outlets should be tight in their boxes.

Ventilated appliances like television sets should be located where air can circulate around them freely. Keep portable electric heaters out of bathrooms and away from combustibles. Moreover, don't put them where they might get tipped over. On that subject, every electric heater should have a tipover-cutoff switch.

Countertop appliances, when not in use, should be unplugged. Locate them away from the sink and route their cords carefully to avoid hot surfaces.

Any problems you find should be corrected right away.

If you are ever shocked by an electrical appliance or even feel a slight buzz while touching it, unplug it and red-tag it (or cut off the plug). Then have it repaired before using it again. Or dispose of it.

If your house has a fuse-type service panel, check to make sure that each fuse is correctly rated for

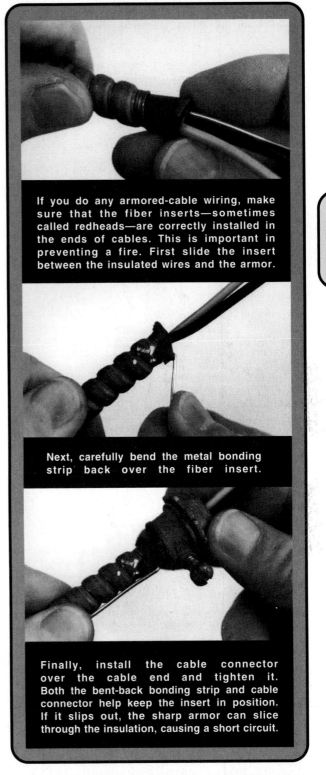

If you do any armored-cable wiring, make sure that the fiber inserts—sometimes called redheads—are correctly installed in the ends of cables. This is important in preventing a fire. First slide the insert between the insulated wires and the armor.

Next, carefully bend the metal bonding strip back over the fiber insert.

Finally, install the cable connector over the cable end and tighten it. Both the bent-back bonding strip and cable connector help keep the insert in position. If it slips out, the sharp armor can slice through the insulation, causing a short circuit.

the wiring in its branch circuit. No. 14 (AWG) copper wires are fused at 15 amperes, No. 12 at 20 amps and No. 10 at 30 amps. It's a good idea to replace the fuses with correctly sized Type S adapters and Type S fuses.

The fact is, you cannot be too careful with electricity.

HOW TO READ A METER

The only way to check how much power you are using is to read your meter. Millions of homes have the dial type illustrated but the utility companies are installing electronic meters with digital readout which can be programmed to provide additional data.

AT SOME TIME, every home owner has the nagging suspicion that he is paying too much for electricity. His first thought is that the meter is "running fast", but upon honest reflection he will probably realize that the weather has been unusually hot and that his air conditioners have been running almost around the clock.

The easiest way to check on your own power usage is to learn how to read the meter and to keep your own record. You'll still pay according to the monthly record of the power company's "meter maid", but at least you'll become aware of the desirability of conservation habits and you'll teach your family to turn off lights and appliances when they're not really needed.

The most common type of residential meter has a glass cover about six inches in diameter, with four (sometimes five) numbered dials. These look like watch faces, but on closer examination you'll spot two important differences: the numbers go from O to 9, not from 1 to 12, and the pointers on adjacent dials turn in opposite directions. The pointers are geared to the drive mechanism (actually, a sort of compound motor that responds to both voltage and current variations) in such a manner that one complete revolution of the right-hand dial moves the pointer of the dial to its immediate left one division. Similarly, one complete revolution of the second dial moves the pointer of the third dial one division. The progression continues to the last dial on the left. In other words, the dials are geared in a one-to-ten ratio, corresponding to numbers from 1 to 10 to 100 to 1,000 to 10,000.

READING THE METER

To take a reading, start with the first dial on the left and in each case note the *lower* figure of the two between which the pointer is resting. In the drawing of a four-dial meter, observe that on dial 1 the reading is 8, on dial 2 it is 2, on dial 3 it is 4 and on dial 4 it is 2: this means that a total of 8,242 kilowatt hours of electricity has run through the meter since it was started, assuming that all dials read O at that time. If another reading of this meter is made perhaps a week later and the total is 8,674, the consumption for that week was 432 kilowatt hours. Always read a pointer as indicating the figure it passed, not the one to which it is nearer.

If the pointers are too close to the marks on the meter for you to figure them out, wait about

DIGITAL READOUT

BETWEEN 8 AND 9 MEANS <u>8</u>   PAST 2 IS <u>2</u>   PAST 4 IS <u>4</u>   NOT YET 2 IS <u>2</u> ON LAST DIAL

8242
LAST READING COULD BE – 8015
YOU USED IN KILOWATT HRS. 227

If you use more than one hundred and less than one thousand kilowatt (KWH) hours the last three digits of the typical dial meter will tell you how much electricity was consumed since the last meter reading.

half an hour and try again. This problem can't arise with meters of the digital readout type which are making their appearance not only because they are easier to read but they are electronic and can be programmed to store additional information such as what time of the day the most power is used, etc.

This data in turn can help the utility company plan their electrical requirements more efficiently. Who knows, with this electronic sophistication eventually our meters will be read at the utility office rather than have a meter reader go from house to house?

This is a typical Con Edison (New York) residential bill similar to those used by utility companies throughout the country. Note the KWH reading of the reading dates (one month apart) and detailed information as to how the total sum was calculated. Also, the computer analyzes usage for the month being billed and compares it with the same time period the previous year.   Other important messages are printed at the end of the bill.

ELECTRIC USE – RATE EL1 RESIDENTIAL

07/19/ reading (Actual).......	8666
06/19/ reading (Actual).......	-8632
Meter reading difference	34
Meter multiplier	x10
Total KWH used in 30 days......	340

CHARGES FOR ELECTRICITY USED

Basic service charge:		$4.73
(does not include usage)		
KWH	COST/KWH	
First 250.0 @ 12.4080¢		31.02
Next 90.0 @ 13.4778¢		12.13
Fuel adjustment @ .7170¢		2.44
Sales tax @ 4.000%		2.01

CURRENT ELECTRIC CHARGES $52.33

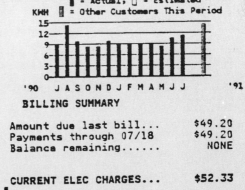

AVERAGE DAILY ELECTRIC USE

■ = Actual, □ = Estimated
KWH ▊ = Other Customers This Period

'90   J A S O N D J F M A M J J   '91

BILLING SUMMARY

Amount due last bill...	$49.20
Payments through 07/18	$49.20
Balance remaining......	NONE
CURRENT ELEC CHARGES...	$52.33
TOTAL AMOUNT NOW DUE...	$52.33

IMPORTANT MESSAGES

In the current bill period, you used 11.33 kWh a day, compared to last year's daily use of 9.00 kWh a day. The average temperature was 76 degrees this period compared to 74 degrees last year.

In comparing this bill with other periods, please note summer rates are higher, as prescribed by the Public Service Commission to reflect higher costs in this period.

Thank you for your payment.

In a small house or apartment, the fuse box is generally installed in the wall of a hallway or even in a closet. In large private homes, it will be found in the garage, a stair well, or in a basement.

In an all-electric house you will find circuit breakers instead of fuses, mounted inside of a steel box as shown. It is a good idea to identify each circuit according to the room or area it serves.

FUSES VS. CIRCUIT BREAKERS

Both protect you from line overloads that could result in fire and burned out motors. But the circuit breaker makes life much easier.

"WHICH ARE BETTER—fuses or circuit breakers?"

The answer depends on circumstances. If a real short-circuit develops in a defective appliance, the line fuse will blow out or the breaker will trip open with the same speed, thus protecting the line against potential fire danger. You unplug the appliance and go to the branch panel to restore the line. If the panel contains fuse sockets, you must, obviously, have a replacement for the dead fuse. But do you? When did you last check your supply, and do you remember where you put it? The answers to these questions can sometimes be downright embarrassing. However, if the branch panel contains circuit breakers you can approach it with a smile on your face, because breakers look exactly like ordinary switches and you can reset the tripped unit merely by pushing its little handle to the reset position and then the "on" position. Incidentally, this also happens if the line is overloaded. So chalk up "convenience" as an advantage for the circuit breaker.

CIRCUIT BREAKERS

Circuit breakers for 120-volt brand circuits are made either as singles or as pairs in one case, with separate on-off handles. For 240-volt lines they are always paired, with joined handles. Thus, regardless of which half tends to open first on an overload, because of slight differences in manufacturing tolerances, the two sections flip open together and the defective appliance is completely disconnected from the 240-volt line. With fuses, there is always the possibility that one of the pair required for 240-volt applications will remain intact after the other blows. This means that one side of the 240-volt appliance is still "hot" with 120 volts to ground.

TYPES OF FUSES

There are two different kinds of screw-in fuses of identical appearance. The first, marked "slow-blow," gets its name from its ability to remain intact on a *momentary* overload in excess of its rated capacity. It was designed specifically for motorized uses, such as clothes washers, air conditioners and stationary power tools, whose motors take a heavy current for perhaps a second after they are started and then drop quickly to their normal running current. If a machine is overloaded and the motor cannot achieve its rated speed, the continuing heavy current will blow the fuse. This is a warning to the owner.

An ordinary fuse (not a slow-blow), is suitable for other household appliances such as lights, dishwashers, disposals, fans, sewing machine, radio/stereo/TV equipment, etc., but it is not practical for the heavier machines because it

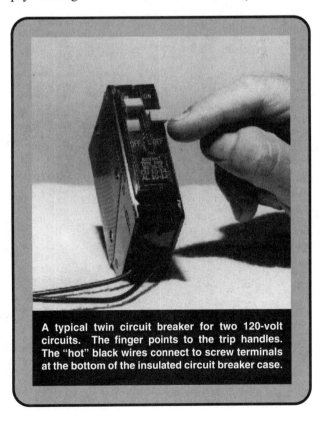

The only way to determine the condition of a suspected cartridge-type fuse is to run a continuity check with a multimeter. There is no visible evidence of failure or "good" with fuses of this kind.

may blow almost the instant the switch is turned on. Of course slow-blows can be used for all purposes, and for this reason many electrical supply catalogs don't even list the ordinary kind. All

The pencil points to the contact spring in the bottom of the circuit breaker that connects to the "hot" side of the current-feeding plate in the breaker box. Breakers for 240 volts have two contacts.

A typical twin circuit breaker for two 120-volt circuits. The finger points to the trip handles. The "hot" black wires connect to screw terminals at the bottom of the insulated circuit breaker case.

standard circuit breakers have the delayed-trip feature built into them.

DISADVANTAGE OF FUSES

From the protective standpoint, a weakness of the fuse system is the ease with which it can be manipulated dangerously by an unthinking home owner. In older houses the capacity of most branch circuits is 15 amperes, whereas in newer

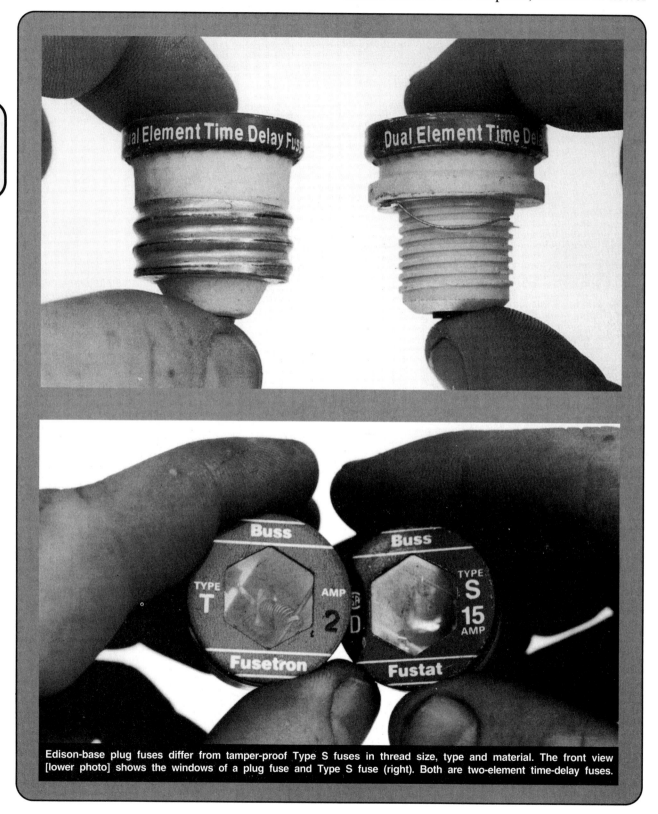

Edison-base plug fuses differ from tamper-proof Type S fuses in thread size, type and material. The front view [lower photo] shows the windows of a plug fuse and Type S fuse (right). Both are two-element time-delay fuses.

models it is likely to be 20. If a 15-ampere fuse blows now and then with too many appliances on the line, some people don't hesitate to screw in a 20-amp fuse instead. And if this "pops out" they'll even try a 25-amp fuse. It doesn't seem to occur to them that they are putting a slow match to their own property. If you know anyone so foolish, try to sell him on the idea of using safer Type S fuses. These resemble regular fuses, but have slightly smaller bodies whose diameters depend on the current rating. They are sold with reducing adapters that go into the fuse sockets, and once in they cannot be unscrewed without virtually breaking the fuse socket. A 15-amp adapter accommodates only a 15-amp Type S, a 20-amp size only a 20-amp Type S, etc., and no nonsense about it. These fuses also have the desirable dual-element action.

TAMPER-PROOF FUSES

Do yourself a good safety turn and replace plug fuses with tamper-proof ones. Tamper-proof Type S fuses, called that in the NEC, fit ordinary fuse-holders using tamper-proof adapters. Once screwed in, the adapters cannot be removed. Type S adapters will not accept fuses of the wrong ampere rating, preventing overfusing. What's more, plug fuses won't fit the adapters at all.

A tamper-proof fuse cannot be readily short-circuited to bypass its protection, thus the name *tamper-proof*.

Type S fuses and their matching non-removable screw-in adapters are widely available. Get them in the proper capacities to suit your house branch circuit wiring. Fuse color indicates ampere rating. One well known brand is Fustat by Bussman.

To install tamper-proof fuses, first turn off the house main disconnect. Thread the tamper-proof Type S fuses into their matched Type S adapters. Then you can carefully remove the Edison-base plug fuses from their sockets and screw the fuse-adapter assemblies into the open fuse sockets without touching the metal adapters. Do the same for all the open fuse sockets.

Once you've switched over your house main service panel to all-tamper-proof fuses, you have the next thing in safety to a circuit-breaker system, and the cost is far less than upgrading to a circuit breaker panel would be.

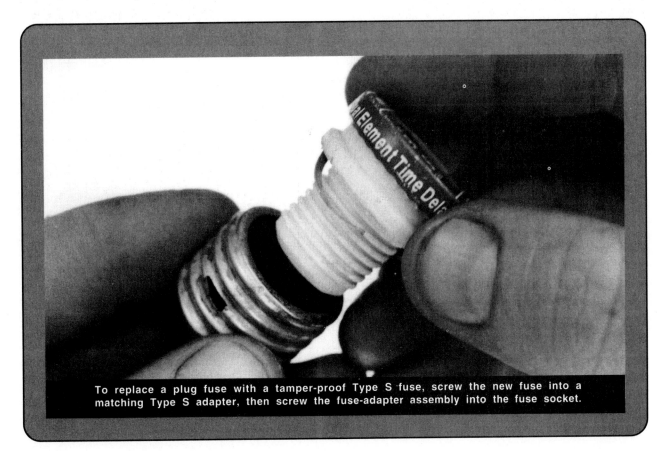

To replace a plug fuse with a tamper-proof Type S fuse, screw the new fuse into a matching Type S adapter, then screw the fuse-adapter assembly into the fuse socket.

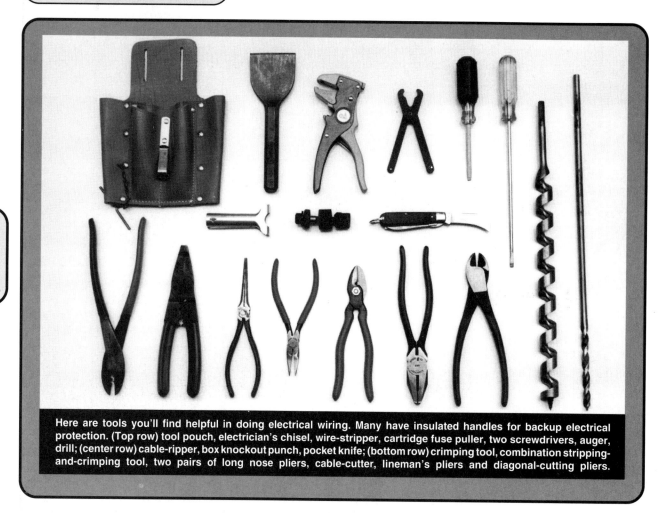

Here are tools you'll find helpful in doing electrical wiring. Many have insulated handles for backup electrical protection. (Top row) tool pouch, electrician's chisel, wire-stripper, cartridge fuse puller, two screwdrivers, auger, drill; (center row) cable-ripper, box knockout punch, pocket knife; (bottom row) crimping tool, combination stripping-and-crimping tool, two pairs of long nose pliers, cable-cutter, lineman's pliers and diagonal-cutting pliers.

TOOLS AND TESTERS

Making electrical repairs requires far fewer tools than carpentry, plumbing or masonry. The right tools will make the job easier.

PRACTICALLY all the small jobs of maintenance and repair of household electrical appliances, installation of new fixtures, and wiring new outlets can be done with the hand tools and supplies that normally accumulate in the basement or garage.

Check the contents of your tool box and see how many of the items shown in the photographs you already have. Wiring tools, however, have insulated handles for electrical safety.

Slip-joint pliers. Also known as gas pliers. For twisting heavy wires, holding parts to be soldered, undoing or tightening nuts, bending sheet metal, etc. The inner surfaces of the jaws are ribbed and slightly concave; they can grip rods and

pipes up to about 5/8-inch in diameter.

Long-nose pliers. For twisting wires under the heads of terminal screws on plugs, outlets, sockets, and for holding small parts. The tips must close tightly so they can pick up and maintain their grip on thin wires, soldering lugs, washers, etc. *An urgent caution about this tool*: use it only for light work, never for tightening nuts. Some long-nose pliers have wire-cutting jaws near the joint.

Lineman's pliers. For the sole purpose of snipping wire. The angled cutting lips come to a fine point, so they can cut very close. If you use side-cutters only on copper wire, they will last a lifetime. If you tighten nuts with them, they'll quickly lose their cutting edges and their alignment. It's almost impossible to repair a damaged tool of this type. Buy a new one and treat it properly the next time.

Wire-stripper. Replaces the common knife as a means of removing insulation from wires without nicking them. Resembles side-cutters, but can be adjusted quickly to bite only through the insulation and to stop at the wire. A great time-saver.

Pocket knife. For scraping wires clean and shiny. Use the *back edge* of the blade, not the sharp side.

Short, stout scissors. For cutting tape, trimming insulation. forming thin washers, etc.

Screwdrivers. An assortment of sizes, both blade and Phillips head.

Soldering iron. You have a wide choice. For most electrical connections, the pencil-type with screw-in tips is inexpensive and adequate. Incidentally, the word "iron" means tool. The working end of a soldering iron is always made of

Wire strippers come in a variety of sizes and prices and do a perfect job cutting and stripping the ends of wires without tearing into the copper. The more expensive models can also crimp connectors. All have insulated handles.

The multimeter does more than just light up when checking a circuit; it measures the resistance and can be used to detect trouble in almost any device that runs on electricity. The unit shown can measure resistance up to six million ohms, AC voltage to 1,000 volts and DC current as low as 1/4 ampere. Many models are available at very affordable prices.

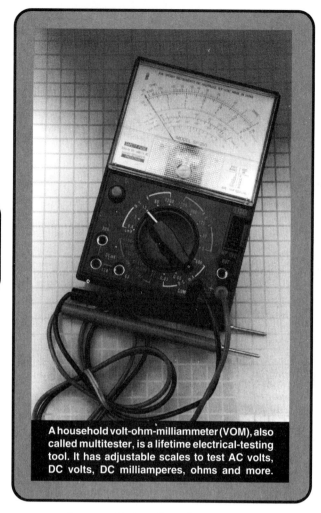
A household volt-ohm-milliammeter (VOM), also called multitester, is a lifetime electrical-testing tool. It has adjustable scales to test AC volts, DC volts, DC milliamperes, ohms and more.

familiar to homeowners who do their own maintenance .

TESTER

You can tell if a plug fuse (the screw-in type) is intact or blown by just looking at it, but something more than observation is needed to check a cartridge fuse. You can't tell by just looking at an appliance cord whether the wires inside are short-circuited or broken. You can't tell from looking whether a bare, exposed wire is "hot" or not, although you can tell very definitely if you are foolish enough to touch it. For serious troubleshooting you need an electrical tool called simply a "tester" or "voltage tester."

A simple neon voltage tester will serve for this. It contains a neon bulb with two insulated-handle leads that can be touched to the circuit for the test. A voltage tester costs very little and is a mainstay of the home electrician's tool box.

copper. Irons of the "gun" type are popular because they heat to operating temperature in a few seconds.

Solder. For electrical work use only rosin-core solder. This produces clean joints with no corrosive after-effect. Under no circumstances use acid-core solder because its flux residue quickly attacks the wire. Do not use solder on house wiring.

Drill. With an assortment of bits, essential for boring holes in floors, ceilings and walls for wires.

Tape. For covering splices in wires and reinforcing insulation on flexible cords of appliances: The usual kind is black and is called friction tape, but plastic tape, which costs a little more, holds better.

Hacksaw. For cutting flexib mored cable and similar jobs.

In addition you will need the basic tools such as a hammer, saw, ladder and wrenches, all

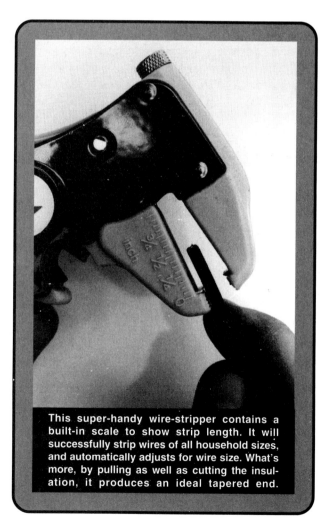

This super-handy wire-stripper contains a built-in scale to show strip length. It will successfully strip wires of all household sizes, and automatically adjusts for wire size. What's more, by pulling as well as cutting the insulation, it produces an ideal tapered end.

To test a receptacle, use one hand to insert one tester lead into the wider neutral (grounded) slotand the other lead into the narrow hot slot. If the outlet is live, the tester should glow. Dead, it should not.

You can also use the voltage tester to check whether the receptacle's D-shaped equipment-grounding hole is actually grounded. Working one-handed, insert a lead into the narrow hot slot and the other lead into the D-shaped hole. The tester should glow, indicating ground continuity.

Connected across the wider neutral (grounded) slot and the D-shaped hole, the tester should not glow, even though the outlet is live, because both of these slots are supposed to be at ground potential.

To facilitate one-handed testing, a professional circuit tester with alligator-clip grounding lead is recommended. The Model 100 Circuitracer (available from Desco Industries, Inc., 761 Penarth Ave., Walnut, CA 91789) is such a tester. Its cost is not great. The Circuitracer is for use on circuits from 60 to 600 volts.

In use the circuit tester's grounding lead is clipped to one wire of the circuit or to a good ground and the test prod is touched one-handed to each of the other wires to see whether any are live, making the light glow (see Electrical Safety chapter). For added safety, a high resistance built into in the Circuitracer greatly limits the amount of current that can flow through its neon tube to ground. This is reason enough to have one.

The Circuitracer may be had with a number of useful accessories, including a battery-powered testing setup for use on unpowered, disconnected circuits, allowing it to be used as a continuity tester (powered test light).

Whatever you do, avoid using a so-called "wireless" tester that relies on body capacitance. When you touch a finger to the metal portion of the tester, it grounds the neon tube through the ability of your body to absorb electrons and feed them into the air—or anything else you're touching. We've seen a number of body-capacitance testers but haven't found one that's UL-listed or safe to use. In fact, we've heard some horror stories connected with them. It's

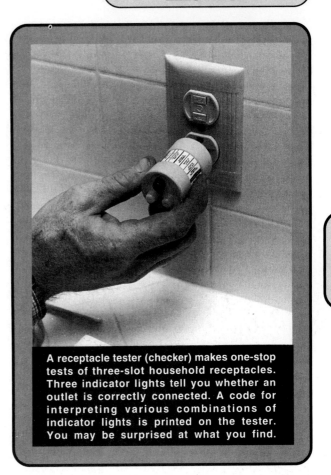

A receptacle tester (checker) makes one-stop tests of three-slot household receptacles. Three indicator lights tell you whether an outlet is correctly connected. A code for interpreting various combinations of indicator lights is printed on the tester. You may be surprised at what you find.

safest to keep your body out of the way of ground seeking-electrons.

CONTINUITY TESTER

There is another type of tester called the "continuity checker," or powered test light. This too looks like a fountain pen, but it contains one or two small flashlight cells in addition to a small lamp connected to a pair of test leads like those on the neon light. It is intended primarily to distinguish between a closed circuit and an open circuit, for example, to tell if a fuse is intact or open, or if the contacts of a switch have welded together or broken off, or if wires enclosed in a common sheath of insulation have shorted together or broken. The lamp merely lights when the circuit is closed or doesn't light when it is open.

CAUTION: never use a continuity checker of any kind on a live circuit, or anything connected to one. With appliances or machines having flexible line cords, always pull the plug first and then think about a test procedure. If a suspected com-

Model 100 Circuitracer makes it easy to do safer, one-handed electrical tests on live circuits. The alligator-clip grounding pigtail holds itself in place while you test with the insulated test prod containing the neon tube. You needn't look away from the test prod to tell whether the tube glows.

ponent is soldered or otherwise connected, undo the connections to isolate it from other parts that might give misleading indications on the tester.

MULTITESTER

An instrument called a multitester, multimeter or volt-ohm-milliammeter (VOM) will perform a whole raft of electrical tests including measure AC volts, DC volts, DC milli-amperes and ohms. VOMs, however, are safest for taking ohm readings on unpowered, discon-nected circuits. Unless the specs say it has at least a 10,000-ampere *interrupting capacity* (AIC), you should avoid using a VOM on a household circuit. (Few household units do.) For this reason it's best to confine a VOM to use on unpowered circuits, or for low-voltage electronic and automotive work. They are also excellent for low-voltage bell-and-chime testing.

TESTING FOR GROUND

The hardest thing to verify is the quality of

a ground. The best you can do is to test with a VOM to see whether there is continuity to ground, for example in metal outlet boxes and equipment-grounding circuits. First you need to find a known ground as a reference. A metal water pipe or metal faucet body is a good bet. If you have trouble finding a good ground, the meter box—the *box* not the meter socket—is almost always well grounded. Don't depend on gas pipes; they're often not grounded.

Using a VOM with its selector set to the Rx1 ohms position, contact one lead to the known ground and the other to the ground being tested. The branch circuit should be turned off for the test. The VOM needle should move all the way to the right, indicating zero-ohm resistance between the two grounds. If it moves part way or not at all, both circuits are not grounded.

A voltage tester can be used for making ground tests, but the branch circuit's power will have to be turned on for the test. For this reason, be extra careful in handling the test prods. Working one-handed, contact one lead to the ground being tested and the other lead into the narrow hot slot of a live receptacle. The tester should glow to indicate ground continuity. If it does not, either the hot slot isn't hot or the ground isn't grounded.

Working this way, the grounding of appliances such as ranges can be checked. Remember, though, that this test says nothing about how *good* the ground is, which cannot be easily checked.

In the powered test-light mode, the Circuitracer is useful for finding the common terminal on a three-way switch. With the tester's grounding clip attached to the switch's common terminal, the other two terminals indicate one on and one off. When the switch is thrown the other way, the on and off indications reverse. A VOM set for reading Rx1 ohms will also make this test. A full-scale ohm reading is equivalent to a glow from the test light. In any case, a switch must be removed for continuity testing.

RECEPTACLE TESTER

A receptacle checker is a great tool to have. Use it to test all the outlets in your house. Plugged into an outlet, it checks for the following: correctly connected wiring; reversed polarity; open-circuited equipment ground; open-circuited neutral (grounded) wire; open-circuited hot; hot and equipment ground reversed; and hot connected to the neutral (grounded) side with the hot slot unwired. It will NOT check for: equipment ground and neutral (grounded) wires reversed; two hot wires connected to outlet; quality of the equipment ground; or combinations of defects. For a valid test, all plugs should be removed from the other branch circuit outlets before testing. Using a receptacle tester, it takes only a few minutes to check out every receptacle in the house.

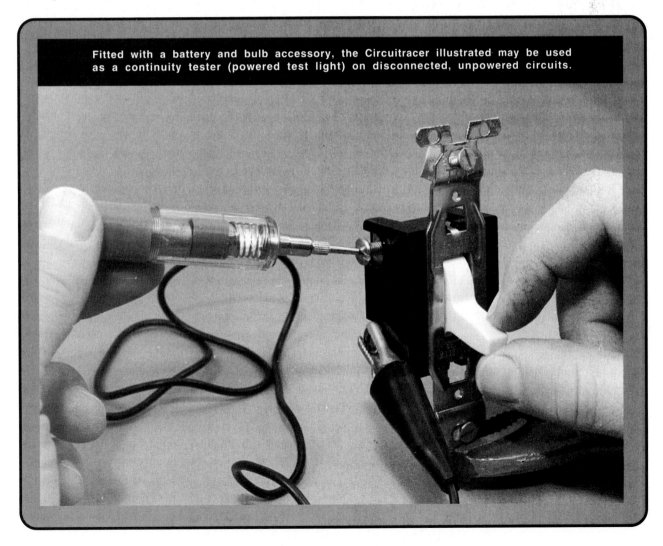

Fitted with a battery and bulb accessory, the Circuitracer illustrated may be used as a continuity tester (powered test light) on disconnected, unpowered circuits.

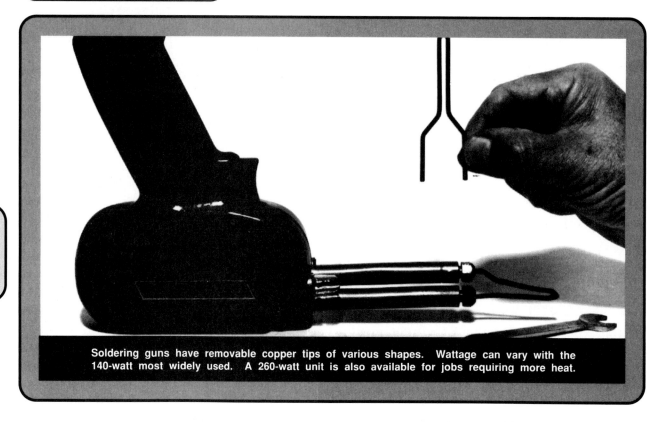

Soldering guns have removable copper tips of various shapes. Wattage can vary with the 140-watt most widely used. A 260-watt unit is also available for jobs requiring more heat.

SUCCESSFUL SOLDERING

A well-soldered splice is the best guarantee for a foolproof electrical connection. Ideal for joining multi-strand cords

SOLDERING is a highly useful operation that you can master with five minutes of practice if you observe a very simple precaution: *Cleanliness.* Your fingers should be clean and dry, so that you don't transfer skin oil to the work being soldered; the metal surfaces that are to be joined must be clean, clear and bright, with no trace of insulation or other previous covering; and the tip of the soldering tool (the iron) must have a shiny coat of simmering solder.

"Solder" is a soft alloy, generally of 60 percent lead and 40 percent tin. The type universally used for electrical purposes is in the form of hollow wire, filled with rosin. The latter is called "flux" and its job is to absorb oxidation products of the metal being soldered as it gets hot enough to melt the solder. Without flux of some kind the molten solder will not adhere to the joint, but merely forms globules that roll away like so many drops of water on a waxed surface.

Both copper and brass (an alloy of copper and zinc) are very receptive to soldering with rosin flux.

Soldering tools are usually called "irons", although the term is a misnomer as the heated tip that does the actual work is a piece of copper. The heat is provided by a coil of resistance within the body of the tool. Depending on size, a straight iron takes from about three to five minutes to reach operating temperature.

Irons are rated by their power consumption in watts. The light-weight, pencil-type iron consumes about 50 watts and uses a variety of screw-in tips with bases like those on Christmas tree bulbs. It is inexpensive, and is entirely satisfactory for 95 per cent of household electrical repair work. Larger models run to 85 and 150 watts.

Soldering tools that look like pistols are called "soldering guns" are popular because they heat up in a matter of seconds instead of minutes.

They are in effect small transformers, with a primary winding of many turns of fine wire connected to the AC power line through a trigger switch on the handle. The secondary winding consists of one or two turns of very heavy wire or tubing. The ends of the secondary are joined by a U-shaped loop of copper wire about l/8-inch square. The step-down action of the transformer produces a low secondary voltage but the current in amperes is high enough to heat the loop quickly to soldering temperature. Tips eventually burn up, and are easily replaceable. A typical gun is rated at 100 watts.

Each time a soldering iron is to be used, it must be "tinned." First clean the tip by rubbing it on emery cloth or with a fine file. Plug it into an outlet, and while it is warming up hold the solder against the point. Some of the flux will run down, followed by molten solder. Let it cook for a few seconds until the flux smoke disappears. Wipe the tip with a clean rag and you are ready to work.

The accompanying pictures show what is probably the common electrical soldering job—splicing two pieces of lamp cord. It should take you less time to do this than to read the instructions.

Here are some useful do's and don'ts:
• After allowing several drops to melt onto a joint, remove the solder but keep the iron in position for a few seconds, to cook out excess rosin·Remove

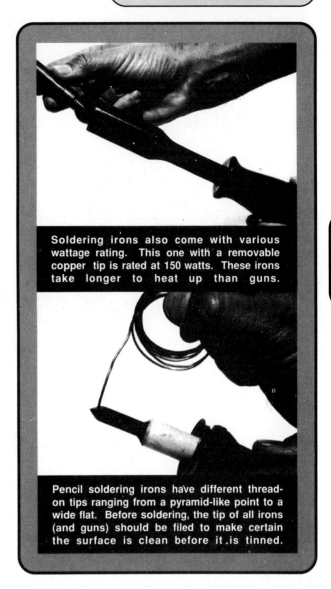

Soldering irons also come with various wattage rating. This one with a removable copper tip is rated at 150 watts. These irons take longer to heat up than guns.

Pencil soldering irons have different thread-on tips ranging from a pyramid-like point to a wide flat. Before soldering, the tip of all irons (and guns) should be filed to make certain the surface is clean before it is tinned.

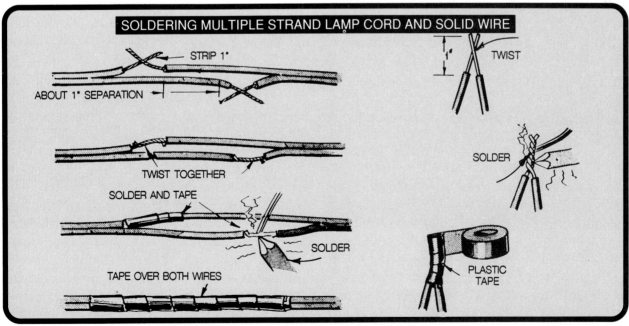

SOLDERING MULTIPLE STRAND LAMP CORD AND SOLID WIRE

STRIP 1"

ABOUT 1" SEPARATION

TWIST TOGETHER

SOLDER AND TAPE

SOLDER

TAPE OVER BOTH WIRES

TWIST

SOLDER

PLASTIC TAPE

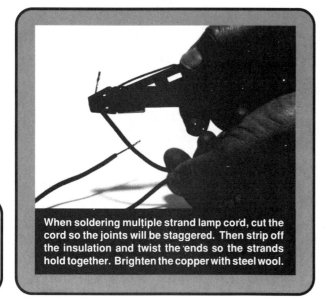

When soldering multiple strand lamp cord, cut the cord so the joints will be staggered. Then strip off the insulation and twist the ends so the strands hold together. Brighten the copper with steel wool.

Twist the two strands together and apply the hot iron to the copper. Once hot, melt some solder on the joint. The solder should flow readily around the twisted wire. Allow to cool before moving.

the iron, but don't disturb the joint for another few seconds. This gives the solder a chance to set thoroughly. If you jiggle the wire too soon, the joint will become undone. Start again, please.

• *Always* position the joint so that the molten solder runs into or along it, not away from it. Hot solder flows as readily as water.

• Keep your fingers away from the joint; it gets *very* hot, and a solder burn can be nasty. If you must hold the two parts of a joint to keep them from separating, use a pair of pliers (locking type pliers are good) or a spring-type wooden clothespin.

CONNECTING WIRES TO TERMINALS

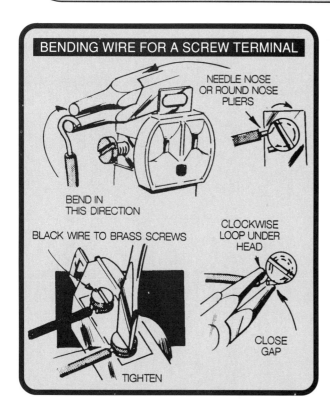

BENDING WIRE FOR A SCREW TERMINAL

NEEDLE NOSE OR ROUND NOSE PLIERS

BEND IN THIS DIRECTION

BLACK WIRE TO BRASS SCREWS

CLOCKWISE LOOP UNDER HEAD

CLOSE GAP

TIGHTEN

In ELECTRICAL WORK one of the most frequent jobs is joining wires or fastening wires to terminals on switches, sockets, outlets, and plugs. A good joint, or connection, is one that is clean and tight. If it is dirty and loose it can heat up and under some circumstances it can cause serious fire damage. All splices and joints of circuit line should be made in a separate junction box if more than four connections are necessary. Otherwise a deep gem or hex box can be used.

MAKING A JOINT

After removing the outer insulation, clean the wire with a strip of emery cloth or the back of a knife. The quickest and simplest joint, (see drawing) is made by twisting the bare ends together and soldering them with rosin-core solder. Leave the tip of the iron against the wires for at least three or four seconds to cook out excess rosin. Wipe the

This is how your joint should look when complete. Check to make certain the lead has taken hold. In some instances you may need to use a little additional rosin core flux, depending upon the wire.

Once the joint is made, spiral tape the single strand with plastic electrical tape. Run the tape around two inches on either side of the soldered joint. Then proceed to twist the remaining wire ends and solder.

• Don't try to solder aluminum or stainless steel with the same solder and flux used for copper and brass. These metals require special solders and fluxes, and the results are not always fully satisfactory. Iron is a little less troublesome, but it needs an acid-base flux that tends to be very corrosive. And never use an acid-base flux for electrical work.

• The insulation on some wires is a flexible plastic that loosens or burns in the presence of a hot soldering iron. Don't let this bother you. After the joint cools, you'll have to tape it anyway.

USING WIRE NUTS

joint with a clean rag and cover with two layers of plastic electrical tape.

WIRE NUTS

Soldering is unnecessary if the wires are snugly clamped by insulated "solderless connectors", as shown. These look like the caps of toothpaste tubes, are threaded on the inside, and simply screw over the bare wires. These wire nuts are easy to remove when wiring must be changed and they are the only practical means of joining aluminum wire. To lengthen flexible cord, make staggered joints as shown.

The trick in attaching wires to screw terminals is to form a hook-shaped loop and to squeeze this under the screw, without overlap, before tightening the latter. The loop should be made in a *clockwise* direction so that it will not be loosened when the screw is tightened.

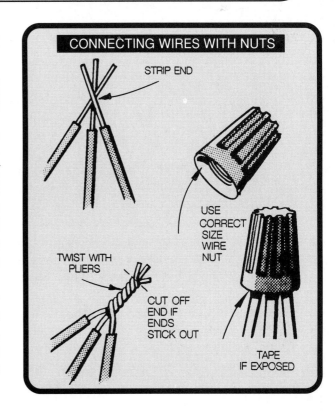

CONNECTING WIRES WITH NUTS
STRIP END
USE CORRECT SIZE WIRE NUT
TWIST WITH PLIERS
CUT OFF END IF ENDS STICK OUT
TAPE IF EXPOSED

THE GFCI GROUND-FAULT CIRCUIT-INTERRUPTER

GFCI stands for Ground-Fault Circuit-Interrupter. This device can save you from dangerous and potentially lethal electric shock. Four types are available.

LEAKAGE OF ELECTRICITY from appliances to persons using them, with an accidental "ground" forming the return circuit to the power line, has long been a problem. The danger is minimal if all the wires and connections inside the metal case are well insulated from the latter and also from each other, or if the case is made of an insulating material. Potential trouble develops when interior insulation dries out or wears away because of vibration and bare wires finally touch the frame. This is called a *ground fault*. If the appliance is fitted with a three-wire line cord terminating in a three-prong plug that fits into a matching outlet, the first such internal contact (a real "short-circuit") will almost certainly blow the fuse or circuit breaker. No one can ignore this danger signal cutting off the power.

UNGROUNDED APPLIANCES

Many of the common appliances found in the home, however, do not have three-prong plugs: irons, coffee makers, toasters, mixers, food processors, can openers, fans, lamps, razors, hair dryers, radios, stereos and TV sets, etc. They can continue to run in perfectly normal fashion even if they have the internal short-circuit just described. But touch them with the juice on and you'll be lucky to escape with just a dazed expression on your face. If you were leaning against a stove, sink, radiator, or refrigerator—grounded—at the time, you wouldn't be reading this right now.

What has been described is extreme but by no means an infrequent occurrence. The internal breakdown in an appliance does not have to be complete; if it is partial, the leakage of current is merely lower. A person doesn't have to be in direct contact with a good electrical ground such as household piping to get a shock. A damp floor or wall is in effect also grounded; not very well, but often well enough to complete a circuit. It takes less power than a Christmas-tree lamp draws to kill.

Some appliances that are absolutely safe electrically when dry can become lethal if water is allowed to seep into them to form a conducting surface between the metal case and energized connections inside. Moisture on any electrical device is bad. Operating any appliance with wet or damp hands is bad—twice over.

THE GROUND-FAULT CIRCUIT-INTERRUPTER

The three-wire equipment-grounding system unquestionably has saved many people from shock. Additional protection is available in the form of of the "ground-fault circuit-interrupter," or in shortened form, merely "GFCI."

The GFCI takes advantage of the fact that the current in a "ground fault" (the accidental path

HOW THE GROUND-FAULT

1

SAFE : CURRENT IN HOT WIRE AND GROUNDED WIRE ARE EQUAL

GFCI "WATCHES" CURRENT FLOW

HOT WIRE

AMOUNT OF CURRENT

GROUNDED NEUTRAL WIRE

BATHER IS GROUNDED IN WATER

between an ungrounded wire and ground) represents an extra load on the power line, which passes through the GFCI. The difference is very slight, but it is enough to unbalance a sensitive solid-state circuit, which kicks the electricity off instantly.

HOW IT WORKS

The question everyone asks about GFCI is, "The short-circuited current has to flow through a person's body to complete the circuit and to trigger the device. Why isn't he shocked just as he would have been without it?''

Let's say right off that a GFCI *does not eliminate shock.* However, it triggers when the body current differential is only 6 milliamperes, which is far below the 50 or 60 figure considered to be really dangerous, and it flips the current off in about 1/40th of a second. The actual amount of energy in the shock (the combination of the small current and the short time that it flows) is so limited that a victim feels hardly more than a slight jolt.

The GFCI has already proved its value as a safety measure. However, it is not and cannot be a substitute for careless electrical habits, such as making changes in power circuits with the current on or for poor maintenance of appliances and machines.

GFCIs take four forms: A receptacle GFCI that replaces a regular wall outlet, an adapter that plugs into wall outlets, fixed units combined with

circuit breakers for permanent installation in branch panel boxes, and GFCI extension cords. GFCIs are required in normally wet areas, such as outdoors, a bathroom, kitchen, laundry, garage, near a swimming pool, etc.

To provide a measure of protection against fatal ground-fault shocks, the NEC in 1968 made three-slot grounding-type receptacles a requirement for new construction. Few older houses have them. Those with ungrounded two-slot, outlets can benefit from ground-fault protection through conversion of their two-slot outlets to three-slot, provided that a means of grounding is available inside outlet boxes. That's not too likely, however. Lacking in-box grounding, failed two-slot outlets *must* be replaced with two-slot outlets.

Happily, the NEC has made one tiny exception to this outlet-replacement rule. Named NEC 210-7(d) Exception, the Code permits an old two-slot outlet to be replaced with a receptacle GFCI, if no means of grounding is available inside the box. And no grounding available is the typical case. So if your house has two-slot outlets, you can probably replace them with safer receptacle GFCIs.

Receptacle GFCIs will give you and family members a high degree of protection against ground faults in power mowers, stereos and TV sets, coffee-makers and toasters, washers and dryers, refrigerators and freezers, plus portable power tools and the like. While someone might *feel* a shock, the GFCI's job is to open the circuit before the shock can be fatal.

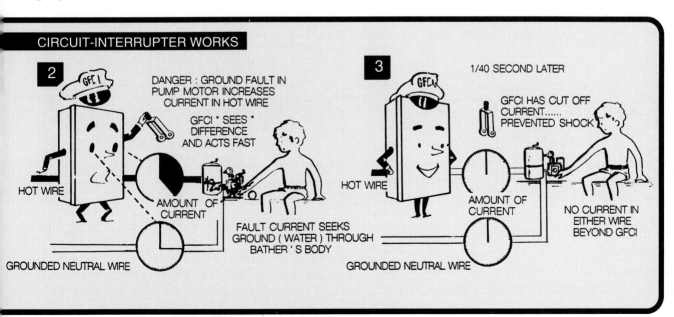

224

ELECTRICAL

224
ELECTRICAL

FEED-THROUGH DESIGN

What's feed-through? Feed-through receptacle GFCIs contain two "line" terminals and two "load" terminals for the black- and white-insulated current-carrying wires. If you locate such a GFCI as the first receptacle in a branch circuit, its fault protection *feeds through* to the outlets downstream from it in the branch circuit. (No equipment-grounding conductors may run between outlets.) It's easy to do, a worthwhile opportunity provided for by the code.

IS A GROUND AVAILABLE?

The first and most difficult step is to see whether the outlet boxes in your house have no means of grounding available. To do it, turn off the power to a receptacle circuit and check at one of the outlets to be sure it's off. Check at *both* outlets of a duplex receptacle, as it could be on two separate circuits. Remove the cover from the outlet and test again. Unscrew and carefully pull the outlet from the wall, testing yet again for no power. (See section on Electrical Safety.)

Then peer into the outlet box with a plastic flashlight so you can see. You're looking for either of the following: (1) a bare or green-insulated wire or (2) a metal outlet box that is served by metal cable or metal conduit. The metal cable/conduit may be tough to tell. Look closely at the box connectors. Most probably the box is served by plastic cable with black-, white- and possibly red-insulated wires but no bare or green-insulated equipment-grounding wires. Plastic cable is easy to spot, since it should protrude 1/4 inch or so beyond the box connectors.

If you have a powered test light (continuity tester) or multi-tester, a better method is to test from a known ground to a metal outlet box to find whether there is continuity. Connect one lead of the tester to the box and the other to a known ground, such as a metal water pipe that's grounded—no plastic pipe intervening, no dielectric couplings, etc. If in doubt use the electric meter box as a ground. There should be no indication of ground continuity: the powered test

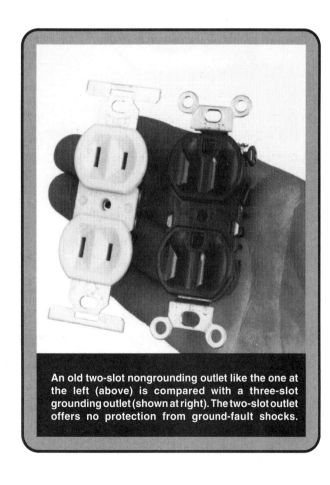

An old two-slot nongrounding outlet like the one at the left (above) is compared with a three-slot grounding outlet (shown at right). The two-slot outlet offers no protection from ground-fault shocks.

Leave an ungrounded replacement GFCI's hex-head green equipment-grounding terminal empty and protected from contact with uninsulated, live parts in the box. If the GFCI's ground is a screw, tighten it; if it's a lead, bend the end over and install a wire nut.

light should not light or the multi-tester ohm reading should indicate infinite resistance when the selector is set on Rx1 ohms.

If no ground is available, the two-slot outlet may be replaced with a GFCI outlet.

If you find either a bare or green-insulated wire or a metal box served by metal cable or conduits, the box has a means of grounding available, and any replacement outlet—GFCI or plain three-slot—must be grounded. The hex-head green grounding terminals must then be provided with equipment- grounding wires. In no case may standard three-slot outlets be installed without grounding.

Be sure to follow the detailed instructions that come with your receptacle GFCI. These offer the very best instructions you'll find for (1) locating the first outlet in a branch circuit; (2) determining which are the feed and load wires in an outlet box; and (3) installing the GFCI. The GFCI outlet also comes with small stick-on labels for identifying it and the downstream outlets as being GFCI protected.

A receptacle GFCI is connected like an ordinary receptacle: the black wires go to the brass terminals (or black leads); the white wires go to the silver terminals (or white leads). If you wish to feed GFCI protection through to downstream outlets, connect the feed (power source or line) wires to the line side of the outlet and connect the downstream (or load) wires to the load side of the GFCI outlet. If you don't wish to feed protection through, either look for a nonfeed-through GFCI outlet without separate line and load sides (hard to find) or, easier, connect all wires to the line side of a feed-through GFCI, leaving the load- side terminals unused.

In any case, remember that your new outlet doesn't offer grounding. But even though it's ungrounded, it still will work, giving 6-milliampere, 40 millisecond trip-off protection against fatal line-to-ground shocks. GFCIs cannot protect against line-to-line (black-to-red, etc.) or line-to-neutral (black- or red-to-white) shocks. In order to work, a GFCI needs some form of ground reference, and it gets this through the neutral (ground) wire.

Even with GFCI protection, don't take chances by using damp or wet electrical equipment or by working near grounds. Common sense is still your best protection.

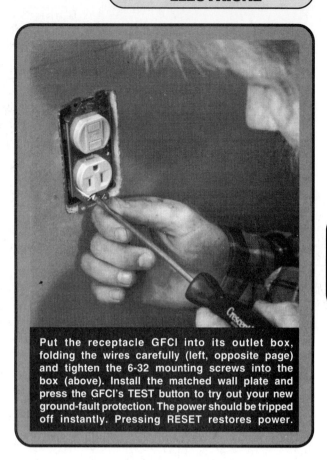

Put the receptacle GFCI into its outlet box, folding the wires carefully (left, opposite page) and tighten the 6-32 mounting screws into the box (above). Install the matched wall plate and press the GFCI's TEST button to try out your new ground-fault protection. The power should be tripped off instantly. Pressing RESET restores power.

When you shop, you may find two kinds of receptacle GFCIs—lead type (at top) and terminal type. Either may be used. Both these GFCIs are the typical feed-through type, offering line and load connections for the black- and white-insulated circuit wires.

When replacing or installing a new switch the wires connected to the terminal are hot so make certain you pull the fuses or trip the circuit breaker before starting the job. Always use an insulated screwdriver.

INSTALLING OUTLETS AND SWITCHES

Switches and even outlets can break because of excessive use over the years. Here is how you can replace both.

Wall switches rarely need replacing but on occasion after years of constant use they may not work, or you may wish to replace what you have with a silent type.

The first step is to flip off the circuit breaker or remove the fuse that controls the circuit to the switch. Next, remove the cover plate by unscrewing its two screws. This will expose the switch. Remove the top and bottom screws that hold the switch in the box. Now, gently pull out the switch to expose the two screws that connect the wires to the switch. Note that one wire is black (or red) and the second wire is white. Normally, the white wire is the ground wire, but if it is used as a ''hot'' line (switches always interrupt a "hot" line), it should be painted black at the end. This is a legal requirement as all "hot" wires must be black or painted black. Loosen the two screws holding the wires in place so you can remove the switch. Do not tamper with any other wires you may find in the box except those connected to the switch. These wires may feed other lights or outlets and have nothing to do with the switch.

When you install the new switch with the same amperage rating, connect it the same way as the old one. Make sure the switch will be in the off position when the toggle is down. If you replace the switch with a silent mercury-type switch, look for the word "Top" stamped on the switch body and install with this word on top. When you make the wire connections, wrap the wires around the screws in a clockwise direction so that tightening the screws will keep the wires wrapped around the shank of the screws.

THREE-WAY SWITCHES

Three-way switches are used to control the same light from two different locations. Replacement of these switches is the same as for conventional switches except they have three connections instead of two—usually one wire at the top of the switch and two at the bottom. Mark the wires so you will know to which screw they go before removing them. If the replacement is a mercury-type switch, install it with the word "Top" at the top. Unlike conventional switches, the toggle position on a three-way switches does not necessarily mean the light is on when the toggle is up, or off when the toggle is down. The On and Off positions of either switch depend upon the On or Off positions of the switch you are replacing.

INSTALLING A NEW SWITCH

In many unfinished basements and attics, rather than install a wall switch to control the ceiling lights, builders often use simple — and economical — pull chains. If you have such a situation and you are planning to finish off the area to make it liveable, here's how to convert the ceiling light so it can be operated by a wall switch.

First turn off the current going to the ceiling light by removing the fuse or flipping the circuit breaker to Off. Next, determine where you want the switch located. A wall switch should always be on the doorknob side of the wall, about four feet from the floor. If the wall is covered with plasterboard, or solid plaster as is the case with

most homes older than 50 years, tap the wall to locate the studs, or drill a series of 1/16-inch holes to find the stud. Trace the outline of the metal box that will house the switch on the wall and drill a hole in each corner and use a keyhole saw to cut away the plaster.

Next you will have to pass a cable (BX or Romex) long enough to reach from the light to the switch position. To do this you will need a long drill and an electrician's snake. Drill the holes as shown in the drawing to pass the cable through. Fish for the cable with the snake. Insert one end of the cable through one of the knockouts in the ceiling box after removing about five inches of the outer protective coating to expose the two insulated wires. Strip off an inch of insulation from each wire. Disconnect the black wire to the ceiling light and connect it to the black wire of the new cable. The white wire of the new cable goes to the black wire that was formerly connected to the ceiling light. Solder and tape the connections or use wire nuts. Note that the white wire from the fuse box to the ceiling light is not disturbed.

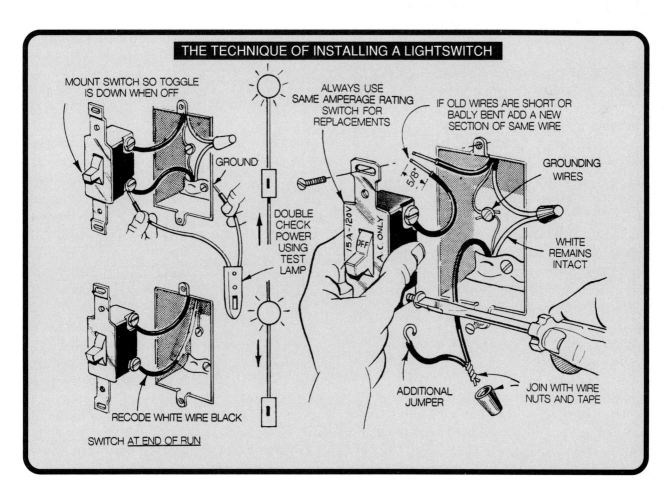

THE TECHNIQUE OF INSTALLING A LIGHTSWITCH

MOUNT SWITCH SO TOGGLE IS DOWN WHEN OFF

ALWAYS USE SAME AMPERAGE RATING SWITCH FOR REPLACEMENTS

IF OLD WIRES ARE SHORT OR BADLY BENT ADD A NEW SECTION OF SAME WIRE

GROUND

GROUNDING WIRES

DOUBLE CHECK POWER USING TEST LAMP

15 A - 120 V

A. C. ONLY

OFF

5/8"

WHITE REMAINS INTACT

RECODE WHITE WIRE BLACK

SWITCH AT END OF RUN

ADDITIONAL JUMPER

JOIN WITH WIRE NUTS AND TAPE

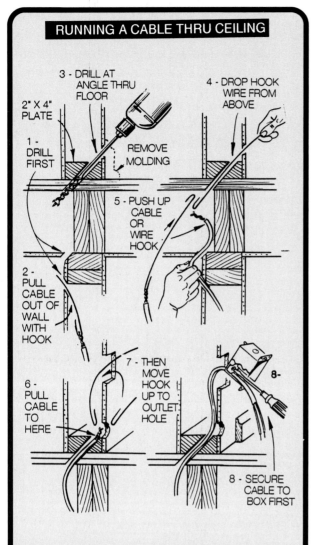

Now go back to the opening in the wall for the switch. Push the cable back into the opening and try the switch box for fit. No need to attempt to attach the switch box to the wall stud; many boxes are available that automatically grab the wall from the rear when the front mounting screw is turned. Pass the cable through one of the knockouts and clamp it in place after first removing about five inches of the outer protective covering. Strip off about an inch of insulation from each wire. Now push the box back into the opening and secure it to the wall by turning the mounting screws which will collapse and press against the back of the wall. The top and bottom tabs on the front of the box rest against the edge of the opening.

Connect the two wires to the switch terminals. Fold the excess wire behind the switch and gently force the switch into the box. Secure the switch to the box with the two screws supplied and then install the cover plate. The cover plate should hide the opening cut in the plaster wall. If it doesn't, patch the hole with plaster. Now replace the fuse (or trip the circuit breaker) and try the switch. It works!

TYPES OF WALL SWITCHES

Many different types of switches are available ranging from decorator switches to sound

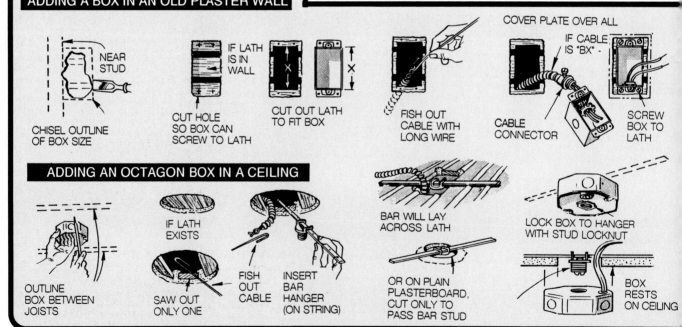

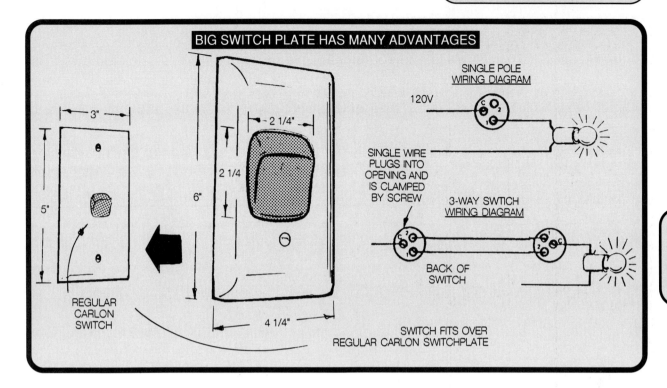

BIG SWITCH PLATE HAS MANY ADVANTAGES

SINGLE POLE WIRING DIAGRAM

120V

SINGLE WIRE PLUGS INTO OPENING AND IS CLAMPED BY SCREW

3-WAY SWTICH WIRING DIAGRAM

BACK OF SWITCH

REGULAR CARLON SWITCH

SWITCH FITS OVER REGULAR CARLON SWITCHPLATE

activated switches but one of the most unusual—and functional— switch is the "Big Switch" illustrated in the drawings. This switch is big—the base plate measures 4 1/4x6 inches, compared to the 2 1/2x5 inch size of a regular switch, and the tripper button is over 2 inches square. This switch is ideal for a child's room; individuals with severe arthritis find it much easier to operate than regular wall switches. Also, if you enter the room with your arms filled with bundles you can easily turn the light on by tapping the switch with your elbow! Available in a few popular colors, "Big Switch" fits over a smaller version by the same manufacturer, which is supplied in the same package, so if the day comes when you no longer need it merely unscrew to reveal the normal size plate and switch.

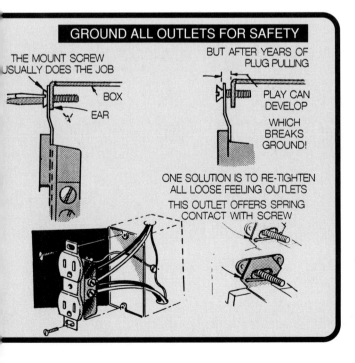

GROUND ALL OUTLETS FOR SAFETY

THE MOUNT SCREW USUALLY DOES THE JOB

BOX

EAR

BUT AFTER YEARS OF PLUG PULLING

PLAY CAN DEVELOP

WHICH BREAKS GROUND!

ONE SOLUTION IS TO RE-TIGHTEN ALL LOOSE FEELING OUTLETS

THIS OUTLET OFFERS SPRING CONTACT WITH SCREW

Replaciing wall outlets is not as common as replacing a switch but on occasion it must be done. Turn off the power, unscrew the plate and remove the switch. Make certain that the outlet is grounded.

WIRING TECHNIQUES

Electrical work requires some knowledge, confidence in yourself, the right tools and supplies—and lots of caution. Here is information that will help.

THE EXPRESSION "new work" can mean two things: (1) wiring, outlets, switches, protective devices, etc., in a house under construction. Or, (2) additional facilities in a completed house already occupied by the owner.

If you are having a house custom-built, your architect will take care of the details of the electrical system in the blueprints that he will turn over to the building contractor. Obviously, you and the architect must get together during the early stages of the planning and decide what you want or should have. For instance, you might think that a 100-ampere service is enough for your anticipated needs, but he will probably recommend 150 to 200 because the labor cost is the same and the materials only cost a little more. Once you approve the overall plans for the house, don't make changes unless you are prepared to pay heavily for them.

Most new houses built since the 1970's have very good electrical systems because builders have learned that this feature is a strong selling point. A typical three-bedroom house of the 1950's had two-wire, 30-ampere service, whereas its later counterpart is more likely to have three-wire, 100- or 150-ampere.

After you have lived in a place for a year or so you may well decide that you want to add a finished playroom or den in the basement, a patio off the kitchen, or some similar improvement. If you can handle the carpentry and masonry work that these projects entail, you can probably do the extra electrical wiring.

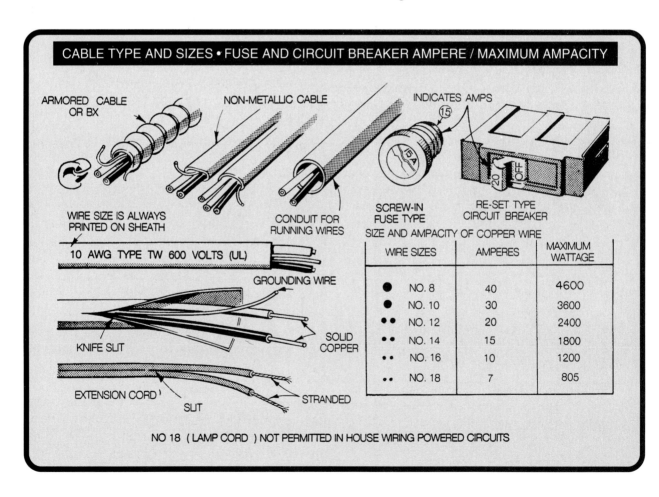

CABLE TYPE AND SIZES • FUSE AND CIRCUIT BREAKER AMPERE / MAXIMUM AMPACITY

ARMORED CABLE OR BX

NON-METALLIC CABLE

INDICATES AMPS

WIRE SIZE IS ALWAYS PRINTED ON SHEATH

CONDUIT FOR RUNNING WIRES

SCREW-IN FUSE TYPE

RE-SET TYPE CIRCUIT BREAKER

10 AWG TYPE TW 600 VOLTS (UL)

GROUNDING WIRE

KNIFE SLIT

SOLID COPPER

EXTENSION CORD

SLIT

STRANDED

SIZE AND AMPACITY OF COPPER WIRE

WIRE SIZES	AMPERES	MAXIMUM WATTAGE
● NO. 8	40	4600
● NO. 10	30	3600
●● NO. 12	20	2400
●● NO. 14	15	1800
●● NO. 16	10	1200
●● NO. 18	7	805

NO 18 (LAMP CORD) NOT PERMITTED IN HOUSE WIRING POWERED CIRCUITS

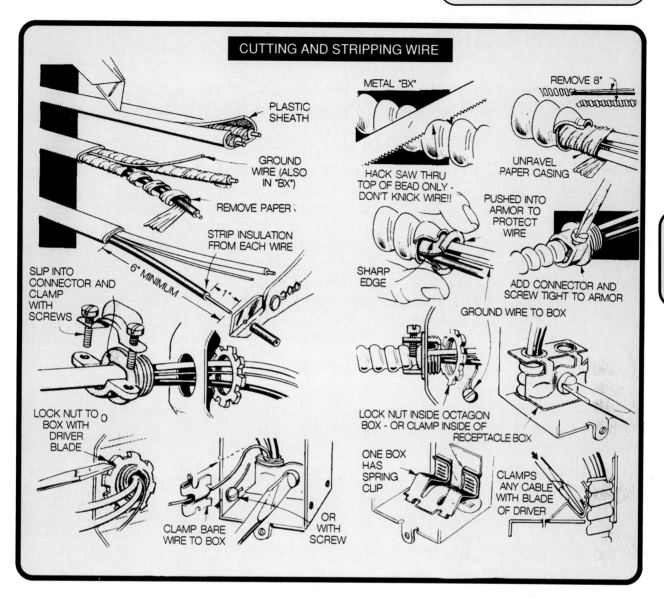

CUTTING AND STRIPPING WIRE

PLASTIC SHEATH

GROUND WIRE (ALSO IN "BX")

REMOVE PAPER

STRIP INSULATION FROM EACH WIRE

SLIP INTO CONNECTOR AND CLAMP WITH SCREWS

6" MINIMUM

1"

LOCK NUT TO BOX WITH DRIVER BLADE

CLAMP BARE WIRE TO BOX

OR WITH SCREW

METAL "BX"

HACK SAW THRU TOP OF BEAD ONLY - DON'T KNICK WIRE!!

SHARP EDGE

REMOVE 8"

UNRAVEL PAPER CASING

PUSHED INTO ARMOR TO PROTECT WIRE

ADD CONNECTOR AND SCREW TIGHT TO ARMOR

GROUND WIRE TO BOX

LOCK NUT INSIDE OCTAGON BOX - OR CLAMP INSIDE OF RECEPTACLE BOX

ONE BOX HAS SPRING CLIP

CLAMPS ANY CABLE WITH BLADE OF DRIVER

A basement house is easiest of all to work on, because the main service panel is often there and any new wiring can be run easily in the basement. However, because live, unswitchable 120/140-volt wires live inside the main service panel, it is recommended that only a professional electrician make connections inside the panel. You can do everything else in installing new branch circuit wiring, having the electrician check your work and make the final hookups inside the panel. Leave several extra feet of cable at the panel location for final connection. The pro will cut off any wiring not needed.

If there isn't space for adding circuits to the main service panel, the electrician can add a branch panel with room for additional circuit breakers. A circuit breaker branch panel may be added to a fused main service panel, no problem.

TYPES OF WIRING

The electrical codes approve a number of wire types for household wiring, all needing some type of protection against impact and abrasion. The wires may be run inside protective pipes called *conduits*. Or they may run inside of protective sheathing called cables. Cables are easier to install.

Plastic-sheathed cable, also known as *Nonmetallic*: This consists of two or three insulated wires, usually with a bare grounding wire, enclosed in a durable molded insulating material. This is called the NM-B or NM-C -cable. The better grade, called Type UF, is thoroughly weatherproof and can be buried in the ground for fused circuits to outdoor lights. Two-wire cable is flat; three-wire is generally round.

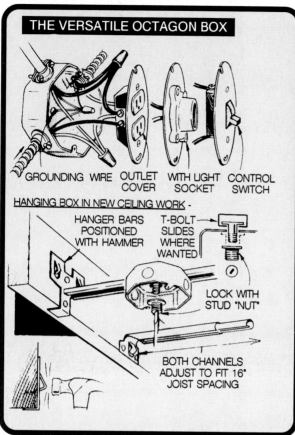

THE VERSATILE OCTAGON BOX

GROUNDING WIRE | OUTLET COVER | WITH LIGHT SOCKET | CONTROL SWITCH

HANGING BOX IN NEW CEILING WORK —

HANGER BARS POSITIONED WITH HAMMER

T-BOLT SLIDES WHERE WANTED

LOCK WITH STUD "NUT"

BOTH CHANNELS ADJUST TO FIT 16" JOIST SPACING

Plastic-sheathed is far and away the most widely used cable for house wiring. It is relatively inexpensive and easy to work with.

Armored Cable, also known as *BX*: Contains two or three insulated wires, usually with a bare bond strip. The latter supplements the grounding function of the spiral, galvanized-steel cover. The steel cover is not waterproof, so the cable is suitable only for dry indoor use. Armored cable makes a less-desirable installation than flexible metal conduit, through which the wires are pulled after installation.

Metal Conduit: This is merely empty metal piping, made in three weights: rigid inter-mediate and thin-wall. As you might guess, the first is stronger than the last. The standard length is 10 feet. Numerous couplings, bushings, straps and other fittings are available for mounting and connecting to electrical fixtures.

The empty conduit is mounted first and the wires pulled through it afterward. If the pipes are fairly short and don't have too many right-angle elbows, the usual No. 14 and No. 12 wires can be pushed through. For longer runs a long, flexible steel tape called a "snake" is needed. This is started at one

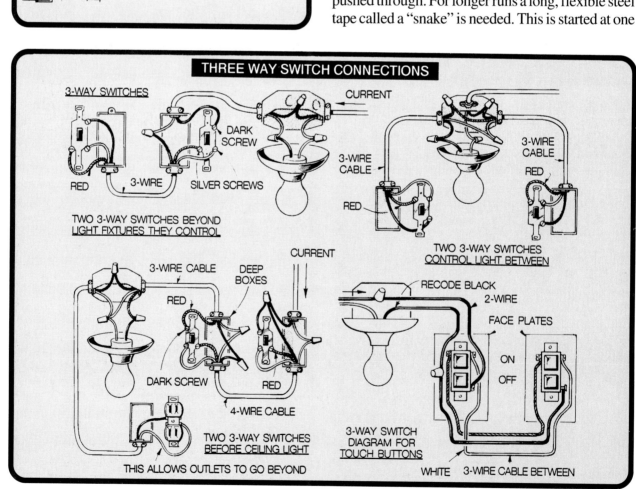

THREE WAY SWITCH CONNECTIONS

3-WAY SWITCHES

CURRENT

DARK SCREW

RED | 3-WIRE | SILVER SCREWS

TWO 3-WAY SWITCHES BEYOND LIGHT FIXTURES THEY CONTROL

3-WIRE CABLE

RED

3-WIRE CABLE

RED

TWO 3-WAY SWITCHES CONTROL LIGHT BETWEEN

3-WIRE CABLE | DEEP BOXES

CURRENT

RED

DARK SCREW | RED

4-WIRE CABLE

TWO 3-WAY SWITCHES BEFORE CEILING LIGHT

THIS ALLOWS OUTLETS TO GO BEYOND

RECODE BLACK
2-WIRE

FACE PLATES

ON

OFF

3-WAY SWITCH DIAGRAM FOR TOUCH BUTTONS

WHITE | 3-WIRE CABLE BETWEEN

outlet or switch box and wiggled until it reappears at the next open box. One wire at a time is twisted around a loop at the end of the snake and fished through. The process is tedious and uncertain, and often very frustrating because the wires tend to snag at 90° turns. For difficult bends special grease is available to make the pull easier. With thin-wall conduit this problem is alleviated to a great extent because the pipe can be bent into a smooth quarter-circle turn about a foot in radius by means of a tool called a conduit bender. Rigid conduit lives up to its name; it doesn't bend, and it must be handled just like piping for water or gas.

The easiest metal conduit to install is flexible metal conduit, called *flex*. Widely available, flex has largely supplanted armored cable (BX) for home wiring in damp and dry locations. Armored cable and flex look much alike, once installed. Between-box runs of flex shorter than 6 feet and protected at 20 amperes or less may serve as equipment-grounding conductors. Longer between-box runs need equipment-grounding wires pulled into the flex, along with the current-carrying wires. These should be the same wire size as the current-

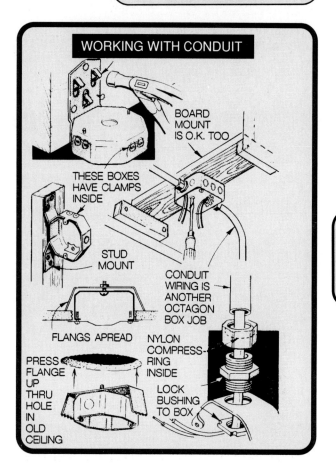

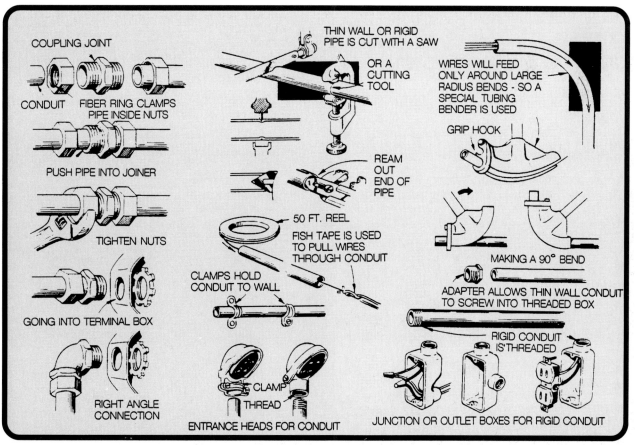

INSTALLING A DIMMER SWITCH

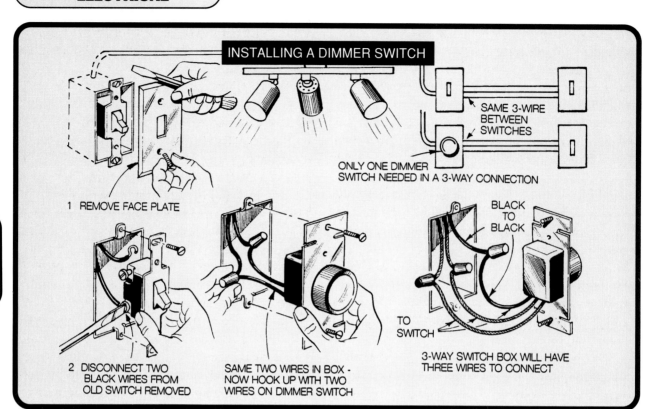

SAME 3-WIRE BETWEEN SWITCHES

ONLY ONE DIMMER SWITCH NEEDED IN A 3-WAY CONNECTION

1 REMOVE FACE PLATE

2 DISCONNECT TWO BLACK WIRES FROM OLD SWITCH REMOVED

SAME TWO WIRES IN BOX - NOW HOOK UP WITH TWO WIRES ON DIMMER SWITCH

BLACK TO BLACK

TO SWITCH

3-WAY SWITCH BOX WILL HAVE THREE WIRES TO CONNECT

CEILING OUTLET BOX CONNECTIONS

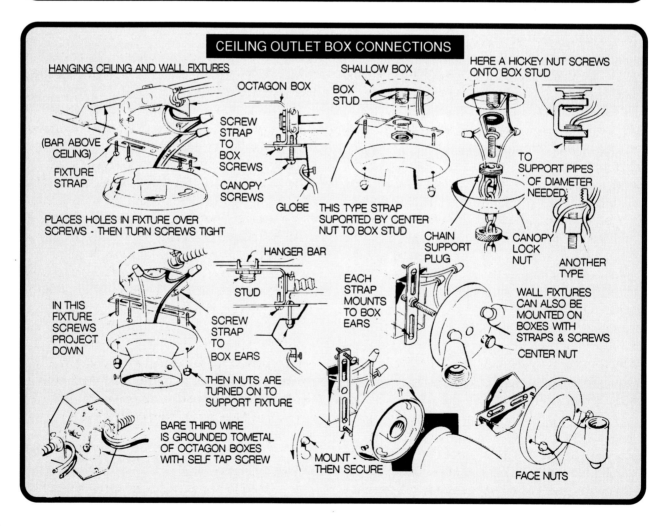

HANGING CEILING AND WALL FIXTURES

OCTAGON BOX

SHALLOW BOX

BOX STUD

HERE A HICKEY NUT SCREWS ONTO BOX STUD

(BAR ABOVE CEILING)

FIXTURE STRAP

SCREW STRAP TO BOX SCREWS

CANOPY SCREWS

GLOBE

THIS TYPE STRAP SUPORTED BY CENTER NUT TO BOX STUD

TO SUPPORT PIPES OF DIAMETER NEEDED

PLACES HOLES IN FIXTURE OVER SCREWS - THEN TURN SCREWS TIGHT

CHAIN SUPPORT PLUG

CANOPY LOCK NUT

ANOTHER TYPE

HANGER BAR

STUD

EACH STRAP MOUNTS TO BOX EARS

WALL FIXTURES CAN ALSO BE MOUNTED ON BOXES WITH STRAPS & SCREWS

IN THIS FIXTURE SCREWS PROJECT DOWN

SCREW STRAP TO BOX EARS

CENTER NUT

THEN NUTS ARE TURNED ON TO SUPPORT FIXTURE

BARE THIRD WIRE IS GROUNDED TOMETAL OF OCTAGON BOXES WITH SELF TAP SCREW

MOUNT - THEN SECURE

FACE NUTS

carrying wires. (Note that the code calls wires and the metal parts of an electrical system *conductors*.)

Plastic (polyvinyl chloride, or PVC) conduit is a nonconductor so that an equipment-grounding wire must be pulled into it.

The easiest working conduit of all (for indoor use only) is electrical nonmetallic tubing (ENT). It, too, needs an equipment-grounding wire pulled in.

The maximum number of wires that may be run in any size of conduit is specified by code. For example, 1/2-inch conduit may contain as many as seven No.12 common Type TW wires and nine No.14 wires. When you buy conduit, ask your dealer how many wires of the size you're using it can hold.

BASIC CODE REQUIREMENTS

Electrical codes establish requirements as to methods of installation, all aimed at building a safe, secure electrical system. Here are some:

Wire splices must be made inside approved boxes. All boxes must be accessible. Wiring devices—such as switches and receptacles—must be mounted in boxes.

Depending on their use, boxes may be junction boxes, outlet boxes or fixture boxes. These come as square, rectangular, round and octagonal (octal). Your dealer can show you a selection. The handiest have mounting brackets permitting nailing or screwing to the framing. Others, called "old-work," "insert" or "remodeling" boxes, are designed for easy mounting in finished walls without any attachment to the framing. One handy fixture box comes with a sliding bracket for nailing to the ceiling joists on either side. Boxes may be metal or plastic, except that metal cables and conduits *must* use metal boxes.

Box capacity in cubic inches is marked inside of every box. The wires, studs, straps, and clamps, etc., used inside a box must not exceed the code-approved quantity (ask your dealer to see box-capacity tables or look for them in the NEC). In the tables, all the equipment-grounding wires together count as one wire.

The code notwithstanding, large boxes are easier to work with, so it pays to use them. Large 4-inch-square, 1 1/2-inch-deep boxes will hold nine No.12 wires before running out of space. Single-gang or two-gang (double) "plaster covers" in various

wall thicknesses may be had for them. Solid box covers are also available for junction boxes (boxes with no devices).

Conduits and cables enter outlet boxes by means of box connectors. These need to match the kind of cable or conduit. Some metal and plastic boxes (the code calls them *nonmetallic*) have built-in clamps for plastic cables.

ELECTRICAL POLARITY

Codes require that the polarity of wiring (equipment-grounding/neutral/hot wires) be maintained throughout a system. This is aided by color-coded insulation on the wires.

Three wires serve the typical 120-volt branch circuit: (1) a bare equipment-grounding wire that is unfused and unswitched back to the grounded bus bar in the main service panel; (2) a white-insulated neutral (grounded) wire, also unfused and unswitched, back to the grounded bus bar; and (3) a black-insulated (or sometimes other color, often red) hot wire. The voltage from black to white is 120 volts.

The typical 240-volt circuit is served by an additional red wire that is also hot. From black to red is 240 volts; black to white or red to white is 120 volts, each.

Both the white- and black-insulated current-carrying wires are called the *line*. These wires must be treated with great deference.

To maintain continuity and polarity, proper outlet box makeup is vital, established by code. How you do it depends on whether the box is end-of-run or middle-of-run. Boxes served by a single cable (or conduit) are end-of-run. Those served by two or more cables or conduits are middle-of-run.

Wire colors (except in a few cable-wired switching circuits) should be spliced black-to-black, white-to-white and bare-to-bare.

At end-of-run receptacles the bare wire always attaches to the back of a metal box with a bonding screw. A 4-inch long bare or green-insulated grounding jumper wire reaches from the box to the hex-head green grounding terminal on the receptacle. (A metal box used with metal conduit may not have any equipment-grounding wire since the conduit serves that purpose. The grounding jumper is still needed, however.)

Middle-of-run, all bare wires are spliced

together with a wire nut, along with two jumper wires. One jumper is attached to the back of a metal box. The other jumper is attached to the receptacle's hex-head green terminal. Plastic boxes need no grounding wires.

End-of-run, the white-insulated wire is connected directly to one of the silver receptacle terminals. Middle-of-run, all the white wires are spliced with a 4-inch white jumper and *it* is connected to a silver terminal of the receptacle.

The black-insulated (or colored—but not white or gray) wires connect to the brass terminals, and each terminal may get a black wire. If there are more than two black wires, splice them together with a black jumper and connect *it* to a brass terminal.

All jumpers should be the same wire size as the current-carrying wires, but may be stranded rather than solid for greater flexibility. Make sure that any wire nuts you use are approved for splicing solid and stranded wires.

Bonding screws have flat, washer-like heads and may be purchased from your dealer. Self-

tapping, they fit into already-tapped 10-32 holes in the backs of metal boxes. Instead of a bonding screw, a green grounding clip may be used. It is pressed over the side of a metal box.

Only hot wires may be switched. For this reason only black (or colored) wires may be connected to switches, not white or gray. An exception in cable wiring, a white-insulated cable wire may be attached to a switch to serve as a hot wire. Nevertheless, it's good practice to *recode* the white insulation black at that point , even though the NEC does not require recoding.

If a switch has a grounding screw, ground it just like a receptacle. Otherwise, the switch may be grounded through contact with its metal switch box.

Polarity in lighting fixtures is maintained by color-matching the branch-circuit and fixture wires as they are spliced. This keeps the body of the fixture at ground potential, the outer screw shells neutral (grounded) and the center socket contacts hot. Then if someone should touch the screw base of a bulb while replacing it, he shouldn't get shocked. (Don't try it, though.)

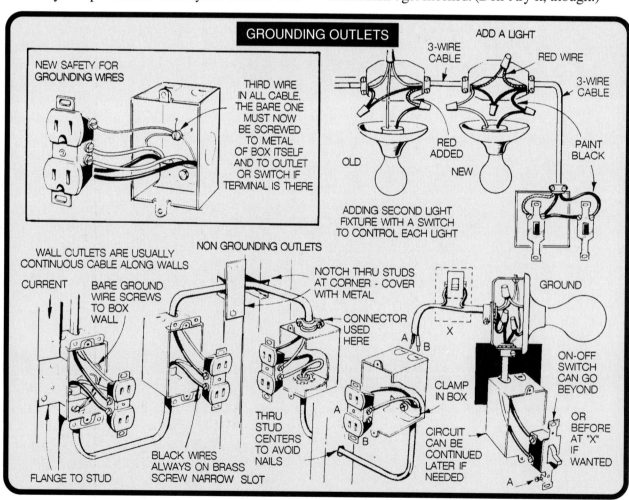

Polarity is carried through to plugged-in appliances (lamps, television sets, etc.) with polarized outlets and plugs. The wide slot of a polarized outlet is its neutral (grounded) slot. The narrow slot is hot. Three-wire grounding outlets are polarized, as are the older narrow/wide two-slot ungrounding outlets. When plugged into a polarized outlet, a polarized plug carries the hot circuit to a lamp's switched center socket contact and to a television set's switched internal circuitry. At the same, it carries the neutral (grounded) circuit to a lamp's unswitched screw shell and to a TV's unswitched chassis.

To maintain polarity, it's a good idea to fit older electrical equipment with correctly wired polarized plugs. Moreover, polarized extension cords, either three-wire grounding ones or two-wire ones having narrow and wide slots, should be used. Otherwise, correct polarity to the appliance cannot be maintained, except by the sheer 50-50 chance of how it gets plugged in.

Cables and flexible metal conduit must be secured to the framing within 12 inches of a box and no more than 4 1/2 feet apart between. Other conduits must be secured within 3 feet of boxes and at 10-foot-maximum intervals between. A cable that runs through holes in framing is considered secured, except at boxes. Wiring that runs close enough to the surface that nailing could affect it, must be protected by metal plates.

Wires have code-set temperature limits, depending on their insulation. Slim, nylon-insulated Type THHN wires can withstand temperatures up to 194° F. (90° C). These wires are superb for use in conduit, as they're so slim and heat-resistant that more of them can be fitted into a conduit. For example, ten No.12 Type THHN wires may run together in a 1/2-inch conduit instead of seven for Type TW wire. Type NM-C plastic cable contains Type THHN wires.

If you have questions about proper wiring methods, check the current electrical code or ask a qualified professional. Also, many dealers are able to advise on electrical wiring.

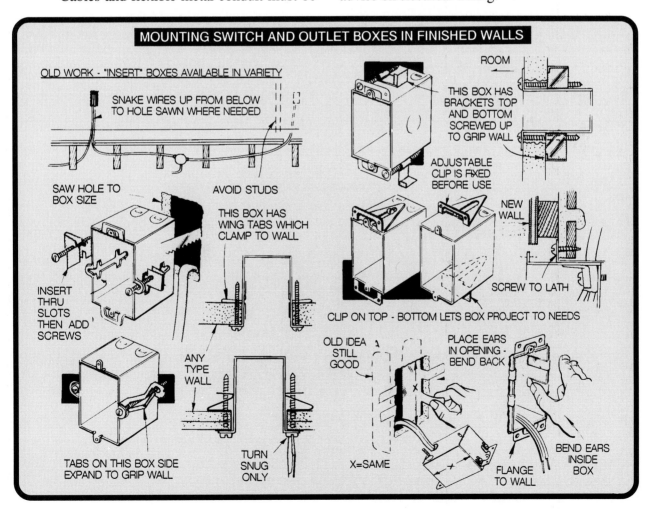

MOUNTING SWITCH AND OUTLET BOXES IN FINISHED WALLS

OLD WORK - "INSERT" BOXES AVAILABLE IN VARIETY

SNAKE WIRES UP FROM BELOW TO HOLE SAWN WHERE NEEDED

SAW HOLE TO BOX SIZE

AVOID STUDS

THIS BOX HAS WING TABS WHICH CLAMP TO WALL

INSERT THRU SLOTS THEN ADD SCREWS

ANY TYPE WALL

TABS ON THIS BOX SIDE EXPAND TO GRIP WALL

TURN SNUG ONLY

ROOM

THIS BOX HAS BRACKETS TOP AND BOTTOM SCREWED UP TO GRIP WALL

ADJUSTABLE CLIP IS FIXED BEFORE USE

NEW WALL

SCREW TO LATH

CLIP ON TOP - BOTTOM LETS BOX PROJECT TO NEEDS

OLD IDEA STILL GOOD

X=SAME

PLACE EARS IN OPENING - BEND BACK

FLANGE TO WALL

BEND EARS INSIDE BOX

WIRING TRICKS YOU CAN USE

Tips from the pros help you to work with wiring faster, better and safer.

THE NEXT BEST THING to having an electrician at your side is knowing a few of the tricks the pros use when they wire.

For example, it takes lots of time to make an end loop on a wire for attachment to a binding-screw terminal. There's a faster way. A screwdriver is the only tool used. Strip 4 1/2 inches of wire instead of the amount normally stripped. The extra length gives you a "crank handle" on the wire end. Then wind the wire clockwise around the fully loosened binding screw using the extra-length handle as a crank.

Tighten the screw down onto the wire (the code calls for 12 lb-in of torque here). See that the wire remains under the screw head and that the insulation comes within 1/4 inch of the screw. The wire should circle the screw two-thirds to three-quarters of the way around but not overlap itself. Once tight, the remaining wire can be bent back and forth until it breaks off next to the screw. Check for tightness.

Be sure to strip 10 to 12 inches of cable so you'll have enough to reach farther into the outlet box, giving you the extra wire for a good crank handle.

Another trick, when running a bare equipment-grounding wire from a metal box to a receptacle simply wrap it one turn clockwise around the green bonding screw in the back of the box on its way to the device. The continuous wire does away with having to make one splice in the box.

RULE-OF-THUMB MEASUREMENTS

Speaking of cable-stripping, electrical work isn't nearly as exacting in the measuring department as carpentry is. Therefore, electricians can adopt rule-of-thumb measurements, literally. For example, from the heel of the hand to the tip of the

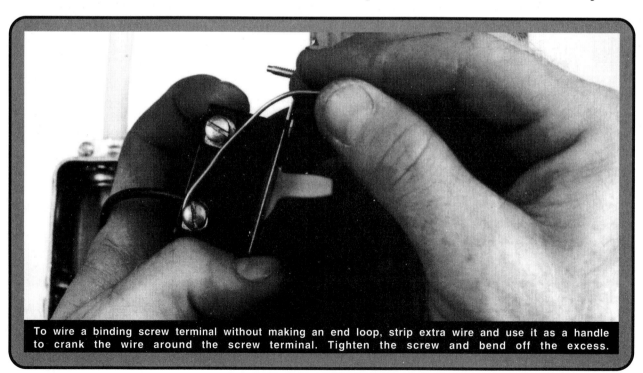

To wire a binding screw terminal without making an end loop, strip extra wire and use it as a handle to crank the wire around the screw terminal. Tighten the screw and bend off the excess.

thumb measures very close to 6 inches, a measurement useful in cable-stripping. For a 12-inch strip, use two hands with the thumbs pointed at each other. And for an 8-inch strip use two hands with the thumbs folded in.

Here's an easy way to strip off flat two-wire-with-ground plastic cable sheathing using a utility knife. Lay the cable flat on a wood surface and run the utility knife down through the sheathing slightly off center. Pull the knife to the end of the cable. The bare equipment-grounding wire will help guide the knife blade straight along the cable without endangering the insulation on the current-carrying wires. Peel the sheathing back and snip it off. Finally, inspect the insulation on the current-carrying wires for damage. The trick doesn't work on round three-wire-with-ground plastic cable.

The NEC requires that splices be insulated equivalent to the original wires. Split-bolt splices, can be insulated only with electrical tape. And the best tape to use is 3M's Scotch 130C Linerless Rubber Splicing Tape. While it takes many turns of thin plastic electrical tape to build up the insulation needed, fewer wraps of the thicker tape do the job. Linerless 130C tape is available in 1- and 3/4-inch widths. You may have to see an electrical pro distributor to find it.

When using Linerless 130C tape, remember that the side inside the roll should be wrapped outside the splice (sticky side out, in other words). Stretch the tape as you apply it, making a 3/4-inch width stretch down to about 9/16 inch. Continue until the required thickness has been built up. It's not required, but you can overwrap the Linerless 130C layers with a cover of plastic electrical tape, winding it in the same direction.

Another method of insulation is heat-shrink tubing. The tube is available in various sizes. You cut off the length needed. In most cases, the tube must be installed before making the splice. Heat-shrinking can be done with a match or propane torch—be careful not to burn the insulation. A heat gun does a better job.

Here's another splicing trick. Wire splices in damp and wet locations—outdoors, basements, garages—can benefit from moisture proofing. Marine Development and Research and 3M make moisture-proofers, dielectric black vinyl liquids

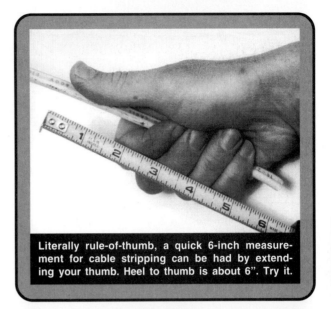

Literally rule-of-thumb, a quick 6-inch measurement for cable stripping can be had by extending your thumb. Heel to thumb is about 6". Try it.

For stripping the insulation from wire ends, use the rule of thumb...nail, that is. Measure the strip against your thumbnail. It gives the typical 5/8-inch strip and it's super-fast.

Heat-shrink insulation protects splices and terminals without taping. The best way to shrink it is with a heat gun. This one has an attachment that concentrates the heat around the insulation.

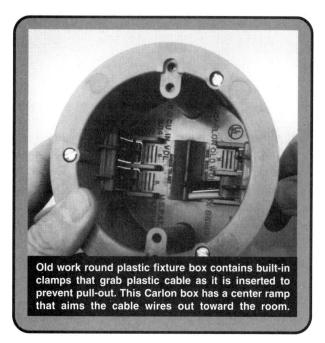

Old work round plastic fixture box contains built-in clamps that grab plastic cable as it is inserted to prevent pull-out. This Carlon box has a center ramp that aims the cable wires out toward the room.

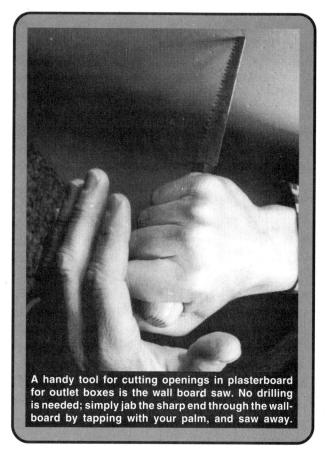

A handy tool for cutting openings in plasterboard for outlet boxes is the wall board saw. No drilling is needed; simply jab the sharp end through the wallboard by tapping with your palm, and saw away.

supplied in brush-top cans. The liquid coats the splice to keep corrosive moisture locked out. To build a thicker coating, two or more coats can be given, with drying time between. Paint it on the inside of taped splices and on the exterior of wire nuts and binding-screw terminals. Don't use it under wire nuts or crimp sleeves, as the coating would prevent a good electrical connection.

PLASTIC BOXES

Nonmetallic outlet boxes, as the codes term them, are of polyvinyl chloride (PVC) or fiberglass. They're light, cost little and work especially well with plastic-sheathed cable. In fact, some plastic boxes contain built-in clamps to hold plastic cable without the need for separate box connectors. Plastic boxes meet the highest house temperature requirements of 194°F (90°C).

Plastic boxes save time because they need not be grounded. Equipment-grounding wires can go directly to devices, fixtures or appliances instead. Grounding jumpers aren't normally needed.

Plastic boxes are available in rectangular, round, flattened round and 4-inch square for receptacles, switches, fixtures and junction boxes. They come from single-gang to four-gang. Square boxes accept plaster rings in either 1/4 inch or 1/2 inch. Some have built-in brackets for attachment to framing. Others have clamps for box support by

If metal outlet boxes protrude slightly from the wall, good grounding by device-yoke contact with the box is assured. Just 1/16 inch of protrusion won't affect wall plate fit.

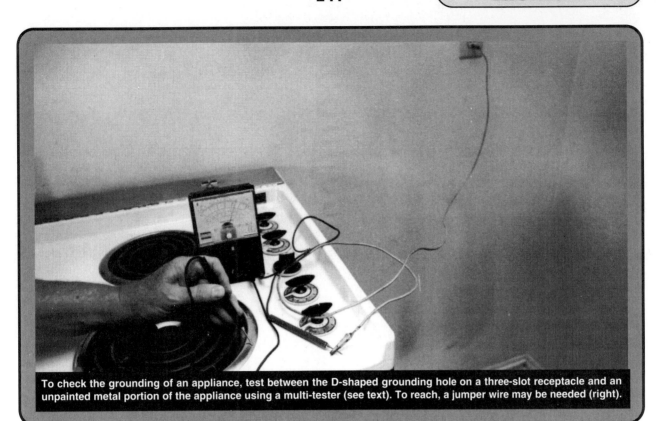

To check the grounding of an appliance, test between the D-shaped grounding hole on a three-slot receptacle and an unpainted metal portion of the appliance using a multi-tester (see text). To reach, a jumper wire may be needed (right).

the wall material ("old work" boxes). Some have pre-installed nails for easy attachment to framing in new construction. Ceiling boxes with sliding fixture hangers are popular.

A good way to fasten outlet boxes to framing is with 1 1/4 inch No.6 drywall screws. Once you do it this way, you'll never nail them again. (Did you ever miss with a hammer and crack a plastic box?) Drywall screws need no pilot holes. They're sometimes called by other names such as multi-use screws, multi-purpose screws, utility screws, self-tapping screws and the like. Drive them with a cordless driver/drill. The same driver/drill fitted with a standard screwdriver bit is the best tool for running the long 6-32 device screws that attach switches and outlets to their boxes.

While on the subject of outlet boxes, you can get more room inside small rectangular switch and receptacle boxes by wiring from the end knockouts rather than the side ones. You'll be glad you did.

Another trick for wiring boxes: route the wiring so the bare and white-insulated wires are on one side and the black-insulated hot wire is on the opposite side. Likewise, install the devices that way. With everything at ground potential on one side and everything live on the other side, an unwanted short circuit is much less likely to develop inside the box.

TESTING FOR GROUND

It's a good safety measure to test home appliances for proper grounding. There's an easy way to do it with a multi-tester. First set the tester's selector to the lowest AC-volts setting, possibly 6 volts. Put one test prod into the D-shaped grounding hole of a nearby three-slot receptacle. (Stay away from the current-carrying slots). Touch the other prod to an unpainted portion of the appliance and read the meter. The reading should be zero volts, indicating that no power is leaking to its body.

That okay, next switch the selector to the Rx1 ohms position, touch the prods together and zero the ohms needle. Test again. The meter should read 0 ohms indicating no resistance from the appliance to ground. An ohm reading of more than 0 means that either the appliance or the receptacle is not well grounded. The fix is likely one for a professional, but don't neglect to have it done.

AMPERAGE REQUIREMENTS

Know the wattage of your appliance or tool and the size of the circuit wire before you plug it in. It's safer for the house and the equipment.

SOME PEOPLE blithely plug appliances into the wall outlets without regard for the capacity of the latter to handle the load. A particular branch circuit might be fused for 15 amperes, but this does not mean that each of the outlets on the line can provide 15 amperes independently of the others when all are being used. It means that the *total* current of 15 amps must not be exceeded. If you are making breakfast and turn on both a coffee pot (about five amps) and a toaster (about ten amps), almost anything else you plug in will probably pop the fuse or circuit breaker.

A little simple arithmetic can help you avoid brownouts. Study the accompanying chart and check off the appliances and machines in your own home. The figures here are for representative products, and are close enough for planning purposes. Of course, you should know what fuses protect what branch circuits, so you should be able to distribute the load to best advantage.

Note that the important figure in each case is the current in amperes that an appliance draws from the line. Fuses and breakers recognize only the current and not the actual working power in watts.

If you plan to install any new current consuming equipment your utility company will be only too happy to advise you if you have adequate power and, if not, how large a service you will need.

Small-Current Class, to 5 amps.
  120 volts (600 watts)
Razor—1/10 amp. (10-15 watts)
All incandescent lamps—1/2 amp. per 60 watts
All fluorescent lamps—1/2 amp. per 40 watts
Fan, 10-inch size—1 amp. (75 watts)
Solid-state radio set—1/10 amp. (7 watts)
Stereo—2 amps. (150 watts)
Food processor—2 1/2 amps. (200 watts)
Refrigerator—3 amps. 250 watts)
Television set—4 amps. (300 watts)
Vacuum cleaner—5 amps. (400 watts)
Coffee pot—5 amps. (600 watts)

Medium Current Class, to 15 amps.
  120 volts (1800 watts)
Portable heater—7 amps. (840 watts)
Hand iron—9 amps. (1000 watts)
Toaster—9 1/2 amps. (1100 watts)
Rotisserie—2 to 13 amps. (1400-1500 watts)
Microwave—up to 1000 watts
Window air-conditioner—6 to 15 amps.
                (600-1500 watts)
Clothes washer—12 amps. (1500 watts)
Dishwasher—13 amps. (1650 watts)

Heavy Current Class, to 50 amps.
  120/240 volts (12,000 watts)
Water heater—11 amps. (2500 watts)
Window air-conditioner—15 amps. (3000 watts)
Clothes dryer—25 amps. (5600 watts)
Central air-conditioner·0—30 amps. (6000 watts)
Range—30 to 60 amps. (8000-16,000 watts)

Home Workshop Tools, to 15 amps.
  120 volts (1800 watts)
Portable drill—1 1/2 amps. (200 watts)
Saber saw—3 1/2 amps. (400 watts)
Drill press—8 amps. (800 watts)
Portable saw—9 amps. (1200 watts)
Bench saw—14 amps. (1680 watts)

AMPERE CAPACITY OF COPPER WIRE			
No. 14	15 amps.	Entrance Line	
No. 12	20 amps.	No. 4	100 amps.
No. 10	30 amps.	No. 1	150 amps.
No. 8	40 amps.	No. 00	200 amps.

HOW MANY WATTS APPLIANCES AND TOOLS DRAW

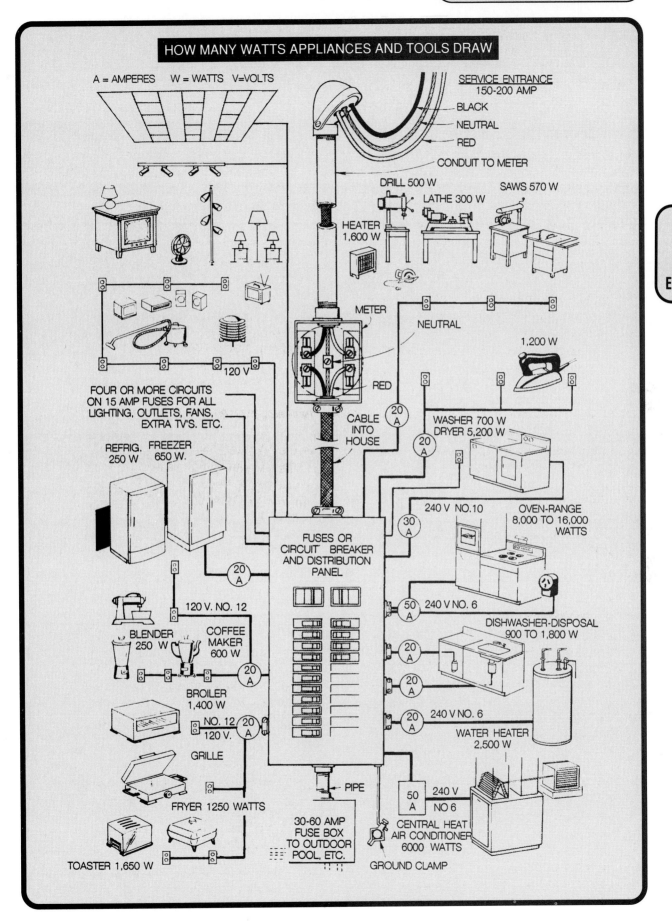

A = AMPERES   W = WATTS   V = VOLTS

SERVICE ENTRANCE
150-200 AMP

BLACK

NEUTRAL

RED

CONDUIT TO METER

DRILL 500 W

SAWS 570 W

LATHE 300 W

HEATER
1,600 W

METER

NEUTRAL

1,200 W

RED

FOUR OR MORE CIRCUITS
ON 15 AMP FUSES FOR ALL
LIGHTING, OUTLETS, FANS,
EXTRA TV'S. ETC.

120 V

CABLE
INTO
HOUSE

WASHER 700 W
DRYER 5,200 W

REFRIG.   FREEZER
250 W   650 W.

240 V NO.10

OVEN-RANGE
8,000 TO 16,000
WATTS

FUSES OR
CIRCUIT   BREAKER
AND DISTRIBUTION
PANEL

120 V. NO. 12

240 V NO. 6

BLENDER
250 W

COFFEE
MAKER
600 W

DISHWASHER-DISPOSAL
900 TO 1,800 W

BROILER
1,400 W

240 V NO. 6

NO. 12
120 V.

WATER HEATER
2,500 W

GRILLE

PIPE

240 V

NO 6

FRYER 1250 WATTS

30-60 AMP
FUSE BOX
TO OUTDOOR
POOL, ETC.

CENTRAL HEAT
AIR CONDITIONER
6000 WATTS

TOASTER 1,650 W

GROUND CLAMP

20 A

20 A

30 A

20 A

50 A

20 A

20 A

20 A

20 A

20 A

50 A

ENT: THE DO-IT-YOURSELF CONDUIT

**The "plastic plumbing" of electrical wiring,
ENT, Electrical Nonmetallic Tubing, is literally a snap to wire.**

CALLED "ENT" FOR SHORT, electrical nonmetallic tubing is light, strong and easy to work with. What's more, it can't corrode. Furthermore, ENT is nonconductive and cannot become accidently energized to give someone a shock. ENT protects the wiring better than most cable wiring does, and the bright blue-colored PVC

tubing and accessories are widely available at do-it-yourself outlets.

ENT is code-accepted for dry and damp locations up to the third floor in walls having at least the fire-resistance of wood-framed walls that are finished with 1/2" gypsum board. This includes most house walls. ENT may be left

ENT can be bent by hand without a conduit bender. Bent, it trains easily to hold the curve. Only minimal measuring is required to install ENT. Highly efficient, few pieces are left over after a job.

Accessory products available for use with Carlon Flex-Plus ENT tubing are (top row, l. to r.) 2"x3" single-gang box, box terminator, snap-coupling, 4"-square box with cover screws; (bottom row, l. to r.) box covers: single-gang flush, single-gang plaster ring and two-gang plaster ring.

Ever try this with rigid conduit? It can't be done. Running 1/2" tubing centered on 2 X 4 framing places it more than 1 1/4" from the face of the framing, enough to be safe from wallboard nails. Larger tubing needs 1/16"-thick metal plates installed for nail-protection.

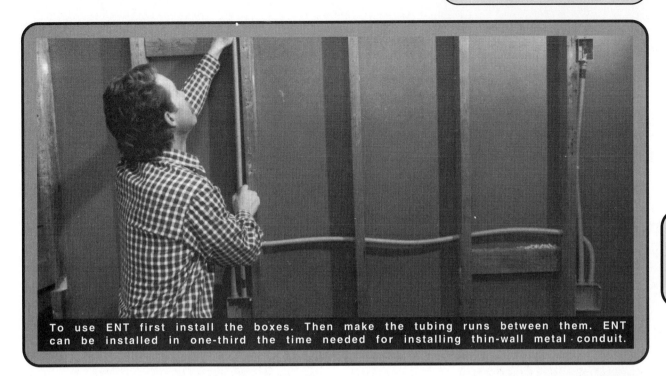

To use ENT first install the boxes. Then make the tubing runs between them. ENT can be installed in one-third the time needed for installing thin-wall metal conduit.

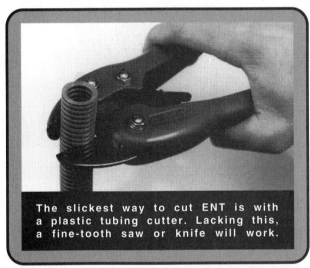

The slickest way to cut ENT is with a plastic tubing cutter. Lacking this, a fine-tooth saw or knife will work.

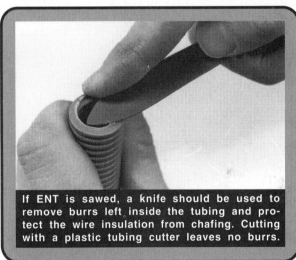

If ENT is sawed, a knife should be used to remove burrs left inside the tubing and protect the wire insulation from chafing. Cutting with a plastic tubing cutter leaves no burrs.

Snap-on couplings lock into the tube corrugations and close over the joint between lengths of ENT, holding them together and protecting the joint.

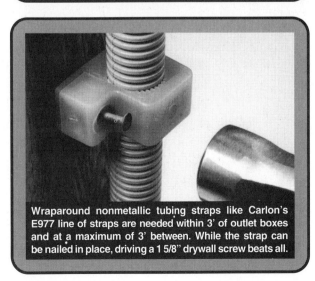

Wraparound nonmetallic tubing straps like Carlon's E977 line of straps are needed within 3' of outlet boxes and at a maximum of 3' between. While the strap can be nailed in place, driving a 1 5/8" drywall screw beats all.

Box knockouts are made by tapping out the prepunched plastic discs with a screwdriver. It doesn't damage the tool's tip.

Carlon Flex-Plus Blue ENT outlet boxes have prepunched mounting straps for fastening to the framing. They also come with screws for quick and easy cover attachment.

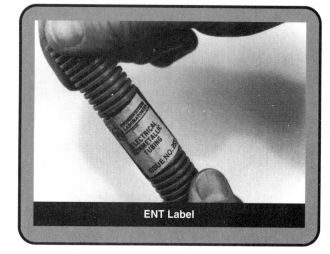

ENT Label

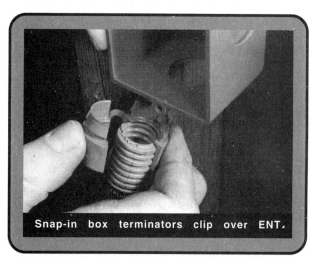

Snap-in box terminators clip over ENT.

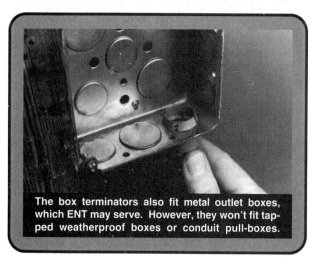

The box terminators also fit metal outlet boxes, which ENT may serve. However, they won't fit tapped weatherproof boxes or conduit pull-boxes.

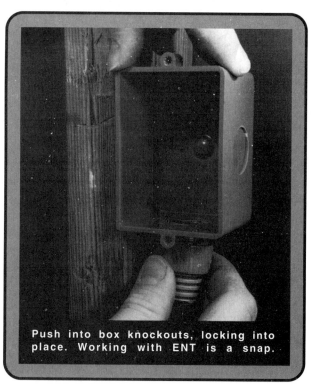

Push into box knockouts, locking into place. Working with ENT is a snap.

exposed, but should not be buried in the ground or used where it's subject to physical damage. Carlon Div. of Lamson & Sessions, Inc., the manufacturer, calls it Flex-Plus Blue ENT.

Like other raceways, ENT tubing lets you use low-cost insulated wires rather than cables. Moreover, any time later, if new wires are needed between boxes, such as for installing a pilot-lighted switch—and the tubing isn't already filled to its approved capacity—you can simply fish additional wires through without tearing into the walls.

Economical, ENT comes in 1/2", 3/4" and 1" diameters in 6- and 10-foot lengths. The 1/2" size will handle most house-wiring needs, especially if slim, nylon insulated Type THHN wire is used.

Carlon PVC boxes offer 1/2", 3/4" and 1" knockouts, with the larger square boxes having the widest selection of knockout sizes. Boxes in the ENT system are not designed to support fixtures. Therefore, metal boxes must be used in those locations. No problem. Flex-Plus Blue ENT works as well with metal boxes as it does with its own PVC boxes. Box fill is the same as for other boxes of identical volume. The cubic-inch volume figure is molded into every box.

Plaster rings for square boxes may be had in flat for surface mounting or in projections of 1/2", 5/8", 3/4" and 1" letting the PVC covers extend through just about any thickness of wall material.

Wire used with ENT must be temperature-rated at 194°F (90°C) or less, which is the temperature rating of the ENT system. Popular Type TW and Type THHN wires both meet this need. Maximum ambient temperature is 122°F (50°C). As with any raceway, the numbers of wires installed in ENT tubing must not exceed that called for in the NEC fill tables for that trade size of conduit.

Because ENT is nonconductive, a same-sized bare or green-insulated equipment-grounding wire must be used in the conduit along with the current-carrying wires. It should be properly connected at every outlet.

Tools needed for an installation are knife, screwdriver, hammer and lineman's pliers. You'll also need a drill with spade bit for boring holes in the framing. Use a 1" bit for 1/2" ENT tubing.

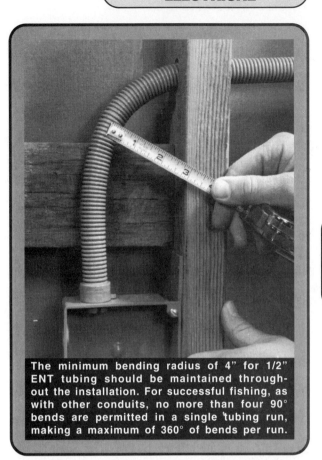

The minimum bending radius of 4" for 1/2" ENT tubing should be maintained throughout the installation. For successful fishing, as with other conduits, no more than four 90° bends are permitted in a single tubing run, making a maximum of 360° of bends per run.

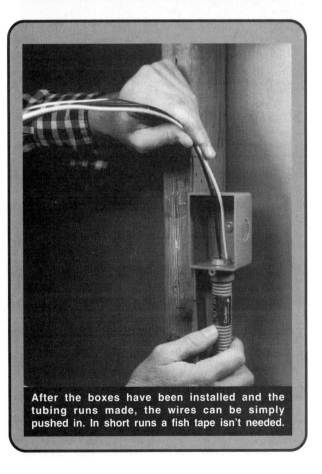

After the boxes have been installed and the tubing runs made, the wires can be simply pushed in. In short runs a fish tape isn't needed.

FLUORESCENT LAMPS

With power costs destined to go higher and technological advances responsible for producing the same light as incandescent bulbs, fluorescent lamps are gaining in popularity. They produce the same light as incandescents at one third the cost and last 8-12 times longer.

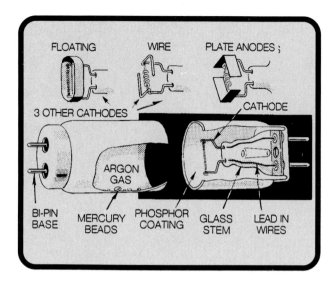

INCANDESCENT LAMPS consist of a wire filament inside a glass bulb. Fluorescents are entirely different in construction, operation and appearance. The first illustration shows their basic internal arrangement, common to all types. The components are as follows:

1) A glass tube, or bulb, internally coated with fluorescent material called phosphors. 2) Electrodes called "cathodes," supported by a glass mount structure, and sealed at the ends of the tube. 3) A filling gas to aid starting and operation—usually argon, or argon with neon. 4. A small amount of mercury which vaporizes during lamp operation. 5. A base cemented on each end of the tube to connect the lamp to the lighting circuit.

Tube. Acts as an airtight enclosure for the mercury, the filling gas, the cathodes, and the phosphor coating. Glass must be free of structural defects and cleaned before lamp assembly.

Bases. Connect- the lamp to the electric circuit, and support the lamp. Lamps for preheat and rapid start circuits use two contacts on each end of the lamp. The bi-pin base is used on all preheat and many rapid start lamps. Some rapid start type lamps, such as high output and Power Groove lamps, use recessed double contact bases because of the higher ballast voltage required with lamps longer than 4 feet. Instant start lamps require only one electrical contact on each end of the lamp; thus the single-pin base is most commonly used. Some instant start lamps use bipin bases with the two contacts connected together inside the lamps.

Mount Structures. Close off ends of the tube and support each cathode. Wires leading from base are sealed off here. These wires are made of special metal, called Dumet wire, which has virtually the same coefficient of expansion as glass. The mount structure also includes a long glass exhaust tube; during manufacture, air is pumped out of the bulb, and the filling gas and mercury are inserted. The exhaust tube is then cut and sealed off so that it fits inside the base.

Cathodes. Cathodes provide terminals for the arc and a source of electrons for lamp current. In some lamps they function alternately as cathodes and anodes, but are commonly called cathodes. In other lamp designs, separate anodes are used because they best fit lamp design requirements. Plate anodes in high output lamps and wire anodes in Power Groove lamps are used to reduce the wattage loss at the lamp ends. Cathodes are usually made of coil-coiled, triple-coiled, or stick-coiled tungsten, like an ordinary lamp filament, except coils are filled with alkaline-earth oxides. These oxides emit electrons more freely, thus minimizing losses and keeping efficiency high.

Mercury Vapor. Droplets of liquid mercury are placed in the fluorescent tube during manufacture. During lamp operation, the mercury vaporizes to a very low pressure (about 1/100,000th of atmospheric pressure). At this pressure, the current through the vapor causes the vapor to radiate energy most strongly at one specific wavelength in the ultraviolet region, 253.7 nanometers. (A nanometer is one billionth of a meter). Higher mercury pressures tend to reduce the production of this ultraviolet line. The mercury pressure during operation is regulated by the temperature of the bulb wall.

Filling Gas. Besides mercury, the tube also contains a small quantity of a highly purified rare gas. Argon and argon-neon are most common, but sometimes krypton is used. The filling gases ionize readily when sufficient voltage is applied across the lamp. The ionized filling gas quickly decreases in resistance allowing current to flow and the mercury to vaporize.

Phosphor Coating. Transforms radiation into visible light. The fluorescent lamp gets its name from the fact that the phosphor coating fluoresces. The chemical make-up of the phosphor determines the color of the light produced. Phosphor particles in fluorescent coatings are extremely small—approximately 0.0007 inch in diameter. Careful control of phosphor particle size is necessary to obtain high lamp efficiency.

Fluorescence is defined as "the property of a material to become self-luminous when acted upon by radiant energy, such as ultraviolet or X-rays." This definition pinpoints the two elements required in a fluorescent lamp: 1. A source of radiant energy. 2. A material that fluoresces.

Many natural and synthetic materials exhibit fluorescence. In fluorescent lamps, a powder having this property is applied to the inner surface of the bulb, which is usually tubular in cross-section. The selection of the phosphors and certain additives, called "activators", determines the characteristics of the emitted radiation; that is ultraviolet, colored light, or various shades of white light.

The source of radiant energy that acts on the fluorescent material is an electric arc which passes through mercury vapor within the tube. A lamp starts when the voltage between the cathodes is sufficient to strike an arc in the filling gas. As the current passes through the vapor, it causes changes in the energy levels of electrons in the individual mercury ions; energy is then released in the form of several wavelengths of visible and ultraviolet (invisible) energy. The latter is radiated to the tube wall, where it activates the fluorescent material and causes it to emit visible light.

The voltage needed to strike an arc through the length of the tube depends to a large extent on the temperature of the electron-emitting cathode. There are three types of starting arrangements.

The cathodes of the preheat lamp are preheated to emit electrons before the arc strikes; this is where the name "preheat" comes from. This type of lamp operation is also referred to as switch-start or starter-start. See circuits 1, 2 and 3.

The preheating process requires a few seconds. It is usually accomplished by an automatic starter which applies current to the cathodes of the lamp for sufficient time to heat them, and then automatically removes the current from the cathodes, causing the voltage to be applied between the cathodes and striking the arc. In some preheat systems, such as fluorescent desk lights, the preheating is accomplished by pushing a manual start button. This is held down for a few seconds. During this time, the cathodes heat. When the button is released, the arc strikes. Preheat lamps are usually identified by wattage, bulb diameter (in eighths of an inch, and color. Thus a lamp marked F15T8/CW is a 15-watt, l-inch diameter, Cool White fluorescent lamp. With preheat lamps designed for appliance service, wattage varies widely depending on the ballast. These lamps are identified by length instead of wattage. For example, F25" T8 is for a lamp 26" long, 1-inch diameter.

Ballasts, also known as "choke coils", are available to operate certain preheat lamps without using starters. These ballasts use the rapid start principle of starting and operation. They are designed around the characteristics of the preheat lamps involved. These ballasts are popularly called " trigger start" ballasts.

To overcome the slow starting of the preheat system, General Electric introduced "instant start" lamps. In addition to lighting as soon as current to the lamp is turned on, instant start lamps also eliminate the need for starters, and thus simplify maintenance. See circuits 4, 5, 6.

Since slimline lamps can be operated at more than one current and wattage, they are identified by lamp length. The number following the F in the designation is the nominal lamp length in inches, rather than the lamp wattage as with most preheat lamps.

The "rapid start" is the most recent devel-

1 - BASIC PRE-HEAT CIRCUIT

BALLAST

LAMP

STARTER

2 - PRE HEAT WITH AUTO TRANSFORMER STEP-UP
OF VOLTAGE AND CAPACITOR

BALLAST

PF
CAPACITOR

LAG-LAMP INDUCTOR

TWO LAMPS AND STARTERS

LEAD-LAMP
CAPACITOR

BALLAST

3 - LEAD LAG PRE-HEAT CIRCUIT

BALLAST

LAMP

CIRCUIT 4 - BASIC INSTANT START

opment in fluorescent types. Rapid start lamps start quickly without external starters such as required for the pre-heat type. Also, ballasts are smaller and more efficient. See circuits 7 and 8.

The new lamps utilize cathodes that can be heated continuously with very low losses. An incidental feature of the system is that it permits dimming and flashing, not possible with other types. Because of these multiple advantages, rapid start fixtures are used in most new lighting installations.

BALLASTS

The "ballast" required for all fluorescent lamp operation is essentially a single winding of wire on a laminated iron frame. In fluorescent circuits the ballast performs two independent functions. First, it momentarily increases the line voltage to overcome the high resistance between the widely separated cathodes, and establishes a conductive arc between them. The resistance of the path then becomes very low, so the ballast is left in the line to limit the current to a safe value. Without the ballast, the tube would draw so much current that it would destroy itself.

DIMMING

The light output of rapid start fluorescent lamps can be adjusted or dimmed by a number of special circuits. All of these incorporate one essential principle: the ballast must keep the cathodes of the lamp energized at the proper voltage regardless of the amount the lamp is dimmed.

Current passing through the lamp or lamps

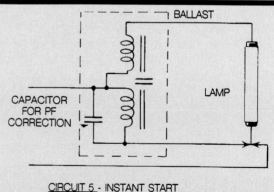

CAPACITOR
FOR PF
CORRECTION

BALLAST

LAMP

CIRCUIT 5 - INSTANT START
WITH DISCONNECT LAMP HOLDER

in the dimming system can be controlled by a number of methods. These include thyratrons, silicon-controlled rectifiers and other solid-state devices, variable inductors, autotransformers, saturable core reactors, magnetic amplifiers, etc.

Dimming systems vary widely in performance. Some systems can dim lamps no lower than 20 percent of normal full output, while others can dim lamps as low as 0.2 percent.

FLASHING

The life of fluorescent lamps is seriously reduced by turning them on and off frequently when ordinary ballasts are used. However, it is possible to flash rapid start type lamps and maintain satisfactory life by using a special flashing ballast.

SPIRALING AND FLICKERING

When a new lamp is first turned on it may occasionally exhibit a condition called spiraling; i.e., the brightness varies from end to end. This condition is often caused by loose materials knocked off the cathode. Normally, it disappears after the lamps have been burned for a few hours.

UNDER AND OVERVOLTAGE

Ballasts are usually designed for operation on 120-volt circuits. In general, operation is satisfactory, with voltage as low as 110 volts, or as high as 125 volts. Similarly, ballasts for 208-volt service operate satisfactorily from 200 to 215 volts; 240-volt service from 220 to 250volts; 277-volt service from 250 to 290 volts; and 480-volt service from 440 to 500 volts.

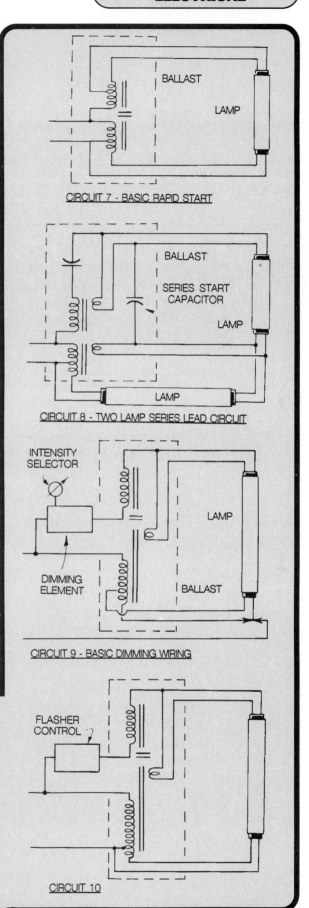

CIRCUIT 7 - BASIC RAPID START

CIRCUIT 8 - TWO LAMP SERIES LEAD CIRCUIT

CIRCUIT 9 - BASIC DIMMING WIRING

CIRCUIT 10

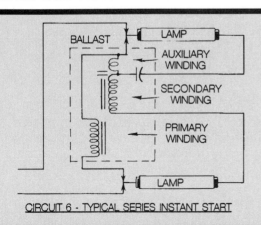

CIRCUIT 6 - TYPICAL SERIES INSTANT START

252

ELECTRICAL

TROUBLE SHOOTING CHART

STEPS IN FINDING TROUBLE

First find symptom here, noting the code number and letter. Then refer to that number and letter in the Sections below.

While the following symptoms apply particularly to preheat fluorescent lamps, most of the appearance factors also apply to the Instant Start, Slimline, Rapid Start, High Output, and Power Groove types as well.

NORMAL END OF LIFE

Lamp won't operate; or flashes momentarily and goes out; or blinks on and off, perhaps with shimmering effect; ends probably blackened. — **1-a.**

SHORT LIFE

— **1-f, 1-q, 2-a, 2-b, 3-a, 3-d, 3-g, 5-a, 6a, 6-c, 7-a.**

IMMEDIATE FAILURE OF NEW LAMPS

— **1-q, 3-d, 3-g, 6-c, 6-f.**

END BLACKENING

Dense blackening at one end or both, extending 2''-3'' from base. — **1-b.**
Blackening, generally within 1'' of ends. — **1-i.**
Blackening at one end only. — **6-a, 6-c, 1-l.**

Blackening early in life (indicates active material from electrodes being sputtered off too rapidly). — **1-q, 2-a, 2-b, 3-a, 5-a, 6-a, 6-c.**

RINGS

Brownish rings at one or both ends, about 2'' from base. — **1-c.**

DENSE SPOTS

Black, about ½'' wide, extending about half way around tube, centering about 1'' from base. — **3-b.**

DARK STREAKS

Streaks lengthwise of tube. — **1-j.**

DARK SECTION OF TUBE

⅓ to ½ of tube gives no light (tubes longer than 24''). — **4b, 4-c, 6-e.**

ENDS ONLY LIGHTED

— **2-b, 6-b, 6-c.**

BLINKING ON AND OFF

Accompanied by shimmering effect during "lighted" period. — **1-a.**
Blinking of relatively new lamp. — **1-q, 1-k, 2-a, 3-a, 4-a, 4-c, 5-c, 6-a, 6-c.**

NO STARTING EFFORT, or SLOW STARTING

— **1-l, 1-m, 1-n, 1-p, 1-q, 2-c, 2-d, 3-a, 3-c, 3-e, 5-c, 6-c, 6-d.**

FLICKER (NOT STROBOSCOPIC EFFECT)

Pronounced, irregular flicker on looking directly at lamp (spiraling, swirling, snaking, etc.) — **1-g, 2-e, 3-a, 5-b, 6-c.**
Flicker suddenly occurring — **1-h.**
Persistent tendency to flicker. — **1-k, 6-c.**

DECREASED LIGHT OUTPUT

— **4-b, 4-c, 4-d, 5-c, 6-c, 7-b,** (During first 100 hours' use — **1-d.**)

COLOR AND BRIGHTNESS DIFFERENCES

Different color appearance in different locations of same installation. — **1-e, 4-c, 7-c.**
Lamps operate at unequal brilliancy. — **4-c, 5-c, 6-c.**

NOISE

Humming sound, which may be steady, or may come and go. — **3-f, 3-j.**

OVERHEATED BALLAST

— **1-q, 3-d, 3-g, 3-h, 3-i, 5-d, 6-c, 6-f.**

RADIO INTERFERENCE

— **1-o, 6-g.**

1. LAMPS

	POSSIBLE CAUSES*	MAINTENANCE
1-a	Normal failure; active material on electrodes exhausted.	Replace lamp (remove old lamp promptly).
1-b	Normal — end of life.	Replace lamp.
1-c	May occur on some lamps during life.	Has no effect on lamp performance.
1-d	Light output during first 100 hours is above published rating, sometimes as much at 10%. (Rating is based on output at end of 100 hours.)	
1-e	Actual slight differences in lamps may be discernible; perhaps wrong color lamp used; possibly lamp outside limits of color standards; or apparent color difference may be only difference in brightness between old and new lamp.	Replace lamps if objectionable. (If warranted, color temperature can be checked in laboratory to determine whether there is a difference, and how much.)
1-f	Mortality laws (Lamps of shorter life are balanced out by those of longer life to give rated average life.)	
1-g	New lamp may flicker.	Flicker should clear up after lamp is operated or turned on and off a few times.
1-h	May suddenly develop in any lamp in normal service.	Should clear up if turned off for a few seconds.
1-i	Mercury deposit.	Should evaporate as lamp is operated.
1-j	Globules of mercury on lower (cooler) part.	Rotate tube 180°. Mercury may evaporate by increased warmth, though it may condense out again on cool side.
1	sibly lamp at fault	Replace lamp. Investigate further if successive lamps blink or flicker in same lampholders.
1-l	Open circuit in electrodes, due to broken electrode, air leak, open weld, etc.	If open circuit is shown by test or inspection as in **3-e**, replace lamp.
1-m	Burned out electrode (might be caused by placing one end of lamp directly across 120 volts).	If open circuit is shown by test or inspection as in **3-e**, replace lamp.
1-n	Air leak in lamp. In test with test lamp (see **3-e**) leak is indicated by absence of fluorescent glow, though electrode lights up.	Replace lamp.
1-o	Lamp radiation "broadcasts" through radio receiver.	Locate aerial and radio at least 10 ft. from lamp; or shield aerial lead-in wire, provide good ground, and keep aerial proper out of lamp and line radiation range.
1-p	Dirt accumulation on 40-watt Rapid Start lamps may cause unreliable starting under high humidity conditions.	Cleaning lamps restores normal ease of starting.
1-q	Wrong lamp type used.	Replace with lamp type marked on ballast label.

FOR FLUORESCENT LAMPS

2. STARTERS

	POSSIBLE CAUSES*	MAINTENANCE
2-a	Wrong type of starter or defective starter, causing on-off blink or prolonged flashing at each start.	Replace with proper starter. Watch Dog (automatic cutout) starters overcome on-off blinking or prolonged flashing.
2-b	Ends of lamp are lighted while rest of lamp is not; starter failure.	Replace starter.
2-c	Starter at end of life.	Replace Starter.
2-d	Starter sluggish.	Replace Starter.
2-e	Starter not performing properly to pre-heat electrodes.	Replace Starter.

3. AUXILIARIES & FIXTURES

	POSSIBLE CAUSES*	MAINTENANCE
3-a	Ballast installed not supplying specified electrical values.	Replace with ETL approved ballast of correct rating for lamp size.
3-b	May occur near end of life on some lamps, but if early in life, indicates excessive starting or operating current.	Check for ballast off-rating or unusually high circuit voltage.
3-c	Remote possibility of open-circuited ballast.	Check ballast.
3-d	Wrong type of ballast used (e.g., AC type on DC power, wrong voltage rating, instant-start ballast in rapid-start fixture, etc.).	Replace ballast with proper type.
3-e	Burned-out lamp electrodes due to: – broken lampholders. – grounding of combination lampholder and starting socket, mounted on metal. – one strand of conductor touching grounded fixture. – improper wiring. – D-C operation without necessary additional resistance. – ground from some other cause.	To determine necessity for replacing lamp, examine electrodes by viewing end of bulb against pinhole of light. (Or test by connecting base pins **in series** with test lamp† on 120-v circuit. Fluorescent glow means intact electrodes, and active electrons.) †Correct Various Test for F. Lamp Size Lamps 60-w 14-w to 40-w. 25-w Small diameter or miniature. 200-w 90-w or 100-w
3-f	Slight transformer hum inherent in ballast equipment; varies in different ballasts. Objectionable amount may be due to improper installation or improper ballast design.	Tighten ballast bolts; where possible use 4 bolts instead of 2; tighten fixture louvers; glass side panels; wedge vibrating parts of fixture.
3-g	Short in ballast or capacitor.	Replace ballast or capacitor.
3-h	High ambient temperature inside fixture housing.	Refer to fixture manufacturer.
3-i	Prolonged blinking tends to heat ballast, and heating is aggravated under high ambient temperature inside fixture housing.	See "Blinking On and Off," under Behavior and correct the cause.
3-j	Overheated ballast.	See **3-g, 3-h, 3-i, 6-f.**

4. TEMPERATURE

	POSSIBLE CAUSES*	MAINTENANCE
4-a	Low temperature (starting difficulty may be experienced below 50°F).	Use ballast and/or starter designed for minimum expected temperature.
4-b	Low temperature operation. (Below 65° F light loss may be 2% or more per degree F.)	Change to enclosed fixture properly designed for expected temperature range; or change to jacketed outdoor type lamp if available.
4-c	Cold drafts or winds hitting tube.	Enclose or protect lamp.
4-d	Where heat is confined around lamp, light loss is 1% per degree F.	Better ventilation of fixture.

5. VOLTAGE

	POSSIBLE CAUSES*	MAINTENANCE
5-a	Too low or too high voltage.	Check voltage with range on ballast nameplate.
5-b	High voltage starting.	Check voltage.
5-c	Low circuit voltage.	Check voltage and correct if possible.
5-d	High circuit voltage.	Check voltage and correct if possible.

6. CIRCUIT

	POSSIBLE CAUSES*	MAINTENANCE
6-a	Loose circuit contact (likely at lampholder).	Lampholders should be rigidly mounted; lamp securely seated.
6-b	In new installation, may be wiring or ground fault.	Check circuit wiring.
6-c	Ballast improperly or incompletely connected.	Study ballast label instructions and check connections.
6-d	Possible open circuit.	Test lamp in another circuit, being sure of proper contact in lampholders. Check voltage from one lampholder to the other. (Use voltmeter or 220-v, 100-w test lamp. Only one connection at each holder should be alive; hence 4 ways to check 2 live ones.) If no voltage indication from lampholders, check circuit leads to holders. If still no voltage, check circuit connection.
6-e	D-C operation without using reversing switches.	Install reversing switches.
6-f	Short in wiring.	Correct wiring.
6-g	Line radiation and line feedback.	Apply line filter at lamp or fixture; sometimes possible to apply filters at power outlet or panel box.

7. OPERATION

	POSSIBLE CAUSES*	MAINTENANCE
7-a	Too many lamp starts.	Average life dependent on number of starts and hours of operation.
7-b	Dust or dirt on lamp, fixture, walls, or ceiling.	Clean.
7-c	May be due to reflector finish, wall finish, other nearby light, room decorations, etc.	Interchange lamps before assuming color difference.

* Service problems may arise from a combination of causes — not always from one single cause.

A decorative chime that strikes eight notes can also be adjusted to strike four notes. Low-voltage wires run to the front entrance and rear door.

Chimes have three connections. The center connection extends straight to one terminal to the transformer. End connections connect to the door button.

DOOR CHIMES BELLS AND BUZZERS

Most homes have melodious chimes to announce the arrival of a guest but you can also use bells and buzzers with the same system of wiring. And the new wireless chimes give you even greater flexibility!

The door chime—of which there are many different styles with different sounds—years ago replaced the old fashioned dry cell powered bell and buzzer combination used to announce a visitor. Surprisingly, some of the very old homes still have this 6-volt battery arrangement and if your home uses this system you can easily update to a chime system, using the same old wiring. All that is needed are the chimes and a new transformer.

The standard operating voltage of chimes is 16 volts. Note in the diagram that the chimes and the buttons are wired to the 16-volt secondary of the line transformer, and that the primary of the transformer is connected permanently to the AC 120-volt source. This is perfectly safe because it draws only a very small current.

Some chimes consist of open brass tubes that are struck by magnetically operated little hammers when the push-button is pressed while others consist of suspended metal strips that vibrate. The chimes peal once when the button is pressed and a second time when it is released.

TROUBLE SHOOTING

Because it is in use for short and infrequent periods, such a door signaling system lasts practically forever. When it does stop working, the trouble in 99 cases out of 100, is a corroded door button. The internal parts of some buttons are made of iron and they inevitably rust. Unscrew a suspected button from the wall and try short

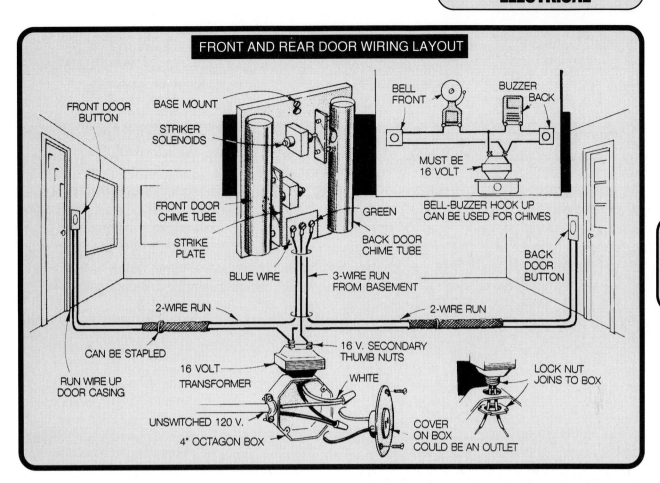

FRONT AND REAR DOOR WIRING LAYOUT

FRONT DOOR BUTTON

BASE MOUNT

STRIKER SOLENOIDS

FRONT DOOR CHIME TUBE

STRIKE PLATE

BLUE WIRE

GREEN

BACK DOOR CHIME TUBE

BELL FRONT

BUZZER BACK

MUST BE 16 VOLT

BELL-BUZZER HOOK UP CAN BE USED FOR CHIMES

BACK DOOR BUTTON

3-WIRE RUN FROM BASEMENT

2-WIRE RUN

2-WIRE RUN

CAN BE STAPLED

16 V. SECONDARY THUMB NUTS

RUN WIRE UP DOOR CASING

16 VOLT TRANSFORMER

WHITE

LOCK NUT JOINS TO BOX

UNSWITCHED 120 V.

4" OCTAGON BOX

COVER ON BOX COULD BE AN OUTLET

If your chimes do not work, check the connections to the transformer. Often these connections vibrate loose. Clean the wire and tighten.

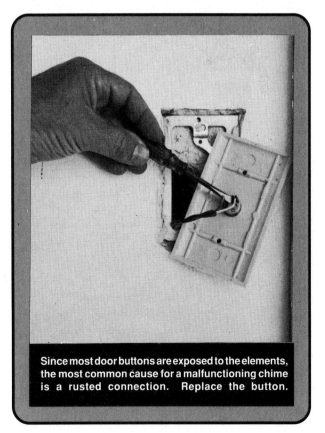

Since most door buttons are exposed to the elements, the most common cause for a malfunctioning chime is a rusted connection. Replace the button.

circuiting the terminals with a clean screwdriver blade; if the chimes come to life, buy a new button. Incidentally, you might as well buy one of the illuminated type. A tiny bulb under the button is connected to the button's terminals, thus connect- ing it to the transformer. Enough current flows through this complete circuit to light the bulb, but not enough to ring the chimes. When the button is pressed, the resistance of the lamp is shorted out by the button's contacts, and the chimes peal.

WIRELESS DOOR CHIME BY DIMANGO

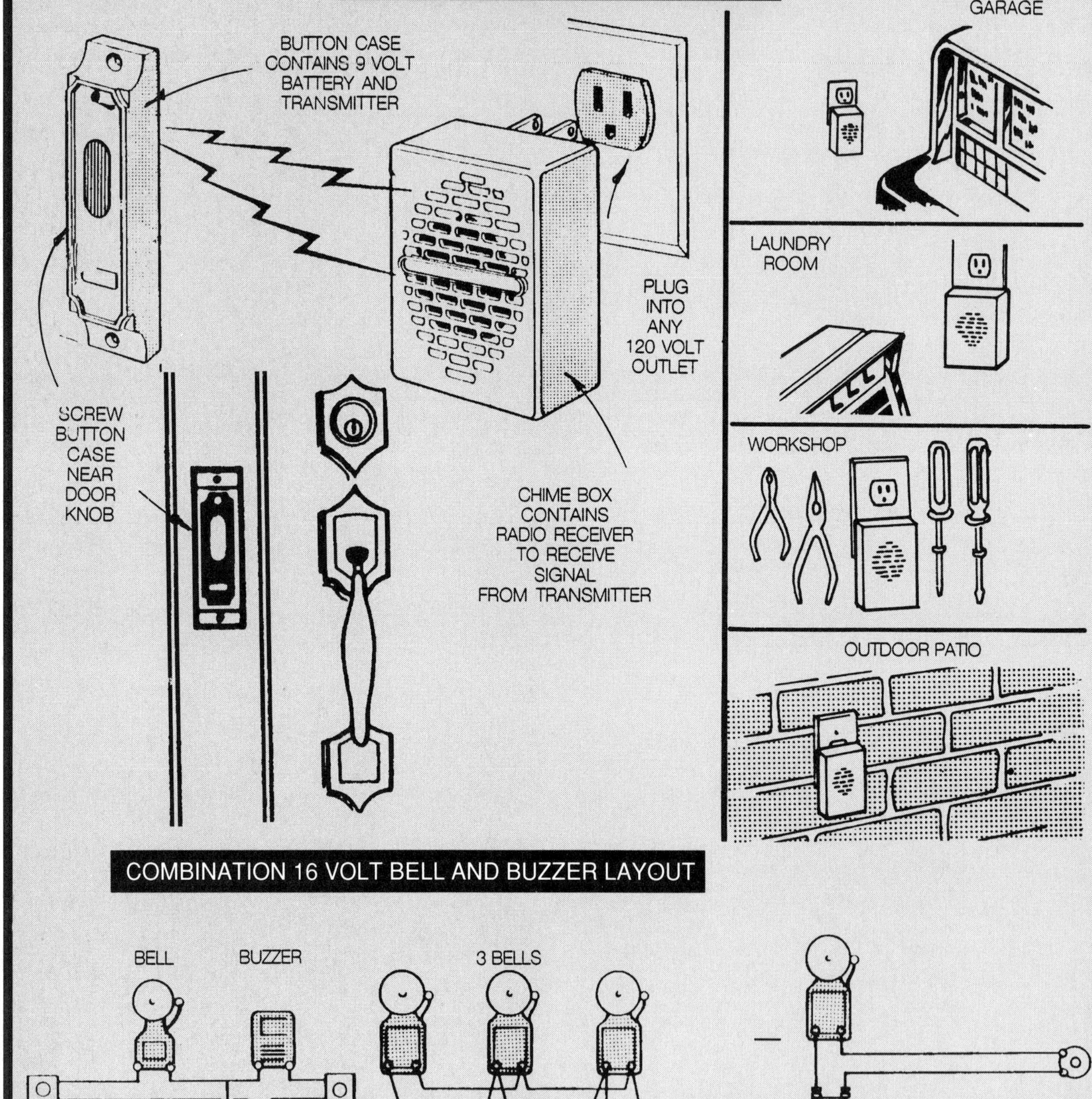

BUTTON CASE CONTAINS 9 VOLT BATTERY AND TRANSMITTER

GARAGE

PLUG INTO ANY 120 VOLT OUTLET

LAUNDRY ROOM

SCREW BUTTON CASE NEAR DOOR KNOB

CHIME BOX CONTAINS RADIO RECEIVER TO RECEIVE SIGNAL FROM TRANSMITTER

WORKSHOP

OUTDOOR PATIO

COMBINATION 16 VOLT BELL AND BUZZER LAYOUT

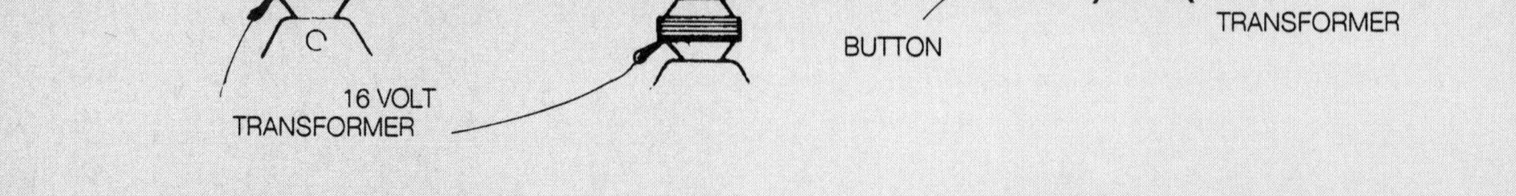

BELL   BUZZER

3 BELLS

BUTTON

BUTTON

TRANSFORMER

16 VOLT TRANSFORMER

CLEANING

If the chimes' box is mounted on a kitchen wall it is bound to accumulate grease from cooking vapors. It therefore should be inspected about every six months and cleaned if necessary. Don't be surprised if you find insect nests in the tubes.

BELLS AND BUZZERS

There are many different communication devices other than the chime, and for factory or garage use horn and gongs are usually installed using 120-volt wiring and no transformer. However, for offices and small shops a wide assortment of bells and buzzers are available, all operating on low voltage. And if you do not have nearby access to make the 120-volt connection the transformer requires, you can hook up a 6-volt dry cell battery.

THE WIRELESS DOOR CHIME

One of the new electronic innovations in door chimes is a chime that is triggered by a button that contains a miniature radio transmitter, as shown in the illustration. The case is slightly larger than a regular button also contains a 9.5 volt battery to power the transmitter, in addition to the button. It is screwed to the side of an entrance door in much the same manner as the regular door chime button is positioned and the chime box contains a miniature radio receiver which can be plugged into any electrical wall outlet in the home.

When someone pushes the button button on the outside wall near the door, a very audible and pleasant sound will come from the chime box! A really great way to install a door chime without resorting to running wires through the wall and ceiling to connect to the 16-volt transformers most chimes require. The battery will easily last one year before replacement is required.

ADD A REMOTE CHIME TO YOUR PRESENT 16-VOLT SYSTEM

The door chime system of most homes usually consists of a wiring arrangement for a side door and the entrance door. When the button is pushed, a different sound is emitted to indicate if the bell on the side or front door was pushed.

Of course, for you to hear the chime you must be in close audible range. But what if you are in the basement, or the bedroom, or even the garage and out of range? How do you know if someone is at the door? You don't—not unless you adapt your present system so when the button is pushed your regular chime operates and simultaneously sends a radio signal to a remote chime box which contains a receiver. The miniature transmitter is wired into the existing chime system and the receiver is plugged into an 120-volt electrical outlet, which can be in the bedroom, workshop, or wherever you are! One of the wonders of miniaturizations and electronics!

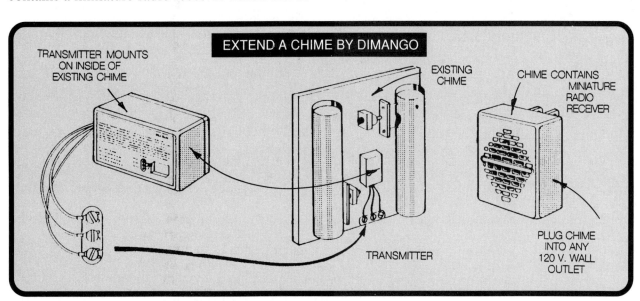

EXTEND A CHIME BY DIMANGO

TRANSMITTER MOUNTS ON INSIDE OF EXISTING CHIME

EXISTING CHIME

CHIME CONTAINS MINIATURE RADIO RECEIVER

TRANSMITTER

PLUG CHIME INTO ANY 120 V. WALL OUTLET

Strip fluorescent lights behind a valance that also contains a drapery rod produces this startling effect, bouncing light off the beamed ceiling. Special ballasts must be used to connect fluorescent fixtures to a dimmer switch.

DRAMATIC LIGHTING

Dimmer switches and hi-low toggle switches make it possible to vary the intensity of your lights to reflect a mood.

To create a dramatic effect in a room, in addition to using unusual shaped fixtures, ceiling and wall arrangements of track lighting to illuminate a specific object or setting, the dimmer switch has made it possible to establish a mood by controlling the amount of regular overhead or lamp lighting. Economical and very easy to install as a replacement in a regular single pole switch box, many home have three or four such switches in various rooms.

Most dimmers made for home use have an on-off switch that is combined with the actual brightness control. In some the AC to the lamp is off when the knob is turned counter-clockwise (to the left) until it clicks. It is on when the knob is twisted slightly the other way. In other models, the switch is push operated. With either type, turning the knob gives any degree of brightness from full to a scarcely noticeable red glow and then to nothing. Most dimmers suitable for home use are rated at 600 watts but commercial units with a 2,000-watt limit are also available. All sorts of dramatic and useful lighting effects with a dimmer switch are possible. For example:

In a dining room, soft light to resemble that of candles, with none of the latters' fire danger. A slightly bright level if the tablecloth is dark, or a lower level if white. Or full brightness if the affair is informal, the guests dressed casually and the overall atmosphere cheerful.

For TV viewing, only enough room illumination to enable you to find your way in and out without stumbling over furniture.

For all-night light in a baby's room, a hallway, a bathroom, etc. Similarly for security purposes, half-bright lights on a porch, over a garage and in a basement, etc.

Real professional effects for amateur theatricals.

Dramatic lighting of works of art such as paintings, sculptures and photographs. Try bright spotlights on these, with all other room lights turned about half-way down.

Various types of dimmers are shown in the accompanying illustrations. The most popular model by far is the one that replaces any standard on-off toggle switch in a wall box. The only tool you need for the job is a screwdriver. After re-

Spectacular lighting ideas can also be applied in the kitchen. Here three low voltage halogen lamps in ultra small ceiling fixtures accent the counter.

INSTALLING A DIMMER SWITCH

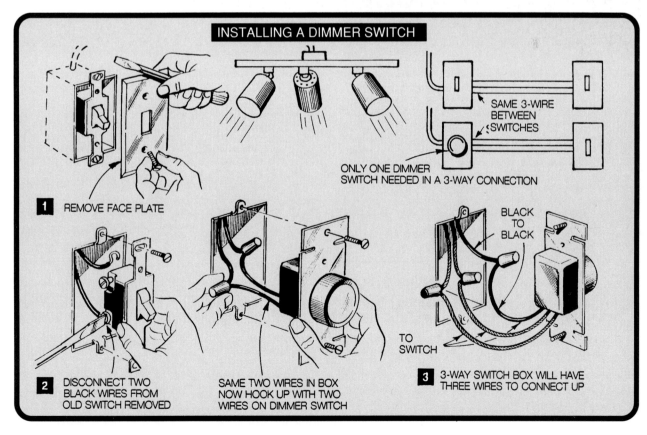

1 REMOVE FACE PLATE

SAME 3-WIRE BETWEEN SWITCHES

ONLY ONE DIMMER SWITCH NEEDED IN A 3-WAY CONNECTION

2 DISCONNECT TWO BLACK WIRES FROM OLD SWITCH REMOVED

SAME TWO WIRES IN BOX NOW HOOK UP WITH TWO WIRES ON DIMMER SWITCH

BLACK TO BLACK

TO SWITCH

3 3-WAY SWITCH BOX WILL HAVE THREE WIRES TO CONNECT UP

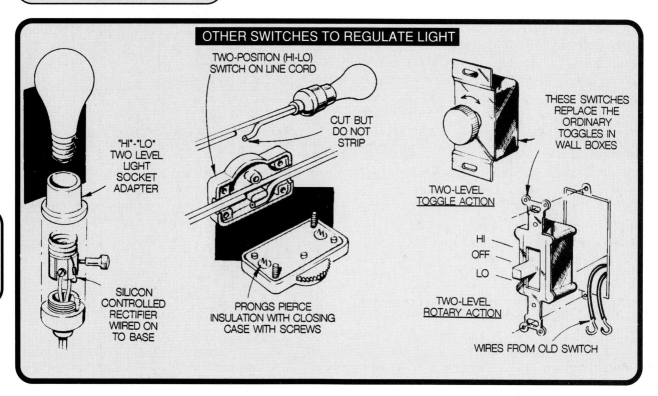

OTHER SWITCHES TO REGULATE LIGHT

"HI"-"LO" TWO LEVEL LIGHT SOCKET ADAPTER

SILICON CONTROLLED RECTIFIER WIIRED ON TO BASE

TWO-POSITION (HI-LO) SWITCH ON LINE CORD

CUT BUT DO NOT STRIP

PRONGS PIERCE INSULATION WITH CLOSING CASE WITH SCREWS

THESE SWITCHES REPLACE THE ORDINARY TOGGLES IN WALL BOXES

TWO-LEVEL TOGGLE ACTION

HI
OFF
LO

TWO-LEVEL ROTARY ACTION

WIRES FROM OLD SWITCH

moving the fuse or opening the breaker on the circuit, you can make the replacement in a few minutes.

It is important at this point to mention that the dimmers obtainable in hardware and electrical stores are almost without exception suitable only for incandescent bulbs, the ordinary screw-in type. Fluorescent lamps are not nearly so adaptable. In fact, conversion is not really practical with existing fixtures because it requires a different "ballast" (the transformer-like part inside the body of the reflector), as well as rewiring. However, full flexibility of control is available in newer styles of fluorescents specifically designed for dimming.

In many homes a wall switch controls only the ceiling lights or a single wall outlet. For control of individual lamps, the simplest plan is to wire a small dimmer into the line cord; this does not involve a change of any kind in the lamp itself. You can buy dimmer-adapters and replacement sockets with the dimmer built in, as well as a handy portable remote-control model that requires no work at all; it just plugs in.

The small dimmers for insertion into lamp cord are usually rated at 200 watts and have a rotary-action switch. It might feel slightly warm to the touch, this is normal.

For some purposes continuous adjustment of illumination is not needed. For example, a simple high-low control is often adequate for a basement or bathroom light. Dimmers of this type look exactly like switches and have three settings: off, high and low.

Perhaps you have the notion that house-lamp dimmers are like the dashboard dimmers of cars. In purpose, yes; in construction no. The latter are rheostats. These are variable resistors which reduce the lights by wasting some of the battery current to them in the form of heat. AC dimmers use solid-state devices called "thyristors." In effect, these are rectifiers that keep some of the AC back, without wasting it, so a bulb doesn't shine as brightly as it would with all of the current.

Speed controls, which are incorporated in many hand power tools such as drills and saber saws, are similar to light dimmers. However, they work only with small fractional horsepower motors of the series type, which can be recognized by the presence of two carbon brushes that make sparking contact with a rotating spool-line section of the shaft, the commutator.

One of the less-recognized features of dimmers is the great increase in the life of bulbs that they make possible. Also, since they burn at lower temperatures than normal for considerable periods, inside blackening of the glass is reduced.

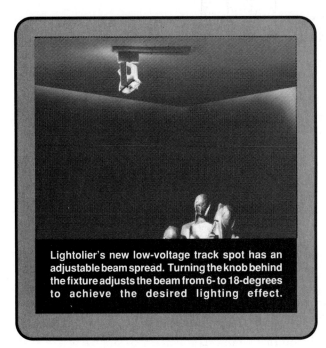

Lightolier's new low-voltage track spot has an adjustable beam spread. Turning the knob behind the fixture adjusts the beam from 6- to 18-degrees to achieve the desired lighting effect.

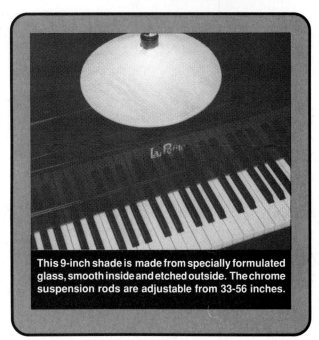

This 9-inch shade is made from specially formulated glass, smooth inside and etched outside. The chrome suspension rods are adjustable from 33-56 inches.

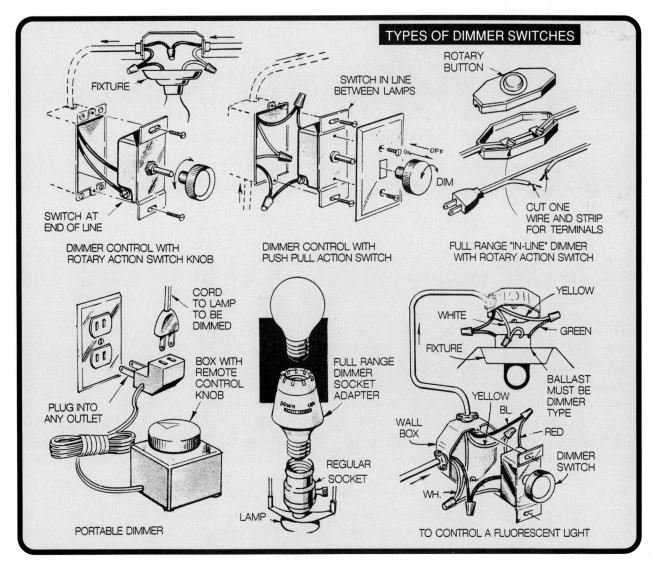

TYPES OF DIMMER SWITCHES

FIXTURE

SWITCH AT END OF LINE

DIMMER CONTROL WITH ROTARY ACTION SWITCH KNOB

SWITCH IN LINE BETWEEN LAMPS

ON OFF
DIM

DIMMER CONTROL WITH PUSH PULL ACTION SWITCH

ROTARY BUTTON

CUT ONE WIRE AND STRIP FOR TERMINALS

FULL RANGE "IN-LINE" DIMMER WITH ROTARY ACTION SWITCH

CORD TO LAMP TO BE DIMMED

BOX WITH REMOTE CONTROL KNOB

PLUG INTO ANY OUTLET

PORTABLE DIMMER

FULL RANGE DIMMER SOCKET ADAPTER

DOWN UP

REGULAR SOCKET

LAMP

YELLOW

WHITE

GREEN

FIXTURE

YELLOW

BL.

WALL BOX

BALLAST MUST BE DIMMER TYPE

RED

DIMMER SWITCH

WH.

TO CONTROL A FLUORESCENT LIGHT

Here is a low voltage lighting arrangement consisting primarily of many individual floodlights on stakes trained upwards on the side of the home. Some fixtures have a 20-watt halogen bulb for intense light output. This group is timer controlled.

LANDSCAPE LIGHTING IDEAS

Lighting your yard is usually for the reasons of security and safety but with the popular low-voltage systems you can also make it beautiful.

EXCITING NEW DIMENSIONS can be added to family living by lighting the areas surrounding the home to enhance their intrinsic charm, beauty and utility at night. Extending imaginative patterns of indoor illumination to outdoor areas—gardens, patios, pools, work and play spots—is not only consistent with good, overall home planning but opens up whole new vistas for more family enjoyment and safety.

Well-planned residential outdoor lighting creates a total home environment combining maximum esthetic appeal with efficiency. It makes the home and its surrounding grounds complementary and endows the entire living area with a distinctive aura of unity and completeness in all seasons. When light is brought outdoors, it reveals the beauty of gardens, trees and foliage. It expands the hospitality and comfort of patios and porches and stretches the hours for outdoor recreation or work. Many homes have underground conduit (or underground cable where the code permits) as an

additional circuit delivering 120 volts. Such a system is permanent and if you change your planting you run the chance of having to relocate the conduit. However, more and more homeowners are using low voltage 12-volt systems which plug into an outdoor receptacle. No need to bury the wire in the ground either; you can run it over the surface where it will be hardly noticed, especially in areas with dense planting. Most low voltage outdoor lighting systems also include a timer to allow homeowners to automatically turn on the lights. Others have a built in computer and a photoelectric cell which automatically turns the lights on at dusk and off at dawn. Remote control switches are also available to control the lights from inside the home. The remote control is battery powered and uses FM frequencies to control the lights from a distance of up to 75 feet.

The accompanying text and illustrations show how to capture the mystery and subtle qualities of night lighting—how to light ground contours and focal points—how to create silhouetted forms and shadow patterns—how to use colored light—and many other ways to make any home more attractive, safer and just plain fun to live in. But perhaps the biggest plug for low-voltage lighting is that you can do-it-yourself and rearrange the positioning of the various lights for maximum effectiveness. Many kits are available for any size yard.

MODELING

Depth and three-dimensional character can be given to exterior objects at night by lighting them from several directions. A large tree, for example, can be modeled by casting light upon it from one or more directions, thereby emphasizing various aspects of its form. More light from one side than the other accentuates the effect. A smaller tree can be lighted from two sides with a spotlight from one side and a floodlight 90° away. The space or distance between the light source & what is to be lighted is extremely important in determining both the area that it lights and the light level. Light from a distance is often much more effective but is not always possible. Light sources placed too close to objects of medium to high reflectivity can create excessive brightness which spoils the effect.

HIGHLIGHTING

Highlighting usually refers to special lighting for patios and other outdoor living areas or for small flower beds that require lighting emphasis. Lighting equipment can be mounted high in trees and aimed down to light a garden area, or mushroom-type fixtures can be spiked in the ground to emphasize certain parts of a garden.

SHADOW PATTERNS

Shadows can be used to create broken or solid patterns and to introduce the excitement of movement from tree branches or foliage. The object which casts the shadow-house, plant, ornament or other-doesn't have to be visible. The elongated shadow of a group of poplars or a row of hollyhocks, for example, can convey the suggestion of another area, with imagination creating the remainder of a visual impression for the viewer. Spotlights create more clearly defined patterns than do floodlights. If either a spot or floodlight is placed very close to the object, a fuzzy shadow pattern will result. This may not be desirable when lighting a single object, but a shadow pattern cast by a solid mass is best if it is fuzzy rather than well defined.

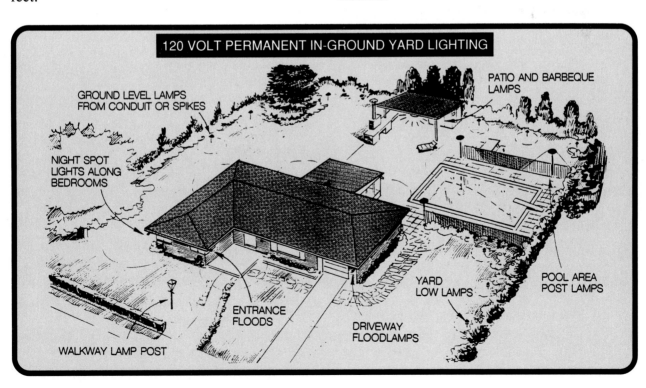

120 VOLT PERMANENT IN-GROUND YARD LIGHTING

GROUND LEVEL LAMPS FROM CONDUIT OR SPIKES

PATIO AND BARBEQUE LAMPS

NIGHT SPOT LIGHTS ALONG BEDROOMS

WALKWAY LAMP POST

ENTRANCE FLOODS

DRIVEWAY FLOODLAMPS

YARD LOW LAMPS

POOL AREA POST LAMPS

SILHOUETTING

Exterior objects having interesting line and form are frequently best lighted so they are seen in silhouette, either as a dark object against a lighted background or a luminous material against darkness. The first method is to light wall, fence or shrubbery *behind* the object with very little light on the front. Silhouetting objects against darkness is achieved by shining light through translucent materials such as certain types of leaves and other foliage.

GRAZING LIGHT

Grazing light can be used to great advantage in emphasizing the textural qualities of tree bark, hedges, masonry, fences and many other outdoor objects. Light sources should be aimed parallel to the surface of objects (four to ten inches out from the surface) since "head on" lighting flattens the appearance of the material and minimizes the desired lighting effect.

TINTED LIGHT

Tinted light is used primarily for emphasis — to bring out the color in flowers, shrubbery and special objects. Generally, light of the same color as the object to be lighted, is a good choice for heightening its color. White flowers highly-saturated colored flowers or gardens with mixed colors look most natural under white light. Low-wattage incandescent lamps being more yellow in tone, tend to deaden the color of grass and foliage. Better foliage color results from using lamps of higher wattage, cool white or daylight fluorescent tubes or with sky blue bulbs.

All colored fluorescent lamps have saturated colors and will cause distortion of the actual colors in nature. Fascinating treatment can be given to objects by mixing red, blue and green light — the objects are seen in white light but surrounding shadows are seen with tints of color.

WIRING

Outdoor lighting equipment can be installed on building structures or anywhere in the yard and garden. Equipment and wiring may either be permanently installed or temporary. All equipment and wiring should be weatherproof. Permanent wiring usually should be run underground. Underground wiring can be enclosed in metal pipe or Type UF cable may be used. Sand or light gravel around the wire will help water drainage, and a board over the wire will protect it from picks and shovels. UF cable must be at least 18 inches below the ground when it is buried directly. Conduit or

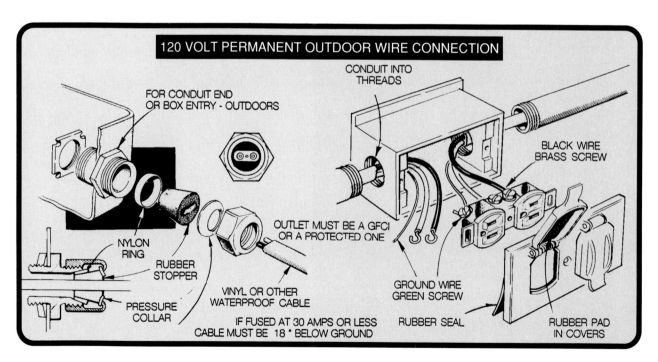

120 VOLT PERMANENT OUTDOOR WIRE CONNECTION

CONDUIT INTO THREADS

FOR CONDUIT END OR BOX ENTRY - OUTDOORS

BLACK WIRE BRASS SCREW

NYLON RING

RUBBER STOPPER

OUTLET MUST BE A GFCI OR A PROTECTED ONE

VINYL OR OTHER WATERPROOF CABLE

GROUND WIRE GREEN SCREW

PRESSURE COLLAR

IF FUSED AT 30 AMPS OR LESS CABLE MUST BE 18" BELOW GROUND

RUBBER SEAL

RUBBER PAD IN COVERS

wire can be run to various areas of the garden to convenience outlets or to permanently installed equipment.

All portable cords and outlets, if used should be grounded. Most portable lighting equipment is supplied with six-foot or longer weatherproof cords. Additional portable cord is available in various lengths. You can get cords designed specifically for outdoor use with suitably molded rubber plugs and sockets. Some lighting equipment also has built-in outlets into which additional units may be connected.

LAMPS

The most useful bulb types are the following:

1. **A-line**. A typical household bulb can be used out of doors mainly in mushroom-type equipment, path-light equipment, lanterns and wall-mounted brackets. The 15- and 25-watt lamps can be used without protection from water. Higher wattages need shielding from weather.

2. **Reflector lamps.** Popular, self-contained spot and flood-lamps, these light sources need protection from weather, too. Available in the following: 30, 50, 75, and 150-watt sizes. Higher wattages are available but are not normally used in landscape lighting. The 75- and 150-watt reflector lamps are available in both spot and flood-light distribution. The 30 and 50-watt lamps are available only in a medium flood distribution.

3. **PAR lamps.** Molded out of heavy heat-resistant glass, PAR lamps are rugged. They are unaffected by rain or snow but must be installed in fixtures having a weather-tight seal at the socket. The 75 watt PAR and the 150-watt PAR are available in both the spot and floodlight distribution. Higher wattages are available for longer throws and where a well-controlled high intensity beam of light is needed.

4. **Quartzline lamps,** available in wattages from 250 watts to 1500 watts, can be used for general lighting such as in sports areas. Their advantages are high efficiency, long life, excellent lumen

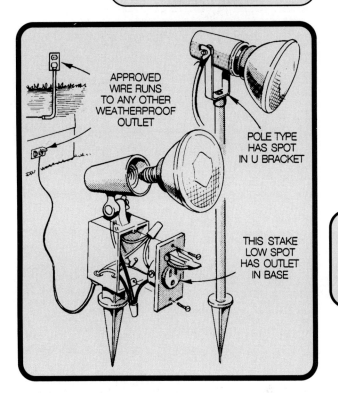

LIGHT BULB COLORS	RELATIVE LIGHT OUTPUT	WHAT THEY WILL DO
White	100%	Good on reds, oranges, yellows. Will gray blues.
Blue-White	40% Sky Blue 39%°	Emphasizes reds, pinks, greens, flesh tones.
Pink	75% Dawn Pink 52%°	Excellent on red foliage—flattering to people but not to green foliage.
Green	17%°	Will exaggerate greens but kill reds and pinks.
Blue	5%°	Will exaggerate blue tones.
Yellow Amber	77%° 57%°	Good on yellow, orange, brown foilage.
Red	7%°	Will exaggerate red tones.

°(100-watt PAR lamp)

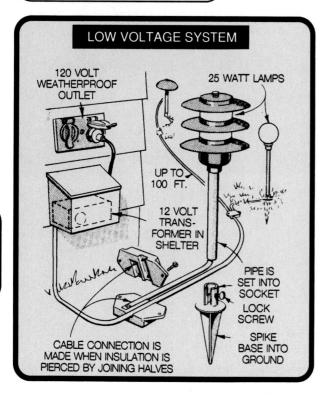

LOW VOLTAGE SYSTEM

120 VOLT WEATHERPROOF OUTLET

25 WATT LAMPS

UP TO 100 FT.

12 VOLT TRANS-FORMER IN SHELTER

PIPE IS SET INTO SOCKET

LOCK SCREW

SPIKE BASE INTO GROUND

CABLE CONNECTION IS MADE WHEN INSULATION IS PIERCED BY JOINING HALVES

Weatherproof controlled; come in various wattage capacities ranging from 36- to 160-watts. Add the total wattage of the bulbs you use to determine the size controller you need. This Toro unit also has a photoelectric cell and timer.

maintenance and good lighting control in fixtures specifically designed for them.

5. **Colored lamps.** A wide array of colors are available in A-line bulbs, PAR and reflector lamps. A-line or ordinary household bulbs come in Dawn Pink in 40, 60, 75 100, and 150 watts and Sky Blue in 60, 75, 100, and 150 watts. Seven colors are available in the 75-and 150-watt reflector lamps and in the 100-watt PAR lamp. Two of the colors are tints, the pink and blue-white. Two colors, the yellow and the amber, are of medium intensity. The red, blue, and green are strong colors which are normally recommended for holiday decorating or unusual specialty effects.

6. **Fluorescent lamps.** Fluorescent lamps can be used in weatherproof fixtures where lines of light are desired. Equipment is available in sizes ranging from 15 watts to 40 watts. For outdoor lighting, use cool white, daylight, blue or deep blue.

7. **Christmas strings.** The outdoor-type Christmas bulbs can be used for outdoor lighting without protection. Normally, the clear and white lamps are the only ones used for garden lighting but color

bulbs can be used for a party effect. Twinkle lights would be annoying and are restricted in their use.

8. **Low-voltage lamps.** The demand for low-voltage lamps for outdoor lighting is growing, because of the low cost when compared to a 120-volt system, the ease of installation, plus the flexibility of the lighting arrangement. The most commonly used low-voltage lamp is the 12-volt lamp, although higher wattage bulbs are available. The 40-watt halogen lamp provides the most light.

OUTDOOR LIGHTING EQUIPMENT

A wide range of outdoor lighting equipment is readily available. Many factors related to mechanical design as well as electrical features are important but lighting effects desired are primary considerations in equipment selection. Both day and nighttime appearance of fixtures should be carefully checked.

Durability is a prime concern in picking outdoor lighting equipment and the cost of fixtures is usually directly proportional to durability. Equipment must be able to stand up under a great

Designed for outlining the perimeter of a driveway, this post light is available in either 11- or 33-inch height. The unit contains a 12-watt bulb.

These walk lights are mounted on stakes about 14 inches high and positioned at about six-foot intervals. Connecting wire runs along the walk edge.

amount of abuse throughout the year— not only against weather but also the destructiveness of lawn mowers, snow blowers, dogs, children— even adults. Fixture design and color normally should blend in with the landscape and should be as inconspicuous as possible, day or night. Most

garden lighting equipment is finished in black or green or matte aluminum. Green blends with most types of foliage and is a very practical color when shielded by garden plantings. Black or dark green equipment mounted adjacent to a tree trunk is inconspicuous in most cases.

Now even decks can have a lighting system. This 7-watt fixture comes with a redwood base and is attached underneath the railing or step overhang.

Accent lighting on deck steps is especially important for safety. The connecting wires are stapled to the underside of the rails.

Exterior lights will discourage an intruder, but also install automatic timers that turn on interior lights when you are away to give the impression that someone is home.

LIGHTING FOR SECURITY & SAFETY

The increased rate of home burglaries triggered the growth of alarm systems. However, exterior lighting is still the best way to deter crime.

AROUND the front entrances, paths and walks, steps, garages and recreational areas of private homes and apartments, lighting installed for convenience and accident prevention provides additional benefits by deterring prowlers and vandals.

An interesting aspect of protective lighting systems is that intruders rarely seem challenged to outwit them. Perhaps it is the passive quality of light which quells the spirit of malicious aggression, or perhaps the rationale is more simply put: where there is light, someone cares, someone is likely to be watching. Law enforcement officials have frequently pointed out that lighting on properties surrounding occupied buildings creates points of visual interest giving occupants a reason to look out. Thus they become watchers, and are feared by the intruder.

In the scheme of community affairs, light-ing is not only beneficial as a deterrent to aggression, but also has value in that a deterred crime incurs no cost for police action and no cost for prosecution. So the crime-deterrent capability of lighting has economic value and ample justification for community-wide "Light the Night" campaigns.

Following are some typical recommendations and brief comments about several universal factors that apply for selecting and using lighting equipment in typical residential areas.

ENTRANCEWAYS

Light Sources—Incandescent lamps from 25-watt decorative types to 150-watt PAR lamps are widely used sources.

Types of Equipment—Usually preferred are wall-mounted brackets in pairs, one on each

The traditional post lantern light is always popular. This one uses a powerful mercury lamp that floors the ground with light. Some post lanterns have a built-in outlet for operating electric tools.

This striking display of plants at the entrance of a house is actually a ground-to-ceiling glass enclosure, accessible from inside the house through louvered door shown at the left of main door.

side of the door. Effective mounting location is 5 1/2 feet above standing level. A single fixture, at the same height, is best located on the lock side of the door; or is also effective centered above the door. Good alternatives also are recessed units in the ceiling or roof overhang. Those fixtures mounted higher above the standing level require higher-wattage lamps; at least 60-watt lamps for side brackets and 75- or 100-watt lamps in above-the-door fixtures.

The luminous quality of fixtures is a factor often overlooked. They can be architecturally compatible for daytime viewing but offensively bright and glaring at night; shielding the light source is essential. Frosted or opal diffusing glass is preferred: clear glass is tolerable only when low-wattage lamps are used and the ambient light level is fairly high.

In ceilings of external entrance-way structures or in roof overhangs, recessed or surface mounted units can be installed. Although overhead units in most cases are out of the direct line of sight on approach, they require light source shielding with some sort of diffusing material; their brightness can be annoying. Recessed fixtures,

often unobtrusive, give high levels of light for the horizontal surfaces underfoot as well as in the vertical plane, that is, on callers' faces.

The best location for a single fixture is centered close to the entrance door. Larger areas can, of course, be covered with multiple fixtures. Square fixtures are usually equipped with one 100-watt lamp, whereas some rectangular types with two lamp sockets offer better end results. In either case, shielding with diffusing material is necessary. Installations that incorporate both decorative wall-mounted fixtures and recessed functional lighting equipment often work best. The visible fixture's brightness and styling are for appearance, and the recessed equipment principally for the light level necessary for seeing and safety.

STEPS, PATHS AND WALKS

Light Sources—Applicable generally are 25-watt to 150-watt incandescent lamps, and mercury lamps in the 50-watt to 75-watt range. The mercury lamps are more efficient, and they have longer life to sustain safety and protection for

Using standard incandescent lamps in strategically located fixtures, this house becomes an attractive picture each evening. The post lantern takes a 100-watt lamp, other fixtures use 75-watt lamps.

greatly prolonged periods between burnouts.

Types of Equipment—There are several types of equipment for mounting below eye level, to light ground areas: ground-spike units and units with louver or lens plate light distribution control for installation in walls adjacent to paths or walks. Overhead units are available for tree or pole mountings. And there are post-top and wall-mounting lanterns designed for both decorative style and functional lighting.

Ground-lighting units installed below eye level normally light, at best, no more than an eight-foot diameter area, coverage being influenced by the size and shape of the reflector. Complete shielding of below-eye-level light sources is obviously necessary. When used alongside stairs, particular attention should be given to shielding because of possible low viewing angles. Spacings are generally considered effective if the semi-dark interspaces between pools of light are not greater than the breadth of the light pools. Louvered or lens plate type equipment designed for installation in walls adjoining paths are effective if mounted 16 and 24 inches above ground and not more than eight feet apart; they are also effective if recessed

in stair risers.

Post lanterns are effective lighting tools provided their design has not rendered them glaringly bright or restrictive in light distribution toward ground levels. Frosted glass diffusion, at least, is usually adequate, heavier diffusion materials are better. Prismatic lens control is best. It is excellent as a light distribution feature. A light distributing reflector built in above the lamp adds to effectiveness, depending on the type of reflector. For wall-mounting units that serve functions similar to post lanterns, the same features apply.

The post lantern is an excellent solution to the distribution of light on ground areas, and the visible lamp is of low-wattage with agreeable brightness. Another variation has a second lamp in the cap above the glass panels. Equipment of this sort is effective along paths and drives when spaced not more than 25 feet apart.

Overhead floodlighting from poles 10 to 20 feet high offers the advantage of widespread light distribution or sharp spot beam control. Floodlighting lamps are effective in shields nine inches or more deep to hide the visible brightness of lamps. Low-voltage bulbs are another choice;

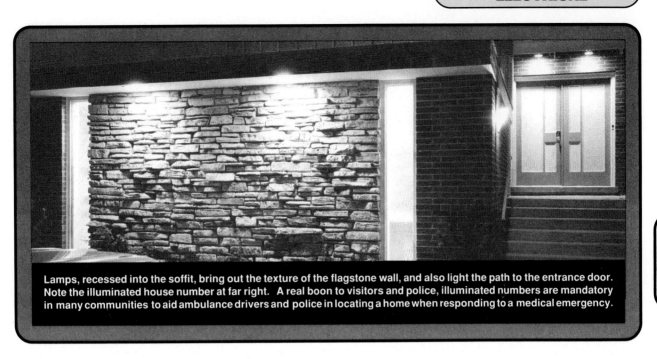

Lamps, recessed into the soffit, bring out the texture of the flagstone wall, and also light the path to the entrance door. Note the illuminated house number at far right. A real boon to visitors and police, illuminated numbers are mandatory in many communities to aid ambulance drivers and police in locating a home when responding to a medical emergency.

they have built-in shielding that minimizes spill-over of light.

Two valuable accessories for security lighting systems are the photo-electric and clock-timer controls, but another popular security product is the Infrared Motion Detector (IMD) which is connected to turn on lights when any motion is detected in the monitoring area. They measure the heat emitted from the body. As an example, if a dog jumps in front of an IMD the lights will not turn on because the detector is programmed only to react to the body heat of humans. They sense motion up to 75 feet away and can cover large areas by tilting the detector. The trick is to install them as high off the ground as possible—under the roof soffit or even in a tree—for broader coverage. Most homeowners install them near the entrance door to turn lights on when a visitor approaches. Many manufacturers produce similar products and all are readily available in home centers and electrical supply outlets. They are very affordable and also very easy to hook up to an existing flood light.

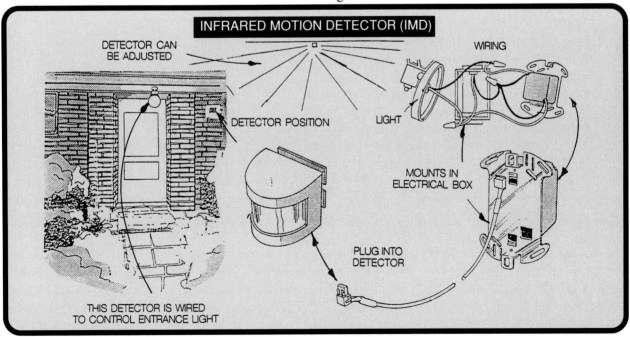

INFRARED MOTION DETECTOR (IMD)

DETECTOR CAN BE ADJUSTED

DETECTOR POSITION

WIRING

LIGHT

MOUNTS IN ELECTRICAL BOX

PLUG INTO DETECTOR

THIS DETECTOR IS WIRED TO CONTROL ENTRANCE LIGHT

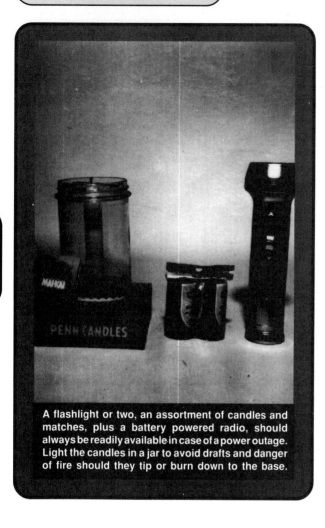

A flashlight or two, an assortment of candles and matches, plus a battery powered radio, should always be readily available in case of a power outage. Light the candles in a jar to avoid drafts and danger of fire should they tip or burn down to the base.

WHAT TO DO BEFORE A STORM

Our tremendous power requirements that cause generator breakdowns, plus electrical and wind storms, can cause power failure. So be prepared!

YOU CAN'T REALLY APPRECIATE how thoroughly electrified our life is until you encounter a "blackout", which is a 100 percent loss of power. Not just a "brownout", which is only a reduction of voltage. However, you might be able to minimize the effects of such occurrences if you heed some of the suggestions given to its customers by the Florida Power and Light Company.

PRELIMINARY CHECKLIST

Know in advance where your service entrance equipment is located so that you can check quickly and safely for a blown fuse or tripped circuit breaker.

Keep an adequate supply of fuses accessible; make certain they are of the proper type and size.

Always have a workable flashlight in your home.

A battery-powered radio can be a valuable asset during a power interruption. Keep yours in working order.

If for some reason your lights go out, check lights and appliances in other rooms and see if your neighbors have power. If you still have power elsewhere in your house, or if your neighbors' lights are burning, chances are you have blown a fuse or tripped a circuit breaker—a warning that your wiring is overloaded or a short has occurred.

TO REPLACE A FUSE

1. If your service entry box is of the fuse type, pull fuse blocks marked Main at service entrance to cut off power while you replace burned fuse; 2. Disconnect the lamp or appliance that you believe caused the fuse to blow; 3. Be sure your

hands are dry, and stand on a dry surface when removing or replacing a fuse; 4. Carefully examine the blown fuse. Usually the mica window is blackened or a gap in the element can be seen; 5. When removing or inserting a new fuse, grasp just the rim between thumb and forefinger; 6. Replace the blown fuse with a new one of proper size; 7. Replace Main fuse blocks for restoration of power.

A TRIPPED CIRCUIT BREAKER

Results from the same cause as a blown fuse. Take the same precautionary measures as prescribed for fuses and carefully follow instructions on the panel to reset the circuit breaker. IMPORTANT. During any power interruption—regardless of the nature or duration—immediately turn off major electric equipment: air conditioners, washers, dryers, television sets, computers, heavy-duty motors. Otherwise, when the electricity comes back, the sudden surge caused by these load demands could blow fuses or trip breakers; in the event a broad area is affected by the outage, the momentary surge could complicate and delay power restoration efforts.

If your neighbors are without power, there has probably been a minor equipment problem. Call your utility company and steps will be taken immediately to determine the source of trouble and restore your service.

POWER INTERRUPTIONS

Brief interruptions of a more widespread nature may occur for such reasons as: equipment malfunction, damage to facilities caused by falling trees, auto accidents, electrical storms; fires in commercial or residential areas which make it necessary on occasion to shut off power as a safety measure.

Widespread outages are immediately "reported" by automatic monitoring equipment. Therefore, it is not necessary in these instances to report loss of service or to seek progress reports via telephone. A battery-powered radio will keep you informed on power restoration efforts. If still without power after all service restoration is announced, you should then report the trouble to your utility.

WIDESPREAD INTERRUPTIONS

During severe storms, electric service may be interrupted as the result of damage, or it may be shut off as a safety precaution. In these circumstances, the outages could be widespread and of extended duration. Inconvenience can be minimized by observing certain precautions as the storm approaches.

CONSERVE REFRIGERATION

Open your refrigerator or freezer only when absolutely necessary and close quickly. Both will stay cold much longer if these precautions are taken. Well-constructed and insulated home freezers, filled with food, will maintain food-preserving temperatures up to 48 hours.

If you need emergency refrigeration, use regular ice in ordinary refrigerators and in the refrigerator section of your combination refrigerator-freezer. Use dry ice only in frozen food cabinets and in the frozen food compartments of combination refrigerator-freezers.

Provide for water. Your water supply may fail. Sterilize your bathtub and other containers by scrubbing thoroughly; then saturate a cloth or sponge with ordinary bleach and swab the container. Let it dry. Then fill with water. Boil water before drinking. These reserves can also be used to operate toilets by partially filling the tank.

Check emergency cooking facilities. Be sure adequate fuel is on hand. Provide an ample supply of canned foods and milk.

Plan for temporary lighting. Check candles, lamps and flashlight batteries and bulbs.

Use telephone for emergencies only. If damage is widespread, your utility company has systematic plans for complete service restoration. Call the company only to report any hazardous conditions you might observe, such as live electric wires. Overloaded switchboards may prevent completion of their essential calls. Report individual trouble if it still exists only after service is back on in your neighborhood.

ELECTRICAL

LAMP REPAIR

Often the socket of a table lamp breaks because of constant switching on and off, or the spring terminal in the socket is corroded and does not make full contact with the bulb. Sometimes you can pull the spring up so it does contact the base of the bulb but by doing so you may break the spring completely. In such instances it is usually best to replace the entire socket.

Lamp sockets are interchangeable and if you take the old socket to an electrical supply house or hardware store you can get an exact duplicate. To take the socket apart, unplug the lamp and examine the brass shell. Near the switch you will see the words "press" which indicate the point where thumb and finger pressure should be applied by squeezing to loosen the outer shell from the base. Once apart, unscrew the two wires. Pull the replacement unit apart to expose the terminals and reconnect the two wires. Then press the outer shell and the base together and screw the socket to the lamp.

If the fault seems to be in the socket, pull the plug from the wall outlet and examine the center contact closely. It may be pressed down too far; raise it with the hooked end of a nut picker.

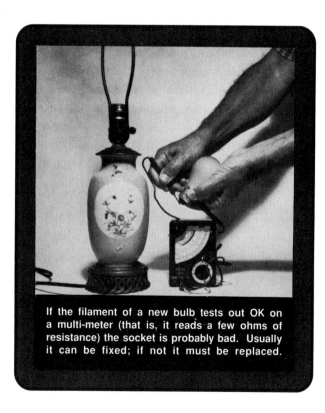

If the filament of a new bulb tests out OK on a multi-meter (that is, it reads a few ohms of resistance) the socket is probably bad. Usually it can be fixed; if not it must be replaced.

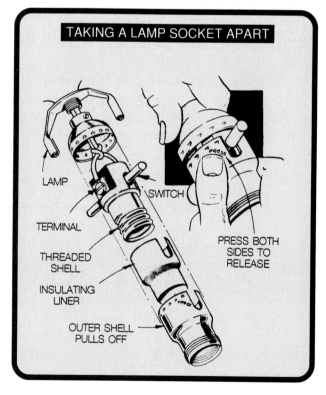

TAKING A LAMP SOCKET APART

LAMP

SWITCH

TERMINAL

THREADED SHELL

INSULATING LINER

PRESS BOTH SIDES TO RELEASE

OUTER SHELL PULLS OFF

HANGING A SWAG LAMP

Hanging lamps, often referred to as "swag" lamps are exceedingly popular because they come in many shapes and forms, are easy to install and can provide a ceiling light by plugging into a baseboard outlet. The chain from which the lamp hangs offers an additional decorative touch while simultaneously concealing the wire.

The swag hooks that you buy where the lamp is sold have a head threaded to take a size 10-24 machine screw. In places along the ceiling where beams or lath can be found the actual fastener is a double screw with machine threads at one end to fit the hook and wood threads at the other end to bite into the beam. If you drill through the ceiling and do not hit a beam, rather than reposition the lamp location use a 10-24 toggle bolt. Thread the swag hook on a length of 10-24 thread stock or use a long bolt with the head cut off. Screw on the folding toggle and push it through a ceiling hole. Pull down while turning the hook so it grabs the underside of the ceiling until it is tight. Now you can hook on the swag chain.

Hanging from a short chain, this swag lamp is most effective in lighting up a corner decorated with pictures. The height of the lamp can be raised or lowered by adjusting the metal chain as required.

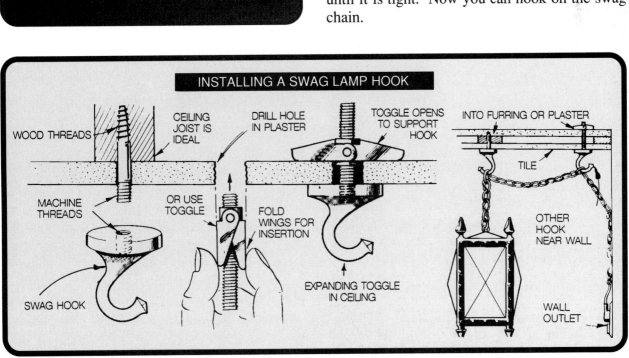

INSTALLING A SWAG LAMP HOOK

INSTALLING YOUR OWN TELEPHONES

Despite the fact that it is perfectly legal to run your own telephone lines inside your home and install your own jacks, millions of families still rent their phones and have the local phone company run new extensions. You can save a substantial amount of money each year if you buy your own phones, run your own lines, and install your own jacks. Here is a basic course on what and how to do it.

The telephone was invented by Alexander Graham Bell, who was born in Edinboro, Scotland, March 3rd, 1847. He was just 27 years old when he uncovered the principle to transmit speech electrically, and just two years later, in 1876, his basic telephone patent was granted. Bell's family life and early education were largely responsible for his interest in communication. His father, Alexander Melville Bell, taught deaf mutes to speak and created "Visible Speech", a code of symbols which indicated the position of the lips, throat and tongue in making sounds. After studying at the University of Edinboro and the University of London, Alexander Graham Bell became a full time teacher and used the Visible Speech system to teach deaf children. He subsequently joined his father in his teaching program and when Alexander Melville was invited in 1871 by the School for the Deaf in Boston to teach teachers how to use the Visible Speech System his son, Alexander Graham, went because his father was not available. The following year he opened a school to teach deaf children and in 1873 young Bell became a professor at Boston University and started to experiment with electricity.

For some 30 years prior to that time the telegraph was the prime method of transmitting messages over long distances and many scientists and inventors were conducting experiments in an effort to find a way to transmit the human voice. The Bell experiments were centered around inventing a harmonic telegraph in which various electrical currents would vibrate thin metal reeds much like those we find in a harmonica. Bell accidentally discovered that when one of the reeds was plucked it would change its vibrations into variations of electrical current which would produce the same vibrations in a receiver located in another room connected by wire. While experimenting with his colleague, Thomas Watson, Bell accidently knocked over a battery—not unlike the present day car battery— spilling some of the acid on his clothing. Impulsively Bell shouted, "Mr. Watson, come here I want you." From the room containing the receiver which was connected to Bell's transmitter Watson rushed into the room and exclaimed, "Mr. Bell, I heard every word you said— distinctly." The rest is history!

In 1880 Bell and two colleagues formed the American Bell Telephone Company and five years later The American Telephone and Telegraph Company (AT&T) was created to handle long distant calls for regional telephone companies. Five years later, in 1900, AT&T absorbed the American Bell Telephone Company and became the parent of a group of companies which eventually comprised 22 Bell System Companies. In 1974, the United States Government filed an anti-trust suit against AT&T which continued for the next seven years. Finally, in 1982, the suit was settled and as part of the settlement in exchange for divesting itself from the 22 Bell System companies, AT&T was permitted to keep its Long Distance Operations, the research organization, Bell Laboratories, and the Western Electric manufacturing division.

This divestiture has changed our telephone system and one of the more meaningful changes is that now all consumers can own their own phones and run their own lines complying, of course, with the regulations established by the Federal Communications System.

YOU AND YOUR TELEPHONE COMPANY

In order to provide you with good service, your local telephone company should be advised of what you plan to do. Work closely with them.

Your telephone is probably the most useful - and trouble free - appliance in your home. In previous years the average home had only one telephone - and many homes still have only one instrument. The reason was logical ... why pay a monthly rental fee for two or more telephones plus an extra outlet charge for each outlet? After all, you can usually only use the telephone from one location so was the second telephone worth the added convenience? It all depended upon your pocketbook!

Most of us will agree that two, three, four or more telephones in a household are certainly more convenient than a single telephone which we often may not hear ringing when in another part of the house. And if we do often the caller hangs up while we are racing to answer the telephone!

Now that we can own our own telephones and save the monthly instrument rental charges and outlet charges by running our own lines, we can enjoy the convenience of a telephone in just about any room in the house for only the cost of the instrument(s), wiring and jacks. Modest one time costs, too!

When the subject of installing your own outlets and buying your own telephone(s) comes up invariably the question arises, "Who will repair the telephone if it doesn't work?" .. or .. "What happens if something goes wrong with the wiring in my home?" In previous years if the telephone or the wiring malfunctioned you merely contacted the telephone company from a pay station or neighbor's telephone and the trouble was corrected FREE. Well, not actually free because you were paying those monthly rental fees! But before you concern yourself with the question about repairs try to recall how many times in the past your phone or line went out because of a fault within your own home!

The current system of modular jacks and plugs has changed the entire picture regarding telephone and wire malfunctions. In previous years all telephones were hard wired, more or less per-

manently connected to the telephone lines in the house. This meant if your telephone did not work the telephone repairman would visit your home and trouble shoot the problem. If the instrument was at fault you received a replacement and if the fault was somewhere in the wiring the trouble was soon corrected at no charge.

With the present day system of modular jacks and plugs you need not be a telephone mechanic to install new telephones, new outlets and trouble shoot them should the occasion arise. If your telephone does not work in your outlet and it does when plugged into an outlet in your neighbor's home you know the problem is not with the telephone, or vice versa. Because you can unplug the telephone if the problem is with the instrument, as a last resort you can bring it to a local repair station. If the problem is in your wiring this too is easy to correct since you know the location of the wires, wire junctions and jacks.

Telephone troubles are not usually in the home but, rather, on the lines leading to your home — a telephone company responsibility. To make possible an instant check to determine where a fault lies, the telephone company now installs what is called a Network Interface from which they can usually determine from the central office where the trouble lies. No expensive house call either. If you agree that having the capability of plugging a telephone in every room of your home, and having as many individual instruments as desired has merit, then determine the cost for such a convenience. Your first step is to get in touch with your local telephone company and discuss your plans. Your customer service person is seated in front of a computer terminal so when your telephone number is punched into the terminal all pertinent data— including when you paid your last bill—appears on the screen. You will be told what your monthly rental charges are, your line charges and details about any other charges that may apply. Then discuss the plan of turning in the rental equipment and running either new lines to

YOU AND YOUR TELEPHONE COMPANY

new locations or new lines to an existing jack. Once you have an itemized listing of your monthly charges you can better evaluate the economic feasibility of owning your equipment and running your own lines.

If you elect to turn in your old rental equipment—as millions of families have—and run your own line, your customer service person will explain the telephone company's responsibility and your responsibility. You will be advised you must have installed by the telephone company (1) A Network Interface, OR (2) A Standard Interface, OR (3) Have an existing jack designated as the Point of Demarcation. The first two will require a telephone repairman. Once you have a

Network Interface or existing jack designated as the Point of Demarcation, i.e., where your responsibility for the telephone and the wiring starts and the responsibility of the telephone company stops, you can add new telephones and wiring. However, you must advise the telephone company of exactly what you plan to do and notify them as to the FCC number (which should be on the back of each new telephone) of the equipment you plan to use.

As you will see in the forthcoming pages, running your own lines is easier than you probably imagined. If you can distinguish between the colors red, green, yellow and black and can follow simple instructions, a new telephone outlet in every room of your home and in your backyard will provide convenience you never thought economically possible.

YOUR ENTRANCE CONNECTION – THE POINT OF DEMARCATION

The telephone line from either a pole or underground conduit first connects to your home to what is known as a protector, a type of fuse installed by the telephone company to protect against lightning. To be effective a ground wire leads from the protector to a water pipe or copper bar driven into the ground. Two wires lead from the protector which is usually mounted on an outside wall of the house in a waterproof box, although in many older installations the protector is located inside the house. From the protector two wires usually identified as the Red and Green (often referred to as "Tip and Ring") connect to either a Network Interface, a Standard Interface, or - in older installations - a (42A) terminal block you can have the telephone company designate as your "Point of Demarcation." Like the Network Interface this means that from this point to the central office the wiring is the responsibility of the telephone company. And all wiring, junction boxes, jacks and phones connected from the same point to locations in the house are your responsibility. This Point of Demarcation block can be

located just about anywhere . . . in the attic, in the basement or any other accessible space. In fact, in some homes it may even be connected to the phone located on a baseboard! However, if you have a flush wall mounted or table telephone the lines leading to the telephone come from a (42A) junction block.

While you can run any number of extensions from a (42A) junction block it is usually advantageous to have a Network Interface installed; all homes built in recent years have a Network Interface. This is a job for the telephone company. The advantages, however, are many: Since the Network Interface has a modular jack you can plug in either a wire junction with a modular plug that has terminals for four separate lines or, if you do not need four lines, you can insert a dual adapter (a plug with two jacks) and run two lines equipped with a modular plug.

The fact that the Network Interface has a modular jack into which a wire terminal or single plug connects means you can easily disconnect the entire telephone system in your home if you are adding new outlets. But the most important feature of a Network Interface is that it is equipped with what is called a "ringer simulator", a clever bit of circuitry that permits the telephone company to check a fault in your line direct from the central office. No expensive house calls necessary! Remember, if for some reason your telephone does not work, and you have tested the phone in another working outlet at a neighbor's home, the trouble could be between the Network Interface and the central office which is a telephone company reponsibility to repair at no cost to you. But if the ringer simulator indicates line voltage is being delivered to the Network Interface you know the

trouble is in your lines and outlets — which is your responsibility. For a few dollars less than the cost of the Network Interface most telephone companies can install a Standard Network Interface which does the same job as the Network Interface but does not have the ringer simulator feature.

Once your Network Interface is installed you can add the station wire for separate outlets and if you have elected to have a (42A) junction designed as the Point of Demarcation you can adapt it to accept a modular jack converter and then either plug in a wire junction with a modular jack or a dual outlet adapter if you only need two lines.

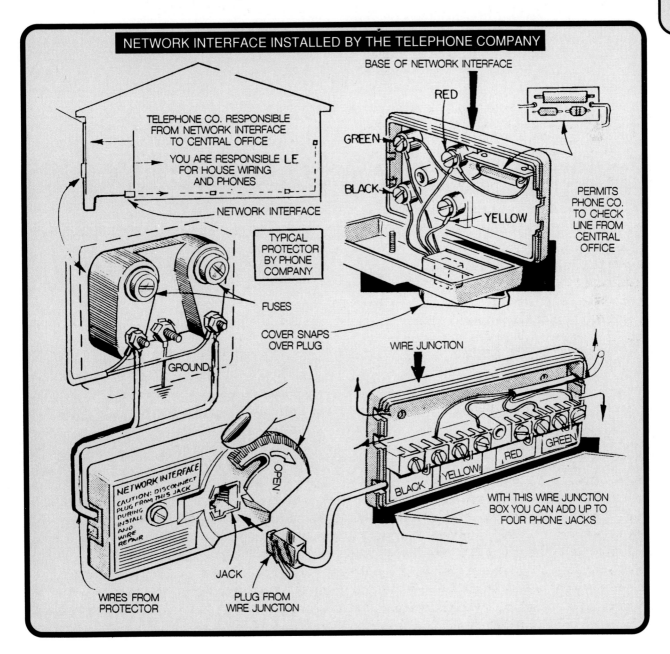

NETWORK INTERFACE INSTALLED BY THE TELEPHONE COMPANY

PULSE & TONE DIALING TELEPHONES

The telephone system in your home is both simple and complex! When you realize each home with one telephone number is connected to the outside world by only two thin wires the system may appear simple. And it is simple when we run new lines to new junctions or jacks, especially since the wires are of different colors which virtually eliminates the possibility of making a mistake when connecting wire to a terminal.

Despite the fact that our telephone uses only two wires, called conductors, some homes may be wired with as many as twelve conductors. Many new homes have six conductor lines. Why the extra wires when you need only two? Spares ... and for future use with other telephone equipment, a Fax machine, or even a new phone with a separate number.

The two wires leading from your home that eventually end up in your central office carry both Alternating Current (AC) and Direct Current (DC). The alternating current (AC) is used to ring the bell but voice transmission uses only direct current (DC).

Two types of phones that send electrical signals to the central office when we dial are pulse dialing and tone dialing. The old and familiar rotary dial is the best example of pulse dialing; when the finger is placed in the hole for the number to be dialed, the dial automatically returns to the stop during which time it opens and closes switches in the phone that break and make the circuit to the central office. The breaking and making of the circuit causes the current in the circuit to stop flowing and start flowing. The on-off current pulses correspond to the digit dialed. Computers in the central office count the pulses and store each digit in switching circuits until all of the numbers are stored. When the pulses of the last digit are counted the complete number is transmitted either by direct wire, microwave or even satellite to the telephone number originally dialed. The revolving rotary dial produces ten pulses per second it rotates and, because the electric signals are pulses, this type of dialing is called pulse dialing. Inciden-

tally, while all phones with rotary dials are of the pulse type, some with the push buttons are also pulse type. By pushing a button, mechanical switches within the phone open and close the electrical circuit.

Far superior than the push button phone is the tone dialing type. Rather than transmit a signal to the central office in electric pulses that correspond to the number being dialed, tones are sent over the telephone line to the central office where the switching mechanism store and relay the number to eventually ring the number being called. One advantage of tone dialing for the consumer is one of speed; it is over ten times faster than pulse dialing!

The type of switching arrangement in your central office that services your phone handles either pulse dialing or tone dialing. If you buy a tone dialing phone you must advise the telephone company because special circuits are required to detect the tone signals and identify the digits. Also available is a combination pulse-tone phone which is often referred to as a pulse tone switchable. This phone can use either pulse or tone circuits.

What actually happens when you make a long distance call? Let us say you want to dial a friend in the San Francisco area (1-415-976-5432). When you pick up the phone your central office is immediately alerted to the fact that the call is coming from your number thru your two wires. You want to make this a direct dial — an operator assisted call will cost more — so you dial 1 which alerts the computer in the central office that a direct dial is coming. You then punch in the area code 415 — one of the 9 area codes in California — and your call is routed to this area. The switching office in California notes the exchange number 976 is located in Berkeley, to which the call is instantly relayed. Finally, at the central office in Berkeley the number 5432 connects and the phone rings. Your call — from your two wires now is connected to your friend's phone — on their two wires! This entire procedure probably requires less than 15 seconds!

SAFETY TIPS WHEN RUNNING YOUR LINES

To determine the safety aspects of running your own lines and connecting them to wire junctions and modular jacks, you should know just what happens when you make a phone call. First, two types of electricity are involved in a telephone call, DC or Direct Current which is supplied by a battery located in your central office which delivers about 40 volts and AC, or Alternating Current which is used only to ring your bell, chime or buzzer. When a call is made to your number in the central office the switching equipment in the central office locates your two wires and sends a pulse of low voltage (90 volts) alternating current. Unlike the voltage of an electrical outlet which is a steady flow that stops only when you switch it off or pull out the plug, telephone voltage is a quick burst that is repeated every five seconds. That is why the ring of your phone is every five seconds. The split second you pick up the handset the alternating current is disconnected and your conversation is powered by direct current from the central office batteries. What is the possibility of a shock? Under normal conditions you can receive a slight shock IF you are holding bare wires or contacts AND someone rings your phone which triggers the pulse of AC current every five seconds. That is why you should always take the phone off the hook whenever doing any wiring. With the phone off the hook it is impossible for the AC voltage to be triggered. Anyone calling your number will receive a "busy" signal but no AC power will flow thru your wires — only DC which will not shock you.

Since accidents can happen— after all, an accident is an unexpected and undesirable event— you should use tools with insulated handles and, when making a bare wire connection, in an instance where you cannot take the handset off the hook to prevent the possibility of the AC voltage being triggered by an incoming call, use rubber gloves. Admittedly, it is awkward to work with rubber gloves if they are bulky but now on the market in home centers, hardware stores and home care surgical supply centers are extremely thin rubber or plastic gloves similar to the type surgeons use.

Very few tools are required to run your own lines and install your own outlets; you probably have most of them to make the wire connections. A screwdriver with an insulated handle with a 1/4 inch blade, a pair of diagonal cutting pliers which are really handy if you have a hard wired system and must cut the existing line near the 42A connection block to which the phone is connected. Also, you need a pair of needle nose pliers if you must wrap wire around the connecting terminals. However, with the AT&T jacks and connecting blocks you do not even need to strip your wires to make a connection; contact is made by piercing the colored insulation to reach the copper. Also handy is what is commonly referred to as the "Telephone Tool" which is fully described on the following pages. With this tool you can quickly cut the protecting sheathing that surrounds the color coded strands of wire without the risk of cutting through the insulation of the color coded solid copper lines. Incidentally, in older homes the insulation of the wire used was much larger in diameter than the type currently used, so the only way it will fit the wire junction or jack terminal posts is by stripping the insulation down to the bare copper with a knife.

SAFETY RULES

(1) Always take the handset off the hook when installing a jack or tapping into a line.
(2) If you have a Network Interface or Standard Interface, unplug your system completely before making a connection.
(3) Use only tools with insulated handles.
(4) If you wear a pacemaker DO NOT make repairs or run lines.
(5) Do not install new lines while a thunderstorm is taking place.

PHONE LAYOUT FOR AN APARTMENT

If your apartment was built prior to 1982, and no telephone improvements have been made, you probably have a single phone mounted on the kitchen wall or in another room a 2-inch square connecting box screwed to a baseboard to which your desk type phone is permanently connected. Your local telephone company will rent you additional phones and run whatever extension lines you request or you can do your own upgrading by planning new outlets as suggested in the illustration. Check with them to compare their charges against the DIY route.

If you do not have a network interface then the telephone company may consider the location of your only phone the Point of Demarca-tion for a modular jack converter. From this modular jack you can run a four or six conductor line from room-to-room. When you come to a solid wall it may be necessary to drill through the wall and fish the line through the hole but you may be able to hug the baseboard and lead the wire around the door jamb and into the adjacent room. Or you may find old painted-over wires already in place. The old wires were usually separate three or four strand wires twisted together, and each strand is much thicker than the type used today. The copper is the same, only the insulation is thicker so you must cut away the insulation and look for the telltale red, green, yellow or black thread that identifies the line.

MODULAR JACK ON BASEBOARD

WALL MOUNTED MODULAR JACK FOR WALL PHONE

RUN 4-WIRE CONDUCTOR LINE ALONG BASEBOARD AND THRU WALLS

MODULAR JACK ON BASEBOARD

BR

KITCHEN

BR

LR

CONVERTED ENTRANCE MODULAR JACK OR NETWORK INTERFACE ON BASEBOARD OR WALL

42A CONNECTING BLOCK

EXISTING "HARD WIRE" ENTRANCE TERMINAL CONVERTED TO NEW MODULAR JACK

WALL MOUNT FOR PHONE IN KITCHEN

CONVENIENT HEIGHT FOR WALL PHONE IS USUALLY 50" TO 60"

PHONE LAYOUT FOR TWO-STORY HOMES

Upgrading the telephone system of a home is usually easier than running new lines in an apartment because you probably have access to the basement or attic that will present various options as to how to run the lines.

If you have a basement, the entrance service and fuse the telephone company originally installed is usually located near the ceiling. To give you the flexibility to run new lines, it is best to have the telephone company install a Network Interface so you can tap into this modular connection and run new lines in any direction. With a Network Interface in place you can connect your old wire to the new interface and then install a modular jack to where the wire connects to the upstairs phone. With one modular jack upstairs, you can run a line along the baseboard or even find a way to thread a wire to the second floor rooms. Of course, with your Interface located in the basement the job of adding new phones to the basement rooms, workshop or even drilling a hole thru the wall to the outside for an exterior jack is especially convenient.

Because of the scarcity of wall space in the kitchen and workshop, these rooms are best suited for a wall mounted phone. With all other rooms, a baseboard modular jack is adequate. And if you want a phone outlet for a patio, pool area or screened porch you should use a weatherproof outdoor jack.

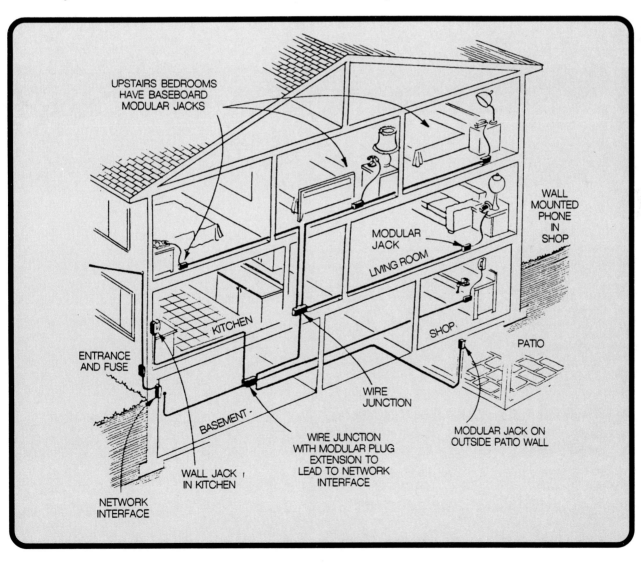

MAJOR ACCESSORIES FOR RUNNING

V isit the telephone section of any home center, mass merchandiser or specialty telephone shop and you will see a wide selection of telephone accessories ranging from different colored and lengths of handset cords, terminal boxes, rolls of station wire and special tools, along with many multi-feature phones, answering machines, etc. All at very affordable prices, too! For most home installation jobs the most widely used accessories are illustrated, together with a description and use for each

(1) The MODULAR JACK CONVERTER - If your home or apartment is "hard wired" (the wire from the phone is connected permanently to the wall), the baseboard terminal to which the phone is connected to what is called a 42A terminal. Unscrew the cover and you will see four screw heads to which wires are connected, and on the corner of the base you will note the letters RGYB, which are used as a guide when connecting the red, green, yellow and black lines. To convert to modular, you need the modular jack converter illustrated which has four color-coded caps (or wires) leading from the modular terminal. Just press the colored cap over the correct screw head, screw on the cover and you now have a modular jack.

(2) The MODULAR JACK - This accessory is just like the modular jack converter except it also has a base and terminals which are labeled red, green, yellow and black. Station wire leading to it connects to the color coded terminals and station wire from the jack can lead to another outlet in another room.

(3) The WIRE JUNCTION - This is a terminal box from which you can lead station wire to many locations, as many of the same color coded wire as each connection will hold. Some wire junctions also come with a modular plug which is usually plugged into the Interface.

(4) The DUAL OUTLET ADAPTER - The two popular types illustrated permit you to insert two lines into one outlet. Three, four and even five outlet adapters are also available.

(5) The WALL JACK - This accessory is screwed

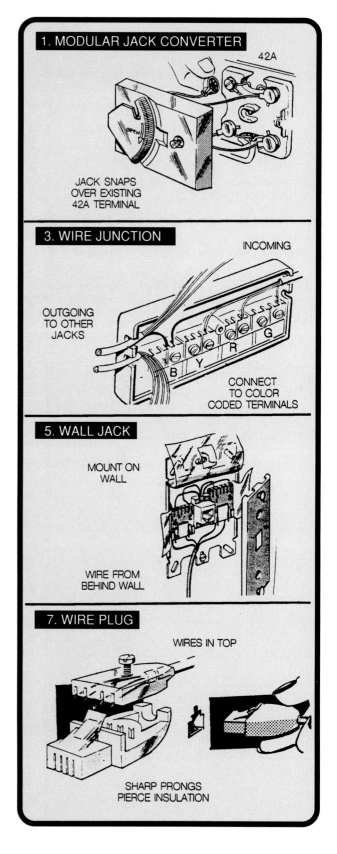

1. MODULAR JACK CONVERTER
42A
JACK SNAPS OVER EXISTING 42A TERMINAL

3. WIRE JUNCTION
INCOMING
OUTGOING TO OTHER JACKS
B Y R G
CONNECT TO COLOR CODED TERMINALS

5. WALL JACK
MOUNT ON WALL
WIRE FROM BEHIND WALL

7. WIRE PLUG
WIRES IN TOP
SHARP PRONGS PIERCE INSULATION

YOUR OWN TELEPHONE LINES

2. MODULAR JACK

PLASTIC BASE

TERMINALS

JACK ON SIDE

4. DUAL OUTLET ADAPTER

TWO OPENINGS

6. FOUR PRONG ADAPTER

OLD TYPE

BARBED PRONGS

PLUG

8. TELEPHONE TOOL

THE BEST TOOL FOR REMOVING STATION WIRE COVERING

9. STATION WIRE

RED

GREEN

YELLOW

BLACK

OUTER CASING

MOST NEW HOMES HAVE SIX CONDUCTOR STATION WIRE

to the wall. A wall phone hangs on the two prongs; the plug from the phone plugs into the jack of the mount. Some wall jacks also have an additional outlet at the bottom into which you can plug a Fax, etc.

(6) The FOUR-PRONG ADAPTER - Before the modular jack made its appearance, homes had four-prong plugs for use with four-prong jacks. To convert such an outlet to modular merely press in the adapter illustrated. The spurs on the legs will keep it securely in place.

(7) The WIRE PLUG - This accessory makes it possible to add a modular plug to station wire so you can run a line from one room to another without directly tapping into the jack.

(8) The TELEPHONE TOOL - The easiest and best way to remove the protective jacket from station wire. This tool has many other uses too, i.e, it helps staple wires to a baseboard, it has a ruler for measuring and a slot for knocking out an entranceway for an incoming or outgoing station wire. With these accessories and a four conductor station wire, you really can upgrade your telephone system!

(9) TYPES OF WIRE - There are three types of copper wire used in our phone system. LINE cord runs from the base of the telephone and plugs into the wall or baseboard jack. Line cords have a factory installed plug at both ends and are available in many lengths. HANDSET cords, as you would surmise, connect the handset to the base of the telephone. Like the line cord, handset cords have four insulated stranded wires so they are flexible, and come in various lengths with a modular plug at each end. STATION wire runs from station to station and connects one junction box or modular jack to the next. The individual solid copper coded strands are encased in a protective jacket. While station wire is available for home installation in three or four strands (although you only need two to make the connection) it is wise to use a four or six strand wire which will give you additional flexibility in years to come to run low-voltage telephone lights, buzzers or even an additional phone or fax number. The slightly added cost is well worth the difference.

CONVERTING A HARD WIRED BASEBOARD OUTLET TO MODULAR

If you have a hard-wired phone , when the telephone company made the original installation they ran a line from their protector (the fuse) to your terminal block which was either on the wall or along the baseboard where it was encased in a 2-inch square box from which the permanent line to your phone led. Take the cover off the box and you will see the familiar 42A terminal block with four screws and the corners of the block labeled in raised lettering RGYB. You can use this block as your "Point of Demarcation" if you call your telephone company. Converting this terminal to modular is extremely simple. You will need a Modular Jack Converter which takes the place of the metal cover you removed. This accessory has a modular jack wired into the side (some versions have the jack on the face) and four color coded

wires with either spade or press on button connectors. They are identified with the letters RGYB and attach to the RGYB screw heads of the terminal. To make this simple installation, take the phone off the hook and cut the four lines that lead from the phone cord, using a pair of side cutter pliers, as shown in the drawing. DO NOT cut any any of the four wires leading to the same terminal from the underside because these come from your protector. If you are using the connector with snap on color coded leads, press the red button over the screw nearest the R mark, the green button nearest the G mark, the yellow button nearest the Y mark and the black button nearest the B mark. Flush wall phones are connected the same way but require a different type built-in modular jack that is flush with the wall.

TAPPING INTO A JUNCTION BOX

The wire junction is merely a connecting block from which you can lead station wire in all directions to install other jacks. A junction box can also be used as a splice box when you want to tap into an exposed overhead basement line. All telephone wire stretches, and if you have at least a sixteen foot run of the four conductor wire encased in a plastic sheath, if you pull it down at the center about 16 inches it will stretch about 2 inches which will be just enough to reach each of the color coded terminals from both sides.

If you cannot make a connection, then two junction boxes mounted about 2 inches apart are the alternative, as illustrated. You can run new lines from either box,

Even the three conductor twisted lines found in old homes can be tapped into using either the stretch wire or the two junction box method. The outside of these lines are not color coded; when you remove the insulation you will find a colored thread next to the wire. Choose the matching color for each terminal.

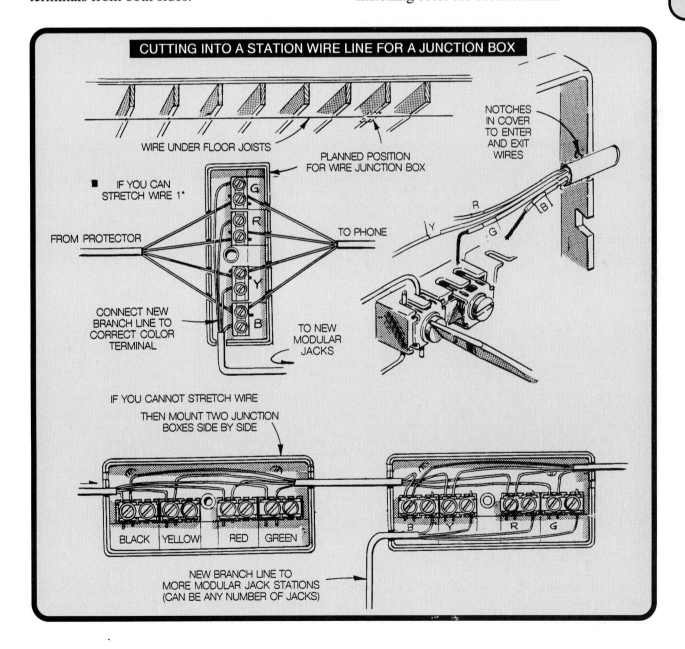

CUTTING INTO A STATION WIRE LINE FOR A JUNCTION BOX

REN -THE RINGER EQUIVALENCE NUMBER

The central office of your telephone company guarantees to supply only a certain amount of ringing power, usually enough to ring five telephones. To guide you when buying and using new telephones, answering machines, automatic dialers and other accessories that require AC current, on the label of the underside of the phone base where the FCC registration number is printed on label is a line, i.e., Ringer Equivalence Number followed by a number. The Ringer Equivalence number is in very fine print and is not always listed as a single digit. A standard phone has a REN number of 1 and your local telephone company guarantees to supply you with 5 REN ... enough power to ring 5 phones. However, some REN numbers are less than 1 and some are more. If the REN is not a whole number the fraction appears as a decimal, i.e., 1.5 is one and one half, etc. Therefore, look carefully for the decimal point when adding up the REN numbers; the print is so fine that what might appear as a 2.8 may be .28!

On some identification labels the Ringer Equivalence line will also have a letter A or B following the number. The A letter stands for a certain single party ringing frequency while the letter B indicates the equipment will respond to a much wider frequency range. When you total your REN numbers disregard the A and B letters.

GLOSSARY OF TELEPHONE TERMS

COUPLER - A device into which a modular plug can be inserted to make the modular plug equipped station wire or line cord wire longer.
DEMARCATION BLOCK - The point established by the telephone company where their responsibility for the telephone services stops and your responsibility starts.
FCC REGISTRATION NUMBER - The manufacturer's registration number assigned by the Federal Communications Commission. All new telephones and accessories should have a FCC number which you are required to report to your local telephone company.
FLUSH JACK CONVERTER - A jack that snaps over an old 42A connecting block to convert the connecting block to modular.
FLUSH WALL JACK - The type of jack that is built into the wall and has station wires leading to it from within the wall.
HANDSET - The part of the telephone you hold. It contains the transmitter and receiver.
HANDSET CORD - The term describing the line that leads from the base of the telephone to the handset.
HARD WIRED - Permanently connected wires from the wall to the telephone. Phone cannot be unplugged.
LINE CORD - The term designates the wire that leads from a jack and connects to the base of the telephone.
MODULAR JACK - The female half of a telephone connecting device.
MODULAR PLUG - The male half of a telephone connecting device.
NETWORK INTERFACE - A connection block installed by the telephone company into which the line from the protector is connected. The station wire in your home connect into this Interface either directly or via a wire junction.

PREWIRE - The term applies to junctions and jacks in new construction.
PULSE DIALING - The mechanical system used to turn current on and off to dial a number.
RINGER EQUIVALENCE NUMBER - A standard ringing power designation, i.e., the telephone company normally supplies a 5 REN to ring your phones; 1 REN is the ringing power of a standard phone.
RINGER SIMULATOR - An electrical arrangement in the Network Interface that permits the telephone company to change the condition of the lines to determine faults.
STATION WIRE - The term designates wire that connects the wire junctions and jacks, i.e., making a station-to-station connection.
SURFACE MOUNTED JACK - The type of jack that is attached directly to the surface of the wall or baseboard.
TONE DIALING - The use of tones rather than turning the current on and off (pulse) to dial a telephone number.
TWISTED STATION WIRE - The older type of station wire that was not wrapped in a jacket. The station wire usually consisted of two or three wires with the same color insulation but containing a color tracer thread under the insulation.
WIRE JACKET - The exterior covering of a four conductor station wire that must be removed when making a connection.
WIRE JUNCTION - A connecting terminal block from which a separate station line can be run.
4 PRONG PLUG - The older plug that fits into a 4 prong jack to connect the telephone line cord to the jack.
4 PRONG WALL JACK - The older jack that connects to a four prong plug.

CONTENTS

290   The Basics of Concrete
294   Tools & Techniques
302   Mixing Concrete
308   Buying Ready-Mix Concrete
312   How Much to Order
316   Using Sacked Concrete
318   The Importance of Curing

BOOK 4   # CONCRETE

Prime Author: RICHARD DAY

320   All About Footings
324   Plain and Fancy Walks
330   Build a Floor
334   Repairing Walks and Drives
336   Pour a Driveway
340   Unusual Surfaces
346   Pattern Stamping
348   Concrete Can Be Colored
350   Making Mortar
352   How to Lay Blocks
360   Building a Retaining Wall
364   Masonry Fences
366   Cement Plastering
368   How to Lay Bricks
374   The Art of Repointing Bricks
376   How to Lay Stone
380   Make a Patio

A patio added onto your home increases its outdoor living space at a fraction of the cost of building that much space indoors. The 4" x 4" post supporting a concrete patio cover should be firmly anchored to the slab, preventing lift-off in a strong wind.

THE BASICS OF CONCRETE

What you should know about concrete, the most universally used building material in America.

CONCRETE IS THE WORLD'S most useful low-cost building material. It is used to build roads and streets, airport runways, office structures, dams., to name a few. Around your house, concrete will make a sidewalk, driveway, patio, pool deck, floors, walls, footings and a host of other projects. You can either hire a concrete contractor for these projects or do it yourself. Do-it-yourself saves money, and working with concrete is not too hard, if you tackle each project in easy-do stages. In fact, working with concrete is fun!

Even if you have no experience with concrete, you can make durable, good-looking slabs and walls the first time. What you need to know is contained in the following chapters.

CONCRETE vs. CEMENT

First understand the difference between concrete and cement. Many people use the two words interchangeably, but they're not. Concrete is to cement as cake is to flour. Concrete is a mixture of ingredients that includes what is called portland cement but contains other ingredients too. Concrete contains portland cement, sand, stones—the term we'll use to mean gravel or crushed stones—and water.

The most important ingredient in the mix

Precast solid concrete slabs 1 1/2" thick set in sand make a home-built patio. These Spanish-motif slabs were cast in a rented form and took just 20 minutes each to make.

is the portland cement, which is manufactured cement made by firing finely crushed rock of the correct composition in huge kilns. On completion it is packaged 94 pounds to the bag and sold by building materials dealers, home centers, etc. One bag holds one cubic foot of cement.

Cement, with water added, is used as a "glue" to hold the sand and stones in a concrete mix tightly together. The whole mass hardens by what is called hydration into something like rock. Unlike most glues though, the process needs no air. Concrete can harden even under water.

A good concrete mix must contain enough portland cement so each particle of sand and stone is coated with the cement-water paste. If too much sand is present, the mix is weakened. A good concrete sand is coarse, containing particles from about 1/4 inch on down to dust-sized ones. The stones (gravel) used in home projects are usually 3/4 or one-inch maximum size but also contain smaller stones as small as the largest of sand particles. Thus, with the sand and gravel mixed together the concrete contains a full range of sizes from the largest to the smallest.

This makes for an efficient mix. If any sizes are either missing or in short supply, the mix requires more cement paste and is therefore weaker.

Usually about 2 1/4 cubic feet of sand and 2 1/2 cubic feet of gravel combine well with a one

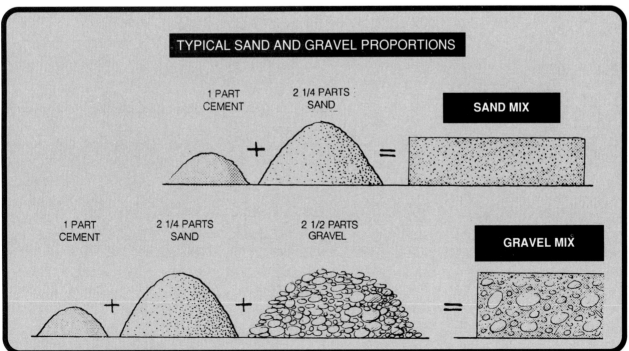

TYPICAL SAND AND GRAVEL PROPORTIONS

1 PART CEMENT   2 1/4 PARTS SAND   +   =   SAND MIX

1 PART CEMENT   2 1/4 PARTS SAND   2 1/2 PARTS GRAVEL   +   +   =   GRAVEL MIX

When you use ready mix, the producer takes care of preparing the mix. All you must do is place and finish it. It helps to bring the truck-mixer in close enough to dump right on the site. Here part of a fence was removed to let the mixer back into a patio jobsite and dump directly on the subbase. Ordinarily, the ready mix driver is not allowed to help you with the pour.

Concrete trucks are classified according to the number of cubic yards of mix they carry. Five yarders serve most homeowners because the smaller size is easier to back into driveways. Some trucks carry up to 12 yards. Trucks carry their own hoses and water; after the placement, troughs must be cleaned and this should be done away from the construction site.

cubic foot (a sack) of cement to make about 4 1/2 cubic feet of concrete. These figures don't compute; that is, 1 plus 2 1/4 plus 2 1/2 don't equal 4 1/2. The reason is that the smaller particles fit in among some of the larger ones taking up space that was empty.

LIQUID AND SOLID

Concrete comes in two states or forms: the plastic, or wet state, just after its ingredients are combined, and the hardened state after the hydration process has taken place. In its plastic state concrete can be shaped by casting it into forms or finished by tooling the exposed surface, or both. While concrete is plastic you can do pretty much anything you want with it, limited only by the time you have before it sets up too hard to work. Some

of the more pleasing and useful shapes and finishes for concrete take the least skill to produce.

TO MIX OR NOT

You can proportion the various concrete ingredients yourself and mix them or you can get them already mixed in several forms. Which way you do it depends on how much money you can spend vs. how much work you want to do yourself. Mixing it yourself will save you about fifty percent of the per-yard cost of ready mix delivered to the job site, which will vary tremendously dependent upon the number of yards ordered. You can easily calculate the savings by determining the quantity of concrete required and comparing the per yard delivered cost with the cost of portland cement, sand and gravel. Mixing by hand in a wheel

When you mix your own concrete, you are responsible for selecting, proportioning, mixing and transporting the ingredients to the casting site. Having a pneumatic-tired wheelbarrow is absolutely necessary.

barrow is hard work so if you have more than a yard to mix consider renting an electric or gas powered mixer which all tool rental shops and many hardware stores make available on a daily rental basis. Or for a big project that will take months of time and work space, scan the classified pages for a used mixer or — a technique we have used in the past — buy a three or four bag mixer and advertise it for sale in the classified section of your local newspaper when your project is complete. Used mixers — cleaned carefully after each mix of concrete — depreciate very little and will often command nearly the same price as a new one!

But perhaps one of the main advantages of mixing your own is that you can mix only as much as you can effectively handle. For small jobs, mixing your own from prepackaged sand or gravel mixes is very handy but it is more expensive than if you purchased the cement, sand and gravel and mixed all the ingredients yourself. Ready packaged mixes are blended mechanically at the factory and generally assure you of getting a stronger mix because the ingredients are thoroughly

mixed. Since we are always trying to save dollars, apply your basic math to figure out the cost differential between the quantity you require if supplied with ready packaged mix as against the cost of separate cement, sand and gravel.

Big projects — a driveway, walks, footings or a full-sized patio call for a ready mixed concrete which comes delivered in a big truck-mixer. The cost is about 50 percent more than buying separate ingredients. The drawback of ready-mixed concrete is that you usually must order at least three cubic yards of mix.

Ready mix trucks have a capacity of anywhere from six yards up although in some areas of the country small two-or-three-yard trucks are serving do-it-yourselfers. All of you have seen ready-mix concrete trucks with a huge revolving drum — they are so large who could possibly miss them? But another type of ready mix truck that produces metered concrete is gaining popularity, especially in areas where homeowners and small contractors require anywhere from one to three yards of concrete. This type truck, with a total capacity of nine yards of dry material and a tank of water, works on a different principle than the usual drum mixer where all contents are mixed by revolving in a drum. Rather, the amount of concrete required is dialed, and the prescribed amount of cement, sand, gravel and water is released and mixed in the pouring trough via screw action! The major advantage is the owner gets the exact quantity of concrete, but another equally important advantage is the concrete is absolutely fresh! Thus, even with a five-yard pour the concrete can be mixed in smaller batches if you cannot handle a full five-yard or larger quantity efficiently. Check your local ready mix firm or your telephone yellow pages for this type of metered mixer for this type of "metered" mixed concrete.

If you just do not have the time and must resort to having a contractor do the job, knowledge of what the concrete will cost will help you when evaluating the price quoted. You can easily make the forms and, once made, you can calculate the area and the depth to determine how much concrete the project will take, call your ready mix firm and get a price; if the job calls for less than 3 yards, find out how much the cement, sand and stone will cost from your masonry supply yard!

TOOLS & TECHNIQUES

The tools for working with concrete are basic hand tools; most likely you have them in your basement or garage.

TOOLS FOR CONCRETE and masonry work are not complicated nor are they expensive. You probably have most of the basic tools because anything you do in building — including concrete and masonry work—calls for hammer, saw, square, chalk line tape measure or rule and a level-plumb combination. You'll need them to build forms, lay out footings, measure for quantities, etc.

For finishing concrete you start with what is called a strikeoff. It's simply a straightedge. Most often the strikeoff is nothing more than a straight 2x4 long enough to reach across the tops of the forms. Its purpose is to shave down the concrete level with the forms leaving no high spots or low spots.

On projects up to about six feet wide, one man can work the strikeoff. Wider ones call for two men, one on each end. The strikeoff is worked by see-sawing it back and forth and with each stroke pulling it farther along. It's tilted toward the direction of travel to give it a cutting edge. Low spots should be filled in ahead of the strikeoff so that a little concrete wells up ahead of the edge. After covering about 30 inches in the first pass, a second pass is made to knock off any high spots that are left and to fill in any low spots. On the second pass the straightedge is tilted backward for a filling rather than a cutting action.

Hammer, saw, tape, pencil, chalk line, square, level are basic tools (above). Finishing tools include sponge float, edger, steel and magnesium trowels and wood float (below).

INITIAL FLOATING

Right after strikeoff comes the use of either a bull float or a darby. You can make these tools, too, as shown in the drawing. The bull float, with its long handle, is best for reaching in where the darby cannot. Otherwise the darby is better. Both tool are designed to fill any voids left by the strikeoff and to push stones slightly below the surface where they're out of the way of further finishing operations.

A bull float is a long-handled, large-bladed flat made of wood or metal. Wood is recom-

---

mended. As the bull float is pushed out over the surface, its handle is lowered to raise the leading edge prevent digging in. On the return strike the handle is positioned to make the blade flat on the surface so it can cut off bumps and fill in holes. If there isn't enough concrete on the surface to fill in all the holes, some should be shoveled into the low spots and bull floating repeated.

A darby is three to six feet long made of wood or metal. Wood is most popular. The handle is best placed low on the tool, as shown in the drawing, to give the most precise control. On the first pass the darby is held with the blade flat to the surface and see-sawed from right to left and back again to slice off lumps and fill in low spots. Then when the surface is level, the darby is swung in arcs one way then the other, always with the leading edge raised. This fills in small holes left by the sawing operation.

When bull floating, darbying or leveling, shape and smooth the surface and also work a little cement paste to the surface. Just-placed concrete can easily be overworked, so finishing should be stopped after the floating just described.

A popular tamping tool called a jitterbug should not be used except on very stiff concrete. You don't need one.

EDGING AND JOINTING

Wait until all surface bleed water has disappeared before starting the rest of the finishing. How long this takes depends on wind, humidity, sun, and temperature. On a hot, dry, windy day with no shade, this initial set can come within minutes and on a cool, damp, or cloudy day, it can take several hours. With air-entrained concrete, which doesn't bleed, you can begin finishing almost right away, as soon as the water sheen (if there is one) has disappeared and the concrete can hold your weight on one foot with no more than a slight depression.

The first finishing step is to edge the slab all around. Done with an edging tool, this breaks the sharp corner to prevent later edge chipping. You can get edging tools in various curves, but most acceptable is the 1/2-inch radius. They come in a large blade and the more popular small-blade

One tool you can make yourself if the straightedge. Here a straight 2 x 4 is see-sawed along "wet screeds" on a sloped concrete garage floor. The 2 x 4 guides are later removed.

For an outdoor slab, magnesium-floating (left) makes a good slip-resistant finish. For indoors, you'll also want to steel-trowel the surface (right). Do it immediately after floating. Then broom the surface if necessary to get slip resistance.

with curved-end edges which measures about 3x6 inches. Material is cast iron, aluminum, stainless steel or formed bronze. Insert the bit of the edger downward into the joint between the concrete and its form and stroke it back and forth until the edge has been shaped, then move forward to the next portion. Flat edgers should be lifted on the leading edge to keep them from digging in. Try not to let the edger leave too much of an impression in the surface that may be tough to remove later. Usually edging is done just before each finishing operation, even the final one.

A jointing tool is like an edger except that the bit is in the middle and it leaves a groove with curves on both sides. The idea of jointing is to divide a slab into panels small enough so when the concrete shrinks on drying the cracks formed will fall conveniently in the joints. These joints are called control joints. To make them work, the bit of the jointing tool must be at least 1/4th the depth of the slab. Thus, for a four-inch slab a 1- inch deep bit is minimum. Any less and the tool is called a *groover*. The grooves made would be for appearance only, not for control of cracking. Cracks likely will then occur at random in and out of the grooves.

Most dealers sell groovers as jointing tools so you should insist on a proper bit depth.

Jointing is done like edging, but to get a straight joint a board is laid down on the surface and the tool guided against one edge. Subsequent jointing will follow the groove without a board.

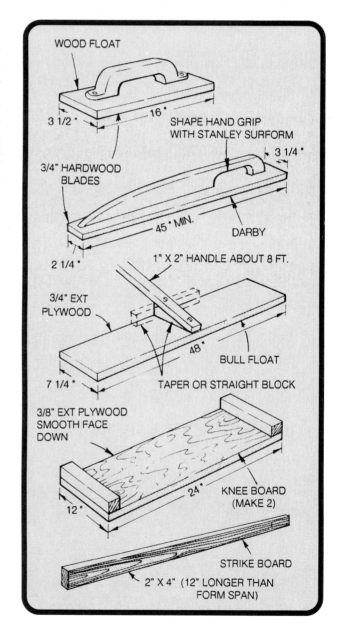

WOOD FLOAT

3 1/2" 16"

SHAPE HAND GRIP WITH STANLEY SURFORM

3/4" HARDWOOD BLADES

3 1/4"

45" MIN.

DARBY

2 1/4"

1" X 2" HANDLE ABOUT 8 FT.

3/4" EXT PLYWOOD

48"

BULL FLOAT

7 1/4"

TAPER OR STRAIGHT BLOCK

3/8" EXT PLYWOOD SMOOTH FACE DOWN

24"

KNEE BOARD (MAKE 2)

12"

STRIKE BOARD

2" X 4" (12" LONGER THAN FORM SPAN)

Darbying, as shown on this page, should follow right after strikeoff. It is done in two steps to smooth the surface and prepare it for floating. The home-made darby above is see-sawed over the fresh concrete surface to slice off high spots and fill in depressions left by the straightedge. In this manner, it is used much like a straightedge. Fashion your darby from 1 x 2s and 2 x 2s so it is both light and easily used.

Next, the darby is swung in large arcs over the previous darbied surface to further smooth it prior to floating. When the slab is large, generally the unreachable center, portions are bull-floated rather than darbied. Darbying and bull-floating with long-bladed tools help to eliminate "birdbaths" from being formed in the soft surface. Once you can use a darby and bull float all your future concrete jobs will be easier.

FLOATING

Right after edging and jointing, floating further pushes large stones beneath the surface and removes any roughness left by previous finishing. It also compacts surface mortar for a tough, hard-wearing layer readying it for the steps to follow. A float may be wood or metal; you can make the wood one yourself. When finishing air-entrained concrete, a magnesium float is best. A wood one tends to tear the surface. Another advantage of a magnesium float is that it slides easily over the concrete.

To use a float, hold it flat on the surface and swing it in seeping arcs one way and then the other. Floating puts an even but not smooth texture on concrete. If you want a surface with good slip-resistance, floating may be the final finishing operation. The finish left by a wood float is rather coarse. That left by a magnesium float would be fine for a sidewalk, driveway, or pool deck.

If you want your control joints to be square with the sidewalk, driveway of whatever you're building, form them along a line snapped between form marks. Control joints are at 5'–10' intervals.

TROWELING

Hand-troweling immediately follows floating. In fact, both tools are carried and one is used to lean on while reaching out with the other. The indentation left is smoothed over before leaving that area.

A hand trowel is a flexible piece of steel, preferably stainless steel, that puts a smooth, dense surface on the concrete. Pros make use of two trowels, a larger one for first troweling and a smaller 3x12 inch one for final troweling. To save money, you can get along with just one, an in-between 4x14 inch trowel.

For initial troweling hold the trowel flat on the surface. Tilting it makes ripples that tend to show up in the finished slab. Move the trowel in sweeping arcs letting one arc smooth out the edge marks of the one before it by lapping half-way. Pick out any stones that intrude into the surface and toss them away.

First troweling produces a good surface for most uses but for an easy-to-clean surface, as in a basement where a non-slip footing isn't as important, you can trowel several times. The time for the next troweling is when pressing your hand onto the surface makes only a slight impression. On the second troweling, hold the trowel blade with its leading edge up slightly to further compact the concrete. If you give a third troweling for an almost glossy surface wait until the concrete has gained additional strength. Hold an even greater tilt on the trowel during this pass. The trowel should then make a ringing sound as you draw it over the surface.

KNEE-BOARDS

To get out onto a large concrete slab and finish it you'll need a set of knee-boards. Make them yourself from plywood as shown. To use, place one in front of the other and step out into the center slab. Lay the knee-boards down about two feet apart so your knees can rest on the board and the toes on the other. Finish the area in front of you, then move sideways to the next area. Skip any spots that can be reached from outside the slab. Always work backwards after a sidewise pass so the impressions of the knee-board are finished over. When you have completed everything unreachable from off the slab, put the knee-boards aside and finish around the slab. Don't toss out your knee-boards after your project is complete; they are a permanent part of your concrete tool kit.

Since the first floating and troweling is a combined operation, take both tools with you. If they are strong, you can rest your hand on one while using the other. Redwood floats are great.

OTHER FINISHING METHODS

If you look over the displays at your building materials dealer, you'll spot a number of different concrete-working tools that look as though they have the same purpose. One is a sponge rubber float. It looks like a dense sponge glued to a wood or metal float. It is used to create a textured, slip-free surface on slabs after magnesium-floating.

Other interesting-looking trowels come two to a set. They're for finishing steps. One finishes the inside corner of the steps, the other finishes the outside corner. It's about the only way to get a complete finish on concrete steps.

Broom-finishes after final troweling can be fairly fine or coarse. To broom a finish, first dampen the broom, then pull it lightly over the surface. Test in a spot to see if you're getting the effect you want. Early brooming and stiff bristles make for coarser finishes; late brooming and finer bristles make for smoother finishes. The broom may be swirled or zig-zagged during its passes for a wavy finish rather than straight lines.

The mason's trowel is shaped somewhat like the palm of your hand but larger. The handle is wood and the blade is steel. Mason's trowels are made in various patterns (shapes) with narrow

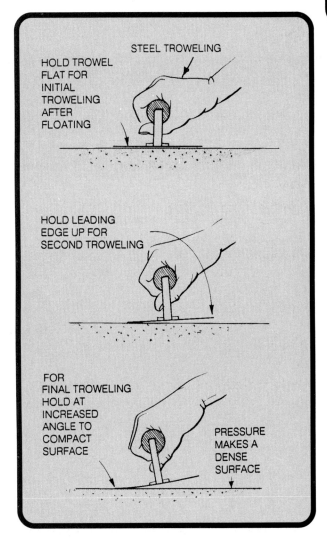

STEEL TROWELING

HOLD TROWEL FLAT FOR INITIAL TROWELING AFTER FLOATING

HOLD LEADING EDGE UP FOR SECOND TROWELING

FOR FINAL TROWELING HOLD AT INCREASED ANGLE TO COMPACT SURFACE

PRESSURE MAKES A DENSE SURFACE

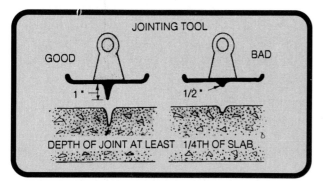

JOINTING TOOL

GOOD   BAD

1"   1/2"

DEPTH OF JOINT AT LEAST 1/4TH OF SLAB

Bull-floating a slab lets you remove the high and low spots left by strikeoff without getting onto the fresh concrete. The long handle reaches to the center of just about anything you'd build.

Whenever you get a spare minute during a concrete finishing project, use the time to clean tools that you're through with. A garden hose fitted with trigger nozzle will do the cleaning job.

Control joints should be formed with a jointer having a bit at least 1/4th of the slab's depth. Use a board as a guide the first time, then tool will follow the joint during later steps.

heel (4-7/8 inch) or wide heel (5-5/8 inch) and in various balances. Choose one that feels comfortable when you hold it. Weekend masons shouldn't get too large a trowel because they tend to tire the wrist and arm muscles.

LEVEL

A mason's level is longer than a carpenter's level, usually four feet long. You needn't buy a long level unless you plan on doing a great deal of masonry work. The greater length lets the level be used as a long straightedge for aligning courses of brick and block.

STRINGLINE

Masonry units are laid straight to a taut stringline. You can use nylon fishing line, if you wish, or buy nylon mason's line.

Handy to have with your line is a pair of line blocks. These are attached to the masonry corners to let you stretch the line without inserting nails in the joints. You can get line blocks in wood, metal, or plastic.

MASON'S HAMMER

A carpenter's hammer should not be used for cutting bricks and concrete blocks. For that

Another way of cutting the all-important deep control joints is with an abrasive wheel mounted in a power saw. The advantage of this is that jointing can be left until after the slab has set hard enough to walk on. Don't wait more than 12 hours, however, or the contraction will cause random cracking before you cut the joints to control it. Sawing too soon tears out stones. Most of our concrete highways use sawed joints but these are cut with diamond blades.

you'll need a mason's hammer. It has a square head at one end for chipping off pieces and a chisel point at the other end for chipping lines across masonry units in cutting them. A 20-ounce head is a good size.

RULE

Some means of measuring the height of each course of brick or block is needed. You can either make a wooden pole (called a story pole) with the course levels marked on it, or buy a special mason's rule. These are available in folding wood or steel tape with the various dimensioned courses clearly marked.

JOINTING TOOLS

The mortar joints in masonry work should be tooled to compact and smooth them. What you use for this will determine how the joints look. V-shaped tools make V-shaped joints. Rounded tools make concave joints. Special raker tools are made for raked joints. For concrete blockwork, the jointing tool should be about 20 inches long. For brickwork only, it may be shorter.

MISCELLANEOUS TOOLS

In addition to the above masonry tools, you'll need a wire brush for cleaning off mortar. If you are to acid-clean your brick or block project to remove all traces of mortar stains, you'll need a pair of waterproof gloves. If you like working with gloves, a pair of vinyl- or rubber-dipped work gloves will save your hands while handling mortar and masonry units. If kept dry, leather gloves are more comfortable because they "breathe." They need not be full leather, just leather-faced for hard wear. Cloth work gloves containing small plastic gripper dots are tough-wearing, yet they are comfortable. The full-dipped gloves tend to make your hands sweat.

A brick chisel, a flat one with a wide face and perhaps 2 1/2 inches across, may be useful for cutting bricks to exact lengths. It is laid across the brick and struck with a mason's hammer for a clean cut.

You may need a mortar box, hoe, shovel, pail, garden hose, wheelbarrow, and some other tools. Often, if you don't have these, you can make-do without them. They help the job go easier, though.

Water is the most critical ingredient in concrete. The less you add, the stronger the concrete will be. Left mix is too wet. Mix in center is just right. Right, too dry.

MIXING CONCRETE

Concrete can be mixed by hand or by power; but large batches should always be power-mixed.

ANY PROJECT REQUIRING up to about three cubic yards is an excellent prospect for mix-your-own concrete.

You can mix by hand or with a concrete mixer. Easiest, of course, to use is the mixer. Home-type concrete mixers come in all sizes from a five-gallon pail to a five-cubic-foot and even larger. The smaller mixers are good for making stepping stones, laying flagstones and other limited-pour projects. All but the smallest mixers are available either electric or gasoline powered. The gasoline-powered mixers cost more but are handiest because they're independent of an electrical outlet.

If you plan quite a few concrete projects over the next few years, it will pay to buy your own mixer. They last, practically without trouble, for a lifetime. The handiest ones are mounted on wheels for easy transporting. Some are designed to be moved about like a wheelbarrow.

MIXER CAPACITY

The actual capacity of any concrete mixer is 60 percent of its drum capacity. Thus, a five-cubic-foot mixer will actually handle batches of about three cubic feet. This size is known as a half-bag mixer because it will handle a half-sack of Portland cement plus the sand, gravel and water. This is a very convenient size because it lets you proportion half-bags of cement, avoiding further measuring. The identification plate on the mixer gives its capacity in cubic feet.

Concrete that is improperly proportioned, mixed, placed and finished can suffer all kinds of troubles from cracking to scaling and dusting. So do it right and you'll bypass these problems.

Start with good materials. Portland cement, though not a brand, is good in all brands. Use either Type 1 or 2. They are suitable for everything you will ever make. Type 3 cement is for high early strength. It hardens quickly to permit early removal of forms. While you could use it, you don't need it. Other types of cement are for highly specialized purposes.

You can also get types 1A and 2A. The A stands for *air-entraining*, that is, this cement when mixed, creates air bubbles in the mix. When trapped within the concrete, these microscopic bubbles act

The amount of water you add to a mix depends on how much free water is in the sand being used to make it. To find out, pick up a fistful of sand, squeeze and release. Dry sand at left contains no free water, falls apart. Average sand (center) stays in tight lump but leaves no water on the hand Wet sand, illustrated right, leaves your hand wet.

To judge sand-stone proportions in a fresh mix, dump same in a pile and pass a trowel or shovel over the top. If the surface shows stones and holes, as at left, it contains too much gravel. If it trowels beautifully with no signs of stones, it has too much sand (center). If it smooths without tearing, as illustrated at right, but shows some stones, it's OK.

as tiny "relief valves" for pressures caused by freezing water within the concrete. Instead of popping off a chunk of the surface, during sub-freezing weather, the freezing water expands harmlessly into the bubbles.

All concrete exposed to freezing should be air-entrained. Air-entrained concrete costs no more. It contains air bubbles. To make air-entrained concrete, you can get an air-entraining agent and add it separately to your mix. Air-entraining agents are not widely available to the home owner so the best place to get it is from a ready mix concrete dealer who is accustomed to supplying air-en-trained mixes to his contractor customers Take a gallon can along with you and for a few dollars he'll sell you a lifetime supply; but ask the dealer for advice on how much agent to add to each batch since different manufacturers require different proportions If it's the most popular brand—Darex— use it at the rate of two tablespoons per bag of cement. A half-bag mix then would get one

tablespoon of *Darex*. One important point; hand-mixing is not vigorous enough to entrain any air, so you needn't expect to make air-entrained concrete by hand.

QUALITY AGGREGATES

Quality in aggregates (sand and stone) is important, too. You should use only sand and stone that are known to make good concrete. Often raw materials dug out of the ground have to be washed, crushed, regraded and reblended to make good concrete aggregates. For this reason, it's a good idea to buy the materials from a ready-mixed concrete producer or from a reputable concrete products dealer.

One way to judge the cleanliness of sand is to put two inches of it in a jar, add water almost to the top and shake thoroughly. Let it stand over-night and measure the thickness of the top layer just beneath the water. If the silt layer is more than

With a good sized half-bag mixer, it's easy to batch cement. Just open the bags with a shovel and pour half a bag into each batch

Clean-up of tools and mixer after a pouring project is important. The best way is with a garden hose trigger nozzle. Squirt right after use.

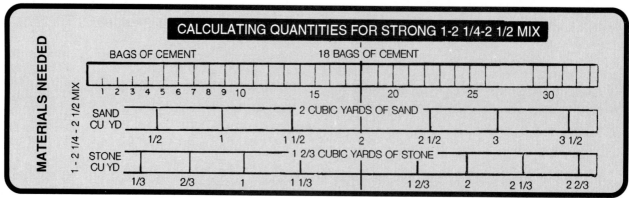

MATERIALS NEEDED

1 - 2 1/4 - 2 1/2 MIX

CALCULATING QUANTITIES FOR STRONG 1-2 1/4-2 1/2 MIX

BAGS OF CEMENT   18 BAGS OF CEMENT

1 2 3 4 5 6 7 8 9 10   15   20   25   30

SAND CU YD   2 CUBIC YARDS OF SAND

1/2   1   1 1/2   2   2 1/2   3   3 1/2

STONE CU YD   1 2/3 CUBIC YARDS OF STONE

1/3   2/3   1   1 1/3   1 2/3   2   2 1/3   2 2/3

1/8-inch thick. the sand is too dirty to make good concrete.

Another way to judge aggregates is to look at the piles. Pick some up. Do they contain mostly one-size particles, or are all sizes present as they should be? Fine sand—the kind you'd want for a child's sandbox—is not suitable for making concrete. It contains few larger, coarse particles and tends to be all one-sized grains. Good concrete sand is coarse, sharp and grainy. In different locales it goes by different.names, but if you ask for *concrete sand,* you should get the correct product. What you *don't* want for making concrete is masonry sand, sandbox sand or beach sand.

Water quality is important. The rule is, if you can drink the water, it's okay for concrete.

When you have all the materials on hand, you are set to mix and pour. In addition, forms, tools, helpers—everything else you'll need to complete the job—should be on hand before you start.

Arrange the piles of sand and gravel handy for shoveling into the mixer. You may find it handy to place all the materials on one side of the mixer and leave the other side free for dumping and hauling. Hook up a garden hose, ideally one with a trigger nozzle both for mixing water and for clean-up. This saves running to turn off the hose. Another way is to let the hose run into a 55-gallon drum with the top removed. Then you can dip buckets of water from the drum as needed.

The more helpers you can muster, the better. However, by yourself you can tackle everything if you plan on doing a little at a time. As a general rule, you can probably handle the mixing, placing, and finishing of one cubic yard in one day. Two workers can do twice as much. If you have three, put one man on the mixer, one hauling and spreading, and the most careful one, finishing.

PROPORTIONING INGREDIENTS

The accuracy you use in measuring out ingredients for your concrete is up to you. The more accurately you work, the better concrete you'll produce. The simplest but least accurate method is by counting the shovels of each ingredient. Most accurate is putting each material into measure-marked cans and emptying these into the mixer. For most purposes, the shovel method works fine. See that shovels of cement, sand and gravel are all about the same size. This isn't as easy as it sounds because damp sand and the cement both tend to pile up on the shovel, whereas gravel tends to roll off. Try filling a wheelbarrow with sand and with gravel to see how shovel quantities compare.

The proportions by volume for a strong concrete mix are shown in the table at left....it provides 1 part portland cement to 2 1/4 parts sand and 2 1/2 parts stones, all measured by volume. This mix makes good footings and foundations as well as slabs and walls of all kinds. When you know how much concrete you need, figure on six bags of portland cement for each cubic yard, then draw a line down the table to find the volume of concrete, sand and stones needed. For example, as shown in the table, a three-cubic-yard project would require 18 bags of cement, 1 1/2 cubic yards of sand and 1 2/3 cubic yards of stones.

For accurate proportioning, use equal-sized shovelfuls of cement sand and stones. To make the 1:2 1/4:2 1/2 mix in a small concrete mixer, for example, you'd add five shovels of portland cement, 11 1/4 (5x2 1/4=11 1/4) shovels of concrete sand and 12 1/2 (5x2 1/2=12 1/2) shovels of stones.

WATER WEAKENS

No matter what size mix you make, the proportion of water should be no more than six gallons of water per sack of cement. Too much water weakens the mix.

Since sand contains some free water, or is so dry that it absorbs some of the mix water, the amount of water you put into a mix depends on the condition of the sand on the day you use it. Average sand is wet, that is, it contains enough water to wet each particle. If you squeeze a handful and release it, average sand is wet enough to stay in a tight lump. Test yours. If the squeeze-test leaves water on your hands, the sand is very wet and the mix water should be reduced, but only by about half a pint in a half-bag mix.

If, on the other hand, the sand is so dry that it falls apart when squeezed and released, mix water should be increased about half a pint over that shown for a half-bag mix.

Incidentally, when ordering your cement, sand and gravel, add at least 10 percent extra to allow for waste and miscalculation. Remember, it is better to have too much than too little.

LOADING THE MIXER

Arrange to have the concrete mixer high enough to dump right into a wheelbarrow. A big rubber-tired contractor-type wheelbarrow is handiest. It holds about five cubic feet and gives a smooth ride without too much settling of the stones.

Load the mixer in this way: first put in about half the water, pouring down the sides of the rotating drum to clean it. Then shovel in half the stones and all of the sand. Let them mix for half a minute, then add all of the cement and the rest of the stones. Also put in the air-entraining agent, if one is being used. Finally, pour in the rest of the water. A good way to measure the water is in a pail, filling to a depth mark taped or drawn on the side or inserting a stick with a depth mark on it. Just remember that water quantity should be consistent.

One concrete mix, called sand-mix, is made without any stones. Use sand-mix concrete for thin sections of 1 1/2 inches or less. It's made using the Strong Mix proportions, but without the stones. Yield, of course, is much less.

Mix concrete at least two minutes after

One of the handiest home-type concrete electric mixer made uses a 5-gallon pail for a drum. Ingredients for concrete or mortar are batched and mixed, then toted to site in same can.

Take care in measuring water. Good way is to find the correct amount for a batch, then mark a stick at the height it comes to in the batch can. Fill to mark each time, keep it just for water.

adding the last ingredient, but don't leave it in the mixer more than half an hour or it may begin to harden. When throughly mixed, the ingredients should fall off the mixer blades cleanly without the mix being sloppy.

Take these precautions when mixing. (1) Don't peer too closely into a rotating mixer drum. The slopping concrete can get you in the eye, a painful experience that will send you to the garden hose to flush out the debris. (2) Be careful when reaching into the turning drum with your hand or a shovel as when trying to retrieve a piece of cement sack or a twig. Shovels and arms can get broken that way. It's best to stop the mixer when removing things from it!

As soon as you dump the last batch of concrete for a project, put some water and several shovels of stones into the drum and let it revolve for 10 or 15 minutes while you place the last batch. This will clean the drum's insides. Likewise, if you stop for lunch do the same thing. Finish the cleaning job with a hose while it turns. Also,

remove cement from the outside of the mixer and from the wheelbarrow. Use a wire brush on stubborn deposits. Stop the drum and make sure no deposits are left in it. Also, when washing down equipment, don't let the cement-laden water run down a drain. It can harden and plug the drain.

HAND-MIXING

Mixing concrete by hand is a little different from machine-mixing. Dump the materials onto a smooth surface. Use a concrete slab or set down a sheet of plywood. First measure out the sand and stones into a heap. Add the cement to a crater formed in the center of the pile. Turn the dry mix until the whole pile is the same even color without streaks and lumps. Usually, turning several times from one pile to another does the job. Crater the heap again and start adding water a little at a time. Keep mixing until the whole pile is the same color and consistency. Adjust the ingredients, if need be, as described for machine-mixing.

Carry concrete from mixer to the pour site in a rubber-tired wheelbarrow. The softer ride keeps the stones from settling to the bottom. Use wood planks as ramps. It's best to wear boots.

To make air-entrained concrete, use an air-entrained portland cement to make your mix. The microscopic air bubbles in air-entrained concrete protect the slab from freezing. See your dealer.

Getting a big truck-mixer in and out of your job requires guiding the driver. Old sheets of plywood often can prevent the wheels from sinking in.

BUYIN

There's more to picking up the phone and ordering mix. Here are some helpful tips you can use...

A PROJECT THAT REQUIRES three-cubic yards of concrete or more is a good candidate for ready mix. Ready mix can be used on smaller projects, too. However, unless you can buy "metered" ready mix in your area you will find most of the drum ready mix producers make a minimum charge somewhere around three cubic yards, so you'll probably pay for that much whether you need it or not.

Ready mix is purchased and delivered to your house just like a piece of furniture. All you do is call up and order it, and don't be surprised if you are scheduled for a specific time and date. The supplier takes care of selecting materials, proportioning them, mixing, delivery, and discharging the mix as nearly as possible to the place where you want it.

On the other hand, using ready mix lets you in for plenty of hard labor. Having that much concrete to place and finish in a short time can be a big burden. Have plenty of help on hand, especially if the weather is hot and dry and the sun will be shining on your project. Concrete sets up quickly under such conditions. Two people can probably handle three to five cubic yards of ready mix in a day. If you are new to concrete, it's better to have three. If the mix has to be wheeled to the site, you'll need three more helpers.

You'll find ready mix producers in the Yellow Pages of your telephone directory. Like other businesses, there are large dealers and small ones, good ones and not-so-good ones. It's hard for the occasional user of ready mix to know the difference. Generally the big producers who serve many concrete contractors know the most about making good concrete. On the other hand, they are the least anxious to bother with a small load. It's practically impossible to get a Saturday delivery from one of them. If you do succeed, you'll probably find the price much higher on that overtime day. The small ready mix producer may be a better bet for you. Choose your man on the basis of the service he offers. Will he bring the mix when you want it? Does he have a wheelbarrow to rent you? What is the farthest he can dump the mix from the rear end of the truck? If you need more distance, does he have an add-on chute?

ORDERING

Ready mix properly ordered is half-way toward being good concrete. Here's how to do it: Read your ready mix producer this statement over

READY MIX CONCRETE

Have enough strong help on hand before the ready mix truck arrives. Once it begins dumping, things can get really hectic. Wear boots and use a square shovel or hoe to move the mix along.

Ready mix is ideal for pouring driveway strips, patios, an area for a basketball hoop, etc. Just figure out the economics and labor involved of mixing your own or pouring in from a truck.

the phone, filling in the blanks as you go:

"Can you deliver___cubic yards of ready mix with one-inch maximum-size aggregate, a minimum cement content of six bags per cubic yard, a maximum slump of six inches and a 28-day compression strength of 4,000 pounds. It should also have (in freezing climates) an air entrained content of six per cent, plus or minus one per cent. And can you bring it at __o'clock on ___?"

Your dealer should be impressed, because usually only engineers know enough to order ready mix this way. It covers all the bases for quality.

Maximum aggregate size depends on the section thickness of your project. This should be as large as possible without being more than one quarter of the section dimension, (i.e., one inch aggregate for a four-inch slab). Slabs five and six inches thick can use 1 1/2-inch aggregate. For building steps, a one-inch maximum size is preferred.

Slump is a measure of the workability (ease of placing and finishing) of the plastic concrete. Concrete with more than six inches slump begins to get sloppy and tends to be weak. Much less slump and you'll have too tough a time placing and finishing.

Specifying compressive strength for ready mix implies to the dealer that you are going to cast test cylinders on the job—very professional—to check up on the quality of his product. The minimum entrained air content ensures weather-resistant concrete because the air bubbles keep water from bleeding to the surface and getting in the way of your finishing operations.

PLANNING YOUR JOB

Be ready before the ready mix truck arrives. Have your project formed and plan so the truck will be close to the forms so you can dump the mix directly into the forms. If you must wheel it in, have ramps ready. Put planks down where the truck will cross over a shallow buried sewer and lawn sprinkler pipes or soft ground. Protect thin-section sidewalks and driveways less than six inches thick from the weight of the truck-mixer by laying down planks or sheets of 3/4-inch plywood. An overhead clearance of about 11 feet is needed for most trucks. Prop up telephone and electric wires if necessary, or plan how you will have the driver avoid them. Have your tools ready and your

There is no finer way to get ready mix in place than with a concrete pump. The trailer-mounted contractor's pump can be positioned practically anywhere that the ready mix truck can dump into its screened hopper. A 2" hose (center) leads to the construction site. The pump takes small-aggregate mix almost as fast as it can be dumped. Almost every community has at least one concrete pumping contractor (see your local Yellow Pages).

helpers on hand.

When the truck arrives, guide the driver into position for the first pour. See that he revs his engine up and mixes the batch for at least two minutes after which time he can start dumping. The driver's job is to control the dumping, nothing else. Most drivers are not allowed to help, even if you are overworked and he hasn't much to do.

Should the mix prove too stiff for you to handle, you can have the driver add water at the rate of one gallon per cubic yard. He does it from a storage tank on the truck but remember that adding water will void the compressive strength minimum that you have specified because *too much water weakens concrete*. Keep in mind that concrete should not be so wet that it flows into place. After adding water, the driver should run the drum at mixing speed for two full minutes before dumping any more concrete. *This is important*!

Most ready-mix producers allow you a specific amount of time per yard for unloading. If dumping the whole load takes longer than anticipated, you have to pay for the additional time. Time starts usually when the driver arrives on the job and runs until he is ready to clean up and leave.

If your project requires more than one load of ready mix, have the two trucks arrive about a half hour apart or have the same truck go back to the plant and get your second load. That gives you a breather between loads. Use it to spread and to begin finishing the concrete.

A good many communities have what is a real do-it-yourself innovation—trailered ready-mix. The best trailer-mixers contain a one cubic-yard mixing drum. The trailer attaches to a hitch installation on your car. At the ready mix plant, you pull the trailer under a chute or hopper and it is filled with mix. The self-contained mixer engine is started and it mixes while you drive home. Once there, you pull the trailer to the dumping site and empty the mixer. While you begin to place the mix, someone can drive back for the next load, if necessary, or clean and return the mixer.

Trailering is ideal for projects up to several cubic yards. The best place to rent a trailer-mixer is from a ready mix producer, because he knows concrete. Cost is about the same as for ready mix.

In many communities "metered" concrete is available. These trucks carry about 9 yards of dry stone, sand, concrete and water and, when you tell the driver how much concrete you need, he sets his dials so the correct proportion of all ingredients is released and mixed in the delivery chute via screw action. Not mixed in a revolving drum most common with a ready mix truck, but mixed as it is sliding down the delivery trough. Thus, you can dial and mix as you pour! Check your yellow pages for a trailer mixer or metered concrete pages or chat with your local masonry supplier who usually knows how the do-it-yourselfer is supplied.

PUMPED CONCRETE

If getting a ready mix truck close to your job site is a problem, use a concrete pumping contractor's services, if available in your area. This is a specialty service, the cost of which varies with the job. A pumper can easily double the cost of a pour but in many instances it is the best route to take. The process is simple, the ready mix truck dumps the mixed concrete into the hopper of the pump. The pumper operator starts the pump and hands you the end of the hose which can be two or

three inches in diameter. Concrete will flow steadily from it like toothpaste from a tube, as you need it!

Using a concrete pumping contractor lets you place all the concrete for a large patio in about 15 minutes, by yourself. There is no additional truck-mixer time charge, and you needn't pester your friends to help. The mix can even be pumped into a basement through an open window. Uphill or down, is no problem, within reasonable limits. When finished, the contractor cleans his own equipment, presents you the bill, and leaves when you pay. It's an ideal way to get ready mix. Some ready mix dealers have pumps. Others let you arrange for pumping separately, getting the ready-mix and pump on the job at the same time.

Ask the pumper you call whether he has a two-inch pump to handle small jobs. Handling a larger hose is difficult and requires extra help.

If you use a pumping service, be sure to order your ready mix with 3/8-inch maximum-size aggregate so it will go through the pump. Often, this is called a *grout and pump mix.* At any rate, your ready mix producer should be told that you plan to pump-place the mix so he can specify it accordingly.

Pumped concrete comes from the hose end like toothpaste from a tube. Make certain the mix does not shift the forms or screens. Direct the mix first on both sides of the wood, then fill in.

This large patio required six yards of mix and took just 20 minutes to pump. Gauging the right amount of mix calls for noting when each square is full before moving the hose to the next square.

HOW MUCH TO ORDER

When that ready mix truck backs up to your job, you cannot help but wonder whether you ordered enough to fill the forms. Remember, it's always better to have a little too much mix than not enough to fill the forms.

How to order or mix the concrete you need without running short or having a big left-over pile for which you have no use.

EARLY IN THE BUILDING PROCESS you must figure out how much concrete you'll need. After you calculate the volume the job requires, round off the figures to the larger quarter-yard or half-yard, rather than down. If you end up with a concrete requirement of 6.3 cubic yards, order 6 1/2, not 6 1/4. A little extra concrete left over after the job may be used to cast step-stones (if you have a form handy) or it can be spread out in a pre-dug hole as a free-form fish pond. One smart home owner uses left-over ready mix to lengthen his backyard walk. He has the forms ready and dumps the excess between them each time he uses concrete. His walk grows a little every year.

For cast-in-place concrete slabs, figure the area covered by the slab. If it's square or rectangular, the job is easy. Simply multiply the length times the width, both in feet, and you have the area in square feet. If it's triangular and one of the corners is a right-angle (90° angle), find the area by multiplying the dimensions of the two sides that meet at the right angle, then take half that amount as the area (see drawing on page 315). If the area is triangular, but without a right angle, you can divide the triangle in two right-angle triangles by an imaginary line. Then figure the areas of these and add them together. Other shapes are estimated as shown in the drawing.

An irregular area, such as a kidney-shaped pool deck, is figured differently. Sketch a miniature of it on squared paper, letting one-inch squares equal one-yard squares. First count up all the whole squares within the area and write that figure down. Then guess at what portion (in tenths) of each of the partial squares is part of the project. Write them down. Add it all up and you have the approximate area in square yards, probably within tenths either way. Using a pocket calculator simplifies the process.

ESTIMATING VOLUME

Now that you know the area to be covered by a slab, you can figure its volume. We recommend starting in square feet. Then, since you want the volume in cubic yards, convert area to square yards. (If it's square feet, divide by nine to get square yards.) Then apply the thickness to find volume. Thickness is nearly always measured in inches, and an inch is 1/36th of a yard, so first multiply the area in square yards by the thickness in inches and then divide by 36 to end up with cubic yards.

If you order materials by weight rather than by volume, remember that sand weighs about 2,500 pounds per cubic yard and 3/4-inch stones weigh about 2,800 pounds per cubic yard.

The chart simplifies figuring how

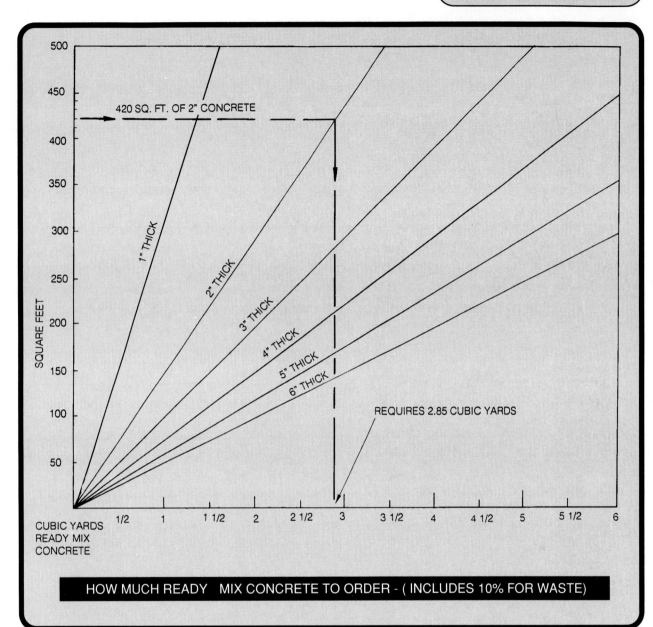

313
CONCRETE

much cement, sand, and stones are required to make the concrete you need for any slab. To use it, all you need know is the size of the slab in square feet and its thickness in inches. Quantities are shown for slabs up to 500 square feet and from one to six inches thick.

For example, suppose your slab measures 12 x 35 feet for a total of 420 square feet and that it is to be two inches thick. Start to the left opposite "Area to Cover" at the 420 square feet level and draw a line horizontally until it meets the two-inch thickness line. Then continue the line straight down, as the dotted line shows the quantities of materials it crosses below the chart are those you

should order, with a ten percent allowance for waste included. The total concrete required in the example is 2.85 cubic yards. If you were buying ready-mix, this is how much you'd order, upping it to an even three cubic yards.

To mix 2.85 cubic yards of concrete yourself, you'd need a bit more than 17 sacks of cement (2.85x6=17.1). The table on page 304 indicates that 1.4 cubic yards of sand and 1.6 cubic yards of stones would be needed with the 127 sacks of cement. It's a good idea to get more materials than you expect to need to avoid running out during a project.

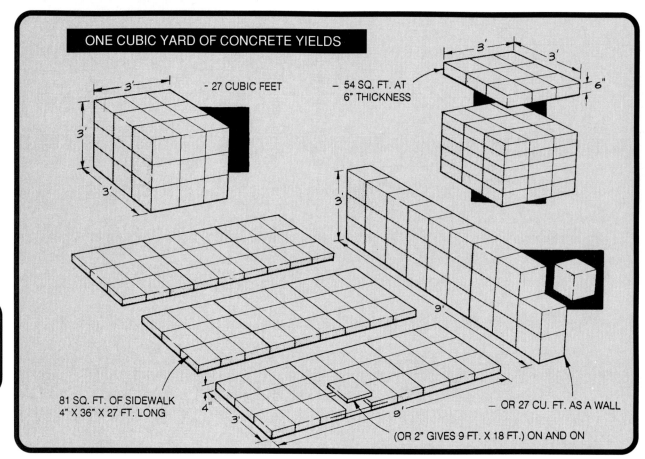

ONE CUBIC YARD OF CONCRETE YIELDS

- 27 CUBIC FEET

— 54 SQ. FT. AT 6" THICKNESS

81 SQ. FT. OF SIDEWALK 4" X 36" X 27 FT. LONG

(OR 2" GIVES 9 FT. X 18 FT.) ON AND ON

— OR 27 CU. FT. AS A WALL

METRICATION

In some countries where this book is distributed the metric system is used,so here is a table of approximations that will help you make the transition most easily:

USEFUL METRIC APPROXIMATIONS

10 millimeters (mm)	3/8 inch
25mm	1 inch
100mm	4 inches
300mm	1 foot
1 meter (1000mm)	3 feet 4 inches
1 square meter (m)	10 3/4 square feet or 1.2 square yard
1 cubic meter (m)	35 cubic feet or 1.3 cubic yard
1 liter	1.06 quart
4 1/4 liters	1 gallon
1 kilogram (kg)	2.2 pounds
45 1/2 kg	100 pounds

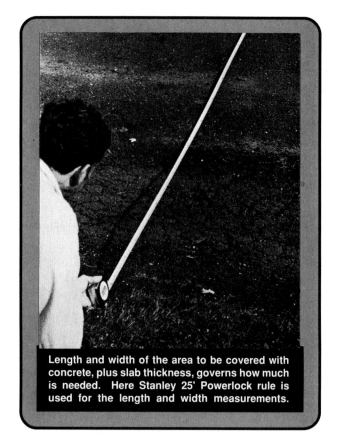

Length and width of the area to be covered with concrete, plus slab thickness, governs how much is needed. Here Stanley 25' Powerlock rule is used for the length and width measurements.

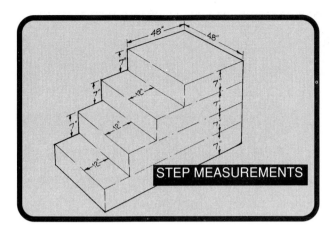

STEP MEASUREMENTS

STEPS

Steps might seem tough to figure, but they aren't. If you'll consider them as separate stacked-up slabs, they calculate easily. In the drawing the steps are composed of four 7-inch-thick slabs, each one 48-inches wide. The topmost slab measures 7 x 48 x 48 inches. The next one down is 60 inches long and the next 72 inches long. The bottom one is 84 inches long. Your figuring would go like this.

$$7 \times 48 \times 48 = 16{,}128 \text{ cubic inches}$$
$$7 \times 48 \times 60 = 20{,}160$$
$$7 \times 48 \times 72 = 24{,}192$$
$$7 \times 48 \times 84 = 28{,}224$$
$$88{,}704 = 1.9 \text{ cu. yd.}$$

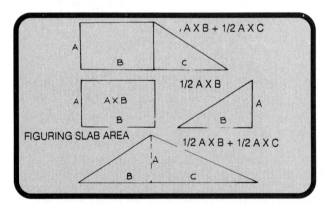

FIGURING SLAB AREA

FIGURING OTHER WORK

Calculating how much concrete to order for a wall is little different. A wall is simply a vertical slab. Multiply its length times its height, both in feet, divide by nine to get square yards, then multiply by its thickness in inches and divide by 36.

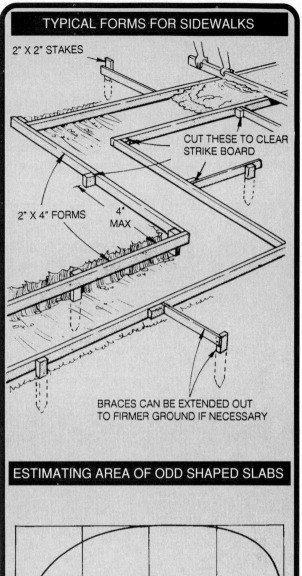

TYPICAL FORMS FOR SIDEWALKS

2" X 2" STAKES

CUT THESE TO CLEAR STRIKE BOARD

2" X 4" FORMS

4' MAX

BRACES CAN BE EXTENDED OUT TO FIRMER GROUND IF NECESSARY

ESTIMATING AREA OF ODD SHAPED SLABS

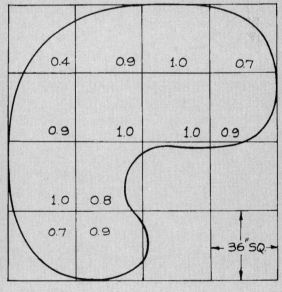

- DRAW TO SCALE ON SQUARED PAPER
- COUNT THE WHOLE SQUARES
- ADD ON THE PARTIAL SQUARES

Prepackaged, sacked mixes come three ways: gravel-mix, which is ordinary concrete containing stones; sand-mix, containing no stones; and mortar-mix, which is used only for°block and brickwork.

USING SACKED CONCRETE

Sacked concrete makes up for its extra cost in time saved. But its best use is for small jobs.

THE PRICE OF PREPACKAGED sacked concrete—the kind where all you do is add water and mix—makes it cost almost twice that of ready mix, but don't let it scare you. It may well be the best way to handle your project. It gets you out of buying, hauling, storing, and handling the separate ingredients for mix-it-yourself concrete. Sacked concrete mixes can be used for any one-of-a-kind small projects. Things like casting a small slab for a few stepping-stones, setting a line of fence posts solidly or even pouring a small walk. Think of sacked concrete as instant concrete whenever and wherever you need it. It is also practical for other projects, up to a cubic yard, if the saving in effort is worth the extra cost.

GRAVEL- AND SAND-MIX

Sand-mix comes in 20-, 40- and 80-pound bags while gravel-mix is usually packaged in 80-pound bags. Some of the larger home centers package their mixes in less than 80 pounds for marketing reasons. As with most everything, the larger bags are more economical per pound.

thin-section projects and for concrete resurfacing. Because it has no stones, it costs somewhat more per bag than gravel-mix. It is sometimes called t*opping.*

You'll find many brands of sacked concrete; all those we've seen produce excellent concrete that works well and hardens as well or better than that you'd make yourself.

Sand mix comes in 20, 40 and 80 pound bags while gravel mix is usually packaged in 80 pound bags. Mortar mix comes in 40 and 80 pound bags and some of the larger home centers package their mixes in less than 80 pounds for marketing reasons. As with most everything, the larger ones are more economical per pound.

Directions for mixing are given on each package. Ingredients are predried, so the exact water content called for on the package works every time. If, to get easier working, you add more water than is specified, you are weakening the mix. On the other hand, if you use less water, you can make a stronger mix.

Because prepackaged concrete is most often hand-mixed, the manufacturers do not incorporate an air-entraining agent because these agents work only if the ingredients are vigorously mixed which is impossible in a wheelbarrow!

The right way to use ready-packaged concrete mix, whether you're mixing a whole bag or not, is to dump the sack and mix it dry again. Then put back what you won't use and save it.

You can mix on a flat surface. Spread out the mix with a hollow spot in middle, add water in the center, and mix, using the proportion of water called for on the sack. Add a little water at a time.

When all the water has been added, the mix will look like this. Troweling should produce a smooth surface without tearing (too dry) or running (too wet). All you need is a little practice.

An excellent project for sacked sand-mix is an outdoor table made by embedding wrought iron legs in the fresh slab. Hardware cloth, 1/2" mesh or chicken wire, reinforces center of slab.

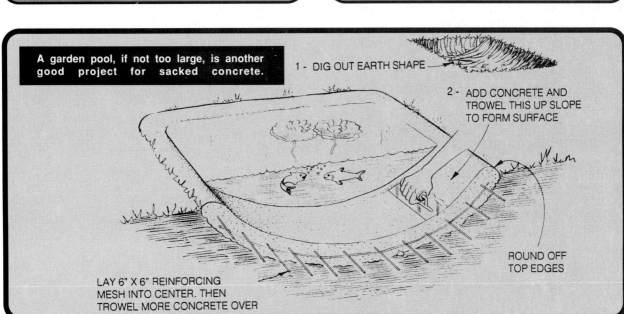

A garden pool, if not too large, is another good project for sacked concrete.

1 - DIG OUT EARTH SHAPE

2 - ADD CONCRETE AND TROWEL THIS UP SLOPE TO FORM SURFACE

ROUND OFF TOP EDGES

LAY 6" X 6" REINFORCING MESH INTO CENTER. THEN TROWEL MORE CONCRETE OVER

Curing can be handled in many ways, but one of the easiest methods, if you have a garden sprayer, is to use white-pigmented membrane curing compound and spray it on. You can start as soon as the slab can be walked on without leaving marks. The pigment helps you to see what areas you've covered, yet weathers away after the curing period is

THE IMPORTANCE OF CURING

The maximum strength of concrete can only be developed by proper curing methods.

CURING IS STRESSED because it is so important. Curing has to do with the love life of the cement gel, the tiny thing that makes concrete harden. The more gels that take place in the hydration reaction, the harder the concrete will get. And the more durable and watertight its surface will become.

Water is the kicker that makes cement gels do their thing, so you want them exposed to lots of it. For a long time, too. That's why the very hardest concrete is cured under water. Yes, concrete will set under water even better than it does on the ground. The next best thing is to keep water present for as long as practical while concrete is setting.

Why not, you ask, just make concrete with a lot more water in the first place? The trouble with that is it won't stay in the mix long enough to do any good. Just long enough to weaken it. The water bleeds out and evaporates, or migrates to the subbase. As it does, it leaves tiny capillary pores all through the mix. Later these form places for water to freeze and crack away the concrete surface.

So the answer to quality concrete is to keep the mix as dry as you can work with it, but let it wet cure.

As we've said, the best way to do this is under water. Since your driveway or patio cannot be built under water, some other means will have to be devised to keep the concrete wet. The accompanying photos show the most practical methods for around-the-house use.

Tests have been made on the hardening of concrete. At first it proceeds at a rapid rate, from the initial set that lets you get onto a slab and finish it, to slabs more than 50 years old. The graph illustrates what happens. Hardness gains fast for the first week or so, then slows down. But concrete really never stops getting harder. Very old concrete—properly made—is the hardest of all.

The tests show another interesting fact: stop the curing and let concrete dry out, and its rapid strength gain stops, too. The loss in strength can never be recovered, even by more curing. This is why it is important to cure every new concrete project you build long enough to let it gain most of its strength. The practical limit is usually about a week, then strip your curing material and your project will be strong and durable.

Garden soaker hose, turned face up, makes a fine concrete curer. Simply snake it around your project, hook it up and turn on the water. Be sure to turn it on often enough to keep surface wet.

Wet-sand.cure is an oldie, but a goodie. Spread it out either wet or dry, then soak it well with water from a garden hose. Except in the driest weather, it should not need any further wetting.

Straw-cure is effective, too, if you sprinkle it occasionally to keep the straw always wet. Spread it out thick enough to hide the concrete beneath soon as you can safely walk on the slab.

Roll out polyethylene plastic sheeting over the newly finished concrete slab and leave it there for a week to effect complete curing. You'll note on unrolling, the poly is wet underneath.

EFFECT OF CURING
TIME ON CONCRETE
STRENGTH

DURABLE
STRONG

PASSABLE

WEAK

VERY WEAK

NO CURING

1   3   7   15   21   28

NUMBER OF DAYS

ALL ABOUT FOOTINGS

The chief requirement for a footing is strength, but there are other considerations too. Here is what you should know.

Big footing-casting jobs are ideal for ready-mix. If the truck mixer must be backed up to an open house foundation, don't let it get too close. If the embankment gives way, you'll have trouble.

A FOOTING (often referred to as a footer) is a below-ground slab of concrete designed to support a wall, column, or other structure. It must be large enough to do the job without wasting concrete; it need not be pretty. Often the excavation it is cast in serves as the form. The top of a footing is merely struck off, perhaps floated once, but left otherwise unfinished. Strength is a requirement; neatness is not. Some footings contain reinforcing steel. The steel need not be there unless the footing is an engineered one. If the steel is needed, then the engineering also is needed. So you may as well omit steel from footings you build.

FOOTING SIZE

All footings serve the same purpose: to distribute concentrated loads from above to as much ground as is necessary to support it. Thus the poorer the ground in bearing capacity, the larger the footing should be to distribute the load. Any footing built on porous or sandy soil should be made extra large. Your building department may have standard footing designs that have been found adequate for your soils. Check with them. If not, ask what size footing they recommend.

For a wall, the footing is often built twice as wide as the wall it is to support. An eight-inch-thick wall thus gets a footing 16 inches wide.

Columns and piers, such as those beneath a porch or deck, concentrate lots of weight on their footings. They carry all of the floor load and all of the roof load for an area half-way to the nearest column on all sides. If a wall is located in this area, they carry its weight too (see the drawing). They also carry what engineers call a *live load* as well as the dead load of the structure. The live load on a floor is furniture and people. The live load on a roof is wind load plus snow. Normal floor live loads are 40 pounds per square foot (psf). Roof live loads vary, but they run from 20 to 50 psf and more, depending on snow conditions. Thus, tremendous loads can be brought to bear on footings. Ordinarily, if you make pier and post footings two feet square, they will be large enough.

Precast footings are used in some deck construction. Dig the hole first, tamp the bottom and set each in place. Top should be 6 inches above the final grade so posts will not touch the ground.

Precast concrete piers come in two sizes —8" and 12"—and in several styles: (left), wood block top for toenailing; hole for pegging (center); and (right) nailing strap. Check your dealer.

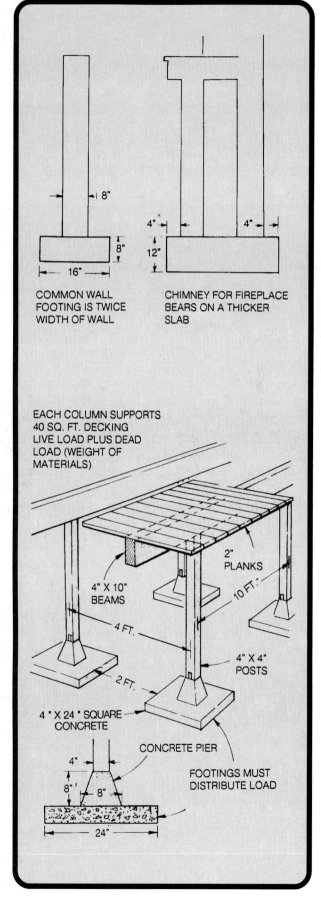

COMMON WALL FOOTING IS TWICE WIDTH OF WALL

8"
8"
16"

CHIMNEY FOR FIREPLACE BEARS ON A THICKER SLAB

4"
4"
12"

EACH COLUMN SUPPORTS 40 SQ. FT. DECKING LIVE LOAD PLUS DEAD LOAD (WEIGHT OF MATERIALS)

2" PLANKS

4" X 10" BEAMS

10 FT.

4 FT.

4" X 4" POSTS

2 FT.

4" X 24" SQUARE CONCRETE

CONCRETE PIER

FOOTINGS MUST DISTRIBUTE LOAD

4"
8"
8"
24"

A long concrete chute made from lumber wasneeded on this job get ready mix to all parts of a footing pour because truck could reach only two sides directly. Pumping the mix would have worked, too.

FOOTING DEPTH

Just as important as the size of the footing is depth. The rule applies to all footings—wall, pier, fireplace. Place footings at least 12 inches below frost depth. Build them on unexcavated soil. No footing should be built on fill. No stones are used underneath a footing, even in poorly drained-soil.

Footings are extended up to the ground depth with concrete or concrete block walls. Concrete piers or pressure-treated rot-proof piers that can be safely buried below ground are used to bring post and column footings out of the ground. For column footings you can buy precast tapered

Footings needn't be pretty or finely finished. Make them strong and just as level as you can, though tie-strips of 1 x 2 lumber hold the tops of the forms firmly together to prevent spreading.

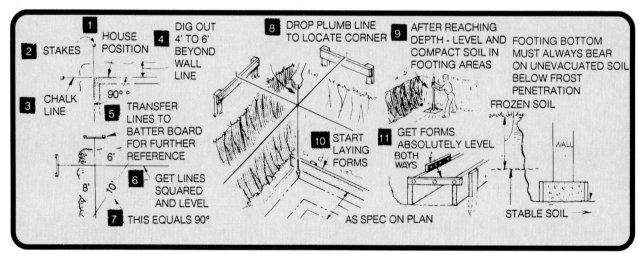

A key, made from an oiled 2 x 4 placed along the center of the footing top after casting, is pried out with a pickaxe as soon as the concrete hardens sufficiently. Key all block and cast walls.

Footing for a fireplace is formed right along with the wall footings. It should be independent of the house footings, however, since rates of settlement may vary. Cast only on undisturbed soil.

piers that do the job expediently. They should have steel nail-strips cast in their tops to anchor a wood post to the pier.

Footings for complicated or very heavy structures should be designed by a professional engineer and be built to these specifications. The same applies to earthquake-prone areas. Such footings will probably contain steel reinforcing rods or bars embedded in the concrete. If they do, be sure the concrete is well compacted around the steel. Ultimate strength of the job depends on a good bond between the concrete and the steel. Steel reinforcing bars should have at least two inches of concrete cover to prevent corrosion.

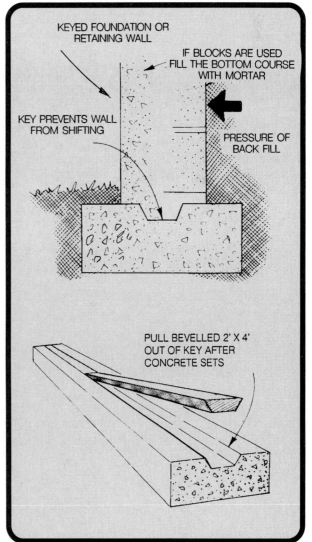

KEYED FOUNDATION OR RETAINING WALL

IF BLOCKS ARE USED FILL THE BOTTOM COURSE WITH MORTAR

KEY PREVENTS WALL FROM SHIFTING

PRESSURE OF BACK FILL

PULL BEVELLED 2' X 4' OUT OF KEY AFTER CONCRETE SETS

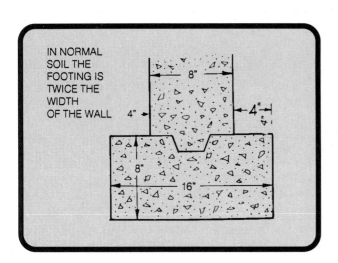

IN NORMAL SOIL THE FOOTING IS TWICE THE WIDTH OF THE WALL

8"

4"

4"

8"

16"

PLAIN AND FANCY WALKS

**A walk is simple to build, but it need not be plain and drab.
Here are a few techniques for the novice and experienced.**

A SIDEWALK IS AN IDEAL project in concrete. It is usually narrow so you can finish without stepping or kneeling on it. It doesn't take much concrete and you can stop for the day installing a bulkhead (see drawing on page 329) between the forms wherever convenient. When you resume work the bulkhead is removed and the resulting keyed joint holds the two slabs together without separation at the joint.

Every concrete project needs forms to contain the concrete while it sets. Sidewalk forms can be 2x4s staked with 1x2 or 2x2-inch stakes driven into the ground as illustrated. Stakes may be up to four feet apart. Front sidewalks are usually built three to four feet wide but a back yard service walk can be as narrow or as wide as you like.

Control joints that create roughly square slabs can be formed by tooling or with leave-in pressure-treated wood forms installed at right angles to the side forms.

DRAINAGE

For proper drainage, a sidewalk should slope 1/4 inch per foot. Place one form higher than the other or finish the walk with a crown. If the walk slopes along its entire length, no slope or crown is needed.

Control joints should divide the sidewalk into slabs (no more than 1 1/2 times as long as they are wide) to prevent in-between cracking. A sidewalk slab should be about four inches thick. Pour the concrete on well-drained soil; soft earth and sod should be dug out. In poorly drained soil, excavate deeper and place a tamped layer of stones (gravel) to within four

Forming a curve is best done by sawing halfway through the plywood and holding the curve with stakes on the inside and outside. Cut stakes off, remove inside ones while mix is wet.

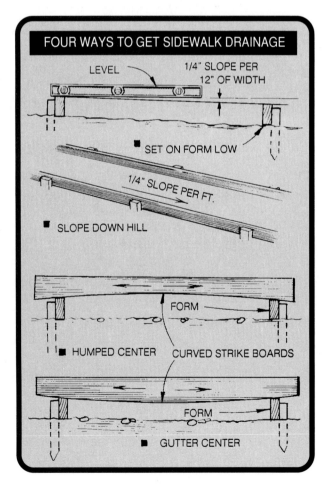

Technique for avoiding sunken slabs is to provide a good subbase. If a slab cannot be cast on unexcavated soil, rake out fill dirt, dampen and compact. Powered compactors can be rented.

inches of the tops of the forms.

If you dig out too deep and have to backfill, do it in layers. Each layer of earth should be dampened and tamped down hard or else backfilled with tamped stones.

HANDLING FRESH CONCRETE

The following tips on handling concrete during placement apply to any project—sidewalk, driveway, patio, footing or wall.

When moved from the mixer—or ready mix truck—to the jobsite, concrete is in danger of segregating. That is, its ingredients may separate, the stones (gravel) moving to the bottom and the water and cement moving to the top. Segregated concrete is weak concrete, so you should prevent segregation. Do it by transporting concrete in a rubber-tired wheelbarrow. Air-entrained concrete is resistant to segregation because the tiny air bubbles buoy up the stones and sand particles and hold the water in the mix. Stiff mixes segregate less, simply because they are stiff. It's tough to keep a sloppy mix from segregating, which is another reason why you shouldn't put too much water in concrete.

FOUR WAYS TO GET SIDEWALK DRAINAGE

LEVEL

1/4" SLOPE PER 12" OF WIDTH

■ SET ON FORM LOW

1/4" SLOPE PER FT.

■ SLOPE DOWN HILL

FORM

■ HUMPED CENTER   CURVED STRIKE BOARDS

FORM

■ GUTTER CENTER

CONCRETE / MASONRY

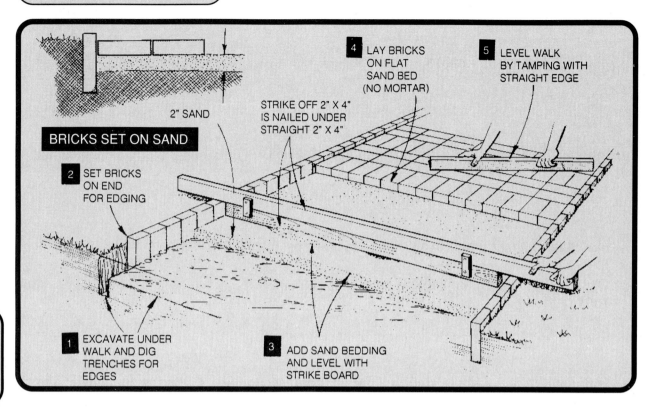

2" SAND

BRICKS SET ON SAND

2 SET BRICKS ON END FOR EDGING

4 LAY BRICKS ON FLAT SAND BED (NO MORTAR)

STRIKE OFF 2" X 4" IS NAILED UNDER STRAIGHT 2" X 4"

5 LEVEL WALK BY TAMPING WITH STRAIGHT EDGE

1 EXCAVATE UNDER WALK AND DIG TRENCHES FOR EDGES

3 ADD SAND BEDDING AND LEVEL WITH STRIKE BOARD

You can lay temporary track for your wheelbarrow with planks. These can cross flowerbeds or even go up stairs. Use them wherever needed.

Don't put too much concrete in the wheelbarrow, it will tend to spill out. Besides, a fully loaded five cubic-foot wheelbarrow is hard to manage. Start small and work up to what you feel you can manage.

Small amounts of mix can be carried to the forms in pails, although that's heavy work. If a wheelbarrow cannot be pushed near the pouring site, a bucket brigade is unavoidable. Hose down buckets and wheelbarrows thoroughly and tip them over after use so that no concrete hardens in them.

DUMPING THE MIX

Dampen the subgrade with a fine spray of water but don't make any puddles or muddy spots. Dump the first load against the form at one end of the sidewalk. Move it into the corner with a hoe or shovel and leave it about a half-inch higher than the forms. If you must walk in the fresh mix, wear rubber boots or old ankle-high shoes. One resourceful homeowner we saw taped plastic gar-

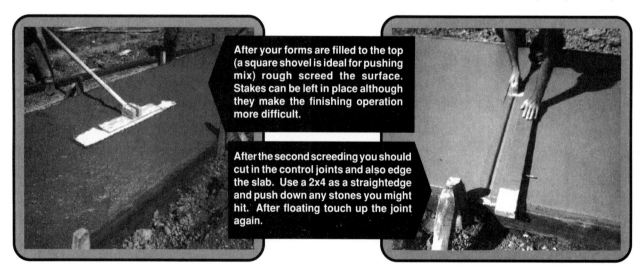

After your forms are filled to the top (a square shovel is ideal for pushing mix) rough screed the surface. Stakes can be left in place although they make the finishing operation more difficult.

After the second screeding you should cut in the control joints and also edge the slab. Use a 2x4 as a straightedge and push down any stones you might hit. After floating touch up the joint again.

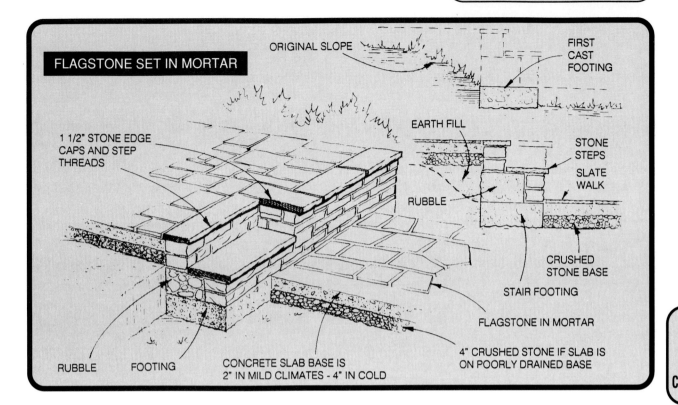

FLAGSTONE SET IN MORTAR

ORIGINAL SLOPE

FIRST CAST FOOTING

EARTH FILL

1 1/2" STONE EDGE CAPS AND STEP THREADS

STONE STEPS

SLATE WALK

RUBBLE

CRUSHED STONE BASE

STAIR FOOTING

RUBBLE   FOOTING   CONCRETE SLAB BASE IS 2" IN MILD CLIMATES - 4" IN COLD

FLAGSTONE IN MORTAR

4" CRUSHED STONE IF SLAB IS ON POORLY DRAINED BASE

bage bags over his shoes up to his knees.

Subsequent loads of concrete should be dumped against the previously placed load. Don't dump them elsewhere and then rake into place.

If you have enough help, someone should start finishing the surface while others bring up more concrete. Strike off, darby, edge, joint, float, and otherwise finish the slab as described in the chapter on tools and techniques.

SIDEWALK TIPS

Like other slabs, sidewalks should be separated from adjacent walls and existing slabs by isolation joints. They're often called expansion joints, though that is a misnomer. The material used is 3/8- or 1/2-inch-thick asphalt-impregnated joint material. Get it from a concrete supplies dealer or from a lumber yard; it comes in strips 3 1/2 inches wide and ten feet long. Fasten it to the

On sidewalks any expansion joint is used at regular intervals. It may tend to rise during the pouring operation so push it back in place with a straightedged ice chipper or spade.

Most common expansion joint material is asphalt impregnated woodchip material 4" x 1/2"thick. If you can't complete your pour in one day finish at point where there is an expansion joint.

wall or existing slab with its top edge about 3/8-inch below the finished level of the slab. During finishing, run the edger along the joint. An isolation joint prevents the new slab from forming a bond with the existing structures and later cracking.

Curved sidewalk forms can be made with 1/4-inch plywood or hardboard bent to shape. The thinner materials will bend to make sharper curves but stakes are needed both inside and outside the curved sections as well as at the transitions between straight and curved forms. The inside stakes can be pulled as soon as concrete has been placed around them.

Sidewalks are well adapted to the use of special finishes and colors. You can apply a magnesium float finish or a rubber float finish. Don't do more than one steel-troweling on a

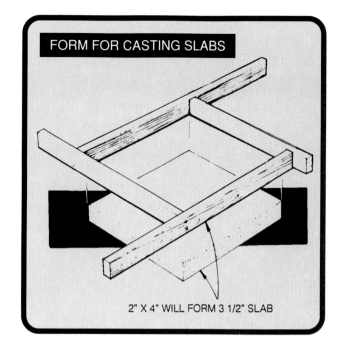

FORM FOR CASTING SLABS

2" X 4" WILL FORM 3 1/2" SLAB

sidewalk unless you plan to broom-finish it later because the steel trowel makes the surface too slick for safe use when wet.

Concrete can withstand a light rain shortly after final troweling, but rain during the finishing process or a heavy rain shortly after finishing can spoil the job. The lesson: don't work when rain is expected.

All concrete should cure slowly, and the best way is to keep it damp or wet for the first week. Do this by covering it with plastic, wet rags, damp sod, hay, or even with a garden sprinkler. A soaker hose left running slowly will also do the job. Or you can buy a spray-on curing that forms a film that prevents the slab from drying out. In a few weeks it will automatically wear off.

These stepping stones are artistic and are cast in a circular form, finished and cured before hauling to your walk site. They are ideal for hillside slopes where building a slab is impractical.

Another interesting and artistic walk treatment. Individual slabs are first poured and finished. Ordinary fieldstone fill in the spaces and the joints between the stones filled with mortar.

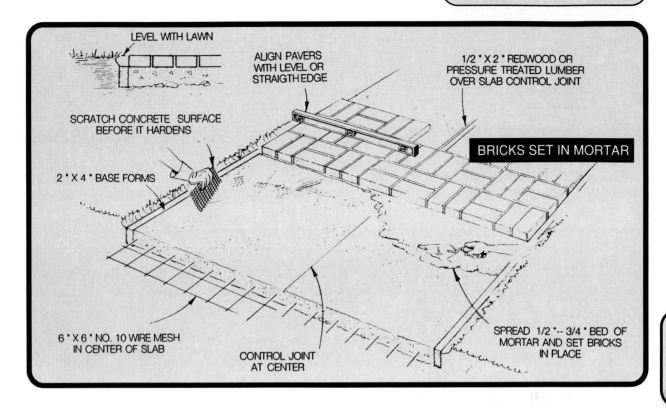

LEVEL WITH LAWN

ALIGN PAVERS WITH LEVEL OR STRAIGTH EDGE

1/2 " X 2 " REDWOOD OR PRESSURE TREATED LUMBER OVER SLAB CONTROL JOINT

SCRATCH CONCRETE SURFACE BEFORE IT HARDENS

BRICKS SET IN MORTAR

2 " X 4 " BASE FORMS

6 " X 6 " NO. 10 WIRE MESH IN CENTER OF SLAB

CONTROL JOINT AT CENTER

SPREAD 1/2 "-- 3/4 " BED OF MORTAR AND SET BRICKS IN PLACE

HOT AND COLD WEATHER PROBLEMS

In hot weather concrete needs special treatment because it sets up fast. Cut the casting area to a half or one-third. Sprinkle the surface after strikeoff with a fine mist of water to slow air-drying and to cool it. You can start at dawn so as to finish before the heat of the day, or start in the afternoon and finish in the cool of dusk.

In cold weather concrete must be protected from freezing. The best policy is not to start a project if an overnight freeze is possible. Concrete can be ruined by freezing. Even if it doesn't freeze, cold concrete is slow to set.

Of course, you can rent kerosene-fired stoves, called salamanders, to prevent your concrete from freezing during cold weather.

Do not apply any deicing chemicals to your slab during its first winter. Spread dry sand instead. Also, your slab should have at least four weeks to dry out before being exposed to a hard freeze.

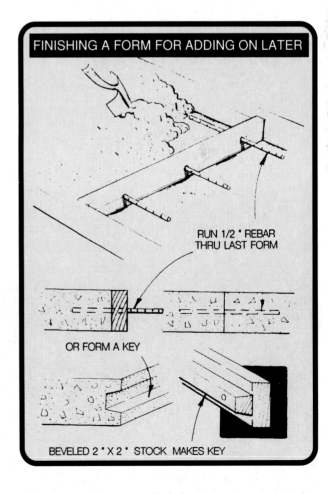

FINISHING A FORM FOR ADDING ON LATER

RUN 1/2 " REBAR THRU LAST FORM

OR FORM A KEY

BEVELED 2 " X 2 " STOCK MAKES KEY

BUILD-A-FLOOR

POURING A CONCRETE FLOOR isn't too different from a concrete sidewalk or driveway, but there are differences. An indoor floor need not be made with air-entrained concrete, even in the coldest climate.

Because a concrete floor is surrounded by walls, unless you are pouring a combination slab and footing and plan to build a wall directly over the edge of the slab as illustrated in the photos, forming it makes use of what are called screeds. Screeds are temporary forms placed around the edges at eight or ten-foot intervals. After strikeoff, the screeds are pulled out and additional concrete is shoveled in to fill the space. This must be done immediately before the mix starts to set. The fresh mix is blended in with the existing mix by "chunking" it with a shovel. Screeds are staked into the subgrade just as though they were forms. To remove them, wade in with rubber boots and use a crowbar or pickaxe to pull out everything, including the stakes.

Ordinarily, the screeds are placed level all the way around. The level line is established using a transit, a line level or a tube level longer than

the diagonal measurement of the floor. Fill the tubing with colored water and, since water will always seek its own level, with one end of the tubing set at the screed height you want, by raising the other end of the tube you will note when the same level is reached. This is a very accurate way for the homeowner to make certain the edge of the slab is at the same level. In fact, one manufacturer makes it even easier; they have a tubing and battery powered electronic device so a beep is emitted when two points far apart are at the same level.

Chalk lines snapped onto the walls indicate the tops of the screeds. If you like, the screeds can be nailed to the wall, with masonry nails instead of being staked to the subgrade. Just don't fasten them so well that they cannot be removed easily later.

At any rate, you'll need a strip of isolation joint material between each screed and the wall. Neglect this and the new slab will bond so tightly to the wall it will crack as it shrinks. The isolation joint material should be set 3/8-inch below the level and should extend through locations where

A floor that will never squeak or rot is a floor that is made out of concrete - and in colors too!

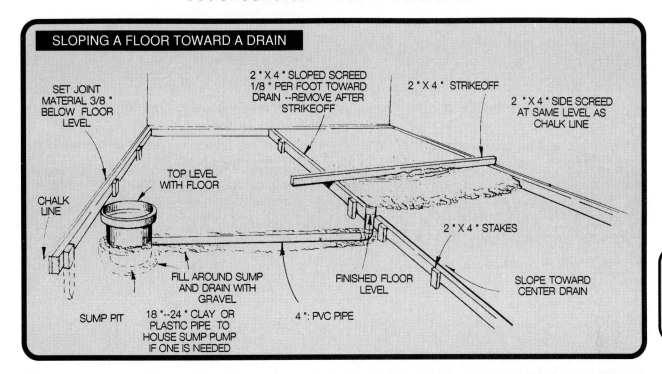

SLOPING A FLOOR TOWARD A DRAIN

SET JOINT MATERIAL 3/8 " BELOW FLOOR LEVEL

2 " X 4 " SLOPED SCREED 1/8 " PER FOOT TOWARD DRAIN --REMOVE AFTER STRIKEOFF

2 " X 4 " STRIKEOFF

2 " X 4 " SIDE SCREED AT SAME LEVEL AS CHALK LINE

TOP LEVEL WITH FLOOR

CHALK LINE

2 " X 4 " STAKES

FILL AROUND SUMP AND DRAIN WITH GRAVEL

FINISHED FLOOR LEVEL

SLOPE TOWARD CENTER DRAIN

SUMP PIT

18 "--24 " CLAY OR PLASTIC PIPE TO HOUSE SUMP PUMP IF ONE IS NEEDED

4 ": PVC PIPE

the new floor slab meets other slabs, such as where a garage floor meets an existing driveway.

DRAINAGE

Every floor must provide for drainage, to either a floor drain or, in the case of a garage floor, to the driveway. A good many garage floors are sloped to drain toward the driveway. The floor drain, of course, must have somewhere to drain. This is usually a dry hole filled with stones, a sump pump pit, a drainage ditch, or whatever other drainage is at hand. A floor drain should not just empty into a stone-filled layer beneath the floor. This encourages rapid settlement of the floor that would soon crack the slab. Naturally, all portions of the floor drain system beneath the floor should be installed before the concrete is placed. Easiest to use is a four-inch PVC pipe and solvent-welding fittings available at home centers.

In areas of heavy rain and poorly drained soil, a basement floor may need inside perimeter subfloor drains to keep water pressure from building up under the floor causing cracks. This is made with perforated pipe placed just inside the forms.

Getting the mix in can be the hardest part of floor-making. In this case a 15' extension trough was rented from the ready mix producer. Move the concrete along with a square shovel.

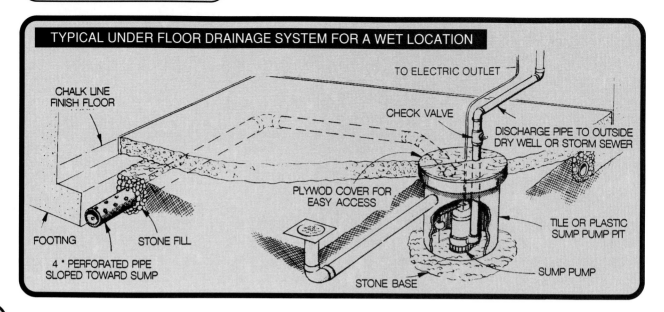

TYPICAL UNDER FLOOR DRAINAGE SYSTEM FOR A WET LOCATION

Place stones around the pipe to keep concrete out. The drain system is usually run into a sump pit located below the floor, where a sump pump can discharge water into the sewer (if permitted) or to the outside.

An 18-inch diameter concrete or clay sewer tile makes a handy sump pit. Install it with the flange up. You can also buy a plastic sump pit. The top of the sump pit should be at floor level. Run floor drains and the underfloor perimeter drainage pipes into the sump above the halfway point so they'll be above water level at all times. Failure to do this will cause bubbling and gurgling.

If a basement laundry or shower discharges into the same sump, floor drains should be fitted with traps. Otherwise gases created in the sump will enter the basement. A toilet should never be connected to a sump.

Steel 1/2" x 10" anchor bolts are wiggled into the fresh concrete mix and are located 4' to 6' apart around the slab edges of this garage slab. These hold the structure to the foundation.

SLOPING A FLOOR

The finished concrete floor should slope evenly toward its drain in the floor or out the garage door. The best way to slope a floor to a more or less central drain is to install additional screeds from the four corners of the walls to the drains sloping them at least 1/8-inch per foot. Like the edge screeds, the sloped screeds are removed after strikeoff. Fill in with extra concrete and chunk it to mix thoroughly with the previously installed concrete. Smooth off with the darby later.

On floors sloped to a floor drain, work the darby with its blade pointed toward the drain. This will maintain the slope, smoothing it without changing it.

Concrete should not come in contact with untreated wood because that encourages rot. Slope of a garage floor should be about an inch for every ten feet, toward the door of course. Get it by sloping the side screeds. In a two-car garage you may need a center screed to keep the strikeoff board shorter than 12 feet.

Floors should be a nominal four inches

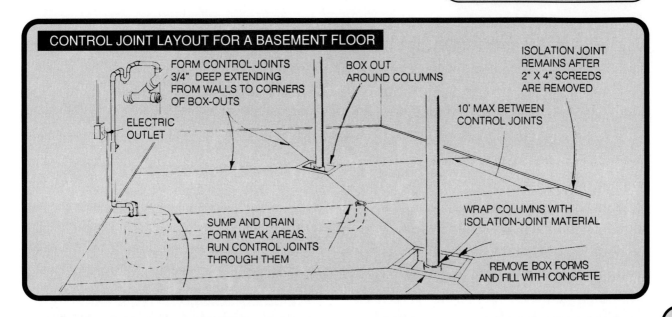

CONTROL JOINT LAYOUT FOR A BASEMENT FLOOR

FORM CONTROL JOINTS 3/4" DEEP EXTENDING FROM WALLS TO CORNERS OF BOX-OUTS

ELECTRIC OUTLET

BOX OUT AROUND COLUMNS

ISOLATION JOINT REMAINS AFTER 2" X 4" SCREEDS ARE REMOVED

10' MAX BETWEEN CONTROL JOINTS

SUMP AND DRAIN FORM WEAK AREAS. RUN CONTROL JOINTS THROUGH THEM

WRAP COLUMNS WITH ISOLATION-JOINT MATERIAL

REMOVE BOX FORMS AND FILL WITH CONCRETE

Floating and finishing a floor slab around the edges can be done best from outside the slab. The out-of-reach center portion of the slab must be done working from knee-boards on the slab.

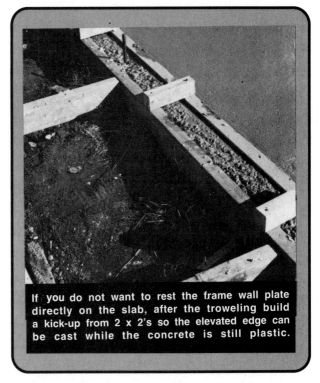

If you do not want to rest the frame wall plate directly on the slab, after the troweling build a kick-up from 2 x 2's so the elevated edge can be cast while the concrete is still plastic.

thick. The subgrade underneath is sloped to maintain this thickness throughout the floor. Any backfilling done beneath the floor should be compacted stones or sand. In poorly drained soil lay a sheet of 6-mil polyethylene over the stones if there's a chance of water coming in contact with the finished floor slab from below. Run it up the walls behind the isolation joints and cut off the excess later.

Ready mixed concrete may be chuted in through a basement window. For a garage floor, the ready mix can usually be dumped directly from the truck onto the subgrade.

Cut control joints into the floor slab to divide it into ten-foot maximum sections. Basement columns and floor drains are weak spots so control joints should run to them as shown in the drawing. For a crack-free floor, box the basement lally columns. Remove the box forms later and add concrete around the columns, finishing it to match the surrounding floor. Few contractors do it this way, but it will ensure a crack-free floor.

Steel-troweling makes the easiest-to-clean basement floor finish. Be sure to cure the floor for at least six days.

REPAIRING WALKS AND DRIVES

Sooner or later the time will come when a little repair work is called for on concrete projects—here's how to do it.

Here's a sidewalk problem that can happen when a tree is planted too close to the walk and the growing roots actually lift the slab. You have two choices: remove the section completely and build a thinner slab or build a ramp-like slope between the adjacent sections to prevent people from stumbling. Or don't plant trees close to the edge of your sidewalk.

THREE THINGS can happen to sidewalks and driveways: (1) they settle unevenly, (2) they crack, (3) they scale. If you build yours carefully, you may avoid all three problems. Also, for homes located in northern areas subjected to snow in the wintertime, never use de-icing chemicals containing ammonium nitrate and ammonium sulfate as these chemicals react with the concrete causing it to disintegrate.

If the paving around your house shows signs of deterioration, your best bet is to resurface it. Cast a whole new slab over the damaged one. It can be done.

THIN-BONDED RESURFACINGS

There are two ways you can do this — with a thin resurfacing that is bonded to the existing slab, and with a thicker, unbonded resurfacing. Which you use depends on how much of a change in elevation can be tolerated. If the old slab has settled considerably and a raise in grade of at least 3 inches is not objectionable, use the thicker unbonded resurfacing. but if only a slight increase in elevation is possible, go the thin-bonded route.

To do it, first acid-etch the surface of the

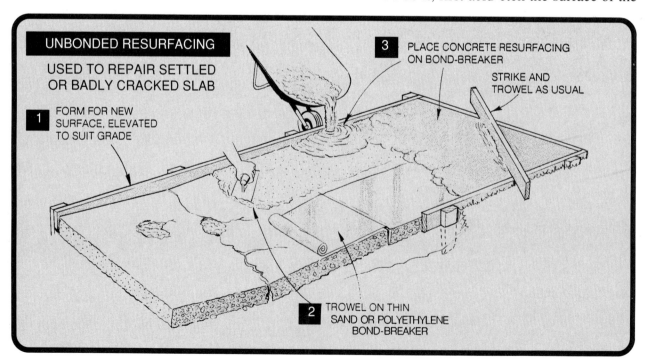

UNBONDED RESURFACING
USED TO REPAIR SETTLED OR BADLY CRACKED SLAB

1 FORM FOR NEW SURFACE, ELEVATED TO SUIT GRADE

2 TROWEL ON THIN SAND OR POLYETHYLENE BOND-BREAKER

3 PLACE CONCRETE RESURFACING ON BOND-BREAKER

STRIKE AND TROWEL AS USUAL

old slab with a 20-percent solution of muriatic acid (one part acid to five parts water). This gives "tooth" to the surface for a better bond. Wear goggles and rubber gloves. Rinse with water until entirely free of acid. Make the form for the bonded topping layer to the desired grade and slope, leaving a minimum of 3/4-inch for the topping layer. If the old slab has not settled, you can use construction adhesive to fasten redwood strips to the edges as forms. Put additional strips over all cracks in the old slab, else the new topping will crack there, too.

Mix the topping using 1 part portland cement and 2 1/2 parts of concrete sand. Or you can use sacked topping mix.

Just before pouring it, scrub a slurry of pure portland cement and water into the base slab with a stiff scrubbing brush and place the topping before it dries white. Strike off, edge, finish, and cure as usual.

If portions of the topping are less than 3 inches, it is recommended that a commercial bonding agent, or adhesive, be used instead of cement slurry Many different types are available from your masonry supply yard or even your hardware store. Clean the surface, brush on the bonding agent making certain the surface is thoroughly covered and follow the directions on the jar. These adhesives work well and can be effectively used for feathering a new surface as thin as a half inch.

The best patches are made with prepared patching mixes. With some you add water, mix thoroughly and brush on; others come in liquid form and must be painted on. After patching, cure the surface.

UNBONDED RESURFACING

Building an unbonded resurfacing is like making a new slab using the old one for a subbase. Form it as usual, making it at least the thickness of a 2 x 4 (3 1/2"). Before pouring concrete, cover the surface of the old slab with a thin bond-breaker of sand or a sheet of 2-mil polyethylene plastic.

Control joints can be placed anywhere since those in the unbonded base slab will not "telegraph" up to the upper slab. Thin-section slabs less than 31/2 inches thick should be jointed into two-foot squares. Otherwise follow the usual jointing requirements. Cure as for any concrete.

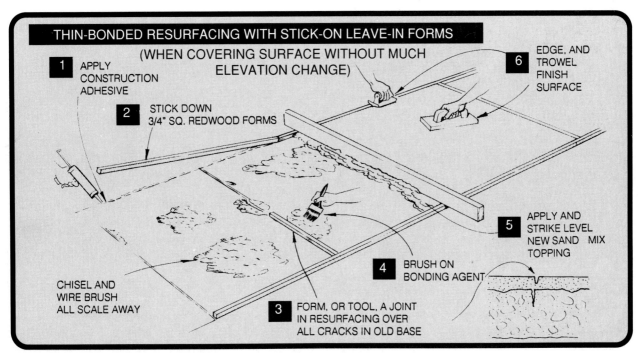

THIN-BONDED RESURFACING WITH STICK-ON LEAVE-IN FORMS

(WHEN COVERING SURFACE WITHOUT MUCH ELEVATION CHANGE)

1 APPLY CONSTRUCTION ADHESIVE

2 STICK DOWN 3/4" SQ. REDWOOD FORMS

6 EDGE, AND TROWEL FINISH SURFACE

CHISEL AND WIRE BRUSH ALL SCALE AWAY

3 FORM, OR TOOL, A JOINT IN RESURFACING OVER ALL CRACKS IN OLD BASE

4 BRUSH ON BONDING AGENT

5 APPLY AND STRIKE LEVEL NEW SAND MIX TOPPING

A concrete driveway is a big do-it-yourself project. But if you have help, and proceed in easy-do stages, you needn't worry. It goes best with labor-saving tools, like a bull float that lets you reach out over the slab's surface to put an initial finish on it.

POUR A DRIVEWAY

Black top—asphalt—is a popular driveway surface installed by professionals. For do-it-yourselfers poured concrete is one alternative but with a little imagination your drive need not be plain.

DRIVEWAYS are simply wide sidewalks but because of their extra width, more concrete is required. A driveway usually calls for the use of ready mix because few people would care to hand-mix enough (even with a power mixer) concrete for a whole driveway. However, if you divide the drive into four-foot squares and do one or two squares each day you bring the job within the reach of your muscles and back.

When most people think of a driveway they picture a plain concrete slab slightly wider than a car and extending from the street to the garage or carport. With a little imagination, a driveway can be much more. It's out there in front. It may as well add to the appearance of your home. For this reason we recommend that you plan your driveway in a special shape and with a colored, textured, or colored *and* textured finish that will set off the house. Leave-in forms of redwood,

cypress, or pressure-treated lumber go well in a driveway.

A good width for a one-car driveway is 10 to 14 feet; make it 14 feet wide if it curves. For two cars parked side by side, the drive should be 16 to 24 feet wide. The drive can be single width, widening to double-width near the garage and should allow a car to swing into either garage stall. Economical strip drives are satisfactory, if they are straight, but the added maintenance of the center area makes them undesirable. They are cheaper initially but the homeowners we surveyed preferred a driveway poured full width.

SLOPE

The maximum slope for an inclined driveway should be a 14 percent grade which is a rise of 1 3/4 inches per foot. Changes in grade from sloping to level should be gradual so that cars with long wheelbases don't scrape as they pass.

Good driveway drainage calls for a cross-slope (side-to-side) of 1/8 to 1/4 inch per foot or else a general slope toward the street. A cross-slope can be made by using a curved strikeoff board or by making one side form higher than the other. If the drive slopes to the garage, you'll have to provide a drain at the garage for the water. The driveway should be one inch lower than the garage floor to keep the water out, then flared up to the garage floor in the last six inches of driveway. In fact, it is a good idea to slope your garage floor slightly (1/8-inch to the foot) from rear to front just in case a sudden rainstorm floods your driveway. Also, the slight slope permits cleaning by hosing the floor.

HOW THICK?

For cars only, a good concrete driveway need only be 3 1/2 inches thick, but no less anywhere else. If you go this route, you'll have to remember that fuel delivery trucks, garbage trucks, refuse, service trucks, and ready mix trucks must be kept off. A five-inch thickness is safer and will handle some truck traffic. However, for regular use by heavy trucks—not just pickups—make the

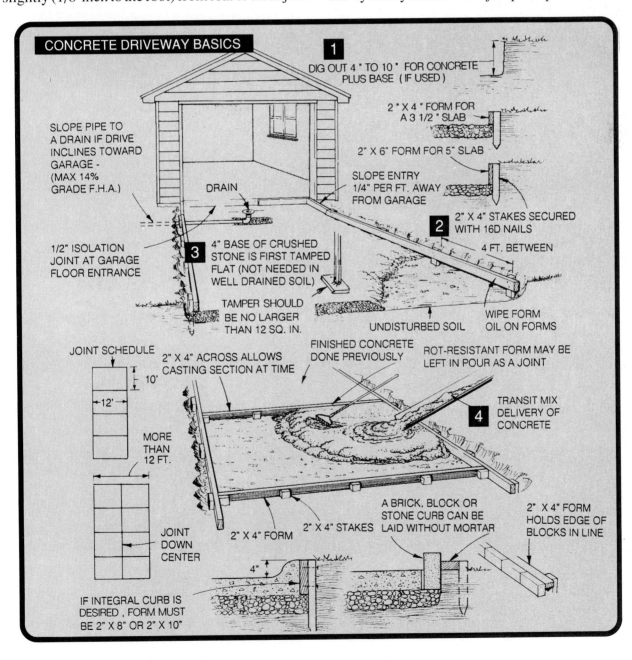

CONCRETE DRIVEWAY BASICS

1 DIG OUT 4" TO 10" FOR CONCRETE PLUS BASE (IF USED)

2" X 4" FORM FOR A 3 1/2" SLAB

2" X 6" FORM FOR 5" SLAB

SLOPE ENTRY 1/4" PER FT. AWAY FROM GARAGE

SLOPE PIPE TO A DRAIN IF DRIVE INCLINES TOWARD GARAGE - (MAX 14% GRADE F.H.A.)

DRAIN

2 2" X 4" STAKES SECURED WITH 16D NAILS

4 FT. BETWEEN

1/2" ISOLATION JOINT AT GARAGE FLOOR ENTRANCE

3 4" BASE OF CRUSHED STONE IS FIRST TAMPED FLAT (NOT NEEDED IN WELL DRAINED SOIL)

TAMPER SHOULD BE NO LARGER THAN 12 SQ. IN.

WIPE FORM OIL ON FORMS

UNDISTURBED SOIL

JOINT SCHEDULE

10'

12'

MORE THAN 12 FT.

JOINT DOWN CENTER

IF INTEGRAL CURB IS DESIRED, FORM MUST BE 2" X 8" OR 2" X 10"

2" X 4" ACROSS ALLOWS CASTING SECTION AT TIME

FINISHED CONCRETE DONE PREVIOUSLY

ROT-RESISTANT FORM MAY BE LEFT IN POUR AS A JOINT

4 TRANSIT MIX DELIVERY OF CONCRETE

2" X 4" FORM

2" X 4" STAKES

A BRICK, BLOCK OR STONE CURB CAN BE LAID WITHOUT MORTAR

2" X 4" FORM HOLDS EDGE OF BLOCKS IN LINE

4"

Double exposed-aggregate driveway with its ends flared into the street says "welcome" to friends. Exposed-aggregate concrete is more difficult and time consuming to place and finish than the usual trowel-finished kind but you can do it if you take the time.

driveway thickness six inches. A four-inch thickness calls for excavating half an inch below the bottoms of 2x4 form boards. The five-and six-inch thicknesses require the use of 2x6 forms.

No steel mesh or reinforcing bars are needed in driveways but using mesh has the advantage of keeping any cracks that may develop from separating. Steel mesh costs about the same as an inch thickness of concrete. The subgrade should be unexcavated earth or compacted stones. The stones are needed only in poorly drained soils, such as heavy clays in wet climates. Prepare the subgrade, measuring down from a straightedge placed across the tops of the forms. Try for a uniform thickness all over, but don't worry too much about spots that are too deep. Concrete will fill them.

CURBS

You can cast integral curbs on your driveway by using 2x8-inch side forms and striking off with a template made of 3/4-inch wood and nailed to the straightedge. The ends of the template are curved to form the curbs you strikeoff. It can even slope the driveway if the slope is built into the template (see drawing). The embryonic four-inch curb left after strikeoff is finished by floating and troweling along the contour.

Dampen the subgrade just before the ready-mix truck arrives to keep the mix from giving up its water to the subgrade. *This should be done with every slab-casting project.*

As in the case of pouring a wall, a keyed joint left at the end of a session of work lets you start again at a later time without destroying the slab's continuity.

To get smooth slab edges, tamp the concrete along the forms with a straight-backed shovel or ice chopper.

Be sure to form a cross-wise control (expansion) joint at least every ten feet along the driveway. A driveway more than 12 feet wide should have another control joint running the full length, usually along the center line, as shown in the drawing.

Depth of the center joint should be about one inch on a four-inch driveway. You'll also need isolation joints at all adjoining walls and slabs, including the garage floor and sidewalk.

A magnesium float makes a good driveway surface; steel-troweling is too smooth. If you use a steel trowel, finish by brooming to make a nonslip surface. Cure for at least six days before stripping the forms. Then the drive can be opened to traffic.

Local building regulations may govern driveway design so check with your building department. Normally the driveway meets the street two inches above the street elevation.

This sprawling poured concrete driveway was formed with isolation joints at 10 feet intervals. One section at a time was poured and the outline of irregular stone tooled in the surface.

Stacked pattern of precast concrete flagstones create a different-looking driveway. The stones can be cast one or more a day in the backyard, cured, then set on a compact sand subbase.

Cast-in-place concrete rectangles help divide a driveway project into "bite-sized" chunks you can easily handle. It's no strain to do one or two squares a day. Grass grows between them.

All -masonry entrance attests to the do-it-yourself skills of the homeowner. This driveway is pattern-stamped, colored concrete that looks like bricks but is actually tooled rectangles.

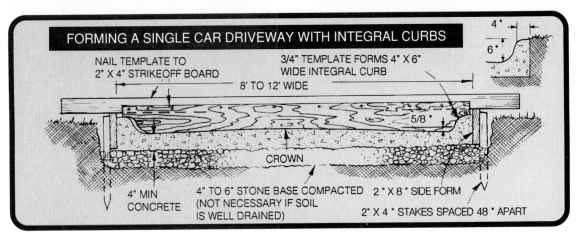

FORMING A SINGLE CAR DRIVEWAY WITH INTEGRAL CURBS

NAIL TEMPLATE TO
2" X 4" STRIKEOFF BOARD

3/4" TEMPLATE FORMS 4" X 6"
WIDE INTEGRAL CURB

8' TO 12' WIDE

4"

6"

5/8"

CROWN

4" MIN
CONCRETE

4" TO 6" STONE BASE COMPACTED
(NOT NECESSARY IF SOIL
IS WELL DRAINED)

2" X 8" SIDE FORM

2" X 4" STAKES SPACED 48" APART

UNUSUAL SURFACES

**Concrete need not be drab or strictly utilitarian.
Here are eight different ways to glamorize concrete.**

Most popular specialty surface for concrete—and among the most attractive—is exposed aggregate. It's made by brushing away surface mortar to expose the colorful stones beneath.

CONCRETE TAKES EASILY to decorative treatment. In many cases special effects are very little harder to get than an ordinary smooth trowel finish. You need not always use a decorative finish, but you should at least consider one for your project. Very often the special treatment is combined with a colored surface to get both color and texture.

Decorative surfaces can be had by tooling during finishing, by imprinting, by brooming or by otherwise texturing the surface

EXPOSED AGGREGATE

One of the prettiest ways to enhance surface appearance is to wash and brush away the surface mortar exposing the stones immediately below. This is called an exposed aggregate treatment and it's particularly attractive if special colored aggregates are used in the mix. A wide variety of textures is possible through the use of different-sized aggregates. You can collect your own gravel along streambeds — with the landowner's permission — or buy what you need from a masonry or terrazzo supply yard. A broad selection is available. What you use depends on the effect you want. Exposed aggregate is excellent for sidewalks, patios and driveways. It is best used with integral coloring in the concrete. If, however, you are located in a northern area subjected to winter freezing, this may not be the best surface because if water collects and freezes between the aggregate and the surrounding mortar, the expanding ice may loosen a stone. So keep this in mind.

A magnesium-float finish gives just the right texture for walking on and not slipping. One of the many non-slip surfaces very easy to make, it is ideal for swimming pool aprons and walks.

Brooming produces a gritty surface texture on a concrete sidewalk. The degree of texturing may be varied at the time of brooming and broom stiffness. Brush only in the pulling direction.

This may look like brick or flat concrete blocks set in place but the surface was actually stamped after the floated surface was hard enough to take the stamp without having the impressions sag.

Another raised brick surface made via the stamping route. A new roller stamp (by Goldblatt) is now available from tool rental houses. Make the impression by rolling rather than foot stamping.

TWO METHODS

You have a choice of making exposed aggregate concrete with either the mixed-in method or the seeding method. Both are about equal in effort. The seeding method lets you use plain ready mixed concrete, perhaps colored. The mixed-in method, if special decorative stones are to be used, requires that you mix the concrete yourself.

To seed in exposed aggregate, form and cast the slab in the usual way, then strike it off. That's as far as normal finishing should go. No floating or troweling is required. Let the surface set up slightly then begin spreading the decorative stones over it. Use your hands or a shovel, whichever seems to work best.

Begin tapping the stones into the soft surface. Use a wood float, a darby, or the edge of a 2 x 4. If the stones sink out of sight, the mix is too soft. Wait until it gets harder. If the stones resist entrance, you have waited too long. Pound them with a brick to force them into the topping. At any rate, the stones should be embedded until they are either flush with the surface or just beneath it. Ideally after embedment, the slab should look as though it had just been floated. In fact, you can run the float over it just to close any openings.

The surface needs time to set up harder before you begin the next step. The rule is to wait until it can hold your weight on knee boards without leaving much of an impression. Start by brushing away the surface mortar with a stiff nylon-bristle push broom. How much mortar you brush away depends on the size of the stones to be exposed. If they are golf-ball size, you'll have to remove more mortar than if they are pea-gravel size.

FLUSHING

After brushing you still can't see the stones — just their forms beneath a thin mortar covering — so flush the mortar covering away with a *fine* spray of water from a hose. This may well be done along with brushing. If the slab has set up hard enough, few stones will be brushed and flushed out.

Brush and flush until the surface has the appearance you want. Don't, however, expose

As soon as the concrete has set enough, decorative stones are spread evenly over the surface in a layer one stone-deep. Use a rake or square shovel. The larger stones are best hand-placed.

more than the upper third of each stone. If you go deeper, you'll be removing mortar that the stone needs to hold it in place. If brushing and flushing remove mortar too fast or loosen many stones, stop and give the concrete more time to set up.

Treatment too soon, while easy work, is tough to control. On the other hand, if you wait too long to brush, the surface mortar will be reluctant to come off and hard brushing will be required. In this case, have a wire brush on hand for emergency exposure of problem areas. You'll find that you can expose surface stones quite well when the concrete is hard enough to walk on without kneeboards. If you use leave-in forms, brush the mortar from them with a wire brush and flush all loose mortar from the slab.

BRIGHTENING THE LOOKS

In a few days the slab should be washed with a solution of one part muriatic acid (commercial strength) poured into ten parts of water. This removes any dulling mortar film from the surface, brightening the aggregates. Cure the slab in the usual manner.

After curing and air-drying, your exposed-aggregate work will still look dull and lifeless compared to the way it did when wet. To give it a constant wet appearance, treat the surface with a non-yellowing concrete sealer. Apply two coats

Then tap and push the stones down into the surface with a float. All stones should be firmly embedded until they can barely be seen under the surface. Float over them to even surface.

Wait a while, then brush and flush off the hardening surface mortar with hose and stiff broom. Brush deep enough to expose the top third of each stone but do not brush any stones out.

Some dealers carry combination brush-and-flush tools such as this one illustrated. Connected to a garden hose, it does two jobs at once, leaving an exposed-ag surface like that at the right.

Using a concrete bonding agent between the courses of an integrally colored two-course job is as simple as brushing the bonding agent on. The colored second course can be poured immediately or done weeks later with a bonding agent. Topping thickness can be as thin as desired, yet it will still bond well to the base slab.

of the sealer but remember the slab should be *DRY* before application!

MIXED-IN METHOD

To make exposed aggregate concrete by mixing-in, simply substitute the pretty stones for the ordinary concrete aggregates in your regular mix. Handle surface exposure the same as for the seeding method.

To save on the amount of costly aggregates needed and on coloring pigment, you can cast a two-course exposed aggregate slab. The bottom course is a regular mix, even a ready mix, without special stones. Strike it off an inch below the tops of the forms and finish by scratching the surface with a piece of metal lath or hardware cloth. This step may be omitted if the topping layer is poured right away. Otherwise, apply a commercial concrete bonding agent to the base slab before pouring the top mix containing a coloring and fancy aggregates. This may be days or weeks later, if you wish. The topping need be only as thick as a single layer of the topping stones but not thinner than a half-inch. Expansion joints in base and topping should coincide.

Using a two-course mix for exposed aggregate you can get rich-looking effects inexpensively because the decorative stones are only surface deep. This system also eliminates most of the mixing, letting you use ready mix for the bulk of the job, and mixing only the topping yourself.

TOOLING

Tooled and imprinted surface textures are applied during finishing. They may be as simple as lines dividing a slab into flagstone shapes or as complex as some of the imprints illustrated. Simple tooling may be done with masonry jointing tools, the edges of trowels and floats, or even with tin cans. A broom drawn over the surface makes a texture all its own. You can get a good-looking swirl finish by moving the float or trowel in short arcs or circles finishing the slab. Pattern-stamp-

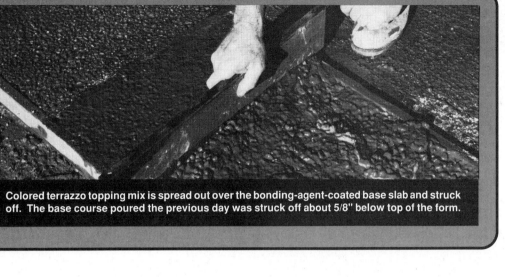

Colored terrazzo topping mix is spread out over the bonding-agent-coated base slab and struck off. The base course poured the previous day was struck off about 5/8" below top of the form.

ing, in the shape of cobble stones, brick and flagging, is done with shaped tools, which you can usually rent. Check with your local tool rental shop or masonry supply yard.

ROCK SALT FINISH

An arrestingly different finish can be made by throwing salt on the surface just after floating and troweling it. Roll or press it into the surface so only the tops of the salt chunks are left exposed. Later, when the concrete has hardened, the rock salt will wash out, leaving random impressions. As you would expect, this type of surface is not recommended in freeze-thaw climates because it opens the surface to scaling damage.

COMBINATIONS

You can choose combinations of any of the tooled, imprinted exposed-aggregate surfaces, along with others, to get any effect you want. Sometimes a driveway, patio, or walk is made of rectangles of exposed aggregate concrete separated by strips of plain concrete, or by brick strips laid in mortar on a concrete base. Rock salt textures go well with tooling, imprinting, and exposed-aggregate. This reduces the amount of coloring and special aggregates you need to cover an area yet gets away from the too-common smooth patio slab.

If concrete is right for around-the-house work, it's even better when done in color and texture.

Brush-flushing the colored terrazzo topping brings out the beauty of its integrally-cast pea gravel. If brushing tends to knock out many stones, give the terrazzo topping longer to set.

Travertine finish is made by spatter-dashing a soupy, tinted topping of cement, water and coloring (lamp black) on the base slab, then troweling it lightly, leaving depressions. Do not use in cold climates.

PATTERN STAMPING

Concrete can be made to look like brick, stone or tile by coloring and pattern-stamping it.

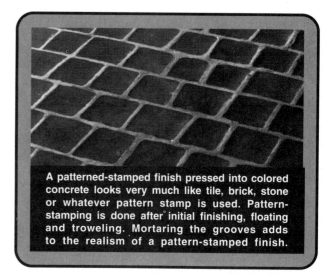

A patterned-stamped finish pressed into colored concrete looks very much like tile, brick, stone or whatever pattern stamp is used. Pattern-stamping is done after initial finishing, floating and troweling. Mortaring the grooves adds to the realism of a pattern-stamped finish.

YOU CAN GIVE a patio, driveway, side-walk or other slab the rustic look of costly pavers by impressing stamped patterns into the surface. You'll need two stamping pads of matching design, such as Brickform's reinforced-plastic pads. Many concrete product dealers carry them or you can rent aluminum pads from a tool-rental dealer. Also get a three or four-pound Stanley Compocast Soft-Face dead-blow hammer for pad-setting. Pounding the pads with an ordinary hammer will crack them. Have plenty of help on hand, not taking on much more than 100 square feet per person per day.

For pattern-stamping you want a cement-rich high-slump mix. If you tell your ready mix dealer what you're doing with it, he can provide the proper mix. You want 1/4" maximum-size aggregate with 7 1/2 percent entrained air, plus or minus 1 percent. (Only 3 percent entrained air will do for a mild climate.) Then ask your dealer to add what's called a *water-reducing retarder* to the mix, plus a little *superplasticizer*. These additives will provide additional open time for stamping. If in doubt your dealer can consult National Ready Mix Concrete Association Publication No. 158.

FORMING THE SLAB

Form the project in multiples of stamp pad size, plus an allowance of 1/16 inch per foot for "float". Float is the distance that pads will separate while they're being impressed. For example, using Brickform's 1 x 2-foot pads, you'd form an 8 x 10-foot patio 8 feet 1/2 inch by 10 feet 5/8 inch. Control joints are created by the pads, provided you impress them the full 1-inch deep.

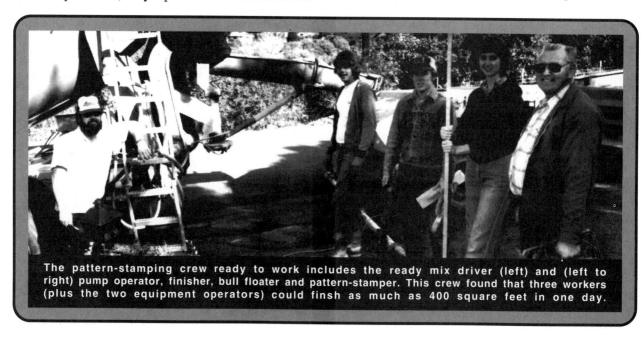

The pattern-stamping crew ready to work includes the ready mix driver (left) and (left to right) pump operator, finisher, bull floater and pattern-stamper. This crew found that three workers (plus the two equipment operators) could finsh as much as 400 square feet in one day.

Stamping pads are leap-frogged across the fresh, colored patio slab, standing on one while the other is lifted and moved.

Careful tapping with a dead-blow hammer sets the pads. Touch-up with a hand grooving tool finishes around the edges.

STAMPING THE PATTERN

Stamping is done after all the normal finishing steps have been completed. It looks best with colored concrete, and a good way to provide that is with the dust-on method (page 348). The concrete is ready for stamping when you can stand on a pad without sinking it. If you must pound hard to embed a pad, work quickly because the surface is getting too stiff for easy stamping. Align the first pad carefully in one corner of the forms and step out onto it. The open side of the pattern should be placed against the form (or house wall). Tap the pad gently, starting in the center, until it is embedded the desired depth. This can be a full 1-inch depth, or as little as half an inch if you provide separate control-jointing in the slab.

Next, align the second pad next to the first, step onto it and tap it in. Standing on the second pad, lift the first pad by its handle, moving it into position for the next stamping. You can move front to back or side-to-side, as long as you align the pads correctly. Pads are designed to interface on all four sides. Continue until you've stamped an entire row. Then go on to the next row, etc.

Be sure to align pads carefully to avoid what's called *straight-line irregularity*, visible as crookedness in your pattern and most readily seen from a distance. Patterns like cobblestone without straight lines have the least irregularity.

Partial pattern lines at form edges can be stamped lightly with the pad overlapping the form, enough to indicate where the lines should go. Then, working from outside the forms, use the hand tool to deepen the lines to match the others.

If you need to stamp around a corner, tool a 45° miter line and stamp up to it from both sides, being careful not to go across. Cure your project the same as any colored concrete slab.

Once cured, a pattern-stamped slab benefits from having its grooves filled ewith mortar. This will make it look like hand-set brick, tile, cobbles, etc. Just mix up some mortar—plain or colored—and spread it in the grooves. A neat way to handle this is to cure the slab by applying membrane curing compound to the slab with a paint roller, not letting the compound penetrate into any grooves. The dried compound will keep excess mortar from adhering to the faces of the "tiles" so that it can be cleaned off easily. If any mortar does remain, acid-etching and brushing will get rid of it.

Stamping pads are made of tough reinforced plastic and may be purchased in a number of patterns. Top of pad is shown at left, bottom at right. The bottom has 1" deep tile-pattern blades. A dead-blow hammer (foreground) helps set the pads to proper depth.

Dust-on method of coloring is economical, putting the color only on the surface of the slab. You can buy the dust-on mix or blend it yourself with cement and sand. Use rubber gloves.

CONCRETE CAN BE COLORED

Concrete need not be natural gray or white. It can be colored before, during and after the pour. Any color.

YOU HAVE A CHOICE of four methods for coloring concrete: (1) use an integral coloring agent; (2) apply a dust-on coloring pigment; (3) apply a stain, and (4) paint the concrete. The first two are done during construction. The last two are done afterward, even long afterward.

INTEGRAL COLORING

The best way to color an exposed aggregate surface or a wall or a cast-in-place or precast item is doing it integrally. For that you'll need to use a coloring pigment. Get only the type made for coloring concrete and mortar. Your concrete supplier should have a selection of colors, including browns, reds, yellow, black, and maybe even green and blue. Cost varies, depending on color. Blue and green cost more than the "earth" colors.

The coloring pigment is added to the portland cement during mixing. (Colored ready-mix can be ordered.) To learn exactly how much pigment to use in creating the color you want, experiment with small samples. Oven-dry the samples before judging them for color tone. Synthetic blacks are potent. About 2 percent of coloring pigment, by weight of the portland cement , is plenty for a dark color. Other colors need greater concentrations, up to 10 per cent by weight of cement, but never more, because the coloring can weaken the mix.

For rich, clean colors (except blacks and grays) make colored concrete with white portland cement rather than the natural gray kind. It costs slightly more but is best to use for colored work. If you have trouble finding white portland cement, try a terrazzo supplies dealer.

To save on the amount of coloring pigment and white cement, use the two-course method explained; add the coloring pigment only to the top layer. Be sure to get the amount of coloring pigment in each batch exactly the same. Measure, don't guess. It's best to weigh out the coloring on a postal scale.

DUST-ON COLORING

For use with ready mixed concrete slabs and on large float-and-trowel-finished slabs that are not getting the exposed aggregate treatment, use the dust-on method. It is preferable because it costs less. A prepared dry color material is sifted onto the surface after the first floating, edging and grooving.

Integrally cast coloring calls for adding color pigment directly to the mix as shown above. For a two-course colored slab, scratch the surface of plain base for a good bond. Add second course.

Concrete stains, as well as oil stains, can be used to color the surface of existing concrete. Vari-colored flagstones tooled into slab get a dark-stain outline. Stains wear very well, apply easily.

You can buy a ready-prepared dust-on but if you mix your own use a 2:2:1 mixture of white portland cement, fine mortar sand and coloring pigment, respectively. You'll need about one pound of dust-on material for each three square feet of surface to be colored.

Apply it in two applications. After the first dusting, trowel the coloring into the surface with a magnesium float. Dust lightly again and trowel that in, too. Finish the surface as normally and cure without plastic sheeting, which makes a spotty appearance in colored concrete.

STAINS

Two types of concrete stains are available: solvent-types (like wood stains) and inorganic acid types. Because of their strong acidity, inorganic stains—which change the color of concrete chemically—are not recommended for do-it-yourself use.

Solvent stains come in all colors. You can even use those intended for wood, though those specifically made for concrete are best. With any stain, follow the label directions. Application is with brush or roller.

PAINT

Concrete is not the ideal surface for painting, but in areas subjected to the outdoor elements it can be painted. When used outdoors on an exposed floor slab, we have found that over the years the chemical reaction of the concrete will in many instances separate the paint film from the concrete surface and bubbles will develop. If you must go the paint route use an acrylic latex or, preferably, an epoxy paint recommended especially for concrete. For poolside use you can also add a non-slip agent to the paint.

MAKING MORTAR

How to prepare a good mortar mix—a most essential ingredient for laying bricks and blocks.

A deep wheelbarrow (4-cubic-foot capacity) often called a "contractor's" wheelbarrow, makes a terrific mortar-mixing box. Dry-blend all the ingredients, first, then add water, and mix with a square shovel or hoe.

MORTAR—the stuff that "sticks" masonry units together—is the weakest part of any masonry wall. Since the wall can be only as strong as its weakest part, you want your mortar to be as strong as you can make it. Unlike ready mixed concrete, you can't buy ready mixed mortar; you must make it yourself, if only to add water and stir.

Good mortar is plastic and workable in the soft state and it bonds well to the masonry units. Like concrete, it hardens after placement. In the hardened state, it should still bond to the units. It must also be tough and weather-resistant. If you start with quality materials and mix them in the correct proportions, you can make good mortar.

BAGGED MORTAR MIX

For small projects the easiest way to make mortar is to buy a packaged mortar mix. Mortar mix is different from gravel-mix or sand-mix concrete. As with them, all you do is add the required amount of water and stir thoroughly. When preparing only part of a bag of mortar mix, mix the entire bag to reblend the ingredients—and then remove the quantity you need; otherwise you may get a variation because of settling during shipping and storage. A 60-pound sack of mortar mix should be enough to lay 15 eight-inch standard concrete blocks or 30 common bricks with 3/8-inch joints.

MIX YOUR OWN

It's less expensive on large projects to make your own mortar, starting with the basic ingredients. Mortar is different from concrete in that its workability and bond are more important than their strength. Therefore, a special cement is made for mortar-mixing, called masonry cement, or *plastic* cement. Neither should ever be used to make concrete. Mix the cement with fine mortar sand (also known as beach sand, sand box sand, and by various other names) in these proportions:

**1 part masonry cement
to 2 to 3 parts damp,
loose mortar sand**

First mix the ingredients dry, then add all the clean drinking water the mix will take without affecting workability. Mortar is the opposite of concrete in this respect. Water is essential for a good bond.

Good mortar spreads easily by trowel, yet doesn't slip off the trowel when picked up. It

Some dealers rent or can sell you plastic treated cardboard or metal mortar-mixing boxes that beat hand-mixing on a concrete floor or plywood base. Mixing is much easier if done with a hoe.

To make colored mortar, dump coloring pigment in with the dry ingredients and thoroughly blend them before adding the water. Use enough of the pigment to get the exact color you want.

351

CONCRETE

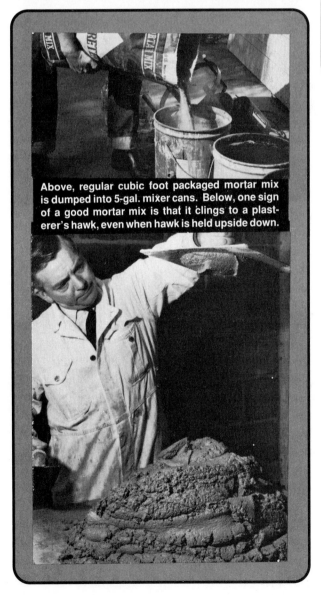

Above, regular cubic foot packaged mortar mix is dumped into 5-gal. mixer cans. Below, one sign of a good mortar mix is that it clings to a plasterer's hawk, even when hawk is held upside down.

clings to the faces of masonry units even when they're inverted.

Mortar than stiffens can be retempered with more water and mixing, but when a batch is more than 21/2 hours old (at 80° working temperature), it begins to set and should be discarded. Colder, it will last 3 1/2 hours.

You can mix mortar by hand in a mortar box, wheelbarrow, or on a concrete slab. Do it with a hoe or square shovel. However, a better mortar mix can be made easier—and faster—in a powered paddle-type mixer which you can rent.

COLORING

Pigments, the same as described for concrete coloring, may be added during mixing to make colored mortar in yellows, reds, browns, greens, blues, and blacks.

If you prefer, mortar can be mixed with portland cement instead of masonry cement by adding hydrated lime as follows:

1 part portland cement, 1 part hydrated lime, 4 to 6 parts damp, loose mortar sand.

Mix the lime with water first to form a lime putty, then add the other ingredients.

HOW TO LAY BLOCKS

Laying concrete blocks, you'll soon learn, is easier and faster than laying bricks or stone.

LAYING CONCRETE BLOCKS is no more difficult than bricklaying. And the wall goes up many times faster because of the large size of the blocks. Concrete blocks are especially good for foundations and large expanses of wall where speed of construction is important. The variety of shapes, sizes, textures and colors is tremendous. Best looking are the sculptured, slump and ground-face units. Ask your block dealer about them.

As with brickwork, concrete blocks may be laid in a variety of bonds. Strongest is the running bond. Each block overlaps the one below half-way. At corners, the blocks interlace like the fingers of praying hands.

A block wall may be 4, 6, 8, 10, or 12 inches thick, according to the width of the blocks used to make it. For most purposes, though, the eight-inch width is used. Standard of the block industry is the 8x8x16-inch concrete block, which builds an eight-inch-thick wall. Blocks measuring 8x8x8 inch eliminate the need for cutting. The four-and six-inch blocks build non-load bearing walls. The 10-and 12-inch blocks are used chiefly for foundations.

Laying concrete blocks is a leisurely job yet it progresses so fast that it's satisfying to do. Setting the corner units is the only part that requires any skill: the rest is simply laying blocks to a taut stringline. And with a little practice you can master the trick of laying corner blocks using only a rule, plumb and trowel for the mortar. It's easy enough if you start off level and square. Most important is the bottom course. It determines job quality.

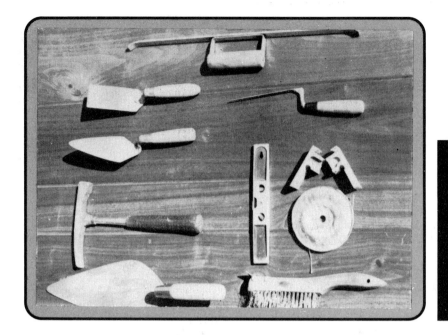

Tools for laying concrete masonry are similar to those for laying bricks and stones. The one special block-laying tool is the 22" long jointer shown at top. Others are: margin trowel, pointing trowel, baby mason's trowel, mason's hammer, level/plumb, line blocks and line, mason's trowel and wire brush.

CORE-FILLING

The cores of concrete blocks can be filled after the wall is up. This is done with concrete containing 3/8-inch maximum-size aggregate. Except in earthquake areas or when blocks are used below-ground, the core may not need to be filled. However, core-filling does make a stronger wall. The four-inch-block cores are open only at one end and cannot be filled.

Most concrete blocks are two-core with squared off ends. Blocks are made of portland cement and aggregates in vibrating forms that consolidate the mix for great strength. Then, to maximize strength, blocks are moist-cured in a warm, steamy curing room. After that, they are dried and, to avoid shrinkage cracks, blocks should be laid dry. While the aggregates used to make blocks may be cinders, more often they are fine stones. thus the term *cinder blocks* isn't applicable to most concrete blocks.

Blocks with square ends can be used in corners. Otherwise, enough full-end corner blocks must be purchased separately. You can also get jamb blocks, lintel blocks, cap blocks, and bond-beam blocks. Moreover, special units are sometimes available for making chimneys and for building pilasters— thick columns in a wall.

Useful for "stretching" a wall is the concrete brick. It's made of the same stuff as a con-

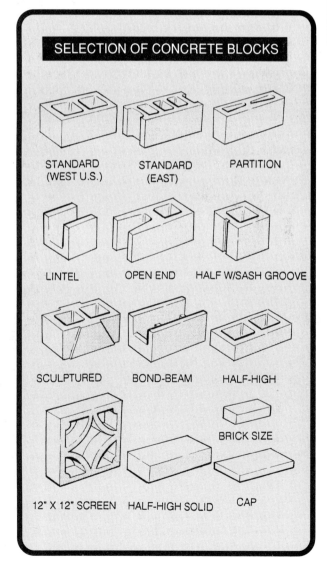

SELECTION OF CONCRETE BLOCKS

STANDARD (WEST U.S.) — STANDARD (EAST) — PARTITION — LINTEL — OPEN END — HALF W/SASH GROOVE — SCULPTURED — BOND-BEAM — HALF-HIGH — 12" X 12" SCREEN — HALF-HIGH SOLID — BRICK SIZE — CAP

crete block but in brick size.

Glamour blocks, such as grille blocks, split-blocks, slump blocks, can be used to build a concrete block wall that matches brick for beauty.

PLANNING

Because concrete blocks are modules of eight inches — anything you lay up with them should also be modular. Otherwise you'll find yourself cutting and piecing all the way up the wall. To avoid this, see that all your dimensions — height, width, length — can be divided evenly by eight inches. For example: (1) an even number of feet, such as two feet or four feet, (2) an even number of feet plus eight inches, such as two feet eight inches, four feet eight inches (3) an odd number of feet plus four inches, such as three feet four inches, five feet four inches. These rules apply to vertical as well as horizontal measurements.

Concrete blocks have tops and bottoms. The top of the block has the smoothest, widest face shells (left). Tapered mold makes the bottom face shells narrower. Always lay blocks top side up.

It's easy to estimate how many standard 8x8x16-inch blocks you need for a project. First calculate the square-foot area of the wall less openings. Then multiply by 1.125. Thus, a wall of 120 square feet would need 135 blocks.

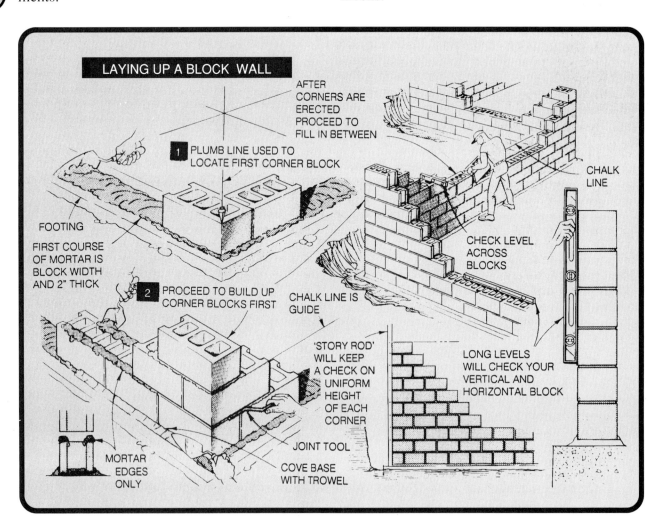

LAYING UP A BLOCK WALL

AFTER CORNERS ARE ERECTED PROCEED TO FILL IN BETWEEN

1 PLUMB LINE USED TO LOCATE FIRST CORNER BLOCK

FOOTING

FIRST COURSE OF MORTAR IS BLOCK WIDTH AND 2" THICK

CHALK LINE

CHECK LEVEL ACROSS BLOCKS

2 PROCEED TO BUILD UP CORNER BLOCKS FIRST

CHALK LINE IS GUIDE

'STORY ROD' WILL KEEP A CHECK ON UNIFORM HEIGHT OF EACH CORNER

LONG LEVELS WILL CHECK YOUR VERTICAL AND HORIZONTAL BLOCK

JOINT TOOL

COVE BASE WITH TROWEL

MORTAR EDGES ONLY

Cutting blocks is quick and easy. First lay the block on a firm surface and tap a line all around, using the chisel end of a mason's hammer. Keep going gently until the block cracks on the line.

Start of a job is to lay out the first course of blocks on the poured footing dry. Space them with a scrap of 3/8" plywood and carefully mark the footing (use a chisel) where each joint falls.

Water tube level with built-in rule at each end is the easy, accurate way to level the corners of a wall. This one connects to a garden hose but masonry supply yards have similar products.

Story pole with marks for height of each course saves measuring for each course. Set the corner block in mortar and tap it down until its top comes to the mark and is level in both directions.

To lay subsequent blocks from the corner butter two strips of mortar onto the end of each block. Chunking it down with the trowel helps make the mortar cling tightly and stick to the surface.

Set the end-buttered block down in mortar as you shove it toward the previously laid block in its course. A stringline stretched between corners guides alignment. Level in both directions.

To go around a corner with blockwork, butter the ends of a block with mortar and gently push against the side of the already-laid corner block; tap it level with the handle of your trowel.

Mortar for the corner is placed so the second-course corner block overlaps the joint in the blocks below. Some masons fill first-course. Interlacing of corner units makes for strength.

LAYING THE BLOCK

Start laying blocks as for bricks on a clean, dampened concrete footing without puddles of water. First lay the blocks dry without mortar to check your modular dimensions and mark where the joints fall. Snap a chalkline between corners. Make a story pole with height marks every eight inches to save measuring corner block heights each time.

TRUE BLOCK DIMENSION

The actual dimension of a block is 3/8-inch less on a side to allow for mortar joints; namely 7-5/8 x 7-5/8 x 15-5/8 inches.

Unlike bricklaying, in which the corners are first built up to several courses, an alternate do-it-yourself method for laying blocks completes the first course before starting the second. This maximizes the laying of easy in-between blocks to a string line and minimizes the tougher laying of corners. You could do the same with brickwork except that it takes a corner brick some setting time until a string line can be stretched from it without pulling loose.

With a concrete block you can usually stretch the line almost right after laying the block because it is heavy. So, lay all corner blocks first, right on the footing in a full bedding of mortar. Use a mason's hammer to tap the block into the mortar, but be careful not to chip the face or corner edge where it will show. While it is handier to tap with the trowel handle, because it's already in your hand, this often brings down a rain of mortar on your hand and on the top of the block being laid.

Concrete blocks have tapered cores leaving one surface with a wider shell than the other (see phot on page 354). Lay blocks with the wide face shell on top. They're easier to hold this way, and it's easier to spread mortar on the wider shell.

Level corner blocks in three directions: (1) plumb above the block beneath, (2) level lengthwise and at the right height, and (3) level crosswise.

Make sure that bottom and side joints have plenty of mortar before setting a block. No masonry should be joined by stuffing mortar into empty joints. That builds no bond and no strength into the wall. Blocks, after the first course, are laid

Control joints to prevent shrinkage cracking of block walls should be continuous up the wall. For a flexible tie, bridge over them with hardware cloth (1/2" squares will do) laid in mortar.

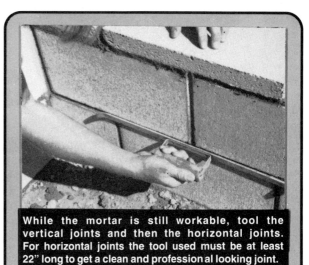

While the mortar is still workable, tool the vertical joints and then the horizontal joints. For horizontal joints the tool used must be at least 22" long to get a clean and professional looking joint.

Top off the wall with a course of cap blocks to hide the exposed cores. If additional strength is needed the cores should be filled. Sometimes a layer of wire block reinforcement is used every 4th or 5th course.

Grille block walls not only give privacy, they break up the wind, letting only a gentle breeze through. This wall was built from 8" blocks with 12" solid cap. Walls can be left unpainted.

Since grill blocks are cast in economical forms, a multitude of shapes are available. This rectangular unit can be used for decorative walls and also for a chimney by threading over the flue tile.

in what's called *face-shell bedding*. Beads of mortar are placed along the inner and outer face shells of the blocks below. The webs between the face shells get no mortar.

USE THE RIGHT MORTAR

If the mortar is too wet, it will be impossible to hold the proper 3/8-inch mortar-joint thickness and keep the block course at the right height. For this reason block-laying mortar needs to be stiffer than brick-laying mortar. If you find your blocks settling too much, add dry ingredients to the mortar in proper proportion to stiffen it up.

Lay the corner blocks for courses so they overlap joints in the ones below. Thus, the corner blocks tie together like the fingers of praying hands.

One difference between blocks and bricks: *blocks are never wetted before laying them. In fact, you must keep them from getting wet before and after laying the wall.* Between work sessions, cover the pile of blocks with polyethylene sheet-

As you lay grille blocks match the pattern of each block with those laid previously. The overall pattern of the wall depends on how each block is positioned. Many designs are available.

ing and lay strips of sheeting over the top of the wall to keep rain out of the cores.

Like all masonry work, block walls should be protected from freezing until the mortar has fully hardened. Either don't work in freezing weather, or plan on covering and heating the wall while the mortar sets.

You can produce a finished appearance at the top of the wall by laying a course of cap blocks. These have no cores and are two inches thick. Foundation walls need no cap blocks since their tops are covered by the structure above.

Curved block walls can be built (brick, too) by laying the units to a plywood template instead of a line. Curved walls make great fences and are self-bracing against the wind. Pilaster spacing should not be more than twice the height of the wall and the blocks should be tied into the wall either by the bond of the units or by installation of hardware cloth ties in every joint. Any free-standing wall more than seven feet high, however, should be of engineered design using grouted, steel-reinforced cores.

The trick to laying grille blocks is to make certain they are absolutely straight. Do not lay more than two or three courses a day and use a taut line with each course. Tool flush joints.

If your house is much above the street, you can have a level front yard by building a retaining wall along the sidewalk. This brick beauty has been set back for a sidewalk planter bed.

BUILDING A RETAINING WALL

A retaining wall should live up to its name. Here are a few facts you should know before you plan to build yours.

A RETAINING WALL is one of the most risky structures you can build, as it can be pushed over by heavy soil pressures from behind. For this reason most building codes limit retaining wall height to four feet unless the design is engineered. If you must go higher, either consult a professional engineer or use a series a four-foot-high walls stepped up the hill. Experts maintain you should have engineering advice, too, on slopes greater than 36 percent. In any case, a building permit is usually required.

To minimize earth pressures on a retaining wall, be sure to provide for drainage so water will not add its pressure to the wall. Wall drainage can be designed in the form of a shaped-earth gutter near the top of the wall and leading beyond it on one or both ends.

Another possibility is to lay a drain tile line along behind the base of the wall and backfilling with a porous stone fill. Sloped to the end on one or both ends, the line will carry water out before hydraulic pressures can build.

Through-the-wall drains, in the form of cast-in tiles, plastic pipe or holes left in the wall at regular intervals can also serve the same purpose. In any case, the water pouring out of them should not be allowed to undermine the wall's footing. Build a paved gutter, if necessary, to catch it and lead it away.

CONCRETE WALL

Strongest, but not the easiest to build, is a massive concrete retaining wall. The drawings show an accepted design built without reinforcing steel. Both footing and wall are cast at the same time. Earth serves as a form for the footing. Plywood, 3/4- or 5/8-inch thick, can be used to form the wall, bracing it on 12- to 16-inch centers with 2 x 4s.

Most of the stress on a set of forms comes from the pressure of the wet concrete pushing outward. This force can be balanced from one wall to another by drilling holes in the form and running tie-wires inside the form between its two walls.

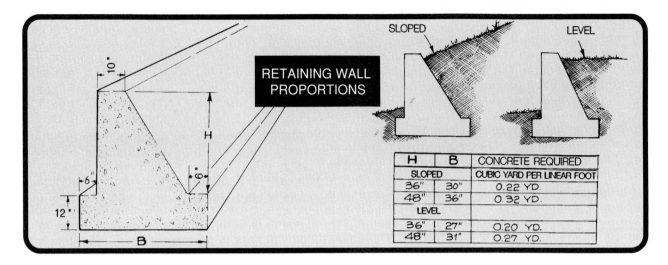

RETAINING WALL PROPORTIONS

H	B	CONCRETE REQUIRED
SLOPED		CUBIC YARD PER LINEAR FOOT
36"	30"	0.22 YD.
48"	36"	0.32 YD.
LEVEL		
36"	27"	0.20 YD.
48"	31"	0.27 YD.

Split concrete blocks make a stonelike retaining wall. Slim split cap blocks cover the hollow cores, which have been filled with ground around reinforcing steel. Poured walls are still strongest.

Concrete is poured around the tie-wires, which are later cut off. Nails or sticks can be used to twist the tie-wires tight. Be careful not to over-tighten the wires or else you may get a pinched-waist form. Short reinforcing bars, or even sticks, are sometimes used to hold the forms in place as the wires are tightened. Many lumber yards and masonry supply houses usually stock special formed and welded "Snap Ties" which serve the same purpose as wires and are primarily used for poured concrete foundations. These ties are usually available for walls 8, 10 and 12 inches thick.

REINFORCED CONCRETE WALL

You can save on concrete by reinforcing your wall with steel. It can have a much thinner section because the bars take much of the stress put on the concrete. Soil must be

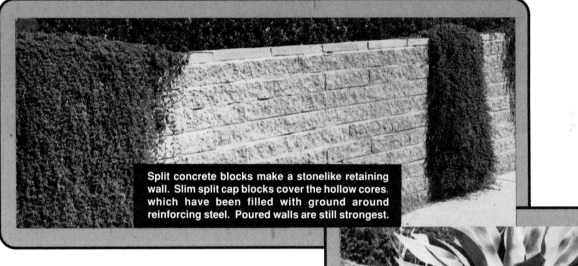

A retaining wall can be as simple as stacked-up pieces of broken sidewalk. These may be found at some city dumps and sledged into right-sized chunks. Check for nearby concrete demolition.

Low retaining wall forms planter for tree. To lay bricks in a circular pattern, make a curving template from 1/4" plywood or hardboard. Stake in place, then lay bricks to top edge. End-wise bricks trim top.

firm to prevent tipover. A reinforced-concrete wall, however, should be designed by a professional engineer. The backfill behind it may be either sloped or level. Install through-the-wall drains six feet apart or closer.

Reinforced concrete must be compacted well around the bars. Tapping on the bars lightly and rapidly with a hammer as you cover them with concrete ensures a firm bond between concrete and the bars.

Where vertical and horizontal reinforcing bars cross each other, tie them together with double loops of 16-gauge wire twisted tight with pliers. You can bend bars with a pipe wrench. Bars must be continuous or else overlapped by at least a foot and secured with wire.

You can get reinforcing bars from a concrete products supplier or building supply yard. They come in 20-foot lengths. Have them cut or bent in half so you can get them home easily.

OTHER MATERIALS

Retaining walls may also be made of concrete block, brick, and stone. Sometimes low stone walls are laid dry without mortar. In spite of its informal construction, such a wall may last for years. A reinforced brick or block wall may be built to the same dimensions as the one shown for reinforced concrete, but make it of eight-inch-thick concrete block or two tiers of four-inch brick with a half-inch space between them for the bars. The cores of blocks and the between-tier space in a brick retaining wall is filled with grout, a mixture of portland cement and sand, using enough water to give it a pouring consistency. The top of such a wall can be finished with a cast-in-place concrete cap or a course of bricks or cap blocks to hide the grout and reinforcing. See the pages on bricks, blocks and stones.

Gaining popularity is the use of interlocking concrete blocks called "modules" designed especially for retaining wall use and rapidly becoming another product available from your local masonry supply yard. While actually cast from concrete at the factory, the face can be sculptured rock, vertical lines or exposed aggregate. Using the modules — which measure 18 inches wide, 4 or 8 inches thick and 24 inches deep — has the advantage in that they can be positioned dry.

Draining should be provided at the base of a retaining wall. A neat way to do it is to lay a concrete block sidewise in the wall. Its cores drain the water off. Perforated pipe is also used.

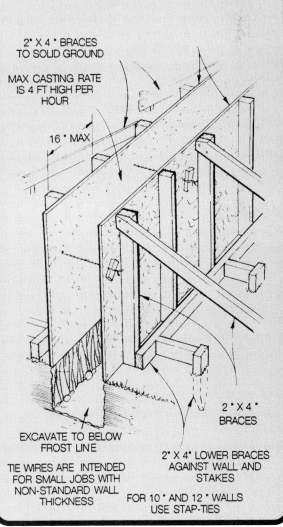

3/4 " EXTERIOR PLYWOOD FORM

STICK OR NAIL

TEMPORARY WOOD SPACER

TIE-WIRE THRU HOLES IN FORM

TWIST STICK TO TIGHTEN TO SPACER

FORMS FOR A POURED WALL

2" X 4 " BRACES TO SOLID GROUND

MAX CASTING RATE IS 4 FT HIGH PER HOUR

16 " MAX

2 " X 4 " BRACES

EXCAVATE TO BELOW FROST LINE

TIE WIRES ARE INTENDED FOR SMALL JOBS WITH NON-STANDARD WALL THICKNESS

2 " X 4" LOWER BRACES AGAINST WALL AND STAKES

FOR 10 " AND 12 " WALLS USE STAP-TIES

DRY STACK PRECAST BLOCKS

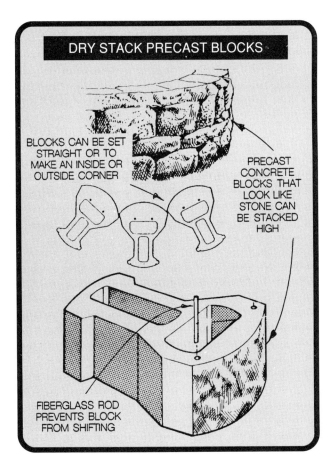

BLOCKS CAN BE SET STRAIGHT OR TO MAKE AN INSIDE OR OUTSIDE CORNER

PRECAST CONCRETE BLOCKS THAT LOOK LIKE STONE CAN BE STACKED HIGH

FIBERGLASS ROD PREVENTS BLOCK FROM SHIFTING

MASONRY FENCES

Build a fence that never rots, never needs painting, never needs any maintenance and will outlast the house.

ORDINARILY, concrete and masonry are ignored in selecting material for fence-building. Yet they make excellent maintenance-free fences. Most are laid on a footing. Once the footing has been poured, you can build your fence with brick, blocks, stones or pour it in place using plywood forms. The easiest to build is a concrete block fence. Special grille block units are available to create a fence that breezes can blow through, yet will tame high winds.

Some concrete block producers make units especially for fence building. These are four inches thick. Pilaster units twice as thick have recesses that hide the joints between sections of the fence at corners. Check with your dealer to see what's available.

FENCES AND THE LAW

Any fence you build must meet local laws. These vary from community to community, so find out what regulations will affect your fence before you start planning. Some govern the length, height and thickness of the fence. Others pertain to setbacks from property lines. Some regulations outlaw fences. Deed restrictions on your title can also govern fences. So can zoning ordinances. Check everything.

Legal problems get even worse if a fence runs along a property line. Sometimes you can build a fence astride the property line without first getting permission of your neighbor. In other cases you can't. Such a fence may become half his even though you pay for it. If you build the fence entirely on your property, you usually needn't get your neighbor's agreement as long as the fence meets all regulations. But you'd better be sure where the property line is—even putting the fence several inches on your side of the line to be clear of any later disputes.

The best bet is to put up a fence that both you and your neighbor agree on. Best yet, get his help in buying materials and construction, and any eventual maintenance.

After the fence is up, you can paint it if you wish. Use exterior latex paint of the desired color. It will give a lasting color on concrete masonry that won't need recoating for a long time.

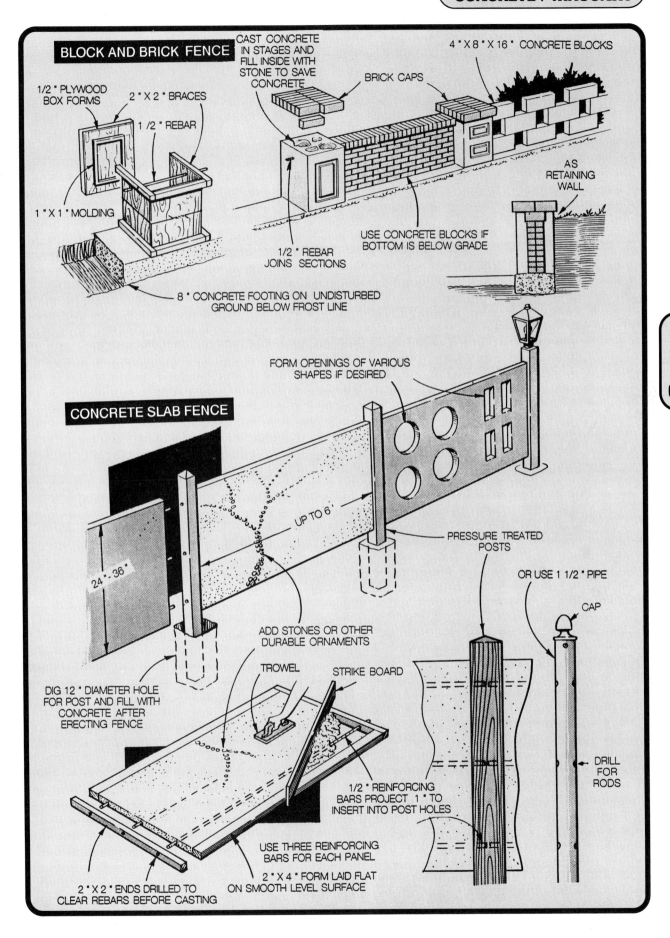

BLOCK AND BRICK FENCE

1/2 " PLYWOOD BOX FORMS

2 " X 2 " BRACES

1 /2 " REBAR

1 " X 1 " MOLDING

CAST CONCRETE IN STAGES AND FILL INSIDE WITH STONE TO SAVE CONCRETE

BRICK CAPS

4 " X 8 " X 16 " CONCRETE BLOCKS

AS RETAINING WALL

1/2 " REBAR JOINS SECTIONS

USE CONCRETE BLOCKS IF BOTTOM IS BELOW GRADE

8 " CONCRETE FOOTING ON UNDISTURBED GROUND BELOW FROST LINE

FORM OPENINGS OF VARIOUS SHAPES IF DESIRED

CONCRETE SLAB FENCE

UP TO 6 '

24 "- 36 "

PRESSURE TREATED POSTS

OR USE 1 1/2 " PIPE

CAP

DIG 12 " DIAMETER HOLE FOR POST AND FILL WITH CONCRETE AFTER ERECTING FENCE

ADD STONES OR OTHER DURABLE ORNAMENTS

TROWEL

STRIKE BOARD

DRILL FOR RODS

1/2 " REINFORCING BARS PROJECT 1 " TO INSERT INTO POST HOLES

USE THREE REINFORCING BARS FOR EACH PANEL

2 " X 4 " FORM LAID FLAT ON SMOOTH LEVEL SURFACE

2 " X 2 " ENDS DRILLED TO CLEAR REBARS BEFORE CASTING

365
CONCRETE

CEMENT-PLASTERING

Troweling cement-mortar onto a masonry wall not only changes its texture and gets rid of joint show-through. it helps waterproof the wall. Applications should be in 1/4" to 3/8" layers, two layers thick for waterproofing. To help the first layer bond well, the wall should be dampened and coated by brushing on a water-cement paste.

Next to brick or stone, a cement-plastered or stucco wall produces a surface that requires little maintenance over the years. Different surfaces and textures are available.

CEMENT-PLASTERING can help you to hide the mortar joints in a masonry wall you've built. It can also be used to help waterproof the outside of a concrete block or cinder block basement wall. You could also apply a sand-cement coating—called stucco—to the outside of a masonry wall above ground, simply for a smooth appearance. Either way, it involves troweling on a layer of mortar onto the vertical wall surface.

BAGGING-IN

One of the easiest treatments to hide the texture and most joints in block-work is to *bag-in* the wall. This fills the joints and closes the block pores with a sand-cement mortar. Tools required are just a soft brush and a burlap bag or a rubber float of the kind used for some concrete finishes.

Make the bagging-in mixture with 1 part portland cement and 1 1/2 to 2 parts mortar sand. Mix dry, then add enough water to make the mix fluid but not runny. Dampen but don't soak the blocks. Use a fine spray from a garden hose nozzle. Apply the mix with the brush, working it into the block pores. Do about five square feet at a time. After applying, go back over the surface with the dampened burlap bag or rubber float and rub off the excess mix up to the high spots on the wall. This should leave a thin, masking coat over the blocks. The rubber float generally gives a finer texture than the burlap.

Dampen the wall again as soon as it's able to take it without washing off the mix. Keep it damp for 48 hours.

STUCCO

A coat of stucco has the same effect as bagging-in but it is thick enough to completely hide the texture beneath. First dampen the wall. Then apply a 1 to 2 1/2 portland cement mortar sand-mix from a plasterer's hawk, using a cement-finishing trowel. You can also use regular masonry mortar. Hold the hawk piled with mortar next to the wall and angled away from it; Trowel the mix upward onto the wall. It should be spread about 1/4 to 3/8-inch thick. Once applied, it can be smoothed by further troweling or texturing. Texture with the trowel, a rubber float, or almost anything that produces an effect you like. Interior surfaces should be smoother than exterior ones. Tin cans, cookie cutters, hand tools, brushes, all make attractive designs in the soft stucco. Cure the same as for the bagged-in coating. Incidentally, while you can proportion your own stucco, a number of fine pre-mixed stucco products are on the market. Many use special colored sand so you need not expect the same white surface when using portland cement; the ready mix stucco is colored.

Plain concrete block planter is decorated with two coats of troweled-on cement-plaster. The first coat was troweled smooth. The second coat was spotted, for texturing, then troweled lightly.

Other methods of texturing cement plaster are numerous. This one is done by pressing the corner of a trowel into the fresh mortar coat. The marks could be subdued by light troweling.

Bagged-in finish is started by brushing the bagging-in mixture onto a block wall. Dampen the wall first and work the mix well into the pores to help smooth and hide them in the finished job.

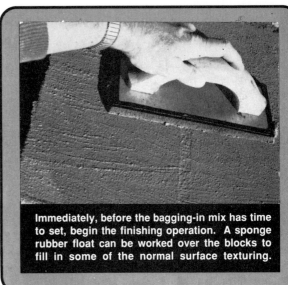

Immediately, before the bagging-in mix has time to set, begin the finishing operation. A sponge rubber float can be worked over the blocks to fill in some of the normal surface texturing.

Old, original bagged-in finish is made by rubbing the wall with a damp piece of burlap sacking. To hide joints as much as possible, rub straight across them at right angles or in circles.

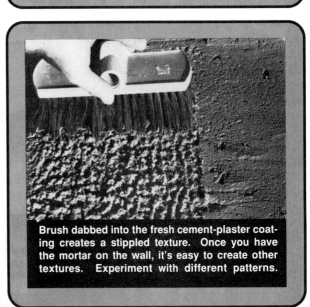

Brush dabbed into the fresh cement-plaster coating creates a stippled texture. Once you have the mortar on the wall, it's easy to create other textures. Experiment with different patterns.

HOW TO LAY BRICKS

The art of laying brick consists of being patient, careful, and following the accompanying instructions.

ONE OF THE MOST satisfying do-it-yourself projects is bricklaying. It moves along reasonably fast. And with just a little care you can do as good a job as a professional, one that your friends won't believe you did. You cannot work as fast as the pro, that's all. Be satisfied with 50 to 200 bricks a day, not the 1,000 a professional can lay.

Bricks come in all colors and a number of shapes. The best way to pick out what you want is to visit a dealer and see what he has. Some dealers have their bricks displayed with the units laid on strips of fiberboard to resemble their appearance in a wall. This is a big help in selection.

If you're going to lay bricks outdoors, you must get either *medium-weathering* or *severe-weathering* bricks. The high-type units called face bricks are made only in these two types. A third type is called non-weathering, and should be used indoors or in protected locations only.

Bricks in *modular* sizes lay up to make either 8- or 12-inch modules. Non-modular bricks don't come out so even. No harm unless you're trying to fit in a modular window or door opening. Then you must do some fancy cutting or joint jockeying.

FIGURING QUANTITIES

The chart on page 372 shows how many of each type of bricks are needed to build 100 square

House first-floor wall of 6"-wide SCR bricks here is laid two tiers thick so that the wall can go a second story high. A single story home, built with SCR bricks, may be only one tier thick.

Plastic mason's line blocks make it easy to handle the taut line at wall corners. Move the blocks up as each new course is completed. Line should be flush with the top.

Corners are the most important part of a wall. Take the most care with them, keeping them absolutely plumb, even.

feet of wall four inches thick. If your wall is to be a bearing wall, (a wall that supports a floor or a roof) then twice as many bricks will be needed. The brick quantities shown allow a customary 5 per cent for waste.

You can also figure mortar quantities from the table. Because the amount of mortar depends on the thickness of the mortar joints, three thicknesses are shown. To make a portland cement-lime mortar. you'll need one sack of portland cement and a sack of lime for each five cubic feet of sand. To make mortar-cement mortar, you'll need a sack of masonry cement for every three cubic feet of sand.

BRICK PATTERNS

Bricks can be laid in many different patterns that a mason calls *bonds*. A single-tier wall built one brick thick can use either a running bond or a stacked bond. For beginners the running bond is much easier to lay, and is therefore recommended. It is also stronger. A two-tier eight-inch-thick brick wall needs crosswise bricks called *headers* laid into the wall about every sixth course in height. The purpose of this is to tie the tiers of the wall together all the way up. The simplest way to get them is to place an entire course of header bricks every sixth or seventh course as you go up the wall. This, however, creates horizontal lines in the wall. You may prefer to use one of the Flemish bonds shown in the drawing. These take in some headers into each course, thereby masking their use. Whatever bond you choose, keep the pattern in mind as you lay each brick.

Buttering the ends of bricks so that the mortar will stay on them takes a little practice. It helps to wipe the trowel down across the mortar at an angle from each side of the brick to taper mortar.

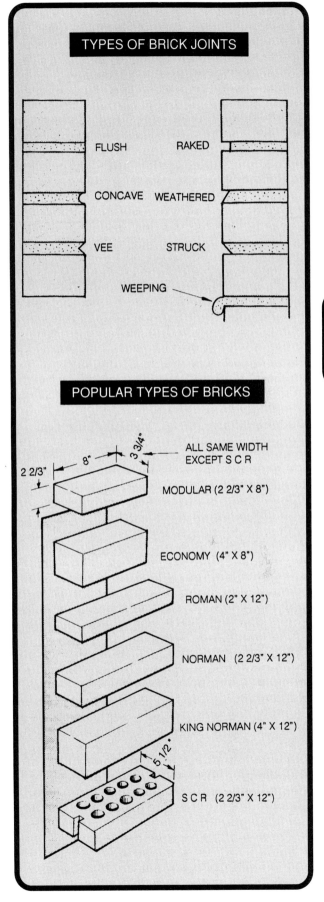

TYPES OF BRICK JOINTS

FLUSH   RAKED

CONCAVE   WEATHERED

VEE   STRUCK

WEEPING

POPULAR TYPES OF BRICKS

3 3/4"
8"
2 2/3"
ALL SAME WIDTH EXCEPT S C R

MODULAR (2 2/3" X 8")

ECONOMY (4" X 8")

ROMAN (2" X 12")

NORMAN (2 2/3" X 12")

KING NORMAN (4" X 12")

5 1/2"

S C R (2 2/3" X 12")

Varying the way you lay the bricks can make all sorts of patterns in the wall. This one is open to let the breeze come through a brick fence while still giving privacy. Adaptable things, bricks!

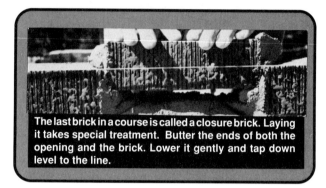

Laying bricks from the corners each way goes quickly. Spread mortar for a full bedding. Then butter a brick's end and set it against the corner brick. Tap level and into careful alignment.

The last brick in a course is called a closure brick. Laying it takes special treatment. Butter the ends of both the opening and the brick. Lower it gently and tap down level to the line.

GETTING STARTED

Have your bricks stacked handy to the job and your mortar-mixing operation ready to go before you start bricklaying. Also, make a *story pole*, a 8-foot straight lxl or lx2 stick with the tops of the brick courses carefully marked starting with the first and reaching up to the top course, if your wall is eight feet high. This saves much measuring.

Bricklaying consists of building up corners first, stretching a line between corner bricks and laying in-between bricks to the line. Start the process by laying out the first course of bricks on the footing, dry without mortar. Dry-laying will show you how the bricks will fit what you're building. Make the end joints—the joints between bricks in the same course—to the desired dimension. The thicker joints are recommended because they allow a greater margin for error in brick placement. Thin mortar joints are difficult to lay accurately. If the bricks don't come out as you wish, you can either adjust the end joints slightly (not much or it will look strange in the finished wall) or you can use part of a brick in the wall, cutting it with a mason's hammer. If everything fits, mark the centers of the end joints on the footing and take up the dry-laid bricks.

BUILT UP CORNERS

All bricks should be soaked with water, but allowed to surface-dry before laying them. One way is to sprinkle the pile regularly all day. Another is to keep a soaking pail full of water and bricks, taking them out a few minutes before laying. If not wetted, a brick's bond will be poor because it steals all free water from the mortar.

Start the operation by spreading enough mortar for one brick on top of the footing in one corner. Place the story pole on the footing at that location and lay the brick on the mortar, tapping it down with the trowel handle until its top is even with the story pole mark for the first course. Take away the story pole and lay your level on the brick lengthwise. Tap the high end down until the brick is level. Lay your level crosswise on the brick and tap until the brick comes level that way, too. Always tap on the side toward the bubble. Finally, check the brick height again using the story pole and again check the level. Adjust if necessary. That's a lot of fuss for one brick, simply because it's a corner brick, but it controls all the bricks in the course. Get it right and the rest will be right.

Now lay several more bricks stretching out

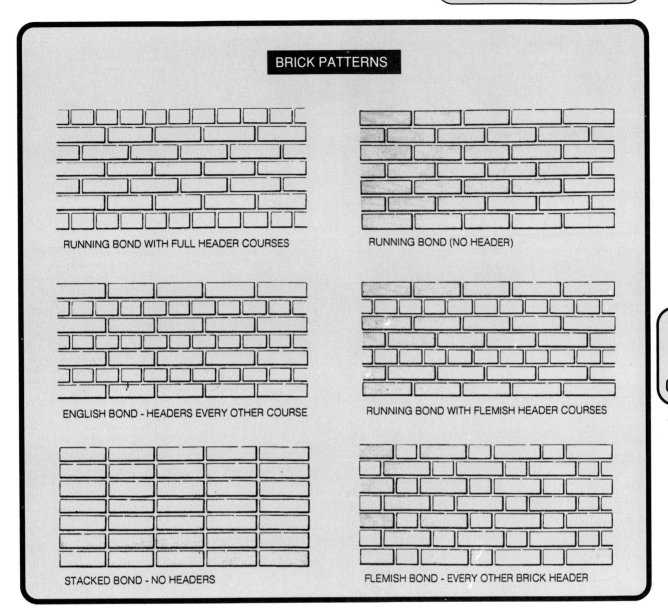

BRICK PATTERNS

RUNNING BOND WITH FULL HEADER COURSES

RUNNING BOND (NO HEADER)

ENGLISH BOND - HEADERS EVERY OTHER COURSE

RUNNING BOND WITH FLEMISH HEADER COURSES

STACKED BOND - NO HEADERS

FLEMISH BOND - EVERY OTHER BRICK HEADER

371
CONCRETE

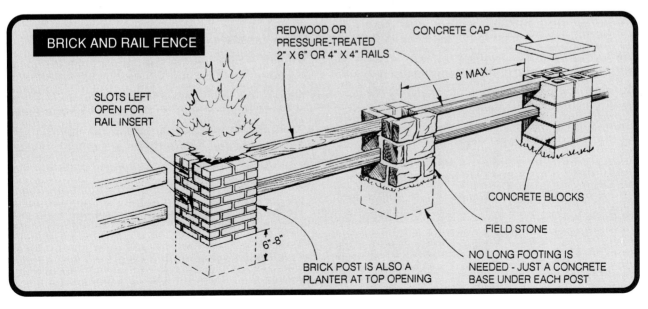

BRICK AND RAIL FENCE

REDWOOD OR PRESSURE-TREATED 2" X 6" OR 4" X 4" RAILS

CONCRETE CAP

8' MAX.

SLOTS LEFT OPEN FOR RAIL INSERT

CONCRETE BLOCKS

FIELD STONE

6"-8"

BRICK POST IS ALSO A PLANTER AT TOP OPENING

NO LONG FOOTING IS NEEDED - JUST A CONCRETE BASE UNDER EACH POST

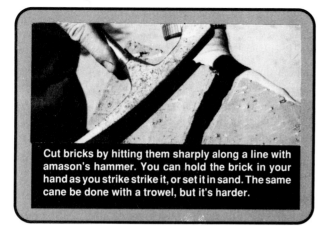

Cut bricks by hitting them sharply along a line with amason's hammer. You can hold the brick in your hand as you strike strike it, or set it in sand. The same cane be done with a trowel, but it's harder.

BRICK AND MORTAR QUANTITY FOR 4" WALLS *				
BRICK SIZE IN INCHES	NUMBER FOR 100 SQ.FT.WALL	CU.FT.MORTAR PER 100 SQ.FT.WALL JOINT THICKNESS		
* ALLOWS FOR WASTE		1/4"	3/8"	1/2"
2 2/3 X 4 X 8	742	40	58	73
2 X 4 X 12	660		67	86
2 2/3 X 4 X 12	495	37	54	68
3 1/5 X 4 X 8	618	35	50	64
4 X 4 X 8	495		43	55
4 X 4 X 12	330	27	39	49
2 2/3 X 6 X 12	495		8.2	106
2 1/4 X 3 3/4 X 8	715	4.2	60	76

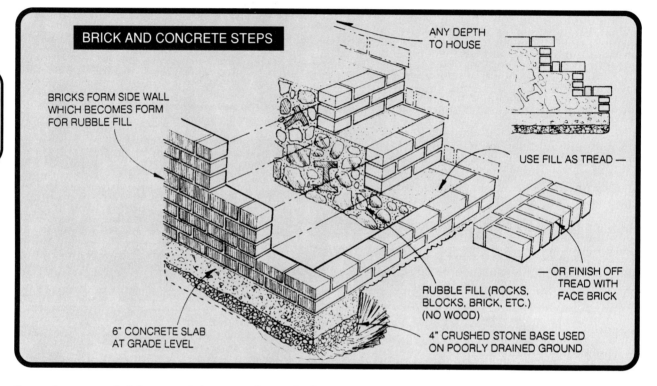

BRICK AND CONCRETE STEPS

BRICKS FORM SIDE WALL WHICH BECOMES FORM FOR RUBBLE FILL

ANY DEPTH TO HOUSE

USE FILL AS TREAD —

— OR FINISH OFF TREAD WITH FACE BRICK

RUBBLE FILL (ROCKS, BLOCKS, BRICK, ETC.) (NO WOOD)

6" CONCRETE SLAB AT GRADE LEVEL

4" CRUSHED STONE BASE USED ON POORLY DRAINED GROUND

from the corner brick toward the opposite end of the wall. Go only as far as your level will reach. In any case, four bricks is plenty. Place the level on the corner brick and tap subsequent ones down to the same level. Use the level placed along the face of the row of bricks to bring all bricks into perfect alignment with each other.

All adjustments must be made while the mortar is soft. Once it dries out, any movement of a brick will destroy its bond. Such a brick should be pulled out, cleaned of mortar, and relaid in fresh mortar.

Lay a row of several bricks at the second corner, aligning them with the level used as a straightedge.

Now build up the corners about four bricks high. If the wall goes around a corner, get started in that direction as well, being sure to maintain your desired bond pattern with the use of overlapping full bricks and half-bricks around the corner.

Instead of headers, metal ties can be used to hold the tiers together. These are embedded in mortar joints and do not show on the wall. There should be at least one tie for each 4 1/2 square feet of wall area. Stagger the ties in alternate courses.

LAYING IN-BETWEEN

Now lay the in-between bricks to a tight mason's line. In the time it takes to lay one corner

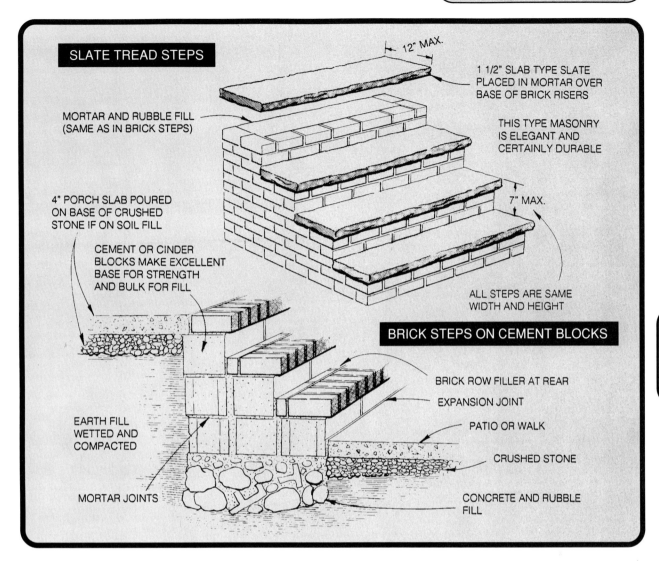

SLATE TREAD STEPS

MORTAR AND RUBBLE FILL
(SAME AS IN BRICK STEPS)

12" MAX.

1 1/2" SLAB TYPE SLATE
PLACED IN MORTAR OVER
BASE OF BRICK RISERS

THIS TYPE MASONRY
IS ELEGANT AND
CERTAINLY DURABLE

4" PORCH SLAB POURED
ON BASE OF CRUSHED
STONE IF ON SOIL FILL

CEMENT OR CINDER
BLOCKS MAKE EXCELLENT
BASE FOR STRENGTH
AND BULK FOR FILL

7" MAX.

ALL STEPS ARE SAME
WIDTH AND HEIGHT

BRICK STEPS ON CEMENT BLOCKS

BRICK ROW FILLER AT REAR

EXPANSION JOINT

PATIO OR WALK

CRUSHED STONE

CONCRETE AND RUBBLE
FILL

EARTH FILL
WETTED AND
COMPACTED

MORTAR JOINTS

373
CONCRETE

brick, you can lay five in-between bricks. Stretch the line between the corner bricks when the mortar has set enough so they can stay put. Spread mortar on the footing between corners and begin laying the first in-between course. Butter one end of each brick before you lay it. Then, as you set it in the mortar, give it a gentle shove downward and toward the adjoining brick. Tap it into alignment with the string and to the proper distance from the next brick using the mason's hammer. In every case the line should be flush with the top of the brick and about 1/16- inch away from it, not touching it. The bricks should be level, too. Check each one with a level until you get adept at judging what's level.

The last brick in the course is called the closure brick. It gets a joint at each end. Do it as shown in the photo by buttering both ends of the opening as well as the closure brick.

Cut off excess mortar that oozes from the joints and return it to the mortarboard. As soon as the first course has been completed, move the line up one course. And so on up the wall.

After tooling the joints in a day's work, brush off all loose mortar from the face of the wall with a soft brush. After a week or more, wet the wall with a hose and scrub it with a 1:9 solution of muriatic acid (one part acid to nine parts water) in water. Use a stiff fiber brush and wooden scraper. Be sure to wear rubber gloves, goggles and old clothes. The acid will remove all traces of mortar on the wall. Rinse it completely before letting it dry out.

For gray and buff-colored bricks, clean with trisodium phosphate "TSP" and *hot* water. Rinse thoroughly as for acid-cleaning.

THE ART OF REPOINTING BRICKS

Preparation is the most important ingredient before you repoint bricks.

Getting the old mortar out of the joint to a depth of about an inch is hard no matter how you do it. Try various chisels to see which works best. Important; always wear safety glasses as you pound.

Dampen the whole prepared wall by sprinkling, then push stiff mortar into each joint. Fill the vertical joints first, next the horizontal ones. Finish by tooling to match the rest of the wall.

ABOUT THE ONLY MAINTENANCE a brick wall needs is an eventual repointing. This is the renewing of the exterior portion of the mortar joints. After many years the mortar begins to weather. It softens, crumbles and some of it may even fall out of the joint. If the process continues long enough, all the mortar will become affected and whole bricks may loosen up, especially in homes located in northern areas. Fortunately, in a well built wall, this takes decades. In fact, many brick homes built a century ago still have perfectly sound, smooth joints. That's why a brick home is by far more maintenance free than a home framed with shingles, clapboard, vinyl or aluminum siding.

Repointing consists of chipping out the old mortar an inch or so deep, and replacing it with new mortar. Do the chipping with a cold chisel or a mason's chisel. Since the mason's chisel contacts a wider area, start with it. If you run into tough spots, try using the cold chisel. A mortar-raking tool also may be used if the mortar has decayed greatly.

If you have much repointing to do, find a tool rental firm that will rent you a tuckpointer's grinder. It has a Carborundum abrasive wheel, spinning 4000 rpm to clean out mortar joints to the desired depth—fast. On smaller jobs, you might try using an abrasive wheel chucked into a half-inch electric drill. Chip away at small pieces of the old mortar, aiming the tool back toward the chipped out portion. It's easier that way. Be careful not to damage the bricks themselves. Clean by blowing the joints out with compressed air from a paint sprayer, a vacuum cleaner, or a brush. *And, of course, use safety glasses.*

POINTING

Tackle the repointing in a ten-foot square area and dampen the brickwork before you repoint a section.

Always work from the ground or from sturdy scaffold; it isn't safe to repoint high walls from a ladder.

Mortar should be the same as that recom-

Always wear goggles or safety glasses when chipping out mortar. You never know when a chip will shoot toward your eye; the risk is much too great. Glasses are least prone to cloud up.

If the mortar is very soft and aged, a wire wheel chucked in your electric drill can put power to work cleaning out mortar joints. The stiffer the brush you use, the faster and better the job.

mended for laying masonry. If you aren't doing the whole wall, but are simply repairing a part of it, try to match the new mortar color to the old by adding a concrete coloring pigment. The joints of a wall laid with mortar colored with lampblack over the years will tend to gray, so if you are repointing such a wall cut down the amount of the coloring else the repointed joints will be much darker than those left untouched. Mortar, when wet, should look somewhat darker than what you want it when dry. Good repointing mortar is stiffer (has less water) than mortar used for laying brick. It should slide off the trowel when turned side-wise.

Place the mortar on a plasterer's *hawk* which is a flat board with a handle underneath. Low cost hawks are available with a round handle and an aluminum platform but you can make your own from a 12-inch-square piece of 1/2-inch thick plywood and a six-inch length of broomstick. Screw the broomstick handle to the plywood rather than using a nail because you do not want the hawk to wobble. Hold the hawk up next to the first joint to be pointed and pack the joint full of mortar with a narrow trowel which has an offset handle to clear your knuckles from the brickwork. Trowel blades are seven inches long and may be a quarter-inch to one-inch wide. Blade width should be no more than the width of the masonry joints.

Fill the vertical joints first, then the adjacent horizontal joints. Later, tool the filled joints to match existing joints. Clean up the same way as for new brickwork.

Plasterer's hawk makes it easier to push mortar into the raked-out joints between bricks. Concentric circles on the hawk plate keep the mortar supply from slipping off when the hawk is tilted.

Finish off the repointing job by tooling the joints. Here a short curved length of copper tubing is used to make a slightly concave joint. Time for tooling is when mortar is "thumbprint" hard.

HOW TO LAY STONE

The ultimate in masonry work is being able to work with stone. Here are some tips on how this can be accomplished.

Rubble rock walls need not be straight and level. Curves and sloping tops are easy. Minimum width for load bearing rubble walls is 16". Laying rock walls requires more mortar than laying brick/block walls.

You can build outdoor projects that will be the making of your house. The inner structure of this massive yard light consists of concrete block. Masonry ties hold the stones in place.

STONE, often considered the ultimate in masonry beauty, need not be the ultimate in cost. Random stones picked up along the road or found in creek beds have a natural "belongs there" look, unlike man-made materials. However, laying rubble stone masonry is more work and takes more skill than laying brick and block. This is because fieldstone doesn't come in standard sizes and shapes with square corners and flat tops and bottoms. If you buy stones, you can get them squared off enough to permit laying with slim joints like brick and block. Then the procedure is not much different than bricklaying. Wall thickness in that case may be the same as for brickwork. Random stone masonry walls, however, must be at least 16-inches thick if they are loadbearing. They have only half the strength of other masonry walls that are built with squared-off units. Also, rubble masonry joints are wider, ranging from a half-inch to one-inch thick. Of course, if you are in an area where you just cannot find stone easily, or the stone you want for a project is only available from a quarry, then a visit to your local masonry supply yard will present a wide selection of granite, limestone, to name a few. Stone can be expensive, and is usually sold by the ton, so solicit the help of your supplier when you buy the stone as to just how much you will need for your project. The cost of freight is a significant part of the overall cost; stone from a nearby quarry will cost less than stone hauled from another state.

Just as in brickwork, stone walls should have headers, stones that reach completely from

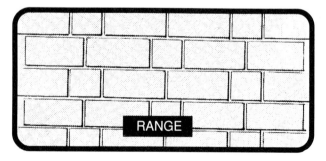

RANGE

the front to the back of the wall. These bond the facing and backing stones into a strong, structural unit.

Stones, even fieldstone rubble, may be laid either coursed or random. Coursed lay-up calls for more chipping to fit them, but it makes a stronger wall. For maximum strength, an equal number of header and stretcher stones should be used in the wall. Avoid, if possible, long vertical joints in the wall.

FITTING STONES

Stone masonry mortar is the same as that used for laying bricks and block. *Shape each stone with a mason's hammer before laying it.* The amount of work you put into this step determines how closely the stones fit and how strong the wall is. Also, it governs how formal the wall will look. A wall built with very little stone fitting has both thick and thin mortar joints and presents a rustic appearance. That's all right if rustic is what you want and if you build the wall at least 16 inches thick so it has sufficient strength.

Fitting is done with both ends of the hammer, whichever gives the results you're after. Most stones will break cleanly to a line chipped around them if you keep chipping along the line with the chisel end of the hammer. Once broken, irregularities in the face can be brought down by swift glancing blows with the head end of the mason's hammer.

To avoid a too-finished appearance in cut stone, a heavy hammer is used to break chunks out of a stone's corners and thus give it a rough look.

LAYING THEM

Because of the roughness of most stonework, you needn't get each cornerstone laid per-

fectly plumb above the one below. Hold the level in plumb position half an inch or so away from the growing stone wall and make the wall generally plumb at the corners. Peaks of each cornerstone may stick out and almost touch the level, but these are ignored. The main body of the stone wall is what counts in positioning it. This is easy because you don't have to be exact. It's harder, too, because it depends on your having a good eye for alignment before you may have had time to develop one! Still, if you're satisfied with each stone as you position it, you should be well satisfied with the entire job.

In stonework, a line is loosely strung between corners to help keep the walls straight. Individual units are not laid to the line as with bricks and blocks.

Lay the corners first, no different than other masonry, using a full bed of mortar. Larger stones should be laid in the lower portion of the wall; the small ones should be laid in the upper part. This looks right because it's the way of nature. Do it the other way around and the wall will look unnatural and top-heavy.

Spread mortar and lay each fitted stone in place among others in the growing wall. Chips of stone may be placed in the mortar to hold the stone from sinking out of position while the mortar sets. In any case, the stone should end up with a full bedding of mortar around it.

Break up stones that are too long for their height and width. Strong stones like granite can be up to five times as long as they are wide. Limit this to three times for soft stones such as limestone and sandstone.

If you're building a rough rubble wall and find that mortar joints are hard to keep filled with mortar to a uniform appearance, you can rake them all out an inch deep. Later, the joints can be filled with stiff mortar to the desired depth. This depth

377

CONCRETE

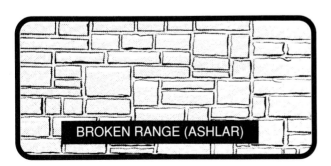

BROKEN RANGE (ASHLAR)

RANDOM RUBBLE

should leave the joints no more than an inch wide. Slim joints make your wall look more stone-like, less mortar-like.

HOW MUCH MORTAR?

Figuring mortar quantities is more of a gamble with stones than it is with conventional masonry. A good rule-of-thumb for squared-off-stone is to allow seven per cent of wall volume — volume not area—for mortar using half-inch joints. Allow twice that if the stones are small or only roughly squared. For rubble masonry, allow up to 35 percent of wall volume in mortar.

Since an acid wash cannot be used to clean stonework because it stains the stones, be extra careful to keep mortar off the faces of the stones. Remove mortar stains when you tool the joints, by using a nylon brush. If stains are stubborn, try using a wire brush.

Some experts recommend cleaning the stones with a laundry detergent and warm water. First wet down the wall with a garden hose, then scrub the detergent in with a brush. Rinse and wash again. Finally rinse thoroughly. Sometimes a jigger of household ammonia is added to the wash water. At any rate, don't clean the stones with an acid solution.

Stones that are flat and layered — slate for example— should always be laid in their natural position—flat. If you lay them vertically the wall will not look right and its strength will be adversely affected.

The amount of wall you can build with a ton of stones varies depending on the material, its degree of finish, and the wall thickness. However, most rubble stones will build from 25 square feet to 50 square feet per ton. Most cut stones will make around 50 square feet per ton. Selected finely cut

Rocks are there for the collecting, along roads, and in fields. Ask the land owner for permission first, then toss them into a pickup. Hand-pick as you go, hosing them clean before unloading.

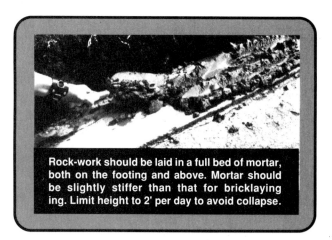

Rock-work should be laid in a full bed of mortar, both on the footing and above. Mortar should be slightly stiffer than that for bricklaying. Limit height to 2' per day to avoid collapse.

Start laying cleaned, shaped rocks into their mortar bed. For best appearance use the larger rocks at the base of the wall. Wear rubber-dipped or leather-faced gloves to protect your hands.

Just as in laying bricks and blocks, tap each rock in place before setting the next one. If the wall is more than one rock thick, some larger rocks should be laid crosswise wall width for strength.

stones can cover more than 100 square feet per ton. Slate, flagstone, and other stones used for paving and flooring cover greater areas.

Outside of building with earth, stone is the most natural, unprocessed-by-man material you can use. You can find it in many places, free for collecting. Many farmers and ranchers would be happy to let you carry off stones from their fields if you ask them. Likewise, stone quarries often consider the rubble left over after selling the good stones to be worthless. For a small cost they might let you take what you want and haul it away. Stratified stones like limestone can often be brought down to lifting size by hammering steel wedges into the natural cleavage lines. Be sure to wear eye-protection. You can also buy the stones you need, rubble or dressed to any degree you like.

RUBBLE

Rubble is raw, unprocessed stone as you find it. It makes fine-looking walls. When laid with straight horizontal joints as in brick and block. it's called *coursed rubble*. Laid without regard to pattern, it's called *random rubble*.

Keep this in mind, too, as you lay stones: stones should work together for size, shape, and color. That is, they should look as though they belong together. There may be a variation in color, but keep it within the natural variation found in nature. Moreover, two stones of the same size and shape should not be laid side-by-side. Separate them with either smaller or larger stones. For strength, stones should extend at least one-third of the way into the wall. In a 16-inch-thick wall no stone should be less than five inches in width. Always lay stratified stones with their cut edges on the face of the wall. The striations, if exposed to the weather, will bring water into the wall's interior—sometimes with disastrous results.

All stones should be dampened before being laid in the wall. To help the curing of the mortar used, it is a good idea to keep a wall damp by sprinkling for a week.

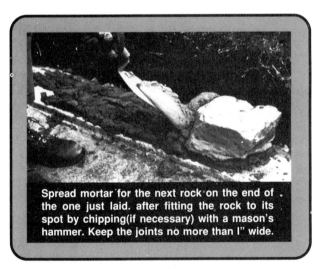

Spread mortar for the next rock on the end of the one just laid. after fitting the rock to its spot by chipping(if necessary) with a mason's hammer. Keep the joints no more than 1" wide.

Set the next rock in place, pressing it into the mortar. In rock-work it is permissible to prop rocks into the desired position with chips of stone. The mortar must surround each rock.

Corners of rubble rock-work are merely "aimed" at being plumb. Since the irregular shapes of all rocks cannot be plumbed like regular bricks and blocks, they need only look plumb.

Since keeping full mortar joints in rough rubble masonry isn't always practical, the joints may require pointing after laying. First, rake the joints, then fill the cavity to the desired depth.

MAKE A PATIO

Making a patio a livable place is like adding an extra family room to your house—at less than half the cost.

The best patios give a snse of complete enclosure, hence the brick wall around this one. The edge of the slab was thickened and steel-reinforced to 12" to form what is called a grade beam to support wall.

AN EXCELLENT PATIO for outdoor enjoyment can be made of concrete, bricks, pre-cast concrete tiles and many other materials. Combinations of these can be used, too. The most popular patio material is probably concrete, although wooden decks have given the homeowner the option of additional outdoor living space up to 8 feet above the ground. A concrete patio can be poured to any desired shape, is practically maintenance-free and can be colored and textured to suit.

A patio should be below the interior house floor level to keep water from coming in under the door. A one-inch difference is enough. Of course, you can have more than an inch difference if you wish. In fact, a patio can be made on various levels to take advantage of sloping ground. The patio should also slope away from the house about 1/4-inch per foot to carry off rain and, if you are in the north, melting snow.

A concrete patio is usually built four inches thick with control joints dividing it into ten-foot maximum size slabs to prevent cracking. The subgrade is prepared the same as for a sidewalk or driveway. Forming is similar, too. A sand or stone surface, if used, should extend a foot beyond the patio edges to prevent undercutting in a heavy rain. Provide some method of draining to keep water from collecting along the edges.

To save on concrete you can build a patio only 1 1/2 inches thick if it is jointed into two foot maximum size slabs to prevent cracking. One way to do this is with a jointing tool. Another way to form the patio into small squares or rectangles is with non-rotting 1x2-inch redwood, cypress, or

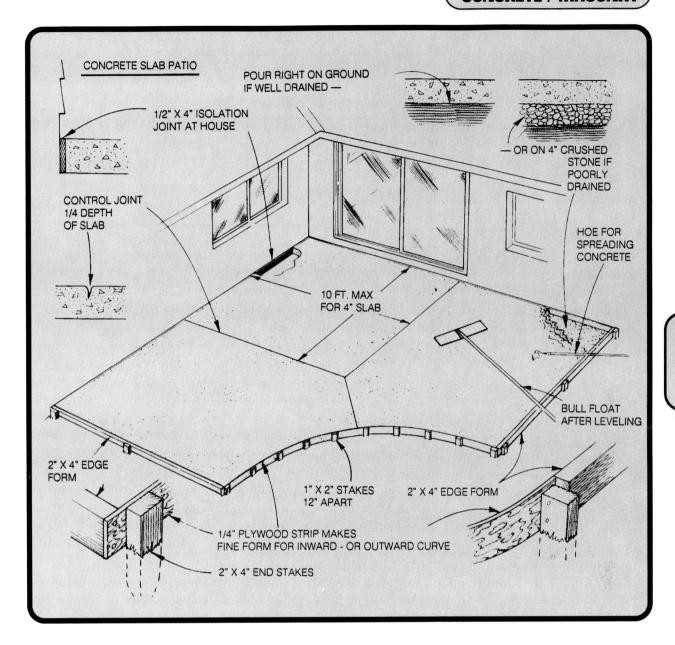

pressure-treated wood. The frames can be partially pre-nailed and assembled in ladder-like strips. If you stagger the adjoining wood form strips, all can be end-nailed. Lay them on the subgrade and stake them temporarily. Level, if necessary, by sliding blocks under the low spots. Since the thickness is only 1 1/2 inches, a load of ready-mix builds a lot of patio.

To prevent the strips from working up or down and spoiling the future appearance of your job, drive 8-penny galvanized nails through the strips at frequent intervals. These will become embedded in the concrete tying it and the strips together.

PREPARATION OF SUBBASE

With a thin-section patio, subbase preparation is important. Tamp it well, or else cast the patio on unexcavated earth. Getting that to proper grade is tough, so a sand fill is recommended. Dampen and compact it. Use a home-built hand tamper made with a 2 x 6 or 4 x 4 with a 2 x 2 handle nailed across it. If you have a large area to do, you may want to rent a power compactor.

An isolation joint should be used at the house wall, at the sidewalk, the driveway and at other adjoining walls and slabs.

If your patio cannot be easily graded by hand, then a front-end loader with a rear blade (above) can do the job. Or you can rent a smaller "Bob Cat" grader and run it yourself.

Once your patio is graded and formed, if you can get a ready mix truck or a concrete pumper within a short distance, the pour can be done in 15 to 20 minutes, depending upon the area.

NO MORTAR BRICK OR TILE

A serviceable patio can be made just out of bricks or precast concrete tiles set on a sand bed. First, construct a non-rotting wood edging or a trench with a row of bricks set on end for an edging. An edge is needed to hold the bricks or tiles together. Dig the sod out down to a level that will place the tops of the units at the desired grade. Set the edging with its top at or above finished patio grade. Then spread a two-inch layer of sand and smooth it to slope away from the house 1/4 inch per foot.

Now you can begin laying the units. Choose any pattern you like, combining different-sized precast concrete tiles, paving blocks or bricks. Bricks you use should be hard-burned bricks that will be able to take the severe weathering they'll be subjected to on the ground. Besides bricks, a fine no-mortar flagstone patio can be laid the same way.

Whatever material you lay, throw damp sand over the finished surface and sweep it into the cracks between, until the sand is flush with the surface. Often the wider joints between flagstones are filled with topsoil or sod to get "living" joints between the flags.

Below, leave in pressure-treated wood (or untreated redwood, cedar, cypress). Work has been positioned, ready for pouring. No other jointing is needed, since the forms make their own.

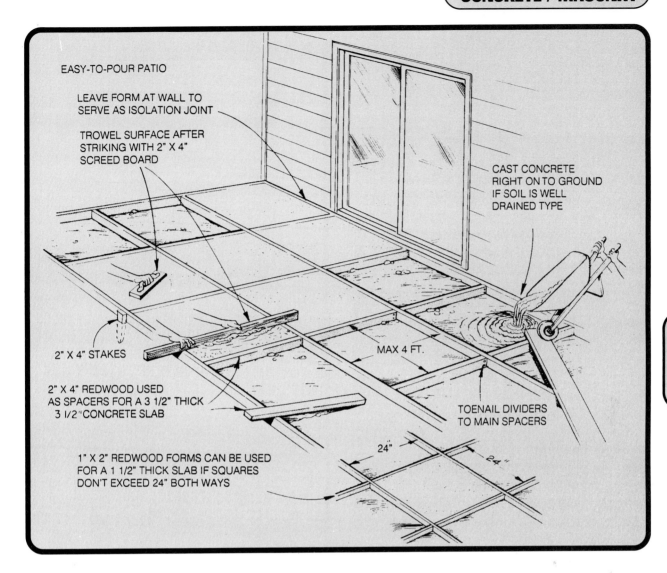

EASY-TO-POUR PATIO

LEAVE FORM AT WALL TO
SERVE AS ISOLATION JOINT

TROWEL SURFACE AFTER
STRIKING WITH 2" X 4"
SCREED BOARD

CAST CONCRETE
RIGHT ON TO GROUND
IF SOIL IS WELL
DRAINED TYPE

2" X 4" STAKES

2" X 4" REDWOOD USED
AS SPACERS FOR A 3 1/2" THICK
3 1/2"CONCRETE SLAB

MAX 4 FT.

TOENAIL DIVIDERS
TO MAIN SPACERS

1" X 2" REDWOOD FORMS CAN BE USED
FOR A 1 1/2" THICK SLAB IF SQUARES
DON'T EXCEED 24" BOTH WAYS

24"

24"

This patio area was made with
concrete patio pavers measuring
4" x 8" x 16". The area was first
leveled and tamped, then 2" of
sand was spread. Just before
laying a group of four blocks
the sand was sprinkled with
portland cement and the blocks
set level. After the patio was
completed the area was hosed
down. Water seeped through the
cracks and the cement and sand
set to give each block a firmer
base. There are many different
sizes and colored blocks available.

If a wood edging is used, you can make a self-leveling strikeoff board that, drawn over the tops of the forms, will smooth off the sand bedding to the right level and sloped for drainage.

CONCRETE AS A BASE

Bricks, tiles, and flagstones may be set on a solid concrete base for a patio surface that needs almost no maintenance. First pour the concrete base almost as though it were a patio itself. Make it three inches thick, float it, and scratch the surface with the edge of a piece of hardware cloth or chicken wire to provide "tooth" for what's to follow.

Some method must be devised to prevent shrinkage cracks that are bound to form in the concrete base from affecting the tiles, bricks, or flagstones. The best way to build the base is with 6x6-inch No. 10 steel mesh laid in the halfway section of the three-inch base slab. This won't prevent cracking, but it will hold the cracks tightly together and, hopefully, keep them from cracking the upper masonry units. Another method is to form control joints in the base slab no more than ten feet apart and match them with the joints above. This is a bit harder to work out. You need to know exactly where the top joints will fall. This is a sure way to avoid unsightly cracks.

The following day spread a one-inch layer of mortar over a portion of the base slab. Begin laying paving units in it right away. Pound them level and align with a mason's hammer, being careful not to chip the top surfaces and edges. A long level or straightedge will help.

USE OF ADHESIVES

You can wait as long as you like between building the base slab and preparing the base concrete for a good bond if you apply a good concrete adhesive or a similar bonding agent. You can also use a bonding slurry made of portland cement and water. Brush it into the pores of the base slab and place the mortar topping while it is still damp.

Stay off the patio for one day while the mortar sets up. If you must walk on it to work, lay sheets of 3/4-inch plywood or planks to work on.

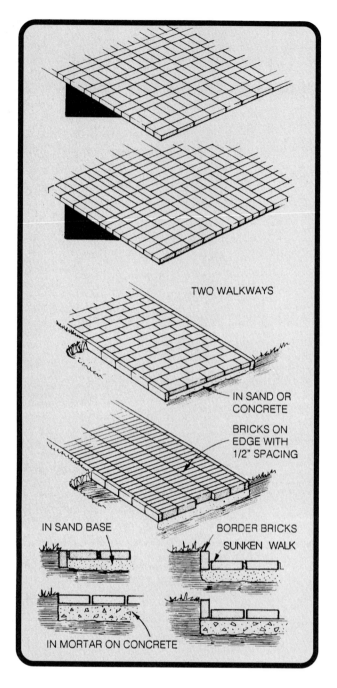

TWO WALKWAYS

IN SAND OR CONCRETE

BRICKS ON EDGE WITH 1/2" SPACING

IN SAND BASE

BORDER BRICKS
SUNKEN WALK

IN MORTAR ON CONCRETE

The next day, fill in the joints with mortar and tool the joints. Hose the area down regularly so the mortar can cure properly. And when filling the joints remember *too much water weakens* so keep your mix stiff. For a formal effect make neat mortar joints, as in a brick wall. A long, narrow trowel made for tuck-pointing may be helpful here. Within several hours remove mortar stains with a brush. Later, get rid of all stains completely, following the directions in the chapter for laying brick, concrete block, or stones, whichever material you are paving with.

CONTENTS

PAINTING

386 The Pros and Cons of Painting Your Home
388 Enemies of Paint
390 Comparing Oil & Latex Paints
392 How to Estimate Paint Quantities
392 Paint when Weather is Right
394 Primers Solve Paint Problems
396 Selecting Interior Paint
396 Solid Color Latex Stains
398 Surface Preparation: Wood, Metal, Stucco
398 Painting Concrete Floors

400 Painting Aluminum/Vinyl Siding
400 Safety Rules when Painting
400 Elastomeric Coatings for Masonry
402 Storing Latex Paint
402 Painting an Older Home
402 Understanding Paint Terminology
404 Diagnosing Paint Failures
404 Future Trends in Paint Technology
406 All About Paint Brushes
412 All About Paint Rollers
416 Three Ways to Apply Paint
418 What Makes Paint Durable?
418 Answers to Painting Problems
420 Unusual Rollers, Mitts and Pads

BOOK 5 PAINTING/ WALLCOVERING

Prime Author: WALTER GOZDAN

385

422 Masking Around Windows and Doors
424 Cleaning Brushes and Rollers
426 Paint with a Roller that does not need a Tray
428 Power Rollers
428 Cordless Roller
430 Power Sprayers

WALLCOVERING

432 History
433 Selecting Ideas
434 Choosing the Right Wallcovering
436 Special Effects
437 Innovative Use
438 Wallcovering Wizardry
442 Home Decorator's Dictionary
444 How to Hang Wallcovering
446 Unusual Glamour Wallcoverings

448 Tools and Equipment Required
450 All About Patterns
452 Working with Adhesives
454 Estimating Number of Rolls
456 Must you Remove the Old Covering?
458 Treating Painted/Unpainted Walls
460 Do You Need a Lining Paper?
462 Hanging Instructions
466 Covering Around Windows and Doors
468 Covering Behind Sinks and Radiators
470 How to Hang a Ceiling
472 Techniques: Pasting the Wall
474 Working with Pre-Pasted Rolls
476 Trimming Untrimmed Rolls
478 Correcting Common Faults
480 Wallcovering Glossary

THE PROS AND CONS OF PAINTING YOUR OWN HOME

Life is full of decisions, especially for homeowners. One of the big decisions is determining whether your home exterior needs repainting. If it does, the next question is usually, "Should I hire a professional or do it myself?"

While the answer to that question will differ from homeowner to homeowner, there are certain considerations everyone should take into account.

To the uninformed, painting may not look very strenuous. But that's an opinion that's often revised after a day of climbing up and down ladders.

Are you in good health? Do you enjoy physical work? Are you afraid of heights? Working two or three stories off the ground can be physically demanding and, for many of us, a little scary as well.

Do you have the proper tools and equipment to handle the job? Without scaffolding, painting even a moderate size home can be a monumental task. Those who've been through the experience will tell you that attempting to paint from a single ladder is a mistake you won't make twice.

And if you don't have the right equipment (or the required skill) to do a professional job, will you be happy with the results?

For many people, the biggest consideration is the time the job will take. Do you really want to spend your vacation, weekends or free time painting the house? Only you can decide.

On the other side of the ledger, there are some sound reasons to undertake the project yourself.

First and foremost is the money you can save. House painting is very labor-intensive. In fact, labor costs often total from 80 to 85 percent of the cost of repainting. That's money you can pocket if you do the work yourself.

Then there are the psychological rewards that can come from successful do-it-yourself

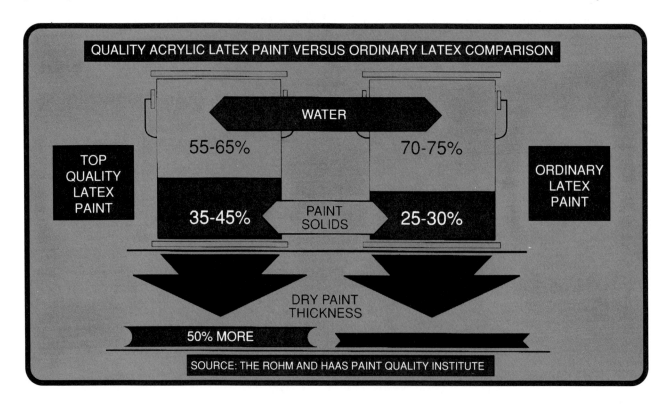

QUALITY ACRYLIC LATEX PAINT VERSUS ORDINARY LATEX COMPARISON

TOP QUALITY LATEX PAINT

ORDINARY LATEX PAINT

WATER

55-65%

70-75%

PAINT SOLIDS

35-45%

25-30%

DRY PAINT THICKNESS

50% MORE

SOURCE: THE ROHM AND HAAS PAINT QUALITY INSTITUTE

projects. For many of us, repainting can be satisfying and a pleasant change of pace from our regular jobs. And there's always the feeling that we'll take just a little more care than would a stranger, since it's our own home we're working on.

If you do not elect to go the do-it-yourself route, call in several professional painting contractors. Here is a proven approach:

SEEK RECOMMENDATIONS. Solicit the names of contractors from friends and neighbors. Ask if they were happy with the work performed.

CHECK OUT CONTRACTOR'S WORK. Don't rely totally on the opinion of others (you may have different standards or expectations). Go out and inspect homes the contractors have painted. Most professionals will be glad to provide the names and addresses of previous customers.

CHECK AFFILIATIONS. Find out if the contractors belong to local or national painting contractor associations. Membership is one indicator of reliability.

NEXT COMES THE MOST IMPORTANT STEPS:

GET ESTIMATES. For a fair comparison, get at least three estimates and make sure the bids are based on the same materials and workmanship.

Some of the things the estimates should include are:

—brand and quality of paint
—details on surface preparation, i.e., whether the bid includes sanding, power washing, caulking and priming
—number of coats to be applied
—the way the paint will be applied, i.e., spray, brush or roller
—breakout of total bid into labor charges and materials cost

INSIST ON A WRITTEN CONTRACT. Make sure the contractor puts into writing (and signs) a document containing all details of the work to be performed. Key items are specifics that appear in the estimate, as well as payment terms, timing for the work to be done, and any warranty or guarantee that applies.

Whether you do it yourself — or hire a contractor - one decision to make is to choose or stipulate the best materials be used. As the chart indicates, the life expectancy of a paint job when top-of-the-line acrylic latex paint is used can be two or three times that of low-grade latex paint that contains more water and less solids, pigment. and binder. With more solids, a thicker film results and the film thickness is directly related to the life of the painted surface!

TOTAL COST OF A CONTRACTOR-APPLIED JOB

85% Labor ▶ 15% Paint

SOURCE: THE ROHM AND HAAS PAINT QUALITY INSTITUTE

ENEMIES OF PAINT

Let's face it. You can't control the weather. However, if you plan to paint the exterior of your home the understanding of how weather can affect paint will help you make better decisions on when to start your paint job.

We expect a lot out of paint, especially when you consider that a coating that is just two or three 1,000ths of an inch thick must stand up to the ravages of nature over the course of many years.

THREE ENEMIES OF PAINT:

Experts agree that the three worst enemies of paint are temperature fluctuations, ultraviolet sun rays, and moisture. Regardless of where your home is located, you are bound to face one or more of these nemeses.

Perhaps the most demanding test for an exterior house paint are temperature fluctuations experienced in freezing climates. This is due to the potentially damaging effects of the freeze/thaw cycle, where the temperature may drop below freezing at night, and then rise above 32 degrees during the daytime.

The freeze/thaw process places extraordinary stress on a coating since the wood surface underneath tends to expand and contract along with the temperature changes. If the paint on top of the surface isn't flexible, this stress can cause it to crack and even flake off.

Severe temperature fluctuation occurs in the Northern U.S. and Canada from late fall through early spring. In the Northeastern U.S., freeze/thaw cycling is particularly frequent. A house in this region can experience from 50 to 70 freeze/thaw cycles during this period.

Tests performed at the Rohm and Haas Paint Quality Institute's main facility in Spring House, Pennsylvania—right in the heart of the Northeastern region—show that top quality acrylic paints tend to be tougher and more flexible than ordinary paint, which allows them to expand and contract in the face of severe temperature swings.

NO FUN IN THE SUN

While painting contractors in regions like Southern California, the Southwest, and Southeast rarely have to worry about the effects of freeze/thaw cycling, they have another enemy to contend with—ultraviolet sun rays.

The downside to the great sunny weather in these regions is that the sun's ultraviolet rays tend to deteriorate a paint's binder. As the binder breaks down, pigment is released in a powdery or chalk-like form.

Heavy UV exposure can result in accelerated fading with many paints and erosion of the paint's protective properties. Since color fade is a touchy subject, it's better to be safe by choosing a paint with superior protection against UV (ultra violet) degradation.

MOISTURE IS EVERYWHERE

Paint's third enemy—moisture—is a particularly difficult problem since it appears in many forms and attacks exterior paint in most regions of the country. Exposure to rain, snow, frost, and high humidity can all take their toll on your paint job. Moisture in any form can cause paint to soften and swell, leading to blistering, cracking, peeling, or flaking. In addition, moist conditions encourage the growth of unsightly mildew, which is particularly common in the humid South.

Because of its superior binder, a top quality paint adheres to substrates better than ordinary paint and reduces the chance of moisture-related blistering. Also, these paints typically contain more mildewcide than lower quality paints.

Q.   Why are certain trim colors, such as red, so tough to cover on the second coat? Would it be best to apply some kind of primer and then an acrylic latex topcoat to cover more easily? What other colors are tough to cover?

A. Difficulty in covering a previously painted surface relates not so much to the color of the earlier paint but to how dark it is. The recoat hiding problem is compounded when a very light color (most noticeably yellow) is applied over a dark one. Multiple coats of paint are often necessary in these cases.

Use of a primer as a first coat may be helpful depending on the hiding of the primer and of the topcoat. Using a poor hiding primer may be no better than using two top coats. Also, tinting the primer to approximate the topcoat can help.

Q. Are acrylic latex primers and topcoats "breathable," allowing moisture vapor to pass through the outside? Doesn't this breathability diminish when second topcoating and subsequent painting is done?

A. Moisture vapor is more likely to pass through acrylic latex paint films than through solvent alkyd types. It is true that application of additional coats will, simply on the basis of increased film thickness, reduce moisture vapor transmission.

However, even with several coats applied, the latex film will be adequately permeable to water vapor and better than alkyd paint films of comparable thickness.

Q. When painting entrance doors and trim, it is important that brush marks not show. What gives a latex paint superior flow and leveling qualities?

A. The best gloss and semigloss acrylic latex trim paints are modified with flow-improvers (known "rheology modifiers") which provide exceptionally smooth finishes.

Not surprisingly, lower-priced ordinary latex paints are less likely to contain enough of these expensive additives to give the same good appearance that results from the use of top line acrylic latex paints.

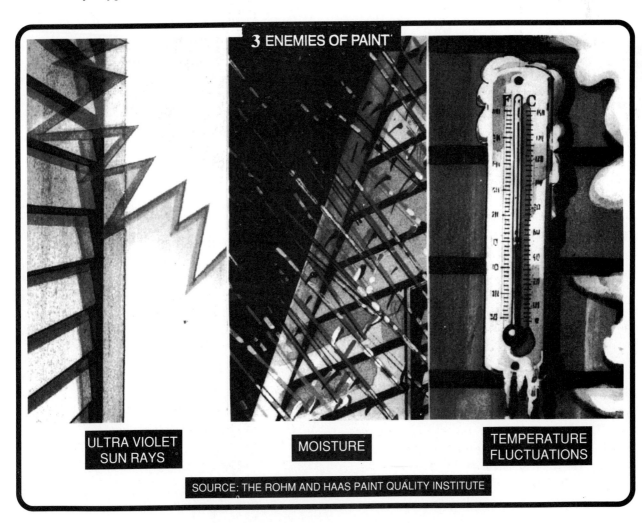

3 ENEMIES OF PAINT

ULTRA VIOLET SUN RAYS

MOISTURE

TEMPERATURE FLUCTUATIONS

SOURCE: THE ROHM AND HAAS PAINT QUALITY INSTITUTE

COMPARING OIL & LATEX PAINTS

More and more, homeowners are switching from traditional alkyd or oil-based paints to latex or water-based paints. Oil paints and latex paints both have three key components: pigment, thinners and binders. While similar pigments are used in both kinds of paints, oil and latex use different thinners and binders, as the chart shows. When choosing your paint consider the following eight important points.

DURABILITY

Good adhesion is probably the single most important property of paints, because it helps prevent blistering, flaking and cracking. Top quality latex paints that contain top quality acrylic binders provide maximum adhesion to most surfaces. Latex paints are also very flexible, so they continue to adhere even when temperature changes cause the surface to expand and contract. This elasticity helps forestall chipping, cracking, peeling, flaking and other common paint failures.

Alkyd paints also have excellent adhesion, and perform better than latex paints over heavily chalked surfaces. But with time, the alkyd can embrittle, sometimes resulting in cracking in just a few years.

COLOR RETENTION

Top quality acrylic latex paints provide superior resistance to bleaching and fading, even when exposed to damaging ultraviolet sun rays.

Alkyd paints fade faster than latex paints. They are

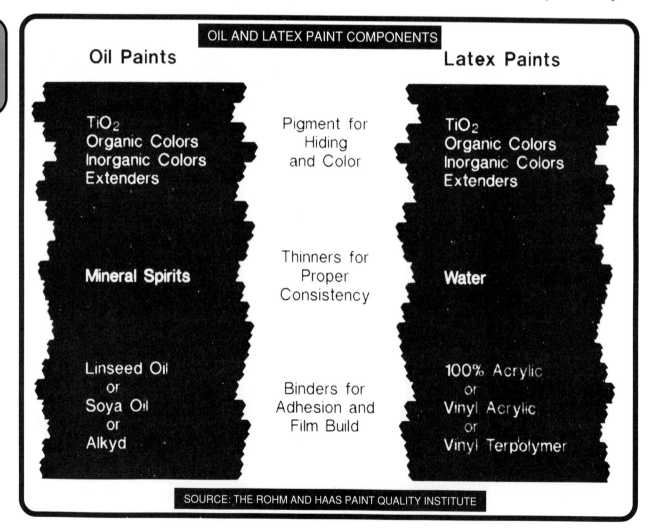

OIL AND LATEX PAINT COMPONENTS

Oil Paints		Latex Paints
TiO_2 Organic Colors Inorganic Colors Extenders	Pigment for Hiding and Color	TiO_2 Organic Colors Inorganic Colors Extenders
Mineral Spirits	Thinners for Proper Consistency	Water
Linseed Oil or Soya Oil or Alkyd	Binders for Adhesion and Film Build	100% Acrylic or Vinyl Acrylic or Vinyl Terpolymer

SOURCE: THE ROHM AND HAAS PAINT QUALITY INSTITUTE

more likely to chalk (develop a powdery substance on their surface), which causes the color to whiten.

EASE OF APPLICATION

Latex paints glide smoothly from the brush or roller onto the surface. Top quality latex paints are especially easy to apply, since recently developed additives provide even application and spatter resistance.

Compared to latex paints, alkyd paints are more difficult to apply, especially when brushing a large area, because they have more "drag." On the other hand, they go on heavier and give more complete one-coat hiding and coverage.

MILDEW RESISTANCE

Top quality latex paints contain mildewcides to discourage mildew and help the paint maintain a fresh appearance.

Alkyd paints, while also containing mildewcides, are derived from vegetable oils which provide nutrients for mildew growth.

VARIETY OF USES

Latex paints can be used on wood, concrete, metal, vinyl siding, aluminum siding, brick and stucco. Alkyd paints should not be applied directly to galvanized metal. They also require special chemical pretreatments before use on new concrete, stucco and other masonry surfaces.

ODOR

Latex paints have little odor and are non-flammable. Alkyd paints have noticeably more odor owing to the solvents and oils they contain.

CLEANUP

Latex paints cleans up easily with soap and water. Alkyd paints require solvents for cleanup, making this chore messy and complicated.

DRYING TIME

Latex paints dry in just a couple of hours, so you can recoat quickly. However, they are vulnerable in case of sudden rain. Drying time for alkyd paints can take up to two days — plenty of time for dirt, insects and people to come in contact with the surface and mar it permanently.

HOW PAINTS DRY AND AGE

	At Application	1 Year	2 Years
Oil Paints	Mineral spirits evaporate and the oil or alkyd oxidizes.	Yellowing/fading begins.	Oxidation continues causing paint to become brittle.

	At Application	3 Years	7 Years
Quality Acrylic Latex Paints	Water evaporates and the acrylic polymer fuses into a film.	Slight tint loss may appear.	No oxidation; protective properties are maintained.

SOURCE: THE ROHM AND HAAS PAINT QUALITY INSTITUTE

HOW TO ESTIMATE PAINT QUANTITIES

The Boy Scout motto "Be Prepared" also applies to do-it-yourselfers and homeowners planning to purchase paint.

You can save time and money by estimating your paint needs before you visit your local paint or hardware store, or service-oriented home center. Below are some tips to help size up your home paint job, and determine the number of gallons required for your project.

BRUSH UP ON MATH

The easiest way to estimate the amount of paint you'll need is to measure each surface area to be painted — multiplying the height by the length or width. Duplicate this calculation with the areas that won't be painted over, like doorways and windows. Then, subtract non-paint areas from the overall surface area to get an estimate of the square footage to be painted.

The next step is to look at the paint can label to determine the spread rate, which is, on average, 400 square feet per gallon. Divide the total surface area by this number to determine the number of gallons you'll need for each coat.

NUMBER OF COATS

A number of factors — like the type of paint, the color you are applying and the nature of the surface — dictate the number of coats you should apply. For example, you will likely need a second coat of paint when covering a dark color with a lighter one. Also, masonry surfaces like stucco are very porous and absorb a great deal of paint. Hence, a second coat is often needed on these types of materials in order to get a uniform appearance.

Applying two coats of top quality acrylic latex paint to provide better durability is recommended. Two-coat coverage stands up to the demands of weather and environment better than one-coat painting.

STORING USED PAINT

If you've overestimated your paint needs, don't be concerned. Age alone won't detract from a paint's properties. However, an improperly sealed container and excessive heat or cold can affect paint. Latex paints should never be stored where they can freeze. Before re-using old paints, be sure to remove any "skin," rust or particles that have accumulated. Mix the paint thoroughly and, if necessary, strain through cheesecloth or a nylon stocking to remove any remaining sediment. Also, unused paint can often be returned for credit as long as it has not been opened and is not a customized color. In the final analysis, taking time to think through your painting projects before you begin will pay big dividends in time and money saved. It's the smart way to paint.

PAINT WHEN THE WEATHER IS RIGHT

Weather plays an important role in our lives. It can affect our moods, our plans — even our house painting! To make sure your painting projects don't get under the weather, here are some proven suggestions.

•Ideal weather conditions for exterior painting are an air temperature in the 60 to 85-degree range, low or moderate humidity, little or no wind, and overcast skies.

•Surface temperature can be 10 to 20 degrees higher than the air temperature, so avoid painting in the glaring sun. High temperatures cause the water in latex paints to evaporate too quickly, which can prevent proper formation of the paint's protective film.

•Remember that metal surfaces such as aluminum siding can be hotter than the air temperature. Painting over these surfaces when they're too hot can lead to paint failures such as peeling or flaking.

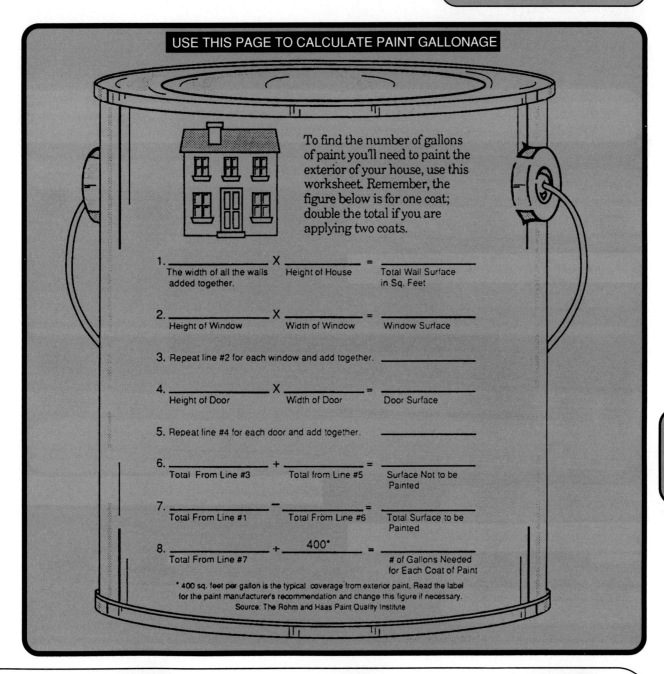

USE THIS PAGE TO CALCULATE PAINT GALLONAGE

To find the number of gallons of paint you'll need to paint the exterior of your house, use this worksheet. Remember, the figure below is for one coat; double the total if you are applying two coats.

1. _____ X _____ = _____
   The width of all the walls added together. Height of House Total Wall Surface in Sq. Feet

2. _____ X _____ = _____
   Height of Window Width of Window Window Surface

3. Repeat line #2 for each window and add together. _____

4. _____ X _____ = _____
   Height of Door Width of Door Door Surface

5. Repeat line #4 for each door and add together. _____

6. _____ + _____ = _____
   Total From Line #3 Total from Line #5 Surface Not to be Painted

7. _____ − _____ = _____
   Total From Line #1 Total From Line #6 Total Surface to be Painted

8. _____ + 400* = _____
   Total From Line #7 # of Gallons Needed for Each Coat of Paint

* 400 sq. feet per gallon is the typical coverage from exterior paint. Read the label for the paint manufacturer's recommendation and change this figure if necessary.
Source: The Rohm and Haas Paint Quality Institute

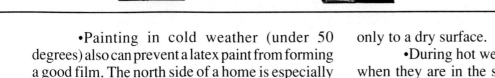

•Painting in cold weather (under 50 degrees) also can prevent a latex paint from forming a good film. The north side of a home is especially vulnerable, since it gets the least sunshine — as a result, the surface to be painted may even be cooler than the air temperature.

•With latex paints, you can paint a surface within a half-hour after it rains if the surface is not visibly wet. This is not the case with oil or other solvent-based paints, which should be applied only to a dry surface.

•During hot weather, try to paint surfaces when they are in the shade. The north and west sides of the home are shaded in the morning; the south and east sides are shaded in late afternoon.

•Avoid painting when it is very windy. Even light wind can cause the paint to dry too fast and affect the protective film. This is especially important if conditions are particularly warm and dry.

PRIMERS SOLVE PAINT PROBLEMS

Without proper information, selecting the right primer for a paint job can be as confusing as choosing the right paint. There are primers for wood, metal and masonry. There are latex and oil-based (alkyd) primers. And there are sealers that aren't exactly primers, but are close cousins.

To avoid confusion, it's necessary to first understand the role of a primer and how it can improve a paint's performance and longevity.

The purpose of a primer is simple: to help create a tight bond between the paint and the surface to be painted. Simply speaking, the primer helps paint get a better "grip" on a bare surface by making the surface more uniform and accepting for a top coat. In addition, the primer helps prevent

stains and tannins from seeping through the paint.

Primers should be applied over surfaces that have never been painted before — like new wood and plaster. When repainting, primers are needed in two instances: when a surface is uneven; or when the surface has been stripped or is worn down to the original substrate.

But primers can also solve some sticky problems that require more than a simple coat of paint. Most can do one or more of the following:
• keep iron and steel from rusting;
• help cover stains and graffiti;
• hide water damage;
• seal off knots and sap streaks in wood;
• prevent bleed-through from "staining

MASONRY

Apply masonry sealer first if surface is very porous; otherwise not necessary. In repaint situation, use sealer if old paint is partly or all removed by scraping or wire brush.

FERROUS METALS

Apply acrylic latex or oil-based corrosion resistant primer (two coats is better) before topcoating.

ALUMINUM, GALVANIZED STEEL

Primer is not necessary unless galvanized surface shows sign of rust -- then remove any white, powdery oxide on aluminum surfaces with coarse steel wool, then dust off before applying the paint.

woods" like cedar and redwood;

•seal porous surfaces like sheetrock, cured plaster and weathered masonry;

•help paint adhere to slick surfaces such as tile and high-gloss enamels.

While primers are effective problem solvers, however, they can hide only so much. If a stain is caused by a leaky water pipe, for example, it is important to fix the leak before using a primer to conceal the stain.

Sealers, although they are similar to primers, are designed to serve a different purpose. They are commonly applied before painting so that the surface will not absorb the paint.

Typically, sealers are used to coat wood or masonry surfaces that have areas with varying degrees of porosity. If a sealer were not applied to these surfaces, the finished job would not look smooth and uniform. Instead, the more porous

areas would look "flatter" than the non-porous areas and the effect would be very unflattering.

Even after deciding that a primer or sealer will improve the final appearance of a paint job, it still is important to choose the right type of product for the project at hand. To that end, it is important to know that there are two general types of primers and sealers: latex or water-based products; and alkyd or oil-based products.

Alkyd products were once the only choice available. But with the development of latex primers and sealers that contain state-of-the-art acrylics, today these products perform just as well as their alkyd counterparts in many applications. And latex products have some big advantages. For example, latex products are easier to work with, since they clean up easily with plain soap and water. And unlike alkyd primers and sealers, acrylic latex products do not have a strong odor.

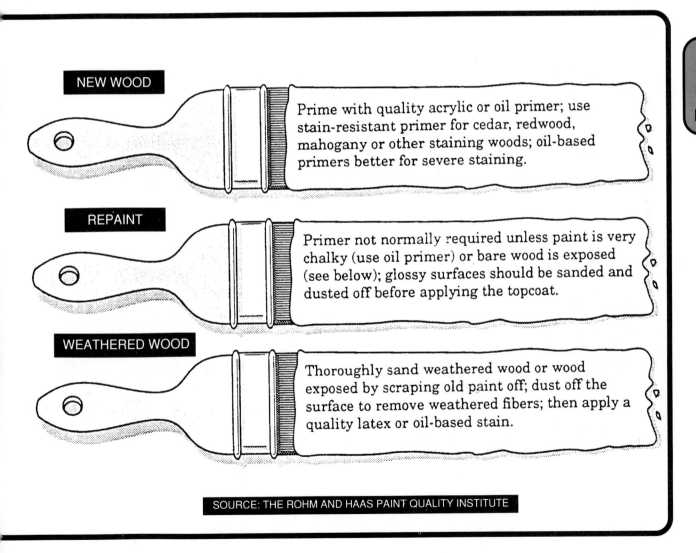

NEW WOOD
Prime with quality acrylic or oil primer; use stain-resistant primer for cedar, redwood, mahogany or other staining woods; oil-based primers better for severe staining.

REPAINT
Primer not normally required unless paint is very chalky (use oil primer) or bare wood is exposed (see below); glossy surfaces should be sanded and dusted off before applying the topcoat.

WEATHERED WOOD
Thoroughly sand weathered wood or wood exposed by scraping old paint off; dust off the surface to remove weathered fibers; then apply a quality latex or oil-based stain.

SOURCE: THE ROHM AND HAAS PAINT QUALITY INSTITUTE

SELECTING INTERIOR PAINT

"To gloss or not to gloss?" That is the question homeowners and do-it-yourselfers often ask when they visit their local paint store. With so many options available, selecting the right type of paint for your latest home improvement project can be a confusing task, especially with interior paints. The following tips along with advice from your local paint retailer, hardware store, or decorating center — will help you get the best results from your next paint job.

•Use flat paints on walls and ceilings, anywhere you want a muted, low-reflecting surface, or where it's important to hide surface imperfections. Flat paints are best suited for the low-traffic areas of your home, because it takes more effort to remove dirt and stains from these paints than from finishes with higher sheen or gloss.

•Eggshell, sheen and satin paints are best suited for areas where a slight luster is desired, such as kitchen and bathroom walls, children's rooms and playrooms, hallways and woodwork — in general, the high-traffic areas of your home. These paints are easier to clean than flat paints, hold up better after repeated washings and provide a shinier appearance.

•Semigloss and high-gloss paints and enamels are most suitable for trim, banisters and railings, shelves, kitchen cabinets, bathroom and kitchen walls, furniture, door jambs and window sills, and surfaces that you want to accentuate. A general rule to remember is: The higher the gloss you choose, the more it will highlight surface imperfections. So it's especially important to properly prepare surfaces where a semigloss or high-gloss finish is applied. Be sure patched areas are thoroughly sanded prior to painting.

•When selecting an interior finish, consider choosing a water-based gloss enamel as an alternative to using an oil-based gloss paint. Water-based enamels have less odor than oil-based paints. They are also much easier to clean up after and are less prone to yellowing and embrittling as they age.

•Select a top quality paint because it will perform better for a longer period of time. They won't yellow; are easier to wash; are stain- and dirt-resistant; and won't show unsightly brush marks. They tend to go on more readily, and hide the surface better than ordinary paints. With the better performance you'll get from using top quality paints, you won't have to repaint as often. That means you'll get more for your money in terms of years of service.

SOLID COLOR LATEX STAINS

America's love for the texture and character of wood has given rise to another love affair—this one with latex solid color stains for home exteriors.

Deep-tone latex stains permit the natural beauty of wood textures to show through on lap siding, textured plywood and other popular building materials. The result is a rich, rustic look that's much in vogue.

But exterior stains can vary in terms of durability. And selecting the most durable type is especially important because of the way exterior stains are typically applied.

Unlike paint, which is often applied in two or more coats on top of a primer, it is common to apply just one coat of latex solid color stain without using a primer. Since it's the only thing standing between the homeowner's biggest investment and the harsh outside environment, that single coat of stain has to be durable.

Stain has to be durable for another reason, too. That's because dark-colored exterior stains are the most popular. As a result, they must resist the fading effects of the outdoor elements.

To get the attractive appearance of textured wood and to keep that appearance for as long as possible, homeowners should use a solid color latex stain.

Top-of-the-line exterior latex solid color stains cost a little more, but the added performance is worth it.

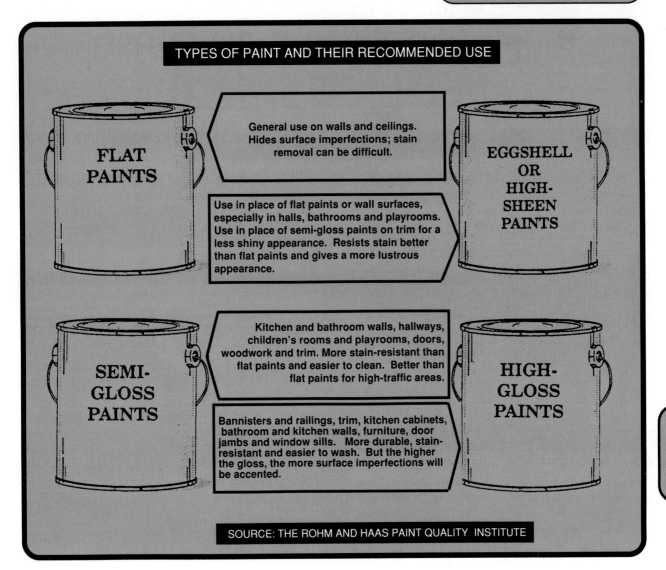

TYPES OF PAINT AND THEIR RECOMMENDED USE

FLAT PAINTS

General use on walls and ceilings. Hides surface imperfections; stain removal can be difficult.

EGGSHELL OR HIGH-SHEEN PAINTS

Use in place of flat paints or wall surfaces, especially in halls, bathrooms and playrooms. Use in place of semi-gloss paints on trim for a less shiny appearance. Resists stain better than flat paints and gives a more lustrous appearance.

SEMI-GLOSS PAINTS

Kitchen and bathroom walls, hallways, children's rooms and playrooms, doors, woodwork and trim. More stain-resistant than flat paints and easier to clean. Better than flat paints for high-traffic areas.

HIGH-GLOSS PAINTS

Bannisters and railings, trim, kitchen cabinets, bathroom and kitchen walls, furniture, door jambs and window sills. More durable, stain-resistant and easier to wash. But the higher the gloss, the more surface imperfections will be accented.

SOURCE: THE ROHM AND HAAS PAINT QUALITY INSTITUTE

Here are some of the benefits these products offer:

Better adhesion. While a textured wood surface is beautiful to look at, coating an irregular surface like wood can be quite a challenge. Top quality stains adhere tenaciously to wood surfaces, adding years to their life expectancy.

Better color retention. These stains resist degradation from the sun's ultraviolet rays which means they'll retain their original color better than other types of stains.

Easier application and cleanup. Compared to oil-based stains, latex stains are a breeze to work with. They go on easily and, being water-based, they can be washed from tools, pans and hands with plain soap and water. And they are low odor, too.

Here are some tested tips:
1 –Spot prime any knots in the wood with a quality latex exterior primer.

Particularly if you are planning to use a light colored stain, consider applying a primer to stop discoloration from the wood. This is especially important if the surface is cedar or redwood.
2 –Since a thicker film of any exterior coating will provide a longer coating life, consider applying a second coat of stain. It will make the job last longer.

SURFACE PREPARATION: WOOD, METAL AND STUCCO

Surface preparation and quality paint are keys to long-lasting paint jobs

Housepainting experts agree that two things are needed to get the most from a paint job: good surface preparation and top-quality exterior paint. But to get the full benefit it must be applied to a sound, well-prepared surface—one that is clean and free of dirt, chalk, mildew and loose, flaking or peeling paint.

Here are preparation tips for commonly painted surfaces:

NEW, UNPAINTED WOOD

Remove any dirt or other contaminants by washing with soapy water. If mildew is present, wipe down the surface with a bleach solution and rinse thoroughly.

Noticeable surface imperfections such as knots should be sanded and spot primed. Then apply a primer over the entire surface. (Your paint or hardware dealer can recommend a quality stain-resistant primer or other product appropriate for your use.)

The coat of primer will provide a sound, stable base for the paint to adhere to. Top-quality latex paint made with 100 percent acrylic will grip the surface tenaciously, helping to protect against future paint failures.

PREVIOUSLY PAINTED WOOD

Remove all loose, peeling or flaking paint by scraping, sanding or wire brushing. If rough paint edges remain, continue sanding to feather them back. Only in extreme cases is it necessary to remove the old paint completely.

Check old painted surfaces for glossy areas. These should be sanded or wire brushed to dull the surface and provide more "grip" for the new paint.

PAINTING CONCRETE FLOORS

In order to beautify their homes or to gain more usable living space, more people today are considering paint as a top surface over their basement, porch or patio concrete surfaces. As a result, not only will these stark surfaces look nicer, but they also are easier to sweep, more resistant to staining, and less dusty. (Note: Do not use conventional paints on garage floors -- a wet hot tire can soften and lift the paint. Consult with your paint dealer as to the best coating for this purpose.)

But to do so you must be familiar with the unique procedures needed to prepare concrete surfaces for painting. Perhaps more than with any other surface being painted, one cardinal rule is—pardon the expression—cast in concrete: surface

preparation is the key to a successful job.

The surface should be sound; free of dirt, oil, powdery dust, and loose chalk; and rough enough to ensure good adhesion of the coating. Special situations encountered in the painting of concrete, especially when new or insufficiently cured, are:

—unbound moisture within the concrete remaining from the original mixing,

—efflorescence (an encrustation of soluble salts on the surface, usually white)

—glazed areas resulting from casting against a smooth form, and

—oily areas left from release agents used on casting forms.

Aging (curing) and the effects of weath-

Areas that are totally bare of paint should be spot primed as though they were new, unpainted wood.

The prepared surface should then be brushed clean of dust and particles left from scraping and sanding. A dry paint brush works well for this.

Mildew is often found on previously painted wood, especially in warm, humid climates and in shady areas. To combat the problem, clean the surface thoroughly with bleach solution, rinse and let dry. Then paint with a top quality acrylic latex paint; nearly all of these products contain mildewcides to fight mildew growth.

NEW, UNPAINTED METAL

As with wood, it is important to provide a clean, sound surface so the paint will adhere well.

Remove any loose scale or rust with a scraper or wire brush. Next, wipe down the surface with paint thinner to remove any dust or debris that remains. (Paint thinner also will remove any protective oil or grease coating that may be present.) Rinse thoroughly. Alternatively, wash the surface with soap and water, then rinse. Apply metal primer for better paint adhesion. Then coat with top quality acrylic latex paint.

PREVIOUSLY PAINTED METAL

Remove loose or peeling paint with a scraper or sandpaper, then sand glossy areas to a dull finish. If necessary, eliminate mildew with a bleach solution. Then wash the surface and wipe clean. Prime areas where bare metal is exposed, then paint.

MASONRY STUCCO, BRICK AND CEMENT

Unpainted surfaces of these types should be thoroughly cleaned with soap and water, and if necessary, wire brushed. Weathered, very porous surfaces should also be treated with a masonry conditioner. When painting fresh masonry or stucco, always use 100 percent acrylic latex paint— it will resist breakdown caused by the alkalinity of these surfaces.

On previously painted surfaces, remove loose or peeling paint. Heavily chalked surfaces should be cleaned with a wire brush, then washed off with water. Very porous surfaces should be treated with a masonry conditioner prior to painting. If the surface shows only minor chalking and dirt, simply clean, then paint.

ering are the most desirable means of preparing concrete for painting. These natural processes allow the concrete to dry out, reduce the surface alkalinity, and add a beneficial roughening to the surface. But, since months or even years are required to properly complete this aging process, it is often impractical to delay painting for so long.

When using acrylic latex-based paints, only four weeks of aging is mandatory, due to their relative water and alkali resistance. However, in the case of oil-based paints, special chemical treatments are necessary before painting if the concrete has aged less than a year.

When removing powdery dust, dirt, and other loose material, bristle-brushing followed by hosing with clean water should suffice. When

necessary, wire-brushing or light sandblasting may employed.

In the absence of adequate weathering, oil contaminants and grease should be removed by etching the surface with a 5 to 10 percent solution of hydrochloric ("muriatic") acid. Always rinse with clean water after any procedure.

Warning: *Muriatic Acid is potent—it has to be if it etches concrete. Follow ALL instructions on the container including avoiding contact with skin, eyes, mouth. Do not breath the vapor. Handle with extreme caution!*

Alternatively, oily contaminants can be removed by mechanical means by rubbing the surface with steel brushes or abrasive stones.

PAINTING ALUMINUM / VINYL SIDING

A common misconception among homeowners is that you can't paint vinyl or aluminum siding. The fact is, it's just as easy to repaint these materials as it is ordinary wood. In most cases, you can even paint your vinyl or aluminum siding just to change its color.

There are two secrets to successfully completing these projects: (1) surface preparation, and (2) the use of a top-quality 100 percent acrylic latex paint.

ALUMINUM SIDING

The color on aluminum siding is a surface coating applied in the factory. It wears and weathers just like ordinary paint, and over time, it too will chalk and fade. That's when to repaint.

Power washing is an efficient and inexpensive way to prepare the surface. Equipment is available at most rental centers. An alternative is

SAFETY RULES WHEN PAINTING

At one time or another, nearly all of us tackle a home painting project. But all too often, we ignore proper safety precautions.
To help ensure that your next exterior painting project is both successful and safe, follow these tips.

Use of ladders: Exterior painting projects almost always involve ladders. And ladder misuse is the cause of many a miscue when painting.

After you remove your ladder from the garage or tool shed, take time to inspect it. Is it in good repair? Are all the rungs intact and free of dirt or paint buildup that could interfere with footing? Be certain.

When raising the ladder to paint, make sure that the base is level and that it sits firmly on the ground. Also check to see if the ground is solid. A ladder can slip in unstable soil or mud.

Keep the angle of the ladder at about 15 degrees. If you are using an extension ladder, stay off the top three rungs; stay off the top two steps of a stepladder. Wrap cloth around the tops of the ladder to protect the siding and prevent slipping.

When applying paint, don't reach out too far. Always keep your hips between the rails of the ladder. And when scraping or doing repairs, use care when applying force, as this can cause the ladder to slip.

Keep your ladder away from power lines, especially if it is made of metal. And never climb

ELASTOMERIC COATINGS FOR MASONRY

At first blush, the idea of a house "moving" might seem preposterous, but houses do move — by expanding or contracting when outside temperatures rise or fall dramatically.

And while these movements are slight, they can create big problems for exterior masonry walls by causing cracks, degrading the appearance of the home and creating hidden water damage.

If your home is made of concrete, cement block or stucco, don't despair. There is a high-tech

exterior wall coating that offers excellent protection against these problems. Elastomeric wall coatings made with 100 percent acrylic literally "stretch" to span cracks and wall imperfections, sealing out moisture and the elements. When the cracks contract, the coatings return to their original shape without warping or wrinkling. Elastomeric coatings provide a flexible, dirt-resistant finish that can be applied to virtually any masonry surface. Besides protecting against wall cracks, these coatings can

to simply wash the siding panels with warm, soapy water to remove dirt, dust and chalk. Then rinse with plain water.Next, apply a top quality acrylic latex house paint. The extra money you spend will translate into better paint performance and better appearance.An important advantage to these acrylic latex paints is their superior leveling, which helps duplicate the original appearance of your siding, whether smooth or textured.Spray painting is faster and easier than brush painting. It often results in a better looking job also. If you've hired a contractor to paint your home, suggest that he consider spray painting your house. Dented siding from backyard baseball? Remember that a glossier surface will tend to highlight surface imperfections. If dents are present, use flat paints rather than semigloss products.

VINYL SIDING

While the color of aluminum siding is contained in the surface coating, vinyl siding's color is blended into the material. As a result, proper surface preparation involves a different technique. Vinyl siding should not be wirebrushed or sanded.

That would mar the surface of the panels. Instead, just as you would with aluminum siding, power wash the siding or use warm, soapy water to remove dirt and chalk. Then rinse.

A tip on color selection: *Never paint vinyl siding darker than its original color. Dark colors tend to absorb the heat of the sun and that can cause vinyl siding to warp and buckle.*

a ladder that is wet.

Proper clothing: When climbing a ladder, be sure to wear non-slip shoes. Tennis shoes or work boots are good choices.

If you are using bleach solution to remove mildew, wear eye goggles and rubber gloves, and avoid working on a windy day. Should bleach solution come in contact with your skin, rinse well with cold water and see the label on the bleach for further instructions.When wire-brushing or scraping old paint, use gloves to avoid cutting or jabbing your hands.

Power equipment: Be especially careful if you are using power tools for your house painting.

If you are using power washing equipment,

keep the nozzle pointed away from you and others. Don't try to clean windows with a power washer; the spray may be powerful enough to shatter the glass. Wear a hood with a respirator and clothes that cover every part of your body if you are spray painting with oil-based (alkyd) paint.

Fire safety: Since oil-based paint is combustible, don't smoke when using it.

If there is wet paint or thinner on your rags or drop-cloths, spread them out to dry; or place them in a tight metal container away from heat sources and materials that can easily catch fire.

Safe painting is largely a matter of common sense. If you question whether something is safe, it probably isn't. Good luck and good painting!

hide unsightly mortar lines that often show through on cement block homes. As for their appearance, when these coatings cure, they tend to conform to the shape of the surface below, forming a non-tacky surface that is highly resistant to dirt pickup. They also resist degradation from the sun's ultraviolet rays, which enables them to retain their original color and texture for years.

Elastomeric wall coatings can be made in almost any shade you desire — dark or light,

vibrant or subtle. In fact, some homeowners apply elastomeric wall coatings for decorative reasons alone. But part of the beauty of elastomeric wall coatings is that they can be specially formulated to meet the unique demands of your local climate and different types of masonry. So there is a formulation just right for your home. If you decide to tackle the project alone, always apply two coats of the elastomeric coating in a thick film using a heavy-nap roller.

STORING LATEX PAINT

If you are like most homeowners, you've got more than a few cans of paint squirreled away somewhere in your house. They may be the "leftovers" from past home improvement projects or reminders of jobs never started.

Either way, it's important to store paint properly so it will work well when you apply it.
•Don't subject paint to extreme cold or heat. Although most paints are formulated to withstand several freeze-thaw cycles, these conditions can cause them to solidify and be ruined. To be safe, if you live in a cold climate, don't leave paint outdoors or in an unheated shed or garage. You should also

avoid exposing paint for any length of time to temperatures higher than 100 degrees.
•Seal paint cans securely before you store them. Once a can of paint has been opened, use a wet paper towel to thoroughly clean paint from the grooves on the rim. That will help the lid fit tightly and form a good seal, thereby protecting your paint.
•Don't open more cans than you need. Avoid the need to reseal paint containers by completely finishing one can before you open another.
•Don't encourage bacteria contamination. When excess bacteria are present, water-based paint can

PAINTING AN OLDER HOME

Many people take great pride in owning an older home. But home ownership necessitates home maintenance. And the owners of older homes have more than their share of that.

One of the best ways to keep an older home looking fresh while accenting its character is with a fresh coat of paint. Of course, paint is also the first line of defense against the harsh elements that can weather a home's exterior.

Here are answers to some common painting questions from the owners of older homes.

Q. What type of paint provides the most durable protection for old woodwork?
A. It depends upon the type of surface to be painted and its condition. With a sound substrate that has

been properly prepared (i.e., scraped, sanded and cleaned), two coats of a top-quality acrylic latex paint provide the best adhesion and, consequently, maximum durability.

However, if the old paint is chalking badly and cannot be thoroughly cleaned, then apply an oil-based primer followed by a top-quality acrylic latex topcoat.

Q. Can latex paint be applied over oil-based paint?
A. Yes, today's high quality acrylic latex (water-based) paints are formulated to provide excellent adhesion to surfaces painted with oil- or alkyd-based paints. But if you encounter a surface with more than three or four coats of oil paint, you may want to apply an oil-based topcoat. Be sure to

UNDERSTANDING PAINT TERMINOLOGY

Do you understand the difference between oil paint and latex paint? Do you know what "acrylic" means? If not, here's a quick primer on paint terms:

Oil Paint. Sometimes called "alkyd" paint, oil

paint is made with pigment, mineral spirits and oil (typically a vegetable oil such as linseed, soya, or a modified oil). The product does emit fumes and makes for difficult cleanup, usually requiring paint thinner or some other solvent.

Latex Paint. All latex paints are made with

get thin and runny, making it all but unusable. To help avoid the problem, stir your paint with a clean wooden or plastic stirrer rather than a soiled screwdriver or stick. Keep the lid on the can, except when actually painting. And when you go to buy paint, remember that top quality latex paints contain added preservatives to ward off bacterial problems.

•Thoroughly stir and test the paint you store. During storage, paint will often separate into a clear liquid layer on top of a denser liquid below. As a result, it is important to stir paint thoroughly before beginning to work. If the paint was stored for more than six months, or if you are doing touch-up work, be sure to spot-check the paint to make sure the color of the fresh paint and the painted surface still match.

•Get rid of rust. If your paint has been in storage for a long time, check to see if rust has formed on the inside can or lid surface. If rust is present, it's best to pour the paint into a clean container before beginning to paint. Otherwise, the rust can affect the color and mar your new paint job.

•Protect the paint can label. The label on a can of paint contains such useful information as brand, color and coverage rate. Don't allow the paint to conceal the label. Even if you discard the can, it's a good idea to keep the label in case you want to match the color at a later date.

After you finish your home painting projects, be sure to store your unused or leftover paint properly; otherwise, the paint can solidify and be ruined. Make sure the cans are sealed tight and, if you live in a cold climate, don't leave the paint outdoors or in an unheated shed or garage. A heated basement or storage room is a better choice.

properly prepare the surface before applying either type of paint.

Q. How can you tell whether the old paint is oil-based or latex?

A. Remove a piece of the old paint with a scraper. Then place it between your fingers and apply pressure. If the paint snaps in half or breaks into pieces, it's probably oil-based. If it is flexible enough to bend between your fingers, then it is most likely a latex product.

Q. What is the best way to remove oil-based paint from old exterior woodwork?

A. Most professional painting contractors use a torch or heat gun to remove old oil-based paint, but some prefer sand blasting. In some cases, chemical paint removers are used. Since all of these methods can be dangerous if proper safety practices aren't followed, consider using a professional painter if you are not thoroughly familiar with the proper procedures.

Q. When is it necessary to strip old paint down to bare wood before painting?

A. If the surface has more than three or four old coats of oil-based paint and you want to use an acrylic latex topcoat, then the old paint should be completely removed. You could, however, add an extra coat of oil-based paint without removing the earlier coats. If the old paint is latex or if there are only a couple of coats of oil-based paint, however, you can use a quality latex paint without removing the old paint, assuming that the surface is clean and stable.

pigment, water and some type of latex polymer. Some of the more popular varieties of latex polymers are:

100 percent acrylic, relatively costly, very durable, used mainly in exterior paints and some premium interior grades.

Vinyl acrylic, used extensively for interior paint, particularly flats; used in some exterior paints.

Vinyl terpolymer, a variation on vinyl acrylic used in some interior semi-gloss and exterior flat paints.

Being water-based, all varieties of latex paint offer easy soap and water cleanup, and are low in odor.

DIAGNOSING PAINT FAILURES

One of the most important steps toward a professional-like paint job on the exterior of your home is to look at the present surface and note any deterioration of the surface so you can in turn understand and prevent those failures from reoccurring.

Generally speaking, *any* change in the appearance or integrity of the paint film is a potential problem. Listed below are some of the more common paint failures and their causes.

ADHESION FAILURES

Since any exposure to moisture (rain, snow, heavy dew) tests the mettle of a paint's adhesion, this property is regarded by many as the most important for excellent paint performance.

Anytime a latex paint film gets wet, it will tend to swell, putting stress on the adhesion bond with the substrate. This is especially so in the early life of the paint, before water soluble components are leached from the paint by rainfall. If the adhesion is not sufficient, blisters can form.

While minor blistering is usually not a problem, future adhesion failures can occur if serious blistering happens early in the life of a paint job. With the bond between the paint and the surface weakened, small ruptures of the film at the blister can result in premature failure by flaking and peeling. Careful surface preparation and use of top quality acrylic latex paint are two prescriptions for preventing adhesion failure and minimizing blistering. Any loose or peeling paint should always be scraped away. Then, the surface should be washed to remove dirt, chalk, and mildew. Any glossy areas should be sanded.

CRACKING/FLAKING

Cracking appears in a paint when the film cannot withstand the expansion and contraction of the substrate. To combat this stress, any coating applied to wood must be sufficiently flexible to withstand fluctuation without rupture or loss of adhesion.

Once again, the best defense against this

FUTURE TRENDS IN PAINT TECHNOLOGY

In recent years, the most significant trend in exterior coatings has been the technological improvements to acrylic latex paints and their increasing popularity among painting contractors and do-it-yourselfers alike.

Since their introduction in 1953, steady advances have made top quality acrylic latex paints the favored alternative to oil-based products for most applications. The reasons are numerous: superior durability, excellent adhesion, longer color retention, faster drying time, and easier cleanup—to name a few.

Today, paint chemists continue to refine and improve the design of acrylic binders and additives formulated into top quality paints. In the future, look for paints with even better brushing properties like improved flow and leveling; greater film build that enhance a paint's durability without

prolonging drying time; and even better adhesion characteristics.

HIGH-GLOSS ACRYLIC ENAMELS SHINE

Although water-based alternatives to high-gloss oil-based paints have been available for years, they traditionally fell short in terms of initial gloss, gloss retention, and brushing characteristics.

However, within the last few years, paint formulators have created new high-gloss acrylic enamels whose flow and leveling properties approach those of alkyd paints.

Moreover, these new acrylic paints exhibit excellent exterior gloss and tint retention. Exposure studies show that acrylic high-gloss retention

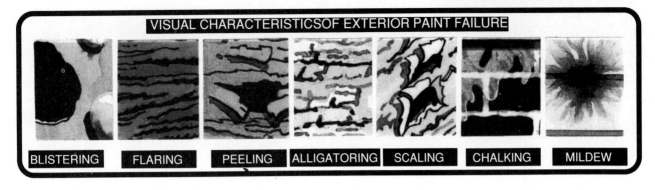

VISUAL CHARACTERISTICSOF EXTERIOR PAINT FAILURE

BLISTERING | FLARING | PEELING | ALLIGATORING | SCALING | CHALKING | MILDEW

failure is a paint film with outstanding adhesion properties. But this trait alone will not prevent cracking

The paint film must also retain its elasticity when weathering in order to withstand the expansion and contraction of the wood. This property is primarily dependent on the proper level of pigment volume concentration in the formulation.

Top-quality paints generally offer the best adhesion and optimized binder level, without excessive levels of extender pigments.

CHALKING

All latex paint films tend to pick up dirt from the atmosphere to some extent. How much dirt pick-up is related to the following variables:- the percentage of the binder (semigloss paints tend to pick up more dirt than flats) in the paint; the exposure direction (north is worst); and location of the home because protected moist areas are prime for dirt pick-up.

Chalking of the paint can help it stay clean, except in areas protected from the cleansing effect of rain. However, excessive chalking can lead to problems — color fading, chalk run-down, and paint erosion.

Ideally, a paint will resist dirt and yet chalk very little. Higher quality paints tend toward this balance more than low-cost paints because of binder types and levels, and extender pigments used.

enamels generally outperform alkyd paints when judged on these two important criteria.

While some alkyds may still initially outshine acrylic paints, the gap is not as noticeable as it was just a few years ago. Expect paint chemists and formulators to continue to make strides in this important area.

ENVIRONMENTAL CONCERNS PRODUCE NEW FORMULATIONS

The composition of tomorrow's coatings may depend as much on concerns about air quality as on performance characteristics. As solvent-based paints dry, they release solvents into the air. Thinners do likewise. These solvents are commonly known as volatile organic compounds (VOCs), or volatile organic solvents (VOSs).

In an effort to reduce the amount of solvents escaping into the atmosphere, several states have enacted or are considering laws which limit the volume of emissions permitted from paints.

To comply with the regulations, paint manufacturers have reformulated oil-based paints to contain higher levels of solids and lower levels of solvents. This is a costly approach. And, it often results in paints that are thicker and more difficult to apply. This increased burden the industry will inevitably result in many reformulations of solvent-based paints in the future. On the other hand, most latex paints have been unaffected by restrictions imposed by VOC/VOS legislation, since they are formulated with a water base and contain relatively low levels of solvents.

ALL ABOUT PAINTBRUSHES

Archaeologists have found rather crude paintings inside caves which date back to the caveman era. Just how these primitive people applied their mixtures of pigments or dyes is not known, but we can assume that it was with some sort of early-style brush using animal hairs.

The first recorded paintbrushes date back to the Phoenicians. Their brushes were made by taking the horn of an animal and placing wild boar hairs in the open end. The hairs were held in place by binding the ends with a twine; hence, the horn served as a handle with the boar's hair serving as the bristle, or painting medium.

Following the original brush styles, which were round due to the shape of the horn, paintbrushes for centuries remained round in shape. Round wooden handles replaced the horns, and better methods of attaching the animal hairs to the handles were developed. Even today, many European-made paintbrushes are round. Here in the

These are just a few of the brushes manufactured by the Wooster Brush Company in Wooster, Ohio. The firm started in the late 1840s when Adam Foss bought an unclaimed package in Cincinnati Express Company office and found it contained hog bristles. In that era many homes and barns weathered away for lack of a protective coating and paint was used mostly on public buildings and the homes of the wealthy. Using the hog bristles found in the shipment, Foss whittled out handles and blocks of wood by hand and fitted the bristles in place to make a brush. People clamored for the products and so he founded the brush manufacturing business in 1851; it is now one of the largest paint brush and roller manufacturers in the world.

United States, all but a few specialized brushes are flat in shape. Until World War II, all paintbrushes were made from animal hairs. Among these were hog bristle, ox hair, sable, camel, and horsehair. The best of the hairs or bristle come from China. The weather conditions and food sources there produce extremely fine-quality hog bristle.

During World War II, Chinese bristle could not be obtained so DuPont developed a synthetic bristle made of nylon. This was the beginning of the use of synthetic bristles or filaments in paintbrushes. More recently, polyester synthetic filaments have been developed; and these make excellent paintbrushes.

Let's take a closer look at the various types of bristle and filaments which are currently used in paintbrushes.

PURE HOG BRISTLE

Today there is an abundance of natural Chinese hog bristle available, and it is widely used in the manufacture of paintbrushes for use with oil-based paints.

Hog bristle is an animal fiber, and as such is porous and will absorb up to 40% of its own weight in water. As a result, it is recommended that pure hog bristle brushes be used only in oil-based paints. Latex or water-thinned paints contain up to 50% water. Hog bristle absorbs water, which causes it to swell, flare out, and become very soft. Within a half hour of painting with latex paint, a hog-bristle brush goes limp and loses its effectiveness as a painting tool.

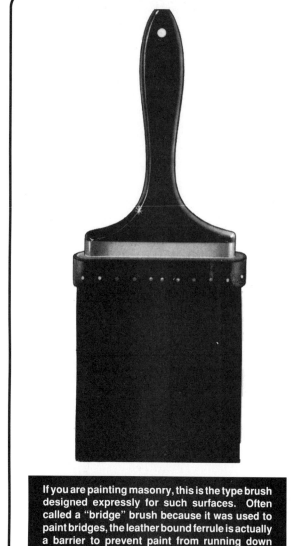

If you are painting masonry, this is the type brush designed expressly for such surfaces. Often called a "bridge" brush because it was used to paint bridges, the leather bound ferrule is actually a barrier to prevent paint from running down the handle when painting overhead.

Brushes are made with various filaments to be used with various types of paint on different surfaces. The early brushes were made exclusively from hog bristles but now nylon and polyester are found in most brushes. This one uses a nylon filament.

REMEMBER, PURE HOG BRISTLE BRUSHES SHOULD BE USED WITH OIL-BASED PAINTS, VARNISHES, AND SHELLAC, BUT NOT WITH LATEX PAINT.

NYLON BRUSH FILAMENTS

The original nylon paintbrushes were poor in quality. The filaments had blunt ends and would not spread the paint effectively. Nylon did possess some outstanding qualities; namely, it would outwear hog bristle 5 to 1. The cost was considerably lower than bristle and it absorbed only 4% of its own weight in water, making it ideally suited for the new latex paints.

Recognizing the good qualities of nylon, brush manufacturers went to work to correct its shortcomings. Tipping processes were developed for the tips or ends of the nylon filaments to enable them to spread paint better. The filaments themselves were given a taper to provide better cutting-in qualities and add a natural taper to the brushes. Within a few years after introduction, nylon brushes had replaced all but about 25% of the hog-bristle.

Their performance and durability had been improved to a point where they equaled the hog-bristle brushes. The popularity of latex water-based paints hastened the acceptance of nylon paintbrushes.

POLYESTER BRUSH FILAMENTS

The most recent development in paintbrush filaments is polyester. Polyester is considered by most experts as the finest filament yet developed for paintbrushes.

The qualities which make polyester such an excellent material for paintbrushes are similar to those which make polyester materials an outstanding fabric for clothing. To help you understand these reasons, let's compare polyester clothing with polyester paintbrushes.

First, polyester absorbs no moisture. Clothing is exposed to body perspiration as well as external humidity. Moisture tends to soften fabrics (wool, nylon, etc.). In the case of polyester, it has no effect. Paintbrushes made from hog bristle or nylon absorb water; polyester brushes absorb no moisture.

Second, heat is a factor that affects clothing fabrics. Nylon, dacron, and rayon are affected by heat — both body temperature and external temperature. The heat factor softens these fabrics. When combined with both moisture and heat, the clothing fabrics become wrinkled.

Polyester is affected by heat but not below 140°, which is uncommonly high. Polyester brushes, therefore, retain their stiffness and resiliency even on days when the temperature may reach 100° or more. Nylon brushes will soften on hot days and tend to become floppy.

You can see why polyester brushes are considered to be the finest.

Nylon and Polyester brushes are recommended for use with oil-based paints, varnishes, shellac and latex based paints.

PAINTBRUSH CONSTRUCTION

To better cope with painting jobs, you should know how a brush is made and what function each contributes to the painting tool.

THE TIPPING

The tip end or working end of the brush is very important for good performance. It is the tips or ends of the bristle which spread the paint on the surface.

Hog bristle, by nature, has split ends, or "flags." These flags make a mass contact with the surface, thus spreading the paint evenly and smoothly.

In the case of nylon and polyester filaments, the split ends or flags are made by machine. As in many cases, man-made processes surpass nature; and this is the case with the nylon and polyester "tipping" process. The filament ends are burst into hundreds of tiny paint fingers to apply the paint evenly to the surface and reduce brush marks.

FILAMENTS

As previously discussed, paintbrushes are made from basically three types of filaments: pure hog bristle, nylon, or polyester.

For applying a stain to a deck or to shingles, a brush made with polyester filaments is the tool of choice. This one is available in widths of 4 and 6 inches and is a full 1 1/4 inches thick.

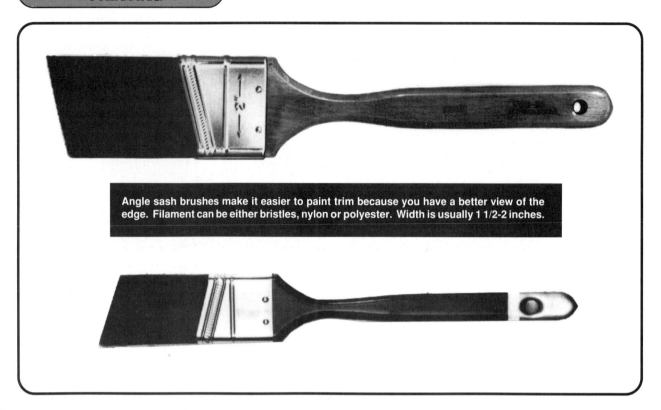

Angle sash brushes make it easier to paint trim because you have a better view of the edge. Filament can be either bristles, nylon or polyester. Width is usually 1 1/2-2 inches.

This is the type brush used to paint masonry surfaces where the paint is heavy and the technique of application is dabbing rather than free flowing. These brushes are also used for texturing a surface.

FERRULE

The ferrule is the metal piece which connects the bristle to the handle. Ferrules are made of rust-resistant metal alloys although there are still a few professional brushes made with leather ferrules. These brushes are very expensive and generally are used only by professional painters.

SPACE PLUGS

Space plugs — Separators inserted in the ferrule during the manufacturing process to separate sections of the filament material. They can be made of either wood, aluminum, or specially treated cardboard. Their purpose is fourfold:

a. To insure a tight bond of the filament in the ferrule.

b. To create "paint wells" within the brush to hold more paint per dip.

c. To add a taper to the brush. This taper allows the painter to "cut in" with a fine point at the end or tip of the brush.

d. To keep the center of the brush open for easier cleaning. The solvents can be forced way up into the brush to remove the paint before it becomes hard in the heel of the brush.

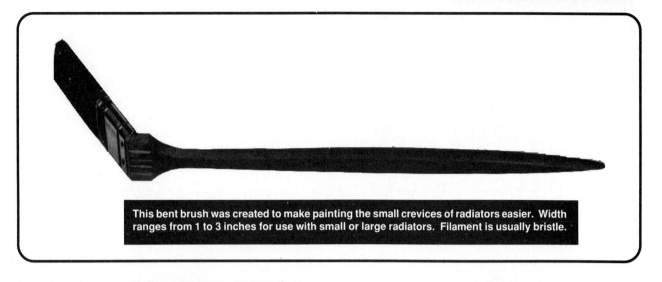

This bent brush was created to make painting the small crevices of radiators easier. Width ranges from 1 to 3 inches for use with small or large radiators. Filament is usually bristle.

SETTING

The setting is the cement which literally "glues" the ends of the filaments inside of the ferrule. Most settings used today are epoxy materials. Poor-quality settings create a shedding problem where the bristle or filaments fall out. Brushes made with quality epoxy settings do not shed.

HANDLES

Paintbrush handles are generally made of wood or solvent-resistant plastic materials. They are attached to the brush by either nailing or crimping them to the ferrule.

Most do-it-yourself-type brushes have plastic handles. These are easier to clean and will not crack or split when left in water or solvents. Wood handles will swell and crack when exposed for prolonged periods of time to water or solvents. In addition, painted wood handles tend to peel or become tacky when exposed to solvents.

Plastic handles are the best quality and the most popular among do-it-yourselfers.

Handle styles and shapes vary, depending on the particular brush and the job it is intended to do. Wall brushes — 3", 3 1/2", and 4" — are generally used on large areas and have large handles for a good, firm grip.

Varnish brushes have smaller handles designed for a comfortable feel when applying enamels or varnish on small to medium areas.

Sash brush handles are generally long and thin, giving "pencil-like" control for cutting-in sash or trim.

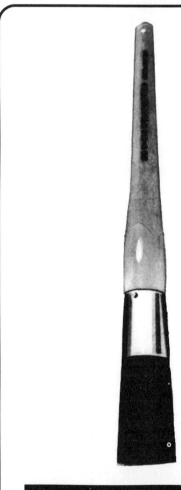

Another specialty brush is an oval sash brush which was created to handle the delicate job of painting window mullions and door trim. The filament is bound in an elliptical shaped ferrule and because of the depth holds more paint. These brushes are usually referred to by number, with Number 2 being 1 3/4 inches wide.

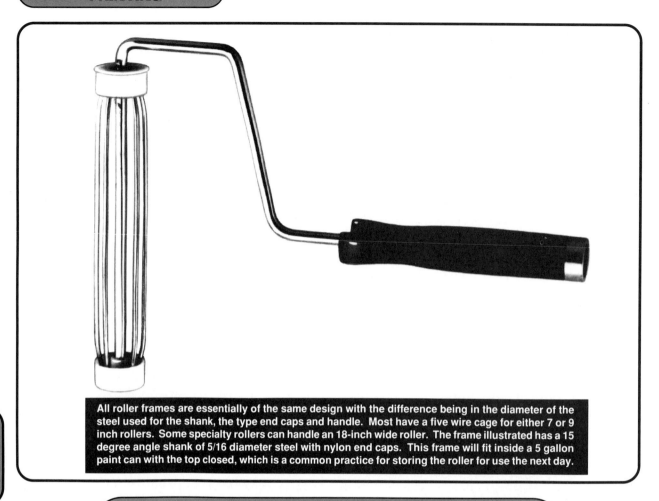

All roller frames are essentially of the same design with the difference being in the diameter of the steel used for the shank, the type end caps and handle. Most have a five wire cage for either 7 or 9 inch rollers. Some specialty rollers can handle an 18-inch wide roller. The frame illustrated has a 15 degree angle shank of 5/16 diameter steel with nylon end caps. This frame will fit inside a 5 gallon paint can with the top closed, which is a common practice for storing the roller for use the next day.

ALL ABOUT PAINT ROLLERS

The first paint rollers were developed in England and they soon caught on in the United States. Today rollers account for perhaps 95% of paint application on interior wall surfaces by the do-it-yourself painter .

Rollers provide a fast, simple, and effective method of applying paint to large areas. Even a rank amateur can obtain professional results with a roller.

The most important part of a paint roller is the core and the roller cover, so let's examine the cores first.

ROLLER COVER CORES

The core, or inner tube of the roller cover provides the foundation. Roller cores are made of plastic, cardboard, and phenolic-impregnated kraft paper.

The finest-quality cores are made of phenolic-impregnated kraft paper. To manufacture these cores, the manufacturer first spirals kraft paper in the form of a tube, similar to a mailing tube. These tubes are then immersed in pressure tanks containing phenolic resins. Under pressure, the phenolic resins are forced through the tube walls. Once this process is complete, the tubes are then placed in large ovens and baked. The end result is a hard core which is resistant to all known paint solvents.Plastic cores, on the other hand, will soften in certain solvents. If the plastic core is not perfectly round, it will "bump" on the surface, resulting in an uneven distribution of paint.

Cardboard cores are used on low-end, inexpensive rollers. They will soften and break up often after a short period of exposure to water or solvents. However, they will generally hold up long enough to do one room.

ROLLER COVERS

The exterior of a roller is referred to as the "fabric". Many roller fabrics exist, each designed for a particular application. The qualities sought in a cover selected for use on a roller cover are:

1. Ability of the fabric to pick up paint
2. Ability of the fabric to release the paint evenly on the surface.
3. Ability of the fabric to recover. This refers to the matting of the fabric after several dips and applications of paint. Can the fabric recover and bounce back? Or, does it tend to mat down and crush after repeated use?
4. Surface finish results—smooth, rough, orange peel?
5. Shedding—does the fabric shed its fibers on the painted surface?

All the above qualities are important to the selection of good-quality and good-performing roller fabrics.

Roller fabrics are made from individual or blended fibers of dacron, polyester, nylon, orlon, rayon, mohair, viscose, lambs wool, etc. Each fiber possesses its own qualities; whether used individually or blended together, they produce high-quality roller fabrics.

The important thing to remember is that each roller is designed and formulated for a specific type of paint and surface.

PILE HEIGHTS

Roller covers come in several pile heights ranging from 13/16" to 1 1/4". The easiest way to determine the proper roller for a given surface is to remember the following:
"THE SMOOTHER THE SURFACE, THE SHORTER THE NAP. THE ROUGHER THE SURFACE, THE HIGHER THE NAP."

If you are painting a smooth kitchen or bathroom wall with an enamel or semigloss paint and want an ultra-smooth finish, use a 1/4"-nap mohair cover or a 1/4"-nap all-purpose cover.

For rough surfaces such as brick or concrete blocks, a 1 1/4" pile cover is recommended.

For flat finishes on walls and ceilings in living rooms, dining rooms, or bedrooms, a 3/8"- or 1/2"-pile cover is usually used.

A quick reference guide can also be found on the roller-cover packaging, where information is usually given regarding both the surface and type of paint for which the cover is designed.

A good-quality roller makes the painting job easier, faster, and produces professional results.

When purchasing a roller cover, keep in mind the type of paint being used and the kind of

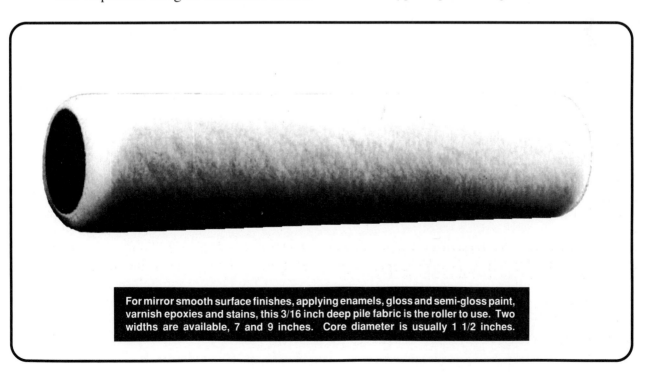

For mirror smooth surface finishes, applying enamels, gloss and semi-gloss paint, varnish epoxies and stains, this 3/16 inch deep pile fabric is the roller to use. Two widths are available, 7 and 9 inches. Core diameter is usually 1 1/2 inches.

surface being painted. Top-quality covers pick up and release more paint per fill and they will provide more uniform coverage with considerably less effort. Inexpensive roller covers tend to mat down. The matting reduces the amount of paint which the cover will pick up and hold per fill, requiring more frequent fillings. Also, a matted cover will make it more difficult to spread the paint evenly on the surface.

APPLYING PAINT WITH A ROLLER

There are various trim tools and roller accessories, but before they are used you should know some of the techniques that apply to the roller. Prior to the first filling of the roller with paint, immerse the roller in water if a latex or water-thinned paint is being applied. This moistening effect aids the roller in picking up a maximum load of paint from the initial filling or loading. This only needs to be done once prior to the first filling or loading.

Most painters use conventional roller trays for loading the roller with paint. The roller should be dipped into the paint and then rolled back on the ribbed bottom of the tray. This process should be repeated until a uniform load of paint has been picked up in the roller cover.

Applying the paint to the surface of a wall, floor, ceiling, etc., is best accomplished by rolling a large W or M pattern on the surface. This widely distributes the initial heavy paint load. By then going back and rolling across the W or M pattern, the paint is evenly distributed on the surface.

Most do-it-yourselfers make the mistake of trying to squeeze the last ounce of paint out of a roller by increasing the pressure on the roller as the paint begins to run out. This pressure causes a matting effect, and it can also cause paint ridges on the painted surface. Refill the roller as it begins to run out of paint, rather than pressing harder to force more paint out of the roller.

ROLLER ACCESSORIES/TRIM TOOLS

To round out the necessary tools for roller painting, let's take a look at the accessories which are designed to speed and simplify roller painting.

ROLLER FRAMES

Basically, there are four types of roller frames:
1. Cage Frame — 4- or 5-wire
2. Solid Cylinder — metal or plastic
3. Floating End Cap — open-style frame
4. Promotion — metal or plastic removable end caps

Most of the better-quality roller frames have threaded handles, providing for the use of an extension handle.

EXTENSION HANDLES

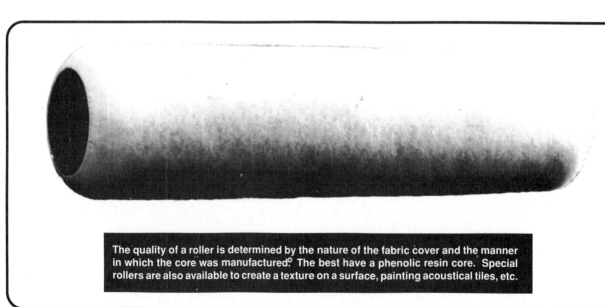

The quality of a roller is determined by the nature of the fabric cover and the manner in which the core was manufactured. The best have a phenolic resin core. Special rollers are also available to create a texture on a surface, painting acoustical tiles, etc.

Extension handles or poles can make roller painting both faster and easier where hard-to-reach areas are being painted.

Extension poles generally range from 11" to 16'. The telescoping poles are adjustable to handle a multitude of painting situations where the use of an extension is desirable.

When painting a room, a 4' extension pole should be used for the ceiling. Also, extension poles make painting a floor faster with less bending and stooping.

Building exteriors, flag poles, basement floors, patios, swimming pools, decks, and fences are all areas which can be painted with less effort through the use of an extension pole.

TRIM ROLLERS AND MITTS

Trim rollers come in various shapes and sizes depending on the trim areas for which they are designed.

The "donut"-shaped trim roller works well in corners or between ceilings and walls.
The conical-shaped trim roller is used for cutting-in woodwork or tight areas around doors or windows.

Three-inch trimmers are excellent on woodwork, screens, or other small areas which are too small for the standard 7" or 9" rollers.

Flat trimmers are generally equipped with wheels or guides for cutting-in corners, ceilings to walls, or walls to woodwork. They cut a sharp, even line quickly and with ease.

PAINTER'S MITT

There are certain irregular or unusual surfaces which are difficult to paint with either a brush or roller. The painting mitt can be quickly adapted to these areas and reduces painting time up to 90%. Wrought-iron railings, fences, etc., can be effectively and quickly painted with a painter's mitt. Pipes, poles, gutters, cables, wire, swing sets, table legs, garden-tool handles, spindles, chair and table rungs, chains, and gate posts are quickly and easily painted with a mitt.

ROLLER TRAYS

Trays are designed to hold the paint and to provide a means of loading the roller. Ribbed bottoms help to level the paint on the cover, removing the excess paint.

Ladder-lock legs on the trays permit them to be used on stepladders when the tray legs snap on the steps of a ladder.

A good-quality metal tray should last a lifetime if cleaned after each use. You can also line the trays with aluminum foil and when the job is finished merely remove the foil and discard. Saves the time and trouble of cleaning the trays and is simple, neat, and inexpensive.

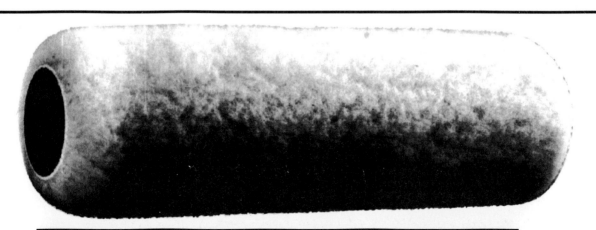

The composition of the fabric cover and the depth of the nap, plus the surface of the material to be covered, determines the roller selection. Nap 3/8 inches deep is used for medium to semi-rough surfaces, 1/2 inch for semi-rough and a longer nap (up to 1 1/4") for very rough areas.

THREE WAYS TO APPLY PAINT

BRUSHES

Before you even open up the paint can make certain the surface you are about to paint is clean and free of peeling paint. If you suspect grease or oil, wash the area with a detergent. Fill all cracks with either a spackle or caulking. Areas that are mildewed should be brushed and washed with a 50/50 mixture of household bleach and water. Shake a new brush to remove any loose bristles before dipping into paint. Dip the brush halfway into the paint and tap it lightly on the inside of the can to remove excess paint. This prevents the brush from overloading and dripping.

ROLLERS

Rollers are a fast, economical way of painting large surfaces. The 9" roller is the most popular size. Select the roller (by length and stiffness of the nap) to match the paint and surface.

SHORT NAP (3/16")
SMOOTH SURFACE—Floors, paneling, boats with enamels, varnish, stain, semi-gloss and gloss paints.

MEDIUM NAP (3/8" or 1/2")
MEDIUM SURFACE—Drywall, sand-finish plaster, textured or grained paneling, and cement block with all flat latex paints.

LONG NAP (3/4" or 1")
ROUGH SURFACE—Cinder block, stucco, brick, and all rough or irregular surfaces.

Fill the paint tray with paint and roll gently over grid of the paint tray, spreading the paint evenly onto the roller.

PADS

Paint pads have earned a place as a tested tool and are excellent for painting certain surfaces and textures. As is the case with a roller, dip the pad into the paint tray and remove any excess paint on the grid of the tray. Start at the top of the surface, painting 2-foot-wide strips, slightly overlapping each strip.

INTERIOR SURFACES

CEILINGS—Select a 3"-4" wide brush. When painting a room, start with the ceiling first. To prevent lap marks, paint across the room width (not the length) of the ceiling in 2-foot-wide sections, slightly overlapping each strip.
WALLS—Select a 3"-4" wide brush. Start in the upper corner of a wall and work down in 2-foot widths to prevent lap marks.
DOORS—Select a 2 1/2"-3" wide brush. Start at the top of the door and work down.
FLOORS—Select a 3"-4" wide brush. Start painting the floor in a corner and work toward the door.
WINDOWS—Select a 1 1/2"-2" wide brush. Use tape along the edges of the glass, or other masking methods. Paint the window in the following order: (**1**) Mullions, (**2**) Horizontal sash, (**3**) Vertical sash, (**4**) Vertical frame, (**5**) Horizontal frame, (**6**) Sill, and (**7**) Apron.

EXTERIOR SURFACES

LARGE SURFACES—Use a 3"-4" wide brush. Start at the top of the surface. Work from the unpainted to the painted area. Paint the underside of lap siding first to prevent the paint from running.
WINDOWS AND TRIM—Use a 1 1/2"-2" angle sash brush. Paint windows in the following order: (**1**) Mullion, (**2**) Horizontal sash, (**3**) Vertical sash, (**4**) Vertical frame, (**5**) Horizontal frame, (**6**) Sill, and (**7**) Apron.
STAINING LARGE AREAS—Use a 4" brush.

Paint a large "W" approximately 2 feet square on the unpainted surface and fill in the unpainted of the W. *Don't paint a large area without refilling the roller cover with paint.* For one coat coverage use plenty of paint on the roller cover. Less paint on the roller reduces the paint film thickness

Cut in the ceiling-to-wall line and the wall-to-baseboard line with a roller trim tool, a pad trimmer, or a 1" or 1 1/2" paintbrush.

the top of the wall in the corner and work down to the floor in 2-foot sections to prevent lap marks Cut the wall line to the ceiling line with a 1" to 1 1/2" paintbrush, a roller trim tool, or a pad trimmer.
WOODWORK—Use a 1" to 1 1/2" angle sash brush for windows and a 2" or 3" paintbrush for the rest of the trim work and baseboard.

INTERIOR SURFACES

CEILINGS—Use a 3/8"- to 1/2"-nap roller. Paint across the width rather than the length of the ceiling in 2-foot sections, slightly overlapping each section. Use a stepladder or attach an extension pole to the roller frame.
WALLS—Use a 3/8"- to 1/2"-nap roller. Begin at

EXTERIOR SURFACES

MEDIUM SURFACES—.Use a 3/8"- to 1/2"-nap roller for vertical siding or cement block. Start at the top and work down.
ROUGH SURFACES—Use a 3/4"- to 1" - nap roller for cinder block, brick, stucco, or irregular surfaces.
WINDOWS AND TRIM—Use a 1" to 1 1/2" paintbrush.

INTERIOR SURFACES

Paint pads will produce a very smooth finish on doors, cabinets, or small areas but are not recommended for walls, ceilings, or other large areas. Use a paintbrush or roller on these areas.

EXTERIOR SURFACES

Paint pads are ideal for painting shakes, shingles, and lap siding.

WHAT MAKES PAINT DURABLE?

The old New York Yankees and the Green Bay Packers share at least one common trait with all top quality paints. Each sports dynasty established a winning tradition and thrived year after year because of the same performance characteristic that separates a quality paint from an ordinary paint — durability.

For obvious reasons, people are interested in a paint's durability. After all, the more durable the paint, the better the performance — and the longer the paint job will last without peeling, fading, or flaking.

When it comes to exterior residential application, two factors stand out in determining a paint's durability: film formation and the quality of the paint's ingredients.

Latex paints are comprised of tiny polymer and pigment particles dispersed in water. After the paint is applied to a surface, the water begins to evaporate, leaving behind the particles.

Without the water to keep them apart, the polymer particles in the latex paint pack together to form a continuous thermoplastic film. This film is permeable to water vapor, and allows excess vapor from the painted surface to escape into the atmosphere.

Oil paint, on the other hand, contains oil or alkyd polymers that are dissolved — rather than dispersed — in petroleum-based thinner.

When an oil paint coating is applied and the thinner evaporates, the polymer binder forms a film which water vapor *cannot* penetrate. As a result, the film can trap moisture in the substrate— causing blistering and peeling.

Oil paints may be adequate for less demanding environments, such as areas that experience little to moderate sunlight. But, for the more rugged climates and conditions — where expo-

ANSWERS TO COMMON PAINTING

Q. Where non-galvanized iron nails were used in siding and have begun to rust, causing a bleeding on the old paint surface, will an acrylic latex cover this stain and prevent further bleed-through, or must something be done before applying the acrylic latex topcoat?
A. Stains caused by rusted nails will bleed through the topcoat of even the most durable of paints unless a stain-resistant solvent-based or acrylic latex primer has been applied first.

If you are painting new exterior construction where non-galvanized nails have been used, it's advisable to spot-prime the nailheads and any knots in the wood prior to applying the topcoat.
Q. Many homeowners want their doors, windows, and shutters covered with a semi-gloss latex paint because they believe it will wear better than a flat latex. Is semi-gloss more resistant to abrasion and wear than a flat latex?

A. Semi-gloss latex paints contain more binder than flat paints, so they do tend to be more durable. In general, the greater the volume of latex binder in a paint, the better its toughness, adhesion, and color retention.

Semi-gloss paints are also more stain-resistant than flat paints, so they'll pick up less dirt than flat latex paints.
Q. Can acrylic latex house paint be applied over gloss alkyd paint on wood surfaces? Is special prep work necessary to ensure good adhesion?
A. Top-quality acrylic latex paints are designed to be used on a variety of surfaces, including bare wood and old gloss alkyd surfaces. For the best painting results, it is advisable to properly prepare the surface to be painted.

Glossy surfaces should be sanded to allow the paint to "grip" the surface. Gloss alkyd paints that are exposed to harsh weather conditions have

sure to the sun's ultraviolet rays, moisture and temperature fluctuations all exact a heavy toll — acrylic latex paints generally demonstrate greater durability.

Another factor to consider with oil-based paints is that they continue to oxidize and embrittle with time, ultimately leading to cracking and flaking.

Because of the mechanism of film formation, latex paints should not be applied when the temperature falls below 50 degrees Fahrenheit. However, oil-based paints can often get by at lower temperatures, thereby extending the painting season.

QUALITY INGREDIENTS

Not surprisingly, top-quality acrylic latex paints contain quality ingredients. Many of these ingredients are key factors in predicting a paint's durability. Among them are the following:
—A binder consisting of 100 percent acrylic polymers. This type of latex binder generally offers the

best durability and adhesion characteristics.
—A high percentage of solids (primarily pigment plus binder). The more solids found in a paint, the thicker the paint's dry film will be—increasing its durability.

Top-quality latex paints contain a high percentage of solids and less water. Ordinary paints often contain more water, which on evaporation leaves a thinner paint film.
—A high content of titanium dioxide. This ingredient gives white and light colored paint its "hiding" power—or the ability to obscure the surface to which it has been applied.

Ordinary paints contain more "extenders" such as clay, silicas, and calcium carbonate. These paints offer less hiding ability.

Note that even within the category of top-quality paints, titanium levels may differ from brand to brand because formulators use other ingredients to aid hiding.

QUESTIONS

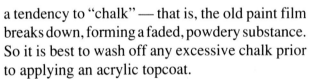

a tendency to "chalk" — that is, the old paint film breaks down, forming a faded, powdery substance. So it is best to wash off any excessive chalk prior to applying an acrylic topcoat.

When painting bare wood surfaces, use an acrylic latex primer before applying the topcoat. This will ensure the best adhesion and long-term durability.

Q. Will acrylic latex house paint stand up to a harsh seashore environment, where there is high humidity, wind-driven rain, and salt? Or must an oil-based paint be used?

A. Acrylic latex paints have demonstrated outstanding durability in the most rugged of environments, including direct sunshine, moisture from rain and snow, and at the seashore.

Due to the superior adhesion of acrylic latex paints, they don't tend to blister, crack or

flake when exposed to rain or high humidity.

Remember that the most important part of repainting is surface preparation. While priming is usually not necessary for some repaint surfaces, when using an acrylic latex paint it is a good idea to prime any bare wood.

For the best seashore painting performance, it's advisable to carefully wash away any salt deposits found on the surface to be painted, along with any "chalk."

Q. Dirt seems to naturally accumulate on shutters, should a gloss finish paint be selected because this will not pick up dirt as much as a flat?

A. Gloss paints are used on trim primarily because they accentuate architectural details and their finish tends to be hard and smooth. By contrast, flat paints have a more porous surface that can collect dirt more readily.

UNUSUAL ROLLERS, MITTS AND PADS

Paint is rolled on, wiped on, sprayed on and dipped on! It all depends upon what you are painting and the area to be covered. For most jobs around the house, either brushing or rolling is the prime method — although not necessarily in that order — and there are certain jobs that require special applicators. Painting iron pipes and wrought iron railings are good examples. To brush the individual vertical members of a railing is very time consuming. A lamb's wool mitt is often used to wipe the paint on, but the process can be messy. These mitts, which fit your hand like a glove, have a nap of about one inch so it can hold enough paint and wrap around the iron column in the wiping process. All mitts come with a polyethylene glove interior; insert your hand into the glove and then into the mitt and dip your hand with the mitt on in a bucket of paint. This method produces

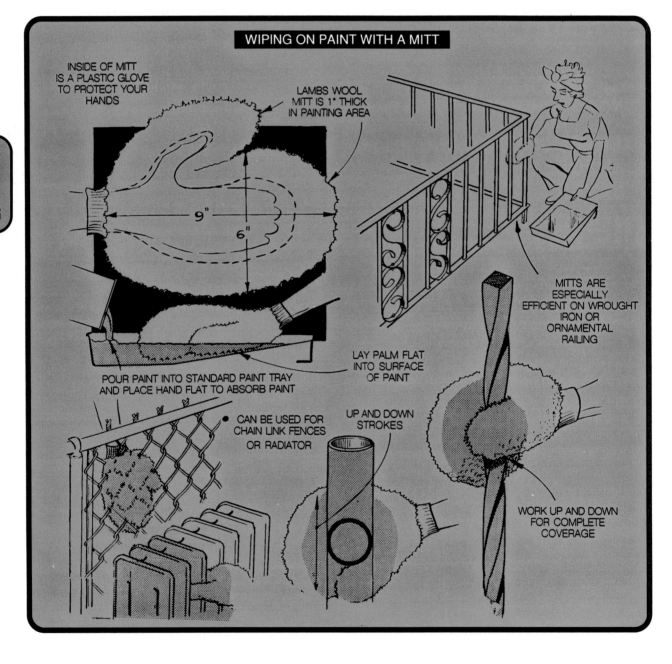

WIPING ON PAINT WITH A MITT

INSIDE OF MITT IS A PLASTIC GLOVE TO PROTECT YOUR HANDS

LAMBS WOOL MITT IS 1" THICK IN PAINTING AREA

9"

6"

POUR PAINT INTO STANDARD PAINT TRAY AND PLACE HAND FLAT TO ABSORB PAINT

LAY PALM FLAT INTO SURFACE OF PAINT

MITTS ARE ESPECIALLY EFFICIENT ON WROUGHT IRON OR ORNAMENTAL RAILING

• CAN BE USED FOR CHAIN LINK FENCES OR RADIATOR

UP AND DOWN STROKES

WORK UP AND DOWN FOR COMPLETE COVERAGE

a good job but there are other ways.

For instance, your railing consists of half-inch square rods, commonly used in wrought iron railing, twin roller tongs is another option. Dip the tongs in paint and when held together the twin rollers apply paint to two sides of the iron; release tension on the handle and the two rollers spring apart. Then rotate the handle and the rollers are in position to paint the remaining two sides, as illustrated. Painting chain link fences has always been a problem and while a mitt can do this job, going the roller route with the special roller illustrated is another choice. Note the roller — also from foam — is undercut to fit between each

diagonal row of the wire link fence. The foam roller can easily depress to apply a coat of paint on both flat and curved surfaces. With this roller you must apply the paint to one side and then approach the fence from the other side and paint the rows that run in the opposite direction.

Many other types of rollers and pads exist, all designed to make a job easier. The miniature rollers illustrated are for getting into tight quarters. They come in a blister pack which, as the roller is removed, serves as a miniature tray. Another convenient wipe-on pad miniature applicator has a blade at the tip that acts as a guide for getting close to the edge you do not want to paint.

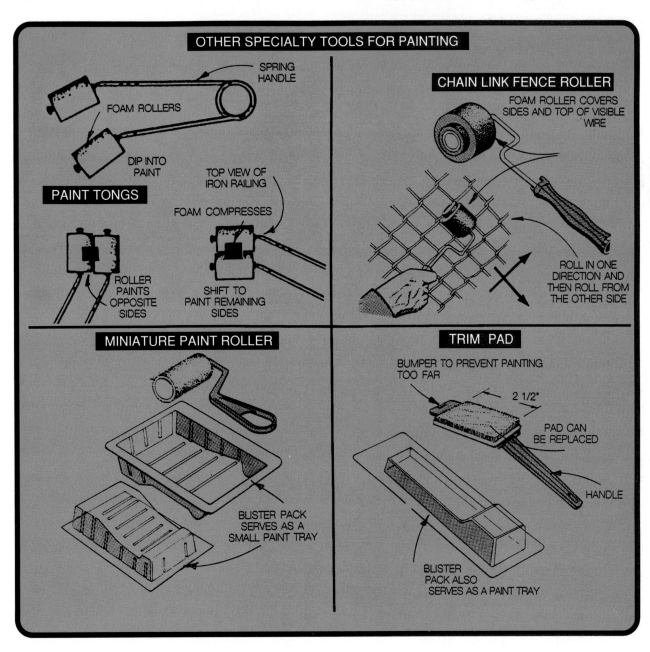

OTHER SPECIALTY TOOLS FOR PAINTING

SPRING HANDLE
FOAM ROLLERS
DIP INTO PAINT
PAINT TONGS
TOP VIEW OF IRON RAILING
FOAM COMPRESSES
ROLLER PAINTS OPPOSITE SIDES
SHIFT TO PAINT REMAINING SIDES

CHAIN LINK FENCE ROLLER
FOAM ROLLER COVERS SIDES AND TOP OF VISIBLE WIRE
ROLL IN ONE DIRECTION AND THEN ROLL FROM THE OTHER SIDE

MINIATURE PAINT ROLLER
BLISTER PACK SERVES AS A SMALL PAINT TRAY

TRIM PAD
BUMPER TO PREVENT PAINTING TOO FAR
2 1/2"
PAD CAN BE REPLACED
HANDLE
BLISTER PACK ALSO SERVES AS A PAINT TRAY

MASKING AROUND WINDOWS & DOORS

When painting door trim, protect the adjacent wall by sticking on a strip of Power-Flo Quick Mask. Pull it off after the paint is dry.

Unless you have the steady hand and eye of an artist when painting trim of a different color than the walls or, when painting the mullions of a window, running a protective strip of paper tape applied to the area you do not want paint has been used for decades. In fact, this is where the term "masking tape" originated! Masking tape does an excellent job and since this type tape is very economical it is widely used. But there are other ways to mask, and each way has certain advantages. For instance, when painting the mullions of a window the special liquid masking solution applied to the glass keeps paint away from the glass; when the wood is painted merely scrape away the film!

For certain situations where masking tape (or the glass mask) cannot be used, a wide masking strip is available. This consists of regular masking tape on to which a strip of polyethylene film has been attached in the manufacturing process. This combination masking tape and polyethylene strip is tightly wound on a roll; unroll as many feet as you need, stick the tape along the edge and then

To protect carpeting or wood flooring from paint splatter, tape the combination masking tape and drop cloth to the edge of the baseboards. The polyethylene is only a half mil thick but will not tear when walked on. It comes folded in a roll. Cut to length, tape it in place and spread to the floor.

COMBINATION MASKING AND POLYETHYLENE CLOTH

QUICK MASK BY POWER-FLO

MASK COMES IN A ROLL 70' LONG

PULL OUT

TEAR OFF DESIRED LENGTH

STICK IN PLACE

UNFOLD POLYETHYLENE

unfold the plastic to cover the woodwork. A few manufacturers produce similar products that unfold 20-23 inches but if you want to protect a complete wall or a piece of furniture while you are painting the rest of the room, wider strips of over 40 inches are available. And if you need to protect a larger area you can always tape a second strip to the edge of the first strip!

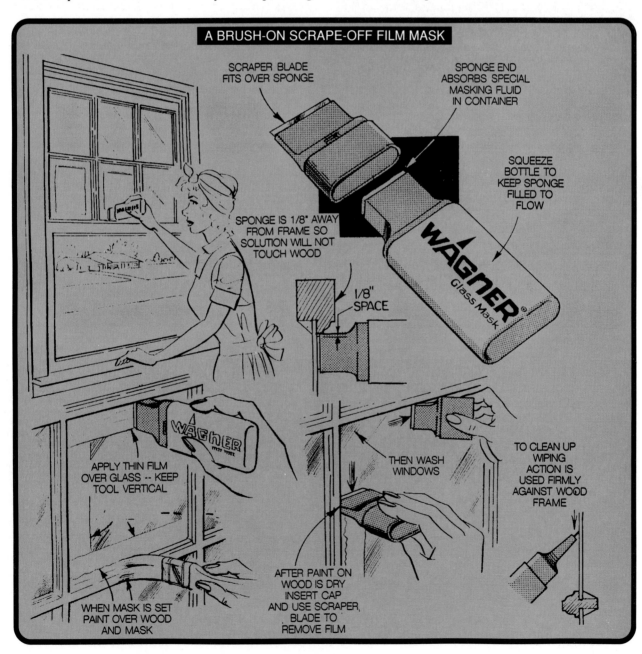

A BRUSH-ON SCRAPE-OFF FILM MASK

SCRAPER BLADE FITS OVER SPONGE

SPONGE END ABSORBS SPECIAL MASKING FLUID IN CONTAINER

SQUEEZE BOTTLE TO KEEP SPONGE FILLED TO FLOW

SPONGE IS 1/8" AWAY FROM FRAME SO SOLUTION WILL NOT TOUCH WOOD

1/8" SPACE

WAGNER Glass Mask

APPLY THIN FILM OVER GLASS -- KEEP TOOL VERTICAL

WAGNER

THEN WASH WINDOWS

TO CLEAN UP WIPING ACTION IS USED FIRMLY AGAINST WOOD FRAME

WHEN MASK IS SET PAINT OVER WOOD AND MASK

AFTER PAINT ON WOOD IS DRY INSERT CAP AND USE SCRAPER BLADE TO REMOVE FILM

CLEANING BRUSHES

BRUSHES

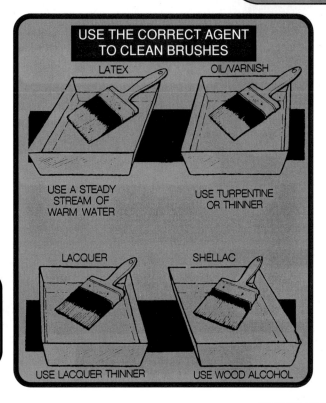

USE THE CORRECT AGENT TO CLEAN BRUSHES

LATEX — USE A STEADY STREAM OF WARM WATER

OIL/VARNISH — USE TURPENTINE OR THINNER

LACQUER — USE LACQUER THINNER

SHELLAC — USE WOOD ALCOHOL

The most important part of cleaning a brush is to use the correct cleaning liquid. With latex paints water, preferably warm water, is the agent. Clean dirty brushes in a sink by running a steady stream of water over the bristles while you massage them with your fingers. Do not be afraid of getting your hands spattered; when all traces of paint in the brush have disappeared merely wash your hands with soap and water. Whip the brush to remove as much water as the bristles have absorbed and lay it flat or, preferably, hang it vertically. Drill a hole in the handle, if necessary, for hanging. Never rest a brush in a jar at an angle because this can create a permanent bend in the bristles.

Cleaning brushes which have been used for oil paint, lacquer, urethane or shellac, calls for using the correct liquid solvent. The paint manufacturers will usually recommend the type cleaner you should use. The illustration suggests time-tested cleaning methods.

ROLLERS

If you use a roller when working with latex paint, here is the best way to clean it. Called Quick Flo, screw it on to a laundry tub faucet or even a garden hose and draw the roller through a few times. A circular jet stream of water on the inside washes away all traces of latex paint in a matter of minutes.

AND ROLLERS

HOW TO CLEAN AND STORE BRUSHES

1

CLEANING

FOR ALL PAINT EXCEPT
LATEX, PLACE A SMALL
AMOUNT OF SOLVENT
IN THE BASE OF
A ROLLER TRAY

WORK OUT
EXCESS PAINT
WITH A
STIFF BRUSH

2

3

TWIRL TO
RINSE

4

COMB
OUT

SHORT
TERM STORAGE

LINSEED
OIL

LONG STORAGE

AFTER BRUSH
IS CLEAN
WRAP IT IN
NEWSPAPERS

STORING

TIE OR
USE A RUBBER
BAND

CUT AWAY PART
OF AN OLIVE
OIL CAN SO
BRISTLES CAN
BE IMMERSED

OR HANG
IN A JAR
OR CAN

Since most paint rolling is done with latex paint, the cleaning process is no different than cleaning a brush that was used to apply latex paint. A steady spray of water will flow away the paint particles. You can ring out the roller by holding it under a stream of water from your faucet and wringing out the nap with your hands. However, the roller cleaner illustrated will do a fantastic job and use less water than the hand method. Connect it to a sink faucet (or a garden hose). The roller cleaner has the same type threads found on garden hoses and most laundry tub faucets but if you want to use it on a regular kitchen faucet replace the aerator with a fitting that has garden hose threads. The working principle is extremely simple; water from the faucet is directed to a circular slot on the inside and the pressure of the stream reaches the core of the roller and floats away all traces of paint.

If you are working with an oil-based paint the cleaning process is really messy and often requires using a great deal of solvent. If you are rolling an oil-base paint, try to do the job in one day and consider using one of the economical rollers you can discard after use. If you want to keep the roller usable for painting the next day find a can with a lid large enough to house the complete roller, set it in the can with a little turpentine, lacquer thinner of whatever solvent is recommended, and replace the lid to make it airtight. Since the vapor cannot evaporate, the roller will be as pliable the next day as it was when you placed it in the can. You can also use this method for storing paint brushes but do not rest the brush in the can. Rather, put hooks in the lid.

PAINT WITH A ROLLER THAT DOES NOT NEED A TRAY!

When the paint roller was first developed in England, amateurs and professional painters alike toasted it as a better way to apply paint. Many thought that it would eventually replace the brush! This, of course, did not happen but the roller way to apply paint has major advantages for certain applications.

Rollers lay down a uniform layer of paint and cover any given area faster than a brush. Rollers, unfortunately, have a common disadvantage — working from a tray to replenish the paint can be messy! But not with the clever paint roller illustrated — a roller with a hollow handle that holds paint and is long enough so you can reach the ceiling without a stepladder by merely pushing the handle upward to feed just the right amount of paint into the roller. The tubular handle contains enough paint to cover a 60 square foot wall!

Loading the paint into the tubular handle is also easy and without risk of dripping excess paint. A special paint can cover is provided with a tube emerging from the top to replace the lid of your paint can. A filling valve is built into the handle of the roller and when the valve is pushed over the tube in the top of the can cover, by pulling the end of the handle up to 16 ounces of paint is sucked into the tube. Just like using a straw or drawing the plunger of a medical syringe. Actually, atmospheric pressure does the work! Appropriately called "Paint Stick," and invented by Power Flo, this unique roller is great for covering large areas — but what do you do about the trim? Use the companion "trimmer" which also holds paint in its hollow handle! This device can be filled using the same can cover with the special tube; or you can remove the pad and insert the tip into any can of paint. Pull the plunger and as it draws back the atmospheric pressure will force paint into the handle. To release the paint on the pad or brush, merely press the button on the handle and the spring-loaded plunger will steadily push out just the quantity of paint you need. The handle can hold enough paint to cover about 50 lineal feet of trim. These innovative tools work exceedingly

Distance from the roller to the end of the tubular paint chamber is three feet, so a person of average height can easily paint a ceiling without using a ladder. The roller is equipped with a spatter shield that clamps in place to control possible dripping. One filling of the tube is enough to paint a 6x10 foot wall.

STEP 2

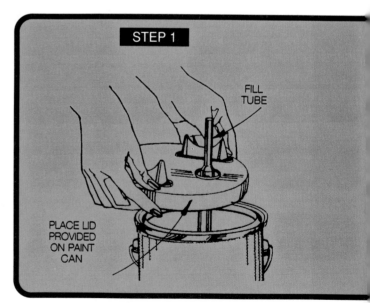

STEP 1

FILL TUBE

PLACE LID PROVIDED ON PAINT CAN

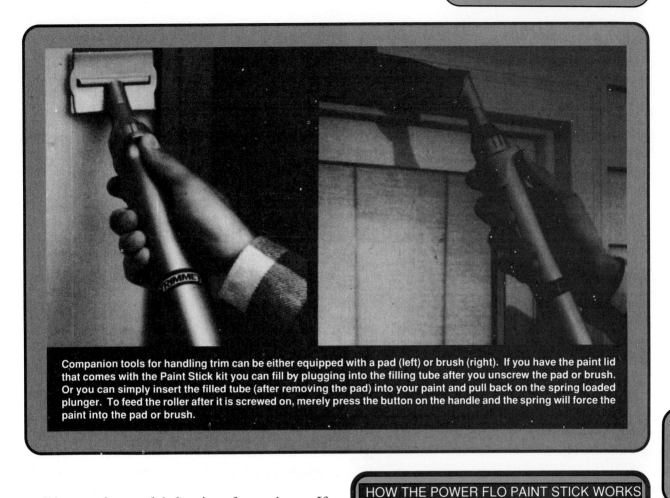

Companion tools for handling trim can be either equipped with a pad (left) or brush (right). If you have the paint lid that comes with the Paint Stick kit you can fill by plugging into the filling tube after you unscrew the pad or brush. Or you can simply insert the filled tube (after removing the pad) into your paint and pull back on the spring loaded plunger. To feed the roller after it is screwed on, merely press the button on the handle and the spring will force the paint into the pad or brush.

well but require careful cleaning after each use. If you use latex paint the cleanup is relatively easy; use plenty of water until all traces of paint are gone. But if you are working with an oil-base paint the clean-up procedure can be as messy as painting with a tray.

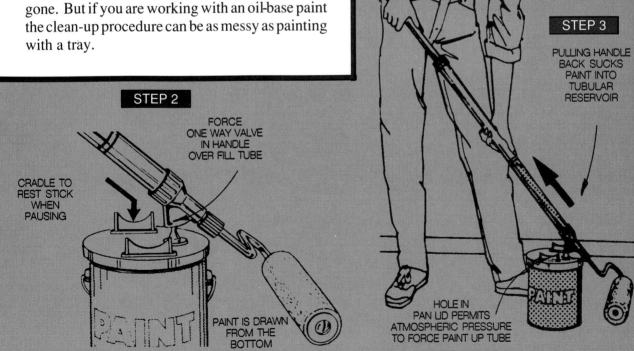

HOW THE POWER FLO PAINT STICK WORKS

STEP 3

PULLING HANDLE BACK SUCKS PAINT INTO TUBULAR RESERVOIR

STEP 2

FORCE ONE WAY VALVE IN HANDLE OVER FILL TUBE

CRADLE TO REST STICK WHEN PAUSING

PAINT IS DRAWN FROM THE BOTTOM

HOLE IN PAN LID PERMITS ATMOSPHERIC PRESSURE TO FORCE PAINT UP TUBE

POWER ROLLER - FLOOR FED, 120 volts

This power roller is only about a foot high, weighs only 10 pounds and plugs into any 120 volt electrical outlet. Paint is pumped from the can through 16 feet of tubing which provides the mobility you need for most rooms. Paint flow is controlled by depressing a button on the handle of the roller.

If you are painting a room or two — or more — and want to go the power route, here is a complete system. Powered by a roller pump that draws less than one amp and plugs into a regular 120 volt outlet. The rolling action of the pump squeezes against a resilient plastic tube which in turn creates a partial vacuum at the intake and pressure on the outlet side. This draws paint into the 18 foot vinyl tube and forces it out into either the standard 9-inch roller, a 3-inch wide roller or an accessory 2-inch sash or trim brush. Locate the unit in the center of the room and move around all four walls, plus the ceiling. You can easily roll a gallon of paint (about 400 square feet) in about 20 minutes. There are three pressure settings, the "High" setting may be used for latex paint that is especially thick and the "Low" setting is recommended for use with the three-inch roller, trim and sash brushes where you do not need the same quantity of paint as when working with the 9-inch roller. The "Medium" setting is used for most applications, and also for cleaning after use. Since this unit is only designed for latex paints or stains, the clean-up procedure — time consuming with all painting chores — is accomplished by running water through the system until all traces of latex have been washed out.

CORDLESS ROLLER CARRIES ITS OWN PAINT

This is a portable cordless power roller. Load it with paint (latex or oil) and sling it over your shoulder. To start, trip the switch on the top.

Cordless power tools have gained tremendous acceptance in the carpentry and related fields because they eliminate the cumbersome power cord necessary with non-cordless tools. And now power painting has entered the cordless era! Fill the container, sling the combination container-pump over your shoulder and start painting. No wires or supply tubes get in your way! The weight of the unit is less than four pounds without the paint and it is powered with four D batteries. Battery life is usually long enough to roll up to 20 gallons of paint, depending upon the paint used. Of course, cleaning is greatly simplified with the use of latex paint, but this unit can also use oil-based paint and stains.

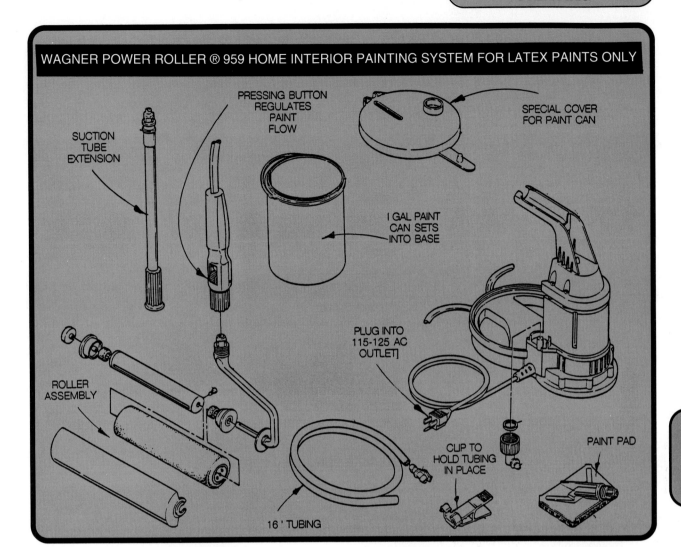

WAGNER POWER ROLLER ® 959 HOME INTERIOR PAINTING SYSTEM FOR LATEX PAINTS ONLY

SUCTION
TUBE
EXTENSION

PRESSING BUTTON
REGULATES
PAINT
FLOW

SPECIAL COVER
FOR PAINT CAN

I GAL PAINT
CAN SETS
INTO BASE

PLUG INTO
115-125 AC
OUTLET]

ROLLER
ASSEMBLY

CLIP TO
HOLD TUBING
IN PLACE

PAINT PAD

16 ' TUBING

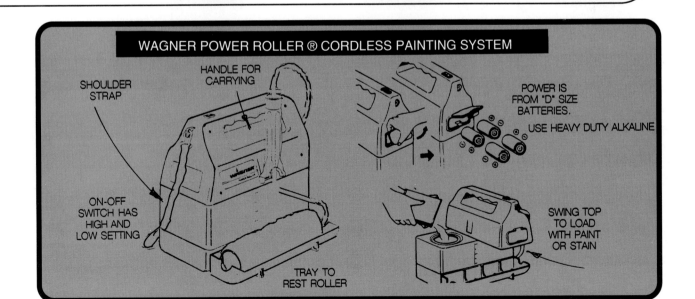

WAGNER POWER ROLLER ® CORDLESS PAINTING SYSTEM

SHOULDER
STRAP

HANDLE FOR
CARRYING

POWER IS
FROM "D" SIZE
BATTERIES.

USE HEAVY DUTY ALKALINE

ON-OFF
SWITCH HAS
HIGH AND
LOW SETTING

SWING TOP
TO LOAD
WITH PAINT
OR STAIN

TRAY TO
REST ROLLER

POWER SPRAYING - FLOOR RESTING TANK

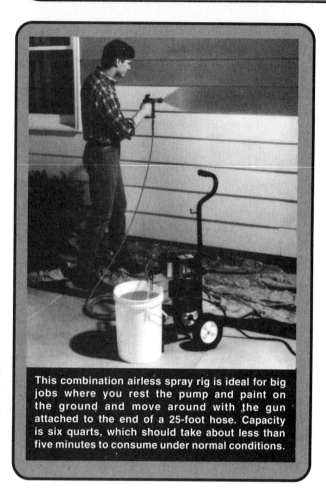

This combination airless spray rig is ideal for big jobs where you rest the pump and paint on the ground and move around with the gun attached to the end of a 25-foot hose. Capacity is six quarts, which should take about less than five minutes to consume under normal conditions.

Spraying has long been the commercial way to apply paint, but more and more homeowners are spraying paint, especially for large jobs. Most spraying equipment uses a compressor tank, but widely popular is the "airless" sprayer which has important advantages. The initial cost is substantially lower because you do not have the usual compressor tank and air pressure regulator. With airless sprayers all you need is a can of paint and a heavy duty extension cord because the pump is built into the base unit. The unit illustrated is driven by a 1/3 HP motor. Spraying pressure is up to 2500 psi which makes possible applying a gallon of paint, stain primer, etc., in about three minutes!

While widely used outdoors where large areas need covering, it can also be equipped for indoor operation for use with a roller. But, of course, the nature of the job should dictate the type equipment and accessories used. With airless however, there is less over spraying resulting in tighter spray patterns which in turn means you can keep the paint going where you want to and not into the air or onto another surface. Generally speaking, airless sprayers will paint much faster than compressor units.

POWER SPRAYING - SELF CONTAINED

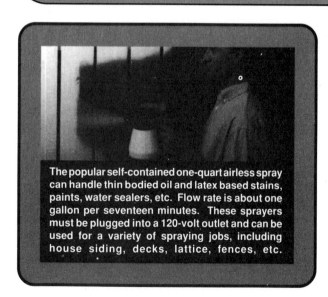

The popular self-contained one-quart airless spray can handle thin bodied oil and latex based stains, paints, water sealers, etc. Flow rate is about one gallon per seventeen minutes. These sprayers must be plugged into a 120-volt outlet and can be used for a variety of spraying jobs, including house siding, decks, lattice, fences, etc.

One of the most popular paint spray units for the homeowner is the self-contained airless gun. Plug it into a nearby 120 volt outlet, pour in your paint and you are ready for just about any paint job. With all paint sprayers cleaning the system after use is absolutely mandatory and in the case of these small guns the job is relatively simple. They come apart easily and because the unit is small, all parts can be soaked in a pan of thinner if you use an oil based paint or water if your paint choice was latex. These sprayers are very versatile in that you have a selection of various tips. For spraying a deck with stain one tip is used; lacquer, latex and oil base paints require a different tip.

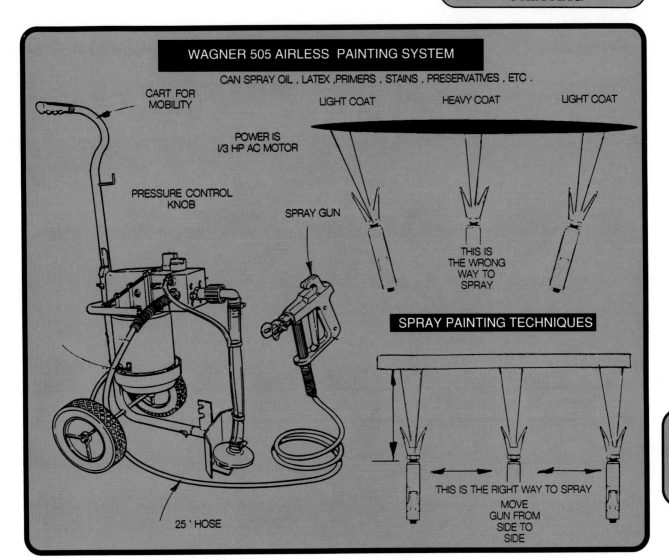

WAGNER 505 AIRLESS PAINTING SYSTEM

CAN SPRAY OIL , LATEX ,PRIMERS , STAINS , PRESERVATIVES , ETC .

CART FOR MOBILITY

POWER IS 1/3 HP AC MOTOR

PRESSURE CONTROL KNOB

SPRAY GUN

LIGHT COAT   HEAVY COAT   LIGHT COAT

THIS IS THE WRONG WAY TO SPRAY

SPRAY PAINTING TECHNIQUES

25 ' HOSE

THIS IS THE RIGHT WAY TO SPRAY

MOVE GUN FROM SIDE TO SIDE

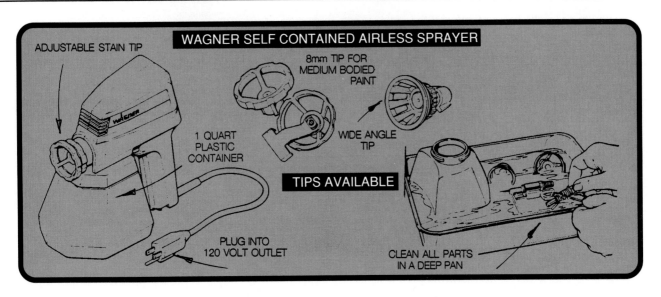

WAGNER SELF CONTAINED AIRLESS SPRAYER

ADJUSTABLE STAIN TIP

8mm TIP FOR MEDIUM BODIED PAINT

1 QUART PLASTIC CONTAINER

WIDE ANGLE TIP

TIPS AVAILABLE

PLUG INTO 120 VOLT OUTLET

CLEAN ALL PARTS IN A DEEP PAN

WALLCOVERING...
A TRADITION IN WELL DRESSED ROOMS

Beautiful walls have long played a prominent role in the decorative history of our homes—and no wonder. Whether it was the ancient artist painting pictures on the walls of his cave, or the pioneer woman stenciling patterns inside her cabin, we've always shared a universal urge to surround ourselves with color, with beauty, with style.

Once there was no such thing as a naked wall; at least, not in a well-dressed room. Walls were there to be decorated, and wallpapers—as they were once called—were carefully chosen and proudly hung, often over linen backings to protect the precious paper from moisture and dampness. Plain, painted or plastered walls were but poor sisters to the beautiful florals and hand-printed scenes our foremothers cherished. Our forefathers, too, according to old records. Thomas Jefferson sent to France for custom-colored wallpapers for his beloved Monticello and George Washington left a recipe for wallpaper paste among his papers at Mount Vernon. Plain, unadorned walls were not for them. Plain, undecorated walls

are not for us, either. Warmth, color, charm and style are what we want, and whatever that means to you, personally, there's a wallcovering to express it Perhaps you're restoring a vintage house and want to recreate an ambiance in harmony with its era. Or you may be faced with square, spare contemporary space and need to make more of less, decoratively speaking. Do it with today's wallcoverings. They're rolled magic, literally, whether you prefer to live in traditional elegance . . . country warmth . . . contemporary sophistication . . . Victorian grandeur. . . or just pleasing prettiness.

And, thanks to modern technology, today's wallcoverings are very durable, inexpensive and easy to install. So, all you have to do is pick your favorites from the wonderful choices in store for you. The many ideas and detailed how-to information on the following pages will help you do that. You will learn all about today's wallcoverings and how to use their magic to work wonders throughout your house.

Left: History often repeats itself on the walls of today's homes. Reproduction wallcoverings instantly evoke the ambiance of any yesteryear you want to re-create. This classic stripe comes from the famed Roycroft Inn in Aurora N.Y. With so many of us interested in period decorating' and romantic restoration, today's wallcovering designers are mining historic houses and museums world-wide for new patterns inspired by old.

ACCENTUATE THE POSITIVE

Walls can do so much more than just hold up the ceiling Make them the start of a fresh new personality for a room. First, choose a wallcovering you love. Then use its coordinating fabrics to dress the rest of the room, from windows to slipcovers such personal touches as tablecloths and throw pillows. It's easy to do since professional designers have already worked out all the color and pattern harmonies so everything blends beautifully. Today's sample books are full of go together wallcoverings and fabrics. Some have special-order home fashion, too, including items like kitchen accessories, tablewear, placemats and more.

BEFORE

AFTER

Pattern adds personality to a plain-Jane room. All dressed up but with nothing much going for it, a so-so living room turns sensational with the added impact of wallcoverings and coordinated fabrics.

WHICH WALLCOVER IS YOU?

Step one toward choosing the right wallcovering for any room: decide what's right for you, your family and the way you like to live. Are you more —or less—formal? Will you be decorating around period furnishings or a particular style of architecture? Do you want to create an ambiance that's elegant and romantic or relaxed and easy-living? The answers will help guide your choice of style, and color in wallcoverings.

Next, the practical considerations. Where is the wallcovering going? Will it be in for an easy life or for heavy duty in a highly trafficked area? These answers will help you chose the right type of wallcoverings for the room. Your options are virtually endless: everything from moderately-priced machine-printed papers to durable fabric and paper backed solid vinyls, to elegant wallcoverings with hand-painted designs.

A contemporary room gets its visual energy from a vigorous geometric, deftly balanced by the quiet solid color of the carpeting and modular sofas and counterpointed by the dotted fabric coordinate on the chairs. A wallcovering pattern like this one is a great disguise for wall and many architectural problems.

Country French flavors an informal living room that's a world away in personality from the room above. Here, a little decorating magic turns a wallcovering border into a "chair rail" that ties two different patterns together. Both take an encore in the fabric coordinates used for the slipcover and throw pillows. Wallcoverings like these add the kind of coziness and warmth that's so right in an informal country room.

MIX PATTERNS LIKE A PRO

Even with all the ready-made color and pattern coordinates in today's wallcovering sample books, there are times you'll want or need to develop your own decorating scheme. In those cases, keep these two pattern pointers in mind: (1) color, and (2) scale. Colors should be alike; scale should not. To implement any mix successfully, you need visual variety ... as in this compatibly-colored large geometric and small dot.

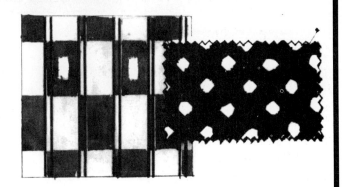

BUILDING A ROOM AROUND A WALLCOVERING

A fail-safe way to decorate a room: start with a favorite wallcovering and borrow its colors for the rest of the furnishings. Here, for example, the background color could be used for woodwork ... a medium-range color for carpeting ... the most outstanding color for accents. Other "stolen" hues will transplant harmoniously onto upholstery and curtains. Other patterns can be worked in as well, following the guidelines above.

ROOM PLANNING IN ADVANCE

Another tip from design pros: plan your room on paper first. Collect swatches of everything you want in the room: wallcoverings, fabrics, paint, carpet, accessories. Pictures of the furniture help, too. Pin them against a neutral background and you'll see at a glance how well they will — or won't — work together *before* you make any purchases.

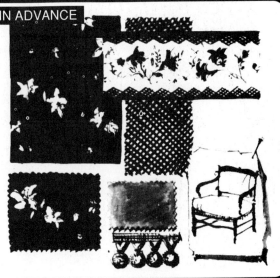

SPECIAL EFFECTS

Pick a pattern and play it off against solid coordinating colors: it's a decorating formula that works every time, and especially well in updated traditional rooms like this one. Here, coordinates in a floral stripe dress walls, window and table, and are repeated in such strategic little touches as the throw pillow on the wing chair. The chair is covered in a color-coordinated solid fabric that matches the table square.

No such thing as too much of a good thing. Make just one decorating decision—which wallcovering/fabric coordinate to use—then spread it all around your room, balancing the pattern with areas of solid color such as the carpeting here. The surprising result of so much uninterrupted pattern: it makes a small space look larger.

INNOVATIVE USE

Look at the whole picture when planning wallcoverings for areas that flow into each other. Coordinates are literally made-to-order for spaces such as this entryway that opens into other rooms. Here, three coordinating wall-coverings co-exist handsomely, accented by a border that does the decorative work of a chair rail.

Personalize small spaces with wallcoverings. Here, a few yards of a wide border frame a tiny kitchen window to give it visual importance far beyond its true size. Leftovers can be used to add delightful accent touches on canisters, cachepots and such.

WALLCOVERING WIZARDRY

Call on wallcoverings to solve all kinds of decorating dilemmas. They can push space around, visually, to raise or lower the ceiling, "cozy-up" cavernous rooms or make small areas look—and feel—more spacious and gracious. Wallcoverings even have the power to iron out architectural uglies in a room and smooth over rough, irregular wall surfaces.

Some pointers to help put this wizardry to work in your rooms:

Low ceiling? Vertical stripes and patterns with a definite upward thrust will make it look higher. To aid the illusion, use light-colored and open, airy designs on the ceiling itself.

Ceiling too high? Bring it down to cozy levels with a dark-colored wallcovering, add a wide border around the top edge of the wall, hang stripes on their sides or choose a horizontal design.

Room too small and cramped? Stretch space in your mind's eye by using small or open patterns—trellis, for example—in light colors. **Room too big or too long?** Reverse the illusion with rich, dark wallcoverings to make it feel warmer, more people-sized.

Too many nooks and crannies or blemishes on the walls? Allover patterns, extroverted textures and embossed or matte finishes can minimize architectural oddities and minimize lumps and bumps, but they will not disappear. A smooth surface is best.

Raise the roof with wallcoverings! Upwardly mobile stripes carry the eye up with them. A mini-patterned wallcovering on the ceiling, plus vertical furniture and long, graceful curtains help bring the eye to the optical conclusion that this room is high and more spacious than it really is.

OFF-THE-WALL IDEAS

Today's wallcoverings don't even need a wall to lead highly decorative lives. You can . . .

Pretty-up a home office file

Personalize a Parsons table

Cover a plywood cornice

Customize a folding screen.

REARRANGING SPACE

Wallcoverings bring down the house! Even in this space-shy age, some rooms are simply too tall to feel cozy and warm. That was once the case in this old-fashioned country bath. The cure: a wide wallcovering border applied well below the ceiling line, plus a dark, warm wallcovering overhead.

Little people are big on color and pattern. Brighten baby's living space with wallcoverings that have coordinating borders. When he or she outgrows the nursery, remove the border and apply something new.

A hit with any miss, this beribboned attic bedroom will remain fresh and feminine from her girlhood into her teens. The vertical pattern of the wallcovering works its visual magic on the low dormer ceiling, making it look high, open and airy. To emphasize the small window, the deep reveal is treated to a charming check, then framed with a wallpaper border.

FOR SPECIAL PEOPLE

For the man — and the boys — in your life: dark-grounded wallcovering coordinates smarten-up his den with colorful yet masculine geometrics. An extra, special touch: bookshelves are lined in the mini-print to better show off his collections.

Theme wallcoverings, relating to hobbies or special interests, put a very personal stamp on any child's room. Siblings who share an interest in sailing will love the nautical theme of this wallcovering and coordinated border. A double helping of the border serves to bring down the high ceiling and to accent the wall-mounted shelf that adds storage space.

WALL COVERING

Home Decorator's Dictionary

Like every field of endeavor, interior design has a language all its own. Here is a glossary of terms to help you talk over your decorating plans and purchases.

A

Abstract: A design not based directly on natural forms.

Adaptation: A design inspired by authentic sources, usually historic or vintage.

Advancing Colors: Warm colors—red, yellow and orange—that make surfaces appear closer or larger. Dark colors have a similar effect.

Allover Design: One that extensively and evenly covers the entire surface of the wallcovering or fabric.

Analagous Colors: Also known as related colors, they have a lot in common. Examples: blue and violet.

Art Deco: Design form from the 1920s and '30s, popularized today by old movie reruns. Look for stylized, often rounded motifs, luscious colors and overall opulence.

Art Nouveau: Means "new art," and it was, back around 1900. Its swirling lines, based on plant tendrils, are now enjoying a revival more than a half-century later.

ASID: American Society of Interior Designers. National organization of professional designers with headquarters at 608 Massachusets Ave., NE, Washington, D.C. 20002.

B

Baroque: Ornate, swirling, elegant style of ornamentation that originally flourished in 16th century Italy.

Biedermeier: Newly popular again, this neoclassic furniture style dates to 19th century Austria. Look for fairly formal, classic designs and slightly overstuffed upholstery.

Bolt: The total yardage contained in a package of wallcovering. It may be a single, double or triple roll.

Booking: When applying paste onto wallcoverings, the procedure of folding pasted surfaces together for easier handling.

Border: A narrow strip of wallcovering often used just under the ceiling or around windows and doors.

Brocade: Elegant fabric or wallcovering with allover design of figures or flowers.

C

Chair Rail: Moulding placed on a wall at chairback height. Wallcovering borders can achieve the same effect by a lot or run number. Order all your wallcoverings from the same color run.

Chinoiserie: Decoration in the Chinese manner.

Coating: A protective layer of vinyl applied to wallcoverings to make them washable and more durable.

Colonial: American furnishings from 1700 to 1781, also known as American Georgian. Think "Colonial Williamsburg" and you've got the look.

Color Run: A wallcovering production run made from the same batch of dyes and inks, assuring that colors will be consistent from roll to roll. Usually identified on the package by a lot or run number. Order all your wallcovering from the same color run.

Colorways: The combination of colors in a pattern. Most wallcovering and fabric patterns come in many different colorways.

Companion Wallcoverings: Also known as "coordinates," these are patterns that harmonize with each other by virtue of a common design motif or color grouping.

Complementary Colors: Colors that lie directly opposite each other on the color wheel and are, therefore, as unlike as they can be. Examples: red and green, blue and orange, yellow and violet.

Contemporary: A style of decorating that is very today, often made of the newest materials. Think sleek, slick and innovative in style.

Cool Colors: Blue, green and violet, or any color to which blue has been added.

Cornice: The horizontal moulding around the top of the wall. Also, a wood frame, upholstered or covered, mounted at the top of draperies as a finishing touch.

Correlates: Wallcoverings and fabrics designed to go together. Also known as "coordinates" or "companions." Because colors won't look exactly the same on different materials, they're said to "correlate" rather than "match."

Country: A nostalgic style that began to sweep the nation a decade ago, bringing back calico, quilt and gingham patterns and small prints.

D

Dado: The wall space between the baseboard and chair rail, often covered with a wallcovering that coordinates with one on the wall above the chair rail.

Documentary: An exact copy of an historic wallpaper.

E

Early American: The furnishings of the first settlers in the New World (1608-1720), a provincial version of 17th-century English styles. Warm, charming, comfortable and closely related to country.

Eclectic: A mixture of furnishing styles from different periods and places, carefully chosen to create highly individual rooms.

Embossing: A raised effect created by impressing a design or texture onto wallcovering, rather than printing it with ink

Empire: Napoleon's style. In America, Empire also revived classic motifs from ancient Greece and Rome, and added a touch of Egypt for good measure.

Euro-roll: A metric-sized roll or bolt.

F

Federal: Elegant, classic furniture that flourished in America after the Revolution until about 1830, often featuring eagles stars and other patriotic motifs.

Flame Stitch: Undulating, multi-colored patterns adapted from a traditional Hungarian needlework stitch.

Focal Point: Anything of major visual interest in a room, such as a fireplace.

Fretwork: Lattice work, usually in geometric designs. borrowed from the Chinese.

G

Georgian: Furnishings from the period when four Georges reigned over England (1715-1780). Designers like Chippendale, Sheraton, the Adam Brothers and Hepplewhite made history.

Ground: The background color on which the pattern of a wallcovering or fabric is printed or embossed.

I

Intensity: The strength of a color. The difference between pink and red is a matter of intensity.

L

Lining: A material applied on a wall as a base to provide a smooth surface before wallcoverings are installed. Fabric linings are used to protect curtains and provide a better hand.

Louis, King: There were three important Louis' in France during the 17th and 18th centuries. Louis XIV lends his name to grandiose, baroque furnishings. Louis XV's style is delicate and curvilinear. Louis XVI means straight lines and classic motifs.

M

Match: The design arrangement that allows for the continuous flow of a pattern on the wall: diagonal, drop, straight across or random.

Matte: A dull finish.

Metallics: Wallcoverings that are printed on foil or metallicized material.

Mission: Decorative style featuring the southwestern flavor originally derived from Spanish missions in early California.

Modern: An approach to furnishings in which the function of an object dictates its form. Frills are eliminated: basic materials are emphasized.

Modular: Furniture with components designed to be combined in different configurations to suit individual needs.

Moire: A watered silk effect on wallcoverings or fabrics.

Monochromatic: All of one color, often ranging from light to dark in value.

Mural: A wallcovering in which the strips are applied to create a single scene, often a landscape.

N

Neoclassic: "New" classics, or classic forms from the past revived and updated for today's living. There's a strong trend toward neoclassic today, in everything from architecture to furniture to wallcoverings.

Neutral Colors: The uncolors: whites, beiges, grays, browns.

O

Object d'Art: The French term we've adopted for any small objects of art such as miniatures and figurines.

Ombre: Striped wallcoverings or fabrics where one color is used in several values.

P

Paisley: Multi-colored, comma-shaped motif borrowed from the town of Paisley, Scotland, renowned for its shawls.

Peelable Wallcoverings: Wallcoverings on which the top layer peels away easily without steaming or scraping, leaving just a thin residue of paper or paste on the wall that can be easily removed.

Post Modern: Literally, "after modern," meaning a return to many of the classic, established forms and furnishings from the pre-20th century era. Empire, Biedermeier, marble and columns are important ingredients in the post modern look.

Pre-Pasted: A wallcovering with adhesive (dry) already on the back. You just dip in water and apply.

Pre-Trimmed: A wallcovering with the selvages already trimmed off the edges to make it easier to install.

Primary Colors: The "Big Three"—red, yellow and blue— from which all other colors are derived.

Provincial: Copies made in the provinces of furnishings popular in the more sophisticated cities. French provincial, for example, was first copied from styles in the court of Louis XV.

R

Railroading: Applying wallcovering or fabric horizontally; rather than vertically.

Receding Colors: Cool colors—blue, green and violet—that make surfaces appear further away or smaller.

Repeat: The vertical distance between identical points in the pattern of a wallcovering or fabric.

S

Scrubbable: A wallcovering that can be cleaned with a soft brush and mild detergent

Secondary Colors: Colors created by mixing equal parts of two primary colors. Orange, green and violet are secondaries.

Shade: Any color to which black has been added.

Single Roll: A length of wallcovering traditionally used as the basis of pricing.

Size: Sealer used to prepare the wall so that the wallcovering adheres better.

Stain-Resistant Wallcoverings: Wallcover-ings on which a coating of plastic or vinyl has been added to make the surface stain-resistant and maintenance-free.

Stenciling: A motif that looks as if it has been applied through cutouts in a stencil. Especially charming in country and early Amerifan rooms.

Strie: Wallcovering or fabric with random stripes only slightly different in color from the background.

Strip: A length of wallcovering cut to fit the height of the wall.

Strippable Wallcoverings: Wallcoverings that can be completely removed from the wall, without steaming or scraping. A boon to do-it-yourselfers and apartment dwellers.

Swatch: A sample cutting of wallcovering or fabric.

T

Tint: Any color to which white has been added.

Traditional: Style of decorating inspired by the past. Sometimes used interchangeably with "colonial."

Transitional: Style of decorating showing the transition from one style to another and containing elements of both.

Tromp l'Oeil: A decorative illusion that "fools the eye" by appearing to have greater depth or dimension.

V

Value: The lightness or darkness of a color.

Victorian: Furnishing style that evolved during the long reign of Queen Victoria in England, characterized by an extravagant eclecticism that has been rediscovered for enjoyment today.

Vinyl: A plastic, flexible wallcovering material usually laminated to a backing of fabric or paper.

W

Wainscot: Wood paneling for interior walls. especially when it only reaches partially up the walls.

Wallcoverings: Flexible wall decorations sold in roll form. Wallpaper: A paper-based wallcovering.

Warm Colors: Red. yellow and orange. or any color to which yellow has been added.

Washable: A wallcovering that can be cleaned with a sponge and mild soap and water.

Waterbox: Tray that holds the water into which pre-pasted wallcoverings are dipped before they are hung.

HOW TO HANG WALLCOVERING

Wallcovering — or wallpapering — has always offered a far greater decorative choice than either paint or wood paneling because of the virtually unlimited selection of colors, designs and textured surfaces. Actually, most of the wallcovering material being hung is not paper, which is why the term "wallcovering" is taking the place of the term "wallpapering." However, I suspect the term wallpaper will never become extinct because of the history behind how it originated. It is interesting to note the early use of wallpaper can be traced over 400 years to the Netherlands and France where artists designed the first patterned wallpaper as an affordable substitute to fine silk and wool cloth tapestries that had been used for centuries to decorate European palaces. The Chinese are credited with first painting landscapes, flowers and birds on rice paper for decorative hanging, but it was the Europeans who first applied it to walls. The first wallpaper strips were actually hand painted and as the demand grew copies were made from carved blocks of wood and printed in much like rubber stamp printing. nt with rubber

Today only five percent of the wall-coverings sold in this country is paper. The rest is vinyl or vinyl coated. Vinyl has many advantages—mainly durability—but some of the more expensive coverings are printed on paper. Equally interesting, of all the wallcovering sold, over 75% is the pre-pasted type.

Even though European countries pioneered wallcovering, only a small percentage of the covering sold today is imported. American manufacturers have adopted the European system and print the measurements of each roll using both our English system and the metric system.

Unlike plywood where you know a 4x8 sheet is an *exact* 32 square feet, the coverage in rolls is really an approximation on the low side because in the process of packaging it is virtually impossible to accurately control cutting the material to the *exact* length. Most manufacturers actually give you more coverage than indicated.

Since running short is often the tendency,

ADHESIVE CAN BE APPLIED
WITH A BRUSH OR ROLLER

PAPER ROLLS ARE USUALLY
PRE-TRIMMED 20 1/2" WIDE

20 1/2"

SOME PAPER ROLLS HAVE
A WASH COAT OF VINYL
ON THE SURFACE

always double check the coverage of the material you are buying. This information is openly displayed on either the label, wrapper, sample book or special instruction sheet packed with each roll.

The width of the covering produced in this country varies, depending upon the type of material. Paper rolls are an exact 20 1/2 inches wide; the vinyl wallcoverings are 27-28 inches wide, while the more exotic grass cloth, mylars and specialty sufaces come in rolls 27-36 inches wide. Wider rolls, usually of vinyl 52 inches wide, are used by the pros.

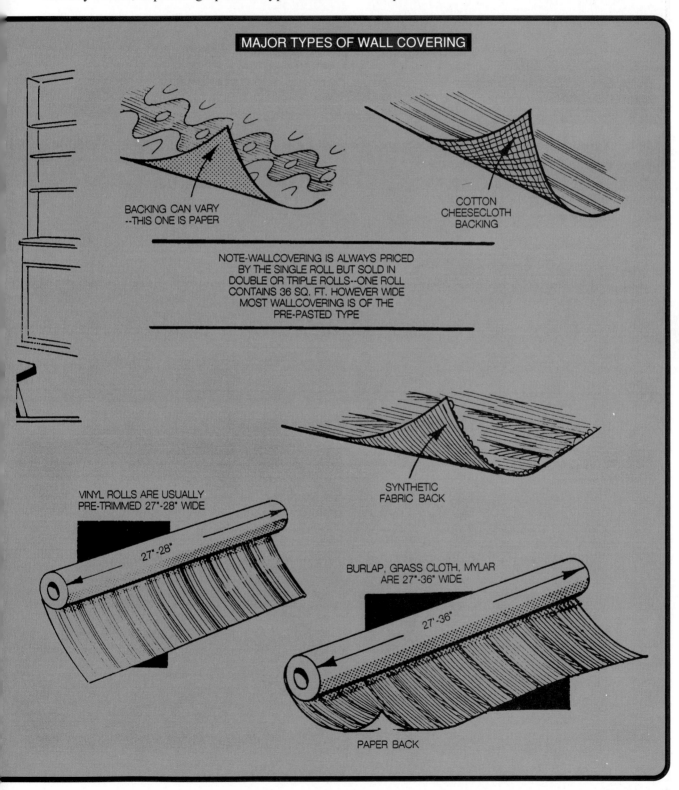

MAJOR TYPES OF WALL COVERING

BACKING CAN VARY --THIS ONE IS PAPER

COTTON CHEESECLOTH BACKING

NOTE-WALLCOVERING IS ALWAYS PRICED BY THE SINGLE ROLL BUT SOLD IN DOUBLE OR TRIPLE ROLLS--ONE ROLL CONTAINS 36 SQ. FT. HOWEVER WIDE MOST WALLCOVERING IS OF THE PRE-PASTED TYPE

SYNTHETIC FABRIC BACK

VINYL ROLLS ARE USUALLY PRE-TRIMMED 27"-28" WIDE

27"-28"

BURLAP, GRASS CLOTH, MYLAR ARE 27"-36" WIDE

27"-36"

PAPER BACK

UNUSUAL "GLAMOUR" WALLCOVERINGS

THE DECORATIVE range of wall covering is so great that literally scores of materials are being used to cover walls and ceilings. Smooth, metallic-like mylar, real foil, silk, grass cloth, cork, canvas, flock, simulated leather, ultra suede, every conceivable range of textiles and even carpeting—to name a few—are generally classified as "glamour" coverings. Most share a common point; they are by far more expensive than regular vinyl or paper coverings and often require considerably more skill to handle. Some of them, especially foils and mylars, require a perfect surface and usually a liner paper.

Each of the aforementioned must use a specific adhesive and be handled in a specified manner. For example, some are best hung by pasting the wall; others, such as fabric and mylar types, must not be subjected to the use of the regular roller for flattening the seams. The taboos are so plentiful—and mistakes often costly—it is best to discuss the handling characteristics with a knowledgeable salesperson at your source of supply if installation instructions are not supplied on the wrapper of each roll. Of all the covering available, working with vinyl is perhaps the easiest because you can shift the covering without the risk of tearing, as is the case with paper. And if you are enchanted with a heavy textured grass cloth, foil, cork, silks, a suede finish or shiny mylar and have not had wall covering experience it is best to consult a pro. Or you may want to gain some experience by covering a wall or two with vinyl or paper, after which time you may be better equipped to handle the exotic coverings.

VINYL GRASS-LIKE

GRASS-LIKE SURFACE ON A FABRIC BACK. USE READY MIXED VINYL ADHESIVE. AVERAGE SKILL REQUIRED.

HEAVY TEXTURED

STRING-LIKE FABRIC ON A VINYL BACK. USE READY-MIXED VINYL ADHESIVE. SEMI-PRO EXPERIENCE REQUIRED.

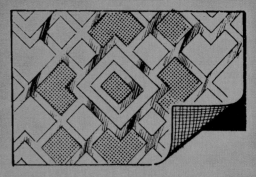

MYLAR

MYLAR SURFACE ON A FABRIC BACK. USE READY-MIXED VINYL ADHESIVE. ABOVE AVERAGE SKILL REQUIRED.

POPULAR GLAMOUR WALL COVERINGS.

GLOSS SMOOTH VINYL

SMOOTH VINYL ON A PAPER BACKING.
USE READY MIXED VINYL ADHESIVE.
ABOVE AVERAGE SKILL REQUIRED.

REGULAR FABRIC

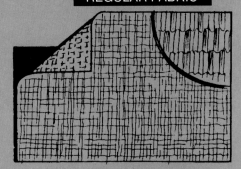

FABRIC ON A PAPER BACKING.
USE CELLULOSE ADHESIVE.
PRO SKILLS REQUIRED.

CORK 1/32" THICK

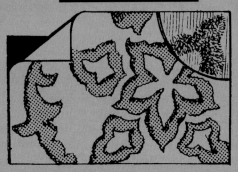

CORK ON A FABRIC BACKING.
USE READY-MIXED VINYL ADHESIVE.
IF PRE-TRIMMED, AVERAGE SKILL REQUIRED.

FLOCK ON VINYL

FLOCK ON A VINYL BACKING
USE CELLULOSE ADHESIVE
AVERAGE SKILL REQUIRED

LINEN TEXTURE

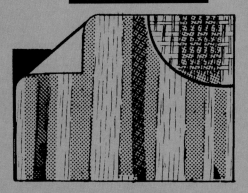

LINEN TEXTURE ON VINYL BACKING.
USE READY-MIXED VINYL ADHESIVE.
AVERAGE SKILL REQUIRED .

SUEDE-LIKE VINYL

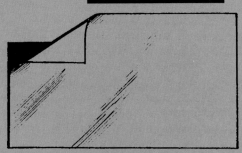

SUEDE-LIKE VINYL SURFACE ON
A FABRIC BACKING. USE READY
MIXED VINYL ADHESIVE.
AVERAGE SKILL REQUIRED

TOOLS AND EQUIPMENT REQUIRED

ONE OF THE really advantageous points about hanging your own wallcovering is that you do not need a collection of expensive tools and equipment. Many common around-the-house items are used—such as a good stepladder, scissors, level, plumb bob, ruler, single edge razor blades, etc. The other items you need are best acquired as part of a regular "paper hanging kit" which is relatively low in cost and literally last a lifetime.

Some not-too-common items can make the job easier. For instance, the combination metal and straight-edge ruler is one; it beats the usual flexible tape or folding ruler because it can also be used when trimming or double cutting. The wide-faced putty knife is a must because it simplifies trimming at the ceiling or base. A good sponge is also a great help.

Of all the equipment needed, perhaps the most important is a flat working surface at the right working height. The kitchen table is much too small, although in a pinch it can be used, but placing a sheet of 3/4-inch plywood on top and then covering the plywood with an old plastic shower curtain provides the best working surface. An ordinary flush door also serves as a good workbench for measuring, marking and, if you do not use pre-pasted covering, applying the adhesive. Most homes have flush doors, and these are not difficult to remove. Pull the hinge pins, remove the lock if necessary and rest the door on your table. The 6-foot-8-inch length is adequate although the door width should be at least 2 feet 6 inches because you probably will be using a wallcovering 20 to 27 inches wide. Prepare the wider specialty covers on the floor.

The flush-door work table has the advantage of being rigid, which is not the case if plywood thinner than 3/4 inch is used. If you cut with a razor and straight edge; make certain you do not cut through the plastic protective sheet and mar the paint job on the door. If you do, you may end up covering the door.

WALLCOVERING

7 FT. LADDER

PASTE BRUSH

PLUMB BOB OR LEVEL

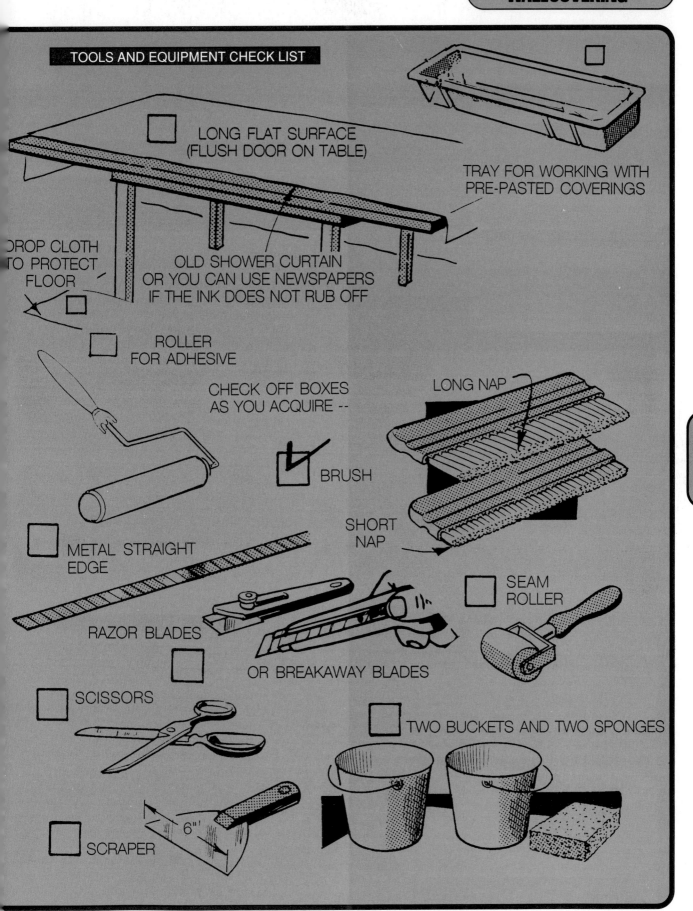

TOOLS AND EQUIPMENT CHECK LIST

LONG FLAT SURFACE
(FLUSH DOOR ON TABLE)

TRAY FOR WORKING WITH
PRE-PASTED COVERINGS

DROP CLOTH
TO PROTECT
FLOOR

OLD SHOWER CURTAIN
OR YOU CAN USE NEWSPAPERS
IF THE INK DOES NOT RUB OFF

ROLLER
FOR ADHESIVE

CHECK OFF BOXES
AS YOU ACQUIRE --

LONG NAP

BRUSH

SHORT
NAP

METAL STRAIGHT
EDGE

SEAM
ROLLER

RAZOR BLADES

OR BREAKAWAY BLADES

SCISSORS

TWO BUCKETS AND TWO SPONGES

6"

SCRAPER

ALL ABOUT PATTERNS

The decision as to the type of wallcovering you select depends upon individual preference and decorating scheme, but you should know the basics about patterns. Wallcovering patterns fall into three different categories: (l) Straight across repeat, (2) Drop match repeat, and (3) No repeat (plain or random match).

The *straight across repeat is* one in which the match is directly across. With a straight across pattern, the repeat distance can vary (most are 9 to 12 inches). Once you decide where the ceiling line interrupts the pattern, measure and cut a floor-to-ceiling strip allowing *2 inches* at the top and 2 inches near the base for trim. Then unroll for another strip so the pattern matches at the top. If, for instance, you must unroll a length that turns out to be more than 4 inches longer than ceiling height to match the pattern, cut all strips to this length and then retrim the base so you are left with 2 inches of excess at top and bottom. Some straight across repeat patterns can be more wasteful than others, but since your estimating made allowances for waste work out on paper just how many strips a roll (or double roll) will yield.

The drop match pattern has the matching point of one side halfway between the matching point of the opposite side. Generally speaking, this provides a less repetitious appearance in large areas because the horizontal design is not the same from strip to strip. The drop match pattern runs diagonally across the wall and is staggered so every other strip is the same. Most drop match coverings are less wasteful than the straight across repeat because the strips can be cut alternately from two separate rolls.

The *no repeat* (plain or random match) coverings obviously do not present a matching problem but if all strips are cut and hung consecutively, if the color differs ever so slightly at the edges, the variation will be very noticeable. Best results are achieved by reversing the strips, as illustrated.

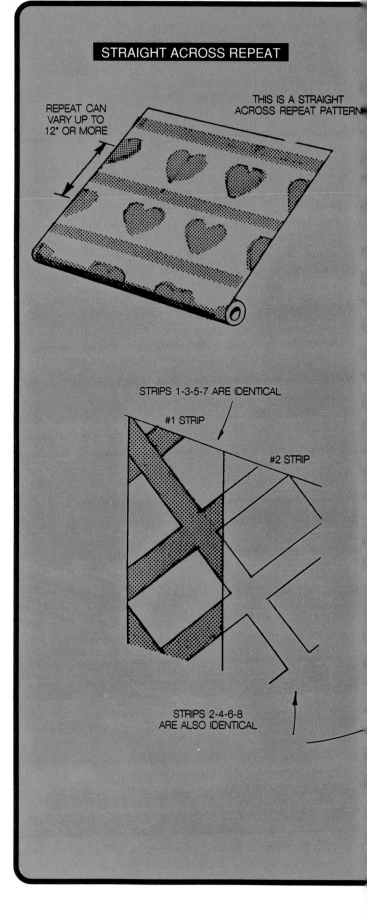

STRAIGHT ACROSS REPEAT

REPEAT CAN VARY UP TO 12" OR MORE

THIS IS A STRAIGHT ACROSS REPEAT PATTERN

STRIPS 1-3-5-7 ARE IDENTICAL

#1 STRIP

#2 STRIP

STRIPS 2-4-6-8 ARE ALSO IDENTICAL

DROP MATCH

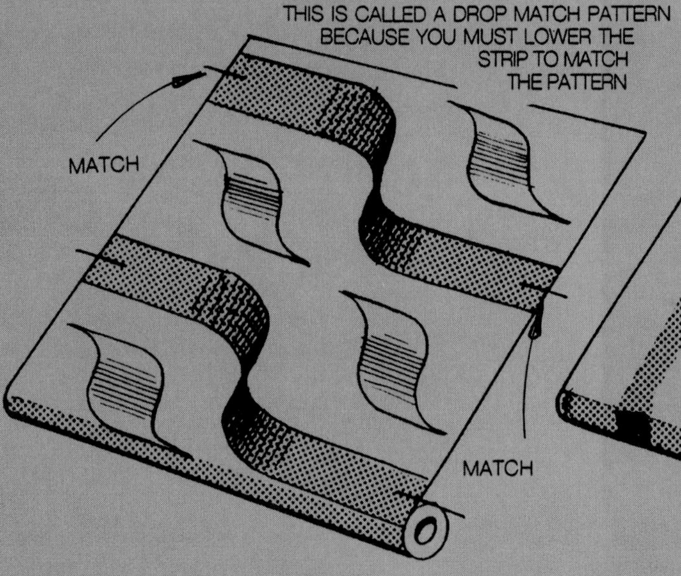

NON-REPEAT OR RANDOM

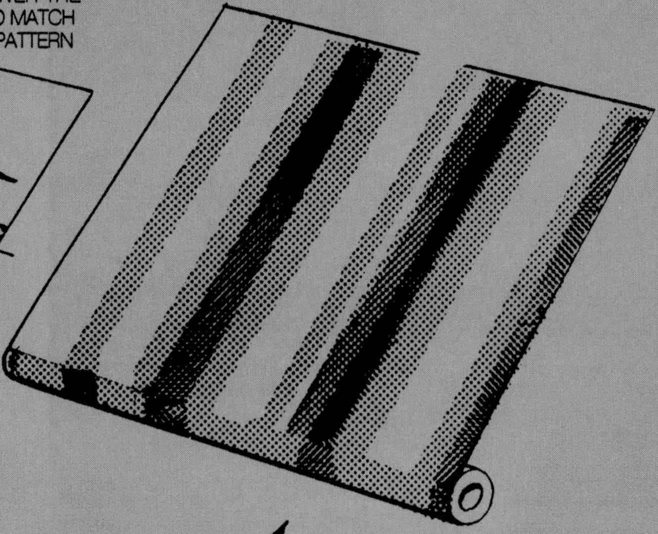

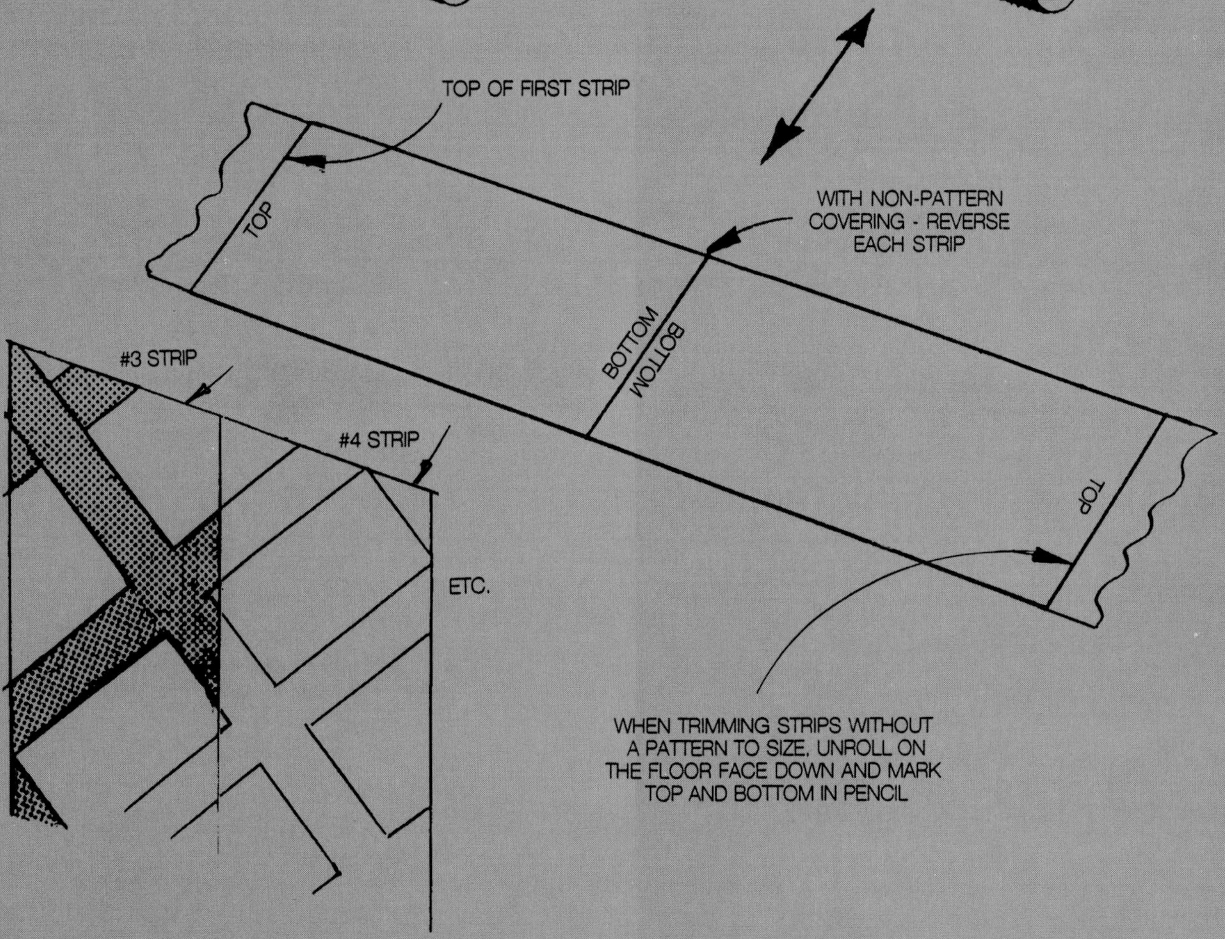

THIS IS CALLED A DROP MATCH PATTERN
BECAUSE YOU MUST LOWER THE
STRIP TO MATCH
THE PATTERN

MATCH

MATCH

TOP OF FIRST STRIP

TOP

WITH NON-PATTERN
COVERING - REVERSE
EACH STRIP

BOTTOM

BOTTOM

TOP

#3 STRIP

#4 STRIP

ETC.

WHEN TRIMMING STRIPS WITHOUT
A PATTERN TO SIZE, UNROLL ON
THE FLOOR FACE DOWN AND MARK
TOP AND BOTTOM IN PENCIL

WORKING WITH ADHESIVES

YEARS AGO wheat flour mixed with water was the standard wallpaper paste, and while wheat paste with special additives (to make it vermin and mildew proof) is still used; cellulose paste is the preferred adhesive for most jobs. However, rather than mix your own we recommend that you use the pre-mixed adhesives recommended by the covering manufacturer. This may be referred to as clear, light duty, heavy duty, etc. These mixes are available in various size pails; if you do not use the complete contents merely snap on the lid and keep the remainder for the next job.

Next to selecting the correct adhesive and a good brush for application, most important is a worktable where the covering can be cut and the adhesive applied. A 5-foot long table is an absolute minimum; preferable is a flush door that can be worked from a waist-high position rather than the 32-inch height of a table. The practice of laying a half dozen sheets of newspaper on the worktable and removing the top sheet after the covering has been pasted is quite common, but in some instances the ink from the newspaper will discolor the covering being pasted. A better method is to cover your work surface with heavy vinyl or even a discarded shower curtain and wipe the surface clean after each strip is pasted. Apply the adhesive initially in a figure 8 pattern. Make absolutely certain the back of the strip is thoroughly covered because any unpasted area will eventually appear as a bubble when the adhesive is dry. Paste one half of the strip first, tuck it over, then apply the adhesive to the other half. "Booking" is the logical name given to this fold-over procedure which greatly simplifies the hanging because it helps spread the adhesive more evenly, soaks the covering to make it more pliable and, of course, does not interfere with scaling your ladder when hanging each strip. Book no more than two strips, allowing the adhesive to soak as recommended by the manufacturer. With pre-pasted covering the booking time should be at least two minutes and care should be taken to assure the adhesive along the edges does not dry out. You will be able to cope with this tendency after you hang the first strip and guide yourself accordingly.

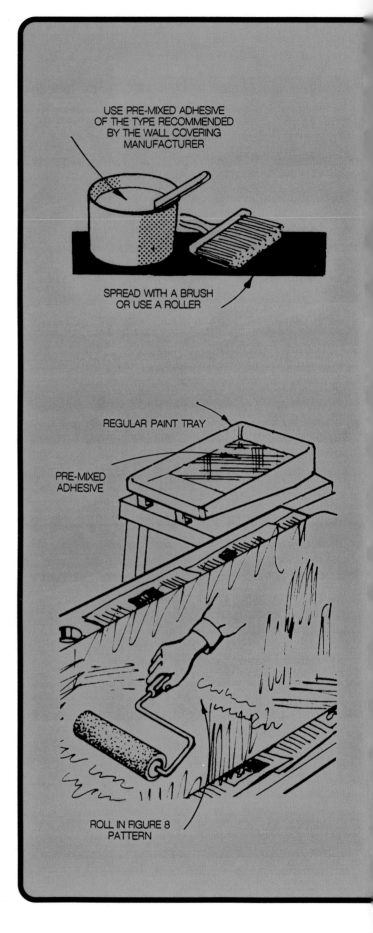

USE PRE-MIXED ADHESIVE OF THE TYPE RECOMMENDED BY THE WALL COVERING MANUFACTURER

SPREAD WITH A BRUSH OR USE A ROLLER

REGULAR PAINT TRAY

PRE-MIXED ADHESIVE

ROLL IN FIGURE 8 PATTERN

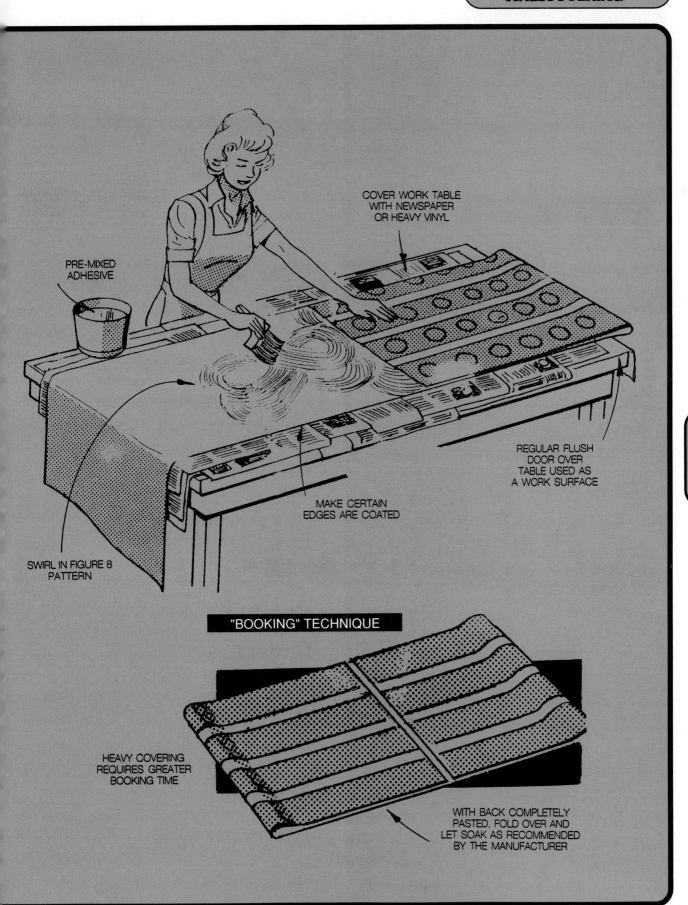

PRE-MIXED ADHESIVE

COVER WORK TABLE WITH NEWSPAPER OR HEAVY VINYL

REGULAR FLUSH DOOR OVER TABLE USED AS A WORK SURFACE

MAKE CERTAIN EDGES ARE COATED

SWIRL IN FIGURE 8 PATTERN

"BOOKING" TECHNIQUE

HEAVY COVERING REQUIRES GREATER BOOKING TIME

WITH BACK COMPLETELY PASTED, FOLD OVER AND LET SOAK AS RECOMMENDED BY THE MANUFACTURER

WALLCOVERING

ESTIMATING THE NUMBER OF ROLLS

BEFORE YOU CAN calculate how many rolls your room requires you must know if the wallcovering you plan to use is labeled American or European because European rolls contain 28 square feet per roll while American rolls contain 36 square feet. All coverings are packaged by what is known as a "bolt" with each bolt consisting of two or three single rolls. Determine the number of rolls required by using the "Magic 22" for European rolls or "Magic 30" for American rolls.

The technique is simple. Measure the perimeter of the room in feet, multiply this number by the ceiling height, and then divide by 22 (European rolls); divide by 30 if you are using American rolls. If the answer comes out to a fraction, say 12.8, then round off the figure to the next whole number. When multiplying room perimeter by the ceiling height, one error many people make is NOT converting a perimeter into the decimal equivalent. As an example, a wall measuring 12 feet 6 inches cannot be multiplied as 12.6. The 12 feet 6 inches is actually 12.5 feet.

Of course, if your walls are broken up with a few windows, a built-in bookcase, a wall-mounted mirror and the like, it is best to make a drawing to scale on graph paper and actually draw vertical lines representing the wallcovering seams. Allowing for the pattern repeat, in this manner you will determine exactly how many strips you need and, since each European single roll has 28 square feet, you can easily convert the number of strips into rolls. A single 20 1/2-inch-wide American roll contains 16 1/2 running feet; a 27-inch roll, 13 1/2-feet if European and 15 feet if American.

Admittedly, this is slightly more complex and time-consuming than the Magic Number method, but in some cases it is preferable—especially in instances where you have expensive rolls and want to keep waste to an absolute minimum. Wall surfaces leading up or down stairs are a prime example where this strip-by-strip measuring technique should be used, as are rooms with a Cathedral ceiling.

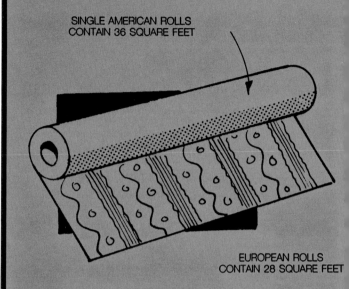

ROLL COVERING

SINGLE AMERICAN ROLLS CONTAIN 36 SQUARE FEET

EUROPEAN ROLLS CONTAIN 28 SQUARE FEET

THE MAGIC 22 TECHNIQUE
FOR EUROPEAN ROLLS
PERIMETER TIMES HEIGHT AND DIVIDED BY 30. PERIMETER 16 + 16 + 10 + 10 TOTAL 52 FEET CEILING HEIGHT - 8 FEET 52 X 8 = 416 DIVIDED BY 22 = 18.9 DEDUCT ACTUAL SQ. FT. OF OPENING – DO NOT DEDUCT SMALL OPENINGS
TOTAL REQUIRED - 19 ROLLS

THE MAGIC 30 TECHNIQUE
FOR AMERICAN ROLLS
PERIMETER TIMES HEIGHT AND DIVIDED BY 30. PERIMETER 16 + 16 + 10 + 10 TOTAL 52 FEET CEILING HEIGHT - 8 FEET 52 X 8 = 416 DIVIDED BY 22 = 13.8 DEDUCT ACTUAL SQ. FT. OF OPENING – DO NOT DEDUCT SMALL OPENINGS
TOTAL REQUIRED - 13 ROLLS

CALCULATING NUMBER OF ROLLS REQUIRED USING THE MAGIC NUMBER METHOD

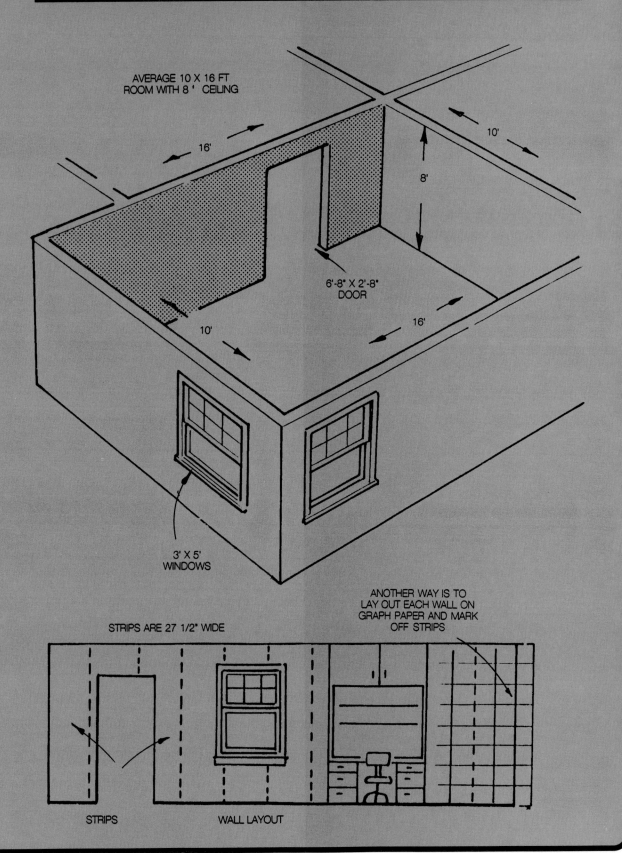

AVERAGE 10 X 16 FT
ROOM WITH 8' CEILING

16'

10'

8'

6'-8" X 2'-8"
DOOR

10'

16'

3' X 5'
WINDOWS

ANOTHER WAY IS TO
LAY OUT EACH WALL ON
GRAPH PAPER AND MARK
OFF STRIPS

STRIPS ARE 27 1/2" WIDE

STRIPS

WALL LAYOUT

MUST YOU REMOVE THE OLD COVERING?

WALLCOVERING to achieve a specific decorative effect can do wonders to beautify a room, and once a room is "papered" it probably will never see paint again. Rather, another covering of a different design is usually chosen come redecorating time.

The pros usually remove all previous covering and make certain the surface is absolutely smooth and free of dents and nicks. Of course, if the existing covering was the strippable type all you need do is loosen a corner at the top and yank in much the same manner as peeling a banana. Then sand the surface slightly to remove any existing sediment.

Many of the older houses have many layers of paper and if the covering is tight there is no valid reason why another layer cannot be added right over the old paper. Any holes or dents should be spackled and then sanded smooth. An occasional bubble or lifting seam should be glued down; slit the bubble and pry some adhesive behind the paper. Press flat.

If you must remove the old covering, you need a few basic tools such as a scraper, a good sponge, a brush and a plastic bucket. Soaking the covering with hot water to which a special paper-removal additive has been mixed can be a little messy, so protect your floors with a tarp and a half-dozen layers of old newspapers to help absorb the water that may drip down. Also, electric powered steam generating strippers are most affordable and can also be rented.

When all traces of the previous covering have been removed, wash the walls (or ceiling) down to remove any loose specks of adhesive. Finally, give the entire area a light sanding and fill in all cracks and holes with spackle. You may require a sealer, a sizing or a primer and, if the surface is not smooth, a liner paper.

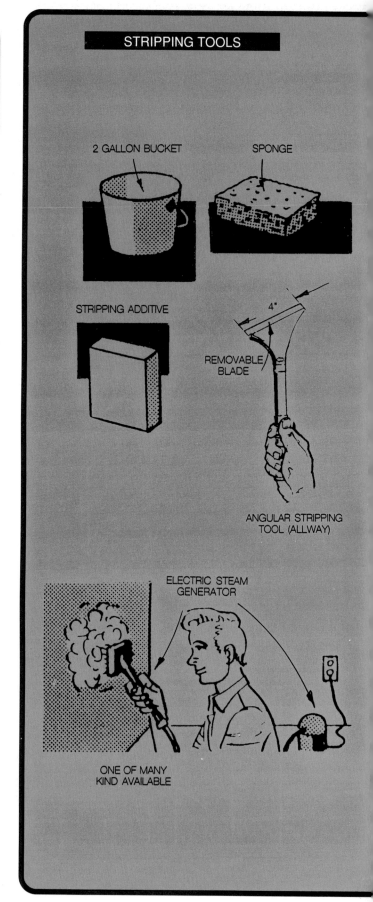

STRIPPING TOOLS

2 GALLON BUCKET

SPONGE

STRIPPING ADDITIVE

4"

REMOVABLE BLADE

ANGULAR STRIPPING TOOL (ALLWAY)

ELECTRIC STEAM GENERATOR

ONE OF MANY KIND AVAILABLE

STRIPPING WALLS OF OLD COVERINGS

AFTER SOAKING WALL
PULL STRIPS OFF
WORKING FROM THE TOP

PAPER
MUST
BE
SOAKED

6" BLADE CAN
ALSO BE USED

IF COVERING IS VINYL
UNLOOSEN TOP CORNER AND
STRIP - THEN SAND LIGHTLY
TO REMOVE TRACE OF ADHESIVE

SPONGE
AND
LET
SOAK

IF SURFACE SHOWS SIGNS
OF MILDEW WASH WITH
50/50 MIXTURE OF BLEACH AND
WATER OR USE A PREPARED
MILDEW REMOVER

PLACE
POLYETHYLENE
TARP OR OLD
NEWSPAPER ON
FLOOR

WALLCOVERING

TREATING PAINTED/ UNPAINTED WALLS

MOST WALLS fall into one of these three categories: (1) Painted over plasterboard or solid plaster, (2) Unpainted—plasterboard or solid plaster, or (3) The same surfaces covered with a paper or vinyl. Here are suggestions for surface preparation:

Painted walls: All chipping and flaking paint should be scraped loose so that when your covering is hung the adhesive will grip the base. If you have plaster walls you probably have a few cracks around the windows or doors from the upper corners to the ceiling. Also, where pictures or mirrors were previously hung, the holes may be enlarged. Remove all loose plaster and fill with one of the non-shrinking vinyl spackle compounds. When dry, any sharp edges left by the spackle should be sanded smooth. Cracks and patched holes should be painted with a prime-sealer. In fact, if the wall was previously painted with inexpensive latex, you run the risk of a poor bond. It is best to paint the entire wall with a acrylic latex primer.

In instances where the wall is extremely slick and glossy, the surface may not accept the adhesive, so this type wall should be washed down with a strong solution of trisodium phosphate. One-third cup to a gallon of water is adequate. Rinse surface.

Unpainted walls: Most homes built in the last 40 years have plasterboard walls, often referred to as dry wall construction. The joints and corners are taped, the nailheads countersunk slightly just to get the head below the surface, and two or three layers of joint compound applied. Inspect these joints; loose tape should be pulled off and replaced. Also, if you note an occasional bubble in the taped joints, slit the bubble and pry joint compound behind the tape. Then press flat. Popped nails should also be driven slightly below the surface and the hole filled with compound. In new construction all dry walls should be painted with a wallcovering primer sealer.

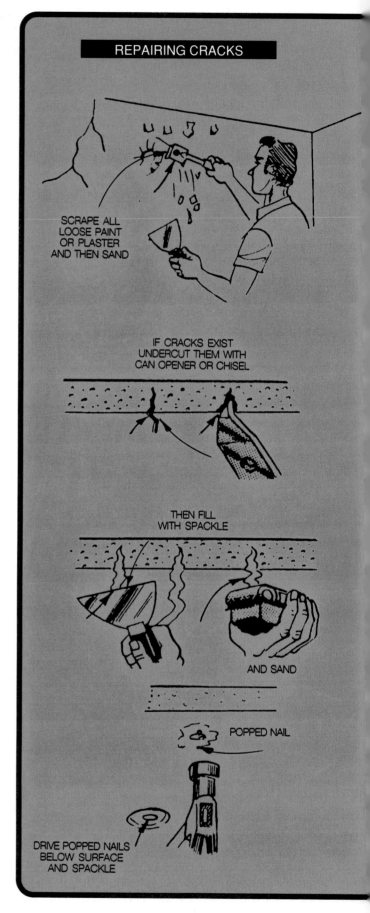

REPAIRING CRACKS

SCRAPE ALL LOOSE PAINT OR PLASTER AND THEN SAND

IF CRACKS EXIST UNDERCUT THEM WITH CAN OPENER OR CHISEL

THEN FILL WITH SPACKLE

AND SAND

POPPED NAIL

DRIVE POPPED NAILS BELOW SURFACE AND SPACKLE

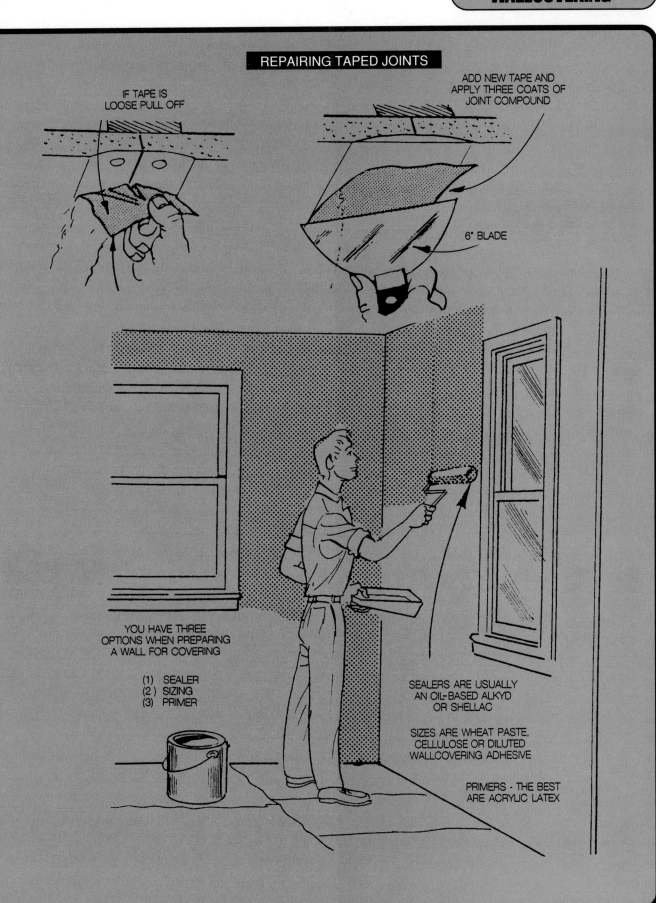

REPAIRING TAPED JOINTS

IF TAPE IS
LOOSE PULL OFF

ADD NEW TAPE AND
APPLY THREE COATS OF
JOINT COMPOUND

6" BLADE

YOU HAVE THREE
OPTIONS WHEN PREPARING
A WALL FOR COVERING

(1) SEALER
(2) SIZING
(3) PRIMER

SEALERS ARE USUALLY
AN OIL-BASED ALKYD
OR SHELLAC

SIZES ARE WHEAT PASTE,
CELLULOSE OR DILUTED
WALLCOVERING ADHESIVE

PRIMERS - THE BEST
ARE ACRYLIC LATEX

WALL
459
COVERING

DO YOU NEED A LINING PAPER?

CERTAIN WALL SURFACES—and certain types of wallcovering—require that a lining paper be applied as a foundation before the finish covering is hung. Lining paper is a plain off-white stock available in various widths. It is inexpensive and helps conceal some of the wall roughness and also absorbs excess moisture that may exist in the covering you are hanging. The more expensive and delicate coverings (metallic foils, some mylars, grass cloth, etc.) are best hung over lining paper.

If your covering requires lining paper, prepare the surface as was previously recommended for regular covering and cut your strips about 1/4 inch short of the ceiling, corner or baseboard. Paste as with regular covering, book and hang. Start a narrow strip, if necessary, to make certain the joints of the finish covering do not fall directly over the lining butt joints. You can hang lining paper both vertically and horizontally, and in all instances the joints are butted. To overlap them would be noticeable when the finish covering is applied.

Lining paper comes in various thicknesses, to cope with the rough surfaces of brick and cinder block walls. However, in the case of a stucco wall which is unusually rough a thin coat of plaster can be applied, but this requires extreme skill. An easier way is to fur out the wall with 1x2-inch strips, screwed 16 inches on centers, and then mount half-inch plasterboard over the complete area. You could use 3/8-inch gypsum board but for the added few cents a square foot the popular 1/2-inch thin grade is well worth the cost because it is stiffer. Finish the joints with a three coat layer of joint compound, and sand the final coat. Then prime the surface with a recommended primer sealer and, after the sealer is dry, the surface is ready for hanging.

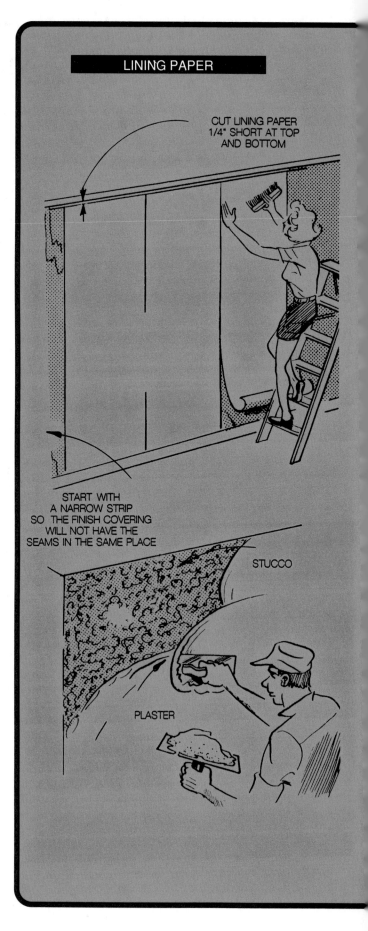

LINING PAPER

CUT LINING PAPER 1/4" SHORT AT TOP AND BOTTOM

START WITH A NARROW STRIP SO THE FINISH COVERING WILL NOT HAVE THE SEAMS IN THE SAME PLACE

STUCCO

PLASTER

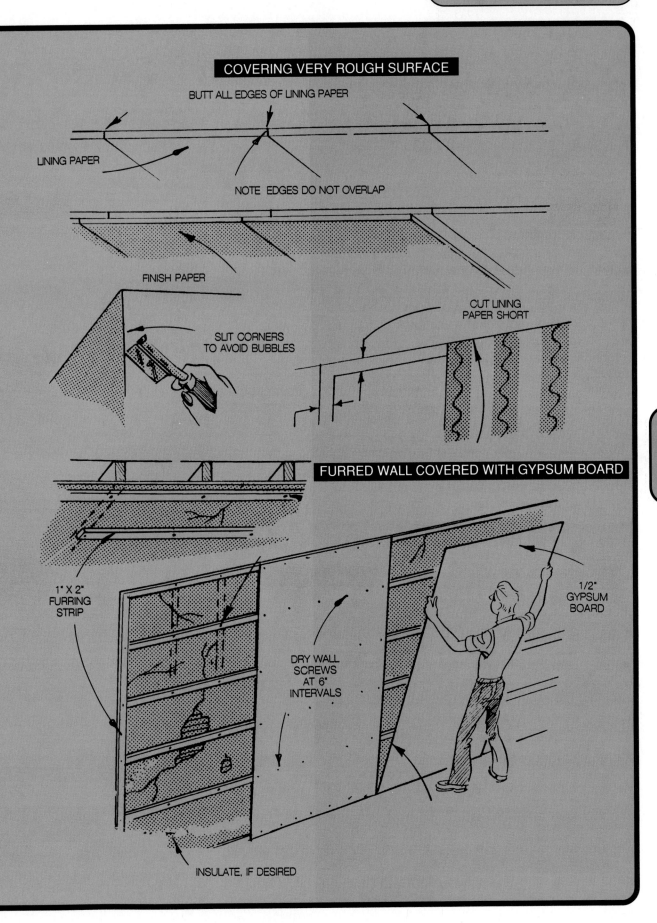

COVERING VERY ROUGH SURFACE

BUTT ALL EDGES OF LINING PAPER

LINING PAPER

NOTE EDGES DO NOT OVERLAP

FINISH PAPER

SLIT CORNERS TO AVOID BUBBLES

CUT LINING PAPER SHORT

FURRED WALL COVERED WITH GYPSUM BOARD

1" X 2" FURRING STRIP

DRY WALL SCREWS AT 6" INTERVALS

1/2" GYPSUM BOARD

INSULATE, IF DESIRED

HANGING THE FIRST STRIP

NEXT TO preparing the wall surface, the most important single step when hanging wallcovering is to make absolutely certain that the first strip is vertical because an ever so minutely slanted horizontal pattern will be very noticeable when the room is complete. If you are using 27-inch-wide pre-trimmed roll—the most popular width—mark off 26 1/2 inches at the ceiling and drop a plumb bob to the floor. Lightly mark points in pencil at about 24-inch intervals behind the string and connect these points with a pencil line, using a straight edge. Do not snap a chalk line because the line will be fuzzy and may even wash away or become faint should the adhesive from the first strip touch the line. The edge must be absolutely straight because the subsequent strips butt to each other rather than overlap.

Whatever the width of your rolls, a full 1/2 inch should be turned into the corner. As you work around the room, in all probability the last strip must be cut to the correct width and set to overlap the first corner. Place the first strip against the wall so the edge touches the pencil line and work from the top down. Since the adhesive is still wet, if you are not precisely on the pencil line you can easily slide the strip so the edge will touch the vertical pencil line. Firm action with your brush, working from the center outward into the corner, will remove any air bubbles.

Now, using your wall scraper as a straight edge, press it into the ceiling corner and trim the excess covering with a single-edge razor blade. Wet covering may tear easily, especially if it is paper, so use a new blade and discard it after a few cuts. Trim the excess covering at the baseboard and then rinse the surface with a large sponge soaked in clean water to remove any excess adhesive. Once you get the "hang" of the first strip, following with the others is both fast and easy.

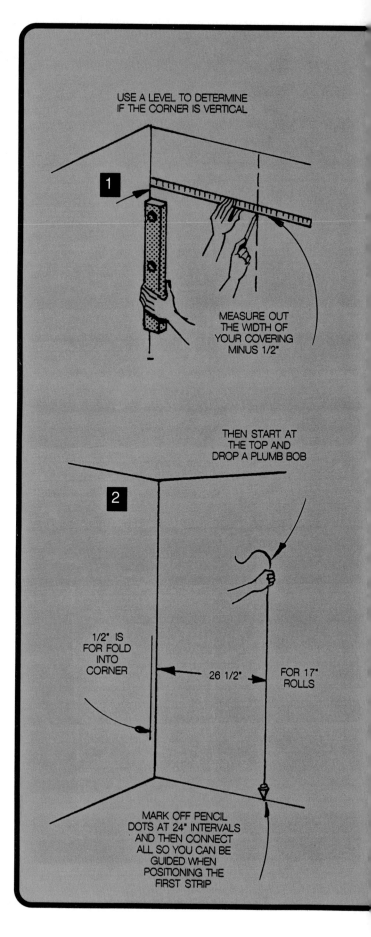

USE A LEVEL TO DETERMINE IF THE CORNER IS VERTICAL

MEASURE OUT THE WIDTH OF YOUR COVERING MINUS 1/2"

THEN START AT THE TOP AND DROP A PLUMB BOB

1/2" IS FOR FOLD INTO CORNER

26 1/2"

FOR 17" ROLLS

MARK OFF PENCIL DOTS AT 24" INTERVALS AND THEN CONNECT ALL SO YOU CAN BE GUIDED WHEN POSITIONING THE FIRST STRIP

HANGING THE MOST IMPORTANT STRIP - THE FIRST STRIP

3 SLIT TOP FOR CORNER FOLD

4

2'-4" EXCESS COVERING AT TOP AND BOTTOM

USE A SHARP RAZOR BLADE AND CUT AT A SHALLOW ANGLE

PUSH SCRAPER INTO TOP CORNER AND USE AS A STRAIGHT EDGE TO TRIM EXCESS

BRUSH FROM THE CENTER TOWARD THE EDGES

FELT EDGE

A HANDY T-SHAPED HELPER PREVENTS A STRIP FROM FALLING

HANGING THE SECOND STRIP

NOTHING IS as satisfying as watching a room rapidly take on a new look—which is exactly what happens when straight runs of a wall are covered. The first strip requires time and patience, but after that the job progresses rapidly. However, there are still a few hurdles you must cross to produce a professional result.

Start the second strip at the ceiling line and carefully butt the joint. Match the pattern at the top and, once about 2 feet of the covering is brushed to the wall at the top, let the rest hang and then slide the strip over for an exact joint. Brush smooth from the center out. Trim the top and bottom, roll the joint with a clean roller and then rinse down the strip, especially at the seams and the areas of the ceiling where you may have smeared adhesive.

Turning inside corners can be tricky, especially if the corner is irregular. The best way is to measure the distance from the corner to the edge of the last strip, add 1/2 inch and cut a booked strip as shown. Then hang each section so the corner joint overlaps. The 1/2 inch allowed for the overlap will also give you the leeway to shift the strip (if necessary) ever so slightly to make it absolutely plumb! Never continue a strip around an inside corner even if it is plumb because any shrinkage of the covering will produce a tear in the corner.

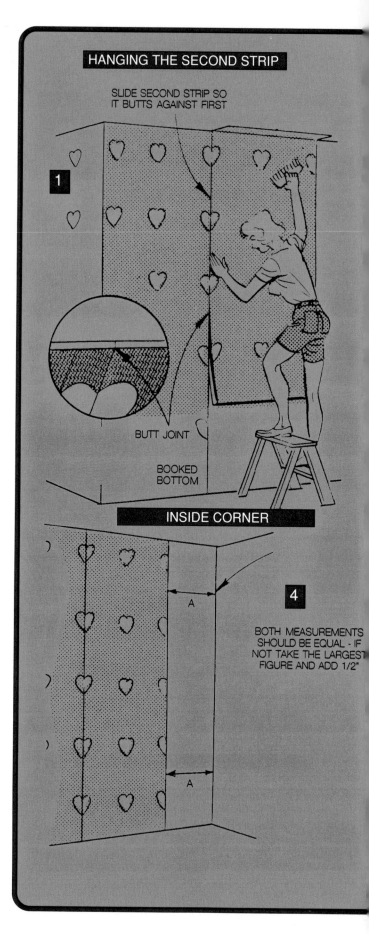

HANGING THE SECOND STRIP

SLIDE SECOND STRIP SO IT BUTTS AGAINST FIRST

1

BUTT JOINT

BOOKED BOTTOM

INSIDE CORNER

A

4

BOTH MEASUREMENTS SHOULD BE EQUAL - IF NOT TAKE THE LARGEST FIGURE AND ADD 1/2"

A

HANGING A COMPLETE WALL

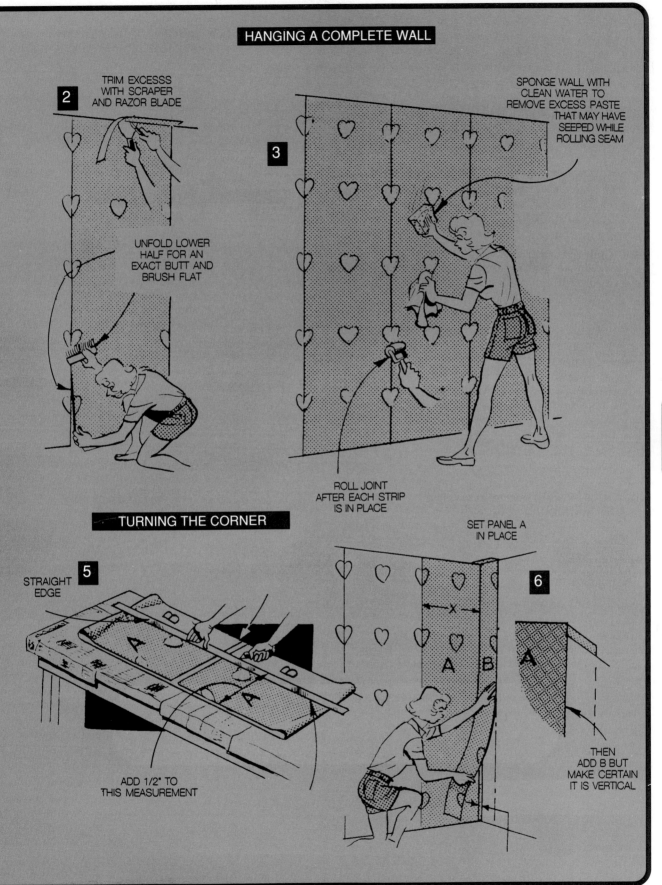

2 TRIM EXCESSS WITH SCRAPER AND RAZOR BLADE

UNFOLD LOWER HALF FOR AN EXACT BUTT AND BRUSH FLAT

3 SPONGE WALL WITH CLEAN WATER TO REMOVE EXCESS PASTE THAT MAY HAVE SEEPED WHILE ROLLING SEAM

ROLL JOINT AFTER EACH STRIP IS IN PLACE

TURNING THE CORNER

5 STRAIGHT EDGE

ADD 1/2" TO THIS MEASUREMENT

SET PANEL A IN PLACE

6 THEN ADD B BUT MAKE CERTAIN IT IS VERTICAL

COVERING AROUND WINDOWS AND DOORS

HOW DO YOU apply wallcovering around a window or door, so it fits perfectly? You make believe the window or doorway does not exist and merely hang a strip as if it were a straight wall!

As you work toward the casing match the pattern with the last strip, butt the joint and permit the wet strip to extend *over* the window casing. Smooth and brush out the flat area near the butt joint and as close to the bulging door or window frame as possible without tearing the covering. Then, at a corner of the window or door molding—which will be very visible through the wet covering—make a diagonal cut with your razor-knife to relieve the pressure. Brush the sides, top and bottom of the wall covering flat against the wall. The wood trim will have adhesive that rubbed off the back of the wall covering so wipe it with clean water and a sponge.

Finally, using your wide scraper as a straight edge, trim the excess covering around the wood trim in exactly the same manner as the ceiling and base excess strips were trimmed.

Turning outside corners that are not absolutely perpendicular can present a few problems unless the corner is plumb. It is always better to roll the covering around an outside corner than to make a seam on the corner because the edge of the covering on the corner will soon loosen. The solution is to work the strip around the corner and if the edge is not absolutely perpendicular lap the next strip over the edge when it is vertical and double cut. With "double cutting" one strip is placed over the other where the patterns nearly match. Then, using a straight edge, a cut is made through both strips of covering. Pull them apart and remove the excess of the lower strip and then press the upper strip in place for a perfect fit. Of course, you must make certain this strip is perfectly vertical before hanging the subsequent strips.

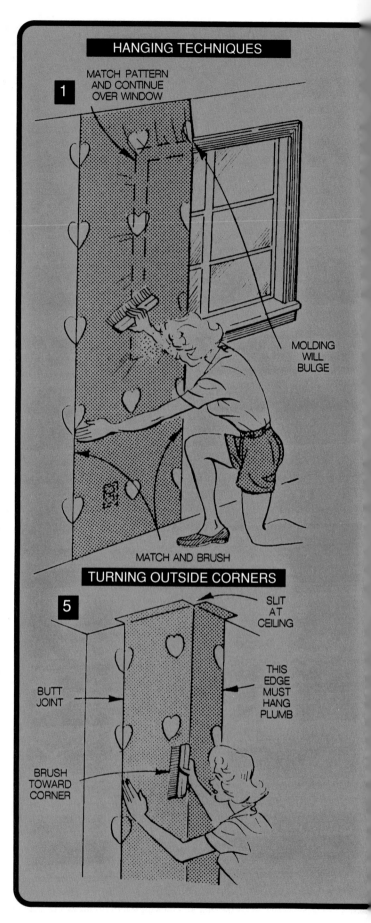

HANGING TECHNIQUES

1 MATCH PATTERN AND CONTINUE OVER WINDOW

MOLDING WILL BULGE

MATCH AND BRUSH

TURNING OUTSIDE CORNERS

5

SLIT AT CEILING

THIS EDGE MUST HANG PLUMB

BUTT JOINT

BRUSH TOWARD CORNER

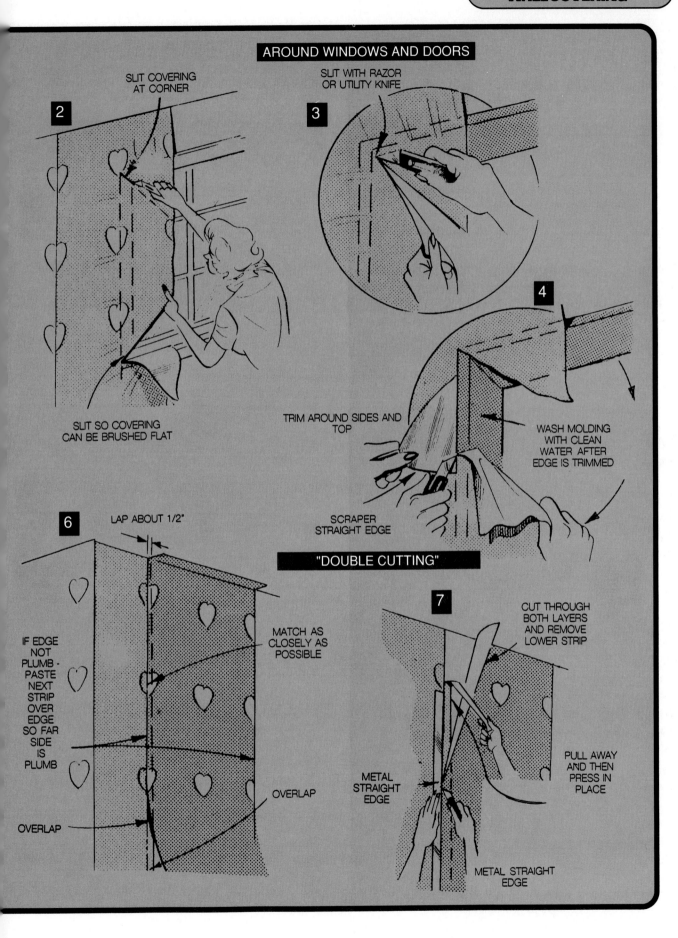

AROUND WINDOWS AND DOORS

2 SLIT COVERING AT CORNER

SLIT SO COVERING CAN BE BRUSHED FLAT

3 SLIT WITH RAZOR OR UTILITY KNIFE

4 TRIM AROUND SIDES AND TOP

WASH MOLDING WITH CLEAN WATER AFTER EDGE IS TRIMMED

SCRAPER STRAIGHT EDGE

"DOUBLE CUTTING"

6 LAP ABOUT 1/2"

IF EDGE NOT PLUMB - PASTE NEXT STRIP OVER EDGE SO FAR SIDE IS PLUMB

MATCH AS CLOSELY AS POSSIBLE

OVERLAP

OVERLAP

7 CUT THROUGH BOTH LAYERS AND REMOVE LOWER STRIP

METAL STRAIGHT EDGE

PULL AWAY AND THEN PRESS IN PLACE

METAL STRAIGHT EDGE

WALL 467 COVERING

COVERING BEHIND SINKS AND RADIATORS

It is not absolutely necessary to hang wall covering completely behind a sink or radiator so the rule of thumb should be to hang as much covering as possible that is visible to the eye when standing in a normal position, then work the hard to get at areas. Of course, it is always desirable to remove the radiator, sink, shelves or what have you and replace them after the wallcovering is hung, but this is often impractical, if not impossible. No two jobs are alike, so you must pre-plan just how to cover these very hard to get at hidden areas.

Radiators are usually a scant 2 inches from the wall, in which case you can use the technique illustrated. Cut the strips to the exact length at the bottom, paste in the usual manner, and then insert the lower end behind the radiator. Smooth upward and brush toward the ceiling. The strip can still be moved slightly to obtain a perfect pattern match; if not, pull it loose and shift it accordingly. Then trim the excess.

Covering behind a sink usually presents a more difficult problem. Make a sketch to note where the water supply lines and drain are located, and pre-cut the bottom as shown in the drawing. Hang the largest section first and then trim the cutout section to fit. Because the wall under a sink is out of view and the many pipes make it difficult to position a large strip of covering, it is always easier to work with small sections, pasting each one in place and double cutting where necessary. The objective is to end up with a nice clean wall and even if the patterns do not match perfectly it is not objectionable since the under section of the sink is out of view. Many supply and waste lines have removable escutcheons that serve as a molding around the pipe and will easily hide a minor miscalculation or a hole that was cut substantially larger than the pipe diameter. If not, you can make your own escutcheon from a scrap of the covering and fit it around the pipe.

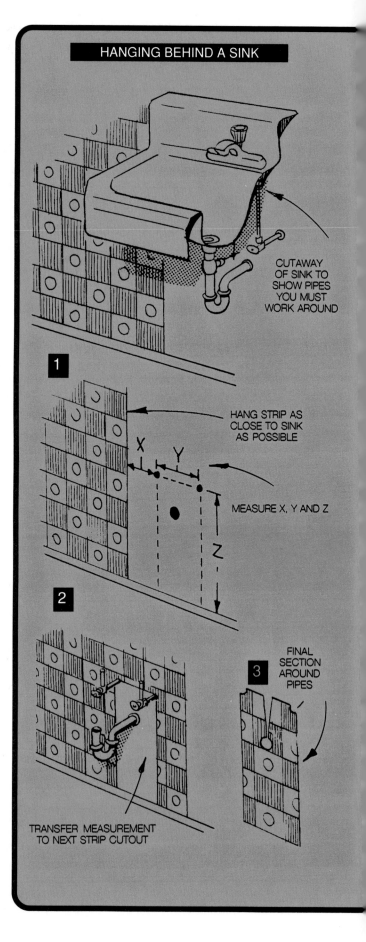

HANGING BEHIND A SINK

CUTAWAY OF SINK TO SHOW PIPES YOU MUST WORK AROUND

1 HANG STRIP AS CLOSE TO SINK AS POSSIBLE — MEASURE X, Y AND Z

2 TRANSFER MEASUREMENT TO NEXT STRIP CUTOUT

3 FINAL SECTION AROUND PIPES

HANGING BEHIND A RADIATOR

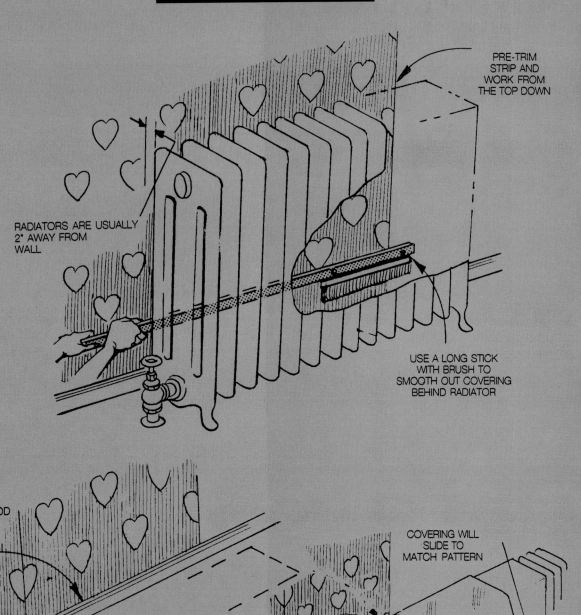

PRE-TRIM STRIP AND WORK FROM THE TOP DOWN

RADIATORS ARE USUALLY 2" AWAY FROM WALL

USE A LONG STICK WITH BRUSH TO SMOOTH OUT COVERING BEHIND RADIATOR

ANOTHER METHOD IS TO WORK FROM THE BOTTOM UP

COVERING WILL SLIDE TO MATCH PATTERN

CUT SO BOTTOM FITS

PRESS IN PLACE AND WORK TOWARD THE CEILING

HOW TO HANG A CEILING

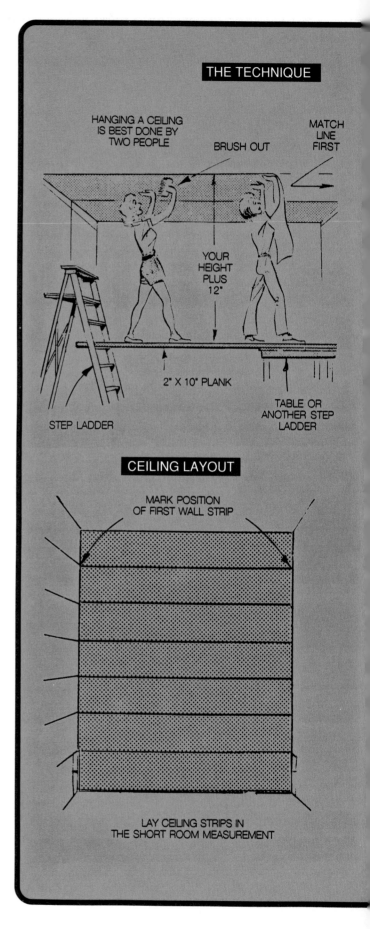

THE TECHNIQUE

HANGING A CEILING IS BEST DONE BY TWO PEOPLE

BRUSH OUT

MATCH LINE FIRST

YOUR HEIGHT PLUS 12"

2" X 10" PLANK

STEP LADDER

TABLE OR ANOTHER STEP LADDER

CEILING LAYOUT

MARK POSITION OF FIRST WALL STRIP

LAY CEILING STRIPS IN THE SHORT ROOM MEASUREMENT

Most homeowners paint their ceiling because they feel covering it with a matching wallcovering pattern is too difficult. Admittedly, hanging a ceiling is more difficult but with a little planning, a good scaffold (two stepladders and a plank) plus a helper to hold one end while you position and brush each strip, you can end up with a pro-like job. The problem with hanging a ceiling is that the force of gravity will cause the sides of the covering to droop and drape over your head. That is why you need more than one pair of hands. However, once you have brushed a good portion of the strip on the ceiling, slipping it into the exact position is easy.

If you plan to have the same pattern covering on both the ceilings and walls, first mark the position of the wall strips around the perimeter of the room so you can match the joints of the ceiling strips with those of the wall. Always run your ceiling strips in the short direction of the room.

To start your first strip, snap a chalk line from one side of the room to the opposite side, coinciding with the lines made when marking off the wall strips. As with hanging walls, first cut all your strips to length allowing about 2 inches excess on both ends to compensate if the room is out of square.

Prepare a work scaffold; a few planks set at a convenient height is preferred. A good rule of thumb is to add one foot to your height and set the planks at this level measured from the ceiling.. Start at one end, unfold a booked strip and smooth the strip so the edge matches the ceiling pencil line. Use the palm of your hand to shift the covering where necessary, and then brush flat to remove any air bubbles and also insure good contact for the adhesive.

The excess covering that extends down the wall should be folded flat on the wall and then be cut away, leaving about a 1/2" deep border. Use a straight edge and a razor to cut thru the covering. You will cut slightly into the plasterboard but the slit will be covered up when covering the wall.

OF HANGING A CEILING

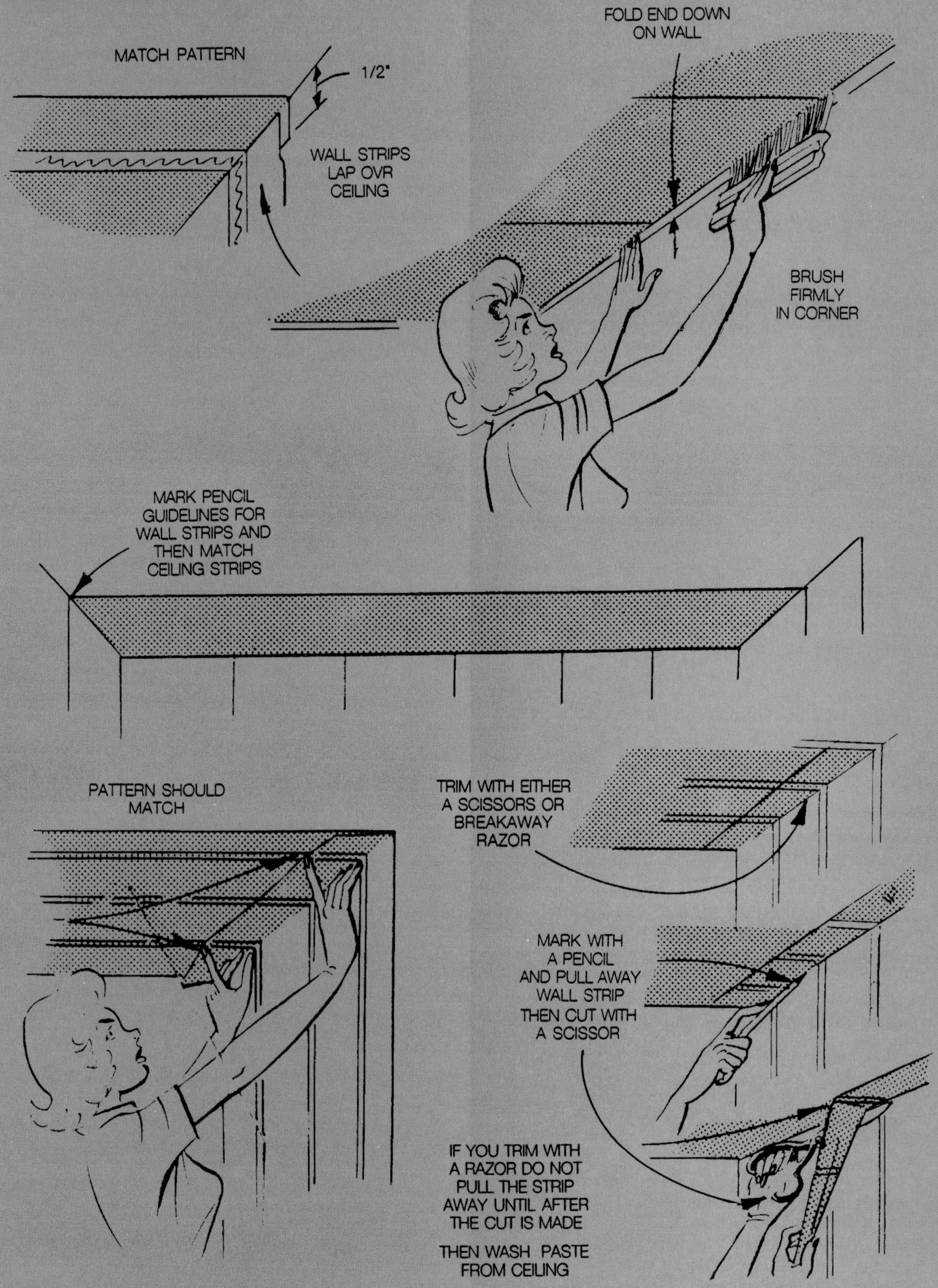

MATCH PATTERN

1/2"

WALL STRIPS LAP OVR CEILING

FOLD END DOWN ON WALL

BRUSH FIRMLY IN CORNER

MARK PENCIL GUIDELINES FOR WALL STRIPS AND THEN MATCH CEILING STRIPS

PATTERN SHOULD MATCH

TRIM WITH EITHER A SCISSORS OR BREAKAWAY RAZOR

MARK WITH A PENCIL AND PULL AWAY WALL STRIP THEN CUT WITH A SCISSOR

IF YOU TRIM WITH A RAZOR DO NOT PULL THE STRIP AWAY UNTIL AFTER THE CUT IS MADE

THEN WASH PASTE FROM CEILING

TECHNIQUES: PASTING THE WALL

WHILE MOST wallcovering is hung by brushing or rolling adhesive to the back of the covering, some types are best hung if the adhesive is applied to the wall. This is especially true with wallcovering that is a extremely rigid and others that are very delicate. The manufacturer of your covering will make specific recommendations as to how their material should be hung. If you choose the pasting-the-wall route as recommended by the manufacturer of your wallcovering and if your covering is tightly rolled or extremely springy, re-roll after cutting each length so it will hang flat against the wall rather than curl up. In fact, if the strip has a tendency to curl, the adhesive may not be effective.

When pasting a wall it is extremely important that the surface be primed or "sized" as recommended so the adhesive will not dry up in spots. This occasionally happens with gypsum board walls where the paper covering will tend to absorb the moisture in the adhesive.

The trick to pasting a wall is not to be sloppy when applying the adhesive. To guide you when positioning the strips, run a faint pencil line where each seam will fall. Since the adhesive is colorless you will be able to see the line and slide the first strip in place. Mark the position of subsequent strips so you know where to stop applying adhesive. Extend the adhesive only about 1/2 inch beyond the pencil line and when you are near the ceiling or baseboard (and even the corner) discard the roller for a brush and carefully brush adhesive on those areas you could not reach with the roller.

After each strip is hung, brush towards the seam and then roll. If you note an edge curling up, pull up the strip slightly, apply adhesive with a brush to the dry area and press the covering back in place. Roll toward the seam to push out any excess adhesive.

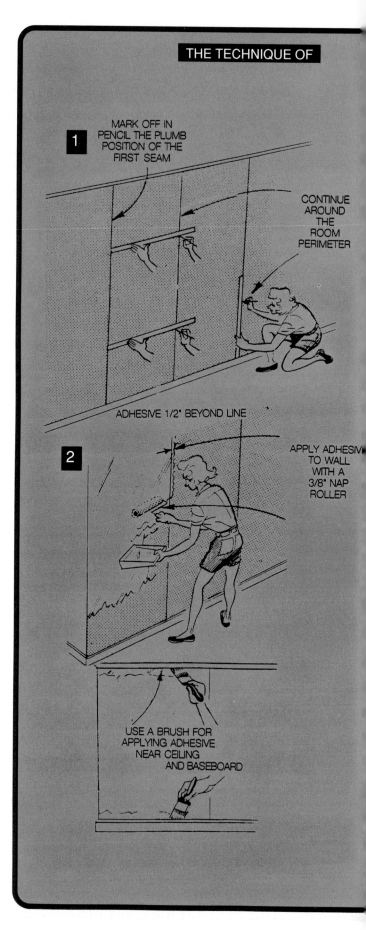

THE TECHNIQUE OF

1 MARK OFF IN PENCIL THE PLUMB POSITION OF THE FIRST SEAM

CONTINUE AROUND THE ROOM PERIMETER

ADHESIVE 1/2" BEYOND LINE

2

APPLY ADHESIVE TO WALL WITH A 3/8" NAP ROLLER

USE A BRUSH FOR APPLYING ADHESIVE NEAR CEILING AND BASEBOARD

PASTING THE WALL INSTEAD OF THE COVERING

3

CUT STRIP ABOUT 4" LONGER THAN ACTUAL CEILING HEIGHT

ABOUT 2"

4

ROLL UP EACH STRIP TO REMOVE CURL

FLUSH DOOR MAKES AN EXCELLENT WORK TABLE

5

STARTING AT THE TOP PRESS STRIP TO WALL

MAKE CERTAIN THE EDGE IS ALONG THE PENCIL LINE

7 FT. STEP LADDER

BRUSH DOWN AND TOWARD BOTH EDGES

WORKING WITH "PRE-PASTED" ROLLS

In an effort to further simplify and make hanging wallcovering more popular, manufacturers have applied to the back of the wallcovering a coating of the type adhesive best for that particular covering. All the consumer need do is to immerse the pre-cut strip in cool water, and allow time for the water to loosen the adhesive. Then book and hang as with a strip that was pasted. So popular is the pre-pasted covering that over seventy-five percent of all covering sold is this type.

Molded plastic water troughs for hanging this type of covering are very economical, but if you rest a trough filled with water on the floor you run the danger of splashing the water when removing the soaked strip which can be quite messy. Using a bathtub is an alternative option that homeowners have used for years but if the room you are covering is too far away from the tub spread some old towels or newspaper on the workroom floor and rest your trough between two bricks so it will not tip or move while you dip and extract each pre-cut length.

A better way is to set up your worktable as you would for pasting each strip (layers of newspapers or a protective sheet of vinyl) and then brush or roll on a "pre-pasted activator" on each strip, available where you purchase your wallcovering.

The use of a pre-pasted activator eliminates the need for a trough or bathtub to soak the wallcovering and also provides additional advantages. For instance, pre-pasted wall coverings often need more working time, better slip and extra adhesion. Activators are used undiluted and give the added protection of a full biocide system with both an in-can preservative to protect the activator in its wet state and a mold and mildewcide to protect the dried film on the wall. These pre-pasted activators are packaged in half gallon and larger sizes. One gallon is enough for 10 single rolls.

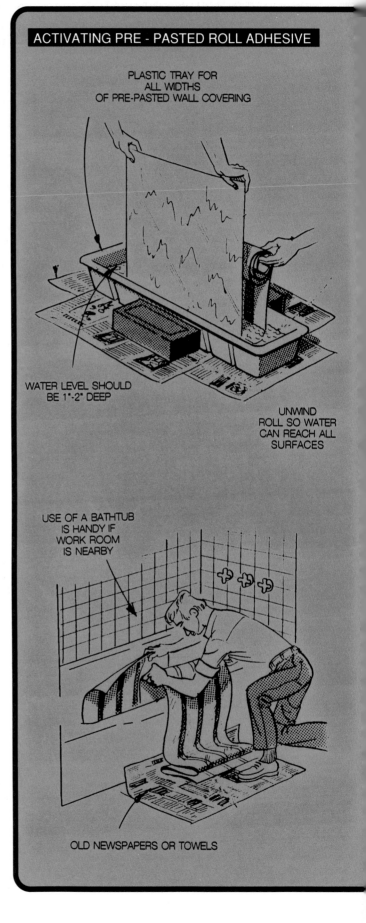

ACTIVATING PRE - PASTED ROLL ADHESIVE

PLASTIC TRAY FOR ALL WIDTHS OF PRE-PASTED WALL COVERING

WATER LEVEL SHOULD BE 1"-2" DEEP

UNWIND ROLL SO WATER CAN REACH ALL SURFACES

USE OF A BATHTUB IS HANDY IF WORK ROOM IS NEARBY

OLD NEWSPAPERS OR TOWELS

APPLYING A PRE - PASTED ACTIVATOR

PRE-PASTED
ACTIVATOR IS
APPLIED
UNDILUTED

USE A BRUSH
OR ROLLER

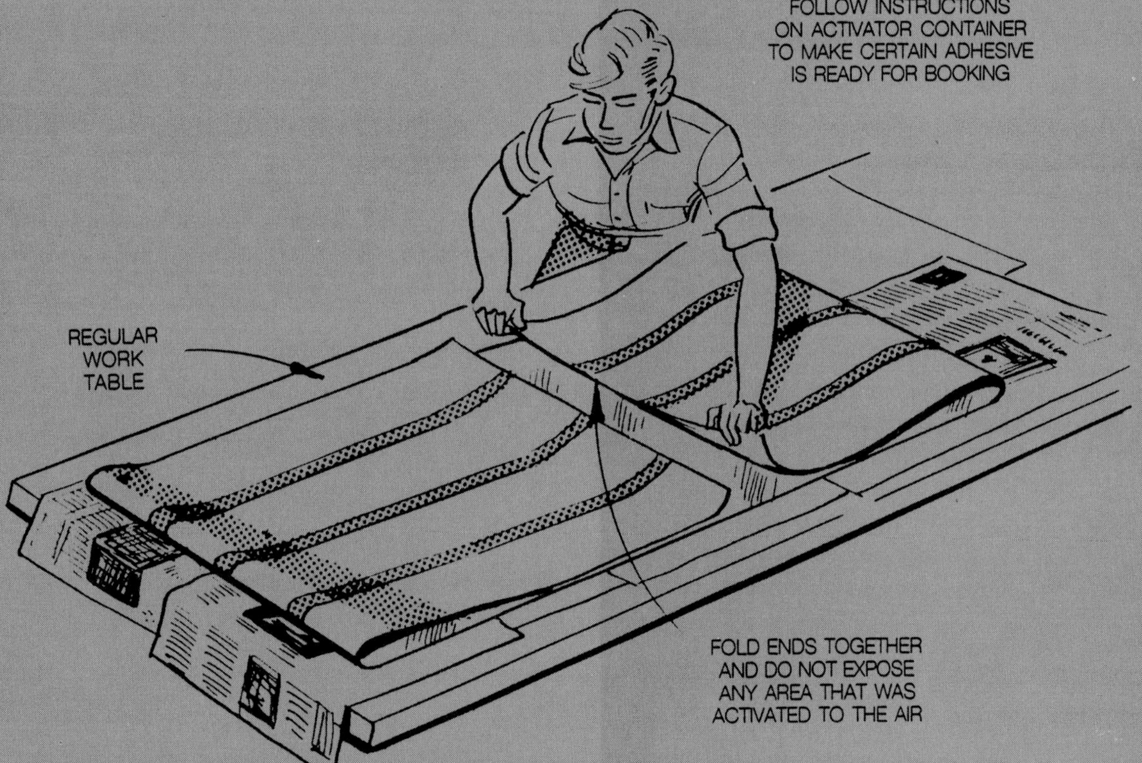

FOLLOW INSTRUCTIONS
ON ACTIVATOR CONTAINER
TO MAKE CERTAIN ADHESIVE
IS READY FOR BOOKING

REGULAR
WORK
TABLE

FOLD ENDS TOGETHER
AND DO NOT EXPOSE
ANY AREA THAT WAS
ACTIVATED TO THE AIR

TRIMMING UNTRIMMED ROLLS

Trimming is a precise mechanical job best done at the factory but if the covering you select comes untrimmed you must do the trimming. A flat plywood covered work table, a steel straight edge at least three feet (four feet or longer is much better), a pair of dividers and a box of straight edge razor blades are your prime tools.

On untrimmed rolls you will see identification marks along the edges that indicate how much should be trimmed. Never attempt to trim a roll with a scissor; rather, use one of the two techniques shown. After each strip has been cut to the proper length, some pros carefully book a strip (depending upon the type covering) and then trim the edges in one sweep. However, we prefer cutting through a single layer by moving a straight edge down the side.

Rather than follow the printed trim marks which can be 1/16" wide, lay the covering on a piece of plywood and use a pair of dividers to pinpoint the edge to be trimmed. Set the divider so it spans the edge just a hair beyond the printed trim mark. If you do not have a pair of dividers, make your own from two push pins driven through a soft wood paint-mixing paddle as shown. Then rest your straight edge against the pins. Place a third pin on the opposite side to hold the straight edge down as shown, and cut a low angle with a sharp razor.

Razor blades will dull quickly and when you notice the cut has a slightly ragged edge, discard the blade for a new one. When trimming it is better not to have the blade mounted in a handle; grasping the straight edge of the blade (which is not sharp) gives you better control over the cut which should be vertical. Also, you will find cutting at a very low angle will produce a better cut because the slicing movement of the blade is used to make the cut rather than just the tip. Experiment a few times and you will note the difference!

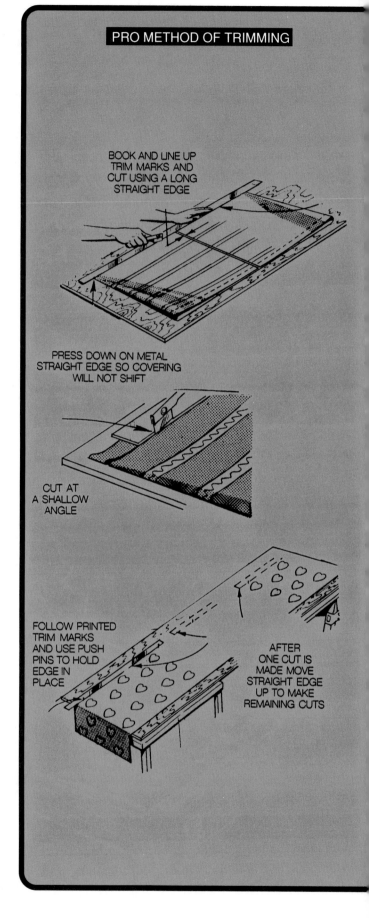

PRO METHOD OF TRIMMING

BOOK AND LINE UP TRIM MARKS AND CUT USING A LONG STRAIGHT EDGE

PRESS DOWN ON METAL STRAIGHT EDGE SO COVERING WILL NOT SHIFT

CUT AT A SHALLOW ANGLE

FOLLOW PRINTED TRIM MARKS AND USE PUSH PINS TO HOLD EDGE IN PLACE

AFTER ONE CUT IS MADE MOVE STRAIGHT EDGE UP TO MAKE REMAINING CUTS

RECOMMENDED TRIMMING METHOD FOR THE HOMEOWNER

PUSH PINS THRU WOOD

DISTANCE FROM EDGE

1 DIVIDERS USED TO MARK OFF TRIM FROM EDGE

REGULAR PAINT MIXER

2

OR MAKE YOUR OWN GUIDE FROM A PAINT MIXER AND PUSH PINS

PUSH STRAIGHT EDGE AGAINST PINS

4

USE PUSH PINS TO PREVENT IT FROM SHIFTING

3

LOCATING HOLES LEFT BY DIVIDERS

WHEN RAZOR REACHES THE END OF STRAIGHT EDGE LEAVE THE BLADE IN THE CUT AND MOVE STRAIGHT EDGE DOWN TO CONTINUE TRIMMING

CORRECTING COMMON FAULTS

BLISTERS, lifting edges and large tears that require a patch are the three most common wallcovering faults. Blisters usually occur either when an area does not have enough adhesive or when the strip was not completely brushed so the adhesive can make a firm contact with the wall. Blisters are most noticeable after the covering is hung and the adhesive has been allowed to dry for a day or so. The remedy is simple: make a slit in the shape of a cross, force adhesive on the inside and press flat. If the covering has a pattern carefully cut on a line so when both sides where the slit was made are back in place the cut will not be visible. Then roll from the outside toward the slit to force out the excess adhesive.

Edges that have lifted are also quite common. In such instances, pull the edge away until a slight resistance indicates you have reached the area that is adhered to the surface; then apply either the wallcovering adhesive originally used or regular white multi-purpose glue. In fact, lifting is so common special adhesives are available in tube form for this purpose. After the adhesive is brushed on both the wall and the edge that lifted, press the wall covering back in place and roll so any excess adhesive will flow from the slit. Wash the area with clean water.

Patching a tear requires the same "double cutting" technique described when turning an outside corner. First, cut a piece of covering slightly larger than the damaged area and paste it over the torn section, making certain the pattern matches. Then, with a sharp razor, carefully cut through the patch and through the wallcovering as shown. Remove the patch and the covering underneath, apply adhesive to the patch and set in place.

Often an outside corner will be nicked to a point where patching the edge is just about impossible. In such instances, clear preformed plastic edging is available. Not only does this plastic hold the patch in place, but it protects the corner from future nicks.

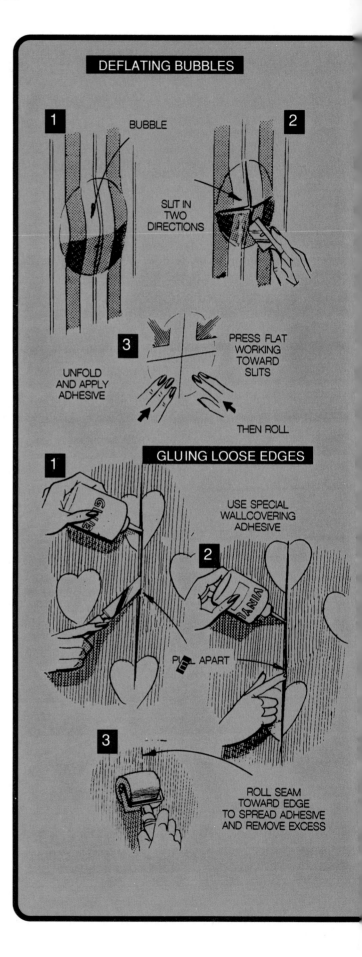

DEFLATING BUBBLES

1 BUBBLE

2 SLIT IN TWO DIRECTIONS

3 UNFOLD AND APPLY ADHESIVE

PRESS FLAT WORKING TOWARD SLITS

THEN ROLL

GLUING LOOSE EDGES

1

2 USE SPECIAL WALLCOVERING ADHESIVE

PEEL APART

3 ROLL SEAM TOWARD EDGE TO SPREAD ADHESIVE AND REMOVE EXCESS

PATCHING VIA THE "DOUBLE CUT" METHOD

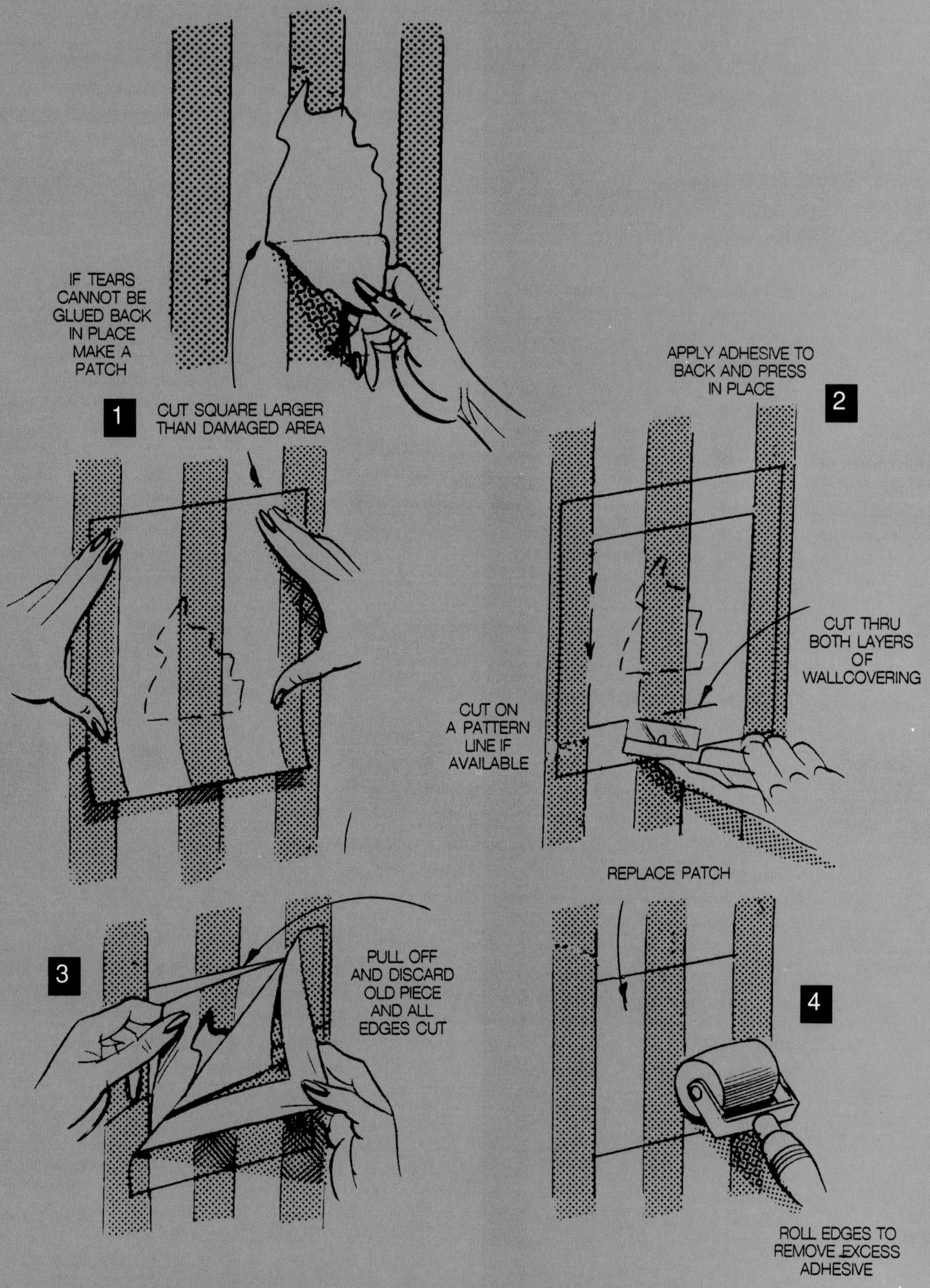

IF TEARS
CANNOT BE
GLUED BACK
IN PLACE
MAKE A
PATCH

1 CUT SQUARE LARGER
THAN DAMAGED AREA

APPLY ADHESIVE TO
BACK AND PRESS
IN PLACE **2**

CUT ON
A PATTERN
LINE IF
AVAILABLE

CUT THRU
BOTH LAYERS
OF
WALLCOVERING

3 PULL OFF
AND DISCARD
OLD PIECE
AND ALL
EDGES CUT

REPLACE PATCH

4

ROLL EDGES TO
REMOVE EXCESS
ADHESIVE

WALLCOVERING GLOSSARY

Abstract: A design that does not directly resemble natural forms.

All-over Design: A design, usually floral in theme, that extensively and evenly covers the wallcovering surface.

Basket-weave Designs: An embossing or printing effect that simulates the over and under look of basket-weaving.

Bolt: The yardage contained in a commercial package of wallcovering: single roll, double roll, or triple roll.

Booking: In the pasting stage, the folding of pasted wallcovering strips surface to surface simplifies handling and to relaxe the material.

Border: a narrow strip of wallcovering often used just under the ceiling or around windows.

Cellulose Paste: A non-staining, odorless adhesive which is often used in hanging natural materials such as silks and linens.

Chair Rail: The molding placed on a wall at chairback height.

Coating: A protective layer of plastic or vinyl applied to wallcoverings to make them washable and more durable.

Color Run: A wallcovering production run made from the same batch of dyes and inks, assuring consistent colors from roll to roll. Usually identified by lot or run number.

Colorways: A given combination of colors in a pattern. Most wallcovering patterns come in two to four colorways.

Companion Wallcoverings: A wallcovering specifically designed, patterned, and colored to harmonize with another, such as a stripe with floral; texture with plaid.

Cornice: The horizontal molding applied to finish the top of a wall.

Correlated: A term used instead of matching to explain variations in tone from one material to the next, i.e., from fabric to wallcovering.

Cove Ceiling: Ceiling which is rounded where it meets the wall.

Dado: The wall space between baseboard and chair rail.

Documentary: A design inspired by authentic sources usually before the turn of the century.

Double Cutting: The technique whereby a top strip overlaps a bottom strip and a cut is made through both strips. Remove the excess from both; the top strip will fit perfectly.

Embossing: A raised effect, fashioned by impressing a design onto a wallcovering, as opposed to printing it with ink.

Ground: The background color on which the wallcovering pattern is printed or embossed.

Lining: A material used as a base on a wall to provide a smooth surface for wallcoverings.

Match: An arrangement of a design for the continuous flow of pattern on the wall; i.e, straight across, diagonal, drop, or random.

Matte Finish: A dull finish.

Moire: A water silk effect on wallcoverings.

Monochromatic: One color, often ranging from light to dark values.

Mural: A walllcovering in which a single subject is printed across several strips.

Peelable Wallcoverings: A wallcovering in which top layer strips away without steaming or scraping, leaving a thin residue of paper or paste on the wall which can be easily removed.

Pre-pasted: A wallcovering pre-treated with adhesive before packaging.

Pre-trimmed: A wallcovering from which edges have been trimmed before packaging so it is ready for installation.

Primer/Sealer: A preparatory coat applied to walls before hanging wallcovering.

Railroading: The horizontal rather than vertical installation of wallcovering strips.

Repeat: The vertical distance between identical points in a wallcovering design.

Scrubbable: A wallcovering designed for cleaning with a soft-bristled brush and a mild detergent.

Seam: A line formed where two strips of wallcovering join together.

Single Roll: A length of wallcovering traditionally used as the basis of price.

Size: Sealer used to prepare the wall for better adhesion before wallcovering is applied.

Stain Resistant Wallcoverings: A wallcovering to which a coating -- a layer of plastic or vinyl -- has been added to make it stain resistant.

Straight Edge: A trimming or cutting guide.

Strippable Wallcoverings: A wallcovering which can be completely removed from the wall without steaming.

Vinyl: A plastic, flexible wallcovering material.

Wallcoverings: Flexible wall decorations prepared and sold in roll form.

Wallpaper: A paper-based wallcovering.

Wall Preparation: The various steps required before the installation of wallcoverings -- cleaning, smoothing, and repairing cracks.

Washable: A wallcovering designed for cleaning with a sponge and mild soap and water.

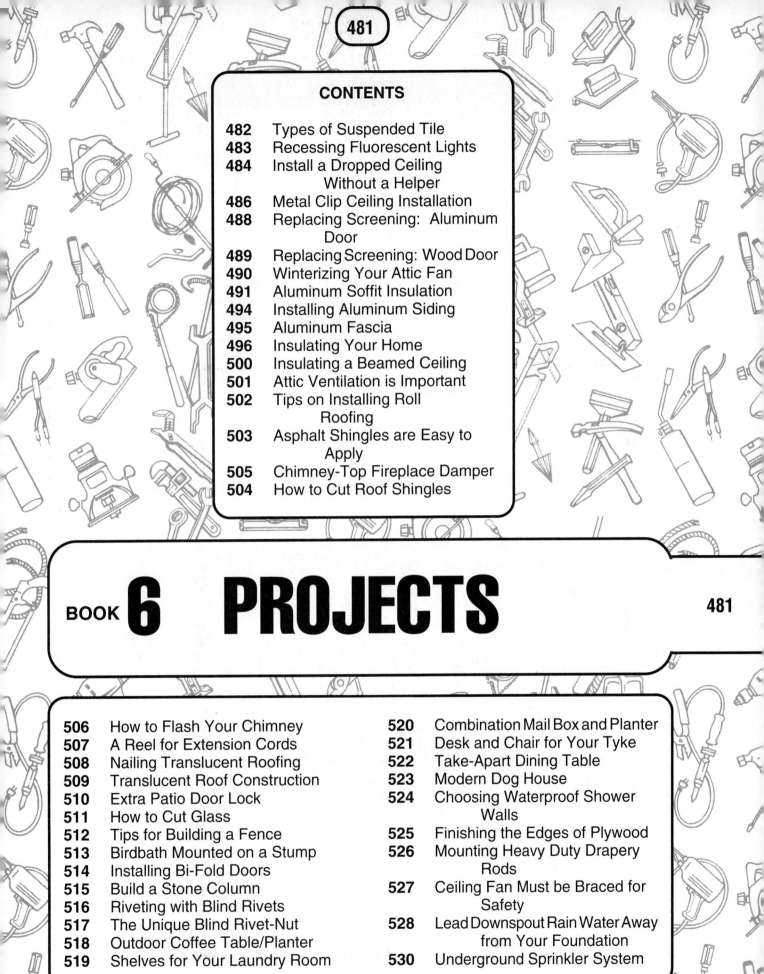

CONTENTS

482 Types of Suspended Tile
483 Recessing Fluorescent Lights
484 Install a Dropped Ceiling Without a Helper
486 Metal Clip Ceiling Installation
488 Replacing Screening: Aluminum Door
489 Replacing Screening: Wood Door
490 Winterizing Your Attic Fan
491 Aluminum Soffit Insulation
494 Installing Aluminum Siding
495 Aluminum Fascia
496 Insulating Your Home
500 Insulating a Beamed Ceiling
501 Attic Ventilation is Important
502 Tips on Installing Roll Roofing
503 Asphalt Shingles are Easy to Apply
505 Chimney-Top Fireplace Damper
504 How to Cut Roof Shingles

BOOK 6 PROJECTS

506 How to Flash Your Chimney
507 A Reel for Extension Cords
508 Nailing Translucent Roofing
509 Translucent Roof Construction
510 Extra Patio Door Lock
511 How to Cut Glass
512 Tips for Building a Fence
513 Birdbath Mounted on a Stump
514 Installing Bi-Fold Doors
515 Build a Stone Column
516 Riveting with Blind Rivets
517 The Unique Blind Rivet-Nut
518 Outdoor Coffee Table/Planter
519 Shelves for Your Laundry Room

520 Combination Mail Box and Planter
521 Desk and Chair for Your Tyke
522 Take-Apart Dining Table
523 Modern Dog House
524 Choosing Waterproof Shower Walls
525 Finishing the Edges of Plywood
526 Mounting Heavy Duty Drapery Rods
527 Ceiling Fan Must be Braced for Safety
528 Lead Downspout Rain Water Away from Your Foundation
530 Underground Sprinkler System

TYPES OF SUSPENDED CEILING TILE

While suspended ceiling tile is available in a wide range of textures and embossed patterns, the actual tiles can be made of different materials. Most tiles are made from either wood or mineral fiber.

You will also find semi-rigid fiberglass tiles covered with embossed vinyl. These tiles are fairly flexible, which can be convenient if you mount your gridwork two inches from the ceiling. Plastic foam tiles are also available.

Since suspended ceilings give the homeowner the option to install recessed ceiling light fixtures, a number of translucent panels are available to cover the lights. And if you must have air circulation from above, a panel made of 1/2-inch plastic squares is used. All suspended ceiling panels fit either a 2x4- or 2x2-foot opening, and are held in place by gravity. If you have a suspended ceiling in a very small room when you open or close the door the change in air pressure may lift the tiles and make a noise. In such cases a piece of double-sided adhesive tape applied to the edge of the T-frame solves the problem.

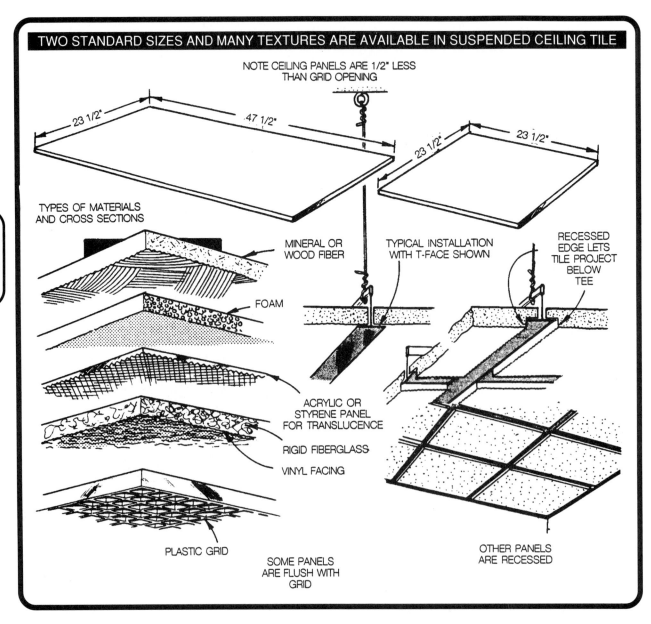

TWO STANDARD SIZES AND MANY TEXTURES ARE AVAILABLE IN SUSPENDED CEILING TILE

NOTE CEILING PANELS ARE 1/2" LESS THAN GRID OPENING

23 1/2"
47 1/2"
23 1/2"
23 1/2"

TYPES OF MATERIALS AND CROSS SECTIONS

MINERAL OR WOOD FIBER

TYPICAL INSTALLATION WITH T-FACE SHOWN

RECESSED EDGE LETS TILE PROJECT BELOW TEE

FOAM

ACRYLIC OR STYRENE PANEL FOR TRANSLUCENCE

RIGID FIBERGLASS

VINYL FACING

PLASTIC GRID

SOME PANELS ARE FLUSH WITH GRID

OTHER PANELS ARE RECESSED

RECESSING FLUORESCENT LIGHTS

Recessing lighting fixtures for your suspended ceiling can be either difficult or simple to install, depending upon the distance between the gridwork and the joists above. Suspended ceilings were initially used in basement renovations where the ceiling height was almost always less than 8 feet. With a suspended ceiling you can install lighting fixtures a few ways: either attach your fixture to the surface of the gridwork, or recess it completely.

The drop-in fixtures designed especially for suspended ceilings represent your best buy in the two-light 48" fluorescent only if you have 5" of space above the gridwork. However, if you must keep the ceiling as close to the beams as possible, a minimum of 2 inches is necessary to place the panels in the gridwork, you can mount individual 40 watt strip fluorescents between the joists.

Keep the tubes about 10" on center and staple aluminum foil to the nearby joists for added reflection. With this type of arrangement you also have the option to use only one fluorescent strip and frame the gridwork so you end up with a 12" x 48" (or 24") recessed light. Of course, you can recess incandescent fixtures between the joists, but we recommend fluorescent lights because they give you more light per dollar. Not only do fluorescent bulbs last up to 24 times longer than incandescent bulbs but they consume 1/3 to 1/2 the amount of electricity for the same amount of light, depending upon the bulb. And the newer fluorescent bulbs give you the same type of light heretofore found only in incandescent bulbs.

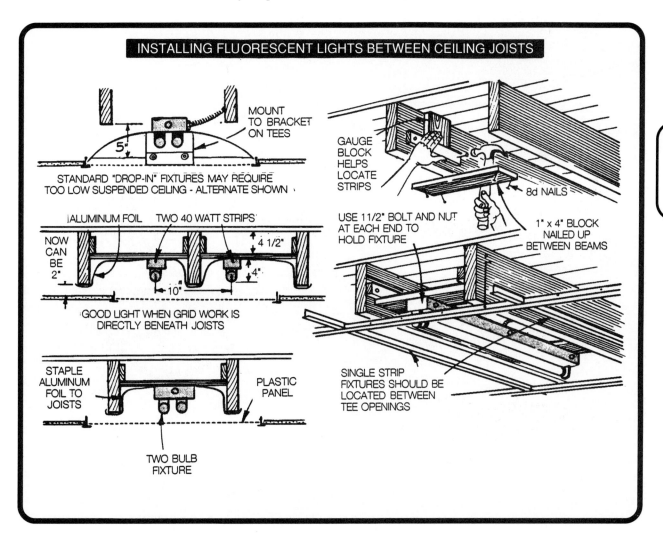

INSTALLING FLUORESCENT LIGHTS BETWEEN CEILING JOISTS

INSTALLING A DROPPED CEILING WITHOUT A HELPER

Slots in the main Ts are punched an exact 24 inches apart to fit the locking prong of the cross Ts. Ceiling panels are a half inch smaller in length and width for easy insertion. Here this 2x4 foot sculptured fiberglass panel is put in place. Note the flexibility.

A second pair of hands will make installing a dropped ceiling easier but if you must do the job by yourself the method illustrated will ensure professional results. A suspended ceiling calls for 10-or 12-foot long wall angles and main Ts, and either 2- or 4-foot cross Ts. Mount your wall angles first and, rather than snap a line along the wall as many manufacturers suggest, once you determine the ceiling height to clear pipes or accommodate lighting make a gauge from a scrap of lumber cut to the distance from the subflooring or joists to 1" below the pipes or electrical outlets you wish to clear. Rather than nail the wall angles in place, plan to use screws. Phillips head screws

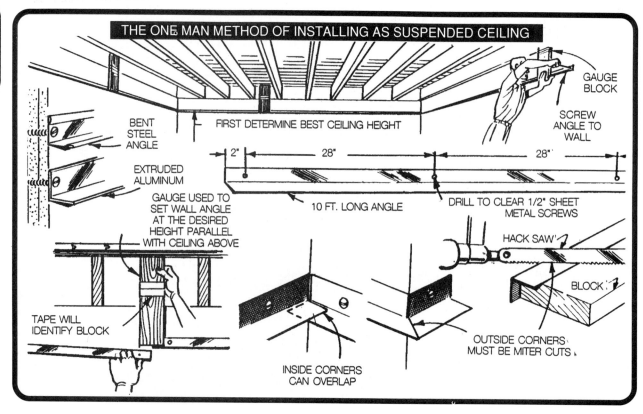

THE ONE MAN METHOD OF INSTALLING AS SUSPENDED CEILING

BENT STEEL ANGLE

EXTRUDED ALUMINUM

GAUGE USED TO SET WALL ANGLE AT THE DESIRED HEIGHT PARALLEL WITH CEILING ABOVE

FIRST DETERMINE BEST CEILING HEIGHT

GAUGE BLOCK

SCREW ANGLE TO WALL

2" 28" 28"

10 FT. LONG ANGLE

DRILL TO CLEAR 1/2" SHEET METAL SCREWS

HACK SAW

BLOCK

TAPE WILL IDENTIFY BLOCK

INSIDE CORNERS CAN OVERLAP

OUTSIDE CORNERS MUST BE MITER CUTS

about 3/4-inch long driven with a cordless screw-driver are ideal. Predrill the wall angle for the screws at about 3-foot intervals and keep the end hole 1-inch from the end. Starting with a corner, use your gauge to position the end hole on the wall. Loosely screw the first wall angle in place and then swing up the other end. Use the gauge when driving the screws home. Follow this procedure as you move around the the room.

　　　With all wall angles in place around the perimeter, locate the center of the room at right angles to the joists and snap a chalk line across the joists. Then screw 1 1/2-inch long screw eyes into the joists at about 4-foot intervals for the wire that will hold the main Ts. Rest the center main T on the wall angle and swing up the opposite end; use the same gauge to keep the main T at the same height as the wall angles. Hang the T with soft iron wire from the screw eye to the nearest prepunched hole in the main T.

　　　With the center main T in place, work at 4-foot intervals (if you plan to use 2x4-foot panels) toward the side walls and install the remaining main Ts. If you plan to use the popular 2x2-foot ceiling panels hang the main Ts 2 feet apart. The side panels closest to the wall will require some cutting.

A wide range of 2x4 and 2x2 floor panels are available with many different surface textures. Thee 2x2 foot panels have a recessed edge which adds another dimension to the normally flat ceiling surface.　All tile can be painted if desired.

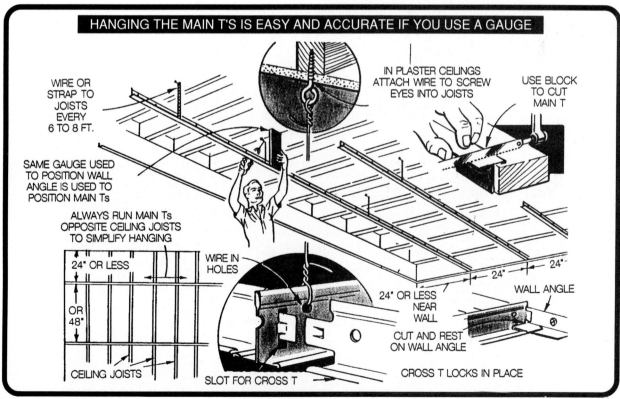

HANGING THE MAIN T'S IS EASY AND ACCURATE IF YOU USE A GAUGE

WIRE OR STRAP TO JOISTS EVERY 6 TO 8 FT.

SAME GAUGE USED TO POSITION WALL ANGLE IS USED TO POSITION MAIN Ts

ALWAYS RUN MAIN Ts OPPOSITE CEILING JOISTS TO SIMPLIFY HANGING

24" OR LESS

OR 48"

CEILING JOISTS

WIRE IN HOLES

SLOT FOR CROSS T

IN PLASTER CEILINGS ATTACH WIRE TO SCREW EYES INTO JOISTS

USE BLOCK TO CUT MAIN T

24"　24"

WALL ANGLE

24" OR LESS NEAR WALL

CUT AND REST ON WALL ANGLE

CROSS T LOCKS IN PLACE

The most popular size ceiling tile measures 12 x 12 inches and comes in a variety of surface textures and pastel colors. However, four foot long simulated wood planks in various widths are also available for those who like the wood plank appearance. These tiles are installed using the Armstrong "Easy Up" that consists of special metal strips and clips that hold the tile in place.

METAL TRACKS AND CLIPS SIMPLIFY CEILING TILE INSTALLATION

The suspended ceiling, often referred to as a "dropped ceiling", is very popular but for those who do not like the metal edging to show and need not gain access to the beams above, individual tiles can easily be installed on either wooden furring strips or metal rails. Wooden furring strips usually 1 x 2 inches in size represent a popular base on which to staple individual tile but an adhesive mounted tile is a good route to take if the ceiling is absolutely flat. However, the technique of using metal "furring strips" attached to the ceiling at right angles, and then adding clips to hold the tile in place, is superior in many ways to the wooden furring strip and stapled tile ceiling. It provides an strip and stapled tile ceiling. It does not wrap or twist and can be removed and replaced if you start from one end.

Tile is available in sealed cartons containing 40 square feet, but the metal tracks, clips and nails come in kit form, consisting of 12 4-foot tracks, 56 clips and 30 nails and 30 drywall screws. The metal tracks are attached through an existing ceiling into the joists or at right angles to exposed floor beams and then the tiles are slipped into place as shown. Aside from providing an inch or so more headroom than would result with a suspended ceiling, with the "Easy Up" system you can also remove and replace the ceiling if, of course, you start from one end.

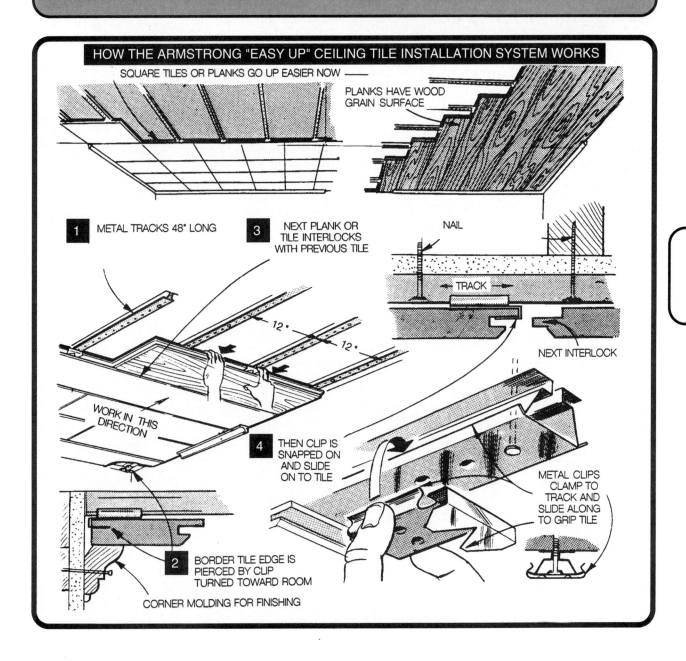

The installation technique of installing a planked ceiling is the same as working with square tile. Once you have determined the size of the border tile, and have installed the first row, work across the room. The clips grab the metal rail. You can use nails to hold the rail against the ceiling but driving 2 1/2 inch drywall screws with a cordless screwdriver is much easier because most homeowners find nailing underhand quite difficult.

HOW THE ARMSTRONG "EASY UP" CEILING TILE INSTALLATION SYSTEM WORKS

SQUARE TILES OR PLANKS GO UP EASIER NOW

PLANKS HAVE WOOD GRAIN SURFACE

1 METAL TRACKS 48" LONG

3 NEXT PLANK OR TILE INTERLOCKS WITH PREVIOUS TILE

NAIL

TRACK

NEXT INTERLOCK

12"

12"

WORK IN THIS DIRECTION

4 THEN CLIP IS SNAPPED ON AND SLIDE ON TO TILE

METAL CLIPS CLAMP TO TRACK AND SLIDE ALONG TO GRIP TILE

2 BORDER TILE EDGE IS PIERCED BY CLIP TURNED TOWARD ROOM

CORNER MOLDING FOR FINISHING

REPLACING SCREENING: ALUMINUM DOORS

Replacing the screening is relatively easy if you have a wooden screen door but if your door is aluminum the job is a bit more difficult. Screening in aluminum doors is held in place with vinyl splines that are press-fitted into a channel built into the frame. The spline serves two purposes. It holds the screening secure and helps make it taut.

First, remove the screen to be replaced and pry out the vinyl spline. Unless your spline is in excellent condition, we suggest you buy a new roll, but make sure it is the same size as the old spline material. Also, you will need a screening tool that has two rollers, a round-edged roller for pressing the screening into the groove before mounting the spline and the concave roller for rolling the spline in place.

Choose screening that is slightly larger than the opening and tape it temporarily in place with either masking or duct tape. Then run the roller in a top groove to seat the screening and follow by inserting a length of spline. as shown. Trim away the excess screening with a sharp utility knife. Easy!

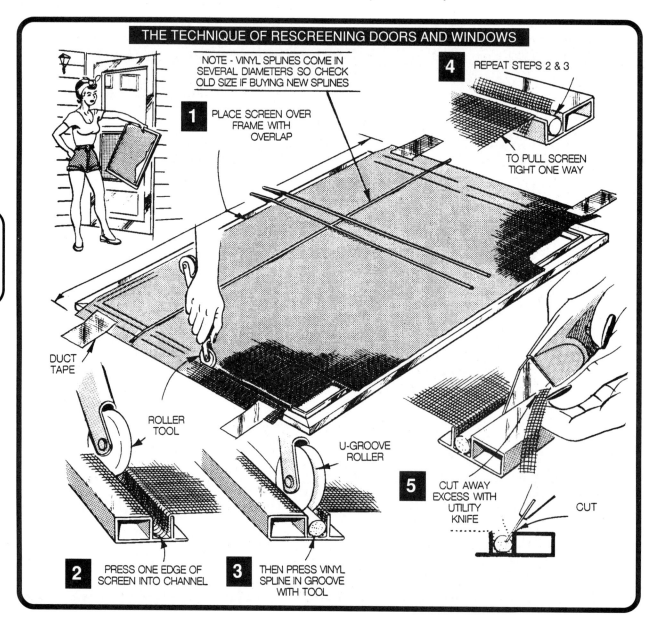

THE TECHNIQUE OF RESCREENING DOORS AND WINDOWS

NOTE - VINYL SPLINES COME IN SEVERAL DIAMETERS SO CHECK OLD SIZE IF BUYING NEW SPLINES

1 PLACE SCREEN OVER FRAME WITH OVERLAP

4 REPEAT STEPS 2 & 3

TO PULL SCREEN TIGHT ONE WAY

DUCT TAPE

ROLLER TOOL

U-GROOVE ROLLER

5 CUT AWAY EXCESS WITH UTILITY KNIFE

CUT

2 PRESS ONE EDGE OF SCREEN INTO CHANNEL

3 THEN PRESS VINYL SPLINE IN GROOVE WITH TOOL

REPLACING SCREEN DOOR SCREENING: WOOD DOORS

Screen doors always take a great deal of abuse, and the usual result is pierced screening that cannot be patched. Replacement requires only a staple gun.   Two types of screening are available: fiberglass, which is very pliable and requires a bit more care to install, and aluminum. The aluminum is just a bit easier to work and costs about 20 to 30 percent more than fiberglass.

Carefully remove all molding and pull the screening off the frame. If your molding was mounted with staples, remove the staples from the molding; the molding will be replaced later. The staples that hold the screening in place need not be removed; hammer them flush with the frame.

Next, choose your screening so it is slightly larger than the opening, fold over and staple the top in place. To produce a tight screen, staple the other end to a 1x3 and tilt the 1x3 down slightly while stapling the end.

Finally, staple the sides, using the extra inch width to pull the screening taut if necessary.

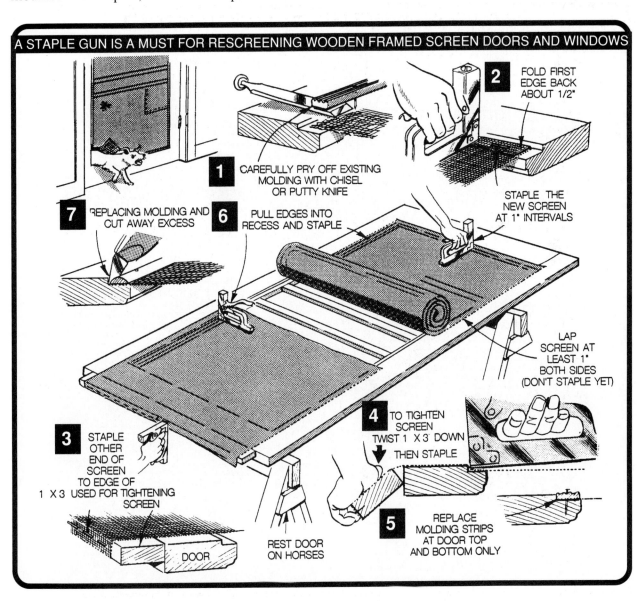

A STAPLE GUN IS A MUST FOR RESCREENING WOODEN FRAMED SCREEN DOORS AND WINDOWS

1 CAREFULLY PRY OFF EXISTING MOLDING WITH CHISEL OR PUTTY KNIFE

2 FOLD FIRST EDGE BACK ABOUT 1/2"

STAPLE THE NEW SCREEN AT 1" INTERVALS

7 REPLACING MOLDING AND CUT AWAY EXCESS

6 PULL EDGES INTO RECESS AND STAPLE

LAP SCREEN AT LEAST 1" BOTH SIDES (DON'T STAPLE YET)

3 STAPLE OTHER END OF SCREEN TO EDGE OF 1 X 3 USED FOR TIGHTENING SCREEN

DOOR

REST DOOR ON HORSES

4 TO TIGHTEN SCREEN TWIST 1 X 3 DOWN THEN STAPLE

5 REPLACE MOLDING STRIPS AT DOOR TOP AND BOTTOM ONLY

WINTERIZING YOUR ATTIC FAN

Before central air-conditioning, huge attic fans were used to provide "whole house" cooling, and these fans are still popular as they provide passable comfort at substantially less cost than central air-conditioning.

If you have such a fan you know the advantages—but you also know the louvres that open up when the fan starts are really not tight-fitting and therefore permit air to infiltrate into the unheated attic space above. Thus, your furnace or boiler must work harder to compensate for this heat loss.

What can you do to block this path of heat loss? One quick way is to cover the entire area with a sheet of vinyl, as show in the illustration.

This fan cover will cut down air infiltration but will only increase the R-value of the area slightly. Since it is impractical to temporarily install ceiling insulation for the winter season above the louvres, rigid foam panels can be mounted in a wooden frame nailed to the underside of the ceiling to achieve the desired R-value.

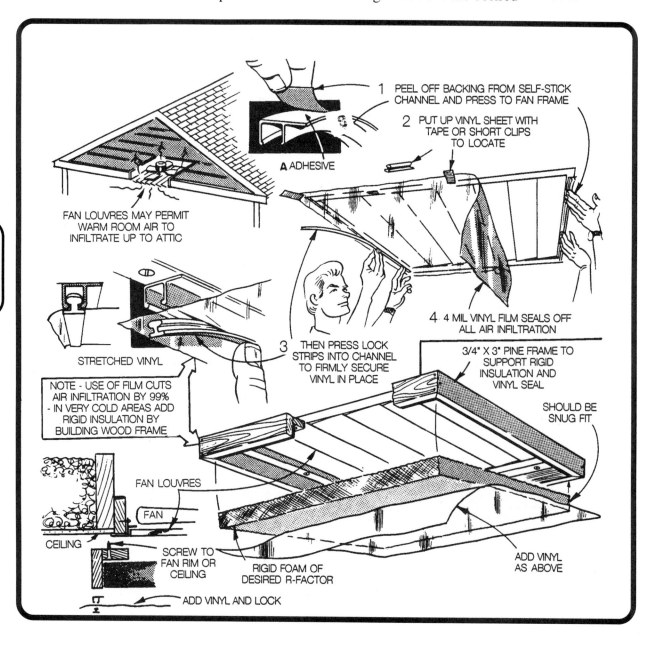

ALUMINUM SOFFIT INSTALLATION: Part I

If you have painted your roof underhang you know what a difficult and time-consuming job that can be, so comes painting time why not install a suspended aluminum soffit?

Aluminum siding and soffit systems have been around for decades but in the past installation was confined primarily to contractors. Manufacturers are now realizing that working with these pre-finished aluminum panels and molding is certainly within the capability of the do-it-yourselfer and are distributing all parts nationally.

Admittedly, installing a soffit (or aluminum siding) is a major home improvement project, but easy-to-use tools, easy-to-follow instructions and the high cost of professional contractors are good motivators! When you consider a soffit requires only three pieces of material — the "Frieze" molding nailed to the side of the house at the correct height, the L-shaped aluminum fascia that is ribbed to maintain rigidity, and the ribbed aluminum panels —the simplicity of the system is apparent. Beats painting!

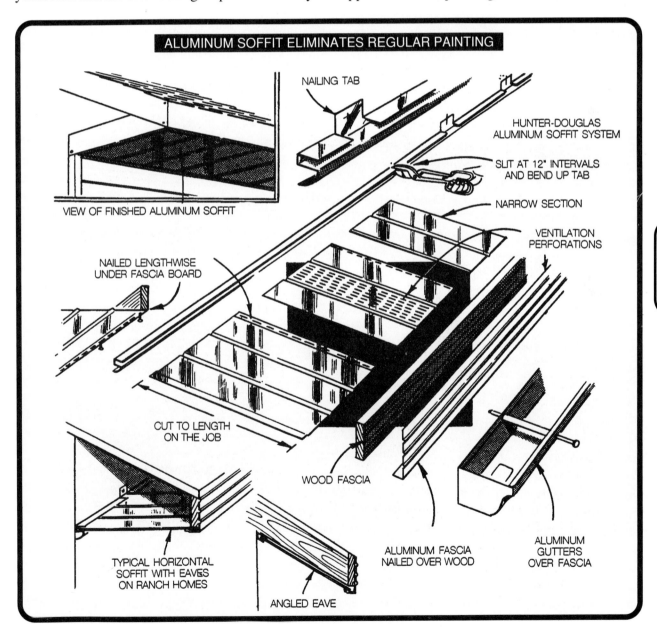

ALUMINUM SOFFIT ELIMINATES REGULAR PAINTING

NAILING TAB

HUNTER-DOUGLAS ALUMINUM SOFFIT SYSTEM

SLIT AT 12" INTERVALS AND BEND UP TAB

NARROW SECTION

VENTILATION PERFORATIONS

VIEW OF FINISHED ALUMINUM SOFFIT

NAILED LENGTHWISE UNDER FASCIA BOARD

CUT TO LENGTH ON THE JOB

WOOD FASCIA

TYPICAL HORIZONTAL SOFFIT WITH EAVES ON RANCH HOMES

ANGLED EAVE

ALUMINUM FASCIA NAILED OVER WOOD

ALUMINUM GUTTERS OVER FASCIA

PROJECTS

ALUMINUM SOFFIT INSTALLATION: Part II

Few tools are required to install an aluminum soffit: a level to make certain the line you snap for the molding along the wall is at the correct height, a utility knife to score flat sections if their width must be reduced, metal snips to cut the molding and fascia, and a fine-tooth plywood blade (mounted backward) for cutting the soffit sections to the correct length.

The sidewall molding and the fascia should always be cut with the snips, and on occasion the soffit panels can be snipped to size. However, a power saw with a jig accessory will make the best cut with the least amount of effort.

The wall molding is 1 1/2 inches deep and the lip of the aluminum fascia is 1 inch. In some instances where you elect not to cover the existing wooden fascia, the soffit panels can be mounted underneath by using a special fascia molding shown at the upper left. Slip the soffit section into the wall molding, insert the other end into the fascia molding and pull out slightly. Gravity and a friction fit hold it in place.

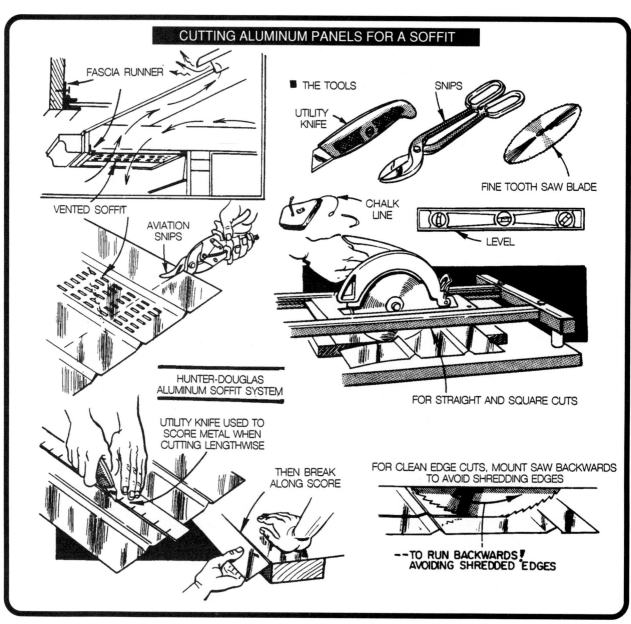

CUTTING ALUMINUM PANELS FOR A SOFFIT

FASCIA RUNNER

VENTED SOFFIT

AVIATION SNIPS

HUNTER-DOUGLAS ALUMINUM SOFFIT SYSTEM

UTILITY KNIFE USED TO SCORE METAL WHEN CUTTING LENGTHWISE

THEN BREAK ALONG SCORE

THE TOOLS

UTILITY KNIFE

SNIPS

FINE TOOTH SAW BLADE

CHALK LINE

LEVEL

FOR STRAIGHT AND SQUARE CUTS

FOR CLEAN EDGE CUTS, MOUNT SAW BACKWARDS TO AVOID SHREDDING EDGES

--TO RUN BACKWARDS! AVOIDING SHREDDED EDGES

ALUMINUM SOFFIT INSTALLATION: PART III

Starting a soffit installation begins with locating the "Frieze" molding on the outside wall at the desired height. This molding comes in a few shapes; the shape shown produces a square look and is used primarily where the existing wood siding will not be replaced or covered.

To mount the Frieze molding, cut and bend up a tab at about 12-inch intervals, as shown. Snap a chalk line along the wall and nail the molding in place with aluminum nails. It is easy to nail right through the aluminum.

Soffit material is available in either solid panels 12 feet long or with small vent holes for homes that have the attic area ventilated via the soffit. Measure from the inside of the molding to the fascia and cut about 1/4-inch less. One end will fit into the molding; the outer end is nailed to the wood fascia base.

Once the underhang is in place, add the aluminum fascia which is available in sizes from 4 to 8 inches wide. The lower edge is L-shaped so it will hide the nailheads.

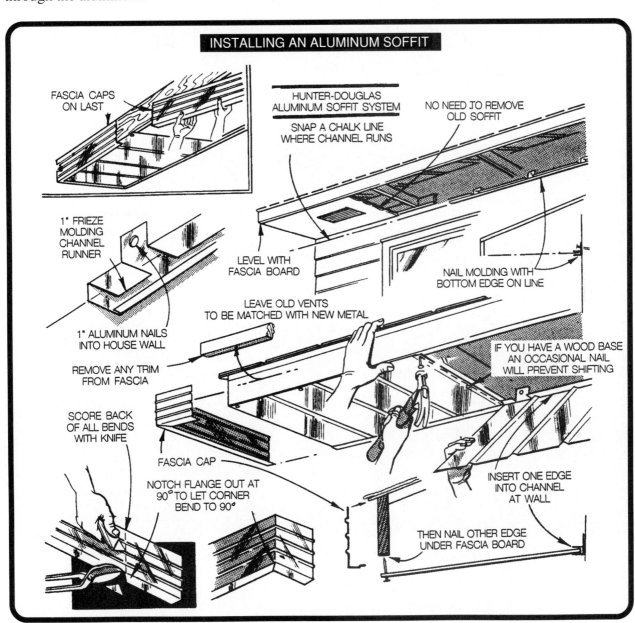

INSTALLING AN ALUMINUM SOFFIT

INSTALLING ALUMINUM SIDING

Aluminum siding has been used in both new construction and remodeling with the installation done almost exclusively by siding contractors. And while the contractor route is still the way to go if extensive two-story scaffolding is necessary, many single-story homes can be re-sided by the homeowner.

Most important in this era of high energy costs, if you are considering aluminum siding you have the opportunity to bring the wall R-value up to R-19 by sheathing the *exterior* with a rigid foam insulation board over which furring strips are nailed. Then add aluminum siding over the furring strips.

Siding is not difficult to install, but you must follow the basic rules. Aluminum expands and contracts at a different rate from the wood frame over which it is applied, so you cannot have tight fits against outside or inside corners, sill or door trims. Always leave at least a 1/8-inch space between the siding and trim, and never drive home the nails that hold the siding in place. Actually, siding should be *hung* to permit expansion and contraction.

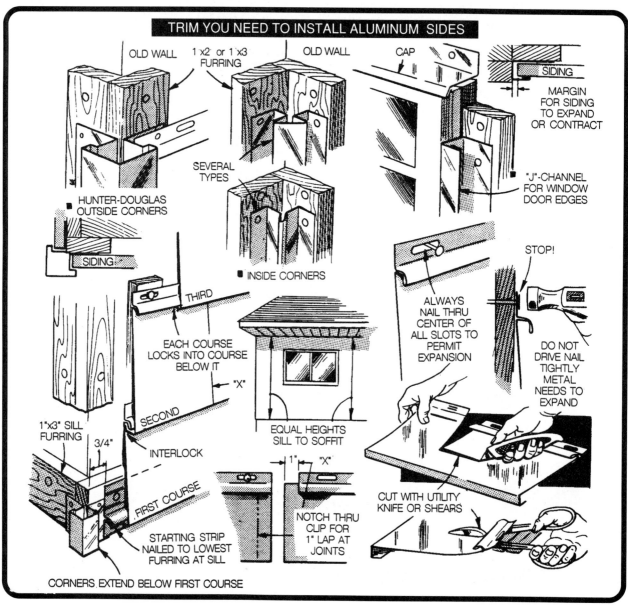

TRIM YOU NEED TO INSTALL ALUMINUM SIDES

OLD WALL

1"x2" or 1"x3" FURRING

OLD WALL

CAP

SIDING

MARGIN FOR SIDING TO EXPAND OR CONTRACT

HUNTER-DOUGLAS OUTSIDE CORNERS

SEVERAL TYPES

"J"-CHANNEL FOR WINDOW DOOR EDGES

SIDING

INSIDE CORNERS

THIRD

EACH COURSE LOCKS INTO COURSE BELOW IT

"X"

ALWAYS NAIL THRU CENTER OF ALL SLOTS TO PERMIT EXPANSION

STOP!

DO NOT DRIVE NAIL TIGHTLY METAL NEEDS TO EXPAND

SECOND

1"x3" SILL FURRING

3/4"

INTERLOCK

EQUAL HEIGHTS SILL TO SOFFIT

FIRST COURSE

1"

"X"

STARTING STRIP NAILED TO LOWEST FURRING AT SILL

NOTCH THRU CLIP FOR 1" LAP AT JOINTS

CUT WITH UTILITY KNIFE OR SHEARS

CORNERS EXTEND BELOW FIRST COURSE

ALUMINUM FASCIA

Aluminum fascia strips go well with an aluminum soffit.

Fascia strips are available in varying widths and lengths and are not butt-joined. Straight runs overlap, but the bottom and top should be snipped away so the ribs of one nestles into the ribs of the overlapping piece.

Inside corners are trimmed at the top and bottom and then carefully bent over a block of wood for a sharp right-angle bend. After the L-shaped end is nailed to the fascia, the adjacent fascia laps over as shown. Note the lower section is cut away at a 45-degree angle to produce a mitered joint at the bottom.

Outside corners are pre-cut as shown and then bent around the corner after the section of fascia is nailed in place. Note the lower lip forms a 45-degree miter. Fascia lengths are nailed to the existing wooden base with l-inch white aluminum nails. You need not pre-drill the aluminum to accommodate the nail; you can easily drive through the layer of aluminum. For nailing through two layers, first punch a hole with an ice pick or awl.

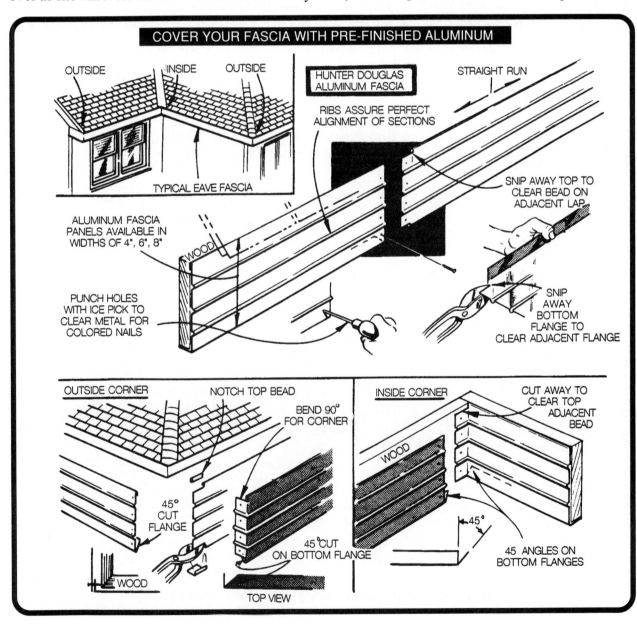

COVER YOUR FASCIA WITH PRE-FINISHED ALUMINUM

OUTSIDE   INSIDE   OUTSIDE

HUNTER DOUGLAS ALUMINUM FASCIA

STRAIGHT RUN

RIBS ASSURE PERFECT ALIGNMENT OF SECTIONS

TYPICAL EAVE FASCIA

SNIP AWAY TOP TO CLEAR BEAD ON ADJACENT LAP

ALUMINUM FASCIA PANELS AVAILABLE IN WIDTHS OF 4", 6", 8"

WOOD

SNIP AWAY BOTTOM FLANGE TO CLEAR ADJACENT FLANGE

PUNCH HOLES WITH ICE PICK TO CLEAR METAL FOR COLORED NAILS

OUTSIDE CORNER   NOTCH TOP BEAD

BEND 90° FOR CORNER

INSIDE CORNER

CUT AWAY TO CLEAR TOP ADJACENT BEAD

WOOD

45° CUT FLANGE

45° CUT ON BOTTOM FLANGE

45°

45 ANGLES ON BOTTOM FLANGES

WOOD

TOP VIEW

INSULATING YOUR HOME

We all know the ultimate short term result of insulating a home is measured in both yearly cost and personal comfort. With our small but steady inflation rate, and as the population and number of homes built increases, over the past three decades we have experienced enormous increases in the cost of energy — oil, natural gas and electricity. In some instances the increase has been sevenfold. For instance, compare the 1957 cost of 15 cents a gallon for oil to the present cost.

And natural gas does not present a more attractive profile either! Nor does coal, or electricity which is our most costly source of heating.

To combat the steady spiral of energy costs over the years we have developed levels of insulation for ceilings, walls and floors, which have been regularly upgraded as the cost of energy increased. The American Building Officials (CABO) recommendations for ceilings, walls and floors are shown in the illustration. While in some

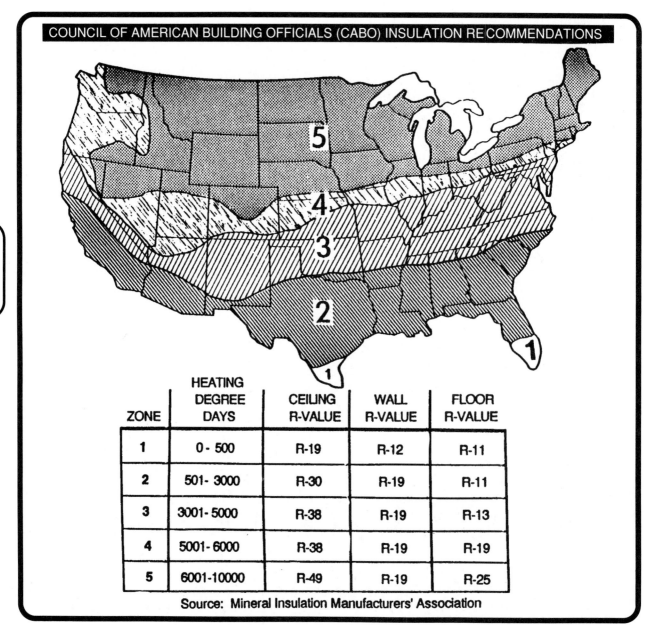

COUNCIL OF AMERICAN BUILDING OFFICIALS (CABO) INSULATION RECOMMENDATIONS

ZONE	HEATING DEGREE DAYS	CEILING R-VALUE	WALL R-VALUE	FLOOR R-VALUE
1	0 - 500	R-19	R-12	R-11
2	501 - 3000	R-30	R-19	R-11
3	3001 - 5000	R-38	R-19	R-13
4	5001 - 6000	R-38	R-19	R-19
5	6001 - 10000	R-49	R-19	R-25

Source: Mineral Insulation Manufacturers' Association

INCH AND TYPE OF NON-RIGID INSULATION REQUIRED FOR VARIOUS R-VALUES

TYPE	R-11	R-19	R-22	R-30	R-38
FIBERGLASS (batts or blankets)	3.5"	6"	6.5"	10"	12.5"
ROCK WOOL (batts or blankets)	3"	5.5"	6"	9"	10.5"
FIBERGLASS (loose fill)	5"	8.5"	10"	3.5"	17.5"
ROCK WOOL (loose fill)	4"	6.5"	7.5"	10.5"	13.5"
CELLULOSE (loose fill)	3"	5"	6"	8"	10.5"

parts of the country other energy codes are followed, the U.S. Department of Housing and Urban Development (HUD) and Minimum Property Standards (MPS) following the CABO recommendations for R-values of insulation produce the most savings.

Of course, it is literally impossible or cost effective to retrofit the nearly 100 million homes we have in the country and bring them up to the CABO levels of insulation, but by anticipating that our energy costs in the long run can only move up, all of us can adopt a simple policy to become more energy efficient as we repair and remodel. For instance, in most homes with open attics it is relatively easy to upgrade the ceiling levels of insulation to the CABO R-values, which incidentally closely parallel the Department of Energy code. With new construction it is especially easy to meet or even exceed these recommendations in walls, but with an existing house if you want to

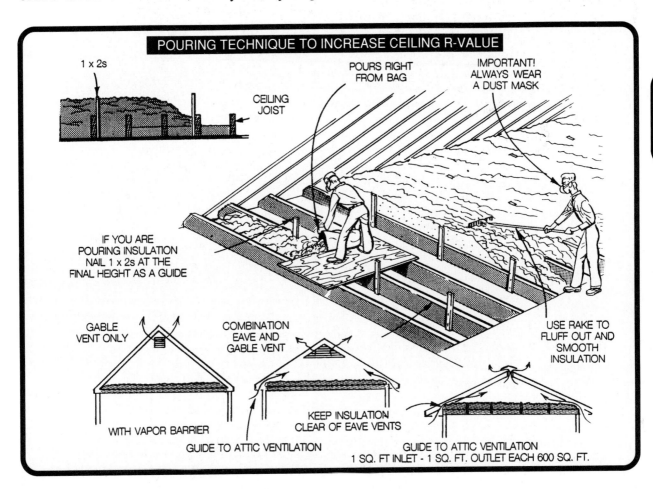

POURING TECHNIQUE TO INCREASE CEILING R-VALUE

1 x 2s

CEILING JOIST

POURS RIGHT FROM BAG

IMPORTANT! ALWAYS WEAR A DUST MASK

IF YOU ARE POURING INSULATION NAIL 1 x 2s AT THE FINAL HEIGHT AS A GUIDE

USE RAKE TO FLUFF OUT AND SMOOTH INSULATION

GABLE VENT ONLY

COMBINATION EAVE AND GABLE VENT

WITH VAPOR BARRIER

KEEP INSULATION CLEAR OF EAVE VENTS

GUIDE TO ATTIC VENTILATION

GUIDE TO ATTIC VENTILATION
1 SQ. FT INLET - 1 SQ. FT. OUTLET EACH 600 SQ. FT.

achieve the recommended levels short of gutting the interior — which is impractical — pumping insulation into the walls is a common practice. However, when going this route you really cannot evaluate the thoroughness of the job. For instance, how do you handle walls with horizontal fire stops when you do not or cannot locate the stops? And what happens to blown-in insulation around pipes, wires and ducts?

To make our homes more energy efficient you must also look at areas other than insulation. Check air infiltration, increase the R-value of windows, use automatic set-back thermostats, install high efficiency boilers and furnaces, live with lower room temperature settings, keep ceilings at a comfortable 8 feet (rather than the 10 feet some new homes feature), insulate basement walls to R-19 by using left-in-place forms made from styrene, just to mention a few additional ways we can conserve energy.

If you have poured insulation in your ceiling —mineral wool or cellulose — you can easily pour additional insulation over the existing level if the level is unfinished. As a guide, nail furring strips at regular intervals to indicate the height you must reach to achieve your desired R-value. Since the R-value of various poured insulation varies on each bag you purchase you should note how many inches are required for a specific R-value. The major consideration when adding loose insulation is that you do not interfere with venting the attic area, which can be easily done if you have a soffit. Use a plastic sheath between the roof joists or a baffle, as illustrated . Of course, if you have a roof gable or a ridge vent you need not be concerned. However, keep the insulation away from any lighting fixtures that may protrude through the ceiling .

Many homes have batt insulation in the ceiling and the R-value can be easily upgraded by

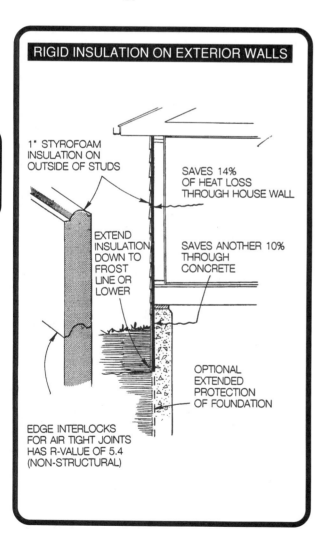

RIGID INSULATION ON EXTERIOR WALLS

1" STYROFOAM INSULATION ON OUTSIDE OF STUDS

SAVES 14% OF HEAT LOSS THROUGH HOUSE WALL

EXTEND INSULATION DOWN TO FROST LINE OR LOWER

SAVES ANOTHER 10% THROUGH CONCRETE

OPTIONAL EXTENDED PROTECTION OF FOUNDATION

EDGE INTERLOCKS FOR AIR TIGHT JOINTS HAS R-VALUE OF 5.4 (NON-STRUCTURAL)

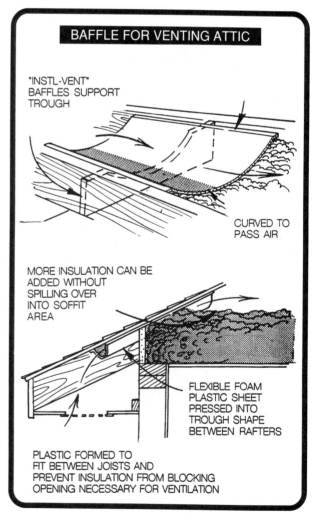

BAFFLE FOR VENTING ATTIC

"INSTL-VENT" BAFFLES SUPPORT TROUGH

CURVED TO PASS AIR

MORE INSULATION CAN BE ADDED WITHOUT SPILLING OVER INTO SOFFIT AREA

FLEXIBLE FOAM PLASTIC SHEET PRESSED INTO TROUGH SHAPE BETWEEN RAFTERS

PLASTIC FORMED TO FIT BETWEEN JOISTS AND PREVENT INSULATION FROM BLOCKING OPENING NECESSARY FOR VENTILATION

adding more batts or pouring loose insulation over the existing batts. Use an unfaced batt available in either rolled or single 4-foot sections because you want only one vapor barrier and that should be on the warm side closest to the ceiling. If you have some vintage batt insulation with a paper cover, it is a good idea to rip off the paper or cut slits in it before laying down your new batts. Rather than run your new unfaced batts in the same direction of the joists, for best results place them at right angles and butt the edges snugly together. Of course, do not block soffit vents, and keep the insulation away from any existing lighting fixtures.

If you have ever worked with insulation you know the mineral fibers scratch, and the dust involved requires you to use a long sleeve shirt, gloves, goggles and, most important, a mask that will filter the smaller fiber particles as you breathe.

Rigid installation also has earned a place in home construction to keep energy costs down.

The three most widely used types are the expanded polystyrene, the extruded polystyrene and isocyanurate. The extruded polystyrene foam has an R-value of 5 per one inch of thickness, expanded polystyrene which has an R-factor of 4 per one inch of thickness and the isocyanurate has an R-value of over 7 per inch. All are used to increase the R-value of walls and ceilings and the expanded polystyrene works well when insulating the exterior of a poured concrete foundation.

You have an excellent choice of insulating materials and only you can decide which fits your particular situation best. In new construction you can use a combination of mineral wool between the studs and rigid panels over the exterior sheathing before the final wall surface is applied. In this manner you can arrive at the desired wall **R-value**. If you are remodeling and are installing siding — aluminum or vinyl — you have the ideal opportunity to nail one of the rigid panels in placed and then attach the siding.

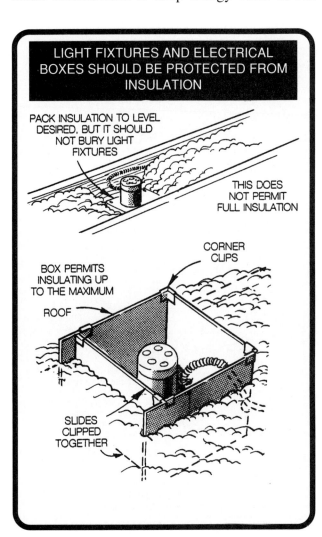

LIGHT FIXTURES AND ELECTRICAL BOXES SHOULD BE PROTECTED FROM INSULATION

PACK INSULATION TO LEVEL DESIRED, BUT IT SHOULD NOT BURY LIGHT FIXTURES

THIS DOES NOT PERMIT FULL INSULATION

CORNER CLIPS

BOX PERMITS INSULATING UP TO THE MAXIMUM

ROOF

SLIDES CLIPPED TOGETHER

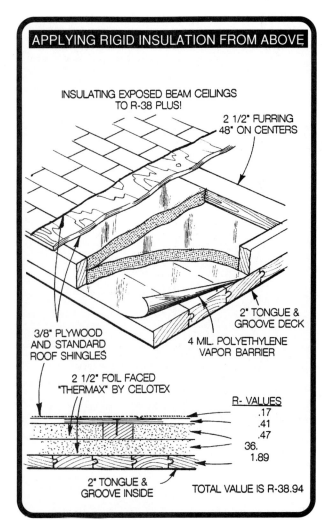

APPLYING RIGID INSULATION FROM ABOVE

INSULATING EXPOSED BEAM CEILINGS TO R-38 PLUS!

2 1/2" FURRING 48" ON CENTERS

2" TONGUE & GROOVE DECK

3/8" PLYWOOD AND STANDARD ROOF SHINGLES

4 MIL. POLYETHYLENE VAPOR BARRIER

2 1/2" FOIL FACED "THERMAX" BY CELOTEX

2" TONGUE & GROOVE INSIDE

R- VALUES
.17
.41
.47
36.
1.89

TOTAL VALUE IS R-38.94

INSULATING A BEAMED CEILING

The naturally finished beamed ceiling—usually 2x6 inch tongue and groove planks spanning beams four feet on centers— has two major advantages, ease of construction and virtually no maintenance. But this type ceiling also has a major fault; the only way to insulate the roof without disturbing the exposed beam arrangement is from the top. If you have this type of exposed beam ceiling here is a way to bring your R-factor up to over R-38.

First add a 4 mil polyethylene vapor barrier over the raw wood and cover the area with two layers of 2 1/4-inch-thick isocyanurate which has an R-value of over 7 per inch of thickness. The reason for using the two thinner layers rather than one thick one is that you can position a nailing strip to hold the lower panels in place and also provide a nailer for the sheathing to serve as a base for your shingles.

Rigid insulation is available in 4x8 sheets from your building supply dealer on special order.

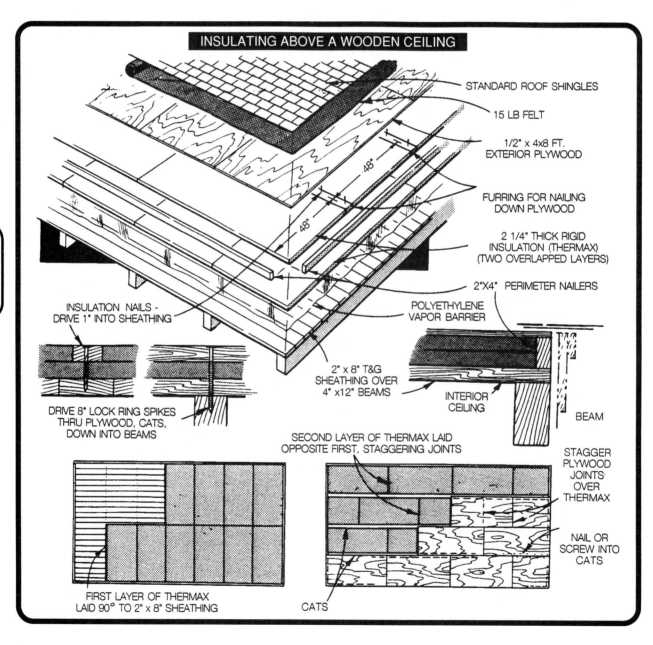

INSULATING ABOVE A WOODEN CEILING

- STANDARD ROOF SHINGLES
- 15 LB FELT
- 1/2" x 4x8 FT. EXTERIOR PLYWOOD
- FURRING FOR NAILING DOWN PLYWOOD
- 2 1/4" THICK RIGID INSULATION (THERMAX) (TWO OVERLAPPED LAYERS)
- 2"X4" PERIMETER NAILERS
- POLYETHYLENE VAPOR BARRIER

48"

48"

INSULATION NAILS - DRIVE 1" INTO SHEATHING

DRIVE 8" LOCK RING SPIKES THRU PLYWOOD, CATS, DOWN INTO BEAMS

2" x 8" T&G SHEATHING OVER 4" x12" BEAMS

INTERIOR CEILING

BEAM

STAGGER PLYWOOD JOINTS OVER THERMAX

NAIL OR SCREW INTO CATS

FIRST LAYER OF THERMAX LAID 90° TO 2" x 8" SHEATHING

SECOND LAYER OF THERMAX LAID OPPOSITE FIRST, STAGGERING JOINTS

CATS

ATTIC VENTILATION IS IMPORTANT

Super insulating an attic area will cut your heating and air-conditioning costs, but unless the attic is effectively ventilated, all sorts of structural problems can develop.

In the summertime the attic heat build-up can make the rooms below very uncomfortable, thereby increasing your air-conditioning costs and, in very extreme cases, even buckle the roof shingles. And in the wintertime, condensation can dampen your insulation, thereby reducing its effectiveness. Condensation can also wet the joists and sheathing which can rot the wood and cause ceiling paint to peel.

There are many types of ventilation systems—from the eave vents to power blowers—but one of the the most effective is a combination of soffit and ridge venting.

Ideally, this ridge venting system is best installed at the time of new construction , but existing homes can be retrofitted by merely cutting through the roof shingles and sheathing. The soffit should also have a continuous ventilating strip that is equal in area to the ridge opening.

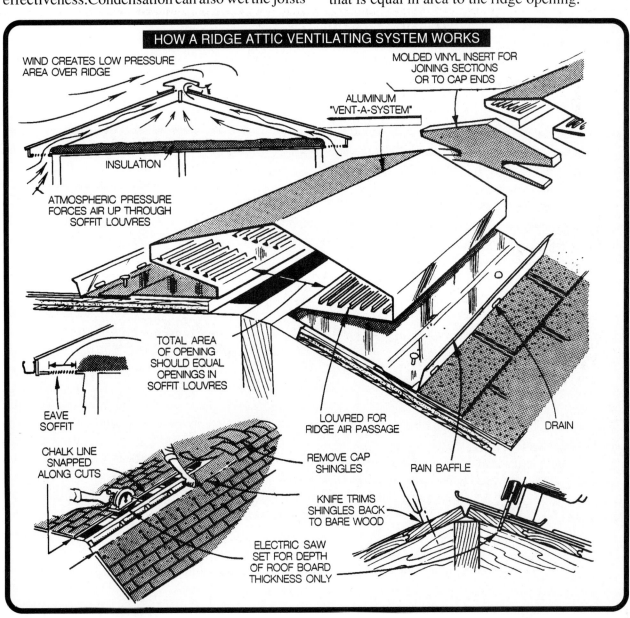

HOW A RIDGE ATTIC VENTILATING SYSTEM WORKS

WIND CREATES LOW PRESSURE AREA OVER RIDGE

MOLDED VINYL INSERT FOR JOINING SECTIONS OR TO CAP ENDS

ALUMINUM "VENT-A-SYSTEM"

INSULATION

ATMOSPHERIC PRESSURE FORCES AIR UP THROUGH SOFFIT LOUVRES

TOTAL AREA OF OPENING SHOULD EQUAL OPENINGS IN SOFFIT LOUVRES

EAVE SOFFIT

CHALK LINE SNAPPED ALONG CUTS

LOUVRED FOR RIDGE AIR PASSAGE

REMOVE CAP SHINGLES

RAIN BAFFLE

DRAIN

KNIFE TRIMS SHINGLES BACK TO BARE WOOD

ELECTRIC SAW SET FOR DEPTH OF ROOF BOARD THICKNESS ONLY

TIPS ON INSTALLING ROLL ROOFING

While mineral surface strip shingles are the most widely used roof covering because of the simplicity of installation (nailing, no adhesive) and long life (up to 20 years, or more in some cases), you just cannot lay asphalt or fiberglass shingles on slopes less than 2 inches to the foot. In such instances you must use roll roofing with either hot or cold asphalt as an adhesive. Roll roofing is manufactured in 36-inch-wide rolls, 36 feet long and weighing anywhere from 60 to 90 pounds per roll. The 90-pound weight has the longest longevity because it is thicker.

While hot asphalt is preferred for dead flat roofs, a "hot mopped" roof is definitely not a do-it-yourself job because of the equipment required; however, a few manufacturers have a cold application technique for dead flat roofs.

Laying roll roofing is actually very simple but a few tricks will help speed the process. While you can install a new layer over an existing roof if it does not have gravel, if you have a bare wooden surface first staple a layer of 15-pound felt over the entire area, overlapping each sheet by about 3 inches. Then cut a strip from the selvage edge of regular roll and nail it in place as the base for a starter strip as shown. The nails should extend at least 3/4-inch into the deck if tongue and groove sheathing was used for the original roof, and through the sheathing if it is plywood. Set the first strip in place, nail down the selvage edge as shown and fold it back. Apply your adhesive (trowel or brushed) as recommended and roll the roofing into the adhesive. Smooth out to eliminate any air bubbles and repeat the procedure with the subsequent layers.

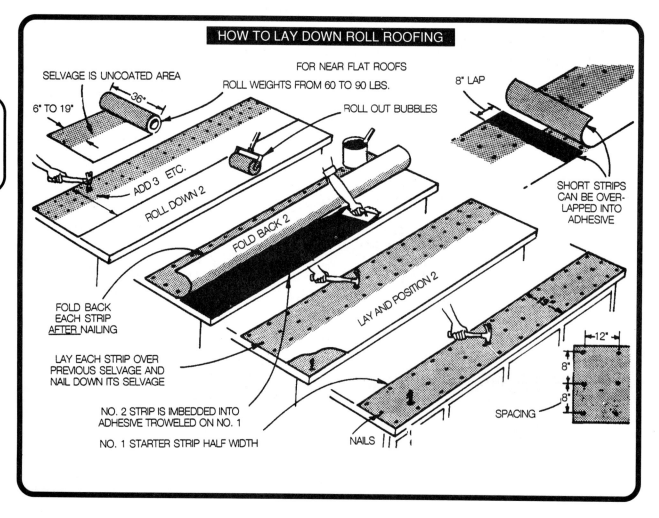

HOW TO LAY DOWN ROLL ROOFING

SELVAGE IS UNCOATED AREA

36"

6" TO 19"

FOR NEAR FLAT ROOFS
ROLL WEIGHTS FROM 60 TO 90 LBS.

ROLL OUT BUBBLES

8" LAP

ADD 3 ETC.

ROLL DOWN 2

FOLD BACK 2

SHORT STRIPS CAN BE OVER-LAPPED INTO ADHESIVE

LAY AND POSITION 2

FOLD BACK EACH STRIP AFTER NAILING

LAY EACH STRIP OVER PREVIOUS SELVAGE AND NAIL DOWN ITS SELVAGE

12"

8"

8"

NO. 2 STRIP IS IMBEDDED INTO ADHESIVE TROWELED ON NO. 1

NO. 1 STARTER STRIP HALF WIDTH

NAILS

SPACING

ASPHALT SHINGLES ARE EASY TO APPLY!

Of all the types of roofing materials—asphalt strip, cedar, slate, ceramic or cement tile — asphalt strips are the most widely used.

Standard shingles weigh approximately 235 pounds per 100 square feet of cover and have a life expectancy of up to 20 years, although some brands are guaranteed up to 25 years. Naturally, heavier shingles made with thicker layers cost more but they also have a longer life. While these shingles come in various shapes, most popular is the rectangular shingle illustrated, which mea-

sures 12x36 inches. Years ago it was not uncommon for a high wind to peel off shingles, but thanks to innovative manufacturing techniques, present day shingles, referred to as "wind-resistant", have a strip of adhesive that holds down the front edge.

Roofing was heretofore confined to contractors who were equipped with elaborate scaffolding, but with the popularization of low-slope single-story homes more and more homeowners find they can handle a roofing job. Just follow the instructions that come with the shingles.

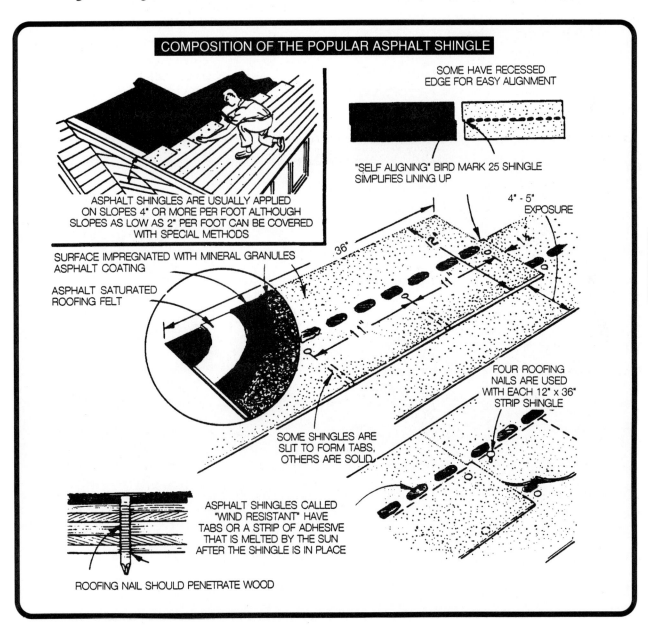

COMPOSITION OF THE POPULAR ASPHALT SHINGLE

ASPHALT SHINGLES ARE USUALLY APPLIED ON SLOPES 4" OR MORE PER FOOT ALTHOUGH SLOPES AS LOW AS 2" PER FOOT CAN BE COVERED WITH SPECIAL METHODS

SOME HAVE RECESSED EDGE FOR EASY ALIGNMENT

"SELF ALIGNING" BIRD MARK 25 SHINGLE SIMPLIFIES LINING UP

SURFACE IMPREGNATED WITH MINERAL GRANULES ASPHALT COATING

ASPHALT SATURATED ROOFING FELT

4" - 5" EXPOSURE

FOUR ROOFING NAILS ARE USED WITH EACH 12" x 36" STRIP SHINGLE

SOME SHINGLES ARE SLIT TO FORM TABS, OTHERS ARE SOLID

ASPHALT SHINGLES CALLED "WIND RESISTANT" HAVE TABS OR A STRIP OF ADHESIVE THAT IS MELTED BY THE SUN AFTER THE SHINGLE IS IN PLACE

ROOFING NAIL SHOULD PENETRATE WOOD

PROJECTS

HOW TO CUT ROOF SHINGLES

Asphalt and fiberglass shingles have mineral granules embedded into an asphalt-impregnated felt base. The granules resist the abrasive action of rain and wind, and also protect the base from the rays of the sun.

The granules form a tough surface which makes cutting difficult. However, the back side of the shingle contains more asphalt and felt and few granules—which is why you should cut all shingles from the back. On a 72-degree day you can nearly cut through the underside with one pass, while on

a 45-degree day a firm slash will merely nick the surface, which is enough to make it easy to break off the shingle along the scored line.

In instances where many shingles must be cut to the same size, a simple jig made from a piece of plywood and nails that serve as stops make the job easy. The jig illustrated has four 8-penny nails that are used to position the shingle. To cut, use a sharp utility knife and a 36-inch metal ruler; clamp the ruler to the plywood and hold the other end against the nail while scoring the shingle a few times.

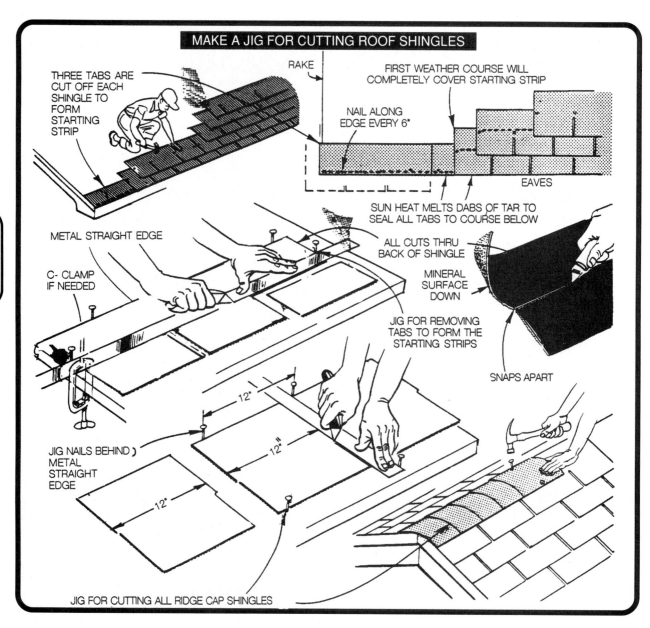

MAKE A JIG FOR CUTTING ROOF SHINGLES

THREE TABS ARE CUT OFF EACH SHINGLE TO FORM STARTING STRIP

RAKE

FIRST WEATHER COURSE WILL COMPLETELY COVER STARTING STRIP

NAIL ALONG EDGE EVERY 6"

EAVES

SUN HEAT MELTS DABS OF TAR TO SEAL ALL TABS TO COURSE BELOW

METAL STRAIGHT EDGE

C- CLAMP IF NEEDED

ALL CUTS THRU BACK OF SHINGLE

MINERAL SURFACE DOWN

JIG FOR REMOVING TABS TO FORM THE STARTING STRIPS

SNAPS APART

JIG NAILS BEHIND METAL STRAIGHT EDGE

12"

12"

12"

12"

JIG FOR CUTTING ALL RIDGE CAP SHINGLES

CHIMNEY-TOP FIREPLACE DAMPER

The three major functions of a fireplace damper are to (1) permit smoke and harmful gases to exit up the chimney, (2) prevent heat from escaping up the chimney when the fireplace is not in use, and (3) prevent birds and other wildlife from entering the home.

The early fireplaces did not have dampers, and many fireplaces built during the past 30 years have dampers that are now virtually ineffective because they warped from excess heat and do not provide a tight seal. These fireplaces are ideal candidates for a retro-fit damper mounted on the top of the chimney where it performs all the functions of a regular damper, but also has the advantage of keeping out rain, birds, squirrels, and other rodents.

The chimney-top damper illustrated is literally glued to the top of the flue with silicone adhesive. A stainless steel cable extends down the chimney and hooks on to a bracket on the fireplace side wall. Release the line and the damper will open because it is spring loaded to stay in the open position; pull the cable and the damper closes for a tight fit.

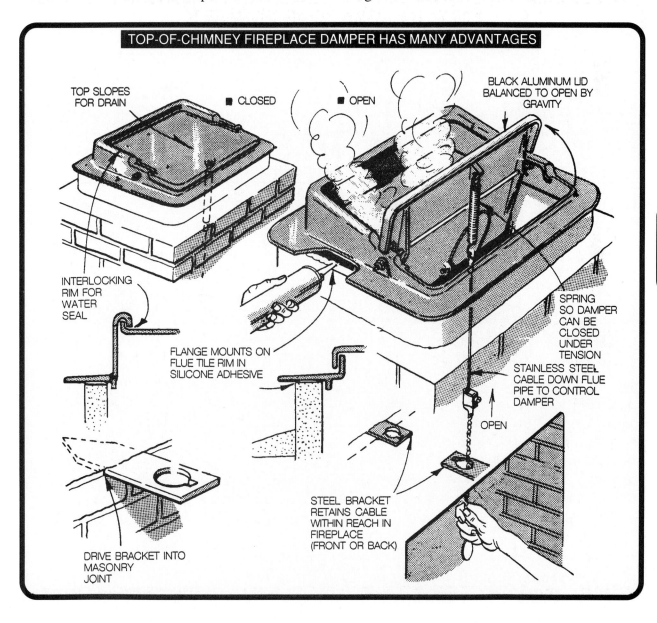

TOP-OF-CHIMNEY FIREPLACE DAMPER HAS MANY ADVANTAGES

TOP SLOPES FOR DRAIN

■ CLOSED   ■ OPEN

BLACK ALUMINUM LID BALANCED TO OPEN BY GRAVITY

INTERLOCKING RIM FOR WATER SEAL

FLANGE MOUNTS ON FLUE TILE RIM IN SILICONE ADHESIVE

SPRING SO DAMPER CAN BE CLOSED UNDER TENSION

STAINLESS STEEL CABLE DOWN FLUE PIPE TO CONTROL DAMPER

OPEN

DRIVE BRACKET INTO MASONRY JOINT

STEEL BRACKET RETAINS CABLE WITHIN REACH IN FIREPLACE (FRONT OR BACK)

HOW TO FLASH YOUR CHIMNEY

Many roofs leak via the chimney flashing—that metal band attached to the chimney and roof—which may have cracked because the foundation settled or, more likely, because the flashing was not properly installed. So if you need to replace your flashing, here is an excellent way to do the job.

Chimney flashing usually (but not always) consists of two elements: (1) flashing nailed to the roof deck to prevent water from seeping under the shingles and down the side of the chimney, and (2) a "counter" flashing attached to the chimney and overlapping the roof flashing. The counter flashing has a short leg that is bent to fit snugly into a groove cut in the brick with a masonry blade.

The roof flashing is first nailed in place. Bend and nail the section that fits on the low side of the sloped roof, then add the two side sections. The high side is positioned last. Then fit the counter flashing via trial and error, and once you have a snug fit remove it so a bead of silicone caulking can be applied into the groove. Push the sections in place.

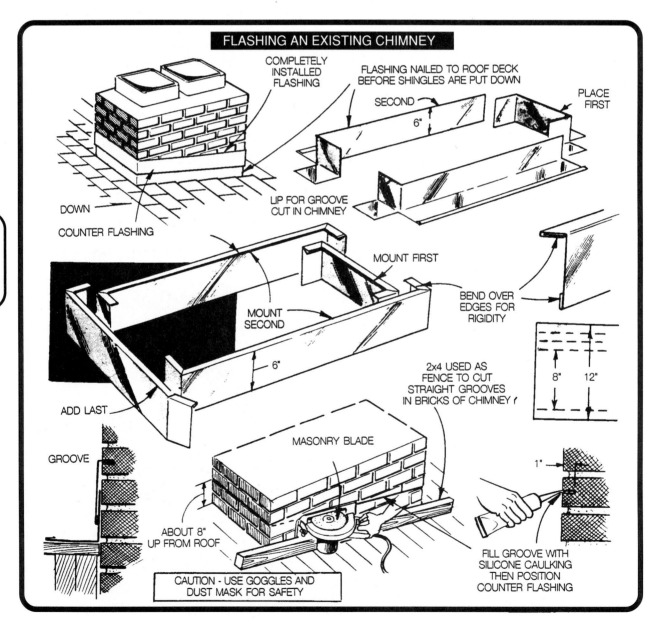

FLASHING AN EXISTING CHIMNEY

A REEL FOR EXTENSION CORDS

Electric extension cords have the nasty habit of becoming tangled after use—but not if you build this very simple and very handy reel my well-organized neighbor Bert Kramer designed. The unit shown has a capacity of up to 150 feet of No. 14 three-wire cord, and by grasping the extended handles and permitting them to rotate in the palms of your hands you can quickly unwind or wind up a cord. Winding or unwinding is a snap.

The two sides are cut from 1/2-inch thick plywood with notches to accommodate the l-inch horizontal members which are glued and nailed to the side pieces as shown. The 12-inch distance between the horizontal strips is adequate. Lumber l-inch square is not a standard size, so if you do not have a table or radial arm saw to rip your own you can drill the side pieces for a l-inch diameter dowel, which all lumber yards stock. If you use the square horizontal members you must then file off the handle corners to make reeling easy. Notch one horizontal member to hold the plug end of the cord.

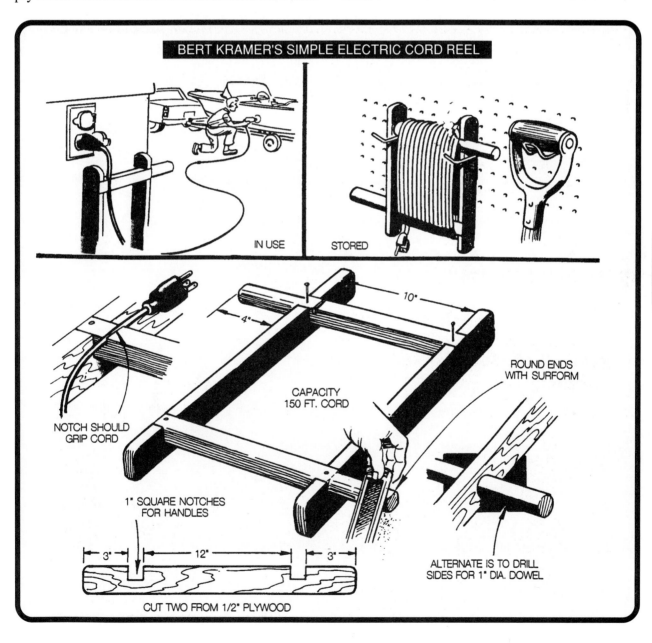

BERT KRAMER'S SIMPLE ELECTRIC CORD REEL

IN USE

STORED

NOTCH SHOULD GRIP CORD

CAPACITY 150 FT. CORD

10"

4"

ROUND ENDS WITH SURFORM

1" SQUARE NOTCHES FOR HANDLES

3"   12"   3"

CUT TWO FROM 1/2" PLYWOOD

ALTERNATE IS TO DRILL SIDES FOR 1" DIA. DOWEL

NAILING TRANSLUCENT ROOFING

If you are installing translucent roofing panels, formed filler strips that are the same shape as the corrugations of the panel, result in the best job because you have a solid nailing base for the panels. The filler strips should be nailed in place with 8-penny common nails driven at a slight angle near one side, (as shown) so they do not interfere with the paneling nails.

Positioning the filler strips must be done by using an actual panel as a guide. Working from one side to the other, nail the top and bottom filler strips to the cross brace. For the center filler strips, run a bead of construction adhesive over the cross braces and set the filler strips in place. Then rest the translucent panel over all strips; those with the construction adhesive can be shifted to fit the panel corrugations. Finally, remove the translu-

cent panel and nail the filler strip to the cross brace.

Paint or stain the entire framing before you start mounting the panels permanently in place. This is important because if you wait until the panels are in place, you run the risk of smearing the underside of the panel with paint or stain. If you paint or stain the framework a few times before the panels are in place, they probably will not need touching up for many years to come.

The nails used to hold the panels to the filler strips are ribbed aluminum and come with a neoprene washer that compresses when the nail is driven home to make it leakproof. It may not be necessary, but check with your instructions that come with the panels you purchase to see if predrilling a hole will eliminate possible cracking around the edge.

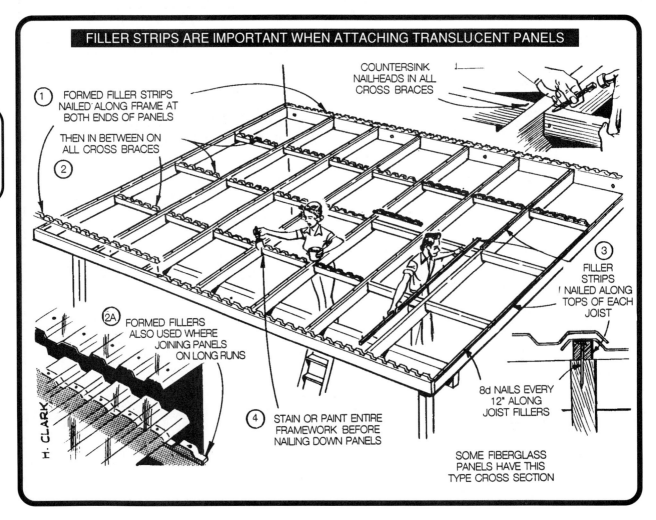

FILLER STRIPS ARE IMPORTANT WHEN ATTACHING TRANSLUCENT PANELS

① FORMED FILLER STRIPS NAILED ALONG FRAME AT BOTH ENDS OF PANELS

② THEN IN BETWEEN ON ALL CROSS BRACES

COUNTERSINK NAILHEADS IN ALL CROSS BRACES

③ FILLER STRIPS NAILED ALONG TOPS OF EACH JOIST

2A FORMED FILLERS ALSO USED WHERE JOINING PANELS ON LONG RUNS

④ STAIN OR PAINT ENTIRE FRAMEWORK BEFORE NAILING DOWN PANELS

8d NAILS EVERY 12" ALONG JOIST FILLERS

SOME FIBERGLASS PANELS HAVE THIS TYPE CROSS SECTION

H. CLARK

TRANSLUCENT ROOF CONSTRUCTION

Corrugated translucent panels can be used for a variety of purposes—from fences to greenhouses—their prime use is for carport, patio and screen porch roofing. They are colorful, weatherproof and transmit light. Panel lengths vary from 8 to 12 feet. fiberglass panels are 26 1/2 inches wide so the framing can be on 24-inch centers. The newer PVC panels, which eliminate the problem many fiberglass panels have of collecting dirt after the surface is worn away and the glass strands are exposed, have metric dimensions; framing should

be on 23-inch centers. The joists used can vary from 2x6s to 2x8s, or even larger, depending upon the slope and snow load. Panels overlap on top, but a 2x4 bridge should be located at about 30-inch intervals as shown.

All translucent panels are relatively easy to work; they can be cut with a fine-tooth saw.

Also, sealing strips should be used wherever panels overlap. Most important: *make sure the rafters are absolutely parallel so the corrugated edges overlap perfectly.*

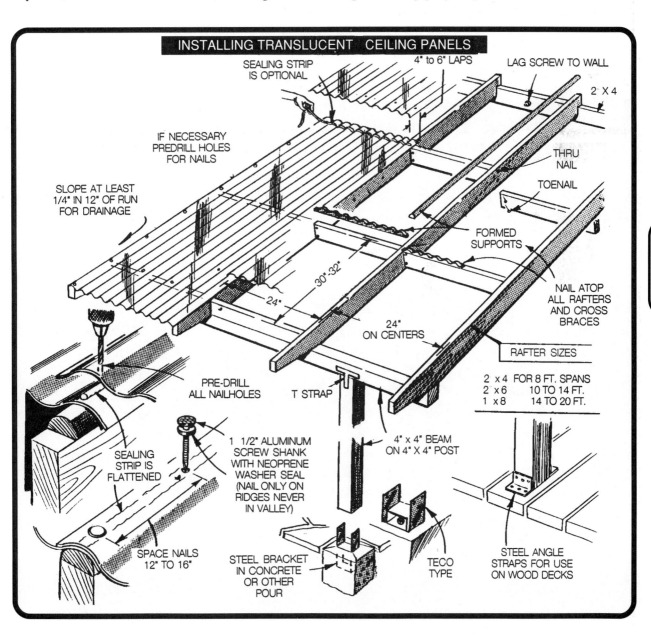

INSTALLING TRANSLUCENT CEILING PANELS

EXTRA PATIO DOOR LOCK

Probably the most widely used technique to lock a sliding door from the inside is to place a broomstick in the sill channel.

A better and very affordable solution is to fit your door with a pin inserted through the frame of the sliding panel and one wall of the stationary frame. All that is required is to drill a 3/16-inch diameter hole through the frame as illustrated, making certain you do not touch either the glass or the corner screw.

The two types of pin assemblies illustrated are available from home centers and hardware stores. The pin is attached to a chain which in turn clamps to the plastic holder that is mounted within easy reach to the frame with a sheet metal screw. The basic model is solid steel and is held in place because of the tight fit. However, wiggling the door constantly might possibly cause the pin to slip out, especially if the hole was drilled at an upward angle, so a more sophisticated model with a spring-loaded ball at the end is available. This tubular pin can be removed only if the inside button is pushed.

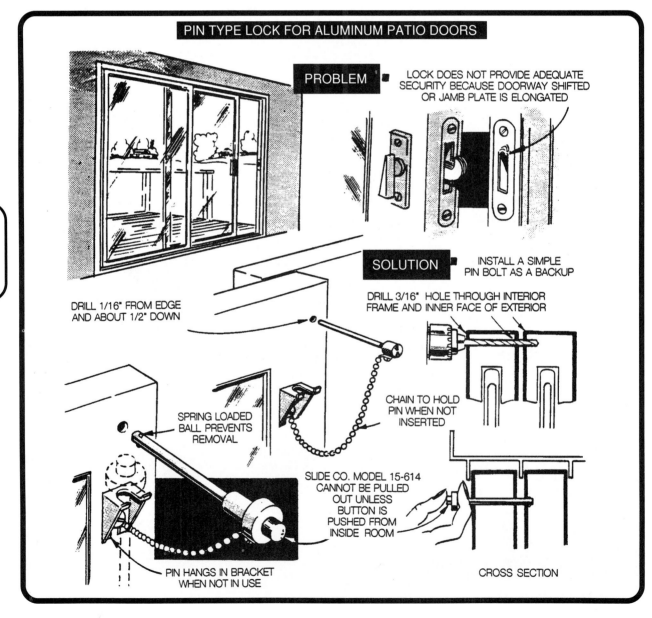

PIN TYPE LOCK FOR ALUMINUM PATIO DOORS

PROBLEM — LOCK DOES NOT PROVIDE ADEQUATE SECURITY BECAUSE DOORWAY SHIFTED OR JAMB PLATE IS ELONGATED

SOLUTION — INSTALL A SIMPLE PIN BOLT AS A BACKUP

DRILL 1/16" FROM EDGE AND ABOUT 1/2" DOWN

DRILL 3/16" HOLE THROUGH INTERIOR FRAME AND INNER FACE OF EXTERIOR

CHAIN TO HOLD PIN WHEN NOT INSERTED

SPRING LOADED BALL PREVENTS REMOVAL

SLIDE CO. MODEL 15-614 CANNOT BE PULLED OUT UNLESS BUTTON IS PUSHED FROM INSIDE ROOM

PIN HANGS IN BRACKET WHEN NOT IN USE

CROSS SECTION

HOW TO CUT GLASS

While most hardware stores will cut single or double strength window glass to your exact size for a small fee, you can cut your own. First, you need a glass cutter, the most common of which is a pencil-like metal holder with a hardened steel wheel at the end. Some cutters have carbide wheels, which do the same job wheels but last much longer, while the longest-lasting cutter is an industrial diamond chip.

Second, you need a flat surface on which to rest the glass. Mark off the line you wish to cut after you wipe the glass surface with a rag dipped in kerosene or paint thinner. Then rest a straight-edge over the glass and dip the cutter in kerosene or paint thinner before drawing it over the glass. Apply a very firm downward pressure and plan to make only one pass; two or three passes are really not necessary and can often result in a ragged edge.

After the cut is made, place a 1/4-inch dowel or pencil underneath the scribe marks at the edge and press down. The glass will snap.

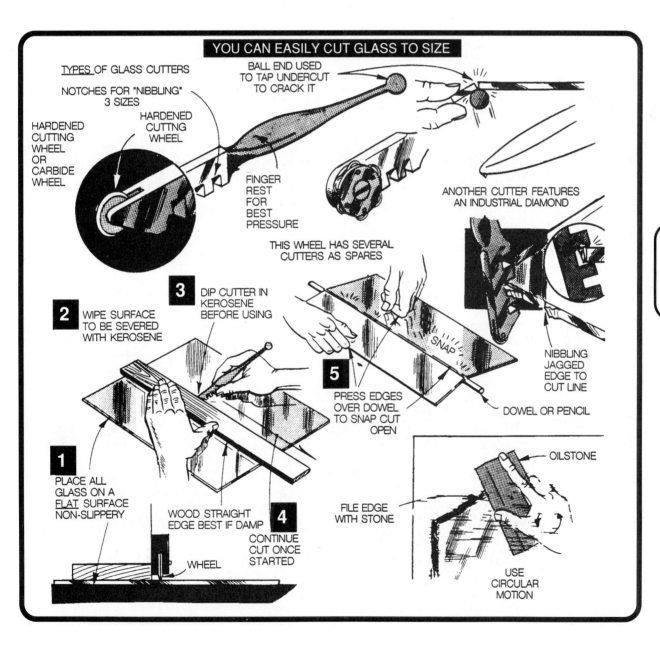

YOU CAN EASILY CUT GLASS TO SIZE

TYPES OF GLASS CUTTERS

BALL END USED TO TAP UNDERCUT TO CRACK IT

NOTCHES FOR "NIBBLING" 3 SIZES

HARDENED CUTTING WHEEL

HARDENED CUTTING WHEEL OR CARBIDE WHEEL

FINGER REST FOR BEST PRESSURE

ANOTHER CUTTER FEATURES AN INDUSTRIAL DIAMOND

THIS WHEEL HAS SEVERAL CUTTERS AS SPARES

3 DIP CUTTER IN KEROSENE BEFORE USING

2 WIPE SURFACE TO BE SEVERED WITH KEROSENE

SNAP

NIBBLING JAGGED EDGE TO CUT LINE

5 PRESS EDGES OVER DOWEL TO SNAP CUT OPEN

DOWEL OR PENCIL

1 PLACE ALL GLASS ON A FLAT SURFACE NON-SLIPPERY

WOOD STRAIGHT EDGE BEST IF DAMP

4 CONTINUE CUT ONCE STARTED

WHEEL

FILE EDGE WITH STONE

OILSTONE

USE CIRCULAR MOTION

TIPS FOR BUILDING A FENCE

There are literally hundreds of different fence designs to please any property owner's taste and pocketbook, but all fences have one thing in common. They need posts. Years ago it was common practice to use ordinary 4x4-inch or 4x6-inch lumber and dip the ends in creosote to discourage rotting. Now pressure-treated posts are readily available because their added longevity is well worth the extra cost. Also, it is always more difficult to replace a post than to set a new one!

Digging a post hole requires some muscle even if you use a sharp two-handled posthole digger; if you have many holes to dig, and the earth is relatively free from rocks, it may pay you to rent a power auger.

There are two basic rules to follow when erecting posts: (1) About one-third of the post should be buried underground, and (2) do not attempt to set each post at its final height. Rather, set each one a few inches above the final height and cut off the top after stringing a line between the end posts, as illustrated.

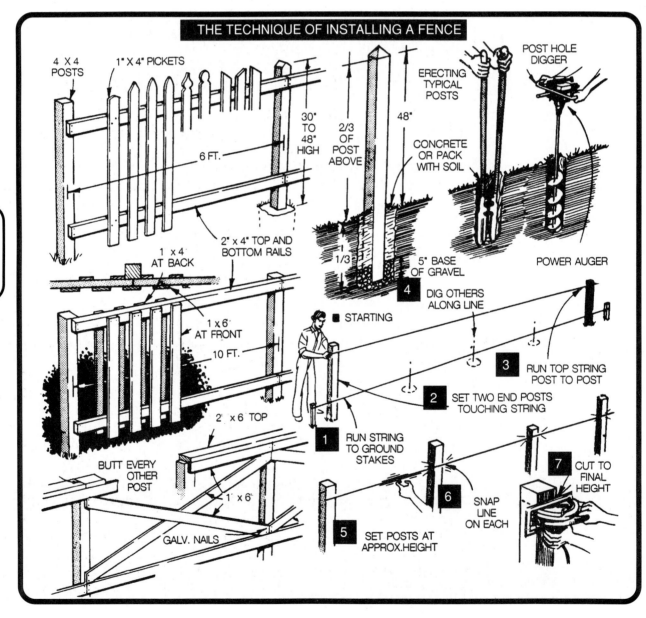

THE TECHNIQUE OF INSTALLING A FENCE

BIRDBATH MOUNTED ON A STUMP

Removing a dead tree stump is always a tough job, and in just about all instances the resulting hole settles and must be constantly top dressed year after year if you want it level with the surrounding lawn.

One way to circumvent this problem is to cut the stump off at a convenient height and rest a concrete birdbath on top. This will work only if the cut you make on the tree trunk is parallel with the ground; a slight slant will cause the birdbath to shift.

The illustrations clearly show how that perfect cut is made. First, nail a length of 1x2-inch furring strip to the tree trunk at the desired height, driving the second nail home only after the 1x2 is level. Then nail in place a second strip, as shown in Fig. 2. Now, with a third 1x2 strip touching the trunk, mark off the angle on both the first and second strips so the ends can be cut and the third strip nailed in place to produce a triangle. Use 8-penny nails.

Depending upon the diameter of the tree stump, use either a regular handsaw or a bucksaw to cut the trunk.

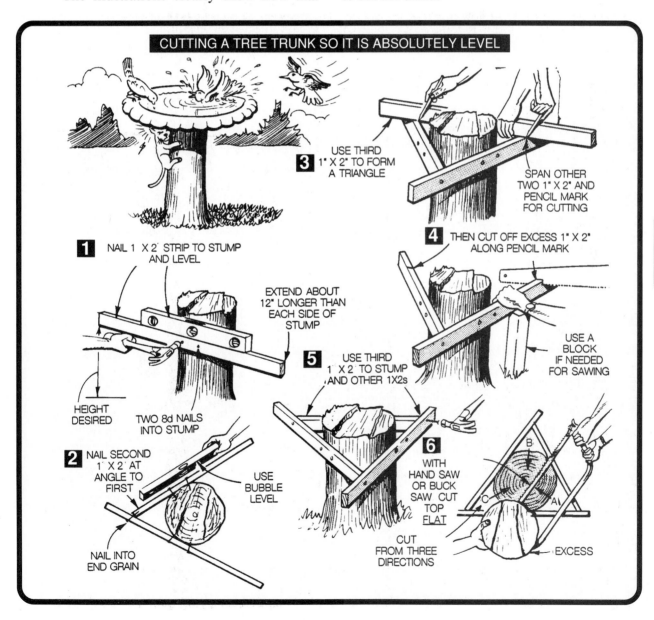

CUTTING A TREE TRUNK SO IT IS ABSOLUTELY LEVEL

3 USE THIRD 1" X 2" TO FORM A TRIANGLE

SPAN OTHER TWO 1" X 2" AND PENCIL MARK FOR CUTTING

1 NAIL 1 X 2' STRIP TO STUMP AND LEVEL

4 THEN CUT OFF EXCESS 1" X 2" ALONG PENCIL MARK

EXTEND ABOUT 12" LONGER THAN EACH SIDE OF STUMP

USE A BLOCK IF NEEDED FOR SAWING

HEIGHT DESIRED

TWO 8d NAILS INTO STUMP

5 USE THIRD 1' X 2' TO STUMP AND OTHER 1X2s

2 NAIL SECOND 1" X 2' AT ANGLE TO FIRST

USE BUBBLE LEVEL

6 WITH HAND SAW OR BUCK SAW CUT TOP FLAT

CUT FROM THREE DIRECTIONS

NAIL INTO END GRAIN

EXCESS

INSTALLING BI-FOLD DOORS

Closet doors are available in four types: (1) swinging doors for openings 24-36 inches; (2) sliding doors (3) accordion doors, and (4) bi-fold doors for openings ranging from 3 feet to as much as 12 feet.

Sliding closet doors have a very obvious disadvantage in that half the closet area is always covered. Folding closet doors, referred to as "bi-fold" because a door section folds in half, have the advantage of affording a view of the entire closet.

Folding closet doors offer much more than closet efficiency; since most of them are made from metal, a wide range of surface designs are available and among these the full-length mirror is one of the most popular for bedroom or bath installation.

Installation of bi-fold doors is simple if you follow these important steps after you have determined the size of the opening. When the diagonal measurements are equal you know all sides are parallel. Once the opening is set, install the top channel and then drop a plumb line so the bottom channel is directly below.

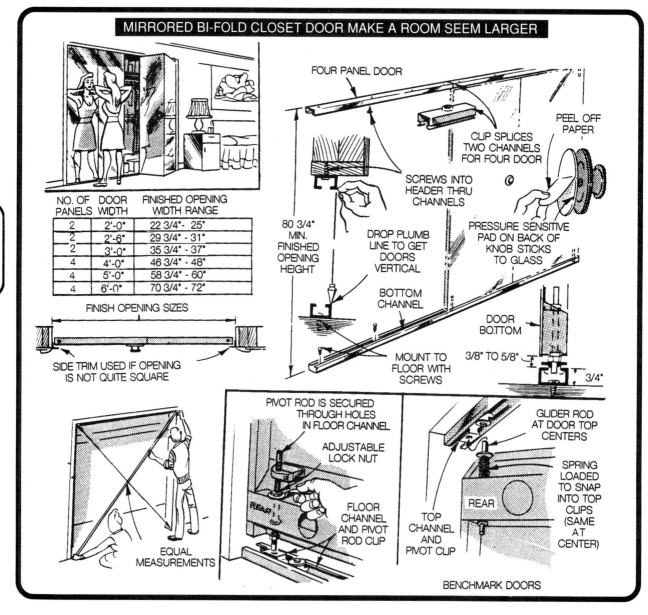

MIRRORED BI-FOLD CLOSET DOOR MAKE A ROOM SEEM LARGER

FOUR PANEL DOOR

PEEL OFF PAPER

CLIP SPLICES TWO CHANNELS FOR FOUR DOOR

SCREWS INTO HEADER THRU CHANNELS

NO. OF PANELS	DOOR WIDTH	FINISHED OPENING WIDTH RANGE
2	2'-0"	22 3/4"- 25"
2	2'-6"	29 3/4" - 31"
2	3'-0"	35 3/4" - 37"
4	4'-0"	46 3/4" - 48"
4	5'-0"	58 3/4" - 60"
4	6'-0"	70 3/4" - 72"

FINISH OPENING SIZES

80 3/4" MIN. FINISHED OPENING HEIGHT

DROP PLUMB LINE TO GET DOORS VERTICAL

PRESSURE SENSITIVE PAD ON BACK OF KNOB STICKS TO GLASS

BOTTOM CHANNEL

DOOR BOTTOM

3/8" TO 5/8"

3/4"

SIDE TRIM USED IF OPENING IS NOT QUITE SQUARE

MOUNT TO FLOOR WITH SCREWS

PIVOT ROD IS SECURED THROUGH HOLES IN FLOOR CHANNEL

ADJUSTABLE LOCK NUT

FLOOR CHANNEL AND PIVOT ROD CLIP

GLIDER ROD AT DOOR TOP CENTERS

SPRING LOADED TO SNAP INTO TOP CLIPS (SAME AT CENTER)

REAR

TOP CHANNEL AND PIVOT CLIP

EQUAL MEASUREMENTS

BENCHMARK DOORS

BUILD A STONE COLUMN

Experienced masons can easily build a stone column using only a level, trowel and mortar, but what does the average do-it-yourselfer do who wants a rustic column for a gate or fence post made from ordinary fieldstone. It is really easy if you use the technique shown.

First, pour a footing that (ideally) reaches the frost line. Undercut the base as shown, keeping the corners square and making sure you are on solid ground. Frame the top with 2x4s and then pour the footing—a 1-2-4 1/2 mix is ideal. Then, using cinder blocks, build a "core" in the center of the footing.   The center core may appear to be wobbly at times, depending upon the height, so take extreme care with the upper blocks. When the mortar has hardened—at least 24 hours—nail a square piece of 1/2-inch plywood the size of the footing, as shown. Then drop a plumb bob and line at each corner. Drive nails in each corner and draw a taut line from the footing upward to the plywood. Set your stones from the outside in.

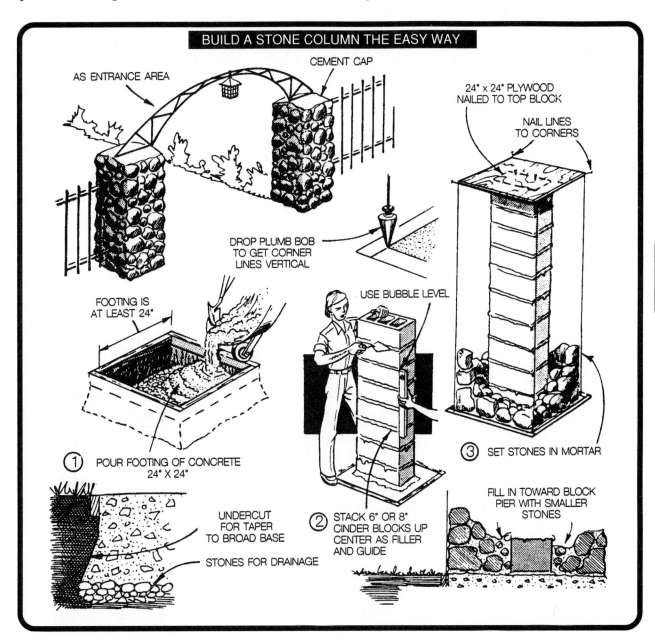

BUILD A STONE COLUMN THE EASY WAY

AS ENTRANCE AREA

CEMENT CAP

24" x 24" PLYWOOD NAILED TO TOP BLOCK

NAIL LINES TO CORNERS

DROP PLUMB BOB TO GET CORNER LINES VERTICAL

FOOTING IS AT LEAST 24"

USE BUBBLE LEVEL

① POUR FOOTING OF CONCRETE 24" X 24"

UNDERCUT FOR TAPER TO BROAD BASE

STONES FOR DRAINAGE

② STACK 6" OR 8" CINDER BLOCKS UP CENTER AS FILLER AND GUIDE

③ SET STONES IN MORTAR

FILL IN TOWARD BLOCK PIER WITH SMALLER STONES

RIVETING WITH "BLIND" RIVETS

"Blind" riveting differs from regular riveting in that you need only work from one side. Developed in England over 50 years ago, this technique of joining two pieces of flat material together was largely confined to industrial applications but now, thanks to a special tool and rivet, we can do it at home.

The technique is simple; a hole is drilled through the two pieces of metal being joined by the rivet. The rivet is then inserted into the hole and the pointed tip (the mandrel end) pushed into the tip of the tool. Jaws inside the tool grip the mandrel; clamping the handle together pulls the mandrel forward to deform the "blind" end of the rivet, as shown. Finally, the mandrel breaks off—but only after the "blind" end has been forced to bulge out and hold the material from the opposite side.

Many manufacturers make similar tools in various price ranges and rivets are available in aluminum, steel and copper in a wide range of lengths for joining materials of different thicknesses. Once a rivet is drawn, the only way to remove it is to drill through the end.

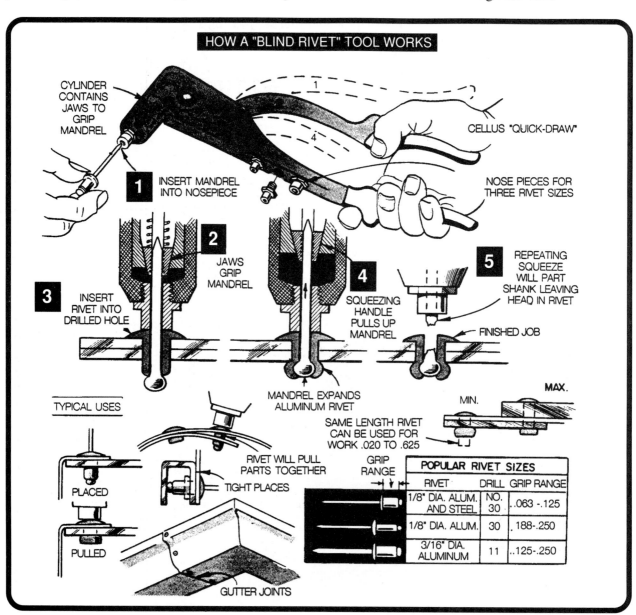

HOW A "BLIND RIVET" TOOL WORKS

CYLINDER CONTAINS JAWS TO GRIP MANDREL

CELLUS "QUICK-DRAW"

NOSE PIECES FOR THREE RIVET SIZES

1 INSERT MANDREL INTO NOSEPIECE

2 JAWS GRIP MANDREL

3 INSERT RIVET INTO DRILLED HOLE

4 SQUEEZING HANDLE PULLS UP MANDREL

5 REPEATING SQUEEZE WILL PART SHANK LEAVING HEAD IN RIVET

FINISHED JOB

MANDREL EXPANDS ALUMINUM RIVET

TYPICAL USES

RIVET WILL PULL PARTS TOGETHER

TIGHT PLACES

PLACED

PULLED

GUTTER JOINTS

SAME LENGTH RIVET CAN BE USED FOR WORK .020 TO .625

MIN.

MAX.

GRIP RANGE

POPULAR RIVET SIZES		
RIVET	DRILL	GRIP RANGE
1/8" DIA. ALUM. AND STEEL	NO. 30	.063 -.125
1/8" DIA. ALUM.	30	.188-.250
3/16" DIA. ALUMINUM	11	..125-.250

THE UNIQUE BLIND RIVET-NUT

"Blind" riveting is the technique of riveting two pieces of metal together when you have access from only one side. Once together, if you want to pull the two pieces apart you must carefully drill out the rivet.

However, if you want to rivet two pieces together and use a threaded bolt so the parts can be unscrewed, a "rivet-nut" is used. The technique was developed in the aircraft industry many years ago but the tool and manner in which the rivet is drawn from the rear is the brainchild of a creative engineer named Alan Martin.

Martin invented a blind riveting tool called "The Brute." How this tool and the rivet-nuts work may seem complicated, but the drawings best tell the story. Rivet-nuts are available in thread sizes ranging from 6-32 up to 1/4-20. A hole is drilled in the base sheet metal to fit the rivet-nut; then the rivet-nut is threaded on the mandrel of the tool and inserted into the hole. Squeezing the handle expands the rear of the rivet-nut and holds it in place, ready for inserting a machine bolt!

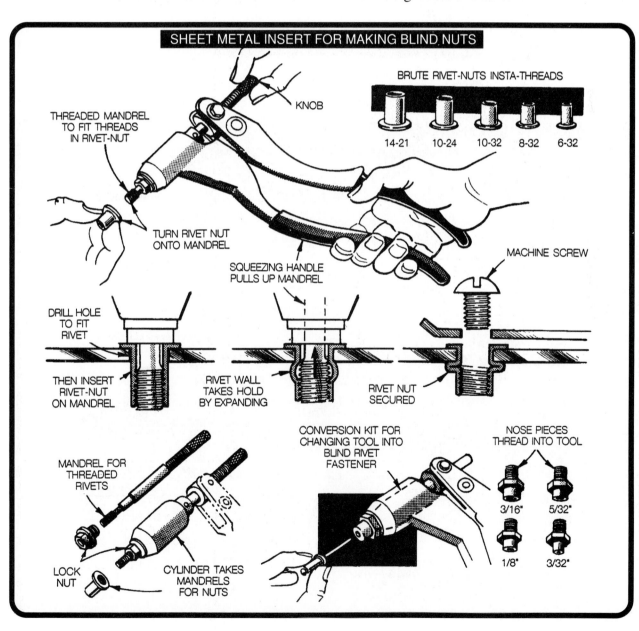

SHEET METAL INSERT FOR MAKING BLIND NUTS

THREADED MANDREL TO FIT THREADS IN RIVET-NUT

KNOB

BRUTE RIVET-NUTS INSTA-THREADS

14-21   10-24   10-32   8-32   6-32

TURN RIVET NUT ONTO MANDREL

SQUEEZING HANDLE PULLS UP MANDREL

MACHINE SCREW

DRILL HOLE TO FIT RIVET

THEN INSERT RIVET-NUT ON MANDREL

RIVET WALL TAKES HOLD BY EXPANDING

RIVET NUT SECURED

MANDREL FOR THREADED RIVETS

CONVERSION KIT FOR CHANGING TOOL INTO BLIND RIVET FASTENER

NOSE PIECES THREAD INTO TOOL

3/16"   5/32"

1/8"   3/32"

LOCK NUT

CYLINDER TAKES MANDRELS FOR NUTS

OUTDOOR COFFEE TABLE/PLANTER

This outdoor coffee table is unique in that the center is cut out to accommodate a 16-inch round planter. The table is 48 inches in diameter built entirely from 2x4s; the legs are cut from a length of 4x4.

First, cut and notch the 2x4 frame sections and fit them together so the tops are absolutely flush. Then clamp one leg to an inside corner and drill with a 3/8-inch diameter spade bit through both the leg and the 2x4 frame in both directions, as shown. After all four legs are in place and

securely bolted, turn the structure upside down and end nail the remaining braces in position with 10-penny nails after the ends have been tapered.

With all braces in place, set the piece right side up and position the 2x4s that will form the top. When all 2x4 pieces have been tacked in place, scribe a circle for both the outside circular curve and the plant hole. A sabre saw is a must for cutting the planter hole, but you can use a regular portable electric saw and make straight out cuts for the outside circle.

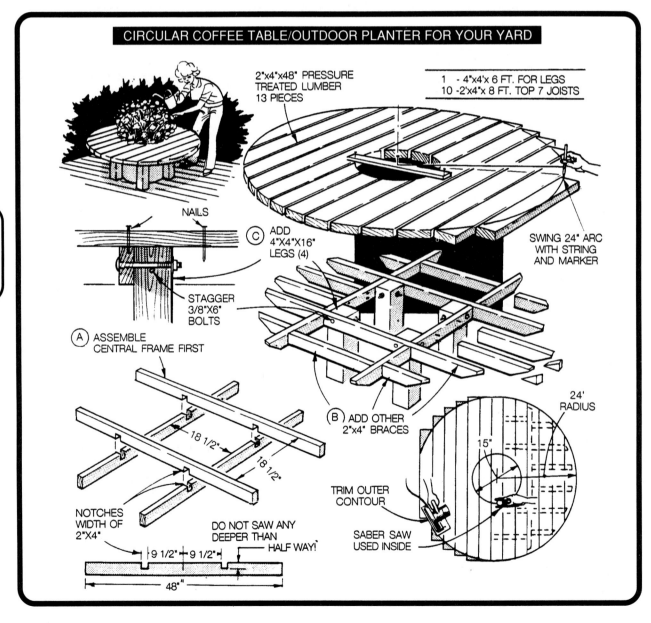

CIRCULAR COFFEE TABLE/OUTDOOR PLANTER FOR YOUR YARD

2"x4"x48" PRESSURE TREATED LUMBER 13 PIECES

1 - 4"x4'x 6 FT. FOR LEGS
10 -2'x4'x 8 FT. TOP 7 JOISTS

NAILS

ⒸADD 4"X4"X16" LEGS (4)

SWING 24" ARC WITH STRING AND MARKER

STAGGER 3/8"X6" BOLTS

ⒶASSEMBLE CENTRAL FRAME FIRST

ⒷADD OTHER 2"x4" BRACES

18 1/2"

18 1/2"

24' RADIUS

15"

NOTCHES WIDTH OF 2"X4"

DO NOT SAW ANY DEEPER THAN HALF WAY!

TRIM OUTER CONTOUR

SABER SAW USED INSIDE

9 1/2" 9 1/2"

48"

SHELVES FOR YOUR LAUNDRY ROOM

Shelves above your washing machine and clothes dryer are an absolute must to accommodate the wash that is folded after it has been removed from the dryer. Many homes have cabinets over these appliances, but shelves offer many advantages. Economy is one.

The unit shown is made from a single sheet of 4x8-foot plywood, 3/4-inch thick, ripped down as indicated in the plan.

Cut all the sections to size as indicated and pre-nail the sides so the 8-penny finishing nails just penetrate the surface. Then apply white glue to the edge of the shelves and drive the nails into the edge. Assemble the top, bottom and the shelves on your floor, and when the diagonal measurements are equal you will know the corners are absolutely square.

Allow the glue to set, fill the edges with paste wood filler, seal and paint. Then mount the shelves as a unit to your wall with lag screws driven into the wall studs or four toggle bolts that grab the wall from the inside.

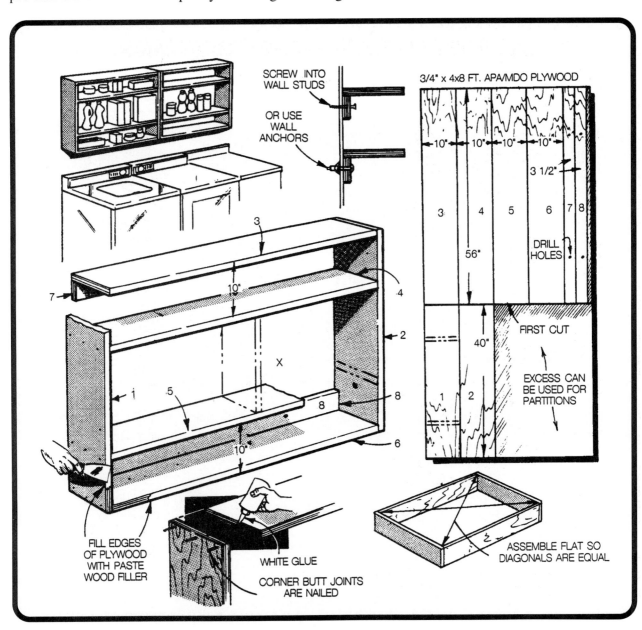

SCREW INTO WALL STUDS

OR USE WALL ANCHORS

3/4" x 4x8 FT. APA/MDO PLYWOOD

10" 10" 10" 10"

3 1/2"

3   4   5   6   7 8

DRILL HOLES

56"

40"

FIRST CUT

EXCESS CAN BE USED FOR PARTITIONS

1   2

FILL EDGES OF PLYWOOD WITH PASTE WOOD FILLER

WHITE GLUE

CORNER BUTT JOINTS ARE NAILED

ASSEMBLE FLAT SO DIAGONALS ARE EQUAL

COMBINATION MAILBOX & PLANTER

Rural mailboxes are mounted on fence posts, garden walls, tree stumps and even links of heavy steel chain welded together, but here is a stand that is not only functional but also contains a flower box. Aside from being imaginative, the planter counterbalances the mailbox so the post will not tilt. How many mailboxes have you seen that tilt forward because of the weight of the mailbox?

Construction is simple; the main post, horizontal arm and angle brace are cut from 4x4-inch lumber while the planter box and shelf for the mailbox is made from 1x6 inch stock. Of course, since the stand and flower box must weather the ravages of time, you should use pressure-treated lumber. To set the pressure-treated post, dig an 8-inch hole with a posthole digger about 30 inches deep and bury the post after the cross member and base for the flower box are in place. Make sure the horizontal arm is level. After the dirt is packed solid around the post you can bolt the mailbox in place, keeping the nuts on the inside of the mailbox.

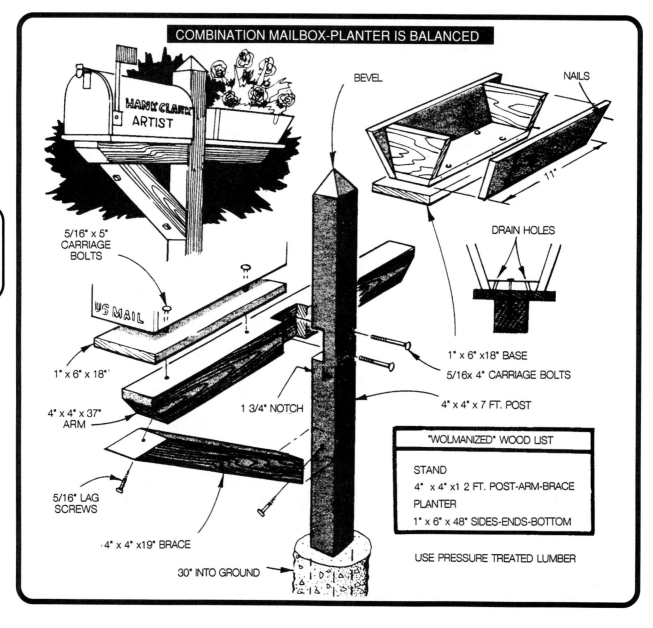

COMBINATION MAILBOX-PLANTER IS BALANCED

5/16" x 5" CARRIAGE BOLTS

1" x 6" x 18"

4" x 4" x 37" ARM

1 3/4" NOTCH

5/16" LAG SCREWS

4" x 4" x19" BRACE

30" INTO GROUND

BEVEL

NAILS

11"

DRAIN HOLES

1" x 6" x18" BASE

5/16x 4" CARRIAGE BOLTS

4" x 4" x 7 FT. POST

"WOLMANIZED" WOOD LIST

STAND
4" x 4" x1 2 FT. POST-ARM-BRACE
PLANTER
1" x 6" x 48" SIDES-ENDS-BOTTOM

USE PRESSURE TREATED LUMBER

DESK AND CHAIR FOR YOUR TYKE

This unusual desk and chair, will serve as a much used piece of nursery furniture. Made from a sheet of 1/2-inch-thick A-B Interior plywood. The bench seat is just 7 inches high and the top 17 inches high so it will fit most 2 to 4 year olds.

Lay out all parts on your plywood as indicated and cut the straight sections with either a bench saw or a portable electric saw fitted with a fence. Parts A, C, D and E are cut square and then the corners rounded with a saber saw. You can make a plunge cut with a circular saw or cut out the inside of Part A with a saber saw because the cuts need not be absolutely straight. Note the side panels of the desk have lengths of 1/2-inch-diameter dowels notched to fit the sides.

The desk top is assembled with 3-inch butt hinges, sides can be folded flat for storage by lifting up the top, which rests on four 3/8- x 2-inch long carriage bolts. The height can be adjusted by repositioning the carriage bolts. The chair—which is in the shape of a seal—is also bolted together as indicated.

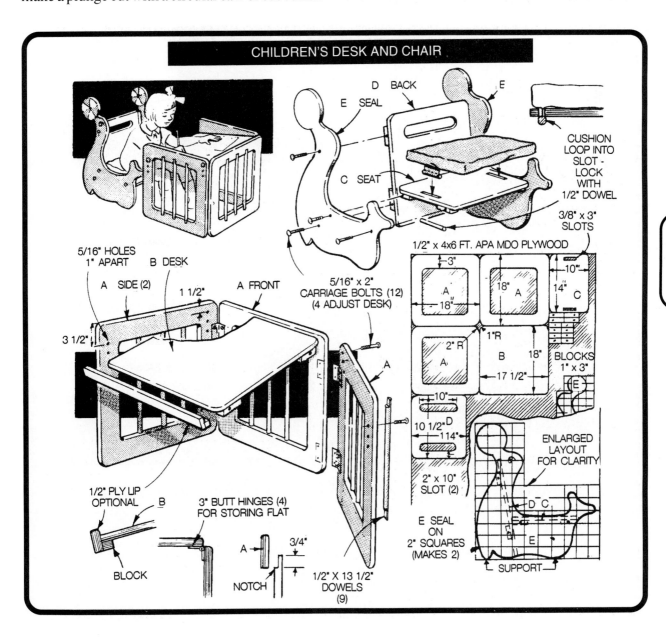

CHILDREN'S DESK AND CHAIR

TAKE-APART DINING TABLE

Here's a plywood table that can either be made as a permanent structure or disassembled and stored along a wall or even under a bed. What's more, it is built entirely from one sheet of 3/4-inch APA plywood, preferably A-C grade or 3/4-inch MDO.

Probably the most time-consuming chore will be laying out all the parts on the plywood. Transfer the straight lines first, using a square and metal straight-edge. The curves shown are made by tying a string to a pencil and swinging the radius indicated.

A bench or radial arm saw is the preferred tool for cutting the straight cuts. Always cut through the line rather than on either side; where parts are notched, cut on the scant side to ensure a tight fit.

Finishing the edges of plywood can be a problem, so sand all edges first and fill with a paste wood filler. If you elect to assemble the table permanently, use finishing nails or wood screws and white glue. If you plan to knock your table down, make certain the notched joints fit snugly together.

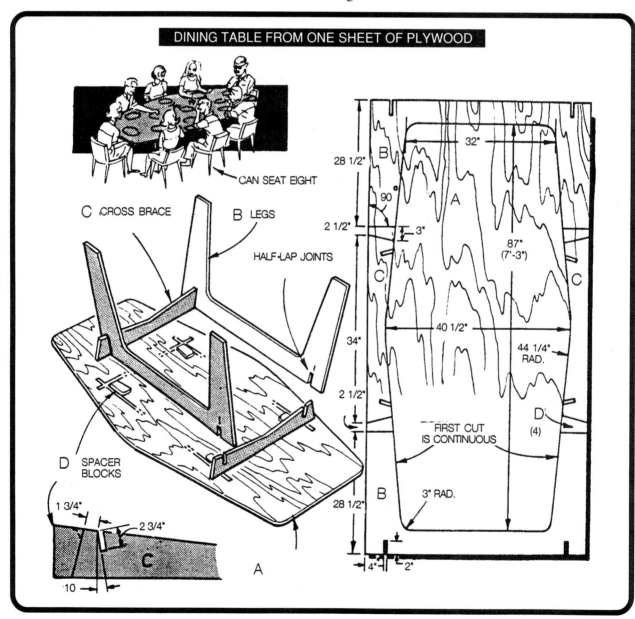

DINING TABLE FROM ONE SHEET OF PLYWOOD

CAN SEAT EIGHT

C CROSS BRACE B LEGS

HALF-LAP JOINTS

D SPACER BLOCKS

FIRST CUT IS CONTINUOUS

BUILD THIS MODERN DOG HOUSE

Here's a dog house that is attractive, functional, economical and very easy to build. Note the raised floor can be insulated from underneath to slow down the body heat loss during those cold winter nights, and the hinged roof makes it easy to sweep out the interior when necessary.

Designed for dogs no larger than 20 inches high, all parts are cut from a single 1/2 inch 4x8-foot sheet of A-B or A-C Exterior or MDO plywood. Because most of the cuts are straight, a table or radial arm saw is the ideal tool to use, but you can do an acceptable job with a portable electric saw and a saw guide to ensure straight cuts. The few curved cuts are best made with a jig or a keyhole saw.

The floor and base are assembled first, the front and back added, and then the sides are glued and nailed in place. Use a waterproof glue and 6-penny finishing nails. The exposed edges of the plywood should be sanded smooth and filled with wood filler before the complete job is painted. Use a sealer for the outside and apply at least two coats of paint.

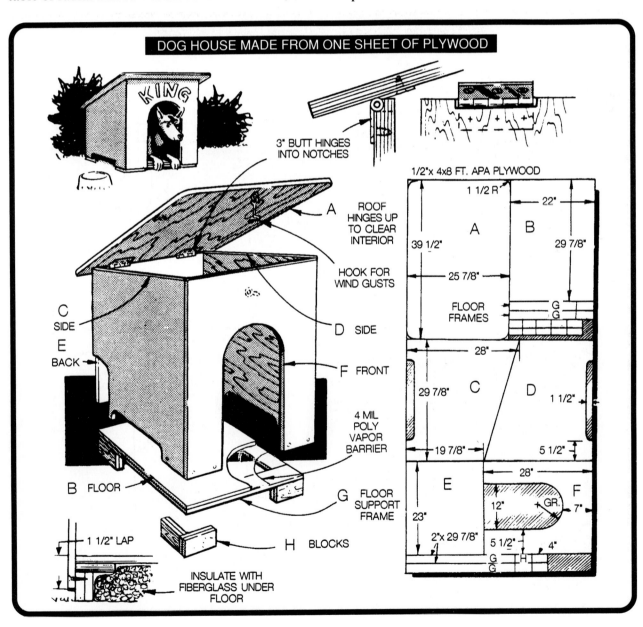

DOG HOUSE MADE FROM ONE SHEET OF PLYWOOD

3" BUTT HINGES INTO NOTCHES

A — ROOF HINGES UP TO CLEAR INTERIOR

HOOK FOR WIND GUSTS

C SIDE

E BACK

B FLOOR

D SIDE

F FRONT

4 MIL POLY VAPOR BARRIER

G FLOOR SUPPORT FRAME

H BLOCKS

1 1/2" LAP

INSULATE WITH FIBERGLASS UNDER FLOOR

1/2" x 4x8 FT. APA PLYWOOD

1 1/2 R

22"

39 1/2"   A   B   29 7/8"

25 7/8"

FLOOR FRAMES   G G

28"

29 7/8"   C   D   1 1/2"

19 7/8"   5 1/2"

28"

23"   E   12"   F GR. 7"

2" x 29 7/8"   5 1/2"   4"

G G

CHOOSING WATERPROOF SHOWER WALLS

If you are building your own shower or bathtub surround you have a choice of wall finish. The oldest and still one of the most popular surfaces is ceramic tile. Since water resistant "tile backer" gypsum board and the newer waterproof Portland cement base panels are available, all you need do is to trowel on a regular ceramic tile adhesive and set the tiles in place one by one.

Plastic-surfaced hardboard is another wall material you can use. Because the sheets are large (up to 4x8 feet) they are very easy to clean.

However, since the inside corner consists of a special piece of plastic or aluminum molding—which was made as small as possible in an effort to make it less visible—you must have a perfect fit.

Pre-formed wall sections made from either ABS plastic, acrylic or fiberglass are the simplest of all to install and have the added advantage of built-in soap dishes and grab bars plus a rounded inside corner. The fact that the panels overlap automatically compensates for any wall discrepancies.

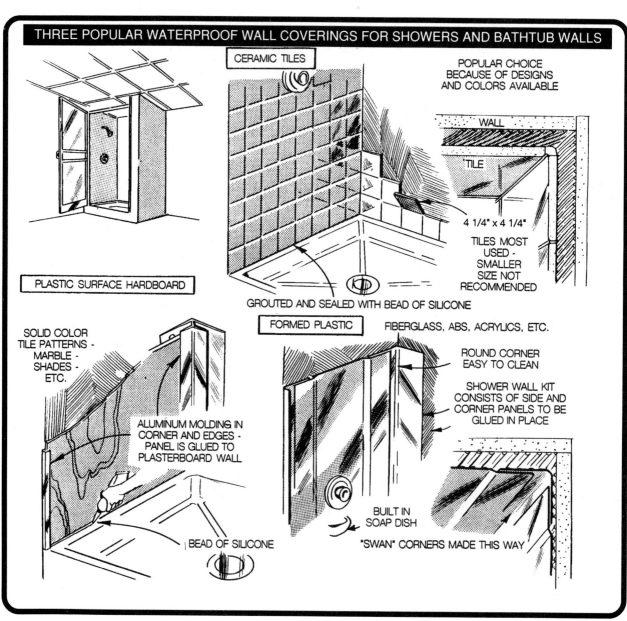

THREE POPULAR WATERPROOF WALL COVERINGS FOR SHOWERS AND BATHTUB WALLS

CERAMIC TILES

POPULAR CHOICE BECAUSE OF DESIGNS AND COLORS AVAILABLE

WALL

TILE

4 1/4" x 4 1/4"

TILES MOST USED - SMALLER SIZE NOT RECOMMENDED

PLASTIC SURFACE HARDBOARD

GROUTED AND SEALED WITH BEAD OF SILICONE

SOLID COLOR TILE PATTERNS - MARBLE - SHADES - ETC.

FORMED PLASTIC

FIBERGLASS, ABS, ACRYLICS, ETC.

ROUND CORNER EASY TO CLEAN

SHOWER WALL KIT CONSISTS OF SIDE AND CORNER PANELS TO BE GLUED IN PLACE

ALUMINUM MOLDING IN CORNER AND EDGES - PANEL IS GLUED TO PLASTERBOARD WALL

BEAD OF SILICONE

BUILT IN SOAP DISH

"SWAN" CORNERS MADE THIS WAY

FINISHING THE EDGES OF PLYWOOD

Because plywood consists of layers of wood glued at right angles to each other, the edge is very porous due to the end grain of the right-angle layers. This is not objectionable for some projects but if you are making a piece of furniture or building shelves you have a few options to conceal this blemish.

A layer of veneer glued to the edge with a contact adhesive is one popular solution. The veneer should be slightly wider than the thickness of the plywood and when glued in place, trimmed with a plane or utility knife. Finally, sandpaper the edge and face to produce a square edge.

Mounting flat or concave molding glued and nailed to the edge is another popular solution. Glue and nail the molding to the edge, countersink the nailheads and fill with wood dough.

But perhaps the most widely used end treatment is to fill the porous surface with paste wood filler, allow the filler to harden and then sand. At least two applications of filler are usually required to hide the end grain.

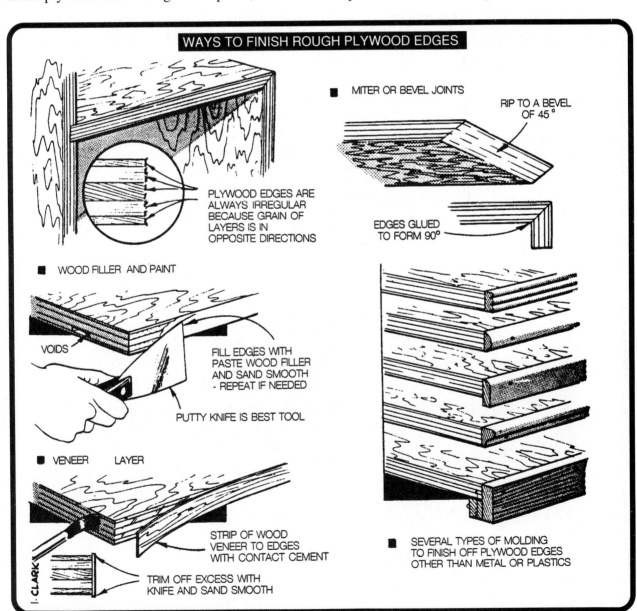

WAYS TO FINISH ROUGH PLYWOOD EDGES

PLYWOOD EDGES ARE ALWAYS IRREGULAR BECAUSE GRAIN OF LAYERS IS IN OPPOSITE DIRECTIONS

■ MITER OR BEVEL JOINTS

RIP TO A BEVEL OF 45°

EDGES GLUED TO FORM 90°

■ WOOD FILLER AND PAINT

VOIDS

FILL EDGES WITH PASTE WOOD FILLER AND SAND SMOOTH - REPEAT IF NEEDED

PUTTY KNIFE IS BEST TOOL

■ VENEER LAYER

STRIP OF WOOD VENEER TO EDGES WITH CONTACT CEMENT

TRIM OFF EXCESS WITH KNIFE AND SAND SMOOTH

■ SEVERAL TYPES OF MOLDING TO FINISH OFF PLYWOOD EDGES OTHER THAN METAL OR PLASTICS

I. CLARK

MOUNTING HEAVY DUTY DRAPERY RODS

Drapery rods are easy to attach to a wall if the brackets are screwed into the wooden window frame or if screws can pass through the plaster (or paneling) into a solid joist or stud. But what happens if you want to position your drapes on either side of a window or doorway and you find a hollow wall behind the bracket?

For very heavy draperies it is best to install a toggle bolt although the wall anchor with arms that flare out from the rear is fine for most installations.

If the names are new to you, an expanding type anchor is a clever device that grips the wall from the rear to prevent the bolt from pulling through. Quite a few different types are available. Despite the fact that most drapery wall brackets have up to four mounting holes, we have found that a single expanding type anchor bolt inserted through the top hole of the drapery bracket and a single regular plaster screw (usually provided) in the bottom hole are all you need for regular

weight draperies ,depending upon the thickness of the wall . Here are some guidelines..

The expanding type anchor bolt is preferable if your wall is anywhere from 1/2- to 3/4-inch thick because once inserted it grips the wall from both sides. Simply mark off the position of the bracket on your wall and pierce the top hole with a wire brad or 6-penny nail to serve as a pilot hole. Then drill a hole to fit the bolt sheathing. The size drill to use is usually stamped on the casing of the bolt. When the anchor is tightened the "legs" will fan out and grip the wall from the inside to prevent the bolt from pulling through. With the top of the bracket secure, drive a screw in the bottom hole.

In instances where the wall thickness is too great for an expanding type anchor, a toggle bolt does the job because the spring-loaded wings or unbalanced arm span the hole from the inside to prevent the bolt from pulling through. The illustration shows both types.

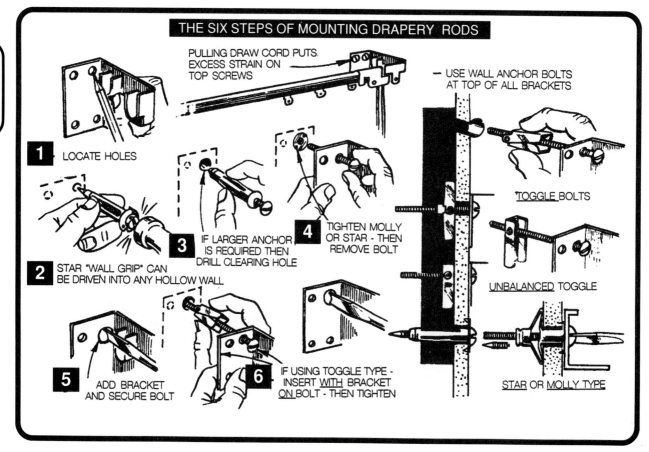

THE SIX STEPS OF MOUNTING DRAPERY RODS

PULLING DRAW CORD PUTS EXCESS STRAIN ON TOP SCREWS

— USE WALL ANCHOR BOLTS AT TOP OF ALL BRACKETS

1 LOCATE HOLES

2 STAR "WALL GRIP" CAN BE DRIVEN INTO ANY HOLLOW WALL

3 IF LARGER ANCHOR IS REQUIRED THEN DRILL CLEARING HOLE

4 TIGHTEN MOLLY OR STAR - THEN REMOVE BOLT

5 ADD BRACKET AND SECURE BOLT

6 IF USING TOGGLE TYPE - INSERT WITH BRACKET ON BOLT - THEN TIGHTEN

TOGGLE BOLTS

UNBALANCED TOGGLE

STAR OR MOLLY TYPE

CEILING FAN MUST BE BRACED FOR SAFETY

When ceiling fans first became popular they were mounted using the same two screws that held the existing ceiling light in place. However, numerous accidents occurred because the outlet vibrated loose so now all fans weighing more than 35 pounds must be attached to a brace that is connected to the ceiling joists.

While a fan brace can be installed from above if the joists are exposed, the fan brace illustrated can be installed from below by inserting it through a 5-inch diameter hole in the ceiling and extending the sides so they dig into the joists. A clamp fits on the brace and the electrical box to which the fan base is connected bolts in place.

In existing construction, rather than loosen the existing ceiling light electrical box and mount it on a brace, it's best to cut a hole next to the electrical box and use the existing outlet as a junction box. Run a line from the existing ceiling electrical box to the fan electrical box. Both the junction box and the new box will be covered by the large base plate of the fan.

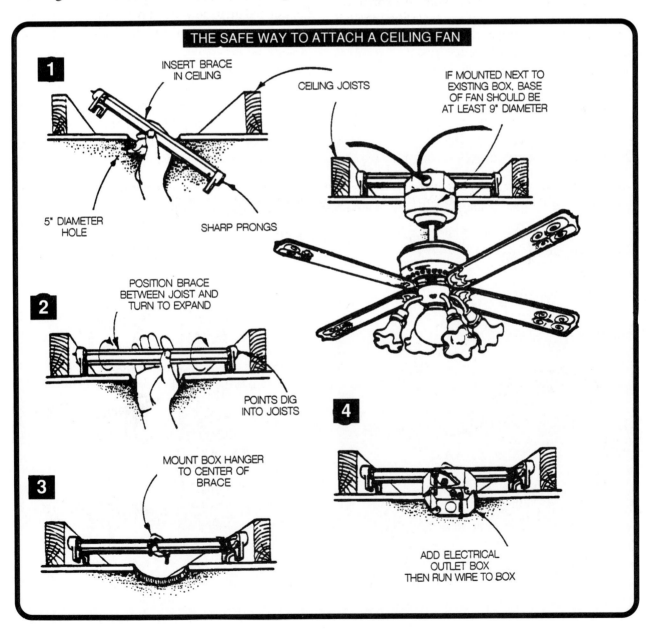

THE SAFE WAY TO ATTACH A CEILING FAN

1 INSERT BRACE IN CEILING — CEILING JOISTS — 5" DIAMETER HOLE — SHARP PRONGS — IF MOUNTED NEXT TO EXISTING BOX, BASE OF FAN SHOULD BE AT LEAST 9" DIAMETER

2 POSITION BRACE BETWEEN JOIST AND TURN TO EXPAND — POINTS DIG INTO JOISTS

3 MOUNT BOX HANGER TO CENTER OF BRACE

4 ADD ELECTRICAL OUTLET BOX THEN RUN WIRE TO BOX

BEFORE

Many homeowners now direct water from their downspout away from the foundations by running a length of leader on the surface of the ground. This represents a distinct hazard.

AFTER

Running PVC pipe under the ground and away from the foundation and into a bubble pot eliminates the hazard and removes the eyesore of an above-grade leader.

LEAD DOWNSPOUT RAIN WATER AWAY FROM YOUR FOUNDATION

Building codes vary when it comes to how rainwater will be distributed; some permit the water to flow over the edge of the roof while others insist on gutters and downspouts leading to a drywell. This wasn't always the case; in many communities, buildings often connected a downspout (called a leader) into the sewer system which is now illegal in nearly all areas.

But when the law mandating the disconnection of a downspout to the sewage system was passed in St. Paul, Minn., a clever inventor named Ken Cotten came up with the idea of not only disconnecting the downspout but leading it away - usually under an adjacent walk — so rainwater would be distributed 8 feet from the foundation and would overflow on to the adjacent grass.

Normally, if a downspout has a short elbow the rainwater will flow directly near the foundation and, unless you have a crack-free foundation, under severe conditions water will seep down and eventually find its way into the basement.

The solution to this common problem is to install the simple underground downspout. It consists of a rectangular plastic pipe into which the most popular 2-1/2-by-3-inch downspout fits. Merely cut off the existing downspout, which is usually aluminum (although we do have extruded PVC downspouts that look like aluminum), slip a fitting in place, and continue running the line in a trench away from the house and into the 8-1/2-inch "bubbler pot" that is set flush with the grass.

This unique kit has one additional feature worth emphasizing. Rather than connecting the house downspout directly to an elbow that leads to the distribution pot, the downspout run is interrupted and a "filter" installed. Thus, leaves and twigs - and if you have a gravel roof, stones - will be prevented from entering the underground pipe.

A clogged drainpipe is a very common condition found in many homes that have their downspout running to a drywell. With the pipe clogged, the rainwater that normally would be distributed into the well flows over the gutters — creating the very condition gutters were designed to prevent!

So if your downspout is clogged - which you can easily conclude if rainwater from the gutter overflows - and you cannot free the clog, you may solve your problem with this kit. Incidentally the bubbler pot cover is large enough so if any debris finds its way past the filter, merely lift off the lid and clean it out. And, lest you think water will collect in the pot and in freezing areas cause a problem, a few drain holes in the pot bottom will permit accumulated water to flow into the ground.

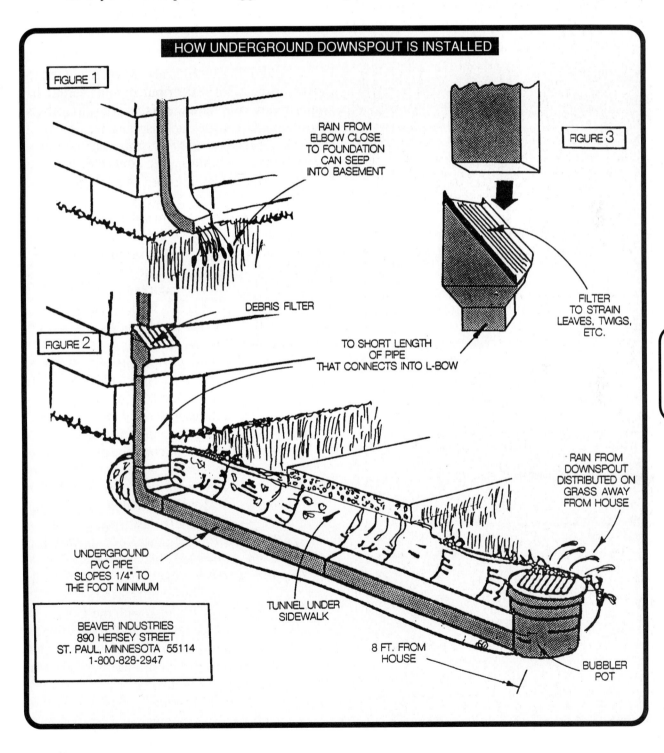

HOW UNDERGROUND DOWNSPOUT IS INSTALLED

FIGURE 1

RAIN FROM ELBOW CLOSE TO FOUNDATION CAN SEEP INTO BASEMENT

FIGURE 3

DEBRIS FILTER

FILTER TO STRAIN LEAVES, TWIGS, ETC.

FIGURE 2

TO SHORT LENGTH OF PIPE THAT CONNECTS INTO L-BOW

RAIN FROM DOWNSPOUT DISTRIBUTED ON GRASS AWAY FROM HOUSE

UNDERGROUND PVC PIPE SLOPES 1/4" TO THE FOOT MINIMUM

TUNNEL UNDER SIDEWALK

BEAVER INDUSTRIES
890 HERSEY STREET
ST. PAUL, MINNESOTA 55114
1-800-828-2947

8 FT. FROM HOUSE

BUBBLER POT

Pop-up sprinkler head (left) is ideal for mounting in the center of the lawn for either full or partial circle coverage. Stream control can also be regulated; radius of coverage can vary from 33 to over 40 feet depending upon make and water pressure. Pop-up adjustable sprinkler heads (right) are great for a perimeter system that requires digging a trench along the side rather than installing sprinkler heads in the center of the lawn.

SAVE WORK AND WATER WITH AN UNDERGROUND LAWN SPRINKLER SYSTEM

Tired of hauling hoses around to water your lawn and flowers? Do you want to water your lawn and garden while you sleep or when the local water pressure is highest? And how can you protect the ever continuing investment you have in your lawn, tree and shrub areas with regular watering while you are on vacation? The answer to all three problem questions is a built-in underground sprinkler system which you can install at a surprisingly moderate cost, depending upon the area you wish to cover, how many heads you need and if you want a manual or timer-controlled system. With a manual system you turn on a single valve when you want to water a specific area; with an automatic system you program the areas you want watered, when you want them watered, and for how long you want them watered! Also, in an era where conservation of just about everything is of paramount importance, underground sprinkler

systems help to save water because you can establish in advance just how much water will be used to adequately supply an area. No over watering!

Most manufacturers produce a wide assortments of timers, heads, valves and other accessories. All of the major manufacturers provide free instructional brochures or booklets which not only describe the timers, valves and sprinkler heads available but also give you graph paper so you can make your own sprinkler plan. Once you have a scale plan of your land made on graph paper, the key to an efficient sprinkler system is to accurately first determine your source of water, the pressure at that source and the amount of water in gallons per minute (GPM) that will be delivered. Few homes have sufficient water to sprinkle the entire yard in one swoop which is why we must break up the areas and water each one separately. A large selection of different type of sprinkler heads — pop up or surface, impulse sprinklers that cover a large area and spray heads, all of which can be adjusted to cover any part of a circle or rectangular shape are available in addition to heads designed strictly to water shrubs, plants and trees. All have a specific GPM rating so once you make a plan of your yard and know how much water is available, you can design individual circuits for the lawn, flower or tree areas, making certain the number of heads required for any one circuit does not exceed the amount of water in GPM at the designated pressure.

Sprinkler heads are available in machined

brass or bronze or molded plastic but for the homeowner the plastic heads are totally adequate and the cost is substantially less than comparable metal units. Here are the four basic categories:

TYPES OF SPRINKLER HEADS

(1) IMPULSE TYPE are designed primarily for lawn areas and cover a wide radius by squirting a revolving stream of water. Two types are available, the flush in-the-ground type that pop up when the water is on and an above grade head that is mounted on a riser. The riser type is ideal for a

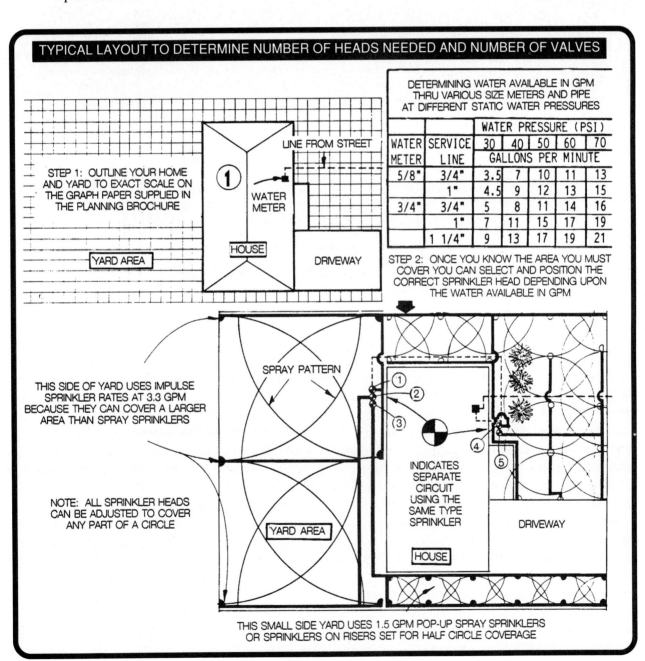

TYPICAL LAYOUT TO DETERMINE NUMBER OF HEADS NEEDED AND NUMBER OF VALVES

STEP 1: OUTLINE YOUR HOME AND YARD TO EXACT SCALE ON THE GRAPH PAPER SUPPLIED IN THE PLANNING BROCHURE

DETERMINING WATER AVAILABLE IN GPM THRU VARIOUS SIZE METERS AND PIPE AT DIFFERENT STATIC WATER PRESSURES

WATER METER	SERVICE LINE	30	40	50	60	70
5/8"	3/4"	3.5	7	10	11	13
	1"	4.5	9	12	13	15
3/4"	3/4"	5	8	11	14	16
	1"	7	11	15	17	19
	1 1/4"	9	13	17	19	21

STEP 2: ONCE YOU KNOW THE AREA YOU MUST COVER YOU CAN SELECT AND POSITION THE CORRECT SPRINKLER HEAD DEPENDING UPON THE WATER AVAILABLE IN GPM

THIS SIDE OF YARD USES IMPULSE SPRINKLER RATES AT 3.3 GPM BECAUSE THEY CAN COVER A LARGER AREA THAN SPRAY SPRINKLERS

NOTE: ALL SPRINKLER HEADS CAN BE ADJUSTED TO COVER ANY PART OF A CIRCLE

THIS SMALL SIDE YARD USES 1.5 GPM POP-UP SPRAY SPRINKLERS OR SPRINKLERS ON RISERS SET FOR HALF CIRCLE COVERAGE

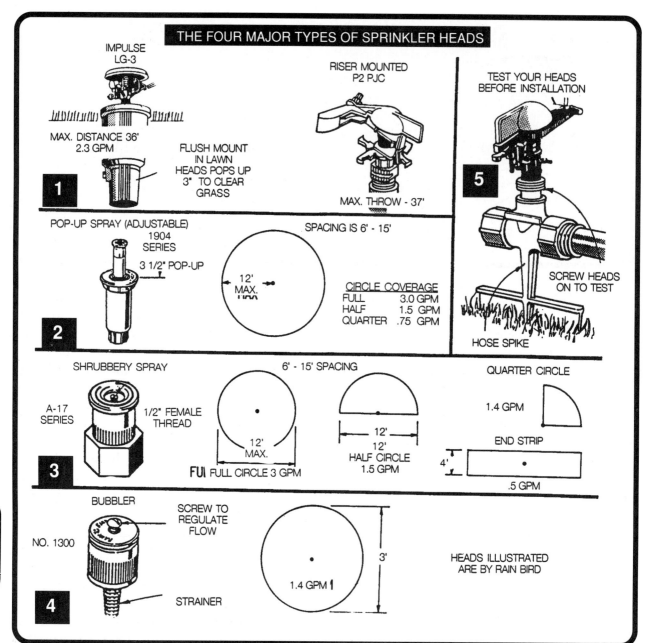

THE FOUR MAJOR TYPES OF SPRINKLER HEADS

IMPULSE LG-3
MAX. DISTANCE 36'
2.3 GPM
FLUSH MOUNT IN LAWN HEADS POPS UP 3" TO CLEAR GRASS

RISER MOUNTED P2 PJC
MAX. THROW - 37'

TEST YOUR HEADS BEFORE INSTALLATION
SCREW HEADS ON TO TEST
HOSE SPIKE

POP-UP SPRAY (ADJUSTABLE) 1904 SERIES
3 1/2" POP-UP
SPACING IS 6' - 15'
12' MAX.
CIRCLE COVERAGE
FULL 3.0 GPM
HALF 1.5 GPM
QUARTER .75 GPM

SHRUBBERY SPRAY
A-17 SERIES
1/2" FEMALE THREAD
6' - 15' SPACING
12' MAX.
FULL CIRCLE 3 GPM
12'
12'
HALF CIRCLE 1.5 GPM
QUARTER CIRCLE 1.4 GPM
END STRIP
4'
.5 GPM

BUBBLER
NO. 1300
SCREW TO REGULATE FLOW
STRAINER
3'
1.4 GPM
HEADS ILLUSTRATED ARE BY RAIN BIRD

perimeter system because it is out of the way and located on the edge of the lawn. The above grade impulse sprinkler covers the same area as the flush pop-up impulse type and costs about a third of the retracting flush head type. Both can be adjusted to cover any part of a circle and the diameter of the circle.

(2) The POP-UP SPRAY does just that; when the water is turned on the head pops up but does not revolve. The only moving part is the center spray tube which slides up only when the water is on; when the water is turned off a stainless steel spring inside the case pulls the head down flush with the surface. The head can be adjusted to cover any part of a circle (square coverage is also available) and the amount of water used depends upon the area covered.

(3) SHRUBBERY SPRAY comes in models that cover a full, half, quarter circle and even a rectangular strip. Unlike the impulse type they have no moving parts, are very economical but must be mounted on a riser. The height of the riser above the ground depends upon what you want to water.

(4) BUBBLER heads are also mounted on a short riser but the circle of spray is directly downward toward the roots and avoids foliage that should not

RAIN BIRD UNDERGROUND SPRINKLER COMPONENTS

be watered. Roses are an excellent example.

The average lawn and garden will require many if not all of these heads and the best way to learn about them is to buy a sprinkler head hose connected spike and screw each head to the top of the spike to see how the various heads work. Once you have examined the type of sprinkler heads you are using you will note how various adjustments are made to control both the distance and coverage properly and after installation if a unit does not work you can usually determine why and solve the problem.

CHOOSING AND USING PLASTIC PIPE

There are a few important points regarding the selection of the pipe you use for your sprinkler system and some timesaving techniques you should consider.

When you tap into your supply line (or hose outlet if it is of the same diameter as the service line) to build a manifold for a series of valves that lead to individual circuits, you should use Schedule 40 PVC plastic pipe with cemented joints or copper tubing with solder joints. However, the pipe leading from the control valves to the sprinkler heads can be either PVC or the flexible "poly" pipe — the short name for polyethylene. Both have advantages and disadvantages of which you should be aware.

Poly pipe is the preferred pipe for most underground sprinkler systems because (1) It is more economical, costing about 40 percent less than PVC. (2) It is very flexible and can be bent

around corners and, because of its flexibility, it is virtually freeze proof — an important consideration when an underground system is installed in colder areas. (3) With poly pipe the heads are connected with what are called insert fittings, which merely slip into the pipe and are usually held in place with stainless steel clamps. Thus, if you make an error on the location of a head all you need do is to cut into the pipe, add an extension called an insert coupling, and the usual clamps.

Some sprinkler supply outlets also sell a hose clamp that must be crimped with a special tool to make a leakproof connection. These clamps are very economical and if your layout is large enough it will be cost effective to buy the crimping tool and the clamps. However, once a clamp is in place it might be a problem if you change your mind as to the location of the sprinkler head. Poly pipe comes in coils of 100 to 400 feet which for some installations may not produce a cost effective installation. Why buy a large coil if you only need 40 feet? For much smaller jobs the semi-rigid PVC pipe used to build the valve manifold is a better selection because it is available in 10-foot and sometimes 20-foot lengths. But care must be taken when adding the heads because once a fitting is cemented in place the only way to correct an error is to saw the pipe and add a coupling — a more tedious chore than correcting the same problem with poly lines.

Since you will be working with both types of plastic pipe, here are a few tested tips. First, cutting poly pipe is easy with a sharp utility knife. Dig the point into the wall and work your way around the perimeter to cut completely through the wall. Insert fittings are molded to produce a very tight fit, and if the pipe is cold it is difficult to push the fitting all the way into the end. Solve this condition by heating the end of the pipe, using a heat gun or even an electric hair dryer. You will find the plastic softens quickly which makes it extremely easy to push the fitting in place. And, when you tighten the hose clamp; do not use a blade screwdriver even though a slot is available in the screw head; use a nut driver, which will not slip off when the clamp is tightened.

Working with PVC pipe requires following a basic procedure. Cut the pipe, using a miter box and a hack saw so you end up with a square cut. Remove the burrs, pre-assemble the fitting and, once it is rotated to the correct position, mark the hub and pipe as shown. Then, when joining, brush on a primer and then a coat of cement. Insert and line up the marks.

ABOUT TIMERS AND VALVES

Once you have determined how many heads you need for complete coverage of your lawn, shrubs and trees, and you have divided the number into separate supply lines to serve a group of heads, you can reach a decision as to the number of individual valves you need for the system. And when you know how many valves you will need you can then select the type of timer to control these valves. Two types of automatic sprinkler valves are available; a type mounted on the side of your house and protected by a shed-type covering or an in-line valve that is mounted underground in a recommended protective concrete box with a cover so you can gain access for maintenance. If you elect not to have an automatic system, manual valves are available. They are just like the automatic valves in that they have the anti-syphon feature but you must turn them on and off.

We prefer the side wall type because of the ease of accessibility. With the exception of the in-line valves, all valves should be of the anti-syphon type so existing water in the sprinkler lines cannot be syphoned into your regular drinking water lines if for any reason you lose water pressure. This is a rare possibility but a possibility nevertheless, so the codes call for sprinkler valves to be of the non-

syphon type.

All sprinkler valves work on low voltage (24 volts) but the timer which controls the valves must be plugged into a 120-volt line The number of valves a timer can control can range from two to seven, or in some cases more. In some instances you may have the timer located in one spot and a few valves in another part of your yard. In such instances merely run underground 18-gauge vinyl covered wire from the timer to the valves. Because the voltage is only 24-volts, there is no danger. The early timers had mechanical tripping arms that turned the trigger switch that actuated the solenoid of a valve, but now this function is usually done electronically. With a digital reading timer you can program the timer to water many times a day for a few minutes and regulate the watering time of each valve. You can even schedule watering every other day every third day, etc. And in the event of rain you can fit your timer with a simple low-cost device that will prevent the system from turning on when it is raining!

When shopping for a timer, consider one that has more stations than you need at the present time because with drip watering systems becoming more and more popular to compensate for escalating cost of water you should be prepared to add valves and additional lines in the future.

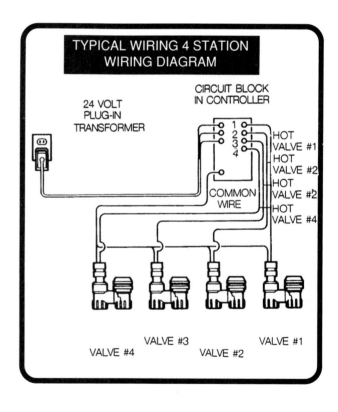

TYPICAL WIRING 4 STATION WIRING DIAGRAM

INDEX

A

42A Junction, telephone installation, 278, 279, 282, 286
ABS, see Acrylonitrile-butadiene-styrene
AC, see Alternating current
Acid-cleaning, see Muriatic acid
Acrylic
  paint
    alkyd (oil-based) comparison, 389, 390-391, see also Paint
    concrete, 349
    definition, 403
    durability, 419
    interior, 396-397
    waterproof shower walls, 524
Acrylonitrile-butadiene-styrene (ABS) pipe, 118-119, see also Pipes, plastic
Activators, pre-pasted wallcoverings, 474
Adapters
  plumbing, 104, 105, 112, 113, 116, 122
  telephone installation, 284, 285
Adhesion, see also Adhesives
  paints, 390, 404
  solid latex stains, 397
Adhesives, see also Cements; Glues
  concrete patios, 384
  contact for plywood, 525
  silicone for damper installation, 505
  wall paneling, 69, 70
  wallcovering, 446-447, 452-453
ADS system, underground drainage, 121
Aerators, faucet, 157
Aging, paints, 391, see also Paint
Air chambers, 100, 113
Airless sprayers, 430-431
Air-entrained concrete, 298, 302-303, 307, see also Concrete
A-line bulbs, outdoor lighting, 265, 266
Alkyd (oil-based) paints, see also Paint
  acrylic latex comparison, 389, 390-391
  definition, 402
  interior, 396-397
  older homes, 403
Alternating current (AC)
  power stations, 194
  telephone bells, 280, 281
  transformers for, 196
Alternators, 195
Aluminum
  electrical conductor role, 196
  wiring, 204
Aluminum siding, painting, 391, 400-401
American Plywood Association (APA), 60, 61
American Wood Preservers Bureau, (AWPB), 88, 89
Ampacity, 230
Amperes
  definition, 195
  requirement calculations, 242-243
Amps, see Amperes
Anchors, deck construction, 90, 92
Angle stop valve, 103, see also Valves
Angles
  right, miter box for, 22-23
  squares for determination, 17
Anodes, fluorescent lamps, 248
Anti-syphon valves, underground sprinkler systems, 534
Apartments, telephone layout, 282
Appliances
  ampere requirements, 242-243
  electrical safety check, 205
  ground testing, 241

Appliances, cont...
  polarity, 237
  testing circuits, 215-216
  ungrounded and GFCI use, 222
Arc, fluorescent lamps, 249
Argon, fluorescent lamps, 248-249
Armored cables, see BX cables; see also Cables, electric
Artificial respiration, 201
Asphalt, roll roofing installation, 502
Attic fans, winterizing, 490
Attics, insulation, 497, 498, 501
Augers
  bits, 21
  posthole digging, 512
  using, 28, 190, 191, 192
Awls, starting holes, 21, see also Tools
AWPB, see American Wood Preservers Bureau

B

Back-siphonage, 103, 168, 170
Backup electrical protection, 201
Baffles, attic insulation, 498
Bagging-in, masonry walls, 366, 367
Ballasts, fluorescent lamps, 249, 250, 251
Basements, wall insulation, 498
Bases, fluorescent lamps, 248
Bathroom sinks, replacing, see Sinks, replacement
Bathtubs, waterproof walls, 524
Batterys, cordless tools, 42, 43
Bells, door, see Door chimes (bells/buzzers)
Belts, sanding, 34
Benches, built-in on decks, 96
Bending
  copper tubing, 129, 131
  electrical nonmetallic tubing, 244
  metal conduit, 233
Bending spring, 131
Bends, 104, 105, 107, 122
Beveling
  chisels for, 20
  electric planes, 39
Bimetallic action, 104, 109
Binders, paint durability, 388, 390, 405, 418-419, see also Paints
Bi-pin base, fluorescent lamps, 248
Birdbaths, mounting, 513
Biscuits, router for, 41
Bits, 14, see also Screwdrivers
  electric drills, 30
  electric shaper, 53
  router, 41
Black iron pipe, see Pipes, black iron
Blackouts, power, 272-273
Blades, see also Knives; Saws
  carbide-tipped, 33, 45
  electric utility saws, 38
  saber saw, 36, 52
Bleach, mildew removal, 457
Bleaching, paints, 390
Bleed-through, 418
Blind rivet-nut, 517
Blistering, paint, 404, see also Paint
Blocks, leveling, 19
Boardfeet, determining, 56-57
Blind rivets, 516
Bolts
  anchor, drapery rod mounting, 526
  carriage
    deck construction, 90, 91, 94, 95
    mailbox/planter, 520

Bolts, cont...
  molly, drapery rod mounting, 526
  toggle
    drapery rod mounting, 526
    swag light installation, 274
Bonding agents, concrete, 334-335, 344, 384
Bonding screws, see Screws, bonding
Bonds, brick, 369, 371, see also Bricks
Booking, wallcoverings, 452, 453, 475, see also Wallcoverings
Box connectors, regulations for, 235
Boxes, outlet, 228, 232, 233, see also Outlets, replacement
Bracing ceiling fans, 527
Branch vents, see Revents
Brass pipe, see Pipes, brass threaded
Bricks
  cutting, 9, 300-301
  fences, 365
  laying, 368-373
  leveling, 19
  paints for, 391
  patios, 382
  repointing, 374-375
  roller covers for, 413
  surface preparation for painting, 399
  walkways, 326, 329
Bridge paintbrushes, 408, see also Paintbrushes
British Thermal Unit (BTU), 108
Broom finishes, concrete, 299, 341, 344
Brushes, solvent-welding, 137-138
BTU, see British Thermal Unit
Bubble pot, 528
Bubbles, deflating in wallcoverings, 478
Buffing, 35, 51
Building drain, waste water, 101
Bulbs, fluorescent and incandescent comparison, 483
Bull floats, concrete finishing, 294-295, 296, 297, 300
Burlap bags, texturing concrete walls, 366, 367
Burrs, wall paneling, 65
Bushings, see Reducers
Buzzers, door, see Door chimes (bells/buzzers)
BX cable, 230, 232, 233, see also Cables, electric

C

Cabinets, making corner joints, 86
Cables
  armored, safety check, 205
  electric, types and sizes, 230, 231-235
  outdoor lighting, 264-265
  running through ceiling, 228
  securing, 237
  stainless steel, damper installation, 505
CABO, see Council of American Building Officials
Canadian Electric Code, 203
Canadian Standards Association (CSA), 203, 204
Cardboard, paint cover cores, 412
Cardiopulmonary resuscitation (CPR), 201
CCA, see Chromated copper arsenate
Ceiling fans, bracing, 527
Ceilings
  beamed, insulation, 500
  insulation, 497, 498-499
  suspended, see Tile, ceiling
Carlon box, 240, 247, see also Outlet boxes
Cast iron traps, cleanout, 102, see also Traps
Cathodes, fluorescent lamps, 248

Caulking, silicone for flashing, 506
  painting, 413, 417, 428
    wallcovering hanging, 470-471
Cellulose, insulation rating, 497, 498
Cement, see also Concrete
  concrete comparison, 290-292
  surface preparation for painting, 399
Cement-plastering, 366-367
Cement mixers, 293, 302-303, 306-307
Cements, plastic pipe, 118-119, 136
Chair, construction of child's, 521
Chalking, paints, 391, 403, 405, 419
Charging, cordless tools, 42, 43
Check valves, well water, 164, see also Valves
Chimney flashing, 506
Chipping, hammers, 8
Chisels
  brick, 301
  butt, 20
  cold, 20
  mill, 20
  repointing bricks, 374
  rip, 29
  wood, 20
Chlorinated polyvinyl chloride (CPVC) pipe,
    water supply, 114, 115, 116, see also
    Pipes, plastic, water supply
Choke coils, see Ballasts
Chop and pry bar, 9
Chromated copper arsenate (CCA), 88, 89,
    92
Cinder blocks, column construction, 515, see
    also Concrete blocks
Circles, cutting, 33, 37
Circuit breakers, see also Fuses
  ampacity/wattage, 230
  electrical fires, 203
  fuse comparison, 208-209
  panel labeling, 203, 208
  tripped, 273
Circuit overload, fire danger, 203-204
Circuitracer, 200, 215, 216, 217
Clamps
  repairing leaks in pipe, 187
  types of, 22, 24
Cleaners, plastic tubing, 136
Cleaning
  concrete tools, 300
  paint, 391, 395
  rollers, 424-425
  surfaces, 397, 398, 399
  brushes, 410, 424-425
  power flo paint stick, 427
  solid latex stains, 397
Cleanout
  accessibility when plumbing add-on rooms,
    168
  plastic pipe, 116
  unclogging pipes, 102
Clogging, see also Pipes
  horizontal pipes, 102
  toilets, 150
Closure brick, 370, 373, see also Bricks
Clothing, painting, 401
Coatings, black iron pipe, 108
Codes, electrical, see Regulations, electrical
Codes, plumbing, see Regulations, plumbing
Coffee table/planter, outdoor construction, 518
Cold water, plastic pipes for, 116-117, see also
    Pipes
Color fading, paint, 388, 389
Color retention, solid latex stains, 397
Colored lamps, outdoor lighting, 266
Coloring
  concrete, 348-349
  mortar, 351
  stucco walls, 366
Columns, construction of stone, 515
Composite board, 60, 61

Compression fitting, copper tubing, 110, 113,
    see also Fittings
Concrete, 290-384
  basics, 290-293
  buying ready-mix, 308-311
  calculating quantities, 304
  cement comparison, 290-292
  chiseling, 20
  coloring, 348-349
  curing, 318-319
  decorative surfaces, 340-346
  floors, 330-333
  painting, 398-399
  footings, 320-323
  forms of, 292
  handling fresh, 325-326
  mixing, 292-293, 302-307
  ordering, 312-315
  paints for, 391
  patio installation, 380-384
  poured driveways and curbs, 336-339
  preplanning, 309-311
  proportion determination, 305
  repairing walks and drives, 334-335
  retaining walls, 360-361
  roller covers for, 413
  sacked, 316-317
  walks, 324-329
Concrete blocks
  fences, 365
  cutting, 300-301
  laying, 352-359
Concrete bricks, 353-354, see also Bricks;
    Concrete blocks
Concrete slabs, fences, 365
Concrete walls, lining paper for, 460
Conductors, electricity, 196-197
Conduit
  securing, 237
  electric wiring, 231, 232-233, see also
    Cables, electric
Connectors, flexible copper, 131
Continuity testers, 215-216, 224
Contour sticks, use for wall paneling, 71
Contractors, painting, 387
Control joints
  concrete block wall installation, 357
  concrete finishing, 296, 300, 301
  concrete floors, 333
  walk and drive resurfacing, 335
  walks, 324-325
Cooking, emergencies, 273
Copper, electrical conductor role, 196
Copper tubing, see Pipes, copper
Cordless rollers, painting, 428-429
Cords, three-pronged, 200
Cores, filling, 353-354, see also Concrete
Cork wallcoverings, 447, see also
    Wallcoverings
Corners, hanging wallcoverings, 464-466, 466-
    467, see also Wallcoverings
Corrosion
  black iron pipe, 108
  brass pipe, 109
  copper tubing, 110
  door bell buttons, 254, 256
  electrical wiring, 204
  faucets, 174
  hot water heater tanks, 142
Council of American Building Officials (CABO),
    496
Countertops, changing when replacing sinks,
    144, 145, 146-147
Couplers, telephone installation, 288
Couplings, 104, 105, 112, 113
  brass, 126
  plastic pipe, 116, 117
  Uncopper, working with, 141
CO/ALR stamp, electrical wiring, 204

CPVC, see Chlorinated polyvinyl chloride
Cracking, paint, 390, 404-405, 419
Cracks, drywall/plaster repair, 457
Creosote, fence posts, 512
Crimping tool, underground sprinkler systems,
    533
Cross-connections, 103
CSA, see Canadian Standards Association
Curbs, concrete, 338-339
Curing, concrete, 318-319
  floors, 333
  painting, 398-399
Curing compounds, 318, see also Curing,
    concrete
Current, shutting off, 197, 198
Curves, router for, 41
Cuts, interval, making with jig saw, 52
Cutters
  cable, 27
  fence, 27
  tubing, 128
Cutting
  bricks, 372
  concrete blocks, 300-301
  copper tubing, 128
  countertops for sink replacement, 146-147
  electrical nonmetallic tubing, 245
  plastic tubing, 136, 140
  rigid plastic pipe, 137
  threaded pipe, 133-134
Cutting oil, threaded pipe, 133, 134

D
Dadoes
  circular saw for, 33
  making with table saw, 45
  plain, 83-84, 86
  radial arm saw, 46, 47
  router for, 41
  stopped, 83-84
Damper, installation for fireplace, 505
Darby, concrete finishing, 294-295, 297
Darex, 303
Deburring tools, plastic tubing, 136
Decay resistance, pressure-treated wood, 88
Decks
  bench construction, 96
  construction of, 90-96
  floor joists, mounting, 93
  hardware and fasteners, 90
  ledger attachment, 91
  lighting, 267, 269-270
  paintbrush for, 409
  pier and post positioning, 92
  plank installation, 94
  safety rail, 95
Decorating, see also Painting; Wallcoverings
  planning in advance, 435
  terminology glossary, 442-443
  wallcoverings, 433-437
  problem areas, 438-439
  special rooms, 440-441
  unusual, 446-447
De-icing chemicals, concrete, 329
Desk, construction of child's folding, 521
Diameter, copper tubing, 127
Dielectric couplings, 104, 109, see also
    Couplings
Dielectric vinyl liquid, moisture-proofing wire
    splices, 239-240
Dies, cutting threaded pipe, 133, 134
Dimmers switches, installation, 234, see also
    Switches, replacement
Dimming, fluorescent lamps, 250-251
Direct current (DC), voice transmission on
    telephones, 280, 281
Dirt resistance
  elastomeric coatings, 400-401
  paints, 396, 397, 405, 418

Dishwasher, water supply, 100
Dismanteling, hammers, 8, see also Tools
Dog house, construction, 481
Door chimes (bells/buzzers), 254-257
Doors
    hanging wallcoverings around, 466-467
    hinges, mortise cutting, 20
    masking, 422-423
    paint applications, 417
    patio, pin lock installation, 510
    planing, 39
    screen replacement, 488, 489
    trimming with planes, 16
Doorways, trimming wall panels, 72
Double cutting, see also Wallcoverings
    torn wallcoverings, 479
    wallcoverings, 467, 468
Dovetails, 83
    double lap, 84
    lap, 84
    router for, 41
    secret (miter), 84
Dowels, joint construction, 85, 86
Downspout, installation of underground, 528, 529
Dowsing, 163
Drag, alkyd paints, 391, see also Painting
Drain cleaners, unclogging, 188, 190
Drain King, unclogging drains, 190, 192
Drain tile, retaining walls, 360
Drainage
    concrete driveways, 337
    concrete floors, 331-332
    retaining walls, 360, 363
    sidewalks, 324-325
    underground, pipes for, 120-121
Drainage fittings, 104
Drains
    bath tubs, installation in add-on rooms, 172
    branch, unclogging, 191
    building, 101
    pop-up, faucet installation, 157
    sinks, installation, 144, 146, 147, 148
    runs for add-on rooms, 166-168
    washing machines, 184-185
Drain-waste-vent (DWV)
    copper tubing, 112-114, see also Pipes, copper tubing
    planning for add-on rooms, 168-169, 170, 171, see also Rooms, piping add-on
    structure of, 100-102
    plastic pipe, 118, 119
Drapery rods, mounting, 526
Dresser tee, 107, see also Tees
Drill points, sharpening, 30
Drilling, wells, 161-162
Drills, see also Tools
    electrical repairs, 215, 247
    types of, 21, 30-31, 43
Driveways, see also Concrete
    installation of concrete, 336-339
    repairing concrete, 334-335
Drop match pattern, wallcovering, 450-451, see also Wallcoverings
Dropped ceiling, see Tile, ceiling
Drying time, paints, 391, see also Paints
Drywall, paint primers, 395, see also Gypsum wallboard
D-shaped grounding holes, receptacles, 200
Dual outlet adapter, telephone installation, 284, 285
Dumet wire, 248
Durability
    elastomeric coatings, 401
    paint, 388-389, 390
    solid latex stains, 397
    wallcoverings, 444
Duroc, 78
Dust bags, electric sanders, 34, 35

Dust-on method, coloring concrete, 348-349
DWV, see Drain-waste-vent

E
Easy up system, 486, see also Tile, ceiling
Economy bricks, 369, see also Bricks
Edges, planing, 17, 39
Edging, concrete, 295-297
Elasteromic coatings, masonry, 400-401
Elasticity, latex paints, 404-405, see also Paints
Elbows, 104, 105, 107, 112, 113
    cast iron pipe, 122
    plastic pipe, 116, 117
Electric hot water heaters, see Water heaters, installation
Electric service, determination, 230
Electrical, 194-288, see Individual entries
Electrical nonmetallic tubing (ENT), 235, see also Cables, electric
    installation, 244-247
Electrical power, testing, 202
Electricity
    basic facts, 194-197
    safety, 198-205
Electrons, movement and electricity, 195
Ells, brass, 126
Embrittling, paints, 390, 391, 396, 419
Emery cloth, sweat-soldering copper tubing, 128
Enamels, see also Paint
    acrylic high-gloss, 404-405
    high-gloss, priming, 395
Energy, costs, 496
Engines, turbine, 194
English bond, bricklaying, 371, see also Bricks
ENT, see Electrical nonmetallic tubing
Entranceways, lighting, 268-269, 271
Environment, paint development, 405
Epoxy paints, concrete, 349, see also Paints
Escutcheons, hiding minor wallcovering mistakes, 468
Expansion joints, see Isolation joints, sidewalks
Exposed-aggregate driveways, 338
    installation, 340-344, see also Concrete
Extenders, paints, 390, 405, 419, see also Paints
Extension cords
    temporary use, 205
    safety, 200
Extension handles, rollers, 414-415, see also Painting
Exterior painting, see also Painting
Exteriors, power paint sprayers, 430-431

F
Fabric wallcoverings, 447, see also Wallcoverings
Fabrics, coordinated to wallpaper, 433, 434, see also Wallcoverings
Fading, paints, 390-391, see also Paints
Fascia, aluminum, 491, 492, 495
Faucets
    bathroom, installation, 146
    fixing, 174-177
    installation, 154-159
    sinks, 149
Federal Communication Commission (FCC), telephone installation, 278, 288
Felt, roofing, 502
Fences
    building, 512
    brick and rail, 371
    chain link, painting, 420, 421
    masonry, 364-365
    painting with mitt, 415
Ferrules
    brass, 127, 131

Ferrules, *cont...*
    leather, 408, 410
Fiberglass
    insulation rating, 497
    roof panels, 509
    shingles, 504
    waterproof shower walls, 524
Filaments, paintbrushes, 409, see also Paintbrushes, construction
Files
    steel, 29
    threaded pipe cutting, 134
    wood surform, 28
Films, latex paints, 391, 418, see also Paints
Filters, underground downspouts, 528, 529
Fireplaces
    chimney-top damper, 505
    footings, 321, 323
Fires
    electrical, 203-204
    painting safely, 401
Fittings
    brass flare, 126
    cast iron pipe, 122
    copper tubing
        flare/compression, 110, 112-113, 127, 130-131
        sizes, 111
    galvanized steel pipe, 107
    no-hub pipe, 125
    plastic pipe, 114-117
    repairing leaks in, 187
    threaded
        installation, 134-135
        makeup, 132-133, 134
        plastic pipe, 138-139
    transition, 139
    vinyl tubing, 120
    winged, 140
Fixtures
    electrical safety check, 205
    lighting
        polarity of, 236
        voltage testing, 202
    placing for add-on rooms, 167, 168, 172
    plumbing, 100, see also Individual entries
Flags, paintbrushes for, 409
Flagstone
    patios, 382
    walkways in mortar, 327
Flaking, paint, 390, 404-405, 419, see also Paints
Flammability, paints, 391, see also Paints
Flange, toilet, 104
Flange bolts, toilet installation, 152, 153
Flare fitting, copper tubing, 110, 113, see also Fittings
Flaring, copper tubing, 127, 129, 130, 131
Flashing
    chimney, 506
    fluorescent lamps, 251
Flat paint, use, 396, 397, see also Paint
Flemish bond, bricklaying, 370, 371, see also Bricks
Flex, 233-234, see also Cables, electric
Flexibility, paints, 390, 404-405, see also Paints
Flickering, fluorescent lamps, 251
Float valves, see Valves
Floating, concrete, 294-296, 298
    curbs, 338
    floors, 333
    sidewalks, 328
Flock wallcoverings, 447, see also Wallcoverings
Floodlights, overhead, 270-271, see also Lighting
Floor pan, installation in add-on rooms, 172
Flooring, nails, 80

Floors, see also Concrete
concrete, 330-333
painting, 398-399
paint application, 417
Flue, checking, 143
Fluorescent lamps, outdoor lighting, 266, see also Lamps, fluorescent
Flush jack converter, 288, see also Modular jack
Flush valves, toilets, 178, see also Toilets, fixing
Flush wall jack, 288, see also Wall jack
Flusher fixer kit, 181, see also Toilets, fixing
Flushing
exposed-aggregate driveways, 342, 343
partial, 182, see also Toilets, fixing
water usage, 150
Flux, see also Soldering; Sweat-soldering
soldering electrical wires, 218
sweat-soldering copper tubing, 127-129
Foils, metallic, lining paper for, 460, see also Wallcoverings
Foliage, lighting, 263-265, 266, 267, see also Lighting, landscape
Footings, 320-323
deck construction, 92
masonry fences, 364
stone columns, 515
stone walls, 378
Forms, see also Concrete
concrete retaining walls, 363
concrete sidewalks, 328
Foundations
pouring and R-values, 497
undermining by rainwater, 528-529
Four-prong adapter, telephone installation, 285, 288, see also Telephones
Framing, chisels for, 20, see also Tools
Freeze/thaw cycles, paint durability, 388, 389, see also Paints
Freezing
concrete block wall installation, 359
concrete curing, 329
copper tubing, 113
Fuels, electric generators, 194-195
Furniture, see also Specific entries
common joints used in, 85
planes for, 16
Furring
aluminum siding installation, 494
ceiling tile installation, 486-487
Fuses, see also Circuit breakers
ampacity/wattage, 230
electric, 209-211
electrical fires, 203, 204
rating check for safety, 205
Future flusher, 182, 183, see also Toilets

G

Gallons per minute (GPM), rating, 530, 531, 532
Galvanized steel armored cables, 232, see also Cables, electric pipes, see Pipes, galvanized steel
Gardens, lighting, 263-265, see also Lighting, landscape
Gas piping, black iron pipe, 108, see also Pipe, black iron
Gaskets, rubber
sink installation, 149
toilet, 153
Gas-fired hot water heaters, see also Water heaters, installation
Gate valves, 112, see also Valves
Gauges
marking, 29
suspended ceiling installation, 484-485
Generators, electricity, 194

Glass
cutting, 511
sanding, 35
Glass mask, painting, 423
Globe valves, 112, see also Valves
plastic pipe, 116
washing machines, 184
Gloves, 201, 301
Glues, see also Adhesives
epoxy, repairing leaky fittings, 187
plywood manufacturing, 61
Gluing, loose edges on wallcoverings, 478
Gouging, chisels for, 20, see also Tools
GPM, see Gallons per minute
Grading, patio installation, 382
Grasscloth wallcoverings, 434, 445, 446, see also Wallcoverings
lining paper, 460
Gravel-mix, prepackaged, 316, see also Concrete
Grazing light, 264, see also Lighting, landscape
Grids, suspended ceiling, 76, 482, 483
Grille blocks, see also Concrete blocks
laying, 359
masonry fences, 364
Grinders, see also Tools
electric, 51
electric drills, 30
Groovers, concrete finishing, 296
Grooves
planes for, 16
router for, 41
Ground
energized circuits and, 198-199
finding, 224-225
testing for, 216-217
Ground faults
dangers of, 199-200
protection against, 223, see also Ground-Fault Circuit Interrupter (GFCI)
Ground spike lighting, outdoors, 270
Grounding
electrical equipment, 199-200
electrical nonmetallic tubing, 247
outdoor lighting, 265
Ground-Fault Circuit Interrupter (GFCI)
installing and safety, 200
monthly test, 202
outdoor lighting, 265
working and installation of, 222-225
Grout, see also Tile, ceramic
retaining walls, 362
Grout and pump mix, 311, see also Concrete
Gutters
aluminum, 491
retaining wall drainage, 360
Gypsum wallboard (drywall; sheetrock)
screws, 80-81
installation, 78-79
over rough surfaces, 461
repairing, 457-458

H

Hacksaw, see also Tools
accessory for drill, 30
electrical repairs, 215
Hammers, 8-9, see also Tools
electric repair, 247
masonry work, 300-301, 372
Handles, paintbrush, 411, see also Painting
Handset, 288
Handset cords, 285, 288
Hangers, see also Supports
copper runs, 129
joist, deck construction, 90, 91, 92, 93
plastic pipe, 138-139
Hardboard
plastic surface, 524

Hardboard, cont...
wall paneling, 62, 67
Hardening concrete, see Concrete, curing
Hardwood, 57-58
Hard-tempered copper tubing, see Pipes, copper Hard-wired telephones, conversion to modular telephone, 286, 288, see also Telephones
Hatchet, 9, see also Tools
Hawks, repointing bricks, 375, see also Bricks
Headers, see also Bricks, laying
bricklaying, 369, 371
stone walls, 376-377
Heating, electricity relation, 195-196
Heat-shrink tubing, see Tubing, heat-shrink
Hiding ability, paints, 390, 391, 396, 419, see also Paint
Highlighting, 263, see also Lighting, landscape
High-gloss paints, see also Paint
acrylic, development of, 404-405
trim, 419
use, 396, 397
Hinges, door, see Doors, hinges
Hog bristle paintbrushes, 407, see also Paintbrushes
tipping, 409
Hole cutter, 30, see also Tools
Holes
cutting in wall paneling, 66
hand drilling, 21
making with drill press, 50
Homes
painting older, 402-403
telephone layout in two-story, 283
Hooks, swag light installation, 274
Horsepower rating, 30, 34, 39, 44, 48
Hose spigots, cross-connections, 103
Hot water
delivery, 142
main, 100
HUD see U.S. Department of Housing and Urban Development
Humidity, paint durability, 388
Hydrochloric acid, see Muriatic acid

I

IMD, see Infrared motion detectors
Infrared motion detectors (IMD), 271
Insert boxes, see Old work boxes
Insert coupling, underground sprinkler systems, 533, see also Sprinkler systems
Insert fittings, underground sprinkler systems, 533, 534
Inspections
electrical, 203
plumbing, 103
add-on rooms, 171-172
Instant-start lamps, see Fluorescent lamps
Insulation
attic, 501
beamed ceiling, 500
dog house, 481
electric wiring
color-coded, 235-236
stripping and splices, 239
rigid vs. poured, 498
types and R-values, 496-497, 499
Insulators, electrical conduction, 197
Integral coloring, concrete, 348, see also Concrete
Interior painting, see Painting
Irrigation, plastic pipe for, 117
Isocyanurate, insulation, 499, 500
Isolation joints (concrete), see also Concrete
curbs, 338
floors, 330
patios, 381
sidewalks, 327-328

J

Jet pumps, see Pumps, water supply
Jitterbug, concrete finishing, 295
Joint knife, 29
Jointer-planer, electric, 54
Jointing, concrete, 295-297, 300
Joints, 82-87
  box, 84
  brick, 369
  compound, repair, 458
  coped, 86-87
  corner, reinforcement, 84
  crossover, 85-86
  dado, 83
  dovetail, 83, 84
  edge-to edge, 86
  keyed in concrete, 338
  lap, 83, 85
  lengthening, 86
  miter, 84-85
  mitered bridle, 85
  mortise, 83, 84
  no-hub, 125, see also No-Hub pipe
  soldering copper tubing, 110
  tenon, 83, 84
  three-way, 86
  Uncopper, 141
Joists
  ceiling
    Easy up system, 486
    fan braces in, 527
    suspended, 484-485
  decks, 91, 93
  roof, insulation, 498
Jumpers, sizing in wiring, 238-239
Junction box, tapping into in telephone
    installation, 287, see also Telephones

K

Keyed footings, 323, see also Footings
Keyed joints, concrete curbs, 338
Keyless chuck, 30
Kilowatt-hour, electricity costs, 195
King Norman bricks, 369, see also Bricks
Kitchen faucets, single-lever, repair, see
    Faucets, fixing
Kitchen sinks, replacing, see Sinks, replacing
Knee-boards, concrete finishing, 296, 298
Knives
  pocket, 213
  utility, electric work, 239, 247
Kraft paper, resin-impregnated for paint cover
    cores, 412

L

Lacquer, solvents for cleanup, 424
Lacquer thinner, paint cleanup, 424
Ladders
  roller trays used with, 415
  safe use in painting, 400-401
  wallcovering hanging, 448
Lally columns, 333
Lamb's wool, painting mitts, 421
Lamps
  fluorescent, 248-253
  outdoor, 265-266
  repair of socket, 275
  soldering cord for, 219, 220-221
  swag, installation, 274
Landscaping, lighting, see Lighting, landscape
Latex paints, see also Paint
  cleaning up tools, 424-425
  definition, 402
  durability, 418-419
  hog bristle paintbrushes, 407
  power paint roller, 428-429
  storage, 402-403
Lathe, electric, 55, see also Tools
Laundry tubs, cross-connections, 103

Laundry/utility faucets, repair, see Faucets,
    fixing
Lavatory
  faucets, repair, see Faucets, fixing
  installation in add-on rooms, 170-171
  wall-hung, replacing, 146, 149
Laws, fence installation, 364
Lead, cast iron pipe, 122, 123, see also Pipes,
    cast iron
Leaks
  checking for in add-on rooms, 171
  faucet installation, 157, see also Faucets,
    fixing
  repairing, 186-187
  sink installation, 148, 149
  toilets, see Toilets, fixing
Ledgers, deck construction, 91
Leveling, see also Bricks; Concrete
  bricklaying, 372
  concrete block walls, 355, 356
  concrete floors, 330
Levels
  concrete finishing, 300
  types, 19
Life Wood, 88, see also Lumber, pressure-
    treated
Light bulbs, life-span and dimming, 260
Lighting
  dramatic, 258-261
  fixtures and insulation, 498, 499
  landscaping, 262-267
  recessed, 482, 483
  security/safety, 268-271
  temporary during power outages, 272, 273
Lights, fluorescent for suspended ceilings, 483
Line blocks, 300
Line cord, telephone installation, 285
Line voltage, rating of electrical appliances,
    196
Linen texture wallcoverings, 447
Linerless 130C tape, 239
Linesman pliers, see also Tools
  electrical nonmetallic tubing, 247
  electrical repairs, 213-214
Lining paper, wallcovering, 460-461, see also
    Wallcoverings
Lintels, 353
Live load, footings determination, 320, 321,
    see also Footings
Locks, pin type installation in patio doors, 510,
    see also Doors
Logs, cutting with chain saw, 38
Low-voltage outdoor lighting, see Lighting,
    landscaping
LP gas, pipe, 108
Lumber, 56-61
  common grading, 56-58
  pressure-treated, 88-89, see also Deck,
    construction
  cutting with circular saw, 33
  fences, 512
  mailbox/planter, 520
  outdoor table/planter, 518
  recommendations, 89
  ripping, 44, 49
  select grading, 56-58

M

Magic 30 technique, wallcovering estimating,
    454-455
Magnesium anodes, hot water heaters, 143,
    see also Water heaters
Mailbox/planter, construction, 520
Main stack, 101
Makeup distance
  plastic tubing, 136
  threaded pipe, 132-133, 134
Mallets, 8, see also Hammers
Marble, sanding, 35

Masking, windows and doors, 422-423
Masonry, see also Painting
  elastomeric coatings, 400-401
  paint primers, 394
  paint sealers, 395
  paintbrush for, 408, 410
  paints for, 391
  surface preparation for painting, 399
Masonry bits, 30
Masonry cement, 350, see also Concrete
Masonry hammer, 9, see also Tools
  concrete finishing, 300-301
Masonry nails, 80
Mason's hammer, see Masonry hammer
Mason's trowels, concrete finishing, 299-300,
    see also Tools; Trowels
Matting, roller covers, 414, see also Painting
Maul, splitting, 9
MDO, see Medium density overlay
Measuring
  rulers for, 18
  squares for, 17
Medium density overlay (MDO), 61
Mercury switches, see Switches,
    replacement
Mercury vapor, fluorescent lamps, 248
Metal
  chiseling, 20
  cutting with saws, 12, 36
  drilling, 30
  electrical conductor role, 196
  painting
  galvanized, 391
  primers, 394
  surface preparation, 399
  sanding, 35
Metal-encased cable, 230, 232-233, see also
    Cables, electric
Metered concrete, 310-311, see also
    Concrete
Meters
  electric, 195, 196
  as ground, 224
  reading, 206-207
  water, 100
Metric conversion table, 314
Mildew, see also Paints
  exterior paint, 388
  removal with bleach, 457
  resistance in paints, 391
Mildewcide
  paint, 388, 391
  wallcovering activators, 474
Mineral spirits, oil-based paints, 390, 391, see
    also Paints
Minimum Property Standards (MPS), 497
Miter box, 22-23, see also Tools
Miters, radial arm saw, 46
Mitts, paint application, 415, 420, see also
    Painting
Mixed-in method, exposed-aggregate
    driveways, 344, see also Concrete;
    Driveways
Model, making using planes, 16
Modeling, 263, see also Lighting,
    landscape
Modular bricks, 369, see also Bricks
Modular jack, telephone installation, 282,
    283, 284, 285, 286, 287, see also
    Telephones
Modular jack converter, telephone installation,
    282, 283, 284, 285, 286, see also
    Telephones
Modular plug, 288, see also Telephones
Modules, retaining walls, 362
Mohair, roller covers, 413, see also Painting
Moisture
  electrical dangers from, 199, see also
    Electric

Moisture, *cont...*
 Ground-Fault Circuit Interrupter (GFCI), 225, see also Ground-Fault Circuit Interrupter (GFCI)
 paint durability, 388, 389, see also Paint
Moisture-proofing, wire splices, 239-240
Moldings
 aluminum frieze, 491, 492, 493
 cutting with miter box, 22-23
 electric shaper, 53
 joints, 87
 planes for, 16
 plywood edge finishing, 525
Mortar, see also Bricks; Concrete Blocks
 bricklaying, 372-373
 concrete block wall installation, 356, 357
 preparation of, 350-351
 stone walls, 377, 378
Mortar-mix, 316, see also Bricks
Mortise
 cutting with chisel, 20
 router for, 41
Mount structures, fluorescent lamps, 248
MPS see Minimum Property Standards
Multimeter, testing circuits, 213, see also Volt-ohm-milliammeter
Muriatic acid
 bricklaying, 373
 exposed-aggregate driveway brightening, 342, 344
 painting concrete floors, 399
 walk and drive resurfacing, 335
Mylar wallcoverings, 445, 446, see also Wallcoverings
 lining paper for, 460

N

Nail pulling, 8, 26, see also Tools
Nail sets, 28
Nails, 80-81
 deck construction, 90, 92, 93
 galvanized, painting, 418
 penny sizing, 80
 wall paneling installation, 69, 70
National Electrical Code (NEC), 203, 211
 electrical insulation, 239
 Ground-Fault Circuit Interrupter (GFCI), 223, see also Ground-Fault Circuit Interrupter (GFCI)
National Sanitation Foundation (NSF) ratings, plastic pipe, 117
Natural gas, pipe, 108
NEC, see National Electrical Code
Neon, fluorescent lamps, 249
Network Interface, telephone installation, 278, 279, 282-283, 288, see also Telephone
Nippers, 27, see also Tools
Nipples, galvanized steel pipe, 107
NM-B cable, see Cables, electric
NM-C cable, see Cables, electric
Nonmetallic cable, see Cables, electric
No-hub pipe
 add-on room plumbing, 169
 working with, 123-125
Notches, rules for, 171, 172-173
NSF, see National Sanitation Foundation
Nylon filament paintbrushes, 408, see also Painting
 tipping, 409

O

Odor, paints, 391, 395, see also Paint
Ohms, definition, 195
Oil-based paints, see also Paint
 cleaning up tools, 424-425
 durability, 418-419
 hog bristle paintbrushes, 407
 latex comparison, 390
Old work boxes, 235, see also Outlet boxes

O-rings
 faucet installation, 157, 174
 toilet installation, 153
Outlet boxes, ceiling wiring, 232, 234, see also Outlets, replacement
Outlets
 grounded vs. nongrounded, 236
 grounding, 229
 mounting in finished walls, 237
 replacement, 226-229
Overflow, installation in add-on rooms, 172
Oxidation, oil-based paints, 391, 419

P

Packing nuts, faucet repair, 174, 176
Pads, paint application with, 416-417, 421
Paint(s)
 acrylic latex-alkyd comparison, 390-391
 acrylic latex-latex comparison, 386
 application
  pads, 416-417
  paintbrushes, 416-417
  rollers, 416-417
 durability, 418-419
 enemies of, 388-389
 estimation quantities, 392-393
 failure diagnosis, 404-405
 future trends in, 404-405
 interior
  eggshell, sheen, satin, 396, 397
  flat, 396, 397
  high-gloss, 396, 397
  selection, 396-397
  semi-gloss, 396, 397
 storage, 392
 of latex, 402-403
 terminology, 402-403
Paint rollers, 412-415
 accessories, 414-415
 cleaning, 424-425
 cover cores, 412, 414
 covers, 412
 pile heights, 413, 415
 frames, 412, 414
 miniature, 421
 paint application with, 416-417
Paint tongs, paint application, 421
Paintbrushes, 406-411
 cleaning, 424-425
 construction of
  ferrule, 410
  filaments, 409
  handles, 411
  setting, 411
  space plugs, 410
  tipping, 409
 historical background, 406-407
 nylon filaments, 408
 paint application with, 416-417
 polyester filaments, 409
 pure hog bristles, 407
 storage, 425
Painting, 386-431, see also Paint(s)
 concrete, 349
 difficult surfaces, 420-421
 extension handles, 414-415
 exteriors, 416-417
 hiring contractor, 387
 interiors, 416-417
 power flo paint stick, 426-427
 power spraying, 430-431
 problem solving, 418-419
 pros and cons for homeowner, 386-387
 roller cover selection, 413-414
 rollers, 414
  cordless, 428-429
  power, 428-429
 safety tips, 400-401
 siding, 400-401
 surface preparation, 398-399

Paneling, 62-73
 calculating, 63
 inside corners, fitting, 73
 molding, 64, 67
 mounting, 67-71
 ripping, 66
 transport and trimming, 65
 types of, 62
PAR bulbs, outdoor lighting, 265, 266, 268
Particleboard
 structural, 60, 61
 wall paneling, 62, 67
Paste brush, wallcovering hanging, 448
Pastes, antioxidant, 204
Patching
 pipe leaks, 186, 187
 torn wallcoverings, 479
Pathways, lighting, 269-270
Patios
 installation, 380-384
 lighting, 263, see also Lighting, landscape
Pattern-stamping, concrete driveways, 339, 341, 344-345, 346-347, see also Concrete
Patterns
 bricklaying, 369, 371
 matching for wallcoverings, 450-451, 471
 wallpaper, 433
PB, see Polybutylene
PE, see Polyethylene
Peeling, paints, 390, see also Paints
Pencil soldering irons, see Soldering irons
Phosphors, fluorescent lamps, 248, 249
Photoelectric cells, 262, see also Lighting, landscape
Pick, 9, see also Tools
Pigments, see also Concrete; Paint(s)
 coloring for concrete, 348
 paints, 419, 390
Pipe dope, see also Pipes
 sink installation, 149
 threaded pipe fitting installation, 134, 135
Pipes, 106-141
 black iron, 108
 brass, threaded, 109
 cast iron, 122-126
 copper
  hard- vs. soft-tempered, 110-112
  tubing, 110-114
 diameters of, 104
 fittings, 102
 galvanized steel, 107-108
 painting with mitt, 415
 perforated
  concrete floor drainage, 331
  water supply, 161
 pitch-fiber, 121
 plastic, drainage, 117-119
 plastic
  solvent-welding, 136-139
  spring water supply, 161
  underground downspout, 528-529
  underground sprinkler systems, 533-534
  water supply, 114-117, 165
 PVC/ABS, 121
 repairing leaks in, 186
 rubber styrene, 121
 running for add-on rooms, 170-171, 173
 threaded, working with, 132-135
 unclogging, 189, see also Clogging
 vitrified-clay, 121
Piping, hot water heaters, see Water heaters, installation
Pitch-fiber pipe, underground drainage, 121
Pitless adapter, 165, see also Adapters
Planes
 bench, 16
 block, 16, 28
 bullnose rabbet, 16
 electric, 39

Planes, *cont...*
  hand, 16
  jack, 16, 39
  jointer, 16
  rabbet, 16
  rocker, 28
  trimming, 16
Planks, deck construction, 94
Planning
  concrete projects, 309-311
  plumbing for add-on rooms, 166, 167
Planter/table, outdoor, construction, 518
Plaster walls, repair, 457-458
Plastering, cement, 366-367, 460
Plastic
  ABS for waterproof shower walls, 524
  boxes, 240-241, see also Outlet boxes
  cement, 350
  cutting with saber saw, 36
  paint cover cores, 412
  sheathed cable, 231-232, see also Cables,
    electric
Pliers, see also Tools
  types, 27
  electrical repairs, 212, 220
Plugs
  dead-front, electrical safety, 202
  polarized, 237
  replacement and safety, 205
Plumb, levels for determining, 19
Plumb bob
  stone column construction, 515
  wallcovering hanging, 448
Plumber's friend, unclogging, 189-191
Plumber's pipe dope, see Pipe dope
Plumber's putty
  faucet installation, 156, 157, 158
  sink installation, 148, 149
  toilet installation, 151, 152, 153
Plumbing, 98-192, see Specific entries
Plunger, using, 191
Plywood, 59-61, see also Wood
  doghouse construction, 523
  edge finishing, 525
  exposure number, 60
  interior for child's desk/chair, 521
  panels, cutting with circular saw, 33
  plies, production of, 60
  sawing, 10
  shelves, 519
  stone column construction, 515
  take-apart dining table, 522
  veneers, groups, 60
  wall paneling, 62
  water resistance, 60
  waterproof, 60
Point of Demarcation, telephone installation, 278-
    279, 282, 286, 288
Polarity, electrical, 235-237
Poly pipe, see Polyethylene
Polybutylene (PB) pipe, water supply, 114-117
    see also Pipes, plastic, water supply
Polyester filament paintbrushes, 409
Polyethylene cloth, masking with, 423
Polyethylene (poly pipe), underground sprinkler
    systems, 533-534
Polyethylene (PE) pipe, water supply, 115,
    117, see also Pipes, plastic, water
    supply
Polyethylene sheeting
  concrete curing, 319
  as vapor barriers, 499, 500
  walk and drive resurfacing, 334,
    335
Polystyrene, insulation, 498
Polyvinyl chloride (PVC)
  conduit, 235, see also Cables, electric
  panels for roofing, 509
  underground downspout, 528, 529
  underground sprinkler systems, 533-534

Polyvinyl chloride (PVC), *cont...*
  water supply, 116, 117, see also Pipes,
    plastic, water supply
Polyvinyl chloride (PVC)/Acrylonitrile-
    butadiene-styrene (ABS) pipe,
    underground drainage, 121
Pop-up drains, types, 145, see also Sinks,
    replacing
Porosity, surface and painting, 392
Portland cement, 290, 302, see also Cement
Post lanterns, 269-270
Posthole diggers, 512, 520
Posts, fence, 512, see also Fences
Potable water, contamination of, 103
Power flo paint stick, use, 426-427
Power spraying, painting, 430-431
Power washing, painting, 400-401
Precast footings, 321, 322-323, see also
    Footings
Preheating, fluorescent lamps, 249, 250
Pre-mixed adhesives, see Adhesives
Pre-pasted wallcovering, see also
    Wallcoverings
  coverage of rolls, 445
  working with, 474-475
Pressure, plastic pipe, 116, 139
Pressure fittings, copper tubing, 112, see also
    Fittings, pipe
Pressure tanks, water supply, 164, 165
Pressure-test, plumbing, 103
Pre-trimmed wallcoverings, coverage of rolls,
    444, see also Wallcoverings
Primers, see also Paintings
  new wood, 419
  paint, 394-395
  surface preparation, 398-399
  trim recoating, 389
  wall repair, 457
Propane torch, sweat-soldering copper tubing,
    129, 131
Prying
  hammers for, 8
  wrecking bar, 29
Pullers
  drive type, 26
  slammer, 26
Pulse ringing telephones, 280, 288
Pumping concrete, 311
  patios, 382
Pumps, water supply, 161, 162, 163-165, see
    also Sump pumps
Punch, nail, 29
Punctures
  copper tubing, 110
  plastic pipe, 114, 119
Putty knife, 29
PVC, see Polyvinyl chloride

Q
Quick flo, 424
Quartzline bulbs, outdoor lighting, 265-266

R
Rabbets
  electric plane, 39
  electric shaper, 53
  planes for cutting, 16
  router for, 41
Radiators
  hanging wallcovering behind, 468-469
  paintbrush for, 411
Radio, battery-operated, 272
Radio receivers, door chimes, 256, 257
Rafters, squares for measuring, 17
Railings
  deck construction, 95
  painting with mitts, 415, 421
Random repeat pattern, wallcovering, 450-
    451, see also Wallcoverings
Rapid-start lamps, see Fluorescent lamps

Rasps
  electric saber saw, 36
  rat-tail, 28
Ratings, plastic pipe, 117, 119
Razors, straight edge, wallcovering hanging,
    462-463, 465, 470, 476, see also
    Wallcoverings
Ready-mix cement, vs. hand-mixing, 292-293,
    see also Concrete
Re-Bar, see also Concrete
  concrete block wall installation, 359
  concrete footings, 323
  concrete walls, 361-362
Receptacles
  grounded, 200
  Ground-Fault Circuit Interrupter, see
    Ground-Fault Circuit Interrupter (GFCI)
  testing, 215, 217
  voltage testing, 202
Recoding, hot wires, 236
Redheads, checking in armored cable, 205
Reducers, 104, 105, 107, 112, see also
    Fittings
  brass, 126
  plastic pipe, 116
Reel, cord, constructing, 507
Reflector bulbs, outdoor lighting, 265, 266
Refrigeration, conservation during power
    outages, 273
Regulations
  electrical, 202-203, 235
  plumbing, 102-103, 114
    add-on rooms, 166, 169, 170
    plastic pipe, 139
Reinforced steel, see Re-Bar
Remodeling boxes, see Old work boxes
Remote controls, 262, see also Lighting,
    landscape
Removing old paint, 403
REN, see Ringer equivalence number
Resin
  impregnated paint cover cores, 412
  plywood manufacture, 60-61
Resistance, electrical conduction, 196
Resurfacing, concrete walks and drives, 334-
    335
Retaining walls, see Walls, retaining
Revents
  add-on-rooms, 169, 170, 171
  traps, 101
Ridge, venting, 501
Ringer equivalence number, 288
Ringer simulator, telephone installation, 279,
    288
Riveting, blind rivets, 516, 517
Rock salt finish, concrete driveways, 345, see
    also Concrete
Rock wool, insulation, 497, 498
Roller covers, nap height, 413, 415
Roller frames, 412, 414
Roller trays, 414
Rollers
  heavy nap, masonry, 401
  screen replacement, 488
  wallcovering adhesives, 448
Roman bricks, 369, see also Bricks
Roof, see also Roofing
  hot mopped, 502
  nails, 80
  squares for measuring pitch, 17
Roofing
  asphalt shingles, 503
  roll, 502
  translucent
    construction, 509
    nailing, 508
Rooms, piping add-on, 166-173
Rope oakum, use with cast iron pipe, 122, 123
Rotary action dimmers, see Switches,
    dimmers

Rotary dial telephones, see Telephones
Rough surfaces, painting, 416, 417
Router, electric, 40-41
RS, see Rubber styrene
Rubber floats, finishing concrete, 299, see also Concrete
Rubber gloves, electrical safety, 201
Rubber styrene (RS) pipe, underground drainage, 121
Rubble, walls, 377, 379, see also Stone walls
Rulers, 18
Running bond, concrete block laying, 352
Rust
    latex paints, 403
    painting problem, 418
R-values
    attic fan winterizing, 490
    insulation, 496-499

S
Safety
    cement mixers, 307
    chimney flashing, 506
    circular saws, 33
    drill press, 50
    electrical check, 204-205
    insulation installation, 499
    muriatic acid use, 399
    painting, 400-401
    radial arm saw, 46, 47
    repointing bricks, 374, 375
    running telephone lines, 281
Salamanders, 329
Sand, concrete mixes, 291-292, 303, 305, see also Concrete
Sanders, see also Tools
    belt, 34
    electric, 34-35
    electric, belt/disk, 51
    electric drills, 30
    finishing, 34
    pad, 34
Sanding
    electric sander, 51
    repainting, 418-419
    siding for painting, 401
Sand-mix, 306, see also Concrete
    prepackaged, 316, 317
Sanitary tee, add-on rooms, 168, 170
Sashes, paintbrush, 410, 411
Satin paint, use, 396-397, see also Paint
Saws
    back, 13
    circular, 32-33
    crosscut, 10
    electric
        band, 49
        bench, 44-45
        chain, 38
        jig (scroll), 52
        miter (shop), 48
        radial arm, 46-47
        saber, 36-37
        utility, 38
    hack, 12
    hand, 10-11
        utility, 12-13
    jig (scroll), 13
    keyhole, 13
    plasterboard cutting, 240
    pocket, 13
    razor, 13
    reciprocating, 38
    rip, 10
    scroll, see jig
Scaffolds, hanging ceiling wallcoverings, 470
Scale
    hot water heater tanks, 142
    resistance in copper tubing, 110
Scallops, electric shaper, 53

Scissors, electrical repairs, 213
SCR bricks, 369
Scrapers, 29
Scraping, surfaces for painting, 398, 399, 404
Screeding, see also Concrete
    concrete floors, 330
    walkways, 326
Screening, replacement
    aluminum doors, 488
    wooden doors, 489
Screens, trim rollers for painting, 415
Screw starter, 26
Screwdrivers, see also Tools
    electrical repair, 213
    types of, 14, 15, 42
Screws
    bonding, 236
    drywall, 79, 80-81
        outlet box installation, 241
    removing with drill, 30
    self-drilling, 81, 90, 94
Sealers
    paint, 395
    wall paneling, 67
    wall repair, 457
Seam rollers, wallcovering hanging, 449, see also Wallcoverings
Seashore environment, painting in, 419
Sediment, hot water heaters, 143
Seeding method, exposed-aggregate driveways, 342-344, see also Concrete
Seepage pipe, see Drainage, underground pipes for
Semi-gloss paint, see also Paint(s)
    durability, 418
    use, 396, 397
Service panels, care in using, 199
Setting, paintbrushes, 411
Sewage disposal fields, plastic pipe for, 121
Sewer gas, release of, 101, see also Revent
Sewers
    street, 101-102
    unblocking, 192
Shadowing pattern, 263, see also Lighting, landscape
Shaper, electric, 53
Shellac, solvents for cleanup, 424
Shelves, construction for laundry room, 519
Shingles, see also Roofing
    asphalt, composition and installation, 503
    paintbrush for, 409
    roofing, cutting, 504
Shocks, electric
    procedures for avoiding, 201
    electric safety, 205
    telephone installation, 281
Short circuits
    about, 197
    testing for, 215-217
Shower control, single knob, repair, see Faucets, fixing
Shower stalls, installation in add-on rooms, 170, 172
Showers, waterproof walls, 524
Shutoff valves, 103, see also Valves
    water main, 100, 101
Shutters, painting, 418, 419, see also Painting
Sidewalks, see also Concrete
    concrete, 324-329
    concrete calculation, 315
    repairing concrete, 334-335
Siding
    aluminum installation, 494
    painting, 400-401
    vinyl, 391
Silhouetting, 264, see also Lighting, landscape
Silicone
    adhesive, damper installation, 505
    caulking, 169, 506
    waterproof shower walls, 524

Silver, electrical conductor role, 196
Single-lever faucets, 159, see also Faucets, installation
Sinks
    hanging wallcovering behind, 468-469
    replacing, 144-149
Siphon-jet toilets, 150, 152
Skilsaw, see Saws
Slabs, odd-shaped, concrete calculation, 315
Slate, treads for brick steps, 373
Sledge, 9
Slipnut tee, 107, see also Tees
Slipnuts, sink installation, 148, 149
Slopes, see also Concrete
    concrete driveways, 336-337
    concrete floors, 332-333
Slow-blow fuses, 209-210, see also Fuses
Smooth surfaces, painting, 416, 417
Snakes
    electricians, 227, 232-233, see also Cables, electric; Switches, replacement
    unclogging drains, 190, 191
Snap Ties, 361
Snips, soffit installation, 492
Sockets, lamp, replacement, 275
Soffits
    aluminum, 491-493
        cutting panels, 492
        installation, 493
        reasons for using, 491
        venting, 501
Soft-tempered copper tubing, see Pipes, copper Softwood, 57-58
Solder, see also Soldering
    copper tubing, 127-129, 131
    electrical repairs, 214, 218
Soldering, 514
    copper tubing, see Sweat-soldering
    electrical wires, 218-221
Soldering guns, see Soldering irons
Soldering irons
    electrical connections, 218, 219
    electrical repairs, 213-214
Solderless connectors, see Wire nuts
Solvent-welding
    plastic pipe, 117, 118
    plastic tubing, 136-139
Sounds, running water, toilet repair, 178-179
Space plugs, paintbrushes, 410
Speed controls, tools, 30, 260
Spiraling, fluorescent lamps, 251
Splices, 82-87
    aluminum screen doors, 488
    bolted, 82, 86
    electrical, 204, 239, 218-221
    fishplate, 82, 86
    half-lap, 82, 86
    scarf, 82, 86
    splayed lap, 82, 86
    V-splice, 82, 86
Spray guns, painting, 430-431
Spray painting, siding, 401, see also Painting
Spring, developing for water supply, 160-161
Spring box, 161
Sprinkler heads, see Sprinkler systems
Sprinkler systems
    plastic pipe, 533-534
    sprinkler heads
        bubbler, 532-533
Sprinkler systems, cont...
        impulse, 531-532
        pop-up spray, 531-532
        shrubbery spray, 532
    timers and valves, 534
    underground installation, 530-534
Squares, 17
Stacks
    vent, washing machines, 184
    installation for add-on rooms, 166, 168
Stain resistance, interior paints, 397

Stainless steel sinks, 145
Stains
    bleeding through, 418
    brushes for, 417
    concrete, 349
    solid latex, 396-397
Stairs, measuring using squares, 17, see also
        Steps
Standard fittings, 104, see also Fittings
Standard Interface, telephone installation, 278
Staple gun
    screen replacement, 489
    ceiling tile, 77
Station wire, telephone installation, 285, 287,
        288
Steam, electricity generation, 194
Steam strippers, wallcovering removal, 456
Steel
    cutting with saber saw, 36
    drilling, 30
    reinforcing concrete, see Re-Bar
Steel mesh, concrete driveway installation,
        338
Stems, faucet types, 175
Stepladders, nonconducting and electrical
        safety, 201, see also Ladders
Steps
    concrete and brick installation, 372
    concrete calculation, 315
    lighting, 267, 269-270
Stone, see also Concrete
    concrete mixes, 291-292, 303
    laying, 376-379
    retaining walls, 362
Storage
    paintbrushes, 425
    paints, 392
    spring water, 161
    water tanks, repairing leaks in, 187
Storms, preparation for, 272-273
Story pole
    bricklaying, 370
    concrete work, 301, 355
Straight across repeat pattern, wallcovering,
        450-451, see also Wallcoverings
Straightedge
    concrete finishing, 294, 295
    wallcovering hanging, 449, 462, 463, 465,
        470, 476
Strand board, oriented, 60, 61
Straps, tubing, electrical nonmetallic tubing,
        245
Straw-cure, concrete curing, 319
Strike board, concrete finishing, 296
Strikeoff, concrete finishing, 294, 296, 297
String wallcoverings, 434, 446
Stringlines, concrete finishing, 300
Strip-by-strip method, wallcovering
        calculations, 454
Stripping
    old wallcoverings, 456-457
    paint, 403
    wire, 231
Stub out, 103
Stucco, 366
    paints for, 391
    smoothing with plaster/or gypsum
        wallboard
        (drywall), 460
    surface preparation for painting, 399
Styrene, insulation, 498
Subbase
    preparation for sidewalks, 325, 326, 327
    preparation in concrete patios, 381
Submersible pump, see Pumps, water supply
Suede, synthetic, wallcoverings, 447, see also
        Wallcoverings
Sump pits, concrete floors, 332
Sump pumps, concrete floor drainage, 332,
        see also Pumps

Sun, paint durability, 388, 389, see also
        Paint
Sunwood, 89, see also Lumber, pressure-
        treated
Superplasticizers, 346
Supports, see also Hangers
    copper runs, 129
    plastic pipe, 138-139
Surface preparation
    painting, 418-419, see also Painting
    older homes, 402-403
    hanging wallcoverings, 456-458
Sweat fitting, copper tubing, 110, 113
Sweat-soldering
    brass pipe, 126-127, 128-129
    copper tubing, 112
Switch plates, types, 229
Switches
    dimmers, 258-261
    electrical safety check, 205
    mounting in finished walls, 237
    replacement, 226-229
    voltage testing, 202

T

Table construction
    ping-pong/dining table, 523
    take-apart dining, 522
Tailpipe connections, sinks, 145, 147, 149
Tamper-proof fuses, 211, see also Fuses
Tamping, concrete finishing, 295, see also
        Concrete
Tank, life in water heater, 142
Tank valves, types, 183, see also Valves
Tape
    electrical for pipe leaks, 186
    electrical repair, 214
Taping, wallboard, 79
Tees, 104, 105, 107, 112, 113
    brass, 126
    cast iron pipe, 122
    plastic pipe, 117
    winged for water-supply lines, 140
Teflon tape, threaded pipe, 134, 135
Telephone Company, working with, 277-278
Telephone tool, 281, 285
Telephones
    installation, 276-288
    pulse vs. dialing types, 280, 288
    use in emergency, 273
Temperature
    concrete, 328, 329
    fluctuations and paint durability, 388, 389
    limit in wires, 237, 247
    paint durability, 419
Tenon
    cutting with table saw, 45
    double, 84
    stub, 84
Terminals, connecting wires to, 220-221
Terrazzo, topping on concrete driveways, 345
Texturing, concrete walls, 366-367
Thermax, 499, 500
Thinners, paints, 390, 424, see also Paint(s)
Threads, galvanized steel pipes, 106
Three-way switches, 226-227, 232, see
        Switches, replacement
Thyristors, 260
Tiles
    ceiling
        arrangement of, 77
        installation, 76, 486, 487
        one man installation, 484-485
        suspended, 482
    ceramic
        waterproof shower walls, 524
    paint primers, 395
    patios, 382
Tilting buckct flush valves, 182, see also
        Toilets

Timers, underground sprinkler systems, 534
Time-delay fuses, 210-211
Tinted light, 264, see also Lighting, landscape
TiO2, see Titanium dioxide
Tip and Ring Connect, telephone installation,
        278
Tipping, paintbrushes, 409
Titanium dioxide (TiO2), paints, 390, 419
Toggle switches, dimming, see Switches,
        dimmers
Toilet tanks, operation, 179, see also Toilets,
        fixing
Toilets
    fixing, 178-183
    installation in add-on rooms, 170
    replacing, 150-153
    traps, 100
    water supply, 100
Tone dialing, 288, see also Telephones
Tooled finishes, concrete driveways, 344-345
Tools
    concrete, 294-301
    concrete block laying, 353
    copper pipe, 126, 127
    cordless, 42-43
    drywall, 79
    electric, 30-41
    electrical wiring, 200, 212-213
    glass cutting, 511
    hand, 8-29
    power, painting safely, 401
    power paint roller, 428-429
    screening, 488
    speed controls, 260
    stripping old wallcoverings, 456-457
    telephone installation, 281, 284-285
    threading for pipes, 109
    wallcovering, 448-449
Topping, 316
Torch, propane for brazing, 514
Track light, dimmers for, 261
Trailered ready-mix concrete, 310, 311, see
        also Concrete
Transformers, electricity, 195, 196
Traps
    bath tubs, installation in add-on rooms, 172
    drum, cast iron pipe, 122
    sinks, installation for, 146, 147, 149
    use and working of, 100
Travertine finish, concrete driveways, 345, see
        also Concrete
Tree stumps, birdbath mounting, 513
Trees, lighting, 263, see also Lighting,
        landscape
Trigger-start ballasts, see Ballasts
Trim
    aluminum siding installation, 494
    painting, 417
        power roller, 428-429
        rollers for, 415
    recoating, 388-389
Trim rings, cutting guide, 146
Trimming, wallcoverings, 476-477, see also
        Wallcoverings
Trisodium phosphate (TSP), 373, 457
Trouble-shooting
    door bells, 254, 256
    fluorescent lamps, 252-253
Troweling, see also Concrete
    concrete floors, 333
    concrete sidewalks, 328
Trowels, finishing concrete, 298, 299
TSP, see Trisodium phosphate
Tube, fluorescent lamps, 248
Tubing
    copper, see also Pipes, copper
        sink installation, 144
        types, 111
        working with, 126-131
    electrical splices, 239

Turpentine, paint cleanup, 424, 425
Type S fuses, tamper-proof, 210-211
Type T fuses, 210-211
T&P valves, see Valves, temperature-pressure

U

UF cable, see Cables, electric
UL, see Underwriters Laboratories
Ultraviolet (UV) light, paint durability, 388, 389
Unclogging, tips on, 188-192
Underwriters Laboratories (UL), 203, 204
Unions, 104, 105, 107
    installation for hot water heaters, 143
    transition for plastic pipe, 140
Urethane, solvents for cleanup, 424
UV, see Ultraviolet light
U.S. Department of Housing and Urban
        Development (HUD), 497

V

Valves
    angle-stop, faucet installation, 156
    brass pipe, 109
    float, toilets, 180, 181
    shutoff for water, 100
    temperature-pressure (T&P), water
        heaters, 143
    underground sprinkler systems, 533-534
Vapor barriers, insulation, 498-500
Varnish
    paintbrushes, 411
    solvents for cleanup, 424
Veneer, plywood edge finishing, 525
Vent stack, 101, see also Stacks
Ventilation, electrical appliances, 205
Venting, attic, 501
Vents
    runs for add-on rooms, 166-168
    soffit, insulation, 498-499
    toilet, 101
Vinyl acrylic paint, definition, 403
Vinyl siding, painting, 401
Vinyl terpolymer paint, definition, 403
Vinyl tubing, uses, 120
Vinyl wallcoverings, 434, see also
        Wallcoverings
    coverage of rolls, 445
Vises, 24, 25
    cutting threaded pipe, 133
Vitrified-clay, underground drainage, 121
VOC, see Volatile organic compounds
Volatile organic compounds (VOC), 405
Volatile organic solvents (VOS), 405
Voltage
    definition, 195
    fluorescent lamps, 250, 251
    testing, 202
Voltage testers
    electric circuits, 214
    electrical power testing, 202
Volt-ohm-milliammeter (VOM), 215-216, 225,
        241
Volume, concrete estimating, 312-313
VOM, see Volt-ohm-milliammeter
VOS, see Volatile organic solvents, 405

W

Waferboard, 60, 61
Walks, lighting, 267, 269-270
Wall jack, telephone installation, 284, 285, 288
Wall thickness, copper tubing, 111
Wallcover primer/sealer, use of, 458, 460, 472
Wallcoverings
    achieving special effects, 436
    correcting common faults, 478-479
    decorating with, 433
        solving problems, 438-439
    estimating, 454-455

Wallcoverings, cont...
    hanging
        first strip, 462-463
        general information, 444-445
        second strip and complete room, 464-
            465
    historical background, 432, 444
    innovative uses, 437, 439
    patterns, 450-451
    special rooms, 440-441
    terminology glossary, 480
    tools and equipment, 448-449
    trimming, 476-477
    types of, 434-435
        unusual, 446-447
Wallpaper, coverage of rolls, 445
Walls
    brick, estimating quantity, 372
    exterior insulation, 498, 499
    paint applications, 417
        power roller, 428
        roller covers for, 413
    pasting wallcoverings, 472-473
    plaster, wall paneling installation, 70
    repairing
        painted, 457-458
        unpainted, 457-458
    retaining, installation, 360-363
    waterproof shower, 524
Washerless faucets, repair, see Faucets,
        fixing
Washers
    replacing in faucets, 174
    tailpipe connections, 145, 147
Washing machines, plumbing, 184-185
Waste arm, 100
Waste pipes, fixture, 100, 145
Water
    bricklaying, 370
    concrete curing, 319
    concrete mixes, 302, 303, 305, 306,
        310
    conserving, 182-183
    electricity generation, 195
    emergency preparations, 273
    latex paint durability, 419
    latex paint thinner, 390, 391
    level in toilets, 182
    locating supply, 163
        connections, 154
        private, 160-165
    paint cleanup, 424-425
    supply lines
        copper tubing, 110-112, see also
            Pipes, copper tubing
        identification, 98
        installation in add-on rooms, 167, 171-
            172
        washing machines, 185
Water disposal, cycle, 101
Water hammer, plumbing system, 100, 106,
        113
    arrester, 139
Water heaters
    water supply to, 100
    installation, 142-143
Water-reducing retarder, 346
Water vapor barriers, paints, 418
Watts
    rating of electrical appliances, 196
    definition, 195
Wax rings, toilet installation, 151, 152
Weather
    painting, 392-393
    wet concrete, 328, 329
Weathering, decks, 95
Weatherproofing, outdoor lighting, 264-266
Wedge bar, 29

Welding, 514
Wells
    plastic pipe for, 117
    water supply, 161-162
Wet-sand curing, concrete, 319, see also
        Concrete, curing
Wet screeds, 295, see also Concrete
Wheatpaste, wallpaper adhesive, 452,
Wheelbarrow, use with concrete, 307
Wind resistance, asphalt shingles, 503
Windmills, 165
Windows
    hanging wallcoverings around, 466-467
    masking, 422-423
    paint applications, 417
    screen replacement, 488, 489
Wire
    bending, 220
    techniques, 230-241
Wire brushes
    concrete work, 301
    for drills, 30
    surfaces preparation for painting, 398-399,
        401
Wire caps, see Wire nuts
Wire junction, 288
    telephone installation, 284, 288
Wire mesh, concrete block wall installation,
        357
Wire nuts
    electrical wiring, 204
    wire-terminal connections, 220-221
Wire plug, telephone installation, 284, 285
Wireless door chimes, 256, 257, see also Door
        chimes (bells/buzzers)
Wireless testers, electric circuits, 215
Wires, color-coded telephone, 284, 285, 286
Wirestrippers, 27, 213, 214
Wiring
    code regulations, 203
    making end loops, 238
    underground sprinkler systems, 534
Wood, see also Plywood
    chisels for, 20
    concrete floors, 332
    cutting, see also Saws
        hand saw, 10
        saber saw, 36
    drilling, 30
    painting
        old, 402
        paints for, 391
        primers for new and weathered, 395
        surface preparation, 398-399
    solid paneling, 62, 67
    solid latex stains, 396-397
Wood alcohol, paint cleanup, 424
Wood filler, plywood edge finishing, 525
Woodwork, painting, 415, 417
Workbench
    building, 74-75
    vises for, 25
Wrecking bars, 29
Wrenches
    basin, faucet installation, 155-156
    pipe, fittings installation on threaded pipe,
        135
    plastic pipe, 138
    sink
        installation, 149
        replacement, 145
    strap, brass pipe, 109
    torque, no-hub pipes, 123
Wyes, 104-105

Y

Yellowing, interior paint, 396
Yields, concrete, 314